FEB 2 7 2001

DATE DUE

FEB 2 3 2010			
FEB 0 2 2010			
MAR 1 8 2010			
APR 1 2 2010			
MAY 1 0 2010			
JUN 0 1 2010			
JUN 0 7 2014			

Demco, Inc. 38-293

*America's
Musical
Life*

BY RICHARD CRAWFORD

Andrew Law, American Psalmodist

William Billings of Boston, with David P. McKay

American Studies and American Musicology

The Civil War Songbook

The Core Repertory of Early American Psalmody

American Sacred Music Imprints, 1698–1810: A Bibliography,
   with Allen Perdue Britton and Irving Lowens

*A Celebration of American Music: Words and Music in Honor of H. Wiley
   Hitchcock,* coeditor with R. Allen Lott and Carol J. Oja

Jazz Standards on Record, 1900–1942: A Core Repertory, with Jeffrey Magee

The Complete Works of William Billings (edited by Hans Nathan and Karl
   Kroeger), editorial consultant

The American Landscape

Music of the United States of America (MUSA), editor-in-chief

An Introduction to America's Music

A HISTORY

America's
Musical
Life

RICHARD CRAWFORD

W. W. NORTON & COMPANY

NEW YORK   LONDON

The text of this book is composed in Fairfield,
with the display set in Liberty.
Composition by PennSet, Inc.
Manufacturing by The Courier Companies, Inc.
Book design by Charlotte Staub

Library of Congress Cataloging-in-Publication Data
Crawford, Richard, 1935–
America's musical life : a history / Richard Crawford.
p. cm.
Includes bibliographical references and index.
ISBN 0-393-04810-1
1. Music—United States—History and criticism. I. Title.

ML200.C69 2000
780'.973—dc21

99-047565

W. W. Norton & Company, Inc., 500 Fifth Avenue, New York, N.Y. 10110
www.wwnorton.com

W. W. Norton & Company Ltd., 10 Coptic Street, London WC1A 1PU

1 2 3 4 5 6 7 8 9 0

For Penelope B. Crawford
wife, mother, musician

Contents

Part Three

THE TWENTIETH CENTURY

Introduction

IN 1969, ADDRESSING THE CADETS at West Point about the genesis of his novel *Invisible Man* (1952), the African-American writer Ralph Ellison explained: "I wanted to tell a story. I felt that there was a great deal about the nature of American experience that was not understood by most Americans. I felt also that the diversity of the total experience rendered much of it mysterious. And I felt that because so much of it which appeared unrelated was actually most intimately intertwined, it needed exploring."[1] Counting myself among those whose grasp of the full implications of American diversity was deficient, I came to feel after reading Ellison's words in 1986 that his comment might well have been addressed to historians of American music. Years of studying the subject had taught me that standard musicological approaches left certain key issues unaddressed. It made sense to be told that an exploration of broader scope might illuminate parallels and intertwinings that give this country's music making its distinctive character.

America's Musical Life: A History seeks to conduct such an exploration by taking performance rather than composition as a starting point. Composers are by no means slighted here. But in a chronicle that begins in the 1500s and seeks at every point to portray the historical conditions in which music has been made, they share the stage with singers, players, conductors, teachers, entrepreneurs, and even writers, not to mention musical creators from overseas.

A historian grappling with the whole of American music cannot avoid encountering generic differences in the way that music has been created, performed, and transmitted—differences that explain why such terms as "classical," "popular," and "folk" music are part of the common vocabulary. While using these familiar labels, however, I have linked them not to an aesthetic hierarchy but to something more concrete and practical: the degree of authority wielded by musical notation.

We begin, for example, with Native American music, which circulated orally. The narrative moves on to trace the musical traditions, oral and written, brought to North America by European settlers, and the impact of the African diaspora. It persistently probes links between musical notation and economic opportunity. And then, in Chapter 12 (on nineteenth-century home music making), I propose a categorical distinction between "composers' music," for works whose notation embodies the authority of the composer, and "performers' music," for works whose notation is intended as an outline to be shaped by performers as they see fit. The first category, ruled by the written directives of composers, is the classical sphere, a realm where works aspire to transcendence: to outliving the time and place of their creation. The second, ruled by performers who shape composers' scores to fit the occasion, is the popular sphere, a realm where works aspire to accessibility: to acceptance by the target audience. With written compositions split into two categories, music that circulates orally may then be considered a third: the traditional (or folk) sphere, often linked with particular customs and ways of life. Tending to preserve each culture's linguistic and musical practices, the traditional sphere is ruled by a belief in continuity.

From Chapter 12 on, then, this book offers an account of three spheres of musical activity, coexisting and sometimes interacting in a nonhierarchical continuum of time and space. The labels are not always crucial to the story: classical, popular, and folk examples are all described here simply as music. Yet the notion of categorical difference is built in to the consciousness of Americans. And because the three spheres have often been seen as hierarchically ordered (from high to low), the crossing of boundaries—as in George Gershwin's borrowing of jazz for concert hall works or the Beatles' use of a string quartet in the recording studio—has often carried a jolt of surprise and excitement. Moreover, as recordings have turned performances into permanent works, the classical sphere has lost its monopoly on the ideal of transcendence. Without such interplay among the categories, American music history—indeed, the experience of many American works— would lose much of its eventful edge.

This story of America's musical life also pays close attention to economics. I trace my own interest in music and money back to the days of writing a dissertation on early American psalmody. After months of copying documents, reading about theological debates, and pondering how to use the tools of musical analysis on hymn tunes, I experienced a breakthrough when I realized that sacred tunebooks were not only religious and artistic artifacts but commercial ones, whose compilers cared about their economic success. Since that moment, early in the 1960s, I have always found it worthwhile to ask how the musicians I am studing have earned their living. Finally, I have grounded this story chiefly in U.S. history, paying particular heed to geographical and social conditions that have struck me as musically influential.

Historians of American music have not always agreed on where the heart of their subject lies. Those who wrote in the 1800s and early 1900s concentrated chiefly on performace. For them, keenly aware of the nation's cultural immaturity, the building of institutions that allowed the works of European masters to be sung and played outweighed other accomplishments. More recently, however, historians have shifted their emphasis toward the creation of music and heightened their interest in musical diversity.

In 1915, the composer Arthur Farwell, writing in the introduction to his *Music in America*, asked a fundamental question: What would a new world "do with the tractable and still unformed art of music?" What would arise from the contact of music with "our unprecedented democracy"? A decade and a half later, John Tasker Howard's *Our American Music* answered with a chronicle of music composed in the United States. For Howard, the encounter between democracy and Old World traditions had produced a wealth of composers and an outpouring of American works for the concert hall. But in the mid-1950s, Gilbert Chase, in *America's Music: From the Pilgrims to the Present*, took a contrary view. Condemning Howard's approach as "genteel," Chase declared that America's most important styles were to be found *outside* the concert hall, where their difference from European music was most striking: in the folk and popular traditions and in the works of composers who borrowed from them.

Histories written since Chase have taken his view as their starting point. No recent historian has questioned the distinctiveness of America's music, nor has any disputed Chase's claim that in popular and folk traditions lie the wellsprings of the nation's truest creative achievements. What has not been widely noticed, however, is that Chase, in overturning Howard's aesthetic hierarchy, opened the door to an older idea that Howard had rejected: the belief of earlier writers that American music history had been shaped more by performance than composition. While Howard had proclaimed composers to be the primary agents of American music history, Chase took his stand with American genres—spirituals, blackface minstrelsy, folk songs and fiddle music, shape-note hymnody, Native American songs, ragtime, blues, and jazz—that relied on the way they were performed. As much as compositional types, these genres were performance traditions that took over and recast any music their practitioners played or sang. Thus, while staking out a fresh perspective, Chase also reaffirmed the judgment of earlier authors that a composer-centered history of America's music would miss the heart of the subject.

In this book, I seek to reconcile Chase's post–World War II perspective with that of earlier historians—George Hood, Nathaniel D. Gould, Frédéric Louis Ritter, W. S. B. Mathews, Louis Elson, W. L. Hubbard, and Oscar G. Sonneck—all of whom were on the scene before a tradition of American works for the concert hall existed. My account also follows Chase's connection between America's democratic heritage and the diversity of its musical life. America's music history was diverse, Chase believed, not only because its composers were stylistically dissimilar but because all categories of musical endeavor belonged to that history. From Ritter's 1883 *Music in America* on, historians had given folk and popular music either a small place in their chronicles or none at all. But from the time that Chase made categories an issue, historians have accepted the idea that different kinds of musicians have found different ways to achieve aesthetic excellence.

A new stage in the recognition of musical categories began in 1969, with the publication of H. Wiley Hitchcock's *Music in the United States: A Historical Introduction*. Hitchcock made popular music a full partner in the saga of America's music: he divided his account of the period 1820–1920 into two complementary streams, and he defined the character of each. Linking classical music to "a body of music that America had to cultivate consciously, music faintly exotic, to be approached with some effort, and to be appreciated for its edification—its moral, spiritual, or aesthetic values," Hitchcock also described a "vernacular" tradition centered on popular idioms. Here, he wrote, one finds "music not approached self-consciously but simply grown into as one grows into one's vernacular tongue, music understood and appreciated simply for its utilitarian or entertainment value."[2] As Hitchcock saw it, the split between cultivated and vernacular traditions grew out of patterns of settlement, immigration, and economics in the early 1800s, then became less distinct after World War I, when new ways of distributing music reshaped the country's musical landscape. Many writers on American music have found Hitchcock's categories useful. Formulated as attitudes toward rather than properties of music, they allow a classification of works that does not proclaim the superiority of one class over another—though admittedly, such classifying is itself a cultivated act.

Although I have not used Hitchcock's terms in this chronicle, neither have I found a way to describe the historical unfolding of America's musical life without recourse to categories.

As this project comes to an end, a consciousness of two facts looms large: the many omissions in my text and the debts I owe other scholars, colleagues, and friends. On the first count, I can only plead that in a work aiming to describe such a complex whole, an author who hopes to be clear must also be selective. Of all the conversations I had while deciding to write this book, the one I recall most vividly was with Charles Hamm, who in 1983 published *Music in the New World*, the most recent full-blown history of the subject. Hamm's encouragement to go ahead with the project gave me a big boost. But it came with a warning that, given the explosion of new work in the field, I would have to digest—as well as new music from the 1980s and 1990s—much more in the way of secondary literature and recordings from older American traditions than he had in writing his account. He was right about that. Yet I also had the advantage of being able to consult *The New Grove Dictionary of American Music* (1986), edited in four volumes by H. Wiley Hitchcock and Stanley Sadie, which brings together information previously unobtainable or scattered. The *"American Grove"* proved a vital reference for writing this work. But more than that, I soon realized, *Grove*'s store of biographical data, work lists, musical analysis, and bibliographical references allowed the general historian's focus to shift away from coverage and toward interpretation. Thanks in part to *Grove*'s presence, I have seen my task as more thematic than documentary: to identify the fundamental patterns in America's musical life, to try to understand what they meant in their own day, and to trace them from the perspective of an observer in the 1990s. With apologies for all the things I would have liked to include but have left out, including for starters such personal favorites as jazz pianists Dave McKenna, Tommy Flanagan, Fred Hersch, and Bill Charlap, those priorities have shaped my choices.

No project that I have ever tackled has made me more aware of scholarship's collaborative nature. Indeed, only in writing these words have I realized what a large role the requests of others have played in its conception. The ground for the enterprise was laid in 1985, when, invited to visit the University of California at Berkeley as Ernest Bloch Professor in the music department, I delivered a series of lectures called "The American Musical Landscape," which began with an overview of the country's music historiography. The next year, Judith McCulloh of the University of Illinois Press asked me to write an introduction for the third edition of Chase's *America's Music*, an assignment that clarified my understanding of Chase's historiographical achievement. While preparing the Berkeley lectures for publication in the early 1990s, I was invited by David A. Hollinger, then on the University of Michigan's history faculty, to write an article on music for the *Encyclopedia of the United States in the Twentieth Century*. I accepted the assignment, intrigued by the problem of tailoring my thinking on the subject to a 15,000-word essay for a nonspecialist audience. And I considered expanding the result into a book, interweaving twentieth-century classical, popular, and folk traditions. At this point, however, Michael Ochs of W. W. Norton approached me with another proposal aimed at general readers: a new history of music in the United States, from the arrival of Europeans in North America to the flowering of hip-hop culture. After six years of writing and revision, supported by constant encouragement and aid from Ochs and Norton's unfailingly professional staff, that book now stands completed. Most of all, developmental editor Susan Gaustad has won my heartfelt gratitude for helping me tell the story as clearly and directly as possible.

I owe special thanks to the University of Michigan's School of Music and Dean Paul C. Boylan for the sabbatical leave and other financial support that helped make the writing of this book possible. A year-long fellowship from the National Endowment for the Humanities also proved indispensable. At Michigan over the past several years, I have used chapter drafts in classes, both graduate and undergraduate, and have learned from the students' responses to them. Advising the dissertations of Jennifer DeLapp, Mark Katz, and Amy C. Beal has also contributed to my knowledge of twentieth-century American composers and issues, and Beal's bibliographical digging eased my access to many sources. In a graduate seminar in 1998, the chance to work with student composers Kevin Beavers, Andrew Bishop, and Stephen Eddins also helped me find a path through music since the 1960s. Tara Browner, a Michigan graduate now on the faculty at the University of California at Los Angeles, shared with me some of her recent unpublished writings on American Indian traditions, for which I am grateful.

Several others at the University of Michigan have proved enormously helpful in the project. Jeffrey Magee, executive editor of the Music of the United States of America (MUSA) series from 1993 to 1997, read and critiqued several chapters and always showed a readiness to discuss my ideas, even when they were barely formed. Mark Clague, his successor, has also provided instructive feedback and an unfailing willingness to lend a helping hand in the project's later stages. Gayle Sherwood, a visiting professor during the years 1995–97, offered aid and encouragement for the chapter on Charles Ives. My colleagues Travis A. Jackson and Albin J. Zak III have also read chapters and made helpful suggestions. In November 1997, I delivered part of a chapter to a musicology department colloquium at Michigan and received constructive responses. Most of all, Tamar Barzel, a student in Michigan's ethnomusicology program, has proved a skillful editor and critic in several different passes through the manuscript—most recently during the summer of 1998. Her judgment and perspective helped me shorten a very long manuscript into more manageable size.

Carol J. Oja, now of the College of William and Mary, and Robert Walser of UCLA generously shared with me some of their work before it was published. Samuel A. Floyd Jr., who directs the Center for Black Music Research at Columbia College in Chicago and with whom I have had many enriching exchanges over the past decade, provided me with much-needed help in the project's early stages. Gena Dagel Caponi, who teaches at the

University of Texas at San Antonio, read a number of the later chapters, always giving me the benefit of her incisive critical eye and ear and her gift for finding connections. And as in the past, I have relied on the good offices of my longtime mentor and friend H. Wiley Hitchcock, who, over more than forty years of encouraging me, has never hesitated to let me know when he thought I could do better. Finally, together with all those named so far, I owe a dept of one kind or another to the following, each of whom has made a positive contribution to this book: Daniel Anker, William W. Austin, Gregory Barnett, Judith Becker, John Beckwith, Crisca Bierwert, John S. Blakemore, Priscilla Blakemore, Marilyn Bliss, Anne Marie Borch, Todd Borgerding, Margaret Boshoven, Horace C. Boyer, David Brackett, Neely Bruce, Martha Dennis Burns, Julia Suzanne Byl, Suzanne Camino, Hui-Hsuan Chao, Dale Cockrell, Nym Cooke, Stanley Crouch, Scott DeVeaux, Michelle Fillion, Jon A. Finson, Suzanne Flandreau, Beth Genné, Judith Guest, Jocelyne Guilbault, Lawrence A. Gushee, Jan M. Hoeper, Paula Higgins, Neil Ryder Hoos, Cynthia Adams Hoover, Joseph Horowitz, John Koegel, Joseph S. C. Lam, Richard Le Sueur, Gustav Meier, Morris Phibbs, Guthrie P. Ramsey Jr., Roger Reynolds, Thomas L. Riis, Ellen Rowe, David Schiff, Wayne D. Shirley, Aaron Siegel, David Warren Steel, David A. Sutherland, Enid Sutherland, Judith Tick, Mark Tucker, Bonnie C. Wade, Glenn Watkins, Anne White, Carl Woideck, and Victoria Zak.

When one has a family, projects like this become family affairs. And my final round of thanks goes to members of mine. Son Bill and daughter Amy Crawford, both voracious listeners, have made me tapes, engaged me in conversations and arguments, and taught me a good deal of what I know about recent popular idioms. Amy also read part of this account and told me where she thought it needed more work. My daughter Anne, an artistically accomplished keyboard player and violinist, edited several chapters, and her sharp eye unerringly found the weak spots in what mine had perceived as a finished product. My daughter Lynn, while not directly involved in this project, inspired me with her own achievements as a writer and mother. My mother, Libby Crawford, who has been writing songs for as long as I can remember, gratified me by approving the chapters I gave her to read. Finally, the musical life of Penny Crawford, to whom this book is dedicated, has done much to shape my idea of what it has meant to be a musician in the United States of America.

Richard Crawford
Ann Arbor and Black River, Michigan
July 2000

PART ONE

The First
Three
Centuries

1

The First Song

Native American Music

AMONG OTHER THINGS, historians search for origins. But if we take history to mean stories about the past that can be supported by facts, the origins of music will always be elusive. Music is an art of sounding, not writing. And the making of musical sounds is a human activity, like dance, that must be much older than written proof of its existence. In Western civilization, with its profound respect for the written record, the origins of music are a subject of speculation. But in many American Indian cultures, the origins of music are a matter of deep-seated belief.

A comparison of Native and Western musical practices reveals different conceptions of history. In literate, record-keeping Western traditions, musicians seldom feel the need to ground their performing in a consciousness of the history of their art. Many Indian people, on the other hand, participate in their music's history through rituals, legends, and parables shared from one generation to the next. They carry with them some understanding of how their singing, dancing, and playing connect with ancestral custom.

The preservation and study of Indian music by Western scholars since the 1880s forms an important part of the story of American anthropology and ethnomusicology (see Chapter 20). In fact, outsiders' accounts date all the way back to the beginnings of European contact. These accounts are usually anecdotal; they are also both fragmentary and rare. Their value is that they preserve most of the factual evidence about Indian music that survives from the remote past. But where do Native historical explanations fit in a modern understanding of Indian music making?

Because it cannot be documented, much of the historical knowledge valuable to a Native musician falls more readily into the category of myth than of fact. Indian musicians carry their beliefs about origins forward because such beliefs are integral to their tradition. A knowledge of origins can supply not merely a colorful dose of background lore but a reason to sing, play, or dance. Blackfoot singers, for example, know that in Blackfoot cosmology music was given to humans to help them solve the problems they must face in life. Thus, they sing with a specific purpose in mind. By the same token, according to the traditional belief system of the Havasupai nation, before humans existed, supernatural beings sang to communicate among themselves. When humans arrived on the earth, they were given music so that they could communicate with the supernatural world. In Havasupai tradition, therefore, singing establishes a sacred context. In the 1970s, Navajo singer Frank Mitchell explained a parallel belief about music, tracing some of his songs back to the origins of the Navajo people:

> According to what I learned, a group came up from under the earth—they must have been some kind of supernatural beings. They were given this area of land within the four sacred mountains. It was in this area that the Navajos had their beginnings.
>
> The whole place was covered with water at that time. Then the water was removed so something could be planted and grow on the earth. The water was all removed to the ocean, perhaps. And from there the first songs and prayers of the Blessingway had their start. They were for the planting of crops. The first thing the Holy People did was to make a song and a prayer for the plants on the earth so the earth would be fruitful. That was the first song and the first prayer to be performed, and they were the first ones that I learned.[1]

European and Native cosmologies could hardly be more different. From the time of their arrival in North America, Europeans have tended to treat human interaction—whether as part of God's plan or outside it—as the chief drama of existence, played out against the backdrop of nature. American Indians, on the other hand, have traditionally held that the central fact of human existence has been its location in a natural world replete with significance. Animals, trees, weather, water, and topography, like supernatural beings, all play a role in human existence too, because all are related parts of the same whole. This is not to say that Native Americans have undervalued human life. Rather, they have experienced it as one strand in a fabric of interconnectedness, not a force claiming dominion over the rest of the natural order. It seems only logical, then, that people holding such beliefs would invest their music making with specific functions, and that music would be judged not by its abstract beauty but by its ability to serve those functions.

All human interaction contains a perception of difference and a perception of similarity. A weighing and monitoring of both is part of the human condition. But when members of two completely separate cultures come into contact on a massive scale, and in circumstances where each is pursuing a different goal, perceptions of difference and similarity can carry vast historical consequences. That was certainly true of the contact between Native peoples and Europeans on the North American continent. And because the history of Indian music making depends heavily on the way Europeans perceived the Natives—on how they compared themselves with the people they were encountering and displacing—the musical information that survives can only be understood in light of those perceptions.

European's perceptions of Natives were formed in a framework of political struggle in which they held the advantage, and which was marked by profound human suffering: for Europeans carried with them to the New World infectious diseases to which Native Americans had no resistance. Estimates hold that chiefly because of disease, Mexico's population dropped by more than 90 percent in the first century of Spanish-Indian contact.[2] The Native population, while trying to cope with overseas invaders, experienced sudden, drastic, and disastrous demographic decline. Biology, then, played a decisive role in the cultural encounters that accompanied the process of settlement.

Economics played another role. North America was colonized by imperial powers eager to tap into New World wealth, whether in gold, furs, agricultural products, or, eventually, markets for Old World goods. And there is evidence that early commercial exchanges were not all weighted in the Europeans' favor. Cultural development in the Old and New Worlds had been so completely separate that each side possessed goods highly desirable to the other.[3] Yet Natives and Europeans held very different positions in the economics of settlement. Europeans had initiated contact in the first place, and the urge to expand their influence placed them in the role of aggressors. It was inevitable that those who resisted their invasion would be considered enemies. Therefore, an imperial relationship was assumed from the start. Because the Europeans, with their biological advantage, superior commercial know-how, and technological skill, prevailed in the New World, their perceptions of the Natives, far more than the Natives' perception of them, set the terms for cultural encounters. And because the spirit of those encounters filtered what was written about Indian music making during that time period, white attitudes toward the Native population deserve attention here.

Two contrasting attitudes have been distinguished in Europeans' perception of Natives, one emphasizing similarity, and the other difference. When Europeans, in taking over and colonizing lands already occupied by others, encountered those they hoped to displace, they were struck most of all by the Indians' resemblance to themselves. Here, in the wilds of a supposedly unoccupied continent, the first European explorers found walking, talking, communicating human beings. Living beyond the reach of Western civilization, these people had developed customs different from the colonizers' own. But their obviously human essence made them fascinating and to some degree sympathetic. At the same time, although it was impossible to deny that Indians shared with Europeans certain traits of appearance and

This French engraving of a Native couple in Florida, appearing in Alain Manesson Mallet, *Description de l'Univers* (1683), reflects the "good Indian" image.

what could pass for language and a certain vocabulary of emotion, their manner of life, customs, dress, and behavior differed so dramatically from white Europeans' conceptions of humanness that they seemed a different order of being altogether.

European reactions to these contrasting perceptions of Natives' "otherness" shaped the history of Indians' lives in North America after European contact. The perception of similarity led settlers to dwell on the Natives' capacity for human virtue as the settlers defined it. If Indians had capacities similar to those of Europeans, then Europeans could supply what Indians needed to reach a fully human state: education to civilize them and religious instruction to save their souls from the damnation that lay in store for heathens. Beginning especially in the Southwest (where the Spanish, moving north from Mexico, had formed settlements) and in the Northeast (where the French had set up trading posts in Canada), Roman Catholic missionaries traveled from the Old World to convert the Natives and to set up mission schools for their education.

The perception of difference, however, suggested an unbridgeable gulf between Natives and settlers; against a scale of European values, the Indians were found wanting. This attitude fueled contempt, which in disputes could provide license to disparage, cheat, brutalize, kill, or remove the Natives from land the settlers wanted to occupy. Yet not even the first attitude left room for much curiosity about the Indians as they actually were. In their contact with the Indians, European settlers showed a consistent inability to grasp the idea that there might be people truly different from themselves. Thus, they tended to equate similarity with good qualities and difference with bad.

Euroamericans' imagery of Indians spans more than four centuries, and any attempt to summarize it risks oversimplifying. Yet the categories of "good Indian" and "bad Indian" were used consistently enough in the past to become paradigms for Euroamerican perceptions. The so-called good Indians were seen to be friendly, modest, dignified, and brave, and to lead simple lives devoted to their families and closely in tune with nature. It was this idealized perception that inspired European attempts to educate and Christianize Native peoples. Settlers who favored the "bad Indian" image tended, when they considered the way Indians lived, to see nakedness and sexual promiscuity, superstition, laziness, cannibalism and human sacrifice, constant warfare, desire for revenge, and cruelty to captives. Nor did Europeans' observations of Indian cookery and personal hygiene do much to raise their opinion of Indian life.[4]

The historical record reflects the destructiveness that followed when dichotomies like the good Indian/bad Indian images took hold. Drawing on observations that made no claim of completeness or balance, neither was more than a notion improvised from a small selection of facts. "Image" is the right word to register their lack of depth. Yet both hardened into beliefs from which flowed courses of action that failed, at every point, to take either the diversity or the uniqueness of Native cultures into account.

MUSIC

Our knowledge about the early history of Native American music depends on reports by non-Natives. The character and usefulness of those reports varies, not only with the observers' own musical knowledge but with their empathy for the Indians. One of the earliest observations was made in the 1530s by a Spanish chronicler who, along with three countrymen, had landed years earlier in Florida and undertaken a long journey west, providing medical treatment to several Natives along the trail. Upon reaching an Indian settlement in what is now western Texas near Big Spring, they were greeted by "all the people . . . with such yells as were terrific, striking the palms of their hands violently against their thighs." (Might another observer have heard the yells and thigh-slapping as music? There is no way of knowing.) The Natives' enthusiasm had been inspired by their guests' reputation as healers. They presented the honored visitors with devices that fit the classification of an idiophone (a musical instrument that produces sound by the vibration of its own substance; by being struck or shaken, for example); one of the Spaniards described them as "gourds bored with holes and having pebbles in them, an instrument for the most important occasions produced only at the dance or to effect cures, and which none dare touch but those who own them. They say there is virtue in them, and because they do not grow in that country, they come from heaven."[5]

Continuing west, the Spaniards found that their fame as medicine men had preceded them. Natives in the Sacramento Mountains of New Mexico gave them more idiophones: a "jingle bell of copper" and two medicine rattles. Another account from New Mexico in 1540 reaffirms the Indians' functional use of musical sound, this time reporting scenes from near where Albuquerque stands today. When a party headed by Captain Hernando de Alvarado approached a Zuñi pueblo in Pecos, they were welcomed "with drums and flageolets, similar to fifes, of which they had many." One Spaniard also described how music served in the Zuñis' ceremonial grinding of corn.

> Three women come in, each going to her stone. One crushes the maize, the next grinds it, and the third grinds it finer. Before they come inside the door they remove their shoes, tie up their hair and cover it, and shake their clothes. While they are grinding, a man sits at the door playing a flageolet,

and the women move their stones, keeping time with the music, and all three sing together.[6]

These reports from the Southwest, less than half a century after Columbus landed in the Western hemisphere, supply some of the first evidence of Native instruments and uses of music. But they say nothing about its sound. On the other hand, when early observers did mention how Indian music sounded, they were more likely to focus on their own response—often negative—than on the sound itself. A case in point is the experience of the Jesuit father Paul Le Jeune with a medicine man in the winter of 1634, as related by nineteenth-century American historian Francis Parkman. Parkman's account makes no attempt to treat the music making on its own terms. Nor is it specific enough to show, as one gathers, that the performance's great length was made possible by much musical repetition. But it does testify to the Hurons' faith that the physical exertion of vocalizing and time beating as part of a healing ritual could help cure a lingering malady.

> The sorcerer believed in the efficacy of his own magic, and was continually singing and beating his drum to cure the disease from which he was suffering. Toward the close of the winter, Le Jeune fell sick, and, in his pain and weakness, nearly succumbed under the nocturnal uproar of the sorcerer, who, hour after hour, sang and drummed without mercy,—sometimes yelling at the top of his throat, then hissing like a serpent, then striking his drum on the ground as if in a frenzy, then leaping up, raving about the wigwam, and calling on the women and children to join him in singing. Now ensued a hideous din; for every throat was strained to the utmost, and all were beating with sticks or fists on the bark of the hut to increase the noise, with the charitable object of aiding the sorcerer to conjure down his malady, or drive away the evil spirit that caused it.[7]

Le Jeune was later to write of the Hurons: "All their religion consists mainly in singing."[8]

Not until later in the seventeenth century did a musically knowledgeable Westerner write down a Native melody heard within the borders of the present United States and describe the circumstances in which he heard it— and these circumstances were very different from those surrounding the Hurons' efforts to drive Father Le Jeune's ailment into submission. The transcriber was another Jesuit priest, Father Claude Dablon, born in France and master of several musical instruments, which, according to a contemporaneous report, he played very well. Dablon and fellow Jesuit Father Claude Allouz had established a mission at Green Bay on Lake Michigan in 1669. In 1670, the two priests visited the present Winnebago County, Wisconsin, where friendly Mascouten, Miami, and Illinois tribes had gathered. Dablon found the Illinois to be polite and their chief especially kind. Sometimes, he reported, "some of the oldest men would appear, dressed as if for playing a comedy, and would dance to the music of some very tuneful airs, which they sang in excellent accord."[9]

The music Dablon transcribed accompanied a dance honoring the peace pipe, or "calumet." Among the Illinois, men and women with the best voices were chosen to sing for the occasion; *berdaches* (transvestites who assumed the dress, social status, and role of woman), "who are summoned to the Councils and without whose advice nothing can be decided," sang as well. According to Dablon, the dancers moved in strict time to the singing, and a mock combat was fought to the slow beat of a drum: "This is done so well—with slow and measured steps, and to the rhythmic sound of the voices and drums—that it might pass for a very fine Entry of a Ballet in France."[10]

Admitting that his transcription failed to do justice to the way the music actually sounded, Dablon wrote: "They give their songs a certain turn which cannot be sufficiently expressed by Note, but which nevertheless endows them with all their grace."[11] Dablon did not explain the double bars that divide the melody into three sections, but one or more of those sections were surely repeated many times in performance. An Illinois calumet dance described by French observers only four years after Dablon made his transcription was long as well as stately. "Everyone, at the outset, takes the

The French-born Jesuit priest Claude Dablon, who in 1670 made this transcription of the music of the Illinois Indians' "calumet" dance in honor of the peace pipe, was a trained musician who sometimes performed for the Native peoples to whom he ministered.

Calumet in a respectful manner, and, supporting it with both hands, causes it to dance, in cadence, keeping good time with the air of the songs," reads the account, which goes on to say that the leading dancer causes the pipe to "execute many differing figures; sometimes he shows it to the whole assembly, turning himself from one side to the other."[12] In other words, the dance had a narrative quality that filled a considerable length of time.

It is not hard to imagine why Dablon took the trouble to preserve this melody in notation, for it shows a clarity and regularity that lend themselves well to visual representation. The three sections are themselves parallel in certain ways. All begin high and move downward; all seem to take aim on one pitch, which then, through repetition, becomes a tonic resting place for that section; and all, by mixing with three-beat groupings an occasional two-beat pair, achieve a gentle, prose-like rhythm.

In the next century, Native music and musical activity were noticed more and more by people who were neither government nor church officials but were fascinated by Indian ways. One example is found in recollections published in 1775 by James Adair, a Euroamerican who described himself as "a trader with the Indians, and resident in their country for forty years" and called his chronicle *A History of the American Indians, Particularly Those Nations Adjoining to the Mississippi, East and West Florida, Georgia, South and North Carolina, and Virginia* (London, 1775). In one passage, the trader recalls a visit paid him by "an old physician, or prophet" from the Chicasaw nation. And he describes the medicine man's performance in detail, though without the help of musical notation.

> When he came to the door he bowed himself half bent, with his arms extended north and south, continuing so perhaps for the space of a minute. Then raising himself erect, with his arms in the same position, he looked in a wild frightful manner, from the south-west toward the north, and sung on a low bass key *Yo Yo Yo Yo*, almost a minute, then *He He He He*, for perhaps the same space of time, and *Wa Wa Wa Wa*, in like manner; and then transposed, and accented those sacred notes several different ways, in a most rapid guttural manner. Now and then he looked upwards, with his head considerably bent backward;—his song continued about a quarter of an hour.[13]

Knowing from experience that the Indians were "tenacious of concealing their religious mysteries," the writer expressed delight in the prophet's song when he learned its purpose: it was the visitor's way of protecting the trader's house "from the power of the evil spirits of the north, south, and west,—and, from witches, and wizards, who go about in dark nights, in the shape of bears, hogs, and wolves, to spoil people."

A round-the-world voyage during the 1780s produced another example of notated Native music, this one from the other side of the continent. In 1787,

William Beresford's 1787 transcription of this trading song from the Norfolk Sound of Alaska was published in Captain George Dixon's *A Voyage Round the World* (London, 1789).

William Beresford, cargo officer on board the *Queen Charlotte,* a ship commanded by Captain George Dixon, wrote: "I shall here write down, in notes, a song which I often heard whilst we lay in Norfolk Sound" in the northern Pacific near the present site of Sitka, Alaska. "It will serve," Beresford explained, "to convey a better idea of the music used on the American coast than any other mode of description can do; at the same time it should be observed that they have a great variety of tunes, but the method of performing them is universally the same." Beresford claimed that the Natives generally sang this song "previous to commencing trade." His notation specifies independent parts for "the Chief (who always conducts the vocal concert)" and the chorus, in which both men and women sing.

According to Beresford, the chief wore a robe when leading this song and carried a rattle made of sticks to which "great numbers of birds' beaks and dried berries are tied." Through the singing, the chief shook the rattle gleefully, believing that it made "no small addition to the concert." Beresford borrows the terms "stanza" and "chorus" to suggest Western analogies to the song he has transcribed. He also confirms that this performance, like many others described by non-Native observers, lasted a long time.

> Their songs generally consist of several stanzas, to each of which is added a chorus. The beginning of each stanza is given out by the Chief alone, after which both men and women join and sing in octaves, beating time regularly with their hands, or paddles: meanwhile the Chief shakes his rattle, and makes a thousand gesticulations, singing at intervals in different notes from the rest; and this mirth generally continues near half an hour without intermission.[14]

From the eighteenth century too come tales of Indian bravery, registered in "death songs" or "war songs" far different in mood from the high-spirited trading songs of Sitka Sound. The circumstances prompting such songs, documented by James Adair in his *History* and other sources, are grim: a warrior is captured by members of another tribe, subjected to grievous physical torment whose painful effects he defies, and eventually killed. The perpetrators seem to be totally lacking in human goodness. First, they do all they can to prolong their victim's pain: they tie him to a stake, poke and beat him with torches, and then, when suffering and desperation threaten to end their sport, cool him off with water, allowing "a proper time of respite," the trader writes, "till his spirits recover, and he is capable of suffering new tortures." Second, the tormenting of the prisoner is staged as community entertainment, with women and children participating. "Not a soul, of whatever age or sex, manifests the least pity," according to this account. "The women sing with religious joy . . . and peals of laughter resound through the crowded theater—especially if he fears to die." This last comment suggests the custom's only redeeming feature: the spectacle gives the prisoner a chance to show courage. "The suffering warrior," the trader writes, "is not dismayed; with an insulting manly voice he sings the war-song . . . [He] puts on a bold austere countenance, and carries it through all his pains."[15]

The notion of a dying warrior who sings stoically in the face of torture and imminent death struck a responsive chord with some European Americans in the years following the War of Independence. In fact, a parlor song about such a victim, *The Death Song of the Cherokee Indians,* appeared in Royall Tyler's *The Contrast* (1787), the first play by an American-born writer known to have been produced onstage. The song, a thoroughly Europeanized composition with several stanzas of text, each sung to the same music—i.e., a strophic song—was set to a tune claimed by an English source to have originated with the Cherokee tribe.[16] Perhaps its rhythmic repetitiveness made that claim plausible to people unfamiliar with Native music.

As parlor songs are inclined to do, *The Death Song of the Cherokee Indians* removes a real-life event from its original context and idealizes it. The circumstances that brought the warrior to the stake in the first place are never mentioned. Tormentors appear, but they are shadowy figures, unable to provoke a response. For the protagonist, a symbol of superhuman courage rather than a believable human being, transports himself to a world of memory and devotion to duty. Even as the flames rise to consume his body, "the son of Alknomook," maintaining a flow of regular two-bar phrases for four full stanzas, "will never complain."

But the *Death Song* comes not from the Cherokees nor indeed any other Indian tribe. It is a product of European culture, inspired by Native imagery of the good Indian variety. Its appearance in a stage play of 1787, a collection of published songs in 1789, and sheet music from around 1799 is a reminder that by 1800 the new nation called the United States of America had its own means to make and sell cultural products. The Native, or rather the image of the Native, provided material for that industry, as did many other creatures and features of the national landscape.

After long contact with Europeans, much of it violently destructive of Native custom, is it still possible today to find Indian musical traditions that are practiced as they were two or even three centuries ago? For historians, no clear answer exists. But for many Natives, the question is unimportant. As they see it, they are still making the music that was passed on to them by parents and elders, who in turn learned it from generations before them— and they sing, play, and dance for the same reasons. They are engaged in preservation, not of historically significant old songs but of a legacy that connects them to the past and to nature, from which they continue to gain physical and spiritual sustenance.

2

European Inroads

Early Christian Music Making

COMMERCIAL AND RELIGIOUS OUTREACH formed the basis for Europe's settlement of North America. The southern branch of the process was centered in Spain, whose king and queen, hoping to extract riches from far-off lands, sponsored the voyage that sent Christopher Columbus to the Caribbean in 1492. Centuries of conflict with Moorish invaders at home, as well as Spain's occupation of the Canary Islands, had given the Spaniards experience in resettling and administering conquered territories and dealing with colonized peoples. Through their "system of conquest," the Spanish had also learned how to produce goods and deliver them homeward from lands they conquered overseas.

The northern branch of settlement, beginning in the 1530s, took two different forms. Canada, whose early history is closely intertwined with that of the United States, was colonized chiefly as a fur-trading venture under the direction of the French crown. Working with the Roman Catholic Church, which sent Jesuit priests to make Christians of American Natives and minister to white settlers, the French turned the St. Lawrence River and its waterways into a delivery system for a business profitable in Old World markets. But the English, who dominated North American settlement south of Canada, lacked any system of conquering and planting. English colonization from Maine to the Carolinas proved more experimental and tentative than that of the Spanish in the Southwest or the French in Canada.[1]

In any case, North American settlement began an unruly process of give-and-take among three continents that brought the peoples native to each into contact—and conflict. We should resist the temptation to think of American history as something that has happened west of the Atlantic Ocean. For the territory that is now the United States was an extension of European empires. In need of a labor force to extract the "new" continent's riches, entrepreneurs in these nations encouraged their own people to settle there; they also brought slaves from Africa to quicken the pace of exploitation. Though geographically removed, for more than four centuries America has been tied economically, politically, and culturally to the Old World, forming a vast transatlantic arena in which the drama of Western expansion has been played out. That fact looms large in the history of this country's musical life.

For all the violence of the Spanish conquest of the Aztecs in Mexico under Hernando Cortés (1519), the invaders did their work with the blessing of the Roman Catholic Church, whose interest lay chiefly in converting the Natives to Christianity. Thus, the first Christian sacred music to take root on the North American continent was that of the Roman Catholic liturgy, brought by priests attached to Spanish missions in the New World. Once they had established their capital in Mexico City, the Spanish set about creating New Spain as a network of settlements ruled from the capital city, with each town formed around a central plaza on which stood a church or cathedral. And in these churches the population, which gradually came to include more and more *mestizos* (people of mixed blood) as well as Spanish and Indians, came to know the Roman rites of worship.

The Roman Catholic liturgy should be understood, first and foremost, as a system in which worship is largely prescribed. One cycle of prescription organizes the entire liturgical year, a second each week of that year, a third each day of the week. A fourth cycle fixes the details of worship in each service: prayers, Scripture readings, music. The church year revolves around two events in the life of Jesus Christ: his birth (the Advent season, leading to Christmas) and his crucifixion and resurrection (Holy Week, Good Friday, and Easter Sunday). Other feasts and festivals, many of them commemorating particular saints (people recognized as holy by the church), as well as occasions for thanksgiving or penance, take place throughout the year.

The weekly cycle of services culminates on Sunday, the Sabbath. Daily events include the liturgy's chief celebration, the Mass of the Holy Eucharist, and the Divine Office, or "canonical hours," which are services of devotion and prayer observed at various times in the day (e.g., vespers at nightfall). The Eucharist is a ceremony in which bread and wine are consecrated by the officiating priest and shared with the people as an obligation or a thanksgiving to God. Some parts of the Mass are spoken, but others are sung to plainsong (Gregorian chant) melodies—not by the congregation but by the priests who lead the worship, perhaps aided by a choir. Among the sung portions are the Ordinary of the Mass, whose five sections keep the same text in all services, and the Proper, whose words change with the occasion.

To make this tightly prescribed routine of worship as impressive and affecting as possible, the Roman Catholic Church has encouraged public display in many forms. Monumental church architecture, bright images and flashing color from stained glass, priestly vestments, incense, vast spaces within which spoken and sung sound can reverberate—all have been welcomed into the Catholic tradition wherever the means to support them has been found. As a part of that heritage, and in the belief that humankind owes God the highest praise it can offer in religious rituals, the church has favored musical elaboration—especially vocal polyphony (singing in two or more independent voice parts) and the use of an organ or other musical instruments. Polyphonic settings of Mass texts, especially the Ordinary, form the heart of a rich sacred music tradition in Western Christianity from the 1400s on. Finally, it should be noted that until the Vatican Council of 1962–65, the Roman Catholic liturgy was carried on throughout the world in Latin, which helped give it an aura of timeless dignity, not to mention the practical advantage of universality: one liturgy and language for one international church.

By the early 1500s, the Spanish had installed the Roman rite in Mexico and were working to Christianize the Native population. As early as 1528, the Spanish-born Franciscan priest Juan de Padilla was teaching Natives near Mexico City to sing plainsong and to participate in liturgical choral singing. In 1540, as one member of a company headed by the explorer Francisco Vásquez de Coronado, Padilla crossed the Rio Grande into New Mexico and began a similar project among the Moquir Pueblo and Zuñi Indians. (Padilla, most likely the first European to teach music to Native Americans, lost his life in 1542 in a battle between Indian tribes on what are now the Kansas plains.) Less than two decades later, in 1559, the Spanish launched a parallel effort in Florida, where the musician and missionary Pedro Martín de Feria taught Natives near the present city of Pensacola how to sing parts of the liturgy in plainsong.[2]

Such examples of priestly endeavor show that the Roman Catholic Church used sacred music not only to maintain and bolster European settlers' faith but to help acclimate the Natives to white settlers' ways. In Texas and especially the territory that is now New Mexico, where the Spanish installed their hierarchical system of conquest, missions were founded and Natives educated in them to participate fully in the missions' musical life. Alonso de Benavides noted in 1630 the presence of "schools for reading and writing, singing and playing all instruments," and by 1680 some twenty-five missions existed across the Southwest.[3]

In the latter 1700s, the missionary effort spread farther west. In 1769, the Franciscan Junipero Serra, himself a trained musician, began the colonization of southern California as a part of New Spain. By the 1820s, a network of twenty-one missions existed in California. The Roman Catholic liturgy, with appropriate music, was carried on in these settlements until 1833, when the government in Mexico City secularized the missions, sold their lands, and sent the priests back to Spain. By 1846, musical activity in the settlements had ceased. While it lasted, however, music making in the California missions, rooted in plainsong but with plenty of polyphonic singing as well, displayed the variety of a well-established colonial practice. Nor were all the texts sung in the missions restricted to Latin and Spanish. Felipe Arroyo de la Cuesta, one of the Franciscan music masters, produced Mutsun dialect versions of familiar Spanish hymns as part of his effort to bring Native languages into the church's purview.[4]

In a development parallel to that of the Spanish Franciscans in the South and West, French Jesuit priests brought Roman Catholic worship to Canada. But the French never tried to install anything like the network of towns that the Spanish introduced to the South. With its long, harsh winters and rough terrain, the northern land proved far less hospitable to settlement. (Explorer Jacques Cartier called Quebec "the land God gave as his portion to Cain," the biblical figure who killed his brother Abel.)[5] The French in Canada found commercial outposts to be the kind of settlement best suited to their needs. In that arrangement, a trading center in Quebec City served as the chief link to the European market. Agents in France received fox, beaver, and mink furs as products of overseas investment, while in Quebec supervising agents monitored the white and Native trappers who fanned out through the vast, thinly settled Canadian wilderness to do their work.[6] Jesuits followed the trappers' routes, helping to carry the flag of the French king into the heart of North America. And the sacred music they brought added to the Roman Catholic Church's authority, a trait that proved useful in the settlement of New France.

In 1671, for example, French colonial officials traveled to what is now Sault Ste. Marie, Ontario, and staged a ceremony for representatives of fourteen Indian tribes who had gathered for the occasion. A group of Jesuit priests was also there to assist. As Francis Parkman described it, the event's climax came at the moment when an official, "holding his sword in one hand, and raising with the other a sod of earth," claimed for France possession of the local fort, plus "Lakes Huron and Superior, the Island of Manatoulin, and all countries, rivers, lakes, and streams contiguous and adjacent thereunto"—in short, the entire eastern Great Lakes region. The moment had been prepared by the raising of a large wooden cross, to which the French sang Vexilla Regis, a Latin hymn, and a cedar post with an engraved plate bearing the royal arms, accompanied by the singing of another hymn, the Exaudiat.[7] The ceremony seems to have been choreographed as a ritual with two audiences: the God to whom all Christian ritual is addressed and whose blessing the French were seeking on their unmistakably secular endeavor, and the Indians. One can imagine that the hilltop setting, the solemn procession, the raising of the cross, the adding of the French king's insignia to the Christian icon, the singing to consecrate both, and the final cannon blast—all described in Parkman's account—combined to dramatic effect. Given the key place of ceremony, symbolism, and music in the Natives' own religious life, it stands to reason that a rite like this one was intended to convince them that, under supernatural guidance, a godlike French king had indeed taken possession of the land.

If the American Southwest and California reflect the northern reach of New Spain, other places—Detroit, St. Louis, and New Orleans are names bearing a French imprint—serve as a reminder of New France's reach southward from Canada. But as important as both of these Roman Catholic realms were to the history of American development, the first Old World settlers to populate the region that is now the eastern United States were Protestants.

The Protestant Reformation changed the religious, political, and economic face of the West. And the feelings of difference that the Reformation kindled led to the kinds of physical and intellectual conflict implicit in the idea of "religious war": a struggle in which all sides remain convinced of their moral superiority. Sacred music seldom plays more than a small role in any such conflict, but as a prominent part of public worship, it does reflect fundamental ideas of the religious outlook it represents. In breaking with the Roman Catholic Church, Protestants took issue with some key premises upon which Roman worship had been founded. As a result, Protestant sacred music may be seen as a critique of music of the Roman Church.

Two Catholic beliefs that Protestant reformers challenged were the notions that (1) carefully prescribed ritual practices fostered true piety, and (2) God was praised most effectively through sacred expression directed at the senses. Reformers actually split on the role of ritual. In German-speaking states, under Martin Luther's leadership, a set of prescribed rituals, inspired by Roman Catholicism but different from it and conducted in the German language, was codified for the Protestants who came to be known as Lutherans. And in England, where King Henry VIII broke with the church in Rome more over politics than theology, the Anglican liturgy likewise preserved much of the Roman, in translated form. (Since 1786, the Church of England in the United States has been called the Protestant Episcopal Church.) Elsewhere in Europe, however, especially under the leadership of John Calvin, reform went further. Fired by the notion of "the priesthood of all believers," Protestant groups in Switzerland, France, and the Netherlands found prescribed liturgy too restrictive, usurping the power of individuals and congregations to decide such matters for themselves. In the same spirit, Reformed Protestants made the Holy Bible rather than church tradition the central authority for theological practice. Protestants have been credited with advancing the cause of literacy by shifting the right to read and interpret Scripture from the clergy to congregation members. Basic to the Reformed vision was that no human power interpose itself between God and the individual believer.

Reformed Protestants disdained the notion that charming the senses in the name of religion could be pleasing to God, an outlook that deeply influenced the church's musical life. For Calvin and his followers rejected the idea that musical skill was worth cultivating in God's service. Protestants assigned music making to the worshipers themselves: to the congregation. And they found a style of singing suited to the abilities of most members. In view of the Catholic practice that it countered, it is hard to avoid describing Calvinist sacred music in negative terms: no part singing, no instrumental accompaniment, and no singing of texts outside those in the Old Testament Book of Psalms. The Calvinist ideal opposed musical professionalism—a stance that Catholics and "liturgical" Protestants, with their priests, choirs, organs, and fondness for polyphonic elaboration, never took. Many of the English Protestants who settled in North America were driven to immigrate, at least in part, by a desire to worship in an environment where no state church existed. And that helps explain why their favored music symbolized a strain of contrary plainness.

The first Protestants whose music making on this continent left a historical trace were a group of French Huguenots who tried in 1564 to found a colony on the Atlantic coast at Fort Caroline, near where Jacksonville, Florida, stands today. Calvinist doctrine had decreed that the Old Testament psalms be translated into vernacular verse and sung strophically to tunes written for congregational singing. It is likely that the settlers sang from the so-called *Geneva Psalter* (*Les Psaumes mis en rime françoise* [Geneva, 1562]) verses by Clément Marot and Théodore de Bèze to Claude Goudimel's melodies. Florida Indians liked the psalm melodies and continued to sing them years after the Spaniards had massacred the French colonists, as a way of testing strangers to determine whether they were friend (French) or foe.[8]

Sacred music making in America reflected the character of the colonizing process that lay behind it. In contrast to the mission approach of the Spanish and the commercial outpost model of the French—each of which incorporated the Natives into the colonial enterprise—the English eventually arrived in numbers so great that in many places they displaced the Indians, often brutally. That process began only in the 1600s, however. Another early encounter of Protestant psalmody with American Natives took place in California in June 1579, and this time the English were involved. Francis Drake, on a mission to plunder Spanish shipping in the Pacific, had anchored in San Francisco Bay and gone ashore with his men when a party of Indians greeted them. Drake's chaplain described the Natives' reaction to the sailors' worship:

> Our generall with his company in the presence of those strangers fell to prayers. . . . In the time of which prayers, singing of psalms, and reading of certain chapters in the Bible, they sate very attentively; and observing the end of every pause, with one voyce still cryed, oh, greatly rejoycing in our exercises. Yea, they took such pleasure in our singing of psalmes, that whensoever they resorted to us, their first request was commonly this, *Gnaah,* by which they intreated that we should sing.[9]

The Indians' "Gnaah" as an imitation of the way the Englishmen sang has survived through the ages as the first musical joke recorded in America.

PSALMBOOKS IN ENGLISH

Drake's men were Anglicans who carried the church's devotional books on their voyage. They must have sung from *The Whole Booke of Psalmes, Collected into Englishe Meter* (London, 1562), versified by Thomas Sternhold and John Hopkins. Adopted by the Church of England, that book remained its congregational psalter until Nicholas Brady and Nahum Tate produced their *New Version of the Psalms of David* in 1696. Sternhold and Hopkins, known as the *Old Version* after the *New Version* appeared but still used well into the 1700s, was charged during its long reign with many lapses, from poetic inelegance to changing the meaning of Scripture for the sake of rhyme. But perhaps the *Old Version*'s greatest contribution lay in turning the psalms into a form of popular poetry, using some of the same simple verse structures in which secular ballads that circulated in oral tradition were cast. These metrical psalms—the texts in the Old Testament Book of Psalms, versified in English and published together in psalters such as the *Old Version*—were to play a key role in American sacred music making through the seventeenth and eighteenth centuries.

The arrival in 1620 of the Pilgrims, a small band of religious separatists who came ashore in Plymouth, Massachusetts, marks a decisive beginning: the start of this continent's continuous settlement by English-speaking Protestants. Thanks to the Pilgrims' record keeping, and that of the Puritan settlers who soon followed them to Massachusetts, we can trace a history of Protestant sacred singing in New England from that time forward. As Calvinist theology dictated, the early New Englanders' psalmody was spare and plain. And although it was European in origin, it claimed a place in American life and eventually a rootedness in American soil that was never won by the sacred music brought from Spain or France. (The former, centered south of the Rio Grande, petered out by the mid-1800s; and the latter, limited at first chiefly to Gregorian plainsong, belongs more to Canadian than to American music history.) The multinational dimension of American music from its very beginnings must always be kept in mind as a fundamental strain in a widely varied whole. Yet although non-English traditions were here first and have been maintained ever since, the Pilgrims' arrival has often been treated as a founding event, and general historians have framed New England psalm singing as the start of a new kind of indigenous musical life.

The Pilgrims at Plymouth sang from a psalter translated by the Reverend Henry Ainsworth, a separatist clergyman who had brought out *The Book of Psalmes: Englished both in Prose and Metre* in Amsterdam in 1612. Its verses and tunes differed considerably from those of the *Old Version*. Yet the so-called *Ainsworth Psalter* shared several traits with the earlier book. Its pocket size made it easily portable; it printed an unaccompanied tune with each psalm text so that those who read music could sing them directly from the psalter; and the number of different tunes Ainsworth printed (39) was far smaller than the number of psalms in his psalter (150). The first and last of these traits are true of all psalters that circulated in New England from that time forward. Indeed, the reason for the disparity between the number of texts and tunes is a fundamental trait of New England psalmody. Because the psalms were cast in standard verse forms, or meters, worshipers could sing many texts to the same tune, proving that music *as an art* played only a secondary role in psalm singing. To those who study music history, the beginnings of New England psalmody mark an early step in music's emergence as an autonomous art on these shores. Yet the settlers themselves would probably have considered it strange that the *musical* portion of their psalmody would some day be singled out for study and comment. For them, psalm singing was first and foremost a way for members of society to praise, glorify, and beg forgiveness from a just, stern, almighty God.

The tunes in Ainsworth's psalter include OLD HUNDRED, also found in the Church of England's *Old Version* and many English and American sacred tunebooks since. OLD HUNDRED traces its origin back to the 1560s and early French Calvinist psalm singing.[10] It was surely melodies like this one that Ainsworth had in mind when he reported, in the introduction to his work, that he had included "the gravest and easiest tunes of the French and Dutch Psalms." For OLD HUNDRED is brief and straightforward enough to be perfect congregational fare, as shown by its continued use in Protestant worship today as the Doxology.

No element is more basic to Western music than melody, and some four and a half centuries of hard, continuous use mark OLD HUNDRED as a good

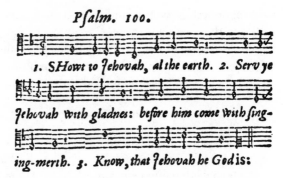

Pſalm. 100.

1. SHowt to Jehovah, al the earth. 2. Serv ye

The psalm tune OLD HUN-
DRED, first published in
Geneva in 1561, supplied the
music for Henry Ainsworth's
version of Psalm 100 in 1612.

Jehovah with gladnes: before him come with ſing-

ing-merth. 3. Know, that Jehovah he God is:

one. As we can see in the example, the melody contains four phrases of
equal length. The phrases' shapes differ, but their rhythm is almost identical, stamping the whole with a unity that singers have been quick to grasp.
The melodic structure of OLD HUNDRED is neatly balanced between con-
junct (stepwise) and disjunct motion (skipping to a note other than adjacent
ones), and between melodic rise and fall. Most of the movement from note
to note is stepwise. But in each phrase at least one skip occurs: a rising
fourth in the first two phrases and a falling third in the next. The last
phrase, however, contains three skips of a third, two falling and one rising.
And it begins with an upward leap of a fifth—the largest leap of the piece,
and to the melody's highest note—while the earlier phrases start either on
the same note as their predecessor or one step away. Thus, the last phrase,
by far the most active, serves as a climax. Each phrase starts off in one direction, then circles back on itself. The upward leap of a fifth beginning the
last phrase feels like a bold gesture, but not for long.

The simplicity of OLD HUNDRED is not typical of the tunes in Ainsworth's
psalter. Indeed, the rhythmic trickiness of the melodies as a group mark the
original Pilgrims as accomplished singers, confirming a later comment by
one that "many of the Congregation [were] very expert in Musick." In fact,
when the congregation in Salem, Massachusetts, voted in 1667 to give up
Ainsworth, they cited "the difficulty of the tunes," as did the Plymouth congregation itself in 1685.[11]

Early New Englanders were more troubled by the psalters' faulty translations of the texts. As the Reverend Cotton Mather wrote: "They beheld in
the translation, variations of, not only the text, but the very sense of the
Psalmist."[12] Intent on following God's word faithfully, a group of clergymen
from the Massachusetts Bay Colony collaborated on a new psalter that
would more closely mirror the scriptural originals. Published as *The Whole
Booke of Psalmes Faithfully Translated into English Metre* (Cambridge,
Mass., 1640), the so-called *Bay Psalm Book* was the first full-length book
printed in the English-speaking colonies. Reprinted often thereafter, this

work supplied New England's congregations with texts for psalm singing well into the next century.

A comparison of the prose beginning of Psalm 23 in the *King James Bible* with the versified form of the same psalm in the *Bay Psalm Book* will help to show how metrical psalmody works in practice.

King James Version	Bay Psalm Book (1651 edition)

The Lord is my shepherd;
  I shall not want.
	The Lord to me a sheperd is
	  Want therefore shall not I.

He maketh me to lie down
  in green pastures;
	He in the folds of tender grass
	  Doth make me down to lie.

He leadeth me beside the still
  waters;
He restoreth my soul.
He leadeth me in the paths of
  righteousness
  for his name's sake.
	He leads me to the waters
	  still;
	  Restore my soul doth he;
	In paths of righteousness,
	  he will
	  For his name's sake lead me.

The *Bay Psalm Book*'s translators, following the example of Sternhold and Hopkins, Ainsworth, and others, set the psalm in four-line stanzas so that it could be sung strophically: with all stanzas of text sung to the same music. (Psalm 23 fills five stanzas in the *Bay Psalm Book* version.) Taking the iambic foot as an accent pattern (short-long, the favored pattern of English verse), the translators also built their stanzas from lines alternating eight and six syllables, a structure familiar enough in English poetics to be called "common meter" and sometimes "ballad meter" (8.6.8.6.). Other verse patterns the new psalter emphasized were "long meter" (8.8.8.8.), the form followed by Old Hundred, and "short meter" (6.6.8.6.).

The *Bay Psalm Book*'s translators placed a high priority on simplifying psalmody for New England congregations. In that spirit, they cast 125 of the 150 psalms in common meter, adding 14 more in long meter and another 8 in short meter. Consequently, all but 3 psalms in the entire psalter could be sung to tunes in one of those three meters.[13] A congregation singing from the *Bay Psalm Book* would therefore need to know only a few tunes—far fewer than the thirty-nine in *Ainsworth,* for example. Although no authority of the time recommended it, in fact the whole *Bay Psalm Book* could be sung to just five different tunes, provided the texts were matched with tunes of the right meters. These numbers point to two conclusions about psalm singing in seventeenth-century New England. First, the tunes of the *Bay Psalm Book* were chosen not to underline the meaning of the words but to provide a musical vehicle for their delivery. And second, the shrinking of the stock of tunes shows that for the Reformed Protestants who settled New England, musical skill was not a high priority.

Psalters like the *Old Version, Ainsworth,* and the *Bay Psalm Book* had been published to serve literate worshipers, equipped to read the Scriptures and ponder their meanings. It was logical for such people to own these devotional books and to sing from them in public worship. But by the 1640s in New England, psalm singing in some congregations required only one singer to have a book. That leading singer (sometimes called the deacon or precentor) would read the psalm, line by line, to the congregation, who would then sing each line back in alternation with the leader. Whether congregations began lining-out, as this practice came to be called, because too few worshipers could read the psalms, buy the books, or sing the tunes as they were written, the custom won acceptance as the clergy realized that without it there would be no congregational singing at all. In 1647, the Reverend John Cotton noted: "Where all have books and can reade, or else can say the Psalm by heart, it were needlesse there to reade each line of the Psalm before hand in order to [sing]." But, he continued, the Scriptures make congregational psalm singing a duty for Christians, not an option; that fact sanctioned the custom of lining-out in cases where people lacked "either books or skill to reade."[14]

Lining-out began, then, as a way of cueing congregation members on the texts they were to sing. Its impact on psalmody was enormous. Lining-out slowed the pace of singing greatly. It also ensured that only tunes the worshipers already knew would be sung, which kept the tune repertory small. In addition, rather than being written down for worshipers, as in the *Old Version* and *Ainsworth,* the music was entrusted to leading singers, each with his own idea about how the tunes should be sung. As one observer of the time wrote, a tune might vary so much from congregation to congregation that " 'tis hard to find Two that Sing [it] exactly alike."[15] Lining-out, with its slow, elastic tempo and tiny stock of melodies, gave birth to a singing style that emphasized melodic elaboration sung full-voice: a style that, eventually labeled "the Old Way" of singing, won the allegiance of many New England worshipers.

But by 1720, some New Englanders were complaining that the lined-out style of congregational singing had fallen away from the Puritan fathers' psalmody, which had been governed by the "rule" of musical notation. The Reverend Thomas Symmes described the process as a giving way to an oral tradition:

> Singing-Books being laid aside, there was no Way to learn; but only by hearing of Tunes Sung, or by taking the Run of the Tune (as it is phrased). The Rules of Singing not being taught or learnt, every one sang as best pleased

himself, and every Leading-Singer would take the Liberty of raising any Note of the Tune, or lowering of it, as best pleas'd his Ear, and add such Turns and Flourishes as were grateful to him; and this was done so gradually, as that but few if any took Notice of it. One Clerk or Chorister would alter the Tunes a little in his Day, the next, a little in his and so one after another, till in Fifty or Sixty Years it caus'd a Considerable Alteration.[16]

Symmes's words appear in a lecture recommending that "Regular Singing," which carried the authority of notated music, replace the mode of singing he described. But they also show that he understood why people enjoyed singing the way they did. In the Old Way, rather than joining others in vocal lockstep, all parishioners were empowered with the freedom—within limits, of course—to praise God in their own musical fashion.

The clergy's objection to the Old Way of singing in and around Boston inspired a burst of rhetoric on the subject: sermons, pamphlets, newspaper accounts, and Regular Singing meetings. But unlike most theological battles of the time, virtually all the published words came from one side only: that of the Regular Singing advocates, chiefly ministers in opposition to a custom of worship that had slipped out of their control. Singers committed to the Old Way made no attempt to justify themselves in writing; they simply continued singing their usual way. In the meantime, the champions of Regular Singing argued that its discipline, order, and solemnity would help to make public worship more pleasing in the sight of God. Following the custom for Puritan ministers of the time, they supported their reasoned opinions with references to the Bible.

In their zeal to discredit Old Way singing, Regular Singing advocates sometimes took a scornful tone:

> Where there is no Rule, Men's Fancies (by which they are govern'd) are various; some affect a Quavering Flourish on one Note, and others upon another which (because they are Ignorant of true Musick or Melody) they account a Grace to the Tune; and while some affect a quicker Motion, others affect a slower, and drawl out their Notes beyond all Reason; hence in Congregations ensue Jarrs & Discords, which make the Singing (rather) resemble Howling.[17]

One Regular Singing advocate went so far as to warn in 1724 that the sound of lining-out could be dangerous to pregnant women. "I am credibly inform'd," he wrote, "that a certain Gentlewoman miscarry'd at the ungrateful and yelling Noise of a Deacon in reading the first Line of a Psalm; and methinks if there were no other Argument against this Practice . . . the Consideration of it's being a Procurer of Abortion, might prevail with us to lay it aside."[18]

For all the criticisms of the Old Way of singing, however, one positive description stands out, though it was written long after the controversy peaked. Published in 1853, the account recollects singing that its author had heard as a boy growing up in the 1780s and 90s, a memory that fits with both earlier accounts of the Old Way and twentieth-century recordings of congregations lining-out hymns. It also carries musical specifics of a kind found in few such descriptions. The author, Nathaniel Duren Gould, was both a knowledgeable musician with more than half a century of experience as a singing-school teacher and an observer with no particular ax to grind concerning the Old Way. By the 1780s, Regular Singing had long been established in New England; musical literacy was relatively widespread. The Old Way survived, but chiefly in the hinterlands and as an old-fashioned practice. Unlike the accounts that came out of the Regular Singing controversy, Gould's statement grants the power that Old Way singing could pack. Gould, who taught his first singing school before 1800, never quite got over hearing in his youth the Old Way of singing God's praise:

> Our memory carries us back some sixty years, to the days of genuine old-style singing,—the days when old St. Ann's, and St. Martin's, and a few similar tunes, were the only ones sung, and when singing schools and singing books were almost unknown. In imagination we recall the sound, as it impressed us in the days of childhood; and we wish that terms were in existence to convey an idea of the tone and manner. Their voices were tremendous in power, issuing from ample chests and lungs, invigorated by hard labor and simple food, and unrestrained by dress. They commenced a note in a cautious and proper manner, carefully swelling it, and with the swell shaking note and word to atoms; and so on from note to note, or word to word. It was no insignificant, tremulous voice, but grand, majestic and heart-stirring; and, when applied to such tunes as Old Hundred, Mear and Canterbury, everything around seemed to tremble.[19]

Gould's words invite a consideration of the Old Way from a point of view far removed from that of the Regular Singing advocates. First he connects the power of the singers' voices to their rugged way of life. Then he describes the style in which they sang, in a tone of respect, even awe. It is as if he is telling his readers, "There were giants in the land." Gould's Old Way singers have been toughened by lives of physical hardship and toil. When they worship God, they reach for a state of mind holding little in common with everyday human interaction. They sing God's praise with a physical force akin to plowing a field, or pulling a stump, or getting through a cold, hard winter. They are single-minded and without self-consciousness. Their voices pour out full-bore, giving each note its own unhurried elaboration.

Gould's singers fix their gaze on the infinite. To borrow a phrase that composer Charles Ives once used to describe the camp-meeting singing of his youth, they sing "as the rocks were grown."

When viewed as a conflict pitting the clergy against the people, rules against customs, and control against freedom, the Regular Singing controversy stands as a colorful, even emblematic episode in New England's cultural history. But in the history of American music, the controversy's outcome is more than that. For it touched off a process of singing reform that was to reshape New England psalmody through the rest of the eighteenth century. The movement toward Regular Singing brought about the formation of singing schools: instructional sessions, usually lasting two or three months, devoted to teaching the rudiments of singing and note reading, with a focus on sacred music. Organized to improve the quality of congregational singing, such schools brought with them the need for instructional materials, and in the 1720s tunebooks began to be published in New England designed for singing-school use. Moreover, singing schools needed teachers. As Americans with some musical skill began to set up singing schools of their own, a fragile institution was founded to support musical professionalism—the first chance for native-born musicians on these shores to earn a living through music. With the wider dissemination of musical learning also came a taste for music more elaborate than unharmonized psalm tunes. By the 1750s, choirs were forming to sing such music in public worship. And by the 1770s, Americans had begun to compose some of the music these choirs were singing.

3

From Ritual to Art

The Flowering of Sacred Music

THE ACT OF JUDGING lies at the heart of Puritanism, in that Puritans, especially in religious matters, follow a moral code stricter than society's prevailing one. Puritanism originated within the Church of England. The term had its beginnings before 1600 as a pejorative label, then became the name of a movement that sparked religious separatism, seized political power, and ruled England during the Commonwealth period. Many of the English who emigrated to North America beginning in the 1620s did so in hopes of finding a form of Christian worship "purer" than what they had left behind. In New England, Puritans mostly followed the strict tenets of Reformed Protestantism, establishing cities and towns in which religious observances and attitudes were built in to the law.

From a modern and secular perspective, the Puritan emphasis on judging has won little sympathy. Today the term is perhaps most often used to signify self-righteous joylessness; H. L. Mencken, for example, defined Puritanism as "the haunting fear that someone, somewhere, may be happy." But we can best understand Puritans' actions by understanding their core belief: human beings are inherently sinful creatures living in a world created by an all-virtuous God. Puritan spirituality, fueled by a perpetual burning desire to be better, sought to narrow this gap. True Puritans, however harsh their judgments of others, were at least as hard on themselves, for they practiced constant self-examination and refused to deny or excuse the selfishness, lust, and mendacity they discovered behind their own thoughts and deeds.

To follow Puritan tenets demanded that one strive, intellectually and morally, toward a goal that could only be achieved through the passive acceptance of the Holy Spirit—*if*, that is, God chose to reward the sinner's effort with such a visitation. Effort was necessary but by no means sufficient for spiritual grace. In their quest to connect the tangible with the unseen world—to learn when to struggle and when to stop struggling against innate corruption—Puritans therefore lived their lives in search of a delicate balance. They understood human existence as part of an epic confrontation between good and evil that stretched from Creation to eternity. For them, the spiritual stakes were always high.

Puritanism provided the theological context for the Regular Singing controversy. In fact, that controversy is probably best understood as one of the religious debates that punctuated early New England life. One participant was Cotton Mather, a leading American intellectual of his time, who published a tract on the subject: *The Accomplished Singer . . . Intended for the assistance of all that sing psalms with grace in their hearts: but more particularly to accompany the laudable endeavour of those who are learning to sing by Rule, and seeking to preserve a Regular Singing in the Assemblies of the Faithful* (Boston, 1721). Mather's analysis reflects the values of Puritan sacred music making. For example, his reminder of why Calvinist tradition favors biblical texts testifies to the dominance of words over music. New sacred verses, he believes, should not replace divinely inspired ones merely because they are more up-to-date. He grants the possible merits of "devout hymns composed by the good men of our own time," but they cannot match "the songs which are prepared for us by the Holy Spirit of God."[1]

Another passage shows how the singing of divinely inspired texts can quicken the consciousness and kindle religious ecstasy. Mather writes of worshipers who seek through singing to achieve a state of oneness with the spirit of those "thro' whom our *spiritual songs* were convey'd unto us" in the first place. When we sing in public worship, Mather counsels, "let us be Inquisitive after those *Motions of Piety*, which are discernible in the Verse now before us." Divine inspiration gives these texts special power, represented by the image of flight: "Let us with a Soul flying away to God," he writes, "try whether we cannot fly *with* them . . . till we feel our selves come into an Holy *Symphony* with the Saints who had their *Hearts burning* within them, when they *sang* these things unto the Lord." Psalm singing was a form of prayer that could lead to rapturous experience: "Behold a lovely Method of getting into those Heavenly *Frames* & *strains* which will assure thee of . . . arriving one Day, to the same state of Blessedness, and those *Everlasting Habitations*, [with] these *Favourites* and *Amanuenses* of Heaven."[2] Rapture was to be reached by contemplating the words while singing them, and heaven's saintly "favourites" were those who first brought these sacred words into human use as God's secretaries.

It might seem that the attitude of almost trance-like absorption achieved by some Old Way singers would lead to the kind of ecstatic flight that Mather's words suggest. But for Mather and his fellow ministers, Regular Singing offered a surer path. The disciplined singing of a sacred text by a congregation of worshipers, they believed, would be pleasing in God's sight. Only a thorough reform of congregational psalmody could produce that result, for an intelligible delivery of verses demanded an approach to singing different from the Old Way. And indeed, reform began in earnest around 1720. Two developments particularly served its cause: psalm tunes were published in fixed, standard versions to protect them from the whim of oral transmission, and instruction in singing these tunes became available to congregation members. As one group of reformers put it, "skilfulness in singing psalms is an acquired gift," adding with irony that "many thousands have attained it, by the Divine Blessing" of learning to sing them.[3]

The publishing of psalm tunes was nothing new to the English-speaking colonies; beginning with the ninth edition (1698), the *Bay Psalm Book* had carried a small appendix of tunes.[4] What *was* new was the format in which published tunes appeared. In 1721, two publications emphasizing sacred *music* over sacred verses were issued, including not only the tunes but instructions on how to sing them. The titles reveal their purpose: John Tufts's

John Tufts's *Introduction*, here in its fifth edition (1726), was an instructional manual with psalm tunes harmonized for three voices.

An Introduction to the Singing of Psalm Tunes,[5] and Thomas Walter's *The Grounds and Rules of Musick, Explained.* Both were published in Boston. And both, together with the small collection of standard tunes they carried, began with an introduction explaining the rudiments of singing: how to use one's voice in the practice of congregational psalmody, including an explanation of the symbols in which the psalm tunes were written.

The publication of Walter's *Grounds and Rules* and Tufts's *Introduction* began a new era in American music history: between them they formed a point of contact between music as an art with a technical basis and a public motivated to learn that technique. Those who aspired to learn could now turn to the singing school, the chief agent of musical reform. As early as 1714, one James Ivers opened a "Boarding School" in Boston in which he offered to teach "Embroidery, and all Sorts of Needle-Work . . . Painting upon Glass, Writing, Arithmetick, and Singing Psalm Tunes."[6] In his essay of 1720, the Reverend Thomas Symmes outlined a more collective approach. Would it not greatly promote the singing of psalms, Symmes asked, if singing *schools* were formed? "Where would be the Difficulty, or what the Disadvantages, if People that want Skill in Singing, would procure a Skillful Person to Instruct them, and meet Two or Three Evenings in the Week, from Five or six a Clock, to Eight, and spend the Time in Learning to Sing?"[7]

Symmes's questions sketch the chief traits of what came to be a major American musical institution of the eighteenth and nineteenth centuries. The earmarks of the later American singing school are here, including its makeshift quality: aimed at beginners, taught in the evenings to avoid conflict with daily work routines, and, though unspecified by Symmes, brief in duration—three months (a "quarter") was typical—and held in any available space. Temporariness is also suggested by the way Symmes characterized the singing master: not a clergyman but a musical person, perhaps recruited by aspiring singers or perhaps deciding on his own to organize a school and advertise for scholars. Moreover, these comments point to another truth sometimes forgotten. The singing school, although growing out of the church's needs, was from the start a social institution distinct from the church.

By the early 1720s, then, the elements of a more disciplined psalmody had been introduced in and around Boston. The story told in most histories from this point traces a pattern of progress: from singing schools to Regular Singing in public worship, to note reading, to the forming of choirs. The inference is that in communities all over New England, such local endeavors merged into a regional trend, crowned eventually by the appearance of native-born psalmodists who were also composers, so that by the 1780s

Americans had a repertory of American music to sing. It is true that in some congregations reform went smoothly. Certain members, perhaps inspired by a "singing meeting" or a sermon preached on the subject, decided to give Regular Singing a try; a singing school was formed; after learning to sing "according to rule," and perhaps demonstrating their skill in public, they persuaded other church members of its superiority; and finally the congregation voted to discard the Old Way and adopt Regular Singing.

In other communities, however, years or even decades went by before Regular Singing was accepted. The rocky path faced by its advocates may owe as much to a democratic form of church government as to Puritan theology, since Reformed Calvinism required no popes or bishops to hand down decrees; instead, each congregation made its own policies. Like other matters of worship, questions about congregational singing were put to a vote of church members, and the majority ruled. Some of the battles fought over Regular Singing were surely sparked more by social issues than musical ones. In Farmington, Connecticut, for example, the congregation in 1727 upheld local independence by voting down Regular Singing as a practice "recommended by the Reverend Ministers of Boston."[8] Moreover, singing schools themselves were acknowledged as social gatherings, providing a rare chance for boys and girls to mingle.

Proponents boosted schools for offering "innocent and profitable Recreation" that would help young New Englanders "to improve the long Winter-Evenings," weaning them away from "Idle, Foolish, yea, pernicious Songs and Ballads," banishing "all such Trash from their Minds." In the view of others, however, schools encouraged youngsters to be "too light, profane and airy," and to "tarry out a Night Disorderly."[9] That those fears were partly justified is shown by a letter written in 1782 to a friend by a Yale undergraduate who seemed to be parodying Goethe's *The Sorrows of Young Werther* (1774), a novel whose sentimental strain was widely admired by youths of the time. "At present," he claimed, "I have no Inclination for anything, for I am almost sick of the World & were it not for the Hopes of going to singing-meeting tonight & indulging myself a little in some of the carnal Delights of the Flesh, such as kissing, squeezing &c. &c. I should willingly leave it now, before 10 o'clock & exchange it for a better."[10]

A comment like this one points to another cause of the Regular Singing controversy. Many who opposed it saw Regular Singing as a secular intrusion into a sacred realm. Walter's book, for example, by explaining the technique of note reading and inviting New Englanders to learn it, introduced a skill that could encompass any music a literate singer might choose, including secular songs. In a theological setting where music's only sanctioned role was to support a congregation's singing of sacred words, some wor-

The title page of Oliver Brownson's *Select Harmony* (Hartford, 1783) shows choir members in a church gallery.

shipers took any emphasis on music itself as a sign of secular influence. The difficulty encountered by Regular Singing reflects a determined resistance to changing a sacred practice.

As the later history of New England sacred music will show, the clergy eventually had cause to regret the course that psalmody took in the latter 1700s. Having endorsed elementary musical learning as a way to gain control over that part of worship, they discovered that Regular Singing led to other changes: the growth of musical literacy, the formation of choirs, and the fostering of independent musical taste. The impact of musical literacy on psalmody eventually carried it as far beyond the clergy's control as had the Old Way of singing.

Singing schools, which taught worshipers the standard psalm tunes and enough about vocal performance to improve the quality of congregational singing, proved so popular that by the 1760s they were becoming a widespread institution in the colonies. And by then, too, another organization devoted to singing, and one new to Calvinist worship in America, had also begun to appear: the meeting-house choir. Indications are that early choirs in New England were formed not at the prompting of clergy or congregation but by the singers themselves. For some, singing schools sparked a wish to sing in a choir. At the end of a singing school session, some of the "scholars" continued singing as a group, sharpening their vocal skills, improving their grasp of musical notation, and performing music that was more challenging than the standard psalm tunes. The singers might then petition for the right to sit together and perhaps to sing separately during public worship. Sometimes their petition was denied, for resistance to any change in worship could be strong, and seating in many New England meeting houses was hierarchical, with seats assigned according to one's standing in the community. Eventually, however, "singers' seats" were designated and the choir invited to sing during the worship service.

Choirs brought new energy and musical diversity to the meeting house. But almost from the moment of their appearance, they also became the targets of complaints, chiefly about the attitude of choir members, which some parishioners found secular and obnoxious. Nathaniel D. Gould's 1853 chronicle of church music offers a vivid account of early New England choirs. Drawing on nearly six decades of personal experience, his comments show that choirs provided for those who sang in them a chance to claim status through musical ability. Such subheadings as "Highest Seats" and "Caste among Singers" point to choirs as hotbeds of social climbing. In Gould's view, sacred music proved vulnerable in meeting-house choirs to corruption for worldly ends, because human nature stood at odds with its proper use. Tippling teachers and singers, choristers who slept through sermons, parishioners who criticized the choir's singing, and—after instruments were accepted in worship—viol players who tuned at distracting length were all characters for whom psalmody had turned into human display drained of sacred content.[11]

Other accounts square with Gould's interpretation. As early as 1764, an observer had already noted the prideful conduct of choir members, referring to one such group in Boston as "a set of Geniuses who stick themselves up in a Gallery." This correspondent went on to observe that the singers "seem to think that they have a Priviledge of engrossing all the singing to themselves . . . by singing such Tunes, as is impossible for the Congregation to join in." Unchecked by sacred or communal purpose, they were most interested in displaying their skill as musicians. Thus, they considered "those plain and easy Compositions" that the congregation sang far too simple, favoring tunes that were more modern, elaborate, and lacking in solemnity. The writer seems to be describing a fugue when he writes of the choir's performance: "Away they get off, one after another, in a light, airy, jiggish Tune, better adapted to a Country Dance, than the . . . Business of Chanting forth the Praises of the King of Kings."[12] Here, then, choir and congregation competed rather than complementing each other. Once musical display won a toehold in the worship service, it took its own course with little regard for the religious framework that had fostered it in the first place.

In view of the long history of singing in New England meeting houses, it may seem strange that the first American tunebook to address the needs of both congregation and choir was published in Philadelphia, where no similar history has been discovered. That collection was *Urania, or A Choice Collection of Psalm-Tunes, Anthems, and Hymns*, compiled in 1761 by James Lyon, a Presbyterian born in Newark, New Jersey, and a recent graduate of the College of New Jersey (Princeton). With its 198 pages of music—chiefly English but also boasting a few new compositions by Americans—*Urania* dwarfed in size every tunebook previously published on American shores. One resourceful Presbyterian in Philadelphia, apparently working on his own, managed to bring out a sacred tunebook more wide-ranging and ambitious by far than any book that forty years of Regular Singing in Boston had been able to inspire.

Philadelphia was the English-speaking colonies' largest city, a dynamic settlement that grew steadily larger, unlike Boston, whose population remained the same from the 1740s to 1775. The religious culture of Philadelphia was also more tolerant and more diverse than Boston's, with substantial numbers of Anglicans, Lutherans, Methodists, Baptists, Roman Catholics, and Quakers as well as Reformed Calvinist "dissenters," including Lyon himself. When Thomas Walter's *Grounds and Rules* had appeared in Boston four decades earlier, an array of well-known ministers publicly declared support. Lyon's book received no such official endorsement; but in the marketplace Philadelphia offered in 1761, none was needed. The key to bringing *Urania* before the public lay in subscription, a business practice designed to scout the public for customers.

A standard practice of the Anglo-American book trade, subscription

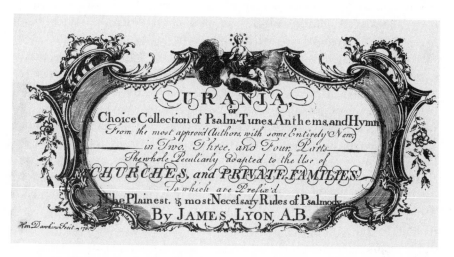

Henry Dawkins engraved this elaborate title page for James Lyon's *Urania* (Philadelphia, 1761).

allowed authors or publishers to propose a work for publication without a heavy investment of their own money. To enroll subscribers, a publisher would offer copies of the book to people willing to buy before publication, at a cost lower than the expected retail price. If enough subscribers could be found, the work would then be printed. We may therefore imagine a possible scenario for *Urania*'s publication. Lyon finished his studies at Princeton in 1759, moved to Philadelphia, and started a singing school there. Finding English tunebooks inadequate, he decided to compile one of his own. Borrowing freely from English collections, he also added a few pieces by local composers, including himself. He then went to work recruiting subscribers, and he arranged for the engraving, printing, binding, and distribution of his tunebook. By June 1762, Philadelphia newspapers were advertising *Urania* for sale.

James Lyon's bold act of entrepreneurship and imagination lie behind this landmark of American music history. Not only did Lyon use commercial means to sell his book—he had compiled a collection designed for broad appeal. For *Urania*'s musical contents offered something for every kind of sacred singer: standard psalm tunes, left textless so that worshipers of any denomination could sing them to their preferred psalter; lots of choir music (including elaborate psalm tunes, through-composed anthems, and set pieces); and some hymn tunes with full texts, apparently geared to home performance, as suggested on the title page: "adapted to the Use of Churches, and Private Families." *Urania* was the first American tunebook to bring psalmody straight into the commercial arena, depending for its genesis and circulation on subscription, advertising, and tailoring its contents to attract customers. From a Puritan perspective, the process bears a distinctly secular flavor. But in Philadelphia around 1760, the Puritan perspective carried no great weight. *Urania* showed how psalmody, a mode of sacred expression, could find a niche in the marketplace. Once Lyon produced and marketed such a tunebook, other compilers began to follow his example.

The absence in New England of any effort parallel to Lyon's suggests how small a role musical learning, as opposed to religious custom, had so far played in the tradition of psalmody. But that would soon change. By the 1760s, singing schools and Regular Singing were finally helping to spread musical literacy and feed interest in more elaborate sacred music throughout the region, as suggested by the roster of church choirs formed in New England after mid-century, especially in Massachusetts. Boston's First Church formed a choir by 1758, followed by many others through the next decade.[13] The notion that some kinds of sacred singing were better left to good singers cropped up even in military ranks. Caleb Rea, a surgeon serving with a Massachusetts regiment in the French and Indian War in 1758 at Fort Frontenac, Ontario, recorded in his diary some observations about the

religious services held for the soldiers. "In his zeal," historian Francis Parkman wrote, Rea "made an inquest among them for singers, and chose the
most melodious to form a regimental choir, 'the better to carry on the daily
service of singing psalms.'" which made "the New England camp . . . vocal
with rustic harmony."[14]

WILLIAM BILLINGS, AMERICAN COMPOSER

In 1770, a young Boston tanner and singing master produced a tunebook
reflecting the vitality that had begun to flow into New England sacred music as Puritan restrictions fell away, music literacy spread, and attitudes
once thought secular grew more acceptable. *The New-England Psalm-
Singer: or, American Chorister*, by William Billings, is a true landmark.
Shorter than Lyon's *Urania*, it still came close to matching that book's variety, with everything from plain congregational tunes to long anthems, able
to tax the skill of any American choir. In musical content, however, the originality of Billings's book far outstripped Lyon's. Containing 127 compositions, all by Billings himself, *The New-England Psalm-Singer* was the first
published compilation of entirely American music and the first American
tunebook devoted wholly to the music of one composer. With its appearance,

Paul Revere's frontispiece for William Billings's *The New-England Psalm-Singer*
(Boston, 1770) encircles a picture of seven singers with a canonic composition: a sacred text apparently performed on a social occasion.

the number of American sacred compositions in print increased tenfold. As Billings's title signified, a region that had long fostered psalmody in the colonies was reclaiming leadership in sacred music.

From a musical and economic point of view, *The New-England Psalm-Singer* traces its origins to the singing schools, which led in turn to the forming of choirs in the 1760s. Both singing schools and choirs supplied customers for Billings's book. But such events in psalmody were themselves symptoms of larger changes in New England culture. By 1770, Boston, if less dynamic than Philadelphia, was also less fixed on theology than it had once been. Almost fifty years earlier, Bostonians had already begun to discuss the state of New England society in financial, political, and social as well as moral terms.[15] The influence of Puritanism may have persisted, but by the time *The New-England Psalm-Singer* appeared in print, the region's moral purpose had found a new focus: resistance to Britain's rule of her American colonies.

The state of mind that led in 1775 to war with England could not have been predicted a dozen years earlier. For in 1763, when the Treaty of Paris put an official end to the French and Indian War, many colonists shared a feeling of pride in a hard-won Anglo-American victory. With the French and Spanish withdrawn from North America, colonial leaders believed, westward expansion could proceed apace. Some even expected more autonomy for the colonies. The British, too, looked for a new relationship with this fast-growing, prosperous part of their empire. But while the Americans saw the departure of the French and Spanish as an opening of fresh new opportunities, British officials regarded the colonies as a source of new obligations—a region needing tighter controls. With the war over, the time had come to reap the rewards of empire, bringing back to England a higher financial return on overseas investments. The first of Parliament's revenue-raising measures—the Stamp Act of 1764, which increased taxes and duties on imports and exports in hopes of enriching the British treasury—began a cycle of escalating grievances. Misunderstandings multiplied. What seemed to the British reasonable steps to govern their colonies some Americans received as impositions of external authority. Such responses brought stronger displays of power from the British. Positions gradually hardened, and extremists took over leadership on both sides.[16]

Boston became the focus of new unrest in 1768 when customs commissioners requested an armed guard to protect them as they performed their duties. British troops arrived in April—the first such military force to be used against citizens of a British American colony. Although an uneasy peace was maintained, some Bostonians viewed the soldiers as an army of occupation. The Boston Massacre of 1770, where British soldiers fired into an unruly mob and killed five colonists, was one of several incidents that inflamed public opinion. Through the years that followed, conflict continued to simmer as the British troops remained. The American public split into factions: "loyalists" who accepted England's right to rule her colonies as she chose, and "patriots" antagonistic toward British rule. In April 1775, war broke out in Massachusetts between the British soldiers and local minutemen. When the smoke finally cleared in 1781, the colonies had won independence.

The New-England Psalm-Singer bore the stamp of its time and place. Unlike Lyon's *Urania,* which broadened British psalmody to include the colonies, Billings's book struck an aggressively American note. In fact, this book and Billings's next, *The Singing Master's Assistant* (1778), must have caught the notice of singers with their local, topical, and personal references. The titles of many tunes, for example, refer to Boston and the surrounding area, including Massachusetts counties (MIDDLESEX, SUFFOLK), cities and towns (AMHERST, HAVERHILL, WALTHAM), and Boston churches (NEW SOUTH, OLD BRICK) and thoroughfares (ORANGE STREET, PURCHASE STREET). Even some of the nongeographical titles carry a topical ring: FREEDOM, LIBERTY, UNION.

Perhaps even more unusual was the persona that Billings offered his readers. Not only did he present his own music, but, in a breezy, confiding author's voice, he took readers through a range of topics, from the rudiments of music to his own philosophy of composing. In contrast to earlier American compilers, Billings doffed the masks of piety and pedagogy, approaching the public as a man of Boston and a musician of the New World, aware of his audaciousness and even willing to share some of his doubts with readers.

Born in Boston in 1746, Billings had attended school only briefly before learning the tanner's trade. As a musician, he seems to have been self-taught. By age twenty-three, he was teaching singing schools, an activity he pursued through much of his life. He also held municipal posts, though not prestigious ones. During the 1780s, he served as Sealer of Leather for the city of Boston, as well as scavenger (street cleaner) and hog reeve (official in charge of controlling roving swine). Billings struggled financially in his later years. The publication of his last tunebook in 1794 was sponsored by local singers as an act of charity toward him and his family.

Billings seems to have believed that composers either were blessed with artistic inspiration or they were not. On "the Rules of Composition," he wrote:

> *Nature is the best Dictator,* for all the hard dry studied Rules that ever was prescribed, will not enable any Person to form an Air [i.e., compose a melody] any more than the bare Knowledge of the four and twenty Letters,

and strict Grammatical Rules will qualify a Scholar for composing a Piece of Poetry . . . without a Genius. It must be Nature, Nature must lay the Foundation, Nature must inspire the Thought.

Confident of the "genius" that linked him with nature's inspiration, Billings then added, in words widely quoted ever since: "For my own Part, as I don't think myself confin'd to any Rules for Composition laid down by any that went before me, neither should I think (were I to pretend to lay down Rules) that any who came after me were any ways obligated to adhere to them, any further than they should think proper." Without such self-assurance, Billings would hardly have admitted to readers eight years later that "after impartial examination" of *The New-England Psalm-Singer* "I have discovered that many of the pieces in that Book were never worth my printing, or your inspection," and urged the public to buy copies of his second and discover for themselves what he now believed to be true: "The *Singing Master's Assistant*, is a much better Book, than the *New-England Psalm-Singer*." Such candor, unique in the psalmody of its time, makes an odd impression even today—especially when we recall that what is being discussed in such cavalierly personal terms is sacred music, which even a few years earlier had still been thoroughly embedded in New England's Puritan religious culture.

For all of Billings's originality and artistry, he has also gained historical attention by launching his career on the eve of American independence, and in a city that played a key role in that drama. Far from disguising his own sympathies. Billings celebrated them. The engraver of *The New-England Psalm-Singer*'s frontispiece was Paul Revere, strongly identified with Boston's patriot faction, as were Edes and Gill, who printed the work, and Gillam Bass, one of its sellers. Like James Lyon, Billings also published his work by subscription. But in an advertisement he apologized for omitting the subscriber list from his book for want of space, an absence that is now a matter for regret. Given Billings's links to Boston's patriots—he was also friendly with the arch-agitator Samuel Adams—it would be interesting to know whether subscribers ran chiefly to like-minded people or to a wider spectrum of Bostonians.

Patriot, composer, vivid personality, William Billings stands as an emblematic figure in American music history. When psalmodists and writers of his own time chose one man to exemplify their tradition, Billings was the natural choice. When later reformers wished to recall the supposedly crude, untutored beginnings of American music, Billings served their purposes too. More recently, when historians of American music have chronicled the beginnings of American composition, or when choirs have performed music of eighteenth-century Yankees, it is to Billings and his works that both have

been most likely to turn. Billings stands foremost among our musical founding fathers, long on talent and historical charisma if short on polish and
solemnity.[17]

When he died in 1800, the Reverend William Bentley, who had known
Billings for thirty years, remembered him in his diary as a "self taught man"
who "may justly be considered as the father of our new England music."
Bentley's obituary noted the composer's lack of "a proper education," his dis-
turbing appearance ("a singular man, of moderate size, short of one leg, with
one eye . . . & with an uncommon negligence of person"), and the air of defeat that marked his life's end ("He died poor & neglected & perhaps did too
much neglect himself"). Yet Bentley could think of no rival who matched
Billings's impact, who "had better original powers," or who could boast
equal fame in the churches. In Bentley's view, Billings "spake & sung &
thought as a man above the common abilities." Earlier he had written of
Billings as owning "more genius than taste." And now his memory of the
psalmodist produced a pungent metaphor: Billings's work showed "inferiour
excellence."

Indeed, the music of Billings, blending energy with untutored directness,
exudes inferior excellence. Take, for example, CHESTER, one of the compositions for which Billings is most remembered and for which he also wrote
the words. CHESTER's popularity in Billings's day can be judged from its frequent reprintings in the tunebooks of other compilers. And long after

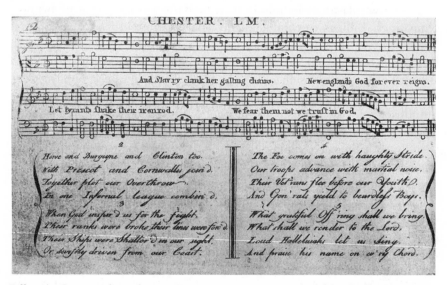

Billings's CHESTER brought a patriotic text into a sacred tunebook. In the version
here, from the *Singing Master's Assistant* (1778), he added four stanzas to the one he
wrote and published in 1770.

Billings's death, CHESTER survived, if not as a hymn in church, as a symbol of the War of Independence and the basis for variations in a twentieth-century instrumental work, William Schuman's *New England Triptych*. Much of the hymn's appeal lies in a melody (in the tenor part), whose profile is shaped by the dactylic rhythm that begins all four of its phrases (♩♪♪). The melody's range also contributes to its character: lying high in the voice, it reaches the top note F in three phrases, encouraging full volume as the rhythm does a fairly brisk pace. It is hard to imagine anyone singing this tune softly or slowly.

Even a quick look at CHESTER shows that voices other than the tenor also claim their share of melodic activity. The bass, for example, moves purposefully in all four phrases, either up or down the scale in support of the tenor tune. The treble (soprano), whose fourth phrase starts with the tenor's first, sings a melody almost equal in interest to the main one. Only the counter voice (alto), whose role is to complete the harmony, lacks tunefulness. CHESTER also illustrates how the method of composition Billings describes in one of his tunebooks worked in practice. He began by writing the tenor, or "first part," which he called "nothing more than a flight of fancy" to which other voices were "forced to comply and conform." He then composed the rest of the voices so that they would partake "of the same air, or, at least, as much of it as they can get." In other words, Billings tried to infuse voices other than the tenor with melodic interest. But because they were composed *after* the tenor voice, "the last parts are seldom so good as the first; for the second part [the bass] is subservient to the first, the third part [the treble] must conform to first and second, and the fourth part [the counter] must conform to the other three." By writing voice parts that kept singers musically engaged while still following accepted harmonic practice, Billings strove to reconcile the claims of nature and art—of inspiration and technique. "The grand difficulty in composition," he wrote, "is to preserve the air through each part separately, and yet cause them to harmonize with each other at the same time."[18]

CHESTER thus presented singers with a confluence of independent, interlocking melodic lines. Billings had tailored those lines to fit metrical verse, a fact important for worshipers and composers alike. As the leaders of the Protestant Reformation had long ago recognized, psalms or hymns in metrical form were as likely to stick in the memory as any other verse, whether one was literate or not. Verse's phrase patterns also provided structures around which composers could invent new melodies. For example, CHESTER, like OLD HUNDRED, is a long-meter tune (8.8.8.8.). In courting nature's inspiration when he wrote the melody, Billings worked within a set of promptings: four phrases, each with eight syllables that were set in alternating pairs of long and short ones (iambic). These fixed features carried implications for the melody's shape: its phrase lengths, its rise, fall, or stasis, the curve it traced through space and time, and the way its harmony moved in the field of influence established by the tonic chord—the chord that, like a magnet, seeks continually to draw other chords back toward itself by way of its closest relative, the dominant. Billings chose a rhythmic pattern for CHESTER that served all four phrases, so the melody features rhythmic if not tune repetition. Finally, that all four phrases begin on a tonic chord implies a single-mindedness confirmed by their destinations: dominant, dominant, tonic, tonic.

CHESTER's text carries a proud, bitter dose of anti-British feeling that actually flirts with blasphemy by enlisting God on New England's side in her quarrel with the mother country. The presence of a text like this in a tune-book indicates that the prohibition against nonbiblical verses was becoming a thing of the past. Breaking down that ban required a long struggle. Especially in the middle third of the century, church members disagreed over whether to continue singing from metrical psalters like the *Bay Psalm Book* or to move to more modern paraphrases—in particular Isaac Watts's *The Psalms of David, Imitated in the Language of the New Testament* (London, 1719), which marinated the Old Testament words in Christian prophecy. By the time Billings's *The New-England Psalm-Singer* appeared, Watts was the psalter of choice in the English-speaking colonies, including New England. In fact, Watts's *Hymns and Spiritual Songs, in Three Books* (London, 1707–9), largely based on Christian ideas taken from Scripture but unmistakably verses "of human composure," as Cotton Mather had put it, also gained currency as the strictures of traditional Puritanism loosened.[19]

In *The Singing Master's Assistant* (1778), Billings added fresh topical stanzas to CHESTER, but he went even further. He composed anthems paraphrasing Scripture to link the plight of present-day Bostonians with that of the Israelites in Egyptian captivity. The Old Testament Psalm 137 begins: "By the rivers of Babylon, there we sat down, yea, we wept, when we remembered Zion." In his LAMENTATION OVER BOSTON, Billings transformed those words to "By the Rivers of Watertown we sat down & wept when we remember'd thee O Boston." And later in the same piece, he took off from the Lamentations of Jeremiah:

> A voice was heard upon the high places, weeping and supplications of the children of Israel (Jer. 3:21).
> A voice was heard in Roxbury which ecchoed thru the continent weeping for Boston because of their danger (Billings).

Texts like these treated Scripture not only as a guide to spiritual inspiration and moral improvement, but as a historical epic that, bringing past into present, offered timeless parallels to current events.

That Billings wrote the verse for some of his musical settings, as well as using prose to personalize his tunebooks, made him unusual if not unique among psalmodists of his time. The notion that in 1770 a local tanner could use a sacred tunebook as a forum for his own efforts as a writer of music *and* verse, and that the verse could convey sentiments like those in CHESTER, shows how far the boundaries of psalmody had stretched since Cotton Mather's day. Then, only divinely inspired texts conveyed by official "amanuenses of heaven" had been allowed; now, an amanuensis of rebellion had opened the tradition up to new expressive territory. With such powerful secularizing events as the War of Independence to deal with in their everyday lives, New Englanders were less and less inclined to look to Puritanism, with its stern, absolute view of human nature, for spiritual guidance, much less temporal leadership.

CHESTER invites discussion of Billings's lack of artistic polish as well as his talent. Note, for example, that the most strongly stressed syllable in the second phrase, highlighted with a melisma (several notes sung on one syllable) in tenor and bass, falls on "clank," perhaps the least euphonious word in the whole stanza. And then there is the matter of parallel fifths between voices, forbidden by "the Rules of Composition" because they restrict melodic independence. Billings, having sworn to uphold that principle, breaks his vow in the very first phrase, where treble and tenor move in a chain of four such intervals. One imagines the prophet of inferior excellence weighing alternatives—the sound of the whole versus the melodic integrity of individual voices—and opting for the first, perhaps because nothing better expressed the obduracy of Britain's "iron rod" than the ring of those descending fifths.

DANIEL READ AND OTHER PSALMODISTS

For all of Billings's fame, he was just one of many New Englanders who composed and published sacred music in the late 1700s, nurtured by the singing school. Like his, their work brings up again the issue of sacredness and secularity. In the years after the revolution, psalms and hymns by Watts and others won acceptance not only as sacred verses for public worship but as popular poetry, understood and loved by the people. Sacred text, in other words, did not always imply sacred function. Singing schools, centered on the skills needed to sing psalmody, were not themselves sacred institutions. Tunebooks like those of Billings and his contemporaries, though overwhelmingly sacred in their texts, were too expensive for church use and their music too elaborate for any congregation. They were intended to serve the needs of singing schools and musical societies. Rather than church music, then, psalmody was more like popular

music. And one tune that proved to be a popular favorite was Daniel Read's
SHERBURNE.

Read, a native of Attleboro, Massachusetts, spent most of his life in New
Haven, Connecticut, where he worked as a comb maker and storekeeper
while compiling tunebooks and composing psalm and hymn tunes. SHER-
BURNE embodies an unceremonious vigor that one can imagine reaching
outside the sacred space of public worship into the secular world. In fact,
the text, though biblically inspired and wholly familiar to Christians, tells a
story of surpassing strangeness. A band of shepherds are working the night
shift. It is a cold evening, the ground is hard, and, as usual in that line of
work, they are bored. Suddenly they see a flash of light. And there stands, or
hovers, an angel, sent by God to report some startling news about His family. (Why pass the news on to these shepherds and nobody else? They don't
have time to ask.) Read's setting, with its homegrown harmony and simple
declamation, seems to encourage the performers to take the role of shepherds—to sing as people who might well have slept on cold, hard ground
themselves, as some of SHERBURNE's early performers doubtless had. For
here, commonplace details and world-changing revelation find common
ground. And when SHERBURNE explodes at its mid-point into chattering
quarter notes and vocal overlappings—an apt facsimile of flashing lights and
disorienting confusion—the singers can hardly help but strive toward ecstatic vocal expression. As people praising God by registering joy in the story

Daniel Read's SHERBURNE, first published in his *American Singing Book* (New
Haven, 1785), sets an anonymous English hymn from the early 1700s. SHERBURNE
became one of the most popular fuging tunes of its day.

and in the act of singing, it hardly seems to matter whether they are inside the meeting house or not.

Cast in two sections, SHERBURNE is a "fuging tune," an Anglo-American form beloved of psalmodists and singers of the period. It is also a piece whose musical idiom typifies a whole generation of Yankee composers, including Read, Lewis Edson, Justin Morgan, Timothy Swan, and others who hailed from the towns and villages sprinkled across the Massachusetts and Connecticut countryside. In addition to their trades (Edson was a blacksmith, Morgan a farmer, schoolmaster, and horse breeder, Swan a hatter), they taught singing schools and wrote music, but without much exposure to the music making of the cities. Their idiom was worked out through the successive writing of different voice parts for unaccompanied chorus, as Billings described. With no tradition of organ playing in worship to draw on, they lacked keyboard skill and a knowledge of standard European harmonic practice. As a result, their music often lacks a clear sense of harmonic direction that a piece like CHESTER shows.

The opening of SHERBURNE shows two harmonic traits that strike the ear as different from anything a European composer of the time would have written. One is the fondness for "open" sounds—harmonies that include only the root and fifth instead of a full triad (root, third, fifth). That sound, which is also heard at the first cadence (on "ground"), is acoustically the simplest of any consonance involving two different notes, which helps to explain why it resonates so well and is easy to sing in tune.[20] The second unusual trait—greater harmonic freedom—can be seen at the end of the first phrase, where, instead of following the expected path to a cadence on A, the fifth scale degree (dominant), finds its destination on B, the sixth (submediant). While there is nothing shocking in that move, an ear used to the formulas of conventional harmony does not expect it. The effect, taken together with the frequent open fifths, is a defamiliarizing one.

SHERBURNE's declamation, given its joyful subject, invites enthusiastic singing. In line with Billings's notion of melodic independence, Read gives all four voice parts, including the counter, an interesting line to sing. The declamation involves groups of quarter notes, each with a new syllable, and sustained notes (especially dotted halves), many of them on either the root or the fifth of an open sound. The quarter notes seem to call for a vigorous, accented delivery that pushes the rhythm ahead like an engine. (One psalmodist, perhaps with pieces like SHERBURNE in mind, cautioned singers to remember that "singing and vociferation are different things.")[21] The sustained tones invite a straight, focused, forward placement of the voice, perhaps even with a "swell"—the gradual increase in volume described in many tunebooks. Read's setting seems to demand accented declamation in the "fuge" ("The angel of the Lord came down"), where the voices sing the same subject (melodic figure) in imitation, and the F-sharp lies high in the tenor and treble range. (By placing the highest note in the melody on "of," an unimportant word on a strong beat, Read breaks an accepted rule of text setting.) As for the sustained tones, if sung with a penetrating quality they can cut, trumpet-like, through the sound of the other voices. More a piece to be sung than listened to, SHERBURNE offers its singers plenty of sheer enjoyment.

The specialization and professionalism found in later American music making are absent from New England psalmody. The composers, who had acquired their own musical learning in singing schools and through personal experience, were writing essentially for peers, friends, and neighbors, and they often continued working at other trades as well. Thanks to subscription and informal interchange, even inexperienced composers could get their music into print. The best performing groups were musical societies— groups of singers from schools and choirs who banded together for the pleasure of exercising their skills. Though all this singing was done for the greater glory of God, much of it took place outside public worship. It is partly the flexibility of boundaries that later became more sharply drawn— between sacred and secular, but also between professional and amateur, composer and performer, creator and publisher—that has led some to call the late eighteenth century a golden age of psalmody.

Yet some religious leaders of the time found the age more gloomy than golden. Looking back on the years 1770–1800, N. D. Gould wrote in 1853: "So far as real devotional music was concerned, the thirty years referred to was a dark age . . . because the tunes were so inappropriate." Compositions like SHERBURNE, popular with choirs but beyond the ability of most worshipers, gained favor, undermining the position of congregational song. "Ministers, Christians, and all good men," wrote Gould, and "men of correct taste in regard to music, looked on, sometimes grieved and sometimes vexed." But their influence had waned. "They had let go their hold, and the multitude had the whole management of it, and sung *what* and *when* they pleased."[22] Only when the clergy reasserted control over psalmody, Gould believed, could its value as religious expression be restored. As Chapter 7 will show, ministers, with the help of community leaders, did just that after 1800.

SACRED MUSIC OUTSIDE THE CALVINIST ORBIT

Psalmody was not the only kind of sacred music that took root on these shores. The Church of England supported a musical life very different from that of the Reformed Calvinists. Anglican worship followed a liturgical cycle

London organ builder John Snetzler completed this chamber organ in 1762. It is now found in the Congregational Church in South Dennis, Massachusetts.

akin to that of the Roman Catholics, with a prescribed church calendar and the content of many services specified. The church was also hierarchical, with tiers of officials from the Archbishop of Canterbury on down. While Calvinist belief endorsed the autonomy of each congregation, in the Anglican system overseas ministers were licensed to preach by the church's Society for the Propagation of the Gospel in Foreign Parts (SPG), centered in London, which also assigned clergymen to specific locations and churches in the New World. Colonial and territorial governors, themselves agents of the crown, were responsible for establishing the Anglican Church in their jurisdiction and ensuring that the rites of the *Book of Common Prayer* were followed. Annual grants from the British Parliament paid part of the salaries of ministers, whose licensing depended on proof of their Anglican orthodoxy.[23] Recognized as the official state church in Virginia, the Carolinas, and Georgia, the Church of England was supported in all three states by tax revenues.

Anglicans in the New World, welcoming visual and musical display, employed anything that might enhance the impressiveness of their services. And that included the organ. Francis Hopkinson, a prominent Philadelphia Anglican and himself an organist, invoked the Old Testament's chief musician in defining his own philosophy: "I am one of those who take great delight in sacred music, and think, with royal David, that heart, voice, and instrument should unite in adoration of the great Supreme."[24] Indeed, much of the history of church music in eighteenth-century North America centers on the organ: either the Calvinists' vigorous opposition to it or the large financial investment required when a church bought one. The cost of importing an organ from overseas, which might run to £300 or £400, was only part of the expense, however, for churches with organs had to find organists to play them. Again, in contrast to the Puritan approach, that usually meant hiring a professional musician, with European background and training.

In a letter written in 1786, Francis Hopkinson warned church organists to remember "that the congregation have not assembled to be entertained with [their] performance." He also counseled: "The excellence of an organist consists in his making the instrument subservient and conducive to the purposes of devotion."[25] But that was sometimes easier said than done, as shown by the Marquis de Chatellux's description of an Anglican service he attended in Philadelphia in 1781.

> The service of the English church appeared to me a sort of *opera,* as well for the music as the decorations: a handsome pulpit placed before a handsome organ; a handsome minister in that pulpit, reading, speaking, and singing with a grace entirely theatrical; . . . a soft and agreeable vocal music, with ex-

cellent sonatas, played alternately on the organ; all this, compared to the quakers, the anabaptists, the presbyterians, &c. appeared to me rather like a little paradise itself, than as the road to it.[26]

That kind of smooth theatricality fed the Puritans' mistrust of musical professionalism and display.

Yet an organ could attract a skilled musician to a community, whose musical life might then be enriched by the organist's presence. In 1737, St. Philip's Church in Charleston, South Carolina, hired as its organist Charles Theodore Pachelbel, a native of Germany and son of Johann, composer of the famous *Canon*. Pachelbel played at St. Philip's until his death in 1750. He also performed in public and taught a singing school in Charleston in 1749, probably to instruct youngsters in the singing of Anglican psalmody—accompanied by organ, unlike the Puritan variety; he may have given private lessons as well. By hiring an organist, St. Philip's was also serving as a patron of sorts, providing a niche for a professional musician whose work would then reach more widely into the community.

Two other Protestant groups led unusually active musical lives. Both were Pennsylvania-based, German-speaking separatist societies that found havens in America, where they pursued their visions of Christian communal living. The first, an early example of a schismatic American community, settled in Ephrata, Pennsylvania. Its founder, Conrad Beissel, was born in Germany, apprenticed as a baker, became a member of a pietist sect, and, after a religious disagreement, immigrated to America in 1720. Twelve years later, Beissel took the name Father Friedsam and founded the Ephrata Cloister. By 1740, the cloister numbered seventy, and at the time of Beissel's death it claimed almost three hundred members, both men and women, celibate and married, who embraced sacred singing with enthusiasm.

Beissel and his followers shared the Puritans' urge for spiritual perfection. But they did not believe that only biblical hymn texts could be divinely inspired. In fact, Beissel himself was a prolific versifier who used hymnody to present his theological ideas. (Two centuries later, German novelist Thomas Mann, who featured Beissel in his 1947 novel *Doctor Faustus*, described his writing style as "high-flown and cryptic, laden with metaphor, obscure Scriptural allusions, and a sort of erotic symbolism.")[27] Beissel produced a number of hymn collections, and during the 1730s Benjamin Franklin printed some of them (texts only, as in many earlier New England psalters). By the mid-1740s, Beissel, though more than fifty years old and untrained in music beyond having played the fiddle as a youth, had also turned into a prolific composer, writing music for his own hymns and for whole chapters of the Old Testament, including two settings of the complete Song of Solomon. He developed his own method of composing, with a novel theoretical basis. Using the soprano line rather than the bass as a foundation, he named the notes of the tonic triad "masters" and other tones of the scale "servants," and he coordinated declamation and harmony by placing accented text syllables on master chords.

Once he began composing, Beissel devoted himself to rehearsing members of the singing school he had formed to sing his music. In search of a soft, polished, otherworldly sound, he held rehearsals that lasted up to four hours. The experience of hearing Beissel's music could be powerful, as described by a visitor to the school three years after the leader's death:

> The sisters invited us into their chapel, and, seating themselves in order, began to sing one of their devout hymns. The music had little or no air or melody; but consisted of simple, long notes, combined in the richest harmony. The counter, treble, tenor and bass were all sung by women, with sweet, shrill and small voices; but with a truth and exactness in the time and intonation that was admirable. . . . The performers sat with their heads reclined, their countenances solemn and dejected, their faces pale and emaciated from their manner of living, their clothing exceeding white and quite picturesque, and their music such as thrilled to the very soul.—I almost began to think myself in the world of spirits, and that the objects before me were ethereal.[28]

Conceived for cloister members alone, Beissel's music was not published. Yet, as if in line with the singing he cultivated, with the hope of being worthy of God's praise, the music was copied by hand, with elaborate decorations, in beautifully illuminated choral books.

The other group of musically inspired separatists were the Moravians, or Unitas Fratrum, followers of the Czech martyr Jan Hus, who crossed the Atlantic in the 1740s and 50s to create their own communities in Pennsylvania (Nazareth, Bethlehem) and North Carolina (Salem). The strong musical emphasis in Moravian community life encouraged the singing of elaborate anthems as well as congregational hymns. Instruments were welcome from the beginning, even for the accompaniment of hymn singing; for the Moravians, musical instruments carried none of the secular taint that so worried the Puritans. As a church elder responded when questioned by a zealous young minister on the propriety of using the same instruments in church that had been used for secular music: "Will you use the same mouth to preach with today which you now use in eating sausage?"[29]

The chief constraints on Moravian musical development were economic, not theological. As community life grew more settled, organs were introduced into the churches. David Tannenberg (1728–1804), a Moravian born in the Saxon town of Herrnhut but a Pennsylvania resident from 1749, became one of the most prolific and skilled American organ builders, with forty-two documented instruments to his credit.[30] Moreover, choral anthems were sometimes accompanied by orchestras formed among men of the congregation. Called "collegia musica," meaning simply groups of people gathered to make music, Moravian instrumentalists also met outside worship services to rehearse and perform chamber and orchestral music, most of it composed in Europe. By 1780, the Bethlehem collegium—four vi-

Conrad Beissel, founder and leader of the Ephrata Cloister in Pennsylvania, wrote both words and music for many hymns, which were skillfully copied in illuminated manuscripts.

olins, one viola, and pairs of violoncellos, flutes, oboes, horns, and trumpets—were skilled enough to perform symphonies by the leading composers
of the day, including Haydn, Mozart, and the sons of J. S. Bach.[31] Like the
singers, collegium members were amateurs who performed in the spirit of
enriching a community musical life dedicated to God's glory.

    Members of Moravian society were divided by age, gender, and marital
status into "choirs": young girls, young boys, older girls, older boys, single
women, single men, married couples, widows, and widowers. Different
choirs often lived together in separate residences, each with its own devo-
tionals and festivals. So pervasive was the Moravians' idea of individuals

This watercolor pictures Moravian bishop Jacob Van Vleck accompanying the
singing of girls who may be students at the school in Bethlehem, Pennsylvania, of
which he was principal.

blending their efforts to achieve a common purpose that a singing chorus could be their metaphor for community structure. Singing was part of daily life, whether during work or at meals. The Moravians' most distinctive instrumental tradition was also rooted in congregational song: a "choir" (actually a quartet) of trombones that played German chorales suited to different occasions in church and community life. When a Moravian died, trombones might announce the event by playing the "Passion Chorale" (*O Sacred Head Now Wounded*) from the church tower, the somber sound heard through the entire settlement.[32]

Some Moravians also mastered the styles of continental composers. Some 10,000 musical manuscripts survive from a tradition that flourished especially from the 1780s through the 1830s, and those manuscripts preserve approximately 7,000 individual works. More than 2,000 were written by Moravian composers working in America: in the eighteenth century, most notably Johann Friedrich Peter, Johannes Herbst, and David Moritz Michael, all born in Europe.[33] At a time when few Americans outside the realm of psalmody were capable of composing at all, American Moravian communities boasted several who wrote music with convincing facility in an up-to-date European idiom.

In 1960, not long after the musical richness of the Moravian archives was recognized, the Moravians were dubbed "the first real composers to work on American soil."[34] But the Moravians now seem more a byway, remote from main currents of music making in the United States. Nevertheless, whatever assessment of long-term influence a present-day observer might reach, the diversity of Protestant sacred music in eighteenth-century America is striking. Each of the four traditions touched on in this chapter carried a different kind of musical significance in its own day. New England psalmody, after a long process of development, produced a tradition of indigenous composing that served the needs of Puritan-inspired, English-speaking Calvinists. Anglican church music created a niche for European-trained professional musicians. The Ephrata Cloister gave rise to a novel musical style. And the religious freedom available in North America allowed the Moravians to set up theocratic communities whose life was shaped in large part by cosmopolitan styles of music making. The variety of ways that Protestants found to praise God through music reflected the diversity of American Protestantism itself.

4

Old, Simple Ditties

Colonial Song, Dance, and Home Music Making

A KEY DIFFERENCE between music making in the Old and New Worlds lies in their economic grounding. In Europe, society's most powerful institutions—the church, the court, and the state—required music for their own purposes, and they hired and supported musicians to supply it. Not all musicians benefited directly from such patronage, but its presence ensured music's place as both a prestigious art and a useful or diverting pastime. In North America, however, no national church existed, nor did any political structure with aristocratic continuity and clout. Privileged places for music were rare on this side of the Atlantic. Lacking sponsorship from society's leaders, music therefore depended heavily on musicians themselves for its support and promotion. Just as the continent's exploration and settlement were sparked by Europeans' hunger for economic gain, so the creation of a diverse musical life on these shores has been largely the work of musicians seeking to market their services. New England Calvinists, placing little value on autonomous art, welcomed only one professional service: that of the singing master—and only after convincing themselves that instruction would improve congregational singing. But Anglicans in the New World admired music as an art enough to invest in organs and hire musicians with the skill to play them. Even more than secular music in these early years, sacred music provided a professional space where musicians managed to find customers.

Customers for music grew in number during the eighteenth century as immigration increased, including more and more musicians from Great Britain who crossed the Atlantic to serve Americans' musical needs. But outside sacred music circles, professional musical life was concentrated during the 1700s to a few cities on the Eastern Seaboard—Boston, New York, Philadelphia, Baltimore, and Charleston chiefly—where immigrant musicians practiced what they had learned in Europe. And that fact points to an overlooked but fundamental condition of America's musical life. From the start of European settlement, musicians here have been able to take for granted the ample supply of music from the British Isles and the European continent, made available through oral tradition and written notation. Given a steady, reliable supply from Europe, there was little if any demand outside the meeting house for music by American composers. Indeed, it apparently mattered little to singers and players on these shores that until after American independence was won, virtually none of the songs, dances, or theatrical works performed here were composed here.

Songs and Ballads in Oral Tradition

An ocean separated early English-speaking settlers from the land of their origin, but not from its language, ideology, popular beliefs, proverbs, verses, or music. Songs from Great Britain were woven into Americans' lives, as suggested by a letter Benjamin Franklin wrote from London in 1765 to his brother Peter back home. Peter had sent Benjamin some original verses, asking that an English composer be hired to set them to music. But in Benjamin's view, the verses called for a tune less sophisticated than a London composer would write. If Peter had given his text "to some country girl in the heart of *Massachusetts*, who has never heard any other than psalm tunes or 'Chevy Chace,' the 'Children in the Woods,' the 'Spanish Lady,' and such old, simple ditties, but has naturally a good ear, she might more probably have made a pleasing popular tune for you than any of our masters here."[1] The songs Franklin names are all ballads: narrative songs in strophic form, with many stanzas of text sung to the same music. Each song tells a vivid story. And together the three suggest the variety found in ballads brought to the New World by English-speaking settlers and sung by them and their descendants thereafter.

Although the origins of most remain unknown, ballads in English-speaking culture circulated for centuries among common people, including the illiterate. Contradicting the belief that artistry depends on literacy and learning, the oral ballad has long fascinated British writers. The poet Philip Sidney, for example, wrote of *Chevy Chase* in 1595: "I never heard the olde song of Percy and Douglas, that I found not my heart mooved more than with a Trumpet: and yet [it] is sung by some blinde Crouder [crowder, or manual laborer], with no rougher voice than rude stile."[2] In 1711, the English essayist Joseph Addison named *Chevy Chase* as "the favourite Ballad of the common People of England." In fact, all three of the ballads Franklin named in his letter originated in Great Britain in the early 1600s or before. That they were still circulating orally in North America in the 1760s, known by country girls and boys and many others, testifies to their hold on the popular imagination.

In a version printed in Salem, Massachusetts, during the eighteenth century, *Chevy Chase* tells a tale of chivalry and slaughter on a British battlefield. The ballad's roots probably lie in a real historical event: the Battle of Otterburn, fought between the English and the Scots in the northwest corner of England in 1388. After a conventional salute to royalty, the first stanza foretells disaster:

> God prosper long our noble king,
>   our lives and safeties all;
> A woful hunting once there did
>   in Chevy-Chace befal.
> To drive the deer with hound and horn,
>   Earl Piercy took his way;
> The child might rue that is unborn,
>   the hunting of that day.[3]

In almost three dozen eight-line stanzas, a grim story unfolds. The English nobleman Piercy. Earl of Northumberland, goes deer hunting in Chevy Chase, a wood claimed by a Scot, Earl Douglas. Knowing that a challenge is likely. Piercy takes an army of fifteen hundred with him. Douglas appears with "full twenty hundred Scottish spears" to interrupt the hunt.

The lines that describe the two leaders' meeting show balladry's descriptive and narrative power in full force. Taking account of Douglas's "milk-white steed," his haughty manner, and the flashing armor of his men, the text pictures the Scots' approach as the English see it. The appearance of Douglas and his men brings the hunt's furious activity to a halt, and the two armies face each other, each soldier knowing that his fate hangs on the leaders' exchange. For listeners and readers, however, the first stanza has already signaled where that exchange will lead.

By bringing their armies to Chevy Chase, Piercy and Douglas have declared their readiness to fight. Humorists from Mark Twain to Monty Python have made fun of this kind of situation. But *Chevy Chase* is a tale of medieval chivalry whose characters *are* knights in shining armor. According to chivalry's code, a knight's honor must be defended. By demanding that Piercy identify himself, Douglas asserts his superiority. By refusing to give his name, Piercy returns the insult. And Douglas's response—"one of us two shall die"—is the proper one in the ritual ruling the exchange.

> Earl Douglas on a milk-white steed.
>   most like a Baron bold,
> Rode foremost of the company,
>   whose armour shone like gold.

> Shew me (he said) whose men you be,
>   that hunt so boldly here;
> That, without my consent do chase
>   and kill my fallow deer?
>
> The man that first did answer make,
>   was noble Piercy he;
> Who said, we list not to declare,
>   nor shew whose men we be;
> Yet we will spend our dearest blood,
>   thy chiefest harts to slay,
> Then Douglas swore a solemn oath,
>   and thus in rage did say:
>
> Ere thus I will out braved be,
>   one of us two shall die.
> I know thee well, an Earl thou art,
>   Lord Piercy, so am I.

Douglas and Piercy join in hand-to-hand combat, each winning the other's respect. But once the two leaders are slain, the armies fall upon each other in a bloody struggle that leaves barely a hundred men alive. Women clean up after the carnage:

> Next day did many widows come,
>   their husbands to bewail;
> They wash'd their wounds in briny tears,
>   but all would not prevail.
> Their bodies bath'd in purple blood,
>   they bore with them away—
> They kiss'd them dead a thousand times,
>   when they were clad in clay.

Even then, however, the killing goes on, for King Henry of England vows vengeance on the Scots.

The view of society inscribed in *Chevy Chase* could hardly be less democratic. The drama's only real characters are the earls Piercy and Douglas. Combat between the two fills several stanzas of description, and the death of each is told in detail. In contrast, "thousands . . . of small account" are polished off in less than a dozen words. Yet it should be no surprise that a ballad like *Chevy Chase*, with its larger-than-life heroes and gory details, should capture the popular imagination in a democracy. For, as later American history shows, the concept of honor—regional honor, for example, in the Civil War—has helped to inspire military effort ever since, even in a society claiming to value the life of every citizen.

Chevy Chase also points up another key trait of balladry: the emotional detachment with which many ballad texts set forth the dramatic events they describe. The strophic form itself is partly responsible, parceling out the story in patterns of metrical verse that, in their stanzas of equal length, formalize the expression. (This trait shows balladry's connections with psalmody, which followed and in some ways copied it.) The tune's function in *Chevy Chase* is also typical of balladry. Rather than providing any kind of commentary on the words, it serves as a more or less neutral framework for their delivery. All the ballad's action-filled events are announced to the same music, and the repetitiousness of structure and tune keeps them all on the same emotional level. Indeed, twentieth-century recordings made by rural singers in the oral tradition tend to share an impassive delivery. Rather than an exercise in animated storytelling, then, traditionally performed ballads come closer to a sober, impersonal ritual.

The Children in the Woods, the second ballad mentioned in Benjamin Franklin's letter, tells a story in which personal emotion plays a much bigger role. The deaths of a rich man and his wife leave their three-year-old boy and his younger sister in the care of an uncle who stands to inherit the parents' estate if the children die before coming of age. Within a year, the uncle's greed overwhelms his sense of family duty. He hires two "Russians rude . . . of furious mood" to take the children into the woods and kill them. But on the way to their planned murder, the little boy and girl prove so charming that one of the would-be assassins repents and kills the other instead. He and the children continue to wander, but soon they grow hungry, and the Russian leaves the youngsters to look for food. He never returns, and they die in the forest.

> Thus wandred these two little Babes,
>   till Death did end their Grief;
> In one another's arms they dy'd,
>   as Babes wanting Relief.[4]

Now "the Wrath of God" descends upon the uncle, who finds his house haunted by "fearful Fiends," his barn destroyed by fire, his cattle dead in the fields, and two sons lost on a sea voyage. He dies in prison after the story of his treatment of the children is discovered.

Both *The Children in the Woods* and *Chevy Chase* may be sung to the tune *Now Ponder Well* (from John Gay's *The Beggar's Opera*). But in another way the two ballads differ sharply. In *Chevy Chase*, the characters' actions are described but never judged; even the English archer whose arrow, shot from afar, hits Earl Douglas in the heart during a lull in his battle with Piercy draws no comment from the narrator. But *The Children in the Woods* is told in an openly partisan voice, with the characters typifying good or evil traits. The father, "a Gentleman of good account," and the mother die with thoughts on their lips only for the babies they are leaving behind. The innocence of the children, "a fine and pretty Boy" and a girl "of beauteous Mould," makes their fate all the more poignant. But the uncle is evil, his promise to guard the children casting his later actions in an even more heinous light. The ballad amounts to a brief morality play. It ends with a two-stanza epilogue: "A Word of Advice to Executors:"

> All you who be Executors made,
>   and Overseers eke,
> Of Children that be fatherless,
>   and Infants mild and meek.
>
> Take you Example by this Thing,
>   and yield to each his Right;
> Lest God by such like Misery
>   your wicked Deeds requite.

While admitting the clumsiness of its verse, Joseph Addison also praised *The Children in the Woods*—"one of the Darling Songs of the Common People"—for authenticity of feeling. He wrote in 1711:

> The Song is a plain simple Copy of Nature, destitute of all the Helps and Ornaments of Art. . . . Because the Sentiments appear genuine and unaffected they are able to move the Mind of the most polite Reader with inward Meltings of Humanity and Compassion. The Incidents grow out of the Subject, and are such as are the most proper to excite Pity; for which Reason the whole Narration has something in it very moving, notwithstanding the Author (whoever he was) has delivered it in such an abject Phrase and poorness of Expression, that the quoting any part of it would look like a Design of turning it into Ridicule. But, though the Language is mean, the Thoughts . . . from one end to the other are natural.[5]

The idea that untutored simplicity could touch the depths of the soul grew familiar in eighteenth-century Europe, helping to raise the interest of sophisticated observers in songs, sayings, and artifacts of "the folk."

The Spanish Lady deals not with a tragedy but with a romance—a male-female encounter that leads to a test of integrity. The emotions expressed show a purity and sternness on a par with the chivalric honor of *Chevy Chase* and the divine retribution of *The Children in the Woods*. By some unexplained circumstance, British soldiers have invaded Spain and taken prisoners. One captive, a Spanish lady who describes herself as "lovely, young and tender," falls in love with her English captor. When the commander of the English orders the release of female prisoners, she is heartbroken. "Leave me not to a Spaniard," she begs. "You alone enjoy my heart." The

Englishman is polite but firm in explaining that he must follow orders, but she debates him all the way. If the English forbid women to be used as spoils of war, she will disguise herself as a page and follow on her own. If he is a poor man, she has money to donate to their cause. If a sea journey to England holds dangers, she stands ready to risk them. Finally, the soldier confesses that he is already married. The news transforms her romantic passion into Christian self-abasement. She tells him:

> Oh how happy is that woman
>   that enjoys so true a friend.
> Many days of joy God send you,
>   and of my suit I'll make an end:
> Upon my knees I pardon crave
>   for this offence,
> Which love and true affection
>   did first commence.[6]

Offering the soldier a gold chain to give his wife, she vows to spend the rest of her days in a nunnery, where she will pray for him (and his spouse). In saying farewell, she also bids him to "count not Spanish ladies wanton." Recognizing her love as a lesser claim than that of a wife for her husband, she proves its moral dimension.

The melody's two-part structure—the final four lines (8.4.8.4.) are set in a higher range, with a character slightly different from that of the first four (8.7.8.7.)—makes it apt for dialogue between the two characters. For example, when she argues against his plea of poverty, the melody neatly supports the conversation.

> [He:]   I have neither gold nor silver
>   to maintain thee in this case.
>   And to travel, 'tis great charges,
>   as you know in every place.
> [She:] My chains and jewels every one,
>   shall be thine own;
>   And eke five hundred pounds in gold,
>   that lies unknown.

BROADSIDE BALLADS

Oral ballads existed outside any professional network. But their influence reached into the world of musicians and customers, and their structure gave other forms of versified expression a starting point. Some oral ballads with unknown authors also found their way into print. (*Chevy Chase, The Children in the Woods,* and *The Spanish Lady* were all published in eighteenth-century America.) And by the early 1700s, songs sung in America to some of the same melodies as the oral ballads were also becoming items of commercial trade.

Verse in the colonial era served as a means of communication. Printed on sheets called broadsides, verses commenting on current events might be matched with a familiar tune and sold in the marketplace, just as sheet mu-

In the Battle of Norridgewock, on the Kennebec River in southern Maine (1724), British troops raided a settlement of Abenaki Indians, an event celebrated shortly after the battle by this Boston broadside.

sic and phonograph records were later to make popular songs widely accessible. Broadside ballads, though, lacked the aesthetic prestige that oral ballads came to enjoy: Their reputation was that of cheap commercial goods.
The Reverend Cotton Mather thus complained in a diary entry in 1713: "I
am informed, that the Minds and Manners of many People about the Countrey are much corrupted by foolish songs and Ballads, which the Hawkers
and Pedlars carry into all parts of the Countrey."[7]

Almost anything could inspire a broadside ballad: the settlement of the
North American colonies, Indian wars, dissatisfaction with English rule,
crime, love, and religion are some of the subject categories, along with humorous and ancient oral ballads. Many that were written with printed circulation in mind reveal a tone closer to the editorializing of *The Children in
the Woods* than to the detachment of *Chevy Chase*. *The Rebels Reward: or,
English Courage Display'd* (1724), for example, promises "a full and true Account of the Victory obtain'd over the Indians at Norrigiwock, on the
Twelfth of August last, by the English Forces under Command of Capt.
Johnson Harmon."[8] Printed in Boston by James Franklin, another brother of
Benjamin, it may have been written by Benjamin Franklin Sr., the younger
Benjamin's uncle.[9] The broadside complements the text with a woodcut
that pictures British soldiers shooting at unclad Indians, most of them in ca-
noes, with their fort in the background. And a printed legend directs: "To
the tune of, *All you that love Good Fellows*." But perhaps the most striking
fact about this song is its timeliness. Advertised for sale less than two weeks
after the battle of Norridgewock (in central Maine), the ballad was composed and distributed under the immediate spell of an event that had just
taken place some 170 miles northeast of Boston as the crow flies.[10]

By the early 1700s, many Jesuit priests in the New World were not only
missionaries to Native tribes but active political agents of the French
government in Canada, which opposed Great Britain's colonizing of North
America. One such figure was Father Sebastien Rale, a French-born scholar
of Indian languages, described in the nineteenth century as "fearless, resolute, enduring; boastful, sarcastic . . . a vehement partisan . . . hating the
English more than he loved the Indians."[11] Father Rale, leader of a mission
settlement of the Abenaki at Norridgewock, on the Kennebec River, had
helped to organize earlier Indian raids on the English settlers. In 1722, after
capturing papers that proved his involvement, the English ordered the
Abenaki to turn Rale over to them, but the Natives refused. Two years later,
convinced that unrest on the border was still being directed from Norridgewock, the English decided to seize Rale and destroy the settlement. Early in
August 1724, they launched their expedition.

Only a modern observer who accepts the English attack as a justified response to provocation could savor the display of "courage" the ballad describes. Writing of the battle, however, the historian Francis Parkman explained that English speakers who lived near the Quebec border considered France's Indian allies "less as men than as vicious and dangerous wild animals."[12] Moreover, partly for religious and partly for political reasons, a deep reservoir of anti–Roman Catholic feeling existed in Protestant North America. *The Rebels Reward* assumes an audience mistrustful of both Indians and Catholics.

Whatever poetic license the author of *The Rebels Reward* may have enjoyed, its plot squares with historical reports. For example, no claim is made that the English needed courage because they were outnumbered. In fact, two hundred of them attacked a village that was considerably smaller. And they surprised the unguarded outpost in mid-afternoon. The ballad suggests that when the English soldiers reached Norridgewock, the community was engaged in a popish ceremony led by Father Rale.

> Full Sixty fighting Indians,
>   with Ralee, their old Priest,
> And Women and Papooses
>   five Score there was at least.
> These all were come together
>   to make their horrid Dins,
> Whenas their Priest pretended
>   to pardon all their Sins.
>
> But you shall be informed
>   how they were forc'd to fly;
> For tho' their sins were pardon'd,
>   full loth they were to die.

The Indians try to escape across the river, but the soldiers pick them off with their muskets until the water is "stain'd with Gore." Then the ballad treats its audience to detailed accounts of the death of its main villains, including Father Rale (the order to capture him is disobeyed, and he is killed in the fight), "Captain" Maug, who dies defying the attackers, and "old Bombazeen," who is shot while running away. From that point on, English hunger for war's booty carries the day. One Indian brave, trapped on a rock in the river, avoids being shot only until a Mohawk employed by the English can finish him off with a knife. The reason is economic.

> Then did old Christians Brother,
>   a Mohawk brave and stout,
> Swim to him with his Knife,
>   and cut him in the Throat.

By which his Scalp was saved,
    which brings good store of Chink [coins],
For if our Men had shot him
    the Rogue would surely Sink.

With the opposition routed, the English soldiers make free use of what remains in the settlement.

Our Men got store of Plunder.
    both, Guns and Blankets too,
And drank the Fryers Brandy.
    which was their Honest due.
Good Powder too, and Kettles.
    which they had long enjoy'd,
Their Houses they were burned,
    and their Canoes destroy'd.
. . . .
They brought away a Squaw,
    and likewise Children three,
Which only were preserved
    our bond Slaves for to be.

The ballad signs off with a tribute to the expedition, giving no sign that the
notion of honor is invoked sarcastically:

Thus did our Honest Soldiers
    their Honour to preserve;
And Harmon's made a Collonel
    which he does well deserve.

In this strongly pro-English ballad, the heroes ambush the Indians; they
show no more mercy to squaws and papooses than to warriors; they hunt
scalps for bounty; they celebrate military success by quaffing brandy; they
take slaves. For actors in a tale purporting to show English courage, the vic-
tors seem more bullying and venal than courageous. But the point here,
rather than judging the ballad or its audience, is to note how it works as a
piece of verbal and musical communication. Telling the story of a fresh
event, a victory over forces that many of its audience members feared, it dis-
penses with shades of gray in celebrating the triumph. *Chevy Chase* chronicles; *The Rebels Reward* editorializes. Having taken a point of view, the
author gloats in the defeat of evil by good, judging the story's actors by who
they are, not by what they do. Finally, by linking his text to a tune whose associations suggest hearty male bonding—the opening words are "You jolly
hearted soldiers"—the author endows the ballad with a spirit like that of a
jovial hunting expedition, as if singing about Norridgewock were almost as
much fun as having been there.

In contrast to oral ballads, many broadside ballads show a cartoon-like quality of exaggeration, sometimes coupled with language or images that make later standards of public taste seem prudish. One example is *The Lawyer's Pedigree*, published in New England in 1755. Rooted in an earthy tradition of English humor, the song denies the legal profession any shred of dignity. It starts by prescribing as the tune of choice *Our Polly Is a Sad Slut*, sung in *The Beggar's Opera* by the corrupt Mrs. Peachum, a receiver of stolen goods (see Chapter 5). And it taps another ready source of ridicule in the anti–Roman Catholic prejudice that existed in Protestant Britain and her colonies, by parodying a much older song called *The Pope's Pedigree*. If the tune association linked lawyers to criminals, the text's background hints that they were also hypocrites, like Catholic clergy whose vows of celibacy did not deprive them of sexual pleasure:

> Thus, as the Story says,
> The pedigree did run;
> The Pope he had a Friar,
> The Friar had a Nun:
> The Nun, she was with Child
> And so her Credit sunk.
> The Father was a Friar,
> The Issue was a Monk.[13]

A song like *The Lawyer's Pedigree* is evidence that the impulse to create stereotypes based on occupation, gender, race, or religion, and to trope them endlessly in a derisive style of humor, has enjoyed a long if not always honorable history in this country. Expressive culture in America—anecdote, verse, song, picture, and stage performance—has drawn heavily on this impulse. In a land full of "others," almost every category of person has been a target for such raillery. And indeed, there is much to be said for banter among social equals and for barbs fired across class lines to deflate pretensions. On the other hand, when people low on the social scale are forced to bear the brunt of it, humor of this stamp can be more bullying than clever.

Broadside ballads followed the twists and turns of public opinion. With more directness than subtlety, they reflected everything from the winds of political change to expressions of national allegiance. British patriotic songs—by the late 1760s being changed by some American colonists into anti-British protests—circulated through broadsides and newspapers, sketching a lively chapter in the period's musical and social history. An observer noted in a diary entry of 1774 that in performing so-called liberty songs, "six, eight, ten or more [men] would put their Heads near together and roar."[14] Patriotism—love of one's country and belief in the rightness of its actions—aroused an uncomplicated passion well suited to the broadside ballad.

In the years before and during the War of Independence, one claim in particular was trumpeted in song after song, sometimes from an American and sometimes from a British perspective: our side is virtuous and right, the other side corrupt and wrong; and if the difference can be settled only through combat, then so be it. In the ideological duel that formed a counterpoint to rising political unrest, two groups of British subjects, the colonizers (loyalists) and the colonized (patriots), used the same stock of British theatrical and patriotic song to tout the superiority of their cause. In fact, the patriotic songs that appeared on broadsides and in newspapers during these years provide their own window on the founding of the American republic.

The Liberty Song, printed in a Boston newspaper in July 1768, illustrates how verse and music were enlisted in a British-American struggle that would soon escalate from debate into warfare. It was a takeoff on *Heart of Oak* (1759), a well-loved song commemorating an English victory over

John Dickinson's *Liberty Song* (1768) defied British authority by setting inflammatory words to the tune *Heart of Oak*, a recent and beloved patriotic song of the English people.

France during the Seven Years' War (1754–61). Perhaps the original song's refrain in praise of perseverance—"Steady, boys, steady"—struck the English as an apt distillation of their national character. Whatever the reasons for its appeal, however, Pennsylvanian John Dickinson chose well when he fired a parody of *Heart of Oak* back at the British. Here is the first stanza of Dickinson's text, typeset to resemble the original:

> Come, join Hand in Hand, brave AMERICANS all,
> And rouse your bold Hearts to fair LIBERTY'S Call;
> No *tyrannous Acts* shall suppress your *just Claim,*
> Or stain with *Dishonour* AMERICA'S Name.
>> In FREEDOM we're BORN, and in FREEDOM we'll LIVE.
>> Our Purses are ready,
>> Steady, Friends, Steady,
>> Not as SLAVES but as FREEMEN our Money we'll give.

Dickinson's patriot thrust hit home. In September 1768, the same Boston newspaper printed a version of *Heart of Oak* upholding the British cause and attacking the patriots, under the heading "Last Tuesday the following SONG made its Appearance" (from a room in Castle William, a British garrison):

> *Come shake your dull Noddles, ye Pumpkins and bawl,*
> *And own that you're mad at fair Liberty's Call,*
> *No scandalous Conduct can add to your Shame.*
> *Condemn'd to Dishonour. Inherit the Fame—*
>> In Folly you're born, and in Folly you'll live,
>> To Madness still ready,
>> And Stupidly steady,
>> Not as Men, but as Monkies, the Tokens you give.[15]

The two parodies of *Heart of Oak* offer the black and white contrasts that one expects from political propaganda. What the words alone cannot convey, however, is the emotional bite that these text-and-tune combinations must have produced in their original setting. Dickinson's pro-American version takes a familiar, much-loved song and twists its meaning; the loyalist version ridicules the new meaning with a strong dose of anti-patriot venom. Americans and English in Boston in 1768 must have received these parodies with some awareness of how they transformed the original. The patriot version is especially potent, for it turns *Heart of Oak*, an anthem of British self-congratulation, into an indictment of her policies. Yet the loyalist version also draws weight from the original, implying that England, which had defeated a potent European rival, stood ready to deal with a minor family disturbance. In both cases, the melody, its ethos, and its associations helped give an edge to political expression.

Patriotic broadside ballads took their melodies not only from English songs but from the vast body of dance music that circulated in Great Britain and her American colonies. It seems likely that the audience for *The Irishman's Epistle to the Officers and Troops at Boston* was expected to take *Irish Washerwoman*, the tune to which those words were sung, as a point of reference. The *Epistle* first appeared in the *Pennsylvania Magazine* of May 1775, only a month after war broke out. In Philadelphia, far removed from the fighting, observers could look beyond the war's grim side and find humor in an event like the hasty British retreat from the colonials.[16] In the second stanza of the *Epistle*, the song's Irish protagonist taunts the British Regulars, gleefully rubbing salt into wounds their pride had suffered:

> How brave you went out with muskets all bright,
> And thought to befrighten the folks with the sight;
> But when you got there how they powder'd your pums,
> And all the way home how they pepper'd your bums,
> And is it not, honies, a comical farce,
> To be proud in the face, and be shot in the arse?

DANCING AND DANCE MUSIC

Dance has functioned for more than three centuries as a lightning rod for American public opinion. Through all the changes in dancing styles since the 1600s, two issues have repeatedly stirred controversy: (1) dance's erotic dimension and efforts to keep it under control, and (2) dance's connection with social class. The first is a reminder that even though dance is being discussed here as a secular activity, it has long been a matter for debate in American religious life. The second testifies that, like clothing and manners, dancing has often served as a marker of social trends and a measure of fashion.

Americans acquired their dances from a variety of sources. Up to the time of the Civil War (1860s), most social dances came from Europe. More recently, they have originated chiefly on this side of the Atlantic, especially among ethnic "others," and most of all African Americans. New dances have tended to be more physically active than the ones they replace, or at least they have been active in different ways, carrying an aura of freshly won freedom by crossing boundaries into formerly suspect territory.

In the story of popular dance's development in America, Puritanism has often been assigned a villain's role. Today, in a social climate that sets high value on personal freedom, past attempts to control dancing styles may seem ineffectual, repressive, or even incomprehensible. Dances once denounced as instruments of the devil now appear quite proper, making objections once raised against them seem old-fashioned or silly. And yet important issues were at stake in the often acrimonious debates that dance has inspired.

The lack of common ground between social dance and the Puritan imagination may be traced to the belief that spirit and flesh, rather than complementary parts of human identity, are contrary forces locked in a perpetual struggle. Occupied with the state of their souls, devout Puritans tried to live their lives in full awareness that they were sinners dependent on the grace of God. Dance that celebrated the human body did so, they believed, only at the soul's expense. Because it fostered a state of mind more conducive to sin than to spiritual contemplation, dance earned the constant vigilance of the Puritan clergy.

While mistrusting the spirit of dance, however, the Puritans acknowledged its force as an agent of discipline. In a tract with a title whose religious passion echoes down through the ages—*An Arrow Against Profane and Promiscuous Dancing; Drawn Out of the Quiver of the Scriptures* (Boston, 1684)—the Reverend Increase Mather, father of Cotton, justified dancing as an effective instrument of social control. If "the Design of Dancing is only to teach children good Behaviour and a decent Carriage," Mather wrote, then he could approve it. "To learn a due Poyse and Composure of the Body is not unlawful, provided it be done without a provocation to Uncleanness, and be not a nurse of Pride and Vanity." And he went on to say that if Christians wished their children to be taught dancing in the proper spirit, "they may send them not to a Blasphemer, but to some Grave Person that will teach them decency of Behaviour, not *Promiscuously*, but each sex by themselves; so neither God nor Man will be offended."[17] To keep uncleanness (i.e., sexuality) at bay, Mather recommends that girls and boys be taught separately, and only by a pious instructor. The one adult Mather refers to in this passage is the dancing master, which shows his reluctance to grant dance's social benefits beyond those of a character-building pastime for youngsters. For those who accepted the Puritans' oppositional view of flesh and spirit, it was hard to believe that men and women could dance together while still honoring and glorifying God.

For non-Puritans, however, dance has not been universally considered a secular activity. Many American Indian tribes, for example, have relied on music and movement together to establish contact with the spiritual realm. African religions brought to North America by slaves also gave dance a crucial role. Even within Anglo-American culture, the Shakers, a celibate sect founded in late eighteenth-century England that endured in this country into the latter 1900s, were known for their sacred dancing.

Anglicans, while sharing the Puritans' view of dancing as secular, did not share their disapproval. In 1714, King's Chapel in Boston hired Edward Enstone from London as its organist, anticipating that his work would also include dance instruction.[18] There were also dancing masters in colonial Boston from the 1670s on, whatever the Puritans thought of them. George Brownell, with whom the young Benjamin Franklin studied writing and arithmetic, advertised in 1713 to teach practical, artistic, and polite skills that included "Writing, Cyphering, Dancing, Treble Violin, Flute, Spinnet," and embroidery.[19] Notices like these are a reminder that dance in early America covered a fairly broad range of accomplishment. At one end of the spectrum were skills taught formally by masters like Enstone and Brownell that prepared people to attend social functions such as balls. At the other was a casual, informal pastime taking place at home and as part of festive occasions.

Dance manuals and musical sources show that Americans of the colonial era performed both couple dances and so-called country dances. Couple dances, including the gavotte, the bourrée, and especially the minuet, were courtly affairs of French origin that called for precise, schooled movements.

From its first publication in 1651, Playford's *The Dancing Master* supplied tunes and instructions for several generations of English-speaking dancers. The dance pictured in this 1725 edition's title page is accompanied by three musicians in the gallery at the left.

To perform such dances well was considered a social accomplishment, possible only through instruction, which itself implies the availability of leisure time and money for lessons. By 1725, however, country dances performed by groups, as in later square dancing, had come into favor in England and the American colonies. Especially popular were "longways" dances, in which a line of men faced a line of women, and the focus, rather than on the movements of individual dancers, was on the patterns traced collectively by the whole group. As their label suggests, country dances claim folk origins, some dating back to sixteenth-century England. But early in the next century, these dances were reworked into courtly and aristocratic amusements. By the time the tunes and instructions for the dances appeared in John Playford's *The English Dancing Master* (London, 1651), the publication most responsible for codifying and circulating them, they were no longer rustic. The frontispiece of Playford's work, dated 1725 in its eighteenth edition, portrays a country line dance in progress.[20]

For all of Great Britain's claim to a democratic heritage, the British Empire, even into the present century, maintained the shape of a society of orders, with an aristocracy, a range of professional and middle-class layers, and a peasantry, each ordained by birth. As an extension of Britain's social structure, American colonial society sought to follow Old World models in formal events like balls and banquets. The courtly French minuet, for example, might begin a ball, danced by the most important guests; other dances with prescribed steps might follow. The rest of the evening was often given over to country dances, whose popularity increased on both sides of the Atlantic through the 1700s. A diary entry from 1774 describes the order of events at one Virginia ball: "About Seven the Ladies & Gentlemen began to dance in the Ball-Room—first Minuets one Round; Second Giggs; third Reels, And last of All Country-Dances. . . . The Music was a French-

Country dancing remained popular well into the 1800s, as shown by this light-hearted stylization of dancers' behavior from a Philadelphia journal of 1817.

when dancing their Silks & Brocades rustled and trailed behind them!"[21] A similar ordering was also found further to the south. When the British replaced the Spanish in Florida after the Seven Years' War, they turned St. Augustine into a settlement that colonial Governor James Grant described in 1771 as "dansing mad." English balls there also began with minuets followed by country dances.[22] Apparently country dances themselves were not free from implications of class hierarchy. One report has it that in 1768, formal balls had to be discontinued for a time in New York "when consorts of General Gage and Governor Moore could not agree on who should stand first in a country dance."[23]

Few if any accounts from the time suggest the erotic power of dance as openly as one set down in 1760 in the diary of future president John Adams. One afternoon, in a tavern in Weymouth, Massachusetts, Adams witnessed a mini-drama centered around dance and secular song. The chief actor was Zab Howard, reputed to be "the best Dancer in the World in these Towns." Adams offers no information about the music he heard. Neither does he search for a moral in the events he observed. But the details that Adams chose to record show that he too felt the electricity Howard's dancing and singing discharged in that informal setting.

> When he first began, his Behavior and Speeches were softly silly, but as his Blood grew warm by motion and Liquor, he grew droll. He caught a Girl and danced a Gigg with her, and then led her to one side of the Ring and said "Stand there, I call for you by and by." This was spoke comically enough, and raised a loud laugh. He caught another girl, with light Hair, and a Patch on her Chin, and held her by the Hand while he sung a song, describing her as he said. This tickled the Girls Vanity, for the song which he applied to her described a very fine Girl indeed.[24]

Adams's vignette captures both the encounter's charm and its hint of danger. An experienced, charismatic male uses song, dance, jokes, and flattery to hold observers in a state of expectation. And in this near-theatrical display of sex appeal, he artfully turns the females present into props, to their apparent delight and that of the assembled company. Depending on how one views it, this Weymouth tavern scene offers either a wanton display of "uncleanness" or a stylized male-female encounter in which eroticism stays within socially acceptable boundaries.

Like the country dances themselves, music for them came from overseas, especially from Anglo-Irish tradition. The music circulated both orally and in written form, including printed collections and manuscripts that musicians copied for their own use. Some of the tunes claimed a lineage reaching back to the mid-1600s and before. As already noted, broadside ballads, which occupied adjacent cultural turf, sometimes borrowed their melodies from dance. The tunes in the dance repertory show a good deal of variety, while sharing common traits with Western dance music in general.

Whatever the period of its composition, dance music can be counted on, first, to move in a steady tempo; second, to be cast in regular melodic phrases of predictable length (usually four or eight bars); and third, to depend on repetition, with repeated sections being called "strains." The tune of *Irish Washerwoman,* which has been traced as far back as Playford's *The English Dancing Master* (1651), is a good example. The following version, preserved in an American copy from around 1795, is cast in two eight-measure strains. The second strain, while resembling the first, occupies a higher range and traces a different melodic curve, though both strains end with the same melodic close. The melody can be sung, of course, but its wide range and frequent leaps point to instrumental origins. In fact, the second strain, and especially the repeated-note figure near the end, invites performance on the fiddle, though it can also be played on the flute, the other favorite dance instrument of the time.

Irish Washerwoman survives in many eighteenth-century copies, domestic and foreign, in print and in manuscript, and several different longways country dances for the tune have turned up in American sources.[25] Since the main requirement of the performers' trade was to support dancers by maintaining a regular flow of rhythm, one imagines that, like dance musicians of other eras, some exercised their imagination by decorating, embellishing, and perhaps also varying tunes rather than simply repeating them verbatim. Beyond the notation in the musical sources, however, no evidence survives of how musicians of the time actually played.

Scholars have also located several different dances to the tune *Black Joke.* A London source from 1742 carries a label that could also be applied to many other country dances: "Longways for as many as will." The instruc-

This American copy of the two-strain dance tune *Irish Washerwoman* is found in a manuscript collection prepared around 1795 for treble instrument.

tions are quite precise—perhaps coordinated with the unusual shape of the tune itself, whose sixteen bars are divided asymmetrically into a first strain of six and a second of ten bars. The instructions read: "Hands round, all four quite round. Hands round, all four back again, clap Hands with your Partner, clap Sides and right & left half round, then lead down and lead up, clap hands with your Partner, & right & left quite round at Top. *Each Strain twice.*"[26]

A manuscript from New Hampshire in the 1780s preserves a different, less detailed dance to *Black Joke* that also contains *College Hornpipe*, another favorite country dance tune.[27] What is especially striking about tunes like *Irish Washerwoman* and *College Hornpipe*, however, is something they shared with oral ballads like *Chevy Chase* and *The Spanish Lady*: their capacity to survive changes of musical fashion. *College Hornpipe*, known also as *Sailor's Hornpipe*, was first published in London in 1766. At least six American editions were printed in the years 1801–25, and in 1870 thirteen of the twenty American publishers in the Board of Music Trade listed editions for sale.[28] Almost half a century later, composer Charles Ives, remembering the fiddling at barn dances he had attended as a Connecticut boy in the 1880s, quoted *College Hornpipe* and other dance tunes in the "Washington's Birthday" movement of his *Holidays* Symphony. Today books of fiddle music still carry *College Hornpipe*. And in animated cartoons of the last several decades, the appearance of a sailor on the screen is likely to call forth a reference to this tune.

HOME AND AMATEUR MUSIC MAKING

The main fact known about music making in early American homes is that it took place. Details giving a comprehensive picture of where, when, how, and at what levels of skill music was performed at home can only be sketched because documentation is sparse. A search of colonial Boston records has turned up evidence that many citizens owned musical instruments: keyboards (especially of the harpsichord type), plucked and bowed strings, wind instruments, trumpets, and drums.[29] Occasional references to their use can also be found; for example, on December 6, 1681, the Reverend Peter Thacher of Milton, Massachusetts, noted in his diary that a group of men "Cut & Carted wood for mee in milton, there was Eleven Carts, 18 Cutters of wood. I made a supper for them. Wee had the Viol afterward." In a later diary, Benjamin Lynde Jr., of Salem, Massachusetts, left a record of dances he attended. Sometimes musicians would be hired for such occasions, but on one March evening in 1730, Lynde wrote that the music was provided by a member of a prosperous merchant family in Salem, William Browne, who also played fiddle: "Fair wind; At night rid on WB's horse; after, he down here playing on his violin."[30] The painting *A Musical Gathering*, most likely an eighteenth-century American work, shows a home ensemble in action and links music making with conviviality.

Colonial American society included a number of people with cultivated tastes, but since it lacked easy access to professional performers, members had to feed their appetite for diversion by entertaining in the home. Both music and dance provided such pastimes. The parallel between couple dances like the minuet and gavotte and music that shows refinement is clear. Both involved social accomplishment, which was linked to class standing, and both required instruction to reach a level of skill that could make a refined impression in performance. Like dancing masters, music masters supplied that instruction, giving lessons in singing or on standard parlor instruments of the day: harpsichord, violin, flute, and guitar. Music masters might be itinerants like John Stadler, who in the late 1760s traveled the Virginia countryside teaching at the estates of such families as the Carters, whose plantation covered sixty thousand acres, or at the Washington family's Mount Vernon. Or they might locate in cities, as did James Bremner—brother of Robert, a prominent Scottish music publisher—who in the early 1760s taught lessons in a Philadelphia coffeehouse.[31] In the years leading up to the War of Independence, evidence of amateur music making increased in the public record, with dealers advertising instruments, accessories, and printed music and teachers offering their services in the

This painting, undated and of unknown authorship but assumed to be North American, shows a punch bowl being brought to a group of players whose instruments include fiddle, oboe, trumpet, cello, and hammered dulcimer.

public press. A musically minded colonial American who could pay for lessons had a decent chance to become a competent amateur performer.

The label "gentleman amateur" carries implications of social class—gentlemen and women enjoy the leisure time and opportunity to perfect musical skills—while also suggesting private performances and perhaps a certain superficiality as well. But in early America, "amateur," rather than referring to someone less skilled or devoted than a professional, signifies one who pursues music simply for love of it, as the Latin root verb (amare, to love) suggests. One gentleman amateur who left a detailed record of music making was Dr. Alexander Hamilton, a native of Scotland who immigrated to America in 1739 and settled in Annapolis, Maryland. Hamilton was a fluent writer of prose who also enjoyed singing and playing the cello. He and his fellow members of The Tuesday Club, a group of Annapolis professional men, met every other Tuesday evening for a meal, conversation, conviviality, and music. One member summed up the club's evenings this way: "We meet, converse, Laugh, talk, Smoke, drink, differ, agree, Philosophize, Harangue, pun, Sing, Dance and fiddle together." A few of the club members composed music; several played instruments, and all sang—one member so well that the others ordered him to sing rather than speak his position in club votes.[32] Most club members were also handy with verse, often providing humorous new words for existing tunes, à la the broadside ballad, and some able to improvise them on the spot.

A far more famous amateur musician than any Tuesday Club member was Thomas Jefferson, author of the Declaration of Independence and third U.S. president. Jefferson, who sometimes pursued music more as an art than a pastime, studied violin and played the instrument through much of his life, owned and maintained harpsichords, and collected a large library of music from which he and others performed.[33] In a 1778 letter to Giovanni Fabbroni, an acquaintance in Paris, he called music "the favorite passion of my soul" and told of his aspirations for building musical performance more fully into the life of Monticello, his Virginia country estate. Confessing envy of European music making, Jefferson saw music in America as standing "in a state of deplorable barbarism" by contrast. He invited Fabbroni to visit him or to send "a substitute . . . proficient in singing, & on the Harpsichord." While granting that "the bounds of an American fortune will not admit the indulgence of a domestic band of musicians," he nevertheless had considered how he might reconcile his "passion for music" with the constraints of his budget. Perhaps the answer lay in importing a domestic staff from Europe.

I retain for instance . . . a gardener . . . a weaver . . . a cabinet maker . . . and a stonecutter . . . to which I would add a vigneron [winegrower]. In a country where like yours music is cultivated and practised by every class of men I suppose there might be found persons of those trades who could perform on the French horn, clarinet or hautboy [oboe] & bassoon, so that one might have a band of two French horns, two clarinets, & hautboys & a bassoon.[34]

Living on a remote country estate, Jefferson imagined a musical environment that would allow him to play and also to retain a "band of music" to gratify his appetite as a listener.

PAINTED BY PINE.

ENGRAVED BY J. HEATH.

Francis Hopkinson of Philadelphia (1737–1791), a prominent patriot during the revolution, was also an active amateur musician who played organ and harpsichord and composed vocal music.

By all accounts, however, there was no more devoted gentleman amateur in colonial America than Philadelphia native Francis Hopkinson, the University of Pennsylvania's first graduate, a lawyer and judge by trade, a patriot, and a signer of the Declaration of Independence. Hopkinson began playing the harpsichord at age seventeen, in 1754, the same year he expressed his love for music in an "Ode" cast in heroic couplets. The poem begins:

> Hark! hark! the sweet vibrating lyre
> Sets my attentive soul on fire;
> Thro' all my frame what pleasures thrill,
> Whilst the loud treble warbles shrill,
> And the more slow and solemn bass,
> Adds charms to charm and grace to grace.[35]

In the 1750s, Hopkinson furthered his musical education by hand-copying arias, songs, and instrumental pieces by many European composers, including George Frideric Handel, Arcangelo Corelli, Francesco Geminiani, Johann Stamitz, Baldassare Galuppi, and Thomas Augustine Arne (music favored by mid-century Londoners). By the early 1760s, he was a good enough harpsichordist to join professional musicians in concerts. As an Anglican, Hopkinson also involved himself in sacred music, serving for a time as organist of Philadelphia's Christ Church, teaching psalmody, and compiling sacred tunebooks for congregational singing. In contrast to the country squire Jefferson, Hopkinson was able to use home music making as a springboard for entry into Philadelphia's musical life, where, given the scarcity of professional performers, his ability and social position would have made him welcome.

Hopkinson combined a creative streak with his performing ability, and he put it to work in the patriots' cause. During the War of Independence's last year he produced *America Independent, or The Temple of Minerva*, a combination masque and oratorio fashionable at European courts of the time. The work, which shows him in a dual role of political balladeer and musical arranger, was performed on March 21, 1781, at the residence of France's minister to the Continental Congress, headquartered in Philadelphia. Predicting the victory of America ("Columbia") in the war, Hopkinson wrote his own verses to fit music composed by others—chiefly Handel and the Arne brothers, Thomas and Michael—and he arranged his patriotic pastiche for soloists and a chorus accompanied by orchestra. To bring *The Temple of Minerva* to a triumphal close, Hopkinson set new stanzas to the tune of *See the Conqu'ring Hero Comes* from Handel's *Judas Maccabaeus*. One stanza praised the Franco-American alliance:

> From the friendly shores of France.
> See the martial troops advance,

>With Columbia's sons unite,
>And share the dangers of the fight,
>Equal heroes of the day,
>Equal honors to them pay.[36]

In the partisan atmosphere of 1781, what inspired one group was sure to offend the other. And indeed, *The Temple of Minerva* drew a quick response in the form of a parody. *The Temple of Cloacina* (a cloaca is a sewer or privy), beginning with an instrumental "overturd" and taking an outhouse for its temple, answered Hopkinson's extravaganza in the loyalist press. In one number, Hopkinson's words, addressed to Minerva, were mocked in an indecent "prayer" to Cloacina:

Temple of Minerva	*Temple of Cloacina*
To th'immortal breath of fame,	To the stinking breath of fame,
Give, oh give, her honor'd name.	Give, oh, give the Yankie name,
O'er her councils, still preside,	O'er her close-stools still preside,
In the field her armies guide.	Wipe with nettles her backside.[37]

The goddesses Minerva and Cloacina offer ample proof that to join the political discourse of the day, even as a gentleman, was to risk involvement in an ideological mud fight.

Francis Hopkinson's musical ambitions reached beyond performances and parodies into the realm of original composition. In 1759, he made his own musical setting of *My Days Have Been So Wondrous Free*, a poem by Thomas Parnell. Cast in two parts, a vocal line with bass accompaniment, this song was modeled on British songs he had copied out on his own. To look at this beginning effort by an "amateur" American composer is to recognize both the talent and the inexperience of the twenty-two-year-old Hopkinson. The setting of the title phrase shows a feeling for graceful melody and apt declamation. The rest of the first section, however, shows a less sure hand. After the shapely opening gesture, the music seems to lose purpose, hovering for several measures, mostly in running eighth notes, between dominant and tonic. But surely, to hold this attempt of the young Francis Hopkinson up for scrutiny is a curious thing to do—especially because he never published the song, nor is it known to have been performed either in private or in public when he was alive, nor do any of his surviving papers refer to it.

Why, then, single out this song for comment? Because of a historical misunderstanding. Nearly thirty years later, Hopkinson published *Seven Songs for the Harpsichord or Forte Piano* (Philadelphia, 1788), dedicated to George Washington, for which he wrote both words and music. A prefatory note declares: "I cannot I believe, be refused the Credit of being the first Native of the United States who has produced a Musical Composition."[38] In 1905, Oscar G. Sonneck, eminent historian of American music, published a study testing Hopkinson's claim. But Sonneck, equating the English-speaking colonies with the United States, concentrated on the year 1759, when both Hopkinson and psalmodist James Lyon, who had composed an ode for Princeton College's graduation, had written their first original music. Does Francis Hopkinson or James Lyon, Sonneck asked, deserve pride of place as America's first composer? After much bibliographical digging and interpretation, he decided in Hopkinson's favor and nominated *My Days Have Been So Wondrous Free* as the first American musical composition. More recently, however, pointing out that no United States existed in 1759, scholars have come to believe that the claim refers to the nation born in June 1788—when the ninth state ratified the Constitution of the United States of America—and to *Seven Songs*, which was published the following November.[39] By that reckoning, Hopkinson's claim holds true if musical composition is taken to mean secular piece.[40]

Historical precedence aside, Hopkinson's collection (it actually contains eight songs, the last apparently added after the title page was engraved) reflects his enduring commitment to the British song tradition, for it surveys the genres that Arne, James Hook, Charles Dibdin, and other London composers wrote for comic opera and pleasure-garden performances. Hopkinson tried his hand at a hunting song, a sea song, a "rondo" whose singer scoffs at the notion that love might enslave him, and a pair of pastoral songs in which shepherds vow devotion to idealized maidens. Like his earlier efforts, the music of *Seven Songs* is set on two staves: a vocal line with supporting bass. Landmark or not, however, the songs seem to have been largely ignored in their own day, though the composer's exchange of letters with Thomas Jefferson in Paris in 1789 shows that Jefferson's daughters, Martha (sixteen) and Polly (eleven), were touched by the "pathos" of one that they played and sang at home.[41]

5

Performing "By Particular Desire"

Colonial Military, Concert, and Theater Music

ARMY COMMANDERS HAVE LONG KNOWN the advantages of musical instruments for outdoor communication. In an account of exploration before
white settlement of North America began, Captain John Smith related: "*The
first Voyage to Virginia; undertaken by Master John White. 1589*. It was late
ere we arrived, but seeing fire through the woods, we sounded a Trumpet,
but no answer could we heare."[1] Trumpets are also mentioned in a report of
a 1621 meeting between Massasoit, chief of the Wampanoag Indians, and
the Pilgrim leader, Governor William Bradford of Plymouth Colony, far to
the north. Bradford was ushered into the meeting "with Drumme and Trumpet after him," at whose sound the Natives were said to have marveled
greatly.[2]

Drums played an important signaling role in early New England life,
summoning citizens to a meeting or to battle, or relaying news. In today's
sonic world, where music's volume is often boosted by electronics, the
sound of fifes and drums being played outside might not seem especially
loud. But early accounts show that they could seem almost deafening. At a
public ceremony to discipline a Continental soldier convicted of thievery in
1775, another soldier wrote that the drums "made such a report in my ears,
when accompanied by such screaking of whifes [*sic*] that I could not hear
the man next to me, or however could not hear what he said."[3]

Military uses for music may be divided into four categories: morale building (or *esprit de corps*), camp duties (which included signaling), public ceremonies, and recreation. On the first count, a soldier in the American Civil
War wrote, after he and his company heard several bands perform: "The
noise of the men was deafening. I felt at the time that I could whip a
whole brigade of the enemy myself." Marshal Maurice Comte de Saxe, an
eighteenth-century European general, understood music's power to impose

its own sense of time and to impart energy that lifts the spirit. Just as "it in-spires people to dance to music all night who cannot continue two hours without it," Saxe recognized that musical sound could help "make the men forget the hardship of long marches."[4]

Music also proved a practical way to regulate camp duties. As armies in-creased in size, they became more cumbersome to control. Techniques of warfare required that large groups of soldiers be moved in an orderly way, and drum cadences proved far more effective than oral commands. By the 1600s, European armies had developed rhythmic and melodic signals such as reveille, retreat, and tattoo. The British military brought these signals to North America, and soldiers here used them in the practice of their trade. Musical signals allowed military leaders to communicate quickly with their men, both in and out of battle.[5]

Military life relies a good deal on ceremonies, which seek most of all to convey a sense of controlled power. Parades that feature uniformed soldiers marching in time to music foster the impression of discipline, linking many individuals in a single mass. Such spectacles seek also to convey an impres-sion of invincibility. With no risk to life or limb, they contribute to any army's goal: to deter wars as well as to fight them.

Finally, a military unit is both a fighting force and a society, and music making has long complemented the military's social side. Musicians who played for marching and other maneuvers also provided musical recreation: concerts, meal-time performances, evening entertainments, sports festivals, and riding exhibitions. In fact, the British and American military in the 1700s fostered two different kinds of ensembles, one strictly functional and the other geared more toward aesthetic ends. "Field music"—which in-volved fifes and drums as in the 1775 ceremony described above—was played by musicians who belonged to the regiments and whose wages were paid out of army appropriations. *Harmoniemusik*, also known as "the band of music" and performed by pairs of wind instruments (oboes, horns, bassoons, possibly clarinets), required more polished musicianship. And the skill re-quired for that ensemble was supplied, in the British army at least, by play-ers hired by the officers and paid out of their own pockets.

The field music, performed by marching musicians, was portable as well as loud, making it an ideal functional medium geared toward building *esprit de corps*, controlling troop movement, and enhancing ceremonies. The band of music, less loud and portable but with a harmonized sound made by upper-, lower-, and middle-register instruments, offered wider musical pos-sibilities; it was most useful for recreation, though it could also be an inspi-rational and ceremonial presence. When American colonists began to form militia units to fight the War of Independence, they followed the British customs they already knew, including the two-part division into field music and *Harmoniemusik.*

Taken together, field music and *Harmoniemusik* prefigure the later history of the wind band as it has developed on American soil. The latter deserves special note as a rare early example on this continent of a secular institution's support of music making. Some bands of music also performed outside a military context—as in 1771, for example, when two Boston musicians, Josiah Flagg and W. S. Morgan, each gave a public concert in which the band of the British Sixty-Fourth Regiment appeared, or in 1774, when the British Fourth Regiment band played in a civilian funeral procession.[6]

By the same token, some bands of music survived beyond the military circumstances for which they were formed in the first place. When George Washington toured the United States in 1789, just before he took office as president, bands welcomed him almost everywhere. These ensembles played the full range of the day's music: marches, patriotic songs, medleys, songs from stage works old and new, battle pieces, rearranged orchestra works, and original compositions. The band's ability to travel and to exist in a variety of forms has made it a uniquely practical ensemble. In that spirit, band performances in early America were given in many different indoor and outdoor settings: coffeehouses, taverns, and theaters on the one hand, and parade grounds and pleasure gardens on the other.

CONCERT LIFE

Early in this century, Oscar G. Sonneck published a chronicle of eighteenth-century American concert life that filled more than three hundred pages, testifying to New World musicians' success in creating a public space where music was presented to paying audiences. For that space to materialize, a concert first had to be imagined and a venue found for it. Next, it had to be organized—date fixed, performers secured, music chosen—and advertised. Finally, it had to attract customers. The first step, imagining concerts, was simpler than it would have been had not most of the musicians been immigrants from Europe. Born and trained in places where secular assemblies were common, concert organizers had only to transplant and adapt to the New World customs already familiar to them from the Old.

Concerts in the 1700s were not necessarily high-toned, formal cultural events; they were more likely to be functions held in modest, often plain rooms with no stage, and with temporary arrangements of chairs that might quickly be pushed aside for dancing when the concert was over. The first known public concert in the American colonies took place in Boston in

1729, in a room that a local dancing master used for assemblies.[7] Not until the next decade did the city gain a real concert hall: a room in a building that in 1754 was acquired and refurbished as "an elegant private concert-room."[8] But such a center made Boston unusual among American cities of the time. In most of eighteenth-century America, concert rooms were concert rooms only as long as the performance lasted. Musicians, having learned to adapt urban environments to their needs, slipped out of the impresario's role when their concerts ended, and their performing sites went back to being drawing rooms, public dancing rooms, taverns or government chambers.

Benefit concerts, which could be put together quickly, were well suited to the conditions of the day's musical life. The benefit concert format allowed local organists, traveling professionals, or newly arrived singers in a theater troupe to star in nearly impromptu shows of their own making. The musician who arranged a benefit took the financial risk, paying the expenses—including heat, light, and publicity—and reaping the profits, if any. Benefit concerts were one-time happenings, which distinguishes them from most subscription concerts, another eighteenth-century approach. The subscription format allowed organizers to hedge their bets: to issue a public proposal and then wait to see whether the response justified going ahead with the plan. One entrepreneur's trial balloon, sent up in Richmond, Virginia, in the 1790s, promised a concert for a certain date, "if a sufficient number of subscriptions are received to defray expences—if not, the money will be returned to those who may have subscribed."[9]

Other types of concerts included the charity benefit given to raise money for a worthy cause, such as aiding residents of the local poorhouse or a family hit by catastrophe. Concerts were also given by musical societies: social organizations formed to promote some aspect of the art. The St. Cecilia Society of Charleston, South Carolina, for example, brought together amateur and professional musicians on a regular basis. The society's membership dues acted in effect as a subscription that supported musical performances, some of them open to the public.

While private concerts were open to only a small circle, the success of public concerts depended on whether their organizers could attract an audience of sufficient size. From the very beginnings of American concert life, much of the burden of audience recruitment fell on publicity, which was dispensed in print as well as by word of mouth. One way to advertise was through handbills, which could be passed from person to person and posted as well. Unlike newspaper announcements, which survive in great numbers, however, few eighteenth-century handbills have been preserved.

The earliest concert ads seldom go beyond the bare facts: Mr. X, for his own benefit, will present a concert at Y hall on date Z; tickets cost U shillings and may be purchased from Mr. V on W Street. After mid-century, however, promoters seem to have lost confidence that a straight factual report would be enough to corral an audience. A plea for customers might be framed as a personal invitation, as when a musician in Charleston announced in 1760 that he had "no Doubt, but that it will be in his Power to give the greatest Satisfaction to those Ladies and Gentlemen who shall honor him with their presence." Some announcements imply that public demand, not the organizer's pursuit of the Almighty Shilling, occasioned concerts. A Philadelphia musician in 1757 headed his ad with the phrase "By particular desire"; a concert there in 1770 was being given "at the request of several Gentlemen and Ladies"; and the next year an ad for another Philadelphia concert stated: "Several Gentlemen, who wish to encourage and reward Merit, have suggested this public Amusement." Others used flattery, boasts, or even warnings to attract customers. One ad cautioned: "This will positively be the only time of his performing, unless by the particular desire of a genteel company."[10]

By the last part of the century, concert advertisements routinely combined vital information with rhetorical flourishes. Stock adjectives studded the verbal formulas of concert publicity: concerts were "grand," physical settings "elegant," repertory and performers "celebrated" and "highly approved," audiences "genteel." An ad for a charity benefit could borrow the rolling cadences of the sermon—"To administer some relief to him whose hope is like a shadow, to raise up him who is bound down with sorrow, and to shew that the fine Arts may and ought to subserve the purposes of humanity"—while more commercial ventures might be described in language suggesting membership in a league of refined taste. More and more intent on persuasion, concert promoters in eighteenth-century America evolved a hyperbolic approach to advertising that by the century's later years marked American concert life as a branch of the theatrical world. One Charleston proprietor proclaimed in 1799 that

> the airy and healthful situation of the Garden; a Military Band, composed of musicians, masters in their profession; elegant illumination in the many avenues and arbours, the low price of admittance, and the particular attention that will be paid to the visitors—are considerations which induce him [the proprietor] to think that he will be highly compensated by a generous public.[11]

Public concerts of the eighteenth century, in both the Old World and the New, emphasized variety and ran more to short pieces than long ones. A few were in three "acts," but most were two-part affairs, each part beginning and ending with as full an ensemble as could be mustered and mixing vocal and instrumental selections. Vocal numbers ranged from solo songs and opera airs to glees for one-on-a-part ensembles. Instrumental numbers included solo keyboard pieces, chamber music, and pieces for orchestra, with "Grand Symphony" meaning one symphonic movement rather than an entire three- or four-movement work. In Philadelphia, for example, in November 1769, John Gualdo, calling himself a "Wine Merchant from Italy, but late from London," announced a "Grand Concert of Vocal and Instrumental Musick" at "the Assembly Room." A local newspaper printed the program on the day the event was to take place:

Act I

Overture composed by the Earl of Kelly
"Vain is beauty, gaudy flower," by Miss Hallam
Trio composed by Mr. Gualdo, first violin by Master Billy Crumpto
"The Spinning Wheel," by Miss Storer
A German flute Concert, with Solos, composed by Mr. Gualdo
A new Symphony after the present taste, composed by Mr. Gualdo

Act II

A new Violin concerto with solos, composed by Mr. Gualdo
A Song by Mr. Wools
A Sonata upon the Harpsichord, by Mr. Curtz
Solo upon the Clarinet, by Mr. Hoffmann, junior
A Song by Miss Hallam
Solo upon the Mandolino, by Mr. Gualdo
Overture, composed by the Earl of Kelly[12]

This concert was typical in its mixing of genres, forces, and sounds. Indeed, variety dictated a concert's pace, for the more different setups a program required, the more time was likely to elapse between numbers. Perhaps some audience members welcomed the chance to socialize during the pauses. For them, at least, the contrasts must have enhanced the atmosphere of entertainment that surrounded public concerts in the colonial and federal eras.

While typical in its format, however, Gualdo's concert was unusual in offering so much original music (none of which has survived). In fact, this benefit for a now-forgotten figure has been called the first "composers'-concert" given in America.[13] As well as writing much of the music on the program, Gualdo seems also to have been its most conspicuous performer. His leading of the concert—"directed by Mr. Gualdo, after the Italian method," read the publicity blurb—and mandolin solo are a matter of record. Since he had earlier advertised himself in the public press as a teacher of violin and German flute, he may well have taken the soloist's role in the flute and violin concertos too. Where Gualdo found his orchestra members is not known for sure, but the singers' names point to a possible source. Nancy Hallam, Maria Storer, and Stephen Wools were all featured members of the New American Company, which in November 1769 was in residence at Philadelphia's Southwark Theater. The calendar shows that the company performed comic opera on November 14 and 17 of that year, but not on the 16th, the evening of Gualdo's concert. Most likely, Gualdo recruited players for his benefit from the New American Company's orchestra.

The program of a concert given nearly thirty years later, on June 25, 1799, in Salem, Massachusetts, provides more musical detail. It also offers a glimpse of how a corps of seasoned troupers might plan a concert as a commercial venture. This performance was a joint benefit for Catherine Graupner, a prominent theatrical singer, and Peter Albrecht von Hagen, instrumentalist and orchestra leader, both active in Boston.

Part 1st

Overture, composed by	Pleyel
Song by Mr. Munto	Dr. Arnold
A Sonata on the Grand Forte Piano for 4 hands,	
by Mrs. Von Hagen and Mr. Von Hagen, jun.	Kozeluch
"By my tender passion," a favourite song in	
the Haunted Tower, by Mrs. Graupner	Storace
Solo on the Clarinet, by Mr. Granger	Vogel
Lullaby, a favourite Glee for four voices, Mrs.	
Graupner, Mr. Granger, Mr. Mallet and	
Mr. Munto	Harrison
Concerto on the Violin by Mr. Von Hagen	Jearnowick

Part 2d

Concerto on the Piano Forte, by Mrs. Von Hagen	Haydn
Columbia's Bold Eagle, a patriotic song, words by a	
gentleman of Salem. Music by Mr. Graupner and	
sung by Mrs. Graupner	
Concerto on the Hautboy, by Mr. Graupner	Le Brun
The Play'd in Air, a much admired Glee in the	
Castle Spectre, by Mrs. Graupner, Mr. Granger,	
Mr. Mallet and Mr. Munto	
Quartetto by Messrs. von Hagen, sen. and jun.,	
Mr. Laumont, and Mrs. Graupner.	
"To Arms, to arms," a new patriotic song, written by	
Thomas Paine, A.M. sung by Mrs. Graupner and	
music by Mr. von Hagen, jun.	
Finale	Haydn[14]

The program follows the standard two-part format, with orchestra works beginning and ending each part and an intermission in between. Soloists supplied variety, and five of the seven belonged either to the Graupner or the von Hagen family. The concert's main singer and co-beneficiary, formerly Catherine Hillier, had immigrated to America in 1794 as part of a London theater troupe; in 1796, she married oboist Gottlieb Graupner in Charleston. Graupner, born in Germany, moved from there to England, where he is said to have played in the concerts (1791–92) for which Joseph Haydn composed his classic *London* symphonies. Graupner had come to America by 1795, and in 1797 he and his wife settled in Boston, where both worked in the city's Federal Street Theater. The von Hagen family—her name was Elizabeth, and both were natives of Holland—had crossed the Atlantic much earlier, arriving in 1774, living in Charleston and New York, and settling in Boston in 1796. Mrs. von Hagen played keyboard, and her husband worked as an orchestra director as well as a performer on keyboard, wind, and string instruments. Their son, Charleston-born Peter Albrecht von Hagen Jr., a prodigy on the violin who was performing in public by the time he was eight years old, was between eighteen and twenty when the Salem benefit concert took place.

With these facts in mind, the Graupner/von Hagen concert may be seen as an event in which Boston's two leading musical families took their act on the road to skim off proceeds from an audience less familiar with their work than Bostonians were. Preceded by their reputation, they traded on it in a program designed to appeal across a broad range of audience tastes. Instrumental selections by leading European composers of the day testified to their artistic seriousness. Vocal selections, both solo and harmonized, showed an intent to engage with the audience's more tender sentiments. And by placing on the concert's second half patriotic numbers of local and recent origin, they evinced a readiness, as theatrical troupers, to rouse Salem's listeners into a state of pride in their American identity.

MUSICAL THEATER

Theater companies enhanced the musical lives of their communities beyond the theater's walls. When a company moved into a particular locale, it arrived with singers and players who were also ready to perform in concerts (as the Philadelphia and Salem programs show), participate in church music, and give music lessons. Company musicians also enlivened the music trades as customers for local dealers, and some involved themselves in publishing and the retailing of musical goods. In the manner of musicians employed by the Anglican Church and the military, theatrical singers and players did not necessarily restrict their activities to one institution.

Like that of Liverpool, York, Edinburgh, and the West Indies, the eighteenth-century American theater was an extension of the London stage.

Some foreign performers toured the New World, then returned to the Old. Others settled here. Not until well into the next century did any appreciable number of American-born singers or players begin to find a place on the stages of America. The plays of Shakespeare, with plots altered, shortened, and interlaced with music, held a central place in the repertory. *Romeo and Juliet, Hamlet,* and *Othello* were particular favorites, their main characters becoming archetypal figures in a network of reference shared by performers and audiences in America from that time forward.

Musical works by Americans filled no larger place in the theater than did American-born performers, which is to say almost no place at all. *The Disappointment* (1767), by Andrew Barton, the first American-composed ballad opera, and *The Contrast* (1787), by Royall Tyler, the first full-length American play produced on these shores, stand as landmarks, though the first was not performed until the twentieth century. In a theatrical tradition carried on by British managers and players, where performances had to pay for themselves, the obstacles against presenting a new work, not to mention knowing how to compose one, discouraged all but a few Americans from trying. New World residents whose musical works were actually produced onstage were all immigrants who had arrived in this country as experienced musicians.

The New Theater in Chestnut Street, Philadelphia, opened in 1793 and was home to theatrical companies thereafter.

Like dance, the theater provoked strong opposition, especially from the Puritan clergy. In opposing theatrical entertainment, however, Puritans were not simply revealing narrow provincialism but tapping into a strain of opinion that may be traced back to the ancient Greeks. In *The Republic*, Plato criticized drama for catering to the ignorant, emphasizing the agreeable over the good, and appealing more to emotions than reason—three flaws all said to undermine public virtue. In fact, the English language itself reflects deep suspicion of the theater. Most expressions borrowed from the arts convey respect or praise, as in "poetic" justice or the "lyric" beauty of a sunset; in contrast, theatrical terms such as "melodramatic," "putting on an act," or "making a scene" usually do the opposite.[15] The immediate background for American objections, though, lies in English Puritan thought of the sixteenth and seventeenth centuries, which treated theater as a generally bad thing, symbolizing a preference for idleness and pleasure over hard work and thrift. From that point of view, the theater was an institution that lured young and old alike away from worthier pursuits, like churchgoing. Moreover, actors and actresses were considered vagabonds who threatened the very stability of society. The habit of imitating others was believed to bring out the worst in the actors' own characters. Faithful to illusion rather than truth, the theater posed social dangers that made it seem corrupt even to some who were devoted to other forms of art.

The antitheatrical prejudice in North America varied with geography and religious persuasion, being strongest where Reformed Protestants held sway. Early settlements under Roman Catholicism seem to have felt no such restrictions; a play about the conquest of New Mexico was performed in the Spanish Southwest as early as 1598, and in 1606 a masque—a theatrical entertainment including music, dance, costumes, scenery, and poetry—in French was presented in Canada's Acadia region. Yet while such diversity is part of the historical record, the London-based English-language theater, especially Shakespeare, was the fountainhead of enduring theatrical activity in America. Efforts to bring the American colonies into that theatrical orbit began in earnest in the mid-1700s with the appearance of English traveling companies in Philadelphia, New York, Charleston, and Virginia (Williamsburg). New England resisted the effort for a time; between 1750 and 1793, a law was on the books in Boston prohibiting theater entertainments there.

The first theatrical performances in America were given in temporary quarters, but by the 1760s theaters were being built to accommodate audiences in seats of varying location and price. A typical theatrical evening lasted four or five hours, usually starting with a long work (a tragedy, comedy, or extended drama with music) and ending with an afterpiece (a short musical work, farce, or masque). Musical interludes were common; so were encores of favorite numbers. Straight plays often began with an over-

NEW THEATRE.

BY PARTICULAR DESIRE. *of Presiden...* ~~George Washington~~

On *Monday Evening*, Jan. 9, *1797*:

Will be prefented, a COMEDY, (in four Acts,) called

THE CHILD OF NATURE.

(From the French of Mad. Genlis, By the Author of Every one has his Fault.)

Marquis of Almanza,	Mr. *Wignell.*
Count Valantia,	Mr. *Moreton.*
Duke Murcia,	Mr. *Warren.*
Seville,	Mr. *Warrell.*
Grenada,	Mr. *Warrell,* jun.
1ft Peafant,	Mr. *Cooper.*
2d Peafant,	Mr. *Mitchell.*
Marchionefs, Merida,	Mrs. *Morris,*
Amanthis,	Mrs. *Merry.*

To which will be added, (for the third time,) a COMIC OPERA, in two Acts, (as performed at Covent Garden Theatre, upwards of 150 Nights,) called

LOCK AND KEY.

Brummagem,	Mr. *Francis.*
Cheerly	Mr. *Darley,* jun.
Captain Vain,	Mr. *Fox.*
Ralph,	Mr. *Harwood.*
Laura,	Mrs. *Warrell.*
Fanny,	Mrs. *Oldmixon.*
Selina,	Mrs. *Harvey.*
Dolly,	Mifs. *Milbourne.*

Box, One Dollar, Twenty-five Cents. *Pit*, One Dollar. And *Gallery*, Half a Dollar.

☞ The Doors of the Theatre will open at 5, and the Curtain rife precifely at 6 o'Clock

Places for the Boxes to be taken at the Office in the front of the Theatre, from 10 till 2 o'clock and from 10 till 4 on the Days of Performance.

Tickets to be had at H. & P. Rice's Book-ftore, No. 50, Market-ftreet, and at the Office adjoining the Theatre.

Ladies and Gentlemen are requefted to fend their Servants to keep places at a quarter before 5 o'clock, and order them, as foon as the Company are feated, to withdraw, as they cannot, on any account be permitted to remain.

No Money or Tickets to be returned nor any perfon, on any account whatfoever, admitted behind the Scenes.

VIVAT RESPUBLICA

This program from Philadelphia's New Theater on January 9, 1797, shows what theatergoers of the time could expect from an evening's entertainment.

ture, included music between the acts, and featured interpolated songs.
Eighteenth- and nineteenth-century Americans seldom formed the silent,
respectful gathering of playgoers that we now expect to find in the theater.
Early audiences were likely to react to the spectacle, responding in public
interchange with the actors and musicians. The work being performed
seems to have been less important to them than the quality of their own experience. If they liked what they saw and heard, they clamored for more; if
not, they demanded an end to it.

In other words, the eighteenth-century musical theater in America was a
branch of what is called show business today. The names of the genres—
ballad operas, pasticcios, and "operas" whose music is mostly original—may
suggest autonomous art forms. But in fact, the goal pursued by theatrical
entertainments was to be accessible to the audience. Performers, composers, and impresarios in this tradition sought most of all to find and please
audiences and to increase their size. Toward that end, their shows featured
plots with characters, whether good or evil, in whose fate spectators could
involve themselves; players with a talent for comedy, singing, or dancing; a
store of melody that was catchy if not already familiar; and a certain amount
of spectacle. In a day when secular public assemblies were rare, the theater,
where stories were acted out onstage by living, feeling characters, gave audience members a chance to experience collectively what Plato had warned
was bad for society: emotions rather than reason.

Accounts of the period portray audiences spurred to outbursts of feeling
not only by the show but by the day's political climate, as on the evening of
November 23, 1793. To set the scene, it should be noted that when the
French Revolution erupted in 1789, most Americans sympathized with its
aims. But when the republic that replaced the monarchy executed King
Louis XVI in January 1793 and then declared war on Britain, Spain, and
Holland, Americans began to take sides. President Washington declared the
American government's neutrality. Powerful cabinet members, however,
went their own way, with Secretary of State Thomas Jefferson supporting
the French cause and Secretary of the Treasury Alexander Hamilton lining
up with the British. By November 1793, France was a political symbol in
American domestic affairs. Some saw her as a nation bravely throwing off
the yoke of tyranny, others as proof that when the people won too much
power, anarchy followed. An eyewitness account of what took place before a
performance in a New York theater illustrates how songs of patriotic stripe
could inflame sentiment in a public assembly.

> One of the side boxes was filled by French officers from the ships of war in
> the harbour. The opposite box was filled with American officers. . . . The
> house was early filled. As soon as the musicians appeared, there was a gen-

eral call for "*ça ira.*" The band struck up. The French in the pit joined first, and then the whole audience. Next followed the Marseillois Hymn. The audience stood up. The French took off their hats and sung in a full and solemn chorus. The Americans applauded by gestures and clapping of hands. We can recall the figure and voice of one Frenchman, who, standing on a bench in the pit, sung this solemn patriotic song with a clear loud voice, while his fine manly frame seemed to swell with the enthusiasm of the moment. The hymn ended, shouts of "Vivent les François," "Vivent les Americans," were reiterated until the curtain drew up, and all was silent.[16]

Favorite works of the British stage proved also to be popular in America, including *The Beggar's Opera* (1728), by John Gay. Essentially a play whose spoken dialogue alternates with songs, this hugely successful work received its first American performance in New York in 1750. What was its appeal for American audiences? Chiefly, one imagines, Gay's plot, characters, and song lyrics, which with comic precision challenged conventional notions of morality and social class. The incongruous title plays on an inversion of high and low. And in fact, *The Beggar's Opera*'s first song confronts that issue head-on as Peachum, a seller of stolen goods, ranks his own line of work on a par with others, including politics, law, and the Christian ministry:

> Through all the Employments of Life
> Each Neighbour abuses his Brother;
> Whore and Rogue they call Husband and Wife:
> All Professions be-rogue one another:
> The Priest calls the Lawyer a Cheat,
> The Lawyer be-knaves the Divine:
> And the Statesman, because he's so great,
> Thinks his Trade as honest as mine.[17]

When word reaches Peachum and his wife that their daughter Polly has secretly married Macheath, a highwayman, they are horrified, not because of Macheath's profession but because Polly tells them she has married for love. (Mrs. Peachum: "Love him! worse and worse! I thought the Girl had been better bred.") As the plot unfolds, Peachum betrays Macheath to the authorities; then the jailed Macheath betrays Polly by agreeing to marry the jailer's daughter to escape from prison. Macheath is finally brought to the gallows and then freed, because although an operatic hero may be threatened with hanging, he must never actually be hanged. As one character says, "an Opera must end happily" if it is "to comply with the Taste of the Town." Thus, mocking operatic customs and blurring the moral distinctions between London society's official leaders and its underworld riffraff, Gay's work offered a social critique with a bite strong enough to be felt across the Atlantic.

If social and moral inversion pervade the plot of *The Beggar's Opera*, the words and music offer another kind of transformation. For in ballad opera, the songs consist of new words set to familiar tunes. As in the broadside ballad, tunes for the stage were chosen not only for their melodies but also for their associations. A good example comes when Polly, pleading with her father to help save Macheath from being hanged, sings a four-line lament in common meter:

> Oh, ponder well! be not severe;
> So save a wretched Wife!
> For on the Rope that hangs my Dear
> Depends poor Polly's life.

The tune for these words is *Now Ponder Well,* familiar in oral tradition especially through its association with the well-loved ballad *The Children in the Woods.* Gay's intent seems clear: to underline Polly's genuine love for her husband, inviting the audience to perceive her as a pure-hearted character in a drama steeped in cynicism.

A different kind of association appears when Mrs. Peachum reviles Polly for marrying. The tune Gay borrows for this song is *Oh London Is a Fine Town*, a satirical attack claiming that the city government's officials are totally corrupt. In a kind of double inversion, Polly is denounced for a breach of her mother's ethics, which are wholly opposed to her own more conventional ones. By marrying Macheath, Polly rejects the career for which she has been groomed. Her parents had long anticipated the day when she would start manipulating the lust of wealthy men, milking their wallets as part of the Peachum family's enterprise. By trading that prospect for love, she has squandered a family asset, leaving her mother in a rage at the "sad slut" she has raised:

> Our *Polly* is a sad Slut! nor heeds what we have taught her.
> I wonder any Man alive will ever rear a Daughter!
> For she must have both Hoods and Gowns, and Hoops to swell her
>   Pride,
> With Scarfs and Stays, and Gloves and Lace; and she will have Men
>   beside;
> And when she's drest with Care and Cost, all tempting, fine and gay,
> As Men should serve a C[u]cumber, she flings herself away.

Yet whatever her mother may say, Polly grasps the sexual politics of her position. Taking the flower as a metaphor for virginity, she sings a song that in its way is no more sentimental than Mrs. Peachum's upside-down view of morality. In Polly's song, a flower in the marketplace, like a woman's virginity, is something that lives and then dies. Living, its beauty and fragility hold the key to her social and economic power. But when severed from its living root, it quickly decays, to be tossed in the street and trampled:

> Virgins are like the fair Flower in its Lustre,
> Which in the Garden enamels the Ground;
> Near it the Bees in play flutter and cluster,
> And gaudy Butterflies frolic around.
> But, when once pluck'd, 'tis no longer alluring,
> To *Covent-Garden* 'tis sent (as yet sweet),
> There fades, and shrinks, and grows past all enduring,
> Rots, stinks, and dies, and is trod under feet.

The tune to which Polly delivers this tough message is a love song written in 1690 by English composer Henry Purcell to the text *What Shall I Do to Show How Much I Love Her?* The gap between its sentiments and those of Polly's song is huge. Purcell's protagonist, in the throes of passion, vows to "love more than Man e'er loved before me"—empty sentiments to a character as versed in the world's ways as Polly Peachum.

English audiences must have felt the sting of *The Beggar's Opera*'s social critique all the more strongly for their knowledge of the tunes, and surely American audience members shared some of that experience. In any case, *The Beggar's Opera* proved a staple of the eighteenth-century theater repertory in this country. The social and moral inversion remained potent enough in the twentieth century to provide a model for Berthold Brecht and Kurt Weill's *The Threepenny Opera*, whose original German version premiered in 1928. Moreover, the air of corruption and depravity that surrounds *The Beggar's Opera* is still strong enough today to show a modern observer why early opponents of the theater could be passionate in upholding their position.

Ballad operas concentrated on words and ideas, sometimes with society as a target. The pasticcio, another popular theatrical genre of the time, put a higher priority on music than on social criticism. A pasticcio that won great popularity on both sides of the Atlantic was *Love in a Village*, based on a play by Isaac Bickerstaff with music supplied and arranged by Thomas Augustine Arne. This work, which premiered in London in 1762 and entered the American repertory after performances in Charleston and Philadelphia in 1766, seeks most of all to provide amiable amusement for its audience. Rosetta, the heroine, has fled her aristocratic home to avoid a forced marriage, taking a post as chambermaid in a country house. Thomas Meadows has left his home for the same reason and is working as a gardener in the same household. Thomas and Rosetta fall in love. Their mutual passion

John Searle's watercolor of New York's Park Theater in 1822 shows the orchestra pit (with orchestra) and tiered seating that allowed theatergoers from different walks of life to attend without mixing socially.

seems doomed to go nowhere until Sir William Meadows, Thomas's father, arrives on the scene and reveals that, from the start, Thomas's intended bride had been none other than Rosetta. Thus, *Love in a Village* moves from complication to a conventional happy ending, obeying the theatrical conventions that *The Beggar's Opera* had mocked.

Except for a handful of new pieces he composed himself, Arne borrowed the music for *Love in a Village* from elsewhere. He did include a few traditional ballad tunes of the kind used in *The Beggar's Opera*, but these were sung by servants or pompous types, implying that they now symbolized old-fashionedness, and were too bare and worn to carry expressions of genuine feeling, especially between lovers. Arne's borrowings drew little on other operas of the time. Instead, they tapped a vein of lyrical song that he and other English composers of the time had created for performances at English pleasure gardens of the 1740s, 50s, and 60s—songs of the kind that Francis Hopkinson emulated as a composer. *Love in a Village* illustrates a truth that successful practitioners of popular musical theater have long acted upon: lyric melodies in a contemporary idiom, sung charmingly from the stage to words of romantic love, can bring an audience into a state of acquiescent pleasure, no matter how conventionalized the dramatic situation, the lyrics, or the musical turns of phrase may be.

Other varieties of musical entertainment included ballet, pantomime, farce, melodrama, and romance. Each resident theater troupe was expected to offer its local audience the full range of theatrical possibilities, from straight play to musical farce. From the 1790s on, with companies established in Baltimore, Boston, Charleston, New York, and Philadelphia, the repertory grew. New works were imported from overseas, while brand-new pieces were created by immigrant composers and playwrights on this side of the Atlantic. As with popular song, a core of theater works came to be standard, while most new works fell quickly into disuse. Established favorites were sometimes updated by replacing original numbers with newer ones or interpolating popular songs. In this tradition of musical theater, local players changed anything in the composer's score that might not please their audiences. Thus, English works were routinely transformed in performance into Anglo-American favorites.

A favorite comic opera of the time was *The Children in the Wood*, with a libretto by Thomas Morton and music by Samuel Arnold. Premiered in London in 1793, it was first performed on this side of the Atlantic in Philadelphia in 1794. The story is based on the ballad discussed in Chapter 4, with more characters added, including a heroine—Josephine, the children's governess—and her beloved, a good-hearted carpenter named Walter. Transferred to the stage, the tale kept its themes of moralism and danger but lost its tragic ending. The parents, Lord and Lady Alford, have not died but are traveling in India, leaving their two young children in the care of Sir Rowland, Alford's brother. In the last scene, everything comes out right. The evil Rowland gets his comeuppance through disgrace and death, and the virtuous parents are reunited with their youngsters, miraculously restored to health after having been found near death in the forest.

While Samuel Arnold's original score carried an overture and ten musical numbers, three of the latter were apparently never performed in America.[18] One was simply dropped and the other two replaced by American substitutes. The first substitute number was written by Benjamin Carr, an English-born singer, organist, and composer, who briefly played Lord Alford onstage and composed a new entrance song for Josephine. The second was provided by a singer named Mrs. Melmoth who played Lady Alford, and who gave herself an entrance song with the words "Mark my Alford all the joys," sung to the tune of *Twinkle, Twinkle, Little Star*. (This melody, known in Europe as *Ah vous dirai-je, maman* since its publication in 1761, was called *Mark My Alford* in America well into the 1800s, proof of *The Children in the Wood*'s popularity.) Arnold's overture, which features an evocatively harmonized version of the original ballad's tune, *Now Ponder Well*, remained intact. And American productions also kept Arnold's *Great Sir, Consider*, a comic duet in which Josephine fends off the romantic advances of Sir Rowland while the butler, oblivious to the seduction being attempted under his nose, tries to inform his lordship that dinner is served.

Perhaps the most dramatic use of music in *The Children in the Wood* also appears in Arnold's original and brings the drama to a head. Josephine, Walter, and a third character are sitting in a room. Walter, whose role overlaps with that of the original ballad's repentant Russian, is troubled because, having lost touch with the children after saving them from assassination, he fears that they have died for lack of food and shelter. Josephine offers to sing a ballad from a broadside she says she bought "of the old blind pedlar who passed by this morning." She introduces her song as *The Norfolk Tragedy*, about "a ghost, a murdered babe." At this point, Walter interrupts with a cry: "No, don't sing that!" But Josephine goes ahead, laying out the tragedy in three stanzas of long meter, which she sings to a folk-like melody that Arnold probably borrowed from oral tradition.

> A Yeoman of no mean degree,
> For thirst of Gain and lucre he
> A pretty babe did murder straight.
> By reason of its large Estate.

At least one American Josephine, a Mrs. Marshall who sang the role in Philadelphia in 1795, performed this song unaccompanied, enhancing its archaic quality, as if it were a voice from another realm.[19] In the song's second stanza, the ghost of the dead child knocks at the window. When these words trigger an actual knocking offstage, Walter is terrified. But after Josephine finishes her song, the door bursts open and the rescued children run to Walter's side and embrace him affectionately. Then, in the company of Josephine and Lord and Lady Alford, the true story of his heroism comes out. A brief finale touts the rewards of virtue and, in fairy-tale fashion, all vow to live happily ever after.

6

$\mathcal{M}$aintaining $\mathcal{O}$ral $\mathcal{T}$raditions
African Music in Early America

WHILE THE CREATION in North America of a lasting democracy stands as a signal achievement, the presence of black slavery glaringly contradicts democratic ideals. Yet by the mid-1600s, the English in America had already found slavery a price worth paying for the economic rewards they desired. When the Constitutional Convention of 1787 mapped out the United States of America's governmental structure, slavery lived on, even though accepting it violated Christian beliefs, English law, and the principles on which the republic was founded. A democratic society that permitted slavery had embraced a paradox that sooner or later would demand resolution.

BLACKS, WHITES, AND SLAVERY

Many white settlers came to America as servants, with the understanding that they would labor under prescribed conditions for a certain period, then be free to follow their own course. Africans, however, from shortly after their first arrival in Virginia in 1619 until Congress halted the legal trade in 1808, were brought to this country as slaves—not a relative but an absolute state that permitted no freedom, fixed no date for the end of bondage, and assumed a hereditary process in which the offspring of slaves were slaves themselves. Slavery in North America predates the U.S. Constitution by more than a century and a half; and the new nation's first policy was to act as if this apparently unbridgeable contradiction had already been bridged, or soon would be, or was less damaging to national life than appearances might suggest. The Founding Fathers recognized the inconsistency in their acceptance of slavery, yet the constitutional debates of 1787–88 show that without that acceptance, some colonies would never have joined the union.

Spanish and Portuguese rule in the southerly regions of the New World

had already established black slavery there by 1500. When the English began their northern settlements after 1600, they found that, for all their historical tendencies in favor of liberty, Negro slavery offered a way to expedite
the settling of the land. Blacks became slaves in large part because certain
opportunities in the New World, such as the growing of tobacco, required a
work force that was cheap and dependent. Only a persistent demand for labor in thinly populated colonies could have brought slavery into existence in
the first place. Yet once established, the presence of slavery seemed to pre-
clude alternatives, though few Americans considered it morally justifiable.
Slavery persisted because it was an integral part of the economic engine
that European settlement built on these shores.

Slavery's evil touched everyone involved. The mental and spiritual burdens slavery imposed on whites (a classic study of the origins of American
racism is called *The White Man's Burden*, after a poem by English writer
Rudyard Kipling) put the moral high ground beyond a slaveholder's reach.
Until well into the nineteenth century, few if any whites seriously made the
claim that the slaves themselves were responsible for their enslavement.
And in regions where blacks outnumbered whites, guilt was mingled with
fear. Slave rebellions in the Caribbean in the 1790s and early 1800s sent
shock waves through North American slaveholders. Although revolts were
rare in the United States, the threat of revolt was seldom absent. And when
slaves did rebel, panic could lead to tighter repression.

In light of the moral shame surrounding slavery, what besides economics
and fear of its aftermath justified its preservation? Some believed that
blacks simply lacked the mental capacity of whites. Others took differences
in appearance and physique as marks of inferiority or fitness for subor-
dination. The idea that blacks and whites could live as equals in the same
society struck even Thomas Jefferson, author of the Declaration of Independence, as unrealistic. History, Jefferson wrote, had already established
between whites and blacks a bond so unequal that reconciliation was impossible:

> Deep rooted prejudices entertained by the whites; ten thousand recollec-
> tions, by the blacks, of the injuries they have sustained; new provocations;
> the real distinctions which nature has made; and many other circumstances,
> will divide us into parties, and produce convulsions which will probably
> never end but in the extermination of the one or the other race.—To these
> objections, which are political, may be added others, which are physical and
> moral.[1]

As a slaveholder who hated slavery, Jefferson also believed that freeing his
own slaves, which he considered doing, would bring him economic ruin
without touching the system. He writes as someone caught in a web of con-

traditions that veered crazily from "the most unremitting despotism on the one part" to "degrading submissions on the other." Jefferson's condemnation of slavery centers less on the slave's yoke than on the white man's burden and the institution's "unhappy influence on the manners of our people" (i.e., whites).[2]

Slave trading was an active business. Approximately 3.8 million slaves were shipped from Africa to the New World by 1750, more than half bound for Brazil and Spanish South America. Of the approximately 1.7 million sent to the British, French, Dutch, and Danish colonies, most went to the West Indies, from which some were carried to the North American mainland. (In 1800, the black population of the United States stood at roughly 900,000.) By mid-century, the flow of Africans was running at between 50,000 and 60,000 per year, more than any other group of people entering the colonies from elsewhere. The slaves came chiefly from West Africa and included peoples with many different languages, religions, and customs. For all their differences, however, these African peoples shared a common outlook toward time, comprised of the past, the present, and the future, and similarities in cultural expression. Their sense of community must have been strengthened by the harshness of slavery in America. Custom and law here deemed Africans' differences from each other insignificant when compared with their differences from whites. Slaves were black and politically powerless. The idea of an "African" component in American society was an American invention.[3]

AFRICAN-AMERICAN CULTURAL EXPRESSION

No fact about black slaves in America is more crucial to this study than their continuing of oral traditions from the African cultures into which they were born. It was once assumed that the forcible removal of African Americans from their homeland had also destroyed their culture. But that view now seems to have underrated black culture's hardiness. It now seems clear that Africa-saturated oral traditions were maintained through slavery; slaves, for example, and black Africans in general, were often described as talented musicians. And where there was music, there was movement. A European observer in Sierra Leone commented in 1796 that music was "seldom listened to alone, but is generally used as an accompaniment to the dance." Accounts of black singing in America often mention dancing too. Indeed, most of what is known about the slaves' modes of expression confirms their origins in Africa. For all the differences among African cultures, the spoken arts, verbal improvising, and an emphasis on broad participation were common to many.[4] The same may be said of the expressive practices of African-American slaves.

One example of an African ritual in the spoken arts was witnessed by William Bosman, a Dutch official who lived on the Gold Coast from 1688 to 1702. For a period of eight days, one group in the region staged a feast "accompanied with all manner of Singing, Skipping, Dancing, Mirth, and Jollity." And the mirth carried a critical edge. For in the ceremonies, Bosman wrote, "a perfect lampooning Liberty is allowed," so that the people "may freely sing of all the Faults, Villanies and Frauds of their Superiors as well as Inferiors without Punishment, or so much as the least interruption."[5] In this ceremony, individuals were being invited to express feelings normally kept to themselves. With the help of song and dance, a cultural space was created within which—openly in the example described here but also covertly, and with the help of metaphor and indirection—Africans fashioned responses to conditions and events in their lives.

Slaves in the New World were known to perform similar rituals, as shown by two accounts from Charleston, South Carolina, in the 1770s. Nicholas Cresswell, an English traveler in the United States, commented in his journal in 1774 after hearing slave music: "In their songs they generally relate the usage they have received from their Masters or Mistresses in a very satirical stile and manner."[6] Two years earlier, a Charleston newspaper described "a Country Dance, Rout, or Cabal of *Negroes*" held outside town one Saturday night, consisting of about sixty people, "provided with Music, Cards, Dice, &c. The entertainment was opened, by the men copying (or *taking off*) the manners of their masters, and the women those of their mistresses, and relating some highly curious anecdotes, to the inexpressible diversion of that company. They then *danced*."[7]

In broadside ballads, Anglo Americans fashioned their own styles of satire as they commented on political events and struggles over power. Yet power takes many forms. In the time of slavery, whites held absolute political and economic power, while slaves found ways, through satiric commentary, to claim a cultural power that white hegemony could neither control nor eradicate. In the two Charleston incidents, blacks burlesqued white manners and pretensions in an ironic mockery that was *performed* in the social realm. The African oral heritage, with its emphasis on spontaneity, improvisation, and quick responsiveness, gave slaves a way to transcend, figuratively if not literally, the officially powerless state in which they found themselves.

Music as Westerners understand it can be hard to separate from other forms of earlier African-American expression. Nor did an African view of the world lend itself to the familiar Western idea that life is split into complementary sacred and secular domains. Like those of Native Americans, African religions find all of life embued with a sacred spirit. Religion extends the world upward in space so that communication with the spiritual world is possible, and time is extended backward to establish contact with ancestors and with the gods. So in a reconfigured and recreated time and space, humans carry on their lives in the presence of both gods and ancestors. Humankind, nature, and divine beings make up a sacred whole, which encompasses what Westerners take to be the secular world.[8] This notion of the universe allowed slaves in America to live in a realm of the imagination far more spacious than the one in which they were held as captive laborers. However dehumanizing slavery may have been, some slaves were able to find practices in the culture they preserved that helped them to endure, and to leave a legacy of their own.

BLACK MUSICIANS IN EARLY AMERICA

Because the black cultural legacy was almost entirely oral, it is no easier to document historically than that of the Indians. Written sources from African Americans themselves are rare before the mid-1800s. Yet a few white observers left comments detailed enough to give some idea of the character of black music making during the colonial period and early republic. Moreover, as blacks became Christians and began to participate in Protestant worship, accounts of their singing appeared in the written record.

Newspapers provide data on black musicians before 1800, not in the form of news or commentary but in advertisements, for chattel slaves were part of the American economy. A slave's market value was increased by the possession of musical skills, as the following ad from a Virginia newspaper in 1766 confirms: "TO BE SOLD. A young healthy Negro fellow who has been used to wait on a Gentlemen and plays extremely well on the French horn."[9] More common, however, are notices about runaways, which sometimes mention musical skill. A Boston newspaper in 1745 carried a notice from an owner in Newbury, a port city to the north, offering a reward for the return of "Cato," who had disappeared a few days earlier:

> about 22 Years of Age, short and small, SPEAKS GOOD ENGLISH AND CAN READ AND WRITE, understands farming Work carry'd with him a striped homespun Jacket and Breeches, and Trousers, and an outer Coat and Jacket of homemade Cloth, two Pair of Shoes, sometimes wears a black Wigg, has a smooth Face, a sly Look, TOOK WITH A VIOLIN, AND CAN PLAY WELL THEREON.[10]

This ad is a reminder that in colonial times slavery was not only practiced in the South. It also outlines the young man's range of accomplishments. But most of all, it was an attempt to keep Cato from gaining his freedom. How many small black fiddlers would have been roaming the Massachusetts countryside in 1745?

Cato's achievements may have been rare, but learning to play a European instrument was not entirely unusual. Advertisements in the *Virginia Gazette* between 1736 and 1780 carried more than sixty references to black musicians, of whom forty-five were violinists or fiddlers. One of them, "a black Virginia born Negro fellow named Sambo, about 6 ft. high" was identified in 1768 also as a runaway who made fiddles and could work "at the carpenter's trade." Some runaways who played fife or German flute were also mentioned, as were a few known for their singing. An ad seeking to locate "a Mulatto fellow named John Jones, about 26 years old" called him "a mighty singer" (1745); another asked readers to be on the lookout for a girl said to be "fond of Liquor and apt to sing indecent and Sailors' songs" when she drank.[11]

The presence of African-American fiddlers shows acculturation going on, with blacks taking up and mastering "white" instruments, presumably in their own way. It also points to a vocation beginning to take shape: that of the black dance musician. Evidence from 1690 has been found in the records of Accomac County, Virginia, of a slave fiddling for a dance at the residence of the Reverend Thomas Teakle while the clergyman was away from home. The dance, starting on a Saturday night, continued through Sunday morning. When Teakle discovered that his house was being used for dancing while church services were being held, he started legal proceedings against the culprits, who turned out to be friends of his daughter.[12] Research has also shown that in the North, music for formal dances in towns and in the country, and for dancing schools too, was routinely supplied by black musicians. In the South, meanwhile, blacks performed for dancing at their masters' balls, assemblies, and special "Entertainments."[13] Many of these players were slaves, which limited their ability to collect payment for their services. But some were free and may be considered tradesmen of sorts. Already in the eighteenth century, then, black dance musicians were meeting a need in white society. They must have been skilled, for only their success could explain why an institution as unbending as slavery would allow the role of black entertainer to take shape in the first place, much less to continue.

REGIONAL DIFFERENCES IN BLACK MUSIC MAKING

The Northern United States

Black music making in North America varied with the conditions in which African Americans lived, and those conditions varied with geography. The most dramatic difference existed between the North, where slavery— sparse to begin with—declined in the later 1700s, and the South, where it was entrenched. By 1786, Pennsylvania and all states north except New Jer-

sey had either abolished slavery or decided how they would do so. And in
the North, blacks formed only a small minority of the population. They
worked alongside whites, though seldom accepted as social equals, and enjoyed some chances to enter the skilled trades.

In both North and South, religion loomed large in black-white relations.
Whites disagreed about whether blacks should be Christianized, especially
if they were slaves. Some believed that religious teaching would help reconcile slaves to their lot in this life and make them more obedient. But others
feared that such instruction, like the ability to read and write, would have
the opposite effect. Generally, however, Christian denominations favored
the conversion of blacks, and the Anglican Church's missionary arm, the Society for the Propagation of the Gospel (SPG), took the lead in that process.
New York's Trinity Church was one place where evangelizing took hold. In
1726, more than one hundred servants, some white and some black, attended catechism classes there that prepared them for church membership
and sang psalms at the end of class. In 1741, Trinity's organist, Johann Gott-
lob Klemm, instructed forty-three Negroes in psalmody. And two years
later, the church's minister wrote that when the clerk rose to lead the congregation in psalm singing, "I can scarce express the satisfaction I have in
seeing 200 Negroes and White Persons with heart and voice glorifying their
Maker."[14]

But the idea of blacks and whites worshiping together was opposed in
many other places. Where more than a handful of blacks joined a white religious society, they were often assigned segregated seating. Because white
church members in general treated race as a social barrier, black Christian
worship in both North and South found its most typical outlet in all-black
congregations. The first of these were formed in the South in the 1770s and
1780s under Baptist preachers. In the North, blacks began in the 1790s and
early 1800s to establish separate congregations, chiefly under Methodist
sponsorship. The founding in 1816 of the African Methodist Episcopal
Church in Philadelphia established a racial division in American Protestantism, each branch with its own ethos and style of expression. According to AME Bishop Benjamin T. Tanner, black worshipers preferred a brand
of Christianity favoring action and fiery preaching over intellectual argument:

> While the good Presbyterian parson was writing his discourses, rounding off
> the sentences, the Methodist itinerant had traveled forty miles with his
> horse and saddle bags; while the parson was adjusting his spectacles to read
> his manuscript, the itinerant had given hell and damnation to his unrepen-
> tant hearers; while the disciple of Calvin was waiting to have his church
> completed, the disciple of Wesley took to the woods and made them re-echo
> with the voice of free grace.[15]

The Reverend Richard Allen (1760–1831), an ex-slave, compiled
for Bethel Church in Philadelphia *A Collection of Spiritual Songs
and Hymns*, the first such book prepared for a black congregation
in America.

In 1801, the Reverend Richard Allen, a founder of the AME Church,
made a signal contribution to black religious music by publishing a hymnal
for Bethel Church in Philadelphia, the first such book assembled by a black
author for a black congregation. It followed the format of metrical psalters
like the *Bay Psalm Book* and Watts's *Psalms of David*: small and easily
portable, devoted to multistanza poetry, and without tunes, for the addition
of printed music would have raised the cost greatly. Among the more than
five dozen items Allen chose for his hymnal are familiar favorites by Isaac
Watts and others. But the hymnal also includes almost two dozen texts that
cannot be traced to any previous author, suggesting that Allen—a self-

educated ex-slave, who worked as a teamster, brickyard worker, woodcutter, shoemaker, and day laborer as well as minister—wrote some or all of them himself.

A few of the unattributed texts are printed with refrains: repeated sections, inserted at the end of each stanza, whose text may show little connection with the subject of the hymn. Being shorter than the stanzas, and normally sung to the same words and music each time they appear, refrains can be learned quickly by ear; they are sometimes sung even by those who do not sing the stanzas. Allen's hymnal also contains a few "wandering" refrains, attached to two or more different hymns. For example, the redeeming power of Jesus' crucifixion is the subject of Hymn No. 1:

> The voice of Free Grace cries, escape to the mountain,
> For Adam's lost race Christ hath open'd a fountain,
> For sin and transgression, and every pollution,
> His blood it flows freely in plenteous redemption.

And Hymn No. 50 tells the Christmas story:

> From regions of Love, lo! an angel descended,
> And told the strange news, how the babe was attended!
> "Go shepherds, and visit this wonderful stranger,
> See yonder bright star—there's your God in a manger!"

Yet the hymnal attaches the same refrain to both hymns:

> Hallelujah to the Lamb who purchas'd our pardon,
> We'll praise him again when we pass over Jordan.[16]

The refrain's words fit Hymn 1 better than Hymn 50. But if a refrain is understood as a unit of text and music that can *contrast with*, as well as support, the meaning of the stanzas, then it seems less incongruous when one is sung with a hymn on a different subject. In both hymns, the changing four-line stanza alternates with the unchanging two-line response, which suggests interaction in performance. Perhaps a group might respond to a leader; or one group might respond to another, the latter, equipped with books, singing both stanzas and refrains, the former bookless and singing refrains only. In any case, Allen's hymnal was the first to put a key trait of oral African-American hymn singing tradition into writing.

Black churches provided African Americans with a setting for carrying on their own kind of musical expression. Holiday celebrations such as Election Day gave them another. Beginning around 1750 in Connecticut, blacks were given a break from their work schedules during local spring elections, and they seized the chance to stage secular festivals paralleling those of white society. They organized parades and games, elected their own "governors" or "kings," and filled the day with singing and dance. A white observer in Newport, Rhode Island, caught the spirit and sound of an Election Day celebration there in 1756, pointing up its difference from anything whites might contrive. His brief comment about the music is one example: "Every voice in its highest key, in all the various languages of Africa, mixed with broken and ludicrous English, filled the air, accompanied with the music of the fiddle, tambourine, banjo and drum."[17]

Another holiday for Northern blacks was the "Pinkster Celebration," held at Pentecost, or Whitsunday, seven Sundays after Easter. (*Pfingsten* is German for "Pentecost.") Pinkster festivities, sometimes resembling a country fair, could fill several days. An account of one such celebration in Albany, New York, probably in the 1770s, recalls a dance that lasted from noon until midnight or later. The ceremony unfolded under the watchful eye of "their venerable sovereign king, 'Charley of the Pinkster hill' "—a native of Angola on Africa's Guinea gulf, Charley was the slave of a successful merchant. As white observer James Eights saw it, the dance consisted of couples whose movements gradually grew more "rapid and furious," fueled in part by their quaffing of "stimulating potions" that seemed to strengthen "all their nerves and muscular powers" and to make perspiration flow "in frequent streams, from brow to heel," before they dropped out when "extreme fatigue or weariness compelled them to retire and give space to a less exhausted set." The music underlying this riot of physical effort came chiefly from a drum fashioned out of a wooden eel pot, over which was stretched "a cleanly dressed sheep skin."

> Astride this rude utensil sat Jacky Quackenboss, then in his prime of life and well known energy, beating lustily with his naked hands upon its loudly sounding head, successively repeating the ever wild, though euphonic cry of *Hi-a-bomba, bomba, bomba*, in full harmony with the thumping sounds. These vocal sounds were readily taken up and as oft repeated by the female portion of the spectators not otherwise engaged in the exercises of the scene, accompanied by the beating of time with their ungloved hands, in strict accordance with the eel-pot melody.[18]

The Reverend Richard Allen's hymns, the Newport Election Day festivities, and the Albany Pinkster celebration all show a fondness for musical forms based on antiphonal, responsorial, or call-and-response interaction, a trait that has been linked to African influence.[19] Indeed, the refrains in some of Allen's hymns create a responsorial structure that suggests how tenacious the African legacy could be. For even in the North, where the black presence was small, blacks and whites in close contact, and Protestant church singing established as a Euroamerican practice, the African custom of responsorial singing survived. The cultural background that black Philadelphians in Allen's congregation brought to the singing of Protestant hymns, in other words, marked the singing with an African-American approach to musical expression.

The Newport Election Day festival of 1756 illustrates another African trait: what has been called the "heterogeneous sound ideal," a preference in either vocal or instrumental music for unblended timbres. In the Newport celebration, singing was accompanied by fiddle, tambourine, banjo, and drum, a combination poorly suited to blending. Yet African musicians are said to prefer a piling up of different-sounding lines to a blending of lines into one homogenous sound. The Newport example, with "every voice in its highest key," singing a babel of African languages mixed with English and accompanied by instruments, also illustrates a third African trait: the tendency to pack a series of musical events as densely as possible into a relatively short time, thus filling all available musical space.[20]

The Albany Pinkster dance exhibits similar African earmarks. First, it makes bodily motion integral to musical performance. Drumming and singing, the musical sounds noted here, are tied so closely to the dancing they accompany that it is hard to say where music stops and physical motion begins. A second trait lies in the way the voice is used. The drummer's repeated cry of *Hi-a-bomba, bomba, bomba* is said to create "a full harmony with the thumping sounds" of the drum, suggesting an approach to singing that is more rhythmic than melodic. Moreover, the women who are not dancing repeat this cry, feeding the rhythmic impulse further and squaring with the precept that African musicians tend to approach singing as well as instrumental playing in a percussive manner.[21] Finally, the account provides clear evidence of a responsorial interaction among at least three different sound sources: the drumbeat, the drummer's vocal cries, and the vocalizing of the nondancing women.

Black Americans were only a marginal presence in the North during the colonial and early federal eras. Yet while evidence about their music making is sketchy, it is enough to show that African influence survived. In the North, too, black musicians enjoyed opportunities not open in the South. For example, Barzillai Lew, a free-born Massachusetts native, served in the French and Indian War as a fifer and drummer (1761), and also in the Revolutionary War. Other blacks also played field music in the colonial military and the Continental army, but the dynastic element in Barzillai Lew's life story is unique. Lew's wife, Dinah Bowman, was herself a musician: the first black woman in history to be identified as a pianist. Barzillai and Dinah Lew, together with their twelve children, supplied music for all formal occasions in the area of Dracut, just south of the New Hampshire border, where they lived. Work for family members was plentiful enough in Boston that some lived there during the winter months. Barzillai Lew's offspring carried on a family tradition that was to last through four more generations, well into the present century. This makes a total of seven generations, for Lew's father, Primus Lew, was also a military field musician, whose service dates back to around 1745.[22] Such continuity would have been unlikely under slavery, which, in an effort to squeeze as much work as possible out of individual slaves, was more inclined to break up families than to preserve them.

Greater Virginia

In the mid-1700s, the region generally known as Greater Virginia, which included parts of today's Maryland and North Carolina, was home to some 400,000 people, of whom 35 to 40 percent were black. Except for the port of Baltimore, Greater Virginia lacked the large and small cities that shaped the economy in the North; it was overwhelmingly rural, with most of the population gathered around the rivers that connected them to the shipping of tobacco, the chief export crop. Though whites in the region imposed one social identity upon blacks, blacks' contact with each other was strong enough to sustain a separate society of their own.[23]

White clergymen in the early 1700s found little sacred content in African-American ideas of the sacred. But the spiritual energy released in the 1730s and 40s by the Great Awakening—a series of religious revivals that swept the colonies from Maine to Georgia—brought a changed outlook, with both clergy and slaveowners more inclined to consider slaves as potential Christians. The Reverend George Whitefield, an English itinerant whose fiery preaching helped to fuel the Great Awakening, accused Greater Virginia's slaveowners in 1740 of purposely keeping "your Negroes ignorant of Christianity," allowing them "openly to prophane the Lord's Day, by their Dancing, Piping and such like." By the next decade, the Reverend Samuel Davies, a Presbyterian minister of Hanover, Virginia, could point to success in his efforts to bring slaves into the Christian fold. "*Ethiopia has also stretched forth her Hands unto God*," Davies rejoiced in 1751, going on to explain that congregational singing was helping to attract slaves to his ministry. "The Negroes," he wrote, "above all the Human Species that I ever knew, have an Ear for Musick, and a kind of extatic Delight in *Psalmody*; and there are no books they learn so soon or take so much Pleasure in." Davies asked a correspondent to send him copies of Watts's *Psalms* and *Hymns*. After the books arrived, he reported that a number of black converts "have lodged all night in my kitchen; and sometimes, when I have awakened about two or three a-clock in the morning, a torrent of sacred harmony poured into my chamber. . . . In this seraphic exercise, some of them spend almost the whole night." In 1758, Davies again praised the singing of black members of his congregation, presumably slaves. "I can hardly express the pleasure it affords me," he wrote, "to turn to that part of the gallery where they sit, and see so many of them with their Psalm or Hymn Books, assisting their fellows, who are beginners, to find the place; and then all breaking out in a torrent of sacred harmony, enough to bear away the whole congregation to heaven."[24] Yet Davies's mention of long stretches of singing, together with the torrential metaphor he used twice, reveal that black members of his flock sang differently from white parishioners, most likely owing to their African heritage.

The spread of the Christian faith seems to have done little to restrain the black population's holiday celebrations. In 1774, Philip Fithian, a Princeton College graduate working as a tutor on an estate in Westmoreland County, Virginia, contrasted the way Sundays were observed in New Jersey and Virginia. A Sabbath in Virginia did not seem to him to "wear the same Dress as our Sundays to the Northward," which were days of religious solemnity. "Generally here by five o-Clock on Saturday every Face (especially the Negroes) looks festive & cheerful—All the lower class of People, & the Servants, & the Slaves, consider it as a Day of Pleasure & amusement & spend it in such Diversions as they severally choose."[25] The slaves could embrace those diversions wholeheartedly on any day of the week. A visitor to Virginia in 1784 expressed amazement that after a full day of work, a slave might

This painting shows plantation slaves observing a holiday by dancing, accompanied by banjo and percussion. The painter, date, and location of the picture are all unknown.

walk several miles to take part in a dance where "he performs with astonishing ability, and the most vigorous exertions, keeping time and cadence, most exactly, with the music . . . until he exhausts himself, and scarcely has time, or strength, to return home before the hour he is called forth to toil the next morning."[26] Perhaps black slaves were willing to endure hardship to attend dances because dancing for them was both recreational and spiritual. Perhaps, in line with African beliefs, they danced not only to relax but to perform their sense of relatedness to community, gods, and ancestors. (A modern student of African cultural expression has dramatized that very point. "If you ask an African why he goes out to listen and dance to music," he writes, "he may tell you, 'I worked hard all day, and now I want to refresh my mind.' ")[27]

South Carolina

Blacks heavily outnumbered whites in South Carolina, which more than any other colony resembled the English planter culture of the West Indies. Regional life was dominated by the capital city of Charleston. Outside the capital, South Carolina blacks lived and worked in large isolated groups. Rice was the main cash crop, grown chiefly through the use of black labor whose Africanness was fortified regularly by fresh slave importations. Blackwhite interaction in South Carolina was limited, but this did not bring slaves any great amount of freedom—especially after the Stono Rebellion of 1739, in which a black revolt left more than twenty whites and an even greater number of slaves dead. One report tells how the rebels emboldened themselves with music and dancing, using the drum to recruit other slaves to their cause:

> On the 9th day of September last being Sunday which is the day the Planters allow them to work for themselves, Some Angola Negroes assembled, to the number of Twenty; at a place called Stonehow. . . . Several Negroes joyned them, they calling out Liberty, marched on with Colours displayed and two Drums beating, pursuing all the white people they met with, and killing Man Woman and Child. . . . They increased every minute by new Negroes coming to them, so that they were above Sixty, some say a hundred, on which they halted in a field, and set to dancing, Singing and beating Drums, to draw more Negroes to them, thinking they were now victorious over the whole Province, having marched ten miles & burnt all before them without opposition.[28]

The rampage ended the day it began. But it also shook the white colonists, who launched an intensive manhunt for conspirators that continued for several weeks. The slaves had come close to overthrowing their masters, who responded with greater repression. In earlier days, a few slaves had enjoyed the freedom to move from place to place, to earn money, raise food, and learn to read. Now, however, controls were tightened: masters who failed to keep their slaves in line faced stiff fines, and slaves were rewarded for informing against each other. Moreover, in hopes of reducing the disproportion of blacks over whites in South Carolina, the importing of slaves was cut in the 1740s to one-tenth the size of the 1730s, which had averaged one thousand per year.[29]

As in Virginia, Christian mission groups in South Carolina struggled with the question of what to do about the black population. One religious conversion ended up robbing the colony of a musician. The redeemed soul was that of "Clarinda," a black fiddler and one of very few female instrumentalists of any race about whom a record survives from these early years. Clarinda's story, published in 1831, was told from a perspective that found fiddling incompatible with her new faith. Born here in 1730, Clarinda was brought up "in a state of ignorance unworthy of a Christian country." Once she learned to play the violin, she "sallied forth with her instrument," usually on Sundays, "in order to draw persons of both sexes together, who, not having the fear of God before their eyes, delighted like herself, in sinful and pernicious amusement." But one day Clarinda "was seized with fits" while dancing herself, "and convulsively fell to the ground." The chronicler observes: "From that moment, she lost her love of dancing, and no more engaged in this vain amusement," becoming instead a preacher and living a pious life until she died at the age of 102.[30]

Clarinda's conversion seems to have taken place without benefit of clergy. Indeed, colonial efforts to Christianize South Carolina's slaves reached very few. In 1779, Alexander Hewatt reported that Negro slaves in South Carolina and Georgia were "kept in heathen ignorance and darkness, destitute of the means of instruction, and excluded in a manner from the pale of the Christian Church." In Hewatt's view, with a few exceptions blacks in these colonies were "as great strangers to Christianity, and as much under the influence of Pagan darkness, idolatry, and superstition, as they were at their first arrival from Africa." An account written more than two decades later by John Pierpont, grandfather of the eminent New York banker J. P. Morgan, details holiday music making on a local plantation. It also confirms the continuing presence in South Carolina of unacculturated Africans, while providing no hint that the slaves celebrated Christmas as a Christian occasion:

> Decr 25th. [1805] Throwought the state of South Carolina, Christmas is a holiday, together with 2 of the succeeding days . . . for the Negroes. . . . On my first waking, the sound of serenading violins & drums saluted my ears, and for some time continued. . . . During almost the whole of the second and 3d afternoons, the portico was crowded with these dancers . . . fiddlers &

drumming. . . . Some of them who were native Africans did not join the dance with the others, but, by themselves gave us a specimen of the sports & amusement with which the benighted & uncivilized children of nature divert themselves. . . . Clapping their hands was their music and distorting their frames into the most unnatural figures and emiting the most hideous noises in their dancing.[31]

Pierpont's comments remain especially valuable for reporting that different groups of slaves on this plantation made different kinds of music, which varied with the closeness of their ties to Africa.

Louisiana

Louisiana, unlike the other environments in which blacks lived and worked, never belonged to the British Empire. Settled by the French in the early 1700s, the territory was controlled by Spain from 1762 to 1800, when it was returned to France, then sold to the United States in 1803 as part of the Louisiana Purchase. With this varied political history, plus its location— linked to the continent by the Mississippi River and to the sea by the Gulf of Mexico—Louisiana, and its chief city New Orleans, acquired an ambiance unique in North America. Most of Louisiana's blacks were slaves, but a good many were not. And the presence of free blacks in sizable numbers made legal and social distinctions less sharp and the possibilities for acculturation greater than elsewhere in the South. While such possibilities as baptism, marriage, manumission (emancipation), and civil rights were not officially available to Louisiana's black slaves, neither were they entirely beyond reach for some. Around 1800, blacks and mulattos in what would become one of America's key musical centers were to be found at most levels of society, mixing freely, even intimately, with Europeans, Indians, and mestizos. This multiracial society, while still stratified, was less rigidly hierarchical than elsewhere on the continent.[32]

During the nineteenth century, the relative openness of New Orleans society allowed musicians of mixed blood to participate in white-organized musical activities, including balls and opera performances. Yet evidence from earlier times also notes what seem to be African-influenced ways. Blacks in New Orleans, for example, were allowed to gather and to dance in public, apparently as a Sunday custom.[33] Some whites found such occasions threatening. A Louisiana planter writing in 1758 confessed:

Nothing is more to be dreaded than to see the Negroes assemble together on Sundays, since, under pretence of Calinda, or the dance, they sometimes get together to the number of three or four hundred, and make a kind of Sabbath, which it is always prudent to avoid; for it is in those tumultuous meetings that they . . . plot their rebellions.[34]

In 1786, a law was passed in the city forbidding slaves to dance in public squares on Sundays and holy days "until the close of evening service." But travelers registered surprise at how New Orleans residents—the "lower sort" of whites and blacks especially—observed the Sabbath. An English visitor who attended a Roman Catholic service in 1797 described its aftermath as something like a release from captivity:

> Scarcely had the priest pronounced his benediction, ere the violin or the fife struck up at the door, and the lower classes of people indulged themselves in all the gaiety and mirth of juvenile diversions. Singing, dancing, and all kinds of sports were seen in every street. . . . The lower sort of people . . . look forward with the highest pleasure for Sunday—particularly amongst the negroes, who in *this* country are suffered to refrain from work on that day. Here, arrayed in their best apparel . . . they would meet together on the green, and spend the day in mirth and festivity.[35]

Another observer also commented on the black population's Sabbath revels in these years: "Sunday, Feb. 24 [1799] . . . we saw vast numbers of negro slaves, men, women, and children, assembled together on the levee, drumming, fifing, and dancing, in large rings." And in 1804, a visitor to the city, after marveling that stores were open even on Sunday mornings, wrote of the local black population: "They assemble in great masses on the levee on Sundays, and make themselves glad with song, dance and merriment."[36]

Although New Orleans was not the only place in North America where blacks carried on such festivities, the city was unique in the way the open expression of Africanness became a regular public custom, governed by law. In 1817, a new statute limited black dancing to Sundays before sundown, and in Congo Square, a spacious common near Rampart and Orleans Streets, known today as Beauregard Square. A remarkable account of what took place in Congo Square early in the 1800s comes from Benjamin Latrobe, an architect and engineer remembered chiefly as the designer of the U.S. Capitol building in Washington, D.C. Working in New Orleans in 1819, Latrobe one Sunday afternoon in February heard "a most extraordinary noise," which sounded to him like "horses trampling on a wooden floor." When he investigated, it turned out to be an assembly of blacks, five or six hundred strong, engaged in some kind of dancing. They had formed themselves into rings, "the largest not 10 feet in diameter." In one ring, two women danced. "They held each a coarse handkerchief extended by the corners in their hands," Latrobe reported, and they danced "a miserably dull & slow figure, hardly moving their feet or bodies." Two drums and a stringed instrument provided the music; in his diary, Latrobe described how they were played:

> An old man sat astride of a cylindrical drum about a foot in diameter, & beat it with incredible quickness with the edge of his hand & fingers. The other

drum was an open staved thing held between the knees & beaten in the same manner. They made an incredible noise. The most curious instrument, however, was a stringed instrument which no doubt was imported from Africa. On the top of the finger board was the rude figure of a man in a sitting posture, & two pegs behind him to which the strings were fastened. The

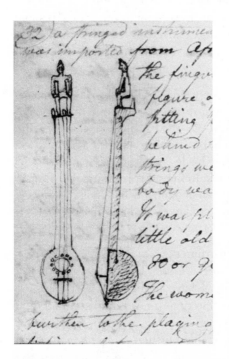

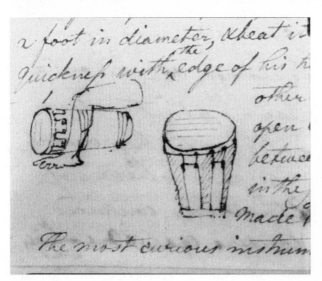

Benjamin Latrobe included sketches of the African instruments he saw played in New Orleans's Congo Square in his journal entry for February 21, 1819.

body was a calabash. It was played upon by a very little old man, apparently
80 or 90 years old.

Singing, though Latrobe declined to call it that, accompanied the dancing,
and the architect recognized it as a form of African call and response: "The
women squalled out a burthen [refrain] to the playing at intervals, consisting of two notes," he wrote, "as the negroes, working in our cities, respond
to the song of their leader." Different rings danced to the beat of different
instruments. Although "most of the circles contained the same sort of
dancers,"

> one was larger, in which a ring of a dozen women walked, by way of dancing,
> round the music in the center. But the instruments were of a different con-
> struction. One, which from the color of the wood seemed new, consisted of
> a block cut into something of the form of a cricket bat with a long & deep
> mortice down the center. This thing made a considerable noise, being
> beaten lustily on the side by a short stick. In the same orchestra was a square
> drum, looking like a stool, which made an abominably loud noise; also a cal-
> abash with a round hole in it, the hole studded with brass nails, which was
> beaten by a woman with two short sticks.

Latrobe also sketched three of these instruments.

Despite the detail he lavished on his description, Latrobe would admit to
finding nothing beautiful in the event. "I have never seen anything more
brutally savage," he wrote, nor "at the same time [more] dull & stupid, than
this whole exhibition." To his ear, the men's singing was simply "uncouth,"
the women's nothing more than a "detestable burthen . . . screamed . . . on
one single note." Perhaps it was the strangeness of the whole affair that
moved Latrobe to give so full an account: for one thing clear to him from
the start was the African origin of what he was witnessing. He guessed that
the singing "was in some African language, for it was not French," and he
commented that "such amusements of Sunday have, it seems, perpetuated
here those of Africa among its inhabitants." At the same time, Latrobe
found nothing menacing in what he had seen or heard. "There was not the
least disorder among the crowd," he wrote, "nor do I learn on enquiry, that
these weekly meetings of the negroes have ever produced any mischief."[37]

THE BLACK PRESENCE IN EVANGELICAL CAMP MEETINGS

The identity of black Americans as a group separate and distinct from
white Americans was taken for granted until well into the twentieth century.
Racial prejudice fed by incomprehension, distrust, and fear defined blacks,
socially and legally, as a category of people with no chance of being assimi-
lated into society as a whole. One result was that social activities in which

whites and blacks engaged as partners or collaborators were few and far between. As white settlement pushed westward, however, a religious institution took shape that proved more hospitable than most white forums to blacks and their habits of expression: the camp meeting.

Evangelical Protestant religion provided the camp meeting's framework. The larger movement from which it sprang was the Second Awakening, successor to the Great Awakening of the 1730s and 40s: a surge of religious renewal that between the 1780s and 1830 touched Protestantism in settled regions while also planting Christianity on the frontier and in the back country. Revivalistic preaching gave energy and purpose to the Second Awakening, and the camp meeting favored that approach. Held in the countryside so they would be accessible to people living in remote areas, camp meetings were gatherings at which frontier farmers and their wives and children camped out for a few days of prayer and singing, in an atmosphere of evangelical renewal. Preachers worked to goad worshipers into confessing their sins and admitting in public that only the sacrifice of Jesus Christ could earn them God's forgiveness, without which they faced damnation in hell's eternal fires. Crowds could be large, sometimes numbering in the thousands, and people might travel long distances to attend.[38]

Beginning around 1800, camp meetings were organized by college- or seminary-educated Presbyterian clergymen. But they were soon taken over by preachers from the Baptist and Methodist faiths, who were required only to be converted Christians. Methodists in newly settled territories seized a prominent place in the religious life by appealing to "the plain folk," wherever they happened to live.[39] In contrast to the Presbyterians, Methodists offered free salvation to all who believed themselves saved by Christ's sacrifice. Although camp meetings were interdenominational and never part of any church's official program of worship, they caught on quickly. A leading Methodist of the day calculated that as many as four hundred camp meetings were held during 1811 alone.[40]

As an *ad hoc* rather than permanent forum, the camp meeting set religion above race and welcomed black participants. Even in slave states, blacks took part, though generally on their own "shouting-ground," where religious meetings were held after the sermon. The camp meeting's egalitarianism, generally applauded today, drew sharp criticism in its own day. In 1819, a tract appeared called *Methodist Error; or, Friendly Christian Advice, to Those Methodists, Who Indulge in Extravagant Religious Emotions and Bodily Exercises* (Trenton, N.J.), written by the "Wesleyan Methodist" John F. Watson. Watson's denunciation of camp-meeting hymnody offers an informative, if slanted, perspective on the early days of an American genre as well as a valuable description of the hymns some years before they found their way into print.

In Watson's view, the Christian gospel deserved a more thoughtful kind of expression than it received in the camp-meeting hymn. The music consisted of "*merry* airs, adapted from old *songs*, to hymns of our composing," and the religious enthusiasm these hymns kindled was no excuse for their shortcomings. "Often miserable as poetry," he writes, they were equally "senseless as matter." Citing Methodist authorities, Watson argues that only "a first rate poet, such as can only occur in every ten or twenty *millions* of men," should try to match words with the great hymn writers of the past. And as for the merry airs, they were "most frequently composed and first sung by the illiterate *blacks* of the society," proof of their worthlessness.

Watson is just as critical of the hymns' manner of performance. His comment that they were often sung "two or three at a time in succession" suggests that many of the hymns shared the same mood. Jumping directly from one hymn to another may have reflected the worshipers' wish to maintain momentum, perhaps to encourage rhythmic movement. That possibility is borne out by Watson's shock at something else he had witnessed: in the clutch of "animal spirits," some worshipers had actually danced the hymns, "with all the precision of an avowed *dancer.*" And "in the *blacks'* quarter," he writes, "the coloured people get together, and sing for hours together, short scraps of disjointed affirmations, pledges, or prayers, lengthened out with long repetition *choruses*. These are all sung in the merry chorus-manner of the southern harvest field, or husking-frolic method, of the slave blacks." Moreover, bodies moved when the black worshipers sang. "With every word so sung," Watson writes, "they have a sinking of one or [the] other leg of the body alternately; producing an audible sound of the feet at every step, and as manifest as the steps of actual negro dancing in Virginia, &c." At this point, Watson's irritation boils over. "What in the name of religion," he exclaims, "can countenance or tolerate such gross perversions of true religion!" Practices like these were "evil," and he found it deeply offensive that they were "only occasionally condemned."

It seems clear that Watson launched his diatribe against the camp-meeting hymn to unmask sacrilege. In the context of music history, however, his words leave a different impression. For Watson seems to have taken aim at traits identified as African: the reliance on oral transmission, the physical movement (or "dance"), and the suggestions of responsorial practice (as in Richard Allen's hymnbook) in the repetitions, choruses, and "short scraps" of tunes. His critique indicates that the camp meeting, rather than establishing a particular kind of hymnody and holding black worshipers to it, allowed them freedom to sing as they saw fit.

What galled Watson most was not the behavior of blacks at camp meetings but their influence. "The example has already visibly affected the religious manners of some whites," he complains. "I have known in some camp meetings, from 50 to 60 people crowd into one tent, after the public devotions had closed, and there continue the whole night, singing tune after tune, (though with occasional episodes of prayer) scarce one of which were in our hymn books." How could several dozen white worshipers sing hymns all night without hymnbooks? Apparently by following the example of blacks, who did not depend on books in the first place. The key lay in the kind of hymns they sang: short, simple statements of music and text, with plenty of repetition and redundancy, and utilitarian in format, designed to invite a group of singers to invent new stanzas or verses. The "endless" stream of hymnody sung by these transported souls seems to have come not from memorizing but from a kind of oral composition they had learned from blacks, using accessible formulas of tune and word.

The formulas Watson criticized lent themselves to quick learning and easy multiplication of stanzas. He cites a chorus called "Go shouting all your days" as an example—"in connexion with 'glory, glory, glory,' in which go shouting is repeated six times in succession." No chorus (or verse either) has yet been found in print with these words, further proof that Watson was discussing an oral tradition.[41] Yet if we use his description to invent such a chorus, it might read:

> Go shouting, go shouting.
> Go shouting, go shouting.
> Go shouting, go shouting;
> Go shouting all your days.

Using the idiom of "merry tunes" of that day, it is easy to compose a tune that fits these words. Perhaps the result supports Watson's claim that such texts are devoid of thought or theological content. But the exercise does suggest something of the process by which camp-meeting hymns drew on oral tradition. Referring to this chorus, Watson asks: "Is there one particle of sense in its connexion with the general matter of the hymn?" But his next rhetorical question recognizes that verbal content has little to do with the impact of sacred songs like these: "Are they [the words] not mere idle expletives, filled in to eke out the tunes?" And he continues: "They are just exactly parallel to 'go *screaming, jumping,* (or any other participle) *all your days! O splendour, splendour.*' Do those who are delighted with such things, consider what delights them?"

It is clear that Watson understood, though he did not appreciate, what was afoot in these hymns. The text functions as the equivalent of vocables to fill out what is essentially a musical structure, in which only one word needs to change from chorus to chorus. "Shouting" might be replaced in later stanzas by "singing," "praying," or even "rejoicing," though probably not "screaming" or "jumping." The camp-meeting worshipers seem to have taken delight in singing spontaneously within an open-ended musical form that their own performance created, through which they were able to capture and extend a moment when mental and physical energy, individuality and group consciousness, and spiritual and worldly concerns came together in the service of a kind of rhythmically animated religious truth that must have felt convincing and encompassing.

On the strength of Watson's comments, it seems fair to say that the camp meeting helped white Protestants learn—or perhaps *re*learn, as people can do in times of spiritual renewal—something that black Protestants' African heritage was perpetually asserting: that sacred expression depended on the spirit in which it was undertaken, and that everything depended on finding a key, whether verbal or musical, to awaken the proper spirit. Without black examples to draw on, white Protestants would likely not have found a musical genre as well suited as the camp-meeting hymn to the informal, participatory atmosphere of evangelical revivalism. The story of the camp-meeting spiritual reflects two complementary processes from which much of the distinctive quality of American music has flowed: blacks infusing Euroamerican practices with African influence, and whites drawing on black adaptations to vitalize their own traditions of music making.

7

Correcting "the Harshness of Our Singing"

New England Psalmody Reformed

AMERICAN HISTORY IS OFTEN CALLED dynamic, and a major source of that dynamism has been immigration, which boomed in the decade and a half before the Revolutionary War. In the mid-1770s, for example, a group of Connecticut men and women decided to move to western Pennsylvania. They were accompanied by Franco-American writer Hector St. John de Crèvecoeur. When the settlers arrived in what Crèvecoeur expected to be a barren wilderness, he was astonished at "the prodigious number of houses rearing up, fields cultivating, that great extent of industry open'd to a bold indefatigable enterprising people." The settlers seemed unworried by the difficulties of the new life they were choosing, scattering themselves "here and there in the bosom of such an extensive country without even a previous path to direct their steps and without being in any number sufficient either to protect or assist one another." On the western frontier, Crèvecoeur marveled, a wide variety of "sects and nations" were to be found. And every spring "the roads were full of families travelling towards this new land of Canaan . . . a strange heterogeneous reunion of people . . . without law or government, without any kind of social bond to unite them all."[1]

The movement Crèvecoeur described was part of a process taking place throughout the American colonies. And in fact there *was* a bond uniting these travelers: the availability of fresh land. The frontier's westward movement brought new settlers into fertile areas of northern New York and Appalachian Pennsylvania while also attracting many more into the territory between the frontier and the Atlantic coast. Statistics measure the quickening pace of settlement. For example, the number of towns founded annually in New England grew from an average of 6 per year before 1760 to 18 per year after, totaling 283 new towns in the period 1760–76, chiefly along the valley of the Connecticut River. Whether they lived in cities, villages, or on the land, few Americans in these years were left untouched by the sense of impermanence that such mobility fostered. The interplay of fixity and change—of things that stay the same over time and things that do not—is one of history's chief concerns. And geography has tended to be a force for change in America. Even before the revolution, travelers knew they had a vast arena to explore, stretching west to the Mississippi and south to the Gulf of Mexico and the Florida Keys.[2]

American dynamism was also fueled by the political revolution and war (1775–81) that ended British control. When the fighting stopped, thirteen principalities remained, linked only by the Articles of Confederation, an agreement overseen by a Continental Congress that held little power to enforce its decisions. With Britain no longer the main target for resentment, rivalries among the colonies, already keen, intensified. State governments were more inclined to work against than with each other. They issued their own paper money and taxed the commerce of other states, built their own navies, and at times even failed to send representatives to Congress. Such disharmony left the collection of colonies dangerously weak and led George Washington to warn around 1785: "We are fast verging to anarchy and confusion."[3]

The Philadelphia Convention of 1787 took place in an atmosphere of crisis. Would its deliberations produce one nation, or a confederacy of sovereign states? The answer, set down in a federal constitution, was that the United States of America was to be both. Granting the legitimacy of competing interests, the makers of the Constitution searched for ways to mediate among them. And thus they built compromise into the governing process to assure that such eternal conflicts as freedom versus order, individual versus community rights, and economic entrepreneurship versus sharing the wealth would be subject to perpetual bargaining. By recognizing the need to distribute political power among federal, state, and local jurisdictions, the Constitution created a government designed to be responsive to the people, yet able to act on its own. The framers' hope was that within its structure, the volatile energy produced by such disruptive forces as immigration, ambition, greed, and free land could be contained and harnessed for the benefit of the nation and its citizens.

PSALMODY, NATIONALITY, AND ANDREW LAW

One of the questions brought to the fore by the winning of political independence was that of nationality: what it might mean to be an American, rather than a British subject living in North America. People living on this side of the Atlantic were not slow to realize that the unique circumstances of their lives offered fresh cultural possibilities, including musical ones. The idea of American musical distinctiveness—for better or worse—first came to light in the field of New England sacred music. And the earliest musician to make an issue of it was Connecticut-born psalmodist Andrew Law.

Law's career revolved around three innovations, all having to do with nationality. First, when he began his work as a compiler, he included compositions by American psalmodists in a repertory that until then had been mostly European. Second, after experiencing a conversion in taste, he advanced the idea that European sacred music was superior to American. And third, Law struggled later in life to popularize the music he favored by simplifying musical notation. All three of these innovations took hold during Law's lifetime, though more to the benefit of rival compilers than of Law himself. The music of American composers did achieve wide circulation; a taste for European psalmody was embraced by many Americans; and a new system of notation akin to Law's did win wide success. Because Law perceived the importance of nationality, and because his changing view of it provides a window on a key period of American musical development, his life and work merit examination here.

Though a devout Calvinist and ordained minister, Law never followed a clergyman's career. Instead, not long after graduating from Rhode Island College (now Brown University) in 1775, he took up the trade of singing master and pursued it for nearly half a century, spending much of his life as an itinerant. His search for schools took him up and down the Eastern Seaboard, from Vermont to South Carolina, and his work as a tunebook compiler spread his reputation further. The image of Law that endures is that of a single-minded evangelical entrepreneur whose zealous ambition centered entirely on sacred music and the singing school. To judge from Law's letters, the main frustration of his career was his failure to profit financially from changes that he himself helped to introduce.

In 1778, despite wartime unrest, inflation, and the scarcity of paper, the twenty-nine-year-old Law and his brother William set up a small tunebook-printing business in Cheshire, Connecticut. From then until he died in 1821, his work in sacred music would have two complementary aspects: the singing schools he taught and the tunebooks he compiled and published. The first dominated Law's activities; the second widened the circulation of his teaching methods and ideas of musical taste. Law's plunge into the tunebook trade led him straight to the issue of nationality: the first tunebook he compiled, *Select Harmony* (1779), reveals him as a champion of American composers, at a time when the notion that Americans could compose music at all was still a new one. In the summer of 1778, he announced a subscription for a new "Collection of Psalm-Tunes and Anthems, from the most celebrated authors in Great Britain and America." Who in 1778 would have qualified as a celebrated American composer? It is true that James

Lyon's *Urania* (1761) and William Billings's *The New-England Psalm-Singer* (1770) had already brought American-composed music into print, and perhaps the prolific, irrepressible Billings did merit the "celebrated author" tag. But by placing the music of Oliver Brownson, Amos Bull, Abraham Wood, and other unknown Americans side by side with that of Billings and of British psalmodists, balancing homegrown and foreign composers in roughly equal proportion, Law implied that the Americans and the British were creative peers, giving a boost to fellow New Englanders who were just beginning to try their hand at composition.

In 1794, Law published under the general title *The Art of Singing* a graded trio of works, each designed for a different clientele: Part I, *The Musical Primer*, aimed at beginners; Part II, *The Christian Harmony*, for singers of moderate skill; and Part III, *The Musical Magazine*, for the most accomplished choirs and musical societies. The books represented nothing less than a conversion in musical taste, laid out in the pages of *The Musical Primer*: "A considerable part of American composition is in reality faulty," Law writes, blaming the harshness of American singing for the deficiencies of American composers. "European compositions aim at variety and energy by guarding against the reiterated use of the perfect c[h]ords"—presumably open fifths and octaves. American composers, on the other hand, dwelled on such chords until their tunes were "all sweet, languid and lifeless," chiefly because the singing was so deficient that "perfect chords" were the only ones that could be sung in tune. *The Musical Primer* announced a program of reform:

> The harshness of our singing must be corrected. Our voices must be filed. Every tone must be rendered smooth, persuasive and melting: and when a number of voices are joined together, they must all . . . be in the most perfect tune. Then, nor till then, shall we sing well, and be able to distinguish between compositions of genuine merit, and those that are merely indifferent.[4]

Once Law declared himself against American composition, he maintained that stance for the rest of his life, systematically removing American music from his tunebooks, replacing it with music from British tunebooks and urging other compilers to do the same. He even linked the European music he now favored with true religious principles. "It will not have escaped your observation," he wrote in 1800, "that very much of the music in vogue is miserable indeed."

> Hence the man of piety and principle, of taste and discernment in music, and hence, indeed, all, who entertain a sense of decency and decorum in devotion, are oftentimes offended with that lifeless and insipid, or that frivolous and frolicksome succession and combination of sounds, so frequently introduced into churches, where all should be serious, animated and devout:

and hence too, the dignity and ever-varying vigor of Handel, of Madan, and of others, alike meritorious, are, in a great measure, supplanted by the pitiful productions of numerous composuists, whom it would be doing too much honor to name.[5]

Having endorsed European principles of composition, Law moved the melody line in his tunebooks from tenor to treble voice, where it could be heard more easily. He also changed the sound of his students' singing. A Salem, Massachusetts, minister wrote in 1796 of a "musical exhibition" by one hundred of Law's singers: "He aims to have his music very soft, & the Treble is the leading part," adding that "not one note of tenour was heard through the Evening."[6] Law also pressured Protestant denominations to adopt his tunebooks. He wrote representatives of both the Methodist Episcopal and Presbyterian Churches, offering to provide a hymnal designed for their use at a price linked to the quantity they purchased. Finally, in hopes of achieving better distribution, he reorganized his tunebook business, appointing agents in cities and towns along the East Coast to advertise and sell his publications and to send him the proceeds of their sales. After Law died, he was given credit in some circles for having championed the cause of "correct taste" in American sacred singing. Yet from 1793 on, his tunebooks lost ground in the marketplace to others that blended American and European favorites in the way that he himself had been the first to do. Not for a dozen more years did his Europeanized ideal of taste begin to take hold in New England psalmody as a whole.

Shortly after the turn of the century, Law made the most radical change of his career. He abandoned standard musical notation, copyrighted his own system in 1802, and the next year began to publish in shape notes—a practice he continued for the rest of his life. Since the Middle Ages, the technique of solmization, which assigns a particular syllable to each pitch in a scale, has been used to teach singers in Western culture how to sing from notation. In modern form, a major scale is sung on seven syllables: do, re, mi, fa, sol, la, ti, [do]. In Law's day, singing masters taught note reading according to a four-syllable system in which a major scale was sung fa, sol, la, fa, sol, la, mi, [fa]. Once singers knew their major and minor scales, could find the keynote fa and the leading tone mi on the page, and had the intervals between syllables ingrained in their voices and memories, they were ready to read music—i.e., to sing from musical notation.

Law's system claimed to simplify the reading of music by assigning a different shape to each of the four standard syllables: a square to fa, an oval to sol, a triangle to la, and a diamond to mi. Singers who could coordinate shapes with syllables were spared having to figure out which syllable to sing. As another "simplification," Law removed the five-line staff, claiming that

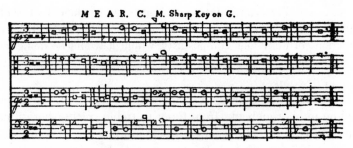

The anonymous British psalm tune MEAR, as printed in shape
notes in William Little and William Smith, *The Easy Instructor* (Philadelphia, [1801]). The shapes represent singing syllables *fa, sol, la,* and *mi.*

his system had no need of any staff at all. Thus a tune printed in Law's notation had a novel look, with a variety of small shapes suspended in space.

Shape notes turned out to be a successful innovation, but not in the form
that Law devised. Although he later claimed to have invented them as early
as the 1780s, he was neither the first to print a shape-note tunebook nor the
first to obtain a copyright on a shape-note system. In Philadelphia in 1798,
the federal government granted William Little and William Smith the right
to publish music with the following characters: a triangle for fa, an oval for
sol, a square for la, and a diamond for mi. (Law's system, patented in 1802,
used the same shapes but reversed the characters for la and fa.) And in 1801,
Little and Smith's *The Easy Instructor,* the first shape-note tunebook, was
published in Philadelphia, beating Law's *The Musical Primer,* 4th ed. (1803),
into print by more than two years. Little and Smith's notation differed from
Law's in one crucial particular: it retained the musical staff.[7]

The Easy Instructor proved a highly successful tunebook that went
through many editions, remaining in print well into the 1820s. And as an
American attempt to improve a familiar Old World technology, shape notation survived even into the twentieth century. When they were first intro-

OLD HUNDRED as printed in shape notes in Andrew Law, *The Musical Primer,* 4th
ed. (Philadelphia, 1803). Law's staffless notation won few customers and is not
known to have been used by other compilers.

duced, however, critics branded shape notes as a symbol of stupidity or backwardness, a crutch for singers too dim-witted to read standard notes or too countrified to have been exposed to them. That response implies that in some locales during the early 1800s, American psalmody acquired values built around notions of social class and geography. Shape-note tunebooks were not published in New England. Moreover, although *The Easy Instructor* was first published in Philadelphia, the book caught on only after a firm in Albany, New York, took it over in 1805. Thereafter shape-note collections, most of them using Little and Smith's system of four shapes on a staff, issued not from major cities but smaller ones in more recently settled regions: upstate New York (Albany), western Pennsylvania (Harrisburg), the Shenandoah Valley of Virginia (Harrisonburg), the Ohio River Valley (Cincinnati), and places farther west and south. The music in most shape-note tunebooks seemed to confirm the belief that such notation was intended mainly for simple country folk. For at a time when reformers in New England were replacing American tunes in their tunebooks with more Europeanized selections, shape-note compilers emphasized native tunes. Moreover, as Americans in newly settled regions began to compose, most took Billings and Company, not British psalmodists, as their models, writing hymn tunes, fuging tunes, and anthems in the manner of their Yankee predecessors and publishing them in shape-note collections.

"ANCIENT MUSIC" AND REFORM

Musical reform was a Northern phenomenon centered in New England. Its promotion of a "correct" Europeanized taste over the music that had gained currency in public worship—much of it American composed—indicates that concerns about religious probity were strong enough to outweigh nationalistic leanings in the region's Protestant meeting houses of the early 1800s.

The clearest account of reform was written in the 1850s by a psalmodist, Nathaniel D. Gould. According to Gould, in the "dark age" ushered in around 1770 by Billings, music-minded individuals, eager to hone musical skills for their own sake, had wrested the control of singing away from congregations and the clergy. By 1800, public worship was plagued by non-singing congregations, aggressively outspoken choir members, and a sprightliness in choral singing that fostered competitiveness and pride. In that state of crisis, true Christians realized that the time had come to regulate and desecularize the singing in worship services. Regulation was achieved by a kind of surgical strike, beginning in 1804 and centered in Massachusetts—especially Salem and western Middlesex County.[8] Clergymen and other community leaders joined forces with "prominent singers" to advocate "ancient music," which they found ideal for kindling a genuine religious spirit among congregation members.

By ancient music, Gould meant the republishing of European tunes composed decades, even centuries earlier, and the introduction of newer tunes whose simple style resembled that of the older favorites. Whereas American-composed psalmody was a recent creation, ancient music had already stood the test of time. Whereas self-taught locals had composed the newer psalmody, ancient music was the work of talented Europeans with Old World training. Whereas some New England psalmody exhibited an infectious rhythmic snap, ancient music moved with a gravity better suited to the solemnity of public worship. And whereas New England psalmody often revealed its composers' ignorance of proper harmony, ancient music embodied true musical science at work.

OLD HUNDRED, with its European pedigree, deliberate, even pace, and wide acceptability, was the quintessential piece of ancient music. "I have been informed," Andrew Law wrote in an essay, "that Handel said, he would give all his oratorios, if he might be the author of OLD HUNDRED."[9] Although Handel is not known to have said any such thing, Law's statement carries a figurative truth. The pious sentiments of Handel's oratorios required many skilled musicians for their expression; but such sentiments lay open to anyone who sang or listened to OLD HUNDRED. In the reformers' view, the skill required to perform complex music raised a barrier between singers and worshipers on one hand, and between singers and Christian truth on the other, that a simple tune like OLD HUNDRED removed. A clergyman of the day put the reformers' position in a nutshell in 1806 when he complained of the mischief created in psalmody "since music has been reduced to an art."[10]

As of 1805, then, ancient music gave reformers a musical rallying point around which they organized to further their mission. New Englanders of that era made a custom of pursuing charitable, civic, educational, and even religious goals by forming voluntary associations devoted to these causes. Debating societies, missionary societies, professional societies, and societies for moral improvement flourished throughout the region.[11] They also served as models for sacred music societies—the Essex Musical Association in Salem and the Middlesex Musical Society, for example—whose channeling of collective effort helped reformers win more public attention and support than an individual like Andrew Law could have hoped to match.

Gould's account names two tunebooks as spearheads of reform: *The Salem Collection of Classical Sacred Musick* (Salem, 1805) and *The Middlesex Collection of Church Musick: or, Ancient Psalmody Revived* (Boston, 1807). Both reached second editions in the year after their appearance, testifying to their success. Two traits distinguish them especially from earlier

American tunebooks: collective and anonymous authorship, and a repertory devoted almost exclusively to ancient music. Between them, *The Salem Collection* and *The Middlesex Collection* contain a total of 185 compositions, and all but 3 are European in origin. In fact, almost the whole repertory of these two books harks back to the 1770s or earlier, before American composers appeared on the scene. Most of the music is also harmonized in block chords, as are OLD HUNDRED and the "common tunes" of the early Protestant Reformation.

The issue of authorship is hardly less important. Most earlier American tunebooks were published under a compiler's name—Lyon's *Urania*, Billings's *The Singing Master's Assistant,* Law's *The Musical Primer*—and their introductions address readers on a more or less personal basis. In contrast, *The Middlesex Collection* was compiled "by the Middlesex Musical Society," and *The Salem Collection*'s introduction reports that its contents were chosen by a committee of the First Congregational Church, "whose names, were we at liberty to mention them, would add authority to the work." *The Salem Collection* also admits to the "humiliating fact" of "a general and most deplorable corruption of taste in our church musick"; such an apology, offered not as personal opinion but a consensus of unnamed experts, was designed to preempt discussion and compel agreement. *The Middlesex Collection* takes a similar approach: "The tunes here introduced," its preface intones, "are recommended by their antiquity, and more by their intrinsic excellence. They are, in most instances, reduced to their primitive style . . . for the spirit and flavor of old wine are always depressed by the commixture of new." Claiming to represent right-thinking Christians through the ages, the compilers implied that the best of all possible sacred repertories had already been in existence for generations. Thus, in these two collections, religious claims and social pressure were combined under an umbrella of cosmopolitan sacralization to discredit a homegrown tradition of psalmody that had taken shape as the United States of America was becoming a nation.

The forces marshaled by reformers, including the clergy, influential laymen, and societies devoted to the cause, proved potent and successful. Sacred tunebooks published in the Northeast after 1805 show a fairly quick drop-off in American musical content and a corresponding increase in European.[12] Some American composers mastered European harmony well enough to begin using it themselves. (Thomas Hastings, in the latter 1810s, was one, followed by Lowell Mason in the 1820s.) And while some compilers who devoted their books chiefly to European music continued the old-fashioned practice of sermonizing, advocating, or disparaging, the force of the ancient music reform lay precisely in shifting the grounds of the appeal from personal opinion to a consensus backed by theological fashion. Addressing the public as an unnamed "we" and making pronouncements that brooked no argument, ancient music advocates won their purpose by launching a social process in the name of religion.

The reformers' approach raises a basic question: To what audience is sacred music addressed? The underlying justification for Christian sacred music through history has been to praise God, and until the mid-1700s sacred musicians in the West focused steadily on God as the receiver of their efforts.[13] Praise could be delivered in more than one form. In a Handel oratorio, for example, God is praised through the composer's artifice and the performers' skill. The elegance and power of the musical statements are offered as exalted human responses to God's greatness. At the other end of the spectrum is the congregational hymn, which requires no great skill to perform. Here the musical offering is deemed worthy of the recipient because of the spirit of urgent humility in which it is sung. And such a spirit, whether confessing sin or making "a joyful noise unto the Lord," was certainly alive among New England choirs and singing schools, for all the criticisms that reformers leveled at them. William Billings's paraphrase of Psalm 148, which urges all manner of creatures to find their own way of praising God, is set to music calculated to push singers and listeners into a mood of wholehearted involvement. The idea that unself-conscious bursts of energetic singing are themselves pleasing in the sight of God finds its embodiment in this Yankee choral work:

> Fire, hail and snow, wind and storms,
> Beasts & cattle, creeping insects, flying fowl,
> Kings & princes, men & angels,
> Praise the Lord.
> Jew & gentile, male & female, bond & free,
> Earth & heaven, land & water,
> Praise the Lord.
> Young men & maids, old men & babes,
> Praise the Lord.
> Join creation, preservation,
> And redemption join in one;
> No exemption, nor dissention,
> One invention, and intention,
> Reigns through the whole,
> To praise the Lord.
> Hallelujah.
> Praise the Lord.[14]

In all three of these sacred expressions—Handel's oratorios, congregational hymns, and Billings's anthem—the singing is directed "out there," toward the ear of God. The reform of early nineteenth-century New England psalmody partakes of a wholly different spirit. For it was centered not on praise but on edification. Rather than God, its main recipients were the people who worshiped God. It is this fact, more than nationality, that beginning in the early nineteenth century divided Protestant music making into two distinct branches.

EDIFICATION AND PRAISE

Edification means intellectual, moral, or spiritual improvement. And a sacred music that is considered a way of "improving" those who use it, rather than a way of addressing the Almighty, grows out of a sensibility different from any discussed so far in this chronicle. To reformers, edification brought an impression of control. Praise, based on faith, eluded explanation; edification, based on reason, thrived on explanation, as shown by the rhetoric of the reformers, who always had a rationale to support their program. Praise tended to accept current practice as its starting point; edification was more inclined to disparage current practice, justifying changes by appealing to outside authorities, whose opinions were presumed to be superior.

Early in the 1800s, a split opened up in Protestant sacred music that was to have lasting reverberations in America. Those who made edification their ideal believed that worship was a solemn affair deserving its own kind of music, separate from secular music in sound, idiom, and style of performance. But Christians who held to praise as an ideal were more inclined to understand sacred expression, music included, as an extension of everyday life than something separate from it. With eyes fixed on God rather than their fellow human beings, they hungered for divine connection. The God they worshiped was more attuned to what was in the hearts of His worshipers than to the piety of their manner or the particular sounds with which they praised Him.

Early historians of American music, from Gould in the 1850s on, viewed sacred music reform positively, whether because it was seen to promote the cause of religion or because it brought a more cosmopolitan outlook into a provincial tradition of music making. Later scholars, however, more committed to the development of *American* musical artistry as distinct from that of Europe, were more likely to blame the reformers for submerging native achievement in a tide of foreign influence. It now seems apt to restore the episode's religious context. As long as Protestant sacred music in New England was ruled by an attitude of praise, questions of moral and spiritual improvement remained secondary, as they had traditionally been in Christian music making. The New England sacred music reform, as a move away from praise toward edification, introduced a bourgeois perspective that when connected with nationality, geography, and social outlook shifted the focus toward human authorities, always ready to provide feedback, and away from God, who provided none. Praise, in other words, encompassed edification, while the latter, recognizing praise as ineffable, focused instead on its own rational agenda.

Since the early 1800s, these two attitudes toward sacred music making have persisted, and new styles geared to one or the other have regularly appeared. Traditions centered on praise, from shape-note hymnody to African-American spirituals and gospel, have resisted the notion that a split between the two was possible, let alone desirable. But in the early nineteenth century, the idea that edification could be effectively pursued through a musical style became a driving force in American sacred music. Its appeal in the churches and meeting houses of the urban Northeast matched the vigor with which evangelical revivalism's music of praise reached out to "plain folk."

The
Nineteenth
Century

8

Edification and Economics
The Career of Lowell Mason

IN 1831–32, French writer and political theorist Alexis de Tocqueville was sent by his government to study the penitentiary system in the United States. In the course of his travels across the country, he also studied Americans, and the result was his *Democracy in America* (1835), a classic analysis of American institutions and "habits of the heart." Tocqueville perceived a big difference between France and the United States in the way society regarded religion. "In France I had seen the spirits of religion and of freedom almost always marching in opposite directions." But in America, "I found them intimately linked together in joint reign over the same land." Religion in America, he observed, "never intervenes directly in the government of American society," but should nevertheless "be considered as the first of their political institutions. . . . I do not know if all Americans have faith in their religion—for who can read the secrets of the heart?—but I am sure that they think it necessary to the maintenance of republican institutions. That is not the view of one class or party among the citizens, but of the whole nation; it is found in all ranks."[1]

Early in the 1820s, a figure appeared on the musical scene whose work illustrates Tocqueville's claim. Lowell Mason is remembered in American music history as the "father" of public school music teaching and also as a sacred music reformer and composer of hymn tunes. While both are true, Mason's grasp of how sacred and secular music were connected proved an even greater contribution.

In the early 1800s, group singing was widely accepted as a Protestant way to praise God and edify congregation members. Americans already sang in group settings other than church and meeting house—in Masonic lodges and private clubs, for example, both male preserves with their own customs. And in the 1790s, musical societies were forming: groups, again chiefly male, established to meet regularly for sacred singing. Most musical societies claimed an idealistic purpose, such as improving the quality of sacred singing or promoting a taste for better music. The proliferation of such groups after 1800 shows Americans' growing appetite for sacred singing in select company.[2]

Gatherings of men and women (or boys and girls) to sing secular or at least nonliturgical music, however, were rare, if they existed at all. It was here that Mason saw untapped musical possibilities, as well as the chance to bridge the gap between sacred and secular. Having begun his career in the field of sacred music, he perceived that techniques of singing-school instruction could be applied outside the sacred realm: classes could be formed, artful use of the voice encouraged, the rudiments of note reading taught, accessible music gathered or freshly composed, and tunebooks published, all with the goal of organizing secular singing as psalmody had long been organized by singing schools and sacred tunebooks. Without setting aside his work in psalmody, Mason widened his interests in the 1830s to include the teaching of secular music. From then on, he devoted his career, in the broadest sense, to making organized musical participation available to Americans on as wide a scale as possible. A talent for organization lies at the heart of Mason's legacy: he brought structure to previously unstructured parts of American musical life.

Tocqueville's comment offers insight into the state of mind that directed Mason's work. To say that Mason secularized his musical enterprise is not quite true, for that claim would imply a distinction between sacred and secular that Tocqueville's observation questions. Rather, Mason expanded his commitment to sacred music to include the elementary teaching of secular music. Instead of treating sacred music as a cause unto itself, he took psalmody as a starting point—an institutional toehold from which he launched a transformation that reached further. It was sometimes said of Mason that although he made his mark in music, he would have succeeded in any field he chose. One reason surely lay in his understanding of the society in which he lived, which enabled him to perceive connection where others saw only disjunction. Or, to put it another way, Mason approached secular singing with a purpose akin to that of psalmody: to edify the singers, improving them intellectually, morally, and spiritually. To his way of thinking, the improvement that edification offered could be a force for freedom; it could break the bonds of ignorance, just as Christian conversion freed sinners from the bonds of ungodliness.

Thus, Mason's deeply held Christian beliefs did not keep him from taking over a slice of the secular musical world. Indeed, the free institution of public schooling into which he moved was itself marinated in the religious spirit. And given that connection, Mason's involvement in both church and public school music seemed natural and complementary. When Mason enlarged his sphere of activity beyond sacred music, he vastly increased his range of potential customers. He also became rich, and many if not all of his contemporaries seem to have considered his earnings the just reward of a good and faithful servant. As the first American musician who recognized the common ground between religion and free institutions, Mason discovered that edification could be big business.

LOWELL MASON, PSALMODIST

Born in Medfield, Massachusetts, in 1792, Mason attended singing school as a youngster, and he also learned to play a variety of instruments: clarinet, violin, cello, flute, piano, and organ. In 1812, he left home and spent the next fifteen years in Savannah, Georgia, working first in a dry goods store and then as a bank clerk. Mason kept up his involvement in music during these years by leading church choirs and studying harmony and composition with Frederick L. Abel, a native of Germany who had immigrated from London to Savannah. It was also in Savannah, while still in his late twenties, that Mason compiled his first sacred tunebook.

Mason's tunebook was noteworthy for its contents, and even more for the circumstances under which it was published. He did not compose the music himself, taking most of it from other publications, including William Gardiner's *Sacred Melodies, from Haydn, Mozart, and Beethoven* (London, 1812–15), which adapted to English hymn texts melodies by European masters. Gardiner's borrowings reflected the belief that if shaped to fit the formulas of hymnody, melodies written by these European composers for their oratorios, operas, and even instrumental works were aptly suited to carry sacred messages. SMYRNA, which Mason took from Gardiner, shows how far outside the meeting house milieu a compiler might go to find a good tune. Mason's intent here differed from melodic borrowing in ballad operas, where knowledge of the original tune heightened listeners' appreciation. Indeed, with SMYRNA, that knowledge would have been distracting. For the melody comes from "Batti, batti, mio Maesetto," sung in Mozart's opera *Don Giovanni* by Zerlina, a young woman pursued by the lecherous Don; her song is an attempt to soothe her fiancé's jealousy. Thus a text that pleads for holy guidance is sung to a melody sparked by an erotic encounter.

When Mason had finished compiling his tunebook, he traveled north to Boston to get it published, for no printer in the South then owned a font of music type. In a letter to a friend in 1821, Mason described his collection as a book with enough psalm and hymn tunes for congregations to sing in public worship, plus some "longer pieces for Country Choirs." He also wondered whether publishers would find the book "too classical—that is—too much of Mozart, Beethoven, etc." That worry aside, however, Mason took pride in the musical know-how his collection displayed. Drawing on his study with Abel, he had harmonized the melodies "according to the modern principles of thorough bass—and I trust every false relation, and every forbidden progression will be avoided."[3] American reformers since Andrew Law had maintained that harmonic correctness separated the sheep from the goats: musicians who understood the principles behind consonance, dissonance, and proper chord progressions and musicians who did not—i.e., Yankee psalmodists. The word signaling the distinction was "science." Music considered scientific differed from music that was merely artful: scientific music required theoretical knowledge; artful music needed only practice.[4]

Mason chose the right sponsor for his tunebook when he approached the Boston Handel and Haydn Society, founded in 1815 to improve "the style of performing sacred music," and to promote more American performances of music by "Handel and Haydn and other eminent composers."[5] The society's leaders found Mason's book much to their liking and agreed to publish it under their name. Appearing in 1822, the *Boston Handel and Haydn Society Collection of Church Music* won resounding success. It lasted through nearly two dozen editions, and proceeds from its sales helped support the society's activities for years to come. But whatever benefits the tunebook brought to the Handel and Haydn Society, it proved to be the cornerstone on which Mason built his career.

What made this tunebook so popular? To start with, Mason created an aura of prestige around it that competing books could not match. The names of Handel and Haydn, famous masters of the art *and* the science of music, probably enhanced the prestige. It must have helped too that Mason's collection was sponsored by a group claiming authority in matters of musical taste. And the book was endorsed by knowledgeable foreign-born musicians, such as Mason's teacher, Frederick L. Abel, and Boston organist George K. Jackson, an Englishman. After revising some of Mason's harmonies, Jackson pronounced the work "much the best book of the kind I have seen published in this country." Mason probably also aided his book's cause by keeping a low profile, omitting his name from the title page. Like *The Salem Collection* (1805) and *The Middlesex Collection* (1807), *The Boston Handel and Haydn Society Collection* was packaged not as the work of an American compiler but as the product of a consensus reached by sacred music experts. For Mason himself, however, the financial arrangement of the book's publication—profits were split equally between compiler and publisher—proved the most brilliant stroke of all. By 1839, when the last edition was published, Mason's share of the proceeds had reached approximately $12,000. Though he was only a part-time musician in the early 1820s, his grasp of the trade's economics already yielded to no one.

Mason had another good reason to keep a low public profile. "I was then a bank officer in Savannah, and did not wish to be known as a musical man," he later wrote, nor had he "the least thought of making music my profession."[6] After working out arrangements for publishing his book, he returned to Savannah, resumed his job in the bank, and continued to lead a Presbyterian choir there. In 1827, however, he moved to Boston as the leader of music in several churches and president of the Handel and Haydn Society. Thus, until he was thirty-five years old, Mason's professional life was centered outside the field of music. By dint of shrewd planning, as well as talent and energy, he was able to enter his new calling at a level of income and prestige unprecedented for a newly professed American musician.

By 1832, just five years after assuming a key role in Boston's sacred music scene, Mason had embarked fully on the teaching of secular music. Yet he remained involved as a church musician, compiler, and hymn tune composer. Showing uncommon talent in the last of these roles, he produced more than 1,100 tunes for congregations to sing.[7] The line between Mason's compositions and his arrangements is not always clear, however, as shown by ANTIOCH, the tune to which Isaac Watts's text, "Joy to the world, the Lord is come," is now sung as a Christmas carol.

When Mason first published this piece in 1836, he attributed the tune to Handel. But he never revealed its source, nor has the melody been found in this form in Handel's compositions. Those who know Handel's *Messiah*, however, will hear echoes of it in ANTIOCH. The tune begins with a four-note motive that shares both melody and text declamation with the *Messiah* chorus "Lift up your heads." (Another parallel occurs in the chorus "Glory to God," where the tenor starts with the same four-note descent.) Later in AN-TIOCH, the melody sung to the words "And heav'n and nature sing" is close to the one played by violins at the start of *Messiah*'s opening tenor recitative, "Comfort ye, my people." From these Handelian fragments, Mason composed a new tune that changed the rhetorical structure of Watts's text. Mason's tune starts high, with a burst of energy underlining the text's rapturous mood. His closing is also vivid, its repetition of the last line suggesting that the birth of Jesus brought the cosmos into a state of sympathetic reverberation. In fact, Mason's setting of the last line, with its word repetition, the dividing of text between upper and lower voices, the tom-tom effect of the repeated notes, and the placing of musical emphasis on the end of the stanza, recalls the fuging tune, a genre long out of favor with New England reformers.

Perhaps no other American wrote so many enduring hymn tunes. Ranging over more than forty years, the tunes vary widely in style. Mason's first success was MISSIONARY HYMN, set to a text by Bishop Reginald Heber, whose clannish sentiments reflect the moral confidence that underlay Christianity's foreign-mission movement in the nineteenth century. Mason wrote this tune in Savannah, publishing it first in 1824 as a song for solo voice and piano, then arranging it as a hymn tune for four voices. While the text had much to do with the number's appeal, Mason's music is both shapely and memorable. The tune's musical quality has been endorsed from two different directions: its appearance in hymnals down to the recent past, and the melody's use as the basis for a fugue subject by composer Charles Ives (in his First String Quartet) more than seven decades after Mason composed it.[8] Ives's borrowing of Mason's tune evokes a sense of the New England past. And the way the melody survives that translation, projecting an air of timelessness as Ives spins it out in instrumental counterpoint, marks it as a statement of substance.

During the 1830s, Mason and his fellow reformer Thomas Hastings took the lead in creating a style of hymnody that preserved some traits of the preceding generation's ancient music, while also appealing to the taste of worshipers in its own day. In a letter of 1837, Hastings wrote with satisfaction:

OLIVET by Lowell Mason, with a text by Ray Palmer, as published in Thomas Hastings and Lowell Mason, *Spiritual Songs for Social Worship* (Utica, N.Y., 1831).

"Europe has no style *strictly devotional* that compares at all with what we are cultivating in this country."[9] OLIVET (1831), which gained acceptance as a setting of Ray Palmer's text "My Faith Looks Up to Thee," embodies that devotional style. Its harmony follows European scientific principles at their simplest, emphasizing tonic and dominant chords and moving in slow harmonic rhythm. Its words are sung in block-chord texture, and only the soprano melody has any clear profile. It can easily be sung by a congregation. And finally, the hymn's steadfast lack of musical elaboration poses no competition for the text. The tune functions as a kind of window, highlighting the words so that their meaning can be understood and felt.

Yet no one would mistake OLIVET for a true piece of ancient music, for its rhythm and structure point to more recent origins. In contrast to the unbroken successions of half or quarter notes favored in ancient music, OLIVET features a rhythmic motive that appears in five of the tune's seven phrases. Before Mason's time, motives like this one were foreign to hymnodic style. And here, rhythmic pattern and harmony are coordinated to serve a highly subjective set of words. In the second half of Palmer's text, the worshiper pleads with God: "Now hear me while I pray. / Take all my guilt away. / Oh, let me from this day / Be wholly thine." The second line is sung to the same music as the first; but it seems more imploring, partly because the bass remains static, and the longer the pedal point (sustained bass note), the greater the expectation that the bass will move. The third line is even more urgent, calling out on the highest note in the whole melody ("*Oh let me from this day*"). By the time a cadence relieves the tension, eighteen consecutive G's that have sounded in the bass help give OLIVET a steadily rising dramatic curve that supports the text's self-dramatizing demands.

As Mason grew older and hymnody more diverse, he kept abreast of new styles. WORK SONG, a late Mason success, was introduced in 1864 when the composer was seventy-two. It was published, in fact, not as a hymn but rather as a vocal number in *The Song Garden,* one of a series of Mason's public school books. WORK SONG, like OLIVET, relies on a rhythmic motive. But here the dotted-rhythm figure proves to be a formula (♩ ♩♩ ♩ ♩) recalling the rhythm of march after march during the eighteenth and early nineteenth centuries. Given the link to the march and the vigor of Annie L. Coghill's text, it is hard to imagine a group of people singing this hymn in anything but a forthright way, and at a brisk, strict tempo. Mason's setting reflects the text's structure: a series of commands phrased in relentless succession and tailored to the tune so that on the downbeat of every second measure, the word "work!" rings out, calling singers to a strenuous life of moral commitment.

LOWELL MASON, TEACHER OF CHILDREN

Like psalmodists before and after him, Mason taught singing schools in hopes of improving teenagers' and adults' musical taste through sacred music performance. Around the time that he moved to Boston, however, a new development was afoot: the tax-supported public school was just beginning to establish itself as a Boston institution. The rise of public schools placed new attention on children, whose potential for making music had never received much notice. Convinced that reform was the road to edification, Mason grasped the advantages of teaching young children to sing *before* their taste was formed and they could develop bad habits. By establishing a secu-

Lowell Mason (1792–1872) not long after he moved from Savannah, Georgia, to Boston.

lar children's singing school, where youngsters could learn to appreciate "good music" as they developed their singing skills, Mason saw a chance to strike a powerful blow for musical improvement in America.

Around 1830, Mason formed the earliest known singing school for children, which he taught free of charge. When he felt the youngsters had learned to sing with discipline and purity of sound, Mason unveiled the results at a public lecture given in 1830 by the Reverend William Channing Woodbridge, a leading educational reformer of the day. The singing "cast a spell" on the audience. As one observer later wrote of public events like these:

> Never shall we forget the mingled emotions of wonder, delight, vanquished incredulity, and pleased hope, with which these juvenile concerts were attended. The coldest heart was touched, and glistening eyes and quivering lips attested the depth . . . of the feelings excited in the bosoms of parents and teachers. . . . A deep and lasting impression had been made on the public mind and the public heart.[10]

Mason's class of children grew quickly: from six or eight at the start to a group of five or six hundred a few years later. And after a year of teaching gratis, he began to collect fees, devoting more and more of his energies from that time on to secular teaching, especially of children.

In 1832, in collaboration with George James Webb, an immigrant musician from England, Mason helped to found the Boston Academy of Music, centered on teaching both sacred and secular singing. Soon he was offering teachers' classes through the academy, and published his *Manual of the Boston Academy of Music* (Boston, 1834; eleven more printings by 1861) to serve them. The introduction of vocal music into public schools had been one of the academy's goals from the start.[11] And so it was that in 1837 Mason took what has been widely considered the most important step of his career: with three assistants, he approached the Boston school board and offered free singing classes in the city's public schools for the coming year. The success of that volunteer experiment led the school board to declare vocal music a regular school subject in 1838 and to hire Mason and his associates as teachers. Mason was also named superintendent of music in the Boston school system, a post he held from 1838 to 1845. He taught music in the Boston schools until 1855.

A key to Mason's economic success was that as he moved from one pioneering project to the next, he compiled, composed music for, and published new tunebooks. Through this entire period, for example, the *Boston Handel and Haydn Society Collection* came out in a new edition virtually every year. And to that sacred collection Mason steadily added others, each aimed at a different clientele, and all now carrying his name. The beginning of Mason's work with children was marked by a new sacred tunebook, *The Juvenile Psalmist* (1829), and a new secular one, *The Juvenile Lyre* (1831). The year after his first venture into the public schools, *The Juvenile Singing School* (1838) appeared. And once he had gained a beachhead in the schools, he published *Musical Exercises for Singing Schools, to be used in connexion with the "Manual of the Boston Academy of Music, for Instruction in the Elements of Vocal Music,"* (1838), a set of several dozen large charts for the use of school practitioners, the newest members of the teaching trade.

By all accounts, Mason was an outstanding teacher with a commanding personality. But what gave him authority as a teacher of other teachers was a systematic method of instruction that led to superior results. In honing his teaching techniques, Mason learned much from William Woodbridge of Boston, who in the 1820s had spent several years in Europe studying educational methods there, especially those of the Swiss educator Johann Heinrich Pestalozzi. Pestalozzi was not himself a musician, but the principles of his approach as conveyed by Woodbridge appealed to Mason, and he based his own method upon them. These principles may seem merely common sense today (though in Mason's day, the notion that learning could be more a collaborative process than a transfer of knowledge was not widely shared):

1. teach children to sing before they learn the written notes;
2. make students active rather than passive learners, by having them imitate sounds and observe their properties;
3. teach one subject at a time, such as rhythm, melody, or expression, and practice each separately;
4. help students master each step through practice before moving on to the next; and
5. teach principles and theories *after* the practice.[12]

According to George F. Root, one of Mason's younger associates in the Boston public school venture, William Woodbridge made Mason a promise: "If you will call together a class I will translate and write out each lesson for you . . . as you want it, and you can try the method; it will take about twenty-four evenings." Mason agreed, and the class was assembled. (Root does not give the year, but it was surely in the early 1830s.) "Speaking to Dr. Mason once about this remarkable class," Root relates, "I asked him what those ladies and gentlemen paid for that course of twenty-four lessons. 'Oh, they arranged that among themselves,' he replied. 'They decided that five dollars apiece would be about right.' 'And how many were there in the class?' He smiled as he answered: 'About five hundred.' "[13] Mason had moved to Boston in 1827 for a yearly salary of $1,500. But in this anecdote, he turns a colleague's suggestion into a sum much larger than that for just twenty-four evenings of classes. Mason was sometimes attacked for being mercenary, overpaid, or both. Root denied that he was either. Admitting that Mason made plenty of money, he nevertheless considered Mason "the most misjudged man in this respect that I ever knew. . . . I do not believe he ever made a plan to make money, unless when investing his surplus funds. In his musical work it was . . . a clear case . . . of seeking first what was right."[14]

LOWELL MASON'S ECONOMICS

Having entered psalmody when it was strictly a subsistence endeavor, Mason turned it into a capital-producing venture, the first of several. Indeed, he seems to have been the first American musician who realized capital—profit in excess of expenditures and wages—from musical work. How he managed that feat is worth considering, for to observe the economics of a musical enterprise is to establish a vantage point on musical life that complements a focus on the music itself.

One way to frame such an inquiry is to consider music as a livelihood offering six different lines of work: composing, performing, teaching, distributing (or publishing), writing about music, and manufacturing musical instruments and other goods. Mason's career was striking in the breadth of its professional involvement: he took part in all of these musical occupations except the last. Yet while he was an active composer, performer (as church organist and choir leader), and writer on music, teaching music and distributing it were the keys to his financial success and his widespread influence.

Long before Mason came on the scene, teaching had been established as the skill most demanded of musicians and a common wage-earning enterprise. But the notion that it could also be a capitalistic one seems to have been Mason's own invention, at least on this side of the Atlantic. The key to that invention lay in the large scope of the projects he tackled, which were often too ambitious and far-reaching to handle by himself. From the early 1830s, when he began children's classes, Mason employed assistants, and by 1844–45 he was teaching singing in six Boston public schools, while supervising ten assistants who taught in ten others.[15] Mason's assistants worked under his direction, taught from his methods, used his books, and were paid by him from funds he collected from the school board. There is reason to doubt that Mason passed on to his assistants all the money the school system paid him. It seems more likely that he took a cut for himself, an act that would qualify him as the first American entrepreneurial capitalist of music teaching. Root, who entered Mason's circle in the late 1830s, had worked under that kind of agreement with A. N. Johnson, his first mentor, with Johnson taking some of the proceeds of Root's teaching in return for setting up his protégé in the trade. Perhaps Mason followed a similar principle with his assistants, young men just beginning their musical careers.

In Mason's day, the distribution of music meant publishing. When Mason entered the book trade, only publishers stood to reap capital from their labors, for profit was linked to financial risk. Mason was never a publisher. Yet in view of the deal he worked out for the *Boston Handel and Haydn Society Collection,* it seems likely that he found ways to collect a larger share of the proceeds from his books than most other authors. That might explain his lack of direct involvement in the publishing trade, though the founding of Mason Brothers, a New York City publishing firm, by two of his sons in the 1850s did draw him indirectly into the business. Indications are that, as with his first tunebook, Mason earned substantial rewards as an author without taking a publisher's risk—good reason to stay out of a trade that already served his interests so well.

How wealthy did Mason become? In 1837, he was sufficiently well-off to manage a European trip of several months that took him to England, Germany, Switzerland, and France. An 1848 list of Boston taxpayers valued his estate at $41,000, making him by far the richest musician in town. And *The Rich Men of Massachusetts,* a book published in 1852, set his worth at $100,000. "His musical productions are in every household," the source reports, "and this also accounts for his wealth, which would have been far greater, were his benevolence less." Mason's tunebooks were regularly updated, and many of them continued to sell for years—especially *Carmina Sacra: or, Boston Collection of Church Music* (1841), which logged sales of 500,000 by 1858. Mason returned to Europe for a longer stay at the end of 1851, remaining there until the spring of 1853 and lecturing in the British Isles on congregational singing and the Pestalozzian method of teaching. When he returned to the United States, it was not to Boston but New York, where he set up new headquarters while he and his family settled in Orange, New Jersey. An article in an education journal in 1857 estimated the total sales of Mason's various publications at over a million copies by that time. In 1869, three years before Mason's death, the Oliver Ditson music-publishing firm bought the assets of Mason Brothers—by this date the holders of all Lowell Mason's copyrights—at which time the plates of Mason's works alone were worth over $100,000.[16]

If Mason's publications produced a fountain of profit that flowed abundantly, he could supplement that income as he chose by taking part in conventions and in so-called normal institutes for the training of music teachers. Moreover, after mid-century, the name Mason stood not only for Lowell but also for a substantial family enterprise. By the mid-1850s, Mason Brothers publishers, set up by sons Daniel Gregory and Lowell, was flourishing. Son Henry was a founding partner in Mason and Hamlin, a firm of reed-organ makers established in 1854, which later entered the piano-making business (1883). And son William, a pianist, composer, and teacher, married the daughter of his father's colleague George J. Webb, becoming a respected piano teacher in New York. By looking to the musical needs of a wide range of Americans, Mason and his family prospered.[17]

Lowell Mason's career traces a path from scarcity to abundance, achieved by targeting new customers while holding on to older ones: first singing schools and congregations (of different Protestant denominations and geographical regions), then children, adult secular singers, and finally teachers, courted avidly as potential advocates for his books. In the 1830s, without discarding the framework of psalmody, he broadened it to include secular edification, thereby welcoming many more customers into the fold of organized singing. Then, having made himself the first American expert on how children learn music, he enlisted and trained the teachers of those children, supplying them not only with ideas and techniques, but with publications to meet their practical needs. By the 1850s, Mason had moved far beyond his predecessors by creating new musical situations and serving them through a growing network of trade that he himself had partly invented.

MASON'S RIVALS, COLLABORATORS, AND LEGACY

Once Lowell Mason began to explore Americans' appetite for edification through music, other musicians recognized that a growing market stood ready to be tapped. By the 1840s, they were entering the territory that his work had opened up. And it is here that the economic implications of Mason's work come most fully into play.

Many of Mason's collaborators and rivals were younger than he was, but one of the most active, Thomas Hastings (whom we met earlier), was eight years his senior. An established psalmodist before Mason came on the scene, Hastings served the cause of scientific sacred music in the 1810s and 20s, through sacred tunebooks and his *Dissertation on Musical Taste* (1822), the first American treatise of its kind. He also composed hymn tunes. In 1832, he moved to New York City, spending the rest of his life as a choir leader and prolific tunebook compiler. Despite their sometime collaboration and complementary goals, Hastings in his later years considered Mason a rival and came to resent his success. A letter he wrote to his brother in 1848 sarcastically dubbed Mason "Friend Lowell," a man who defined doing good as being in a position to "multiply and sell books," and wishfully—and falsely, as it turned out—claimed a decline in Mason's public support.[18] New York University awarded Hastings an honorary doctorate in music in 1858, an accolade it had conferred on Mason three years earlier.

Hastings's promotion of scientific sacred music did much to carry forward that branch of Mason's musical endeavor. But three younger men, all students of Mason's, rang fresh changes on his legacy of organized musical participation. William B. Bradbury (1816–1868), a native of Maine, enrolled in the Boston Academy of Music and sang in one of Mason's church choirs in the early 1830s. After several years as a music teacher in Maine and New Brunswick (1836–40), Bradbury took a post as organist and choir leader in a New York Baptist church. There he established classes for children similar to Mason's in Boston. His first tunebook, *The Young Choir* (1841), continued that emphasis, and it was followed by others aimed at Sunday schools, which, especially after the founding of the American Sunday School Union, gathered strength as an institutional complement to public worship for adults and public schools for children. The sales of Bradbury's tunebooks are said to have reached more than two million copies.[19] Among the popular hymn tunes composed by Bradbury are WOODWORTH ("Just as I am") and CHINA ("Jesus loves me! this I know"), the latter published in 1862.

Setting a text by Anna B. Warner, CHINA became perhaps the most popular children's religious song. Its message of unconditional acceptance and pentatonic tune (its five-note scale lacks the fourth and seventh degrees), with a refrain based on a rhythmic motive, made it easy to learn and hard to forget. The song captures perfectly the voice of childhood innocence as imagined within the edifying framework of American Victorianism. Here is the refrain:

> Yes, Jesus loves me.
> Yes, Jesus loves me.
> Yes, Jesus loves me.
> The Bible tells me so.

This Sunday School hymn's vitality is proved by its staying power and widespread appeal. (An editor of the modern Baptist hymnal reported a remarkable cross-cultural borrowing. On a 1954 visit to a Buddhist temple in Hawaii, he heard children singing, "Yes, Buddha loves me.")[20] Bradbury also showed something of Mason's knack for business. In 1854, he joined with two collaborators to found a piano-making firm in New York, and in 1861 his publishing company opened in the same city.

The career of Isaac Baker Woodbury, born in 1819 in Beverly, Massachusetts, extended Mason's legacy in a different direction. A blacksmith's apprentice as a boy, Woodbury received early instruction in Mason's classes, then traveled to London and Paris in 1838–39 to further his studies. When he returned, he sang with the Bay State Glee Club, a traveling vocal troupe that performed in New England towns. Centered in Boston and working as a private teacher, organist, and choral conductor, Woodbury joined forces with his cousin, Benjamin Franklin Baker, in arranging teachers' conventions that competed with Mason's. He traveled widely as a teacher and solo singer (baritone), working out of Boston through much of the 1840s, then moved to New York in 1848.[21] In the 1850s, he contracted tuberculosis and spent his last three years battling the disease before dying in Florida at the age of thirty-nine.

Woodbury published almost thirty tunebooks, split equally between sacred and secular music. In New York, while serving as organist and musical director of the Rutgers Street Church, he continued his teachers' conventions, edited a music periodical, and also gave *soirées* in theaters at which he sang secular songs, some of which he composed himself.[22] Thomas Hastings, writing in a musical journal in 1835, called it an "evil tendency" when listeners, having heard performers sing in churches, grew "less scrupulous" and followed them "into the concert rooms, the opera, and, on special occasions, even to the Theater!"[23] From that point of view, a choir director who wrote secular ballads and sang them onstage compromised both his religious and pedagogical authority as a teacher of other teachers. But by the later 1840s, boundary lines were being redrawn. When Lowell Mason recognized that secular singing could be pursued in an edifying spirit, he laid the groundwork for the shift that allowed Woodbury to move comfortably between a religious and a theatrical setting.

A third musician who carried Mason's message in new directions was George Frederick Root, whose autobiography offers a detailed look at Mason's influence on one admirer's musical life. Born in 1820 on a Massachusetts farm, Root grew up hoping to be a musician. Yet he never played organ or piano until he went to Boston at eighteen; nor, though he was to win national fame as a teacher of vocal music, was he naturally gifted as a singer. "I had occasionally joined in the base of simple church tunes," he later recalled, "but was never encouraged by listeners to continue my performances long." They would say, "George, you'd better [get] your flute."[24] Within weeks of moving from his hometown of Sheffield to Boston in 1838, he was ordered by his first mentor, A. N. Johnson, to begin teaching an even ranker beginner. And after a brief struggle to make his "clumsy fingers" negotiate a keyboard, he was playing the last hymn in church services, apparently so the regular organist could leave to play another service. Root later explained his quick acceptance into professional ranks as more a matter of opportunity than talent. And he gave Mason credit for creating that opportunity.

> If my getting on so fast in a city like Boston seems unaccountable, I must explain again that music [in 1840] was in a very different condition then from what it is now. It was just emerging from the florid but crude melodies and the imperfect harmonies of the older time. Lowell Mason had . . . just com-

menced what proved to be a revolution in the "plain song" of the church and of the people, and his methods of teaching the elementary principles of music were so much better . . . than anything . . . seen [before] that those who were early in the field had very great advantage.[25]

In Root's autobiography, Mason is a key figure: his respected mentor, model, and eventually colleague. Root auditioned successfully for the Boston Academy Chorus in 1838, and by 1840 he was teaching as one of Mason's assistants in the Boston public schools. The following year, Mason hired him as an instructor in one of his teacher-training conventions, and three years later Root moved from Boston to New York, where he led a church choir and taught from Mason's books in various schools, including "young ladies" academies and the New York State Institution for the Blind. After nine months of musical study in Paris (1850–51) and some breakthroughs in his own career, Root enlisted Mason in 1853 to be one of his collaborators at the first of several three-month normal institutes in New York City.

One of Root's key insights is evident in his autobiography's discussion of the musical hierarchy that took shape in America during the 1840s. Shortly after moving to New York, Root formed a vocal quintet with four other singers and rehearsed the group to near-perfection. "I could carry out every conception I had in the way of expression," he recalled: "increasing, diminishing, accelerating or retarding, sudden attack or delicate shading, with the utmost freedom, being sure that all would go exactly with me." When the quintet sang Mendelssohn's *Hunting Song* for Theodore Eisfeld, conductor of the New York Philharmonic Society, Eisfeld was impressed enough to invite them to sing in the Philharmonic's next concert. "The papers said only pleasant things of our performances," Root recalled, and "from that time on I had the good will and friendship of the best musicians in New York." Root relished that approval so much that when his New York colleagues Bradbury and Woodbury urged him to compile instructional tunebooks because they were "doing well in that line," his reaction was disdainful. "I am ashamed to say it," he confided, "but I looked then with some contempt upon their grade of work. My ladies' classes and choirs were singing higher music, and my blind pupils were exciting the admiration of the best musical people of the city by their performances of a still higher order of compositions." It was under the spell of this admiration that Root compiled his first tunebook, a collection of church music. Its loftiness of approach was something he later remembered with embarrassment: "For scientific but uninteresting exercises," he admitted, the book "could not be excelled." Root's attempt failed because he had yet to realize "what people in elementary musical states needed."[26]

Root's failure showed that two alternatives lay open to him as a musician. Either he could devote his career to the art of music, or he could try to serve the musical needs of his fellow citizens. Root chose the latter course. His reasons for doing so shed light on the structure of American music making at mid-century. Root granted that a hierarchy of musical genres did exist, with European masterworks rightfully at the top. Indeed, he was a lover of the classics and he respected the notion that music must develop and change over time. Beethoven and Wagner were for him the two musical geniuses of the century; Handel's *Messiah* and Mendelssohn's *Elijah* were masterworks that sustained him throughout his life. But as well as being a responsive musician with a strong streak of idealism, Root was also a practical man who had a clear sense of his own abilities. "A majority of the music-loving world," he knew, enjoyed only an "elementary" state of musical knowledge. Would he be selling out if he turned his efforts toward serving the majority?

Mason convinced Root that he would not. In the first place, beginners' love for music was no less genuine than that of connoisseurs, and in the second, beginners' taste ought not to be despised. As Root came to understand, "all must pass" through the same levels of the hierarchy of musical genres, and only a few would reach the top. Moreover, the journey need not be one from bad to good music but from simple music to more complex and scientific compositions. Thus, Root decided, an American musician who sought to satisfy elementary musical needs would be taking on the challenge best suited to his abilities and his situation. In a sentence that could make a fitting summary of his career, Root wrote: "I am simply one, who, from such resources as he finds within himself, makes music for the people, having always a particular need in view."[27]

In the 1850s, when he began writing popular songs, the trajectory of Root's career as a musician of the people moved beyond the realm in which Lowell Mason worked. At the same time, Root throughout his career toiled in the name of edification—a dynamic, powerful ideal in the first half of the nineteenth century. Yet not everyone invested in it. Indeed, part of its dynamism sprang from the forces it opposed. In sacred music, edification's opposite number was "praise": the belief that the Almighty—*not* fellow human beings—is the proper recipient of sacred expression. It is therefore time to trace that impulse as it developed in different regions of the United States before the Civil War.

9

Singing Praises

Southern and Frontier Devotional Music

In 1933, George Pullen Jackson, a New England–born professor of German at Vanderbilt University in Nashville, Tennessee, published a book— *White Spirituals in the Southern Uplands*—about a remarkable tradition he had encountered among "plain folk" in the region. From the time he settled in Nashville in 1918, Jackson noticed a practice of sacred singing that was being carried on outside the churches. Gathering on weekends, groups of Southerners staged all-day "singings," and they brought their own books: thick, oblong volumes of psalm and hymn tunes, fuging tunes, and anthems set mostly for four-part chorus with the melody in the tenor voice. They seated themselves according to voice part—soprano (treble), alto (counter), tenor, and bass—in a rectangle with an open space in the middle. Into that space stepped a succession of singers from the ranks, each leading the group in two or three pieces. Typically, before singing the words of a selection, the group would negotiate the notes on four syllables: fa, sol, la, and mi. Jackson, who found the singers' note-reading ability astounding, learned that most of them had attended singing schools. The sound of the singing, he admitted, took some getting used to. The singers tended to vocalize full blast at all times, making no attempt to blend. As Jackson put it: "A minimum of attention is paid to individual voice quality. . . . The song is the thing—the mass effect." Who, after all, was "going to tell Sister So-and-so not to step on it quite so hard, or that she should place her tone differently, anyway? And why, in the name of good sense, should she bear the audience in mind when there is none?"[1]

Jackson's mention of an audience points to a key difference between the tradition he had discovered and the singing promoted by Lowell Mason and his disciples: the latter always included a human audience, which it tried to please. Mason taught singers to cultivate the attitude of self-awareness that goes along with edification, for only by paying attention to the conscious-

156

ness, including one's own, whose improvement is sought can edifying progress be measured. In contrast, singers in Jackson's Southern tradition sought a state of mind in which vocal sound poured out of the performer toward the ear of God. When Jackson declares that "this is democratic music making" in which "all singers are peers," he is pointing to the attitude of *praise* that ruled the singing. The singers made music to glorify God. According to their understanding, the power of the music and the absorbed concentration they brought to their singing made it worthy of the recipient, no matter *how* it sounded. Reflexiveness and the human audience played no role in this spiritual endeavor. For when human judgments of musical quality begin to be made, Jackson warns, "at that moment, this singing of, for, and by the people loses its chief characteristic."[2]

In 1930, some two hundred men, women, and children attended a singing in Mineral Wells, Texas—"all country folk, of course," Jackson writes, and of "the same type, precisely, that I had met" at other such conventions. "This was evident from their work-browned faces and their absence of 'style.'" The singing that filled the morning from nine o'clock to noon went as usual at such gatherings. But after a noontime meal, a novel event took place: a contest in which some fifteen children took turns as leaders. Judged chiefly on their ability to conduct and to sing the sol-fa syllables, they all received a cash prize. (Vocal quality was not considered.) Once the prizes were distributed, the contestants formed a reception line and the other singers filed by to congratulate them. Jackson writes:

A song was started:

> If a mother wants to go,
> Why shouldn't she come along?
> I belong to this band
> Hallelujah!

This photograph was taken on August 9, 1930, in Mineral Wells, Texas, at the convention of the Texas Inter-State Sacred Harp Musical Association.

One of those exhortational folk-spirituals of infectious tune, compelling
march movement, and a never-ending series of verses (made by substituting
"father," "brother," "sister," etc., for "mother") known to all. At first the happy
children received merely a warm hand-shake and pat on the shoulder from
the men and a kiss from the women. But by degrees the wave of emotion
rose, swept on by this song and then by another one spliced on, and by the
really parental joy in those children who had so beautifully proved that they
could carry on their fathers' and mothers' beloved art—until the warm con-
gratulatory reception became a veritable and ardent "love feast." The little
ones were smothered with kisses and hugs. Tears streamed down the cheeks
of young and old. And one patriarchal fat man, looking on, crying, laughing,
sweating, and fanning, shouted intermittently.[3]

Jackson was deeply impressed by the singers' emotional catharsis. It
came not from spectators but from participants, moved by the sacred cause
that had brought them together, the effort of a day of singing, and the sight
of the tradition's continuity embodied in the youngsters. Singing the old
tunes connected young and old alike in a family of God's people. And it was
in response to those feelings that the old man shouted: "a short staccato
whoop or yell or yip," Jackson writes, that signaled total release from emotional restraint. Such religious ecstasy had been common during the earlier
religious "awakenings" and camp meetings, summoned by evangelical
preaching. Here, it was the entire event that seems to have preached the
sermon to the transported old singer.

Conversations at Mineral Wells and elsewhere helped Jackson understand what these gatherings meant to the singers. "Every time I go to one of
these singings," one veteran confided, "I feel that I am attending a memorial
to my mother," and that, when one of her favorite pieces was sung, it was
"as if heaven itself hovered over the place." Pleasure in making music was
also part of the attraction. But in the end, the spiritual environment seems
to have left the deepest impression. As Jackson noted, many of the people
imagined heaven as "a place where they will meet again those beloved
singers who have gone before, and sing again with them, endlessly."[4]

NEW ENGLAND AND THE UPLAND SOUTH

Although Jackson first regarded these singings as a local phenomenon,
his research revealed them to be the tip of a historical iceberg. Rather than
keeping pace with religious and musical change, people in the Upland
South (which includes the Shenandoah Valley and parts of Maryland, Virginia, West Virginia, Kentucky, Tennessee, North and South Carolina, and
Georgia, but not the coastal areas) had preserved a tradition dating back to
New England in the 1700s.

In New England, the purpose of politics was to create a better society. Government was to be a positive force for good and politics a concern of all citizens. That ideal matched the edifying impulse brought to music by Lowell Mason and fostered an interventionist mode of government action geared to problem solving. The New England ideal stood sharply at odds with the political culture of the Upland South, whose main goal was to keep things as they were. Southerners accepted social hierarchy and paternalistic leaders as a normal condition. Ordinary citizens were not expected to be active in political life. Instead, power was held by an elite whose right to govern was often inherited through family ties or social position.[5]

Jackson, well aware of differences between his native and adopted regions, pointed to them throughout his book. For example, he noticed the different priorities of Northern and Southern tunebook compilers. In the North, with its belief in improvement, compilers gave the public "what they *should* sing." But in the South, compilers encouraged singers "to sing what they like."[6] Where urban life tended to dominate Northern culture, cities in the Upland South were small and relatively few. Southern industries were restricted to processing products drawn from the local countryside. High value was placed on family connections, maintained across generations and geographical distance. The region was populated chiefly by people of English, Scotch-Irish, and German background: people with strong cultural ties *before* they migrated. Their identity was closely tied to religious affiliation. African Americans were relatively few in number and more widely scattered than in coastal regions of the South, where plantations made slavery an economic advantage.[7]

For all their cultural difference, however, New England and the Upland South were home to the same musical tradition, though at different times. When reform took hold in the North in the early 1800s, most locally composed music was replaced by music tailored for more cosmopolitan tastes. Yet long after the music of Billings and Company had all but disappeared from the composers' native region, it remained alive and well in the South. Moreover, it continued there in a practice of sacred singing that revolved around oblong tunebooks and singing schools teaching the four-syllable New England system of note reading.

With historical perspective, the Southern practice looks more like a transformation than a simple survival of the Northern practice. Psalmody was sung in New England during the latter 1700s by a wide variety of Americans: not only rural people but city dwellers, college students, and Calvinist churchgoers of all ages, who sang in the name of artistic performance as well as religious affirmation. In the Southern uplands, however, choral psalmody and hymnody took root among rural plain folk with stern views of religion and generally old-fashioned ways. Perhaps nothing confirms the

Southern branch of psalmody as a countrified tradition more clearly than
the musical notation in which it circulated.

SHAPE NOTES AND SOUTHERN HYMNODY

Many Southern tunebooks used the four-shape notation that William
Little and William Smith's *The Easy Instructor* had introduced in the early
1800s. As noted in Chapter 7, soon after shape notes were invented, musical
reformers branded them a crutch needed only by ignorant or countrified
singers. (In 1835, Thomas Hastings dismissed them as "dunce notes." The
subtitle of Jackson's study—"The Story of the Fasola Folk, Their Songs,
Singings, and 'Buckwheat Notes' "—includes another disparaging label.)
Reform took its stand with musical science, and where science was valued,
shape notes came to symbolize the unscientific.

That attitude did not stop their spread, however, especially in regions
where the reformers' message failed to penetrate, such as New York State,
New Jersey, Pennsylvania, and the Ohio River Valley. After 1810, as the frontier pushed westward, new shape-note collections began to appear in cities
and towns farther and farther from Boston and Philadelphia. And while favorites from New England at first dominated the shape-note repertory, new
tunes by local composers were also welcomed. The new pieces were seldom
scientific. In fact, composers in newly settled locales wrote music with even
less connection to European hymnody than the tunes of their New England
forebears. A pair of examples from the 1810s shows two different ways in
which shape-note compilers set their stamp on American sacred music.

IDUMEA, composed by Virginia native Ananias Davisson, first appeared in
his *Kentucky Harmony* (Harrisonburg, Va., 1816). While there is no way to
recover the sound of plain-folk vocalism in the Shenandoah Valley in the

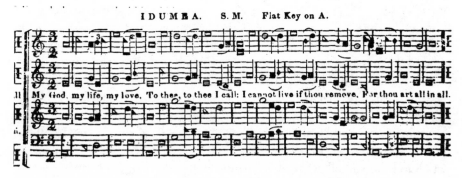

The hymn tune IDUMEA as first published in Ananias Davisson's *Kentucky Harmony*
(Harrisonburg, Va., 1816), which uses Little and Smith's shape notation. Davisson
was also the composer.

mid-1810s, Davisson's composition suits the full-throttle singing style of Jackson's Upland Southerners. In fact, IDUMEA strikes both ear and eye as an emanation from that vocal approach: perhaps people in Davisson's neck of the woods were singing that way long before he composed this piece. Set in a slow three beats to the bar, the hymn revolves around whole-note consonances into which the voices are invited to lock. Davisson's setting of the text's imploring words emphasizes the strength of the downbeats (beat 1), leaving the upbeats (beat 3) weak in comparison. In the top three voices, every strong beat receives a whole note. Weak beats, except for the first note in each phrase, are sung to quarter-note pairs.

Davisson's harmonies encourage the voices' tendency to alternate between decorating and homing in. Many of the whole notes are sung on open fifths, the most resonant harmonic interval and the simplest to sing in tune. On the other hand, many of the weak-beat quarter notes involve harmonic collisions, as we find on the upbeat of IDUMEA's first full measure. If the notes on that upbeat were as important as those on the downbeat, it would make sense to sing them conscientiously as written, as trained choral singers would do. But Southern shape-note singers let their voices slide over the upbeat notes en route to the next downbeat. Dissonances, Davisson writes in his introduction to *Kentucky Harmony,* "answer a similar purpose to acid, which being tasted immediately before sweet, give[s] the latter a more pleasing relish."[8] In that spirit, the hymn alternates the two flavors.

The contour of IDUMEA's vocal lines fits the Southern singing style. The tenor melody, ranging through a series of arch-shaped phrases, seems written to absorb all the sound the singers can make, especially in the high G's that climax the second and third phrases. The other voice parts follow suit: all have the range of at least an octave, and all give the singers a melody line built around whole notes inviting the fullest resonance. In fact, Davisson's wish to endow all four voice parts with melody apparently outweighed his concern for standard part writing, which he violates by sometimes allowing parallel octaves and fifths. Together with the tenor voice's pentatonic melody—using a scale from A to A but omitting B and F, the second and sixth degrees—the harmony, part writing, and likely performance style give IDUMEA the sound of a piece from an earlier age.

IDUMEA was a new composition added by a local psalmodist in 1816 to the repertory as the New England tradition moved south. MORALITY, however, an example from another shape-note collection, raises a broader issue that was responsible for sharp controversy in its day. Setting religious words to a tune borrowed from a secular song, this composition is a "folk hymn," a term coined by Jackson to describe "songs with old folk-tunes which everybody could sing and with words that spoke from the heart of the devout in the language of the common man."⁹ While folk hymns during the 1800s flourished in the South, their origins lay in New England.

The first third of the nineteenth century was a time of unmatched religious ferment in the United States. Evangelical critics attacked established Protestant (Congregational and Presbyterian) clergymen as antidemocratic, charging that they had parlayed education and theological training into positions of influence they did not deserve and personal comforts that a true Christian would spurn. Folk hymnody may be seen as a symptom of the religious struggle.

Even as Northern publishers in the early 1800s brought out new hymnals with verses in the language of "the common man," Congregational and Presbyterian leaders questioned the need for them. In their view, proven sacred verses were already in place. Moreover, the new verses were appearing in hymnals compiled by people with no theological training. New Hampshire layman Joshua Smith, for example, and doctor-turned-preacher Abner Jones, and Elias Smith, the "Christian" denomination's fiery leader. Having founded a new sect, the latter Smith won followers by preaching that since all Christians were equal in the sight of God, the most learned minister's ideas should carry no more weight than those of the humblest believer. Plain people, Smith reminded his flock, had long been denied the right to have their opinions heard. His solution was to produce pamphlets, books, songs, and newspaper articles that railed against social distinction. They also brought Smith into disrepute with established clergymen. One commented in 1805 that the press had "lately vomited out many nauseous things from this writer" and another called his writings "the most wretched trash that ever issued from the press."¹⁰ Furthermore, borrowing familiar tunes that everybody could sing ran counter to the spirit of reform, with its emphasis on dignified, European-influenced, scientific music, that seized the clergy of New England's leading denominations after 1805.

In that setting, Vermont composer and compiler Jeremiah Ingalls's *The Christian Harmony, or Songster's Companion* (Exeter, N.H., 1805) was unique. Where most New England compilers drew their texts from standard hymn collections, Ingalls also tapped the evangelical vein of Smith, Jones, and Smith. While tunes with refrains, common in secular singing, are rare in New England tunebooks, Ingalls included a number of refrain-based compositions in his.¹¹ Moreover, Ingalls's book contains far more folk hymns than any other New England collection of its day. At least 30 of *The Christian Harmony*'s 137 compositions are set to identified secular melodies or instrumental airs. And for 30 more pieces, Ingalls apparently either borrowed Anglo-American folk melodies or wrote tunes himself in a folk-like style.¹² The free-spirited climate of Ingalls's book is reflected by a composition he called INNOCENT SOUNDS, set to words by English Methodist

Charles Wesley that gave religious sanction to folk hymnody. As Wesley's text tells it, the devil long ago took over the domain of good tunes, only because the religious faithful were too timid to claim them for their own. It was time to recapture the best tunes for God by replacing their secular words with sacred ones.

> Who, on the part of God, will rise,
> Innocent sounds recover;
> Fly on the prey, and seize the prize,
> Plunder the carnal lover:
> Strip him of every moving strain,
> Of every melting measure;
> Music in virtue's cause retain,
> Risk the holy pleasure.

The music to which Ingalls set Wesley's stanzas is as sprightly as the title of the borrowed melody suggests: *Merrily Danc'd the Quaker.*

George Pullen Jackson declared Ingalls's *Christian Harmony* "perhaps the first book to record the revival tunes": the catchy, informal music that came into use at camp meetings and other religious conclaves sparked by the Second Awakening. And he argued that, anticipating a trend in nineteenth-century sacred music, the book deserved a place in history.[13] Yet in 1805 New England, *The Christian Harmony* was a failure. Booksellers' ads don't mention it, virtually no other compilers, Northern or Southern, borrowed its tunes, nor do other tunebooks carry attributions to Ingalls's work or any of its music. And no second edition was published. Rather than starting a trend, Ingalls's collection was ignored, then forgotten until Jackson's research uncovered it in the twentieth century.

New England's religious climate holds the most likely explanation for *The Christian Harmony*'s failure to dent the tunebook market. The book's contents made it a risky venture to start with, for the best-selling tunebooks were those that emphasized standard psalm and hymn tunes. By featuring folk hymnody, with its unorthodox texts, secular tunes, and revivalistic leanings, Ingalls probably alienated members of mainstream denominations who feared the rising evangelical tide; and they were the people most likely to support singing schools and buy tunebooks. Perhaps *The Christian Harmony* was intended to appeal especially to the Christian sect of Elias Smith, whose influence in 1805 was growing in rural New England, where Ingalls himself lived. If that was the case, he miscalculated, as Smith and his followers were unlikely customers for any book of harmonized choral music at all. Tunebook buyers were willing to spend money to learn to read music, and to connect choral singing with their spiritual lives. It seems unlikely that many evangelicals of that day, who made a point of their low social estate while disparaging formal education, could be counted in that number.

Yet if folk hymns suggested religious controversy in New England, they carried no such hint in the hinterlands to the south, when in the next decade the folk hymn MORALITY appeared in *Wyeth's Repository of Sacred Music, Part Second* (Harrisburg, Pa., 1813). The text is a six-stanza religious ballad that meditates on the transcience of human affairs. The tune, "duetto" for melody and bass rather than a setting for four voice parts, is one that we have encountered earlier as a parlor song, sung to the words of *A Death Song of an Indian Chief,* a.k.a. *Alknomook* (Chapter 1). In the economy of the shape-note tunebook, a good tune, whatever its associations, was too precious a thing to waste.

PLAIN FOLK, PRAISE, AND THE SACRED HARP

As different views of sacred singing's functions came to the fore in the early 1800s, vocal genres grew more diverse. We saw in Chapter 8 that edification could reach into the secular realm when a Christian entrepreneur like Lowell Mason pursued it. The edifying impulse has proved highly adaptable in America: it is a means without an end, for improvement is a never-ending process. But praise is neither a process nor a matter of degree. It is a state of consciousness from which God may be directly addressed. Hence, those who sing in a spirit of praise strive most of all to enter that state and to remain in it as long as possible.

The religious sensibility joined most closely to praise is a fundamentalist one. Jackson found the shape-note tradition most vibrantly alive among members of the Primitive Baptists, a Southern sect. Like the singing tradition itself, the Primitive Baptists by the early 1930s had been driven into places religiously, culturally, and geographically remote. And with every change in church activities and tenets suggested by a group of worshipers, another group would elect to stay "on the old paths." Whether the conflict dealt with the use of an organ in the service, foreign missionary work, salaries for preachers, or the foot washing ritual, new brands of Baptists had been springing up for more than a century. While perhaps only such single-minded dedication could have sustained it in the modern world, shape-note singing in the early 1800s was something different: a fresh blend of old and new, carried into recently settled territory by singing masters who taught from tunebooks tailored for the pious recreation of plain-folk Christians who lived there.

Three regions of shape-note publication were formed in the years after 1810. The first stretched westward from Pennsylvania and the Shenandoah Valley to Cincinnati and St. Louis. The second, carried on by Germans, sometimes in their native language and sometimes in English, lay between the Shenandoah Valley and Philadelphia. The third was farther south, chiefly South Carolina and Georgia. Regional differences aside, however, the Southern shape-note tradition bore the stamp of the revivalistic impulse that, already noted in New England, touched many regions of the country in the early 1800s. In fact, the shape-note tradition reveals the power of revivalism, not only because it encouraged the kind of worshipful singing that qualifies as praise, but because it indicates a leveling of the class consciousness that seems to have marked Ingalls's *The Christian Harmony* in New England. Revivalism opened the medium of print to any American who had a message to deliver. Printing enabled an author like Elias Smith of New Hampshire or Ananias Davisson of Virginia to reach an audience directly, in the spirit of plain-folk interchange. Americans of any social stripe could become authors, poets, composers, even prophets with their own religious following. Easy access to print countered class-based snobbery. The same was not true in England, where even into the late 1800s tracts and pamphlets issued from the Religious Tract Society were written in a condescending style, as though for children.[15]

The idea of author and book buyer (i.e., singer) as social peers is manifest in the two tunebooks that brought shape-note hymnody to the deep South: William Walker's *The Southern Harmony* (New Haven, Conn., 1835) and Benjamin Franklin White and Elisha J. King's *The Sacred Harp* (Philadelphia, 1844). Both were printed in the North for lack of suitable type where their authors lived. The earlier book, compiled in Spartanburg, South Carolina, sold 600,000 copies by 1866. And *The Sacred Harp*, compiled in Hamilton, Georgia, has been one of the great successes in American publishing history. Although co-compiler King died before the book appeared in print, it went through three revisions and a number of editions under White's supervision, was revised further after his death, and is still in print today, used at singings around the country. No hint of Victorian condescension can be found in this compilation by a pair of Georgia plain folk. In fact, the stories that circulated about the authors help to show why *The Sacred Harp* may be considered an icon of Upland Southern culture, a book meriting Jackson's description "of, for, and by the people."

Elisha J. King, a Georgia native and Baptist singing-school master, was a talented musician who has lived in memory through his association with the book. Benjamin Franklin White, the senior partner, was a native of Spartanburg, South Carolina, who moved to Hamilton in Harris County, Georgia, around 1840. (He and William Walker were brothers-in-law, having married sisters.) The youngest of fourteen children, White received only three months of formal schooling, yet still managed to become editor of *The Organ,* the official newspaper of Harris County. Having begun to study music on his own, White "would sit for hours at a time," Joe S. James wrote in

1904, "and would watch and listen to birds as they sang from the branches of the trees, and learned as much or more from these observations than he did from other men's works."[16]

A surge of interest in local history and biography took place in the United States after 1850, as the evangelical temperament combined with a respect for elders. Biographers related the life stories of early Americans as tales of virtue in action. They also recognized that access to education and gentility varied from region to region. As the *National Cyclopedia of American Biography* put it in 1893: "In the West there are men with rough exteriors who have done more for the prosperity and growth of their communities than has been done by many more noted personages in the East." B. F. White fit this mold. Prominent as a singing master and editor, he also became a civic leader despite his lack of schooling, serving as Hamilton's mayor and clerk of the county court. In 1845, White founded the Southern Musical Convention, dedicated to shape-note singing. His rough exterior did not prevent his gaining a place of influence in the Upland South, a traditionalistic and paternalistic society, where such influence was more often inherited than won.

Another convention of evangelical biography was to interpret lives as dramas, ending with a deathbed scene in which the subjects made their transition to the afterlife. While saying nothing about what caused E. J. King's death at twenty-three, his obituary notice reports that he "died in the full triumphs of faith," adding: "Several days previous to his death his conversation was upon religious subjects entirely." Likewise, as White lay dying at seventy-nine, he was said to have "recounted all the mistakes as well as the good that had followed him throughout his life. He summed it all up in the words, 'The end has come and I am ready,'" departing from this world only after singing the melody of SOUNDING JOY, which he had composed to words by Isaac Watts.[17]

If these recollections seem formulaic, formula was part of their power. They reflect the evangelical belief that a well-lived life deserves a fitting end, with the chief actor teaching one final lesson. Perhaps the lesson taught by White's life was that to achieve eminence in the culture where *The Sacred Harp* flourished was to be remembered as a typical figure, not an innovative one. White's virtues, as local biography perceived them, were those of an exemplar who embodied an established way of life, and a leader committed to the old paths and content to walk therein. Missing from the tale of his accomplishments is any hint that they divided him from his fellow citizens. Joe S. James's account confirms that point by explaining how the compilers relied on their friends' and neighbors' taste in singing. Between White's house and the street, James writes, "there was a beautiful grove of oak, hickory and other large trees, and in the yard was an old-fashioned well of pure water." People would gather there and "in this grove, veranda and house sing the songs long before they were published in book form."[18]

The Sacred Harp emphasized old favorites over new pieces. Familiar numbers in the third edition (1859) include OLD HUNDRED, Daniel Read's SHERBURNE, Lowell Mason's MISSIONARY HYMN, and the folk hymns MORALITY and PLENARY, the latter a setting of Watts's funeral hymn "Hark! from the tombs a doleful sound" to the tune of *Auld Lang Syne*. A more recent favorite is NEW BRITAIN, a three-voice harmonization of the hymn *Amazing Grace*. Although the tune's composer is unknown, it seems to have originated in the Shenandoah Valley, appearing first in print in Clayton and Carrell's *The Virginia Harmony* (1831). NEW BRITAIN, in triple time with whole-note downbeats and decorations on the upbeats, resembles Davisson's IDUMEA closely. In *Spiritual Folk Songs* (1937), Jackson printed a solo version transcribed from a performance he heard in Nashville in 1936. "The tune is slowed and many graces are introduced," he notes, pointing to a trait this performance shares with choral singing in the shape-note tradition. Jackson calls the example "an excellent illustration of the widespread southern folk-manner in the singing of hymns of this sort."

WONDROUS LOVE is a striking example of a Southern folk hymn. Its secular antecedent, Jackson writes, was a song about the pirate Captain Kidd, a link that becomes clear if one sings the tune to the following words:

> My name was Robert Kidd, when I sailed; when I sailed
> My name was Robert Kidd, when I sailed;
> My name was Robert Kidd, God's laws I did forbid,
> So wickedly I did when I sailed, when I sailed,
> So wickedly I did when I sailed.

Jackson's comments give WONDROUS LOVE an aura of age and romance: "The 'Captain Kidd' tune was already a very old and widely sung melody when it was picked up nearly 250 years ago and associated with the tale of the wild pirate who was executed in England in 1701."[19] But he does not document the path linking the Captain Kidd ballad to its sacred transformation.

WONDROUS LOVE also shows a kinship with the revival spiritual (see Chapter 6). Although it lacks a separate refrain, repetitions of text and music saturate the piece with a refrain-like spirit. The form is unusual, scanning poetically as 12.9.6.6.12.9 while inviting text repetitions, though not the way a more square-cut meter would. The first stanza's many incantations of "Oh! my soul" and "for my soul" to the same short-short-long rhythmic motive creates an exclamatory, awestruck mood. Just as important is the way the melody begins: with the first five words sung three times, each at a

The anonymous folk hymn WONDROUS LOVE, as published in the
1860 edition of White and King's *The Sacred Harp*.

higher pitch, and climaxing on the highest note of the piece—precisely at
its midpoint—which is sustained for emphasis. The melody's downward
movement in the second half of the piece balances the trajectory of the first
half. That rhetorical shape allows the text's main argument to unfold over a
whole stanza, while hammering home, measure by measure, an emotional
response to the miracle of Christ's sacrifice. By the stanza's end, only one
phrase—"that caused the lord of bliss"—has gone unrepeated.

Also striking is the way the three voices move in WONDROUS LOVE. Instead of preserving independence, they lock together again and again in parallel fifths and octaves, forfeiting the counterpoint that makes earlier New
England and Southern psalmody satisfying to sing and listen to. But if the
effect of intertwining voices is lost, that of a rugged hortatory power is
gained, especially in the second phrase (repeated as the last phrase), where
every interval between tenor and bass except the final one is a fifth. And the
impact is heightened by the sound of Southern singers' voices. WONDROUS
LOVE endures as an emblematic statement of a singing tradition that has
distilled the attitude of religious praise into an untutored, uncompromising,
heartfelt utterance.

HYMNODY OF NORTHERN REVIVALISM

Revivalism formed the core of American Protestantism before the Civil
War; its impulse was felt both on the frontiers of Kentucky and in New
York's high society.[20] Old-line Calvinism, harking back to the Protestant Reformation, had held that only a certain number of professed Christians were
actually elected—that is, predestined for salvation—while other souls

burned in hell for their sins. The Second Awakening of the early 1800s introduced into some quarters, though not mainstream Congregationalism and Presbyterianism, the alternative of "free grace," which opened the possibility of salvation to all sinners and granted human effort a larger place in religious life. With the rise of revivalism in the North came a sense that the devotional poetry of Isaac Watts, more than a century old and still dominant in hymnals and tunebooks, could no longer encompass the new religious sensibilities. As Presbyterians and Congregationalists searched for new hymns, their first step was to shift emphasis from an intimidating God to joyous salvation, substituting welcome for dread.[21]

Revivalism in the North left a decisive mark on two tunebooks that appeared in 1831: *The Christian Lyre,* compiled by Joshua Leavitt, a Congregational minister in New York City, and *Spiritual Songs for Social Worship,* compiled by Thomas Hastings and Lowell Mason. Leavitt's collection was the first American tunebook to take the form of a modern hymnal, with music for every hymn (melody and bass only) and the multistanza hymns printed in full, under or beside the music. Some of the music was original; the rest came from a variety of sources—New England psalm tunes, rural folk hymns, Western revival songs, the chorale "O sacred head now wounded," the tune to *La marseillaise,* and even popular songs in sacred makeovers, such as *Home, Sweet Home.*[22] The hymns Leavitt chose suggest a theological position influenced less by old-fashioned Calvinism than by the more welcoming approach of camp-meeting revivalism. And Leavitt's book flourished in the marketplace, selling tens of thousands of copies. Its format and contents were copied by later revival songsters and hymn collections for the next several decades.

In copying Leavitt's format, Hastings and Mason's *Spiritual Songs* managed also to compete with it successfully. Wherever customers were to be found in the name of moral improvement, Lowell Mason was there; Northern revivalism provides another example. And it was entirely in keeping with the musical reformer's stance that Mason and Hastings announced their intent to provide music that could not, like Leavitt's, be called "insipid, frivolous, vulgar," or "profane." *Spiritual Songs* contained four hundred hymns and tunes, many of them original, including a number by Hastings himself. The texts, by Watts as well as later writers, summarized the main evangelical themes of the day more fully than any earlier revival hymnal, including the theme of millennialism.[23]

As we have seen, sacred tunebooks, from Walter's *Grounds and Rules* (Boston, 1721) to *The Sacred Harp,* were published to serve singing schools, musical societies, singing conventions, and even meeting-house choirs, but not worshiping congregations. The oblong shape, vocal pedagogy, and varied musical forms (including fuging tunes, anthems, and set pieces) are all

traits that separate such books from hymnals used by congregations. Well
into the 1800s, most congregational hymnals were word books: metrical
psalters or hymn collections printed without music. Some congregations
still relied on a small stock of tunes learned by rote, and some did not sing
at all, turning music in worship services over to a choir or organist. In either
case, there was no need to print tunes in hymnals. Leavitt's *The Christian
Lyre,* and Mason and Hastings's *Spiritual Songs,* however, were intended for
congregations. Their success may be taken as testimony of revivalism's lev-

TOPLADY by Thomas Hastings, with a text by Augustus Toplady, as published in
Thomas Hastings and Lowell Mason, *Spiritual Songs for Social Worship* (Utica,
N.Y., 1831).

eling impact in the social sphere. The disdain in which turn-of-the-century mainstream Protestants had held evangelicals gradually subsided as revivalism, with its informality and emphasis on conversion, brought fresh democratic energies into religious life. That process in the 1820s and 30s was embodied in the career of Charles Grandison Finney, the day's most compelling revivalist preacher.

A lawyer from Adams, New York, Finney experienced religious conversion in 1821 and thereafter devoted himself to Christian evangelism. He began preaching as a volunteer lay missionary in towns along the Erie Canal in New York, the region he called the "burned-over district." In Finney's image, Methodist circuit riders had swept through the territory like a succession of forest fires whose heat left spiritual desolation behind: "souls hardened," as he put it, "against proper religious tutelage."[24] It was to reach such spiritual hard cases that Finney forged his preaching style. (His powers of persuasion must have been awesome; the Presbyterian Church ordained him in 1824, even though he refused formal training as a minister and admitted that he had never read the Westminster Confession.)[25] Finney's appeal lay in part in the simple parables he drew from his own experience as a horseman, marksman, and sailor. He was also a talented singer. Determined to make religious life congregation-centered, Finney preached in a lively, colloquial style that drew his listeners in, and the result was a great harvest of converts and a growing reputation.[26]

Revivalism had begun in plain-folk circles, but Finney often preached to the merchants and professionals, the ordinary well-off farmers, successful artisans, schoolteachers, minor government officials, clerks, shopkeepers, industrial entrepreneurs, and managers who made up the middle class.[27] His preaching also appealed to some members of the gentry (he smoothed the rough edges of his address as he preached to people higher on the social ladder). He was thus able to modify old-line institutions in the direction of democracy.

As Finney and others brought the appeal of revivalism to middle-class Americans, Leavitt, Mason, and Hastings were ready with a supply of congregational music suited to the new sensibility. (Leavitt, in fact, once wrote Finney that *The Christian Lyre* had been inspired by his preaching and urged him to scatter copies through his congregation.)[28] Hastings, a staunch advocate of musical science and a writer of hymn texts himself, gave special attention to fashioning a musical style that would encourage congregational performance. His hymn tune TOPLADY, sung to the text "Rock of ages, cleft for me," shows how an arch musical reformer responded to the expressive challenge of revivalistic worship and its drive for more participation.

Like Mason's OLIVET, published in the same collection (see Chapter 8), TOPLADY exemplifies the devotional style Hastings and Mason had worked out by the early 1830s. Repetition is the tune's lifeblood, both in overall structure (**aba**) and in smaller details. The middle section is nothing more than a two-bar melodic figure sung twice. Both **a** and **b** sections are based on the same two-bar rhythmic motive, with only one tiny change. From a rhythmic point of view, one stanza of TOPLADY consists of the same two-bar motive repeated five times, and over three stanzas, eighteen presentations of the motive are heard. The melody, which lies high and remains mostly within the range of a major sixth, carries all the musical interest, supported by a second treble and bass that stay within the range of a fifth. The text's message of immovability feeds off a static bass that stresses the tonic and dominant pitches.

TOPLADY, OLIVET, and other new numbers in *Spiritual Songs* are nonsectarian, and they lack the religious ecstasy that was considered fundamental to revival song. Indeed, the congregation-centered ideal that Hastings and Mason pursued was far removed from the God-centered one emphasized in this chapter. But the style of hymnody they created by blending elements of European science and American revivalism has endured in Protestant hymnals to this day. Its success proves that in American religious life, music accompanied by an edifying rationale can carry a middle-class appeal missing from music devoted to praise, whose advocates, rather than explaining themselves, simply sing.

10

Be It Ever So Humble

Theater and Opera, 1800–1860

THE GLAMOUR OF THEATER in the United States was an illusion created by players (most of whom were English by birth) at work in a blue-collar vocation. During the regular season, company members received a weekly salary reflecting their marketability onstage. In 1798–99, the Old American Company paid its top performers $25 per week during the season, while those at the low end of the scale received as little as $4; most players lived in boarding houses where a week's meals and lodging cost anywhere between $2.50 and $9.00. A typical stage performer could expect to make an annual income of around $300. By way of comparison, standard weekly pay for an American workman in the 1790s ranged between $6.00 and $7.50 for six days of labor, or a yearly wage of $300 to $375 (no parallel statistics are available for women, since few were part of the acknowledged work force). Stage players enjoyed one economic advantage over laborers, however. In addition to salaries, they were rewarded with benefits: performances whose beneficiary kept whatever proceeds topped expenses. While a star's benefit might net as much as $500 or more, a decent yield for nonstarring players was around $100—one-third of a typical yearly income.[1]

Female actors, however, fared less well financially than their male counterparts. In an age when most theater works idealized the virtues of their heroines, an actress could not count on being treated with respect, onstage or off. Her husband, male companion, father, or brother signed contracts and collected her salary. No matter how important her role, her name always followed those of male actors on the bill. She was fair game for frank, even impertinent commentary on her personal life and appearance, and was expected to perform as long as possible during pregnancies. Only actresses who played leading roles received a benefit night of their own; the rest shared the proceeds of their husbands' or male companions' benefit.[2]

Stock companies in America took residence in a theater for a fixed period of time, offering an assortment of tragedies, comedies, operas, pantomimes, melodramas, and the like for several nights per week throughout their stay. The most prominent companies sometimes played whole seasons (October to June) in one theater; other troupes devoted themselves to touring. Company managers leased theaters from their proprietors, usually members of the community's economic and social elite. In turn, the manager ran the company's day-to-day operations, took the financial risk, and reaped the profits if any. Managers had to pay the rent, the players' salaries, and all other expenses required to stage and promote a theatrical season. John Hodgkinson, an actor and singer who managed the Old American Company for several seasons in New York, offered this description in 1797 of a manager's duties:

> I had to cast and arrange the Business [staging] of every Play brought forward. I had the various Tempers, Rivalships, and Ambitions of thirty or forty People to encounter and please. I kept all the Accounts; I made all Disbursements, and was made, in all Money Transactions, solely responsible. My professional Labours were extreme, and I never finished them for the Evening that I did not attend to take the State of each Night's Receipts. Nay, instead of enjoying my comfortable Hour of social Intercourse with my Family, on my Arrival Home, I had a Check Account to take, and to make the regular Entries in my Books. I wrote and corrected every Play-Bill for the Printer. I planned and copied every Scene-Plot for the Carpenter. I attended every Rehearsal, to give Directions. I went through a varied and extensive Line of Characters on the Stage. I found principally my own Wardrobe for them; and my Salary, for all this, was twenty Dollars per Week, paid only when we performed![3]

Hodgkinson's co-manager, William Dunlap, later corrected one part of this statement. While Hodgkinson did pay himself just $20 per week as an actor, a wardrobe allowance of $5 and an additional $30 for managerial duties brought the total to $55. But his main point remains true: company managers, responsible for both artistic results and the financial bottom line, led hectic lives. Critics expected at least some classics like Shakespeare, while audiences tended to prefer popular pantomimes and melodramas. Staging a new success from London brought prestige to the company, but new productions were more expensive than older ones. It was also up to the manager to determine the length of each evening's entertainment and the work load of individual players, keeping in mind the demands on actors who rehearsed new roles during the day while performing at night. Finally, managers could be sure that their decisions would be debated and sometimes denounced by performers, critics, and audience members.[4]

The chief American companies spent the season in cities like Boston,

New York, Philadelphia, Baltimore, Charleston, and New Orleans. Smaller companies were formed from their ranks for summer touring, which gave players year-round work. A memoir by actor-dancer John Durang describes what life was like in such an outfit. Between 1808 and 1816, Durang toured with a small company to Lancaster, Harrisburg, Lebanon, Reading, Carlisle, Hanover, Yorktown, Chambersburg, and Gettysburg, all in Pennsylvania, and Fredericktown, Hagerstown, and Petersburg in Maryland—all towns where regular theatrical performances were unavailable. Preparing seven or eight nights of varied entertainment, Durang's troupe ran through the repertory, then moved on to the next town, where they repeated it. They adapted the regular season's "tragedys, comedys, farces, and operas" for smaller forces, and also offered their audiences dancing, pantomimes, acrobatics, and even plays in German.[5]

MUSIC IN THE THEATER

Music played an integral role in the theater: it was a necessary part of dramatic representation. But while music could enhance drama, it could also work against the illusion that actors and actresses actually *were* the characters they were portraying. Few singing performers have managed to bring acting and singing together convincingly, and Anglo-American performers of the early 1800s were no exception. They often did their duty to song while standing still, staring out over the footlights at the audience. Soprano Ellen Westray Darley, who began her career in the mid-1790s, was praised for her portrayal of "sentimental young ladies" and called by one Boston critic "beautiful and accomplished" and one of the "most fascinating beings who ever graced the stage."[6] But in 1806, as Rosamunda in *Abaellino, or the Great Bandit,* she was still clasping her hands together and striking a concert singer's pose during her songs. A versifying critic, granting the charm of her looks and her voice, begged for more animation:

> With folded hands see Rosamunda stands:
> Ah me! how pretty are her folded hands!
> Enchanting attitude, which Nature draws—
> Pit, boxes, gallery, bellow out applause.
> With varied voice, which can all hearts control,
> With various movements to entrap the soul,
> With air, face, person, shape and blooming age,
> With powers to grace with novelty the stage.
> Do not, lov'd actress, while each heart expands,
> Forever bore us with your folded hands.
> But if this gentle hint won't make you screen 'em,
> Oh, take the gentle poet in between 'em.

Another critic complained about the way singers acted during the instrumental introductions to their songs. "In modern *opera*," he wrote, "the Song is announced by some studied phrase which drops from the lips of the performers, and which is well understood to be preparatory to the exercise of the lungs." Then begins the orchestra, while "the singer in dumb suspense, awaits" the introduction's end. "This interval is on every occasion a *mighty melancholy* one," the writer continued. "From the doleful manner in which [the singer] paces the stage, during the interval of the symphony one would imagine he was listening to his *requiem*."[7]

Into the 1810s and 20s, stock companies in America were still playing such venerable English works as *The Beggar's Opera* (1728), *Love in a Village* (1762), and *The Children in the Wood* (1793). But newer works by the likes of Henry Rowley Bishop, music director at a famous London theater, were also entering the repertory. As well as composing operas, Bishop gained a reputation for his English adaptations of operas by non-English masters, including Mozart's *The Marriage of Figaro* (1786) and Rossini's *The Barber of Seville* (1815). One of Bishop's own works, *Clari, or the Maid of Milan,* was set to a libretto by the American actor and writer John Howard Payne. First performed in London in May 1823, *Clari* received its American premiere six months later at New York's Park Theater. A melodrama adapted from a French pantomime, *Clari* provides a revealing glimpse of the Anglo-American musical stage in the early 1800s.

The plot of *Clari* has been traced to the story of Beauty and the Beast. (Beauty saves her father's life by consenting to live with the Beast, who, freed by love from the spell that made him repulsive, turns out to be a handsome prince.) In Payne's version, the evil Duke Vivaldi lures Clari to his castle by promising to marry her. An evening entertainment there features a play in which a nobleman carries off an innocent peasant girl: a parallel to Clari's real-life situation. When the father in the play-within-a-play curses his daughter for failing to protect her virtue, Clari rushes on to the stage, pleading both the peasant girl's innocence and her own. Later, Clari escapes from the duke and finds her way home, only to be reviled as impure by Rolamo, her own father, in a rebuke that stuns her for its unfairness. But Duke Vivaldi, changed (*à la* the Beast) from villain to virtuous suitor, arrives to assure Rolamo that Clari remains chaste, then asks for her hand in marriage. Payne's work ends with a solemn tableau. Rolamo takes Clari's hand, "and unites it to the Duke's. They both kneel. Rolamo extends his hands over them. His eyes turn upward and streaming with tears and, with a choked voice, [he] exclaims, 'Heaven bless ye.' "[8]

The sentimentality of the last scene may seem simply a contrivance to make the audience weep. Yet *Clari* is revealing for what its characters say about power relations in society. Father and daughter are reconciled, but strictly on the father's terms. Within the play, both Clari and the duke have been severely tested, and both have shown virtue superior to Rolamo's. Clari has preserved her chastity under pressure. The duke, rather than forcing himself upon Clari, has backed off and changed character in hopes of winning her love. Rolamo, however, has merely granted that Clari did not de-

Home, Sweet Home by Henry Bishop, with a text by John Howard Payne, was introduced onstage in the melodrama *Clari, or the Maid of Milan* (1823) and became perhaps the most popular song of the nineteenth century.

serve his earlier rebuke; yet instead of being called to account for denouncing his daughter, he maintains his authority, and in the end it is he who blesses the young lovers. Rolamo's power derives from his position as a father, not from his actions. Just as the story of Beauty and the Beast sanctions a social order with aristocrats (i.e., the prince) at the top, *Clari* supports a patriarchal order governed by stern father-figures like Rolamo. *Clari* held a place on the American stage into the 1870s, enduring long after Andrew Jackson's election as president in 1828 brought a flood of anti-aristocratic, anti-patriarchal expression to the fore, both inside the theater and out.

One of the songs in *Clari* may explain the work's public appeal more than any specific message in its plot. Bishop and Payne's *Home, Sweet Home,* written to catch the heroine's emotion as she returns after being abducted, is woven into the opera as a theme of remembrance. Recognized as powerful from the time it was introduced onstage, *Home, Sweet Home* became perhaps the most popular song of the nineteenth century. Shortly after the New York premiere of *Clari,* a critic credited the song and its singer with creating an ineffable theatrical mood, calling the song "the most beautiful and tender we have ever heard" and the actress's performance "as she listened to the echoing music that welcomed her home . . . the truest, tenderest acting we have ever beheld."[9]

Trying to explain a hit song's appeal can be a daunting task. But there is little question that *Home, Sweet Home* made its impact through a potent combination of words and music. The music is simple: a melodic range of an octave; a repetitive structure of four-bar phrases (**aabbcb**); harmony limited to basic chords in the key of E major (tonic, dominant, and supertonic or subdominant). But perhaps what gives *Home, Sweet Home* its enduring character is the way these simple elements construct a feeling of stability that manifests the idea of home. The song's rhythmic motion is only one of many stable features. Sixteenth notes pervade the accompaniment, their flow broken only—and for dramatic effect—by the **c** phrase and the final cadenza. Bishop's harmonic structure supports that continuity, not only because it is restricted to so few chords but because its dwelling on the tonic gives the song a rooted, static quality. The bass sounds the tonic pitch on more than half of the forty-eight beats in this twenty-four-bar song. And the harmonic rhythm—the rate and pattern of change in harmony—could hardly be more regular. Phrase **a** fixes the pattern, repeats it, *and* provides the model for phrase **b**. All **a** and **b** phrases begin with two bars over a tonic bass note, move to the dominant for one bar and then return, settle on the "home" pitch (E) for two more bars, then loop back after a bar of dominant harmony.

The melody that rides the surface of this harmonic foundation is hardly more adventurous. In fact, while its own shape is graceful enough, one of the tune's chief traits is its gravitation toward G-sharp, the third scale degree. Harmonized by the bass's E, this euphonious, restful tenth becomes the song's home sonority. Bishop's melody also makes clever use of the tonic note E. In phrases **a** and **c,** it is the bottom note, the point where **a** begins and ends. In the **b** phrase, it is the top note, marking the piece's only surge of melodic energy, a gesture that quickly settles back into mid-range stability. Like the walls of a house, the pitch E provides both the melody's upper and lower boundaries and the harmony's bedrock, domesticating any hint of restlessness that the accompaniment's sixteenth-note flow might suggest.

The single-mindedness of *Home, Sweet Home* makes the **c** section ("Home, home, sweet, sweet home") stand out, breaking the continuity of both accompaniment and text declamation. Payne's words, turning from explanation to eulogy, trigger a contrast in which musical time, strictly metered to this point, suddenly becomes elastic. Bishop's melody invites the singer to linger over "home," drawing out the "o" vowel and the double "e" on "sweet," as though enraptured. If a movie camera were suddenly to zoom in from medium distance, the visual effect might be akin to the aural one that Bishop and Payne achieve at this point. Perhaps it is no coincidence, either, that Payne's last line, rather than trying for poetic eloquence, makes a simple affirmation of fact: "There's no place like home."[10]

Much was made during the nineteenth century of *Home, Sweet Home* as an expression of nostalgia by Payne, who lived the life of a wandering actor and playwright and died overseas. Whatever the impulse behind them and whatever their quality as verse, many Americans found in these words an apt reflection of their own feelings. As a piece of music originating elsewhere, the song could not be copyrighted in the United States. Therefore, many American music publishers rushed their own editions into print in the years 1824–25. The economic weight that a hit song like this one could carry is revealed by its great popularity in both print and public performance. By 1870, American performers of virtually every stripe could buy a sheet-music version of the song—now nearly half a century old—in a form tailored to their own level of skill. Seventeen major music publishers offered a solo song version with keyboard accompaniment. Pianists could choose from among the dozens of fantasies and sets of variations for sale, as well as waltzes, polkas, marches, and arrangements for four hands. Singers interpolated the song into opera performances, seeking to touch the hearts and win the affection of audience members for whom it was already a kind of anthem.

Home, Sweet Home won a popularity in its day parallel to that of more recent recorded hits. The chief difference was that in the days before music could be recorded and played back mechanically, styles changed more slowly and it took a hit song longer to wear out its welcome. The song was a favorite among soldiers during the Civil War and a standard recital piece for vocalists even into the twentieth century. To note the settings and circumstances in which it was performed is to take in much of America's musical landscape: the operatic and concert stage, the parlor, the dance hall, the parade ground, the battlefield, the campfire. From the early 1800s to the recent past, Americans have treasured songs especially for their melodies. As a well-loved melody, *Home, Sweet Home* lies close to the heart of musical experience as most Americans of the 1800s understood it.

ITALIAN OPERA IN AMERICA

On the night of November 29, 1825, New York's Park Theater witnessed an epoch-making performance of Rossini's *The Barber of Seville,* marking the debut of a newly arrived opera troupe headed by the tenor Manuel García. The audience that had gathered to hear Count Almaviva serenade his beloved—"In the smiling sky / The lovely dawn was breaking"—actually heard "Ecco ridente in cielo / Spunta la bell'aurora," and the implications of this fact reverberate through the later history of music in the United States.

When we consider all the new things the García troupe brought to New York, it becomes clear why their visit deserves its place as a landmark event. The Park theater was the first in the United States to offer audiences performances in a genre they were unfamiliar with: operas sung by European-trained singers in the original Italian, including recitative—the declamatory vocal style used in Italian opera to carry on the plot. In Maria García, the troupe also introduced New York's first star female singer. Though only seventeen, "the Signorina," as she came to be called, already performed at a level that would soon make her internationally famous. Perhaps even more important, the audience recognized and accepted her as a star, an altogether superior figure, and since that day, star performers have loomed large on the American scene. In contrast to English custom, the Garcías played only one work per evening instead of two. A lively discussion in the press of Italian opera followed. More than a new musical form, opera was a social phenomenon that raised questions about economics, manners, and social class.[11]

García rented the theater for two nights a week, sharing the stage with an English stock company already in residence. His troupe remained through the summer of 1826, giving a total of seventy-nine performances of nine different operas. Rossini's works dominated the repertory, with three operas (*The Barber of Seville, Tancredi,* and *Otello*) accounting for almost two-thirds of the performances (forty-seven); Mozart's *Don Giovanni* received ten. An orchestra of twenty-six—fourteen strings, a piano, a bassoon, and pairs of flutes, clarinets, horns, trumpets, and timpani—accompanied the works at no small cost. Veteran theater manager William Wood wrote in 1855 that the large gate receipts brought in by musical entertainments were almost always outweighed by expenses. "I am not certain," Wood confessed, that works "devoted to music and dancing . . . are ever profitable to a manager, under any circumstances."[12] By all accounts, the Garcías' opera season was neither the smashing success its financial backers had hoped for nor a failure. Rather, it marked the start of a long struggle of entrepreneurship in New York. For although Italian opera was introduced as an elite form of artistic endeavor, members of New York's upper crust were not able to carry its financial burden on their own.

A key figure in New York's early operatic history was Lorenzo Da Ponte, who wrote the librettos of Mozart's *The Marriage of Figaro, Don Giovanni,* and *Così fan tutte,* then emigrated to this country in 1805 as a teacher of Italian. It was on Da Ponte's advice that a merchant colleague traveled to England in 1825 and hired García's troupe for the Park Theater. Several years later, Da Ponte also helped to find sponsorship for an opera season staged by a visiting Italian impresario; then he and others backed the building of New York's first Italian opera house, which opened in 1833. A new opera company was launched by a restaurant owner in 1844, and three years later 150 wealthy New Yorkers collaborated to give the Astor Place Opera House its own home; all such efforts, however, failed to win a permanent place for opera in the city. Then in the 1850s, at the Academy of Music, Bohemian-born impresario and conductor Max Maretzek finally devised a workable plan. Under his leadership, operas by Rossini, Donizetti, Bellini, and Verdi, as well as other European masters, performed in a large hall (4,600 seats) at varying prices ($1.50 top, for boxes, ranging down to 25 cents for the least desirable gallery seats), attracted an ample base of public support.[13]

It took almost three decades, then, to establish Italian opera in New York. And on the eve of the Civil War, New York and New Orleans were still the only American cities with resident opera companies of their own. Nevertheless, it seems no exaggeration to call opera the most potent force to hit the American musical world in the nineteenth century. One reason lies in the musical and dramatic nature of opera itself. Another was that the operatic stage provided a showcase for star performers.

Italian opera relies on the drama inherent in the notion of larger-than-life characters, dressed in finery and with strong, sometimes beautiful voices, pouring out their emotions—love, rage, grief, exultation—on a grand scale, to music suited for such displays. Singers like Maria García Malibran earned adulation and moved audiences by making public spectacles of themselves. Their skill at communicating the human passions with utter conviction surely helped opera cut across social and class lines, attracting a wide range of listeners.

Another factor in opera's popularity must have been the environment in which performances took place. By most accounts, audiences of the period were anything but silent and passive. "We (the sovereigns) determine to have the worth of our money when we go to the theatre," a Boston correspondent wrote in 1846. "We made Blangy dance her best dances twice; we made Mrs. Sequin [sic] repeat 'Marble Halls' . . . and tonight we are going to encore Mrs. Kean's 'I Don't Believe It' in *The Gamester.* . . . Perhaps we'll flatter Mr. Kean by making him take poison twice."[14] But the audience's lack of decorum is less the point here than its expectations, which were those of people ready to respond in public interchange with stage players. Rather than modern spectators, they were participating witnesses who cheered favorite performers on, abused others, and expected calls for encores to be obeyed.

To speak of such ingredients as stars and interaction with audiences is to recognize that opera is both a form uniting drama, spectacle, and music into one convincing whole *and* a bundle of elements that can be pulled apart, changed, and recombined. The programs given around 1840 at New York's Olympic Theater show opera's adaptability. Managed by a pair of Englishmen, the Olympic offered light entertainment and specialized in opera burlesques for a ticket price of 12 1/2 cents. *The Roof Scrambler,* a travesty of Bellini's *La sonnambula,* was a particular hit there, as were later *Mrs. Normer* (Bellini's *Norma*), *Sam Parr, with the Red Coarse Hair* (Ferdinand Hérold's *Zampa, or The Red Corsair*), and *Fried Shots* (Carl Maria von Weber's *Der Freischütz*).[15] In works like these, performers twisted opera's archetypal characters—the sleepwalker of *La sonnambula,* the madwoman of *Lucia di Lammermoor,* the magician of *Der Freischütz*—for comic effect, with the help of music freely adapted from the original scores. Offstage, the melodies, titles, subjects, leading characters, and plot elements of famous operas supplied hit musical numbers for the sheet-music trade, for home performers to sing and for pianists and wind bands to play. (Bishop's *Home, Sweet Home* was an example from the English tradition, Bellini's *Ah! Don't Mingle*—"Ah! non giunge," from *La sonnambula*—from the Italian.) As a theatrical form, opera struggled for a toehold on these shores. But as a frame of reference and a cornucopia of song, it enriched and vitalized the theater and indeed the musical scene as a whole.

Opera's bountiful store of melody came to be a major contribution to America's music making. Performers of operatic music included not only opera singers but those who sang and played its melodies in other settings. The poet Walt Whitman celebrated opera's adaptability in "Italian Music in Dakota," a poem picturing a regimental army band stationed at the edge of a vast wilderness. Melodies composed to be sung in a packed theater, Whitman reflects, may also be played for the ear of nature. Against a background of "rocks, woods, fort, cannon, pacing sentries, endless wilds," strains evoking "*Sonnambula's* innocent love" and "*Norma's* anguish" are sounded, "in dulcet streams" and without words, by flutes and cornets. To the poet's imagination, the melodies lose little of their beauty and none of their impact. "Electric, pensive, turbulent, artificial," they seem to him even more

Maria García (1808–1836), Spanish mezzo-soprano, came to the United States with her father's opera troupe in 1825, married Eugène Malibran in 1826, and returned to Europe in 1827, having achieved stardom on these shores. Highly acclaimed in Europe, she died from injuries suffered in a riding accident.

"at home" in this desolate setting than when sung in "the city's fresco'd rooms." Whitman fancies nature listening "well pleas'd" to the band's twilight performance. His recognition of melody as the final distillation of operatic experience provides another illustration, and an eloquent one, of how and why Italian opera won a solid and enduring place in the lives of nineteenth-century Americans.[16]

OPERA STARS AND COMPANIES

In March 1826, on the night before her eighteenth birthday, María García married a supposedly wealthy but soon-to-be bankrupt merchant in New York. Several months later, the rest of the company left for an engagement in Mexico, and she, as Madame Malibran, stayed behind. Her performances had already received high praise; but now the young mezzo-soprano made the leap from singer to star and won the New York audience's hearts. With her chance to sing Italian operas gone, she learned English ones, showing skill as both actress and singer whenever she stepped onstage. Comparing her with other cast members in a Bowery Theater production of early 1827, a critic wrote: "It was to the credit of the Signorina (foreigner as she is), and to the rebuke of the other performers that she not only knew her own part perfectly, but prompted the others, and directed the whole stage arrangement." Beyond superior talent, however, Malibran projected an aura that connected with critics and audiences alike. She was lauded for good taste, dignity of deportment, lack of exaggeration, charm, simplicity, ease, and grace—the first woman of the stage whom the American public accepted as "respectable."[17] By the time she left for Europe in the fall of 1827—she was earning $500 per night in New York while still turning a profit for theater owners and managers.

A charismatic star like Malibran could make audience members feel that she was playing directly to them. Stars overshadowed other players—a fact that stock companies had always tried to minimize through ensemble organization: teams of actors and actresses, offering a varied bill of plays and operas with lead roles passed around. Before Malibran, singers of star quality on the American stage had remained within the company's structure, receiving higher pay than lesser players but still under the manager's control. Like John Hodgkinson in the 1790s, managers of the 1820s set the company's agenda and called the shots. The audience appeal of a star like Malibran, however, shifted the focus of public attention toward herself and away from the company. The power of managers declined, and that of public opinion grew.

From the 1820s on, theatrical performance revolved more and more around stars, which meant that finding and presenting them became a key part of a manager's business. One could write the history of musical performance in America by tracing variations on the category of star: a singing actress like Malibran; a concert singer like Jenny Lind; an operatic tenor like Enrico Caruso; a conductor like Arturo Toscanini; a jazz musician like Louis Armstrong; a rock-and-roll singer like Elvis Presley. All of these individuals redefined their initial role as a performer in a way that left its mark on those who came after them. Each managed in performance not only to connect with audiences but to amaze them—to fill them with wonder and hence to assume a public image that was larger than life. In the nineteenth and early twentieth centuries, no other star-producing forum equaled that of the operatic stage.

The advent of Madame Malibran and Italian opera did not put English stock companies out of business. But it did help usher in the "vocal-star troupe": the company specializing in opera whose performances were built around one or more outstanding singers. The American years of Elizabeth Austin provide an example.

Elizabeth Austin and the Vocal-Star Troupe

Toward the end of 1827, Austin, a popular singer of English opera in London's theaters, traveled to the United States in the company of her musical director and agent, and between 1828 and 1835 she toured the country's eastern half. In small towns she sang concerts; in larger cities she sang operas with stock companies, sometimes as the featured soloist but more often teamed up with other well-known singers. Under the second arrangement, two, three, or four star vocalists traveled together, playing the chief roles in productions staged by local companies, many of which also toured. Austin spent her American career chiefly in such cities as New York, Boston, Providence, Philadelphia, Baltimore, and Washington. And she made at least one trip in 1834 to New Orleans.

An American critic of the day described Austin's soprano voice as being of "perfect bird-like softness," ranging over nearly three octaves with a "remarkable purity and sweetness." Trained in England, Austin mastered the florid Italian school of singing better than any other English singer to visit the United States before her. As well as age-old English favorites, her repertory included more recent English works by Bishop and Stephen Storace, and also European operas such as Mozart's *The Marriage of Figaro* and *The Magic Flute,* Daniel-François-Esprit Auber's *Masaniello,* Rossini's *The Barber of Seville,* and Weber's *Der Freischütz,* always in English. But most of all, Austin shone brightly in America as the star of Michael Rophino Lacy's *Cinderella, or The Fairy and the Little Glass Slipper,* an adaptation of Rossini's *La Cenerentola* that also included music from three of Rossini's other operas. She launched the work in New York's Park Theater in 1831;

and Cinderella, whose acting demands were modest but whose coloratura fit her voice well, became her signature role.[18]

Lacy's *Cinderella* enabled Elizabeth Austin to become a star in America by transforming Rossini's *Cenerentola* into a hybrid: an English comic opera with Italian music. Recitative was turned into spoken dialogue, difficult ensemble numbers were cut, and complex arias became strophic songs. Some writers of the day questioned the practice of adapting operas to the talents of particular performers and the tastes of particular audiences, but others applauded it. *Cinderella* made an attractive theatrical package on its own. In fact, John Sullivan Dwight, one of America's most high-minded critics, preferred the adaptation to the original. After a Boston performance in 1853 of Rossini's opera, Dwight wrote: "The plot of this Rossini 'Cenerentola' was extremely meagre; it was emptied of all the charm of the nursery story; it had not even half the interest of the English version of Rophino Lacy."[19]

Promoting a Star: Jenny Lind's American Tour, 1850–52

Star making requires not only outstanding performance and charismatic personality but also imaginative promotion. And one of the most ingenious selling jobs in history took place in 1850 when the impresario P. T. Barnum presented Swedish soprano Jenny Lind to the American public. Believing that a concert tour of the United States could be lucrative for both him and Lind, Barnum first courted her through transatlantic correspondence. When Lind resisted his overtures, Barnum opened his pockets. Perhaps in hopes of discouraging him, she set the figure for an American concert tour at the then-astronomical sum of $187,000, paid in advance; Barnum managed to raise the money. Then, having secured her services, he set about creating a demand for them.

Like all great promoters, Barnum drew on his ability to read the public. Well before Lind's arrival, he launched a publicity campaign blending three elements: claims of the singer's virtuous Christian character, the prestige of opera singing, and the audience's susceptibility. The campaign succeeded. Lind's ship from Europe was greeted by a crowd of thirty thousand when it landed in New York Harbor on September 1, 1850. And Barnum made the tumult of that occasion part of Lind's American saga: the first of a series of mob scenes, orchestrated by him and his agents, that greeted her arrival wherever she went. From reports of huge, enthusiastic gatherings and from his image of Lind as a consummate artist who practiced personal humility, Barnum conjured the belief that Americans wanted desperately to see and hear her. He fostered the impression that Jenny Lind tickets were always at a premium by auctioning off, with great public fanfare, the first pair of admissions to Lind's first concert in a city. Thus, cities as well as individuals were perceived as competing to show their devotion to Lind and her art. In

New York, the first pair of tickets sold for $225; in Boston, a local singer named Ossian E. Dodge won the honor of paying $625 for the same privilege, a victory that gained him wide publicity, helping to boost his own performing career. By stratagems like these, Barnum convinced Americans that if they wanted to experience for themselves what everybody was talking about, they had better rush out and buy tickets while tickets could still be had.

In another masterstroke of promotion, Lind fed "Lindomania" by announcing that she would donate to charity her share of the receipts from her first American concert. It is hard to imagine better testimony that Lind was indeed the kind of woman that Barnum's publicity claimed: in the midst of feverish excitement that could have been milked for even greater economic gain, here was a great star thinking of people who needed the money more than she did! Thus Lind's arrival, her persona, travels, deeds and foibles, and perhaps most of all, Americans' embrace of her visit were received not simply as an artistic enterprise or a commercial venture. They were *news*, reported throughout the country. Avid expectation, a certain amount of curiosity, and more than a hint of competitiveness—Can *we* appreciate Jenny Lind as well as others who have heard her?—were among the feelings that moved people to buy tickets and that also helped shape their reactions to her performances.

Swedish soprano Jenny Lind (1820–1887) made her first American appearance under the sponsorship of P. T. Barnum before a packed house at New York's Castle Garden.

During Lind's stay in the United States (1850–52), her picture was used to advertise a variety of products, most notably sheet music.

Once in the hall, what did Jenny Lind's audiences actually hear? Surviving programs from her American tour reveal that the concerts followed a standard format whose key ingredient was variety. They began with an overture by the orchestra that accompanied the tour. Nor did she sing before tenor Giovanni Belletti, a troupe member, had warmed up the crowd. When Lind finally did step on to the stage, it was usually to sing an Italian aria that showed some aspect of her singing technique. An instrumental solo might follow, providing more contrast while perhaps also suggesting a parallel between vocal and instrumental virtuosity. Then Lind returned to wind up the first half with another selection. The second half showed even more diversity: another overture, more arias by Lind and Belletti, and perhaps a second instrumental solo. Among Lind's standard offerings here was Bellini's "Casta diva," whose long lines and sustained tones gave the singer a chance to display her voice's legato beauty and richness. *The Bird Song,* written expressly for Lind by German composer Wilhelm Taubert, was a crowd pleaser of another kind. A Boston critic of 1851 called the piece "a delightful imitation" of "feathered warblers," calling for "sustained notes and ventriloqual passages." Listeners with an interest in singing technique—in how "the different muscles of the throat and respiratory organs" were "brought into action" by Lind's "management of the breath"—would find *The Bird Song* instructive, the critic wrote.[20]

But the main difference in the second half was the presence of songs that most audience members already knew. *Home, Sweet Home,* for example, appeared on a Washington concert program in December 1850, which closed with *Hail Columbia,* offering patriotic sentiments to an audience that included President Millard Fillmore, Henry Clay, and Daniel Webster. Other such numbers that Lind might sing included Scottish songs (e.g., *Comin' thro' the Rye*), Irish poet Thomas Moore's *The Last Rose of Summer,* and songs from her native Sweden. These anonymous folk ballads and simple art songs by known composers were eagerly anticipated by Lind's American audiences. A Boston critic wrote that people "who would sit unmoved during the exercise of her matchless powers in the scientific productions of Mozart, Bellini, etc.," went into raptures of delight when she sat down at the piano and rendered the "folk songs."[21] Such songs gave audiences a chance to measure the sound of her singing voice and to test critics' claims of its purity and beauty against their own experience.

P. T. Barnum convinced many Americans that a powerful experience lay in store for them; then, through Lind's artistry and his own planning, he met their expectations. The tour's success may be judged by the unlikelihood of Barnum's achievement. By peddling recitals of a foreign opera singer, he created a cultural sensation that was also a commercial bonanza, involving not only concert tickets, sheet music, and pianos, but such Lind-endorsed products as gloves and stoves. Having taken a major financial risk, Barnum saw it pay off handsomely: he turned a profit of more than $500,000 on his connection with Lind.

The last chapter in the story of Jenny Lind's stay in America introduces a subject that could not be discussed in public at the time, but may shed further light on her appeal to American audiences. As well as an outstanding artist and admirable, upright person, she was perceived as an erotic symbol, a respectable Victorian woman subjecting herself in the name of art to intense public scrutiny. Commentators of Lind's day, virtually all of them male, emphasized again and again that she was unmarried, presumably a virgin.

Lind's stock took a sudden dive when, in 1852, she married her accompanist, Otto von Goldschmidt, who came into the union with three strikes against him: he was younger than Lind, he was not a celebrity in his own right, and he was a Jew. In the eyes of the public, Lind's vaunted purity had been compromised and her staunch Christian faith called into question. Having fulfilled her obligation to Barnum in the previous year, Lind toured for a time with Goldschmidt, though less successfully. Then in June 1852, she returned to Europe.[22]

OPERA IN NEW ORLEANS AND SAN FRANCISCO

Opera performance in the United States before the Civil War was centered in the Northeast, where two traditions existed. The English tradition was the more deeply rooted and widespread of the two. From origins in the theatrical stock company, it had grown to include traveling musical troupes whose repertory included not only English operas but Italian, French, and German works in adapted forms. Foreign-language opera, however, had also gained a presence, beginning with the Garcías and continuing with other troupes who brought Italian and even French opera to American audiences.

Between 1827 and 1833, almost the only non-English operas sung in New York, Philadelphia, Boston, and Baltimore were presented by the company of the Théâtre d'Orléans from New Orleans, under manager John Davis's leadership. The company's summer tours brought to Northern audiences operas by French composers and carried on a tradition that could trace its local roots back to 1796, when a performance of a French opera composed by André-Ernest-Modeste Grétry was given in a theater on New Orleans's Rue de la St. Pierre. New Orleans, Louisiana's first city, was home to many French and Spanish citizens—often called Creoles in these years, whatever their race—whose cultural ties to the United States were tenuous at best and whose disdain for Americans impelled them to try to remain culturally distinct. And for French speakers, distinctiveness required preserving their language. In New Orleans, presenting French operas in their original language became a successful means of asserting a French identity.[23]

John Davis's company set a standard of high quality and lavish expense that was remarkable for a community the size of New Orleans. (The city's population grew from 12,000 in 1800 to 46,000 by 1830.) In 1822, three years after taking over the company's management, Davis traveled to France and brought back with him actors, singers, instrumentalists, and dancers, the latter for the ballets that French opera required. From the 1822–23 season on, opera in the Théâtre d'Orléans was played by a resident company whose personnel were imported; the orchestra was good enough to impress Northerners on the company's summer tours. Davis also sought out fresh repertory, giving American premieres of many stellar works including Rossini's *The Barber of Seville*, performed (in Italian) at the Théâtre d'Orléans more than two years before the Garcías introduced it in New York. His push to bring new operas into the company's repertory shows that he was an ambitious entrepreneur with a sophisticated audience to please. (Davis maintained a successful business career while running the theater, allowing him a financial independence that many managers lacked.) Davis's program was expensive. By the mid-1820s, it was costing $50,000 per year to maintain his troupe, inspiring a search for more revenue, which led to the Théâtre d'Orléans company's touring: first to Havana, Cuba, in 1824, and later to the Northeast. When Davis retired in 1837, he was succeeded by his son, who kept the troupe in a flourishing condition into the 1850s. The theater closed after the Civil War.

One reason Davis maintained such a lively, innovative company at the Théâtre d'Orléans is because he had a competitor. James Caldwell, an English immigrant and erstwhile actor, had arrived in New Orleans in 1820 as head of a touring company from Virginia. In 1824, Caldwell began to play English-language opera at the 1,100-seat Camp Street Theater in the city's new American section. Compared with Davis's audiences, Caldwell's could be rough and ready, especially at first. "They average about six rows in the course of an evening's entertainment and have a gouging match by way of interludes," one observer remarked after a night at the Camp Street Theater in the mid-1820s. As time passed, however, Caldwell's audience learned to behave with more restraint as he offered them a wider range of works in English, including *The Barber of Seville*, Mozart's *The Marriage of Figaro*, Rossini-Lacy's *Cinderella*, and in 1826 Weber's *Der Freischütz*. In 1835, he heightened English opera's local prestige by staging *Robert the Devil*, an adaptation of Giacomo Meyerbeer's spectacular grand opera, at the Camp Street Theater before the Davis company could mount its own production of *Robert le diable* in French. Later that year, Caldwell built the large and elegant new St. Charles Theater and soon thereafter began to present Italian troupes there.

Local opera, then, flourished in New Orleans in both foreign-language and English forms. And both maintained a strong position in the city's public life to the time of the Civil War and after. Managers also used the population's love for social dancing to attract audiences. The Théâtre d'Orléans had its own ballroom, and a ticket to the opera—unless it was for a cheap gallery seat—might also entitle the holder to attend a ball after the performance. A newspaper notice in 1836 reported: "Spectacles and operas appear to amuse our citizens more than any other form of public amusement—except balls."[24] As well as enticing customers into the theater, social dancing provided work for members of the opera orchestra, which also raised the quality of musical performance in general, tuning the ears of dancers to more elegant music and making the public familiar with dance music from operas that they might also see played onstage.

New Orleans also became a favorite stop for English touring companies: the Seguins (1842, 1844, 1845), a troupe headed by soprano Anna Bishop (1848), another group led by soprano Anna Thillon (1853), and the Pyne and Harrison English Opera Company, which visited the St. Charles Theater for three weeks in early 1856. Audiences at the St. Charles around 1850 were a diverse lot. Kept apart from each other by the separate entrances that led to boxes, pit, and gallery, these French, Spanish, Italian, German, and American customers included the city's most fashionable and wealthy citizens, and also housewives, clerks, salesmen, shopkeepers, prostitutes, longshoremen and steamboaters, quadroons, and slaves whose masters had given them passes that exempted them from the eight o'clock curfew.[25]

Meanwhile, as local companies and traveling troupes were offering operatic performances in the eastern half of the United States, opera also gained a foothold on the continent's western edge. Thousands of miles separated San Francisco from the cities of the American Midwest. Communication by railroad, transcontinental telegraph, even regular overland mail was established only after 1859, making the region until then like a maritime colony of the East as well as a western frontier settlement. Until the mid-1860s, the "colony" could be reached most easily from the East by two seagoing routes, both long and expensive: transshipping across the isthmus of Panama or rounding Cape Horn. With the sea as their lifeline to goods and information, San Franciscans doted on shipping news. By local custom, when any sizable ship reached the wharf, a cannon was fired from Telegraph Hill—a sound disruptive to theatrical life because it sent most customers scurrying for the exit.[26]

With Spanish-Mexican, French, Italian, German, English, Irish, and Scottish immigrants all included in the city's population, no one group dominated the city's musical life, as did French speakers in New Orleans and, more and more in these years, Italian and German speakers in New York and Philadelphia. And one other thing about early San Francisco's population was unique: men greatly outnumbered women. In the 1850 census, only 8 percent of California's population was female, many of those said to be women of ill repute. This state of affairs can be explained by the discovery of gold in northern California early in 1848, when San Francisco was a village of 500. By 1851, 30,000 people lived there, most of them men drawn by the prospect of getting rich quick. Thus, San Francisco changed overnight from backwater to boomtown—a place where an expensive cultural form like opera could flourish. Life in the days of the Gold Rush was more elemental than genteel, with violence a common occurrence; Western audiences could thus identify more than most with the murders and betrayals portrayed on the operatic stage.[27]

The city's first theater opened in October 1850. By the beginning of 1853, though fires had burned three theaters to the ground, four more were open and operating. On February 12, 1851, a small troupe headed by an Italian tenor formerly employed at theaters in Peru and Chile staged the city's first opera, a severely cut performance of Bellini's *La sonnambula*. In 1852, noted sopranos began to arrive, each remaining in the city for a substantial stay: Eliza Biscaccianti from Boston; Irish-born Catherine "Kate" Hayes, who offered seventeen "concerts-in-costume" in which she sang arias and scenes from well-known operas; English singer Anna Thillon, who in 1854 starred in a series of opera performances—the city's first real professional season—devoted chiefly to English adaptations; and English soprano Anna Bishop, who, traveling with harpist and conductor Nicholas Bochsa, gave a total of forty opera performances as well as many concerts in eighteen months. The most accomplished singer to perform in San Francisco during the mid-century period, Bishop was forty-four years old when she arrived in in 1854, and had already led a life with an operatic sweep of its own. Married in 1831 to composer Henry Bishop of *Home, Sweet Home* fame, she left him and three children behind in 1839 when she eloped with Bochsa and began a touring career that took her to every continent except Antarctica, involved a shipwreck, and ended with a public appearance in New York at the age of seventy-three (1883). Bishop's California performances included works by Rossini, Bellini, Donizetti, and Weber, all in adapted form. She also starred in a "Grand Biblical Spectacle" called *Judith*, compiled by Bochsa from works of Giuseppe Verdi, especially *Nabucco* and *Macbeth*.

Finally, in November 1854, a troupe of performers calling themselves the Italian Opera Company arrived in town and played a season of opera in Italian. Adding a corps of local singers and players to their number, the company, which boasted *two* prima donnas, gave fourteen performances, half of them devoted to operas by Verdi (*Ernani* and *Nabucco*), the rising star of the Italian opera world. Thus, San Francisco, a city whose first opera theater was not built until 1850, in half a decade progressed to full performances of works by a major living composer in their original language.

A San Francisco impresario with unusual credentials played the key role in establishing opera as an enduring local presence. Born in New York City in the early 1820s, Thomas Maguire drove a hack, ran a livery stable, and managed a saloon there before becoming a forty-niner and moving to San Francisco. He made his fortune in the West not by striking gold, but by running a successful saloon and gambling parlor and by building and renting out theaters. In 1856, Maguire opened the elegant new Maguire's Opera House, in which he booked popular entertainment. In 1859, he brought to California an Italian troupe headed by Eugenio and Giovanna Bianchi to take up residence there. Interested more in the power of what could happen onstage than the financial bottom line, Maguire set his prices low: $1 and 50 cents at a time when the going local price for opera tickets ranged from $3 to $1. Maguire later calculated that during the 1860s, he lost $120,000 on opera.[28]

In 1860, he replaced the Bianchis with a new organization: the Maguire-Lyster Company, fashioned out of the traveling Lyster English Opera Company and a complement of Italian singers or English singers who performed Italian opera in its original tongue. This accomplished company featured two "wings," one Italian and the other English; Maguire provided an orchestra of twenty-five players for both wings. Instead of being alternated with minstrels, acrobats, and other popular entertainment, as opera usually was, the Maguire-Lyster Company played opera every night, and to substantial crowds.

That year, 1860, in San Francisco has been termed an *annus mirabilis* (year of wonders) in the annals of opera. A total of 145 performances were given in Maguire's Opera House, which seated 1,700. It has been estimated that attendance averaged 1,500 per performance, making a total of 217,000 seats sold in a city of 60,000. By comparison: in New York today (population 8 million), the Metropolitan Opera, whose house seats 3,800, would have to build an additional fifty-two houses to accommodate a similar audience over 145 evenings. No American city, at any time, has shown a passion for operatic performance equaling that of San Francisco in 1860.[29]

EPILOGUE: NEW YORK IN THE 1850S

Opera enjoyed a more prominent place in America during the antebellum (pre–Civil War) years than it has in this century, as shown by customs that long ago fell by the wayside: unruly, witnessing crowds; free adaptation of and interpolations into composers' scores; sheet-music circulation of opera tunes as popular music; and widespread informal performances. These customs, however, provide only a partial glimpse of operatic life as a whole. Theodore Thomas, German-born but American-bred and the country's leading conductor of the 1800s, wrote a memoir late in life that recalled New York at mid-century as a place where one could hear "the most brilliant, finished, and mature vocalists of the world, such as Jenny Lind and [Henriette] Sontag, besides a large number of eminent Italian singers, among them Mario, Grisi, Bosio, Alboni, and others. I doubt if there were ever brought together in any part of the world a larger number of talented vocalists than were gathered in New York between 1850 and the early sixties."[30]

These words dramatize a point worth stressing: Czech-born Max Maretzek's formation in the 1850s of a company at New York City's Academy of Music to perform operas in Italian, including the works of Verdi, marks the start of an operatic tradition in the city that may be traced continuously up to the present day. This is not to overlook differences that separate New York's later Metropolitan Opera (founded in 1883), the country's premiere opera company in the twentieth century, from its ancestor. The Academy troupe relied to a large extent on touring. Moreover, its focus on Italian opera made for a relatively narrow range of works. But many of the Academy's principles endured: a commitment to hiring the best possible singers and players; the presentation of full works in their own languages, with due respect for the composer's score; a range of ticket prices so that the company could survive in the marketplace; and a consideration for the endeavor as a dignified artistic enterprise, if not one reserved for the city's wealthy elite.

11

Blacks, Whites, and the Minstrel Stage

IN THE EARLY 1850s, Samuel Cartwright, a Louisiana physician, wrote an essay on diseases that were said to afflict black slaves, including "drapeto-mia" (running away), "rascality," and "dysaesthesia aethiopica." He described the symptoms of the latter as follows:

> From the careless movements of the individuals affected with this complaint they are apt to do much mischief, which appears as if intentional, but is mostly owing to the stupidness of mind and insensibility of the nerves in-duced by the disease. Thus they break, waste, and destroy everything they handle; abuse horses and cattle; tear, burn, or rend their own clothing. . . . When driven to labor by the compulsive power of the white man, [the suf-ferer] performs the task assigned to him in a headlong, careless manner, treading down with his feet or cutting with his hoe the plants he is put to cultivate; breaking the tools he works with, and spoiling everything he touches that can be injured by careless handling.[1]

Except for the phrase about "stupidness of mind," these words could sug-gest that the writer was describing canny slaves who avoided work by con-vincing the master they were too dumb for the job. But Cartwright intended no such ironic spin. As a leading advocate of the theory of "polygenesis" (which he claimed was supported by the Bible), he was arguing that each race was a separate and distinct *genus* rather than a variety of one species. In the southern United States, some accepted the theory as proof that Africans were biologically inferior to Caucasians, and that servitude was their natural destiny. Cartwright also claimed to find in the black race "a pe-culiar instinct protecting it against the abuses of arbitrary power." Because blacks could endure greater suffering than whites, they could not be over-worked. Slave owners needed to worry not about mistreating their slaves but about giving them too much liberty. For liberty, Cartwright argued, brought on such ailments as dysaesthesia aethiopica, which rendered slaves useless.[2]

It is obvious today that polygenesis was nothing more than a pseudoscientific theory to support racial prejudice. But its existence also points to deep conflicts in the feelings Americans held about race in the early and middle 1800s. That such a notion was advanced to explain black and white difference while slavery itself was ignored indicates that slave owning forced its own pathology on those who engaged in it. But it also shows the fascination of white Americans—a mixture of curiosity, fear, love, and loathing—with the image of the African-American slave. That fascination formed a key ingredient of blackface minstrelsy, nineteenth-century America's most popular form of entertainment.

Minstrelsy, which originated with white entertainers pretending onstage to be black, has been called a racist and exploitative institution, where the appropriation of black artistry brought fame and fortune to the borrowers. There is no question that race was fundamental to the minstrel show: taking for granted the superiority of Euroamerican culture, white minstrels relied on black-influenced song, dance, and humor to give their performances vitality. It is also true that white minstrels did not share profits with their African-American models. Yet neither racism—the belief that one's own ethnic stock is superior—nor economic exploitation fully explains minstrelsy's significance in its own time. For while entertaining audiences with jokes, skits, and music, minstrel performers also dealt with social disparities in American life: between appearance and reality, theory and practice, the surface and the inside.

Take, for example, the issue of social and political power. In a society that ranked people by race, whites were assumed to hold supremacy. And in the South, the line was drawn with stark, official clarity between white masters and black slaves. Yet the reality was not so simple. Who held the real authority when slaves failed to do their masters' bidding? Clearly, even a master's power was finite, but where did its limits lie? Samuel Cartwright preached that masters accepted false limits when they mistook slaves for thinking human beings. Other Southerners, however, saw slaves as more complex creatures. "So deceitful is the Negro," one owner wrote, "that as far as my own experience extends I could never in a single instance decipher his character. . . . We planters could never get at the truth." Another found black slaves in general enigmatic and "never off guard." "He is perfectly skilled at hiding his emotions. . . . His master knows him not."[3]

Blackface minstrelsy played on ambiguities like these. A black stage character could appear profoundly stupid at one moment and cunning and wily the next, able to frustrate the white man's designs. For the audience, the fascination lay in the disguise itself: in the questions that were raised and the contradictions exposed when minstrels darkened their faces for "Ethiopian" impersonation. On one level, the mask enabled white stage minstrels to amuse audiences by imitating characteristic black ways of talk- ing, moving, dancing, laughing, singing, and playing musical instruments. On another level, white minstrels learned that blacking up freed them to shed conventional manners and behave onstage in ways that polite society found uncivilized. And they could also comment critically not just on black- white interactions but on society in general: on politics, culture, and social class. The minstrel persona offered white entertainers and audiences a chance to visit and explore expressive territory that would otherwise have re- mained private.

The spectacle of performers freed from social inhibition could bring ec- static pleasure to audience members. In 1843, H. P. Grattan, an English ac- tor, visited Buffalo, New York, and there, as part of an audience filled with boatmen, he watched a three-man minstrel troupe led by E. P. "Ned" Christy perform. "So droll was the action, so admirable the singing, so clever the instrumentation, and so genuine was the fun," Grattan later wrote, "that I not only laughed till my sides fairly ached, but . . . I never left an entertainment with a more keen desire to witness it again." For Grattan, "the staple" of this event was "genuine negro fun," which he described as "the counterfeit presentment of the southern darkies" whose dancing and singing they "endeavored to reproduce."[4] Aware that he was not seeing the real thing, Grattan found his disbelief overcome by the minstrels' skill as en- tertainers.

The freedom displayed by performers extended to near-demonic behavior not to be found in other kinds of theater. An English observer in 1846 de- scribed minstrels as "animated by a savage energy," their "white eyes roll[ing] in a curious frenzy."[5] The frenzy was widely believed to have been inspired by black slaves themselves, who, as another observer wrote in 1857, were apt to "let themselves go" in "dervish-like fury . . . all night long, in ceaseless, violent exertions of frenetic dancing."[6] The explicit messages of minstrelsy's songs and humor, then, were only a part of its total environ- ment, which sought to overwhelm audiences with sheer anarchic energy. In their challenge to civilized decorum, blackface minstrels of the 1840s and early 1850s hold traits in common with rock-and-roll musicians from the 1950s on.

Three elements, then—the black mask, the chance for social commen- tary, and the creation of a zone of unbridled pleasure—interacted to give blackface minstrelsy its impact and multilayered richness. Whites' view of African Americans was not so much the focus of minstrelsy but its jumping- off point. Minstrelsy's main subject was something both closer to home and more convoluted: white Americans' responses to the conditions of their own lives, delivered from behind a mask fashioned from their view of African-American culture.

The desire for self-expression had made American blacks into virtuoso mask wearers. Whites found that the more closely they observed black ways, the harder it was to know what African Americans were really thinking and feeling. Blackness itself could be a mask—a way blacks dealt with an adversarial society that had placed them in an underdog's role. That was the reality behind ex-slave Frederick Douglass's description of the gap between slaves' behavior and their feelings:

> The remark is not infrequently made, that slaves are the most contented and happy laborers in the world. They dance and sing, and make all manners of joyful noises—so they do: but it is a great mistake to suppose them happy because they sing. The songs of the slave represent the sorrows, rather than the joys, of his heart. . . . In the most boisterous outbursts of rapturous sentiment, there was ever a tinge of deep melancholy.[7]

In spirituals and the blues, two indigenous forms of music making, African Americans explored the depths of that massive contradiction. If white entertainers failed to reach a similar depth or master black performing styles, neither was their intent in the first place. What they did do effectively was tap into a recognizably black ethos by adapting black habits and techniques. The title of one study of early blackface minstrelsy captures in an arresting phrase the white entertainers' relationship to blackness: "love and theft."[8] Finding in black expression an ecstatic spirit that existed nowhere else, the minstrels loved and were moved by it, and they stole it for their own use—the first if by no means the last salute to black artistry that borrowed its tricks and sold them to theater audiences without benefit to their originators.

Stereotypes bring a familiar story along with them. When characters of American Indian, Irish, or Scottish descent appeared on nineteenth-century American stages, their stories were immediately ripe for elaboration because the audience expected them to behave in certain ways. Black characters were by far the most varied and potent ethnic stereotypes offered. Minstrel characters of the 1840s and later might be portrayed as thinking, feeling individuals or thick-skinned fools. Their capacity as tricksters might be suggested by references to animal characters, as in African folklore. Their love lives might be held up for ridicule or their pretensions exposed. And more than a half century of English and American "negro impersonation" lay behind these shows—a tradition that included not only traits borrowed from African-American culture but stage representations with their own histories.

Among the blackface characters found onstage before the 1840s, when the minstrel show became a full evening's entertainment, one of the most prominent was the stylish, sophisticated Zip Coon.

The late 1820s and early 30s saw the creation of two stage characters who enjoyed a long life: Jim Crow and Zip Coon. Around 1828, an actor named Thomas D. "Daddy" Rice made theatrical history through his response to something he claimed to have seen in Cincinnati. As Rice later told the story, he was so struck by a crippled black stable groom's singing and weird dancing that he memorized the first and tried to copy the second. He then got hold of clothes like those the stablehand wore. And finally, blacked up as "Jim Crow," he began doing an impersonation between acts of the play in which he was appearing. Audiences responded enthusiastically, and Rice soon won fame as an "Ethiopian delineator." The Jim Crow character became a bumptious Southern plantation hand who strutted the stage, unaware that his raggedy naïveté made him a buffoon. Rice wrote a signature song for Jim Crow, born a slave in "Tuckahoe," who wandered the country, rubbing elbows with people all the way up to President Andrew Jackson, who in one edition "ax me wat I do." (Jim's advice to the president parodied the day's political jargon: "I put de veto on the boat, / An nullefy de shoe.")[9]

The character Zip Coon was as urban and stylish as Jim Crow was rural and untutored. Like Jim Crow, Zip Coon was boastful, and he appeared in exaggeratedly fancy clothes. The adventures outlined in the song *Zip Coon*—sung by singing actor George Washington Dixon—include romance:

> O its old Suky blue skin, she is in lub wid me
> I went the udder arter noon to take a dish ob tea;
> What do you tink now, Suky hab for supper,
> Why chicken foot an posum heel, widout any butter.
> O ole Zip Coon he is a larned skolar,
> O ole Zip Coon he is a larned skolar,
> O ole Zip Coon he is a larned skolar,
> Sings posum up a gum tree an coony in a holler.[10]

But this romance has more obstacles to overcome than the unappetizing supper Suky puts on the table. One is that Zip seems too wrapped up in himself to be a serious lover. Another is that the music of *Zip Coon*, the two-strain fiddle tune known as *Turkey in the Straw*, fails to evoke even a hint of love's tenderness.

Coal Black Rose, a song from the 1820s, depicts a black romance that disintegrates into deceit and violence. The song is sung by Sambo, who is wooing the heroine:

> Lubly Rosa, Sambo cum,
> Don't you hear de Banjo—tum, tum, tum;
> Lubly Rosa, Sambo cum,

Don't you hear de Banjo—tum, tum, tum;
    Oh Rose, de coal black Rose,
I wish I may be cortch'd if I don't lub Rose,
    Oh Rose, de coal black Rose.

When Sambo shows up unexpectedly at Rose's cabin, she asks him to wait outside in the cold while she builds a fire. Then she lets him in. The two sit warming themselves until Sambo spots Cuffee, a rival suitor, trying to hide in the dark room's corner. And during the fight that follows, he changes his song's refrain:

    Oh Rose, take care Rose!
I wish I may be burnt if I don't hate Rose,
    Oh Rose, you blacka snake Rose![11]

Although nothing in either *Coal Black Rose* or *Zip Coon* suggests the idealized kind of romantic love that other songs of the time were starting to celebrate, recent commentators have suggested that exaggerated postures of minstrel stage movement were understood as references to sexuality. In the verse of *Coal Black Rose,* as Sambo stands freezing outside Rose's cabin, he pleads: "Make haste, Rosa, lubly dear, / I froze tiff as poker waitin here." And on the cover of the sheet music, which shows a squat, unlovely Rose, looking less like an ingenue than a fullback, Sambo holds his banjo in a way that anticipates the phallic implications of rock and roll.[12] Sex was not something that many white Americans of the period discussed openly, whatever their social class. But by projecting bodily urges onto black stage characters, "Ethiopian delineators" provided a way to approach a forbidden subject that must have been on the minds of *some* audience members.

THE FIRST MINSTREL SHOWS

In the spring of 1877, an article in a New York theatrical newspaper looked back a third of a century to recall how four young entertainers—Billy Whitlock, Dan Emmett, Dick Pelham, and Frank Brower—formed the first blackface minstrel troupe:

All four were one day sitting in the North American Hotel, in the Bowery, when one of them proposed that with their instruments they should cross over to the Bowery Circus and give one of the proprietors (Uncle Nate Howes) a "charivari" as he sat by the stove in the hall entrance.[13] Bringing forth his banjo for Whitlock to play on, Emmett took the violin, Pelham the tambourine, and Brower the bones. Without any rehearsal, with hardly the ghost of an idea as to what was to follow, they crossed the street and proceeded to "browbeat" Uncle Nate Howes into giving them an engagement, the calculation being that he would succumb in preference to standing the horrible noise (for they attempted no tune) they were making with their instruments. After standing it for a while, Uncle Nate said: "Boys, you've got a good thing. Can't you sing us a song?" Thereupon Emmett, accompanying himself on his violin, began to sing "Old Dan Tucker," the others joining in the chorus. The four minstrels were as much surprised at the result as was Uncle Nate. After singing some more songs for him, they returned to the North American, where they resumed their "horrible noise" in the reading room, which was quickly filled with spectators. . . . [Later on they] rehearsed a few songs in Emmett's room.[14]

The first engagement won by this act of self-promotion took place in New York on February 6, 1843. And in Boston a month later, the four staged the first full-length minstrel show, billing themselves as the Virginia Minstrels. The performing customs they established were followed by many of the minstrel companies that sprang up in the wake of their success.

The Virginia Minstrels arranged four chairs onstage in a semicircle, with tambourine and bones at either end and fiddle and banjo in between, and filled their programs chiefly with short musical numbers. They divided an evening's entertainment into two parts, the first including a would-be topical address, delivered in dialect and full of malaprops. It soon was customary for a minstrel show's first part to concentrate on the Northern urban scene, with the second shifting to the South and often closing with a lively plantation number. But however standardized the overall form, the flow of events in any given minstrel show lay in the performers' hands. Minstrelsy was variety entertainment. Each skit, song, and dance was a self-contained act.[15] Ad libbing, topical comments and gibes, and responsiveness to the audience's mood were all part of the format, giving customers and players a sense of collaboration, geared to the moment. The flexible form fit well with blackface performers' calculated lack of inhibition.

By the mid-1840s, minstrelsy was sweeping the nation. In 1844, only a year after the Virginia Minstrels' debut, a blackface troupe called the Ethiopian Serenaders was invited to play at the White House. In later years, Presidents Tyler, Polk, Fillmore, and Pierce, not to mention vast numbers of other Americans, were entertained by blackface minstrels. Within a few months of their debut, the Virginia Minstrels toured the British Isles, where audiences also welcomed blackface entertainment. Spurred by popular demand, countless minstrel troupes were formed: the African Melodists, the Congo Minstrels, the Gumbo Family, the Southern Singers, the Sable Minstrels, the New Orleans Serenaders. Both professional and amateur companies appeared wherever an audience could be found, especially along the Mississippi and in the cities of the Northeast, and the growing railroad system made touring easier. But for all the companies that toured, the center of blackface entertainment was in New York City, permanent home to the leading companies and where most major developments in the form occurred. As companies there vied for audiences, competition forced weaker performers to the sidelines or the hinterlands. By the 1850s, at least ten minstrel houses were open in New York, and a few companies enjoyed consecutive runs of ten years or more.[16]

Beyond its subject matter and entertainment appeal, minstrelsy proved to be the first musical genre to reverse the east-to-west transatlantic flow of performers to North America. Until Americans began to perform on stages in styles that they themselves had invented, a vast majority of stage performers on these shores were immigrants, chiefly from the British Isles.[17] As the presence of many amateur troupes suggests, American minstrels carried no fixed pedigree and emerged from no particular course of formal training. Minstrelsy had little need for musicians who had mastered European performing techniques and repertories. What it required were those who, like the four Virginia Minstrels, could step into the voice and the character of an "Ethiopian" stage darky and entertain an audience with comic turns, dancing, and the singing and playing of popular music.

Daniel Decatur Emmett, who spent more than half a century in the minstrel trade, is a case in point. Born in 1815 in Mount Vernon, Ohio, Emmett received little formal education, but his mother taught him popular songs when he was a boy, and he learned to play the fiddle on his own. At thirteen, Emmett apprenticed himself to a local printer. At nineteen, he enlisted in the army and began a stint at Jefferson Barracks, Missouri, where he mastered the fife and drum. Discharged in 1835, Emmett joined a circus in Cincinnati and within a few years began his career as a writer of black dialect songs. Although he never claimed direct borrowing from African Americans, as had "Daddy" Rice, Emmett may well have been influenced by the Snowdens, a black music-making family of Knox County, Ohio, where he was born. Emmett learned to play minstrel-style banjo in 1840–41 from a white circus performer.[18] Touring with circus companies, Emmett met Frank Brower, a Baltimore-born comedian, singer, dancer, and bones player, and in 1842 the two men appeared in blackface on various New York stages before joining Whitlock and Pelham in the Virginia Minstrels.

Biographical data on the early years of the other three members is scarce, but all shared with Emmett a flair for and a willingness to perfect "negro" impersonation, and hunger for a niche in show business. New York–born William M. "Billy" Whitlock, like Emmett, was a printer's apprentice in his home city before he learned to play the banjo in 1838. From then on, he worked as a blackface performer, both in local variety shows and on tour with circus companies. Whether or not this touring brought him into contact with Southern blacks, Whitlock did take banjo lessons with Virginia native Joel Sweeney, the first known white banjo player, who learned the instrument from slaves on his father's farm. Tambourine player Dick Pelham, another New York native, made his reputation chiefly as a dancer. In 1841, he and his brother joined together in an act where, as Negro servants, they accompanied a song called *Massa Is a Stingy Man* with innovative steps and body contortions. Brower, the youngest troupe member and already a good comic dancer, is said to have learned his steps by imitating the movements of older blacks.[19]

That minstrel skills could not be gained through formal study is confirmed by the makeup of the original minstrel band: violin, banjo, tambourine, and bones. Only the violin was a European instrument with established methods of instruction and a repertory of composed music. Yet the violin led a double life in the British Isles and North America. As the fiddle, this bowed string instrument stood at the heart of Anglo-American dance music, with its jigs, reels, and hornpipes and its characteristic ways of playing them. Like their country counterparts, minstrel fiddlers like Dan Emmett held their instrument loosely and more or less in front of themselves, rather than clamping it firmly between chin and shoulder like a concert violinist. As a minstrel-band fiddle, the violin was less a singing, lyric voice than an astringent, rhythmic one, played with little or no vibrato. Perhaps standard violin technique and sound were themselves targets of the minstrels' parody.

African Americans were fiddling long before minstrel shows, but it is hard to know how much their own playing styles influenced white minstrel fiddlers. When it comes to the banjo, however, whites clearly followed the lead of blacks. Originating in Africa, the early banjo was fashioned from materials found in nature: a large hollow gourd with a long handle, strung with catgut. West African slaves were playing this instrument in the New World before 1700, and black use of it is amply documented through the eighteenth and early nineteenth centuries. No record of white banjo playing exists before Joel Sweeney began learning from slaves in Virginia, probably in the late 1820s; in the next decade, Sweeney began passing on their playing technique to other white performers, such as Billy Whitlock. The early minstrel banjo, which gave the ensemble its distinctive character, did not sound like a modern banjo. Its body was larger, the rim was thinner, the fingerboard had no frets, and its five gut strings (the modern banjo has four metal strings) were tuned well below the instrument's modern pitch. The resulting sound was fuller and suited to its role as a melody instrument.[20]

That two of the early minstrel band's four members played small, portable percussion instruments testifies to the group's emphasis on rhythm, sound, and body movement over melody and harmony. The characters named Mr. Tambo and Mr. Bones were free to move as they performed.

The sound of the bones, which resembles that of castanets, is made by holding a pair in either hand and clicking them together with the fingers, allowing a skilled player to produce complex rhythmic patterns. Playing the bones requires a certain amount of arm flailing, which a good dancer like Frank Brower could choreograph into motions that entertained the customers. First made from animal rib bones and classified technically as idiophones, the bones have a history reaching back to 3000 B.C.E. in Egypt. Although attempts have been made to trace minstrel bones playing to black Africa, no such link has been found. The tambourine, an ancient percussion instrument of Near Eastern origin, is a combination idiophone (the metal jingles) and membranophone (the drum head, which makes sound through the vibration of a membrane). It could be struck with the fingers for accents and also shaken to provide a layer of shimmering sound.

Through observation, imitation, and practical experience, mixed here and there with instruction, young American performers like the Virginia Minstrels honed the skills they needed to create a new theatrical profession. And then, in the minstrel stage's atmosphere of willed pandemonium, they perfected their singing, playing, dancing, and bantering in dialogue with audiences that looked to them for both diversion and social comment.

SONGS OF THE MINSTREL SHOW

The advent of the minstrel show brought a need for a new musical repertory. Instrumental music was important to minstrelsy, but customers came especially to hear songs, and vocal music dominated performances. *Old Dan Tucker,* which Daniel Emmett and his colleagues sang to convince Nate Howes to hire them as a minstrel unit, illustrates one way in which early minstrels translated raw energy into song.

The first published version (1843) raises the question of authorship. Why, when the cover proclaims the piece as one of "Old Dan Emmit's Original Banjo Melodies," are only the words attributed to him? The absence of a composer's name indicates that Emmett did not write the music; perhaps it was taken from oral sources or was the result of a collaboration.[21] Wherever it came from, the tune sounds like a stomping Anglo-American dance laced with black elements. Its melodic idiom fits with that of *Jump Jim Crow, Zip Coon, Coal Black Rose,* and other early blackface favorites. Rather than a harmonized melody, the tune seems more like a musical framework in which words are declaimed to a strict, driving beat. *Old Dan Tucker* fills twenty-eight bars: an eight-bar instrumental introduction and a four-bar coda frame a sixteen-bar vocal statement split equally between verse and refrain.

The introduction sets a raucous mood. Although arranged here for piano

The cover of Daniel Emmett's *Old Dan Tucker* notes that the song is "arranged for the piano forte by Rice," suggesting that Emmett himself lacked experience in the world of parlor music.

(i.e., for home use), the music was clearly not conceived with a keyboard instrument in mind. The right-hand melody is better suited for banjo or fiddle, and the obsessive repetition of the opening four-note figure signals that rhythm will overshadow melody in this song. The return of that figure after each refrain suggests a stage performance where two contrasting sounds are pitted against each other: the twanging, minstrel-band timbre of the introduction and coda, perhaps backing dance movements, and the more conventional, song-like sound of the vocal sections. The change in register and material—from high, circular, continuous figuration to a voice line with oom-pah chords—emphasizes the division; and the piano's melodic right hand in the refrain marks off that section from the verse.

The verse of *Old Dan Tucker* seems designed for singers who are also playing instruments while jumping around onstage. Nearly three-quarters of its syllables are sung on the same note, indicating that text declamation, not tune, is the animating force. Rhythmic drive is so important that the phrase endings are given no time to settle in. Verse leads directly into chorus; the refrain ends on its last bar's last eighth note so that the instrumental coda can start with a clean entrance on the next bar's downbeat. Here is double support for the message of the refrain, whose explosive beginning features both syncopation and call and response, the song's chief Africanisms. "Get out de way!" shouts the chorus, with an offbeat jolt that makes this entry a climactic point of arrival; and the instruments answer by continuing the refrain's catchy melody. At the end of the chorus, it is the voices that get out of the way for the instruments' energetic return.

Dan Tucker seems like a blackface version of the frontiersmen whose exploits are told in Anglo-American folklore. Not one to blend into a crowd, Tucker stirred things up whenever he came on the scene. In a day when temperance organizations were starting to gain influence, he still enjoyed his liquor:

> Ole Dan Tucker an I got drunk,
> He fell in de fire and kick up a chunk,
> De charcoal got inside he shoe
> Lor bless you honey how de ashes flew.

And in a society where middle-class status, churchgoing, and table manners were often thought to go together, Tucker had his own way of behaving in company:

> Tucker was a hardened sinner,
> He nebber said his grace at dinner;
> De ole sow squeel, de pigs did squall
> He 'hole hog wid de tail and all.[22]

An independent, lively, disrespectful dissident, Dan Tucker held genteel standards of decorum in contempt. It seems to have been his independent spirit that moved a New York journalist in 1845—asking the question "Who are our national poets?"—to nominate blackface characters Jim Crow, Zip Coon, Sambo, and Dan Tucker. Granting that black slaves were the origina-

Stephen C. Foster (1826–1864), born near Pittsburgh on July 4, the nation's fiftieth anniversary, wrote more songs that won enduring popularity than any other American songwriter of the nineteenth century.

tors and white minstrels the imitators, this writer marveled at Americans' reception of "negro" songs. He found nothing less than genius in the work of poets able to put "sayings into the mouths of all, so that they may become household words, quoted by every one," like proverbs. "At no time does the atmosphere of our planet cease to vibrate harmoniously to the immortal songs of the negroes of America," wrote this correspondent. Taking the phrase "Get out ob de way, old Dan Tucker!" as an example, he observed wryly: "At this present moment, a certain ubiquitous person seems to be in the way of the whole people of these United States simultaneously."[23] The way *Old Dan Tucker* flaunted social niceties allowed it to tap into an ethos where plain folk could define themselves against the cultural and moral elite.[24]

At about the time Emmett and the Virginia Minstrels were transforming the world of popular entertainment in New York City, a teenage youth in Allegheny, Pennsylvania, was getting together with friends to stage amateur minstrel shows just for the fun of it. And at twenty-four, with several hits already to his credit, Stephen C. Foster embarked on a songwriter's career, one of the most significant in this country's history. One of his early minstrel-show hits was *Gwine to Run All Night,* or *De Camptown Races* (1850). This song, also in verse-and-refrain form, resembles *Old Dan Tucker* in several other ways, as if Foster took the earlier song as a model. Foster follows Emmett's suggestion of the minstrel-band sound by contrasting the registers of the instrumental (high) and vocal (lower) sections. Foster's song, cast in "black" stage dialect, also deals in comic exaggeration and hyperbole ("De Camptown race track five miles long," "De blind hoss sticken in a big mud hole / Can't touch bottom wid a ten foot pole"). And, like its predecessor, *De Camptown Races* features both call and response and syncopation.

But if *De Camptown Races* can count *Old Dan Tucker* as part of its pedigree, Foster wrote his song in a different melodic idiom. While the music of Emmett's song is driven and aggressive, Foster's is jaunty and tuneful. In contrast to Emmett's introduction, which is chiefly sound and rhythm, Foster's is melodic, beginning with the shapely tune that dominates the verse and ends the refrain. Foster's melodies bear up well under constant repetition. The opening tune is one of three catchy melodic bits, the others being the syncopated response ("doo-dah!") in the verse and the five-note ascending figure that begins the refrain ("Gwine to run all night"). Foster's song also offers a wider range of sound than Emmett's: the introduction's minstrel-band opening gives way to solo-song texture (with band references in the piano supporting the "doo-dahs!"), which then yields to a four-voice chorus in the refrain section.

Though we might take the differences between *Old Dan Tucker* and *De Camptown Races* as a matter of different composing styles, they also reflect changes in minstrelsy between 1843 and 1850. A song like *Old Dan Tucker,* with its rough spirit, represented the dominant voice of early minstrelsy: the black mask, linked with muscular, unlyrical music, that invited white entertainers to mock genteel social customs with fierce intensity. In the next few years, however, blackface minstrels vastly increased their audience, in part by broadening their musical repertory. Rip-roaring comic songs like *Old Dan Tucker* were still sung, but so were sad songs, love songs, sentimental songs,

Edwin P. Christy (1815–1862) led one of the nation's most successful minstrel troupes and introduced many of Foster's songs to the public.

and even opera parodies. By mid-century, the noisy, impromptu entertainments cooked up by Dan Emmett and the Virginia Minstrels were a thing of the past. Moving from the fringes of respectability into the center of American show business, minstrelsy evolved toward a more restrained and balanced kind of spectacle. In that setting, a comic song like *De Camptown Races,* with a tune strong enough to hold performers to the prescribed notes, proved a means of channeling unruliness into a more controlled mode of expression.

One person who helped to widen minstrelsy's audience appeal was the impresario and performer E. P. Christy. Born in 1815 in Philadelphia, Christy spent time as a young man in New Orleans, where he later claimed to have studied the Negroes' "queer words and simple but expressive melodies." He perfected his blackface imitation as a traveling comic singer in the 1830s before founding his own troupe, Christy's Minstrels, in Buffalo in the early 1840s. Working as the group's manager, he also performed as interlocutor (master of ceremonies), played banjo, and sang. Christy's troupe toured upstate New York and elsewhere for several years before opening in New York City in April 1846. A critic complimented their first performance there, not only for "very fine" instrumental music but for "chaste, refined, and harmonious" singing, suggesting that the troupe put more emphasis on polished musical sound than unruly antics. Offering family entertainment at cheap prices (25 cents for adults, half that for children), Christy's Minstrels took up residence at New York's Mechanics' Hall for a run of more than seven years (February 1847–July 1854) and 2,792 performances—evidence that Christy had discovered the kind of successful formula for which popular performers search.[25]

Christy's Minstrels, by exploiting the whole range of company member's talents, came to be the most successful minstrel band in America. By the time they began their long New York run, the Christys had grown into a six- or seven-man troupe. They presented their shows in a three-part structure: first a group of songs, often featuring the character of the Northern black dandy; then an "olio" (hodgepodge) section including stump speeches and other novelties; and finally a large-scale burlesque skit set in the South. Programs opened with an overture for full band, which also played marches and dances through the evening. Other instrumental numbers might include a duet for fiddle and bones, a banjo duet, an accordion solo.

The Christy company also presented a wide variety of vocal music, including not only high-spirited, stomping numbers but sentimental songs, glees (secular songs composed for several voice parts in harmony), and arrangements of opera numbers such as the "Phantom Chorus" from Bellini's *La sonnambula,* a company specialty. Christy's Minstrels were one of several companies that tried, in effect, to embrace all of popular vocal music, solo and choral. They began to do so at about the same time Stephen Foster was composing his first songs. Christy must have recognized that

Foster, with his gift for melodic invention, was writing songs that appealed to the very audiences his company was trying to court. And Foster knew that there was no better way to promote sheet-music sales of his blackface songs than to have them sung onstage by a famous company like Christy's. Thus, though they seem not to have met in these years, Christy and Foster became collaborators of a sort in 1850.

When in 1848, Foster's songs first made a hit on minstrel stages, he was working in Cincinnati as a clerk. Success persuaded him to move in 1850 to Pittsburgh, close to the family home, and to launch a career as a full-time songwriter. At that time, he entered into an agreement that gave Christy's Minstrels exclusive first-performance rights to his new songs. The link was a prestigious one for the little-known Foster, but it likewise benefited Christy and his company, for their singing of Foster's popular *Oh! Susanna* and *Old Uncle Ned* had already helped the group gain its sovereign position.[26]

In 1851, Foster even allowed Christy to claim authorship of *Old Folks at Home,* a song of unparalleled impact and appeal. The following year, though, he wrote Christy asking permission to restore his own name to its rightful place on the song's cover. Foster's letter, quoted often since, starts by reminding Christy that he had once thought of "omitting my name on my Ethiopian songs, owing to a prejudice against them by some, which might injure my reputation as writer of another style of music." This statement implies that despite minstrelsy's dominance in New York City's popular music scene in 1852, Foster recognized that it was still short on social prestige. For all his quick success in composing for the minstrel stage, Foster's wider ambition made him wary of being limited by that association. His claim for his own accomplishments, based on having written some fifteen blackface songs, must have seemed overblown to Christy, who for the past decade had been working in the trenches to elevate minstrelsy's tone:[27] "I find that by my efforts I have done a great deal to build up a taste for the Ethiopian songs among refined people," Foster wrote, "by making the words suitable to their taste, instead of the trashy and really offensive words which belong to some songs of that order." But Foster was leading up to something even more likely to leave Christy fuming:

I have concluded to reinstate my name on my songs and to pursue the Ethiopian business without fear or shame and lend all my energies to making the business live, at the same time that I will wish to establish my name as the best Ethiopian song-writer. But I am not encouraged in undertaking this so long as "The Old Folks at Home" stares me in the face with another's name on it. As it was at my own solicitation that you allowed your name to be placed on the song, I hope that the above reasons will be sufficient explanation for my desire to place my own name on it as author and composer.[28]

We discover Christy's response from two directions. First, we know that he refused Foster's request because until the copyright expired in 1879, sheet-music printings of *Old Folks at Home* continued to name Christy as author and composer. And second, Christy scrawled an epithet on the back of Foster's letter: "vacillating skunk"!

Given Foster's secure place in American music history, he has sometimes been portrayed as the injured party in this matter: a young composer trying to rectify an error in judgment and reap the just rewards of his labor. But from the perspective of a member of the minstrel trade, his letter smacks of both condescension and naïveté. In the first place, the letter seems to ignore that Foster had already benefited from the association with Christy's far more famous name. (The royalty of 2 cents per copy went to Foster even though his name was not on the cover.)[29] Second, it is easy to imagine a professional like Christy being offended by the suggestion that the source of his bread and butter—not to mention Foster's own—was somehow beneath the younger man's dignity. Finally, after trading on Christy's fame for more than a year, here was Foster, who in an earlier letter to Christy had called himself "a gentleman of the old school," proposing to renege on a done deal.

Foster's exchange with Christy reveals the mid-century minstrel show as an arena where social status and professional codes of ethics were still being contested. And the song that prompted the exchange itself reaches into

Foster's *Old Folks at Home* (1851) shows his reliance on a single four-measure melody and the simplicity of the piano accompaniment, accessible to inexpert players.

expressive territory that Dan Emmett and his ilk never visited. Foster's shapely, lyrical melody in the mouth of a sympathetically treated black slave, spoke for many members of his white audience. Foster's character, a displaced slave, sings of loneliness and longing. The vagueness of background and absence of narrative help to shift attention from the slave's plight to his isolation, which in turn broadens the song's message beyond slavery. The singer is alone, with no other singers to keep him company (as in the usual harmonized chorus), and with no evident plan to return to the home for which he claims to long so intensely. Together the words and tune effectively convey the emotional weariness that isolation can bring.

There is little in the music to mark *Old Folks* as a minstrel song. In fact, its character owes much to songs introduced to an earlier generation of Americans by Irish poet Thomas Moore.[30] In form, the melody follows *De Camptown Races,* with one four-measure statement filling five of the six phrases in the vocal section—i.e., twenty of its twenty-four bars—and both phrases of the eight-bar piano introduction. Yet for all the song's repetitiveness, the composer's craftsmanship (or inspiration) gives the repeated phrase extraordinary life. The key lies in the way Foster coordinates rhythm with melodic intervals. The long note at the beginning leads to four short notes; small values follow large in a way that foreshadows the arrival of middle-sized ones—quarter notes—after the eighths. (The piano introduction shows that Foster conceived the song's main rhythmic cell as a half note, four eighths, and four quarter notes.) The first half-dozen pitches lie close together too, setting up the octave leap on beat 2 of the second measure. By placing the leap on the weak second beat rather than the strong first or third, Foster de-emphasizes its surprise, making it part of the larger gesture of "Swanee River," which lifts the phrase so that its midpoint hovers high above its beginning. At this point, the ear also anticipates that the line will move downward, filling in the gap, as it does on "far far away." Indeed, this part of the melody is uneventful, balancing the activity of the first two bars. The varied rhythms, octave leap, and unhurried descent of the whole phrase are so neatly fused into one gesture that Foster can repeat these four bars again and again without their growing stale.

Only in the refrain does a new musical gesture appear, with the voice's major-seventh leap above its previous note. By carrying the melody for these words higher than the rest of the song, Foster dramatizes the psychic ache that is his real subject. In *Old Folks at Home,* the sweetness of the melody and the barely moving harmonic support of the accompaniment underline the dreamlike nostalgia expressed in the text. If sentimentality is the evoking of emotional states so that they can be experienced and enjoyed rather than acted on, then this is a prime example of a sentimental song.

Historical commentators concur that many white Americans, including

MECHANICS' HALL
472
BROADWAY, ABOVE GRAND STREET.

OPEN EVERY NIGHT

FRONT SEATS INVARIABLY RESERVED FOR LADIES

BRYANT'S

MINSTRELS

Bryant Brothers............................Proprietors and Managers

MONDAY EVENING, APRIL 4th, 1859
PROGRAMME—PART FIRST.

Instrumental Overture.....................................Bryant's Minstrels
We're the boys for pleasure...........Operatic.....................Company
Me and Eliza..Jerry Bryant
Bonny Mea...T. B. Prendergast
Yes, in a Horn...J. Unsworth
Medley Chorus, popular Ethiopian airs...........................Company
Only 19 Years Old..Dan Bryant
Finale—Masquerade Waltz...Full Band

PART SECOND. VARIETIES.

Pas Seul, Burlesque..H. Leslie
FADDEN MAC FADDEN ....by the........MAC DILL DARROLLS
Violin Solo...P. B. Isaacs
Tambourine Duet.......................................Jerry and Dan Bryant
Favorite Ballad..Little Arthur
WE COME FROM THE HILLS
Emmett, Prendergast, Jerry and Dan Bryant.
Flutina Solo..Neil Bryant

BURLESQUE ITALIAN OPERA

Mlle. Pickle Hominy, Prima Donna.......................Madame Very Angry Prendergasto
Count no-Count MacCaffery, Primo Tenor.....................Sig. Dani Brignole Bryanto
Signor Houlihan Stuffinleown, Primo Basso...................Sig. Unsero Lynexiani
Heer's (well) Formed, Baritone..............................Heer Jerro La Ratchie Bryanto
Sig. Sardinera, " Others"...............................Sig. Excelcorio Emmittiani
Two Distinct Orchestras, Efficent Chorus, &c...........the whole under the direction of.........
Mons. Max Mush-tic-stray-cow-celman, Signors Innocenti and Bros. Hobbo

PART THIRD—PLANTATION.

Local Banjo Song..J. Unsworth
THE SURPRISE PARTY...CARROLL, JERRY and DAN BRYANT
Wooden Shoe Dance...R. Sands

After which Mr. Dan Emmett's new and original
PLANTATION SONG AND DANCE,

DIXIE'S LAND
Introducing the whole Troupe in the Festival Dance.

The whole to conclude with
"OUR AMERICAN COUSIN" BILL

Which has been brought from "Laura Keene's Theatre," AND WILL
BE PLACED ON THIS STAGE WITHOUT ANY ALTERATIONS.

NOTICE CHANGE OF TIME:
Doors open at quarter to Seven.   Curtain will rise at quarter to Eight o'clock.

ADMSISION   -   -   25 CENTS

HERALD PRINT.

Easteners gone west and rural folk newly arrived in cities, looked behind the black mask and stage dialect of *Old Folks at Home* and heard some of their own melancholy feelings expressed. Some consider *Old Folks* an amalgamation of the minstrel song and the home song, exemplified by Bishop's *Home, Sweet Home.* Foster's blackface singer was now reaching out to join lonely white singers and listeners dreaming of home. To be sure, the idea of a real slave pining for a return to captivity was improbable. But in the home song's metaphorical world, to place the longing in the mouth of a lonely black character was to give an especially poignant twist to a familiar subject.[31]

More than that, however, Foster's amalgamation of minstrel and home song signaled the direction in which minstrelsy was heading by mid-century. Unlike Emmett, Foster played piano and conceived his songs at the keyboard. As a player of melody instruments (fiddle and banjo), Emmett seems to have composed without a full command of either standard harmonic practice or the tools of the songwriter's trade. The sheet music of *Old Dan Tucker* points to his need for an intermediary, noting: "Arranged for pianoforte by Rice." In contrast, Foster, raised in relative affluence and growing up in a home where music was regularly made in the parlor, wrote his own accompaniments and aimed his music at singers and players like the members of his own family. This is not to exaggerate his training or technical command as a composer. Yet Foster's inventions are rooted in a smooth, connected, though limited harmonic idiom. And in songs like *De Camptown Races* and *Old Folks at Home,* he showed an uncanny knack for writing minstrel music that suited the talents and tastes of parlor performers. In the early 1840s, Dan Emmett brought songs drawn from the circus and countryside into urban American theaters. Now, around 1850, Foster had found an idiom that that seemed equally at home in the parlor and on the stage.[32]

BLACKFACE MINSTRELSY IN THE 1850S

During their first decade of existence, minstrel shows presented a range of black characters, from shrewd tricksters to sensitive, displaced slaves, each representing some facet of white anxiety about, or appreciation of, black ways. The second decade, however, beginning around 1853, introduced a more limited, stereotyped portrayal of black characters. The reasons for the change are complex.

During the minstrel show's early years, antislavery sentiment increased in the North. The human dimension of blacks was coming to be understood more fully there, in part because of minstrel stage portrayals. For, as well as being demeaning to blacks, minstrel representations helped undermine the myth that African Americans were genetically equipped for nothing better than servitude. But even as Northern opinion questioned the link between blacks and slavery, Southerners hardened their position. Sectional conflict between North and South grew more intense, chiefly because of the slavery debate. As the frontier moved west, bitter controversies took place over whether slavery would be allowed in newly settled territories, which might then become states of the Union. These and other conflicts of the early 1850s put white Northerners on the spot, increasingly aware that economic self-interest and the moral principles informing their view of slavery often stood at cross-purposes. For many Northerners, the only way to preserve the Union seemed to be to overlook their own misgivings and compromise with slaveowners.[33]

Against this background, minstrelsy, which had sought to cultivate a gray area between black and white ideological extremes, retreated from controversy and embraced what minstrels must have considered an apolitical stance. Portrayals of black characters left realism behind in favor of sentimentality, with contented Negroes fondly recalling the good old days on the plantation. Compared with that idyllic portrait of Southern black life, minstrelsy's picture of the North was more varied, but it led in the same direction. Some Northern stage blacks were shown as pretentious dandies and fops in the tradition of Zip Coon, trying and failing to make a mark in the fashionable world. Others were dim-witted fools, fit only to be objects of ridicule. And then there were the ex-slaves, free in the North but, in the words of Stephen Foster, "still longing for old plantation" and its comfort and security. Unhappy blacks—indeed, the very notion that any blacks, even as mistreated slaves, had *cause* to be unhappy—gradually disappeared from minstrel stages. By the mid-1850s, the minstrel show's ideological core was simply a rationalization that, if it did not endorse the beliefs of Southern slavery advocates, did not contradict them either. According to that rationalization, the plantation was blacks' rightful home, the only place they would be truly happy and well cared for.[34]

Politics, the economy, regional pride, and religion were all involved in the rising tension between North and South. And from 1852 on, so was literature. For in that year, Harriet Beecher Stowe's openly polemical novel *Uncle Tom's Cabin: or, Life Among the Lowly* was published. Stowe sought in her work, she explained, "to awaken sympathy and feeling for the African race, as they exist among us; to show their wrongs and sorrows, under a system so necessarily cruel and unjust as to defeat and do away the good efforts of all that can be attempted for them."[35] A huge literary success in the North, with 300,000 copies sold in the first year and 1,200,000 in print by mid-1853, *Uncle Tom's Cabin* was banned as subversive literature in some regions of the South. There is no question that it promoted sectional conflict. Abraham Lincoln, on meeting Harriet Beecher Stowe for the first time in the

1860s, is supposed to have greeted her as "the little lady who started the war."

Uncle Tom's Cabin probably won an even larger audience as a play. In a day when copyright laws allowed stage adaptations, dramatic versions based on Stowe's book began to appear on American stages within weeks of its publication, bringing characters like Uncle Tom, the saintly, trustworthy slave, and Simon Legree, the hard-fisted, hard-hearted slave driver, to life for audiences. In standard melodramatic fashion, Stowe's novel draws sharp distinctions between the forces of good and evil, and the stage versions followed suit.

Uncle Tom's Cabin became a cultural force without precedent in American life. Looking back to his youth, novelist Henry James remembered the book as one whose subject, tone, and characters allowed it to be adapted easily to almost any circumstances: "If the amount of life represented in such a work is measurable by the ease with which representation is taken up and carried further, carried even violently further, the fate of Mrs. Stowe's picture was conclusive: it simply sat down wherever it lighted and made itself at home," where "multitudes" of customers "flocked afresh" to see it. Stowe's work seemed to strike a chord everywhere.

As a work very much in the public eye, not to mention one whose leading character was black, *Uncle Tom's Cabin* was fair game for minstrelsy's machinery of parody and burlesque. And the process was under way by 1854, when Christy and Henry Wood's Minstrels used Stowe's characters in a plantation sketch they called "Life Among the Happy." By all accounts, this performance featured plenty of dancing, singing, and high spirits, ending with the "Grand Characteristic Dance, 'Pop Goes the Weazle.'" It made little use of Stowe's plot and managed to omit any reference to the cruelty and suffering of slavery, which had moved Stowe to write her novel in the first place. It simply capitalized on the vogue for Uncle Tom and Company by borrowing their names, attaching them to stereotyped characters, and conducting business as usual on a happy Southern plantation. This sketch, like other Uncle Tom parodies, and indeed other minstrel entertainments of the latter 1850s in general, did not engage with the issue of slavery, treating it as an accepted fact of American life. As North-South enmity grew and the country's future hung in the balance, battle lines were apparently so firmly drawn that slavery was no longer a matter for joking onstage.

A vivid symbol of the new landscape in which black characters moved can be found in the career of ex–Virginia Minstrel Frank Brower. In 1854, Brower began playing Uncle Tom in blackface, complete with a characteristic dance called the "Uncle Tom jig," and he made that role a personal specialty. There is no evidence that Brower was much interested in Tom as

Stowe had drawn him. For in the novel, Tom's master introduces him as "a good, steady, sensible, pious fellow. He got religion at a camp-meeting, four years ago; and I believe he really *did* get it. I've trusted him, since then, with everything I have,—money, house, horses,—and let him come and go round the country; and I always found him true and square in everything."[36] In contrast, the character Brower played in a stage sketch of 1863 was aging, hard of hearing, and stupid. To Stowe's audience, and indeed to many Americans in this year of Emancipation, Uncle Tom was a powerful symbol of spirituality, morality, and humanity. But on the minstrel stage, at least as played by Frank Brower, he was a simple, feeble old man who came to dancing life at the sound of banjo music.[37]

12

Home Music Making and the Publishing Industry

THE REFORMS OF SACRED MUSIC launched in the 1720s and early 1800s and the efforts of Lowell Mason and his colleagues in the 1830s to teach children to sing all may be linked to the goal of edification. And because they centered around churches and schools, both formal institutions, their course is not hard to trace. In contrast, the creation of a musical market-place in American homes has left a sketchier trail. By the mid-nineteenth century, a substantial music business existed in this country to meet the de-sires of women and men, playing and singing at home, for recreation and entertainment as well as edification. The publishers who fashioned that business did so by coordinating three separate forces: the artistic production of composers, the social aspiration of amateur singers and players, and their own commercial ambition.

The spread of home music making in America belonged to a larger trend in the early 1800s, which saw a growing middle class embrace ideals of re-finement and gentility. More and more families set aside a room in their house for activities separate from the workaday world: for reading, conversa-tion, games, and music. But home music making was different from reform movements, launched in the name of an idealistic purpose and couched in moral rhetoric; it was a business from the start, with producers and con-sumers. Producers taught Americans that they could have music in their homes if they made it themselves. Their customers, sparked by artistic in-terest and social aspiration, learned how to become active, participating mu-sical consumers. The business was built around sheet music: not costly to publish or purchase, tailored to the skills and tastes of buyers, and hence an ideal artifact for a democracy. The sheet-music trade was the economic agent that, more than any other, turned the American home into a market-place for music. And although technology has introduced many changes over the years, the same principle—distributing music in cheap, accessible units—has sustained the music business ever since.

Until well into the nineteenth century, the drive for financial profit seems to have been a side issue on the American musical scene. Money was needed to sustain musical activity but hardly a primary reason to engage in it. In home music making, however, economics was always the driving force. As the sheet-music trade blossomed, a gap in sensibility opened between its tough-minded business ethic and the emphasis on sentimental feelings offered by many of its products. Unlike musical reformers, who argued for change on moral grounds, the merchants who established the home music market stood ready to publish what consumers would buy.

The sheet-music trade required several agents: composers (and arrangers) to create the music; publishers to produce and disseminate it in salable forms; teachers to give lessons in performing it (and also peddle it to their students); and manufacturers of musical instruments to play it. Each played a necessary role, but publishers were the chief architects.

Alexander Reinagle (1756–1809), a native of Portsmouth, England, came to America in 1786, settled in Philadelphia, and during fifteen years with the New Company directed musical productions there and in Baltimore. Most of his music was destroyed in a fire in 1820.

ALEXANDER REINAGLE AND THE MUSIC BUSINESS

The home music-making business, a flourishing enterprise by the 1850s, may trace its beginnings to a specific year in the life of one immigrant musician: the English-born composer and performer Alexander Reinagle in 1787. When the thirty-year-old Reinagle arrived in the New World in the spring of 1786, no such thing as an American *music* publisher existed. Virtually all the composers then working in America were psalmodists whose music reached the public in sacred anthologies brought out by firms that also printed books and newspapers. Until 1787, all secular sheet music and instrumental music was imported, chiefly from England. In that year, however, the first American-published sheet music issued from the Philadelphia shop of engraver and metalsmith John Aitken. At first, Aitken had no competitors. But six years later, as musical artisans in New York, Boston, and Baltimore began to publish sheet music, the United States had its own music-publishing trade. The trade's earliest stage is worth a closer look, even though Aitken's output between 1787 and 1792 totaled only sixteen items.[1]

Signs point to Alexander Reinagle as the instigating partner in Aitken's publishing venture. For one thing, twelve of Aitken's sixteen published works were composed by, arranged by, or printed for Reinagle. For another, when Reinagle took the post of music director for the New Theater in Philadelphia's Chestnut Street in 1793, Aitken stopped publishing sheet music, though he did resume the work some years later. Reinagle's entrepreneurial tendencies had come to light soon after he landed in the New World. A newspaper notice from mid-1786 advertised for pupils "in Singing, on the Harpsichord, Piano Forte, and Violin" and proclaimed Reinagle's readiness "to supply his Friends and Scholars with the best instruments and music printed in London." This notice suggests that he may even have immigrated as an agent of the London music trades, looking to extend their reach to the former colonies. But whether on his own or representing other interests, within a year of arriving on American shores, Reinagle had begun to take part in all four of the professional roles involved in the sheet-music business. He composed and arranged music for home use; he gave lessons to singers and players; he involved himself in the distribution of music; and he plugged the work of London instrument builders.[2]

Reinagle's activity indicates that the American music business in the mid-1780s was still so elementary that one musician could take on almost the whole enterprise himself; that unspecialized condition lasted into the early 1800s. The publishing and selling of music remained chiefly in the hands of musicians working to make ends meet. Oscar G. Sonneck, pioneer historian of American music, made that point long ago in a comment on New York's professional musicians around 1800, numbering about fifty and

Reinagle, Sonata No. 1 for fortepiano (Philadelphia, 1786–94?), page 1. This work was not published until 1978.

virtually all of them performers from the British Isles: "With their revenues from teaching, selling, [and] copying music," and from performing in theater orchestras and public concerts, Sonneck observed, the professional musicians in New York at that time managed "to eke out a living."[3] More-

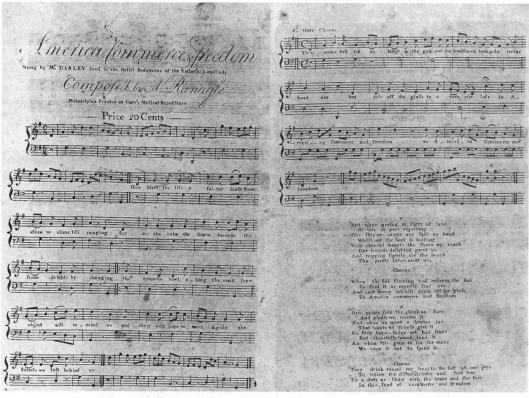

Reinagle, *America, Commerce, and Freedom*, from *The Sailor's Landlady* (Philadelphia, 1794) in its original sheet-music printing.

over, those who began publishing sheet music in 1793 were mostly musician-engravers who, like Reinagle, worked at more than one of what would later be separate occupations.

Although publishers created the American sheet-music business, only after they grasped the home market's economic potential did a substantial business begin to take shape. While there is no way to know precisely when that recognition dawned, two works of Alexander Reinagle show that by the early 1790s—almost half a century before the mass marketing of sheet music became a fact of life—he was already distinguishing music that could be sold to home buyers from music that could not. The first is a piano sonata he composed in Philadelphia, probably between 1786 and 1794. This work, most likely written for Reinagle himself to play in public concerts, reveals a command of the keyboard idiom of eighteenth-century European masters such as C. P. E. Bach and Joseph Haydn. The second piece, a song called *America, Commerce, and Freedom,* was sung in a stage work of 1794.

Aesthetic judgment and historical hindsight would rank Reinagle's sonata as a more impressive piece of music than his song. But the music trade had its own take on quality: *America, Commerce, and Freedom* was published soon after it was composed, but nearly two centuries elapsed between the piano sonata's composition and its publication.[4] Why would a song go straight into print and a piano sonata by the same composer stay in manuscript? Because when this music was written, there was a market in the United States for songs and almost none for piano sonatas. Songs—short, melodious, simple to perform, and carriers of verse—combined traits that appealed to amateur performers. And theatrical performances enhanced their appeal: after hearing a song sung onstage, audience members could buy a copy and perform it at home. But mastering a sonata required a good deal more skill, practice, and most likely lessons. Besides, skilled players could buy imported music by Old World masters like Handel, the sons of Bach, and Haydn himself. Who needed a piano sonata by Alexander Reinagle? Reinagle's own answer remains elusive; there is no sign that he tried to get his sonatas into print.

In Reinagle's two compositions may be read the divided heritage of composing as an occupation in the United States. In writing the sonata, Reinagle was acting as a member of the composing *profession,* whose ideal is tied not to economic outcome but to intellectual control, including a composer's right to control performances through written scores. In contrast, Reinagle's role in *America, Commerce, and Freedom* was more like that of a tradesman working to please customers. Composed for a particular moment in a stage drama, the song was expected also to appeal to amateur performers at home and at the keyboard.

Reinagle's two pieces offer perspective on what has been the most important (and contentious) issue in American music historiography: the perception of a Great Divide between so-called classical and popular music or, in another familiar pairing, between music in the cultivated tradition and music in the "vernacular" tradition.[5] Some have seen such categories as a device used by elite-minded critics and historians to impose an aesthetic hierarchy supporting their own classical preferences. Indeed, by calling the sonata a more impressive piece of music than the song, I may seem already to have endorsed such a hierarchy. The comparison is not made to assign value, however, but rather to focus on the different relationship each piece creates between the composer, the performer, and the written score. That difference makes the aesthetic implications of the Great Divide secondary to a practical question: how have American performers approached composers' scores?

NOTATION, THE GREAT DIVIDE, AND AMERICAN MUSICAL CATEGORIES

Before the advent of the phonograph, musical notation was the key to musical commerce. Not until a piece was written down and circulated in print could it become a commodity to be bought and sold. But musical notation may be used for other purposes too. In Reinagle's sonata, notation embodies the authority of the composer. Performers who played pieces like this one followed the composer's instructions closely, though certain liberties—adding embellishments, for example, or making their own decisions about repeat signs—could still be consistent with a respectful attitude toward the score. In contrast, the score for Reinagle's song is much less prescriptive. From the song's beginning to the instrumental tag the top line of the keyboard part does nothing but double the voice; and the lower line is a stripped-down, elementary bass whose only flash of independence is the eighth-note motion near the end, when the title line is sung. Not a single chord appears until the last two beats of the piece, a curious way to write for an instrument with chord-playing ability.

It is hard to imagine many players, in Reinagle's day or since, performing the keyboard part of *America, Commerce, and Freedom* exactly as written. Some would surely add chords, decorate the melody, or enrich the bass. Others might double the bass line with a cello if one were available, or substitute guitar for keyboard, or extend or cut out the instrumental tag. Still others might sing the song unaccompanied, at a fast or slow clip, or move it to a different key. Significant departures from the score would be unacceptable in the sonata, but expected in the song. The score of *America, Commerce, and Freedom* was published and sold as an outline to be filled in and realized by performers according to their abilities, tastes, and moods.

Given where the authority lies, Reinagle's piano sonata may be called a piece of *composers' music* and his song a piece of *performers' music*. Performers' music, while offering composers little control over performances, gave them access to customers in the marketplace. In contrast, composers' music offered artistic control but few if any customers, at least in Reinagle's day. From an economic standpoint, early American writers of composers' music were strictly on their own, while writers of performers' music worked at the behest of theater managers and publishers. By writing both kinds of music, Alexander Reinagle exercised the full range of his artistic and economic opportunities.

Reinagle's clear distinction between genres shows that the roots of musical categories in America lie in practical conditions more than two centuries old. Yet to frame the discussion of categories solely around composers would be misleading, for performers have traditionally held more power to shape day-to-day musical life. The field of opera is a case in point.

It is a striking fact that although many Americans in the antebellum years took opera to their hearts, most of them encountered operas not as integral works of art, faithful to a composer's score, but in altered form: as pastiches, arrangements, translations, truncations, excerpts, and single numbers. Adaptation—the tailoring of the music to suit particular audiences and circumstances—was the key to opera's popularity in America. In other words, a prestigious genre of composers' music made an impact in the United States only after it was transformed into performers' music. We saw in Chapter 10 how English composer Rophino Lacy turned Rossini's *La Cenerentola* into his own *Cinderella,* to make the original accessible to English-speaking audiences. Other musicians in England and America then borrowed and adapted parts of both *Cinderella* and *Cenerentola* in ways that made them accessible to still other audiences. The *Cenerentola* that flourished in America's performance environment, though dependent on Rossini's inspiration and skill, was not the work written down in his score but a family of varied musical numbers derived from it, put together by arrangers, conductors, performers, and managers to appeal to their audiences.

Composers' authority counted for little in the musical theater, for there, the key to success lay in capturing a general audience's attention. Composers, performers, and arrangers in search of accessibility were obliged to keep the marketplace always in mind, as did Reinagle when he included *America, Commerce, and Freedom* in *The Sailor's Landlady,* and Lacy when he revised *La Cenerentola.* Because the attitude surrounding composers' music discouraged such tailoring, theatrical music in the first half of the nineteenth century must be considered performers' music.

Until after the Civil War, the ethos of accessibility dominated the public performance of virtually all music in the United States. Indeed, perhaps no development in musical performance was more important than the appearance of a new attitude in opposition to accessibility, which may be called authenticity. In contrast to accessibility, authenticity centered on composers' music, privileging works over occasions. Rather than a strategy, it was an ideal that placed ultimate authority in composers' scores. Performers who followed the ideal of authenticity believed that compositions were animated at the time of their creation with a certain original spirit and that players and singers were duty-bound to be guided by that spirit. Authenticity placed composers above performers and above arrangers and adapters too, who were considered performers' agents and hence purveyors of accessibility. Taking audience enjoyment as a secondary issue, authenticity judged performances on their faithfulness to the work as the composer was thought to have conceived it.

For composers, then, the Great Divide lay in deciding whether to write composers' music, with authoritative scores, or performers' music, intended more as a springboard for the interpretations of singers and players. For performers, the divide ran along overlapping but not identical lines; opera performers, for example, seeking accessibility were not obliged to approach composers' music with authenticity in mind. For both composers and performers, the attitude in toward a work's notation was all-important. To what extent did composers expect deference to what they wrote down? Were performers more dedicated to seeking the essence of the work in the composer's notation, or in communicating it to listeners? The answers to these questions reflected the existence of different kinds of musical works, which came to be grouped under such labels as "classical" and "popular."

To connect composers' music with authenticity and performers' music with accessibility is to make a start toward mapping the shape of musical life in the United States during the past two centuries. Again, the crucial difference between the two lies in notation, the authority it carries and the spirit in which it is interpreted. Composers' music, rooted in high esteem for authenticity, constitutes the classical sphere, built around an ideal that may be called *transcendence*: the belief that musical works, like poems, novels, plays, and paintings, can achieve a permanent artistic stature; that such works form the basis for a worthwhile, healthy musical life; and that performers have a duty to sing and play them in a way that reveals their superior traits—i.e., by following the composer's notation closely. Performers' music, in contrast, constitutes a popular sphere whose chief premise is *accessibility*, investing authority most of all in the audience.

While the classical and popular spheres are grounded in notation, a great deal of music in U.S. history has relied on oral transmission. Much unwritten folk music reflects the foreign origins of the classical sphere and the functional emphasis of the popular. But its invention, circulation, and preservation are different enough from either to make it a separate domain: the "traditional" sphere. Musical sound is usually not the main focus of those who sing and play within the traditional sphere, where music making tends to be connected with particular customs and ways of life. In its drive to preserve linguistic, cultural, and musical practices, the traditional sphere is ruled most of all by a commitment to *continuity*.

The idea of three spheres—classical, popular, and traditional—offers an image of American music making that is richer and more flexible than the familiar binary view of classical versus popular music (or the cultivated tradition versus the vernacular, or highbrow versus lowbrow). The binary image suggests a two-dimensional continuum, encouraging discussions that concentrate on either "high" or "low" genres but seldom the whole spectrum, implying that differences between the two are more important than connections. In contrast, three spheres of musical activity coexisting in a three-dimensional space suggest a freedom of movement *and* a connectedness that over time has brought those spheres into contact with each other. And in the interactions that have taken place lie the wellsprings of American musical distinctiveness.

The historical contrast with Europe is striking. There an aesthetic hierarchy sanctioned by church-, court-, and state-backed authority has long provided standards against which other music making has been measured. But the United States has lacked a place for music where political, economic, and aesthetic authority overlap. The popular sphere and commercial interests have therefore enjoyed more clout in America than in Europe. Their dominating tendency has been held somewhat in check by the prestige of the classical sphere on the one hand and the traditional sphere's resistance to economic control on the other.

It is true that many musicians have pursued transcendence, accessibility, or continuity separately and for its own sake. Yet it is also striking how often these goals have collided, intersected, coexisted, or blended. What kind of cultural transaction is taking place when a composer in the classical sphere "borrows" from the popular or the traditional sphere? or when a traditional melody is notated and performed as if it were a composed piece? or when a widely accessible popular genre sustains itself until it enters the performing milieu of the classical sphere? or when a recording makes a performance a candidate for transcendence? Circumstances like these, all involving some kind of boundary crossing, have been commonplace in American music history. Much of the music thought to be most fully American plays on, or has refused to be confined by, the boundaries of the spheres, which would seem to show that the boundaries really do exist. Such borrowings and crossovers are by no means unique to American music; they constitute an important force within Western art music during the nineteenth and twentieth centuries.[6] But they are not so central to the musical profile of European countries, where the realm of composers' music has enjoyed an intellectual position more commanding than that of the classical sphere in North America.

SHEET MUSIC AND HOME MUSIC MAKING

A glance at the publication history of two revered patriotic songs, *The Star-Spangled Banner* and *America* ("My country, 'tis of thee"), illuminates the home music marketplace of the early 1800s. Both songs made their first printed appearance as broadsides, single sheets of lyrics without music. The second, set to the melody of *God Save the King*, the English national anthem, was then printed, words and music both, in 1832 as AMERICA in a tunebook compiled by Lowell Mason. And only after that was a sheet-music version published as *My Country! 'Tis of Thee*, with four stanzas of text. This pattern illustrates how sheet music, appearing on the American scene only in the 1780s, complemented older forms of song publication rather than replacing them. Even after sheet music established itself, songs continued to circulate in broadsides, songsters (books of song lyrics without music), and anthologies (collections of musically notated songs). But if there is any question why sheet music dominated the home music trade, an economic comparison provides the answer. A broadside, the oldest form of all, might sell for a couple of pennies at most. Songsters were pocket-sized, seldom exceeding 25 or 35 cents. But sheet music, printed on folio-sized pages, designed for music racks in parlors and definitely not to be carried around, normally sold for 12 1/2 cents (a shilling) per page. So a two-page piece like *The Star-Spangled Banner* could bring in 25 cents per copy in sheet-music form, more than ten times what a broadside version would bring, and far more than its per-piece yield in any songster or anthology. A large sheet-music collection required a substantial outlay of cash. (Some owners considered their sheet music such prized possessions that they gathered pieces together in bound volumes.)

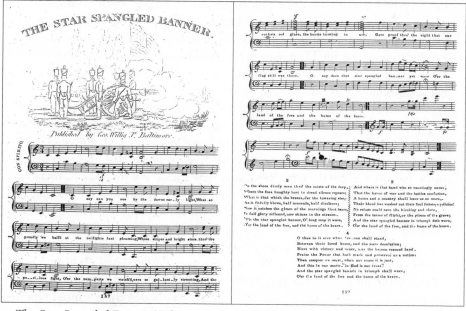

The Star-Spangled Banner (Baltimore, 1814) in its first sheet-music edition.

Earlier in this chapter, sheet music was described as inexpensive and thus ideal for a democracy. That statement holds true for the years after 1845, applies less well to the period 1825–40, and does not apply at all to the years before 1825, when sheet music was something of a luxury. (Besides the cost of printed music, performing from sheet music also required lessons, leisure time to take them, and access to accompanying instruments.) Perhaps it would be better to say that having started out as a costly enterprise supported by the few who could afford it, home music making by the mid-1800s was a pastime accessible to many Americans. While the retail price of sheet music stayed roughly the same, a growing economy increased people's access to consumer goods in general. And the relative cost of music lessons and keyboard instruments also dropped. Having produced no more than 600 pieces between 1787 and 1800, the trade by the late 1820s was turning out that many titles per year, growing to 1,600 annually in the early 1840s and 5,000 in the early 1850s. The threefold leap between 1840 and 1850 reflects a burgeoning of demand.[7]

The economics of sheet-music publishing depended on a variety of factors, including copyright law. As first written, the law protected only authors who were American citizens or residents. Foreign compositions could be reengraved and printed by any American publisher without permission or payment. (Foreign hits like *Home, Sweet Home* were issued by many different publishers because no edition of the song could be copyrighted.) Therefore, it was cheaper for publishers to print foreign music than American music, which required them either to purchase rights from the composer or pay a royalty on copies sold.[8] This fact of economics should not be overlooked when nineteenth-century musical taste is being considered. The American appetite for European music owed much to the notion that Old World culture was superior. But the dollars-and-cents advantage to publishers also promoted the circulation of foreign music.

While there was money to be made in the sheet-music trade, publishers' statements tended to stress its financial riskiness. Indeed, it was a condition of the trade that all but a few of its products lost money. A notice of 1859 from the house of Oliver Ditson & Co., a highly successful firm, painted a bleak picture for composers: "So much new music is now issued, that the sale of each piece is exceedingly limited, unless it is particularly striking or original in its character." Turning a profit was no simple matter: "Not one piece in ten pays the cost of getting up; only one in fifty proves a success." The cost for engraving and printing one hundred copies of a two-page song varied from $12 to $17 depending on title-page design. At a retail price of 25 cents, the publisher would have to sell at least sixty copies to break even on an item that cost $15 to print. Thereafter, copies could be printed much more cheaply, as the main expenses—engraving the plates for the music and lithographing or engraving the title—were already paid. But not many songs of the period sold even one hundred copies, and that fact sparked a double-barreled warning from the Ditson firm. First, authors should not be surprised if their manuscripts were rejected; and second, those whose works *were* published might be required "to purchase a certain number of copies, to help defray the first expenses and introduce them to the public."[9]

An industry statement from a dozen years later (1871) gave more specifics but in no more upbeat a tone. "Only . . . one song in a thousand on the average ever reaches a sale of one thousand copies," this report claimed, "and a composer whose compositions will generally average a sale of five hundred copies, without including his special hits, is considered a success." The report referred to the massive *Board of Trade Catalogue,* issued in 1871 by twenty major American music publishers, as a point of reference. Of the 80,000 items listed there, "there are at present only about twelve hundred good selling pieces, such as would warrant any dealer in ordering twenty-five copies at a time; and less than a hundred of which he could order two hundred copies without running too great a risk of their proving so much waste paper on his shelves."[10]

Success in the trade depended on exceptions: the composer whose name helped to sell copies; the stage hit that transferred well to the parlor; the vocal or instrumental number that the public took to its heart. When one of their pieces struck pay dirt, publishers did all they could to exploit it, packaging the title and melody in as many different arrangements as possible. The size and nature of the sheet-music repertory suggest a trade in which competition saturated the market in the hope of capitalizing on a fad, a current event, or the appeal of an old favorite melody. An analogy might be drawn to farming and the "broadcast" method of sowing seed: scattering them generously and in all directions while trusting that a few will germinate and bear fruit. The enormous outpouring of sheet music during the century's second half testifies that, whatever the risks, publishing it could be a lucrative enterprise.

MEN, WOMEN, AND PIANOS

The growth of the sheet-music business influenced the market for musical instruments, especially keyboard instruments. Harpsichords, their piquant sweetness of timbre made by quills plucking strings stretched over a soundboard, dominated the 1700s. They were replaced late in the century by the fortepiano, in which hammers struck the strings and players could achieve more nuanced volume. By the 1820s, the pianoforte had come into wider use. Capable of playing melody and harmony at the same time, like its predecessors, the pianoforte was equipped with a heavier construction that allowed players to produce more sound. This incarnation of the keyboard became *the* parlor instrument of the nineteenth and twentieth centuries, assuming shapes and sizes that fit different spaces: square pianos, uprights, spinets, consoles, and grands.

The pattern of growth in American keyboard manufacturing paralleled that of the sheet-music trade. At first an import and a luxury reserved for the few, keyboard instruments by the 1840s were accessible to more and more people. (By then, the reed organ, or melodeon, which makes sound by pushing or sucking air through chambers with vibrating reed tongues, was also being produced and sold by a number of American firms.) In early days, most harpsichords and fortepianos were made overseas and purchased by residents of the Northeast. But the climate there was rugged, varying greatly over the course of a year, and European-made instruments were not built to withstand its rigors. The year 1825 marks the start of an indigenous American piano trade, when Alpheus Babcock of Boston obtained a patent on a one-piece metal construction from which, he predicted, a piano frame "stronger and more durable" than one with a wooden frame or case could be built. Babcock had recognized that when weather changed, his frame would expand or contract equally with the strings, and thus "would not be put out of tune by any alteration in the temperature of the air."[11]

In this way, Americans began building pianos that held together and stayed in tune in American climates. As demand for pianos grew, manufac-

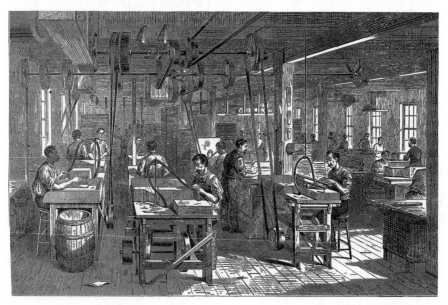

This engraving from 1887 depicts the Action Room of the Chickering Piano Manufactory in Boston.

turers competed to make them more cheaply, with Jonas Chickering of Boston beginning in the 1830s to mass-produce metal-framed instruments. By 1851, some 9,000 pianos per year were being made in the United States; Chickering, the leading firm, produced 10 percent of that total. Piano making was big business in America. When fire destroyed the Chickering firm's Boston plant in 1852, it was rebuilt on a scale that made the Capitol in Washington the only larger building in the United States. That confidence proved justified, for piano sales grew through the rest of the century at a pace much faster than the population. It has been estimated that one out of 4,800 Americans bought a new piano in 1829; in 1910, a year in which 350,000 pianos were produced, one out of 252 bought one.

As well as accompaniment, pianos were also solo instruments, and a great deal of sheet music was published for piano alone. As Reinagle's example suggests, a search for composers' music in the published repertory before 1825 turns up very little. Players looking for sonatas, whether by Europeans or composers living in America, had to rely on dealers who sold imported music. The few larger works that found their way into print were arrangements of overtures and "battle pieces." Much more typical was the dance or dance set, the standard instrumental form of the era. Keyboard sheet music of the early 1800s commonly presented such pieces—marches, minuets, waltzes—set for treble and bass, the melody in the top line and a supporting harmony below: performers' music easily accessible to unskilled players. Between 1820 and the Civil War, three kinds of piano pieces, mostly pictorial, dominated the repertory:

(1) variation sets, based on the melodies of popular songs, hymn tunes, or opera arias (from the 1830s on);

(2) dances, including waltzes, polkas, galops, cotillions, marches, and quicksteps; and

(3) a small amount of abstract music, especially rondos.[12]

When Americans began to publish sheet music in the late 1700s, customers came from the ranks of the affluent. And growing affluence in a newly independent nation brought with it a code of gentility that encouraged the serious cultivation of leisure pastimes. To call Benjamin Franklin, Francis Hopkinson, and Thomas Jefferson "gentleman amateurs" in music is to recognize not only their love for the art but their practice of it as part of everyday life. The activity of a well-ordered American house around 1800 involved a mixture of business and pleasure, including the making of music. A change took place in the nineteenth century, however, when business moved out of the house. The process began at the top of society when governors and other state officials began conducting their business in state capital buildings. Even more dramatic was the shift in the location of commerce and industry to office buildings. As power once dispersed among private dwellings came to be concentrated elsewhere, the home became more a center for family and cultural activity.[13] In the usual Victorian-age picture of family life, husbands left home in the morning, spent their days in the hurly-burly of a competitive marketplace, then returned in the evening to domestic sanctuaries prepared by their wives. In removing their own work from the home, men gave up their involvement in much that happened there, while domestic affairs came to be considered women's work. Home music making was deeply influenced by this change.

Males continued to dominate society as a whole, and women still depended on men for money to run their households. But in the new situation, women in domestic settings were no longer neglected. Instead, they were given responsibility for raising children, managing day-to-day household affairs, and beautifying their surroundings in sight and sound. In the eighteenth century, men like George Washington and Benjamin Franklin involved themselves in domestic affairs right down to the matter of choosing household furniture. In the nineteenth century, responsibility for decorating the house to please both eye and ear passed into the hands of women.

Many women took pride in that role. Elizabeth Cady Stanton, best known as an early advocate for women's rights, recalled that her husband had informed her after their marriage "that his business would occupy all his time, and that I must take entire charge of the housekeeping." She relished the opportunity. "It is a proud moment in a woman's life," she later wrote, "to reign supreme within four walls." To Stanton, women faced the kind of challenge that an artist does in painting a picture:

> Surely a mother and child, tastefully dressed, and a pretty home for a framework, is, as a picture, even more attractive than a domestic scene hung on the wall. The love of the beautiful can be illustrated as well in life as on canvas. There is such a struggle among women to become artists that I really wish some of their gifts could be illustrated in clean, orderly, beautiful homes.[14]

In transforming their homes into artistic statements of sorts, women lavished special attention on the parlor, where, in a middle-class setting, the appearance of polished gentility masked a good deal of anxious striving. And two musical industries, the sheet-music and the piano trades, strove mightily to serve the parlor's refined ethos. Their mission was rooted in the assumption that, in America as in England, parlor piano was a female activity.[15] Piano music published from the 1840s on may thus be seen as music for a feminine instrument, its character shaped by the trade's view of women's musical taste and capacities. Was this an accurate view? It is impossible to tell. For one thing, the publishers and composers who dominated the sheet-music business were all male. For another, only players skilled enough to explore the European classical repertory had an alternative outside the publishers' construction of feminine preference. But although it is not known whether many women would actually have chosen the music they were supposed to like if they had had a choice, sources of the time outside the field of music offer a clear picture of the female sensibility that this music was tailored to please.

Women were thought to have a natural affinity for genteel culture. One eighteenth-century guidebook distinguished women "from the robust Make of *Man* by that *Delicacy*, express'd by *Nature* in their *Form*." And another claimed that "superior delicacy" and "natural softness and sensibility" made women generally complaisant and disposed them toward a taste for beauty. That theme was repeated and elaborated in countless nineteenth-century sources.[16] An attraction to certain objects of beauty, such as flowers, was widely held (and not only by men) to be part of women's nature; something was thought to be wrong with women who did not feel it.

If we took piano sheet music as an index of what drew women of the time to music, we would conclude that females especially loved its power to evoke feelings and make associations. Piece after piece testifies that women were emotional creatures, and seems geared toward touching the player's or listener's imagination or emotions. That emphasis, however, was not only an American phenomenon; it also reflected an attempt in Old World education to cultivate sensitivity among students.[17] Music publishers sought at every point to capitalize on such sensitivities. And one way to do it was to issue piano music based on familiar melodies. The *Board of Trade Catalogue* (1871) carries many such pieces, including variations, fantasies, and arrangements of various kinds. The size of this category is a reminder of something nineteenth-century music publishers never forgot: the emotional and associative power of melody.

In the popular sphere, especially, melody was the ingredient that kept customers coming back for more. Sheet-music publishers squeezed their song hits for all they were worth. For example, the *Board of Trade Catalogue* lists no fewer than forty-nine different piano versions of *Home, Sweet Home* under "Rondos, Fantasies, Variations, &c." (one is labeled "Variations and Tremolo"). The technique of repackaging familiar tunes was recognized as a way to create communities of feeling, especially among women. The stock ways of dressing up familiar tunes in fantasies and variations now seem hackneyed—less musical than industrial. But that view disregards two key points. First, it sells short the pleasures, in a society where all music was "live" music, of rehearing favorite melodies. And second, it overlooks that in the nineteenth-century parlor, music's purpose was more social than artistic, and that touching the heart was among the highest social purposes of all. Composers and arrangers of parlor music, fully allied with the popular sphere's credo of accessibility, were far more concerned with the feelings of players and listeners than with any concept of artistic originality or integrity. And for some players, the presence of a familiar melody was enough to make a musical experience worthwhile.

Dance music, the second large category of piano composition, stressed rhythm over melody. Each popular dance had its own tempo, meter, and characteristic way of moving. As in later times, the advent of new dances sometimes signaled important social changes: the rise of an ethnic group, for example, or a shift in the relationship between the sexes. If the new dance caught on, money could be made by tapping its popularity, as happened with the polka. A dance originating among Bohemian peasants, the polka is said to have arrived in Vienna from Prague in 1835, Paris in 1840, and London in 1844, creating a stir wherever it appeared, perhaps because of the novel hop it introduced into social dancing.[18] The dance was introduced to America in May 1844 on a New York theater stage and for a time enjoyed considerable vogue. There was, however, some resistance. In 1845, the New York lawyer and music lover George Templeton Strong reported with sour disapproval his first encounter with the polka at a fashionable ball. "It's a kind of insane Tartar jig," he wrote, "performed to disagreeable music

This political cartoon capitalizes on the advent of the polka in 1844 to comment on the prospects of Democratic presidential candidate James K. Polk, who won election later that year.

of an uncivilized character." Strong complained that he had lost sleep that night because of one polka tune that had lodged in his brain. Haunting him "like an evil spirit," the tune "came jerking and creaking into my head whenever I began to subside into a doze."[19] But for every polkaphobe like Strong, there seem to have been many more who loved the dance. One reason Stephen Foster's bumptious *Oh! Susanna* (1848) caught the spirit of its time so well is that it borrowed the still-novel and fresh polka rhythm. The *Board of Trade Catalogue* reports that some 3,600 different polkas were published between the mid-1840s and 1870.

How did the sheet-music trade package the polka for parlor consumption? The main strategy was to give fanciful titles to pieces, in the hope of turning routine musical material into something picturesque. Only ten of the catalogue's 3,600 polkas are called simply *Polka*. Many more bear headings like *Polka artistique, Polka brilliante, Polka de concert, Polka di bravura, Polka fantastique, Polka gracieuse, Polka militaire,* and *Polka sentimentale,* suggesting either that the use of foreign languages—especially French— would attract refined customers or that the trade was working to teach refinement to provincial Americans. Female names abound among the titles, from Ada to Zenobia, with nine different titles referring to Jenny Lind. The supposed feminine floral fetish is reflected in the polka's celebration of every conceivable blossom, especially the rose. Long lists of polkas named after precious metals and jewels could also be made, not to mention birds, places, moods, and experiences of romantic love; now and then, titles with industrial or masculine associations crop up, such as the *American Petroleum Polka,* the *Ninety-seventh Regiment Polka,* and *Uncle Tom's Polka.* All these titles (and perhaps their title-page designs) were intended to catch the attention of the prospective buyer.

It is not easy to find *musical* grounds for calling a piano dance piece *Griselda Polka* rather than *American Petroleum Polka.* But nineteenth-century American parlor culture was not much concerned with issues of art or musical substance. Publishers were anxious above all to sell their products. With the help of the piano industry, they tailored a growing repertory of piano sheet music for what they took to be the taste of mostly female amateur pianists to play in the parlor. Yet for all the piano's prominence, it was merely an adjunct to the singing voice, the favorite home instrument of all. For in the nineteenth century, as in the days of Alexander Reinagle, the heart of the sheet-music trade lay in the solo song with keyboard accompaniment. And, from early in the century through the Civil War, songs written and published for parlor performance provide insight into the way Americans viewed themselves.

13

From Ramparts to Romance

Parlor Songs, 1800–1865

ON THE EVENING of September 13, 1814, Washington lawyer Francis Scott Key was onboard ship during a naval battle. Two years earlier, the United States had declared war on Great Britain, chiefly over trade and maritime disputes; in August 1814, British troops had invaded Washington, setting fire to the Capitol building and the White House; and now the British fleet was bombarding Fort McHenry, which guarded the city of Baltimore. Called to the scene to negotiate the release of a friend captured by the British, Key later recalled the moment when the firing suddenly stopped. He spent the rest of that night pacing the deck in suspense, unsure whether the fort had surrendered or the British had abandoned their attack. Finally, "in the dawn's early light," he saw the American flag, still flying over the fort.

Key wrote a poem about the experience. A week after the battle, his verses were published in a Baltimore newspaper as "Defence of Fort M'Henry." The second stanza of what is now known as *The Star-Spangled Banner* captures a mix of physical detail, threat, and triumph:

> On the shore, dimly seen through the mists of the deep,
>> Where the foe's haughty host in dread silence reposes,
> What is that which the breeze o'er the towering steep,
>> As it fitfully blows, half conceals, half discloses?
>>> Now it catches the gleam of the morning's first beam,
>>> In full glory reflected now shines on the stream—
>>>> 'Tis the star-spangled banner, O! long may it wave
>>>> O'er the land of the free, and the home of the brave.

As the national anthem (since 1931), this song now carries a ritual status that complicates any attempt to view it objectively, though that status has not forestalled criticism. Some have questioned the truth of the phrase "the

240

land of the free"; some have complained that the melody's wide range makes it hard to sing; and composer-performer Laurie Anderson has invited Americans to ponder what it means to have a national anthem that asks so many questions. But *The Star-Spangled Banner* did not begin life as a national anthem. First of all, it was a response to an event, appearing in a newspaper, then on a broadside, then in sheet music. Like most songs of its kind, it borrowed a familiar tune, this one from an English drinking song. John Stafford Smith's *To Anacreon in Heaven*, composed in the 1770s for a London men's club, tells of an ancient Greek poet known for his verse in praise of the muses, wine, and love. Key's use of "Anacreontic" meter reflects the shared heritage of language and culture that linked the United States to Great Britain. On that level, his borrowing was no political act but simply the use of an artistic device lying close at hand.

Like Reinagle's *America, Commerce, and Freedom*, *The Star-Spangled Banner* was written to celebrate the virtues of the United States and to enlist others in that celebration. Key's subject is the American flag's symbolic force. His poem dramatizes that force by putting the flag at the center of a battle—a real-life peril that must be overcome. The foe fires off rockets and bombs, but the defenders hold firm, and the flag waves on. The poet's point of view gives the scene immediacy. He writes as if his readers were there, standing at his elbow and sharing his anxiety. In the dark, no one onboard can tell why the fighting stopped. Not until the sky begins to lighten is the answer known. Then comes the poet's rush of patriotic feeling: victory has been won by determined fighting and superior virtue. As Key proclaims in his fourth stanza: "Then conquer we must when our cause it is just, / And this be our motto—'In God is our trust!' "

Key's poem embodies a patriotic state of mind into which singers are invited to step. The Americans in the song have thrown off the yoke of monarchy and are now defending themselves against further oppression by a foreign king. As people of a nation dedicated to freedom, citizens can translate into music their belief in that ideal. Knowing the cost at which personal freedom has been purchased, Americans—free individuals all—stand ready to unite for what is right, even if war is the outcome. And that image then becomes part of the nation's living mythology. Approached this way, a patriotic song is a hymn addressed not to God, though God's blessing is invoked, but to each other, as co-holders of a collective ideal of nationhood.

We are likely to associate *The Star-Spangled Banner* with massed crowds and public occasions, but its appearance in sheet-music form by November 1814 reveals a parlor-song lineage. Patriotic songs were one of several genres that found their way into the home circle, where, among other subjects, romantic love was also being explored. Indeed, one noteworthy group of early nineteenth-century American songs is centered on an age-old mythic view of love. Harking back to the Middle Ages, when love between knights and ladies was ruled by an explicit, courtly code, songwriters in the British Isles and America—for these songs belonged to an international tradition—surrounded courtship with an aura of archaic romance.

Songs based on the lore of medieval chivalry began to appear early in the 1800s and increased in number through the next two decades.[1] Their vogue was largely due to British writers—especially Sir Walter Scott, whose medieval romances (such as *Ivanhoe*) and imitations of old ballads kindled a fascination for what seemed a picturesque way of life. Composers working in this country set texts by Scott and others that center on courtship in the days of yore, sometimes with sheet-music covers picturing medieval scenes. For example, Benjamin Carr, an English-born composer, organist, and publisher who settled in Philadelphia, brought out in 1813 a setting of a text by Scott about Allen-a-dale, a minstrel usually linked to Robin Hood and the 1300s. ("Minstrel" here means the class of medieval entertainer from which the blackface variety took its name.) The text reads in part:

> Allen-a-dale to his wooing is come;
> The mother, she asked of his household and home;
> "Though the castle of Richmond stand fair on the hill,
> My hall," quoth bold Allen, "shows gallanter still;
> 'Tis the blue vault of heaven, with its crescent so pale,
> And with all its bright spangles!" said Allen-a-dale.[2]

The mythic layers here include a scene from folklore, set in the deep past and using an elevated style of diction, and a high-flown dismissal of a parent's practical question. (As an artist, Allen implies, he is not concerned with such mundane matters as the ownership of property.) Carr's music features a tuneful melody in 6/8 time that seeks to narrow the gulf dividing this song from the lives actually lived by Americans who were expected to buy it.

Composers of the next generation found other ways to set texts of chivalric courtship to music. John Hill Hewitt, born in this country in 1800 to a family of immigrant musicians, took an unusual approach in *The Minstrel's Return'd from the War* (composed 1825 in Greenville, S.C.; published around 1833 in New York). Choosing as his central character a minstrel-knight of medieval times, Hewitt wrote a text that seems inspired by Scott's telling of the crusades.[3]

> The minstrel's returned from the war,
> With spirits as buoyant as air;
> And thus on his tuneful guitar,
> He sings in the bower of his fair.
> The noise of the battle is over,
> The bugle no more calls to arms,

　　A soldier no more but a lover,
　　I kneel to the power of thy charms!

Hewitt's music begins like a march, in 4/4 time and with a melody more declamatory than supple. The music suggests that even while strumming out tender love songs, the knight cannot shake the memory of war. Although the melody eventually turns serenade-like, the march motif proves prophetic. In the fourth stanza, summoned by the sound of the bugle, the song's hero lies mortally wounded on the battlefield.

　　By the mid-1830s, however, Hewitt and other Anglo-American songwriters were matching another kind of music to the imagery of archaic romance: an Anglo-Italian style akin to Henry R. Bishop's in *Home, Sweet Home.* Models were widely available in sheet-music form, not only from English contemporaries but in songs by Italian opera composers, which were being sung onstage, published for parlor performers, and heard in instrumental versions. Italian opera brought to Anglo-American song a new source of grace and intensity, as well as a tone of accessible elevation. The gently arched shape of its melodies lent itself well to even vocal production as well as turns, trills, and other kinds of ornamentation. One example of a song that fuses historical imagery with Italianate melody is Hewitt's *The Bridesmaid* (1836), in which the heroine watches anxiously for her knight to appear. Her description of his arrival is full of archaic images:

　　Be still—be still, my throbbing breast,
　　I hear the bugle sounding;
　　I see a warrior's snowy crest—
　　A war steed proudly bounding.
　　He comes—I know his gallant mien,
　　His helmet, sword and spear;
　　I know him by his doublet green
　　My own brave Cavalier!
　　True to his word at eventide,
　　He's come to claim me as his bride.[4]

As she awaits her beloved, she sings in the rounded, arching phrases of Italianate melody.

　　Granting that courtship is a time of heightened feelings, readers may still wonder why songs featuring brave knights and protected damsels appealed to Americans. The United States, after all, was a democracy, not a society of orders in which the many labored for the comfort and pleasure of the few. And when Andrew Jackson—champion of the common people—was elected president in 1828, many believed that what remained of earlier aristocratic privilege would be swept away. Yet the chivalric courtship song persisted through the Jacksonian era and beyond. Why would Americans want to sing songs based on a myth that contradicted the ideals and realities of everyday life?

The question points to an element common to the two eras: both courtly love and nineteenth-century courtship were based on separation of the sexes. Within courtly love's idealized realm, men and women acted as virtually different species, each governed by its own rules. In fact, chivalric courtship songs grew popular in America at a time when business was disengaging from home life. As people moved from farms into cities, and as urban homes were turned into female domains, men and women found themselves more and more separated. The distancing of men from women and the redefining of roles made an impact on the language and decorum of romance. It now became possible to imagine men as gladiators who jousted in the public arena by day, then returned to the "bowers," where they sang and were sung to. (Mark Twain once ironically counseled young men that they must seek permission before saving a young lady from a fire. An imperiled damsel might be expected to fling herself into any rescuer's arms first and ask questions later, but if she had read the etiquette books, she would certainly want to know her savior's social pedigree. According to Twain, he could set her worries to rest by addressing her as follows: "Although through the fiat of a cruel fate, I have been debarred the gracious privilege of your acquaintance, permit me, Miss [here insert name, if known], the inestimable honor of offering you the aid of a true and loyal arm against the fiery doom which now o'ershadows you with its crimson wing. [This form to be memorized, and practiced in private.]")[5]

As the sheet-music business reached into more middle-class homes, the chivalric courtship song faded, though not without leaving its mark. As early as the 1820s, songwriters had begun adapting the courtship song for democratic customers, taking separation, not medieval romance, as their main subject. Male lovers and their ladies might be separated by shyness (love might be undeclared), the social code, physical distance (journeys often sparked love songs), and even death, the ultimate separation. Almost all of these songs take a man's point of view, and they dwell on the emotional fallout of separation. Elevated speech, Italianate melody, and an image of pure, nonfleshly love became standard ways to express a yearning for the beloved in song, even while knights, steeds, banners, castles, and other medieval trappings were discarded. This new kind of courtship song, however, does *not* show lovers coming together, touching (except perhaps for a formal handshake), enjoying each other's company in free conversation or banter, or developing anything like a friendship, let alone an erotic attachment. Even when physically together, they view each other as if through a screen that holds them always apart.

Stephen Foster was a leading American master of the translated courtly love song. His first published composition (1844), set to a poem by George Pope Morris, provides a good example of the type:

> Open thy lattice, love listen to me!
> The cool balmy breeze is abroad on the sea!
> The moon like a queen, roams her realms of blue,
> And the stars keep their vigils in heaven for you.
> Ere morn's gushing light tips the hills with its ray,
> Away o'er the waters away and away!
> Then open thy lattice, love listen to me!
> While the moon's in the sky and the breeze on the sea!

Foster's song is a serenade, a genre that originated in the Middle Ages.[6] The melody traces a graceful curve in 6/8 time, and the rhythm, as in some Italian arias, invites the singer to be flexible. Marked "delicatamente," the accompaniment suggests the strumming of a guitar. In the poem, although the physical distance between the lovers may be small, society's code of conduct keeps them apart: the man camps at the woman's window while she stays protected inside. And that tension feeds the singer's romantic fantasy. He pictures a seaside setting with the two lovers sailing off into the sunrise. He also fancies that nature joins him in celebrating his beloved's charms, the stars keeping vigil just for her. The *bel canto* setting for Morris's imagery suggests that Foster entered the songwriting trade with a grasp of the earlier courtship song's conventions, which he then used in his own ways.

In 1851, Foster set a text by Charles G. Eastman sung by a suitor enduring another kind of separation. In *Sweetly She Sleeps, My Alice Fair*, the poet hovers over the woman he loves while she slumbers, unaware of his presence. Although the separation here could be ended by a word, a gentle nudge, or even a discreet clearing of the throat, there is no sign that the singer considers waking the fair Alice. He seems content to gaze in admiration, noting how her face meets the pillow and her hair seems to glow as if lit by sunshine; his only action in the whole song is to warn the wind and the birds not to disturb her. Foster's music supports the song's static image. The melodic structure, with two lines per section, circles back to repeat the beginning (**aabcaa**). The first, third, ninth, and eleventh lines of the twelve-line stanza are sung over the same bass note, a repeated B-flat; and the **a** sections are accompanied by the continuous movement of quiet block chords, as in a lullaby. Yearning in this song is not for change but for fixity, with Alice's admirer trying to preserve as long as possible the picture of her lying at rest, à la Sleeping Beauty.

One of Foster's most enduring songs of courtship, *Jeanie with the Light Brown Hair*, deals with permanent separation: Jeanie, "the lost one that comes not again," has either gone away for good or died. In the text, which

Cover art such as the winsome portrait on Stephen Foster's *Jeanie with the Light Brown Hair* (1851), rare before the 1830s, was by mid-century a regular feature of sheet music.

Foster himself wrote, the bereft lover is left with only recollections of the look, the grace, and the sound of Jeanie to sustain him.

> I dream of Jeanie with the light brown hair,
> Borne, like a vapor, on the summer air;
> I see her tripping where the bright streams play,
> Happy as the daisies that dance on her way.
> Many were the wild notes her merry voice would pour.
> Many were the blithe birds that warbled them o'er:
> Oh! I dream of Jeanie with the light brown hair,
> Floating, like a vapor, on the soft summer air.

In later stanzas, the lover recalls Jeanie's smile, her songs again, and her fondness for flowers, describing her as if she were more sprite than woman. But he reports nothing that Jeanie ever said or thought, and her character in the song remains that of a wraith-like spirit who inspires dreamy reveries. Jeanie trips through meadows, singing, dancing, and plaiting flowers, apparently self-absorbed and all but oblivious to her suitor's admiring presence.

Yet Foster's music makes this insubstantial scenario work. The first section (lines one and two of the text) is strong enough to bear plenty of repetition. And the composer takes advantage of it, using a familiar principle of musical form: statement, restatement, contrast, and return, or **aaba**. (The **a** theme is also heard in the piano introduction.) In writing this well-balanced melody, Foster drew not on the Italian style but on Irish melody of the kind popularized by poet Thomas Moore in several volumes of Irish song published in both the British Isles and America. The tune begins relatively high in the singer's range, the elevation and sustained note on "I *dream*" capturing in one stroke the sense of floating in fantasy that the song portrays. (The sensitive male protagonist is ready to be carried on a tide of remembrance.) The accompaniment's repeated F-major chord in quarter notes acts as a rhythmic foil for the vocal line, which, after pausing briefly on "dream," pushes ahead in eighth notes, then falls into phase with the piano on "light brown hair." It would be hard to find a better match of music and words than Foster's next gesture, in which the upward leap on "vapor" encourages the singer to produce a lighter-than-air sound. The gesture reinforces the dreaming mode of the first line, revealing the song to be a gentle, subli-mated reverie of a soul almost purged of passion. Its bold melodic reach—the high F stands a sixth above the previous note—recalls Thomas Moore's *The Last Rose of Summer* and its style of Irish melody, where flights of feel-ing and imagination are highlighted by unexpected leaps that are then filled in by falling movement, mostly stepwise. Foster's "borne like a *vapor*" closely resembles Moore's " 'Tis the last *rose* of summer," the key word given out on the high note and seeming to linger even after the line moves on.

The bold, complementary melodic curves and flexible declamation of *Jeanie*'s first four bars show a plasticity that stands at the center of Foster's art. But the rhythm and harmony also contribute to the overall effect. The declamation's pushing ahead of then synchronizing with the repeated chord's quarter-note rhythm in the first two measures has already been noted. By starting line two of the text on the downbeat, Foster gives "borne" the emphasis due the song's first active verb—an emphasis he supports with the first chord change since the voice entered. That chord change starts a harmonic process that moves away from the tonic, just as the summer air carries the dream of Jeanie. "Vapor" is sung to a B-flat (subdominant) chord, and the phrase-ending melodic cadence ("on the summer air"), enlivened by the song's first dotted-eighth-and-sixteenth figure, is sung to harmonies that change every beat. Thus, in just four bars of singing, Foster has taken a fa-miliar premise—a suitor dreaming of his absent lover—and set it to music so strong and distinctive that both performers and listeners are eager to learn what will happen next.

In their role as makers of myth, songwriters cultivate the ability to set a scene quickly. But to fulfill that promise, they must also sustain interest through the rest of the song. In *Jeanie*, for example, each **a** section begins with the same two-bar statement, then diverges from it. And the **b** section creates a blossoming effect, beginning softly and leading to a brief vocal ca-denza in which the singer ascends to the register of "I dream" and the main melody's return. Most of the song is built from such precisely balanced ele-ments and aptly shaped phrases that it seems to impose a mood of restraint on the performers. But the cadenza offers the singer a chance for a bit of vo-cal freedom in the Italian manner.

OTHER SONGS OF SEPARATION AND YEARNING

To judge by their songs, Americans of the 1800s were keenly aware of be-ing removed from things they wanted. The song of yearning that flourished then was largely a creation of the Irish poet Thomas Moore, who, as we have seen, was one of Foster's chief models. Moore once laid out his fa-vorite subject in a four-stanza lyric. The first stanza is especially worth quoting because it crystallizes an attitude that many Americans took to be artistic, and its spirit lies behind any number of beloved nineteenth-century songs:

> My harp has one unchanging theme,
>   One strain that still comes o'er
> Its languid chord, as 'twere a dream
>   Of joy that's now no more.

The idea of "joy that's now no more" proved to be hugely popular: here was a myth into which anyone could step, for all had experienced disappointment and unrealized hopes. Moore's example helped songwriters to become connoisseurs of regret.[7]

While later songs about triumphs of technology—steam engines, bicycles, balloons, and automobiles—praise the advantages of progress, many pre–Civil War songs tend to prefer the past. Stephen Foster's *The Voice of By Gone Days* (1850), for example, announces that then was better than now and claims the sound of that older voice as a tonic for the "weary hearted":

> Youthful fancy then returns,
> Childish hope the bosom burns,
> Joy, that manhood coldly spurns,
> Then flows in memory's sweet refrain.

Soon the singer's belief is explained: his beloved has died—or rather, as Foster euphemistically puts it, he is haunted by the memory of a "fair and gentle being of my early love" who, "beloved of angels bright," has gone to join "their bless'd and happy train."

Poets and songwriters searched for subjects that would trigger yearning, and not all the subjects they found were as general as Moore's lost joy or Foster's retreat into the past. One favorite device was to focus memory on an inanimate object. In 1818, Samuel Woodworth published a poem called "The Bucket" that was later sung to more than one tune of the same meter. In the 1840s, it was linked with *Araby's Daughter*, a melody by English composer George Kiallmark, and that connection proved enduring. Kiallmark's tune is straightforward and dance-like, well suited to the structure of Woodworth's poem, whose words and syllables fit it neatly. Rather than recounting a vague "dream" in the manner of Moore and Foster, the text of *The Old Oaken Bucket* recalls a past way of life:

> How dear to my heart are the scenes of my childhood,
>   When fond recollection presents them to view!
> The orchard, the meadow, the deep-tangled wild-wood,
>   And every loved spot which my infancy knew!

> The wide-spreading pond and the mill that stood by it,
>   The bridge, and the rock where the cataract fell,
> The cot[cottage] of my father, the dairy-house nigh it,
>   And e'en the rude bucket that hung in the well—
> The old oaken bucket, the iron-bound bucket,
> The moss-covered bucket which hung in the well.[8]

By setting the bucket in a specific landscape, Woodworth offers a glimpse of a farm boy's youth, complete with a reference to physical labor. In the second stanza, the text recalls the boy's "exquisite pleasure" when, fresh from strenuous work in the fields, he quenched his thirst by drinking cool water from the bucket. This memory spurs him in the last stanza to declare a preference for the homely, moss-covered bucket over the civilized elegance of a "full blushing goblet." The poem suggests that Woodworth himself knew the satisfaction that a long-awaited drink can bring a thirsty worker.[9]

A less convincing song about an object is Henry Russell's *Woodman, Spare That Tree* (1837), set to a text by George Pope Morris. The English-born Russell was both a songwriter and a public performer of his songs. He perfected his art in the United States, where he spent part of the 1830s and 40s. His claim to have studied in Europe with Rossini and Bellini has been questioned,[10] but he did master Italian *bel canto* song and seems to have developed a commanding presence as a ballad singer. An accomplished keyboard player, Russell accompanied his singing on a small upright piano, which allowed him to face the audience and deliver his songs with dramatic nuance and directness. In his autobiography, he stresses the importance of clear diction, and his reputation was that of a performer whose words could always be understood. Russell named as his main inspiration not another musician but an orator, the statesman Henry Clay. Moved by Clay's power to hold an 1835 audience in his spell, Russell later wrote: "That speech of Henry Clay affected me to a singular extent. . . . I don't think I should be talking extravagantly, if I declare that the orator Henry Clay was the direct cause of my taking to the composition of descriptive songs."[11]

While some of Russell's songs won popularity as sheet music for parlor use, all carried the theatrical stamp of their creator, which some Americans found too flamboyant for their taste. Teacher, composer, and songwriter George Frederick Root, for example, had hardly an unkind word for anyone in his autobiography, but when he came to Russell, his tolerance wavered. Root was nineteen when he first heard Russell sing in Boston in 1839, and the younger man was impressed:

> He had a beautiful baritone voice and great command of the keyboard—played his own accompaniments, gave his concerts entirely alone, and in a year in this country made a fortune. Some of his [songs], like "The Maniac"

and "The Gambler's Wife," were exceedingly pathetic, and always made people cry when he sang them. He looked so pitiful and so sympathetic—"he
felt every word," as his listeners would think and say.

Then, however, Root discovered that Russell's sincerity was an act. "When
he retired to his dressing room," Russell "was said to have been much
amused at the grief of his weeping constituents." Root could neither accept
nor forgive such cynicism. "Good taste," he declared, "requires that the
singer should treat respectfully the emotion he excites."[12]

Root's comment is a telling one, not only about Henry Russell but about
his own moral code as a song composer. Like many of his contemporaries,
Root committed himself to serving the taste of "the people"—not the relatively few who thought themselves musically knowledgeable but the larger
mass who enjoyed music that touched their hearts. He stood ready to embrace sentimentality or any other emotional coloring that would reach such
an audience. But, as his comment on Russell shows, he felt an obligation to
respect the taste of the audience that supported him. Root detected an unhealthy sophistication in Russell's readiness to manipulate his audience's
emotions, as if from a position of superior artistic taste, and that perspective
puts Henry Russell's popular songs into focus.

Morris's poem for *Woodman, Spare That Tree* is written in the voice of a
man addressing a woodcutter who is ready to swing into action:

> Woodman spare that tree!
>   Touch not a single bough;
> In youth it shelterd me,
>   And I'll protect it now;
> 'Twas my forefather's hand
>   That placed it near his cot,
> There, woodman, let it stand,
>   Thy ax shall harm it not!

Russell directs that the song be sung "With much feeling and Expression."
After an unusually long piano introduction, the melody is cast in four sections, **aabc,** the last starting on the same note as **a** and sounding like an expansion of it. One can imagine Russell performing this song in public, his
face miming emotions during the introduction to prepare the audience for
his vocal entrance.

The threat of loss hangs over *Woodman, Spare That Tree.* The first is the
ruin of the tree itself: the prospect that an ancient, majestic living thing will
fall in an act of quick destruction. Second is that if the tree goes, the site
of family memories will cease to exist. Morris's third stanza recalls the
speaker's links with the old oak:

WOODMAN! SPARE THAT TREE!

A BALLAD

Lith.ᵈ of Endicott N.Y.

THE WORDS COPIED FROM THE   NEW YORK MIRROR, WRITTEN BY

GEORGE P. MORRIS,

BY WHOM THIS SONG IS RESPECTFULLY DEDICATED TO

BENJAMIN M. BROWN, ESQ.

THE MUSIC BY

Henry Russel.

New York, Published by FIRTH & HALL, Nᵒ 1, Franklin-Sq.

George P. Morris's melodramatic tale of a threatened oak is suggested by the cover of this 1837 song by Henry Russell, though the tree looks a bit undernourished above its trunk.

When but an idle boy / I sought its grateful shade;
In all their gushing joy / Here, too, my sisters played.
My mother kiss'd me here; / My father press'd my hand—
Forgive this foolish tear, / But let that old oak stand!

Finally, the poet gives the scene added poignancy by writing as if the tree were human: "My heart-strings round thee cling, / Close as thy bark, old friend!"

Morris's poem is not a narrative but a piece of rhetorical persuasion. Russell apparently played the scene for all it was worth, sometimes offering a spoken prologue tying the song to a real-life incident. Some editions print a long letter from Morris to Russell claiming the speaker as "a friend, who was once the expectant heir of the largest estate in America, but over whose worldly prospects a blight [had] recently come." Thus, a document included with the sheet music adds a twist to the poem's theme of threatened loss: the ex-owner of the property on which the oak stands now finds himself dependent on a woodcutter's whim. (According to Morris's letter, the woodman wanted only the $10 worth of firewood the tree contained, and a deal was quickly struck to save it.) The song's text leaves the tree's fate unresolved, and Russell used that uncertainty to create suspense in concerts. His autobiography reports that after one performance, a man in the audience rose and "in a very excited voice, called 'Was the tree spared, sir?' 'It was,' I said. 'Thank God for that,' he answered, with a sigh of relief."[13]

The theme of yearning and loss also pervades some blackface minstrel songs—*Carry Me Back to Old Virginny, Darling Nelly Gray, In the Evening by the Moonlight, My Old Kentucky Home, Old Black Joe,* and *Old Folks at Home* are a few examples. And favorite parlor songs on the same subject include *Ben Bolt; I'll Take You Home Again, Kathleen; Listen to the Mocking Bird; Lorena; Sweet Genevieve; When I Saw Sweet Nelly Home;* and *When You and I Were Young.* But patriotic songs, more light-hearted minstrel songs, and operatic numbers found their way into American parlors as well, along with religious, comic, and topical songs. Moreover, the early and middle 1800s were a time when long-standing customs came under attack. Movements took shape to abolish slavery and to reform the way Americans worshiped, their drinking habits, and the treatment of women in society. Rather than catering to sentimental impulses, some popular songs of the period urged citizens to act in the social realm.

THE HUTCHINSON FAMILY AND SONGS OF SOCIAL REFORM

The leading singers of activist songs in the pre–Civil War years were the Hutchinsons, children of Jesse and Mary Leavitt Hutchinson of Milford, New Hampshire, who began singing together for musical enjoyment and then found that they could make a career out of it. Their reform music has caught recent historians' attention, partly because it anticipates the work of such later folk protest singers as Woody Guthrie, Pete Seeger, and the young

From 1842 until sister Abby married in 1849, the Hutchinson Family singers toured the United States and Great Britain, entertaining and edifying audiences with their songs.

Bob Dylan. But the Hutchinsons should first be considered as professional entertainers. They succeeded by singing music of the day for paying audiences; it was not yet possible to make a living by singing songs about society's ills.

The Hutchinsons were inspired to enter the public arena by a concert some of them attended, given in 1840 by four members of the Rainer family. These singers had come to America in 1839, advertising themselves as the Tyrolese Minstrels and performing quartet arrangements of Swiss songs in native costume. Their tour caused a sensation. Publishers quickly brought out the Rainers' songs in sheet music, and American family groups imitated them, with the Hutchinsons as the prime example. By mid-1842, the Hutchinson Family Singers, a quartet made up of brothers Judson, John, and Asa and their thirteen-year-old sister Abby, had launched a career as a touring ensemble. Their travels, beginning in New England, took them down the Eastern Seaboard to New York, Philadelphia, and even Washington, where in 1844 they sang in the White House for President Tyler. In 1845–46, they spent a year performing in the British Isles, then returned and continued to tour the United States. The Hutchinsons' heyday ended in 1849 when Abby married and left the troupe. Various brothers continued to sing in public even as late as the 1880s, when John Hutchinson claimed to have participated in twelve thousand concerts during his career. But the family never regained the prominent place they held in American musical life during the 1840s.

Entering a field dominated by foreign musicians, the Hutchinsons stressed their American origins. Yet, especially at the start, their repertory included plenty of music by Europeans: glees (part songs) from standard tunebooks and solo songs and ballads by popular composers such as Henry Russell. As time passed, the Hutchinsons sang more music on American themes, accompanying themselves with violin, cello, and later harmonium and guitar. The combination of an unaffected stage manner and the uncultivated (but carefully rehearsed) sound of their vocal blend gave the troupe a public image of authenticity. In fact, they seemed to play themselves onstage, taking on personas that audiences found genuine for members of a small-town New Hampshire family. When a New York critic in 1843 praised their singing as "simple, sweet, and full of mountain melody," he was noticing strengths consistent with who they really were.[14]

For a polished trouper like Henry Russell, a clear line separated professional from personal behavior. For the Hutchinsons, that distinction was not so clear. In fact, the lack of firm boundaries, which accounted for much of the family's appeal, also helps to explain how they were drawn into supporting reform causes. For example, John Hutchinson took a nondrinking pledge in 1841, and from that time forward, the family made a point of staying in temperance hotels when they toured. Through the 1700s and early 1800s, the drinking of alcohol had been considered part of the American way of life. An English traveler had commented in 1819: "You cannot go into hardly any man's house without being asked to drink wine, or spirits, *even in*

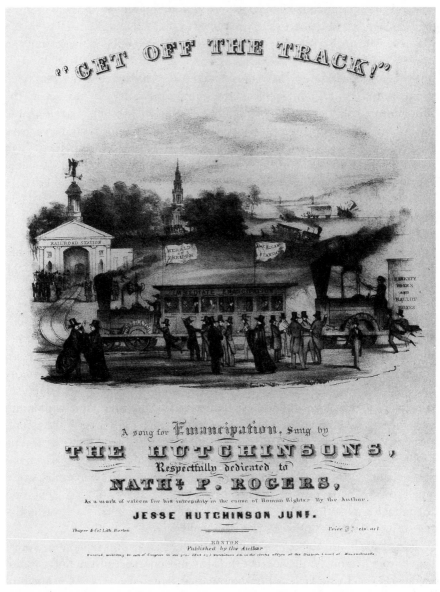

The Hutchinsons' emancipation song *Get Off the Track*, sung to the tune of the minstrel hit *Old Dan Tucker*, made a strong impression at abolitionist meetings and rallies in the North.

the morning."[15] One reason was that other drinkable liquids were not always easy to find in the early 1800s. The fouling of some rivers, ponds, and wells was starting to give water a bad name. Milk was easily available only to farmers, and tea and coffee were considered luxuries until the 1840s. But fermented or distilled liquids were widely available and cheap. One estimate puts the per capita consumption of drinking-age Americans in 1830 at nearly three times the rate measured in 1975.[16]

During the 1830s, however, more and more Americans recognized that drinking alcohol could be destructive. Connecting strong drink to poverty, immorality, lack of family responsibility, and neglect of women and children, reformers mounted an antidrinking campaign. Their campaign succeeded: by 1845, the consumption of alcohol had dropped to one-fourth of what it had been in 1830. Drawn to the cause by personal conviction, the Hutchinsons found their own niche in the temperance movement. They began early in their career to include antidrinking songs in their concerts, and a few were published in sheet-music form, helping to bring the message of sobriety into American parlors. In *King Alcohol,* they set their own verses to the folk melody *King Andrew* and harmonized it for three voices. To compare the Hutchinsons' harmonization with one that might have appeared in a tune-book by Lowell Mason or Thomas Hastings is to recognize that the two came from different musical worlds. The smooth, scientific part writing of those psalmodists would never have allowed parallel octaves and fifths between treble and bass, nor the unorthodox harmonic movement of the Hutchinsons' setting, whose sound stamps it as the product of untutored musicians.

The Hutchinson Family Singers also plunged into the fight against slavery. In the spring of 1843, they appeared at an antislavery rally in Boston's Faneuil Hall, joining with leading abolitionists: William Lloyd Garrison, Wendell Phillips, and ex-slave Frederick Douglass, who became a close friend. (John Hutchinson sang over Douglass's grave when he died in 1895.) According to one eyewitness, slavery that day found no more forceful foe than the Hutchinsons. "Speechifying, even of the better sort," he wrote, "did less to interest, purify and subdue minds, than this irresistible Anti-Slavery music."[17]

One of the group's most effective rallying cries was *Get Off the Track!,* sung to the tune of *Old Dan Tucker* and trading on that minstrel song's rough appeal. The sheet music, published in 1844, billed the piece as "A song for Emancipation." Its cover pictures a locomotive labeled Liberator ringing its Liberty Bell and pulling a car named Immediate Emancipation; the car is already packed with passengers, but more people race to jump on. In the background are two derailed trains representing proslavery forces. One can imagine Americans who shared the song's sentiments joining in with verve in their parlors—especially on the chorus, where Emmett's "Get

out de way!" shout turns into "Get off the track!" But when sung by the
Hutchinsons themselves, the song's impact could be overwhelming. An account written after the New England Anti-Slavery Convention in May 1844
describes one such performance:

> And when they came to that chorus-cry, that gives name to the song, when
> they cried to the heedless pro-slavery multitude that were stupidly lingering
> on the track, and the engine "Liberator" coming down hard upon them, un-
> der full steam and all speed, the Liberty Bell loud ringing, and they standing
> like deaf men right in its whirlwind path, the way they cried "Get off the
> track," in defiance of all time and rule, was magnificent and sublime. They
> forgot their harmony, and shouted one after another, or all in confused out-
> cry, like an alarmed multitude of spectators, about to witness a terrible cata-
> strophe. . . . It was the cry of the people, into which their over-wrought and
> illimitable music had *degenerated*,—and it was glorious to witness them
> alighting down again from their wild flight into the current of song, like so
> many swans upon the river from which they had soared, a moment, wildly,
> into the air. The multitude who heard them will bear me witness, that they
> had transcended the very province of mere music.[18]

These words dramatize a key fact about the Hutchinsons: although they
published a number of original songs, their talent lay more in performance
than composition. When the Hutchinsons faced an audience, they knew
how to involve spectators in their music and ideas—to make them believe
in the emotional truth of what they were hearing. Their personal charisma,
however, did not survive translation to the printed page. None of the compositions bearing their name found their way into anthologies of popular
song that appeared in the late nineteenth and early twentieth centuries. For
all the fame they enjoyed, and their willingness to take controversial public
stands, the Hutchinsons themselves outlived their songs.

SONGS OF THE CIVIL WAR

When war erupted in 1861 between the Northern and Southern states,
the sheet-music industry responded with vigor. The songs of the Civil War,
fueled by patriotic feelings and commerce, brought together in a new cause
many of the elements discussed so far in this chapter: myth making, sentimentality, yearning, reform, and loss.

The Civil War was the seminal event of nineteenth-century American
history, a critique of the country's true nature as a political structure. For the
United States owes its birth more to the grievances of individual colonies
than to any shared sense of nationhood. In 1788, thanks to compromises on
slavery and the distribution of power, the original thirteen states managed to

agree to a federal constitution. From that time forward, states or regions repeatedly questioned the federal government's right to dictate policy. As the West was settled, arguments over slavery intensified, leading to more compromises. Through the 1840s, Congress admitted free and slave states in roughly equal numbers. But by mid-century, antislavery sentiment was strong in the North, and so was the South's fear that the growing Northern population and political strength would destroy the balance of power between regions. Common ground between North and South seemed to shrink during the 1850s. By the decade's end, national debate was dominated by hard-liners eager to provoke a crisis.

In November 1860, Abraham Lincoln was elected president. In December, South Carolina seceded from the Union, and by February 1861 it had been joined by six more slave states—Florida, Georgia, Alabama, Mississippi, Louisiana, and Texas—which declared themselves the Confederate States of America. During his first days in office, Lincoln sought conciliation. The seceded states, however, acted like a foreign power, taking over customs houses, arsenals, and federal forts in their region. In April 1861, when the federal government in Washington tried to supply Fort Sumter, near Charleston, South Carolina, state troops bombarded the fort and forced it to surrender. Declaring that insurrection had occurred, Lincoln sent out a call for troops to suppress it. In response, Virginia left the Union, followed by Arkansas, Tennessee, and North Carolina.

The war was on. By the time it ended in April 1865, more than 600,000 men had been killed and a million more wounded, the slaves were free, and the Union forces had prevailed. The bravery and resourcefulness of the Southern army kept the final outcome in doubt for more than three years, despite the North's superior numbers and industrial capacity. The South, involved in a "War Between the States," battled to win independence, whereas the North, engaged in a "War of Rebellion," sought the South's unconditional surrender. In the end, the Civil War proved to be the "War of National Unification" that Lincoln had pursued. Once the shooting stopped, a process began that has proved no simpler than resolving differences between North and South: defining citizenship so that more than 4 million ex-slaves and their descendants, marked by ethnicity and culture as different from whites, could find independent, politically equal places in American life.

The issues at stake in the Civil War—nationhood itself and the rights of citizenship—gave epic stature to its events. Heroes and villains emerged: Abraham Lincoln, Jefferson Davis, Ulysses S. Grant, William Tecumseh Sherman, Robert E. Lee, and "Stonewall" Jackson. The conflict, the biggest shooting war ever waged on American soil, was fought in the full glare of publicity, which meant that its course could be followed by citizens at home. Daily newspapers carried dispatches from the front; photographs showed war scenes more realistic than the lithographs and engravings that had illustrated earlier wars. Finally, the Civil War unleashed destruction on an unprecedented scale. Both sides believed they were fighting for an American cause, but with totally different ideas of what "American" meant. Each side sought to have its own definition prevail, by killing those who disagreed.[19]

Song provided a way for North and South to define their ideals. On April 19, 1861, two days after Virginia left the Union, a prosecessionist mob in Baltimore attacked a regiment of Union troops from Massachusetts, and in the fighting that followed lives were lost on both sides. The incident inspired one of the first enduring songs of the war. James Ryder Randall, a young professor of English and native Baltimorean, wrote the words just after the attack:

> The despot's heel is on thy shore,
>> Maryland!
> His torch is at thy temple door,
>> Maryland!
> Avenge the patriotic gore
> That flecked the streets of Baltimore,
> And be the battle-queen of yore,
>> Maryland! My Maryland!

Randall's poem, immediately published in newspapers, calls on the memory of past state heroes as away of urging fellow Marylanders to resist federal tyranny. His appeal is cast in elevated language familiar from the earlier courtship song, with some biblical diction mixed in:

> For life and death, for woe and weal,
> Thy peerless chivalry reveal,
> And gird thy beauteous limbs with steel,
>> Maryland! My Maryland![20]

In October 1861, Randall's words appeared in a sheet-music version, set to the German Christmas song *O Tannenbaum*, and the link between text and tune held from that time on.

Maryland, My Maryland is less patriotic than chauvinistic. Patriotic expressions reflect a love of country and concern for its well-being, but Randall's song is short on love and long on vengeance. Expressing total allegiance to one side and implacable hatred of the other, it calls fellow countrymen names—"tyrants," "vandals," "Northern scum"—that undercut the two sides' common ground. Its tone, found in both Northern and Southern songs, surely helped to create an emotional climate in which merciless war could be waged.

Maryland, My Maryland also suggests that the experience of the war was shot through with complexities and ambiguities. For Maryland was a border state, neither clearly Northern nor Southern in character but separating the national capital from the rest of the North. In 1861, its governor was pro-Union and its legislature prosecessionist. In the end, Maryland stayed loyal to the Union. But the obvious conflict behind its decision was repeated in many other border states and communities, sometimes turning neighbors and even members of the same family into adversaries. The middle ground between "Yankee Land" in the far North and "Secession Land" in the deep South bred mixed loyalties; many young men from the North headed south to join the Confederate army, and many from the South went north to join the Union forces (some Plains Indian tribes sent men to both sides).[21]

A huge gap opened between the war's idealistic slogans and the human suffering it caused. In May 1864, the Northern army under Grant and the Confederates under Lee had just finished a fierce, bloody battle in Virginia, and one Union nurse wrote to another:

No words can express the horrible confusion of this place. . . . The wounded arrive . . . two, three days on the way, plunged in quagmires, jolted over [rutted roads], without food, fainting, starving, filthy; frightfully wounded, arms gone to the shoulder, horrible wounds in face and head. I would rather a thousand times have a friend killed on the field than suffer in this way. . . . There is no . . . use in trying to tell you the story. I can scarcely bear to think of it.

Elsewhere in the same letter, however, she wrote in a very different vein.

Yesterday a squad of rebel officers was marched on board a boat lying by ours . . . strong, well-fed, iron looking men, all of them. There's no "give in" in such . . . men as these. Our soldiers from the front say the rebels stand—stand—in solid masses, giving and taking tremendous blows and never being shoved an inch. It is magnificent![22]

This disjunction is especially striking because the writer seems unaware of it. For her, the cause of war remained an exalted one even after she had experienced its human results, touching and binding wounds and tending the maimed and dying with her own hands.

Just as this army nurse could respond to a noble military ideal *and* feel revulsion for the suffering caused by its pursuit, war songs are much more likely to celebrate or grieve than to comment. Conventions for dealing in song with both war's glory and its pain were already well established. The music trade was set up to produce and sell songs of patriotic or chauvinistic stripe, like *Maryland, My Maryland,* and songwriters also discovered that they could sentimentalize grief over wounded and dead soldiers as they had missing lovers or the longing for home. No change in musical or expressive style was required to satisfy the public's appetite for war songs.

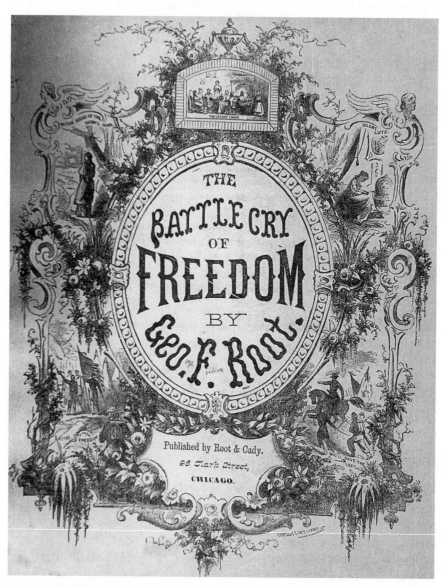

George F. Root wrote both words and music to *The Battle Cry of Freedom* (Chicago, 1862), whose cover offers a variety of wartime vignettes while also plugging other Root and Cady Civil War hits.

Perhaps the most lasting of all Union contributions, the *Battle-Hymn of the Republic*, with words by Julia Ward Howe, unself-consciously combines moral totalism and musical catchiness. Written in a biblically inflected voice, Howe's verses celebrate a cause born of righteousness. It is glorious, she preaches, to fall in step beside an omnipotent God, marching into battle at the head of a virtuous (Northern) army. As with *Maryland, My Maryland*, vengeance is the subject, but here the agent is divine, not human. Howe's poem, which celebrates the birth and sacrifice of Jesus while also conveying the steely, unforgiving tone of Old Testament prophecy, was first published in January 1862. A few months later, these words, with the "Glory, Hallelujah" refrain added, were published in sheet-music form, sung to a Methodist hymn tune of the late 1850s.[23] The music's character and the added refrain take the edge off the harsh message of Howe's words. To be sure, the tread of repeated quarter notes in the accompaniment shows that God's marchers mean business; but the cry of joy at the end of each stanza emphasizes camaraderie and high spirits over revenge. Like many enduring American songs, this one was made by several hands—poet, composer, arranger—some of them unknown.

More is known about the origins of *The Battle Cry of Freedom* (1862), by George F. Root, whose Union songs helped Root and Cady of Chicago, his brother's publishing firm, become successful. "When anything happened that could be voiced in a song," Root later recalled, "I wrote what I thought would then express the emotions of the soldiers or the people." One advertisement called these songs "munitions of war." Root explained: "If I could not shoulder a musket in defense of my country, I could serve her in this way."[24] *The Battle Cry of Freedom*, a recruiting song for the Union army, offered a potent mix of soul-stirring ingredients: the flag, the collective cheer, the notion of fighting for a high ideal, the blunt statement of the Union's goal in less than ten words ("Down with the traitor! / Up with the Star!"), and a refrain that, like "Glory, Hallelujah," could easily be learned on the spot.

The Battle Cry of Freedom moves in a way similar to *The Battle-Hymn of the Republic*, with repeated quarter notes in the accompaniment measuring out the tread of soldiers' marching feet. But Root's piece is musically richer, with three distinctive, memorable ideas: "Yes, we'll rally round the flag," "Shouting the battle cry of Freedom," and in the refrain, "The Union forever, / Hurrah, boys, hurrah!" Every musical phrase in the song is a statement or variant of one of the three, so melodic energy stays at a high level throughout. Dotted rhythms on weak beats tie the three melodic phrases together; and the syncopation in the chorus on the song's highest pitch (G) casts the word "forever" into relief with a climactic jolt. When these musical details, supported by harmony that goes beyond Root's usual "land of tonic, dominant, and subdominant," are linked to the resonant phrases in the text, there is little mystery why *The Battle Cry of Freedom* became one of the

Union's most popular martial songs. It was also taken over by the Confederates and adapted for their use.

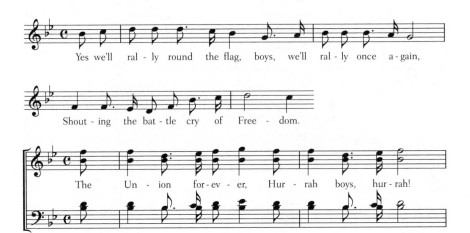

Yes we'll ral - ly round the flag, boys, we'll ral - ly once a - gain,

Shout - ing the bat - tle cry of Free - dom.

The Un - ion for - ev - er, Hur - rah boys, hur - rah!

The signature song of the Confederacy and the postwar South also originated in the North. *Dixie*, composed by Ohio-born minstrel Dan Emmett
and introduced on a New York stage in 1859, found its way the following
year to New Orleans, where it created a sensation.[25] Its text appeared immediately in broadsides, and a sheet-music version was issued there with no
attribution to Emmett. A year before the Civil War broke out, then, *Dixie*
had already caught on with the public as a favorite Southern song in a key
Southern city. Here are the first stanza and refrain as they appeared in the
original sheet music:

> I wish I was in de land ob cotton,
> Old times dar am not forgotten,
>   Look away! Look away! Look away! Dixie Land.
> In Dixie Land whar I was born in,
> Early on one frosty mornin,
>   Look away! Look away! Look away! Dixie Land.
>
>   Dan I wish I was in Dixie,
>   Hooray! Hooray!
>   In Dixie Land, I'll take my stand,
>   To lib an die in Dixie.
>   Away, Away, Away down south in Dixie,
>   Away, Away, Away down south in Dixie.[26]

What made *Dixie* a Southern favorite? Its Northern origin may make it
seem a strange choice. We might also wonder why white people fighting
to preserve slavery would express their solidarity in the comic dialect of a

minstrel-show slave. And why would a song lacking the standard paraphernalia of patriotism or chauvinism—no war, no enemy, no revenge, no Southern cause—command such allegiance? While these questions may not yield definite answers, Emmett's song seems to have offered a myth of the South so inviting that Southerners in vast numbers stepped immediately into it. The first winning element in the myth is the song's title, which popularized an unforgettable colloquial nickname for the whole region, though Emmett did not invent the name. It has been suggested that "Dixie" originated among show people in the North as a white person's nickname for blacks, then gradually came to signify the whole South.[27]

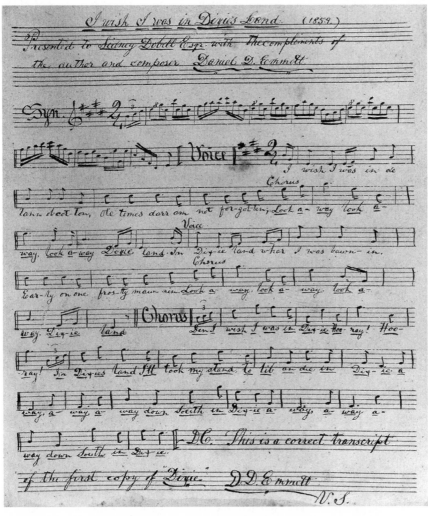

This manuscript of Daniel Emmett preserves *Dixie* (1859) in the composer's own hand.

Emmett's text shows the South in a genial light. Dixie is a land whose sons and daughters relish the memory of "old times" there. If they leave, they long to return, whether to the heat that grows the summer's cotton or a "frosty mornin' " in winter. Dixie is also an egalitarian kind of place where people don't need to worry about their prepositions ("In Dixie Land whar I was born in") and can speak the English language as they choose, for the song's dialect could easily be adapted to the speech of the many Southern whites who were neither slave owners nor aspired to the aristocratic status of the plantation owner. It is a place, too, that merits loyalty, no matter what outsiders may say ("In Dixie Land, I'll take my stand, / To lib and die in Dixie"). In short, avoiding patriotic solemnity, the words and images of *Dixie* picture the South as a place to love, and they support that view with concrete, homey details.

The tune of *Dixie*, however, is probably most responsible for the song's electric appeal. Neither a march nor a hymn, as are many national songs, *Dixie* is a dance written to accompany the jaunty strut of a minstrel-show walkaround—a number to which the performers cavorted in what was taken to be the manner of Southern plantation hands. Emmett's tune, whose form can be diagrammed **aabc**, is strenuous to sing. The range of all four of its sections is wide: a tenth (E to G-sharp) in the first, second, and fourth, and a ninth (F-sharp to G-sharp) in the third. It balances fast declamation with sustained notes, especially in the verse. And the placement of those sustained tones invites loud singing, as does the pounding strictness of the rhythm. (It is hard to imagine *Dixie* being sung with a flexible beat.) "Away," "hooray," and "look away"—the latter an internal refrain in each stanza—all sound pretty much the same; and as the sustained "a" sound is heard fourteen times in a single stanza and refrain, it seems conceivable that people who know the tune but not the words can join in simply by singing "ay" in strategic places.

When combined with its words, the tune of *Dixie* kindles the kind of enthusiasm that has long made Southerners want to hoot and holler, wave banners, and throw hats in the air. But even without the words, the tune could stand on its own, as shown by a recollection involving President Lincoln. On April 10, 1865, the day after Lee's surrender to Grant at Appomattox brought the war to an end, Lincoln was serenaded at the White House by a crowd of jubilant citizens and several bands. After bantering briefly with the crowd, he announced:

> I propose closing up this interview by the band performing a particular tune which I will name. Before this is done, however, I wish to mention one or two little circumstances connected with it. I have always thought "Dixie" one of the best tunes I have ever heard. Our adversaries over the way attempted to appropriate it, but I insisted yesterday that we fairly captured it. [Ap-

plause.] I presented the question to the Attorney General, and he gave it as his legal opinion that it is our lawful prize. [Laughter and applause.] I now request the band to favor me with its performance.[28]

But *Dixie* was never really included in the North's spoils of war. By 1865, it was so firmly linked to the South, its challenge to national orthodoxies, and the mood of unconquered defiance that was to linger long after the Confederate army surrendered that it could not be reclaimed by the nation as a whole.

As well as inspiration, patriotism, and revenge, many songs were written about the human tragedy of the Civil War. Some were set on the battlefield. In one standard type, a wounded soldier utters noble or touching words: a wish for his side's success, a poignant recollection about his family, a prayer. Many songs about loss dwell on the feelings of those who, rather than fighting the war, remained at home. Root's *The Vacant Chair* is set in the household of a soldier who has died in battle. His family marks his absence by keeping a place for him, even though he will not be returning ("We shall meet, but we shall miss him / There will be one vacant chair"). Even more popular was *Weeping, Sad and Lonely, or When This Cruel War Is Over*, with words by Charles C. Sawyer and music by Henry Tucker. This song about war's duty and the conflict it brings is sung by the beloved of a Northern soldier who is away at the front. She addresses him as if in a letter:

> Dearest love, do you remember
> When we last did meet,
> How you told me that you loved me,
> Kneeling at my feet?
> Oh! how proud you stood before me,
> In your suit of blue,
> When you vow'd to me and country,
> Ever to be true.
> Weeping, sad and lonely,
> Hopes and fears, how vain (yet praying)
> When this cruel war is over,
> Praying! that we meet again.[29]

The singer goes on to confess that "many cruel fancies" haunt her. She imagines her soldier wounded, calling for help, and she grieves over the possibility that no one will comfort him. In the last stanza, however, she reassures herself that, fighting in a noble cause, he will receive the protection of angels.

Tucker's music is simple and straightforward, with six sung four-bar phrases (**aabcda**) and a unity stronger than that diagram may suggest. The rhythmic pattern of **a** (♩ . ♪ ♫♫ ♩ ♩) also appears in phrases **b** and **c**.[30]

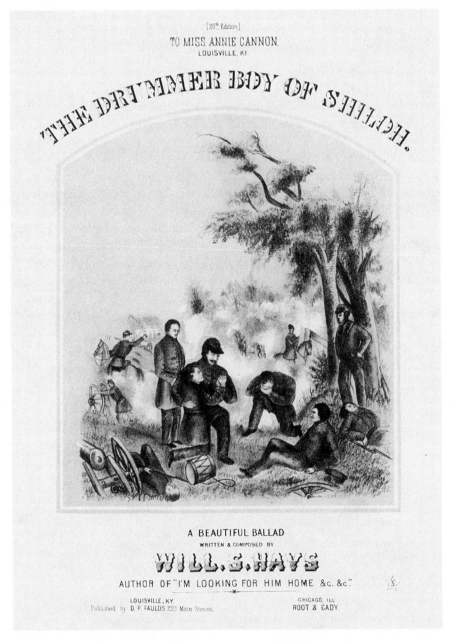

The cover of Will S. Hays's *The Drummer Boy of Shiloh* (1863) pictures the final prayer of a wounded noncombatant on the brink of death.

And since the introduction anticipates the main melody (**aa**), that pattern appears in every phrase except **d,** which Tucker makes the climax of the song by starting the refrain with it.

Weep- ing, sad and lone - ly, Hopes and fears, how vain. Yet pray- ing,

When this cru- el war is ov - er, Pray - ing! that we meet a - gain.

One may imagine a parlor performance of the time, with singers gathered around a piano or harmonium. One singer or perhaps the whole group in unison might sing the stanzas. But when phrase **d** arrives, they divide into four-part harmony to declaim "Weeping, sad, and lonely" in a new quarter-note tune. The sensuous effect of the chords shifts the emphasis from message to music; and if the refrain is repeated *pianissimo* as the sheet-music directs, and the singers blend their voices at an even softer level, it is the vocal *sound* that commands the ear of participants and listeners alike.

The means used here are so simple that we may be tempted to underestimate the composer's craftmanship, as if the song's popularity were an accident. It is no accident, however, that the refrain offers striking musical contrast at the very moment when the text's mode of address changes: vocal harmony replaces unison, and a new rhythm supplants the one heard in every previous phrase. It is also there that the words of an individual to her soldier boyfriend turn into a collective lament of families, households, and larger communities. The return of the **a** melody to end the refrain then offers a note of hope for all who count themselves victims of the war's cruelty: this terrible conflict will not last forever.

Few songs of the Civil War try to deal with the connection between patriotic glory and human suffering. But one exception, *Tenting on the Old Camp Ground*, by Walter Kittredge—"adapted and sung by the Hutchinson Family," according to the sheet music, and arranged by M. F. H. Smith—looks beyond the standard language of heroism. Its center of gravity is the refrain, where, rather than raising their voices in ecstatic, comradely shouts, soldiers sing in four-part harmony about war weariness. The song's arrangement adds a layer of drama. It opens with reveille in the piano (four bars), followed by a loud, jaunty, four-bar "tempo di marcia" (march time), which is repeated. But after the voices enter, that mood gradually loses steam, for the melody lacks a martial character. Behind it, the piano now plays two rather than four chords per measure, as in a slow march; brief fills between phrases suggest military signals from the field, as if in the distance. The last two lines are sung quietly to rolled, sustained piano chords:

> We're tenting tonight on the old Camp ground,
>   Give us a song to cheer
> Our weary hearts, a song of home,
>   And friends we love so dear.
>   Many are the hearts that are weary tonight,
>   Wishing for the war to cease;
>   Many are the hearts looking for the right
>   To see the dawn of peace.
>   Tenting tonight, tenting tonight,
>   Tenting on the Old camp ground.[31]

Each of the four stanzas, then, starts in a bumptious, almost swaggering vein and ends in a more contemplative one. The final stanza, dropping all pretense of male bravery, pictures the aftermath of battle:

> We've been fighting today on the old Camp ground,
> Many are lying near;
> Some are dead and some are dying,
> Many are in tears.

And Kittredge, marking the final two lines *ppp* (as soft as possible), draws out the refrain in a last epiphany of grief: "Dying tonight, dying tonight, / Dying on the old Camp ground." Imagination combines here with the idiom of the sentimental song to create a mood of numb resignation: an authentic human response to the Civil War.

Union General William Tecumseh Sherman once wrote: "War, like a thunderbolt, follows *its* laws and turns not aside even if the beautiful, the virtuous and charitable stand in its way."[32] And what was the primary law of war? In Sherman's words, "to produce results by death and slaughter." The men fighting for those results could be both the mourners of *Tenting on the Old Camp Ground* and agents of war's thunderbolt. One Rhode Island volunteer, for example, recalled what happened when a small group of Union soldiers entered the house of a Confederate family in Fredericksburg, Virginia, and listened as a private played "really fine music" on the piano. "As he ceases playing, another says, 'Did you ever see me play?' and seizing his rifle, he brings it down full force upon the keyboard, smashing it to splinters." That action signaled other soldiers to go on a rampage, destroying the remaining furniture in the house.[33]

It was in response to incidents like this one, as well as to battles in the field, that a song like *Tenting on the Old Camp Ground* explored the gap between the heroic and the sentimental, pondered what war could lead decent men to do, and thus reached a level of understanding that neither standard approach could manage.

14

Of Yankee Doodle and Ophicleides

Bands and Orchestras, 1800 to the 1870s

THE HISTORY OF THE American wind band is one of changing makeup, broadening repertory, and diversifying functions—led not by composers but by performers. Responding to various social needs, from military functions to popular entertainment, band musicians have pursued the goal of accessibility within a framework colored by military discipline. The band uniform symbolizes that framework. Indeed, the image of musicians in paramilitary garb signals that artistry is not the only impulse they serve, perhaps not even the primary one.

The armed forces have long provided bands in this country with an institutional base. As the 1800s dawned, the military was still using wind instruments according to customs borrowed from the British army, with fifes and drums performing field music, while bands of music (oboes, clarinets, French horns, and bassoons, ideally in pairs) played so-called *Harmoniemusik* for listening (see Chapter 5). After the revolution, the size of the army was drastically reduced. But in 1792, Congress passed an act ordering every able-bodied white male citizen between eighteen and forty-five to join his state militia. Field music was required for each battalion, and bands of music were also maintained, though these were essentially civilian groups.

The wind band's public appeal is fundamental to its history. Indeed, the idea of a band that only connoisseurs can appreciate seems a contradiction in terms. A reminiscence printed in a Boston music journal of 1838 suggests the excitement that followed bands in the early days of the Republic. "Full well do I remember when I first heard the sound of a *Clarinet, French Horn* and *Bassoon*," the writer confided about a performance he heard around 1800. "It was at a regimental muster, where I went with my father." According to this report, news that the militia commander had hired the Boston Band to play was greeted with keen anticipation.

At length the wished-for day arrived, and a glorious day it was, most clear and bright. . . . we saw a brilliant company of light-horse prancing over the plain. When they had arrived within half a mile of the parade ground, they slackened pace, and the music struck up *Washington's March*. . . . The march was continued until the company came in front of the public house, when it halted, and Capt. Taylor gave orders for *Yankee Doodle*. This fairly bewitched the crowd, and they rent the air with huzzas.

The band continued to play outdoors long enough to get through several tunes, including one that inspired an old townsman to break into a sprightly dance, delighting the crowd. From the excitement described, one might imagine the Boston Band as a large ensemble. But in fact they numbered only four: oboe, clarinet, French horn, and bassoon—all men of an older generation and considered outstanding performers in their day.[1]

However humble its forces, the Boston Band thrilled the townspeople at that long-ago muster by playing familiar tunes to fit the occasion. *Washington's March* and *Yankee Doodle* carried a patriotic charge, and in line with the day's festive spirit, the bandsmen had also offered dance melodies like *St. Patrick's Day in the Morning*. These were all well-known pieces that could be whistled, hummed, or played on fiddle, flute, keyboard, or by an ensemble of almost any size. For two centuries and more, American bands have been stoking enthusiasm by presenting tunes that listeners already know in ways they can readily appreciate.

Bands have courted audiences not only through their repertory but also through their sound. And nineteenth-century performers maintained that sound's appeal by keeping pace with the changing technology of wind instrument making. The Boston Band in 1800 was continuing a tradition of European wind music that reached back at least half a century. But the addition by 1850 of two new instrumental families transformed the sound of the wind band. The first was the percussion, especially the so-called Janissary instruments of triangle, tambourine, cymbals, and bass drum, which by the 1830s were standard in American ensembles. The second was the brass, now freed from earlier limitations. In the 1700s, brass instruments were nothing more than long coiled tubes. By changing lip pressure, players of these older horns could sound only the so-called partials above the fundamental pitch of the tube's harmonic series. In 1810, Joseph Halliday of Dublin, Ireland, found that by cutting holes in the side of a bugle and fitting the holes with keys, he could change the tube's effective length, hence its fundamental and partials. The result was a brass instrument that could play any note in any scale. Halliday's bugle helped to inspire the making of ophicleides, an entire family of keyed brass. And within a few years, German instrument makers introduced valves rather than keys, taking fuller advantage

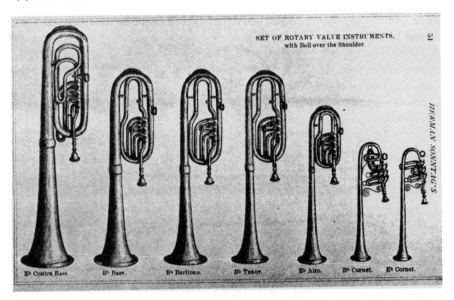

Saxhorn instruments like these were advertised in dealers' catalogs until the late nineteenth century.

of the brass tube's natural resonance. By the 1820s, a wide variety of brass instruments—the keyed bugle, bass ophicleide, cornet, trumpet, and French horn—were capable of playing melodies. Moreover, their volume suited them better for outdoor use than the instruments of the older *Harmoniemusik* ensemble. By mid-century, the brass band had become the typical American wind ensemble.

Adolphe Sax's invention of the saxhorn in Paris in the early 1840s furthered the brass band's vogue. The saxhorns, a family of instruments modeled after the upright tuba, brought to the multitimbred wind band the possibility of homogeneous sound. A brass band with cornets, percussion, and saxhorns ranging from alto down to bass could achieve a uniform blend. Dominating wind ensemble music by the mid-1850s, saxhorns formed the core of the typical Civil War band. The instruments were well suited for military parades, their straight, over-the-shoulder bells carrying the sound clearly to marchers and listeners. Not everyone, however, found saxhorns an improvement. William R. Bayley, writing in 1893 after sixty years in the business, admitted that recent band instruments were "much better made and easier to learn" than those of his youth. Yet Bayley missed the sound of bands in the pre-saxhorn age—fifteen-piece ensembles with sharply contrasting instrumental colors: "two E-flat bugles, 1st and 2nd French horns (without valves), the post horn, and E-flat trumpet. We had the brilliant tone of the slide B-flat trombone and the F-bass trombone for bass, ophecleide [sic] (brass), and the serpent (a wooden instrument with keys), cymbals, snare and bass drums." These instruments of varied construction offered a palette of different tone qualities more interesting, to Bayley's ear, than the saxhorn-dominated blend that prevailed in the later nineteenth century.[2]

REPERTORY

By the middle nineteenth century, bands in America were serving functions that had nothing to do with the military. Bands might be heard in theaters, private halls, hotels, resorts, parks, hospitals, or churches; they were hired to perform at sporting events, fairs, store openings, dinner parties, club meetings, and even funerals.[3] In all these settings, music served as an adjunct to some other purpose. But bands also played concerts, and here they followed the long-standing custom of varying the sound from number to number.

During the 1850–51 season, for example, the American Band of Providence, Rhode Island, presented a four-concert series in a local hall.[4] Conducted by W. F. Marshall, the group numbered sixteen: an E-flat bugle played by "leader" J. C. Greene, plus a bugle in B-flat, cornet in E-flat, post horn, trumpet, three percussionists (side drum, bass drum, and cymbals), and eight saxhorns (two alto, two tenor, one baritone, and three bass). On at least two of the concerts, the band was also joined by a singer and a pianist, both apparently local performers. The program for the evening of February 3, 1851, was arranged in two parts with six numbers on each.

Part I

Elfin Quick Step—Band	W. F. Marshall
Song of America—Miss Carpenter	Carl. Lobe
Cornet solo—(accompanied by orchestra)—	
Mr. J. C. Greene	Romaine
Pas de Fleurs—Band	Max Maretzek
Romanza—"Sounds so entrancing,"—Miss Carpenter	Andreas Randel
Overture—Donna del Largo—Band	Rossini

Part II

Grand Wedding March—From Mendelshon's Opera—	
"Midsummers Night Dream,"—arranged expressly	
for the Band, by W. F. Marshall	Mendelshon
Song—"Let the bright Seraphim,"—Miss E. B.	
Carpenter,—with Trumpet Obligato by	
Mr. J. C. Greene	Handel

Septette—From Amille—("Rest Spirit, Rest,")—
    Miss Carpenter   Rooke
Polka—Band   A. Dodsworth
Cavatina—" 'Twas no vision,"—From I. Lombardi—
    Miss Carpenter   Verdi
Evergreen Gallop—Band   Labitzky[5]

The program leaves little doubt that the American Band sought to edify its audience as well as entertain it. One indication is that composer attributions are given for every piece. It is true that a few gaffes undermine the attempt at cultural uplift: calling Shakespeare's *A Midsummer Night's Dream* an opera rather than a play; misspelling "obbligato," "galop," and several proper names (Mendelssohn, Dodworth, Amilie); and transforming Rossini's *Lady of the Lake* (*Lago*) into *Lady of the Width* (*Largo*). Yet the presence of works by such European masters as Rossini, Mendelssohn, Handel, and Verdi underlines a commitment to artistry. Composers working in America were represented too: Max Maretzek, Czech-born conductor and impresario, who had come to the United States in 1848 to conduct Italian opera in New York; Allen Dodworth, English-born wind player, bandmaster, and dancing teacher also living in New York; and the band's own conductor, whose *Elfin Quick Step* began the program.[6]

Contrasting with the American Band's program, one that survives from an Ohio ensemble's concert a few years later emphasizes performers, not composers. On April 14, 1858, at Western Reserve College, "A. James, The Great English Harpist" and singer W. Milton Clark joined the Tallmadge Cornet Band and Orchestra in a performance whose first half included the following:

Prairie Flower Quickstep   Band
Akron Gallopade   Orchestra
Blue Bells of Scotland—Harp   A. James
Song   W. Milton Clark
Passage from Verdi   Orchestra
Solo—Harp   A. James
Song   W. Milton Clark
Zitti Zitti   Orchestra
Mountain Echo   Band[7]

With Verdi the only composer named and several titles unspecified, the Tallmadge Band's program looks artistically less ambitious than that of the American Band. Yet both groups offered a variety of sound, changing the performing medium from number to number, even including an orchestra. Indeed, nineteenth-century band concerts embraced virtually all the musical genres that American audiences of the time were likely to hear, including marches, patriotic songs, popular songs, programmatic pieces, solo pieces, transcriptions of orchestra works, and dance pieces. Except for programmatic pieces, each type is represented on the two programs quoted here. That variety also reflects the band's role in community musical life. As the main focus for music making outside churches, wind bands offered a framework in which local musicians could present themselves to a ticket-buying public.

It is obvious that the band's military background links it to the march, and that band instruments are well suited to the march's character. When the American sheet-music business began in the 1790s, marches were among its standard issues—not in wind-band versions but in arrangements for keyboard, upon which the parlor trade in sheet music depended. Stately grand marches such as *The President's March*, many of them making use of fanfare-like melodies and a characteristic dotted-rhythm motive (♩♩♩♩), dominated the form through the 1820s. In the 1830s, the quickstep came into prominence, its sprightlier, more flowing melodic style reflecting the brass's new aptitude for playing melody. And marches served as dance music for so-called country dancing, including the cotillion and the quadrille. By including both Mendelssohn's *Wedding March* and a quickstep by its own conductor, the American Band recognized that the march could encompass both enduring compositions and fresh ones. Moreover, the title *Elfin Quick Step* is a reminder that marches could also be character pieces, depicting a particular mood, scene, or event. Both the Rhode Island and Ohio programs began with marches, a rousing way to open a concert.

The band's military background also helped to make patriotic songs favorite concert fare. Bands had long been a natural medium for such favorites as *The Star-Spangled Banner, Yankee Doodle,* the French *La marseillaise,* and *Hail Columbia,* a favorite patriotic lyric from around 1800, set to the tune of *The President's March.* The Providence singer's performance of Lobe's *Song of America* indicates that the stock of patriotic songs grew through the mid-century years and that they were sung as well as played in public. The 1860s, when the Civil War urged patriotic passion to the fore, also brought a fresh crop of patriotic songs. Band performances of such numbers as *The Battle-Hymn of the Republic, The Bonnie Blue Flag, The Battle Cry of Freedom,* and *Dixie* popularized their melodies and enhanced the band's inspirational role.[8]

Popular songs are missing from the American Band's program, though they may have been sung or played as encores. Nevertheless, band arrangements of songs sung in the parlor were common: new hits like Foster's *My Old Kentucky Home* and Pierpont's *Jingle Bells*; older favorites like *Auld*

The E-flat cornet part of Holloway's *Wood Up Quickstep* (1834) illustrates the virtuoso technique demanded of star soloists in the nineteenth-century American band.

Lang Syne and *Home, Sweet Home*; and medleys of Irish and Scottish songs
(*The Last Rose of Summer, Annie Laurie*). The harp rendition of *Blue Bells of
Scotland* on the Tallmadge Band's concert provides one example. And the
second half of that concert ended with the band playing the *Gentle Annie
Quickstep*, featuring a tune Stephen Foster wrote in 1856—a reminder that
quicksteps, made up of several strains, might borrow a popular-song melody
for one of them.

Bands also played works intended to be descriptive or narrative. Under
such titles as *The Night Alarm* or *An Alpine Storm*, such program music di-
verted and pleased both European and American audiences for many generations. *The Battle of Prague* was a perennial favorite in the United States.
Written in the 1780s by Bohemian composer Franz Kotzwara, this work was
still well enough known a century later for Mark Twain to call it a "venerable shivaree" in a hilarious account of an amateur pianist's performance.[9] A
number of American composers modeled battle pieces of their own on *The
Battle of Prague*. In this format, short movements depict different scenes in
the conflict, inviting listeners to imagine the action: camp maneuvers, the
call to arms, the cavalry charge, the thrill of combat, the moans of the dying,
the victory call. Program music could also be inspired by less dramatic
events; for example, John Holloway's *Wood Up Quickstep* (1834) is said to
represent the refueling of a wood-burning steamboat.

Solo pieces like *Wood Up*, written to exhibit a star performer's virtuosity, formed another staple of the band repertory. In the Providence concert, J. C. Greene's cornet solo with orchestra accompaniment provides one example and Miss Carpenter's singing of Handel's florid aria *Let the Bright Seraphim* with Greene's obbligato another. The presence of A. James on the Tallmadge concert also implies that some virtuoso display was unveiled there, at least enough to justify the label "The Great English Harpist." Band programs of the time routinely included instrumental soloists. No fewer than five were featured in an 1835 "Grand Concert" by the Boston Brass Band: a trombonist, flutist, violinist, clarinetist, and keyed bugle player.

The keyed bugle, the wind band's first virtuoso instrument, allowed performers to play with boldness *and* delicacy. Leading players of the time, including Richard Willis, black bandleader Francis Johnson, and Edward Kendall, became well-known figures in concert life. The growing prominence of valved brass from the 1830s on helped make the cornet a rival to the keyed bugle; musical duels between soloists were sometimes even staged. With technical prowess expected of them, soloists tended to play music that showed off their high range, fast passagework, wide leaps, and sustained notes. A common vehicle for virtuosity was the theme and variations, which grounded display in familiar tunes and formal repetition. Virtually any melody, from dance tunes to opera arias, could be varied in this way, and tunes by Auber, Bellini, Donizetti, and Giacomo Meyerbeer were especially popular with nineteenth-century brass soloists. Their arching phrases provided an ideal showcase for breath control and beauty of tone. Moreover, widely known through stage, concert, and parlor performance, operatic melodies lent themselves well to virtuosic variation. Their place in the band repertory marks the cornet (or keyed bugle) soloist as the wind band's star performer.

Bands also performed wind arrangements of classical orchestra works, as we saw from the American Band's program. Overtures by Rossini and eventually Wagner were common, as were selections from operas and symphonic works by Mozart, Verdi, Mendelssohn, Weber, Liszt, Meyerbeer, and Bellini, included on programs to balance lighter fare. As the century neared its end, prominent American musicians were crediting the band with raising public taste. Composer and sometime bandmaster Victor Herbert wrote in the 1890s: "The important part that military bands have taken in the development of musical knowledge in America can not be overstated." Herbert found Wagner's music especially well suited for the band because of the prominent role it gave to wind instruments.[10] And John Philip Sousa, who for several decades led America's most famous wind ensemble, claimed in 1910 that bands had helped make Wagner "less of a myth to the people at large than Shakespeare."[11]

The American Band's program also shows the importance of dance music in the band's concert repertory. A group that played marches in a parade one day might serve as a dance ensemble the next. Bands that played for dancing were expected to accompany new dances as they found their way into American ballrooms. But dance music also lent variety to concert performances. As well as the opening quickstep and the wedding march, the American Band featured a polka, galop, and "Pas de Fleurs" on its concert. And more than half the numbers on the Ohio concert's second half were dance pieces.

My Mary Ann Quickstep	Band
Laclede Waltz	Orchestra
Song	W. Milton Clark
Solo—Harp	A. James
Capt. Shepherd's Quickstep	Orchestra
Song	W. Milton Clark
Solo—Harp	A. James
"Our" Quadrilles	Orchestra
Gentle Annie Quickstep	Band[12]

Given the twentieth-century separation of bands and orchestras, their overlap in earlier days may seem curious. But "orchestra" carried a broad range of meanings in the 1850s. Except for the New York Philharmonic Society, which numbered around sixty and played only a few concerts per season, full symphony orchestras simply did not exist in America. The largest orchestras were the ensembles that accompanied operas and dramas in theaters and chamber orchestras of twenty to thirty strings and winds. At the other end of the scale stood the "social orchestra," an ensemble of perhaps five or fewer players that accompanied dancing or played in domestic settings. The label was nonprescriptive. In the mid-nineteenth century, Elias Howe of Boston published social-orchestra music for two violins (one for melody and the other for rhythmic background), a cello, and a fourth instrument that could be a clarinet, flute, cornet, harp, or piano.[13] In *The Social Orchestra* (1854), Stephen Foster arranged melodies from "the most popular operatic and other music of the day" into ensemble pieces "suitable for serenades, evenings at home, &c."[14] *The American Collection of Instrumental Music* (Boston, 1856) offered dance pieces arranged in a similar way: marches, quicksteps, waltzes, country dances, quadrilles, cotillions, polkas, hornpipes, and mazurkas.

These collections and the concert programs quoted earlier reveal common ground between bands and orchestras of the time. They also suggest that bands enjoyed more public appeal than orchestras and a firmer institutional base. That point is confirmed by a November 1856 program of the

Manchester Cornet Band of New Hampshire, which shared the concert with an orchestra, several vocalists, and a pianist. The band's prominent place on the program, leading off and ending each half, is proof of its local prestige. It was clearly under band sponsorship that Manchester's citizens heard the music on this ambitious concert, most of it composed originally for orchestral and theatrical performance.[15]

ORCHESTRAS AND ENTERTAINMENT

In the mid-nineteenth century, American concert life was transformed when European impresarios recognized the United States as a market for concert performers. Customers would be plentiful, these entrepreneurs realized, if musical artistry could be packaged and delivered as entertainment. Social changes and technology made that step possible, in the form of a touring circuit that served as a new musical marketplace. Networks of canals and railroad lines now connected distant cities. The telegraph, invented in the mid-1830s, simplified communication, allowing artists to change touring plans without forfeiting concert engagements. After 1840, the growth of leisure time and the rise of the music-teaching profession encouraged the making of music in middle-class homes. As more Americans learned to play and sing, the audience for accomplished musicians grew. Concert halls, opera houses, and assembly rooms appeared in more and more cities, including even smaller ones such as Utica, New York, and Toledo, Ohio. While money for some halls was raised by local civic groups, others were built with borrowed funds by entrepreneurs who hoped that box office receipts would justify their financial risk.

The decade of the 1840s saw these elements fused into a network for marketing entertainment, which might be anything from a lecturer or concert pianist to a minstrel troupe or a team of acrobats. Before Jenny Lind's landmark tour in 1850–51, violinists Ole Bull, Henri Vieuxtemps, and Camillo Sivori and pianists Leopold de Meyer and Henri Herz had traveled the United States in search of monetary gain. Most were managed by European impresarios, for they knew best how to seek out foreign-born artists with the skill, presence, and reputation to attract audiences on the American circuit.

Typically, a manager contracted with a star performer (as did P. T. Barnum with Jenny Lind) to give a specified number of concerts for a specified amount of money. But under that arrangement, performers earned their fees only by assigning artistic control to the manager, who was ready to do whatever necessary to round up an audience. In a country where many potential concertgoers had never attended a concert, adversarial feelings between impresarios and their artists were common. Pianist Louis Moreau Gottschalk complained: "The artist is merchandise that the impresario has purchased, the value of which he enhances as he chooses. You might as well reproach certain pseudo gold-mine companies for announcing dividends that they never will pay as to render an artist responsible for the lures of his contractor."[16] Some impresarios were sophisticated music lovers and even musicians, but their role invited a thoroughly commercial approach to concert giving. Pianist Henri Herz reported impresario Bernard Ullman's definition of music as "the art of attracting to a given auditorium, by secondary devices which often become the principal ones, the greatest possible number of curious people, so that when expenses are tallied against receipts the latter exceed the former by the widest possible margin."[17] One of Ullman's own wisecracks seems to confirm that cynical statement. Asked by a New Orleans concertgoer what kind of music his artists were going to perform, the manager replied: "Financial music."[18]

Under the guidance of managers like Bernard Ullman, concert musicians began to perform on an entertainment circuit that put little stock in artistic edification. By the 1840s, impresarios had seized power in a hierarchy ruled by economic muscle. That hierarchy helped to define and encouraged what audiences seemed to like about concerts, including virtuoso display; wide variety (relatively short pieces that mixed sounds and styles); compositions based on familiar tunes, especially patriotic ones; descriptive instrumental music (program music); established favorites; and dance music, especially dances currently in vogue. As customers applauded their use, these elements hardened into consumer-tested devices that governed a formulaic approach to concert programming. Performers on the circuit were not given to taking artistic risks. Many grew weary of repeating the same pieces and of manipulating audiences into predictable responses. But as long as customers seemed to respond to them, managers held performers to standard routines. Ullman and Company, it should be remembered, were Europeans who knew the United States only through the prism of the concert hall. Yet it was their reading of American taste, formulated under economic pressure, that fixed the customs governing this branch of concert life.

The American concert circuit began to diversify almost as soon as it was set up. And orchestras joined soloists as touring attractions. In 1847–48, four different orchestras reached New York from German-speaking regions in Europe, where political unrest was causing mass immigration. The first to appear was the Austrian Steyermark ensemble, which came by way of Boston, having arrived there in 1846, twenty men strong. Recalling the group's visit a half century later, a Boston clarinetist named Thomas Ryan wrote that they performed "mostly light dance music, overtures, potpourris, and solos." Striking dress, including "the picturesque Steyermark country uniform," and a certain amount of stage business also enhanced their ap-

This unusually detailed lithograph shows twenty-one of the twenty-four original players in the Germania Musical Society, which toured the United States from 1848 until it disbanded in 1854.

peal. Ryan remembered the "little clinking, cymbal-like bits of metal attached to the heels of their long boots," which during some pieces they knocked together to produce "a clear, lively sound which 'took' with the audience." The Steyermarkers "did everything with great 'chic' or 'snap,'" Ryan recalled—"a new thing to our people."[19] Their playing seems to have been no less impressive than their appearance. In December 1847, a New York critic commented: "Even the Philharmonic might learn from these Styrians."[20]

The fall of 1848 brought to New York a thirty-two-piece ensemble led by Hungarian-born bandmaster and dance composer Josef Gungl, followed soon after by twenty-four musicians from the Saxon city of Dresden, traveling as the Saxonia Band. But more than any of these groups, the Germania Musical Society left its mark on the American scene. Having formed in Germany an ensemble that claimed devotion to democratic principles, the Germanians advertised their New York debut in October 1848:

The Germania Musical Society from Berlin, composed of 25 instrumental and solo performers who have made themselves well known on the continent of Europe and England for their precision and skill in execution of the best works of the celebrated masters, as Beethoven, Mendelssohn, von Weber, and Strauss, Lanner &c. &c. respectfully announce to the citizens of New

York that they have just arrived in this country and that they will make their first appearance at Mr. Niblo's, Astor Place, on Thursday evening next.[21]

Playing for audiences of up to three thousand in the principal American cities, the Germanians featured symphonies, overtures, and concertos by the likes of Haydn, Mozart, Beethoven, Mendelssohn, Liszt, and Wagner on programs more substantial than those of other orchestras. But these musicians, who played over nine hundred concerts in North America before disbanding in 1854, could hardly have survived for six years on an exclusive diet of classics. Indeed, their own list of featured composers includes not only Beethoven and Mendelssohn but Johann Strauss and Joseph Lanner, both dance conductors who specialized in the Viennese waltz. The Germanians' concert programs during their first two months in New York were devoted mostly to light music by Gungl and Strauss, sprinkled with overtures by Mozart, Auber, Donizetti, Rossini, and their specialty, Mendelssohn's Overture to *A Midsummer Night's Dream*.[22] Some selections were intended as crowd pleasers. For example, *Up Broadway*, composed by the group's leader, offered a tone portrait of sounds encountered on a journey along that New York thoroughfare. As Thomas Ryan remembered it, the potpourri included Barnum's Museum, with a band "of six or eight brass instruments, which, as all old New Yorkers know, played all day long on a high balcony . . . nearly opposite the Astor House," a parade of firemen, a dance hall, a church, a pair of bands converging in Union Square, an eruption of fireworks, and a playing of *The Star-Spangled Banner*.[23] Mixed with Beethoven symphonies, Strauss waltzes, and the *Midsummer Night's Dream* overture, a novelty like *Up Broadway* was a repertory staple for all audiences that, together with polished ensemble playing and frequent tours, helped create the group's formula for success.

The Germanians made Boston their American headquarters. There, Ryan wrote, "subscription lists twenty feet long (no exaggeration) could be seen in the music stores for a series of twenty-four Saturday evenings, and the same number of public rehearsals on Wednesday afternoons."[24] Stays in Boston alternated with time on the road, and occasionally the orchestra performed with soloists, including the best in North America: singers Jenny Lind, Henriette Sontag, and Catherine Hayes and violinists Ole Bull and Camilla Urso. In 1854, the ensemble toured what was then the American West, with concerts in Pittsburgh, Louisville, Cincinnati, St. Louis, Chicago, Cleveland, Milwaukee, and Minneapolis. Programs varied, but they always included works by Classical and Romantic era masters, which many audiences were hearing for the first time. Even after the orchestra broke up, its influence continued, for many of the members settled in American cities. Ex-Germanian Carl Bergmann led the New York Philharmonic Society for two decades (1855–76), and Carl Zerrahn served as conductor of the Boston Handel and Haydn Society from 1854 until 1898.

Another landmark orchestral tour came from outside the Germanic orbit. In the summer of 1853, French-born conductor Louis Jullien, accompanied by twenty-seven instrumentalists, sailed from England to the United States. When he reached New York, he recruited another sixty players. Then, at the helm of this impressively large orchestra, he began a series of New York concerts that lasted into the fall. Size was not the only unusual thing about Jullien and his orchestra. For he himself was the star performer: a conductor who had spent nearly twenty years in Paris and London polishing his personal charisma and charming audiences through instrumental performance.

Jullien's orchestra had won fame in Europe before traveling to America. Its reputation for flashy amusement reflected the personality of the leader, whose full name was enough to amuse almost anyone: Louis George Maurice Adolphe Roch Albert Abel Antonio Alexandre Noé Jean Lucien Daniel Eugène Joseph-le-brun Joseph-Barême, Thomas Thomas Thomas-Thomas Pierre Arbon Pierre-Maurel Barthélmi Artus Alphonse Bertrand Dieudonné Emanuel Josué Vincent Luc Michel Jules-de-la-plane Jules-Bazin Julio César Jullien (the names of all thirty-six godfathers/members of the musical society in the provincial town where he was born in 1812). Jullien enrolled at the Paris Conservatory in 1833, then dropped out three years later and began to organize popular concerts—promenade concerts, as they came to be known in England—that featured overtures, instrumental solos, and plenty of dance music, well played and at a cheap ticket price. The atmosphere at these concerts was informal; audience members were free to sit, stand, or stroll while the music was being played. With Philippe Musard in Paris and Johann Strauss in Vienna, Jullien belonged to the first generation of conductors who achieved success by making themselves into intriguing public figures. A Parisian of the day advised: "If you want to see a handsome man, go and eat an ice in the *Jardin turc* at Jullien's feet."[25]

Around 1840, Jullien moved from Paris to London, where he won an immediate following. Although his musicians also played in three other London ensembles, Jullien's leadership produced not only better entertainment but better musical results. One feature of Jullien's programs was their reliance on quadrilles: four-couple contradances consisting of five sections in 2/4 or 6/8 time. Quadrilles were popular with dancers of the day, creating a lively market for newly composed quadrille music. At the same time, their foursquare phrases provided molds into which familiar tunes could be fitted: popular songs, operatic numbers, even sacred works. Thus the quadrille was both a dance form and a musical form, with the finale sometimes used to create a colorful climax.

Jullien's orchestra successfully imported his London formula to the

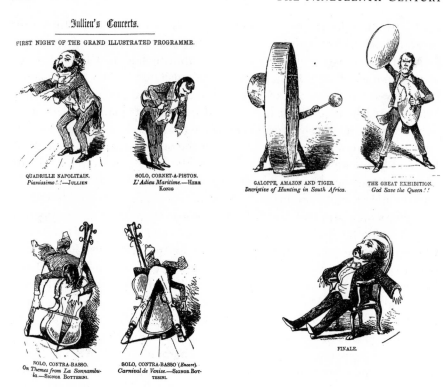

Jullien's Concerts.

FIRST NIGHT OF THE GRAND ILLUSTRATED PROGRAMME.

QUADRILLE NAPOLITAIN.
Pianissimo!!—JULLIEN

SOLO, CORNET-A-PISTON.
L'Adieu Maritime.—HERR
KOXIO

GALOPPE, AMAZON AND TIGER.
Descriptive of Hunting in South Africa.

THE GREAT EXHIBITION.
God Save the Queen!!

SOLO, CONTRA-BASSO.
*On Themes from La Sonnambu-
la.*—SIGNOR BOTTESINI.

SOLO, CONTRA-BASSO (*Encore*).
Carnival de Venise.—SIGNOR BOT-
TESINI.

FINALE.

Conductor Louis Jullien's New York concerts created an enthusiasm that, as these fanciful cartoons show, stopped short of artistic reverence.

United States, remaining for almost ten months and playing more than two hundred concerts, including a Southern tour with stops in New Orleans, Mobile, and Charleston. The conductor made a vivid impression wherever he appeared, and critics scrambled for new ways to describe him: "emphatically a superior mind," "true genius," "Autocrat and Grand Emperor." One New York writer likened him to a military hero: "Have we a Napoleon amongst us?" he asked. "Yes—the Napoleon of music, who, after conquering Europe, has invaded the realms of Yankee Doodle and Hail Columbia, with fiddles, fifes, trumpets, drums." Another journalist described how the conductor mimed the musical sounds. "Talk of descriptive music!" he exclaimed. "Why, here, the very whisk of the horses' tails, as they rush into the fight, is perceptible; and if you are not bright enough to understand all this musical language—look at the index, M. Jullien, who acts it out."[26]

Even those who criticized Jullien granted that his orchestra played well. The critic John Sullivan Dwight warmly praised a New York performance he heard in October 1853: "To hear the great works of the masters brought out in the full proportions of so large an orchestra, where all the parts are played by perfect masters of their instruments, is a great privilege and great lesson." Dwight admired the dance music too. Jullien's "quadrille, waltz and polka compilations," he wrote, "are all set in most brilliant frame-work, and treated with a consummate mastery of brilliant instrumentation, which make them absolutely exciting."[27] Jullien also performed compositions of his own on the tour, including the *American Quadrille*, based on *Yankee Doodle, Hail Columbia, Hail to the Chief*, and *The Old Folks at Home*. In a "monster concert" given just before the orchestra's return to Europe, the New York audience heard his *Fireman's Quadrille*, whose final section featured a real blaze, complete with clanging bell and a battalion of firefighters rushing in to quench the flames.[28]

Chapter 15 will trace how, after the Civil War, symphony orchestras were formed and encouraged to concentrate on composers' music, the authority of scores, and the ideal of transcendence. Indeed, the orchestra as a local institution would become the linchpin of the classical sphere's growing prestige in the United States in the latter nineteenth century. Before the Civil War, however, orchestras, like bands, depended for their existence on the musical marketplace and their ability to offer concerts with plenty of audience appeal.

PATRICK S. GILMORE, BANDMASTER

Wind bands never wavered in their commitment to performers' music and audience accessibility, even while raising their level of artistry and professional status. A key figure in steering the wind band's course after 1850 was Patrick S. Gilmore, a bandmaster who, cutting loose from military affiliation, proved that the band could succeed as an independent ensemble in the public arena.

Born in Ireland in 1829, Gilmore immigrated to the United States in 1849 as a cornetist. Settling in Boston, he went to work for publisher John Ordway, who in 1850 formed a minstrel company in which Gilmore performed as a cornet and tambourine player. Gilmore also composed popular songs in these years, and he learned another side of the music business by serving as an agent for Ordway's troupe. In the early 1850s, Gilmore began to lead bands, including the Salem Brass Band, which he took over in 1855. The next year, Gilmore engaged the keyed-bugle virtuoso Ned Kendall in a public competition. Neither was judged to have won the contest, but with a shrewd gift for promotion, Gilmore parlayed his challenge into public recognition for himself and the cornet. That an unknown young bandleader could play a famous keyed bugler to a draw seemed to signal that the bugle's days as a featured instrument were numbered.

In 1858, Gilmore resigned from the Salem Brass Band and founded

Patrick Sarsfield Gilmore (1829–1892), Irish-American bandmaster.

Gilmore's Band, which made its debut at the Boston Music Hall in April 1859. Following the Dodworth Band in New York City, Gilmore's was a professional ensemble, with the leader in charge of both its artistic and business sides. Gilmore conducted the band, selected and bought uniforms for his thirty-two players, chose the music, booked engagements, and handled all other details, musical and nonmusical. He also collected the profits. With a repertory tailored for each function, Gilmore's Band performed for concerts, parades, public ceremonies, dances, and social entertainments.

The outbreak of the Civil War in April 1861 interrupted the successful routine of Gilmore's Band, which became part of the 24th Massachusetts Volunteer Regiment. When all volunteer military bands were mustered out of the Union army in August 1862, Gilmore and his musicians returned to Boston, playing concerts to sustain public morale. One of the most popular

Civil War songs, *When Johnny Comes Marching Home*, was published in that city in 1863, "introduced and performed by Gilmore's Band," as its cover proclaimed. With both words and music attributed to the otherwise unknown Louis Lambert, the song is now thought to have been written by Gilmore himself. In 1864, he accompanied a band to New Orleans, where he organized a giant musical celebration for the inauguration of a new governor: a "Grand National Band" boasting some 500 players and a chorus of 5,000 schoolchildren. The ceremony featured patriotic songs, including *The Star-Spangled Banner*. And according to one account, the singing of *Hail Columbia*, a musical symbol of the Union cause, was "punctuated by thunderous roars from a battery of cannons, one of which boomed on each beat of the drum, reinforced by the pealing of bells in neighborhood churches."[29]

Gilmore's grandiose streak was soon to find an even grander focus. In June 1869, mindful that the war's end had not soothed the bitterness between North and South, he organized a National Peace Jubilee in Boston; a musical event of unprecedented scope. Gilmore assembled vast forces: an orchestra of 500, a band of 1,000, a chorus of 10,000, and many famous soloists. Over a five-day span, an ambitious program of concerts took place, including symphonic music, oratorio excerpts, band music, and the singing of schoolchildren. The program for one of the concerts reveals that, for all his emphasis on gargantuan effects, Gilmore varied his selections to show off their sound contrasts to greatest effect. The concert began with a huge orchestra featuring more than four dozen trumpeters on the solo part of an overture by Auber. A choral hymn followed, and then a newly composed march for band and orchestra combined. Next came a soprano aria, which scaled down the volume so that the following number—Verdi's "Anvil" Chorus, with a hundred Boston firefighters socking real anvils—could roar forth in all its splendor. Gilmore then relied on the patriotic familiarity of *Hail Columbia* to avoid anticlimax.

Testimony to the jubilee's success came from one who had first opposed it: the Boston critic John Sullivan Dwight, editor of *Dwight's Journal of Music* and a champion of music as edifying art rather than entertainment. Dwight began his detailed review by admitting his initial reservations about the whole undertaking. Who was Gilmore, after all? Certainly not a "great musical man" or one "who fellowshipped with artists." Instead, Dwight described the bandleader as "a man of common education," Irish by birth, good natured and generous:

> an enthusiast of rather a sentimental type; chiefly known as caterer in music to the popular street taste, dispenser of military and of patriotic airs, exceedingly fond of demonstrations, restless getter up of "monster concerts," in which classical works of genius were pressed into damaging promiscuity with

The Coliseum for Gilmore's National Peace Jubilee of 1869 was built specially for the event and dismantled after it was over.

> musical *mix pickel* for the million; bountiful in advertising patronage (sure road to favor with the press); one of the glibbest, most sonorous and voluminous in all the wordy ways of "stunning" and sensational announcement.

Gilmore, as the disapproving Dwight saw it, had seemed determined "to 'thrust' greatness upon us by sheer force of numbers." And that approach had made "disinterested music-lovers" like himself anxious about "the honor and the modesty of Art." Implying that cultural events should be led by the most cultured people, Dwight found it unnerving "that our whole musical world, with all the musical resources of the nation" should be marshaled by a man like Gilmore.

Yet Dwight did not allow such reservations to overcome his respect for what Gilmore had accomplished. First, the bandleader had used advertising, about which Dwight confessed himself squeamish, to plant the seed and catch public attention. And then, with consummate tact, Gilmore had unveiled his genius at lining up financial support.

> At the critical moment Business stepped in to the rescue; Business, with the money guaranty, with organizing skill, with ready way of rushing its big en-

terprises through. The application of Dry Goods and Railroad methods saved the whole. The work was well laid out among responsible committees. The word went forth that now the enterprise was on its feet. Conversions became numerous; subscriptions, too; whole business streets were canvassed, and it demanded courage in the unbeliever to say no. The huge Coliseum went up as by magic.

Having acknowledged Gilmore's superior entrepreneurship, Dwight turned his attention to the jubilee itself. The coliseum built for the occasion held 50,000 people, performers included. And in the critic's view, the spectacle of "so many beings met and held together there in full sight of each other, and in perfect order" formed the most indelible memory of all. "What but music," he asked, "could secure such order?" The choral singing he found generally impressive.

> In the great chorus there was far more unity, precision, light, and shade in rendering, than almost any one of musical experience could have believed possible. And it grew better as the thing went on. It gave one a proud joy to know that so many thousands of singers, with only one rehearsal of the whole, could sing so well together. It told of musical enthusiasm, of *esprit du corps*, of good native average of voices and of talent, good instruction, thorough and inspiring drill in separate bodies.

While Dwight found things to criticize in the performances, he saw the whole event as an impressive demonstration of "the musical resources of our people." As a result, "tens of thousands of all classes (save, unfortunately, the poorest)" had been given the chance to experience music and to respect it, perhaps "for the first time . . . as a high and holy influence" and "the birthright of a free American," and not "a superfluous refinement of an over-delicate and fashionable few."[30]

The National Peace Jubilee of 1869 was the high-water mark in the influence of the band in American life. For it was a bandleader who conceived and organized this event, an artistic and financial success for which an entire region pooled its musical resources on a huge scale. While the sheer numbers of musicians involved was remarkable, so was the participation of all manner of music makers: European-born conductors, solo singers and players, church musicians, whole choirs, public school teachers, orchestra players, bandsmen, and children—not to mention the Boston Fire Department. Gilmore, the only musician in Boston with ties to such a wide community, was the catalyst that made the enterprise work.

During the 1870s, however, the notion that such diverse elements as edifying music, entertaining music, and mammoth spectacle could be democratically intermixed lost ground to the view that edifying music deserved a forum all its own. As the prestige of European concert music grew, its need to support itself in the marketplace declined. Orchestras began to attract patronage; the orchestra and band went their separate ways. When the United States celebrated its centennial in 1876, symphony conductor Theodore Thomas, a champion of art over entertainment, was hired to oversee the music, which turned out to be an unhappy choice. In Boston in 1869, Pat Gilmore had staged a gigantic display of musical democracy. But in Philadelphia in 1876, no similar unity of purpose could be discovered, even though the occasion called for it. With aesthetic opinion, now backed by patronage, insisting on the priority of music *as an art*—claiming that priority, in fact, as proof of the nation's growing maturity—it was no longer possible for a bandleader to rally the whole spectrum of the country's musical forces.

15

From Church to Concert Hall
The Rise of Classical Music

ON CHRISTMAS NIGHT IN 1815, a concert took place in Boston's Stone Chapel that marks a new stage in Americans' recognition of music as an art. Some months earlier, the Boston Handel and Haydn Society had been formed to improve sacred music performance and promote the sacred works of eminent European masters. And now the society was giving its first public performance for a paying audience. Attended by an estimated one thousand customers, the program included excerpts from Haydn's *The Creation* and Handel's *Israel in Egypt*, as well as the "Hallelujah" Chorus from *Messiah*, sandwiched around a more varied menu of numbers. According to a Boston newspaper, the concert "electrified" the crowd. "Those who are judges of the performance," read the report, "are unanimous in their declaration of [its] superiority to any ever before given in this town." And the writer added: "Notwithstanding the sanctity of the place and day, the excitements to loud applause were frequently irresistible. . . . We have no language to do justice to the feelings" evoked by hearing these works "from the fathers of sacred song."[1]

There are good reasons to treat this concert as a landmark event, perhaps none more important than the role it gave to composers. While reformers of psalmody had long been touting European musical science as a positive force, their interest lay in congregational, not choir, singing and certainly not in the complexities of oratorio. (In this period, "oratorio" was used to mean both performances of particular oratorios, such as Haydn's *The Creation*, and a concert of sacred music.) The Boston Handel and Haydn Society set out to establish a place for Handel and Haydn *as composers of oratorios*, placing fresh emphasis on music itself. In other words, they performed a selection of composers' music, where the score provided the authority. Their effort testified that works other than hymn tunes could outlive the time and place of their origin. And such transcendence formed the ideological cornerstone for an approach to music making that was just starting to blossom. The Handel and Haydn Society's concert put musical science—which could mean correct harmony *or* musical complexity—on display in a new context. Audience members heard words familiar from Bible reading and churchgoing sung to music whose complexity enhanced their grandness, and they responded with an enthusiasm that no Protestant church congregation could have registered. Hearing the music of Handel and Haydn, Boston audiences could experience the evocative power of musical sound that was artistic as well as sacred.

The blend of worldly and spiritual elements made the society's first concert unusual. The spiritual elements included the performance in a church, on a holy occasion, of music sung to sacred words. Secular elements included the concert setting itself, the emphasis on particular composers and the sound of their music, the price of admission ($1 per ticket), the presence of both an orchestra and organ, and the applause that punctuated musical numbers. In the spirit of a festival honoring Handel and Haydn, the concert brought sacred music to listeners who paid their way into the church, listened rather than sang, and responded by clapping rather than praying.

The Handel and Haydn Society's debut concert began a tradition of oratorio performances that laid the groundwork for a concert life new to the United States. Toward the end of his life, the pianist William Mason, eldest son of Lowell, remarked that while New York had "received its musical culture from abroad," Boston was "a self-developing musical city."[2] Mason attributed the difference largely to his father's work. And indeed, although the elder Mason was not a founder of the society, he later became its leader, and his blend of artistic idealism and economic practicality had much to do with its influence. The Handel and Haydn Society's success with oratorio began a process in Boston that would lead to the construction of a public space where music could be presented as an independent art, free from the need to be linked to Christian ideology or worship.

CONGREGATIONS, CHOIRS, AND ORATORIOS

By 1820, the Boston Handel and Haydn Society was giving several concerts per season. Income in these years came from membership fees and concert-ticket receipts, with a bit more from rental of the hall the society leased for its own rehearsals and functions. Expenses included the payment of performers (the organist, some vocal soloists, and members of the orchestra, who were mostly professionals), the purchase of instruments, lease for the hall, and the cost of music. When income failed to meet expenses, members were expected to make up the deficit out of their own pockets.

As noted in Chapter 8, Lowell Mason visited Boston in 1821, approaching the society with a manuscript tunebook he had compiled in Savannah, Georgia, and proposing that the society publish the book under its name, with the proceeds split equally between author and publisher. *The Boston Handel and Haydn Society Collection of Church Music* (1822) proved a financial windfall for the partners, enriching each by about $12,000. The book's success helped the society maintain its concerts for chorus and orchestra while also expanding their repertory. By 1827, when the thirty-five-year-old Mason moved to Boston as the society's president, the Handel and Haydn Society was Boston's foremost musical organization.

The income from the book's publication was surely unexpected. Yet by publishing Mason's tunebook, the society was pursuing one of its goals: to raise the standard of singing in public worship. Whatever the musical distance between Handel's oratorios and the hymn tunes published in Mason's book, both involved choral performance, the era's ultimate form of democratic music making. Psalmodist Thomas Hastings neatly described the pleasure that singing in a choir could bring: "The conscious blending of voices in melody and harmony—the simultaneous enunciation of the cherished themes—the mutual kindling of emotions—and the union of effort towards the right expressions of sentiment, are among the sources of musical enjoyment, which are but imperfectly understood by the silent listener."[3] The Handel and Haydn Society channeled that impulse toward sacred concerts, intended to show Bostonians how far beyond congregational singing sacred choral music could reach. The singers performing Handel's and Haydn's scientific music were amateurs; few had been trained beyond the singing school. Most were evangelical Protestants of middle-class background.[4] The sacred subject matter of oratorios most likely drew them to choral singing in the first place. But once enlisted in the name of God, choristers were then required to sing demanding voice parts artistically and on pitch, with decent vocal quality and clear pronunciation.

Chapter 7 noted how reformers of psalmody took up the cause of European standards and "correct taste" as early as the 1790s. By around 1805, reformers were using Handel's name to symbolize musical correctness. Like a wand being waved, his spirit might be called up to bless the stance taken by reformers, from Andrew Law to Lowell Mason, in favor of "chaste" European-style hymnody over the more rough-and-ready tunes of Billings and his New England compatriots. Some reformers also linked a European musical standard, in the name of religion, to refinement and gentility. But in the Handel and Haydn Society, the two composers were more than symbols of refinement; they were the authors of works that singers and listeners were coming to know through experience. Members of the chorus could seek religious exaltation—praise directed to the ear of God—while trying to improve their singing and broaden their aesthetic horizons. Thus the society provided a forum for musical aspiration of a kind new to Americans, through a medium that fostered artistic skills in the name of religion, not refinement. Sacred subject matter, citizen involvement, and self-financing came together to ground what might have been an elite enterprise in democratic values. The Handel and Haydn Society's survival provides a glimpse of the way Boston became a self-developing musical city. Building on a tradition of Protestant psalmody, Bostonians by 1820 had found a place for European sacred music of high artistry, performed chiefly by amateurs.

Like oratorio societies, church choirs also brought the aesthetic pleasure of sacred choral music to singers and listeners alike. Singing teacher and composer William Bradbury, a younger colleague of Lowell Mason, made that point in a church musicians' credo he set down in the mid-1800s. Bradbury urged congregation members with "more musical talent than the rest" to form choirs and sing in each service, with the rest of the congregation as "silent listeners." Volunteer choirs, Bradbury wrote, should sing "new and beautiful music appropriate to the occasion," performed "with as much taste and skill" as the choir's "study and practice" would allow.[5]

Recognizing that sacred choral singing could be both beautiful *and* worshipful, psalmodists nevertheless remained wary of its aesthetic side. Thomas Hastings cautioned against sacred singing in which aesthetic appreciation outran religious control. "No one thinks of attending a religious meeting when he goes to the oratorio," wrote Hastings. "He goes to a musical feast." As for church choirs, they needed to be schooled in actually *feeling* the truth of the sacred ideas they uttered in song. In 1861, Hastings, then in his late seventies, was still active in the business, leading a choir at a Presbyterian church in New York City. One imagines that he spent as much rehearsal time expounding spiritual messages as he did polishing the choir's singing. For if choirs strove only for a pleasant sound, Hastings wrote, "why, then, let us have at once the *prima-donnas* of the drama for our leading singers."[6] Indeed, by the time of the Civil War, many of New York's churches were in fact employing "quartet choirs": usually a soprano, alto, tenor, and bass, some of whom were opera or concert singers.[7] Professional singers brought into churches a technical skill and mastery of aesthetic effect that amateurs could not match. But, evangelical leaders warned, some also displayed an insincerity that could blunt the religious impact of performances during public worship. Nevertheless, there is little question that performances by accomplished singers in church helped pave the way for music to be appreciated more widely as an art.

Trinity Church on New York City's Wall Street.

CHURCH ORGANS AND ORGANISTS

In the early 1800s, more and more congregations bought organs—the largest financial investment in music that Americans of that era were consistently ready to make. Only the organ's sacred function can explain the outlay, for organ playing in church was considered a ritual offering to God. Yet, like oratorio singing, organ playing could carry its own aesthetic force. Extolling the organ "for fulness, majesty, richness, modulation, and condensation of sound," one enthusiast wrote in the mid-1830s: "Perhaps no work of man's device can claim equal power of exciting and arresting the feelings."[8] Indeed, the organ's sound and its power to affect the emotions—testifying not only to God's greatness but to the power of music as an art—complicated church leaders' efforts to control its expression.

The eighteenth-century practice of Anglican (i.e., Episcopal) churches hiring their organists from England continued in the nineteenth. Many of the most active composers in America during the early years of independence, including Rayner Taylor, Benjamin Carr, James Hewitt, and George K. Jackson, were organists. And until after the Civil War, those performing in larger city churches—Samuel P. Taylor, Henry C. Timm, George J. Webb, and Charles Zeuner among them—were also mostly immigrants. A list of native-born organist-composers after the Civil War confirms the instrument's important place in American musical life: John Knowles Paine, Hor-

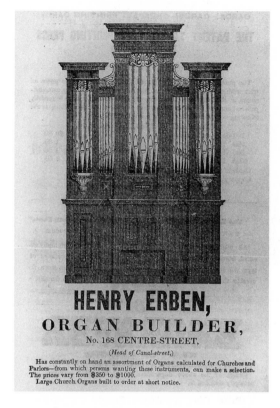

HENRY ERBEN,
ORGAN BUILDER,
No. 168 CENTRE-STREET,
(Head of Canal-street,)
Has constantly on hand an assortment of Organs calculated for Churches and
Parlors—from which persons wanting these instruments, can make a selection.
The prices vary from $350 to $1000.
Large Church.Organs built to order at short notice.

The business card of Henry Erben (1800–1884), one of New York's leading organ builders of the nineteenth century.

atio Parker, George W. Chadwick, Arthur Foote, Dudley Buck, and Charles Ives.

As affluence grew during antebellum years, so did the grandeur of American organs. In 1846, Brooklyn builder Henry Erben completed a large instrument for New York City's Trinity (Episcopal) Church at a cost of $10,500. That expense proves the congregation's commitment to sacred music, enhanced further by the hiring of Edward Hodges, holder of a doctorate in music from Cambridge University, as organist. The Trinity organ, then the largest in the United States, impressed both ear and eye. One description noted the swell box's extraordinary power and the organ's majestic height, "60 feet above the pavement of the church."[9] A New York observer who visited Erben's shop while the organ was being built confessed amazement at the size of the lowest pipes—"big enough for a small family and room for boarders," he joked, wondering whether Hodges intended "to save house rent" by living in one of them.[10]

Like church organs themselves, organ playing different greatly from place to place. In the 1820s and 30s, as more meeting houses and churches acquired organs, finding people to play them was not always easy, especially in smaller towns. Bemoaning the "difficulty of procuring good organists," singing teacher N. D. Gould described the results of unsatisfactory organ playing: "Complaints are made; the organist is mortified, if not provoked; stays away from church,—no organist. The waiting eyes and ears of the congregation are disappointed."[11]

Yet organists were as likely to draw criticism for showing off as for being incompetent. In the view of Thomas Hastings, organists often abused their role and the power of their instrument. In some churches, he wrote, the organ

> seems to be employed as a labor-saving machine, just as if it could supersede the necessity of vocal cultivation. In others, it serves as a kind of musical deluge, to overwhelm the jargon of a thousand dissonant voices. In others, still, it serves as an object of splendid attraction, that the vacant seats of a congregation may be the more readily supplied with wealthy occupants; or as an instrument upon which the performer is to advertise the liberality of the donors, the ingenuity of the builder, or the marvellous powers of the executant.

The urge to display their skills led some organists to become virtual "dictators" over public worship. Hastings complained especially about voluntaries played before and after the worship service and interludes between hymn stanzas. A voluntary, he wrote, should establish or maintain a worshipful aura through unity of mood. But some organists used the occasion to uncork an arsenal of affects, including "everything in turn that is learned, magnificent, grave, lively, comic, and grotesque." Following the same impulse during hymns, they sometimes buried the singers' voices in "massive peals of legato harmony." The end of each hymn stanza, Hastings lamented, brought a "moment of liberation," when the instrument was "allowed to burst forth in all the rhapsody of execution, as if exulting in its emancipation from an unwilling captivity!" And service-ending voluntaries provoked "the same disposition to exult and revel at will in all the intricate mazes of melody and harmony."[12]

The opening of Henry Erben's giant instrument for Trinity Church brought the organ's dual heritage of worship and artistry into conflict. At Erben's request, two days were given over to a public display in which local organists were invited to play anything they chose. The invitation, a local newspaper reported, brought a "suffocating jam" of people flocking to the church gates. When the gates were opened, the crowd streamed into the church with "such a buzz and a chatter, and a running about, up the pulpit stairs, into the vestry, and over the barriers of the chancel" as had never been seen before. Not everyone was there for the music, though: inside the church, "we found that the organ was in full blast, and the audience in full march, examining the various parts of the building, most being busily engaged in conversation upon various topics, with only here and there a group listening to the organ." The music included opera arias, "marches from military bands, and waltzes from the ballroom. These were interspersed with chromatic improvisations, and complicated fantasias, and voluntary variations on popular airs, or, perhaps, here and there, a *Kyrie Eleison* from a mass, or a fugue from an opera." Calling the event as a whole "a farce," the report ended by charging that it had turned the house of God into "an exhibition room."[13]

This moment in the life of Trinity Church dramatizes the public impact of the church organ, an instrument that delivered more than just sacred experience. Like oratorio singing and church choirs, organ playing fostered performing skill and an aesthetic sense that sacred expression could not wholly contain. By the 1840s, thanks partly to opera and partly to the church, the sounds of compositions by European masters were no longer inaccessible to Americans, especially city dwellers. Certain European repertories were being recognized as worthy of respect and their composers as gifted creative artists. In short, the groundwork was being laid for a concert life rooted in the musical idealism that underlies the classical sphere. In the self-developing musical city of Boston, that concert life began to take shape in 1815 with the Handel and Haydn Society.

CLASSICAL INSTRUMENTAL MUSIC COMES TO BOSTON

In the 1800s, as affluence and leisure time increased, the audience for music grew, and promoters and musicians found ways to turn Americans into listening customers. Just as churches fostered sacred music, other kinds of music were linked to the theater, the military, the school, and the parlor. But one kind of Old World music could claim no tie to entertainment, religion, education, or domestic culture: classical instrumental music. Originating in the latter 1700s, this music placed special emphasis on works of sonata design: written for certain combinations of instruments, in three or four independent movements, and with no descriptive program. Haydn, Mozart, and Beethoven, for example, raised the symphony, a sonata for orchestra in three or four movements, to prominence in the concert hall. And they fashioned works in a similar mold for the drawing room and parlor, including the string quartet (a sonata for four string instruments), the duo sonata for violin and piano, and the solo sonata for keyboard instrument alone. Immigrant musician Alexander Reinagle, who composed four keyboard sonatas in Philadelphia during the 1780s, was just one of many composers in the Western world who wrote such works under the influence of these classical masters.

John Sullivan Dwight (1813–1893), a member of Harvard College's class
of 1832 and an 1836 graduate of Harvard's Divinity School, became
Boston's leading writer on music with the founding of *Dwight's Journal
of Music*, which he edited from 1852 until 1881.

In the hands of Haydn, Mozart, and Beethoven especially, the sonata became the chief exemplar of composers' music: a serious, discursive form,
with themes presented, repeated, altered, and developed over long stretches
of time. If other kinds of music sought to teach, entertain, or praise God,
classical instrumental music invited an aesthetic contemplation of tonal
and thematic play. A growing appreciation of its artistic substance in Europe
after 1800 eventually carried over to the United States so that, in the
post–Civil War era, a whole concert life took shape around it. In the early
1800s, however, classical instrumental music was still new to America, and
its character posed difficulties for performers and listeners alike.

Beethoven's First Symphony may serve as an example. Set in four movements, this work, compared to others heard in Boston in the early 1800s, was long and hard to play. It required competent musicians and time for them to rehearse. With no tradition of instrumental ensemble performance in town, there was no chance for audiences to learn the symphony through repeated performances, as they might learn *Messiah* or *The Creation*. The lack of words, singing voices, programmatic narrative, and indeed any literal reference at all left listeners to appreciate the work for its musical events alone. By the 1830s, a few American musicians and writers, following Europeans, were starting to recognize Beethoven as a great master, although describing the nature of his mastery was difficult. His music certainly *sounded* expressive—one could hear a wide range of moods and affects, from serious to playful. But before Americans could embrace Beethoven's symphony, reasons for listening to it were needed, and so was an institutional framework to support its performance. We can observe how these obstacles were dealt with in Boston by tracing the path that led to the first performance of Beethoven's First Symphony there in 1841.

One leader in the effort to prepare Bostonians for Beethoven was John Sullivan Dwight, who would become the city's most prominent music critic by the 1850s. Rather than a practicing musician, Dwight was an ardent music lover whose interest in transcendental philosophy combined with a fascination for German poetry. In 1838, he brought out an English translation of poems by Johann Wolfgang von Goethe and Friedrich von Schiller, finding in their work a spiritual quality of yearning and aspiration that taught him "how life, and thought, and poetry, and beauty, are the inheritance of Man, and not of any class, or age, or nation." By then, he had already informed a group of student instrumentalists at Harvard College that Handel, Mozart, and Beethoven were thinkers on a par with Socrates, Shakespeare, and Newton and was praising instrumental music as "a language of feeling" that had reached "its highest external development" in works for orchestra. In 1841, Dwight described Beethoven's instrumental slow movements as music aspiring to a realm beyond language and even worship, with an ability "to hallow pleasure and to naturalize religion."[14] The critic's articles and addresses of the latter 1830s and early 1840s helped pave the way for classical instrumental music, especially Beethoven's, by pronouncing it a uniquely eloquent, ecumenical kind of spiritual utterance.

Institutional support for instrumental music came first from the Boston Academy of Music. Founded in 1833 to further the teaching of sacred and secular singing, the academy boasted Lowell Mason as its first professor, with George J. Webb as his second-in-command. The new organization caught on quickly with the public. Revenues from membership dues, classes for children and adults, and contributions were enough by 1835 to refurbish the Odeon Theater, supply it with a new organ, and set up academy headquarters there, at a cost of almost $17,000. In the mid-1830s, the academy began broadening its purview to include the cultivation of instrumental music, thanks largely to its president, Samuel A. Eliot. Like Dwight, Eliot—a member of Harvard's Class of 1817, Boston's mayor in 1837–39, and among the city's wealthiest citizens—was no practicing musician but an interested layman and music lover.

Early signs of the new direction are found in the academy's annual report of 1836, which reminded readers that the group's interests went beyond the promotion of sacred singing. Not only did the new headquarters contain a concert hall seating 1,500, but the academy had appointed an instrumentalist as the third professor after Mason and Webb. By the end of the decade, the academy's leaders seem to have viewed singing instruction as merely one stage in a farther-reaching project to enrich and diversify Boston's musical life. "As efficient an orchestra" as possible was to be engaged.[15] Indeed, it was the orchestra of the Boston Academy of Music that gave the local premiere of Beethoven's First Symphony on February 13, 1841.

Although reviews of the concert are lacking, indications are that the Boston public was ready for Beethoven. The academy orchestra followed it with more performances of classical works, and other orchestral concerts began to be given in town as well. In 1842, a local newspaper reported that only a few years earlier the music of Haydn, Mozart, and Beethoven, "with no other attractions offered, would hardly have drawn an audience of fifty persons. Now, we see the hall filled an hour before the commencement of the performances . . . which speaks well for the increase of correct musical taste in our good city." The same report praised the Academy of Music's role in bringing about "this great revolution in musical taste." The academy's 1843 report even suggested a link between musical taste and personal virtue. Calling classical orchestra music "an intellectual and social enjoyment" of a high order, it noted that music's ability to stimulate "the mind and the best feelings." If Bostonians rejected such a force for good, the report warned, that would be "a very discouraging and painful symptom of the character of our population."[16]

This last comment may suggest that the academy's leaders championed instrumental music as an emblem of social exclusiveness. Indeed, scholars in recent years have suggested that, even more than a disinterested love of art, the force that stood behind the establishment of many nineteenth-century musical institutions was a wish to exercise social control by excluding others, because of their class or ethnic background. A few studies have interpreted the founding of the Boston Symphony Orchestra in 1881 in that light.[17] But however it may apply to the post–Civil War era, the notion of

social exclusivity does not apply to the Boston Academy of Music in the
1840s, a populist organization financed by its hundreds of members and devoted chiefly to work in which they participated: sacred singing, choir music, and elementary musical learning. The notion of bringing *all* worthwhile
music making, from elementary to sophisticated, into the academy's field of
endeavor reflected a larger political outlook, which has been described as
republicanism in Thomas Jefferson's mold. According to the republican
view, society was both hierarchical, in that authority was vested in the best-
qualified citizens, *and* egalitarian, in that all members of society were free to
earn their place in the hierarchy. The parallel to the academy's musical program seems clear. Just as social exclusivity would disconnect those at the
top of the hierarchy from the root of their social authority, so would a specialized cultivation of classical instrumental music compromise the whole-
ness and variety of the music making the academy had embraced.

The Boston Academy of Music's sponsorship of instrumental music complemented the ideas of John Sullivan Dwight, for whom one of music's
highest missions was to provide a common rallying point for all people.
Dwight believed "in the capacity of all mankind for music," because music
supplied "a genuine want of the soul."[18] Just as, a generation earlier, the
Handel and Haydn Society had given local citizens a chance to hear oratorios, the academy was now introducing the symphonies of Mozart and
Beethoven to the public. In the early 1840s, with Dwight's idealistic notions
in the air and an appetite for instrumental music apparently growing,
Samuel Eliot and his compatriots had reason to hope that, given a choice,
American listeners would come to understand and prefer "music of the
highest class."[19]

NEW YORK AND THEODORE THOMAS, CONDUCTOR OF THE CLASSICS

In April 1842, a number of New York's leading musicians gathered to discuss the founding of an orchestra whose members, in contrast to the city's
many pickup ensembles, would be permanent. The constitution that resulted from the group's early meetings called for a structure of "actual" and
"professional" members who performed and associate members who attended rehearsals and concerts. The new ensemble, named the New York
Philharmonic Society, was founded, therefore, as a cooperative venture
whose playing members were less interested in financial gain than in the
chance to play the best symphonic music. The United States's oldest professional orchestra, the society gave its first concert in December 1842, offering a mix of vocal and instrumental works by Weber, Johann Nepomuk

Hummel, Rossini, Mozart, and Johann Wenzel Kalliwoda and led by three different conductors. The concert's first number, a full performance of Beethoven's Fifth Symphony, announced the kind of orchestra the Philharmonic Society intended to be.

An orchestra like the New York Philharmonic Society emphasized symphonic works and sought to edify players and audiences alike. Playing only four programs per season, the Philharmonic could be no more than a complement to any musician's livelihood. As a commercial attraction, it was no match for some of the touring orchestras that appeared in the city. Yet its survival shows that the ensemble filled a need on the local scene. Moreover, the Philharmonic's early history is intertwined with the careers of many influential American musicians, including the redoubtable conductor Theodore Thomas.

In the fall of 1853, Louis Jullien's orchestra caught New York's fancy as Jenny Lind had done a few years earlier. Appearing almost nightly with a crowd-pleasing blend of overtures, instrumental solos, and dance numbers, Jullien managed a run of almost one hundred concerts before needing to look beyond the city for audiences. One of the violinists Jullien recruited in America was the eighteen-year-old Thomas, a New York resident since his family had immigrated there from Germany in 1845. Theodore Thomas, who would become this country's premier orchestra conductor of the nineteenth century, had little good to say about Jullien in later years. For Jullien's approach was very different from that of Thomas, whose musical philosophy, grounded in history and a reverence for the classics, took root in America during the latter 1800s and remains a force almost a century after he died.

Thomas's outlook, rooted in a lifetime of making music, deserves a preview here because it represents the classical sphere's core values clearly, and it also shows the difficulty of establishing their position on American shores. First and foremost, Thomas viewed himself as an agent in the work of raising musical standards to secure the symphony orchestra's place in the United States. His autobiography brims with statements of that mission. In 1874, for example, he wrote: "Throughout my life my aim has been to make good music popular," trusting his belief "that the people would enjoy and support the best in art when continually set before them in a clear, intelligent manner." Where most performers were obliged to respect audience taste enough to gratify it, Thomas labored to elevate public taste to the point where it would be worth gratifying. Where most performers centered attention on concerts they were about to give, Thomas was forever imagining what performances might be like in the future—after public taste had risen. Thomas trusted that audiences would come to understand things his way. As a contemporary put it: "He was sure that he was right, and he was

Theodore Thomas (1835–1905), German-born American conductor and one of the most powerful classical musicians in the nineteenth-century United States.

sure that the people would see he was right." Or, as a New York admirer told the guests at a banquet honoring Thomas in 1891: "Like the old warrior who hurled his javelin far into the ranks of the enemy, and fought his way forward to recover it, Thomas flings his baton higher and higher toward the pure and awful peaks, and we all gladly press after, up, up, into a more inspiring air and a broader and grander horizon."[20]

Thomas, however, was a young lion before he could become an old warrior. In 1854, at nineteen, he joined the first-violin section of the New York Philharmonic Society. Within a few years, he also was serving as concertmaster of the Italian opera orchestra at New York's Academy of Music. And he had joined forces with pianist William Mason and cellist Carl Bergmann to launch a chamber music series. Although Thomas kept playing violin in public into his fourth decade, a talent for leadership set him apart from the beginning. His autobiography describes the role of an opera orchestra's concertmaster in the 1850s. Such groups were

> generally engaged and formed by some man . . . who was supposed to know the better musicians, and had some business capacity. This man would receive, besides his salary from the manager, a percentage from every man in the orchestra. . . . As concertmeister, I had both power and responsibility, and I dispensed with this middle man, and began by making all engagements with the members of the orchestra myself.[21]

Thomas, then, mastered not only the artistic but the business side of his trade. There is no question that artistic idealism fueled his long career, but he was an idealist with a payroll to meet.

In May 1862, Thomas conducted his first professional orchestra concert in New York's Irving Hall, an event for which he took the financial risk himself: booking the hall, choosing the players and the program, conducting the rehearsals, supervising the advertising and ticket sales, and paying players from the proceeds while he kept the rest. Soon he also began to conduct the Brooklyn Philharmonic Society, formed in 1857 as a parallel to New York's. But it was as conductor of the Theodore Thomas Orchestra (1865–90) that he accomplished one of the more complex balancing acts in the history of American music, by controlling both its artistic and economic arms.

To call art and economics separate arms of activity is to recognize the conflict between them. The assumption that economic interests run counter to aesthetic ones—that the marketplace is a foe of artistic values—has been basic to many Americans' understanding of their country's musical development. The Germanic outlook certainly shares that assumption. In fact, the strength of its commitment to artistic idealism can make money matters seem crass, as if in a Victorian parlor one were suddenly to begin discussing the mechanics of childbirth. By that token, artists known to keep an eye on the box office have sometimes been suspected of low artistic integrity. But Thomas's career challenges the notion that art and economics are separate things, for without a musical marketplace the Thomas Orchestra could never have survived. The conductor's great achievement was to discover within that marketplace an audience for the symphony orchestra, which in turn allowed him to create for his men a musical livelihood new to America: that of symphony orchestra player.

Thomas found his audiences by blending idealism with a strong pragmatic streak. Three related factors dominated his concerns during the Thomas Orchestra's early years: how the ensemble played, what it played, and where it played. The quality of the playing demonstrated the conductor's pragmatic idealism in action. On the podium, Thomas was a taskmaster who strove for precise, polished performances. Since much of the music

Thomas programmed was hard to play, good performances relied on skilled players and time to rehearse them. In an age of makeshift ensembles, however, the best players were the most in demand; and to recruit them, Thomas had to provide good wages, which hinged in part on the quantity of work he could provide them. Thus, as well as performing the classics in concert halls, theaters, and auditoriums, from 1865 on the orchestra also made a specialty of outdoor concerts. A summer series in Central Park Garden proved especially popular with the public: 1,227 programs in an eight-year period (1868–75), or more than 150 performances per summer on the average. At Central Park and in other outdoor series he conducted, Thomas followed Louis Jullien's example, though without the flashy showmanship. Customers were served a mixture of symphonic movements with overtures, dances, and lighter selections in settings where they felt relaxed and comfortable—snacking, drinking, and socializing. Such "concessions" to public taste, Thomas believed, chipped away at barriers between audience and orchestra. At the same time, thanks to all that performing, the Thomas Orchestra came to play better and better, soon outstripping all other American ensembles, with their changing personnel and fewer concerts.[22]

Still, however popular Thomas may have become with New York audiences, he was able to stay in business only by touring. In 1869, the Thomas Orchestra made the first of many journeys down the so-called Thomas Highway of the United States and Canada, which included Montreal, Maine, Georgia, New Orleans, San Francisco, and many places in between. Through the early 1870s, the orchestra sometimes spent more than half the year on the road. While the rigors of that life may have worked hardships on Thomas and his men, few listeners or critics questioned the quality of the playing. Russian pianist and composer Anton Rubinstein testified at the end of an 1873 tour with Thomas that, in the whole world, only the orchestra of the National Conservatory of Paris was the Thomas Orchestra's equal in personnel—"but, alas, they have no Theodore Thomas to conduct them."[23]

Even as Thomas was tailoring programs to fit the tastes of different audiences, his belief in the superiority of certain classical works never wavered. Performers and listeners alike, he believed, were tested and measured by the great symphonic compositions. And the moral authority of the music reached beyond the concert hall. Thomas once explained why he discouraged the telling of risqué stories, and why he never read "trashy" books or attended "trashy plays": "When I come before the public to interpret masterworks, and my soul should be inspired with noble and impressive emotions, these evil thoughts run around my mind like squirrels and spoil it all. A musician must keep his heart pure and his mind clean if he wishes to elevate, instead of debasing his art."[24] In listening to music by Beethoven and

The Music Hall in Cincinnati, Ohio, opened for the city's third May Festival in 1878, under the direction of Theodore Thomas.

other great composers, Thomas wrote, "faculties are called into action and appealed to other than those [the listener] ordinarily uses," absorbing attention and freeing listeners "from worldly cares." He shared John Sullivan Dwight's view that instrumental music held an advantage over vocal music, whose meanings were fixed by the words. Addressed chiefly to the "imagination and intellect," Thomas thought, instrumental music invited listeners to make their "own interpretation to the extent of [their] experience."[25]

Differences in listening experience were precisely what divided Thomas's audiences. "Symphonic music," he once wrote, "is the highest flower of art," and "only the most cultivated persons are able to understand it." Thomas noted the challenge posed by "the orchestra, with its unlimited palette, whereby the modern composer paints every shade and gradation of tone color," and admitted that "the complexities of symphonic form are far beyond the grasp of beginners." The Central Park Garden concerts of the 1860s and early 70s were aimed at such beginners. Featuring music with "very clearly defined melody and well-marked rhythms, such . . . as is played by the best bands," they were meant to prepare novice listeners "for a higher grade of musical performances." As he grew older, however, Thomas came to believe it "a waste of time for a great symphony orchestra to do this work, which could be equally well accomplished by smaller and less costly organizations."[26] On the other hand, when the audience gave a symphony orchestra its attention, the impact could be breathtaking, even for inexperienced listeners. In 1877, the Thomas Orchestra paid a visit to a Mississippi River town, playing works by Mendelssohn, Charles Gounod, Camille Saint-Säens, Robert Schumann, Hector Berlioz, and Liszt. "Life was never the same afterward," a writer who heard that concert as a boy later recalled, for audience members had been shown that "there really existed as a fact, and not as something heard of and unattainable, this world of beauty, wholly apart from everyday experiences."[27]

Thomas's understanding of how the musical marketplace worked made him increasingly eager to end his dependence on it. And indeed, the Thomas Orchestra was no model for the symphony orchestra's establishment as an American institution. Relying on concert receipts for support, Thomas toured from necessity, not choice. In Europe, most orchestras were local organizations financed by local resources and addressed to local audiences. But before a similar situation could arise in the United States, three elements had to come together: (1) a belief in the artistic importance of the symphony orchestra; (2) civic pride, centered in the feeling that an orchestra enriches community life; and (3) wealth, donated in recognition that the marketplace cannot support an orchestra of the first rank.

The first of these elements, fostered by the Germanic outlook, reflected the belief that classic orchestral works ranked among the supreme achievements of humankind, and that music was a composer-centered art. Indeed, the recognition of the composer as primary agent in musical art helped to create a consecrated aura around the classics, which in turn fed the process of "sacralization" that scholars have identified in American cultural life from the 1870s on.[28] Thomas was a prime mover in establishing the ritual elements in a symphony orchestra concert: an atmosphere of attentive restraint; a code of behavior and dress for both players and audience; and an assumption that performers approach their task with fealty to the scores, sparing no effort to honor the composers' artistic intentions. Just as liturgy ruled the public worship of a God whose presence, though unseen, was always felt, so musical scores filled in for composers who, though most likely absent, were celebrated in concert performances. Thus, symphony orchestras, understood as agents of artistic ritual, brought prestige and valuable experience to the life of a community.

Beginning in the 1880s, orchestras were formed where money was available to free them from dependency on the marketplace. A landmark event took place in Boston in 1881, when banker Henry Lee Higginson founded the Boston Symphony Orchestra, which he himself ran for nearly four decades, hiring and firing conductors and players—all under personal contract to him—and collecting the receipts, making up deficits out of his own pocket. The Chicago Symphony Orchestra, founded a decade later, used a different approach. Fifty backers, each pledging an annual donation of $1,000 for three years, formed an Orchestral Association, which in turn hired a musical director. Other cities followed schemes of their own; in New York, the Philharmonic Society kept its cooperative status and musicians' control until around 1910, when a board of directors was organized to assume financial responsibility. By that time, Philadelphia, St. Louis, Cincinnati, Minneapolis, and Pittsburgh had all started orchestras following Chicago's model.

Theodore Thomas, who had done more than anyone else to inspire this trend, continued to lead the Thomas Orchestra, and in 1877 was also chosen music director of the New York Philharmonic Society, a post he held until 1891. Here was an association that had come full circle, for Thomas, a Philharmonic member in the 1850s, had during the 1860s and 70s been the conductor of its chief rival. The years under Thomas's leadership proved successful ones for the Philharmonic, both economically and artistically. Even as conductor of two New York–based ensembles, however, Thomas dreamed most of all of a permanent orchestra: one that offered its musicians full-time employment, with funding independent of the marketplace and not supplied by Thomas himself. When asked by Chicago businessman Charles Norman Fay if he would consider moving to Chicago to take up such a post, Thomas is said to have replied: "I would go to hell if they gave me a permanent orchestra."[29] In response, Fay organized a group of financial backers who then invited Thomas to become the new Chicago orchestra's music director with complete control of its artistic affairs. A season of twenty-eight weeks was projected, with two concerts per week, plus eight weeks of touring. The orchestra would consist of eighty-six players, of whom sixty-two were to be regular members, under contract to the Orchestral Association; the rest were to be engaged on a temporary basis. The association could hire out the orchestra for opera performances, with or without Thomas as conductor. For an annual salary of $15,000 Thomas agreed to give up other conducting engagements and to allow the Chicago Symphony Orchestra to use the library of scores and parts he had accumulated through a lifetime.

And so, from 1891 to the end of his life, Thomas conducted his own permanent orchestra. The Chicago Symphony's articles of incorporation described the music director's duties in language that Thomas might have written himself: "The Musical Director is to determine the character and standard of all performances . . . make all programmes, select all soloists, and take the initiative in arranging for choral and festival performances." He was also given "the power and responsibility for the attainment of the highest standard of artistic excellence in all performances given by the Association." Thomas's wife, Rose (the sister of Charles Norman Fay), later recalled that this provision gave him special joy. "All my life," he told her, "I have been told that my standard was too high, and urged to make it more popular. But now, I am not only to be given every facility to create the highest standard, but am even told that I will be *held responsible* for keeping it so! I have to shake myself to realize it."[30]

As music director of the Chicago Symphony Orchestra Thomas won the autonomy he had long desired. Although he faced such obstacles as financial shortfalls, complaints about programming, the continuing need to tour, and the lack of a suitable concert hall, for the most part the orchestra succeeded. On December 14, 1904, Thomas conducted the inaugural concert in Orchestra Hall, the ensemble's new home, built under his own supervision and with the help of donations from eight thousand Chicagoans. But illness immediately overtook him. Ten days later, he laid down his baton after a concert for the last time, and he died of influenza on January 4, 1905.

If Thomas's life was one of constant struggle, many of his triumphs had national impact. By the time he died, a classical sphere based on composers' music was well established in America, and a number of cities boasted symphony orchestras, some with halls built specially for them. In the new century's early years, musical life in centers like New York, Boston, Philadelphia, and Chicago was sometimes said to be catching up with that of European cities, where an infrastructure of musical activity existed: performing groups, concert halls, conservatories, and enough public interest in these institutions to support them financially.

Critics and historians of the day often pictured the United States as a young nation whose musical life was starting to blossom along Old World lines; and part of any mature musical culture, they recognized, was musical composition. A nation whose composers could write music worthy of standing next to the classics was surely ready to take its place among musical nations of the West. If the United States was now on the brink of realizing that status, Theodore Thomas, in the mind of at least one composer, had helped to position it there. When Thomas died, the Boston composer George W. Chadwick wrote that of all conductors in America, Thomas alone had treated American composition "as a dignified and serious effort":

> Not, on the one hand, as the work of incompetent amateurs to be scoffed and sneered at; nor, on the other, as an infant industry to be coddled and shielded from all opposition. He produced the works of American writers

side by side with the classic, and also the modern masters, so that they could be compared with their contemporaries, and could stand or fall by their own intrinsic value—the only position a real artist cares to occupy.[31]

Chadwick was speaking in 1905 on behalf of a generation whose members had come of age after the Civil War. He saw himself and his compatriots as pioneers within the cosmopolitan musical life that had taken root in the United States, emanating from Europe, especially Germany. Yet well before Chadwick and his generation came upon the scene, several musicians had presented themselves to the public as American composers. Their careers show that the classical sphere as defined by advocates of the European masters was a bit too narrow and exclusive to contain the burgeoning new democracy's musical energies in the earlier and middle nineteenth century.

16

From Log House to Opera House

Anthony Philip Heinrich and William Henry Fry

AMONG THE MUSICIANS who played in the New York Philharmonic Society's first concert in December 1842, one member of the viola section could lay claim to being the nation's chief composer of orchestral music. Anthony Philip Heinrich, a sixty-one-year-old Bohemian-born American who had chaired the society's founding meeting in April, had by 1842 written at least a dozen such works, most of them still unperformed. We might guess that a new ensemble like the Philharmonic would have been eager to play new American compositions, but that was not the case. Perhaps the Philharmonic was prejudiced against home-grown art, as two American-born composers were to charge in the 1850s. Or perhaps Heinrich and his music were simply too eccentric to be championed by a fledgling orchestra. Whatever the reasons, the New York Philharmonic Society was founded and grew to its early maturity almost entirely apart from any engagement with music by American composers.

THE LOG-HOUSE COMPOSER OF AMERICA

Born near the German border of northern Bohemia in 1781, Heinrich began his life in affluence, thanks to a family business. Though he learned to play violin and piano as a boy, he grew up intending to be a merchant, with music as a sideline. An energetic traveler throughout his life, Heinrich visited the United States in 1805 and returned in 1810, hoping to establish his business here. After economic collapse in America and the Napoleonic Wars abroad wiped out his family's fortune, Heinrich, at the age of thirty-six, decided to embark on a musical career—in the West, rather than in the cities of the Eastern Seaboard. From Philadelphia, where he had played in a theater orchestra, he traveled in 1817 to Pittsburgh, hoping to direct the same kind of ensemble there. When that prospect fell through, he continued westward down the Ohio River as far as Kentucky, where he decided to settle. The journey, more than seven hundred miles through rough, sometimes untracked terrain, created a lasting impression. Apparently under the spell of this encounter with the North American wilds, Heinrich made a decision that shaped the rest of his life. Not only would he seek his fortune in music; he would be a composer.

More than one music historian has connected Heinrich with the Romantic spirit that came to dominate European musical composition in the early 1800s.[1] Musical Romanticism can be characterized as a preference for the original, unique, extreme, expressed in rich harmonies and innovative textures and tone colors.[2] These features are all found in Heinrich's music. Indeed, if self-reliance fosters originality, then Heinrich was a true original. Living by himself in a wilderness log cabin near the village of Bardstown, Kentucky, and with no access to formal musical learning, he had only his own intuition to rely on when he began to compose. Romantic artists also drew inspiration from nature, a lead that Heinrich followed wholeheartedly in such orchestra works as *The Wild Wood Spirits' Chant* (1842) and *Manitou Mysteries* (1845).

Heinrich's prose, preserved in letters, prefaces, and critical writings, adds to his image as a colorful character, "vegetating in my Bardstown log house" and living "upon roots, milk and bread, quite solitary." Occasionally his isolation was broken. One evening after midnight, Heinrich was "playing on the violin a dead march in honor of my poor departed wife," when suddenly "a negro prowling about" burst into his cabin. The startled composer was asked to keep playing, for the violin's "sweet sounds" had drawn the guest there in the first place. "I began again the dirge which pleased him amazingly," he recalled. When the visitor tried to pay him, Heinrich refused, then repeated the dead march. "This adventure with the negro," he concluded, "at dead of night, in the lonely forest, seemed to me rather poetical. I liked the good ear, taste and generosity of the sable visitor exceedingly."[3]

Heinrich left no account of how he learned to compose; apparently, he simply started writing music. In the spring of 1818, attracted by Heinrich's "well known seclusion in a retired loghouse," a young Bardstown man "interrupted my studious application on the violin," and asked for a musical setting of "How Sleep the Brave," a poem about military heroism. "I took pencil and instantaneously reciprocated," Heinrich recalled, suggesting a mind well stocked with musical ideas that needed only to be written down. From that time on, music poured out of him: at first songs and compositions for violin and piano, then more piano music, and from the 1830s music for orchestra and even oratorios. In 1820, Heinrich published *The Dawning of Music in Kentucky* (Op. 1), a collection of vocal and instrumental pieces. In

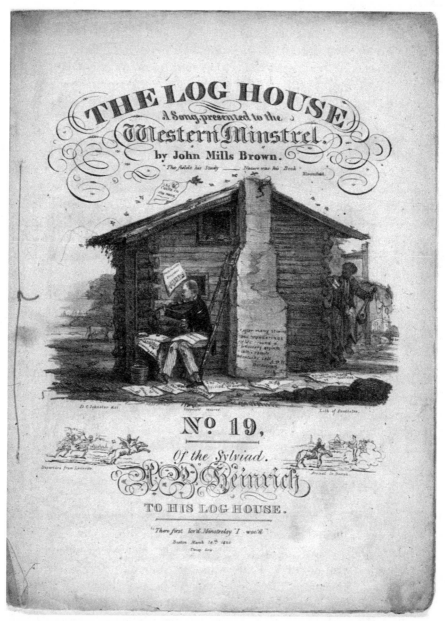

This image of Anthony Philip Heinrich (1781–1861) as the Loghouse Composer of Kentucky is found in his *The Sylviad*, Op. 3, a collection of pieces for keyboard, voice, and other instruments.

a review, the editor of a Boston music journal registered amazement at what Heinrich had achieved. As he put it, an ex-businessman nearing forty years of age had suddenly declared himself a composer, and had then written music that showed "vigour of thought, variety of ideas, originality of conception," and "classical correctness," not to mention "boldness and luxuriance of imagination."[4]

In 1823, Heinrich left Kentucky for Boston. Now a composer of some experience, he served briefly as organist at Boston's Old South Church, probably played in theater orchestras, and did some teaching. He also took part in at least two concerts that featured his music. In the meantime, a new collection of his work was published: *The Sylviad, or Minstrelsy of Nature in the Wilds of N. America* (Op. 3; Boston, 1823). The Boston journal that had praised Opus 1 also endorsed this latest offering. All the composer's works, the reviewer wrote, "abound in boldness, originality, science, and even sublimity; and embrace all styles of composition, from a waltz or song up to the acme of chromatic frenzy." The review concluded with the suggestion that Heinrich "may be justly styled the *Beethoven of America*, as he is actually considered by the few who have taken the trouble to ascertain his merits."[5]

These comments confirm what Heinrich's scores suggest: that he was a "difficult" composer whose fondness for complexity made it hard for him to find an audience, despite a populist streak in both his persona and his music. Dubbing himself the "loghouse composer," Heinrich reveled in that homespun image, which he furthered in written comments full of jokes, puns, and self-deprecation. His music often quotes well-known national tunes, and his instrumental works are more descriptive than abstract, many of them inspired by an image or story found in the American landscape. Heinrich was the first American composer to celebrate the customs of North America's native peoples. Beginning in 1831 with *Pushmataha, a Venerable Chief of a Western Tribe of Indians*, he tried to catch some of the mystery of Indian life in a series of works for large orchestra. But if these compositions marked the peak of Heinrich's artistic ambition, the technical difficulty of his works put them beyond the reach of all but a few performers.

Widespread complication is found not only in Heinrich's orchestra music but in a chamber work like *The Yankee Doodleiad: A National Divertimento* (from Op. 1) for three violins, cello, and piano. Ending with virtuosic variations on the revolutionary-era song *Yankee Doodle,* this work begins with *Hail Columbia,* whose melody Heinrich decorates with an acrobatic violin part that leads to an elaborate cadenza. After a brief pause, violins 1 and 2, with cello support, pump out a plain version of *Yankee Doodle*, with violin 3 and piano adding unusually intricate decorations. Most variation movements of Heinrich's day introduce their theme straightforwardly, before the elaborations begin; with Heinrich, elaborations and embellishments are there from the start.

Even when Heinrich wrote songs with popular sheet-music circulation in

Heinrich's *The Yankee Doodlediad* illustrates the technical demands he often placed on players, even in pieces based on familiar melodies.

mind, he did little to simplify his musical style. In 1829, during a stay in England, he sought advice from veteran Irish songwriter Thomas Moore on achieving the commercial success that had so far eluded him. After examining some of Heinrich's songs, Moore told the composer that their harmonic complexity lay "so far beyond the capacity or powers of execution of any of our ordinary amateurs of music" that few would buy copies. They seemed to Moore more like learned exercises than songs. Proclaiming the American's compositions "too good for the world—particularly our English world," Moore advised him: "You must throw a good deal more singsong into your works before you can expect them to succeed."[6]

Moore's words suggest what the notion of Heinrich as the Beethoven of America might have meant in the 1820s. To John Rowe Parker, the Boston writer who assigned Heinrich that label in 1823, Beethoven symbolized not just artistic greatness but a nonconforming, exploratory approach to composing. "It is to be expected," he wrote, that Beethoven "will extend the art of music, in a way never contemplated even by Haydn or Mozart." Parker called Beethoven's symphonies "romances of the wildest invention," adding that "his genius seems to anticipate a future age." Caring little for the performer's convenience, Beethoven crowded "zig zag notes" even "into subservient parts" showing his disdain for "the fetters of established forms of accompaniments." Hence, wrote Parker, "the comparative difficulty of Beethoven's music, the danger even for the experienced player to trust to the forebodings of the ear, the necessity of the eye being forever on the watch, and the impossibility of executing many of his works at sight, however great the reward of perseverance in mastering these obstacles."[7]

For Parker, then, Beethoven was a genius whose music could be unpredictable, even sometimes overloaded. And here is where he found parallels with Heinrich:

> There is enough in his well-stored pages to gratify every taste and fancy. There is versatility for the capricious, pomp for the pedant, playfulness for the amateur, learning for the scholar, business for the performer, pleasure for the vocalist, ingenuity for the curious, and puzzle for an academician. He seems at once to have possessed himself of the key which unlocks to him the temple of science and enables him to explore with fearless security the mysterious labyrinth of harmony.[8]

Heinrich was to live for almost forty years after these words were published. Although his orchestral performances were few and far between, his dedication to composing for orchestra continued into the eighth decade of his life, audiences or no audiences. When his music *was* performed, however, its uniqueness was recognized. After hearing one of Heinrich's symphonic movements in 1836, a reviewer in Graz, Austria, declared the composer's muse "a daughter of Nature, but not of that Nature whose quiet, idyllic grace possesses us all unconsciously." Heinrich, this writer fancied, "has sought out Nature in her workshop where she produces her mighty works . . . where great lakes plunge with deafening roar to the depths below,

and the tornado, with its crashing strength lays bare the impenetrable secrets of the primeval forests."[9] Perhaps these thoughts were triggered as
much by Heinrich's American subject matter as by the character of his music.

After an 1846 benefit concert for the composer in New York, another
critic offered this explanation for the strangeness of Heinrich's work: "Heinrich is undoubtedly ahead of the age; and we believe that his music will be
far more popular long after he is dead than now." And in a letter written the
same year, the composer himself described his music as "full of strange
ideal somersets and capriccios," adding: "I hope there may be some method
discoverable, some beauty, whether of regular or irregular features. Possibly
the public may acknowledge this, when I am dead and gone. I must keep at
the work with my best powers, under all discouraging, nay suffering circumstances."[10] Here Heinrich pictures himself as a composer striving not to
please audiences but to meet an obligation to the art of music. As concert
repertories in the early 1800s were formed around works by composers both
living and dead, the idea took hold that the true worth of a musical composition could only be judged at a chronological distance. If music was a
changing art and composers artists obliged to follow their creative instincts,
then those unappreciated today might tomorrow be perceived as giants.[11]
By mid-century, American concert life included a sphere whose priorities
were shifting away from easily accessible music. As works by Haydn,
Mozart, Beethoven, and other long-dead authors still spoke to present-day
audiences, a composer like Heinrich had reason to feel that his own music's
fate lay in the hands of posterity.

WILLIAM HENRY FRY: AMERICAN COMPOSER

No native-born American composer of the nineteenth century wrote an
opera that entered the standard repertory. In fact, with only a few exceptions, opera in America before the Civil War, governed by accessibility, revolved around works that London audiences favored. English companies
performed English operas or adaptations of foreign ones, and stars of other
nationalities—Maria Malibran and Jenny Lind, for example—came to the
United States by way of London. Nevertheless, from the 1790s on, composers in this country had begun adding works of their own to the American
stage repertory: Benjamin Carr's *The Archers* (1794), John Bray's *The Indian
Princess* (1808), and Rayner Taylor's *The Ethiop* (1813), all by men who had
immigrated from England. Two operas from the 1840s and 50s loom larger,
not only as through-composed works in the grand-opera manner but because both were home-grown efforts: *Leonora* (1845), with music by

Philadelphia-born William Henry Fry, and *Rip Van Winkle* (1855), composed by George Frederick Bristow, of Brooklyn, New York.

As one of four sons of a Philadelphia newspaper publisher, Fry was born in 1813 into a well-to-do family. He attended Mount St. Mary's Academy in Emmitsburg, Maryland, then studied music with French-born Leopold Meignen, said to be a graduate of the Paris Conservatory, who had settled in Philadelphia. In 1833, an opera orchestra in Philadelphia played an overture composed by the twenty-year-old Fry. And soon he embarked on his life's main vocation: writing about music, which he did between 1837 and 1841 for his father's newspaper, the Philadelphia *National Gazette*. He also continued to compose, though that brought him little or no income.

In the early 1840s, Fry concentrated his musical energies on opera, leading up to the premiere of *Leonora*, which took place at Philadelphia's Chestnut Street Theater on June 4, 1845. *Leonora* was a Fry family enterprise: William wrote the music and brother Joseph the libretto, brother Edward acted as impresario, and the whole family covered half the production costs. The Frys intended *Leonora*, based on an English play, for the Seguin Opera Company, headed by English singers Anne and Edward Seguin. The Seguins had arrived in America in the late 1830s, formed a troupe in 1841, and watched it blossom into a company that held a virtual monopoly on English opera performance in the United States until late in the 1840s. Soprano Anne Seguin sang the role of Leonora well enough to win the composer's gratitude; Edward Seguin sang the lead bass role, and company singers took the other major parts. The chorus, some seventy members strong, and the orchestra of fifty were trained by T. Y. Chubb, brought from New York to Philadelphia for the occasion. Leopold Meignen, Fry's first composition teacher, conducted the performance.

The *New York Herald* sent a correspondent to Philadelphia for *Leonora*'s premiere. His breezy account of a night at the opera, short on musical specifics, was also short on respect for the Frys' endeavor. Headlines set the tone for the review: "Grand Opera by Fry and Brother—Excitement among the Quakers—Great rush to the Theater . . . The commencement of the new musical revolution—Awful commotion among the flats and sharps—The great speech of the great Fry—Terrible time among the professors, &c, &c." The review went on to treat the thirty-two-year-old composer with scorn, inviting readers to chuckle over his provincial effort. "The long agony is over," it announced. "The child is christened, and 'Alleghania' has at last an opera of its own—musical taste is on the ascendant, and native Mozarts yet unborn shall lisp with gratitude, in after ages, the mighty name of Fry." After a summary of *Leonora*'s plot and its musical underlining, the writer continued: "All were delighted with the music, it was so much like an old acquaintance in a new coat." In fact, "some of 'the cognoscenti' said that it was a warm 'hash' of Bellini, with a cold shoulder of 'Rossini,' and a handful of 'Auber' salt—whilst others congratulated Mr. Fry upon his opera being so much like *Norma*, an evident proof that the same grand idea may consecutively strike two great minds."[12]

The *Herald* review also quoted at length from a post-performance speech Fry delivered in front of the curtain. Because Americans had so completely neglected "the science of music," the composer complained, "no national standard" exists. Fry confided that as a boy he had already decided to write an opera

> because I thought that it was the only thing Americans had never tried, whilst we had become proficients in every other art and science, particularly locomotives, the only thing which every American understands. (Great laughter, bravoes, and applause.) So I looked around to find someone to teach me, when I alighted upon the gentleman who so ably led the orchestra tonight. (Blushes on the modest face of the susceptible Meignen.) Under that gentleman, a graduate of the Conservatory of Paris, I studied every great composer, from Palestrini up to Rossini, and then I stopped. I then wrote an opera, and since then I have written several operas [*Leonora* was Fry's third], which circumstances or ill luck, it matters not, has prevented them from being brought out.

Fry refused to make excuses for his work. "This opera," he proclaimed, "has been written according to the highest rules of art, and is to be judged by the severest criticisms of art." And he added: "For your favors to myself personally, I thank you; for my opera I ask nothing; the dignity of art disdains all favors."[13]

When Fry claimed to be following art's "highest rules" in *Leonora*, he was challenging the operatic form that then dominated the American stage. Most English operas, with their combination of sung numbers and spoken dialogue, seemed to him corruptions of the true operatic ideal, which lay neither in melodies nor plots but in presenting a staged drama through continuous singing. Following the model of Italian composers, whose use of recitative led to "a proper uniformity of style," Fry had composed *Leonora* as a grand opera with every word "sung throughout, and accompanied by the orchestra." "There is no better reason," Fry wrote, "why a tragic or serious singer should be required to speak on the stage, than a tragic actor to sing." Fry saw his own work as drawing on "the genius of melody" as a universal dialect, which claims, indeed, supremacy over words."[14] Thus, when he declared *Leonora*'s historic importance, Fry was referring not to artistic inspiration but to a musical/dramatic approach. His continuously sung opera, he believed, could carve out a place for English-language works in the true operatic tradition.

Fry's beliefs about opera offer perspective on a public stand he took some years later in New York City as music critic for the *Tribune* (1852–64). Although he used his post to crusade on behalf of American composers, later historians, while agreeing with Fry's advocacy, have sometimes wondered how it fit with the style of his own music. The *Herald's* review of *Leonora* had noted that, except for being set to English words, Fry's music sounded much like that of the European composers he admired, especially Bellini. An aria sung by Montalvo, the villain of *Leonora*, features a Bellini-like, arching vocal melody that unfolds over a rhythmic and harmonic accompaniment. In the example shown below, arranged for voice and piano, an introduction sounds the first two phrases of the melody so that the singer enters with a tune listeners have already heard. Melodies like this one distill emotional statements into the sound of beautiful singing. In fact, they made stars of singers like Jenny Lind, who mastered this smooth, vocally conceived *bel canto* style. Fry believed that such lyric moments, experienced in the context of a continuously sung work, were fundamental to the dramatic impact of an opera. And an American composer who helped to perpetuate opera in its true form deserved a hearing and a place of respect, even if his American music had an Italian sound.[15]

Fry's project as an American opera composer, then, was to master European techniques of opera writing so that audiences could experience them in the English language. Thus, he made no attempt to disguise his models. The idea of an opera named after its female heroine brings to mind the most popular such work of Fry's day, Bellini's *Norma*. And it was no coincidence that in 1841, four years before *Leonora* was premiered, Fry and his brothers had staged a scrupulously respectful performance of *Norma* in Philadelphia. Knowing that Americans had so far heard the work only in bits and pieces or stage adaptations, the Frys based their version on Bellini's original score, in an English translation by Joseph Fry. They then enlisted patronage from other Philadelphians and threw in some of their own money too so that they could hire the best singers, the largest opera orchestra yet assembled (led by the conductor of the Chestnut Street Theater), and the foremost American scenery painter, Russell Smith.[16] The Frys' production of *Norma* succeeded well enough to be repeated a dozen times, and at the end of its run a benefit performance was staged for the translator. As for *Leonora*, in 1845 it also created enough of a stir to receive twelve performances at the Chestnut Street Theater and four more by the Seguins in Philadelphia the following year.[17] It was then laid aside until 1858, when, in what were to be the last performances in the composer's lifetime, a revised *Leonora* was sung in New York City—this time, ironically, in an Italian translation.

In 1846, Fry sailed for Europe, spending several years in Paris as a correspondent for the New York *Tribune*. An experience there taught him, in case he had not learned it already, how low American composers stood in the artistic pecking order. Hoping to hear *Leonora* again, he offered to pay members of the Paris Opera for a rehearsal, but the director refused. "In Europe," he told Fry, "we look upon America as an industrial country— excellent for electric telegraphs, but not for Art . . . They would think me crazy to produce an opera by an American."[18]

Fry returned to the United States in 1852, settling in New York as the *Tribune*'s music critic. He quickly made his presence felt by giving lectures on music in one of the city's best concert rooms. "The aim of these Lectures,"

AH DOOMED MAIDEN.

ARIA,

FROM FRY'S GRAND OPERA, LEONORA.

AS SUNG BY MR. SEGUIN.

ARRANGED WITH A PIANO FORTE ACCOMPANIMENT

Arranged for voice and piano, Fry's aria *Ah Doomed Maiden*, from his opera *Leonora* (1845), sets English words to a melody inspired by Italian bel canto singing style.

Fry is pictured here (top row, at the left) in a daguerrotype from the 1850s with other members of the staff of the *New York Tribune*, for which he wrote.

an advertisement read, "will be to present, in a condensed but clear form, an illustrated history of the rise, progress, and present state of all departments of instrumental and vocal music; whether sacred, dramatic, symphonic, classic, romantic, or national, or of those various kinds of music which it would be difficult to class specifically." By "illustrated," Fry meant that he had hired the services of an orchestra, a chorus, a band, and several vocal soloists to demonstrate his points, which helps to explain why delivering his lecture series cost him $10,000.[19]

Fry's lectures caused a stir. They were quoted widely in New York's newspapers, and they drew large crowds—an average of two thousand according to one estimate.[20] The last lecture, given early in 1853, closed with Fry denouncing American musical life, which he compared unfavorably with the literary scene. He praised writers Washington Irving and James Fenimore Cooper, and noted that a book "written by an American lady"—Harriet Beecher Stowe's *Uncle Tom's Cabin*—was being read more widely in Europe "than any since the Bible was first printed." His point was that a nation with such famous authors ought to start paying attention to its composers, whose excellence might also be revealed if their music could only be heard. The mention of Stowe's controversial novel drew a mixture of cheers and hisses; but Fry knew how to work a crowd. "I like to hear hissing," he told his audience. "No speaker or artiste is good for anything until he is soundly hissed."[21]

Fry then defined two major problems that the United States faced in the field of music: the ignorance of American audiences and the weak presence of American composers. Because of the first, musical appetites were being satisfied by inferior forms. "As a nation," Fry proclaimed, "we have totally neglected Art. We pay enormous sums to hear a single voice, or a single instrument . . . [but] we will pay nothing to hear a sublime work of Art performed." Since no financial base existed to support composers, only musicians of independent means like Fry himself could afford to take composition seriously. Thus, even in the largest cities, barely one or two could be found, and outside the cities none at all. Furthermore, the few American composers who did exist lacked creative boldness. Having long ago won political autonomy, Fry counseled, the United States now needed "a Declaration of Independence in Art." He warned his countrymen and women:

> Until American composers shall discard their foreign liveries and found an American school—and until the American public shall learn to support American artists, Art will not become indigenous to this country, but will only exist as a feeble exotic, and we shall continue to be provincial in Art. The American composer should not allow the name of Beethoven, or Handel or Mozart to prove an eternal bugbear to him, nor should he pay them reverence; he should only reverence his Art, and strike out manfully and independently into untrodden realms.[22]

Fry's raising of the issue of musical nationalism introduces a subject that has long been debated: what constitutes "American music"? Twentieth-century composer and critic Virgil Thomson once said that to create American music, one needed only to be an American and to compose. In other words, American music is defined by nationality, not any particular sound or style. Fry's idea of musical nationalism, like Thomson's, had nothing to do with style. When Fry urged American composers to "discard their foreign liveries and found an American school," he was encouraging them to work in the musical forms favored by concert hall and opera house. Throughout his career, Fry insisted that American composers needed all the help they could get, and that performers and audiences should give their music a hearing simply because they were Americans.

On December 15, 1853, Fry the music critic compared the quality of Louis Jullien's orchestra to "the Apollo Belvedere, the Parthenon, the Cologne Cathedral, or any other historical world's wonder."[23] Ten days later, Jullien conducted Fry's new *Santa Claus* Symphony, whose title page reads: "Santa Claus, written expressly for Jullien's orchestra, and performed with the greatest applause, for the first time, on Christmas Eve, 1853." The symphony contained several movements, but rather than following classical sonata principles, it was structured by a narrative program, which interpreted the musical sounds and even named some of the players. According to Fry's program, for example, the "quaint" sound of "the Bassoon of Mr. Hardy" represented Santa Claus himself:

> It gives an air in double-time like the trot of horse, accompanied by sleigh bells, and the cracking of a whip. The trotting and bells grow louder, and suddenly SANTA CLAUS reins up his steed with a jerk, imitated by a rasping sound on the stringed instruments. SANTA CLAUS then flies down the chimney to the soft notes of the flutes; the LULLABY is again heard hinting at the children, while harp-like notes on the Violins show the click of the toys as they are thrown in the stockings of the happy little sleepers. SANTA CLAUS then retakes his sleigh as the flutes mount up, and the retreating music of pattering hoofs and tinkling bells dies away. A few whirring notes on the kettle drums speak of the wind-tossed snow, and then is heard in the highest regions of the Violins with the fluttering ecstasy of hovering angels, the Christmas Hymn, *Adeste Fideles*.[24]

When a New York critic called Fry's symphony "a good Christmas piece but hardly a composition to be gravely criticized like an earnest work of Art," the composer fired off a long, heated reply, sparking a controversy that continued for months in local newspapers and music journals. As the question of what place orchestral music by American composers should occupy in concert life was debated in public, Americans were being invited, perhaps for the first time, to think of concert life as a form of national expression. Was it enough for them simply to hear the music of European masters? Or, since European works made up virtually the whole orchestra repertory, should they also hear the efforts of American composers? Should the concert hall, in other words, be ruled solely by cosmopolitan aesthetics, or should a place also be reserved for home-grown talent, whatever it produced?

No one in New York at the time was better equipped to make the case for the need for American composers than William Henry Fry, who called the New York Philharmonic Society "an incubus on Art" (an incubus is an especially malevolent kind of evil spirit) because it had never "asked for or performed a single American instrumental composition during the eleven years of its existence." We might wonder why, if a famous orchestra like Jullien's had played Fry's music, the Philharmonic's indifference rankled so deeply. The Philharmonic, after all, was strictly a local enterprise that played a few concerts per season to a limited audience, while Jullien's touring gave many more Americans a chance to hear Fry's music. Better than any testimonial, however, Fry's complaint indicates where the Philharmonic Society stood in

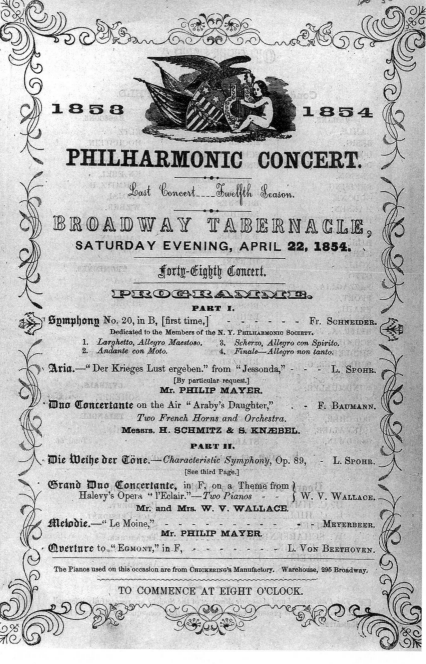

This program from an 1854 concert by the New York Philharmonic Society shows what the group's concerts were like in the mid-nineteenth century, when Fry and Bristow were arguing for more American music. (Schneider's Twentieth Symphony, coming from inside New York's German-speaking circle, was not what the two American composers had in mind.)

New York's musical life. In slightly more than a decade, the ensemble had established a regular interaction between the city's orchestral musicians and an audience. With its corps of associate members committed to hearing and rehearing the masterpieces of symphonic literature, the Philharmonic had won a place in New York's musical infrastructure. Its artistic continuity gave a weight to its musical choices that reduced traveling ensembles, Jullien's orchestra included, to secondary importance. Fry, who had written his *Santa Claus* Symphony with Jullien and his audiences in mind, attacked the Philharmonic because its commitment to music as art and not entertainment made it a symbol of the obstacles that he and his fellow American composers faced. His comments suggest how it felt to be an American composer in the 1850s.

Fry's attack drew a quick rebuttal from a Philharmonic Society member, which was answered sarcastically by Brooklyn native George Frederick Bristow, himself a composer, an officer of the orchestra, and one of its violinists. Bristow backed up Fry's indictment:

> As it is possible to miss a needle in a haystack, I am not surprised that Mr. Fry has missed the fact, that during the eleven years the Philharmonic Society has been in operation in this city, it played once, either by mistake or accident, one single American composition, an overture of mine. . . . This single stray fact shows that the Philharmonic Society has been as anti-American as if it had been located in London during the Revolutionary War, and composed of native-born British tories.[25]

From the time of its founding, Bristow claimed, the Philharmonic Society's directors and players had carried on "little short of a conspiracy against the art of a country to which they have come for a living." In Bristow's view, some immigrant members of the orchestra were biting the hand that fed them. The Germans were especially to blame. "If all their artistic affections are unalterably German," railed Bristow, "let them pack up and go back to Germany, and enjoy the police and the bayonets . . . where an artist is a serf to a nobleman." He ended his diatribe with a barrage of rhetorical questions: "What is the Philharmonic Society in this country? Is it to play exclusively the works of German masters, especially if they be dead? . . . Or is it to stimulate original art on the spot?"[26]

The New York Philharmonic Society devoted itself to cosmopolitan values and works by European composers; and when other symphony orchestras were founded, they followed suit. The artistic and technical demands of the repertory made it only natural for their rosters to be filled with foreign-trained players, and for conductors from overseas to lead them. Under the banner of art, symphony orchestra concerts became an intense, absorbing experience for more and more listeners.[27] Music critics helped listeners understand and interpret the music they were hearing. Music-loving citizens worked hard to make local orchestras the focus of civic pride. And in this process, American composers played virtually no role. In New York, for example, Bristow wrote symphonies inspired by Mendelssohn; but with Mendelssohn's own symphonies available, the Philharmonic found no reason to perform Bristow's. Fry and Bristow advocated *American* orchestra music on ideological grounds; but their appeal made little headway against the Philharmonic's cycle of supply and demand. Rooted in what seemed a limitless supply of European masterworks, the orchestra fostered a demand for performances of more. It was no wonder that Bristow turned elsewhere, winning some success in 1855 with his opera *Rip Van Winkle*, based on a tale set in upstate New York by American author Washington Irving.

A late twentieth-century observer of this debate can hardly help but take the side of Fry and Bristow. But those who were working to establish a place for the orchestra in America knew very well the precariousness of their endeavor. To perform untested music—and American works fit that category—was considered a risk, and the fragile economic status of orchestras made such artistic gambles seem foolhardy. The American symphony orchestra took root in a state of mind that tried to balance the economic risk of performance by playing only music of high quality. In that framework, it was not until later in the century that American composers began to find a place.

17

A New Orleans Original

Gottschalk of Louisiana

LOUIS JULLIEN'S SUCCESS with New York audiences in the fall of 1853 frustrated the efforts of other performers seeking public attention, including the Louisiana-born, Paris-trained pianist and composer Louis Moreau Gottschalk. Gottschalk, who had given a number of successful concerts in New York earlier that year, returned there in hopes of launching another such series. But the public stir created by Jullien's arrival undermined that plan. In fact, Jullien had hired Gottschalk's manager for *his* promotional staff, leaving the pianist scrambling to organize his own concerts. Amid the public enthusiasm for Jullien, Gottschalk booked a concert hall for October 13, but he neglected to advertise or change his program from one he had already played the previous spring, and only a third of the tickets were sold.[1]

Despite this fiasco, however, the twenty-four-year-old Gottschalk was already emerging as the top American attraction on a concert circuit set up by European impresarios to market virtuoso classical performers as high-class entertainers. Part of his appeal lay in original compositions that gave his appearances a unique flavor. Writing chiefly for piano, Gottschalk developed as a composer in regular contact with paying audiences, whom he was expected to please. And some of his music survived in performance long after his death.

A diary entry from June 1857 offers striking images from Gottschalk's personal history. Having spent several months in Cuba, he was bound by ship for St. Thomas when his vessel passed within sight of the island of Santo Domingo. Gottschalk's first-ever glimpse of the Haitian coast brought to mind stories he had heard as a child. His mother was descended from an official of the French colonial regime that ruled Santo Domingo until the slave rebellion of the 1790s overthrew it. "When very young," Gottschalk recalled, "I never tired of hearing my grandmother relate the terrible strife that our family, like all the rest of the colonists, had to sustain" when the slaves overwhelmed them. That memory led Gottschalk's imagination to a scene from his boyhood. "I again found myself before the large fireplace of our dwelling on the Rue des Remparts at New Orleans," he wrote, where, "in the evening, the Negroes, myself, and the children of the house formed a circle around my grandmother. We would listen, by the trembling fire on the hearth, under the coals of which Sally, the old Negress, baked her sweet potatoes." Just as memorable as their grandmother's stories for the children was the lore passed on by Sally, the Gottschalks' longtime slave. "We listened to Sally so well that we knew all of her stories by heart," he recalled, "with an interest that has lasted till today and still makes me find an inexpressible charm in all these naïve legends." For Gottschalk, the "picturesque language," "exquisite originality," and "simple and touching melody" of Creole ballads he had learned in his youth went "right to the heart" and conjured up a "dream of unknown worlds."[2]

Not only did Gottschalk remember his past; he relied on it as an artistic source. Born of an English-Jewish father and a mother who was culturally French by way of Haiti, raised Roman Catholic in a cosmopolitan city and a household where blacks and whites mingled freely, Gottschalk recognized the artistic possibilities in his cultural heritage. In the annals of American composition, he is known for bringing indigenous, or folk, themes and rhythms into music written for the concert hall. His shipboard reflections show that this practice was rooted in respect for the unique appeal of supposedly primitive forms of expression. Gottschalk's journal, published as *Notes of a Pianist*, reveals him as an observant, culturally responsive man with a keen interest in the human condition. His comments on travel, personal encounters, performances, and experiences with music introduce the reader to an artist who approached life with an appealing blend of empathy and skepticism. That impression helps one appreciate Gottschalk's music.

GOTTSCHALK AND HIS MUSIC

Born in 1829 into a household that valued his innate musical talent, Gottschalk also had the good fortune to grow up in a lively, vital musical environment. The population of New Orleans stood at about 46,000 in 1830, supporting several full-time theaters, all with their own orchestras, and half a dozen dance halls—a mecca for musicians seeking employment. Local music stores sold instruments and sheet music, and they also published the work of local composers. A touring circuit that connected New Orleans with New York and Havana, Cuba, brought many performing musicians, including Europeans, to town. The city's streets and saloons were home to such informal music makers as fiddlers and banjo pickers, and

Louis Moreau Gottschalk (1829–1869) was painted by French artist J. Berville around 1843, shortly after he arrived in Paris to continue his musical training there.

minstrel troupes began to appear in the 1840s. Organists played and choirs sang in Roman Catholic churches. And army bands offered a range of music, from military to recreational. Thus, New Orleans, with its mingling of

French, Spanish, and free black residents, enjoyed a highly diverse musical life, from artistically elegant to functional and homespun.

Gottschalk's career was rooted in this musical richness. His mother took him to the opera, and he also picked up his musical vernacular in front of the hearth and around the city. He began playing piano at three and was soon taking lessons from French-trained F. J. Narcisse Letellier, a singer with a local opera company. The concertmaster of another opera orchestra taught him violin. Gottschalk sailed for France just after turning thirteen, well prepared for further musical education in Europe. His father, who took an active part in the boy's musical career, had hoped that he would study at the Paris Conservatory. But the director rejected Gottschalk without an audition, and with a condescending snub: "America is only a land of steam engines." Soon, however, he was accepted as a piano pupil by Camille Stamaty, a student of Frédéric-Guillaume Kalkbrenner, then the leading piano teacher in Paris. His general education was supervised by private tutors who helped kindle a lifelong love of literature, including poetry, plays, and novels. A frequent concertgoer, Gottschalk also studied composition with Pierre Maleden, teacher of Camille Saint-Saëns. Most of all, as the center where the world's leading pianists displayed their art, Paris proved the ideal place for Gottschalk to prepare for a virtuoso's career. There he came to know the playing of such renowned artists as Franz Liszt, Frédéric Chopin, and Sigismond Thalberg firsthand, and to measure his own skill and public appeal against theirs. When he made his own public debut as a pianist in Paris shortly before his sixteenth birthday, both Chopin and Thalberg were in the audience.[3]

Gottschalk's playing won approval from critics and audiences alike. And he had also begun to compose. Starting with dance-based pieces such as the *Polka de salon* (Op. 1), he paid homage to Chopin in a series of mazurkas and waltzes. Then in 1849, he based four new compositions on melodies he had learned in America: *Bamboula, La savane* (The Tropical Plain), *Le bananier* (The Banana Tree), and *Le mancenillier* (The Manchineel Tree), all of them published in Paris under the name "Gottschalk of Louisiana."[4] These pieces established Gottschalk as a musical representative of the New World in the Old. And they provide a telling glimpse of a young American creative artist, discovering an approach suited to his own talents as both a public performer and a publishing composer.

La savane (Op. 3), subtitled "Ballade Creole," sustains a plaintive mood by dwelling on one simple, square-cut melody—identified as West Indian and linked to the song *Lolotte*. Listeners who know the Appalachian folk song *Skip to My Lou* will recognize Gottschalk's tune as a close relative, but in minor rather than major mode. *La savane* begins with twenty measures of "prelude," an introduction with an improvised flavor. (In concerts,

Gottschalk and his contemporaries often did improvise their preludes and transitions from one number to the next.) By hinting repeatedly at tunefulness and then breaking off, this section whets the appetite for something more continuous that listeners can settle back and enjoy. The prelude, marked "Con Malinconia" (With deep sadness), introduces the unusual key of E-flat minor and plays with a six-note figure based on a descending triad (5-3-3-1-3-5), punctuated with silences. The seven-note figure that dominates *Lolotte* never appears, but it too outlines an E-flat-minor triad (3-2-1-1-3-3-5). Thus, Gottschalk's introduction foreshadows the mood, key, and primary tones of the borrowed melody upon which *La savane* is based.

Lolotte is a thirty-two-bar melody with four eight-bar sections, each built from two-bar figures. A seven-note figure (**a**) is heard three times in each section, followed by a five-note cadence formula (**b**), so that the whole melody presents the same eight-bar section four times. *Lolotte* offers just enough tonal variation to avoid monotony: after two identical sections in E-flat minor, the third moves to G-flat major, and the fourth begins there, then returns to E-flat minor in its last four bars. Gottschalk directs that the melody be played "molto semplice sempre legato" (with great smoothness and simplicity), and if listeners do not find it beautiful—a tuneful gem glimmering over a soft harmonic background—*La savane* will fail, for the melody provides the work's musical substance. By never changing key, register, or character, the composition maintains a simplicity that catches and holds the ear from the start. But with each repetition, the accompaniment grows faster and more complex, bringing into focus a trait typical of Gottschalk's music: it is difficult for the player but easy for listeners. While Gottschalk demands flashy technique, he keeps the volume low to create an aural screen through which the simple melody may always be heard.

With the rhythmic speedup of its accompanying figures—from quarter notes to eighth notes, triplet eighths, and sixteenth notes—*La savane* resembles classical theme and variations form. But most variation sets decorate their theme and leave its form intact. Gottschalk keeps the melody's notes unchanged while he plays with the form, which he shortens from

Seven banjos, a tambourine, several pairs of bones, and a free-flowing pennant spell out the title of Gottschalk's piano piece *The Banjo* in its first edition (New York, 1855).

thirty-two bars to twenty-four and even sixteen. When decoration finally subsides, the basic eight-bar section of *Lolotte* has been repeated no fewer than twelve times. And now Gottschalk presents it once more, changing melody notes to signal that the end has arrived. Listeners who have been lulled into daydreaming by *La savane's* gentle redundancy may be jolted by the last chord, marked "subito fff"—the only loud sound in the whole composition.

By fall 1851, having completed a program of formal training and established himself as a composer, Gottschalk was concertizing throughout Spain, playing compositions that borrowed rhythms and tunes from patriotic Spanish airs or indigenous folk music. At the end of 1852, he was ready to leave Europe, and the first concert he played after landing in New York took place in February 1853. Together with works by Liszt, Verdi, and others, plenty of Gottschalk's own music appeared on this program, including *Le bananier* (Op. 5), *Dance ossianique* (Op. 12), and a "Grand Caprice and Variations" for two pianos on *The Carnival of Venice*. As with other pianists of the time, Gottschalk's concerts seldom took the form of solo piano recitals, except where other skilled musicians were unavailable. He was joined in his American debut by a flute soloist, several singers, a pianist, and an orchestra.

A different side of Gottschalk's creative personality appears in *The Banjo* (subtitled both "An American Sketch" and "Grotesque Fantasie"), published in New York City in 1855 during his first years of touring the United States. Again, seeking material with immediate impact, he borrowed from the musical vernacular, choosing two attention-grabbing elements: the sound of the banjo and Stephen Foster's well-known minstrel song *De Camptown Races*. And he brought them together in a piano piece that catches something of the spirit of the blackface minstrel stage, a dominant force in urban musical culture since the 1840s.

As in *La savane*, Gottschalk devised for *The Banjo* a musical form that blends conventional and unconventional elements, with the goal of delighting listeners. To speak of the conventional is simply to recognize that since the late 1700s, when musicians in America began to compose, they have followed formal principles developed in Europe and accepted as norms throughout the Western world. Gottschalk himself followed these principles in many of his works, but *The Banjo* is a distinctly unbalanced piece. Its brief introduction, based on Foster's tune (8 bars), is followed by a long section that imitates the banjo's sound (162 bars), then a shorter section presenting Foster's tune and ending in a noisy burst of pianistic effort (54 bars). One might argue that if Gottschalk had wanted balance, he could have brought back the banjo imitation in a three-part form (**ABA**) or expanded the second section of his two-part form. But neither would have produced the sheer excitement of this *Banjo*. Perhaps he took a staged minstrel performance for a model: a brief opening gesture to catch the crowd's interest; a long stretch of intricate, buzzing figuration; and a climactic finale, performed with the vigor of a company walkaround.

The beginning of *The Banjo*'s first section is also unconventional. Gottschalk introduces his banjo sound in measure 9 with three performance directions that together create a unique mood. "Tres Rythmé" calls for rhythmic emphasis; "Con Spirito" demands a lively rendition; and **p** means that the playing must not be loud. The "picking" style of banjo performance stands behind this sound. As a plucked instrument with gut strings, capable of rhythmic energy but not much volume, the banjo of Gottschalk's day called for close listening. And here it is as if the audience is invited to lean toward the music, concentrating on the details of the hushed evocation of the tenor banjo. The technique is clever and the spirit ear-catching. Upbeats and downbeats are divided between hands, with staccato marks urging crisp attacks and releases so that nothing is blurred or covered up. But at this moment, there is no danger of anything being covered. For, instead of a melody, Gottschalk offers a sound: a texture that itself suggests an accompaniment to another melody.

By delivering tunelessness where melody is expected, Gottschalk surprises his listeners. Some might be inclined to wait expectantly for a "real melody" to appear, while others *make* melody out of what the composer offers. Whatever the response, it is hard to imagine a listener of Gottschalk's day expecting anything like this beginning. He composed *The Banjo* at a time when Italianate vocal melody was coming into its own in America, not only in songs but in band music and dance music too. For most listeners, melody was the lifeblood of music. Hence, *The Banjo*'s withholding of melody until later in the piece—or perhaps its invitation to hear the picking sound *as* melody—sets it apart from other music of the era. In fact, though separated by distance, time, and a host of artistic conventions from direct African influence, *The Banjo*'s African-American lineage is unmistakable. Gottschalk's emphasis on rhythm and sound over melody—especially the pulsating, captivating, wholly original music that follows the introduction—shows him drawing on African roots to create a work obviously not cut from European cloth.

The Banjo's overall form may be unusual, but its phrase-by-phrase unfolding is straightforward. Indeed, on that level, Gottschalk's piece may be considered a lively, stylized work for piano, rooted in the conventions of dance music: a strict tempo, regular phrase structure, and lots of repetition. The beat and the four-bar phrases carry listeners comfortably ahead. And the music is at once familiar (Foster's song), novel (the banjo imitation), and ingenious enough (the variety of banjo sounds) to hold their attention. Finally, the contrast between *The Banjo*'s final roar and the delicacy of its picking sections dramatizes the vastly different capabilities of the grand piano—a technological marvel of the age—and the banjo itself, still in some quarters a homemade instrument in 1855.

Some of the most popular piano compositions in nineteenth-century America were programmatic ones whose music was supposed to tell a story. Gottschalk contributed to this genre too, achieving great commercial success with a piece called *The Last Hope*, which was published with an attached anecdote that locates the music in a framework of extreme sentimentality. While staying once in the Cuban city of Santiago, Gottschalk had met a charming older woman who felt for him an affection that was deep, yet with the purity of maternal love. "Struck down by an incurable malady," and alone without her family, this woman found her only solace in listening to the playing of Gottschalk, "her dear pianist" and "most powerful physician."

> One evening, while suffering still more than usual—"In pity," said she, making use of one of the ravishing idioms of the Spanish tongue—"in pity, my dear Moreau, one little melody, the last hope!" And Gottschalk commenced to improvise an air at once plaintive and pleasing,—one of those spirit-breaths that mount sweetly to heaven, whence they have so recently descended.

Forced to travel to another city for a concert engagement, Gottschalk returned to Santiago a few days later to hear the church bells tolling. "A mournful presentiment" froze his heart. He arrived at "the open square of the church just at the moment when the mortal remains of Senora S—— were brought from the sacred edifice." And that was "why the great pianist always plays with so much emotion the piece that holy memories have caused him to name 'The Last Hope.'"[5]

The goal of this story is obviously to claim *The Last Hope* as a spiritual utterance with more depth than the standard parlor fare. By evoking Gottschalk's presence, the story frames the piece as the "voice" of the composer, reaching out to soothe a kindred soul in distress. Perhaps these traits help to explain why a piece as hard to play as this one was published in 1854 in sheet-music form. Gottschalk recalled in 1862 being slipped a note during a concert that read: "Would Mr. G. kindly please 36 young girls by playing *The Last Hope*, which they all play."[6] Whatever its attraction for those three dozen fans, there was a wide circle of amateur pianists with their own reasons for buying the piece. A look at the sheet music suggests one of them: Gottschalk was an admired concert performer, and the sheet music makes available a detailed transcript of his piano technique. Indeed, *The Last Hope* is notated with a precision that specifies how virtually every note is to be played. By following the fingerings, marks of articulation and expression, dynamics (loud and soft), and use of the damper pedal, a performer with the technical skills to do so can reproduce the composer's intentions scrupulously.

The first page of Gottschalk's *The Last Hope* for piano illustrates the precision with which he specified how the music was to sound.

Like the opening of *La savane*, the first page of *The Last Hope* is clearly a preparation. Two musical fragments are heard, the first perhaps the end of a melody, the second a brief, delicate, broken-chord gesture in the high treble, as if responding to the organ-like chords of the first. Then another figure is taken up briefly and elaborated, but to no particular effect. Page 2 presents what sounds like a new beginning: two sustained B-major chords, again followed by the high-treble gesture, and then a second try at a melody, which soon dissolves into passagework. The composer is still preparing, and the piece is nearly two minutes old. Finally, on page 3, the long preparation finds a satisfactory outcome when Gottschalk launches a real melody: an arching sixteen-bar tune (**abac**), punctuated by the high-treble gesture. When the melody is finished, Gottschalk does what composers of attractive tunes usually do: he repeats it. He then seems most concerned with preserving the mood he has created. During the four-page coda-like section that follows, he affirms and reaffirms the key of B major through almost continuous treble passagework, a nine-measure trill on B, and an increasing emphasis on the treble register. Growing ever softer, *The Last Hope* comes to an end in a high-register whisper.

This description summarizes the events of *The Last Hope* as a work of abstract instrumental music, concerned with the play of themes, motifs, textures, and keys. But the sheet-music publication of *The Last Hope* indicates that its events are determined by the program: the title, subtitle ("religious meditation"), and the story of Gottschalk and the Señora. Once a listener has the program's explanation in mind, the piece becomes a showcase for a melody whose spiritual and moral significance have already been proclaimed.

Connecting specific images to the sounds, the program sets the scene in an aristocratic Cuban parlor or drawing room, with the Señora on her sickbed and Gottschalk at the piano. The opening pages of preparation become a narrative, as Gottschalk searches for a melody to fit the solemn occasion. Once he finds it, the melody becomes an avenue for spiritual consolation. (Indeed, if Gottschalk composed this melody to carry a message of religious significance, he hit the mark; set to sacred words, it has been sung as a Protestant hymn ever since a nineteenth-century tunebook compiler borrowed it for that purpose.)[7] The program also connects the high-treble gesture to the story. Gottschalk the character plays chiefly in the low and middle registers, where he sets his melody of consolation. But the pianist who performs *The Last Hope*, constantly reaching up to the top of the keyboard to play that figure, also perpetuates the idea that Gottschalk and the Señora are seeking through music to transcend the earth, visiting the heavenly plane of spirituality that hovers over the scene. (One modern-day pianist has irreverently dubbed this gesture "the heavenly flutter," like a rustle of angels' wings.) Musical sound is an avenue for the apotheosis of the Señora's soul, soon to be released from earthly pain.

Although sentimental narratives like this one do not connect with modern sensibilities, *The Last Hope* is clearly a more effective piece with its program than without. If called simply *Adagio* or *Klavierstück* (Keyboard Piece), and with no program, the piece could boast little in the way of musical substance beyond its appealing sixteen-bar tune: certainly enough for the singing of a hymn but thin for a five-minute instrumental work.

GOTTSCHALK AND THE CLASSICS

Nothing was more fundamental to Gottschalk's artistic vocabulary than the piano's sound. Explaining why he favored pianos made at the Boston factory of Jonas Chickering, he once wrote: "I like their tone, fine and delicate, tender and poetic," adding that Chickering pianos allowed him to achieve "tints more varied than those of other instruments." These words point to the heart of Gottschalk's musical philosophy, which held sound to be as important to a piece of music as were colors to a painting. "We often see fine pictures admirably drawn," he wrote, that still "appear cold to us," because "they are wanting in color." Technical skill, though essential to piano playing, was never enough. "Many pianists whose thundering execution astonishes us still do not move us," he counseled, because "they are ignorant of sound"—the surest means of touching listeners' hearts. Sound carried the essence of music. Painters could learn to draw and musicians to play the right notes, if they worked hard enough. But a command of sound, which expressed music's spiritual side, depended on intuition. "Color and sound are born in us," Gottschalk wrote; they were "the outward expressions of our sensibility and of our souls."[8]

Gottschalk's belief in the primacy of sound distanced him from the outlook he called Germanic. The contrast is shown by a comparison of his priorities with those of the Boston critic John Sullivan Dwight, who, like Theodore Thomas, championed the European classics. Dwight once advised performers to play with "no show or effect" so that "the composition is before you, pure and clear . . . as a musician hears it in his mind in reading it from the notes."[9] In other words, the way musical works sounded in performance might actually prevent listeners from experiencing them as their composers intended. Those who shared this outlook tended to think of music primarily as a composer's art. By suggesting that a piece might just as well be heard by an accomplished score reader in private as in public performance, Dwight was urging concertgoers not to glorify performers at the expense of the composers. A public performance, he reminded them, was a collaboration in which players and singers brought a composer's creation to an audience of listeners. Performance always involves interpretation; and the Germanic outlook directed performers to look to the score, not their personal whims or the mood of the audience, for interpretive guidelines.

In Dwight's first review of a Gottschalk concert, in the fall of 1853, he admitted that the pianist's tone was "the most clear and crisp and beautiful that we have ever known," but then summarily dismissed Gottschalk as an artist. "Could a more trivial and insulting string of musical rigmarole," he asked about one of the pieces, ever "have been offered to an audience of

Louis Moreau Gotschalk as depicted by a cartoonist for the journal *Ba-ta-clan*, published in Rio de Janeiro, June 19, 1869.

earnest musical lovers?"[10] While sound for Gottschalk was nothing less than the essence of music making, for Dwight it was a trivial issue. The critic may never have asked the question posed years later by composer Charles Ives—"My God, what has sound got to do with music?"—but he shared Ives's attitude. Dwight took the sonic beauty of Gottschalk's playing as an attempt to hide artistic emptiness.

In this clash of priorities, Gottschalk knew precisely where he stood. In 1862, he wrote: "Music is a thing eminently sensuous. Certain combinations move us, not because they are ingenious, but because they move our nervous system in a certain way."[11] In other words, for all the ingenuity preserved in composers' scores, music does its work in performance, occasion by occasion. Performers and composers can have no worthier goal than to form emotional links with their listeners. Gottschalk's belief in music's sensuous nature stands behind his work as a composer.

From his New York debut in 1853 until early 1857, Gottschalk traveled the United States, establishing himself as a presence in concert life and a prominent American composer. He soon came to regret that, following his father's advice, he had rejected P. T. Barnum's 1853 offer of a guaranteed yearly income of $20,000 for concert touring. But he did negotiate a fee for endorsing Chickering pianos. And he signed a contract to publish new piano works through a New York firm headed by William Hall. Gottschalk's touring and personal charisma thus made him a star, profiting not only from concert performances but also from the selling of musical goods. Complaints in his journal, however, suggest the price he and other stars paid for the rewards that came their way, including schedules crammed too full of concerts and train rides; hotels that roused guests with an alarm bell and served indigestible food; bizarre audience behavior; and constant demands that the same few popular numbers be endlessly repeated.

But these were hazards of the profession. More frustrating to Gottschalk, because it concerned his identity as an artist, was the disparagement he received for being both a performer and a composer. Some critics took the pianist to task for playing his own compositions in public. But what, Gottschalk asked rhetorically, if he had not been a composer at all? Any musician "who had manufactured a polka or a valse would have thrown it in my face that I played only the music of others." Or, if his compositions had been less catchy and original, he might have been accused of copying. Fame, he recognized, made him a target for criticism, regardless of the course he took. Whatever his detractors might say, composing was fundamental to both Gottschalk's musical nature and his career, and the public *liked* his music. Being "cast in an original mold," he could hardly "abdicate his individuality," even if he tried.

As Gottschalk saw it, critics who championed the classics were especially apt to exaggerate their authority, and this habit placed living composers, especially American, at a disadvantage. He knew, for example, that the very idea of classic works depended on who was defining them and how. In any discussion of the subject, Gottschalk wrote, he would insist on "reserving the right to ask you what you understand by the classics," for the label could be used as a "convenient club with which you knock on the head all those who annoy you." Fearing also that a preoccupation with the classics would reduce musical diversity, he asked, "Because the apple is a fruit less delicate than the pineapple, [would you] wish that there should be no apples?" Ready to grant the artistic worth of music that performers and critics had already consecrated, he still doubted that such works could be the exclusive diet of a healthy musical life. The classics, he wrote, flipping to another page of the menu, could be the roast beef "on which the people who begin to feed at the banquet of civilization must be nourished." But once listeners are "sufficiently fortified, should you refuse them the little dainties of the dessert," especially when these offerings "seem to stimulate your taste" and refresh a palate "dulled and overheated by too rich food?"

All in all, Gottschalk believed, the classics were being set off from other music in a way that gave their advocates more intellectual cover than they deserved. "If we are yet to proclaim an art and to form our taste," he wrote as if to a critic, "I understand that you would like better a tame interpretation of consecrated chefs-d'oeuvre than an original that is not yet consecrated and whose place in art you dare not yet designate." The thought of that state of mind led to another food analogy: "There are some individuals who like only dried fruit," he wrote. "They even like it a little moldy, and if they find dust in it they are transported." In contrast, Gottschalk likened new compositions—works not yet classified or categorized, and with sound their only credential—to a "fruit in flower," free of mold and dust, and exuding "the perfume that opens to the sun and betrays a young and vigorous growth." But, just as the flavor of a freshly picked plum comes without the guaranteed sweetness or shelf life of a prune, so the aesthetic reward of a new composition involves risk when compared with a classic.[12]

Sixteen years of life remained to Gottschalk after he returned in 1853 from Europe, and, although he never left the Western Hemisphere again, he spent less than half of that time in North America. After touring the United States and Canada until 1857, he passed the next several years in the Caribbean, with long stays in Puerto Rico, Martinique, Guadeloupe, and especially Cuba, where he played many concerts, staged festivals, and even for a time managed the opera in Havana. Early in 1862, he returned to his native land, winning a warm reception for his second New York debut performance on February 11. A strenuous tour followed, with Gottschalk calculating at one point that he had given eighty-five concerts in four and a half months and traveled fifteen thousand miles by train in a country where long-simmering sectional conflict had erupted into civil war. (An ardent foe of slavery, he supported the Northern cause.) Among at least a dozen new compositions he introduced in 1862 was *The Union* (Op. 48), a war-inspired fantasy on national songs, featuring *The Star-Spangled Banner, Hail Columbia,* and *Yankee Doodle.*[13]

Gottschalk toured eastern North America until early 1865, when he sailed for California by way of Panama. Arriving in San Francisco in late April, he

Gottschalk in full maturity.

played concerts there and in Oakland, San Jose, Sacramento, and Stockton. The month of June found him inland, performing in the mining towns of Nevada, including Virginia City, where he stayed eleven days and played three concerts and which he declared "the saddest, the most wearisome, the most inhospitable place on the globe."[14] Not long after his return to the coast, however, Gottschalk was involved in an incident whose outcome made San Francisco seem even less hospitable than Nevada. That it involved a young woman will surprise no reader of his journal, which carries a recurrent motif in which his eyes sweep the audience during a performance and light upon a woman whose beauty so distracts him that he flubs the passage he is trying to play.

From early in his performing career, a strong mutual attraction existed between Gottschalk and the women who formed a large part of his audience. But in California in September 1865, the pianist went too far. By failing to return a local schoolgirl to her residence on time after an outing with another couple, he offended local propriety to the point that vigilante justice was threatened. Though Gottschalk stoutly denied any wrongdoing in the matter, he also took the precaution of fleeing by sea to South America, and there he spent the rest of his life, performing in Lima, Peru (1865–66), Santiago and Valparaiso, Chile (1866–67), Montevideo, Uruguay, and Buenos Aires, Argentina (1867–68), and Rio de Janeiro, Brazil. He died in Rio of pneumonia, aggravated by extreme exhaustion, on December 18, 1869, after organizing and performing in a monster concert involving some 650 musicians. His death was marked by a hero's funeral.

No other American-born musician of the 1800s matched Gottschalk's impact, which continued long after he died at the age of forty. Biographies were written, and the journal was edited and published in its original French. With the composer no longer alive to perform it, his music took on a life of its own. Editions of his works were published in North and South America, Europe, and Cuba. As late as 1915, no fewer than fifty-five of his piano compositions were still available in sheet-music form, not to mention those brought out as rolls for player pianos. Thereafter, however, the music dropped out of the concert repertory, and Gottschalk was gradually forgotten. In the 1970s, when dance impresario Lincoln Kirstein suggested that the New York City Ballet stage a work called Cakewalk using Gottschalk's music, the only one in the company who had even heard of the composer was George Balanchine, the great choreographer, who recalled hearing his music in his native Russia.[15]

Gottschalk poses a challenge for historians and students of American music. On the one hand, there is no denying the wide swath that he cut in the international musical life of the 1850s and 1860s and later. Acknowledged as a superior pianist, he also won praise as a composer from both critics and listeners in Europe, South America, the Caribbean, and North America. His music delighted and moved audiences then, and it still sounds original today. On the other hand, Gottschalk is not widely performed nowadays, when the repertory of the concert hall and the teaching studio render what may be taken as history's judgment: the true verdict on musical quality. According to this line of thinking, whatever may be admired in Gottschalk's personality or approach to composition and however unusual his place in history, the proof is in the pudding, and the music has simply not been good enough to survive. A case may also be made, however, that

According to this Rio de Janeiro cartoon, when Gottschalk died in Brazil in December 1869, he was mourned on three continents.

Gottschalk's eclipse has had more to do with historical fashion than the worth of his music. His artistic pedigree is unique, blending the grass-roots flavor of New World rhythms and melodies with the elegant sounds and textures of French pianism. That blend, however, went unappreciated by those who shared the Germanic outlook that gained strength after the Civil War. Once Gottschalk was no longer around to play it, his staunchly non-Germanic music lost its place in an American concert hall wary of music that, in the composer's own words, was "not yet consecrated."[16]

ON CATEGORIES AND *THE LAST HOPE*

We could make a case for Gottschalk's *The Last Hope* as a piece of composer's music in the classical sphere. It calls for a well-developed performing technique, and its notation is a fully realized representation of the composer's intent. Moreover, it is based on materials that are heard in much composers' music of the middle 1800s. Yet we can also find good reasons to argue against that classification. One is the work's program: not only the extreme sentimentality of the story but the way it puts musical rhetoric in the service of emotional expression. Another is its marketing in sheet-music form to emphasize emotional content. In *The Last Hope*, the program makes the piece accessible in a highly explicit way, supplying literal meanings that then are supposed to elicit emotional responses. Gottschalk's piece may therefore be described as a detailed musical work that favors accessibility over transcendence—a sentimental tearjerker that requires a formidable technique to play.

The two pieces by Alexander Reinagle discussed in Chapter 12 divide neatly into composers' music and performers' music (the classical and popular spheres) in a way appropriate to the time in which they were written. *The Last Hope*, however, seems to call the categories into question, suggesting that changing historical conditions brought different emphases into play. In contrast to Reinagle's music, *The Last Hope* was created to find a niche in a world of commercial sheet music, related to the concert hall but also linked to the development of home music making, which was aimed chiefly at women and supposedly feminine tastes. Thus, it combined familiar elements with ones that had barely existed half a century earlier.

Gottschalk's personal memoirs reveal the commercial roots of *The Last Hope*. He wrote this "melancholy" item, he recalled, for a publisher (Firth & Pond of New York) who had advised him to try "to copy the style of the pianist Gockel, of whom a certain piece—how I do not know—had just obtained a great run." In Gottschalk's view, *The Last Hope* seemed "to unite the conditions requisite for popularity," and he received $50 when it was published in 1854. Later, however, he struck a deal with the New York house of William Hall to publish all his new works in the United States. Wishing also to bring out Gottschalk's earlier compositions, Hall asked the head of Firth & Pond if he would give up the rights to *The Last Hope*. "Willingly," was the reply. "It does not sell at all; pay me the fifty dollars it has cost me, and it is yours." As things turned out, Hall had the last laugh on this transaction. According to Gottschalk, writing in the late 1860s, more than 35,000 copies had been printed in America by then, and the piece "still produces yearly to its publisher, after a run of more than twelve years, twenty times the amount that it cost him."[17]

In the marketplace for sheet music in mid-nineteenth-century America, composers' music and performers' music intersected and blended in ever-changing ways. Gottschalk composed *The Last Hope* for a pianist with more than a little technique, and he wrote his score out in meticulous detail. At the same time, he gave the work a program and a lyric melody that boosted its accessibility, attracting buyers whose fingers would never be equal to the task of playing all of it as written. Some parts of the piece were written to make a good effect even under clumsy fingers (i.e., much of the opening and the melody, when it arrives); others would sound good only when played gracefully and with delicate touch (i.e., the last four pages). While performers must have tried to defer to the composer's wishes, they *had* to defer to their own technical limitations. In other words, the categories of composers' and performers' music are concerned not only with musicians' intent but with their abilities; a work conceived and written down as composers' music might well be played as performers' music. As in many other instances across the American musical landscape, home performers, acting as consumers in the marketplace, found ways of controlling the categories and using them to their own advantage. A piece like *The Last Hope* shows them enjoying some of the classical sphere's prestige without abandoning their democratic appetite for accessibility.

18

Two Classic Bostonians

George W. Chadwick
and Amy Beach

IF BEETHOVEN, MOZART, AND HANDEL were cultural figures on a par with Socrates, Shakespeare, and Newton, then there was good reason for Americans to know their music. But to be known, the music had to be performed. And performances required skilled singers and players, schools and conservatories for training them, suitable concert halls and theaters, and a public willing to support a musical infrastructure of considerable cost. Nineteenth-century Americans struggled to build and maintain that infrastructure. The concert hall brought Old World art to American shores, and its leading figures came from Europe, whether they were touring artists (Jenny Lind), permanent residents (Theodore Thomas), or entrepreneurs (Bernard Ullman). From overseas, too, came the concert hall's aesthetic ideals and musical repertory. Without these Old World elements, the concert life described in earlier chapters could never have taken shape.

Yet though classic works set the tone of concert life, new music was being composed, and American audiences wanted to hear it. In the century's later years, for example, Richard Wagner's works hit the American musical world with mighty force. Conceived for the stage, Wagner's music dramas were also full of moments suited for concert performance. As Wagnerian excerpts entered the repertory, audiences heard fresh proof of the modern symphony orchestra's range and power. They also observed the composer's skill at catching an emotion in a gesture or a sound and then, through musical development, working it into a monumental climax. Wagner's impact convinced some listeners that music as an art was progressing toward larger scope, heightened expression, and perhaps even more social inclusiveness, for the composer's cult status brought new customers to the concert hall. The story of Wagner's music in America has its place in a chronicle of democratic encounters. In fact, some commentators of the day went so far as to claim that Wagner's ability to communicate with "the people" made his music a kind of ultimate in democratic art, more expressive of the United States than of Old World autocracy.[1]

The latter 1800s also saw a growing number of Americans writing composers' music for the concert hall. Until now, most American composers in the classical sphere had worked as isolated individuals. But in the century's later years—called "the Gilded Age" by Mark Twain to suggest a culture whose cheap core was hidden under glittering surfaces—there emerged in and around Boston the first real group of American composers since the Yankee psalmodists or the Moravians of a century earlier. Several deserve to be remembered, including John Knowles Paine, George W. Chadwick, Arthur Foote, Horatio Parker, and Amy (Mrs. H. H. A.) Beach, all native New Englanders. And to that group may be added New York–born Edward MacDowell, who lived and worked for a time in Boston, and Charles Martin Loeffler, born in Germany but a resident of the Boston area from 1882 until his death in 1935. Historians have referred to them collectively as the Second New England School, the Boston Classicists, or even the Boston Academics, suggesting artists inclined to follow established rules.

In 1907, Chadwick wrote an article that looks back on the years 1890–97 as a kind of golden age. Singling out Paine, Foote, Parker, MacDowell, and Loeffler, Chadwick recalled how it had felt to be part of this group, connected by interest and age. "They knew each other well," he wrote, and most were members of the same Boston social club. "Many a night after a Symphony concert, they "gathered about the same table" in the Tavern Club, bantering in friendly exchange, "rejoicing in each other's successes, and working for them too." They also tried to protect each other against egotism, standing "ever ready with the cooling compress of gentle humor or sarcasm" when "a head showed an undue tendency to enlarge." Chadwick's image of these years portrays a community of equals who had fashioned an "invigorating atmosphere of mutual respect and honest criticism," in which "they worked with joy and enthusiasm, knowing that if only their work was good enough it would be pretty sure of a hearing sooner or later."

Beginning in 1892, the brotherhood also included Theodore Thomas, who, traveling between Chicago and his summer home in New Hampshire, often stopped in Boston to enjoy this circle of the "boys," as he called them. From then on, Chadwick writes, Thomas "was often with them in the spring and autumn, to their great delight and edification." Artistic and social bonds nourished comradeship; there were few places in America where serious musicians could gather regularly and informally to share such conversation. Chadwick recalled an evening when Thomas "sat with them until two in the morning, with the score of Beethoven's ninth symphony in front of him, pointing out with reverent care the details of orchestral nuance as he had worked them out, his eyes flashing with enthusiasm as he lived the music over in his mind."[2] The fraternal bonding pictured here excluded Amy Beach, for social custom would not have encouraged the wife of a local physician to spend her Saturday nights with male colleagues at the Tavern Club. Nevertheless, those colleagues respected her work. In 1896, after a successful Boston Symphony Orchestra performance of Beach's *Gaelic Symphony*, Chadwick pronounced the composition fine enough to make her "one of the boys."[3]

The friendship of Theodore Thomas and the playing of Beach's symphony point up the Boston composers' connection to performance. Several were skilled players themselves, chiefly pianists or organists. And their compositions—operas, oratorios, symphonies and other works for orchestra, chamber music, sacred and secular choral music, solo songs, organ works, and piano music—were heard regularly in Boston, some on the programs of such local ensembles as the Boston Symphony Orchestra, the Kneisel Quartet, and the Handel and Haydn Society. Arthur Foote reported that in the orchestra's early days (1890–1905), local composers were often invited to conduct their own works. He remembered these occasions as "good fun" and the players as having been kind even to those who lacked experience as conductors.[4] Some works were repeated, and a few—Parker's *Hora novissima*, Chadwick's *Melpomene* overture, Foote's *Serenade for Strings*, and MacDowell's Piano Concerto in D minor, among others—found a place in the day's standard repertories. As Chadwick noted in his article, Boston performances could be stepping stones to performances in other American cities and in Europe as well. For not only did these composers' links with performers cross the sea, but some of their music was published in England and Germany as well as the United States.

The account in Chapter 15 of Theodore Thomas stressed his allegiance to the classics and determination to elevate the taste of American audiences. But as an American conductor leading the Thomas Orchestra, the Brooklyn Philharmonic, the New York Philharmonic, and finally the Chicago Symphony Orchestra, Thomas also programmed American works, including a good deal of music by the New Englanders. One reason he, the Boston Symphony's various conductors, *and* the city's main chamber musicians felt at home with this music was that the Boston composers' music was written within an international idiom whose roots lie in Germany. Thomas could sit half the night with composer friends talking about Beethoven's Ninth because they shared musical ideals rooted in the procedures, style, and sound of Beethoven.[5]

Yet emulation was not their goal. Rather than wanting their music to be German in style, they strove to master the idiom favored in the Euroamerican concert hall. If their training emphasized harmony, counterpoint, and orchestration, it was because such technical command was judged essential in guiding the creative imagination. Their drive to succeed as *composers*, not just American composers, won Thomas's respect. New York critic James Huneker reported an exchange that followed the Brooklyn Philharmonic's world premiere in 1889 of MacDowell's D-minor Piano Concerto, with the composer as soloist and Thomas as conductor. "Very good for an American," Huneker had remarked, to which Thomas replied, indignantly if not idiomatically: "Yes, or for a German either."[6] Thus, the Boston composers' careers and compositions reflect a will to chart an artistically responsible course: upholding standards, displaying professional craftsmanship, winning the respect of performers, and communicating with audiences. Their encounter with democracy was marked, most of all, by a refusal to give in to it—if giving in required any compromise with artistic seriousness.

During the "golden" years of 1890–97, Paine was professor of music at Harvard, Chadwick a faculty member at the New England Conservatory of Music (he became its director in 1897), Parker organist and choirmaster at Trinity Church (from 1893; in 1894, he was named professor of music at Yale but kept his Boston church post until 1902), MacDowell a piano soloist and private teacher (Columbia University named him its professor of music in 1896), Foote organist at the First Unitarian Church and also a piano teacher, and Loeffler assistant concertmaster of the Boston Symphony Orchestra. Beach's husband supported her musical career until his death in 1910. Since there was no possibility of earning a living by writing composers' music, members of the Boston group composed as an avocation. That they supported themselves chiefly through teaching and church work suggests a disciplined, rational attitude toward composing and a clear sense of stylistic limits. Yet, like the idea of artistic seriousness, neither these professional callings nor the Germanic approach itself dictated more than broad outlines of attitudes and practices. The musical differences among composers in the Boston group testify to the range of creative freedom they enjoyed.

It was no coincidence that the "self-developing musical city" of Boston should be home to creative musicians like these. For Boston's unique aura left a mark on those who lived and worked there. Chadwick's article quotes Theodore Thomas as having once said that "the prestige of Boston as a musical city" stemmed largely from Harvard University's influence. Since instruction in musical performance was not available at Harvard, Chadwick speculates that Thomas must have been referring to "the refining influence of the fine arts, and that broad, general culture which Harvard offers in such large measure."[7] Perhaps Thomas made this statement to distinguish Boston from New York, where he lived from 1845 until 1891. By 1850, New York was the nation's chief city: its center of finance, commerce, intelli-

This photograph pictures Boston's Quincy Market district in the 1880s with historic Faneuil Hall in the background.

gence, and to some degree culture. And by 1890, with the Philharmonic Society, Walter Damrosch's New York Symphony Orchestra, opera companies including the Metropolitan, and choral societies, plus many foreign-born residents (especially Germans) who relished music and supported it, New York City enjoyed a concert life wider and more varied than Boston's. New York was also the capital of American show business, dependent on a popular music trade centered in "Tin Pan Alley," where rival music publishers carried on a relentless quest for hit songs. In short, New York during these years was bursting with musical energy, vitality, and variety. But it was also an unruly, fiercely competitive place, with commercialism always in the air. According to Horatio Parker, "the serious musician" in New York was "treated as a mere entertainer," whereas in Boston and in "cities of the West," such musicians had a better chance of finding positions commensurate with what they had achieved as artists.[8]

As the capital of New England, which styled itself "schoolmaster to America," Boston had long enjoyed leadership in American education and social reform. Indeed, a financial connection has been discerned between Gilded Age New England's concern for moral character and its tradition of philanthropy. Laws in Massachusetts, for example, encouraged philanthropic giving by allowing wealthy citizens to form endowment trusts—in contrast to New York, where the law actually discouraged such trusts. Despite all the wealth accumulated in New York, the city lacked universities and cultural institutions comparable to Harvard or Yale, the Massachusetts General Hospital, or the Boston Athenaeum. To that list could be added the Boston Symphony Orchestra, whose private endowment is further proof that in the late 1800s, New England's cultural influence on the nation remained strong.[9] In the spirit of following a course of action because it was right, Boston came to be a center of American musical creativity in the Gilded Age.

Writing in 1904, two years before John Knowles Paine died, a historian of American music called him "the Nestor [a venerable king in ancient Greece] of the American composers in the great classical forms": the wise elder who blazed a trail followed by others. And indeed, Paine's commitment to composers' music inspired other Americans. Born in 1839 into a family that ran a music store in Portland, Maine, he was taught there by a German musician who had come to America with a traveling orchestra in 1848 and stayed in Portland after the group broke up. Paine was already a competent organist when he traveled to Berlin in 1858 for two years of study. Returning to the United States, he settled in Boston as organist of a local church. In 1862, he was named instructor of music at Harvard. In the years that followed, Paine composed steadily, lectured at Harvard on music, and organized a well-received Berlin performance of his own Mass in D. In 1875, Harvard established a professorship in music and hired Paine to fill it. There, while continuing to compose, he set up a music curriculum that emphasized intellectual training rather than performance. In a city that by tradition still looked to Harvard for leadership, Paine and his students made the university a force in American music as the century drew to a close.

Three members of the Boston group stand out especially: George W. Chadwick, for his contribution to American orchestra music; Amy Beach, the nation's first notable female composer; and Edward MacDowell, whose fame in his own day eclipsed that of any American contemporary, and whose music is still occasionally heard.

CHADWICK: YANKEE COMPOSER

During the last two decades, Chadwick's music has enjoyed a modest revival in performances and recordings, so that the earlier image of a proper Bostonian with a German bias has lost ground to that of a "Yankee composer." The label seems to fit. Born in 1854 in Lowell, Massachusetts, to parents who may have met at a New Hampshire singing school, Chadwick grew up in circumstances that were far from prosperous. He left high school two years short of graduation and went to work for his father, a businessman who opposed his son's wish to be a musician. While still working in Lowell,

The orchestra of the New England Conservatory in 1915, with its conductor George W. Chadwick pictured as an inset.

Chadwick managed in 1872 to enroll at the New England Conservatory, where he studied organ, piano, and harmony. Though he had never completed a systematic curriculum, in 1876 he was appointed professor of music at Olivet College in Michigan, apparently on the strength of personality and talent. And with money he had saved, Chadwick sailed in 1877 to Germany, where he studied privately and at the Leipzig Conservatory. In the summer of 1879, he traveled to France with painter Frank Duveneck and "the Duveneck boys," a group of vagabond American artists who inspired characters in William Dean Howells's novel *Indian Summer* (1884). After a summer of travel, Chadwick spent a year in Munich studying with Josef Rheinberger. In 1880, he returned to Boston, took a job as a church organist, and taught privately until 1882, when he joined the faculty of the New England Conservatory, an association that lasted until just before his death in 1931.

In later life, Chadwick sometimes voiced regret that his musical training had not begun sooner. But perhaps the need to improvise a musical education gave him confidence to follow his own creative path. Chadwick's teachers at the Leipzig Conservatory pegged him from the start as an out-of-the-ordinary student. In June 1879, his *Rip Van Winkle* Overture for orchestra, performed on a graduation concert, was reviewed by a Leipzig critic as "uncontestably . . . the best of this year's compositions."[10] Salomon Jadassohn and Carl Reinecke, with whom Chadwick studied, both signed an evaluation that reads in part: "Herr Chadwick possesses a completely exceptional talent for composition, as is sufficiently demonstrated by his work . . . [which is] far beyond school work. The lessons with him were always a pleasure."[11] An American audience also had a chance to hear *Rip Van Winkle* in December 1879, when the overture received its Boston premiere. Again the response was warm. In later years, Chadwick reflected: "I think I may say without egotism that the whole Boston movement in composition really dates from the performance of my Rip van Winkle overture" in Boston. "It was the keystone of my entire success in life and brought me Horatio Parker, Arthur Whiting, F. S. Converse & Henry Hadley for pupils who went to Rheinberger from me and by my advice."[12] Chadwick seems to have known from the start how to communicate in a concert hall, a talent that helped raise him to a position of leadership in Boston's musical life.

In Chadwick's case, "Yankee composer" means a musician fully at home in European genres but approaching them through an American sensibility. Chadwick's biographers choose as his most representative works the Second Symphony, the Fourth String Quartet, *Symphonic Sketches, Tam O'Shanter* for orchestra, an opera called *The Padrone,* and a number of the songs. Traits of his style include a fondness for pentatonic and gapped scales, distinctive rhythms from Anglo-American psalmody, African-Caribbean dance syncopations, parallel voice leading, and skillful orchestration; all except the last distinguish Chadwick's music from German prototypes. And so does his sensitivity, in setting words to music, to characteristic English rhythms. From these traits, Chadwick evolved a personal approach that allowed him to write cosmopolitan music with an American twist.

Recently Chadwick has been credited with the creation of an American symphonic style.[13] The claim may seem grandiose for a composer who wrote only three symphonies, all of them forgotten by later generations. But the more one learns about Chadwick, the less far-fetched it seems. For one thing, as well as his trio of symphonies, he composed between 1879 and 1923 five overtures, two symphonic poems, a *Symphonic Ballad,* a Sinfonietta, the four-movement *Symphonic Sketches,* and a number of smaller orchestra pieces. For another, Chadwick felt a deep connection to the symphony orchestra. Active as a conductor from the early 1880s on, he led the orchestra at the New England Conservatory for many years. A rehearsal incident reported by a student violinist reveals the depth of his attachment: "One day nothing went well. Suddenly Chadwick laid down his stick and surveyed the scene with a curious mixture of sorrow and anger. . . . His eyes roamed the stage; then he slumped heavily in his chair and shouted: 'Do you want to know something? This orchestra is my life blood—do you understand? My life blood! You're hardening my arteries—that's what you're doing.' "[14] Yet the best test of this claim lies in Chadwick's orchestra music itself—for example, the Second Symphony (1886).

Chadwick does not seem to have begun this work with a symphony in mind. He wrote it in pieces: first a Scherzo for orchestra in 1884; then an Overture in B-flat, "Introduction and Allegro," first performed in 1885; and finally the whole four-movement work, starting with the Overture (the first movement) and the Scherzo (the second), and followed by third and fourth movements linked thematically to the first. The first two movements, then, were both written to appeal on their own. Reviewing the premiere in 1886, one critic found the work

> so unexpected in character that one hardly knows how to take it. . . . We, for one, cannot remember any music of this character being written in the symphonic form. . . . The light, almost operatic character of the thematic material; the constant changes of rhythm; the frequent solo passages—not merely incidental phrases for this or that instrument, but often full-fledged solos of considerable length—all contributed to make the work fall short of what may be called symphonic dignity.[15]

Although the writer's comments are more general than specific, it is not hard to link them to particular moments in the Second Symphony. For example, the complaint about the thematic material's "light, almost operatic character" may apply to the melody that closes the first movement's exposition. And the jaunty rhythm of a melody late in the second movement anticipates a prominent theme in Dvořák's *New World* Symphony (1893); Victor Herbert's operettas were also to tap this vein of dreamy mood and vivid orchestral color.

By "constant changes of rhythm" the critic may have been referring to tempo shifts such as the one at the end of the first movement, where acceleration and hemiola (in triple time, a pattern of three accented beats instead of two within a two-measure unit) figures may disorient listeners; or the lift-off effect at the end of the fourth movement, where Chadwick changes meter four times in eleven pages of score; or the fast-paced last movement's quotation from the slow-moving third movement. Perhaps the rhythm of some of the themes themselves struck him as too syncopated, varied, or complex. One of the "frequent solo passages" takes place in the first movement's recapitulation, where one trumpet plays a melody that recalls a band concert in the park more readily than it does a symphony.) But whatever the particulars, it is clear that for this critic, the unconventional features of Chadwick's symphony overshadowed the conventional colorful chromatic harmony, four-movement structure, standard formal plans within movements, even cyclic form (more than one movement featuring the same thematic material) in the up-to-date European manner. To Chadwick's biographer, this music sounds like an American response to an Old World aesthetic challenge, the first example of a distinctively American symphonic style. But to a critic of the composer's own day, the Second Symphony was a blow to the integrity of symphonic form itself.

There is no evidence that Chadwick regretted the Second Symphony's unrestrained tone, but he stopped composing symphonies after finishing his third in 1894, and from then on his orchestra writing took other forms. The *Symphonic Sketches* (1904) follows the standard four-movement plan (fast-slow-fast-fast) but gives programmatic titles to each of the movements: "Jubilee," "Noel," "Hobgoblin," and "A Vagrom Ballad." Here, rather than offering abstract musical development, Chadwick translates specific images into music. An eight-line verse linking sound, color, and mood serves as a prologue to the first movement:

> No cool gray tones for me!
> > Give me the warmest red and green,
> > A cornet and a tambourine,
> To paint MY jubilee!
> > For when pale flutes and oboes play,
> To sadness I become a prey;
> Give me the violets and the May,
> > But no gray skies for me!

Symphonic Sketches seems to have been accepted and judged at face value. For critic Henry Taylor Parker, who reviewed a performance in 1908, the work was a set of unmistakably American mood pictures by "the most American of our composers." Parker's review emphasized expressive features over formal ones. He heard in "Jubilee" echoes of "Negro tunes," and he fancied that the work unfolded in an American farmhouse setting. He also delighted in the music's "high and volatile spirits . . . the sheer rough-and-tumble of it," concluding: "The music shouts because it cannot help it, and sings because it cannot help it, and each as only Americans would shout and sing."[16]

"Jubilee" alternates a boisterous Allegro with more pensive and restrained music in a seven-part design (**ababab a**). And Parker took its mood swings as further proof of Chadwick's nationalist stamp. It is an American trait, he wrote, "to turn suddenly serious, and deeply and unaffectedly so, in the midst of its fooling to run away into sober fancies and moods, and then as quickly turn 'jolly' again." The slower section, reduced to short score in the example, shows Chadwick's New World sensibility in full bloom.

As Gottschalk did in *The Banjo*, Chadwick takes Foster's *Camptown Races* as a starting point, which can be heard not just as a quotation but as an example of three important New World elements: habanera rhythm (2/4 at a moderate-to-slow tempo—a familiar accompaniment figure in Cuban song and dance), prosodic syncopation (the short-long rhythm [♪♩] in the melody's second measure, drawn from the rhythm of such English words as

"river" or "money"), and gapped tetrachord (the melody is built from a four-note scale [1-3-5-6] in which skips outweigh stepwise motion). This brief passage is followed by a singing theme in the violins that, in combination with an Afro-Caribbean dance figure, brings to twentieth-century minds images of the empty plains and prairies of the Old West.[17] As long as Chadwick's music remained unheard, it was possible to infer that he, like other Boston composers, was cast aside after World War I because his works echoed German models, which had fallen out of favor. But the sound of this passage is far from Germanic. If Chadwick was able, long before any such convention was established, to write music instantly recognizable today as a musical metaphor for the wide open spaces of the movie Western, then Teutonic influence can hardly be blamed for his music's failure to crack the concert-hall repertory.

But does Chadwick really deserve credit for creating an American symphonic style, or is it enough simply to note that he found a personal style of writing for orchestra that now sounds American? The first implies a histori-

Chadwick (left) trades hats with composer Victor Herbert in
this 1890 photograph taken in Springfield, Massachusetts.

cal process in which other concert-hall composers followed Chadwick's
lead, which none did. The second, on the other hand, may seem to reduce
to a private quirk Chadwick's musical response to an issue that was to occupy many of his contemporaries and even more composers and critics after
World War I: the role of nationality in American music. However his style is
classified, it does seem to have fallen victim to attitudes like that of the
critic who reviewed the Second Symphony in 1886. The ideal of elevation
that ruled the concert hall, together with the notion that artistically serious

music ought to be grave and dignified, apparently conspired to make Chadwick's style seem unsuitable. Could the standard Old World forms of concert music accommodate a playful, sometimes informal American mode of orchestral expression? Or did such music risk trivializing Americans' quest to find a place of honor among the world's musical nations? In Chadwick's case, these questions led to direct answers: no and yes.

Yet although the concert hall found no lasting place for his music, the world of popular entertainment was soon to welcome a style of orchestral writing like his. A photograph taken in Springfield, Massachusetts, in 1890 of Chadwick and another man wearing each other's hats seems to comment on his place in American music. Chadwick, staring glumly to his right, looks engulfed by the top hat he wears, while the large, handsome figure facing him dwarfs the homburg perched on his own head. The second man is Victor Herbert, Irish-born composer, conductor, and cellist, who had moved from Germany to New York City in 1886 and would become a dominating figure on the American scene. If we read this photo as a glimpse of historical destiny, then it seems fitting that Herbert cuts the more impressive figure. Having arrived in this country as an orchestra player and composer for the concert hall, he soon outgrew that setting, connecting with a much larger American public through the concerts he conducted—he took over Gilmore's Band when Patrick S. Gilmore died in 1892—and the operettas he began composing in 1894.

The two men caught here in a moment of comic role playing occupied common musical ground but served institutions with different goals. Chadwick's concert hall, centered on works, was devoted chiefly to an elevated art of music; Herbert's musical theater, centered on occasions, was intent on bringing pleasure to its audiences. And it was through composers like Herbert that the American style Chadwick helped to invent found its niche. That niche grew with the changing times. The leaders of the Hollywood film industry probably had no idea who George W. Chadwick was when sound films began in the 1930s to be accompanied by orchestras. But they chose a musical style close to that of the Second Symphony and the *Symphonic Sketches*: rooted in German Romanticism, tuneful in Chadwick's Yankee manner, colorfully written for the instruments, and easily accessible to a general audience.

AMY BEACH AND AMERICAN MUSICAL DEMOCRACY

Amy Marcy Cheney was born in 1867 in West Henniker, New Hampshire. It did not take Mrs. Cheney, a brilliant pianist according to her daughter, long to discover Amy's talent for music. At the age of one, the child could sing forty tunes exactly as she heard them, and before she was two, she could improvise harmony to her mother's lullaby.[18] Beach's mother obviously had a prodigy on her hands. But she was determined neither to push her daughter into music nor to exploit the child's talent in public. When she finally began to give Amy piano lessons at six, progress was swift, and before long the young girl was studying with a respected piano teacher in Boston. At sixteen, she made her public debut as a pianist, playing a concerto with an orchestra in Boston in 1883. Two years later, she married Dr. Henry H. A. Beach, a forty-two-year-old Boston widower, physician, and amateur musician. And for the next twenty-five years, she lived an active, well-rounded musical life centered in Boston.

Amy had been writing music since she was four, and in her early teens she had taken a year's worth of lessons in harmony and counterpoint from a local teacher. As a woman, she found avenues for further formal study closed to her, so she acquired scores, books, and treatises on counterpoint, fugue, and orchestration and essentially taught herself to compose. After her marriage, she concentrated more on composition than performance, though she still played in public, chiefly in and around Boston and often in benefit concerts for charity. (In later life, even after a long performing career, she is said to have thought of herself as a composer who performed mostly her own music rather than a concert pianist.) Beach composed until well into her seventies, writing many songs, choral pieces, works for keyboard, some chamber music, a piano concerto, a symphony, and even an opera. In 1895, her mother, always Beach's main musical adviser, moved in with the childless couple after Amy's father died, taking over some of the household chores and leaving Beach free to compose.[19]

Beach's settled life in Boston came to an end when her husband died in 1910, followed by her mother early the next year. In the fall of 1911, at the age of forty-four, she seized an independence she had never enjoyed before: sailing for Europe, hiring a manager, and beginning to play more often in public. When World War I forced her return to the United States in 1914, she set up a cross-country concert tour. After a brief stay in California (1915–16), she established in 1916 a new home base in Hillsborough, New Hampshire. A close friend of the widow of Edward MacDowell, who had died in 1908, Beach from 1921 on spent time each summer at the MacDowell Colony in Peterboro, New Hampshire, where she found it easy and natural to compose. Beginning in 1930, she made New York City her winter home. When Beach died in New York in 1944, she left behind more than three hundred compositions and a record of pioneering achievements, as both a performer and a composer: she was the first American-trained concert pianist, part of the first generation of professional American female instrumentalists, and the first woman to compose large-scale works for the concert hall. And although this aspect of her work has been uncovered only through persistent research, Beach was also one of the first to use folk melodies to help create a distinctively American style.[20]

If democracy means a social condition of equality and a respect for individuals within the community, then the list of Amy Beach's achievements points to an undemocratic condition. Although women had taken an active part in this country's music making during the eighteenth and early nineteenth centuries, except for a few families of professional musicians (most of them foreign-born), they led their musical lives within severe limits. Women were perceived as "the weaker sex," and this perception, in addition to placing social restraints on upper- and middle-class American girls and young women, divided musical activity into categories deemed suitable or unsuitable for females. If Beach's generation was the first to produce professional women instrumentalists, that was because singers had previously been the only women encouraged to develop their performing skill. If Beach was the first American-trained concert pianist, that was because the parents of talented males like Gottschalk and MacDowell recognized European grooming as essential for their sons' future livelihood, whereas Beach lived until middle age under the protective wing of others, with no thought of following a professional performer's career. Finally, if she was the first American woman to compose successfully in large-scale forms, that was because the men who controlled such opportunities had resisted the idea that a female composer could meet the demands of the symphony, concerto, oratorio, or opera. These points may seem obvious today, but a century ago they were not.

"Can a woman become a great composer?" asked Louis Elson, Boston critic and music teacher in his *History of American Music* (1904). "Will there ever be a female Beethoven or a Mozart?" In Europe, Elson reported, these questions had been answered "quickly and in the negative," and he cited Carl Reinecke, Chadwick's teacher at the Leipzig Conservatory, as a source. Reinecke had once told Elson that "up to a well-advanced point in the interpretation of the ideas of others, the female student often outstripped the male; but in the highest realms of musical performance, where individuality needed to be blended with the text of the composer, there was a timidity that militated against progress." And Elson had also heard similar views from other European teachers.

Yet Elson himself did not believe men's capacities in music superior to women's. "We venture to believe," he wrote, "that it has been insufficient musical education and male prejudice that have prevented female composers from competing with their male brethren in art." And what was his evidence? First and foremost, the career of Amy Beach. In America, Elson wrote, "the female composer was in the field" at the same time as "our Chadwicks, Parkers, and MacDowells; and America can boast at least one

This program of the Handel and Haydn Society of Boston places Amy Beach, composer of a new Mass in E-flat (1892), in the company of the European masters.

female composer who can compare favorably with any woman who has yet entered creative musical art."[21] For all its affirmative tone, this statement seems to give with one hand and take back with the other. Seemingly ready to declare Beach the artistic equal of her male colleagues, Elson ends up ranking her only among women. Nevertheless, as a Boston critic and a member of the New England Conservatory's faculty, he had observed Beach's musical development firsthand, dispelling any doubt that a woman could function at the highest levels of musical endeavor. As a child with near-miraculous talent, she had shown the energy, confidence, and character to acquire professional skills that made her a peer of male colleagues. And with Beach as Exhibit A, Elson could survey the scene and find other female composers capable of challenging the stereotype.[22]

Thus, the career of Amy Beach, undercutting the essentialism at the heart of antifemale prejudice, served in her own day as a symbol of what a woman musician could do if given the chance. Well-known and tireless as both a composer and a performer, she set an example that must have inspired other American women to take their talent seriously. But Beach's contribution to musical democracy took two forms beyond the symbolic: (1) her interest in borrowing thematic material from outside concert-hall traditions, and (2) the life she led as a composer-pianist, especially from 1914 on, when she devoted herself chiefly to bringing music in the classical sphere to the American people. Because the first belongs to a subject taken up more fully in the next chapter, it will not be discussed here. The second, however, leads to a perspective on Beach that has sometimes been overlooked.

As a composer-pianist, Beach wrote music chiefly for the kinds of programs in which she herself performed. Yet it was large-scale works that distinguished her from female predecessors who by the 1890s had already composed a substantial repertory of songs and piano pieces. Most of her large-scale works, including the Mass in E-flat (1892), the *Gaelic* Symphony (1896), and the Piano Concerto (1900), were written before she was thirty-five, a period that coincides generally with the so-called golden years of the Boston group as Chadwick recalled them. The Boston Handel and Haydn Society premiered the first of these compositions, and the Boston Symphony Orchestra introduced the other two, reflecting Beach's esteemed position in the city. New York critics also reviewed the premiere of the Mass in February 1892, sung to a packed house; one called the performance "the event of the season in musical circles."[23] Moreover, the symphony's premiere in Boston was followed soon by performances in Buffalo and Brooklyn, New York, and the next year by the Chicago Symphony Orchestra under Theodore Thomas.

It is not hard to understand why Beach's Mass was warmly received. Philip Hale, one of Boston's most astute critics, commented on the work's "long breath," and the "knowledge, skill and above all, application, patience and industry" of its composer. He praised Beach for not following "closely an illustrious predecessor," as one might have expected a young, self-taught American composer to do, but having "ideas of her own" which "she has not hesitated" to carry out.[24] The Gloria movement displays Beach's lyric imagination and her fearlessness about putting a personal stamp on a time-honored form. In setting the words sung by angels on the night of Christ's birth—"Gloria in excelsis Deo; et in terra pax hominibus bonae voluntatis" (Glory to God in the highest, and on earth peace, toward men of good will)—she began with a ringing tenor solo, followed by a chorus alternating freely between counterpoint and octaves, with a dance-like declamatory rhythm in 3/4 time and even a hint of an oom-pah-pah accompaniment. Though there is nothing in this music to suggest that an American wrote it, listeners must have appreciated the sheer delight in music making that Beach invoked to underline the text's joyous message to the world.

Although Beach taught herself to compose in large forms, it was on a composer-pianist's smaller scale that she did most of her work. During many years before the public, she did play occasional solo recitals, but more commonly she was joined by other musicians (chiefly singers but sometimes violinists), and she often appeared as an assisting artist on other musicians' programs. As a practiced collaborator, Beach was accustomed to fitting her style to the genre and the occasion. On May 11 and 12, 1892, for example, in a concert of the Cecilia Society, one of Boston's leading choral groups, she premiered *Fireflies* (Op. 15, No. 4), a short piano piece that calls for a delicate touch and the ability to play streams of thirds smoothly in the right hand. Beach's goal here was apparently to add variety to the program. For *Fireflies*, a night scene with flashing pianistic colors and quick movement to suggest the insects' unpatterned glimmerings, contrasts sharply with the sound and spirit of the Cecilians' choral fare. *Fireflies* became a kind of signature piece for Beach.

Another invitation five years later led to a different kind of composition. On January 4, 1897, the Kneisel Quartet programmed Beethoven's String Quartet, Op. 59, No. 2, a string quartet in E-flat by Mozart, and the premiere of Beach's Sonata for Violin and Piano in A minor (Op. 34), played by violinist Franz Kneisel with Beach at the piano. It takes only the first two-dozen measures of this sonata to suggest how well the music must have fit the program: in effect, three generations of chamber music in an Austro-German style, by a German, an Austrian, and an American. The principal melody, announced quietly and in the piano's middle range, makes no attempt at catchiness but seems more a gesture out of which something more sharply defined will grow; in fact, thematic play and development dominate

Amy Beach (1867–1944).

the movement. Beach included this violin sonata in concerts of her own over the next several decades. Her scrapbooks show that it was still being played in the 1940s, especially in concerts featuring her music or that of other female composers.

These glimpses of works from the 1890s suggest that Beach's musicianship and practicality enabled her to tailor her music for a variety of situations. It is worth remembering here that despite the prejudice she faced as a female, compared with most other American musicians (male or female), Beach lived a privileged life. Her mother spotted her talent from the start and fostered it. Although the lack of systematic training in composition was a handicap, she was given the leisure and opportunity to develop her creative powers on her own. Once she married, a secure social position allowed her to play and to present her music in prestigious situations. Free from the need to make a living or to run a household, she was one of very few Americans able to devote herself to writing and performing music at a professional level without having to depend on the economic outcome. Her music found an audience, too, as is shown by the substantial royalty checks she received in later years.

Not only did Beach prefer to be thought of as a composer rather than a concert pianist, there is evidence that she resisted the social status that being a professional musician carried with it, especially for a woman. Until 1911, when she made her first trip to Europe, Beach's musical career was structured as that of an extraordinary amateur, free from any need to grapple

with the pressures of the marketplace. Her appearances had been before select audiences, including many friends and acquaintances. When she returned to America from Europe in 1914, however, the niche she had once
filled in the Boston scene no longer existed. Therefore, becoming in effect
her own manager, she began to fashion a career that involved more playing
in public, for nonexclusive audiences away from the major musical centers.
In the opinion of eminent pianist and teacher Ernest Hutcheson, a contemporary, both Beach and Marian MacDowell, wife of composer Edward Mac-
Dowell, "were remarkably good concert pianists who had succumbed to the
tragic mistake of playing mainly to second-string audiences instead of aiming only for the more discriminating concert and recital audiences," such as
those in New York's Town Hall and Carnegie Hall.[25] As a male performer
and disciple of elevated art, Hutcheson could assume that artists were duty-
bound to pursue the most prestigious goal available to them. By that token,
anyone able to follow a top-level career in performance who passed up the
chance to do so was guilty of an artistic sin on a par with moral failure. But
Beach gave no sign that she saw her career in these terms. Devoted to musical elevation, she now served it at another level. She continued to accept
recital engagements and an occasional performance with orchestra, but she
built the heart of her performing career around the local musical organizations that grew up in the late 1800s and early 1900s.

Musical energy abounded in the classical sphere in those days, much of
it centered on amateur performance and a growing audience of appreciative
listeners. Organizations were formed to tap this energy, from choral societies to teachers' associations, to organists' guilds. Beethoven clubs, Mac-
Dowell clubs, even Beach clubs sponsored meetings, musicales, and
concerts, celebrating the art in general and sometimes a respected composer or performer in particular. Beach herself was active in the Music
Teachers' National Association (MTNA), which promoted the cause of
American composers by sponsoring performances, and the National Federation of Music Clubs, which awarded prizes for new compositions. She was
also among the first members of the New Hampshire Music Teachers' Association, dedicated to performing music by native and contemporary composers. In that environment, demand for traveling artists, especially pianists,
ran high, though fees were modest. Beach intended much of the music she
wrote either for such groups as these or for church use. (Shortly after her
mother's death in 1911, Beach joined the Protestant Episcopal church,
which loomed large in her life from then on.) It was no accident that her
first concert after her return from Europe in 1914 took place at Boston's
MacDowell Club, where she presented two groups of songs composed overseas. "An audience of some 700 people rose *en masse* as she stepped upon

the platform," a press account read, "and after an address, Mrs. Beach was showered with flowers."[42]

As we can see from this brief announcement, the composer was still being called "Mrs. Beach" in the city that had fostered her musical career from the start. Although Beach signed all her music "Mrs. H. H. A. Beach," she called herself "Amy Beach" when she was in Europe from 1911 to 1914, but then decided to revert to her married name when she returned to the United States. When asked about her choice of name, she replied that it was only "proper" for married Bostonian women to be known as "Mrs. so-and-so."[26]

As a woman who declined the label of professional musician, Beach had no need of a separate professional name. "Mrs. Beach" defined herself socially first and artistically second: a "nice" and "proper" married Bostonian woman who also happened to be one of the nation's leading composers. The name she chose was therefore as unique as the role she embraced: that of a social aristocrat—at least insofar as an American could be one—with the skills of a professional musician and the artistic attitude of an enlightened amateur (i.e., a lover of music). "Mrs. H. H. A. Beach" may seem today an odd, quaint, or perhaps even disrespectful way of referring to Amy Beach. Yet by keeping her distance from a professional world in which she was superbly qualified to excel, Beach reminds the present-day observer that the social and artistic priorities of one era are not necessarily those of another.

19

Edward MacDowell and Musical Nationalism

BORN IN NEW YORK IN 1860, trained in Europe, and associated with Boston only from 1888 until 1896, when he lived there, Edward MacDowell won a reputation that made him more a national than a local figure. Yet Chadwick included him in his list of the "boys," even though his musical orientation ran against the classic strain of nineteenth-century German Romanticism—from Beethoven and Schubert through Mendelssohn, Schumann, and Brahms—that inspired most of the Bostonians. Rather than being drawn to symphonies and string quartets, concerned with the logic of sonata design, MacDowell identified with the "New German School" of Franz Liszt and Richard Wagner, which emphasized programmatic implications and musical narrative over abstract problems of tonal play.

As a child, MacDowell was an avid reader whose parents encouraged him to develop his artistic flair, which included a talent for drawing.[1] Although not wealthy, MacDowell's family sent him to private school; then in 1876, after his gift for music proved uncommon, his mother took him to Europe for more specialized training. He was accepted at the Paris Conservatory but grew disenchanted with French instruction and moved on to Germany two years later. Studying piano in Wiesbaden and then in Frankfurt, he also took composition lessons from Joachim Raff. Among the highlights of this phase of his life were chances to play in 1879 and 1880 for Franz Liszt. After securing a post as piano teacher at the Darmstadt Conservatory, where he taught from 1881 to 1882, MacDowell had an experience that changed the way he thought of himself as a musician. In July 1882, when he played his First Piano Concerto at a concert in Zurich that Liszt attended, the encouraging response from both the older composer and the audience surpassed anything MacDowell had imagined. "Until then," he later wrote to an American friend,

I had never waked up to the idea that my compositions could be worth actual study or memorizing. . . . *Inside* I had the greatest love for them; but the idea that any one else might take them seriously never occurred to me. I had acquired the idea from early boyhood that it was expected of me to become a pianist, and every moment spent in scribbling seemed to be stolen from the more legitimate work of piano practice.[2]

Now MacDowell directed more and more attention to composing. By 1884, German publishers had issued some of his works, and pianist Teresa Carreño, with whom he had studied as a boy in New York, was programming MacDowell's music on her American concerts. In the same year, he married Marian Nevins, an American and a former piano student, and the couple settled in 1885 in Wiesbaden, where MacDowell taught piano and composed. Three years later, having lived nearly half his life in Europe, the twenty-seven-year-old MacDowell and his wife moved to Boston, where he launched an American career centered on composing but funded chiefly by piano teaching and playing.

In the spring of 1889, MacDowell premiered his Piano Concerto No. 2 in D minor with the Theodore Thomas Orchestra in New York, followed a month later by a performance with the Boston Symphony. In July, he presented the work again at the Paris Exposition Universelle in a concert of American music conducted by Frank van der Stucken.[3] When the respected New York critic H. E. Krehbiel called the concerto "so full of poetry, so full of vigor" that it deserved placement "at the head of all works of its kind produced by either a native or adopted citizen of America," some observers began to perceive the young composer as American music's Man of Destiny.[4] MacDowell premieres were now eagerly anticipated, and more resounding claims were made for his achievements. In 1894, he played his Second Piano Concerto with the New York Philharmonic Society; the conductor, confirmed Wagnerite Anton Seidl, declared MacDowell superior to Johannes Brahms as a composer. And two years later, at a concert in New York's Metropolitan Opera House, he played his First Piano Concerto with the Boston Symphony Orchestra in a program that also introduced his Second (*Indian*) Suite to great critical acclaim.

This concert proved a turning point in MacDowell's career. Now reckoned as one of the country's leading musicians and even "the greatest musical genius America has produced," he was offered a prestigious post: the first professorship of music at Columbia University in New York City. In the fall of 1896, he plunged wholeheartedly into teaching and the life of the new music department he intended to build. But the job at Columbia proved so demanding that he found little time for composition, except during school vacations. Though he continued to write piano music, songs, and choruses, no more orchestra works appeared. MacDowell took his first sabbatical leave in 1902–3, touring the United States and Canada as a pianist. Returning to his post in the fall of 1903, he found himself in conflict with Columbia's new president over the music department's place in the university. When no resolution could be reached, MacDowell resigned in 1904 amid a commotion publicized in the New York press. Emotionally drained and embittered by the experience, and perhaps still feeling the effects of a traffic accident earlier in the year, he soon suffered a crisis in health. By December 1904, he was showing signs of serious mental illness, which gradually worsened into a state of near-complete physical and mental helplessness. He died early in 1908, at the age of forty-seven, and was buried near his summer home in Peterborough, New Hampshire, which, through Marian MacDowell's dedicated efforts, was made into an art colony in his memory.

While MacDowell's musical gifts were decidedly uncommon, it is also true that he arrived on the scene at an opportune moment. For around the time that he moved to Boston from Germany, a quickening public interest in the history of music in America was preparing the ground for the advent of a "great American composer." Historical studies published in 1889 and 1890 traced a growing appetite for music and the building of an infrastructure to support it: ensembles, conservatories, concert halls, and opera troupes. The only missing element was a composer whose distinctive voice would signal that the nation was approaching musical maturity. Enter the young, handsome, charismatic—and modest—Edward MacDowell, seemingly born to the role: impeccably schooled, with European training and reputation; an excellent pianist who performed his own music superbly in public; an artist of broad range who also wrote poetry and showed a knack for drawing. And his music had a sound of its own. All of these traits combined to make MacDowell a fitting subject for the first book-length biography of an American composer, and perhaps the first to be considered an agent in a historical process.

Edward MacDowell: A Study, written in 1906 by music critic Lawrence Gilman and revised in 1908 after the composer died, presents likenesses at several stages of MacDowell's life, from a self-portrait drawn at fourteen to a frontispiece showing him in solemn maturity. And the author tries to illuminate both the outer and the inner man. In view of the grimness of MacDowell's last years, it is striking that Gilman recalls especially his "inextinguishable humour": the "fugitive twinkle" in his "light and brilliant blue" eyes, and the "low, rich chuckle" when he was amused, which was often. Gilman's blend of physical description and character analysis seems to announce: Behold, a true specimen of American artistic manhood! At the same time, his portrait of the artist as a hero—"a fusion of Scandinavian and American types"—also implies the tragic side of MacDowell's history.[5]

Edward A. MacDowell (1860–1908).

For readers of the book have always known that the composer never fully realized the hopes inspired by his early success.

MacDowell obviously profited from the favored role that was thrust upon him, but eminence brought pressures too, and they seemed to increase with the years. From a distance, MacDowell's christening as a historical figure and his acceptance of the Columbia post seem to have been a catch-22—a reward for creative artistry whose duties eventually swamped his creative vocation. After the *New England Idylls* (1902), the composer began several new works but finished none of them. His illness was partly to blame, but so was the habit of second-guessing himself. As a painstaking craftsman, profoundly self-critical, MacDowell indulged his mania for revising compositions out of an urge to improve them that, in a sympathetic contemporary's words, "found no rest until he had given them that finish of detail which is so characteristic of his art at its best."[6] But that state of mind was not the self-assured one that might have been expected of a great American composer. Perhaps a few more Saturday evenings at the Tavern Club in Boston would have eased the burdens of his New York years.

MacDowell and Musical Nationalism

Not long after his return from Germany, MacDowell found himself part of a debate about the character and future direction of American music. As an anointed leader expected to carry the banner of national art, he could scarcely have ducked the issue, even though he placed little stock in the idea of musical nationalism. MacDowell saw art as a realm that should be kept free of politics. For him, the customs that ruled musical practice stemmed from a history of purely artistic choices, and the idea that they might become subject to policy decisions struck him as ominous. That is why in 1891 he announced his opposition to programs devoted completely to American music (even though he had performed in one in Paris two years earlier). When the Worcester (Massachusetts) Festival proposed to include his First Suite for orchestra on an all-American concert, MacDowell tried to block its performance—unsuccessfully, as it turned out, for the work was already published. In the same year, he explained his new position to a Chicago colleague: "Whenever an exclusively American concert is given, the players, public and press seem to feel obliged to adopt an entirely different standard of criticism from the one accepted for miscellaneous concerts. Some people would run down an American concert *before* hearing the music—and others would praise it (also *before* hearing it)."[7] In other words, all-American concerts were political events. By exempting works from the standard of criticism that European music had had to face, organizers of such concerts encouraged musical protectionism. In the long run, Americans would compose robustly for the concert hall only when their work was good enough to *earn* performances through a competitive process of selection based on aesthetics. MacDowell held to that position for the rest of his life.

By taking a position above politics, MacDowell might be seen as trying to further his own cause; for music by America's leading composer was sure to be performed, all-American concerts or not. On the other hand, MacDowell knew that his reputation gave him clout that might be used to improve the status of colleagues. In 1903, for example, a San Francisco music critic reported having caught the composer off guard by calling him "Dr. MacDowell."

> "Don't call me Doctor!" he protested, all but blushing. "Why not," I asked. "You are a doctor of music aren't you?" "Yes, I know, but it sounds so stiff, it's an honorary degree conferred by an American University, by two of them in fact . . . [and] when I took them I was thinking of American music, that is, music in America. I thought they might help . . . make people think that music is recognized in this country as well as any other. Those who could do so much for music think it such a trivial thing."[8]

MacDowell and his wife, the American pianist Marian Nevins MacDowell (1857–1956). They established that after his death, their summer home in Peterborough, New Hampshire, would be set up as the MacDowell Colony, a working retreat for composers, writers, and artists.

Beyond musical politics, however, lay musical style. And here MacDowell aspired, both for himself and for American music, to the universality that European classics had achieved. His return from Europe set him on a search for an artistic profile that would be both personal and American. In fact, he may well have been the first American composer to grasp the connection between universality and nationalism. In nineteenth-century Europe, music in the classical sphere was given a nationalist slant by borrowing from folk music, especially in newly emerging nations such as Hungary, Bohemia, Poland, and Russia. Cultural nationalism was based on the idea that each nation should have its own language, folklore, music, flag, and government institutions, while remaining part of cosmopolitan Europe and being aware of each other's developments. Indeed, rather than being viewed as opposites, nationalism and universality were closely connected in

European musical thought. It was in fact their nationalistic traits that brought composers like Frédéric Chopin and Modest Musorgsky international recognition.[9]

These ideas help to situate MacDowell in the discussion of nationalism that in the 1890s surfaced in the United States. To claim an identity as an American composer was a key step in his career. In early 1896, shortly before he took the Columbia professorship, MacDowell sent a complimentary letter to Hamlin Garland, an American writer whose essays on literature, painting, and drama he had just read. "I wish to tell you," wrote MacDowell, "that I am proud of the book with every other true American. It must find an echo in every heart, and I wish to thank you for having said so eloquently what many of us feel, but have never been able to express save in the most timid manner."[10] It is easy to see why Garland's artistic principles appealed to an Edward MacDowell in a nationalist frame of mind. Garland defined literary realism as "the truthful statement of an individual impression corrected by reference to fact." Following the example of impressionistic painters, he strove to register a "personal impression of a scene" rather than simply describing it. Seeking to fuse hard facts with strong feelings, Garland believed that an author should not merely "write of things as they are," but "of things as he *sees* them."[11]

Garland was insisting that emotional vigor was as important to a realist as to a romantic. In fact, precisely *because* it was centered on personal impressions, an art of the commonplace and the "probable" could also tap an artist's full emotional range. MacDowell's letter led to a meeting between the two men, and Garland later recalled how closely his own ideas about American art matched the composer's. MacDowell told him "that he was working toward a music which should be American." Garland also remembered him saying: "Our music thus far is mainly a scholarly restatement of Old-World themes; in other words it is derived from Germany—as all my earlier pieces were."[12] And so MacDowell resolved to be an American composer in the way that Musorgsky was a Russian composer and Dvořák a Bohemian one: by treating his own country as the equivalent, musically speaking, of a peripheral European nation, and bringing the American landscape and indigenous American materials into his own European-based style. He perceived, in other words, that the road to universality led through nationalism.

MacDowell's *Woodland Sketches* (Op. 51; 1896), written the year he met Hamlin Garland, reveal one way in which he claimed an American composer's identity. The work consists of ten short piano pieces whose titles refer to the American landscape and connect with the composer's personal experience. Though raised a city boy in New York, MacDowell developed a taste for the rural while in Germany. And shortly after he and his wife

moved to Boston, they began spending summers in the countryside near Peterborough, New Hampshire, where in 1896 they bought a parcel of land
with a farmhouse on it. MacDowell relished life in the country, which gave
him the seclusion he needed to compose while offering physical pastimes to
vary the routine: fishing, golf, and hiking. With such titles as *To a Wild Rose*,
By a Meadow Brook, and *A Deserted Farm*, the individual pieces of the
Woodland Sketches register MacDowell's impressions of the New England
countryside—perhaps moments experienced on a hike. Listeners thus have
reason to accept the inspiration as American and to think of the music as a
response to the challenge of nationalism.

The *Woodland Sketches* may be approached in a variety of ways. For example, we could set aside the titles and deal with the music in formal terms.
To a Wild Rose, the collection's first piece and MacDowell's best-known
composition, is in a simple three-part (**aba**) form: statement, contrast, and
return. The beginning gives the piece its character: an eight-bar melodic
curve built from a motive of two eighth notes and a quarter, and avoiding
both stepwise motion and the tonic pitch A until its last note.

The harmony of *To a Wild Rose* saves it from blandness. MacDowell usually favors thick chords, enriched with sevenths, ninths, and nonharmonic
tones. But here he keeps the texture transparent, never piling more than five
notes in any chord. He also supports the melody's gentle movement with a
simple harmonic progression. Yet dissonance becomes a factor as early as
the composition's second chord, where the right hand moves to the dominant, while the left hand remains on the tonic, adding a D as if from a voice
that was not there before. This mild harmonic clash asserts a freedom that
MacDowell uses only sparingly; it also prepares the ear for more dissonant
moments. The more complicated harmony of the middle section, with the
help of a *crescendo*, a *ritard*, and changes in texture, range, and harmonic
rhythm, moves away from the manicured neatness of the opening statement. Yet the harmony that fills the end of the b section, while seeming
ready to leave the key of A major, is actually built on its seventh scale degree
so that, after a brief pause, MacDowell can return easily to the main melody
and the tonic key.

There is, however, no reason to think that MacDowell wanted listeners to fix their attention on the formal elements of his music. In fact, he once complained that "we are too often willing" to attribute the power of music "to the mere pleasing physical sensations of sound."[13] Musical sound, proportion, and structure for him were simply means of bringing composers and listeners together in a state of intimate communication. He admitted that it was hard to put into words exactly what instrumental music like the *Woodland Sketches* communicated, but that was because music is much more specific than words. In the past, MacDowell thought, music had been restricted to an imitation of nature (as with storms or birdcalls), a stimulant "to fire the blood, or a sedative to lull the senses." Now, however, thanks to such recent composers as Richard Wagner, it was "a *language*, but a language of the intangible, a kind of soul-language. It appeals directly to the *Seelenzustände* [frame of mind] it springs from, for it is the natural expression of it, rather than, like words, a translation of it into set stereotyped symbols."[14]

The closest MacDowell came to describing this new language further is found in a lecture he gave at Columbia, published under the title "Suggestion in Music." The modern system of tonality, he wrote, opened up resources unavailable to composers of earlier times. Present-day composers could use harmonies "lying outside of the key in which a musical thought is conceived," creating "a sense of confusion or mystery that our modern art of harmony and tone colour has made its own."[15] Thus, in a piece like *To a Wild Rose*, harmonic dissonances bring to MacDowell's sound image of a woodland flower just enough tonal ambiguity to cast an aura of mystery around it. It is not crucial, MacDowell says, for listeners to picture an actual flower; rather, the music portrays the *composer's personal response to the idea* of coming upon a wild rose in its natural surroundings. In Hamlin Garland's realistic terms, MacDowell took a commonplace experience, rendered in music a personal impression of that experience, and invited performers and listeners to share in the unique frame of mind that the music embodies.

MacDowell's Columbia lectures, which were published after his death, reflect his belief that had he appeared earlier on the musical scene, he would have lacked the tonal vocabulary to write music with the expressive truth he achieved in the *Woodland Sketches*. Composers before Wagner, MacDowell wrote, had communicated chiefly through "melodic speech." But the new harmonic vocabulary had added to the older resources of melody "the shadow languages of speech, namely, gesture and facial expression." This combination allowed a more nuanced, complex, and evocative kind of musical communication than ever before. For, just as the "shadow languages of speech may distort or even absolutely reverse the meaning of the spoken word," he wrote, so could "tone colour and harmony change the meaning of a musical phrase." By adapting Wagner's tonal language (developed for his music dramas) to wordless piano music, MacDowell had shown its usefulness in an everyday American context. Still, he cautioned, melody must not be neglected in favor of harmonic effect. For in the long run, it is "the line, not the colour, that will last."[16]

To a Wild Rose's tune offers "melodic speech" catchy enough to balance the harmony's power of suggestion. And if we were to hold a real wild rose up against MacDowell's musical image, correspondences would be easy to find. The dainty one-measure melodic motive matches the idea that a flower is formed from many petals; and the symmetry of a three-part musical design, returning to music previously heard, seems consistent with a rose's circular shape. Furthermore, the flashes of dissonance and harmonic ambiguity undercut the atmosphere of serene loveliness enough to remind listeners that roses have thorns, and that a rose's delicacy and perfection will be short-lived. *To a Wild Rose* fuses beauty (the tuneful surface) and truth (the dissonant undercurrent) in a musical image that celebrates the life and mourns the impending decay of a woodland flower.

The musical style of *To a Wild Rose* is rooted in European practice and no American melodies are quoted, yet the native lineage of this work is also clear. For all the years he spent in Europe, MacDowell was a born-and-bred American, and the New England countryside inspired the *Woodland Sketches* shortly after he told a colleague that he was "working toward a music which should be American." What, then, constitutes distinctively American music? Is it a matter of style? nationality? indigenous quotation? the composer's intent? subject matter? performance history? the commentator's position? some combination of these factors and others?

The question of what is authentically American in music has sparked interest and controversy since the 1890s. So many different criteria have been used to measure musical Americanism—aesthetic, stylistic, historical, political—that there seems little prospect of finding a definition satisfactory to all. From one perspective, MacDowell's career and music show America's dependence on Europe; from another, the American identity of a piece like *To a Wild Rose* seems indisputable; and from still another, both MacDowell and this small piano piece reflect an interweaving of European and American traits that contradicts either label. While none of these views is wrong, neither does any of them tell the whole story. Conundrums such as this have led one music historian to propose a parallax perspective, which recognizes that because each vantage point yields its own insight, different answers to the same question are not only inevitable but can be highly informative.[17] Applying this perspective allows us to keep the question of Americanism in music open in a way that encourages reflection and comparison where partisanship and dispute have often prevailed.

NATIONALISM AND THE INDIAN SUITE

Since musical borrowing is a standard approach to nationalism, an earlier work whose themes MacDowell found in American sources also deserves discussion. Several years before the *Woodland Sketches*, in an effort to compose music that did *not* sound German-inspired, MacDowell wrote an orchestra piece based on Native American melodies. The notion of writing an Indian work dated back to his years in Germany, where in 1887 he had considered an orchestral tone poem about Hiawatha, Henry Wadsworth Longfellow's mythical Indian hero. Although he abandoned that project, the idea remained with him in 1891, when he told Henry F. B. Gilbert, one of his composition students in Boston, that he was "curious to see some real Indian music." Gilbert brought him a copy of Theodore Baker's *Über die Musik der nordamerikanischen Wilden* (On the Music of the North American Indians, 1882), a doctoral dissertation written at the University of Leipzig, which contained a number of transcribed Native melodies. There MacDowell found the themes he used in composing his Second (*Indian*) Suite.

Clearly, it was the expressive possibilities he sensed in Indian life rather than the music itself that first attracted MacDowell. Yet once he began composing with Indian melodies, he believed that no one would hear the outcome as European music. In fact, he considered the *Indian* Suite's sound and style so unusual that he delayed the first performance for several years, admitting after the 1896 premiere his doubts that "this rough, savage music" would "appeal to our concert audiences."[18]

MacDowell's suite contains five movements: *Legend, Love Song, In Wartime, Dirge,* and *Village Festival.* Each is based on a theme MacDowell found in Baker. The quiet, tender second movement quotes a melody that Baker labels an "Iowa love song, sung by young warriors when out riding." And MacDowell drew a theme for *Village Festival,* his fifth movement, from Baker's transcription of "a song for the Iroquois women's dance."

The composer once told an interviewer that of all his music, the *Dirge* in the *Indian* Suite pleased him the most. MacDowell was not alone in judging this movement a success. Calling the *Dirge* "overwhelmingly poignant," Gilman ranked it "the most profoundly affecting threnody in music since the 'Götterdämmerung' *Trauermarsch*" by Wagner; and Arthur Farwell, who worked extensively with Native American melodies himself, praised its "sheer imaginative beauty."[19] MacDowell's *Dirge* is for a son who has died.

Since the preceding movement is about war, listeners are invited to think that he has been slain in battle.

The movement makes a strong impression in part because of the composer's ingenious handling of musical continuity. There is nothing tuneful about the theme he fashioned from the Kiowa melody. Although here and there he coaxes it into the four- and eight-bar parallelisms of Euroamerican tonal music, he never uses it to create momentum or sweep. Furthermore, while rich in harmonic implication, the *Dirge* never settles into a key for long. We hear sections in G minor and E major, but other sections suggest a key only to move away from it, and still others show no clear sense of key at all. The *Dirge* maintains its continuity of mood chiefly through the recurrence of the theme (especially its rhythmic pattern), the generally soft volume, the sparseness of events, and MacDowell's refusal to sustain any continuous flow that might obscure the halting character of the motif. By accepting the severe restrictions of the theme he has made from the borrowed intervals, the composer allows its brevity and harmonic ambiguity to mold the movement's character.

By the time MacDowell's *Indian* Suite was premiered in January 1896, the American visit of a famous European composer had brought the issue of nationalism into the public arena. The visitor was Bohemian composer Antonín Dvořák, who arrived in the United States in 1892 as director of the National Conservatory of Music in New York and remained until 1895. Dvořák had been invited by Jeannette Thurber, a patron who, in setting up the National Conservatory, hoped to encourage the growth of national musical culture—if possible, with funding from the U.S. government. She also expected the composer to found an American school of composition. While Dvořák's success in that endeavor is debatable, he did become a strong public advocate for musical nationalism in America. He showed particular interest in melodies native to the United States—especially plantation melodies of African Americans and tunes of American Indians. By the spring of 1893, he had apparently decided that the former would make a better source. On May 21, he was quoted in the *New York Herald* as saying that after eight months in America, he was "now satisfied . . . that the future music of this country must be founded upon what are called negro melodies. . . . There is nothing in the whole range of composition that cannot be supplied with themes from this source."[20] As if to show how composers on this side of the Atlantic might proceed, during his American stay Dvořák wrote his Symphony No. 9 (*From the New World*), inspired in part by African-American melody, plus two "American" chamber works that may or may not reflect New World influence.

Edward MacDowell—surely one of the best-informed Americans on the subject, having finished his own *Indian* Suite more than a year before the well-publicized premiere of the *New World* Symphony in December 1893—took a dim view of the attention that Dvořák's pronouncements received. Rather than bringing his objections into the public arena, however, he kept them more or less private. In fact, we know about them only because they were published, long after the controversy peaked, in Gilman's biography and in "Folk-Song and Its Relation to Nationalism in Music," a lecture he gave at Columbia.[21] "Purely national music," wrote MacDowell, "has no place in art, for its characteristics may be duplicated by anyone who takes the fancy to do so." After giving examples, such as "the Viennese Strauss family adopting the cross rhythms of the Spanish," he came to the heart of the matter. "We have here in America been offered a pattern for an 'American' national musical costume by the Bohemian Dvořák—though what the Negro melodies have to do with Americanism in art still remains a mystery."[22] MacDowell objected to the foreign intrusion: a visitor who presumed to tell his hosts what to do in a situation they knew better than he did. But beyond Dvořák's meddling, his prescription for national music seemed shallow to MacDowell. "Music that can be made by 'recipe,'" he wrote, "is not music, but 'tailoring.' To be sure, this tailoring may serve to cover a beautiful thought; but—why cover it?" In other words, rather than granting that borrowing a melody and engaging with it musically could be a complicated process, Dvořák seemed to be offering a prescription that could lead simply to arranging "folk" melodies in fancier grab—hardly a foundation for a national art.

MacDowell next raised the question of which indigenous traditions, if any, American composers ought to tap. First he denied that national music *needed* to be based on quotations from national melody. Then he criticized Dvořák's choice. "If the trademark of nationality is indispensable," asked MacDowell, "why cover it with the badge of whilom [former] slavery rather than with the stern but at least manly and free rudeness of the North American Indian?" These words indicate that MacDowell saw musical nationalism primarily as a way of celebrating a nation's virtues. Music based on plantation tunes might be easy to identify as American, but what would it say about the nation's history and character? On the other hand, the music of American Indians pointed toward a heroic past, an unspoiled continental landscape, and an American people of admirable, independent spirit.

MacDowell ended his criticism with an idealistic plea. The goal of musical nationalism should be elevating: to echo the "genius" of the nation. And that could only be achieved by composers "who, being part of the people, love the country for itself" and who "put into their music what the nation has put into its life." In America, furthermore, European musical influence was so strong that both composers and the public needed to seize "absolute freedom from the restraint that an almost unlimited deference to European thought and prejudice has imposed upon us. Masquerading in the so-called nationalism of Negro clothes cut in Bohemia will not help us. What we must arrive at is the youthful optimistic vitality and the undaunted tenacity of spirit that characterizes the American man. This is what I hope to see echoed in American music."[23]

MacDowell's words connect him to a key aspect of European nationalism: the wish for nationally inspired music to be universal in its impact. About the *Indian* Suite's *Dirge* movement, he wrote that the Indian woman's lament over the loss of her son "seems to tell of a world sorrow." And Gilman reported that when MacDowell composed the *Dirge*, he "was moved by the memory of his grief over the death of his master," Joachim Raff, who had died in 1882 while MacDowell was his student in Germany.[24] National elements thus provided a convention through which he could find his own expression of a universal state of mind—in this case, the emotion of grief. What gave that expression validity, he believed, was that it came from a sensibility reflecting America's "youthful optimistic vitality" or its "undaunted tenacity of spirit." A true national art was one that framed American virtues in a way that any music lover, American or European, could understand.

The *Indian* Suite, MacDowell once told an interviewer, was "the result of my studies of the Indians, their dances, and their songs," adding that he had used and developed "themes which came to me from these people."[25] Yet there is no evidence that MacDowell had any direct contact with the lives, activities, or music of Native American people. Rather, his "study" seems to have consisted of reading and consulting his own imagination, which pictured the heroic Indian in an ancient setting long vanished from the earth. This image was held by many others and had been widely circulated by Henry Wadsworth Longfellow's popular epic poem *The Song of Hiawatha* (1855). What is peculiar to MacDowell is that the image seems to have served nationalistic goals in the 1890s in the same way that a distanced view of the Middle Ages had fired his imagination during his European years. Here is how Gilman described MacDowell's idea of the medieval world that inspired many of his compositions:

> While he was enamored of the imaginative records of the Middle Ages, he had little interest, oddly enough, in their tangible remains. He liked, for example, to summon a vision of the valley of the Rhone, with its slow-moving human streams flowing between Italy and the North . . . where the bishops had been lords rather than priests. But this was for him a purely imaginative enchantment. He cared little about exploring the actual and visible memorials of the past: to confront them as crumbling ruins gave him no pleasure, and, as he used to say, he "hated the smells."[26]

By the same token, the smells of the reservation were not for MacDowell, who seems to have been able to read, or to imagine, everything he wanted to know about Indian life.

To an age like our own, alert to the pitfalls of cross-cultural borrowing, MacDowell's willingness to settle for armchair ethnography may seem less than admirable. Although his orchestral suite pictured Native Americans as an ancient people now vanished, MacDowell had access to their melodies only because the people themselves had kept them alive. Dispossessed of most of their territory, depleted in numbers, and more and more segregated on reservations by government policy, they still maintained many of the traditions that their ancestors had practiced before them. But just as medieval ruins held no fascination for MacDowell, neither did the remnants of past Indian civilizations; it was their representation of the universal that attracted him. The Euroamerican present to which MacDowell addressed his *Indian* Suite drew strength and cultural distinctiveness from those "stern" and "manly" forerunners in the primeval past. If Longfellow used trochaic tetrameter and dozens of Ojibwa words to remind readers that Hiawatha's world was a mythic one, so MacDowell's distancing use of "ancient Indian" lore, melodies included, allowed him to imagine the virtues of Native American life that resonated best with his own artistic understanding of the spirit of the American nation.

20

Travel in the Winds

Native American Music from 1820

A NOVEL BY BLACKFOOT INDIAN AUTHOR James Welch, set in the Montana Territory in 1870, traces the coming of "Napikwans"—white settlers—to the region and their impact on the Native peoples who lived there. Toward the end of the book, Fool's Crow, the main character, is summoned in a dream to take a religious journey. After days of travel and fasting, he is shown a vision of his people's future. First he sees them decimated by smallpox, "the white-scabs disease." Then a band of whites appears, riding north to occupy the land where he and his people now live. In the next episode, he is shown that land, his eyes filling "with wonder at the grand sweep of prairie, the ground-of-many-gifts that had favored his people." But then he notices that the blackhorns, the big-horned sheep on which he and his people depend for food, are missing.

As the vision unfolds further, he sees "something that seemed not to fit in the landscape": a square dwelling built by whites. Outside that square a few tipis are pitched, with people "standing around the tipis and the buildings . . . huddled in worn blankets," an altogether pitiful people he does not recognize. Next he is shown a scene of starvation involving two people he recognizes: a boy's body is being carried by a scrawny brave, who stumbles under the meager weight of his load. Fool's Crow's vision now fades until the only thing visible to him is the tanned yellow hide on which the images have appeared, as if on a screen. "He had seen the end of the blackhorns and the starvation of the Pikunis. He had been brought here," Welch writes, "to see the fate of his people. And he was powerless to change it, for he knew the yellow skin spoke a truth far greater than his meager powers, than the power of all his people."

Fool's Crow interprets his vision as proof that, for some reason he cannot fathom, he and his people are being punished. He decides that it is his duty to return to his people and try to prepare them for the future, knowing that "if they make peace within themselves," they will still be able to "live a good life in the Sand Hills," where those who have held to virtuous ways go after their life in this world is over. In this happier place, they will be free from interlopers, disease, and starvation. The Indian brave's vision tells him that the Pikunis will not vanish but survive. Yet, he reflects, "I grieve for our children and their children, who will not know the life their people once lived. I see them on the yellow skin and they are dressed like the Napikwans, they watch the Napikwans and learn much from them, but they are not happy. They lose their own way." Nevertheless, Fool's Crow foresees that the generations to come will still "know the way it was" through stories handed down to them, and will understand "that their people were proud and lived in accordance with the Below Ones, the Underwater People—and the Above Ones."[1]

Fool's Crow's vision touches on many elements of American Indian life during the last two centuries: the spread of Euroamerican civilization across the continent; the disruption of traditional Native ways; the survival of Indian peoples in a society alien to their own; and their struggles to adjust to minority status. The upheavals of Indian history in North America—the forced migrations, constant warfare, ravages of disease, and cultural debilitation—square with Fool's Crow's idea that his people were being punished. In fact, so harsh was the Indians' lot that in 1865, as the Civil War ended, most whites assumed that Indians were heading for extinction as their race gave way to a superior one. Yet more than 300,000 American Indians were still alive in 1865. In some regions, Apaches, Nez Percé, Sioux, Cheyenne, Modocs, and Kickapoos hunted, traveled, threatened settlers, and stole livestock. These tribes were subject to military action, unlike the Seminoles in Florida or groups of Cherokees in North Carolina, who lived in isolation and were generally left alone. Other Indian populations survived in federal reservations and in small, out-of-the-way enclaves.

As Euroamericans extended their settlements across North America, few of them quarreled with the assumption that Indian difference, long a source of conflict, was a national problem. The main difference was perceived as racial. Compared with whites, Indians seemed primitive and savage: they had to be incorporated into society or separated entirely from it. Those in the first camp included missionaries who considered savagery a stage of development that education and the Christian religion could correct. From this perspective, culture, not race, was the barrier. The second camp consisted chiefly of people who were battling Indians for land and resources. As they saw it, their rivals should be quarantined: removed from their homelands, and settled on reservations that would keep them permanently apart from whites.

By the end of the Civil War, Indian peoples had long been under heavy pressure to change or disappear. Yet even as Indian life was being destroyed, Euroamericans were finding that the beliefs, tales, songs, dances, and material arts of these ancient civilizations were worth preserving. The preservation effort, carried on chiefly by non-Indians, offers twentieth-century observers their best window on Indian music making in the past. But we also need to recognize its limitations: first, the incompleteness of the data that have survived; second, the difference between oral expression *in* its natural habitat and outside it; and third, the contrast between Native and non-Native perceptions of Indian ways.

By the 1880s, when the rise of modern anthropological thinking sparked the first serious efforts to preserve and study American Indian music, only a severely truncated view of the subject was possible. It has been estimated that when European settlement of North America began in earnest, between one and two million Indians lived in the territory that is now the United States. Aboriginal peoples were also much more diverse before the forced migrations and tribal decimations of the 1800s. (The concept of "Indian" in North America is a Euroamerican conflation of many different peoples into one ethnic group.) At one time or another, North America has been home to as many as a thousand tribal units, most of them with their own language, and roughly sixty different language families. Yet in only about 10 percent of those units is enough known about the culture to allow any reliable description of its music.

The second issue has to do with recognizing the different forms in which Indian music can exist. Oral circulation among Native peoples themselves is faithful to the music's original spirit. But more widespread has been the practice, led by non-Natives, of by creating musical artifacts, in the form of either transcriptions (sung texts written in words or syllables and musical notation) or recordings, beginning in 1890, when scholars first used cylinder machines to capture the sound of Indian music. Writing and recording allow music that exists only in Indian performance to be heard in other contexts, repeated as desired, and studied. Indian forebears are known to have sung, chanted, prayed, told stories, and taken part in rituals that determined *in the moment* the forms their expression took. But once a song is reified in writing or on record, it takes on a fixed identity that it may never have enjoyed in performance. Only in that form may it be analyzed according to the traits that scholarship emphasizes.

The third issue, the gap between Indian and white attitudes, is related to the second. In the face of the changes that white settlement forced upon them, Indians had strong reasons to maintain the way of life in which their musical practices were embedded. Euroamericans, on the other hand, had strong reasons of their own to assume the superiority of their literate culture

to the nonliterate ones of the Indians. Better technology and growing numbers had enabled them to seize territories where Indians had once lived.
And nineteenth-century thinking endorsed the notion of whites as a more
fully evolved species, ordained to replace "the red man" in the natural order.
Yet at the same time, white Americans' interest in the products of Indian
culture showed a recognition of the Natives' uniqueness. Occasionally
whites included music in their commentaries on Native life; a handful went
as far as writing down sung words, which were then translated into English
and published. A glance at what was preserved before the idea of studying
tribal traditions took hold dramatizes the key role of white perception in stories of early Indian music making. Until the very end of the 1800s, almost all
knowledge about Indian music was filtered through the observations of non-
Indians.

There is no denying the fascination that Indians and their culture held
for some nineteenth-century Americans, especially those who saw them in
their natural surroundings. In 1822, Lewis Cass, then the governor of the
Michigan Territory, quoted from a Miami Indian song in a journal article on
Indian customs: "I will go and get my friends—I will go and get my
friends—I am anxious to see my enemies. A clear sky is my friend, and it is
him I am seeking." Aware that these words bore little resemblance to any
song his readers would know, Cass commented on their performance:

> The manner in which these words are sung cannot be described to the
> reader.—There is a strong expiration of the breath at the commencement of
> each sentence, and a sudden elevation of the voice at the termination. The
> Chief, as he passes, looks every person sternly in the face. Those who are
> disposed to join the expedition exclaim *Yeh, Yeh, Yeh*, with a powerful tone
> of voice; and this exclamation is continually repeated during the whole cere-
> mony. It is, if I may so speak, the evidence of their enlistment. Those who
> are silent decline the invitation.[2]

Cass's account squares with what are now understood as timeless Indian
practices. One of the song's traits, said to be typical of nonliterate societies,
is that its music has a specific purpose: in this case to recruit volunteers for
a mission of war. The text's brevity does not mean that the performance was
short. Many commentators of the time reported Indians' tendency to repeat
bits of text and music incessantly, and noted the long stretches of time that
performances could fill.[3] Vocables (nonsemantic syllables, such as "yeh")
are also found in many Indian songs. Typical too was the text's emphasis on
a natural image—the clear sky, personified as a friend—rather than a narrative or literal description. Finally, like many who heard Indian songs, Cass
was struck by the unusual quality of the singing.

Henry Rowe Schoolcraft, a leading observer of Indian life during the first

Old Bear, a Medicine Man, by George Catlin (1832), oil on canvas.

half of the nineteenth century, accompanied Lewis Cass in 1820 on an expedition to the Upper Mississippi and Lake Superior, winning an appointment in 1822 as Indian agent for tribes in that region. In 1823, Schoolcraft married Jane Johnston, a half-blood Native who was the granddaughter of an Ojibwa chief. His sustained contact with Indians led in 1839 to the publication of *Algic Researches,* the first major study of Ojibwa culture. And he followed that in 1845 with a combination memoir and ethnographic study, *Onéota, or Characteristics of the Red Race of America,* which included an item called *Death Song,* collected from Ojibwa sources. The text, printed

without music, is a vivid statement in eighteen lines: the words of a brave
lying wounded after a battle, gazing at the sky, where he sees "warlike birds"
who may represent his fellow warriors as they enter the territory of their
foes. Schoolcraft identifies the adversaries as "the Dacotahs or Sioux," said
to be hereditary enemies of the Ojibwa (or Chippewas). The text concludes:
"Full happy—I / To lie on the battlefield / Over the enemy's line." The
neatly constructed poem, however, turns out to be a compilation by Schoolcraft—part of it "taken from Tsheetsheegwyung, a young Chippewa warrior,
of *La Pointe*, in Lake Superior" and the rest of the lines "actually sung on
warlike occasions, and repeated in my hearing. They have been gleaned
from the traditional songs of the Chippewas of the north."[4] Armed with literary experience and a sense of what his readers might find poetic, Schoolcraft thus combined several sung moments into one song: evidence that the
wish to document Native life lagged behind the urge to arrange it for literate consumption. Nevertheless, the Ojibwa *Death Song* preserved an image
of Indian stoicism maintaining a theme from the past that would resonate
into the future.

Observers like Schoolcraft and Cass were not the only agents through
which Indian songs found their way into print. In 1847, George Copway
(Kah-Ge-Ga-Gah-Bowh), an Ojibwa born in Ontario whose parents were
converted to Methodism by missionaries and who himself became a
preacher in Illinois, published a memoir that included the five-line *George
Copway's Dream Song*:

> It is I who travel in the winds,
> It is I who whisper in the breeze,
>   I shake the trees,
>   I shake the earth,
> I trouble the waters on every land.

According to Copway, he received this song at the age of twelve from the
god of the winds himself, who appeared to him in a dream in the form of a
person walking on air, and gave him an explanation of the song and its
power. Copway's father, when he heard of the dream, told him: "My son, the
god of the winds is kind to you; the aged tree, I hope, may indicate long life;
the wind may indicate that you will travel much; the water you saw, and the
winds, will carry your canoe safely through the waves."[5] The notion of songs
as personal possessions, received in dreams by their owners, has not been
rare among Indian peoples. Also commonplace are the supernatural framework and the belief that songs are carriers of prophecy.

Whites' views of Indians entered a new phase after 1855, which saw the
publication of Longfellow's *The Song of Hiawatha*, in twenty-two sections,

George Copway.

or cantos, as the poet called them, based on Henry Schoolcraft's researches. Selling thirty thousand copies during its first six months in print, *Hiawatha* would become the most popular long poem ever written by an American. At a time when white settlement had largely wiped out traditional Indian ways of life east of the Mississippi, the poem introduced dramatic, elevated images of that life as it had existed earlier. Longfellow ascribed to Indians virtues admired by Victorian-age Americans, including manliness, courage, and integrity. Moreover, these virtues seemed as well matched to primordial times as were the industry, will, and technological knowledge of nineteenth-century Euroamericans to taming the North American continent for modern habitation. If Indian customs were no longer useful, that fact proved the truth of the "vanishing Indian" syndrome: having prepared the way for white settlers, Native peoples had fulfilled their destiny and would now disappear, lingering only in memories built around historic preservation and myth.

The Song of Hiawatha's Introduction places the poem in a mythic realm by attributing it to oral tradition. Longfellow claimed as his source a Native bard named Nawadaha, who, in the poet's presence,

> Sang the Song of Hiawatha,
> Sang his wondrous birth and being,
> How he prayed and how he fasted,
> How he lived and toiled and suffered,
> That the tribes of men might prosper,
> That he might advance his people.[6]

These few lines suggest how *Hiawatha* captured the public imagination: they set the scene for a gripping story told in unrhymed trochaic tetrameter, whose eight-syllable lines Longfellow borrowed from the *Kalevala*, the national epic of Finland. Combined with a stock of Ojibwa words and names, the meter of *Hiawatha* establishes an atmosphere of remoteness that fits the epic tone and gives his tale an aura of dignified fantasy.

At a time when most North Americans lived outside cities, Longfellow addressed his work to a public whose idea of nature was based in experience. Readers, even if their view of the natural landscape was less romanticized than the poet's, would have perceived the primeval forest as American, just as the Mediterranean and its coastline were classical in such epics as *The Odyssey* and *The Aeneid*. And the notion of ancient Indians dwelling in a wilderness that could be dangerous as well as picturesque suggested an epic sweep and grandeur worth poetic treatment on a large scale. Longfellow hailed readers in an inclusive spirit that invested the American out-of-doors with romance:

> Ye who love the haunts of nature,
> Love the sunshine of the meadow,
> Love the shadow of the forest,
> Love the wind among the branches,
> And the rain shower and the snowstorm,
> And the rushing of great rivers
> Through their palisades of pine trees
> And the thunder in the mountains,
> Whose innumerable echoes
> Flap like eagles in their eyries;—
> Listen to these wild traditions,
> To this Song of Hiawatha.

Recent opinion has judged its romantic, benign image of Hiawatha and his people to be no truer than the older stereotype of Indians as savages. The poem's conclusion, especially, has won no praise from Native peoples.

In the last scene, Hiawatha orders his people to welcome the Christian missionaries, and then "sails (or rather paddles) into the sunset." Lacking a tragic vision, Longfellow missed a crucial literary fact: in epic sagas, people who do not win are destroyed, whereas *Hiawatha* ends with a reconciliation between Indians and Europeans.[7] Nevertheless, *Hiawatha's* popularity and staying power make Longfellow's poem the central source for understanding how Americans east of the Mississippi viewed Indians from the mid-nineteenth century on. Just as movies and television shows today can leave lasting impressions of unfamiliar subjects in the minds of viewers, so *Hiawatha* had a powerful impact on people's opinion of Indian culture, music included.

The latter 1800s witnessed two responses to the Indian presence that hardly existed before the Civil War. One, connected to show business and popular entertainment, and taking white preconceptions as its framework, trivialized Indianness. The second response was a scientific interest in Native life, rooted in idealistic curiosity and requiring trained workers and institutional funding.

Show-business Indians, based on familiar images, grew more widespread as contact between Indians and white Americans decreased. Parodies of Longfellow's *Hiawatha* were standard fare. Another popular form was the "Wild West" show staged by William "Buffalo Bill" Cody, a plains hunter turned showman. In Cody's shows, which began in 1882 and included real Indians, whites were the good guys and Indians the enemy, a conflict carried over into other popular forms, including pulp fiction, dime novels, and, later, Western movies. As in minstrel shows, variety shows, vaudeville, and other entertainments featuring ethnic characters (non-Anglo-Americans), this strain of representation emphasized Indian stereotypes: the savage foe of the Anglo-Saxon hero, the noble Red Man, and the beautiful Indian maiden, as well as lesser figures including thieves, drunkards, and half-breeds. Blind to ambiguities, this response to the Indian presence assumed that Euroamericans knew all they needed to know about the ethnic characters whose portrayals kept them entertained.

The second response rejected that assumption. Rooted in the belief that cultural difference demanded attention, it took place chiefly at the U.S. government's initiative. In 1879, Congress directed that the Bureau of American Ethnology be created at the Smithsonian Institution in Washington, to find out more about the peoples with whom the army was still at war. During the 1880s and 1890s, anthropologically minded scholars created in the nation's capital a flourishing intellectual community with more than twenty scientific and literary societies whose members were chiefly federal workers hired to do research. Much of that research was focused on Native peoples, including sending field workers to document life in tribal settings. The drive to learn more about Indians gave a strong push to the study of Native music. Anthropologist Franz Boas, writing in 1888 in the newly formed American Folklore Society's journal, explained that primitive societies could only be understood through comprehensive inquiry.

> The habits and ideas of primitive races include much that seems to us cruel and immoral, much that it might be thought well to leave unrecorded. But this would be a superficial view. What is needed is not an anthology of customs and beliefs, but a complete representation of the savage mind in its rudeness as well as its intelligence, its licentiousness as well as its fidelity.[8]

More than a devotion to music as an art, then, a mission to explore Indian culture stands behind the scholarly effort that, by the century's end, reckoned Indian music making within its purview.

In 1882, the year Buffalo Bill staged his first Wild West show, Theodore Baker, an American music historian, published *Über die Musik der nordamerikanischen Wilden* (On the Music of the North American Indians), his doctoral dissertation at Leipzig University. Baker's work, the first real scholarly treatment of American Indian music (and supplying themes for Edward MacDowell's *Indian* Suite, as we saw in Chapter 19), relied chiefly on transcriptions of songs sung by Seneca performers in the summer of 1880, when he visited their reservation in New York State. Baker supplemented these songs with others written down at the Carlisle Indian School in Pennsylvania. Based on direct though limited contact with Indian singers, Baker's study was also useful for summarizing bibliographical sources on the subject. More than a decade passed, however, before a steady flow of Native musical studies began. A leader in that effort was Alice C. Fletcher, whose 1893 report on the music of the Omaha tribe was the first of her many important scholarly contributions. Emphasizing the subject's scientific interest, Fletcher and others gathered accurate data about the music, taken more or less on its own terms. By the early twentieth century, reports and monographs on American tribal music were appearing regularly. Their contents were likely to include transcribed melodies with text; information on where, when, and from whom the melodies were collected; comments on the performance setting and style; an explanation of the ritual or ceremonial context; and sometimes an interpretation of its significance.

If the intellectual climate of the late 1800s fostered curiosity about Indian music making, technology transformed its study. It was no coincidence that work on Indian traditions intensified after researchers started recording the music on Thomas A. Edison's cylinder phonographic machine. The recordings of Indian music begun around 1890 and continuing through the next century are the basis of a collection at the Smithsonian that is the largest and most important in the world.[9] The effort of these scholars and

An Indian singer records Native vocal music on a cylinder machine.

others to preserve and understand what remained of North America's oldest musical traditions seems all the more noteworthy when two further obstacles are considered. The first was the sheer foreignness of Indian music to people outside Native cultures. Traditional Indian music has virtually no connection in sound, style, or aesthetics with the European- and African-based traditions that have dominated music making in this country. To be attracted to Indian music making required an open-minded willingness to cross severe cultural barriers. The second obstacle was that musical fieldwork, while carried on in the name of objective, scientific fact gathering, proved to be a delicate human endeavor. Its requirements were demanding, including language ability, a keen musical ear, and the winning of Native informants' trust. Field workers were cultural aliens who had to earn the right to participate in Native life as witnesses. In overcoming these two obstacles, scholars of Indian music helped to establish fieldwork as the methodological basis of a new field that emphasized ethnography, recording, transcription, and cultural and musical analysis. They stand among the key founding figures of ethnomusicology, an academic discipline that only in the 1950s would gain a foothold in academia.

Because the credentials for studying the music of any one Indian nation were themselves hard to acquire, scholarship centered on tribal studies.

Then as tribal research accumulated, some scholars began grouping Indian peoples geographically, seeking connections within particular regions. Following the lead of anthropologists, authorities have sometimes divided Indian peoples into six culture areas: the Plains, the Plateau (northern Rocky Mountains), the East (subdivided into Northeast and Southeast, roughly by the Mason-Dixon line), the Southwest (including California), the Great Basin (centered in Nevada), and the Northwest Coast. They have then identified musical traits common to tribal traditions in each area. Authors following this scheme have also advised caution when comparing tribal practices: one tribe's music may have been recorded in the nineteenth century, while the music of another was collected fifty years later and may have changed substantially from its earlier state.[10]

But for all the mystery surrounding the subject, Indian music collected and studied since the 1880s has not proved to be highly complex and allows for some generalizations about its style:

1. *Vocal texture.* Indian music is monophonic: sung by one voice or a number of voices in unison, except for drones, an overlap between independent groups of singers, or an occasional (rare) ostinato figure.
2. *Musical instruments.* Indian music is vocal. Voices are accompanied by instruments, classified scientifically as idiophones (rattles, sticks, and pieces of wood beaten together), membranophones (drums with skin heads), and aerophones (whistles and flutes). Independent instrumental music is rare or nonexistent.
3. *Musical forms.* Indian music is highly repetitive, its form shaped by the ceremony or activity of which it is part. The music's reliance on brief melodic fragments or phrases repeated over and over makes much of it sound static to Western ears.
4. *Scale systems.* Scales of three, four, five, or six notes are common.
5. *Sung texts.* While words in everyday language are sometimes sung, many songs feature syllables that seem to have no meaning (vocables) or words taken from other Indian languages.[11]

Many stories could be told about the effort that began in the latter 1800s to collect, preserve, and disseminate Indian music, and the stories would vary greatly according to the examples chosen. An Omaha song collected by Alice Fletcher in 1884 offers its own window on the intellectual and artistic climate in which this new musical study took shape.

Born in 1838, Alice Fletcher studied in Cambridge, Massachusetts, at Harvard's Peabody Museum of Archaeology and Ethnology during the 1870s. In 1881, she traveled to Nebraska for her first fieldwork with the Omaha people. There, direct contact with Indians gave Fletcher a first-hand look at the sorry conditions in which many of them lived, turning her into a strong

Alice Cunningham Fletcher (1838–1923), pioneer collector of music of Plains Indian nations, confers with Chief Joseph of the Nez Percé tribe.

advocate for Indian reform and education. Fletcher's shift in outlook was also influenced by her affiliation with the Bureau of American Ethnology (BAE) in Washington, through which she administered grants of land to tribes in the western states, including the Pawnee, Arapaho, Dakota, Winnebago, Nez Percé, Omaha, and Cheyenne. Fletcher did not at first think of her research as primarily musical. But she soon recognized the key role of music in Indian rituals and began collecting melodies, which she wrote down from Indian singers.

Fletcher's work owed much to her collaboration with Francis La Flesche, who was younger by some two decades and of mixed Omaha, Ponca, and French ancestry. La Flesche combined a thorough knowledge of traditional Omaha religion and ceremony with an education at a mission school on the Omaha reservation where he grew up. In 1881, he began working as a clerk and translator for the Bureau of Indian Affairs in Washington. On a trip home to Nebraska that summer, he met Fletcher on her first visit. The two became friends and from then on worked together to document Omaha traditions. In fact, *The Omaha Tribe* (1911), a monograph coauthored by Fletcher and La Flesche, has been praised as the first truly ethnomusicological work, by virtue of its integration of Omaha music and Omaha culture.[12]

Alice Fletcher's transcription of this traditional Omaha song was taken from a performance by her assistant, Francis La Flesche, in 1884.

Song of Approach, shown above, dates from an early stage of the collaboration. The musical source for this melody, identified elsewhere as *The "Wa-Wan," or Pipe Dance of the Omahas*, was La Flesche himself, who had learned the song in his youth. Now he sang it for Fletcher's transcribing hand, which carefully notated not only pitches, rhythms, and syllables but also the singer's phrasing and accents.

If Fletcher's early work paid special heed to the ritual use of melodies she collected, her interest in the melodies as pieces of music grew over time. Like several other scholars of her era, she was intrigued by the question of where Native music belonged in the full range of human music making. In 1888, in an article called "Indian Music" that she never published, Fletcher wrote: "The Indian Scale is different from our own; but there are songs that come very near to our scales and yield very readily to our keyboard. . . . I am sorry that it is impossible for me to exemplify to you the Indian scale. It could only be done by the violin. There is no notation in common use that would make it feasible to describe it."[13] The differences that caught Fletcher's ear were pitches sung by Indians that fell outside the twelve chromatic notes comprising an octave on the piano. Experience as a transcriber had taught her that rather than singing out of tune, Indians sang and heard music according to a logic that had so far eluded non-Indians.

In the year Fletcher drafted her article, she established contact with John Comfort Fillmore, a European-trained American classical musician and teacher with a strong taste for theorizing. Fillmore considered music an art that evolved, like life itself, according to a unified scheme. All music, Western and non-Western, written and nonwritten, seemed to him to share a common harmonic basis. As Fillmore heard them, Indians' deviations from major and minor scales reflected not an alternative system but "an underdeveloped sense of pitch discrimination" likely to mature in the future.[14] Moreover, although Indians neither sang nor played in harmony, Fillmore heard harmonic implications in their melodies. When he first tried to har-

John Comfort Fillmore's reworking and harmonization of the Omaha *Song of Approach* for voice and piano appeared in Fletcher's *A Study of Omaha Indian Music* (1893).

monize Omaha melodies that Alice Fletcher had collected, he wrote in 1894, he found that "that no satisfactory scheme of chords could be made without employing the missing scale tones." The experiment convinced him that though Indian melodies seldom used all notes in a standard major or minor scale, they were grounded in incomplete forms of these scales. Moreover, when Indians heard their songs played in unison or octaves on a piano or organ, "they are not satisfied without the addition of chords."[15] Fillmore took their reaction as further evidence that Indian musics embodied an arrested stage of music's evolution.

Alice Fletcher agreed with Fillmore's evolutionary hypothesis, at least at this point in her career. When *A Study of Omaha Indian Music* was published in 1893, only four of the collection's ninety-three melodies were left without accompaniment. The rest appeared with Fillmore's harmonizations, chiefly in major mode. The example on the previous page shows his version of the *Song of Approach* that Fletcher had transcribed from La Flesche in 1884.

Differences between the two examples are striking. Beyond the decisions to turn a vocal piece into an instrumental one and to harmonize a one-line melody, there is no bigger change than the continuous eight-note rhythm in the piano's left hand, creating the throbbing character that whites came to associate with Indian music. Fletcher had marked accents on many strong beats (one and three in 4/4 time), but she also left some unmarked. In contrast, Fillmore's left hand accents every beat of every measure; he also overrides the momentum-breaking pause in the third line. Fillmore got rid of the two notes (F-natural and D-natural) foreign to the major scale. In the first six bars of his version, the melody follows Fletcher's quite closely. But from that point on, he has taken the material from the last five bars of Fletcher's original, made a related melodic figure out of it, and used that as the basis for the rest of the piece.

Starting with Fletcher's transcription, Fillmore imposed on it a pounding, percussive continuity, as if to emphasize the idea of primitivism that surrounded Indian music and culture at the end of the 1800s. However remote its connection with Indian practices, Fillmore's approach was tuned to the sensibility of his time, for *A Study of Omaha Indian Music* proved widely influential. Fletcher, La Flesche, and Fillmore's volume of harmonized Indian "folk songs" turned out to be a popular source for composers in search of Native music to use in works that they fashioned for parlors and concert halls.

EPILOGUE

This chapter began with a vision of Indians and their culture being overrun by whites. Alice Fletcher's 1893 volume may look like a crowning symbol of that very process, if an unintended one. For her research, rooted in a genuine desire to know the culture of the Omaha people, led to the publication of the melodies she had collected, not in original unaccompanied form but as a selection of music arranged for pianists.

Chapter 19 traced how, in the 1890s, Edward MacDowell tapped the growing stock of Indian music accessible to literate musicians to create music for the concert hall that bore an American stamp. The example of MacDowell and others—Amy Beach was one—who followed his inclination to borrow has sometimes been taken to suggest, first, that the primary value of Indian music has been the use to which non-Indians have put it, and second, that the arranging or appropriation of indigenous musics for literate performers stems from feelings of cultural superiority or violates rights of cultural ownership, and in either case deserves to be condemned. The first of these suggestions is obviously false. The second, more widely held today, invites a bit more historical perspective.

It is true that later collections by Fletcher, Frances Densmore, and other scholars in the field discarded the idea of harmonized melodies in favor of unaccompanied ones. In 1893, however, when Alice Fletcher's monograph appeared, the idea of music as a branch of scientific study was just coming into existence. Music first and foremost was a performing art; amateur players and singers were enjoying a booming musical culture rooted in participation. When Fletcher referred to the piano and the violin in her 1888 article draft, she was assuming a common framework with her readers. Indeed, it is probably more accurate to see her harmonized Omaha melodies of 1893 as evidence of respect and practicality than a mark of cultural condescension. Having uncovered a previously unknown stock of American music, she published it in a form that amateur musicians could enjoy.

As composers grew more interested in the possibilities of Indian music—especially Arthur Farwell, who in 1901 founded the Wa-Wan Press in Massachusetts and began to publish compositions based on Native melodies—scholars de-emphasized participation in favor of preservation. Natalie Curtis, a collector writing in 1907, went so far as to say that the preservation effort had been undertaken on behalf of the Indians themselves: "The older days were gone; the buffalo had vanished from the plains; even so would there soon be lost forever the songs and stories of the Indian. But there was a way to save them to the life and memory of their children, and that was to write them even as the white man writes. The white friend had come to be the pencil in the hand of the Indian."[16]

How Indians were supposed to respond to white friends who offered written copies of songs and stories as a substitute for the life that had sustained them is not known. But Curtis's comment about a gap in knowledge of earlier Native musical life sounds a theme familiar in this chapter. In-

This photograph of the performers collectively called "The Drum" was taken at a modern Indian pow-wow.

deed, assembling information about Indian music history in the 1800s dramatizes nothing more vividly than the elusiveness of Indian perspectives on that history. Almost everything after the vision that opens this chapter has been seen through Euroamerican eyes. And a believer's faith is a very different thing from an observer's respect for that faith. In transactions between nonliterate subjects and literate agents, the latter hold the power to name, describe, disseminate, and therefore control.

As the twenty-first century dawns, the "vanishing Americans" have reestablished a presence on the American scene. Native peoples, once members of many independent, isolated cultural units, have formed themselves into a minority within a large, culturally unrelated population. If many tribal cultures have broken down, Natives in the modern age have substituted for them a "pan-Indian" consciousness grounded in racial difference.[17] Moreover, the creation of that consciousness has been no simple matter but a tough-minded, complex process involving both pragmatism and spirituality.

As Indians have managed to reconstruct a sense of peoplehood, even while the life that once supported it was being destroyed, music has helped to provide continuity. It seems right to end this chapter, on a subject whose story has depended so heavily on the person telling it, with a statement from an article written by Tara Browner, a scholar of Choctaw background. The vision of the Blackfoot author James Welch with which this chapter begins predicted that future generations of Native people would still "know the way it was" through stories handed down to them. From the evidence in this scholar's account, respect for the past combined with a need to adapt to changing circumstances have inspired a blend of tradition and modernity. Describing song types, Browner starts with ceremonial and ritual songs for worship and healing. She then moves on to

> social and war dances, animal songs, work songs, songs to proclaim social status, lullabies, and many other genres. Rarely "composed" in the Western sense, songs in their entirety most often came to life through a dream or vision, with the singer serving as a musical conduit and caretaker. Contemporary traditionalists use the term "made" (or occasionally "caught") to describe songs acquired through personal creation, which are then learned and preserved by individuals via oral tradition, or through the medium of cassette tapes. With the exception of ethnological transcriptions, Indian music has bypassed the stage of printed notation, moving directly from oral tradition to dissemination by modern recording technology.

The last paragraph of this survey describes the Indian musical present as an amalgam constructed from elements that, while some may seem contradictory, have been pulled together in a way that feels to participants like a cultural whole.

> Many traditional dances are still preserved and performed regularly in seasonal ceremonies according to a calendric cycle. At the same time, the contemporary Pan-Indian pow-wow has become a major force for music and dance innovation among today's Indian populations, especially those with far-flung tribal memberships. Pow-wows provide a gathering place for Indian people to celebrate their culture through music and dance, and fertile ground for change, as members of diverse tribal groups interact and share music, dance styles, and dance regalia. Cassette and video tapes are sold featuring the newest songs and dance footwork, resulting in stylistic mixtures impossible only a few decades ago. Consequently, a new Pan-Indian culture, with regional music and dance layered upon [a] Plains Indian framework, is

shaping an overarching "Indian" identity. Pow-wow dance styles in urban areas and outside of the Plains regions tend toward the generic, with personal interpretation of the various categories (Traditional, Fancy, Grass, and Jingle). The spread of competition pow-wows offering large prize moneys, where "different" is frequently equated with "better," escalates the rate of change in dance and regalia styles at urban events. Reservation elders, however, continue to ensure the preservation of older forms for the younger generations, continually revitalizing the pow-wow with tradition.[18]

Joy Harjo, a contemporary Indian poet of Creek ancestry, has written that the urgent message she and other Native poets must continue to deliver is "the fantastic and terrible story of all our survival, / those who were never meant / to survive."[19] At the same time, pow-wows, with their competitive dancing, generic blends of Indian expression, and relaxed, welcoming atmosphere, today provide a leading public forum for Indian culture's survival. Poetry and pow-wows both belong to contemporary Indian life. The obligation to keep outraged memory alive while adjusting, adapting, and coming together with other Indians has marked the consciousness of modern Native Americans with a profound tension, fueled by loyalty to older ways that the society in which they live has dismissed.

21

Make a Noise!

Slave Songs and Other
Black Music to the 1880s

SLAVES WERE "generally expected to sing as well as to work," recalled Frederick Douglass, born a slave on Maryland's eastern shore around 1818. "A silent slave is not liked by masters or overseers," he explained. "'*Make a noise,*' '*make a noise,*' and '*bear a hand,*' are the words usually addressed to the slaves when there is silence amongst them. This may account for the almost constant singing heard in the southern states."[1] Douglass's statement points to the unique conditions in which blacks made music in nineteenth-century America. Aware that slaves' bodies were easier to control than their minds, masters could command singing to track their workers' whereabouts and monitor their mood. When slaves sang of brutality, injustice, or liberation within white hearing, they often disguised their meanings; it has long been understood that what slaves sang about was not always obvious from the words of their songs.

Douglass escaped from slavery in 1838, but he never forgot the way his fellow slaves sang. Beginning life on a large plantation, which he left in 1826 at the age of eight, Douglass recalled that at the end of each month, a few slaves from outlying farms traveled to "the great house farm" to pick up the next month's food supply. "These were gala days for the slaves," he wrote, "and there was much rivalry among them as to *who* should be elected to go." Not only was it an honor to be chosen, but it gave the messengers a break from the monotony of work and took them "beyond the overseer's eye and lash." Douglass continued: "Once on the road with an ox team, and seated on the tongue of his cart, with no overseer to look after him, the slave was comparatively free; and, if thoughtful, he had time to think." During these journeys, the slaves "who visited the great house farm were peculiarly noisy and excited." There was no difficulty keeping track of where they were, for "while on their way, they would make the dense old woods, for miles around, reverberate with their wild notes." Douglass recalled that their songs always included "some expression in praise of the great house farm; something which would flatter the pride of the owner, and, possibly, draw a favorable glance from him.

> I am going away to the great house farm,
>   O yea! O yea! O yea!
> My old master is a good old master,
>   O yea! O yea! O yea!"

To this flattery the ox-cart drivers would also add new words—"jargon to others, but full of meaning to themselves." And the "wild notes" they voiced "were not always merry because they were wild. On the contrary, they were mostly of a plaintive cast, and told a tale of grief and sorrow."

Looking back on his earlier years, Douglass could recognize "a tale which was then altogether beyond my feeble comprehension"—a tale that lay more in the singing than in the words. "They were tones, loud, long and deep," he wrote, "breathing the prayer and complaint of souls boiling over with the bitterest anguish. Every tone was a testimony against slavery, and a prayer to God for deliverance from chains." Slavery itself had drawn "wailing notes" like these from human throats, and Douglass could think of no more eloquent proof of its injustice.

> If any one wishes to be impressed with a sense of the soul-killing power of slavery, let him go to Col. Lloyd's plantation, and, on allowance day, place himself in the deep, pine woods, and there let him, in silence, thoughtfully analyze the sounds that shall pass through the chambers of his soul, and if he is not thus impressed, it will only be because "there is no flesh in his obdurate heart."

To a slave, Douglass concluded, songs "represent the sorrows, rather than the joys of his heart; and he is relieved by them, only as an aching heart is relieved by its tears."[2]

Douglass's words introduce a realm where singing was a tool in an existential struggle. In 1850, almost one out of every six Americans was of African descent. The mid-century national census identified 3.6 million people—just over 15 percent of the population—as black, with 434,000 (about 12 percent) free and the rest slaves. Concentrated in the South, most heavily on cotton and rice plantations, blacks were nevertheless present throughout the country. Yet white Americans everywhere basically agreed that blacks were inherently inferior, and even among slavery's opponents, few whites endorsed the notion of black-white equality. This attitude must be kept in mind in any discussion of black music making during the 1800s. Black Americans preserved African cultural practices not only out of prefer-

In 1853, Lewis Miller sketched this Negro dance in Virginia, picturing stately-looking movements accompanied by fiddle, banjo, and bones.

ence but because whites discouraged their participation in Euroamerican life. With avenues for open exchange limited, they were forced to rely on exchanges with each other, and a strong African heritage was thus maintained.

Whether the opposing force was slavery, segregation, physical intimidation, social or political exclusion, or personal prejudice, black life and culture in this country have been shaped in large part by the opposition blacks have faced. Indeed, African-American musicians have often taken the South and white oppression as reference points in their performances and compositions. One measure of their success was the gradual recognition by whites, even across barriers that racial separation had built, that black music was becoming part of the nation's music history.

TRADITIONAL BLACK MUSIC MAKING

A few free black Americans made a mark in the music professions between 1800 and the Civil War. But most African-American music in these years was made by slaves, and knowledge of it depends on accounts written by whites. For example, working in Georgia during the summer of 1841, New Englander Lewis Paine visited a local plantation on a holiday and witnessed slaves dancing to a unique kind of accompaniment.

Some one calls for a fiddle—but if one is not to be found, some one "pats juber" [juba]. This is done by placing one foot a little in advance of the other, raising the ball of the foot from the ground, and striking it in regular time, while, in connection, the hands are struck slightly together, and then upon the thighs. In this way they make the most curious noise, yet in such perfect order, it furnishes music to dance by. . . . It is really astonishing to witness the rapidity of their motions, their accurate time, and the precision of their music and dance. I have never seen it equaled in my life.[3]

Georgia-born poet and musician Sidney Lanier referred to the same custom in a later discussion of poetic theory. Patting juba could substitute not only for fiddling but drumming, which was banned in many slave states. An 1845 Georgia law also kept loud instruments of any kind out of slaves' hands for fear they would be used to call together conspirators. Slaves got around that prohibition by dancing to the accompaniment of sticks, bones, tambourines, and hand clapping.

Travelers in the South were also struck by the way slaves sang while they worked. Work songs help workers fulfill their tasks by pacing their activity, coordinating their movements, and rallying their spirits. All these situations were noted by observers of African Americans in nineteenth-century America. For example, an 1857 portrayal of black workers loading a steamboat in Mobile, Alabama, on the Gulf of Mexico credits music with synchronizing the workers' efforts:

> The men keep the most perfect time by means of their songs. These ditties, nearly meaningless, have much music in them, and as all join in the perpetually recurring chorus, a rough harmony is produced, by no means unpleasing. I think the leader improvises the words . . . he singing one line alone, and the whole then giving the chorus, which is repeated without change at every line, till the general chorus concludes the stanza.[4]

The singing described here follows responsorial practice traceable to Africa; with its strict rhythm and short phrases, responsorial singing encouraged improvisation, especially by the leader.

Slaves sometimes sang work songs that needled their masters. The author of a report published in 1841 told of a clergyman who made his slaves work on Sunday and found himself a target of scorn in a corn-shucking song. The setting for these songs was competitive. Ears of corn, fresh from the harvest, were heaped in two large piles; two groups of slaves raced to shuck their pile first, and the rival groups sang to promote speed and high spirits. The tale of a preacher more intent on planting tobacco than keeping the Sabbath unfolded between leader (L) and chorus (C), as the piles of unshucked corn grew smaller:

L: The parson say his prayers in church.   C: It rain, boys, it rain.
L: Then deliver a fine sermon.   C: It rain, boys, it rain.
L: He cut the matter short my friends.   C: It rain, boys, it rain.

L: He say the blessed Lord send it.	C: It rain, boys, it rain.
L: Now's the time for planting bacco.	C: It rain, boys, it rain.
L: Come, my negroes, get you home.	C: It rain, boys, it rain.
L: Jim, Jack, and Joe and Tom.	C: It rain, boys, it rain.
L: Go draw your plants and set them out.	C: It rain, boys, it rain.
L: Don't you stop a moment, boys.	C: It rain, boys, it rain.
L: 'Twas on a blessed Sabbath day.	C: It rain, boys, it rain.
L: Here's a pretty preacher for you.	C: It rain, boys, it rain.

"We are told," writes the author of the report, that this disgraced minister "was actually sung out of the neighborhood."[5]

Few observers took the trouble to record the precise words sung by slaves. Even fewer tried to write down their music. One of the first to transcribe a slave melody was James Hungerford, in a novel he published in 1859. This book contains a passage based on a visit Hungerford made to a plantation in southern Maryland in 1832, where he heard and notated a "boat song." In the novel, a slave named Charley and several black oarsmen take a group of white visitors on a tour of local waterways. As sunset approaches, the company falls silent, and Charley is asked to "give us a song to enliven us a little." He obliges, with the other oarsmen answering "in chorus, all timing the strokes of their oars to the measure." The song Charley strikes up is about a slave being "sold off to Georgy." Hungerford's comments suggest that he transcribed it to show that "negro songs—that is, such as they can compose themselves—are mostly without rhymes," for "they can not do better" than to make "the vowel-sounds at the ends of the lines agree." Yet although Hungerford found Charley's song crudely made, he did not deny its impact. "The tone of voice in which this boat-song was sung was inexpressibly plaintive," he writes. With "such a melancholy tune, and such affecting words," the singing "produced a very pathetic effect. I saw tears in the eyes of the young ladies, and could scarcely restrain my own." This was the wrong mood for the occasion, however, and one of the passengers cuts Charley and his companions off after three stanzas:

"Confound such *lively* music," he exclaimed; "it is making the girls cry, I do believe. And with such slow measure to sing to, we shall scarcely get into Weatherby's Creek tonight."

"De boat-songs is always dat way, marster," said Charley—"dat is mo' er less."

"Well, try to find something better than that," said the major; "I am sure that it is impossible for any thing to be more low-spirited in words, or tune, or manner of singing."[6]

White observers came to recognize black Americans' talent for making songs out of their life experiences. But even when they sang Euroamerican melodies, African Americans had their own way of performing them. William Mason, Lowell Mason's concert-pianist son, heard an example sung by a group of black laborers shortly after the Civil War. As Mason told the story to a Chicago music critic, it seems that he was "sitting upon a hotel piazza watching some negro roustabouts unload the cargo of a steamer. As they worked they whistled or sang one melody, which seemed to him exactly like Verdi's anvil chorus [from *Il Trovatore*], until a certain point was reached." But then,

> they uniformly turned aside and ended Verdi's melody improperly. Hearing this for an hour or more finally awakened a missionary spirit in the conscientious musician, and he strolled down to the wharf to give the dusky singers a lesson, and secure artistic justice to Verdi's music. But when he began to teach them the correct interpretation, he seemed to them to be spoiling their melody, which upon farther investigation proved to be Geo. F. Root's *"Tramp, Tramp, Tramp, the Boys Came Marching."*[7]

Different observers often cited the same performing customs. "The style of singing among the Negroes, is uniform," wrote a man who had lived in Jamaica in the late 1700s. And then he described the responsorial approach, giving the singers credit for rhythmic and tonal precision. A Russian visitor to a black Methodist church in Philadelphia around 1812 confirmed that performances by black singers and players were apt to go on for a long time. In every psalm, this observer wrote, "the entire congregation, men and women alike, sang verses in a loud, shrill monotone. This lasted about half an hour. . . . Afterwards . . . all rose and began chanting psalms in chorus, the men and women alternating, a procedure which lasted some twenty minutes."[8] Comments like these, acknowledging unique ways blacks performed music, lead to a consideration of their source: the cultural heritage of Africa. When black Americans embraced a white institution like the Christian church or black musicians entered show business, they did so without breaking their links to African-based music making.

Of all the different kinds of black music that emerged in the nineteenth century, none matched the impact of the "spiritual" songs. Whether as an American musical repertory, a legacy of sacred folk music, a source of argument about origins, or a case study of cultural interaction, the black spiritual provides an excellent example of how African cultural memory and Euroamerican written traditions intersected to create a new American form. In fact, the circulation of spirituals after the Civil War gave many white Americans their first hint that if the United States was a nation with its own distinctive music, the ex-slave population was in large part responsible.

Song of the "Contrabands"

Shortly after hostilities between North and South broke out at Fort Sumter, South Carolina, in April 1861, refugee slaves began seeking protection at Fortress Monroe, Virginia. Their masters demanded the slaves' return, but the fort's commander refused, calling them "contraband of war"—property that, in effect, had been captured. The now freed blacks were put to work in the fort, but the military could not meet their needs in shelter or clothing, let alone other social services. In August, the American Missionary Association proposed a campaign of contraband relief, and in early September the Reverend Lewis C. Lockwood, a YMCA employee, arrived at Fortress Monroe as missionary to the ex-slaves. Lockwood's first encounter with Southern black worship left a lasting impression, especially the singing. "They have a prime deliverance melody, that runs in this style," he wrote in his first report from the field. " 'Go down to Egypt—Tell Pharoah / Thus saith my servant, Moses— / Let my people go.' Accent on the last syllable, with repetition of the chorus, that seems every hour to ring like a warning note in the ear of despotism."[9]

Lockwood's report was published in October in a Northern abolitionist newspaper. In early December, the same paper carried more proof of the impact the freedmen's singing had made on their missionary: a transcription of *Let My People Go. A Song of the "Contrabands,"* in twenty stanzas of regularized English. "The following curious hymn," the notice reported, came from Lockwood, who had taken down the text *"verbatim* from the dictation of Carl Hollosay, and other contrabands." According to the same notice: "The air to which the hymn is sung is in the minor key, and very plaintive." Soon that air was also available to the public, for a sheet-music version of *Go Down, Moses* was advertised for sale before the year was out.[10]

The printed circulation of the spirituals had begun. And it involved three parties, each with a different stake in the process. White opponents of slavery like Lockwood took the lead, eager to document the spirituality and creativity in the black soul. Also interested were music-business figures like the New York publisher Horace Waters, whose issue of a spiritual song showed a readiness to take up the freedmen's cause if there was money in it. The third party was the "contrabands" themselves. During the war and for some time after, the spirituals' circulation depended on white advocates. The link with the music business went nowhere, for sheet-music versions never won much commercial success. Therefore, the main story of how slave songs moved beyond slave communities is revealed chiefly in the black singers' interaction with Northern white clergymen and teachers.

There is little to praise in the first printed version of the *Song of the Contrabands,* for Thomas Baker, whose arrangement for voice and keyboard is

22 JUBILEE SONGS.

Go down, Moses.

1. When Is-rael was in E-gypt's land : Let my peo-ple go,

Op-pressed so hard they could not stand, Let my peo-ple go.

Go down, Mo - ses, way down in E - gypt land,

Tell ole Pha - roh, Let my peo - ple go.

2 Thus saith the Lord, bold Moses said,
   Let my people go ;
If not I'll smite your first-born dead,
   Let my people go.
Go down, Moses, etc.

3 No more shall they in bondage toil,
   Let my people go ;
Let them come out with Egypt's spoil,
   Let my people go.
Go down, Moses, etc.

4 When Israel out of Egypt came,
   Let my people go ;
And left the proud oppressive land,
   Let my people go.
Go down, Moses, etc.

Theodore Seward's arrangement of *Go Down, Moses* was published in *Jubilee Songs* (New York, 1872).

the earliest sheet-music publication of any black spiritual, turned the slave song into a parlor ballad in 6/8 time. It seems likely that Baker, a violinist who had come to America in 1853 with Jullien's orchestra, had only the melody from Lockwood to work with and knew nothing of the song's original context. Theodore F. Seward, who later put *Go Down Moses* in the form that won lasting renown, had little knowledge of its original context either, but he retained at least some of the traits that had impressed listeners when the slaves sang it. Seward's arrangement (first published in 1872) manages to resemble white hymnody while keeping a flavor apart from it.

By taking a story from the Bible as a commentary on their own lives, the slaves fashioned a spiritual song of sober dignity and moral force. And just as God delivered Israel from bondage, so, the song predicted, would blacks be delivered. In the 1872 version, which adds several stanzas to the twenty that Lockwood published in 1861, *Go Down, Moses* starts like a ballad telling a story. But during its course, the voice shifts from stanza to stanza: from the narrator (in verses 1, 4–7, 9–11, and 16) to Moses (2–3), to God himself (8, 12–15), to a slave protagonist (17–24). The overall form is familiar from white Methodist hymnody: strophic with a refrain. Within each verse, the singing is responsorial, a leader alternating with a chorus. *Go Down, Moses* takes its implacable force from this repeated response and chorus, which embody the voice of God, who orders his prophet Moses to confront Egypt's ruler. And the message, sung six dozen times in harmony during a complete performance, is a flat command: "Let my people go." The slaves' confidence that, as God's people, they would soon be free links this solemn litany to their joyous "Jubilee Songs" (spirituals that rejoice in the expectation of better things to come) despite its different mood.[11]

By the time *Go Down, Moses* had passed through the likes of Lockwood, Baker, and Seward, it bore the earmarks of white Christian hymnody, though its subject and mode of address remained the freedmen's own. White foes of slavery had long argued that no human with an immortal soul deserved a life of forced servitude. Growing contact with blacks was showing sympathetic whites that racial differences might owe more to environment than to innate capacity. And they found no evidence of the slaves' human capacity more striking than the spirituals: songs whose ethical, religious, and aesthetic worth seemed obvious. By singing about their experience in ways that condemned slavery, affirmed faith in God, and tapped the depths of the human soul, the slaves were revealing their fitness to live as free Americans. In the struggle against slavery and its aftermath, then, *Go Down, Moses* and other spirituals signaled the involvement of Southern black people in what was to be a long campaign for equality.

BLACK SPIRITUAL SONGS

Slave Songs of the United States (New York, 1867), collected and published by William Francis Allen, Charles Pickard Ware, and Lucy McKim
Garrison, is the first of many anthologies in which black spirituals are preserved. It was the work of three Northern antislavery activists, all connected
with efforts during the Civil War to educate freedmen on the Sea Islands
near Port Royal, the harbor commanding the approach to Charleston. Compiled before folklore and ethnomusicology were academic disciplines in the
United States, the collection shows respect for the songs' unlettered, untrained creators. And the compilers made a good team, though they never
worked together in the field. Before arriving at Port Royal, Massachusetts
natives Allen and Ware knew little of black Americans or their music, but
their duties there gave them sustained contact with both. Allen taught in a
freedmen's school for more than eight months (1863–64), and Ware, his
younger cousin, worked as superintendent of several plantations on St. Hel-
ena Island from 1862, when he graduated from Harvard College, until 1865.
Garrison's music credentials were the best of the three. Born in Philadelphia, she took piano lessons from prominent local teachers, studied violin as
well, and began teaching piano out of her home at the age of fifteen. The
scholarly expertise behind *Slave Songs* was chiefly Allen's; Ware supplied
the largest number of transcriptions; while Garrison—with help from her
husband, Wendell Phillips Garrison, literary editor of *The Nation*—collected and edited transcriptions and saw the work through the press.[12]

Slave Songs contains 136 melodies with texts, arranged geographically.
Four regions of the South were canvassed: "South-Eastern Slave States, including South Carolina, Georgia and the Sea Islands" (82 songs), "Northern
Seaboard Slave States, including Delaware, Maryland, Virginia, and North
Carolina" (20), "Inland Slave States, including Tennessee, Arkansas, and
the Mississippi River" (9), and the "Gulf States, including Florida and
Louisiana: Miscellaneous" (25). Each song's transcriber is named in the index, and so is the location where it was collected. Facing up to the difficulty
of transcribing the music, the introduction admits that the published
melodies "will convey but a faint shadow of the original." Allen explained:
"The voices of the colored people have a peculiar quality that nothing can
imitate; and the intonations and delicate variations of even one singer," let
alone several, "cannot be reproduced on paper." Moreover, although sung by
many singers, the spirituals were published as unharmonized melodies—not
because the freedmen sang in unison but because their singing was too
complicated for musical notation to capture. "There is no singing in *parts*, as
we understand it," Allen wrote, "and yet no two appear to be singing the
same thing."[13]

Using the conceptual tools available, *Slave Songs* sought to record faithfully what the compilers took to be a valuable part of slave culture. Anyone who compares the song texts with the "standard" English in the 1872 version of *Go Down, Moses* will recognize the difference in approach. Yet Allen's introduction never judges the quality of the ex-slaves' English. The compilers, encountering a culture profoundly different from their own, still recognized it *as* a culture and worked in that spirit to set down this repertory of "old songs . . . before it is too late," knowing that associations with slavery were making the freedmen reluctant to sing them. It was chiefly in their differences from white hymnody that the uniqueness of the spirituals lay. If readers had trouble fitting texts and melodies together, Allen referred them to the singers' own practice. "The negroes keep exquisite time in singing," he wrote, "and do not suffer themselves to be daunted by any obstacle in the words."[14] Rhythm, in other words, took precedence over the placement and meaning of the texts. In contrast to other responses to slave music, this comment is an early example of cultural relativism, which declines to make cultural difference a measure of quality in either direction.

Slave Songs contains chiefly sacred songs, for the compilers had found secular music more difficult to come by. Among the varieties of spiritual song they heard, the "shout"—a hymn of exalted spirits with a strong rhythmic drive—proved most foreign to white customs of worship. A description in *Slave Songs*, quoted from a New York newspaper of 1867, reports that a "true shout" takes place "on Sundays or on 'praise'-nights through the week, and either in the praise-house or in some cabin in which a regular religious meeting has been held. Very likely more than half the population of the plantation is gathered together. Let it be the evening, and a light-wood fire burns red before the door of the house and on the hearth." From outside the praise house, observers may hear the formal part of the meeting. Its sounds include "vociferous exhortation or prayer" from the presiding elder and hymns lined-out from the hymnbook, their "wailing cadences" casting a mood "indescribably melancholy . . . on the night air." The shout begins only when the regular meeting is over. The room is rearranged, with benches "pushed back to the wall," and "old and young, men and women, sprucely-dressed young men, grotesquely half-clad field-hands—the women generally with gay handkerchiefs twisted about their heads and with short skirts—boys with tattered shirts and men's trousers, young girls bare-footed, all stand up in the middle of the floor." When the singing of the shout "sperichil" begins, the shouters begin walking, then

> shuffling round, one after the other, in a ring. The foot is hardly taken from
> the floor, and the progression is mainly due to a jerking, hitching motion,
> which agitates the entire shouter, and soon brings out streams of perspira-

tion. Sometimes they dance silently, sometimes as they shuffle they sing the chorus of the spiritual, and sometimes the song itself is also sung by the dancers. But more frequently a band, composed of some of the best singers and of tired shouters, stand at the side of the room to "base" the others, singing the body of the song and clapping their hands together or on the knees. Song and dance are alike extremely energetic, and often, when the shout lasts into the middle of the night, the monotonous thud, thud of the feet prevents sleep within half a mile of the praise-house.[15]

The shout as performed here, Allen told his readers, was apparently not to be found north of South Carolina. Moreover, the shouters did not look upon their physical actions as dancing, a worldly pastime. "Dancing in the usual way is regarded with great horror by the people of Port Royal," Allen explained, "but they enter with infinite zest into the movements of the 'shout,'" a sacred activity. The Euroamerican-American (i.e., Christian) elements in the meeting described here include preaching and praying, lining-out hymns, and a belief in life after death that marks spirituals in general, including *I Can't Stay Behind*, a shout published in *Slave Songs*.

As no white American congregation of the time is known to have pushed back the benches after prayer meeting, formed a ring, and stomped, clapped, and sung half the night away in sanctified ecstasy, Allen was surely on the mark when he concluded: "This remarkable religious ceremony is a relic of some native African dance."[16]

Ring dancing was and is found in many parts of Africa. In the time of slavery and later, the ring shout provided the main context in which transplanted Africans recognized common values.[17] Lacking the means to translate memory into written form, people of African descent embodied their fundamental practices in *cultural* memory, preserved in the ring-shout ritual. Given the separateness that white oppression fostered, the ring shout was apparently seldom encountered by whites, and was perceived as no threat when they did happen upon it.

The ring did more than form the context in which shout spirituals were created. It allowed all the elements of African-American music to be together in one place, including calls and hollers; call and response; additive rhythms and polyrhythms; heterophony, blue notes, bent notes, and elisions; hums, moans, and vocables; off-beat melodic phrasings and parallel intervals and chords; constant repetition of rhythmic figures and melodic phrases; game rivalry; hand clapping and foot patting; and a rock-steady pulse.[18] Spirituals now a century and a half old were thus conceived within the same African-based performance tradition as blues, jazz, soul, and hiphop, a tradition that also touched and vitalized country music and rock and roll. Apart from the astonishing continuity that this notion reflects, it is hard to think of another body of performing techniques so readily updated and refreshed, from generation to generation, without growing dated or stale.

In slave culture, spirituals were created, fostered, and maintained by singers steeped in these underlying elements, many of which cannot be written down. William Francis Allen admitted the gap between practice and notation in his introduction to *Slave Songs*. But whereas Allen, Ware, and Garrison compiled their work to document a declining oral practice, an effort began in the early 1870s to turn black spirituals into a repertory of written music that could circulate much more widely. Before that could happen, vocal arrangements de-emphasizing the songs' African content had to be made. The 1872 publication of *Go Down, Moses*, which put the text and music into a form accessible to white singers and listeners, is one example of the result.

As the war ended, missionary societies in the North stepped up efforts to educate the Southern freedmen. Among the schools newly organized for blacks was Fisk University in Nashville, founded in 1865 with a white faculty. Housed in a former army hospital barracks and dependent on donations from the North, Fisk needed more income than the missionary societies supporting black schools in the South could supply. Then in 1870, the choir formed at Fisk under the direction of Northern-born faculty member George L. White performed at a national teachers' convention in Nashville, to such enthusiasm that White began to imagine a fund-raising tour of the North by a select group of Fisk singers, emphasizing spirituals. School authorities agreed, and in the fall of 1871 the group set out by train on their bold venture. They met racism almost everywhere they went, and at first the cost of touring outstripped receipts. But two events helped to change that. First, the Fisk Jubilee Singers performed in November at Oberlin, Ohio, for a convention of Congregational ministers, and many were deeply touched by what they heard. Second, when the Singers reached New York, they were welcomed and endorsed by the area's leading clergymen, including the Reverend Henry Ward Beecher—brother of Harriet Beecher Stowe—and himself a top attraction on the American lecture circuit. With the clergy behind them, the Jubilee Singers were a sensation in New York and New England, where they netted $20,000 in three months. Having far surpassed the college's financial expectations, they continued to tour for the next seven years (1871–78), including journeys to the British Isles and the European continent. Their performances during those years enriched Fisk University by a total of $150,000.[19]

Black spirituals were enlisted to bridge two separate spheres: the past of Southern slaves and the present of Northern urban Protestants. The Jubilee Singers' differences—their skin color, the uniqueness of their songs, and apparently the way they sang them—were mediated by dress, smooth concert

The Jubilee Singers of Fisk University, Nashville, Tennessee, photographed around 1880.

staging, the familiar atmosphere of the churches and meeting houses where concerts were given, and the Singers' civilized image. Another mediating force was also in play from 1872 on, when Theodore Seward's arrangements were published and began to be sold at the concerts. Set in book form like a hymnal, the spirituals could now be sung by whites in the North. As the Fisk singers' chronicler put it: "Hills and valleys, parlors and halls, wherever they went, were vocal with Jubilee melodies"—melodies tailored to gratify the taste of many who would have found their original form incomprehensible.[20] Although director George L. White had learned the spirituals from his students in the first place, his idea of how they should be sung in public, with very little dialect and much precision, ruled the Jubilee Singers' performing style.[21]

Black spirituals in written form proved irresistible to many. Even after heavy editing and with African-American elements watered down, their heartfelt conception gave them the benefit of simple directness. In fact, the "universal" elements in the black spiritual have had much to do with its enduring appeal. As pictured in the songs, the slave's place in the world overlaps somewhat with that of the sinner in the Christian cosmos. Both view life as a hard journey, and both hope to find eternal peace when death brings release from this "vale of tears." One difference is that while Christian sinners are weighed down chiefly by a sense of their own wrongdoing, slaves suffered more acutely from the wrongs of others. Nevertheless,

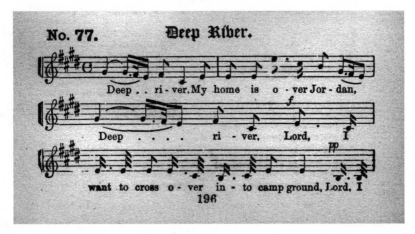

Deep River, opening measures, as printed in J. B. T. Marsh, *The Story of the Jubilee Singers* (Cleveland, 1892).

whether guilt-ridden or oppressed by outside forces, white sinner and black slave held in common a sense of standing alone in a world that was both temporary and hostile. Black spirituals appealed to widely diverse audiences by communicating persuasively how it felt to live in that state.

The singer of *Deep River* contemplates the Jordan as a boundary between a life of toil and an afterlife of rest in heaven's "campground." The drawn-out descent of the first syllable and the energy required by the octave leap on "over" suggest an arduous journey ahead, for the river is a dark abyss and

Swing Low, Sweet Chariot, opening measures, as printed in J. B. T. Marsh, *The Story of the Jubilee Singers* (Cleveland, 1892).

the way home strenuous. Beginning with a brief melisma (three notes on one syllable) that makes the beat slightly ambiguous, this song also invites performers to take a free tempo, a rare quality among spirituals.

More typical is the beginning of *Swing Low, Sweet Chariot*: by placing the second word on the longer note and weaker beat, the song establishes rhythm as a force from the start, opening the door to syncopation. Few popular songs or white hymns of the day can match the declamation's variety, for each of the first three measures presents a different rhythmic pattern. As it happens, the first and third match music with text as these words might actually be spoken. But the second, with its musical accent on a weak syllable (char-i-OT), bears out Allen's dictum that in black spirituals, words must bend to rhythm. In contrast to *Deep River*, the two-note melisma here requires rhythmic strictness, because it comes at the end of a word, *after* the beat is established. Death here is empowering. The song's gentle propulsion breathes confidence that life's journey is almost over and heaven within easy reach.

Another classic spiritual, *Sometimes I Feel like a Motherless Child*, packs so much poignancy into its opening line that elaboration is hardly needed. Yet it establishes a beat with its first melodic gesture so that it unfolds in strictly measured time, if at a slow tempo. The first stanza repeats that line twice, then fills out the stanza with repetitions of "A long ways from home." As in parlor music of the day, "home" is a key notion in many spirituals. To the slaves, though, home was not the domestic institution that songs like *Home, Sweet Home* celebrate but rather an *idea* of home.[22] It might be eternal, as in *Deep River* and *Swing Low, Sweet Chariot*: or it might be in the world, as in *Got a Home in That Rock* or even *Steal Away* ("Steal away home"), where it refers to freedom; or it might be either one, as in *Sometimes I Feel like a Motherless Child*.

A spiritual about the sufferings of Jesus invites listeners to imagine his torment. *He Never Said a Mumblin' Word* reviews the events of the Passion, including Christ's judgment before Pontius Pilate, the crown of thorns, the whipping, the nails, and two stanzas' worth of flowing blood. While one can picture onlookers cringing at all this brutality, the victim silently, stoically accepts his fate:

> O they took my blessed Lawd,
> Blessed Lawd, Blessed Lawd,
> O they took my blessed Lawd,
> An' he never said a mumblin' word,
> Not a word, not a word, not a word.

In this spiritual, words seem to fail the singers. Faced with a crime so enormous, they can only register numbed amazement by repeating the same words over and over again.

For all their saturation in woe, however, spirituals also cultivated a strain of joyful hope. The upbeat energy of *Didn't My Lord Deliver Daniel* shows the slaves' confidence that freedom would soon be theirs. Inspired by God's Old Testament miracles, this song is made irresistible by the momentum of syncopated rhythm, turned loose to shape the declamation of the words. The hero is the Hebrew prophet Daniel, thrown into a lions' den for flouting a royal decree, who survives under God's protection. The refrain highlights the prophet's name through three devices. First, it is repeated several times; second, it is almost the only word of more than one syllable whose natural accent falls on a strong beat; and third, the accent is heightened by sounding as if it is delayed, for the last syllable of the first "deliver" is a sixteenth note longer than we might expect. Such poetic lines as "D'liver Daniel, d'liver Daniel" and "And why not a ev-e-ry man" signal that music, not text, is the dominant force.

The song's chief traits include a driving metronomic pulse, off-beat melodic phrasing, pendular thirds (G/B-flat), and the frequent repetition of verbal, melodic, and rhythmic figures—foundational elements of black American music. And one imagines that performances by slaves or freedmen off the concert stage might also have invoked the ring shout's ecstatic spirit through the use of hand clapping, foot patting, call and response, cries, hollers, heterophony, and other such devices. But whether employing such African-based oral practices or not, black spirituals as a whole testify to the uncanny power of music. As the first historian of black American music wrote in his discussion of spirituals in 1878: "The history of the colored race in this country" proved that "no system of cruelty, however great or long inflicted, can destroy that sympathy with musical sounds that is born with the soul."[23]

BLACK PROFESSIONAL MUSICIANS

The end of the Civil War brought freedom to Southern slaves and a widening range of professional opportunities, including musical ones. Free blacks in the North and in the special environment of New Orleans, however, had been finding niches in the American music business for decades. The careers of these professionals reflect both the racial bias they faced and the working hypothesis of this chapter: black American music makers, even when they entered the white-run music business, maintained their connection to African-based performing styles.

Francis "Frank" Johnson, one of the most prominent black musicians in pre–Civil War America, worked in a setting far removed from that in which the spirituals were created. Once thought to have been a native of the West Indies, Johnson was born in Philadelphia, which he made his permanent

Francis Johnson (1792–1844), composer, bandleader, and trumpeter of Philadelphia.

headquarters. An account from 1819 calls him the "leader of the band at all balls, public and private," the "sole director of all serenades, acceptable and not acceptable," and the "inventor-general of cotillions." Johnson, who played violin and keyed bugle and published more than two hundred songs, dances, operatic arrangements, and other compositions, worked in an urban milieu of military bands, dance orchestras, concert ensembles, and musicians versatile enough to please more than one audience. As a player of two different instruments, Johnson recruited others who could also double. One of his groups won praise in 1837 for the ease with which the musicians "laid down the fiddles" and "took up the key'd bugles and other wind instruments."[24]

Between the 1810s and 1840s, band instrumentation in the United States changed from the *Harmoniemusik* combination (oboes, clarinets, French horns, and bassoons in pairs, plus percussion) to a brass ensemble, and Johnson's band followed suit. In these years too, the keyed bugle was the virtuoso instrument of the band. Johnson mastered it so well that during a trip to London in 1837–38, he received from Queen Victoria a silver bugle in appreciation. After attending promenade concerts on this London trip, Johnson returned home to stage his own, in the vast space (70 by 235 feet) of the Philadelphia Museum's Grand Saloon, attracting crowds in the thousands.[25] Introduced in Paris by Philippe Musard (1833), then popularized in

London by others, including Louis Jullien, the promenade format mixed an informal atmosphere, refreshments, and music aimed at a diverse audience: overtures, current dance music (especially waltzes by Johann Strauss), and quadrilles that featured popular melodies from songs and operas. As the first to stage promenade concerts in the United States, Frank Johnson introduced a format suited to the use of instrumental ensembles for popular entertainment.

According to the author of the 1819 Philadelphia notice, Johnson added to his other talents "a remarkable taste in distorting a sentimental, simple, and beautiful song, into a reel, jig, or country-dance."[26] This statement may mean only that Johnson was uncommonly good at adapting song melodies to dance forms, a skill he put to good use in the quadrilles that later played a key role in promenade concerts. But another spin might also be put on these words: "distorting" may mean that Johnson and his musicians, who were also black, enlivened the music with rhythmic complexities as a way of exercising their African heritage.[27] They won their place in a white musical world not only by matching white rivals' skills but by bringing something unique to their performances: they interpreted at least some of the music they played within an oral tradition based on African-American foundational elements that the ring shout had preserved. In other words, Johnson and his men treated notation not as composers' music but as performers' music.

It is not easy to imagine experienced dance musicians—especially African Americans who are heir to a rich tradition of oral performance—playing the same strains over and over again from written music, without embellishment. Johnson's musicians were accomplished professionals: they read music, played both wind and string instruments, and were able to perform in a variety of styles. A comment from late in the leader's life also suggests that the ensemble's members were less than genteel in their personal behavior. A member of the abolitionist Hutchinson family singing group commented in 1842, after meeting "the old Fellow" Johnson and his men in a Massachusetts railroad station: "They are a *Rough* sett of Negroes."[28] While this says nothing about their playing, it suggests an attitude that tempts a modern observer, after weighing the admittedly meager evidence, to believe that musical freedoms relating to ring-shout techniques were also part of their performing vocabulary.

Another niche that began in this period to open up to blacks was the popular musical stage, on which William Henry "Juba" Lane became a full-fledged star. Born around 1825, possibly in New York, Lane won fame as a teenager when English novelist Charles Dickens saw him perform during his American tour of 1842 and called him "the greatest dancer known." Lane became the first black member of a white troupe when he joined Charley White's minstrels in 1846 as a tambourine player and a jig dancer.[29] In 1849

Elizabeth Taylor Greenfield (1824?–1876), ex-slave and concert singer, on the eve of her departure for Europe.

he went to England, touring with Richard Pell's Ethiopian Serenaders, where his performances wowed English critics. One of them, admitting that he could not have imagined what dance steps such as the "Virginny Break-down," the "Alabama Kick-up," the "Tennessee Double-Shuffle," or the "Louisiana Toe-and-Heel" might look like, confirmed that these dances really did exist. For if they did not, he asked: "How could Juba enter into their wonderful complications so naturally? How could he tie his legs into such knots, and fling them about so recklessly, or make his feet twinkle until you lose sight of them altogether in his energy?" On top of all this physical virtuosity, another critic called Juba "a musician, as well as a dancer." He seemed to coax "marvellous harmonies" from the tambourine, which he played so well, this writer claimed, that he would not have been surprised to hear Juba play a fugue on it. Another observer compared Juba's tapping steps to the Pell troupe's bones player. "This youth," he wrote, "dances demisemi, semi, and quavers [thirty-second, sixteenth, and eighth notes] as well as the slower steps."[30]

During these years, a few African-American musicians also began to appear on the concert stage, most notably Elizabeth Taylor Greenfield, also known as "the Black Swan." Born a slave in Natchez, Mississippi, around 1824, she was taken as a young child to Philadelphia, where she grew up free in a Quaker household. She received some singing lessons as a girl and learned to play harp, piano, and guitar on her own. But it was her voice that caught listeners' attention: an instrument of extremely wide range and unusual timbre. In 1851, she settled in Buffalo, New York, where, under the sponsorship of the Buffalo Musical Association, she made her concert debut. After two years of touring in the northern United States and Canada, she traveled to England in the spring of 1853. Harriet Beecher Stowe, who was visiting at the time to promote antislavery sentiment, helped introduce Greenfield to socially prominent patrons there. The singer also met George Smart, organist and composer for Queen Victoria's Chapel Royal, with whom she studied during her English stay. Stowe's vivid account of a concert in a private residence in 1853 indicates that Greenfield, whether because of her limitations or the audience's, was unveiled not as an artist but as a vocal phenomenon:

Miss Greenfield's turn for singing now came, and there was profound attention. Her voice, with its keen, searching fire, its penetrating vibrant quality, its *timbre* as the French have it, cut its way like a Damascus blade to the heart. She sang the ballad, "Old Folks at Home," giving one verse in the soprano, and another in the tenor voice. As she stood partially concealed by the piano, Chevalier Brunsen thought that the tenor part was performed by one of the gentlemen. He was perfectly astonished when he discovered that it was by her. This was rapturously encored. Between the parts, Sir George [Smart] took her to the piano, and tried her voice by skips, striking notes here and there at random, without connection, from D in alto to A first space in bass clef. She followed with unerring precision, striking the sound nearly at the same instant his fingers touched the key. This brought out a burst of applause.[31]

After singing for Queen Victoria in 1854, Greenfield returned to the United States. From that point on, her musical career included concertizing, teaching in Philadelphia, and staging programs in the 1860s with an opera troupe. As the first black American concert singer to win acclaim on both sides of the Atlantic, Greenfield was able to parlay her English training and public experience into something of an American career as a vocal star.

If Greenfield worked to carve out a public niche, another black professional took a more anonymous approach. Justin Miner Holland, freeborn (1818) on a farm near Norfolk, Virginia, headed north at the age of fourteen in search of musical instruction. Settling in Chelsea, Massachusetts, he studied guitar with a Latin-American musician there, and flute and music theory with band musicians in Boston. After several years at the Oberlin Conservatory in Ohio, he opened a studio in Cleveland in 1845, and there he spent the rest of his life teaching, composing, and making arrangements for the guitar, his favorite instrument. The first historian of African-American music wrote in 1878 that Holland's published guitar arrangements then numbered more than three hundred pieces. As well as original guitar music, Holland also composed variation sets on familiar melodies such as *Home, Sweet Home* and *The Carnival of Venice.*[32] Many publishers also commissioned him to arrange pieces for guitar, which Holland preferred to do indirectly. The Brainerds in Cleveland and John Church in Cincinnati were the only publishers who knew his race and were indifferent to it. Holland, then, was the exception that proves the rule: a black American musician whose African roots seem to have played little or no role in his professional life and which, in fact, he sometimes found it an advantage to conceal.

22

Songs of the Later Nineteenth Century

By 1850, the Euroamerican settlement of western North America was well under way. With some 10 million Americans, or 44 percent of the population, participating in this westward expansion, tales were told and written, pictures painted, and songs composed to recount their experiences on the land.

The songwriters, poets, and publishers who worked in the sheet-music trade, always ready to capitalize on any event or trend that might sell songs, took note of Western settlement. In a song published in 1845 called *To the West*, English-born singer-songwriter Henry Russell and Scots poet Charles McKay, who never left the British Isles, portray an ideal landscape:

> To the West! to the West! to the land of the free,
> Where mighty Missouri rolls down to the sea,
> Where a man is a man, if he's willing to toil,
> And the humblest may gather the fruits of the soil.

Sung to a lilting waltz, McKay's words picture the West as if it were a stage set. A later stanza promises broad rivers "thousands of miles" long and "green waving forests . . . as wide as all England, and free to us all": a land of benign fertility. This West is a vast oasis where people may be sure that their dreams will be fulfilled. Like many other songs for the mid-century stage and parlor, *To the West* is steeped in Victorian values and the sensibility of melodrama. Behind it lies a state of mind that draws a firm line between good and evil. Good people, like the would-be pioneer who sings this song, are proper Victorians who work hard, remain sober and conscientious, and are willing to delay gratification. The song finds virtue in the pioneering impulse, and is not much concerned, given its claim that the Missouri River flows into the ocean, with map reading.

The idealistic mindset of *To the West* places everything else in the background. Its moral framework is asserted so confidently that nature seems unimportant; so does the question of how a traveler might actually get there. In contrast, John A. Stone's *Sweet Betsey from Pike* traces the journey itself. First published in 1858 in a San Francisco songster (a collection of song lyrics without music), *Sweet Betsey* relied from the start on oral tradition, for it was to be sung to *Villikins and His Dinah*, a popular four-line waltz tune with a refrain made from vocables. In eleven stanzas, *Sweet Betsey* offers vignettes of a couple's journey across the continent, starting with a sketch of their traveling party:

> Oh, don't you remember sweet Betsey from Pike,
> Who crossed the big mountains with her lover Ike,
> With two yoke of cattle, a large yellow dog,
> A tall shanghai rooster and one spotted hog.
>> Tooral lal looral lal looral lal la,
>> Tooral lal looral lal looral lal la.

Sweet Betsey's narrative emphasis recalls the traditional ballad, but Stone found a nontraditional way to treat love and journeying. In the second stanza, the couple stop for the evening on the banks of the Platte River. Ike's admiration of Betsey's beauty may be typical ballad fare, but the heroine's aching feet are not:

> One evening quite early they camped on the Platte,
> 'Twas near by the road on a green shady flat,
> Where Betsey, sore-footed, lay down to repose—
> With wonder Ike gazed on that Pike County rose.

Troubles mount as the journey continues. Wagons break down, and the food supply dwindles:

> The shanghai ran off, and their cattle all died;
> That morning the last piece of bacon was fried;
> Poor Ike was discouraged, and Betsey got mad,
> The dog drooped his tail and looked wondrously sad.

Turning south from the Platte, they enter Utah territory near the Great Salt Lake. Here they encounter Mormons, religious dissenters from New York who had been hounded out of every place they had tried to settle until Brigham Young led them in the 1840s to these deserted plains. In *Sweet Betsey*, Young, who was famous outside Mormon circles for practicing polygamy, casts an approving eye on the heroine, who flees to avoid becoming another of his wives, said to number between two dozen and fifty-five:

> They stopped at Salt Lake to inquire the way,
> When Brigham declared that sweet Betsey should stay;
> But Betsey got frightened and ran like a deer,
> While Brigham stood pawing the ground like a steer.

Heading across the desert west of Salt Lake, Betsey is hit by a spell of craziness, but Ike humors her out of it, and they continue their journey arm-in-arm:

> They soon reached the desert, where Betsey gave out,
> And down in the sand she lay rolling about;
> While Ike, half distracted, looked on with surprise,
> Saying, "Betsey, get up, you'll get sand in your eyes."
>
> Sweet Betsey got up in a great deal of pain,
> Declared she'd go back to Pike County again;
> But Ike gave a sigh, and they fondly embraced,
> And they traveled along with his arm round her waist.

After trekking through mountains, Betsey and Ike finally reach the mining town of Placerville, California, in the High Sierras. They celebrate their arrival by attending a dance, Ike in "a pair of his Pike County pants" and Betsey "covered with ribbons and rings." Betsey accepts a local miner's request for a dance—with words that no fair damsel from traditional balladry or "lady" in a Victorian song would ever have uttered:

> A miner said, "Betsey, will you dance with me?"
> "I will that, old hoss, if you don't make too free;
> But don't dance me hard; do you want to know why?
> Dog on you! I'm chock full of strong alkali!"

Betsey and Ike become husband and wife, but their marriage fails, presumably because Betsey is beautiful, women are scarce in mining towns, and female nature is inconstant, or so the thinking went:

> This Pike County couple got married of course,
> And Ike became jealous—obtained a divorce;
> Sweet Betsey, well satisfied, said with a shout,
> "Good by, you big lummux, I'm glad you backed out!"[1]

Betsey's character locates her outside the world of sheet music, where most heroines embody Victorian virtue. On the Overland Trail, whose men have little in common with the blushing swains of antebellum parlor song, only her determination, physical toughness, and self-reliant spirit allow her to survive. Her relationship with men turns out to be as important to the song as the journey itself. Sexual repression is nowhere to be found. As an unmarried couple traveling for months through a largely deserted landscape, Betsey and Ike seem to face no barriers to lovemaking. Further, Betsey mocks Victorian sheet-music norms by toying with male attention. She falls out of love with Ike, runs away from Young, and, responds to the Placerville miner with an earthy outburst. "Dog on you!" may be a euphemism for "Damn you!," but it's also trail talk, not proper female discourse. Nor is Betsey's confession that she's "chock full" of a desert laxative what one expects to hear from the belle of the ball. As a female protagonist who is comely, physically strong, morally independent, and talks like a man, Betsey is too complex for Victorian-age sheet music, which establishes character in black and white terms. *To the West*, with its stagy calls for departure, brings a ranting tone to what promises to be a static encounter between virtuous humans and idealized nature. *Sweet Betsey*, on the other hand, relates a dynamic experience. When people set out to explore the world, the song counsels, there is no predicting what may happen.

To the West, an independent piece of sheet music by a songwriter who was also a famous singer, was designed for a market that could be lucrative for both publishers and composers. A customer who paid thirty cents for a copy would most likely have access to a piano, and might also be willing to pay for piano and singing lessons. But pianos, music lessons, even musical notation had no more to do with *Sweet Betsey from Pike* than did the spirit of cultural uplift that infused the sheet-music business. It is likely that *Put's Golden Songster*, an entire collection of lyrics, sold for less than did Russell and McKay's single song. To sing *Sweet Betsey*, one needed only to know the tune *Villikins and His Dinah*, whose many repeated notes fit the delivery of a comic text, and whose refrain places nonsense vocables where a didactic message is expected. Appearing in a cheap songbook whose format flouts the very idea of elevation, *Sweet Betsey* declared a lineage that squares with

Ike's antiromantic response to the couple's arrival in California. Standing "on a very high hill," he grandly proclaims, as if looking down at the Promised Land: "Sweet Betsey, my darling, we've got to Hangtown."

To the West and *Sweet Betsey from Pike* deal with only one phase of the violent American expansion that took place during the first half of the nineteenth century. Settlement proceeded not only through St. Louis and towns along the Missouri River, but also through port cities like New York, Philadelphia, Baltimore, Boston, and Salem. Another song in *Put's Golden Songster*, set to the tune of *Pop Goes the Weasel*, confirms that fact, though not in an upbeat way:

> You go aboard of a leaky boat,
> > And sail for San Francisco;
> You've got to pump to keep her afloat,
> > You have *that*, by jingo.
> The engine soon begins to squeak,
> > But nary thing to oil her;
> Impossible to stop the leak
> > *Rip* goes the boiler.

Later stanzas move from mechanical troubles to complaints about the food, drunken crew members, and unhealthy conditions aboard ship:

> Cholera begins to rage.
> > A few have got the scurvy;
> Chickens dying in their cage—
> > Steerage topsy-turvy.

The song fails to say where the voyage began; it transports passengers only as far as Panama, where a rail trip carries them to the Pacific Ocean and another vessel.

On land, meanwhile, miners, loggers, homesteaders, Mormons, farmers, soldiers, and cowboys settled the West; all contributed to the large body of song that accumulated during the process. Circulating orally and in the semi-oral format of songsters, broadsides, and newspapers, songs about the West were also composed by songwriters in the sheet-music trade. We have already seen how songs on the same subject could take sharply different approaches, and that point is further confirmed by cowboy songs. In the first book written about the range-cattle trade of the West and Southwest (1874), cowboy life was reported to be "hard and full of exposure." But it was also "wild and free, and the young man who has long been a cow-boy has but little taste for any other occupation. He lives hard, works hard, has but few comforts and fewer necessities." According to the author, cowboys often slept in the open because they were too lazy to pitch a tent. Many found life in cow camp so dull that they sought out "frolic and debauchery" to enliven their days. A typical cowboy, this observer added, "has little, if any taste for reading" and "enjoys a coarse practical joke or a smutty story." He "never tires riding; never wants to walk, no matter how short the distance he wants to go. He would rather fight with pistols than pray; loves tobacco, liquor and women better than any other trinity."[2]

These comments set the stage for a pair of songs from the 1870s that picture cowboy life in different ways. Written in 1873 to *Captain Jinks*, a well-known English tune, *The Captain of the Cowboys* faces up to the life's hardships, though its diction is more literary than one might expect from a ranch hand:

> I do that work which I think to be,
>   think to be, think to be
> Consistent with the dignity
> Of a captain among the cowboys.

The third stanza serves inexperienced cowpokes a stern warning:

> If a visit to Blackjack Ranch you pay,
> By way of advice, just let me say,
> You'd better not come on branding day,
>   If beauty is your portion;
> For what with dust and what with blows,
>   what with blows, what with blows,
> A dirty face and a broken nose
>   Will likely change your notion.[3]

The second song, this one with its own melody, paints a picture far removed from dust and broken noses. And so deftly does it suggest an idealized West that it has since come to be the best-known of all Western songs:

> Oh, give me a home where the buffalo roam,
> Where the deer and the antelope play;
> Where seldom is heard a discouraging word
> And the skies are not cloudy all day.
>   Home, home on the range,
>   Where the deer and the antelope play;
>   Where seldom is heard a discouraging word,
>   And the skies are not cloudy all day.

A half dozen more stanzas follow, all reinforcing the image outlined in the first. One stanza notes without regret the Indians' removal ("The red man was pressed from this part of the West"). Others celebrate nature's unspoiled beauties: clear air, balmy breezes, colorful wildflowers, the calls of birds, glittering stars, and landscapes with "white rocks and the antelope flocks / That graze on the mountain-tops green." The West of *Home on the Range* is the stuff of legend: a place "where the graceful white swan goes gliding along / Like a maid in a heavenly dream."

When this song is placed in the context of nineteenth-century American song as a whole, it seems likely that its appeal owes much to the idea of home. To begin with, the key word is cleverly emphasized, sung at the melodic peak of the first stanza's first phrase and again on the refrain's first two downbeats and highest note. "Home" reverberates through the song as it does through Bishop and Payne's *Home, Sweet Home,* in whose debt it surely stands. Moreover, *Home on the Range* turns the age's chief domestic icon into a notion broad enough to encompass the wide open spaces. Few would take literally the song's image of wild deer and antelope cavorting under cloudless skies, entertaining ranch hands who are incurable optimists. Yet the connection of life on the range to a vision of home elevates the cowboy into a mythic figure, and the song offers a peek into his dreams. The attractive **aaba** waltz tune provides a perfect vehicle for imagining the West as an idyllic stage for heroes. To the superior male beings who live there, the song suggests, home is not just a domestic arrangement but a state of mind: a reward for mastering a perilous environment.

Home on the Range is evidence that the romanticized image of the cowboy in song existed as far back as 1876, when the song was first published. This song's mythical hero is a close relative of the cowboy who later crooned cows to sleep on the movie screen. But songs from less commercial environments offered other perspectives. For example, life in the West is widely assumed to have fostered the positive trait of rugged individualism, but songs about people trying to go it alone on the frontier dwell chiefly on loneliness and misery. The image of lone rangers forging heroic lives from prairie solitude is not reflected in most songs that Westerners themselves actually sang. In fact, as the songs would have it, only when settlers organized themselves into groups—the Mormons, the Wobblies (members of the Industrial Workers of the World, a radical labor union), or the grangers (the Grange was an organization created in 1867 to further the interests of farmers)—did they succeed in bettering their lot.[4]

SPANISH SONGS OF THE SOUTHWEST

Long before westward expansion began, parts of the Southwest and southern California had been settled by people moving northward from Mexico. And there Spanish-language singing traditions flourished, separate and distinct from the English-language ones discussed so far. Mexican-American song of the late 1800s can be glimpsed through the work of

Writer and folk song collector Charles F. Lummis (1859–1928), photographed in Los
Angeles with his daughter Turbesè and son Jordan (1903).

Charles F. Lummis, a Massachusetts native who crossed the country on
foot in the mid-1880s and fell in love with the culture he encountered in the
West. Lummis came to believe that life in California "before the gringo" ar-

Composer Arthur Farwell (1872–1952), photographed in the early 1900s by Charles Lummis when Farwell was transcribing songs that Lummis had collected.

rived had been "the happiest, the humanest, the most beautiful life that Caucasians have ever lived anywhere under the sun." And he demonstrated his esteem for the singing he heard there by collecting Hispanic folk songs. Lummis described what he found to enjoy in these songs: a "fascination, a naiveté, and yet a vividness and life," and "a certain resilience and wilfulness." So reflective of their culture were they that only a Spanish word— *simpatica*—could express their character.[5]

A journalist by trade, Lummis started collecting folk songs in Spanish soon after he arrived in Los Angeles in 1885. And a few years later, he was collecting in New Mexico. "For months I hung by night around the sheep camps of Don Amado," Lummis recalled, "squatting with the quiet Mexican herders in the little semi-circular brush shelter by a crackling fire of juniper. March and spring nights are chill up there at 7,000 or 8,000 feet." Affection for the singers marks his vivid memory of those evenings:

> There were few good voices but all had what is more important than a good voice, the will to sing and express their emotion. And beyond that, an invariable sense of time and rhythm which only our best musicians can match. And they were such human, friendly folk! Glad to sing a song over and over until I had it note-perfect and then to repeat the words while I wrote them down. They were greatly pleased when I could sing their songs back to them. . . . So we sang and talked and smoked cigarettes under the infinite stars of a New Mexican sky or the even more numerous flakes of a mountain snowstorm.[6]

In the early 1900s, Lummis obtained a wax cylinder machine to record songs and hired trained musicians to help transcribe his recordings. One who joined the project was American composer Arthur Farwell. Visiting Los Angeles in early 1904 on a lecture tour, Farwell was invited to the house Lummis had built with his own hands, and there he encountered "a little world of Spanish-Californians and Indians." Farwell was enchanted. "I not only heard many of their songs," he later wrote, but "I swam in the musical atmosphere of them—the suave or vivacious songs of the Spanish settlers and the weird, somber, and mysterious songs of the dwellers of the desert."[7] As founder of the Wa-Wan Press in Newton Center, Massachusetts (1901), dedicated to music by American composers, Farwell had already published a number of Indian melodies harmonized by himself and others. After receiving a grant from the Archeological Institute of America, he spent the summers of 1904 and 1905 in Los Angeles transcribing the melodies Lummis had recorded. Almost two decades passed before the collaboration produced a tangible result. And by any measure, *Spanish Songs of Old California* (Los Angeles, 1923) was a meager outcome after so much work—fourteen songs out of the three hundred recorded and transcribed.[8] Yet the modest volume is worth comment, both for the music it contained and the format in which it appeared.

In the manner of folklorists, Lummis named the singers he had recorded. He paid special tribute to Doña Manuela García of Los Angeles, noting that "in all my collecting, throughout Spanish America, I have not found another such golden memory."[9] Anyone seeking authentic versions of these melodies with their complete texts, as remembered around 1905 by a Los Angeles-born, Spanish-speaking singer in her middle thirties, will find them here.[10] Only later research verifies that fact, however, for the compilers say little about details of preservation. In fact, they neglect to explain why, although the songs were recorded with guitar and sung in Spanish, the published versions have piano accompaniments, with English translations underlaid. The reasons were obvious to them and their public: Lummis and Farwell were more interested in having these songs sung than in preserving them for study.

By the time *Spanish Songs of Old California* was published, Farwell, who had worked as a music critic, held academic posts, and supervised municipal concerts for New York City, was involved in a national movement to encourage community singing by amateur singers. In his historical survey of music in America (1915), Farwell had posed a provocative question: What would "a new world" founded on democratic ideals "do with the intractable and still unformed art of music?" Community singing, which involved large-scale participation by citizens, was part of his answer. And to show that musical democracy could overcome barriers of region, culture, and language, Farwell had already included some of these Hispanic songs in that effort:

> To the vast community singing movement of America, the meaning and value of these songs is beyond all power to estimate or predict. The Spanish Californian songs come to this great movement as a veritable new lease [on] life. In community song movements under my direction they have been sung, and are being sung, by large numbers of people year after year with increasing enthusiasm and delight, even under the difficulties of their hitherto unpublished condition. Their power to animate and thrill the people in community singing is remarkable.[11]

Such comments link *Spanish Songs of Old California* to a time when musical scholarship, not yet an independent specialty, was still considered an accessory of performance. A musician like Farwell could grapple one day with the difficulties of transcribing a Hispanic folk song and another day conduct an accompanied, translated, choral version of the same song, confident that the two activities complemented each other. For Farwell and Lummis, preserving a song was first and foremost a step toward singing and enjoying it.

Nothing in the American songs considered so far in this chronicle prepares an observer for *La hámaca* (The Hammock), the first number in the songbook. The singer, who could be a woman or a man, lies in a hammock, fanned by a soft sea breeze, musing about how sweet life can be when one is in love. The swing of the hammock is suggested by a habanera rhythm (♪♩♪), while the voice mixes sustained tones with triplets that sinuously disengage from the bass.

The thirty-two-bar song is cast in two sections; the melodic structure might be diagrammed **aabb** or, at a phrase-by-phrase level, **ababcdce.** Rather than circling back toward its opening statement, as do many of the day's English-language songs, the melody moves away from it, erupting in

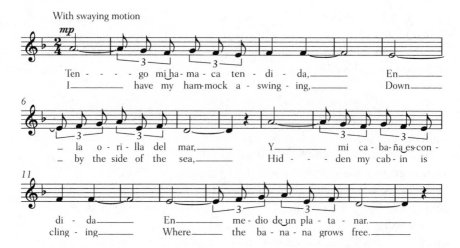

With swaying motion

Ten - - - - go mi ha-ma - ca ten - di - da,_____ En_____
I_____ have my ham-mock a - swing - ing,_____ Down_____

_ la o - ri - lla del mar,_____ Y_____ mi ca - ba - ña es con -
_ by the side of the sea,_____ Hid - - - den my cab - in is

di - da_____ En_____ me - dio de un pla - ta - nar._____
cling - ing_____ Where_____ the ba - na - na grows free._____

the last four bars into a blaze of triplet motion. The music suggests what the text's rather sultry second stanza claims: when savored this deeply, love becomes unsettling as well as pleasurable.

El capotín (The Rain Song), sung in accented 3/4 time, presents three stanzas of text and a refrain that sets vocables to repeated eighth-notes, mimicking the sound of falling raindrops:

Con el capotín-tin-tin-tin,	With the capotín-tin-tin-tin,
Questa noche va llorer,	For tonight it's going to rain,
Con el capotín-tin-tin-tin,	With the capotín-tin-tin-tin
Que sera al amancer.	And maybe at dawn again.
Con el capotín-tin-tin-tin	With the capotín-tin-tin-tin,
Questa noche va llorer,	For tonight it's going to rain,
Con el capotín-tin-tin-tin	With the capotín-tin-tin-tin,
Que sera al amancer.	And maybe at dawn again.

The song also plays with phrase lengths. The verse (**A**), which sets up a norm of four-bar units, is followed by a chorus (**B**) whose phrases are all six bars long. The source of the extra length is not the waltz-like **B** melody, which continues in the vein of the verse, but the two-bar rain figure. Tacked on, like a parenthesis, to the start of each phrase, this figure unbalances the song's syntax with a recurring asymmetrical hitch. The text turns out to be as much about love as the weather. Fearing that his passion is not returned, the singer pleads for an end to his misery:

No me mates, no me mates,	Do not kill me, do not kill me,
Con pistola ni puñal,	With a pistol or a knife!
Matame con tus	Kill me, rather, with thine eyes,
ojitos,	love,
O esos labios de coral.	With those red lips take my life.

But the music continues its sprightly course, as if brushing this outcry aside as the posturing of an overheated lover.

La hámaca and *El capotín* offer glimpses of a sensibility different from anything found in nineteenth-century American sheet music. It is hard to imagine a song in English from this period whose main character is content simply to lie in a hammock in broad daylight, contemplating his or her love life. To abandon oneself to the sensuous pleasure of the moment is foreign to the ethos of the English song, as is the closeness of love and death. Mexican-American folk songs were also musically distinctive, with their flexible rhythm, melody, and form. For Lummis and Farwell, the attraction lay not in any abstract wish to represent Hispanic culture to English speakers, but in the qualities of the songs themselves. Spanish-language songs, they believed, could enrich the artistic and emotional experience of English-speaking Americans, for such songs conjured up "a world of romantic adventure" with "a mood of its own, thrilling with picturesqueness," and far removed from the Victorian values that dominated English-language song of the post–Civil War years.[12] The songs that Lummis recorded and that he and Farwell published treat love as one of life's great mysteries. And at the heart of that mystery lay an idea of beauty that transcended verbal explanation.

SHEET MUSIC AND ITS OFFSPRING

After the Civil War, the sheet-music trade showed little interest in the central issues of the day. The hardships of war widows and ex-slaves and the bitterness of Southern whites may have been acute social realities, but they were not the stuff from which song hits could be fashioned. Composer and publisher George F. Root noted that when the war ended, sales of "war songs stopped as if they had been shot," for "everybody had had enough of war."[13] Instead, songwriters returned to subjects and sentiments popular in the 1820s and 30s: brief, nostalgic or cautionary dramas or vignettes.

Moreover, rather than trying out new musical forms, postwar songwriters took elements from older songs and cast them into prescribed formulas. The verse-and-chorus form of Stephen Foster and contemporaries remained as prominent after the war as it had been before. And the key to popular-song composition still lay in inventing a brief, catchy musical statement, usually four bars long, and then imprinting it on listeners through repetition. Following the dictum that the main statement must be heard early and often, postwar songs presented it in the introduction, the verse (usually more than once), the chorus, and the piano tag, if there was one. Thus, formal ingenuity counted for little; redundancy was welcomed and embraced.

Silver Threads Among the Gold (1873), with words by Eben Rexford and

Silver Threads Among the Gold, set by Hart P. Danks to words by Eben E. Rexford (1873), shows that melodic economy was still being practiced by popular song writers after the Civil War.

music by Hart P. Danks, is a good example of the standard recipe for post–Civil War popular songs. The four-bar piano introduction prefigures the main statement: a pair of two-bar phrases with a complementary curve, the first starting high and moving downward, and the second reversing direction. Both emphasize leaps of a sixth—unusually wide for a signature interval, but written to sound more flowing than strenuous. Sung legato and at a moderate tempo, the gently flowing melody fits the subject: the ripeness of married love. The beginning "Darling, I am growing old," a flat, truthful declaration, is immediately softened by the poetic title line, which turns human hair into skeins of gold and silver. To a person viewing life from this song's perspective, the passing of time brings a mellowing and deepening of affection. Musical form contributes to the comfortable atmosphere. The four-bar main statement supplies the a section of the verse, which unfolds in an **aaba** structure; the chorus repeats the verse's second half (**ba**) in four-part harmony; and the piano introduction and tag contribute the main idea as well, for an overall thirty-two-bar structure of **aaababaa.** The words of the chorus also repeat the four lines that begin the first stanza. All this repetition makes for a structure in which love is a force of stability, like home itself: a haven shielding partners from the ravages of time.

The easy melodic flow of this hit number comes at the price of an unbalanced text delivery.[14] Danks's melody places six of the first line's seven syllables in the first measure, leaving only one syllable for the second. And that pattern continues, so that stop-and-start declamation pervades the whole song, with piano accompaniment filling in the gaps. In the chorus, Danks enhances material sung in the verse with richer texture (four voices) and broader phrases.

Two enduring songs of the era celebrate the consumption of alcohol. Written in the voice of a two-fisted drunk, *The Little Brown Jug* (1869) may have been intended to expose the shamelessness of drinkers the temperance movement was sworn to reform. This song follows the sheet-music formula of unison verse and harmonized chorus. Its use of melody is especially economical, for the composer Eastburn (songwriter-publisher Joseph Eastburn Winner) hammers home a single four-bar phrase, almost unchanged, from start to finish. Perhaps four bars of bone-simple music are supposed to be all the singer can remember as he wallows in a destructive romance with the bottle:

'Tis you who makes my friends my foes,
'Tis you who makes me wear old clothes;
Here you are, so near my nose,
So tip her up, and down she goes.
    Ha, ha, ha, you and me,
    "Little brown jug" don't I love thee;
    Ha, ha, ha, you and me,
    "Little brown jug," don't I love thee.

The text of *There Is a Tavern in the Town* (1891) might make us think this is a love lament. Sung by a spurned female, the words dwell on a carousing ex-lover who now "drinks his wine 'mid laughter free, / And never, never thinks of me." But the music fails to support a doleful mood. The opening, and especially the shouted response, mark this song as a male group effort. *Tavern* belongs to a genre that was just coming into prominence in the 1890s: the college song that arose with the advent of school glee clubs. Made from two complementary melodies (**ABA**), *Tavern* is sung in unison. But glee clubs also featured harmonized, hymn-like alma maters as well as convivial numbers like this one, which seems to invite performance by boys of all ages, with full glasses in their hands.

INDUSTRIALIZATION AND THE RISE OF GOSPEL MUSIC

The postwar years brought many changes. In the years between the Civil War and World War I, the United States became the world's leading industrial nation. And as industry advanced, agriculture declined, a trend typical of modernization. By 1910, when manufacturing jobs were on the rise, farm workers made up only 31.4 percent of the labor force, compared with 52.5 percent in 1870. Changes in the nation's economic and social structure touched all facets of American life, music included. Industrialization brought more people into urban areas, for industries were concentrated in cities. As that trend continued, the popular-song trade came more and more to be ruled by the tastes of city dwellers.

Industrialization did more than shift workers from the countryside to the city; it changed the nature of work and, in the process, alienated many workers. A machinist testified in 1883: "The different branches of the trade are divided and subdivided so that one man may make just a particular part of a machine and may not know anything whatever about another part of the same machine." By this man's testimony, even long experience on the job taught few skills, for workers themselves functioned as interchangeable parts of a vast industrial process. "There is no system of apprenticeship," he explained. "You simply go in and learn whatever branch you are put at, and you stay at that unless you are changed to another."[15] Wages for such workers were low and job security nonexistent. Thus, while industrialization brought great wealth to a few and raised the country's standard of living, it also made the lives of many workers more uncertain. Chronic unemployment became part of the everyday experience of the unskilled. Such working conditions form the background for a key religious development of the postwar years: the Protestant urban revival movement, which also borrowed from the popular song and sheet-music trade.

Evangelical revivals aimed at bringing the gospel—the glad tidings of Jesus and the kingdom of God—to unchurched Americans of all social and economic classes. One of the movement's leaders was Dwight L. Moody, who, though he lacked any formal training in theology, became a renowned preacher. Born in 1837 in Massachusetts, Moody moved to Chicago in the mid-1850s, where he prospered in the shoe business. He then began Christian work with the YMCA (Young Men's Christian Association) and in 1864 founded a nondenominational Protestant church. Moody's preaching emphasized God's love for sinful humans and soft-pedaled such subjects as hellfire and the wrath of God. Ruled by a pragmatic standard, he wished only to deliver messages "fit to convert sinners with."[16] Moody cultivated sentiment over theological doctrine. He also followed Sunday schools and

Singer, compiler, and gospel hymn writer Ira Sankey (1840–1908), at the reed organ, is pictured with Fanny Crosby (1820–1915), who wrote the words for more than nine thousand hymns, including many gospel favorites.

the YMCA in favoring simple, popular hymns like William Bradbury's *Jesus Loves Me.*

In the early 1870s, Moody was invited to hold evangelical meetings in Great Britain. He took with him as his musical director Ira Sankey, who not only led group singing but sang solos, accompanying himself on the reed organ. In the spirit of Moody's sermons, Sankey composed and sang music calculated for broad public appeal. The impact of these meetings was enormous. By the end of 1873, they had kindled in Scotland something of a national revival and made Moody and Sankey famous, leading to evangelical tours of the United States. Singing played a key role in the work of changing sinners into Christians. Moody and Sankey and other traveling evangelists found in "gospel" hymns, sacred songs in popular musical dress, an ideal way to give their audiences personal access to Christianity's profound spiritual truths. Communicating directly with worshipers, gospel hymns helped revivalists tap unguarded emotions, promoting a desire to connect with God in an attitude of praise, with little concern for edification.

The career of Philip P. Bliss shows clear links between gospel hymnody and the popular-music trade. Bliss, a man of stentorian voice and handsome appearance, moved in 1864 from Pennsylvania, where he was born in 1838, to Chicago, where for the next four years he worked as a "song booster" for the publishing firm of Root and Cady. His duties included promoting the company's copyrights in and around Chicago, holding music teachers' conventions, and giving concerts of Root and Cady's music, accompanied by his wife at the piano. In the late 1860s, Bliss came to the attention of Dwight L. Moody, who enlisted him to sing at prayer meetings. Already an experienced song composer, Bliss now demonstrated a knack for writing words and music in the informal gospel vein. At Moody's urging, Bliss became a singing evangelist. But serving God and mammon amounted to much the same thing professionally: Bliss continued to travel and promote the sheet music and books of sacred songs that he and others had written and that were on sale at every service.

By 1875, evangelical revivalism was not only a religious force to be reckoned with but a successful business in the United States. "As he stood on the platform," wrote a fellow preacher about Moody shortly before the evangelist's death, "he looked like a business man; he dressed like a business man; he took the meeting in hand as a business man would."[17] Moody's entrepreneurial sense helped win support from leading citizens wherever he held his meetings. Philadelphia department-store founder John Wanamaker, New York financiers J. Pierpont Morgan and Cornelius Vanderbilt, and Chicago industrialist Cyrus McCormick and meatpacker George Armour were some of the men who lent their names to the committees that organized Moody's local visits. Crowds of over ten thousand flocked to his meetings, where they heard huge choirs that had been carefully trained by Ira Sankey.

In 1876, gospel hymnody lost one of its leading composers when Philip P. Bliss died in a train wreck. But by then, Sankey had gathered the hymns he had used in Britain, added some by Bliss and others, and brought out *Gospel Hymns* (1876), a collection that was to be a best-selling hymnal until well into the twentieth century. With copies of this new work being sold at Moody's meetings, royalties of some $360,000 were paid during the book's first ten years in print. To deflect any hint that they were more interested in money than saving souls, Moody and Sankey channeled proceeds from the hymnal into church work.[18]

Two hymns from the collection, *Beautiful River* and *Sweet By and By*, reflect the gospel approach that Moody and Sankey promoted. Baptist clergyman Robert Lowry wrote the words and music of the first, inspired by a scene from the Book of Revelation. Sounding a lot like a march, *Beautiful River* exudes comradeship:

> Shall we gather at the river,
> Where bright angel feet have trod
> With its crystal tide forever
> Flowing by the throne of God?
>> Yes, we'll gather at the river,
>> The beautiful, the beautiful river
>> Gather with the saints at the river,
>> That flows by the throne of God.

The last verse promises, "Soon we'll reach the silver river, / Soon our pilgrimage will cease," breathing confidence about the end of life's journey. Yet *Beautiful River* also lends itself well to the subject of baptism. Whatever the author may have had in mind, no anxiety about Judgment Day clouds the sunny picture offered by this hymn.

Sweet By and By, in contrast, is a daydream of heaven by a composer and lyricist outside the revivalist circle. New Hampshire native Joseph P. Webster, the composer, studied music with Lowell Mason in Boston in the early 1840s, toured for a time as a professional singer, worked for a music publisher in Chicago in the 1850s, and eventually settled in Elkhorn, Wisconsin. He published some four hundred songs and hymns during his lifetime, including *Lorena* (1857), a Civil War favorite. *Sweet By and By*, Webster's best-known hymn, was composed in 1867 to words by Elkhorn resident (and pharmacist) S. Fillmore Bennett. The music sustains the reverie caught by Bennett's text, in part by avoiding any tonal complication: there are only three chords (tonic, dominant, subdominant) and not a single sharp or flat. At the same time, unbroken rhythmic flow is equally important. Webster instructs performers: "With much feeling and in perfect time." This is an unusual, if not a contradictory, direction. For bending the tempo is a standard way to emphasize feeling in a sung text. Moreover, with regular eighth notes in the piano accompaniment and a dactylic rhythm (♩♩♩) dominating the vocal parts, *Sweet By and By* joins strict tempo and smooth declamation—again an unusual pairing. Only the dotted rhythm that dominates the chorus and begins each phrase of the verse enlivens the song's tranquil surface.

Sweet By and By follows a familiar formal plan: piano introduction, unison verse, harmonized chorus. Unlike most secular songs of the day, however, its main interest lies in the chorus. Both verse and chorus are eight measures long; but the length of the chorus, which introduces the title phrase and main message, is doubled by a repeat. An echo effect between male and female voices invites singers and listeners to savor a rosy view of the future. And a softening on the repeat allows the chorus to fade gently away at the end, perhaps suggesting the eternal peace that lies waiting.

In the sweet by and by, We shall

In the sweet by and by, In the sweet by and by, We shall

In the repeat, diminuendo gradually to the end.

meet on that beau - ti - ful shore, In the sweet by and

meet on that beau - ti - ful shore, by and by, In the sweet by and by, In the

by, We shall meet on that beau - ti - ful shore.

sweet by and by, We shall meet on that beau - ti - ful shore.

Where *Beautiful River* finesses Judgment Day, the words of *Sweet By and By* retreat even further into theological vagueness, turning the Christian idea of life after death into a euphemistic phrase, a "beautiful shore" where singers will meet when their days on earth are over. Suggesting a point of view that overlooks or readily pardons sin, these words must have struck some believers of the day as falsely optimistic. Yet the air of serene confidence that radiates from this hymn brought to evangelical revivalism an image of trust in the future that must also have disarmed the doubts and fears of many.

During the latter nineteenth century, labor unions proved a valuable weapon to workers in their struggle with managers over control in the workplace. Joining forces to seek higher wages and better working conditions, workers found that the threat of striking could be an effective bargaining tool. Given the unequal balance of power, it is no surprise that they explored many ways of boosting morale and confirming solidarity. Singing was one. And labor songs, written for jobs ranging from mining to farming, are another musical legacy of the post–Civil War years.

Leopold Vincent's *Alliance and Labor Songster* (1891) was compiled for use at meetings of the Farmers Alliance, which by 1890 claimed more than three million members. One example from that collection, *The Right Will Prevail,* sung to the tune of *Sweet By and By,* illustrates the uncompromising tone that labor songs usually took:

> When the Workingmen's cause shall prevail
>> Then the class-rule of rich men shall cease,
> And the true friends of Labor will hail
>> With a shout the glad era of peace.
>>> Right will reign by-and-by,
>>>> When the Workingmen come into power;
>>> Right will reign, by-and-by,
>>>> Then the gold thieves shall rule men no more.[19]

Readers will recognize here an impulse for parody that dates back to the broadside ballads and patriotic songs of the 1700s. Here, the author transformed *Sweet By and By*—surely chosen because it was well-known—a gentle affirmation of heavenly peace, into an attack on capitalists. One can only speculate about the full range of meanings this song carried in 1891. For most, the use of *Sweet By and By* must have signified confidence. Just as believers could count on going to heaven, workers, who thought their cause the more virtuous, would ultimately prevail over bosses. On the other hand, if triumph was to be postponed into some vague "by and by," perhaps others took this version more cynically, in the spirit of a later parody that promises workers: "There'll be pie in the sky when you die."

Some labor songs were set to original music. But those that borrowed familiar music, like *The Right Will Prevail,* circulated more easily and traded on built-in references. Since labor songs were militant, they were often sung to melodies whose original texts also drew clear lines between right and wrong. Civil War songs were favorites. (Many labor songs were based on the *Battle-Hymn of the Republic* and on Root's *Battle Cry of Freedom* and *Tramp, Tramp, Tramp.*) So were gospel hymns. Alfred Green's *Workman's Hymn,* a

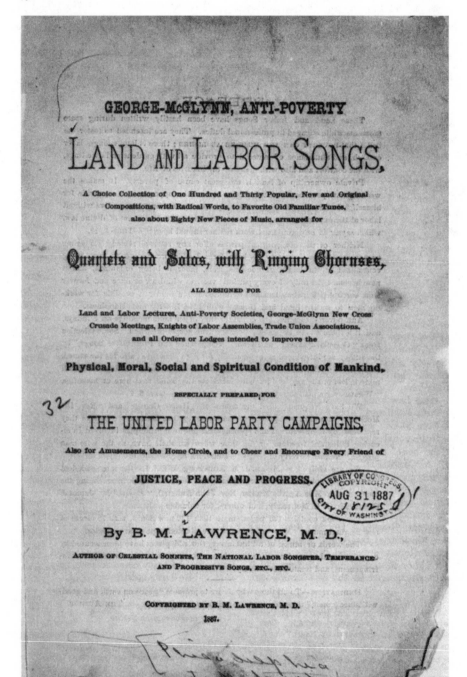

Songsters like this one, published in 1887, circulated pro-labor messages cheaply, relying on familiar music for much of their impact.

parody of Philip P. Bliss's *Hold the Fort*, appeared in a labor newspaper in 1877. One of the stanzas reads:

> See the Oppressor's host advancing
> Money leading on—
> Workingmen around us falling
> Courage almost gone.
> > Hold on friends, the time is coming
> > When workmen with one will
> > Shall claim the birth-right free from heaven
> > Just pay for their skill.

The melody to *God Save the Queen*, sung in the United States to "My country, 'tis of thee," also served the labor movement. As part of a campaign to shorten working hours, the following lyric was published in 1865:

> Ye noble sons of toil,
> Who ne'er from work recoil,
> > Take up the lay;
> Loud let the anthem's roar
> Resume from shore to shore,
> Till Time shall be no more.
> > Eight hours a day.

Finally, management was not the only target of the nineteenth-century labor press. In 1893, the Philadelphia *Journal of the Knights of Labor* used a famous hymn to launch a bitter attack on Christian outreach. Claiming that religion was being used as a cover for violence and economic exploitation, this derisive parody of Arthur Sullivan's *Onward, Christian Soldiers* reads like something out of the tumultuous 1960s. Here is the first stanza of *Modern Missionary Zeal*:

> Onward! Christian soldiers;
> > On to heathen lands!
> Prayer book in your pockets,
> > Rifles in your hands.
> Take the happy tidings
> > Where trade can be done;
> Spread the peaceful gospel
> > With a Gatling gun.[20]

Later stanzas, which accuse missionaries of plying Indians with liquor and then stealing their land, are no more complimentary. Thoughts like these proceeded not from the music business, still a bastion of Victorian values, but from what amounts to an underground press. Taking the work of the popular-music trades as a starting point, the labor movement mocked establishment beliefs through such ridicule. And in turning "respectable" messages back on the powers that be, labor songs reveal another face of American musical democracy: one that, rather than affirming the established social order, gives it a critical look and invites citizens to imagine that it could be otherwise.

23

Stars, Stripes, and Cylinders
Sousa, the Band, and the Phonograph

In August 1898, a newspaper in Wayne Country, Pennsylvania, carried a poem that declared the Keystone Band of Lake Como, in the state's northeast corner, one of the town's chief assets.

> The grand old town of Como lies resting 'neath the hills,
> While its waters run on daily, in quiet rippling rills;
> And its sights and scenes are glorious—in fact, are simply grand,
> But there's one thing does excel all else—it's the music of its band.

The poet, a summer resident of Lake Como, said nothing about the bandsmen's dedication to music. But he recognized one benefit of membership: the boys in the band got plenty of female attention:

> And Como's lovely maidens go on practice nights to hear
> The band boys in their club room, and fill the place with cheer;
> 'Tis then the boys will play their best, and show that they've got sand
>   [courage, grit],
> By the music they will give you, they try "to beat the band."[1]

Local pride stands behind this glimpse of an amateur group that played for summer picnics, winter entertainments, and civic occasions as they arose. The music, the poet implies, reflects life in Lake Como, where such things as pretty scenery and the joys of innocent romance were commonplace. People outside Lake Como may not have thought much of the Keystone Band, but the group was valued at home because of a tradition of self-sufficiency that grew out of the isolation of rural towns. A local band affirmed local self-respect. In newspapers of the time, there are next to no critical reviews of any band performance.[2]

The Keystone Band stands in a line that began in the 1700s with local

Photographed around 1887, this band from Baraboo, Wisconsin, seems to have used a camping trip as an occasion to play.

Lookout Mountain, Tennessee, is the site of this 1864 photograph of a Civil War brass band's performance.

militia bands, blossomed during the Civil War into a national patriotic movement, and continued as an amateur pastime even after an elite professional strain of wind band performance emerged. The professional band, led in the postwar years by Patrick S. Gilmore and John Philip Sousa, brought polished musical performances to the ears of more Americans than any other ensemble. But behind bands like Sousa's lay a vast network of amateur groups that, like church choirs, were part of many Americans' musical experience, as both performers and listeners. Nourished by the spread of music teaching, the growth of the music instrument business, and an appetite for music at local functions, the amateur band provided amusement for people in towns and villages. When band members described the character of that amusement, they often mentioned fellowship and cultural uplift. As the constitution of Farr's Band of Princeton, New Jersey, noted in 1892: "We the undersigned citizens of Princeton, seeking relaxation from the cares and burdens of life and deeming a social organization for the cultivation and practice of music as leading to a higher and better appreciation of the same, do hereby resolve to band ourselves together for this purpose."[3]

Between the Civil War and World War I, the wind band enjoyed its heyday in the United States. One reason is that the amateur band seems to have been well matched to the character of life in both towns and cities. As technological progress brought more leisure time to the general population, civic functions multiplied: parades, picnics, dedications, store openings, as well as concerts, dances, and other social functions. By playing music that the public enjoyed, at a volume that could be heard outdoors, a band enhanced the atmosphere of these occasions. In cities, the performers at such events might be professionals who played in theater orchestras during the winter season and added more outdoor work in the summers. But in villages and towns, local players of all ages were recruited to form amateur bands. Band instruments were inexpensive, and the repertory required only modest technique; enough to keep a beat and sustain a melody line. To imagine what a town band like the Keystoners sounded like is not easy in an era when recording and broadcasting have made the sound of note-perfect performances seem normal. Perhaps a school band or a composition like Charles Ives's *Country Band March*, which parodies a group struggling with rhythm and tuning, provide hints. In any case, the playing of amateur town bands reverberated across the land during these years: bearers of a tradition of democratic music making that gradually faded in the twentieth century.

SOUSA, AMERICAN BANDS, AND THE MARCH

Band concerts were not new in the late 1800s, but earning one's living by playing in them was. Patrick S. Gilmore led one of the first such outfits un-

John Philip Sousa in his uniform as leader of the U.S. Marine band.

til he died in 1892. And in that year, John Philip Sousa formed the band that set the professional standard from that time forward. Sousa is a key figure in American music history. As a prolific composer for the stage and concert hall, he put his unmistakable stamp on a well-known popular form: the march. As a conductor, he thrilled audiences with a blend of showmanship and polished performance. When Sousa came on the scene, the American

Sousa's southern Michigan itinerary covered approximately 450 miles in seven days, and the band played fourteen concerts in that period.

wind band was already a leading purveyor of music to the public, a role he magnified in the years before World War I. But by the time his performing career ended in 1931, the professional band was a thing of the past, and a new amateur incarnation, the school band, had begun to flourish.

Born in 1854 in Washington, D.C., the son of a trombonist in the U.S. Marine Band, Sousa began playing violin as a boy. He studied in a local conservatory of music and at age fourteen entered the Marine Band's apprenticeship program. Discharged from the Marine Corps in 1875, he settled in Philadelphia, played violin in theater orchestras, worked on his composing, began conducting in earnest in 1879 with a performance of Gilbert and Sullivan's *H.M.S. Pinafore*, and returned to Washington in 1880, at the age of twenty-five, as leader of the U.S. Marine Band. During his dozen years in that post, Sousa also composed vigorously, especially marches and operettas. When he moved to New York in 1892 to form his own band, he found a ready supply of competent professionals to choose from. The first Sousa band contained forty-six members, including some who left Gilmore's band when the leader died; by the 1920s, Sousa's band numbered about seventy, with some forty reed players, twenty-five brass, and five percussionists.

Sousa and his men proved a popular draw at fairs and expositions, settling in for weeks at a time. An Atlanta newspaper reported in 1895 that the band had already "pulled many expositions out of financial ruts" and had "actually saved the Midwinter Fair in San Francisco" by attracting large crowds to the fairgrounds.[4] The band also spent half the year or more touring North America by rail. European trips were organized in the early 1900s, and a world tour in 1910–11. With concerts seven days a week and often twice a day, Sousa's tours were not for the faint of lip. Here is the itinerary for a week's swing through southern Michigan in 1913:

Sat. 9/27	Kalamazoo	M[atinee] & E[vening]	Fuller Theater
Sun. 9/28	Detroit	M & E	Detroit Opera House
Mon. 9/29	Port Huron	Matinee	Majestic Theater
	Mt. Clemens	Evening	Bijou Theater
Tues. 9/30	Pontiac	Matinee	Howland Theater
	Flint	Evening	Stone Theater
Wed. 10/1	Bay City	Matinee	Washington Theater
	Saginaw	Evening	Academy of Music
Thurs. 10/2	Owosso	Matinee	Owosso Opera House
	Lansing	Evening	Gladmer Theater
Fri. 10/3	Adrian	Matinee	Croswell Opera House
	Ann Arbor	Evening	Whitney Theater[5]

As this schedule also shows, Sousa's band played in the same theaters that housed operettas, musical comedies, and the variety shows known as vaudeville.

In a realm where amateurs had set the standard, few audience members had heard anything like Sousa and his men. Playing shiny instruments and dressed in military-style uniforms, they affected an impressive spit-and-polish demeanor and played, under an exacting leader, as if they were a single, well-tuned instrument. The band's appeal in concerts was also well served by the leader's approach to programming. Sousa liked to begin concerts with a classical work such as an overture. (Wagner's to *The Flying Dutchman* was a favorite that he arranged for band.) When the number ended, Sousa would acknowledge the applause, but rather than leaving the stage, he would turn back to the musicians, tell those closest to him the name of the first encore—perhaps a popular song arrangement or a Sousa march—and give the downbeat before the applause had died away. While the encore was being played, a large show card placed on an easel at the right of the stage identified it to the audience. It might be followed by another encore; or Sousa might move on to the next number printed in the program. Not knowing what music to expect, the audience was kept in a state of anticipation. And so were the players: Sousa liked to mix encores to keep the musicians alert, and they often had to scramble to find the correct number in their encore books.[6]

The second scheduled number typically featured one of the band's solo stars: cornetist Herbert L. Clarke, for example, or trombonist Arthur Pryor. Next came another full ensemble piece, such as a suite by Sousa himself. A vocal selection usually followed, perhaps a familiar operatic song or aria sung by the band's soprano soloist; and a rousing instrumental number completed the first half. Except for the last, all these selections were encored. And the second half continued in a similar vein. From a variety of music—classical and popular, vocal and instrumental, loud and soft, solo and ensemble—Sousa the conductor wove collages of sound on the spot, responding to the occasion and the atmosphere in the hall.

Sousa also varied the moods on each program. As he told an interviewer in 1911, Shakespeare found nothing incongruous in following a tragic scene with a comic one. Therefore, he had "no hesitation in combining in my program clever comedy with symphonic tragedy, rhythmic march or waltz with sentimental tone pictures." The opinions of professional colleagues carried little weight with Sousa. "I learned very early in life," he once said, "that if musicians depended upon musicians for their support there would be no musicians." Since art could survive only by pleasing people, musicians had to "heed the wishes of the masses" if they hoped to succeed.[7]

Sousa began tailoring encores to audience taste even before he formed his own band. In 1889, the secretary of the navy ordered him and the Marine Band to Fayetteville, North Carolina, to help celebrate the hundredth anniversary of that state's ratifying of the U.S. Constitution. There the crowd, prepared to listen politely but coolly to this government band, was instead whipped into an emotional and enthusiastic frenzy as the band launched into *Dixie*. The spontaneous outburst brought tears to Sousa's eyes. In a different vein, in 1901 the Sousa Band played a concert in Columbus, Ohio, shortly after President William McKinley, a native of that state, died in office. The last number before intermission had just been played when Sousa "again raised his baton" and, according to the local newspaper:

Instantly a profound hush fell upon the audience, for something not on the program was coming. . . . Then softly in strains sweeter than Apollo's lute, in harmony that seemed to have its source in realms celestial, there stole upon the ear that wondrous creation of the Christian hymnology, "Nearer My God to Thee." The audience hardly breathed for with one wave of the master-hand they were suddenly lifted from the midst of the grandest band concert ever given in the Ohio capital and set down beside the catafalque of the dead president. Tears welled in nearly every eye as that divine hymn was played. It seemed as if its matchless beauty had never been realized before. And midst the solemn, breathing sound, faint as the distant echo from some sacred shrine, there came the tolling of the funeral bell. No words can picture the effect.[8]

Sousa even used encores to comment on audience behavior. At one matinee concert, he muttered to the band: "If they're going to act like children, we'll give them children's music!" And he ordered up the *Mother Goose* march, a medley of nursery-rhyme tunes. From that time on, the story goes, a restless or inattentive audience might lead some bandsman to remark: "The Old Man's about ready to give 'em 'Mother Goose'!"[9]

Spontaneity and showmanship aside, Sousa's band possessed the skill to give a good account of classical works originally written for orchestra. Sousa liked to say that as well as entertaining audiences, he hoped to educate them too. The technical demands of classical selections also helped keep his musicians engaged. Wagner, whom Sousa once called "the Shakespeare of music," was a particular favorite. And the band also played Sousa's arrangements of Grieg's *Peer Gynt Suite*, Richard Strauss's *Don Juan* and *Death and Transfiguration*, and even Debussy's *Prelude a "L' après-midi d'un faun,"* not to mention older works like Bach's Toccata and Fugue in D minor.

Although Sousa made no attempt to hide his distaste for syncopated dance music (including ragtime) in its native setting, which he judged sleazy, he was willing to mix it into concerts. Audiences seemed to love it, and Sousa believed that his band's performances raised the music above its origins. The concept of "high" and "low" stood behind a hierarchy of musical values assumed by many musicians and critics of that day, including Sousa. In 1899, he likened a syncopated tune to a low-born woman made respectable by the band's attentions. "We play a common street melody with just as much care as if it were the best thing ever put on a program," Sousa wrote. "I have washed its face, put a clean dress on it, put a frill around its neck, pretty stockings. It is now an attractive thing, entirely different from the frowzly-headed thing of the gutter."[10]

Sousa's qualms about syncopated music provide background for a look at his best-known compositions. From the standpoint of musical form, a Sousa march, like a Strauss waltz, is a sharply drawn miniature, conventional in makeup but varied in detail. As a dance-based form, the march follows dance-music traits: a steady beat, regular phrase structure, and repeated

This cartoon from 1907 depicts Sousa's "characteristic poses" on the podium.

sections. But Sousa believed that he invested these traits with special artistic and ethical force. For example, the beat of a Sousa march was not just steady; it was "military." And in that idea lay the distinction that Sousa made between the march, where males walked a disciplined, "honorable" path, and the cakewalk or ragtime, where male and female bodies moved in more uninhibited ways. For Sousa, military purpose raised the march above other forms of popular music. Discussing *The Man Behind the Gun* (1899), inspired by the Spanish-American War, Sousa told a reporter: "A composition in march tempo must have the military instinct." Then he claimed that "few of the great composers have written successful marches" because "they lived in an atmosphere of peace," and "the roll of musketry had no meaning for them."[11] While this statement may be faulty history, it offers a revealing glimpse about what the march meant to Sousa.

Growing up in the nation's capital, Sousa was seven years old when the Civil War began and twelve when it ended. He also spent his teens and early twenties connected with the Marine Band, which his father served and he himself would soon conduct. Steeped in a military ethos, Sousa felt deeply the military cost of the freedom that Americans enjoyed. That knowledge proved an inspiration throughout his life as a composer, for his marches affirm the link between armed struggle and peacetime ease. Sousa's capturing of a martial tone in marches like *The Gladiator*, *The Thunderer*, and *The Gallant Seventh* summoned others to celebrate Amer-

ica's fighting spirit—not because war was virtuous but to show that democracy was grounded in American sovereignty, won and preserved through military effort. Patriotic sentiments grew in America as the United States came
to be recognized as a power among nations. And patriotism was Sousa's
great subject, the source from which his most characteristic and enduring
music flowed. For him, the most potent symbol of patriotism was the American flag. In fact, Sousa's best-known march *The Stars and Stripes Forever*,
glorifies the flag, and its words deliver a warning to potential enemies:

> Let despots remember the day
> When our fathers with mighty endeavor
> Proclaimed as they marched to the fray
> That by their might and by their right it waves forever.[12]

In all, Sousa composed 136 marches, three-quarters of which follow a
standard musical form that he adopted around 1880, though he did not invent it: (1) an introduction, most often four or eight measures long, and
preparatory rather than melodic; (2) a first strain, usually a sixteen-bar
melody, repeated; (3) a second strain, presenting another sixteen-bar
melody, also repeated; (4) a third strain, or "trio," in a new key (often the
subdominant) and with a new melody, often the most tuneful and longest of
the piece, repeated one or more times in alternation with a contrasting, usually nonmelodic "break" strain; and (5) sometimes a fourth strain, with another new melody. This form points up a crucial difference between Sousa's
marches and other dance music. By nature and function, dance music is
continuously repeatable; but Sousa wrote marches with the idea of making
the last strain the climatic one. Sousa's marches pack with eventfulness a
musical space that seldom exceeds three minutes. Three full-blown themes,
sometimes four, are heard. Rather than returning to the beginning ("da
capo"), the march moves toward a musical climax in a new key. Starting
simply and often softly, a typical Sousa trio increases in volume and complexity, blossoming into the sound of the full band. Throughout, Sousa
marches feature plenty of contrapuntal interplay between instruments.

The Sousa band and others of the era consisted of three instrumental
sections—trumpets, trombones and euphoniums, and clarinets—that might
carry a melody, with the rest (saxophones, French horns, tuba, and percussion) filling in the texture. In peak moments of a Sousa march, such as the
last strain's final appearance, the main tune might well be joined by a countermelody (a melody composed to accompany the main tune) or sometimes
two. The main tune might show up in any of the three melodic voices, or
perhaps some combination such as trumpets doubled by trombones at the
octave. That left the other sections free to present countermelody. The mu-

sical space, chopped into units of predictable length, brims with melody and counterpoint—a prime reason Sousa's marches are still relished today.

Catchy tunes are another key feature; some were written by Sousa himself, but more than a quarter of his marches quote melodies that were already well-known or composed for another purpose. The *Revival March* of 1876, for example, is built around the gospel hymn *Sweet By and By*; *Ancient and Honorable Artillery Company* (1924) features *Auld Lang Syne*; and *The Pride of Pittsburgh* (1901) quotes famous melodies by composers born in or around that city—Stephen Foster's *Come Where My Love Lies Dreaming* and Ethelbert Nevin's *Narcissus*. In several other marches, Sousa recycled melodies composed for his operettas—for example, the *El Capitan* march (1896), whose last strain borrows the melody that concludes *El Capitan* the operetta, written the previous year. By far Sousa's most successful stage work, *El Capitan* toured North America for four years and played another six months in England. So the *El Capitan* march tune won popularity in both vocal and instrumental versions. Moreover, as with other popular music of the day, Sousa and his publishers milked the marches for commercial gain by arranging them for an astonishing variety of combinations. Published in both band and orchestra arrangements, the *El Capitan* march was also available for piano (two, four, or six hands); banjo; guitar; guitar duet; mandolin; mandolin and piano; mandolin, piano and guitar; mandolin and guitar; two mandolins and piano; two mandolins and guitar; zither; and two zithers. Sousa obtained a separate copyright for each of these versions, most of them aimed at the vast market of amateur performers.

But while Sousa often borrowed from himself and others, he also drew from a reservoir of melodic inspiration that served him well in his marches. Indeed, as an active theatrical composer, he was uniquely endowed among march writers with melodic creativity. *Semper Fideles* (Always Faithful, 1888), dedicated to the U.S. Marine Corps and using its motto as a title, contains four memorable sixteen-bar melodies, all but the trio interconnected. The first and second strains, though their tunes differ in character, share a formal parallel: after twelve bars of driving duple rhythm, a four-bar "break" allows call-and-response dialogue between treble and bass instruments. The third strain, (trio), in F instead of C, borrows a melody Sousa had composed in 1886 for trumpets and drums. In the character of a bugle call with plenty of sustained notes and slow harmonic rhythm, it proves an excellent foil for countermelodies, one in the lower brass and the other in the upper woodwinds. Sousa follows this complex texture with a fourth strain whose melody, played *fortissimo* (very loud) and doubled at the octave, resembles the second strain closely enough to recall it. By channeling the energy of three independent melody lines into one, the fourth strain achieves louder volume, hence greater weight than the third. Thus, in *Semper Fideles* Sousa engineers a musical climax in part by referring back to elements from earlier strains.

The Washington Post (1889) and *Manhattan Beach* (1893), like *Semper Fideles*, are also four-strain marches, but the form is handled differently in each. *The Washington Post*, also in 6/8 time, was a great success with dancers. In fact, it was so well suited to the two-step, a fast ballroom dance introduced in the late 1880s, that in Europe the two-step was actually called the *Washington Post*.[13] *Manhattan Beach* (1893), a four-strain march in cut time (2/2), achieves a different kind of climax. The trio is quiet throughout, with a smooth, songlike melody accompanied by clarinets in quick, low-register arpeggios that suggest the undulation of waves on the surface of the sea. This delicately colored section is followed by a fourth strain in "patrol" form. Beginning softly, the music builds to a peak by the end of the sixteen-bar strain, then reverses the process on the repeat, as if a band were passing in review and marching off into the distance. After sketching a vivid aural image of the ocean, *Manhattan Beach* breaks with custom by fading into silence where maximum volume is expected.

In *The Stars and Stripes Forever* (1897), Sousa composed an American classic by inventing a memorable, songlike melody and then playing it off against instrumental interludes of a completely different character. This march's center of gravity lies so firmly in its trio that the first two strains seem, at least in retrospect, like an introduction. Cast in two halves in A-flat, the trio's melody fills thirty-two bars. It relies on a four-note motive that moves mostly stepwise and lends itself to circular melodic shapes. This melody (**abac**) traces its own climactic curve through four eight-bar sections. Not until the last of these sections do we hear an A-flat as the root, or main note, of a tonic triad. And at that point, having long avoided the tonic, Sousa finds two ways to emphasize it. First he sets A-flat at the top of an octave leap and sustains it as the melody's highest note. Then he introduces a new motive centered on the tonic and moving in quarter notes, bringing the tune to a resolute close in a rush of activity.

Sousa follows the trio with a break strain that is virtuosic for the lower brass, unusually active in rhythm and harmony, and without a hint of melody—intended, it seems, to wipe out the trio's lyric mood so that its return will sound fresh. The device works, partly on the strength of the new strain's disruptive, slashing character, and partly because the piccolo section adds a striking countermelody to the trio's repeat. After the break strain is heard again, the trio tune returns once more, this time with percussion in full cry and a low-register countermelody to balance the piccolos on top. *The Stars and Stripes Forever* goes out with the band's full artillery blazing: a

deft blend of lyric melody, historical reference (the piccolo sound recalls fifes), and military clamor.

While Sousa's achievements loom large, other bandleaders of the day also deserve mention. Some were star soloists who went on to form bands of their own, as did Herbert L. Clarke and Arthur Pryor from Sousa's ranks. David Wallis Reeves, cornetist and composer, led the American Band of Providence, Rhode Island, for more than three decades, training a group of amateur players to near-professional skill. As well as military and concert bands, professional groups included circus bands and even family bands (complete with wives and daughters) that toured on entertainment circuits; in amateur ranks, lodge bands, industrial bands, ethnic bands (German, Italian, African-American, even Native American), children's bands, and institutional bands (including prison groups) also flourished. (Around 1912 trumpeter and singer Louis Armstrong was learning to play the cornet in a reform-school band in New Orleans.) New Hampshire–born Helen May Butler, a violinist and cornetist, organized and led a professional Ladies' Military Band during the new century's early years. A tally of concert performances by Butler and her various groups between 1900 and 1913 yields 203 appearances in Boston, 110 in Buffalo, 126 in St. Louis, and 130 in Charleston. Presenting "music for the American people, by American composers, played by American girls," Butler and her musicians bucked stereotypes of the time by showing that women could endure the rigors of

The Sousa Band played in many settings, including this elegant one at Willow Grove, outside Philadelphia.

touring life and please enough paying customers to survive in the music business.[14]

Sousa's example had a particularly strong impact on the career of Alton Augustus Adams, born in 1889 in the Virgin Islands. Adams, who first heard Sousa's band on phonograph recordings and was thrilled by the sound, later recalled:

> Assiduously I would put into band and orchestral scores the immortal "Stars and Stripes Forever," "El Capitan," "Right Forward," "Semper Fideles," "Manhattan Beach," "King Cotton," and others so well known throughout the musical world, so as to clearly analyze and study their content—harmonic progressions, instrumental arrangements, and those original patterns of bass movements so characteristic of their unique style. For many months, each night until the wee hours of the morning, this was my musical menu. This experience was imperatively necessary because of my never having experienced the benefits of formal musical tutorship and guidance.[15]

At twenty-one, Adams organized the St. Thomas Juvenile Band, and seven years later the United States took over the Virgin Islands, recently purchased from Denmark. By that time (1917), Adams's band was so good that the U.S. navy appropriated it—the first black band and bandmaster in that branch of the military. After Adams's navy band toured the United States in 1924, offers of employment came his way, but Adams felt that his talents were needed more on the islands. Proposed for membership in the American Bandmaster's Association in 1928, he was denied admission. Bandleader and composer Edwin Franko Goldman wrote Adams some years later, urging that he reapply and explaining what had happened the first time:

> You will probably be surprised to hear from me but the fact that you were blackballed [voted against in a secret ballot] by the ABA at its annual meeting some years ago is still on my mind. President Frank Simon and I have just discussed this matter again and we feel that you should be a member of this organization. . . . Mr. Sousa and I were both for you the last time but it seems there were a few southern members who caused the blackballing.[16]

Adams's career and the example of Helen May Butler and her Ladies' Military Band serve as reminders of the barriers that until recently restricted musical collaboration in America to patterns ruled by fixed views of race and gender. In the half-century before World War I, many Americans came together to play in bands—some to make a living, but most in the name of fellowship, recreation, functional need, patriotism, or education. Bands were primarily social organizations, carried on by people of like mind and station. Therefore, bands followed society's standards of likemindedness, being mostly all-white, all-black, all-male, or all-female ensembles. Behind Goldman's letter lies what is now called a "professional" attitude, in which the *quality of the music making* outweighs all other factors. Independent of race, gender, or social status, a professional attitude takes musical ability as something that can be judged objectively and that ought to serve as the standard for musical opportunity. Those who hold a professional attitude tend to think of musical ability as the most important likemindedness of all. Although widespread today, and familiar in other branches of musical endeavor long before the 1930s, this belief was slow to take root in the world of the wind band.

Alton Augustus Adams's career also illustrates the impact of phonograph recordings, which, by rendering music repeatable and portable, exerted a broad effect on musical experience. Within a dozen years of Edison's invention of the phonograph in 1877, an industry had taken shape around the recording of music. And because American companies marketed recordings of Sousa and his bands, Adams, a youth on a remote Caribbean island, had access to a professional band's sound long before he heard any such group in person. In fact, Adams's place of birth and the segregation of opportunity in his day make it hard to imagine how else he could have learned what the Sousa band records taught him. Recordings, not teachers, were Adams's "democratic" carriers of knowledge, the springboard that allowed him to jump geographical and social barriers and eventually to challenge the band world's white hegemony. Yet while Adams and many others reaped the ben-

Published in 1891, this photograph shows the U.S. Marine Band recording in the Washington studio of the Columbia Phonograph Company.

efits of phonograph recordings, some musicians in turn-of-the-century America found them a mixed blessing at best—among them John Philip Sousa, who came to see the phonograph as a threat to the health of American music making.

SOUSA AND THE PHONOGRAPH

By around 1890, when recording began to be a factor in the music business, bands were important dispensers of popular music. And through the next two decades, as technology improved and the record business became a stronger economic and artistic force, bands kept their hold on public attention and grew alongside the industry. Sousa played a conflicted role in this partnership. As the leader of two famous bands, he took part in the making of records. Before mid-1892, Sousa conducted the U.S. Marine Band in more than two hundred recordings; and the Sousa band made more than four times that many between 1897 and the early 1920s. Yet Sousa himself conducted very few of his own band's recordings; he also denounced the phonograph publicly. As an artist-businessman, he faced a choice. Should he block the band from recording altogether because he questioned the phonograph's impact on musical life? Or should he use the medium to keep the band's name before the public, while also collecting profits from record sales? In choosing the second course, Sousa recognized the power of recordings to attract audiences to his concerts. (Indeed, until the 1960s, when popular performers began to win hugely profitable recording contracts, most of their income came from personal appearances, not record sales.) Sousa quelled his own doubts by turning the band's recording sessions over to other conductors, chiefly band members.

What were Sousa's qualms about recordings? For one thing, he disliked making them. Recording technique around 1890, when Sousa was first involved, was so primitive that little thought could be given to artistic playing. A photo of the Marine Band making cylinder recordings shows ten Graphophone machines arranged in front of the band. After the title of the work was announced, the band would then perform it in an arrangement that lasted less than two minutes; new wax cylinders were then placed on the machines, and the whole process was repeated. In this mechanical way, ten recordings of a composition could be made every few minutes.[17]

Sousa mistrusted a process that so openly placed music in the service of technology. He also deplored the record companies' refusal in those early days to pay composers for the use of their works. But more than that, Sousa considered phonograph recordings an assault on the ecology of musical life. Testifying at a congressional hearing in 1906, he claimed that the phonograph was starting to discourage many Americans from singing and playing themselves, a trend that could "ruin the artistic development of music in this country." He remembered growing up in Washington at a time when, "in front of every house in the summer evenings you would find young people together singing the songs of the day or the old songs." But now, he complained, "you hear these infernal machines going night and day." In Sousa's view, the change was bad for the art of music, which ought to develop "from the people." "If you do not make the people executants," he told the congressmen, "you make them depend on the machines."[18]

A generation later, Sousa could look back on a time of robust growth for amateur performance in America. Music teaching was widespread and accessible to many. A vast range of music and musical information was published and available. The instrument business, from pianos to winds and strings, was booming. Amateur choral societies existed in virtually every sizable city. Glee clubs, choruses, and banjo and mandolin clubs flourished on college campuses. The piano was the parlor instrument par excellence, and many could play it. And amateur bands flourished as expressions of a wide range of social values, including local pride. The growing appetite for music was being fed chiefly by amateur singers and players for their own enjoyment and edification. Whether or not he ever put it in these terms, Sousa apparently pictured musical life in America in the shape of a pyramid whose wide base and narrow top suggested proportions of amateur to professional musicians. What worried him about the phonograph was its encouragement of consumption without participation. For that, he feared, would erode the base of amateur performers whose love and understanding of music sustained the work of professional musicians, right up to the highest levels.

Sousa's principle that music develops "from the people" offers a window on how he perceived the musical life of his day. Yet "the people" were no monolithic bloc but a vast array of individuals whose own singing, playing, and musical taste were influenced not only by the traditions they inherited but by the professional performers they heard. It may have been true in 1898 that most American villagers had never heard an ensemble better than their own town's band. But by the time the United States entered World War I, that was much less likely. Tours by Sousa and other professional outfits, plus the growing circulation of phonograph recordings, brought the sound of polished playing to more and more American communities and listeners.

And bands were only part of the tide of professional music making that swept across the nation in the century's early years. Theaters were built in which local audiences could gather to watch performances and listen to music. Railroads now linked American communities large and small, creating a national market for consumer goods, and entrepreneurs explored ways of bringing musical entertainment to more customers. Already by the mid-1890s, 200,000 miles of railroad tracks connected some 5,000 theaters in 3,500 communities across the country. From the turn of the century, this transportation network was brought increasingly into the service of an entertainment industry centered in New York City. By the early 1900s, popular entertainment was well on its way to becoming modern "show business," which turned the amusement of audiences into a profitable, capitalistic enterprise. And the workings of this new entertainment industry depended on a new approach to creating and marketing popular song.

24 ☙

After the Ball

The Rise of Tin Pan Alley

ONE PARTICIPANT WHO LEFT a vivid account of older ways yielding to new in the entertainment business was song publisher Edward B. Marks. In 1934, drawing on forty years' experience, Marks brought out a memoir that describes fundamental changes around 1890, when New York publishers were transforming the popular-song trade, and 1900, when theatrical consolidation was making show business a national enterprise. Marks's dates provide the framework for a discussion of the world of musical commerce in which he and his colleagues worked, competed, and sometimes prospered.

New York City's magnetic pull in the field of entertainment during the nineteenth century's later years turned it into the capital of popular-song publishing in the United States. "Tin Pan Alley," the nickname given the publishing district that took shape in New York around 1890, is also an apt metaphor for an approach new to the trade: unelevated in tone, noisy with the sound of song pluggers vying to sell songs, and shameless in the pursuit of commercial advantage. Tin Pan Alley's economics, like its ethos, differed from that of older publishing firms. The flagship American music publisher of the nineteenth century, for example, was Oliver Ditson & Co. of Boston. Founded in the 1830s, Ditson's business grew spectacularly from the late 1850s on, and by 1890 the company had bought the catalogues of more than fifty other publishers and taken a hand in setting up new firms in Philadelphia, New York, Chicago, and Cincinnati. Ditson published many popular songs, but they made up only a fraction of the firm's catalogue, whose contents included piano pieces, choral music, instruction books for different instruments, song collections for school and church, chamber music, and piano-vocal scores of operas and oratorios. Ditson's store in Boston sold all these items and shipped them around the country to other retail outlets.[1] As the century's end approached, the company had grown into a colossus that

The T. B. Harms firm, whose 1891 Broadway location is pictured at right, became the leading publisher of stage music after the turn of the century.

took pride not only in financial strength but in service to the edifying art of music. Ditson would eventually collapse under the weight of its lofty goals and its own inventory.

In contrast, M. Witmark & Sons of New York City, founded in 1884, traveled light. Undistracted by thoughts of duty or edification, Witmark originated in a hunger for profit and a personal snub. As the story is told, in the mid-1880s the Primrose and West minstrel troupe hired a fifteen-year-old boy soprano named Julius Witmark. The youth struck a deal with New York publisher Willis Woodward that for a share of the proceeds, he would sing *Always Take Mother's Advice,* a song in Woodward's catalogue, as often as possible during the troupe's upcoming national tour. Witmark made good on his part of the bargain, and the song enjoyed strong sheet-music sales. But all he received from Woodward in the way of reward was $20 and a dismissive pat on the shoulder. Julius and his brothers retaliated by opening M. Witmark & Sons, using their father's name because they were all under legal age.[2]

Catching the flavor of Tin Pan Alley's commercial origins, this anecdote also illustrates how its location in New York City allowed songs to be promoted through a four-step process. First, a theatrical troupe is in New York recruiting personnel, looking for new material, and planning to tour. Second, a New York music publisher enlists a troupe member to plug one of his songs. Third, that song becomes a hit, thanks in part to the singer's efforts. And fourth, the publisher reaps the rewards from sales of the sheet music, for he has copies on hand wherever the troupe plays; and amateur performers buy copies for their own use. The differences between this approach to music publishing and that of an old-line firm like Ditson, located in Boston and involved with every kind of music, are clear. While not opposed to advertising, the Ditson company tended to let the natural workings of the marketplace decide the fate of individual numbers. The new Tin Pan Alley firms, however, published *only* popular songs, pouring their energy and money into promoting them.

Song plugging was a way of life for Tin Pan Alley's publishers. Before 1900, songs were plugged most effectively by blackface minstrels—long a mainstay of popular entertainment and still going strong at the century's end—and in two New York settings: variety houses and drinking establishments such as beer gardens, saloons, and dance halls. After 1900, the advent of musical comedy and vaudeville changed the balance, giving those forms of stage entertainment a bigger role in a popular song's economic success or failure.

Edward B. Marks began his memoir in the 1890s with a striking claim: "The best songs came from the gutter in those days."[3] And by the time he explained the workings of the trade, the reader knew what he meant. Marks saw the songwriters of early Tin Pan Alley as a seedy, dissolute breed, indifferently trained as musicians. Some were addicted to gambling, others to chasing women, and many to strong drink. Most were careless businessmen who, instead of retaining rights to their songs and collecting royalties, often sold them to a publisher for ready cash, which they then squandered. (Ten or fifteen dollars was a standard rate for a song.) Songwriters wrote "according to the market," Marks charged, and yet at the same time believed themselves superior to the public "to whom they pander."[4] Most seemed content to leave the selling of their wares to publishers, who had the capital and took care of business, and performers, who were loved by audiences and therefore courted by publishers.

Publishers were also a mixed lot. In pre–Tin Pan Alley years, Marks recalled, the leading figures had been old-school gentlemen. But to survive in the "particularly insane business" of the 1890s and later, it helped to be "more of a Bohemian." Some publishers came to the trade through songwriting, performing, or both. Marks himself—stage struck, he confessed, but untalented as an actor or singer—parlayed a modest gift for writing song lyrics into a position in the publishing business.[5] A salesman at heart, he also relished day-to-day life in the trade: the personal associations, rivalries, adventures, and risks that fueled a high-energy enterprise, where the possibilities of financial bonanza or ruin were always present.

Marks entered the song-publishing business in 1894. And for years thereafter, like his competitors, he spent evenings keeping the songs in his catalogue before the public in New York's nightspots. That meant visiting an average of "sixty joints a week" to arrange plugs, while Joe Stern, his partner in the firm of Joseph W. Stern & Co., dropped in at some forty more. On one typical evening round in 1897, Marks was accompanied by an assistant,

"Louis the Whistler," who carried printed "chorus slips, which we distributed among the tables, so that everybody could sing with the orchestra." Singing customers were the surest sign of a plug's success. "When there was a real singer in the joint," Marks explained, "we induced him to sing a solo chorus. Then Louis whistled a second chorus. Finally, we tried to get the crowd in on a third." Aided by the familiarity of verse-and-chorus form, the songs' simple vocabulary of word and tune, and liberal doses of alcohol for the musicians, Marks did what he could at each stop to ensure that "our classic was firmly planted in as many domes as were within hearing distance."[6]

The first stop on Marks's circuit this particular evening was the Atlantic Gardens, a music hall and beer garden run by a German family and featuring an orchestra of women.[7] The visit began on a sour note, for when Marks entered the hall, another publisher's song was being performed. Undaunted, Marks struck up a conversation with the orchestra leader, while Louis the Whistler went to work distributing copies of Stern & Co.'s *Elsie from Chelsea* while "accidentally" sweeping competing chorus slips to the floor. Fortified with two complimentary bottles of Bass Ale, house singer Jenny Lindsey then stood up and sang a spirited verse and chorus of *Elsie from Chelsea*. And the audience responded as Marks had hoped. When Lindsey reached the second chorus, "Louis picked it up and whistled," joined by "a fair number of the men in the crowd." *Elsie* had caught the customers' attention, and "it was a cinch," Marks now felt, "that some of the women would want it for their pianos tomorrow."[8]

Now it was on to the London, a variety theater on the Bowery between Canal and Houston Streets. Things went badly here. Every act Marks interviewed "had too many songs—and most of them our competitors'." So the pluggers beat a quick retreat, taking the elevated railway uptown to Blank's Winter Garden at Thirteenth Street and Third Avenue. There a dollop of whiskey for the bouncer bought Marks a performance of Stern & Co.'s *The Handicap March*. The pair then walked to Fourteenth Street and the 10:30 show at Tony Pastor's prestigious variety house, where Marks had previously arranged for *The Little Lost Child*—a new number for which he and Stern had high hopes—to be sung. Arriving a bit early, Marks sent his card to the dressing room of Lottie Gilson, who was starring there.

> "Ed," she said, when I was admitted to her room, "I thought you were going to call for me after the show last Friday and treat me to pigs' knuckles at Luchow's."
> I gasped. I apologized. I had clean forgotten it.
> "Wait, and see the show," said the deadly Miss Gilson.

Sitting in Pastor's audience after that exchange, Marks was not sure what to expect. It was true that Lottie Gilson had agreed to sing *The Little Lost*

Child, on whose cover she was pictured. But that was before Marks had failed to appear for their Friday night date. Gilson, "who could get that tear in her voice" and "usually had her audience bawling after the first chorus" of a sentimental number, dashed his hopes. As Marks squirmed in discomfort, she sang to the hushed, darkened house "the sob hit" of rival publisher T. B. Harms's catalogue: *She May Have Seen Better Days.*[9]

In need of a drink by this time, Marks and his sidekick fled across the street to Theiss's Alhambra, a concert saloon offering what Marks delicately called "feminine conversation." Concert saloons were New York's first nightclubs, offering a combination of the theater and the brothel in the atmosphere of the saloon.[10] The Alhambra's large orchestra, plentiful wine, and attractive female companions for male customers created a mood of romance that pulled in a lively out-of-town trade. Marks's memoir freely admits the song trade's reliance on lust and alcohol. And he made no attempt to hide the feeling of condescension he bore non–New Yorkers in general, though he welcomed their business. "It meant a lot to have our numbers carried out to the sticks in the subconsciousness of a tipsy country cousin," he mused, adding: "The train of association whereby 'Annie Rooney' eventually appeared on the piano in a small town banker's house would have shocked many a fine community."[11]

The evening's next stop was the Prospect Garden Music Hall: an attempt, Marks said, to import the English music hall to New York. As he and Louis entered, a comedian was just finishing a song called *Oysters*, which stood at "the limit of suggestiveness in those pre-Harlem days." "They're all very fine and large, / They're soft and fat and prime," sang the comedian, with gestures implying "that he meant women's busts." Marks was then approached by a tenor whose picture appeared on the cover of a new Stern-published song and told that the vocal arrangement of it was "no good." As an apparently sure plug slipped away, Marks felt that he was in the midst of "a night dedicated to disaster." But he had two more stops to make: the Haymarket, a concert saloon at Thirtieth Street and Sixth Avenue, and The Abbey, on Eighth Avenue between Twenty-Sixth and Twenty-Seventh—a friendly place in an Irish neighborhood. The latter took the sting out of some of the evening's disappointments. Maude Nugent, who had written *Sweet Rosie O'Grady*, a Marks and Stern number, was singing that night. Here Marks was joined by Stern, who was just finishing his own nightly rounds. As the evening drew to a close, the partners basked in "the satisfaction of hearing two or three dozen choruses of 'Rosie,' and assured by this that we had the makings of a tremendous hit, we went home aglow with optimism."[12]

As Marks and his competitors were scrambling to peddle their songs in Tin Pan Alley's marketplace, the structure of the larger amusement world

In the early 1900s, venues across the country, such as the Grand Theater in Buffalo, New York, offered variety entertainment for low prices.

was changing in ways that affected the popular-song trade. Aware that vast audiences could now be reached outside New York, theatrical producers began sending more of their shows on regional and national tours. In August of each year, local theater owners from around the country went to New York and competed to lure "direct from Broadway" companies and musical attractions to their towns. Each owner negotiated with several producers, hoping to set up long runs of shows in their region's largest city, plus "run-out" performances in smaller communities nearby. As the number of shows on the road increased, booking agents emerged as middlemen to coordinate their touring. In 1896, six of these agents joined together to form the Syndicate, a group that controlled most major theaters in New York and many outside. By 1906, the Syndicate boasted a network of some seven hundred theaters nationwide, and touring on its circuit was coming to be an orderly process, directed from New York.

The trend toward centralization meant that New York–based arbiters now had a larger say in deciding which shows traveled where, and when. And that apparently suited most theater owners well. But the new arrangement paid little heed to local custom or initiative. As well as scheduling, the Syndicate controlled the content of shows, even down to such details as the removal or interpolation of songs. As the contact between amateurs and

The powerful manager B. F. Keith opened the Gaiety, his first major vaudeville theater, in Boston in 1894.

professional stage performers increased across the country, the Syndicate was making the musical theater more profitable by standardizing it as an art form and a business.[13]

Consolidation also took place in variety entertainment, known after the turn of the century as vaudeville. Its roots lay in New York's music halls, concert saloons, beer gardens, and variety houses where Marks plugged his wares. And vaudeville also owed much to the city's ethnic mix, which grew more diverse as large numbers of immigrants arrived by boat from Europe. In the form that crystallized around 1900, vaudeville combined a wide range of performers—comedians, jugglers, acrobats, actors, animal trainers, singers, and instrumentalists, of every nationality—into an evening's entertainment at cheap prices. A standard vaudeville format called for nine acts, each running approximately fifteen minutes. Shows often began with a "dumb act" while latecomers straggled in and from there built to a climactic eighth act that featured the star. A particular group of performers might play a given theater for one night or as many as several weeks, depending on the community's size and the main star's drawing power.

As the Syndicate had done for musical theater, the Keith-Albee organization brought order to vaudeville when in 1906 it formed the United Booking Office of America, connecting thousands of performers and theater managers. In 1927, Keith-Albee combined with the Orpheum circuit, which played a similar role in the West. While large booking agencies like these controlled the money, they held no monopoly over the trade. One smaller circuit in the South, the Theater Owners Booking Association (TOBA), brought black talent to black theaters and audiences, a market that Keith-Albee and Orpheum never tried to serve. Vaudeville czars held power over performers who played their circuits, and the influence of big-time organizations was especially strong. Harpo Marx considered the head of the Keith-Albee empire "more powerful than the president of the United States."[14]

In what was fast becoming national show business, stage performers were considered the most effective boosters of sheet-music sales, and song publishers competed fiercely for their attention in New York City. Novelist Theodore Dreiser, whose brother, Paul Dresser, was a prominent songwriter and publisher, wrote a piece in 1900 describing the atmosphere in which publishers wooed star singers:

> In Twenty-seventh or Twenty-eighth Street, or anywhere along Broadway from Madison to Greeley Square, are the parlors of a score of publishers. . . . Rugs, divans, imitation palms make this publishing house more bower than office. Three or four pianos give to each chamber a parlor-like appearance. The walls are hung with the photos of celebrities, neatly framed. In the private music-rooms, rocking-chairs. A boy or two waits to bring *professional copies* at a word. A salaried pianist or two wait to run over pieces which the

singer may desire to hear. . . . And then those "peerless singers of popular ballads," as their programs announce them, men and women whose pictures you will see upon every song-sheet, their physiognomy underscored with their own "Yours Sincerely" in their own handwriting. Every day they are here, arriving and departing, carrying the latest songs to all parts of the land. . . . One such, raising his or her voice nightly in a melodic interpretation of a new ballad, may, if the music be sufficiently catchy, bring it so thoroughly to the public ear as to cause it to begin to sell. . . . In flocks and droves they come, whenever good fortune brings "the company" to New York or the end of the season causes them to return, to tell of their successes and pick new songs for the ensuing season. Also to collect certain pre-arranged bonuses.[15]

By the time Dreiser wrote these words, Tin Pan Alley publishers knew well the riches that a popular song could produce.

In 1892, banjo player/songwriter Charles K. Harris, living in Milwaukee, wrote a narrative ballad that became the hit of the decade. Harris recalled later that the song took shape from an idea that had popped into his mind: "Many a heart is aching after the ball." With that line as a starting point, he fashioned a story in three long verses (sixty-four bars), each followed by a thirty-two-bar chorus. Then, since his own grasp of musical notation was shaky, he solicited the help of a local arranger to provide a score and a piano accompaniment. Disenchanted by earlier experience with New York publishers, whose royalty payments he had found too small, Harris decided to publish the song himself. His strategy for plugging *After the Ball* proved excellent. A road company was playing a Broadway show in Milwaukee, and Harris arranged a meeting with the cast's leading baritone. The singer agreed to sing the new song in the show, and his first performance drew a five-minute standing ovation, with six encores of the chorus. After Harris promised the singer $500 and a share of the income from sales, from then on his song was sung in every performance of the show.

More than any American popular song before it, *After the Ball* triggered an economic bonanza. Orders for the song began to pour in as the road company moved toward New York. Oliver Ditson ordered 75,000 copies, and John Philip Sousa programmed an arrangement of the song for his band at the Chicago World's Fair (1893). Before long, Harris was earning $25,000 a month from sales, and on the strength of his success decided to open a popular-song publishing business in New York, where he moved permanently in 1903.[16] While New York was not the only place where popular songs were being written, its marketing power held the key to big-time success.

After the Ball tells of a couple who bring an untested romance into the public arena, with disastrous results. An old man recalls the evening "long years ago" that doomed him to a life of loneliness. "Bright lights were flash-

Once Charles K. Harris's *After the Ball* (1892) became a hit, Harris brought out an edition with an illustrated cover suggesting the perils of romance on public display.

ing in the grand ballroom," as he and his sweetheart danced to an orchestra's "sweet tunes." When she grew thirsty, he went to get her a drink. Returning with a glass of water, he found her kissing a stranger. And in the shock of that moment, he dropped the glass, which shattered irreparably. So did his heart. Only years later did he learn that the stranger, rather than a rival, was his sweetheart's brother—a fact she had tried to explain but that he, in that instant of imagined humiliation, had refused to hear.

The cover of *After the Ball* pictures a dance floor filled with men and women dressed in formal finery. Some couples whirl vigorously, others are locked in close embraces, while those on the edge of the dance floor seem occupied with gossip and flirtation. The picture suggests the display of personal charms in a competitive public arena. Such outwardness separates *After the Ball* from earlier songs of courtship and love. Moreover, it is a waltz, and a century ago the waltz, a dance that called for partners to embrace, could carry lustful overtones. It is true that many waltz songs of the day—*Take Me Out to the Ball Game*, for example—struck a mood of innocent fun; but this story depicts a realm where the erotic overtones of courtship are made public. Privacy, permanence, and moral purpose yield to appearance and social flash, at the cost of risk for the people involved. Harris's song dramatizes that risk.

Although its melodramatic pretext may now seem flimsy, *After the Ball* struck a responsive chord in its time. Perhaps audience members and amateur performers found appeal in the story or the proverb-like moral delivered by the chorus:

> After the ball is over, after the break of morn—
> After the dancers' leaving; after the stars are gone;
> Many a heart is aching, if you could read them all;
> Many the hopes that have vanished after the ball.

But it is the music that brings emotion to a tale that might otherwise be taken as a cautionary sermonette. The melody supplies a continuity and lilt that embody the ball's public face: the mask behind which personal tragedies can unfold. While the serene, arching, musical profile maintains the illusion of calm control, the words portray feelings as fragile as the glass dropped by the song's disappointed lover.

The text declamation of Harris's music artfully separates the verses' exterior narrative from the chorus's interior reflection. The long melody of the verse is held together by a four-bar rhythmic cell that goes on through its entire sixty-four bars: ♩. ♩ ♩ | ♩.♩ . or ♩♩. ♪♩ ♩| ♩. ♩ . The chorus shifts to a more concentrated, catchy tune ($\mathbf{aa^1a^2b}$) based on a new four-bar rhythmic motive whose arrival is a welcome contrast. Until its last phrase, the chorus dwells on this figure as single-mindedly as does the verse on its rhythmic cell. But then Harris drops the chorus figure and, returning to that of the verse, brings the song's two sections together in a satisfying conclusion on the title line.

As the opera and minstrel stage had done in an earlier day, musical comedy, vaudeville, and variety now provided the sheet-music business's main

Af - ter the ball is o - - ver, af - ter the break of morn,_____ Af - ter the dan - cers' leav - ing; af - ter the stars are gone;_____ Ma - ny a heart is ach - ing, if you could read them all;_____ Ma - ny the hopes that have van - ished af - - - ter the ball._____

marketing arm. But for all the changes in songwriting that took place—new subjects, fresh cover designs, more stars' endorsements, a growing emphasis on female glamour—Tin Pan Alley's ultimate goal remained the same as that of publishers and songwriters in the day of Stephen Foster and George F. Root: to sell sheet music to home performers in quantities as large as possible.

From that perspective, it seems clear that the 1890s began a time of discovery for home performers that blossomed after the turn of the century. Traveling theater and variety troupes, like minstrel companies and bands, multiplied amateurs' contact with professionals, revealing new customs and ways of approaching songs. Musical amateurs' ideas of tempo, voice production, pronunciation, rhythmic emphasis, and general overall mood were surely influenced by hearing professional performers onstage. And by using stage singers not only to plug songs but also to endorse them on sheet-music covers, the trade boosted them as star vocalists. *When You Were Sweet Sixteen*, by James Thornton (1898), pictures his wife Bonnie and singer/publisher Julius P. Witmark, assuring the public that both had sung the song "with success." *Meet Me in St. Louis, Louis* (1904), by Andrew B. Sterling and Kerry Mills, lists a whole lineup of show-business notables including comedian and singer Gus Williams, who is pictured. Songs linked with popular musical shows note that connection, as, for example, in *Under the Bamboo Tree* (1902), by black songwriting team Bob Cole and the Johnson brothers, J. Rosamond and James Weldon. The cover claims this love song about two black characters in Africa as "a successful interpolation" by white singer Marie Cahill, (pictured) in *Sally in Our Alley*. Finally, the entire cover of *Somebody's Sweetheart I Want to Be*, by Cobb and Edwards (1905), is given over to a likeness of Lillian Russell, the most glamorous female star of the time, with a comment connecting this "Peerless Prima-Donna" with the song.

The names and pictures on these covers were clearly intended as marketing icons. But they also reflect the many different song types that were being performed on American stages around the turn of the century: airs from opera and operetta, Victorian parlor songs, Tin Pan Alley numbers of every description, songs in foreign languages, ragtime and "coon" songs, religious songs, spirituals, and minstrel songs. Each carried its own style of singing. Moreover, each performer had his or her own techniques and mannerisms, and many stars owed their fame to a personal way of approaching songs. As in earlier days, popular songs were performers' music that offered outlines to be filled in according to each performer's personality and skill.

Below is a chronological list of sixteen popular songs that can be seen as a cross-section of what was most popular during the years 1892–1905. Each won great commercial success, selling a million or more copies of sheet music in the years following its publication, and most have remained familiar into the latter twentieth century. All are in major keys and share a familiar musical form: a brief piano introduction, followed by a verse and a chorus. All but three are waltzes, all but two were published in New York, and all but one (*Daisy Bell*, by an English songwriter) are American in origin:

The Bowery (1892)	Charles H. Hoyt and Percy Gaunt
After the Ball (1892)	Charles K. Harris
Daisy Bell (1892)	Harry Dacre
The Sidewalks of New York (1894)	Charles B. Lawlor and James W. Blake
The Band Played On (1895)	John E. Palmer and Charles B. Ward
Sweet Rosie O'Grady (1896)	Maude Nugent
When You Were Sweet Sixteen (1898)	James Thornton
My Wild Irish Rose (1899)	Chauncey Olcott
You Tell Me Your Dream (1899)	Seymour Rice and Albert H. Brown
A Bird in a Gilded Cage (1900)	Arthur J. Lamb and Harry Von Tilzer
In the Good Old Summer Time (1902)	Ren Shields and George Evans
Sweet Adeline (1903)	Richard H. Gerard and Harry Armstrong
Meet Me in St. Louis, Louis (1904)	Andrew B. Sterling and Kerry Mills
My Gal Sal (1905)	Paul Dresser
Wait 'till the Sun Shines, Nellie (1905)	Andrew B. Sterling and Harry Von Tilzer
In the Shade of the Old Apple Tree (1905)	Harry H. Williams and Egbert Van Alstyne[17]

Echoes from this generation of songs may still be heard in America. "Sweet sixteen" remains a common phrase; lines like "a bicycle built for two" (from

Daisy Bell) and "East side, west side, all around the town" (from *The Side-walks of New York*) are also familiar; *And the Band Played On* was recently used as the title of a memoir about the discovery of AIDS in the United States; and *Sweet Adeline* is both the anthem of male barbershop-quartet singing and the name borne by its female branch (as in "Barbershoppers" and "Sweet Adelines"). Many Americans can still sing, whistle, or quote at least the title lines of some or all of these songs. At the same time, the songs carry the antique aura of a bygone age. The image of a woman as *A Bird in a Gilded Cage* (because "her beauty was sold for an old man's gold") goes be-yond the bounds of acceptable melodrama a century later. And some slang has lost its currency, as has "tootsie wootsie" for "sweetheart" in both *Meet Me in St. Louis, Louis* and *In the Good Old Summer Time*.

The songs on the list explore a wider range of moods than the era's popu-lar nickname, the Gay Nineties, might imply. *After the Ball*'s cautionary element is echoed more lightheartedly in *The Bowery*, which warns of the dangers lurking in a notorious New York district where "they say such things, and they do strange things." This song, *The Sidewalks of New York*, and *Meet Me in St. Louis, Louis* (which refers to the international fair of 1904) are the only numbers that are geographically located. But three oth-ers, like *Sidewalks*, also reveal glimpses of life in Irish neighborhoods similar to New York's: *The Band Played On, Sweet Rosie O'Grady*, and *My Wild Irish Rose*. Edward Marks called the years between the Civil War and the early 1890s "the heyday of the Irish-American in the theater," and a time when conventions of Irish ethnicity established themselves in song.[18] All four Irish songs are happy, or at least optimistic. High spirits also pervade *Daisy Bell, In the Good Old Summer Time*, and *Wait till the Sun Shines, Nellie*, with only the last clouded by a hint of difficulty. (Nellie, the girlfriend of Joe, is worried because she's bought a new gown to wear to a picnic, which is threatened by rain. Joe reassures her with the song's title line.)

The darker side of romance is visited in five songs besides *After the Ball*, all dealing with the separation of sweethearts. *When You Were Sweet Sixteen* and *Sweet Adeline* tell of lovers parted by some unnamed cause; the singer hopes for reunion and a return to earlier happiness. But in three other songs, reunion is impossible. In *You Tell Me Your Dream*, a widower reflects on a happier time when he and his now-departed wife were children—kin-dred spirits who shared dreams and fancies. The nostalgic *In the Shade of the Old Apple Tree* imagines a tree that is both trysting place and gravesite, harking back to the days of Henry Russell and his songs about old armchairs and mighty oaks. Two sweethearts fell in love under that tree, and when she died in his absence (he was in "the city"), that is where she was buried.

The least orthodox parted-lovers song is Dresser's *My Gal Sal*, in which death has cut short an unusual friendship. As described by "Jim," who sings

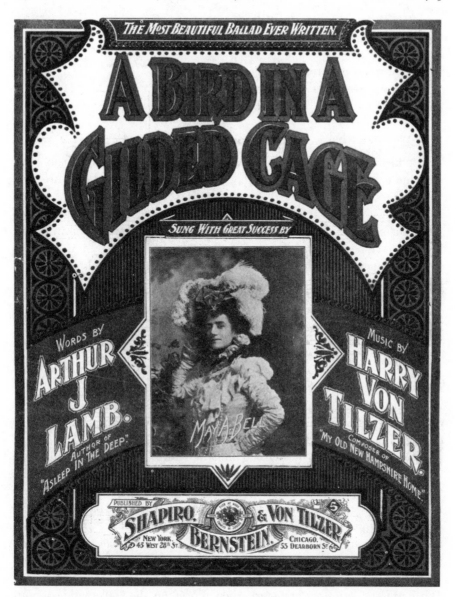

After photographic images became cheap enough to use, pictures of professional singers such as May Bell were used to plug sheet-music editions of songs such as this well-known hit.

this song, Sal was a person of mature years and plenty of experience. The chorus sketches her character:

> They called her frivolous Sal,
> A peculiar sort of a gal,

With a heart that was mellow,
An all 'round good fellow,
Was my old pal;
Your troubles, sorrows, and care,
She was always willing to share,
A wild sort of devil,
But dead on the level,
Was my gal Sal.

The kind of woman a man would describe in the language of male comradeship is rare in Tin Pan Alley song. But then, *My Gal Sal* overturns the
romantic conventions that ruled the day's songs about women. While
mourning the loss of "the best pal I ever had," the verse also mentions Sal's
"face not so handsome," separating her from the ranks of beautiful song
heroines. We never learn why some call her frivolous, or why Jim hails her
as wild. Singers and listeners are free to imagine her misdeeds, though excessive drinking and extramarital sex are implied—according to Tin Pan
Alley's code of social conduct, these are signs of depraved character in a
woman. Yet by calling "old pal" Sal "A wild sort of devil, / But dead on the
level," this song treats her behavior as if it were that of a man, who might
not be condemned for such appetites.

Gender reversal or not, the earthiness of *My Gal Sal*, published in 1905,
might have been impossible in a Tin Pan Alley song even a decade earlier. It
was not that songs had previously ignored the possibility of sex outside marriage. Rather, songs touching the subject treated their female characters as
irretrievably stained and dishonored. Between the Civil War and 1890, Edward Marks observed, "sniffly songs for the strayed sister, whom her virtuous co-females delighted to pity," were quite popular, not because they were
taken to heart, but because they appealed to prurient interests. In these
numbers "dishonor was always presented as the equivalent of death, which
usually accompanied it in some form about the fifth verse."[19] No songs on
the list of sixteen fit this category. But *A Bird in a Gilded Cage* is a close relative. Its female subject dishonors the institution of matrimony by marrying
"for wealth, not for love." Moreover, in the second and last verse, she dies.
The narrator pictures a cemetery, then muses on the "tall marble monu-
ment" marking the unfortunate woman's grave:

And I thought she is happier here at rest,
Than to have people say when seen:
[Chorus:] She's only a bird in a gilded cage,
A beautiful sight to see . . .

The contrast between *My Gal Sal* and *A Bird in a Gilded Cage* points to
the gap between the lives of those who lived and worked on Tin Pan Alley

and the moral outlook of most of the songs they put before the public. Marks's memoir touches often on this split. He notes, for example, that the "particularly innocent" songs of "the late seventies and eighties" rose "from the flamboyant rough-and-tumble of the Bowery," their character determined not by origins but final destination: the home piano. New York in the 1890s, he went on to say, "had curiously mixed standards of propriety. Gambling houses and houses of prostitution stood openly row on row; yet public entertainers were held within far narrower bounds than today."[20]

If Dresser's *My Gal Sal* distanced itself from the straitlaced moral code of earlier songs (though not from their old-fashioned musical style), its way may have been paved during the 1890s by songs from another ethnic group that overturned some of the trade's inhibitions. The group was African American: a new generation who brought fresh energy and subject matter to the music of Tin Pan Alley. In the years after Emancipation, blacks had begun to find places on the minstrel stage. As the century drew to a close, minstrelsy was featuring black troupes as well as white, not to mention African-American stars who blacked themselves up in burnt-cork masks. The minstrel tradition put the crop of young black performers and songwriters who appeared on the New York scene in the 1890s—Will Marion Cook, Ernest Hogan, Bert Williams and George Walker, Bob Cole and the Johnson brothers (James Weldon and J. Rosamond) among them—in a bind, being too rigid to accommodate their full range of talents yet with black character types too widely accepted for a black entertainer to ignore. Moreover, during the 1880s, a new kind of black character had emerged that made some older stereotypes seem almost benign: the "coon," a shiftless black male who could also be dangerous.

The lyrics of "coon" songs feature references to watermelon, chicken, ham, alcohol, gambling, and other demeaning stereotypes of African-American life.[21] Having caught on with audiences, coon songs were part of the legacy these black artists inherited when they entered show business. The Gay Nineties were also a time when black Americans felt increasingly under political siege, with racial segregation established as law in the South and lynching on the increase. As James Weldon Johnson saw it, "the status of the Negro as a citizen had been steadily declining for twenty-five years; and at the opening of the twentieth century his civil state was, in some respects, worse than at the close of the Civil War." Johnson found morale among black Americans low, for "the movement that Frederick Douglass had so valiantly carried forward had all but subsided."[22]

Any African American who worked in show business was faced with the conflict between pleasing an audience and knowing that many standard crowd-pleasing devices reinforced the racial divide. Black performers brought to their stagecraft an empathy and understanding of African-

The cover of this ragtime song shows that in 1899, when it was published, this new syncopated genre was associated with black characters.

American culture as a whole, yet the appeal of stage stereotypes—at least to white audiences—lay partly in their open ridicule of black people's capacities and character. Entertainers dealt differently with the conflict. According to Marks, "even men like Williams and Walker were outwardly resigned to all sorts of discrimination. They would sing 'coon,' they would joke about 'niggers,' they accepted their success with wide-mouthed grins as the gift of the gods." But the Johnson brothers were different: "emphatically new Negro," as Marks perceived it.

> Their father was a minister—and they combined a clerical dignity, university culture, and an enormous amount of talent. . . . Rosamond Johnson, benevolent, mellow-voiced, industrious, and his brother, who was to become the national leader of his race . . . wrote songs sometimes romantic, sometimes whimsical, but they eschewed the squalor and the squabbles, the razors, wenches, and chickens. . . . The word "coon" they banished from their rhyming dictionary, despite its tempting affinity with moon. . . . "We wanted to clean up the caricature," says Rosamond Johnson.[23]

Together with racist conventions and a grim political outlook, however, the new generation of entertainers also inherited the cakewalk, a dance—or perhaps more precisely, a style of moving onstage—of singular, unforgettable vigor. Rooted in African tradition, the cakewalk originated in a contest held during slavery times in which couples competed to show the fanciest strutting, and the winners received a cake or some other prize. Long parodied in minstrel shows, the cakewalk was now being performed to music with an electrifying, driving rhythm that made syncopation the norm rather than the exception. During the 1890s, the distinctive musical style that accompanied cakewalking earned the label of "ragtime." And ragtime proved widely appealing, a dominant presence in turn-of-the-century popular music and so influential that it was thought by many to embody the day's progressive sensibility. By the century's last years, for example, white songwriters were using rag-style syncopation in songs of their own, such as Theodore A. Metz's *A Hot Time in the Old Town* (1896), Kerry Mills's *At a Georgia Camp Meeting* (1897), and Howard and Emerson's *Hello! Ma Baby* (1899). On the list of sixteen, the number most influenced by ragtime is *Wait 'till the Sun Shines, Nellie* (1905), whose verse relies on a rag-derived syncopated motive. Composer Harry Von Tilzer's use of it is formulaic, restricting offbeat accents to the measures' first two beats. The rhythm lends a pleasing, slightly tentative quality to the verse, underscoring Nellie's fretfulness, which is shouldered aside by the chorus's confident arrival in striding, foursquare march time.

By no means did Tin Pan Alley encompass ragtime, nor did the style originate there. Yet the publication of ragtime songs, written in standard verse-and-chorus form, shows that white Americans as well as black bought them in sheet-music versions. Edward Marks comments on the racial prejudice in early Tin Pan Alley: The "older, more dignified publishing houses" did not welcome black songwriters, he reports. In contrast, firms like M. Witmark & Sons and Joseph W. Stern & Co. won success in the marketplace by publishing coon songs and ragtime numbers, whether of black or white authorship. Stern "bought so much stuff from colored writers in those days," says Marks, that "sometimes we wondered whether we were running a publishing house or a vaudeville theater."[24]

Besides Williams and Walker and the Johnson brothers, another black showman who won Marks's respect was Ernest Hogan: "a tremendous performer—perhaps the best colored comedian next to Bert Williams." Hogan's most famous song, *All Coons Look Alike to Me*, published by the Witmark firm, is both demeaning to its black characters and unquenchable in musical liveliness. The subject is a courtship that, by saying nothing about love on either side, makes both parties seem unsympathetic. In the verse, the male protagonist tells ruefully how Lucy Janey Stubbles has dumped him for a "coon barber from Virginia." The experience leaves him feeling "confused" and "abused." But it is hard to work up empathy for a man who would choose such an unashamed materialist for his "honey gal." Her sneering dismissal in the chorus mocks the very idea of love, except perhaps as a ploy to corral a partner for display in public and sex in private.

The cover of this song shows a slim, pert Ms. Stubbles appraising several black men who, apart from their grotesquely distended lips, look entirely different from each other. It is clear from this picture that she is not literally saying she cannot tell her suitors apart. Rather, the difference that really matters—a willingness to spend money according to *her* wishes—cannot be seen by the naked eye. In an era when songs tended to idealize, sometimes even spiritualize, romance, an outlook like this, no matter how thickly layered with irony, allowed sheet-music buyers to glimpse a realm of male-female relations beyond the limits that Tin Pan Alley had explored.

The chorus made this song famous, and not as a song about courtship. For Hogan coined a slogan in the title line that, detached from the song, could be turned into a racial slur, dismissing a whole people in one jeering epithet. Most accounts of Hogan's life note his regret at having fueled the fires of prejudice with this song, though he is supposed to have reminded critics that "the coon is a very smart animal."[25] Set to a strong, memorable tune, however, and promoted by Tin Pan Alley's effective marketing, the title line spread across the United States and abroad. Separated from the words, the tune was durable enough to stand up to instrumental performance. In January 1900, for example, New York's Tammany Hall played host to ragtime pianists from across the country, gathered for the Ragtime Championship of the World Competition. The three pianists who reached the fi-

The piano accompaniment to the final "choice" chorus of Ernest Hogan's *All Coons Look Alike To Me* (1896) is a fully realized rag, in contrast to earlier choruses, where the piano plays only chords in quarter-note rhythm.

nals were required to demonstrate their skill by "ragging" *All Coons Look Alike to Me* for two minutes in front of the judges.[26]

Its title aside, Hogan's music makes an especially strong impact in the second, or "choice," chorus printed in the sheet music, where the accompaniment approaches the style that would soon emerge in piano ragtime. But more than that, its vitality and strut make an independent impact that, in the end, seems to outweigh the force of the racist words. Tapping into a vein of high-spirited energy, whatever the emotional cost, the music resists self-pity and the notion that even rampant racial prejudice and political oppression could defeat the spirit of people capable of inventing music this joyful, appealing, and complex. As the new century began, white Americans were finding themselves beholden to blacks for music that seemed, more than any other, to catch the modern spirit.

PART THREE

The Twentieth Century

25

To Stretch Our Ears

The Music of Charles Ives

BY AROUND 1900, AMERICANS had begun seriously to assess the history and development of the nation's musical life.[1] And their writings, viewed as a whole, recognize a truth that has informed most studies of American music history ever since: musically speaking, the United States has been both an independent democracy *and* a colony—an extension of Europe. Indeed, the colonial impulse lies behind the classical sphere, which involves both the performance of European masterworks and the creation of new American composers' music. At the same time, the democratic impulse, stemming from the public's appetite for functional music (music for worship, instruction, recreational singing and playing, and entertainment) *and* from musicians' pragmatic need to make a living, gave rise to a booming, varied popular sphere devoted to performers' music. A third sphere existed as well, in which music circulated orally rather than in writing. Here, in traditional, or folk, music making, embedded in social custom and ritual, the foreign provenance of the classical sphere and the functional emphasis of the popular were often combined.

That a qualitative distinction separated different kinds of music from each other was recognized as far back as the eighteenth century in the works of Alexander Reinagle (see Chapter 12). And by the latter 1800s, most historians and commentators on music recognized the existence of classical, popular, and folk music as a hierarchy, with classical music on top, popular on the bottom, and folk somewhere in between. Historians writing in those years tended to view the United States as too young a nation to have won high standing in the art of music, which meant music in the classical sphere. Taking Europe as the standard, they pointed out that only since the

Civil War had Americans begun to muster the resources and the will to build a proper foundation: a concert life in the Old World mode, with such masters as Beethoven and Wagner at its center. That foundation had been laid in some cities. And a few home-grown composers, including George Chadwick, Horatio Parker, Amy Beach, and especially Edward MacDowell, were writing works that seemed candidates for the concert repertory. When concert halls and opera houses in the Western world began programming American works alongside European, *then*, the historians believed, the United States would have earned full membership in the family of Western musical nations. In the meantime, promise outweighed fulfillment.

As some writers of the time saw it, American composers were also hand-icapped by the lack of a traditional base in folk music. American Indian music was distinctive, to be sure, and so were "Negro" slave songs. But neither could represent the whole United States, as did the unwritten songs and dances of many European countries. From this point of view, the musical life of Old World nations, especially Germany, seemed an organic whole, like a healthy tree or plant, rooted in common people's song and bearing fruit in classical works for the concert hall and opera house. American musical life seemed fragmented, even weed-like, by comparison. There was no doubt that amateur performance was flourishing, but it was taking place in the popular sphere, for recreation and entertainment, and was seemingly led by commercial interests. Concerned chiefly with music as an edifying art, turn-of-the-century historians found little artistic value in music making driven by the profit motive.

These writers concentrated on the classical and the traditional spheres, which defined themselves historically, rather than the popular, with its ready embrace of novelty and its dedication to accessibility and economic success. Indeed, as a rising standard of living made avid consumers of more and more Americans, some commentators denounced commercialism as the curse of the age and a corrupting influence. From their point of view, accessibility was simply a strategy for commercial advancement. Yet the classical sphere's pursuit of transcedence also hinged on economic support. And since the marketplace could not provide it, money had to be found else-where, whether in the form of patronage or through the establishment of professions that left room for the cultivation of classical music. American musicians in the classical sphere have generally avoided talking about money in connection with what they do, as such discussions risk bringing price tags into a realm where the idea of pricelessness is revered. A strong note of regret stands behind the words of composer Roger Sessions, who wrote in 1948 that no fact about music in America was "more obvious, more pertinent, or more all-embracing in its implications than the fact that music here is in all its public aspects a business."[2]

Around 1900, then, linking artistic importance to idealistic aspiration, historians judged popular music insignificant, despite the vast amount of music making it inspired. Today things look different. With several centuries of American musical activity now chronicled, it is clear that the classical and the traditional spheres have existed on the periphery of the commercially driven, audience-oriented popular sphere, centered on performers' music. Commanding opportunity, financial capital, and cultural power, music in the democratic popular sphere has played a key role—indeed a decisive one—in shaping musical life in the United States. Even before 1800, in the marketplace that crystallized within the popular sphere, musicians and customers with varying needs and interests began coming together to shape the professions of music—performer, teacher, composer, distributor, manufacturer, and writer—and to create what is now recognized as "American music."

As the twentieth century began, the classical sphere enjoyed high prestige in America but not much economic security. Nevertheless, its champions had brought their enterprise to a promising state. The labors of conductor Theodore Thomas and others had helped convince patrons that, as nineteenth-century Boston critic John Sullivan Dwight had preached, a great composer such as Beethoven was indeed the musical equivalent of a great dramatist such as Shakespeare. Belief in the music's universality was the cornerstone on which the classical sphere built its edifice. So important to humankind was the experience classical music offered, it was thought that citizens should not be denied the chance to hear it performed, even though the performances could not pay for themselves.

With subsidies won by appeals to civic pride and the ideal of transcendence, symphony orchestras were formed in major American cities. New York's Carnegie Hall, designed for classical performances, was built in 1891, Boston's Symphony Hall in 1900, and Chicago's Orchestra Hall in 1904. In New York, resident companies performed whole seasons of grand opera, and the Metropolitan Opera Company also toured other cities. Traveling virtuosi—singers, pianists, and violinists—brought their art to communities large and small. Performers who specialized in European classical music were among the day's leading celebrities. (Italian tenor Enrico Caruso, widely known to Americans through his recordings and live performances, could earn a handsome sum for appearing in a *silent* film.) Metropolitan daily newspapers employed well-informed critics like Henry E. Krehbiel, W. J. Henderson, and Philip Hale to discuss such serious musical issues as the merits of a new symphony by Mahler or an opera by Puccini; the significance of Wagner's works for American listeners; the place of American composers and performers in American musical life; the advent of musical modernists, such as Debussy and Richard Strauss, and the meaning of their work for the future of the art. Whatever it may suggest about the size and makeup of the listening audience, the sophisticated level of musical discussion in newspapers shows the respect in which turn-of-the-century Americans held classical music.

In an age when almost all musical performances were heard live, the charisma of performers added to the aura of transcendence that surrounded the concert hall and opera house. Behind these performances, audiences knew, lay a long apprenticeship, a fact that reflects the key role of teaching. Only musicians who had mastered their medium's technique—in tone quality, range, intonation, and agility—could present such music convincingly to the public. And performers were expected to convey a work's spiritual essence: the truth behind the notes. Artful performance of music in the classical sphere was recognized as a high calling.

Through much of the nineteenth century, Americans had reason to believe that the tools needed for such performances could be gained only in Europe. Those who possessed them, after all, were either Europeans (the soprano Jenny Lind, the violinist Ole Bull, the pianists Sigismond Thalberg and Anton Rubinstein, all of whom toured the United States successfully) or Americans who had studied there (the composer-pianist Louis Moreau Gottschalk). But toward the end of the century, a new development undermined that belief: the performance of classical music began to be taught seriously in the United States. Conservatories of music, founded chiefly to teach beginners, added more European-trained musicians to their staffs. Other skilled teachers set up private studios. And the growing ranks of amateur performers included singers and players of classical as well as popular pieces. Musical transcendence could be pursued in the home parlor as well as the concert hall.

In his study of American democracy, Alexis de Tocqueville wrote in the 1840s that rather than being "indifferent to science, literature, and the arts," as some Europeans had charged, Americans cultivated them "in their own fashion" and brought "their own peculiar qualities and defects to the task."[3] The way teaching functioned in the classical sphere helps to illustrate Tocqueville's point. For since the 1700s, one thing Americans have wanted dearly from musicians has been instruction in singing and playing. Teaching has been the American musician's bread and butter, and by 1900 it allowed many performers and composers in the classical sphere to pursue the musical passions closest to their hearts.

Colleges, universities, and conservatories provided teaching posts for many of the nation's leading composers of the day: Paine at Harvard, Chadwick at the New England Conservatory, Parker at Yale, and MacDowell at Columbia, all appointed between 1875 and 1896. As professors, they still composed, as they were expected to do, with such works as Chadwick's lyric drama *Judith* (premiered 1901), MacDowell's *New England Idylls* for piano (1902), and Parker's *Mona* (1910; premiered at the Metropolitan Opera, 1912) among the results. Yet it was not composing that earned these musicians a living. They were paid to be educators who organized curricula, taught harmony, counterpoint, orchestration, composition, and the history of music, and graded students' work. When they joined the teaching profession, they struck a bargain in which they traded freedom for economic security and took on pedagogical tasks they may not have relished; MacDowell, for one, found the demands of teaching burdensome. They and their generation set a precedent that many later musicians have followed. The United States can boast neither a long tradition of aristocratic patronage nor a horde of citizens with an appetite for classical music, European or American. But Americans *have* believed deeply in both the practical and the edifying power of education. And so it was more in education's name than in the name of art that music in the classical sphere won a beachhead in the academy, which has served ever since as an unofficial but powerful patron.

CHARLES E. IVES, AMERICAN COMPOSER

There is good reason to think that Horatio Parker, with whom Charles Ives studied composition at Yale College, would have been astounded to learn that his pupil, who gave up professional music making at the age of twenty-seven and made his living in the business world, is considered today the outstanding American composer of his era and a noteworthy figure in the history of music. Not that Ives's music is as familiar to the general public as a popular song or such concert hall favorites as Gershwin's *Rhapsody in Blue* or Copland's *Fanfare for the Common Man*. Nor, except for a few songs for voice and piano, has his music found a solid place in the concert repertory. Rather, many concertgoers are acquainted with unique elements of Ives's musical personality. For one thing, certain aspects of his style are unmistakable; for another, what has come to be known as the Ives legend is alive and well in concert-hall lore.

The most obvious markers of Ives's style are easy to spot by ear. Listeners hearing an unexpected dissonant patch, or a patriotic melody or hymn tune quoted in a concert work, have little doubt whose music they are listening to. The Ives legend, based on fact but wrapped in layers of inference that research has partly chipped away, pictures him as an aggressively *American* composer who began early in life to experiment and who, working in isolation, "discovered" a number of modern musical techniques before such famous European composers as Stravinsky and Schoenberg. A sympathetic

Charles Ives (1874–1954) attended the Hopkins Grammar School in New Haven, Connecticut, where he pitched for the school baseball team. He is pictured here with battery-mate Franklin Miles (1894).

critic in 1934 described Ives as a genius, "largely self-taught, a business man rather than a professional musician, tied to no schools and refusing to propagandize his own music"; this image has survived to the present.[4] It stresses idiosyncrasy, a fundamental quality in his music and his life. Ives's unique, solitary circumstances stand out, even as he was steeped, saturated, indeed marinated in history.

Charles Edward Ives was born in 1874, the son of a Danbury, Connecticut, musician whose family stood high among the town's leaders. George Edward Ives, Charles's father, had studied music privately in New York City, led a Danbury band during the Civil War, then returned to his hometown to work as a performer and teacher of music and an employee in family-owned businesses. Charlie Ives, as family members knew him, showed uncommon talent on the keyboard, began composing at eleven, played snare drum in his father's band, and took his first post as a paid church organist at fourteen. In 1894, the year Charlie enrolled at Yale College as a freshman, his father died, a loss that he mourned for the rest of his life. After a musically active, academically ordinary career at Yale, which included a year of composition study with Horatio Parker, Ives graduated in 1898, moved to New York City, and began a career in business that led him into life insurance and estate planning. As partner in the firm of Ives and Myrick (founded in 1907), he became known as an innovator in the insurance world, and was quite well-off when he retired on New Year's Day 1930. In the meantime, he continued his involvement with music—professionally as a church organist until he gave up his post in 1902, and avocationally as a composer.

Unconnected with New York's public musical life, Ives composed prolifically in private, at least until 1917, when a long illness brought both his business and musical lives to a temporary halt. Three years later, he printed, at his own expense, the highly original, large-scale Piano Sonata No. 2 (*Concord*) and *Essays Before a Sonata*, a prose companion piece of substantial length. In 1922, his self-published *114 Songs* appeared in print. Neither of these items drew more than fleeting notice from critics, performers, the public, or even advocates of modern music.[5] By the early 1920s, Ives was no longer composing new works. But for many years he continued reworking his music, which was starting to be performed. In the 1930s, younger American composers began to discover him, delighted to find an older figure whose music spoke with a voice so original: full of modernisms, yet firmly in the American grain. Anticipating that some might ask the question "Who is Ives?," he began an autobiographical account, published long after his death in 1954 as *Memos*, a major source of the Ives legend. Highlights of Ives's later years included the first performance of the *Concord* Sonata in 1939 by pianist John Kirkpatrick, to enthusiastic reviews; a Pulitzer Prize for composition in 1946 for his Symphony No. 3 (composed some forty years earlier); and the publication of *Charles Ives and His Music* by composer Henry Cowell and his wife Sidney Robertson Cowell, in the year after Ives's death.

George E. Ives (1845–1894), father of Charles Ives, was a town
musician and bandmaster in Danbury, Connecticut.

Why speak of an Ives legend but not a Gottschalk legend or a Mac-
Dowell legend? The answer has to do with more than artistic greatness.
Gottschalk, MacDowell, and other American composers, whatever mysteries may surround them, arranged for their music to be performed in public
(or played it themselves) and carried on their careers in the light of public
response. Ives did not. From June 1, 1902, when he left the organ bench at
New York's Central Presbyterian Church, composing and performing were
for him private matters. The next fully public acts of Ives's musical life were
the publications of 1920 and 1922. During the almost two decades in between, he had written a large body of music unlike that of any other composer, living or dead, much of it radically forward-looking in style yet rooted
in American musical traditions and celebrating American life. As interest in
that music slowly grew through Ives's later years, and more people wondered who Ives was, he himself—though reclusive, ill, and old before his
time—provided answers in autobiographical writings, letters, and conversations. Implicit in "Who is Ives?" is another question: What circumstances

and influences could have shaped such a character and such music? As long as Ives's music remained private, these questions remained unasked; when it finally began to be heard, only the composer himself was in a position to answer them. Hence the Ives legend, with Charles Ives as chief narrator.

In response to a 1930 request for information about "early musical background, education, home influences, etc." for a book on American music, Ives wrote two paragraphs detailing his father's career and ideas about music, adding: "I feel that, if I have done anything that is good in music, I owe it almost entirely to him and his influence."[6] By writing about his father rather than presenting a list of teachers and institutions where he had studied, Ives sent a clear message: his musical outlook had been formed in early boyhood, and its roots lay in the initiation he had received into his hometown's musical life. George Ives had been a performer and teacher of woodwind, brass, and keyboard instruments. Bands, orchestras, choirs, and even the throngs at outdoor religious meetings had performed under his leadership. He considered music a spiritually precious thing and conveyed his love for it to the youngsters he taught, especially his son. No respecter of hierarchies, he considered the work of both J. S. Bach and Stephen Foster "great music and not trivial music." Finally, for all his involvement in practical, everyday music making, he also had a visionary streak, centered in acoustics.

Ives's autobiographical *Memos*, which he worked on between 1931 and 1934, mentions an acoustical experiment of George's in which violin strings were "stretched over a clothes press and let down with weights," intended to produce quarter-tone subdivisions of the scale. Ives admits that his father's "interest in sounds of every kind" had occasionally "led him into positions or situations . . . that made some of the townspeople call him a crank whenever he appeared in public with some of his contraptions." George Ives's teaching methods could also be unconventional. On the one hand, "Father knew (and filled me up with) Bach and the best of the classical music, and the study of harmony and counterpoint etc., and music history." On the other,

> he would occasionally have us sing, for instance, a tune like *The Swanee River* [Foster's *Old Folks at Home*] in the key of E♭, but play the accompaniment in the key of C. This was to stretch our ears and strengthen our musical minds, so that they could learn to use and translate things that might be used and translated (in the art of music) more than they had been.[7]

The image of Charles Ives and his brother "stretching" their ears through this exercise is a memorable part of the Ives legend. Such schemes, though they may not have been much fun for the performers, helped Ives develop an acute sense of aural perspective. He learned early that euphony was not the only kind of harmony worth hearing; that two key levels sounding at the same time offered wide possibilities for focusing one's ear; and that even the most familiar Stephen Foster song could be defamiliarized.

Ives was careful to separate musical exercises and experiments from compositions. Of George Ives's "Swanee River" exercise, he writes: "I don't think he had the possibility of polytonality in composition in mind, as much as to encourage the use of the ears—and for them and the mind to think for themselves and be more independent—in other words, not to be too dependent upon customs and habits."[8] But George's exercises surely made an impact on his son's composing. Charles's radical ideas took shape "in small studies of particular technical games," including "whole-tone chords harmonizing whole-tone scales" and "a melody harmonized with seventh chords rising in whole steps." Beginning in his teenage years, Ives used these as problem-solving exercises to find new tonal combinations. Each exercise contained its own sound perspective. And as Ives matured as a composer, these perspectives served both his technique and his imagination.[9]

George Ives himself left such composing to his son. After noting in the *Memos* that his father's interest in the acoustical side of music "took all his extra time," Ives explains: "He did but little composing—a few things or arrangements for bands—in fact he had little interest in it for himself, and it was too bad he didn't, *for it would have shown these interests, and they would have been in some keepable form.* He didn't write text books . . . and he didn't write many letters. He left little behind except memories of him in others" (emphasis added).[10] Most striking here is Ives's endorsement of his father as a *potential* composer. By sounding so sure about the traits of his father's (hypothetical) music, Ives reveals how closely George Ives's identity and his own were by then intertwined in his mind. Radical principles attributed in Ives's writing to his father are sometimes "quoted" in a voice that sounds very much like the Charles Ives of the *Essays* and *Memos*, and they also seem to refer to his own compositions. It is no wonder that Henry and Sidney Cowell concluded that "that the son has written the father's music for him."

Taking this thought one step further led to the idea that the works Ives composed after his father's death were the result of a kind of posthumous collaboration.[11] Although Ives wrote in 1907 that "father died just at the time I needed him most," he knew by the time he enrolled at Yale that in the family's eyes, he had already surpassed his father's achievements. Moreover, recognizing as a teenager that his own musical powers outstripped George's, he harbored feelings of guilt that remained unresolved when George Ives died, six weeks after his son entered college. Over the years and to a large degree subconsciously, Ives transformed his father, an inspiring and remarkable teacher, into a visionary (though unknown) musical hero who had long

Charles Ives, of the insurance firm of Ives and Myrick, photographed in Battery Park, New York City, around 1917.

ago anticipated his son's audacities as a composer. By this token, Ives's "giving up" professional music making in 1902 was an important crossroads. It left him free to pursue composition in a way that fully embraced George Ives's legacy to him: European masterworks, American vernacular music making, and acoustical experiments.

This view of Ives combines biographical research and psychological expertise in an attempt to explain the mysteries in the life of a unique American artist. Any such attempt, however, requires a certain amount of speculation. As research on Ives continues, other hypotheses may be advanced. But it is one thing to ponder the mysteries of Ives's life and career and quite another to deal with his music.

IVES'S SONGS

114 Songs, published by Ives himself in 1922, ends with a rambling two-page "Postface" that must have drawn reactions as puzzled as those that greeted the songs themselves. "Some have written a book for money: I have not," Ives confides in this breezily worded text. "Some for fame; I have not. Some for love; I have not. Some for kindlings; I have not. I have not written a book for any of these reasons or for all of them together. In fact, gentle borrower, I have not written a book at all—I have merely cleaned house." The housecleaning turned up songs written throughout Ives's life as a composer, from start to finish—or nearly so, for he completed very few works after the song collection appeared. The variety of musical styles is enormous. Ives's exploration of such new harmonic styles as tone clusters did not lead him to drop older ones. Even parlor-song harmony remained in his arsenal as a composer throughout his career. A consideration of a half-dozen songs completed between 1897 and 1921 will suggest something of their diversity and their connectedness. They are a song in march form; a sentimental song in two contrasting parts; a religious song in two stanzas, based on a pair of oscillating chords; a very short two-part song not included in 114 *Songs*; a cowboy song setting a strophic text in several stanzas; and a true Ivesian synthesis in which a song is made out of a piece first composed for chamber orchestra.

Although these six songs exhibit great differences in sound, each is unmistakably Ivesian. Indeed, according to Ives's musical philosophy, sound could never reflect more than a part of a musical composition's essence. "My God! What has sound got to do with music!" he bursts out in *Essays Before a Sonata*. This paradoxical but revealing blast was Ives's response to the attitude that composers should tailor their music to what performers can already do well. "It will fit the hand better this way—it will sound better," a violinist is supposed to have told Ives, provoking these often-quoted words. A bit later in the same paragraph he writes: "That music must be heard is not essential—what it *sounds* like may not be what it *is*."[12] With statements like these in mind, it is clear that any discussion of the music must be on the lookout for Ivesian traits that reach beyond the realm of sound.

The Circus Band sets a text by Ives himself that views a small slice of town life through a boy's eyes. A circus has come to town, and the company parades down Main Street to the strains of a marching band. The musical form is commonplace, but not for a song. For the vocal line is laid over a rousing march in the piano. Ives shows here that he can write a conventional, three-strain march—two sixteen-bar strains of cut time in A major and a 6/8 trio in F—but he also makes clear that a conventional march is not quite enough for the task at hand. For example, the eight-bar introduction to the trio starts with a strange thumping sound made by densely packed chords in no particular key: Ives called this sound piano drumming, an effect he worked out as a boy while practicing drum parts on the piano. The sixteen-bar interlude, or break strain, jumps from F into D minor, then clouds the new key with chromatic streams of parallel chords. These moments are unexpected in a street march, just as march form challenges the norms of the art song. In the context of the song, however, neither the

An 1873 issue of *Harper's* magazine carried this etching of the circus coming to town, suggesting the excitement captured in Ives's song *The Circus Band* (1897).

thumping nor the chromatic sliding disrupt the procession of regular, foursquare phrases. Even if listeners wonder where the music is heading, they have a pretty clear sense of when it will get there.

The heart of *The Circus Band* lies in the way voice and instrument are connected. The band (i.e., piano) makes the music, carrying the parade past a thrilled singer who responds to the spectacle. In the first strain, the vocal line moves up from mid-range to an outburst on "Ain't it a grand and glorious noise!" Later, the boy gets so excited that he falls behind the accompaniment and is left scrambling to make up beats. And at the start of the last trio, Ives turns the pianist briefly into another parade watcher, as if representing the band were not already enough. As a countermelody in octaves starts in the left hand, the accompanist is supposed to shout: "Hear the trombones!"

Memories is also about the impact of musical experience. The singer is a young girl or boy, buzzing with excitement at being in a theater just before the curtain goes up. *Memories* is actually two songs, proceeding in different tempos and keys and depicting two opposite moods. The first anticipates what will follow the curtain's rise; the second muses dreamily over a melody heard onstage. In part A, marked "Very Pleasant," to be sung "as fast as it will go," the words tumble breathlessly from the mouth of the singer, who prods her companion, whistles along with the precurtain music, and shushes the crowd when the curtain rises to a thunderous half-cadence. But part B, marked "Rather Sad," is as reflective as A is outgoing. Whatever the spectators may have been hoping for, they hear "a tune as threadbare as that 'old red shawl.'" And in this Ivesian frame within a frame, the singer does not just listen to the music, like the boy in *The Circus Band*, but performs it, even while critiquing its quality and connecting it to a personal past:

> It is tattered, it is torn,
> It shows signs of being worn,
> It's the tune my Uncle hummed from early morn.

The song ends in a deep reverie about the singer's uncle, "shuffling down to the barn or to the town, a-humming." The emotional shift between the two parts of *Memories* is as sharp as Ives's labels suggest: from keen anticipation to wistful indifference for what is actually happening onstage. After accompanying the B melody with languid eighth notes outlining chords that last for three or four bars each, Ives quickens the harmonic rhythm briefly—as if for just a moment the singer had joined a barbershop quartet—before *Memories* melts away in a hummed final cadence. By imagining a scene that calls for an old-fashioned sentimental song, then composing a worthy example, Ives proved that in the hands of a composer who still believed in its expressive power, the "worn" idiom was not yet worn out.

In *Memories* and *The Circus Band*, Ives turns popular nineteenth-century forms and styles to his own use. In *Serenity*, he creates a modern musical frame for a familiar nineteenth-century hymn. When sung to the hymn tune WHITTIER, the verses of Quaker poet John Greenleaf Whittier seem homey and comforting. But the calm stillness of Ives's setting is far from homey. Calling *Serenity* "a unison chant," Ives gives the voice a line more incantatory than melodic: narrow in range and to be sung "very slowly, quietly and sustained, with little or no change in tempo or volume throughout." Except for one measure at the end of each stanza where hymnbook harmony appears, the accompaniment consists of two dissonant chords (B-F-A-C and C♯-G-B-E) not related by any standard tonal scheme. They are simply repeated until a listener accepts their connection, though it lacks any of the rootedness of orthodox harmony.

The stillness that Ives conjures up with this combination of words and music is no more stable than the mysterious tonality and wisps of quoted material that echo in the song. In Ives's setting, words that convey a sense of religious ease when sung to WHITTIER take on a different cast. Hovering, rather than moving with purpose, the music turns the "calm of hills above" into a suspended moment rather than an enduring condition. Just as nature can be calm, the human soul can be relieved of "strain and stress." But the music's immateriality suggests that both are temporary. The best that humans can manage are moments of hushed contemplation, tuned to glimpsing a "beauty of [God's] peace" that cannot be sustained.

It takes Ives less than a minute in *Soliloquy* to portray nature as either tame or untamable, depending on whether one is indoors or outdoors. The first half of Ives's text reads: "When a man is sitting before the fire on the hearth, he says, 'Nature is a simple affair.'" Like the words of *Serenity*, these are chanted quietly, mostly on one pitch that hangs above an oscillating pair of unrelated low-register chords. The second half shows the claim to be false: "Then he looks out the window and sees a hailstorm, and he begins to think that 'Nature can't be so easily disposed of!'"[13] Here Ives dispels the settled calm of the first half: the voice jumps wildly from note to note, and the piano abandons any sense of key or regular pulse. But analysis reveals that this chaos is carefully planned. The voice part's first phrase contains all twelve notes of the chromatic scale without repetition. And the piano part is built from major sevenths and minor ninths, intervals that emphasize disjointedness. Then the music turns around, and everything is repeated backward. Ives is experimenting here with techniques—composing with pitches in chromatic series, reversing the order of musical materials, and inverting intervals—that Arnold Schoenberg and his students, working in Vienna, later used to systematize composition. With its use of two different styles set side by side, however, *Soliloquy* is clearly not a piece in search of a system. Rather, it shows Ives, bent on making an expressive point, finding a methodical way to represent the uncontrollable force of nature in action.

In *Charlie Rutlage*, Ives sets a five-stanza saga of death on the range that he found in a collection of cowboy songs. The melody begins simply and diatonically, as if a strophic song were being launched, supported by piano in a guitar-like, "boom-chick" accompanying style. But suggestions of strophic balladry soon fall away as music is turned loose to express the events of the text. Ives's setting, which tries to do justice to both the high drama of Charlie's death in a cattle roundup (his horse falls on him) and the cowboy ballad's deadpan ethos, tests the limits of the art song.

To portray the song's violent climax, Ives asks the performers to step into new roles. For example, partway through the second stanza he turns the singer into a narrator. Writing out the rhythm of the words with no pitches, Ives makes it seem as if the vocalist, so absorbed in telling the tale, forgets to sing. And by the time the singer starts speaking, the piano has abandoned the guitar-like background of the beginning. The left hand plays a chromatic descending eighth-note figure, punctuated irregularly (every two or three beats or so) with low octaves. The right hand plays something completely different, even settling for a time into a four-beat quotation of the cowboy song *Git Along, Little Dogies*. Rhythmically out of phase with each other, the pianist's hands also clash harmonically to produce a dense, racing, almost opaque instrumental support for the urgent voice-over. Given the subject, the piano's near cacophony evokes the dust, confusion, and noise of a cattle drive, and the cowboys' struggle to influence the movement of huge animal bodies, rushing mindlessly ahead. As the moment of Charlie's death approaches, Ives urges the pianist on: "faster and faster—louder and louder." And when the fall of Charlie's horse crushes him to death, a long piano glissando leads to clusters of tones played with the fists. "The notes are indicated only approximately," Ives writes. "The time, of course, is the main point."

Ives once remarked that he never wrote anything he couldn't play on the keyboard. It is well to remember this comment when considering *Charlie Rutlage*, for Ives's abilities at the piano surely lie behind the conception of this song and of other compositions too. John Kirkpatrick, the pianist who premiered the *Concord* Sonata, once said of Ives's performing: "It was a deft, flitting kind of playing, often seeming to be all over the keyboard all at once."[14] And composer Elliott Carter, who was introduced to Ives as a teenager, visited him at home, and sometimes accompanied him to concerts, took away from these encounters a vivid impression of Ives at the keyboard. As Carter recalled:

> Ives had an amazing ability to sit down at the piano and mimic things they had just heard in concert—long stretches of Ravel or Stravinsky orchestra pieces played (and expertly faked) from memory after one hearing, with a continuous overlay of jokes and sarcasm at the expense of the composers. After playing a Stravinskyan polychord Ives might growl, "Anybody can do that," and rip off "My Country 'tis of Thee" with each hand in a different key.

Carter discovered that Ives often played Bach, Brahms, and Franck for the "spiritual elevation and nobility" he found in them. But when he played his own music, "a gleam would come into his eyes as fiery excitement seized him, and he would smash out a fragment of *Emerson*, singing loudly and exclaiming with burning enthusiasm. . . . It was a dynamic, staggering experience, which is hard even now to think of clearly."[15]

If *Charlie Rutlage* draws from that well of Ivesian virtuosity, it also shows that the composer could pull back from the brink of emotional overload when a text demanded it. Charlie dies in the fourth verse of a five-verse text. For the last verse, by bringing back the beginning tune and its guitar-like accompaniment, Ives restores life on the range to normal, minus one "good cowpuncher." The change from sung beginning to spoken middle section and back shifts the focus in a way that may remind listeners of a standard film device. It is as if Ives, starting with a panoramic shot of the ranch, zooms in on one tragic incident, then returns to the apparent tranquility of the wide-angle opening view. Hopeful that Charlie has been welcomed at heaven's "golden gate," the song ends with the standard "Amen" chord progression.

Ives left a description of the experience that inspired *The Housatonic at Stockbridge*, a song, he recalls, that

> was suggested by a Sunday morning walk that Mrs. Ives and I took near Stockbridge, the summer after we were married. We walked in the meadows along the river, and heard the distant singing from the church across the river. The mist had not entirely left the river bed, and the colors, the running water, the banks and elm trees were something that one would always remember. Robert Underwood Johnson, in his poem, *The Housatonic at Stockbridge*, paints this scene beautifully.[16]

After the couple returned from their trip, Ives sketched the first part of a composition for strings, flute, and organ. He completed it some years later, and then in 1921 fashioned it into a song for voice and piano, using Johnson's poem. Another comment by Ives shows a sound picture taking shape in his mind, including the very hymn tune that was being sung that morning. "Housatonic Church across River sound like Dorrnance," Ives jotted down in a note to himself, adding: "River Mists, leaves in slight breeze river bed—all notes & phrases in upper accompaniment . . . should interweave in uneven way, riversides colors, leaves & sounds—*not* come down on main beat."[17] (The hymn tune DORRNANCE, by American composer Isaac Woodbury, was first published in 1845.)

The Housatonic at Stockbridge reflects something of Ives's inspiration and working habits. Conceived first as an instrumental piece, it affirms Ives's fondness for having his music be *about* something: for connecting the sounds to specific images or ideas. "Is not all music program music?" he asked rhetorically, meaning music with an extramusical subject.[18] And in that spirit, the instrumental movement was inspired by particularities: *this* place on *that* riverbank at *this* moment. That Ives could attach to this work, long after it was composed, a poem so well suited to its form and atmosphere shows how effectively the first version caught the spirit of his subject. And speaking of versions, with no performances looming and no publication deadlines to meet, Ives was freer than most composers to tinker with his compositions, refining details and arranging them for different performing media, sometimes over a period of many years.

The Housatonic at Stockbridge shows Ives working to unite a place, a visual image, a memory, and a poem that addresses a river as if it were a living thing; a look at his response to that challenge will shed light on his distinction between what music *is* and how it sounds. *The Housatonic at Stockbridge* employs the principle of textural layering that Ives used in *Charlie Rutlage*, but with a different purpose. In the cowboy song, two clashing layers are piled up to suggest a cattle drive's roar of chaotic energy. Here, however, it is as if an independent song is overlaid with a semitransparent aural screen. Just as one can see a river's banks and track its moving current through morning mist, so the added layer of sound blurs the song's outlines without hiding them. The piano introduction establishes the effect of foreground and background. While the songlike left hand is solidly anchored in C-sharp major, the right—printed mostly in notes smaller than normal—plays a stream of very quiet, disjunct eighth notes in no particular key. Ives's score says that the small right-hand notes, played in the orchestra version by muted strings, "may be omitted, but if played should be scarcely audible." Ives also directs that the right-hand layer "be listened to separately or subconsciously as a kind of distant background of mists seen through the trees or over a river valley, their parts bearing little or no relation to the tonality, etc. of the tune."

Another musical trait of *The Housatonic at Stockbridge*, this one evident to ears attuned to European concert music, is unity through motivic repetition. The song's vocal line is built around a motive of four (sometimes three) repeated notes followed by a descending major third. To suggest how thoroughly that figure pervades the melody, here is the full text, with underlining showing words and syllables sung to the motive:

> <u>Contented river!</u> in thy dreamy realm
> <u>The cloudy willow</u> and the plumy elm:
> Thou beautiful! <u>From ev'ry dreamy</u> hill
> What eye but wanders with thee at thy will,
> <u>Contented river!</u> And yet overshy
> <u>To mask thy beauty</u> from the eager eye;
> Hast thou a thought to hide from field and town?
> In some deep current of the sunlit brown.

> Ah! There's a restive ripple, and the swift
> Red leaves September's firstlings faster drift;
> <u>Woulds't thou away,</u> dear stream? <u>Come whisper near</u>!
> I also of much resting have a fear:
> <u>Let me tomor</u>row thy companion be,
> By fall and shallow to the adventurous sea!

The mist starts to lift just before "Ah! There's a restive ripple." Here the right hand's eighth notes, now printed full-sized, merge with the left hand's somewhat more dissonant idiom as the river's flow toward the sea grows more turbulent. Through the last six lines of text, the song builds to a climax on the final word, sung to the highest note in the whole vocal line. But then, in another kind of layering that Ives was fond of using to end movements or pieces, the loud sounds cut off abruptly, leaving soft ones echoing in the background, as if they had been there all along. And the soft sound heard here is that of the motive, now played rather than sung, affirming the song's melodic coherence.

Quotation—the borrowing of a preexistent melody, whether for general atmosphere, comment, humor, surprise, musical unification or some other purpose—plays a key role in this song. From DORRNANCE, the hymn tune he heard on his walk, Ives borrowed not just a few notes but the first eight bars, which he presents freely in four "stanzas" that provide the vocal line of the entire song.[19] Because quotation is known to be a standard Ivesian technique and DORRNANCE was part of the personal experience commemorated in *The Housatonic at Stockbridge*, one may be tempted to overlook the larger question of why Ives, composing in the classical sphere, repeatedly quoted melodies from the popular and traditional spheres. Clearly, by incorporating a popular hymn tune into an art song, he was at least questioning if not rejecting the musical hierarchy of his day. Moreover, by hanging on to that tune—or some version of it—as the music around it grows more and more complex, Ives seems to be claiming a connection between modern idioms and old-fashioned hymn tunes. But what kind of connection?

In a nutshell, Ives quoted to infuse his compositions with spiritual power. Believing that melodies gained such power through performance, and that the most unself-conscious, enthusiastic, and full-hearted performers were plain folks who sang and played not as avowed musicians but simply in the course of their daily lives, he often quoted melodies that they loved and sang in their own way—in other words, music in the popular or traditional spheres. This view of Ives helps explain his fondness for hymn tunes that most trained musicians scorned as emblems of bad taste. Long before questions of taste had occurred to him, he had heard these melodies in their natural habitat, and under his father's leadership:

I remember, when I was a boy—at the outdoor Camp Meeting services in Redding, all the farmers, their families and field hands, for miles around, would come afoot or in their farm wagons. I remember how the great waves of sound used to come through the trees—when things like *Beulah Land, Woodworth, Nearer My God to Thee, The Shining Shore, Nettleton, In the Sweet Bye and Bye*, and the like were sung by thousands of "let out" souls. The music notes and words on paper were about as much like what they "were" (at those moments) as the monogram on a man's necktie may be like his face. Father, who led the singing, sometimes with his cornet or his voice, sometimes with both voice and arms, and sometimes in the quieter hymns with a French horn or violin, would always encourage the people to sing their own way. Most of them knew the words and music (theirs) by heart, and sang it that way. If they threw the poet or the composer around a bit, so much the better for the poetry and the music. There was power and exaltation in these great conclaves of sound from humanity.

The gap Ives cites between written and sung hymns relates to his distinction between music and sound. It is clear that sung versions, not written ones, inspired his quotations. He found in the spontaneity and freedom of the singing, which was too passionate to be bound by prescription, the spiritual power he came to call "substance." In the same passage, Ives wrote: "It was the *way* this music was sung" that made it "big or little."

> It wasn't the music that did it, and it wasn't the words that did it, and it wasn't the sounds (whatever they were—transcendent, peculiar, bad, some beautifully unmusical)—but they were sung "like the rocks were grown." The singers weren't singers, but they knew what they were doing—it all came from something felt, way down and way up.[20]

The "it" referred to here is substance, the all-but-indescribable force of the spirit that he tried to engage in his own music. While he never defines substance in so many words, Ives's essay offers many examples of "manner," the label under which he grouped technical skill, standard musical customs and forms, academic knowledge, and even sound itself.

One of Ives's best-known anecdotes reveals his distinction between substance and manner. "A nice young man" who was a conservatory-trained musician asked George Ives:

> "How can you stand it to hear old John Bell (the best stone-mason in town) sing?" Father said, "He is a supreme musician." The young man (nice and educated) was horrified—"Why he sings off the key, the wrong notes and everything—and that horrible, raucous voice—and he bellows out and hits notes no one else does—it's awful!" Father said, "Watch him closely and reverently, look into his face and hear the music of the ages. Don't pay too much attention to the sounds—for if you do, you may miss the music."[21]

In other words, the difference between music and sound, substance and manner, lay in attitude. Substance was a matter of spiritual striving, of investing one's whole soul into the making of music, regardless of talent or skill. Thus it was not to be found in these hymns as compositions; rather, it came out of the spirit in which they were performed. To say that hymns were sung "like the rocks were grown" was to suggest that the singers' feelings were so deeply grounded in belief and nature that they approached the geological. Hymns tapping such emotional depth could hardly be trivial, no matter what the professors said.

For Ives, quotation was often a matter of letting the borrowed melody suggest what might have given its performances substance in the first place. Following the camp-meeting singers' lead in *The Housatonic at Stockbridge*, Ives paraphrases DORRNANCE rather than quoting it literally. The voice begins by following the melodic outline of the hymn tune's first eight bars, but by the third time through, Ives's paraphrase has broken away from the tune's original form.

In this composition, Ives uses musical complexity to evoke substance. Convinced that "man as a rule didn't use the faculties that the Creator had given him hard enough,"[22] Ives places tough demands on listeners, as if coaxing them to feel that their effort would bring its own rewards. In his setting of lines 5 through 8 of Johnson's poem, five things are going on simultaneously:

1. In the left hand, the key of C-sharp major is firmly established in 4/4 time, with pitches outside the key also played against it.
2. The right hand, written in small notes, creates a quiet layer of aural mist with a three-beat unit centered on B, and interweaves with the left hand in an "uneven way" by "*not* coming down on the main beat."
3. The vocal melody, over a C-sharp pedal point in the bass, gravitates toward E major and is coordinated with the left hand.
4. The hymn tune DORRNANCE, neither quoted literally nor imitating an actual congregation, is paraphrased with more and more freedom as the song continues.
5. The vocal line is unified motivically, first by the four- (or five-) note motive described earlier, then by the five-note figures from the second and third measures of DORRNANCE.

These musical traits are joined to poetic lines that call the river's appearance a "mask" for its true nature, further evidence of Ives's belief that a "transcendental" reality lies behind what the senses can perceive. In other words, this passage's complexity is a means to an end. By carrying listeners along on a tide of sometimes complementary, sometimes contradictory sounds, images, ideas, and words, Ives aims to bring them into proximity with the spiritual current he calls substance.

And yet   o - ver-shy   To mask thy beau - ty   from the ea - ger eye;

Hast thou a thought to   hide___ from field and___ town?   In some deep___

This page from Ives's *The Housatonic at Stockbridge* (1921) was printed in his self-published *114 Songs* (1922).

The Housatonic at Stockbridge, with its simultaneous musical layers and hymn-tune quotation, is a song with more than one voice. When Ives recommends that the piano's right hand be listened to separately, as background, it is as if he is thinking of his composition as a convergence of musical impulses from different sources and directions. Listeners may identify DORRNANCE, or they may hear the unifying motive, reminiscent of Beethoven's Fifth Symphony, a work Ives admired and quoted in several compositions. More than one voice can also be heard in the other five songs discussed, and not only because of musical complication. In *The Circus Band*, Ives gives different voices to the vocalist (the bystander) and the pianist (the band), then varies the pianist's voice with drumming and one joyous shout. The whistling and shift in persona of *Memories*, the separate musical and textual quotation in *Serenity*, the total change in musical style during *Soliloquy*, and the cinematic zooming in *Charlie Rutlage*—all these devices require listeners to shift or to question their aural point of view as the song unfolds.

If Ives's goal as a composer was to carry listeners beyond the experience of manner and into that of substance, then changes in voice work toward that end. Nonblending layers, quotations, changes in frame of reference all involve shifts in aural perspective, hence of voice, showing that the music exists in the sound *and* the perspective from which it is heard. To experience these shifts—to hear the different voices—is to perceive the sound of Ives's songs as if it were a façade behind which a deeper spiritual current flows: the transcendental region of substance. Each change, each new layer or voice, offers an aural glimpse of what lies on the other side of the sound.

IVES'S OTHER MUSIC

Songs offer an accessible window on Ives's music and musical thought, but they make up just one of the genres to which he contributed, the others being

1. *Orchestral music*: four numbered symphonies, the *Holidays* Symphony, two three-movement sets, one long overture, and the unfinished *Universe Symphony* for large orchestra; also many pieces for small orchestra.
2. *Chamber music*: some fifteen compositions, including four sonatas for violin and piano, two string quartets, a trio for piano, violin, and cello, and several shorter pieces.
3. *Keyboard music*: about forty works, mostly for piano (a few are for organ), with two piano sonatas and many shorter compositions, including one for two pianos tuned a quarter-tone apart.
4. *Choral music*: sacred works, including a large concert cantata and a number of anthems and psalm settings; secular works, including a few part songs from college years and unison chorus—and orchestra—versions of solo songs.[23]

Ives's instrumental compositions reveal many of the same traits as his vocal works. Quotations, layering, and changes of voice abound. Again, Ives's impatience with hierarchical boundaries can lead to jarring juxtapositions—quotations from Beethoven symphonies, for example, next to fiddle tunes and gospel hymns—and opaque overlappings. In *Putnam's Camp*, the second movement of *Three Places in New England* for orchestra, Ives creates the illusion of two bands, each playing a different piece, marching toward each other. In *The Unanswered Question*, a single trumpet repeatedly intones the same angular figure over a string ensemble's consonant, organ-like chords while four flutes respond with growing agitation to the trumpet's calls. Harmonic dissonance in *Putnam's Camp* comes to a head in a roar of cacophony, while in *The Unanswered Question* clashes between layers come and go, each time yielding to the serene euphony of the string background. In fact, however, as in *The Housatonic at Stockbridge*, listeners may find it useful to think of layering as a visual metaphor related to aural perspective.

Ives suggests something like that himself in a "conductor's note" to the Fourth Symphony's second movement (published in 1929):

> As the eye, in looking at a view, may focus on the sky, clouds or distant out-lines, yet sense the color and form of the foreground, and then, by bringing the eye to the foreground, sense the distant outlines and color, so, in some similar way can the listener choose to arrange in his mind the relation of the rhythmic, harmonic and other material. In other words, in music the ear may play a role similar to the eye in the above instance.[24]

Thus, Ives's layering presses listeners to choose their own points of focus among the possibilities he offers them instead of hearing everything as part of the same foreground. Sounds that stretch the ears and minds of listeners helped the composer follow the lead of his intellectual heroes, Ralph Waldo Emerson and Henry David Thoreau, in probing hidden unities and mysteries of human existence.

A work in which Ives thoroughly explores that terrain is the Piano Sonata No. 2, printed in 1920 with the *Essays Before a Sonata* but composed between 1909 and 1915. The sonata, Ives writes, "is an attempt to present (one person's) impression of the spirit of transcendentalism that is associated in the minds of many with Concord, Mass., of over a half century ago. This is undertaken in impressionistic pictures of Emerson and Thoreau, a sketch of the Alcotts, and a *scherzo* supposed to reflect a lighter quality which is often found in the fantastic side of Hawthorne." Thus the *Concord* Sonata reflects two familiar Ivesian traits: his practice of working on compositions for long periods of time and his preference for program music.[25] The sonata is the ultimate Ivesian synthesis. By honoring a group of New Englanders in an esteemed European form, Ives declared the universality of both. By commemorating literary Americans linked to transcendental philosophy, he suggested their impact on his own outlook. By infusing a traditional form with multivocal elements, combining sonata-style thematic development with quotation and layering, he proclaimed their compatibility and his own command of the composer's craft. By accompanying his sonata with an explanatory treatise, he admitted that a composer of music like this had some explaining to do. And by having these items printed rather than adding them to his stock of unpublished manuscripts, he made a bid for public recognition.

For all its American subject matter, there is no denying the place of the European musical past in the *Concord* Sonata's pedigree. Indeed, the spirit of Beethoven's late sonatas animates at least the first three movements. *Emerson*, reflecting Ives's admiration for the eminent philosopher, essayist, lecturer, and poet, is a long, imposing, and varied first movement, drafted as part of a piano concerto that Ives never finished. The second movement, named after novelist and short-story writer Nathaniel Hawthorne, is a racing, fantasy-like scherzo that pulls some startling musical jokes. *The Alcotts* is shorter and simpler, somewhat reminiscent of the parlor and inspired by the family of Bronson Alcott, philosopher and organizer of a Utopian community (and father of Louisa May Alcott, author of *Little Women*).

Only with the fourth movement, *Thoreau*, does Ives break with the usual character of the European sonata. Instead of taking the decisive tone of a typical finale, the movement begins softly, mixes dreamy reflection with livelier moments, and fades away at the end. Yet rather than seeming anticlimactic, the quiet last movement brings the sonata to a satisfying close. In its final measures, the sound of Thoreau's flute across Walden Pond echoes a theme that listeners have already heard, chiefly in fragments, in *Emerson*, *Hawthorne*, and *The Alcotts*. Ives took from European Romanticism this "cyclic" way of unifying a large work by presenting the same theme in more than one movement.[26] Some traits of the Romantic-era sonata Ives did *not* follow: characteristic key structures, for example (much of the sonata is atonal or polytonal); patterns of repetition (Ives repeats few phrases and no sections literally); and standard formal outlines (such as **ABA**, theme and variations, rondo, and sonata-allegro). But while the European cyclic principle is fundamental to this work, Ives discovered a way of his own way to use it.

By this stage of his career, Ives had found the major-minor tonal system limited in expressive scope. He recalls an all-Beethoven recital he heard around 1915:

> After two and a half hours of the (perhaps) best music in the world (around 1829), there is something in substance (not spirit altogether) that is gradually missed—that is, it was with me. I remember feeling towards Beethoven [that he's] a great man—but Oh for just one big strong chord not tied to any key. . . . The more the ears have learned to hear, use, and love sounds that Beethoven didn't have, the more the lack of them is sensed naturally.[27]

In that spirit, Ives begins *Emerson* with a burst of sounds that were unavailable to Beethoven, the unmetered rhythm lacking any pattern of accent. Within this dense, amorphous-sounding texture, however, one soon hears a different voice: a quotation from Beethoven's Fifth Symphony, sounded very quickly in a short left-hand tattoo. A moment later, the borrowed phrase throbs out in left-hand quarter-note octaves. The motive is heard repeatedly through the movement's opening pages, but always overlaid and partly obscured by something different in the right hand. As *Emerson* unfolds, the Beethoven motive returns often enough to give listeners a sense that it has a place in Ives's larger design. That place is not revealed, however, until the end of the third movement, where it blazes forth as the climax of the work's main theme.

To follow the path of this theme—or rather of its bits and pieces, which remain mostly separate until *The Alcotts*—through the *Concord* Sonata is to feel a growing sense of the continuity Ives built in to a work whose sounds and styles are so diverse. In the first movement, the opening four-note motive (a) is heard often, sometimes together with the Beethoven quote (b), usually with other material swirling around it, and seldom as anything more than a fragment. In the second movement, both motives are woven into the texture from time to time, perhaps most tellingly just before a prominent quotation from the hymn tune MARTYN, which echoes softly in the background, as if overheard from far in the distance—a new voice from another realm, which is then abruptly dismissed. (It is surely no coincidence that MARTYN begins with four notes resembling the start of Beethoven's Fifth.) *Hawthorne* has some boisterous moments, as when *The Red, White, and Blue (Columbia, the Gem of the Ocean)* is quoted, or when a band marches through the landscape toward the end of the movement. It also achieves an unusual, shadowy effect in a passage where "group chords" in the right hand are played softly, with the help of a "strip of board 14 3/4 inches long and heavy enough to press the keys down without striking." Thus, abrupt shifts in mood, sound, and voice take this movement into expressive territory seldom visited by sonatas.

The opening of *The Alcotts* with the Beethoven motive, harmonized in B-flat, gives the impression that a moment of thematic revelation is at hand. Ives has hammered at that motive, off and on, through two long movements, always on the way to making another musical point. But now it is part of a rounded statement in a stable key: the motive is presented, repeated, digressed from, then returned to, in a conventional structure (**aaba**) that a sonata theme might take. Yet the sense of arrival turns out to be an illusion. Indeed, this movement illustrates Ives's feeling "that music, like other truths, should never be immediately understood; there must always remain some further element yet to be disclosed. A complete musical statement, in all its clarity and simplicity, like any absolute truth, is an ultimate,

not a beginning." That may be why Ives often reserves clear thematic statements for the culmination of a work, as he does in *The Alcotts*.[28] Through
much of the movement, Ives seems to be seeking a proper role for that
Beethoven figure, which thunders forth impressively in C minor (the original key of the Fifth Symphony) as a climax to the first half. But two cun-
ningly placed dissonances undermine that moment's finality. Each is made
by a single high note, sounded softly but pointedly against the resonance of
these thickly voiced chords, reminding listeners how little it takes for Ives to
suggest a contrasting layer of sound. Finally, after a digression in a quieter
vein, it is as if Ives discovers what he has been after all along: a thematic
statement in which the Beethoven motive is heard in C *major* and given a
proper melodic lead-in, starting with motive **a**. The a and **b** motives are now
linked in one melody that has been seeking to find its destined form and
voice since the first movement.

Having triumphantly assembled and uncovered his main theme, Ives begins the fourth movement quietly, with soft, dissonant material attached to
no key in particular. His program takes Thoreau through an Indian-summer
day at Walden Pond. Ives describes in words, and occasionally suggests in
music, the philosopher's search—not for food, shelter, or physical work, but
for harmony with nature. Thoreau has awakened feeling restless, and only
after part of the day is gone does he recognize what is wrong: rather than adjusting himself to the particular "mood that the genius of the day calls for,"
he has taken his own tempo. Realizing "that he must let Nature flow
through *him* and slowly," Thoreau's state of mind then begins to change.

> He releases his more personal desires to her broader rhythm, conscious that
> this blends more and more with the harmony of her solitude; it tells him that
> his search for freedom on that day, at least, lies in his submission to her, for
> Nature is as relentless as she is benignant. He remains in this mood, and,
> while outwardly still, he seems to move with the slow, almost monotonous
> swaying beat of this autumnal day.

As the day nears its end and light begins to fade, Thoreau recognizes that he
has completed no work. But he is now so perfectly tuned to his surroundings that when a church bell rings in Concord, some distance away, he
hears it as "a melody . . . imported into the wilderness"—a sound with "a
certain vibratory hum, as if the pine needles in the horizon were the strings
of a harp which it swept. . . . a vibration of the universal lyre."[29] In the final
measures, the sound of Thoreau's flute is heard over the pond at evening,
playing the theme from *The Alcotts* as a gentle, lyric layer over a quiet, dissonant background. Thus a large, often stormy piano work ends in a meditative mood that suggests nature itself as the ultimate maker of music. Just

Ives was photographed by W. Eugene Smith around 1947, when
he was in his early seventies.

as Thoreau stops battling the forces of nature and seeks to merge his consciousness with theirs, so the atmosphere of *Thoreau* seeks to bring listeners
into an attitude of attentive, anticipatory acceptance.

The end of the *Concord* Sonata suggests a remarkable statement Ives
made a few years later in the "Postface" to 114 *Songs*, reflecting some of his
more idealistic beliefs: that human beings were not separate from nature
but part of it; that music was progressing, not declining, as an art form; that
its progress would be understood best not by musical specialists but by people singing, playing, and composing in the course of their daily lives; and
that a key to music's progress lay in its growing ability to explore spiritual
connections between nature and humanity—between outward appearance
and inward reality. "The instinctive and progressive interest of every man in
art," Ives predicted,

will go on and on, ever fulfilling hopes, ever building new ones, ever opening new horizons, until the day will come when every man while digging his potatoes will breathe his own epics, his own symphonies (operas, if he likes it); and as he sits of an evening in his backyard and shirt sleeves smoking his pipe and watching his brave children in *their* fun of building *their* themes for *their* sonatas of their *life*, he will look up over the mountains and see his visions, in their reality, will hear the transcendental strains of the day's symphony resounding in their many choirs, and in all their perfection, through the west wind and the tree tops![30]

Ives knew from experience the resistance that his music would have to overcome to be accepted in the concert hall. But in visionary moments like this one, he could imagine a future in which his works could help society's members attune themselves to an elusive spiritual dimension of human life in an interconnected universe.

Because Ives's music came to public knowledge long after it was written, the story of its discovery and performance belongs to a later time. Indeed, the Ives legend, with its themes of experimentation, isolation, neglect, and Americanism, evolved gradually as works were taken up by performers, published, recorded, and put into historical context. From the 1930s on, Ives's profile was recast more than once, as "new" works were discovered and views of them and him were adjusted to fit the perspectives of composers, critics, and historians at that particular time. Thus, Ives's contributions to American musical culture include a substantial body of music, some of it radically individual in style; an original aesthetic philosophy; and a symbolic presence that has served as a barometer of attitudes toward American composition during the last two-thirds of the twentieth century.

26

Come On and Hear

The Early Twentieth Century

In 1903, Broadway song and dance man George M. Cohan wrote a patriotic number, *I Want to Hear a Yankee Doodle Tune*, that included the following lines:

> Oh, Sousa, won't you play another march?
> Yours is just the melody divine.
> Now you can take your *William Tell*,
> Your *Faust* and *Lohengrin* as well,
> But I'll take a Yankee Doodle tune for mine.

Cohan could be sure that his audience would recognize *William Tell*, *Faust*, and *Lohengrin* as the names of famous operas. And opera in the early 1900s still supplied some of the melodies that many Americans sang, played, and listened to. The most glamorous musical genre available, opera was also part of the general public's common culture.

Opera's prestige also made it an agent of social exclusion. When author Edith Wharton published *The Age of Innocence* (1920), a novel of manners in post–Civil War New York City, she set the opening scene in an opera house. The book's first two paragraphs mix historical fact and irony to suggest how society used the opera as an arena for social display:

> On a January evening of the early seventies, Christine Nilsson was singing in Faust at the Academy of Music in New York.
>
> Though there was already talk of the erection, in remote metropolitan distances "above the Forties," of a new Opera House which should compete in costliness and splendour with those of the great European capitals, the world of fashion was still content to reassemble every winter in the shabby red and gold boxes of the sociable old Academy. Conservatives cherished it for being small and inconvenient, and thus keeping out the "new people" whom New

York was beginning to dread and yet be drawn to; and the sentimental clung to it for its historic associations, and the musical for its excellent acoustics.[1]

Public interest in Nilsson's first New York performance of the season reflects the artist-celebrity status of opera stars. The performance of Charles Gounod's *Faust* is a reminder that the opera repertory in America was almost exclusively European (Italian and French chiefly), and so were most of the day's star singers. Wharton also comments wryly that in the "flower" aria, as the heroine pulled out petals to learn whether "he loves me" or "he loves me not," Nilsson sang " '*M'ama!*' and not 'he loves me,' since an unalterable and unquestioned law of the musical world required that the German text of French operas sung by Swedish artists should be translated into Italian for the clearer understanding of English-speaking audiences."[2]

The possibility of a new opera house became fact in 1883, when the Metropolitan Opera opened, at first with a repertory like that of the Academy of Music. Backed by wealthy patrons, the new enterprise achieved a firm financial footing in the later 1880s by specializing in German opera, especially the music dramas of Richard Wagner, under the direction of such German-born conductors as Leopold Damrosch, his son Walter, and Anton Seidl, who had worked with Wagner himself. From the start, the Metropolitan company toured widely after its New York season, with stops in Brooklyn, Philadelphia, Chicago, St. Louis, Washington, Baltimore, and Cincinnati during its first year of existence. In the 1889–90 season, with a few Italian operas back in its repertory, the company traveled as far as San Francisco and Mexico. Ten years later, in a tour of twenty-three cities, including New Haven (Connecticut), Utica (New York), and Portland (Maine), the Metropolitan Opera spent five months on the road. In 1906, the company was caught in the San Francisco earthquake, bringing an abrupt end to its April tour when sets, costumes, and most of the orchestra's instruments were lost.

Through much of the twentieth century, the opera repertory in the United States has resembled the symphony orchestra's, emphasizing works of classic reputation rather than new ones. But that emphasis has not necessarily made opera a prim institution, for intrigue, sex, and violence have always coexisted with drama and spectacle on the operatic stage. Probably the most notorious pre–World War I example was Richard Strauss's *Salome*. Based on a story from the Bible, Strauss's version had been recast by the flamboyant English poet Oscar Wilde to show the decadence of the royal court in which a holy prophet was beheaded.

First performed in Germany in 1905, *Salome* had its American premiere at the Metropolitan Opera in New York in 1907. The event shocked critics and audience members alike, assuring instant fame for the opera. A New York newspaper's headlines caught the occasion's sensational tone:

Stranded in San Francisco by the 1906 earthquake, some members of New York's Metropolitan Opera Company try on California hats for size.

4000 Survive The Most Appalling Tragedy Ever Shown on the Mimic Stage—Composer Who Out-Herods Richard Wagner Conquers Every Hearer of His Incomparable Score—The Last Touch of Genius that Germany's Tone-Poet Achieves by the Dramatic Dynamite of Britain's Unforgiven Oscar Wilde Such a Rehabilitation as No Music Ever Gave a Poet Before—And in a Half-Hour Horror of Death's-Head Embrace the Young American Star, Olive Fremstad, Wins Her Place Among the Greatest Dramatic Singers in the World.[3]

Emphasizing the scandalous moral climate of *Salome*, this notice leaves little doubt about turn-of-the-century opera's place in the public eye. The involvement of Wilde, who before his death in 1900 had served a prison term in England for homosexual activity, and the reference to the soprano's "death's-head embrace" warned the public of the jolt they could expect. Yet the notice also indicates that opera provided a showcase for performers who, like Olive Fremstad, could sing, act, and move gracefully onstage.

As *Salome* was exploring human depravity at the Metropolitan Opera, a more accessible kind of musical drama was coming into its own on Broadway. *The Merry Widow*, a Viennese import by Franz Lehár, made its New York debut in 1907. And from then until World War I broke out in 1914, operetta, sometimes called comic opera, dominated the popular musical stage. Featuring operatically trained singers, elaborate musical numbers, and plots carried by spoken dialogue, operetta was a European form that settled easily into formula. Prague-born Rudolf Friml, a leading American operetta composer, once said that the formula depended on "old things: a full-blooded libretto with luscious melody, rousing choruses, and romantic passions."[4] *The Merry Widow* had all these ingredients. Its romantic story revolved around royalty, duty, and the course of true love. In its English adaptation, a prince in a small, impoverished, Middle European nation is ordered to court a rich young widow to keep her fortune from leaving the country. Reluctant at first, he soon falls in love and woos the widow for herself, not for her money. American audiences took *The Merry Widow* to their hearts. Within a few months of its arrival in New York, several road companies were playing it on theatrical circuits; five thousand American performances were given during 1907–8 alone.[5] Songs from the operetta sold widely, both in recorded form—on cylinders, phonograph records, piano rolls—and as sheet music.

Composer and cellist Victor Herbert was one of the Americans who competed successfully with the Hungarian-born, Vienna-based Lehár and the English team of W. S. Gilbert and Arthur Sullivan, whose operettas had long been favorites on the American stage. Born in Ireland, trained in Germany, an orchestra member through his early years, and active as a composer of classical works, Herbert acquired a musical orientation very different from his younger contemporary Charles Ives of Connecticut. Yet both men turned away from classical concert culture—Ives to pursue musical transcendence on his own, and Herbert to please audiences with operettas that delivered appealing music of high professional quality.

Herbert crossed paths with many of the leading musicians and institutions in the United States. He played cello in the Metropolitan Opera orchestra and with the New York Philharmonic Society, soloed with the Theodore Thomas Orchestra, served in the late 1880s as Anton Seidl's assistant conductor in a summer concert program, and taught at the National Conservatory of Music while Antonin Dvořák was serving as director (1892–95). After Patrick S. Gilmore died in 1892, Herbert became conductor of Gilmore's band. From 1898 until 1904, he conducted the Pittsburgh Symphony Orchestra, and then he formed the Victor Herbert Orchestra, which specialized in light music. Respected by his colleagues, Herbert lived at a time when the restructuring of popular entertainment and the rise of recording were changing the music business. He worked for the passage of the 1909 copyright law that secured composers' royalties on the sale of recorded cylinders, discs, and piano rolls. And in 1914, he helped to found the American Society of Composers, Authors, and Publishers (ASCAP), a performing-rights organization devoted to ensuring that composers were paid for performances of their music. Victor Herbert was as fully involved in public musical life as Charles Ives was detached from it.

If operas belong to the classical sphere and musical shows and revues to the popular, operetta stands somewhere in between. Opera composers, using the full range of musical resources in a drama that could be romantic, tragic, or comic, pursued the goal of transcendence. In contrast, Broadway-style book shows and revues, reflecting the concerns, foibles, and fantasies of plain Americans, featured song, dance, and comedy accessible to present-day audiences. Like musical shows but unlike opera, operettas depended on speaking to carry the plot—usually involving high-born characters who search for true love and find it, a glamorous version of Broadway's boy-gets-girl scenario. Yet operetta took its emotional tone from opera and relied on operatically trained singers. The characters reveal that they are living in an exalted state by singing songs, duets, and choruses built around ringing high notes: clear evidence of the ardent passion that pervaded opera. Victor Herbert could write an operetta in 1910 (*Naughty Marietta*) and an opera in 1911 (*Natoma*) without changing his musical rhetoric, although they posed different creative challenges and were received with different expectations.

Herbert composed forty operettas between 1894 and his death three decades later. *Babes in Toyland* (1903), *The Red Mill* (1906), and *Naughty Marietta* (1910) were among the most successful and longest-running in his own day. And the latter fits Friml's description of the form's ingredients perfectly: old things (set in 1780s New Orleans), a full-blooded libretto (Marietta, a disguised noblewoman, finds her destined lover through music), luscious melody (*I'm Falling in Love with Someone*, *Ah! Sweet Mystery of Life*), rousing choruses (*Tramp, Tramp, Tramp*, *The Italian Street Song*), and romantic passions (a jilted mulatto beauty's plight exposes Louisiana's racial caste system).

Naughty Marietta opens at dawn on the central square of New Orleans. To hear the city wake up in Herbert's orchestration is to realize that he was a master of orchestral effect. Moreover, two vocal numbers from the work point up his ability to bring musical richness from the classical sphere into comic opera without sacrificing immediate appeal. In *I'm Falling in Love with Someone*, Herbert borrows opera's musical rhetoric for the familiar song form of verse and chorus, thirty-two bars each. Until a patch of harmonic complication appears in its last eight bars, the verse could be that of a popular song. But the chorus moves quickly into deeper waters. Instead of sailing straight into the tune, Herbert writes an expressive effect into the score: a hushed tone (**pp**) and a free tempo through the first two bars, as the title line is sung in a mood of slightly stunned astonishment. After regular waltz time sets in, a melodic leap of a ninth ends the first eight bars with a gesture far beyond the vocal intensity expected from any popular song. In the second half of the two-part chorus (**aba^{1}b^1**), impassioned vocalism pushes even further, as the leap of a ninth, heard again, is then topped by a cadence high in the tenor's range. The message of this theatrical love song may be personal, even intimate, but it is written to be heard in the farthest reaches of a large hall. And the journey from a quiet, mid-range *pianissimo* to this ringing climax takes only thirty-two bars.

The *Italian Street Song*, for soprano and chorus in C major, is a distillation of energy, bravura singing, and mindlessness. Its function in the drama is to create a festive atmosphere by displaying the heroine's acrobatic singing skills. A verse in 3/8 time introduces a fast 2/4 chorus in three sections (**ABA**) whose first section must have been planned as a hit, for it is also heard in the overture and returns as the finale of Act II. Since the text is mostly vocables—"zing, zing, zizzy zizzy zing"—the number's impact lies entirely in the music. The infectious melody is based on a two-bar rhythmic motive: two quarter notes and a half note, which dominate the opening twenty-bar section, sung by the soprano. The chorus joins in on the repeat, followed by a contrasting middle section in A minor and a return of the melody, now with Marietta disengaged from the chorus and singing her own florid, virtuosic decorations as the now-familiar tune is repeated underneath them. This spirited show piece, with orchestral introduction, soprano solo, soloist-and-chorus interaction, and virtuosic conclusion, illustrates Herbert's knack for compression, for the whole number lasts barely two minutes. Like much of Herbert's music, it is striking, memorable, and too brief to overstay its welcome.

For all of operetta's popularity, however, it lacked the prestige of opera, where a keen interest in American efforts was being supported in those years. During the long tenure of Italian-born Giulio Gatti-Casazza as manager of the Metropolitan Opera (1910–35), the company produced no fewer than seventeen new American works, of which Frederick S. Converse's *The Pipe of Desire* (1910) was the first. In 1911, the Met held a competition for an American opera, won by Horatio Parker's *Mona*, which was produced in 1912. In 1918, Charles W. Cadman's *Shanewis*, featuring Native American melodies and based on a story involving Indian cultural conflict, could also be seen on the Met stage. Of these works, however, the Met gave only the last as much as a second staging. Even Victor Herbert's *Natoma* (1911), an Indian tale introduced with great fanfare there, failed to make a lasting mark.

Though popular musical shows from the century's first two decades are no longer performed today, a few of their songs are still known, including some with a spirit new to Tin Pan Alley and the Broadway stage. For example, just after the turn of the century, George M. Cohan, an actor, singer, songwriter, and playwright of New England/Irish descent, revealed a talent for songs with a patriotic flavor. In *Little Johnny Jones* (1904), Cohan's *The Yankee Doodle Boy* ("I'm a Yankee Doodle Dandy") made a strong impression, as did *You're a Grand Old Flag* in *George Washington, Jr.* (1906) and the later World War I song *Over There* (1917).

What gave a number like *You're a Grand Old Flag* its marketplace appeal?[6] An important part of the answer lay in the rising nationalism of the century's last years. Through much of the 1800s, the U.S. post office was the only national institution that touched most Americans directly. Journalism was widespread but local, and nothing like national mass media existed. Few colleges offered courses in American history. In the 1890s, however, the situation changed. Hereditary associations such as the Sons of the American Revolution (1889) and the Daughters of the American Revolution (1890) were founded, and they set to work on such projects as renovating Mount Vernon and preserving Independence Hall in Philadelphia. More than ever before, the flag became an object of veneration. For in these years, the Pledge of Allegiance was created, Flag Day invented, and a campaign launched to make *The Star-Spangled Banner* the national anthem. One association helped to pass laws against flag desecration in twenty-nine states. By 1898, the flag, the Declaration of Independence, or both were posted in more than 35,000 schoolrooms and the Pledge of Allegiance regularly spoken in a majority of them.[7]

This patriotic outpouring, which took place chiefly among native-born, middle-class white people, has been traced to three developments of the 1890s: immigration, industrial unrest, and a war overseas. The second was described in Chapter 22, which noted how industrialization changed the nature of work, alienating many workers in the post–Civil War years. Moreover, an economic depression from 1893 to 1897, widening the gap between rich and poor, also spurred efforts to organize labor, an attempt some saw as un-American. During the 1880s, more than 4.8 million immigrants came to the United States, mostly from southern and eastern Europe: Italy, Germany Austro-Hungary, the Balkans, and the Russian Empire. Few of these new arrivals spoke English. And they greatly increased the number of American Catholics (6.3 million in 1880; some 20 million by 1920) and Jews (250,000 in 1880; 2 million in 1910). The figures point to differences of language, religion, and culture between the new immigrants and the English-speaking, Protestant, native-born whites who had always dominated American political life. The Spanish-American War of 1898 added to the sense of change, partly because foreign wars fuel patriotic feelings but also because this one involved race. Many of those "liberated" in Cuba and the Philippine Islands were people of color, and political leaders spoke of the need to raise colonials to the presumably superior standard of white civilization.

By all indications, then, perceived challenges to America's identity, whether by anticapitalists, newcomers from foreign shores, or "lesser" races, brought patriotism to the fore.[8] And the energy and passion at the heart of this patriotism flowed at least as much from the will to exclude as the desire to affirm. Against this background, George M. Cohan's *You're a Grand Old Flag* shows its stripes as a popular song by taking an affirmative, inclusive stance. It combines older and newer elements in a way that seeks to tap the emotions triggered by one of the day's hottest issues, but without offending anyone.

Cohan's ingredients are worth noting. First, although the United States lacked an official national anthem, it could claim a core of widely known national songs from the 1700s (*Yankee Doodle, Hail Columbia*) and 1800s (*The*

Illustrator Norman Rockwell provided this memorable cover for George M. Cohan's World War I hit *Over There*.

Star-Spangled Banner, America, Columbia the Gem of the Ocean, and Civil War songs). Second, the multistrain march with songlike trio—for example, Sousa's *The Stars and Stripes Forever* (1897), which capitalized on the flag worship of the day—was prevalent in the popular sphere. So was syncopation: all four of the chorus's eight-bar sections contain at least one rhythmic jolt that would have been unlikely before the advent of ragtime. *You're a Grand Old Flag*, written in march time and blending patriotic references from older songs, the martial fervor of Sousa, and the pizzazz of current, dance-based popular song, treats a national symbol with easy, respectful familiarity. Cohan's approach to the flag recalls that of the gospel hymn to Christianity: heartfelt, demystifying, and down-to-earth. In the verse, the character admits that he cannot resist a marching band ("Any tune like 'Yankee Doodle' / Simply sets me off my noodle"). This confession leads to quotes from Dan Emmett's *Dixie*, on behalf of the South, and Henry Clay Work's *Marching Through Georgia*, a Northern favorite. And Cohan's chorus endorses national accord by quoting *Auld Lang Syne*. Anyone willing to rally round the American flag is welcome to join in.

Cohan's song is an expression of patriotic esteem whose informality erases distance between singer and symbol. Naming no adversary, the song must have carried for some Americans the ecumenical spirit that the lyrics express. Yet it is likely that some for whom the flag symbolized a nation under siege projected adversaries onto the apolitical surface that Cohan provided. Present-day singers and listeners may also find a similar tone and style in many college "fight songs." Linked with hotly partisan words, these songs emerged around the turn of the century with the rise of intercollegiate sports. And even a century later, in an age that still takes fanhood seriously, they seem to have lost none of their power to register undying devotion to a cause—in this case, victory in an athletic contest.

African-American Traditions and Popular Music

Most black American musicians, at least until the recent past, grew up in black communities, absorbing habits that bore the firm stamp of African-American tradition. Black folk culture extended the practices of the ring shout into an era when musical dissemination took place in written as well as oral form. And black American folk culture offered a unique approach to the making of music: one based on what community members and recent commentators have called "signifying," which makes each performance an occasion for spontaneous commentary, musical and otherwise. Syncopation played off against a strict dance beat, the free bending of pitches (especially a major scale's third and seventh degrees), the exploring of varied instrumental and vocal sound qualities and techniques, and a freedom from fixed repetitions—these are all ways for performers to remake pieces of music in their own image. As earmarks of a distinctive approach to singing and playing, they form one common heritage for many black musicians: "Omni-Americans" who can also draw on a pool of European traditions. As a set of traits that can also be isolated, borrowed, written down, and published, they have also shown their value in the marketplace by being freely accessible to anyone's use.

Chapter 21 noted how the so-called coon song and the cakewalk of the 1880s helped to form the next decade's ragtime songs. And it was during the 1890s that black showmen and composers like Will Marion Cook, the Johnson brothers, and Bert Williams and George Walker began staging shows of their own in New York theaters. A violinist and composer born in 1869 in Washington, D.C., Cook had attended the Oberlin Conservatory in Ohio (1884–87), studied violin in Berlin with Joseph Joachim (probably 1887–89), and then returned to the United States and courses in counterpoint and harmony at New York's National Conservatory (ending in 1893). Writing in the 1930s, James Weldon Johnson described Cook as "the most original genius among all the Negro musicians" and noted his "excellent" classical training. But Cook found the classical sphere closed to him because of race and, in Johnson's phrase, "had thrown all these standards over."

Forced into show business, Cook lavished his skills on shows with black

Will Marion Cook (1869–1944), brought the skills of a classically trained musician to an African-American musical theater that boomed in New York from the mid-1890s until the early 1910s.

casts that, though now forgotten, contain music still worth hearing. His *Clorindy, or the Origin of the Cakewalk*, presented during the summer of 1898, required a black chorus to dance vigorously while singing. *In Dahomey* (1903), the first black-produced show to run at a regular Broadway theater, made an even greater impact. After a warm reception in New York, this show played for seven months in London, including a performance at Buckingham Palace, then toured England and Scotland before returning to the United States for more performances. According to Johnson, Cook "believed that the Negro in music and on the stage ought to be a Negro, a genuine Negro," rather than trying to do "what the white artist could always do as well, generally better."[9] These opinions point to a key question of the so-called Harlem Renaissance that followed World War I: In the fight against racial prejudice, should black artists and intellectuals show their mastery of "universal" (i.e., Euroamerican) modes of expression or embrace African-American cultural roots? As Johnson saw it, Cook did the latter. And in that spirit, *Swing Along*, a number from *In Dahomey*, uses syncopation and dialect to celebrate black folk culture's vigor.[10] (Sung in the show by a chorus, the number discussed here is an adaptation for solo voice and piano, published in 1912.)

The text for *Swing Along*, which Cook himself wrote, begins:

> Swing along chillun, swing along de lane,
> Lif yo' head and yo' heels mighty high,
> Swing along chillun, 'tain't a-goin' to rain,
> Sun's as red as de rose in de sky.
> Come along Mandy, come along Sue,
> White fo'ks a-watchin' an' seein' what you do,
> White fo'ks jealous when you'se walkin' two by two,
> So swing along chillun, swing along.

Cook's setting, based on the syncopated rhythm of the coon song, the cakewalk, and ragtime, celebrates African-American body movement. The same rhythmic motive (♪♪♩) begins the first three sections of this sixteen-bar melody. A brief instrumental transition leads to the next section, but not in strict tempo. Indeed, the first strain's infectious drive does not prepare listeners for the number's rhythmic flexibility as a whole.

The second strain continues the mood of the first—in 4/4 time instead of 2/4, which broadens the rhythmic motion considerably:

> We'll a swing along, yes a swing along
> An' a lif' a' yo' heads up high,
> Wif pride an' gladness
> Beamin' from yo' eye.
> We'll a swing along, yes a swing along,
> From a early morn till night.
> Lif' yo' head an' yo' heels mighty high
> An' a swing both lef' an' right.

Like the first, the second strain also presents a sixteen-bar tune, but one that moderates rhythmic snap with vocal lyricism.

Cook now brings the first strain back on the heels of the second, with no transition. He then shortens its last phrase, marked with a *ritard*, and elides it with a varied return of the second strain's "swing along" motif. But after another pause, forward momentum yields to the dramatic gestures and production-number tone of Broadway, as the voice rises to a high-note climax.

Filling some ninety measures, *Swing Along* proves that in the hands of a musician like Will Marion Cook, folk-style speech, syncopated dance music (and dancing), sophisticated harmony, and near-operatic vocalism could be compatible. Cook's number draws on the "genuine Negro" elements of black folk culture, but it also carries the cosmopolitan stamp of a composer at home in a theatrical idiom whose roots can be traced through operetta to grand opera itself.

Black book shows and revues flourished on Broadway through the century's first decade, but they lost momentum in the second, after the death of several major stars. The rising success of motion pictures contributed to the declining fortune of black shows, for many theaters previously open to them now ran movies. A theatrical newspaper explained in 1916: "Even if a colored company played nightly to capacity in the second and third-class houses now available, the low prices of admission would not support a company of fifty or sixty people."[11] The black musical stage suffered another loss in 1910 when white producer Florenz Ziegfeld hired Bert Williams for his prestigious annual revue, the *Ziegfeld Follies*. Combining spectacle, music, dance, and comedy, these shows were lavishly produced and won a racy reputation for featuring scantily clad women. Ziegfeld gave Williams a starring role in the *Follies*, which he filled until his death in 1922. The producer has been praised for integrating the musical theater and Williams recognized for being too talented to be denied a place in big-time—i.e., white—show business.[12] At the same time, however, Williams's absence deprived the black musical theater of one of its chief attractions.

A vivid tale of the black folk tradition's impact in another setting appears in the autobiography of W. C. Handy (1873–1958), an Alabama-born trumpet player, bandleader, composer, and music publisher, who came to be called "the Father of the Blues." Handy's story takes the form of a confessional. Proud of his skill as a note reader, he had also acquired a music encyclopedia and "picked up a fair training in the music of the modern world," including a belief that "the correct manner to compose was to develop simples into grandissimos and not to repeat them monotonously." But for Handy the more important catalyst was an encounter in the century's early years, when he and his band had been hired to play a dance in Cleveland, Mississippi. Partway through the evening, "an odd request" in the form of a note reached the bandstand: play more of "our native music." "This baffled me," Handy

Alabama-born W. C. Handy as a youth of nineteen (1892), when
he played with a cornet band in Evansville, Indiana.

admitted, for he and his bandsmen "were all musicians who bowed strictly
to the authority of printed notes. So we played for our anonymous fan an
old-time Southern melody, a melody more sophisticated than native." That
number triggered a second request: "Would we object if a local colored band
played a few dances?" Happy to be offered a paid break, Handy and his men
agreed, and three young instrumentalists, with "a battered guitar, a mandolin and a worn-out bass," took over the stage.

They struck up one of those over-and-over strains that seem to have no very
clear beginning and certainly no ending at all. The strumming attained a dis-
turbing monotony, but on and on it went, a kind of stuff that has long been
associated with cane rows and levee camps. Thump-thump-thump went

their feet on the floor. Their eyes rolled. Their shoulders swayed. And through it all that little agonizing strain persisted. It was not really annoying or unpleasant. Perhaps "haunting" is a better word.

Handy could not imagine that anyone would find this music appealing, but he was wrong.

A rain of silver dollars began to fall around the outlandish, stomping feet. The dancers went wild. Dollars, quarters, halves—the shower grew heavier and continued so long I strained my neck to get a better look. There before the boys lay more money than my nine musicians were being paid for the entire engagement. Then I saw the beauty of primitive music. They had the stuff the people wanted. It touched the spot. Their music wanted polishing, but it contained the essence. Folks would pay money for it. The old conventional music was well and good and had its place, no denying that, but there was no virtue in being blind when you had good eyes.
That night a composer was born, an *American* composer.[13]

Once he witnessed their impact, Handy began listening more carefully to local tunes, writing some of them down and making them part of his band's repertory. In 1912, he published the *Memphis Blues*, the first blues number in sheet-music form. And in 1914, the *St. Louis Blues* appeared: the most widely popular and enduring commercial success of all blues songs, published under Handy's name but perhaps containing melodies that he had first heard from untutored singers and players.

If Handy had invented his story to dramatize the music business's discovery of another facet of black folk tradition, he could hardly have caught its spirit better. For in near-mythic fashion, the tale touches on fundamental themes: the improbable artistic source, the authenticity of unschooled musicians, the link between musical learning and hierarchical aspiration, and the folk tradition's readiness to be exploited for money. The story suggests that the strains Handy heard in Mississippi were a localized folk style, for although born in the South, he had not encountered music quite like this elsewhere in his travels. Finally, as one who spent much of his life in the music-publishing business, he admitted freely that the Clevelanders' shower of coins had sparked his determination to become the kind of American composer he turned out to be. The marketplace's discovery of the blues is an episode in American music history that would have enormous repercussions after World War I.

Scott Joplin and the Rise of Ragtime

If W. C. Handy could bring music from the black folk tradition into the popular sphere in the 1910s, perhaps one reason was that the pianist and composer Scott Joplin had already paved the way. Joplin, born in 1868, must have absorbed the traditional elements in his music as he grew up, the son of an ex-slave and his free-born wife, near the Texas-Arkansas border. Julius Weiss, a German-born music teacher in Texarkana, Texas, gave the youngster free piano lessons, exposing him to European art music and leading him to an appreciation of music as an art form.[14] Joplin played violin and cornet as well as piano. At sixteen, he began singing in a vocal quartet. He also traveled in his early years as a minstrel troupe member, and in 1893 spent time in Chicago during the World's Columbian Exposition. Chroniclers of popular music have often cited this gala celebration as crucial in introducing the music soon to be called ragtime to a large audience, for more than 20 million attended the fair. Whether Joplin, Ben Harney (a pioneer ragtime pianist who passed for white), or other black musicians actually performed on the fairgrounds or somewhere outside them, many visitors were thrilled by the new syncopated music. When the fair ended in October, Joplin traveled to St. Louis and from there to Sedalia, a central Missouri town where he lived from 1894 to 1901.

By the time Scott Joplin settled there in 1894, Sedalia was a city of 14,000, a railroad hub with a thriving community that centered the region's commerce and transportation. Sedalia was also full of travelers in search of entertainment. To provide such diversions, the city boasted at least two musical ensembles, two theaters, four baseball teams, five newspapers, twenty churches, twenty-eight secret and benevolent societies, and five paramilitary organizations, as well as pool halls, saloons, and dance halls.[15] In Sedalia and elsewhere, certain musical styles were coming to be linked with the good times that drew men to such places, and that is where musicians who mastered these styles found work. Whether run by whites or blacks, musical venues tended to promote contacts across the racial divide. At a time when Jim Crow legislation was on the rise and lynchings more and more common in the South, no such incidents were reported in Sedalia. Black residents had their own churches, businesses, newspapers, baseball teams, fraternal societies, musical ensembles, and institution of higher learning: the George R. Smith College. Finally, Wood's Opera House, with segregated seating for blacks and whites, housed traveling entertainment: minstrel troupes, operetta companies, and wind bands (including Sousa's), all brought to town by the railroad.

Scott Joplin lived in this environment during his late twenties and early thirties. He enrolled in music courses at George R. Smith College, played briefly with the Queen City Cornet Band, sang with a group called the Texas Medley Quartet, played piano at local dances, and worked for a time as a pianist in two of Sedalia's brothels. During Joplin's years in Sedalia, the

Scott Joplin (1868–1917), the King of Ragtime.

city was also home to two black social clubs where members could go for drinking, entertainment, and social exchange. Joplin was a member of one, the Maple Leaf Club, to which the *Maple Leaf Rag*, his most famous composition, was dedicated.

When in 1896 the first distinctively syncopated songs were published under the "ragtime" label, the style was already familiar to those who knew black folk tradition. But for those who did not, ragtime brought the novelty of a fad—the kind of popular mania for being fashionable that a new, aggressive culture of consumption triggered during the 1890s. Once ragtime numbers appeared in print, their impact was quickly felt. Popular songs grew more likely to offer saucy, unsentimental glimpses of love as well as simple syncopation, which was soon to appear even in a patriotic number like Cohan's *You're a Grand Old Flag*. By the fall of 1898, ragtime songs were appearing on the musical stage. In the meantime, instrumental ragtime began to circulate in mechanical reproductions—cylinder recordings and piano rolls—as well as sheet music, and in arrangements for ensembles like Sousa's band.

The music is thought to have been named for its "ragged rhythm"—the syncopation whose musical accents cut across duple meter's alternating strong and weak beats. But a more recent theory proposes that ragtime was named, by its black practitioners, for the hoisting of handkerchiefs (rags) to signal a dance—thus ragtime.[16] The term seemed demeaning even to Scott Joplin, the declared "King of Ragtime." In 1908, for example, Joplin wrote: "What is scurrilously called ragtime is an invention that is here to stay." And he added: "Syncopations are no indication of light or trashy music, and to shy bricks at 'hateful ragtime' no longer passes for musical culture." Joplin made these comments in the *School of Ragtime: 6 Exercises for Piano*, which sought to bridge the gap between the music's oral and written forms. Ragtime's "weird and intoxicating effect," a product of oral roots, was now open even to neophytes, Joplin explained, if they were willing to master the notation through slow, careful practice. *School of Ragtime* explains syncopation as unusual groupings of sixteenth notes against a strict beat. By removing ties and adding dotted lines between staves, Joplin shows how a strict observance of the ties will lead to "giving each note its proper time." Further comments clarify the distance between performances in the oral tradition and "Joplin ragtime," which reflects the authority and control of composers' music, as opposed to performers' music. His works, he notes, have been "harmonized with the supposition that each note will be played as it is written," for only in that way can "the sense intended" be achieved.[17]

In publishing their piano works, Joplin, ragtime composer James Scott, and others were pursuing three related goals: to give the music a salable form, to expand its range of customers, and to raise its status. As long as piano ragtime stayed in the oral tradition, those who mastered it had only their skill as performers to sell; and as long as syncopated styles were linked in the public mind to seamy surroundings, their artistry had little chance of being appreciated. With *Gladiolus Rag*, published in New York by Joseph W.

Stern in 1907, Joplin and his publishers tried to reposition ragtime in the sheet-music marketplace by playing down its African-American roots. Where the cover of the earlier *Maple Leaf Rag* had pictured two strutting black couples, the cover of *Gladiolus Rag* (named, like *The Chrysanthemum*, *Sunflower Slow Drag*, and *Heliotrope Bouquet*, after a flower) shows an attractive young white woman wearing a floral necklace and clad in an ample, swirling gown draped with blossoms. Dancing, she glances back in the artist's direction over one bare shoulder in a way that suggests feminine urbanity more than sexual flirting. The music begins with the delicate tracery of a wide-ranging melody whose chief accented note is a "blue" (flatted) third. Supported by colorful harmony and a deftly placed syncopation, the example shows Joplin's fertile melodic inspiration at work.

The piece is marked "Slow march tempo," and Joplin adds a warning like one he applied to many other piano rags: "Do not play this piece fast. It is never right to play 'Ragtime' fast." How were sheet-music buyers expected to interpret a package that combined flowers, dancing, female charm, and a bit of flesh with syncopation and a restrained but strict tempo? If *Gladiolus Rag* was intended as a pitch for the black folk tradition or a challenge to the prevailing musical hierarchy, these motives were well disguised. Yet from today's perspective, one cannot mistake Joplin's demonstration, first, that black music making could evoke grace and beauty, and second, that the classical sphere held no monopoly on elegant musical expression.[18]

There is probably no theme in twentieth-century American music history more familiar than that of musicians in the popular and traditional spheres contesting the classical sphere's artistic rule. Songwriter George Gershwin's move in the 1920s into the concert hall, the rise of jazz concerts from the 1930s on, the appearance in the 1960s of "classical rock"—these are only a few examples of "crossover," a phenomenon that confirms the existence of separate musical spheres by playing with boundaries and mixing previously separate styles, techniques, values, and modes of presentation. Such boundary crossings have multiplied with time. And they have often been described in a way critical of the classical sphere and its champions for being too ready to judge music by its category. A familiar image is that of popular and folk musicians tweaking the nose of a stuffy classical establishment.

On the other side of the divide, however, popular music's emphasis on ephemeral pleasures has provoked responses by some classical artists and critics. To cite one pointed example, *The Waste Land*, T. S. Eliot's famous poem of 1922, includes the line, "O O O O That Shakespeherian Rag." By linking the transcendence of Shakespeare with the banality of ragtime song, Eliot's line targets the Western world's trivializing of culture and human experience in the wake of World War I. But if Eliot is deploring cultural contamination from below, Scott Joplin sought respect as just such a boundary crosser: a black composer-performer earning a living in the popular sphere, steeped in the traditional sphere, and seeking his music's acceptance in the classical sphere. Joplin found the cards as heavily stacked against his aspiration as they were against his contemporary Will Marion Cook. Nevertheless, having learned to respect classical music's artistry in his youth, he believed that styles inspired by black folk tradition could stand beside the European ones that had inspired classics in the past. Finding himself in no position to take a provocative stance on behalf of his music, he and his publishers did what they could to emphasize its dignity.

The instrumental ragtime music that Joplin wrote evolved from the connection of syncopated rhythms to the form and the duple beat of the march. The four-bar phrases, sixteen-bar strains, and repetitions of all sections offered a structure that Joplin and his compatriots filled with the flexible, decorative embellishments and jolts that manifest African-American folk tradition. Working as a performer in settings where music often provided background for other activities, Joplin composed with a gift for melody and a passion for detail that rewards close attention.

Published in 1899 as a piano piece by John Stark in Sedalia, Joplin's *Maple Leaf Rag* is a landmark in American music history. It won great commercial success, reportedly selling more than a million sheet-music copies—a remarkable total for a piece so hard to play.[19] And its place in the repertories of later pianists, including Ferd "Jelly Roll" Morton (from New Orleans), James P. Johnson (from New Jersey), and J. Russel Robinson (from Indiana), testifies to its artistic endurance.[20] That no earlier piece by a black composer is known to have sold so many copies is evidence of its appeal to whites as well as blacks. In fact, as music based on black oral tradition that was widely distributed in written form, the *Maple Leaf Rag* must have introduced many white buyers to the challenges and complexities of that tradition—complexities that the *School of Ragtime* would attempt to explain.

Perhaps the key to Joplin's piano rags is that the music seems meant to be experienced as an interplay of content and form. The *Maple Leaf Rag*, for example, contains four strains, each sixteen bars long, each repeated at least once, and with the left hand generally providing a foursquare foil for the right hand's rhythmic trickiness. The form is so familiar from marches and other dance music that we listen with confident expectations of what will happen next. The strict beat never flags, nor does the regular procession of phrases toward their destinations. But the melodies, harmonies, and sounds that articulate this flow are full of variety and surprise. Marches and rags usually ease into the melody through an introduction, but the *Maple Leaf*

Joplin's *Maple Leaf Rag* (Sedalia, 1899), the most famous piano rag of its day, is said to have sold more than one million copies in sheet-music form.

Rag plunges right into the first strain. Likewise, piano ragtime is usually propelled by a left hand that alternates an octave on the beat and a chord after it; but here, Joplin delays that loping figure until the second strain.[21] Also unusual in the first strain is the dynamic plan: a loud beginning, a drop of volume, and a *crescendo* back to the level of the start. The last six bars play on the lowered and raised third in blues-like fashion, in an age before the blues took formal shape.

Like many marches, the *Maple Leaf Rag* is a four-strain piece with a trio in D-flat, the subdominant. In contrast to marches, however, the first strain, not the trio, carries the main melody, and it returns after the second strain before moving on to the trio, creating a form of **AABBACCDD**. The fourth strain's move back to the tonic key of A-flat reconfirms the opening as the composition's core.

Like many songwriters of the time, ragtime writers often sold their works to publishers outright: a catchy, promising piece might bring the composer between $25 and $50. Joplin, however, signed a royalty contract with publisher John Stark for the *Maple Leaf Rag*, and it seems likely that money from his biggest hit helped support him in later years as he moved beyond ragtime into more ambitious endeavors.

Joplin left Sedalia for St. Louis in 1901 and traveled through the Midwest for several years. In 1903, he applied for copyright on an opera, *The Guest of Honor*, which a black touring company performed in Illinois, Missouri, Kansas, Nebraska, and Iowa; the work, however, has disappeared.[22] Four years later, Joplin settled in New York City, where he worked as a composer, arranger, and teacher until he died in 1917. A second opera, *Treemonisha*, written to his own libretto and completed in 1911, occupied much of Joplin's energy during his years there. Taking place in a rural setting near Texarkana, the story seems laced with elements of autobiography. It centers on Treemonisha, a girl of eighteen who hopes to lead her community out of ignorance, superstition, and misery by teaching them the value of education. Joplin called his work a grand opera. "I am a composer of ragtime music," he explained, "but I want it thoroughly understood that my opera 'Treemonisha' is not ragtime. In most of the strains I have used syncopations (rhythm) peculiar to my race, but the music is not ragtime and the score complete is grand opera." *Treemonisha*, however, never found a place in the milieu whose ideas it tried to express. Joplin announced plans for a performance in 1913 by "a company of forty singers, supported by an orchestra of twenty-five musicians," but the performance never took place.[23] In fact, not until the 1970s did his opera receive a full theatrical staging.

According to publisher Edward B. Marks, Joplin told "the other colored song writers" that he would be dead for twenty-five years before people recognized his accomplishments.[24] He was right that posterity would remember him, though public acclaim arrived only after 1970, when a ragtime revival began with Joplin as its central figure. New recordings of his music were made, including some by classical pianists. His rags were republished. *Treemonisha* was performed and recorded. Ragtime orchestras were formed, including a successful one at the New England Conservatory in Boston, one of the nation's venerable institutions. And an Academy Award–winning film, *The Sting*, was released (1973) with a score made up of Joplin's composi-

tions. Although Joplin in his own lifetime never had the cultural or economic clout to secure a niche for himself outside the popular sphere, his
music now enjoys its own kind of classic status.

IRVING BERLIN AND JAMES REESE EUROPE

Scott Joplin's years in New York overlapped with the start of the longest
songwriting career in American history: that of Irving Berlin, a Russian-
Jewish immigrant. For observers who consider Joplin the King of Ragtime,
there is irony in Berlin's reputation during the 1910s as America's chief ragtime composer. But although we think of ragtime today as music for the piano, a sampling of over two hundred ragtime-related books and articles
published between 1896 and 1920 turns up only twenty-one that refer to piano music.[25] The big ragtime successes were songs, and Irving Berlin won
his reputation by writing such ragtime hits as *Alexander's Ragtime Band*.
These songs suggest how, during the 1910s, the social identification of ragtime shifted away from its African-American roots toward the expression of
a new consciousness: a sense that Victorian culture's days were numbered
and that ragtime was both a symptom and a celebration of its decline.

"For some time after the introduction of ragtime" in the 1890s, an observer wrote in 1916, "only songs having to do with the negro were looked
upon as being ragtime numbers." And that was also true of Berlin's early
songwriting years, up to and including *Alexander's Ragtime Band* (March
1911). But the summer of that year marked a turning point for Berlin. For in
That Mysterious Rag, published in August, no black protagonist is implied,
nor do black characters appear in any of Berlin's later ragtime songs. Moreover, at that very time Berlin began to use the word "syncopated" instead of
"ragtime" to describe his own songs in that vein.[26] Syncopated rhythm from
black folk culture, introduced by ragtime and then absorbed into the vocabulary of Tin Pan Alley song, came to symbolize the spirit of social liberation
that appeared in New York society and quickly spread elsewhere. And one
mark of that new sensibility was the craze for dancing that surfaced in the
early 1910s.

Since the mid-1800s, recreational dancing had not enjoyed much social
prominence in the United States, being reserved chiefly for private functions such as formal balls or banished to dives that encouraged illicit behavior—the kinds of places that respectable women did not frequent. But
starting in 1912, public dance halls opened in large numbers, and so did hotel ballrooms and dance floors in cafés, restaurants, and cabarets. A flood of
new dances fueled the explosion. An observer of the time estimated that between 1912 and 1914, "over one hundred new dances found their way, in and
out of our fashionable ballrooms." Dancing in earlier days had been a formal

activity of learned steps and motions of the feet. But the new dances, many of them infused with syncopation and bearing such names as the fox-trot, turkey trot, Texas tommy, bunny hug, and lame duck, encouraged more spontaneous movement. Rather than defining the dance by its steps alone, women and men now began to move their whole bodies to the beat. And the new songs emphasized rhythm over melody, mimicked by Eliot's "O O O O That Shakespeherian Rag," with its four accented beats and the implied syncopation of the added syllable. Popular music was now an extension of dancing as well as singing, playing, and listening.[27]

A journal of 1914 remarked wonderingly on the place that dancing now filled in New York's social life. Even "in the midst of this money-getting machine-made age," people were ready to give up some of their business hours so that they could "not only dance in the evening, but in the after-noon and in the morning." Dance teams such as Vernon and Irene Castle and Maurice Mouvet and Florence Walton became cultural icons whose dress and personal style, as well as their graceful movements on the dance floor, were copied. F. Scott Fitzgerald's *The Perfect Life*, a story of young movers and shakers of New York society, points to the new atmosphere that dancing brought to the social scene:

> The afternoon was already planned; they were going dancing—for those were the great days: Maurice was tangoing in "Over the River" [featuring an onstage cabaret], the Castles were doing a stiff-legged walk in the third act of the "Sunshine Girl"—a walk that gave the modern dance a social position and brought the nice girl into the café, thus beginning a profound revolution in American life. The great rich empire was feeling its oats and was out for some not too plebeian, yet not too artistic fun.[28]

Irving Berlin played a larger role in this transformation than any other songwriter. A force in the profession for almost half a century, he became a trendsetter in the 1910s, when he mastered the carefree new sensibility—more through effort than inheritance. Emigrating with his family from Russia to New York City at the age of five (1893), he grew up in a Jewish neighborhood on the Lower East Side and, lacking formal education, seems to have acquired his skill with words and music on his own. Starting as a singing waiter, he began working his way into the world of Tin Pan Alley. While still a teenager, Berlin published songs for which he wrote words, music, or both. Possessing an acute business sense as well as talent, tenaciousness, and a quick mind, he won such success that after a dozen years in the trade he established his own publishing firm, Irving Berlin Music, Inc. (1919). Describing his working method, Berlin once explained: "I get an idea, either a title or a phrase or a melody, and hum it out to something definite." But if "humming out" sounds like a casual process, Berlin's perfec-

Irving Berlin (1888–1989), photographed between 1913 and 1919, when he and Ted Snyder were partners in the firm of Berlin and Snyder, music publishers on Tin Pan Alley.

tionist streak and ferocious work habits made it anything but that. A long-time friend recalled in the 1970s having sat "beside Irving at his tiny piano" and listened while he composed. "He would go over and over a lyric until it seemed perfect to my ears. Then he'd scrap the whole thing and begin over again. When I asked Irving what was wrong, he invariably said, 'It isn't *simple* enough.'"[29]

To highlight the variety of Tin Pan Alley song genres and Irving Berlin's command of them, the editor of the songs Berlin wrote between 1907 and 1914 has divided them into groups: (1) ballads, (2) novelty songs, (3) ragtime and other dance songs, and (4) show songs. Ballads stood the closest in style and mood to the older Victorian songs; a novelty song sketched a brief, comic story, with no specified style; ragtime numbers include all songs with that word in their titles or that mention ragtime in their texts; and show songs were performed in a stage production in Berlin's day.[30] Subgenres are found within these four types, especially the first two (e.g., high-class, romantic, march, and domestic ballads). And some songs fit in more than one category, as with a novelty song that was performed onstage.

To look chronologically through Berlin's songs is to sense that one is reading a social barometer. Tuned to the marketplace—and sheet music was still being published chiefly for amateur singers and players—these songs reflect *both* the cutting edge of fashion and the entrenched culture that was under siege. The years 1912–17 have been described as both the end of Victorian calm and the beginning of a cultural revolution;[31] and Berlin's early work seems to embody both designations, mixing old-fashioned waltz songs and ballads like *God Gave You to Me* and *When I Lost You* with such novelties as *My Wife's Gone to the Country (Hurrah! Hurrah!)* and *If You Don't Want My Peaches (You'd Better Stop Shaking My Tree)*. Ethnicity was a key subject, for immigrants poured into New York's melting pot until 1914, when war broke out in Europe. The popular theater maintained familiar black stereotypes from the minstrel show and added other nationalities, each with its own built-in story. Thus, as well as coon songs with black characters, Berlin's early work includes songs with Italian, German, and Jewish protagonists, and even a few "rube" songs involving gullible country folk. In *Sadie Salome (Go Home)* (1909), written with Edgar Leslie, Berlin combines the notorious Dance of the Seven Veils from Strauss's *Salome* with a slice of Lower East Side neighborhood life. The main characters are Sadie Cohen, who leaves "her happy home to become an actress lady," and Mose, who loves her. But when Mose goes to the theater to watch her perform, he is horrified to find that Sadie has become a stripper.

If *Sadie Salome (Go Home)* reflects Berlin's flair for topical humor, three songs from 1911 show him celebrating the spirit of those who were ready to end American Victorianism once and for all. *Alexander's Ragtime Band* responds to the charisma of black musicians and the excitement of their playing. *That Mysterious Rag* recognizes the style's haunting, distracting traits and removes it from a racial setting. And in *Everybody's Doing It Now*, ragtime is an infectious dance music—a fad uniting younger Americans in a spirit of uninhibited fun.

Though *Alexander's Ragtime Band* may at first seem free of racial connotations, the name Alexander was associated with black characters in minstrel shows, and the song uses words in ways that audiences then considered part of black speech patterns.[32] And though the song lacks ragtime syncopation, it begins in C and includes a chorus in F, just as the trio strain of a typical rag moves into the subdominant key. The song's muscular, declamatory urging—"Come on and hear / Come on and hear / Alexander's Ragtime Band"—conveys the buzzing excitement that black influence brought to American popular song. Most of all, Berlin's song registers the impact of black musical performance. Alexander and his band can take conventional tunes like the "bugle call" from *A-Hunting We Will Go* and the first phrase of Stephen Foster's *Old Folks at Home* and make them sound "like you've never heard before."

Just thinking about Alexander and his bandsmen is enough to make the singer, who could be either black or white, bubble with high spirits. Had Americans ever before looked forward so eagerly to listening to music?

That Mysterious Rag, the turning-point piece that Berlin wrote a few months after *Alexander*, confirms the impact of ragtime but treats it as something more to be feared than relished. Going beyond aesthetics into pathology, the text tells of a melody so malignantly unforgettable that even sleepers are not immune. "If you ever wake up from your dreaming," warns the verse, "A-scheming, eyes gleaming, / Then if suddenly you take a screaming fit, / That's it!" Once planted in the brain, the music takes over, as if the victim were bewitched, invaded by a parasite, or besotted with a drug. The chorus, cast in an unusual twenty-four-bar structure, lays out symptoms:

> That mysterious rag.
> While awake or while you're a-slumbering,
> You're saying,
> Keep playing
> That mysterious drag,
> Are you listenin'?
> Are you listenin'?
> Look! Look! You're whistlin'
> That mysterious rag.
> Sneaky, freaky, ever melodious
> Mysterious rag.

And, in a novel moment of diagnostic finger-pointing, the eighth line's first two words are to be spoken by the singer. It would be hard to find another Berlin song with one-syllable words so awkwardly stretched or natural declamation so bent out of shape. Perhaps, by making "that" the first word of the chorus, then extending the three-letter word "rag" over eight beats and two whole notes, he was hoping to suggest the demented state into which an obsessed listener could slip.

And if you care to hear the Swa - nee Riv - er played

Although *Everybody's Doing It Now* contains relatively little syncopation, this song emphasizes rhythm at least as much as the other two, for it is dominated by the three-note dotted-rhythm figure to which "doin' it" is delivered. The title, a pun daringly racy for that day, refers to ragtime dancing. The verse notes the music's energizing effect: "Ain't the funny strain / Goin' to your brain? / Like a bottle of wine, / Fine." And the chorus tells us that this electric new musical style—"Hear that trombone bustin' apart?"—was driving dancers to throw restraint to the winds:

> See that ragtime couple over there,
> Watch them throw their shoulders in the air,
> Snap their fingers, Honey, I declare,
> It's a bear, it's a bear, it's a bear,
> There!

At the same time that Irving Berlin was offering ragtime as an emblem of up-to-date fashion, a black musician working in New York was reminding the public of the music's African-American roots, though he shared Scott

Joplin's dislike of the "ragtime" label. And these efforts helped James Reese Europe win a place in the city's musical infrastructure for other black musicians as well as himself. Born in 1880 in Mobile, Alabama, but raised in Washington, D.C., Europe learned to play piano, and he studied violin with Joseph Douglass, grandson of the abolitionist Frederick Douglass. Aspiring to be a well-schooled musician, he also showed a keen interest in music theory, orchestration, and conducting. Around 1903, Europe moved to New York and within a few years was serving as conductor of *The Shoofly Regiment* (1906), a show by Bob Cole and the Johnson brothers. In 1910, Europe joined with others to create the Clef Club, a booking agency for African-American musicians and ensembles: the first real effort to harness the city's black musical talent. The club's roster of players in its peak years numbered more than two hundred, ready to form a dance orchestra at a moment's notice. Annual concerts at Carnegie Hall in 1912–15 added to the Clef Club's prestige, though Europe resigned in 1914 and founded the Tempo Club, a rival group. Equally important in showing the power of black music making, however, was Europe's association with the dance team of Irene and Vernon Castle, for whom he served as musical director and conductor beginning in late 1913.[33]

Europe's protégé, bandleader and singer Noble Sissle, remembered that before his mentor came into prominence, the white New York social elite had favored Viennese waltzes, rendered by "gypsy bands playing violins, mandolins, cellos, and things." But after members of white society were introduced to Europe's music, they immediately began "hiring the Clef Club to come and play." As Sissle recalled: "The Clef Club used to go on after the gypsy band finished playing, and whatever was the last waltz the gypsy band played, the Clef Club would start off by playing it in ragtime. All of a sudden, people commenced getting up and trying to dance it. And this was the beginning of the Negro taking over New York music and establishing our rhythms." While the work of composers such as Joplin and Berlin was fundamental to the ragtime takeover, Sissle's account points to the importance of performers who mastered the new style and white society's infatuation with their music. "We played in parlors, drawing rooms, yachts, private railroad cars, exclusive millionaires' clubs, swanky hotels, and fashionable resorts," he continued. "We played everywhere—from the Everglades (in Palm Beach) to the Green Brier Hotel (in White Sulfur Springs) to the Metropolitan Club (in New York) to Newport's finest." Being appreciated in settings like these was no small matter. "I think we boys who came to New York and were in the music profession at that time lived through the happiest and most interesting time in the development of American music," Sissle said many years later. "We were snatched away from all walks of life, from all en-

James Reese Europe (1881–1919) conducts an ensemble of members of New York City's Clef Club (1914).

vironments, and suddenly found ourselves playing and singing at the homes of the Vanderbilts, the Goulds, the Wanamakers." James Reese Europe and his men were hired for such occasions because they were the best performers of the music their high-toned customers wanted to hear. "The wealthy people," Sissle explained, "would not take a substitute when they could buy the original."[34]

When the United States entered World War I in 1917, Europe was asked to organize a band for the Fifteenth Infantry. Nicknamed "the Hellfighters," the ensemble was sent to France to bring troops a taste of home. We have a detailed account from Noble Sissle of a concert the band gave in Nantes on February 12, 1918, which was a huge success (with the French people as well as the American soldiers) and no less a triumph of programming than were the performances of Sousa's band. In the first half, Europe's men showed their versatility and musicianship with a march, some overtures, and vocal selections, "all of which were heartily applauded." Sissle described the concert's second half as an interaction between performers and audience. Sousa's *The Stars and Stripes Forever* was the first number after intermission, and applause broke out even before the music stopped. After an arrangement of Southern plantation melodies came *The Memphis Blues*. For this number, Europe and his men struck a new attitude. After a "soul-rousing crash" of cymbals, "both director and musicians seemed to forget their surroundings." Cornet and clarinet players began to bend their notes rhythmically, the drummers fell into syncopated time, while the trombones "sat patiently waiting for their cue to have a 'jazz spasm.' . . . The audience could stand it no longer, the 'jazz germ' hit them and it seemed to find the vital spot loosening all muscles and causing what is known in America as an 'eagle rocking it.' "[35]

When the war ended, Europe and the Hellfighters left the army together and toured the United States, billed as "65 Musician Veterans of the Champagne and Argonne." In March and early May of 1919, a smaller contingent of the band recorded some two dozen sides in New York under Europe's direction, playing mostly popular songs. But the Hellfighters' saga ended abruptly in Boston on May 9, when a crazed member of the band stabbed Europe before a performance. He died later that day. The loss of this eminent musician was not taken lightly: Europe was the first black to be honored by the city of New York with a public funeral.

James Reese Europe's death at thirty-nine came at a time when he seemed ready to build on the foundation he had laid before and during the war. When Europe died, he was one of the most respected band leaders in the United States, poised to challenge the leadership of white conductor Paul Whiteman in the world of the 1920s jazz ensemble. "He was not ashamed of being a Negro or being called a Negro," a New York newspaper read, "believing instead of worrying and arguing about what he should be called, the proper thing was to dignify the term *Negro*, just as he helped dignify Negro music." And a Chicago paper praised the bandleader as "a dynamic force that did things—big things," adding: "His death comes as a big loss to the musical world, but a still greater loss to the race of which he was proud to be a member."[36]

Epilogue

On April 8, 1920, Charles Tomlinson Griffes, thirty-five years old and director of music at the Hackley School for Boys, north of New York City on the Hudson River, died in New York Hospital of an abscessed lung. Though not widely known, several compositions by Griffes had been performed in New York in recent years: in 1917, *Sho-Jo* (a stage pantomime) and *Five Poems of Ancient China and Japan* for voice and piano; and the following year, a new piano sonata. *The Pleasure-Dome of Kubla Khan* was played in 1919 by the Boston Symphony Orchestra, and so was the *Notturno für Orchester*, by Leopold Stokowski and the Philadelphia Orchestra. As these titles suggest, Griffes's imagination was far from provincial. If his older contemporary Charles Ives built a composing life around the experience of a New England boyhood, Griffes constructed his around a cosmopolitan consciousness. He left a substantial body of work at his death, including many art songs, a smaller number of piano pieces, and works for chamber ensemble, ballet, and orchestra. His career is evidence that for all the ferment that surrounded social dancing, ragtime, and the music of Tin Pan Alley and Broadway in the 1910s, an environment also existed for composers in the classical sphere who were interested neither in writing operas nor in grounding their work in folk and popular music.

A native of Elmira, New York, Griffes took piano lessons with local teachers, then traveled in 1903 to Germany for more concentrated study. Enrolling at the Stern Conservatory in Berlin, he developed as a pianist while his interest in composition grew. For a time he was a student of Englebert Humperdinck, composer of the well-known opera *Hansel and Gretel*. Returning to the United States in 1907, he took the post at the Hackley School that he filled for the rest of his life—not a highly prestigious job, but one that supported him in an environment that provided leisure time and a chance to promote his music in New York.

Griffes brought back from Europe a number of songs for voice and piano that he had composed to German texts. He continued to explore that vein until around 1911, when his style moved away from German Romanticism toward an approach freer in form. Griffes's inspiration in these years seems to have come more from France than Germany, and especially from Claude Debussy and Maurice Ravel, whose music suggests a parallel with French impressionist painting and poetry—emphasizing sound and color over line, standing ready to dissolve standard syntax, and seeking to evoke fleeting impressions through evanescent images.[37] Traits in Griffes's music from these years include a fondness for parallel chords, whole-tone scales, augmented triads, and pictorial and descriptive titles (e.g., *The White Peacock* for piano). By 1916, Griffes was composing music inspired by the culture of the Far East. *Sho-Jo*, a one-scene pantomime, evokes this culture through delicate harmonies and orchestration and the use of muted strings. The piano sonata of 1917–18 finds him working in yet another style, this one dissonant and more abstract.

It is clear from Griffes's career alone that the classical sphere was open to composers for whom attempts to "sound American" would have been unnatural. By the 1910s, ample opportunity existed for well-made American works to be performed in concert halls by skilled professionals, whatever their stylistic stripe.

27

The Jazz Age Dawns
Blues, Jazz, and a Rhapsody

CHAPTER 26 TOLD W. C. Handy's tale of encountering primitive but crowd-pleasing music in Mississippi, which he began arranging for his note-reading bandsmen. In 1912, Handy published in Memphis, Tennessee, the first of many blues numbers that poured from the pens of songwriters in the 1910s and early 1920s. Thus began the printed history of what may be the most far-reaching contribution of African Americans to twentieth-century musical culture: the sensibility embodied in blues music.

The hardscrabble conditions in which the blues began have been traced to the Deep South, in small towns and rural regions, Mississippi Delta plantations, and industries that demanded heavy manual labor, including mining, logging, and railroad building. Lacking education, property, and political power in a segregated society, the creators of the blues were locked in a cycle of hardship that ensured their rural isolation even as they tried to escape it by moving from job to job. African practices, preserved orally in the ring shout, were more likely to continue here than in less isolated surroundings, and early blues drew on them heavily. Yet singing the blues was from the start a deeply personal pastime that arose from the singers' American experience. While African songs were mostly about social units, the blues dealt with the lives of individuals, the standard focus for Western art.

Since the 1500s, the word "blues" has been associated in English with a melancholy state of mind. But African-American blues songs take a unique attitude toward separation and loss, described by black writer Ralph Ellison as "an impulse to keep the painful details and episodes of a brutal experience alive in one's aching consciousness, to finger its jagged grain, and to transcend it, not by the consolation of philosophy but by squeezing from it a near-tragic, near-comic lyricism."[1] Where the sentimental song creates a realm of passive emotional longing, the blues' determination to probe real suffering brings singers, players, and listeners to a perspective on pain that might even include laughter. For black novelist and critic Albert Murray, the blues tradition is one of confrontation and improvisation, and he explains why improvising, which requires on-the-spot invention, is fundamental to the blues sensibility. A musician or dancer who "swings the blues" is "making an affirmative and hence exemplary and heroic response" to the human condition. "Confronting, acknowledging, and contending with the infernal absurdities and ever-impending frustrations inherent in the nature of all existence," Murray says, the blues performer extemporizes *by playing with the possibilities that are also there.*[2] Ellison, Murray, and others have seen the blues' embrace of the full range of human experience as quintessentially democratic and instructive to all. Indeed, it is hard to think of another kind of expression that has brought so many people artistically face-to-face with human weakness and human strength at the same time.

Before it began to be written down and published, the blues, like ragtime, took shape in oral tradition. The African-derived work song, related to collective physical tasks such as harvesting, hauling, rock breaking, and chopping, may be an ancestor of the blues—especially songs with a dialogue between leader and group, or two groups singing in alternation. And "field hollers," sung by solitary workers, are said to have supplied the basic vocal material for early folk blues. Hollers, highly embellished expressions of (usually) work or love, have been traced back to the time of slavery. But the 1890s seem to have been the time when the blues began to take recognizable shape. As the bitterness of Southern whites toward blacks after Reconstruction led to segregation laws, black communities were forced to create their own identity, and in these settlements black sacred and secular music flowered.

Early blues was accompanied by instruments, especially banjo and guitar, which provided a foundation of harmony and rhythm. Several performing techniques rooted in folk culture and refined by professionals who brought the music into the popular sphere came to be earmarks of blues performance. One had to do with pitch: the so-called blue third and seventh scale degrees in major mode, shaded or flattened for expression. Such tone bending, natural to singers, also suits the guitar, on which the finger may easily be slid along a string. A second blues trait was a rasping singing style; performers might also slide a bottleneck or a knife along the guitar strings to produce the kind of whining tone sometimes heard from African stringed instruments. A third technique was a regular exchange between voice and instrument(s): a call and response in which the singer's vocal statements provoked instrumental answers in a free, eventful dialogue.

These techniques are improvisatory, reflecting the blues feeling of singers and players who used them as a way to play with the possibilities in any performance. In fact, blue notes can only be suggested by musical notation, and changes in vocal sound are not notated at all. Nor was it in the spirit of traditional blues performers to plan responses to a singer's call, for who could anticipate what any particular moment might demand? To write down a blues song goes against the idea that blues is a spontaneous kind of music. Yet during the 1910s, sheet music remained the chief vehicle for putting popular music into marketable form. Once Handy introduced the blues song successfully into print, a new notated popular genre was born, one that applied poetic images from African-American folk tradition to the troubles of human existence. And for all its flexibility, the blues exhibited some stable traits as well. One was a three-line poetic stanza made from a couplet and a single rhyming line: statement, restatement, response. Many blues lyrics were strophic songs with stanzas in that form: three four-bar phrases making a twelve-bar stanza likely to be supported by a standard harmonic progression. By the latter 1910s, blues conventions included not only a mood and certain performing customs but also a poetic style and form, a musical form, and a characteristic pattern of harmony.

Handy's *St. Louis Blues* (1914), the most popular blues song of its time and one of the first to be published, illustrates one approach to putting the blues sensibility into print. The composer, who also wrote the words, later described his song as "the wail of a lovesick woman for her lost man" but told in "the humorous spirit of the bygone coon songs." And he said he had used "Negro phraseology and dialect" to enhance the mood, believing that this language "often implies more than well-chosen English can express." For example, he recalled once hearing a drunken woman muttering as she stumbled down the street: "Ma man's got a heart like a rock cast in de sea." Handy borrowed that image for the chorus of his song:

> Got de St. Louis Blues jes blue as ah can be,
> Dat man got a heart lak a rock cast in the sea,
> Or else he wouldn't gone so far from me.

He also made frequent use of the lowered (minor) third in a major key (one whose third degree is major), producing blue notes. This reflected the practice of "the primitive Southern Negro," Handy claimed, who "was sure to bear down on the third and seventh tones of the scale, slurring between major and minor."

The harmonic progression in the illustration is the now-familiar twelve-bar blues. The first four-bar phrase revolves around a tonic chord; the second is divided into two bars of subdominant (mm. 5–6) and two of tonic (mm. 7–8); and the third begins with two bars of dominant (mm. 9–10), returning to tonic in measure 11 and preparing to begin the same cycle again. Performers since Handy's time have embellished this scheme with substi-

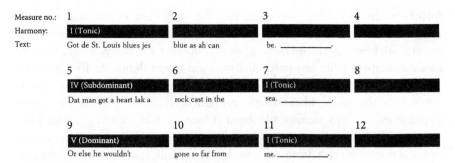

Measure no.:	1	2	3	4
Harmony:	I (Tonic)			
Text:	Got de St. Louis blues jes	blue as ah can	be. _____.	

	5	6	7	8
	IV (Subdominant)		I (Tonic)	
	Dat man got a heart lak a	rock cast in the	sea. _____.	

	9	10	11	12
	V (Dominant)		I (Tonic)	
	Or else he wouldn't	gone so far from	me. _____.	

This diagram summarizes the twelve-bar blues harmonic progression, which under-lies the first strain and chorus of Handy's *St. Louis Blues*. The words underlaid here are those of the chorus.

tute chords while maintaining its pillars: tonic harmony, in one form or an-other, in measures 1, 7, and 11; subdominant in measure 5; and dominant in measure 9.

According to Handy's autobiography, he tried to make the *St. Louis Blues* a hit by departing from well-worn paths rather than following them. His starting point was "real" emotion, "cut to the native blues pattern." He also hoped "to combine ragtime syncopation with a real melody in the spiritual tradition." Since the tango was then a popular new dance in Memphis, Handy included a second section with a tango beat, and he used that mate-rial for his introduction as well. Finally, he added a third section, labeled "chorus" and based on the *Jogo Blues*, a number he had published separately in 1913.[3] The result was a song that fit none of the day's standard popular song forms. To be sure, the printed version of the *St. Louis Blues* is a strophic song with three stanzas, but sixty-four bars at a deliberate tempo makes for an unusually long stanza. The first twelve-bar section, in G major, is followed by a written-out repeat (**AA**); the sixteen-bar tango strain, in G minor, presents a new eight-bar statement plus its repetition; and the twelve-bar chorus in G major is also new and repeated, producing a stanza in a form equivalent to a three-strain rag (**AABBCC**).

The three strains give *St. Louis Blues* a narrative shape usually missing from folk blues. Starting with a confession of misery, it then describes the "St. Louis woman" who has stolen away the singer's man, and ends by defin-ing the woeful tale as a blues experience. Handy's two blues strains (**A** and **C**), supported by the same harmonic progression, differ in character. The first presents the melody that Handy said was in the style of a ragtime-infused spiritual. The second, busier and dominated by a blue-third scale degree, features a continuous eighth-note rhythm, a drone bass, and an os-cillation between tonic and subdominant that anticipates later piano boogie-woogie. Recalling Handy's description of Mississippi blues as "over-and-over

Gertrude "Ma" Rainey (1886–1939) was a Georgia native and one of the first "classic" blues singers. The Georgia Jazz Band, with which she is pictured here, includes pianist Thomas A. Dorsey, later a leader in the field of gospel music.

strains" with no clear beginning or ending, one may be struck by this number's musical variety. Aiming the *St. Louis Blues* at note-reading musicians like himself, Handy wrote a song that combines the spirit of Southern folk blues with an expressive range fit for stage performance.

During the decade after the publication of Handy's *St. Louis Blues*, the blues developed on three different fronts. The Southern folk blues, rooted in regional customs and the primal source of all blues performance, was the most basic. This "down-home" oral practice probably continued with relatively little change, though there is no way of checking that assumption for lack of recordings before the mid-1920s.[4] In the meantime, some blues songs by literate musicians like Handy found their way into the entertainment business, in part through black "songsters": musicians of the post-Reconstruction era who performed popular songs in informal settings, accompanying themselves on banjo or guitar. The impact of early Southern blues singers who worked in medicine shows, performed by street entertainers selling patent medicine, may be likened to that of street evangelists who popularized gospel songs at roughly the same time. At any rate, they spread the blues as they traveled, as did a number of wandering singers. The experience of presenting blues to paying audiences gave such performers a growing professionalism and sophistication.

In 1920, Mamie Smith, a theater and cabaret singer, made history with her recording of *Crazy Blues*, accompanied by a small ensemble she called her Jazz Hounds. The success of this recording, the first by a black singer of a blues song, surprised its producers: 75,000 copies were sold in a few months' time, chiefly in black neighborhoods. Mamie Smith's success brought competitors into recording studios; making records of blues songs was suddenly a profitable business. Classic blues singers such as Gertrude "Ma" Rainey, Edith Wilson, Bessie Smith, Ida Cox, and Alberta Hunter, professionals working in vaudeville and the musical stage, were able to sing virtually any kind of song. Dressing and acting the part of "queens" of the blues, they were usually accompanied by piano or a small jazz group, the piano marking the beat and the horns responding to the singer's "calls," filling in the spaces in the vocal line. Like the singers, their accompanists were entertainment professionals, trained on the black stage circuit, or perhaps talented youngsters such as Louis Armstrong. Presented as a species of popular song and first marketed as "race" records, meaning black musicians performing black music for black listeners, this strain of the blues must have appealed to audiences across racial lines. Bessie Smith's first recording, *Down Hearted Blues* (1923), sold 780,000 copies within six months of its issue.

A third strain of blues song emerged from Tin Pan Alley shortly before 1920, spurring a blues fad from 1919 to 1924. Some numbers were syncopated fox-trots, including *Jazz Me Blues* and *Chasing the Blues*. Others, such as *Wang Wang Blues* and *Wabash Blues*, were simply pop songs. And still others were "real blues": songs with three-line poetic stanzas and twelve-bar choruses, set to blues harmonies, and steeped in human melancholy. Tin Pan Alley disconnected the idea of the blues from its racial origins, sometimes using the word simply as a trendy way to talk about gloom.

As a young songwriter, George Gershwin worked Tin Pan Alley's blues vein often in the early 1920s. Two songs from 1922 show different aspects of his early blues impulse. The thirty-two-bar chorus of *Yankee Doodle Blues*, with lyrics by Irving Caesar and B. G. DeSylva, celebrates the glories of America ("I love every mile"), but only after a verse made up of two twelve-bar blues statements has (lightheartedly) outlined the woe that can accompany a trip overseas. *I'll Build a Stairway to Paradise*, written for *George White's Scandals of 1922* to a text by DeSylva and Arthur Francis (a.k.a. Ira Gershwin, George's brother), on the other hand, refers more inventively to blues traits. The verse contains a trademark convention of Tin Pan Alley blues songs: a succession of repeated chords in a marching, quarter-note rhythm, appearing in the accompaniment's lower reaches as if hinting at a suggestive kind of dancing or body movement. Then Gershwin begins the sixteen-bar chorus with a four-bar phrase whose harmony sounds like the start of a twelve-bar blues progression. Not only does it linger on the tonic chord for four bars, emphasizing the flat-seventh scale degree as a blue note, with the throbbing quarter-note rhythm responding in blues-like fashion to the voice's call, but the first two bars of the next phrase move to the subdominant. Only when dominant rather than tonic harmony is implied in the chorus's seventh bar does a listener recognize that this is not to be a blues chorus. Yet the quarter-note throb returns to underline the next announcement: "I've got the blues, / And up above it's so fair." By the early 1920s, then, American audiences knew something about the blues, and George Gershwin, for one, had shown himself to be at home composing in a blues idiom.

THE RISE OF JAZZ

The origins of the syncopated dance music called jazz have been a matter for much speculation. But virtually all authorities agree that the city of New Orleans played a key role and that its African-American citizens took the lead. Two related factors make it impossible to be more precise about the emergence of jazz: (1) the difficulty of defining what, in these early years, separated jazz from ragtime and blues, two styles that preceded and nourished it; and (2) the lack of recordings to document the beginnings of a music that took shape in oral form. Early in the 1910s, James Reese Europe and his orchestra were playing fast ragtime for dancers in New York, recording some of it as early as 1913. Yet when the Original Dixieland Jazz Band, a group of white New Orleans musicians, first played in New York City in 1916, then recorded *Livery Stable Blues* and *Dixie Jass Band One-Step* there in 1917, the music they offered was accepted enthusiastically as something new and different. Not until the early 1920s were black jazz musicians given a chance to make records; once they were, however, black players from New Orleans, including King Oliver, Jelly Roll Morton, Louis Armstrong, and Sidney Bechet, came to be recognized as the new style's premier figures.

Among the traits that made New Orleans musically unique were its mixed French and Spanish heritage, a long-standing devotion to opera, the presence of many free blacks in antebellum years, and their relative freedom to assemble for various festivities. To these may be added the availability of education and musical training and the forming of many black fraternal groups, some with their own bands for parades and funerals. Although New Orleans gave black residents a wider range of social opportunity than most other American cities, it would be wrong to imagine that blacks and whites mingled freely in the post–Civil War years. During Reconstruction, the white majority refused to share power with black citizens, and later in the century the city's economy grew stagnant and race relations deteriorated. *Plessy v. Ferguson*, the 1896 Supreme Court case that led to legalized segregation throughout the South, stemmed from an incident on a New Orleans railroad car. And a long-established caste system based on color and language split New Orleans's black citizens into French-speaking, lighter-skinned Creoles who lived downtown and darker-skinned English speakers, many of them migrants who had moved from the country into uptown New Orleans neighborhoods.

In the early 1900s, then, three distinct groups of New Orleans musicians—one white and two black—were playing the ensemble dance music from which jazz evolved. While they shared instrumentation, repertory, and some audience members, contact among them was limited. Bass player Pops Foster recalled in later years that "if you didn't play any blues you didn't get any colored jobs, and if you didn't play lancers [quadrilles] you didn't get Cajun [Creole] jobs." And he added: "White jobs didn't care what you played." All in all, white audiences had access to the full array of the city's music, black and white; uptown black musicians could play in some downtown venues but not in others; black audiences were subject to strict segregation, restricted to all-black venues; and downtown Creole musicians and listeners occupied a shifting but marginal position between the polar opposites of black and white.[5]

The origins of jazz have long been thought to lie in New Orleans, but how the new musical style actually took shape has remained a matter of doubt. It seems likely that jazz grew out of ragtime dance music as musicians in the city began playing it early in this century. Dances imported from Paris in the 1840s, such as the polka, the schottische, the mazurka, and the quadrille, had long dominated the New Orleans scene. In the 1890s, however, new dances began replacing them, especially the two-step, a simple walking and sliding movement well suited to ragtime. Later, between 1911 and 1914, the two-step was complemented by sexier new dances such as the turkey trot, which featured flapping arm movements and enough contact between partners' bodies to warrant criticism from the Vatican, and which called for a new, earthier accompaniment.[6]

Another trait may also have played a role: the remarkable expressiveness with which black New Orleans musicians played dance music. Even before 1900, visitors to the city mentioned local musicians' aptitude for melodic playing. Perhaps some players' melodic inventions, together with an altered rhythmic emphasis, brought a different character to their performance of ragtime. Yet pinpointing when, where, and how jazz first diverged from ragtime, and from blues as well, is difficult if not impossible, for even in these early years "jazz" refers to a way of performing that was improvised, not written down. Both ragtime (from 1896) and blues (from 1912) were independent, written forms *as well as* performing styles; jazz, in contrast, was an unwritten performing style that only in the 1920s began to be set down in

The Piron and Williams Orchestra of New Orleans, c. 1915. Members include (standing) Jimmie Noone, clarinet; William Ridgley, trombone; Oscar Celestin, cornet; John Lindsay, bass; (seated) Ernest Trepagnier, drums; A. J. Piron, violin; Tom Benton, mandolin-banjo; Johnny St. Cyr, banjo; and (in front) Clarence Williams, piano.

notation, so the sounds of jazz before the first jazz recordings (in 1917) remain a matter of speculation. How did black, white, and Creole playing styles in pre-1917 New Orleans compare? How closely did King Oliver's jazz band's 1923 recordings, made during a long Chicago engagement, relate to the way Oliver sounded before he left New Orleans in 1918? These are just two of the many unanswered questions that surround the beginnings of jazz history.

The first "hot" players in New Orleans between 1900 and 1920 did not call their music jazz. In fact, only when they went north did New Orleans musicians learn that the label was being applied to what they thought of as a distinctive local way of playing ragtime.[7] "Jazz, that's a name the white people have given to the music," clarinetist and soprano saxophonist Sidney Bechet claimed toward the end of his career. Bechet traced the music he learned growing up to the historical experience of African Americans, including Omar, his slave grandfather. "All those people who had been slaves," he explained, "needed the music more than ever" after Emancipation.

It was like they were trying to find out in this music what they were supposed to do with this freedom: playing the music and listening to it—waiting for it to express what they needed to learn, once they had learned it wasn't just white people the music had to reach to, nor even to their own people, but straight out to life and to what a man does with his life when it finally *is* his.

In Bechet's view, "ragtime" caught that spirit, because "it comes out of the Negro spirituals, out of Omar's way of singing, out of his rhythms." Bechet believed that to call this music jazz trivialized it. "Jazz could mean any damn' thing," he told his interviewer: "high times, screwing, ballroom."[8] Actually, the word first appeared in print in San Francisco in 1913 in reference to baseball, meaning pep and enthusiasm. In any case, its suggestion of speed and excitement helped it catch on as a musical label when New Orleans musicians took their music to other parts of the country.

A typical turn-of-the-century New Orleans dance ensemble was led by a violinist, joined by several wind instruments, plus a rhythm section of drums, guitar, and double bass, the last usually bowed rather than plucked. Playing by ear, they favored old-fashioned dance tunes (schottische, mazurka, and quadrille), performed in a polyphony that allowed the wind players little chance to rest. Larger dance orchestras included violin, cornet, clarinet, trombone, drums, double bass, guitar, and sometimes piano. Following the national trend of replacing guitar and double bass with the banjo and tuba, New Orleans bands also dropped the violin and adopted the saxophone family. Melody, at first shifted from one instrument to another, was by the early 1920s generally assigned to the cornet player, who was now likely to be the band's leader.

By that time, the New Orleans jazz ensemble's three melodic voices—cornet, clarinet, and trombone—had assumed different roles and performing styles. Joe (King) Oliver and other cornetists born in the city before 1895 played the lead melody without much variation, and stayed in the middle register. Against the cornet lead, the clarinetist played a countermelody, often in eighth notes and over a wide range of the instrument. Clarinets were sometimes missing from pre-1920 New Orleans ensembles, but never trombones, which played in what was called the "tailgate style," with frequent smears—slurs over several pitches—and a mixture of countermelody in the tenor range and doubling of the bass line. The players' drive for expressiveness may be heard in the earliest recordings made by Oliver, Bechet, and others, which incorporate blue notes and portamento—purposeful sliding from one note to the next—into an expressive melodic style.[9] Proof of the New Orleans players' impact came from Ohio-born jazz clarinetist Garvin Bushell, who with New York–bred cornetist James "Bubber" Miley—later a key member of Duke Ellington's band—heard Oliver in Chicago in 1922.

It was the first time I'd heard New Orleans musicians to any advantage, and I studied them for the entire week we were in town. I was very much impressed with their blues and their sound. The trumpets and clarinets in the East had a better "legitimate" quality, but the sound of Oliver's band touched you more. It was less cultivated but more expressive of how the people felt. Bubber and I sat there with our mouths open.[10]

Well before these black New Orleaneans began recording, however, the American public had encountered jazz as a riotous new form of popular entertainment. In late 1916, the Original Dixieland Jazz Band was hired at Reisenweber's restaurant in New York, one of the sumptuous Broadway eateries that opened up for dancing after 1910. Made up of five white New Orleans players (cornet, clarinet, trombone, drums, and piano), the group caused a great stir in the restaurant, at private parties, and on the vaudeville stage where the cornetist and trombonist blew into the bells of each other's horns, the clarinetist muted his instrument with a tin can, the trombonist moved his slide with his foot, and the music was played at faster and faster tempos. Working hard to create excitement, the ODJB also mocked musical decorum on its 1917 Victor sides—the first recordings made in the name of jazz. *Livery Stable Blues* featured rooster sounds from the clarinet, cow moos from the trombone, and horse neighing from the cornet. In the hands of the ODJB, jazz was introduced as a nose-thumbing, almost anarchic parody of standard music making, and the public found the result hilarious.[11]

In the years after World War I, jazz was seen in some circles as a symptom of civilization's decline. Many community leaders had opposed ragtime, and now they made jazz a target, though with no agreement about whether the music should be suppressed or just ignored. One complaint linked jazz with the illegal liquor trade that sprang up after Prohibition became law in 1919. Though its goal was to raise the country's moral standard, the measure only succeeded in delivering control of the liquor business into the hands of criminals, who bribed police to keep them from interfering. There was no stopping the urban nightlife that emerged in the 1910s to support dancing. But as places where alcoholic drinks were illegally sold and where jazz was heard, nightclubs and cabarets now operated on the other side of the law. With its eccentric sounds, earthy rhythms, and the encouragement of brazen dance styles, jazz came to be linked in the public mind with the moral drift that educators and the clergy had been deploring since the war's end.

In wartime, it had been relatively simple for Americans to unite against the common German foe. But peace brought new complexity and social unrest. As in the 1890s, the nation's ethnic makeup again became a pressing issue. But now migration, not immigration, was the chief concern—specifically the movement of African Americans from the Southern countryside into the cities of the North. Between 1910 and 1920, for example, as

Chicago's total population grew by 24 percent, the number of black residents in the city jumped 148 percent. Flocking to the cities to find better, higher-paying jobs, Southern blacks changed the culture of the areas where they settled. And they met resistance from whites, ranging from personal prejudice to organized opposition. The Ku Klux Klan, whose constitution pledged "to unite white male persons, native-born Gentile citizens of the United States of America," was reorganized in 1915, and by 1924 its membership reached 4.5 million. It was hardly a coincidence that in 1924, the year of the Klan's greatest popularity, criticism of jazz also reached its peak.[12]

THE ADVENT OF MUSICAL MODERNISM IN NEW YORK

As blues and jazz were making their way into public consciousness, another development was taking place in New York City: the movement to introduce modern music into the concert hall. In the years before World War I, several modern European composers—the Austrian Arnold Schoenberg, the Russian Igor Stravinsky, and the Hungarian Béla Bartók, among others—had broken decisively with key aspects of the Romantic tradition, whose arching melodies, goal-directed harmonies, and faith in certain aesthetic ideals had dominated Western concert halls and opera houses for two generations and more. The new works of these composers, tending to favor shorter thematic gestures, dissonant harmonies, and discontinuous rhythms, were not written with Romantic notions of aesthetic beauty in mind. Although their variety of style and sound was greater than in works of previous historical eras, more than a few critics and audience members, taking strangeness and singularity as cues, lumped such works together in a "modernist" category and then rejected them. Composed, at least in part, to critique styles and customs of the classical sphere, these works also received a chillier welcome from performers than did music rooted in Romanticism, like the symphonies of Jean Sibelius or the works of Sergei Rachmaninoff. Until the first generation of American-born modernists came of age during the 1920s, the establishment of modern music in the United States was chiefly a matter of introducing works by contemporary European composers. Charles Ives and Charles Griffes are exceptions that prove the rule.

Between the mid-1910s and the mid-1920s, the United States grew from an outpost where new European works were seldom heard into an important international center for the presentation of new music. This change, an unsystematic process of trial and error, may be glimpsed in the way the music of Schoenberg and Stravinsky was received in America.[13] Slow to win acceptance in Europe, Schoenberg's music was even slower to make its way in the United States (hostility during World War I toward everything German probably also played a role here). Just as some early twentieth-century visual artists turned from representation toward abstraction, Schoenberg by 1910 had declared the major-minor tonal system obsolete and abandoned it for atonality, and few early listeners showed a genuine appetite for these atonal sounds. In 1914, the Boston Symphony Orchestra gave Schoenberg's *Five Pieces for Orchestra*, composed in 1909, its American premiere—an event that Harvard faculty members were was still talking about when the composer Virgil Thomson arrived there to study in 1919. According to Thomson, Schoenberg's piece had "scandalized the hell out of" the Harvard Glee Club's influential director, Archibald T. Davison, while outraging Boston's critics too. Not until after the atonal song cycle *Pierrot Lunaire* was premiered in 1923 was Schoenberg's music heard with any frequency in New York, and then it was more likely to appear in modern-music concerts organized by societies of composers and other interested parties than in more standard venues like symphony or chamber-music programs.

Stravinsky's music, emphasizing rhythms and instrumental sounds without precedent in the world of classical music, was quicker to win acceptance. Even before *The Rite of Spring*'s American premiere in 1922, his orchestra works surfaced from time to time on American programs. New York saw performances of two ballets, the *Firebird* and *Petrouchka*, as well as the suite from *Pulcinella* and chamber works. In another sign that the aesthetic preferences of American listeners in these years were turning away from Germany, new music by French composer Erik Satie and Russian composer Alexander Scriabin enjoyed a vogue in the United States, with Satie's work being the subject of articles in the fashionable magazine *Vanity Fair* in the early 1920s.

Musical modernism also made an impact in America through the efforts of Europeans who settled here. Two who deserve special comment are Leo Ornstein, who arrived from Russia in 1907, and Edgard Varèse, who came to New York from Paris in 1915. A pianist and composer, Ornstein presented a series of recitals at New York's Bandbox Theater in 1915, including compositions by living composers unlikely to be heard in piano programs of that day: Schoenberg, Scriabin, Debussy, Ravel, and Cyril Scott. In the spring of 1916, Ornstein played four "Informal Recitals" emphasizing modernist works at the home of Claire Reis, a patron who would be a powerful advocate for modern music in New York until after World War II. In the latter 1910s, a number of New Yorkers considered Ornstein the embodiment of musical modernism.

The better-known Edgard Varèse planned to make a career in the United States as a conductor, specializing in new music and lesser-known works of the past. In 1919, he founded the New Symphony Orchestra as an alternative to New York's reigning ensembles. But he quickly resigned after critics attacked the group's first concert, which featured New York premieres of works by Debussy, Bartók, and Alfredo Casella. Two years later, Varèse founded the International Composers' Guild. He announced its birth in a manifesto that put the plight of modernist composers squarely before the public: their dependency on performers, coupled with a fear that performers would duck the challenges that new music posed to their technique and imagination. As early as 1917, as if predicting the arrival of electronic sounds and the control they would bring to composers, Varèse had written: "I dream of instruments obedient to my thought."[14] Now, four years later, he criticized performers for sometimes being more interested in judging new music than understanding it. "Not finding in it any trace of the conventions to which [they are] accustomed," he wrote, they might refuse to perform new music, "denouncing it as incoherent and unintelligible." Even when mainstream groups programmed new compositions, such works were "carefully chosen from the most timid and anemic of contemporary productions, leaving absolutely unheard the composers who represent the true spirit of our times."

It was to serve the latter that Varèse formed the International Composers' Guild, "to centralize the works of the day, to group them in programs intelligently and organically constructed, and, with the disinterested help of singers and instrumentalists, to present these works in such a way as to reveal their fundamental spirit." The guild arranged performances of Schoenberg's *Pierrot Lunaire* and Stravinsky's *Renard* as well as more works by these two masters, plus others by Austrian composers Alban Berg and Anton Webern, before disbanding in 1927. In the meantime, a group of American composers seceded in 1923 from the guild and formed the League of Composers, with Claire Reis as executive director and their stated goal "to bring the entire range of modern tendencies before the public."[15]

The creation of the International Composers' Guild and the League of Composers brought a new situation to the United States. Except for composer-performers like Louis Moreau Gottschalk and Edward MacDowell, earlier classical composers had played only a small role in the nation's musical life. In the 1850s, W. H. Fry and G. F. Bristow had based arguments for their music on nationality, holding that American works had a right to be heard in the country of their origin; that argument may still be heard today. In the 1890s, Edward MacDowell had refused to allow performances of his music in all-American concerts, finding such events more political than artistic, but his stance was unusual; much home-grown music during and after MacDowell's day was performed on such occasions. Yet the public role seized in the 1920s by composers in America went beyond that of nationalists seeking a niche in the existing order, for the music they favored and composed challenged that order. European in origin, the new approaches to composition and the resistance they met drove composers to band together, regardless of nationality, in the name of modernism.

In 1941, the composer Aaron Copland reviewed some of these developments in *Our New Music*. Copland's preface—which, like the book that follows, covers only the classical sphere—calls the "violent upheaval" in twentieth-century music evidence of revolutionary change. Following the example of earlier revolutionaries, such as Beethoven and Wagner, contemporary composers, Copland said, were developing their own kind of music. And in the 1920s, New York was the scene of great activity in modern music circles. Copland listed almost three dozen American composers who participated.[16] As one who saw himself as part of a lively creative scene, Copland made his list broad and inclusive. But one famous name is missing: that of George Gershwin. And what makes its absence conspicuous is that Gershwin's *Rhapsody in Blue*, introduced in 1924 at a concert organized to show the many faces of the new modern music called jazz, struck some Americans as *the* embodiment of the true spirit of their time in a modern musical idiom.

GERSHWIN AND THE *RHAPSODY IN BLUE*

George Gershwin was born in Brooklyn in 1898 to parents who had immigrated from Russia to the United States earlier in the 1890s. His boyhood was marked by an interest in athletics and an indifference to school. Music was seldom heard in the Gershwin household until 1910, when the family bought its first piano so that older brother Ira could learn to play it. But George soon took over the instrument. He progressed quickly in lessons with neighborhood teachers and about 1912 was accepted as a pupil of Charles Hambitzer, a musician known for a discerning ear. Hambitzer recognized genius in Gershwin and sought to open the world of classical music to his pupil, taking him to concerts and assigning him pieces by composers such as Chopin, Liszt, and Debussy. In 1914, however, Gershwin turned to a musical world closer to home when he dropped out of high school and went to work for Jerome H. Remick & Co., a Tin Pan Alley publishing firm. Hired as a song plugger, Gershwin spent endless hours at the keyboard, which improved his playing, though he no longer took lessons. In 1915, he cut the first of the more than a hundred recordings he made for player piano on perforated paper rolls. He also gained experience as a vocal accompanist and began to compose songs and piano pieces of his own, though with no encouragement from his employers. And he aspired to rise in the music business: from Tin Pan Alley's emphasis on single songs to the Broadway musical stage, where composers like Victor Herbert and Jerome Kern, the latter a particular hero of his, were writing scores for entire shows.

George Gershwin (1898–1937), pianist, songwriter, and composer.

In 1917, Gershwin left his job with Remick, finding work as a rehearsal pianist for a show by Kern and Herbert. His flair for composition was noticed, and in early 1918 Max Dreyfus, the head of T. B. Harms publishers, offered him $35 per week for the right to publish songs he might compose in the future. Before the year was out, three Broadway shows featured songs by Gershwin. And soon he composed his first Broadway score for a show called *La La Lucille*, which opened in May 1919 and received 104 performances. Several months before his twenty-first birthday, Gershwin could claim a Broadway show on the boards, a reputation as a good pianist, several independent songs in print, and a publisher eager for more.

Swanee, a song quoting Stephen Foster's *Old Folks at Home* and closely identified with singing star Al Jolson, was Gershwin's first big hit, yielding some $10,000 in composer's royalties in 1920 alone. For Broadway, under contract to the producer George White, he wrote the music for five annual revues, called *George White's Scandals*, in 1920–24. He also wrote songs for other Broadway shows. The first of his shows for which his brother Ira wrote the lyrics, *Lady, Be Good!* (starring dancer Fred Astaire and his sister Adele), included *Fascinating Rhythm* and *Oh, Lady Be Good*, both of which became part of an enduring repertory of standard American popular songs.

In November 1923, Canadian mezzo-soprano Eva Gauthier presented in New York's Aeolian Hall a "Recital of Ancient and Modern Music for Voice." Starting with English Baroque composer Henry Purcell, Gauthier ranged into the present with songs by modernist composers Bartók, Schoenberg, Darius Milhaud, and Paul Hindemith, and half a dozen songs billed as jazz by Jerome Kern, Walter Donaldson, Irving Berlin (*Alexander's Ragtime Band*), and George Gershwin (*I'll Build a Stairway to Paradise, Swanee*), who was her accompanist for that part of the program. According to one critic, the jazz songs, heard side-by-side with standard recital fare, "stood up amazingly well, not only as entertainment but as music." And the audience, which "began by being slightly patronizing," "ended by surrendering completely to the alluring rhythms of our own folk music."[17]

Gershwin's accompaniments made an unforgettable impression. Rather than reading fixed musical texts, he elaborated them freely, in a way that sounded tailored for the moment. And the audience responded with delight. Later commentators would question the "jazz" label for this kind of music making. Yet Gershwin's freewheeling approach to performance—he played *in the style of* an improvisation, though most details were planned—owed much of its spontaneity to jazz, and it brought to the concert hall an immediacy and sense of fun not often heard there. Once the distinctive sound and vigor of American popular music was heard on the concert stage, alternatives to international modernism began coming to mind. Perhaps music like Berlin's and Gershwin's would inspire concert works that were modern yet accessible to listeners, *and* unmistakably American at the same time.

On February 12, 1924, at a concert in New York's Aeolian Hall by Paul Whiteman's Palais Royal Orchestra, George Gershwin played the featured piano part in the premiere of his *Rhapsody in Blue*, a "jazz concerto" commissioned for the occasion. Billing his concert "An Experiment in Modern Music," Whiteman caught the attention of New York's leading music critics, who were intrigued enough to attend an event they normally would have ignored. With discussions of jazz very much in the air, it is no surprise that the unveiling of a new jazz concerto by an up-and-coming young songwriter attracted plenty of public notice. What *is* surprising, however, is that Gershwin's piece lived up to the ballyhoo of preconcert publicity. Bringing together three separate strands of musical development—the rise of blues as a popular song form, the spread of jazz as an instrumental music, and the push for artistic modernism in the classical sphere—the *Rhapsody in Blue* has since come to be reckoned both an American classic and a piece emblematic of its time.

Whiteman, born in 1890 and a classically trained violinist and violist from Colorado who had played in the Denver and San Francisco symphony orchestras in his teens and twenties, had entered the dance orchestra business on the West Coast in 1918. After making two recordings in 1920 that sold more than a million copies each, he relocated in New York, enlarged his orchestra, and, with the help of arranger-composer Ferde Grofé, popularized a dance-orchestra sound based on a reed section (chiefly saxophones) and a brass section, sometimes with supplementary strings (including his own violin). It is one of the ironies of American music history that a man called Whiteman came to be known as "the King of Jazz" by performing popular songs enlivened with the flavor of a black-derived style. What Whiteman called jazz was more an arranger's than a player's art, including the occasional use of syncopation, blue notes, "hot" solos or moments of ensemble playing, offbeat sounds (i.e., instrumental smears, "talking" muted trumpets), and varied restatements—all introduced into a precise, polished approach to playing.

Whiteman's audiece at the Aeolian Hall concert received program notes that granted the jazz label's ambiguity and claimed progress in the music's recent development:

> The experiment is to be purely educational. Mr. Whiteman intends to point out, with the assistance of his orchestra and associates, the tremendous strides which have been made in popular music from the day of the discordant Jazz, which sprang into existence about ten years ago from nowhere in particular, to the really melodious music of today, which—for no good reason—is still called Jazz. Most people who ridicule the present so-called Jazz and who refuse to condone it or listen to it seriously, are quarreling with the name Jazz and not with what it represents.

The long, miscellaneous program ranged widely. It opened with an ODJB-inspired *Livery Stable Blues* and closed with Edward Elgar's *Pomp and Circumstance*, which would be played at many school graduations in the years to come. In between came a spruced-up version of Edward MacDowell's old piano favorite *To a Wild Rose* and a brand-new orchestral suite by the redoubtable Victor Herbert. Following vaudeville's custom of saving the prime attraction for the next-to-last place on the program, the *Rhapsody in Blue* filled that slot. Whiteman's well-promoted, well-attended "Experiment in Modern Music" capitalized on a vital issue of the day, and it set the stage for Gershwin to enter the public's consciousness in a new role.

The concert was by no means the first to present black dance music, ragtime, or jazz in concert settings, for that had been happening at least since the early 1910s under the leadership of Will Marion Cook, James Reese Europe, W. C. Handy, and others. Moreover, many composers before Gershwin wrote concert works with jazz traits. In 1923 alone, Louis Gruenberg, Cole Porter, Wallingford Riegger, Ernest Schelling, and Emerson Whithorne—as well as Darius Milhaud, whose *La Creation du Monde* proved the most lasting—all wrote such pieces for orchestra. Why did the *Rhapsody in Blue*, then, have so much greater an impact? One reason was that Whiteman's publicists cleverly cultivated New York's critics. A second had to do with performance quality. Whereas most earlier jazz-oriented scores had been introduced by pickup orchestras of classical players, Whiteman's concert aimed to show that his "modern jazz-band dance orchestra" could also play complex concert works with skill and panache. From the premiere in February to the end of 1924, the group gave eighty-four performances of the *Rhapsody in Blue*, plus a recording in June with Gershwin at the piano. In fact, the work proved so successful that between 1924 and 1926 Whiteman commissioned pieces in a similar vein from John Alden Carpenter, Ferde Grofé, Leo Sowerby, and Deems Taylor. He also discussed possible commissions of jazz-oriented concert works with George Antheil, Ernest Bloch, Charles Wakefield Cadman, Leopold Godowsky, Percy Grainger, John Powell, and even Stravinsky himself.[18]

To a listener, *Rhapsody in Blue* is both an unfolding of themes and a parade of references. From the opening clarinet smear through the blues-tinged melodies to the syncopation that enlivens tunes and transitions, the work claims African-American folk music, appropriated and transformed by the composer, as part of its pedigree. Gershwin's experience as a writer of popular songs also leaves its mark on the harmonic idiom and thematic structure, with phrases and periods cast in the four-, eight-, and sixteen-bar units of popular song. Finally, the *Rhapsody*'s title and its length, as well as cadenza-like passages, sections of near-symphonic development, and the soaring character of the final theme, show the influence of piano concertos by Grieg, Tchaikovsky, and other European composers. They also reflect Gershwin's early classical training on piano and his on-and-off private study of music theory and classical composition from 1919 until late in life. Gershwin's references are not borrowed tune quotations, like those of Charles Ives, but evocations of different musical styles. And it is precisely in the way these references are joined that the *Rhapsody*'s eclectic essence shines through: this is the work of a composer who believed in the artistic worth of all three spheres of American music.

The start of the piece establishes a blues connection through a clarinet melody (the main theme) whose expression owes much to blue notes, both the natural (raised) and flat (lowered) third and seventh degrees.[19] After an upward sweep on the dominant of B-flat, with its A-natural leading tone, the theme emphasizes A-flat, the blue seventh, and also plays on both D-natural and D-flat, creating a blue third.

Although the opening lacks a solid beat, triplets and offbeat accents promise the rhythmic energy that Gershwin made a trademark of his concert music. In its next appearance, the main theme is treated as a three-bar statement, answered by a brief blue-note figure—a stylized call-and-response surely inspired by the blues.

This section's closing theme also emphasizes the blue third and seventh in

E-flat.

The blues scale's presence, and the freedom of sound, pitch, and rhythmic inflection that Whiteman's soloists show on the original recording give the work's opening measures the character of the day's most prominent African-American folk style.

based on the major-minor tonal system, with most triads enriched by sevenths, ninths, or other nonharmonic tones. Another common element lies in the *Rhapsody*'s melodic structure. The melodies of Gershwin's concert works share with popular songs a trait that helps to imprint them firmly on the listener's memory: they restate their first phrase before moving on to a contrasting phrase. For example, the start of the main theme is distinctive, memorable, and extended through fourteen bars by contrasting material. In its next appearance, the opening three-bar "call" and two-bar "response" make a five-bar unit that will not quite fit into standard popular-song form. Neither of these statements seems to invite restatement. But a change takes place when the theme moves from orchestra to piano. Here Gershwin states *and* restates the five-bar phrase, following it with a contrasting four-bar phrase and a return. The result is a melody in a standard form (**aaba**) that makes a songlike impression on the ear, though slightly off-center because it fills eighteen bars instead of the usual sixteen. From this point on, listeners are more likely to hear the **a** phrase as the start of a full-blown theme than a separate five-bar statement, for the rest of the melody is now expected. And something similar happens to the closing theme, which Gershwin makes the start of a sixteen-bar **aaba** pattern. As melodies like these well up from within the musical flow, the *Rhapsody in Blue* takes on something of the character of a medley or a Broadway overture.

Although the final theme of *Rhapsody in Blue*, like earlier themes, relies on restatement, two traits mark it as more symphonic (and classical) than songlike (and popular). The first is its start-and-stop rhythmic profile. A melody in a popular vein would be unlikely to follow a quarter-note beginning with tones sustained as long as these. The second is that the phrase beginning in the melody's seventeenth bar is a development of the theme's opening gesture, not the contrast one expects in a song. Rather than being rounded off with a return, this theme has no real destination. Its last four bars are a turnaround leading back to the start of another twenty-four-bar statement.

In addition to combining elements from the different spheres—bluesdrenched melodies cast in popular-song forms, symphonic themes harmonized as if they were numbers out of a Broadway orchestra pit—Gershwin also finds different ways of setting one style against another. For example, the opening is jazz in the Original Dixieland Jazz Band vein, with the clarinet, then the muted trumpet giving out the melody, in sounds that seem to mock the standard approach to playing these instruments. But by giving a straight-faced response to the trumpet's comic call, the piano's entrance signals that not all jazz references will be played for novelty or laughs. After a blaring full-orchestra statement of the main theme's "call," the piano again leads away from parody, this time toward virtuosity and the more serious tone one expects from a soloist in a tuxedo. Here, rather than exploring organic formal links, Gershwin behaves more like a film director cutting from one scene to another in ways that highlight their disconnection.

Ninety measures into the *Rhapsody in Blue*, another unexpected move takes place. After a triumphant full-orchestra statement of the main theme, Gershwin turns with little preparation to a brand-new theme in the trumpets: a brash, squarecut tune with a syncopated, Latin-flavored accompaniment. The new theme is catchy and striking, but it lasts only sixteen bars. And when it yields to the return of the closing theme, it disappears, never to be heard again. Within the intellectual framework of organic form, such a waste of thematic material is a serious flaw. But in the heat of performance, a sudden shift like this one can bring fresh excitement as the music veers off in a new direction. Gershwin makes such moments work by keeping a tight hold on his listeners' attention. Recognizable, satisfying melodies give *Rhapsody in Blue* continuity, for listeners are expected to welcome their return. At the same time, Gershwin's wide range of sources and near-cinematic approach to form give the work an aura of slightly disjointed spontaneity.

Introduced with fanfare and performed often, Gershwin's *Rhapsody in Blue* played a role in defining American musical modernism in the mid-1920s. To several New York critics who aligned themselves more with Stravinsky's diatonic approach than Schoenberg's chromatic one, Gershwin emerged from the *Rhapsody in Blue*'s premiere as the American composer who most closely resembled Stravinsky. Older composers and critics, born in the 1870s and 80s, also responded favorably; they saw Gershwin as the man most likely to carry American composition beyond its unimpressive past. Both groups approved in principle the idea of an American concert music based on an American vernacular style.

Younger composers who had to compete with Gershwin responded less heartily to his success. In 1925, Virgil Thomson wrote that though he found the *Rhapsody in Blue* "enormously superior to anything that the better educated musicians have done in that style," the work was "at best a piece of aesthetic snobbery" with "scraps of bully jazz sewed together with oratory and cadenzas out of Liszt." George Antheil, who liked the direction Gershwin had taken but found the result mediocre, promised a jazz symphony of his own that would outshine Gershwin's effort.[20]

Gershwin's rhapsody met its toughest opposition from critics who wrote for journals with an intellectual mission—especially Paul Rosenfeld, music critic of *The Dial* from 1920 to 1927. Rosenfeld treated Gershwin and the *Rhapsody in Blue* as threats to the position he had staked out in support of a more uncompromising modernism. While Rosenfeld surely deserves credit for bolstering a cause that would never resonate with the larger public, his comments also reveal a fully hierarchical view that placed the classical sphere securely above the popular. And he branded Gershwin with the popular label, even though works like the *Rhapsody in Blue* were composed to call such labels into question. In the effort to define the qualities of American modernism, Rosenfeld rejected Gershwin in favor of Aaron Copland, also Brooklyn-born and of Russian-Jewish heritage, just two years younger than Gershwin, and in the mid-1920s the composer of works inspired by jazz. The parallels between the two young composers brought differences in their backgrounds into focus. For while Gershwin was honing his professional skills in front of mass audiences, Copland had spent several years of study in France (1921–24) under the tutelage of harmony teacher Nadia Boulanger, an experience that also introduced him to the modern music scene in France.

Copland's jazz-inflected Piano Concerto, premiered in 1927, allowed Rosenfeld to compare what he claimed to be Copland's elevation of jazz into art with Gershwin's refusal (or inability) to do more than leave it at the level of popular entertainment. For Rosenfeld, true modernism carried a purity of essence and intention found only in high art. And he found in Gershwin's music no underlying concept to channel his natural talent. On the other hand, Copland had transformed jazz, a "product of second-rate feelings," into real art, with "a whole, very clear, positive, and well-balanced" structure.[21]

For a young composer like Copland, the drive to create American-sounding modernist music was intense. Yet he and his colleagues also sought to be recognized in an international arena of classical composition. They all sought a delicate balance between elevation and accessibility, hoping to strengthen modern music's place in the concert hall through works that embodied their own carefully calculated approach to modernism. But while Copland and his compatriots walked that tightrope, Gershwin's *Rhapsody in Blue*, followed by the *Concerto in F*, had already won large, enthusiastic audiences, plus a fair share of critical approval. If the gap between the classical and popular spheres remained a defining condition for Copland and his compatriots, Gershwin had declared it closed, except as a source of musical variety and surprise.

28

The Birthright of All of Us

Classical Music, the Mass Media, and the Depression

GERSHWIN'S RHAPSODY IN BLUE WAS received, in part, as a challenge to the prevailing musical hierarchy. Earlier line-drawing efforts may help to put its challenge into perspective: the separation of band and orchestra repertories after the Civil War; the establishment of the symphony orchestra as a vehicle for classic works; the impulse toward concert-hall rituals that historians have called "the sacralization of culture." Behind these earlier endeavors lies a belief in the authority of composers and the transcendence of certain works, a resolve to perform them in a respectful setting, and the notion of the classical sphere as controlled by an elite, whether of wealth, social class, or taste. Exclusiveness played a role in the argument that pitted Copland against Gershwin. Finding in his jazz-oriented works an intellectual rigor that Gershwin's more accessible *Rhapsody in Blue* lacked, Copland's champions declared them truly modern, hence fit for listeners with elite taste.

One way to learn how the modernist impulse fared between the two world wars is to look at the symphony orchestra. A marvel in its range of instrumental possibilities, the orchestra had long been the medium through which composers addressed the public at large. And the local financing of American orchestras made them a focus of local pride, reflecting their community's love of art. Given the orchestra's prestige, there is no more powerful role in the performing world than that of conductor. Indeed, the agreement that Theodore Thomas struck in 1891 with the Chicago Symphony Orchestra—he was to make all programs, select all soloists, and arrange for choral and festival performances, as well as conducting rehearsals and concerts—can be taken as a model for the conductor's role. Conductors are the ultimate line drawers: it is they who decide most often which works will be performed, which excluded.

In the latter 1800s, Thomas and other conductors of German background established the American symphony orchestra as an ensemble grounded in European classics. They emphasized works written by German-speaking composers because they judged them to be the best music. At the turn of the century, the orchestra in the Western world was a cosmopolitan medium, growing and changing to meet composers' demands. Living composers were writing music that explored and extended its expressiveness: symphonies, symphonic poems, concertos, overtures, and ballets. As composers outside the Germanic circle won more advocates, conductors in America programmed them. Audiences came to accept works by Tchaikovsky, Dvořák, Richard Strauss, Brahms, Rimsky-Korsakov, Debussy, Jean Sibelius, and other more recent composers, with their fresh approaches to melody and form. Like Theodore Thomas, some conductors were also friendly to the cause of American composers, but their music had yet to find more than a small place on concert programs. By the century's early years, the American symphony orchestra belonged to an international tradition, rooted in older classics but responsive to more recent developments too.

As some composers saw it, the advent of modernism after World War I placed the concert hall in a reactionary position. Aaron Copland claimed in 1941 that in writing their new music, he and his compatriots were following in the footsteps of "revolutionaries" like Beethoven and Wagner, who "sought new expressive possibilities in music—and found them."[1] From that point of view, narrow-minded performers had caused a crisis by closing concert repertories to new works that embodied "the true spirit of our times," as composer Edgard Varèse had put it. Yet the symphony orchestra was not much affected by modernist composers' music or their sense of crisis. From its perspective, the classical sphere seemed healthy, thanks in large part to a strong economy.

The years 1890 to 1930 saw a major change in American society from a Victorian culture based on thrift to one more consumer-oriented and ready to spend. Musical life benefited from that shift, with growing investment in musical instruction, growing opportunity for amateur vocal and instrumental performance, and at the professional end, the establishment of permanent orchestras in such cities as San Francisco (1911), Los Angeles (1919), Seattle (1926), and Kansas City (1934). Symphony orchestras were supported by a combination of box-office receipts and private gifts. The role of affluent citizens was crucial; yet orchestras survived, even flourished, because members of the general public also bought tickets.

Because historical chronicles emphasize what is new, the rise of modernism in the 1920s and the appearance of more American-born classical composers than ever before have loomed large in accounts of American music history. So has the wealth of vernacular music produced in the popular sphere in those years. Alongside these changes, however, the prestige of classical performers and composers remained a key element of musical life. Earlier chapters described the cult of personality that made soprano Jenny Lind a national sensation in the mid-1800s and pianist Louis Moreau Gottschalk a Civil War–era matinée idol. Similarly, in the early 1900s, tenor Enrico Caruso of the Metropolitan Opera became a recording star and one of the most famous people in the world. These performers were able to produce sounds that transported listeners, providing emotional excitement and grist for the publicity mill that glorified them. Appearing in public under the sponsorship of institutions and impresarios, they sang or played repertories chosen to display virtuosity—a sovereign command of musical technique and expression. Such traits distinguished them from conductors, who were also being fitted for the mantle of star performers and who demonstrated *their* virtuosity by leading others in the making of musical sounds. The fascination of watching conductors perform lay in the spectacle of many players being molded into a force subject to one will.

Orchestra conductors had to balance the demands of a threefold obligation: to composers (both past and present), to audiences, and to the art of music itself, whose advocate they were expected to be. Music in the classical sphere was a written practice, and conductors felt obliged to follow composers' intentions as conveyed in their scores, and within a shared tradition of performance practices. But in deciding whether or not to program music outside the repertory's norms, they had a delicate course to steer. For their choices were formed in the gap that had opened between the creators of "revolutionary" new works on the one hand, and on the other, listeners for whom the orchestra repertory was expected to be a cross-section of "the best that is known and thought" in the realm of music.[2] Each side rallied around a valid premise. An art that excluded the new *did* risk its connection to present-day life; and concerts that left audiences baffled *did* put public support at risk. In mediating between these positions, conductors constructed their own vision of the orchestra's art.

Like other performers, symphony conductors were publicly defined as charismatic artists. Yet a successful conductor also had to assume the role of an administrator willing to grapple with tough issues. Was music in a state of crisis or not? Were modernist composers really the legitimate heirs of Beethoven and Wagner? And even if they were, should the U.S. concert hall continue to identify with Germanic music? Did American composers deserve a larger place on concert programs? Was jazz a healthy source of inspiration for new American music? Questions like these, hotly debated by musicians and critics, were far from academic for conductors, who based their programming on the answers.

Serge Koussevitzky (1874–1951), conductor of the Boston Symphony Orchestra from 1924 to 1949, in action.

The careers of three illustrious conductors—Arturo Toscanini, Serge Koussevitzky, and Leopold Stokowski—who led major American orchestras during the first half of the century show that the questions being raised could be answered in different ways, with lines drawn accordingly. The Italian-born Toscanini first came to the United States in 1908 as principal conductor at the Metropolitan Opera, a post he held until 1915, when he returned to Italy. In 1920–21, he toured this country with the orchestra of the La Scala opera company in Milan. He served as that house's artistic director from 1921 until 1929, when a Fascist takeover of the Italian government caused him to resign. Toscanini had conducted the New York Philharmonic Society as a guest in 1926–28 and was then named permanent conductor, a post he held until his resignation in 1936. By late 1937, the National Broadcasting Company had created an orchestra expressly for Toscanini, now seventy years old. And from then until he retired in 1954, he conducted the NBC Symphony in concerts, tours, radio and television broadcasts, and on recordings.

Toscanini's reputation outstripped that of any other classical musician before his day or since. During his years at the Metropolitan and with the New York Philharmonic, he was often proclaimed the "greatest conductor of all time," and the promotional forces behind the NBC Symphony helped spread this message.[3] In performance, Toscanini was noted for his energy, the command he brought to the podium, his demands for perfection, and his uncanny musical memory. Adding to the legend were his abiding hatred for political fascism and his towering rages when rehearsals went badly. Toscanini conducted the music of virtually every major Classical and Romantic composer (he was noted particularly for his interpretation of Italian

This photograph of conductor Leopold Stokowski (1882–1977) was taken in Hollywood in 1937.

and Wagnerian operas and Beethoven symphonies), as well as works by such modern masters as Richard Strauss, Debussy, Ravel, and Prokofiev.

Serge Koussevitzky, a native of Russia and virtuoso double-bass player, began conducting in his early thirties and assembled an orchestra that in the summers between 1910 and 1914 traveled the Volga River, playing concerts that emphasized works by Russian composers. After World War I, he left Russia and settled in Paris for several years, forming an orchestra that included in its programs new scores by French and Russian composers, including Ravel's orchestration of Modest Musorgsky's *Pictures at an Exhibition*, Arthur Honegger's *Pacific 231*, and works by Prokofiev and Stravinsky. In 1924, at the age of fifty, he was named conductor of the Boston Symphony Orchestra, a post he held until 1949. Aaron Copland, whose music the Russian conductor championed, later wrote that Koussevitzky brought with him from Paris not only skill on the podium but also "his passion for encouraging whatever he felt to be new and vital in contemporary music."[4] That included works by living American composers such as Roy Harris, Walter Piston, Samuel Barber, Howard Hanson, Edward Burlingame Hill, and William Schuman, not to mention commissions of works by Stravinsky, Paul Hindemith, Honegger, Prokofiev, Ravel, Bartók, and other leading European figures. In the summer of 1940, the Berkshire Music Center opened at Tanglewood, a Massachusetts estate, with Koussevitzky as director and Copland as assistant director. And in later years, contemporary composers including Hindemith, Honegger, and Olivier Messiaen taught there as guests. Koussevitzky has been praised for the emotional power he brought to performances (sometimes taking decidedly untraditional liberties) his command of Russian music (especially Tchaikovsky's symphonies), and works of such French composers as Debussy.

The London-born Leopold Stokowski came to the United States in his early twenties (1905) to be organist at a New York church. But he quickly moved into conducting, and in 1909 was named music director of the Cincinnati Symphony Orchestra. In 1912, Stokowski began a twenty-five-year stint as conductor of the Philadelphia Orchestra. If Toscanini was identified as a servant of the composer's score, Stokowski was known for showmanship. Tall and striking, he made his Philadelphia string section famous for their singing sound. In 1940, he appeared onscreen in Walt Disney's *Fantasia*, with animated characters including Mickey Mouse—the first conductor to achieve the status of entertainment star. Stokowski was also interested in musical technology. Starting in 1917, he and the Philadelphians made the first of many recordings for Victor, including a version of Stravinsky's ballet *The Firebird*; twelve years later, the NBC network featured him and the orchestra in the first commercially sponsored radio broadcasts. A staunch champion of twentieth-century music, Stokowski, still on the podium at age eighty-eight, conducted over two thousand first performances—most by American composers. Among the premieres were works by Varèse, Ives, Copland, George Antheil, Henry Cowell, Griffes, and Alan Hovhaness, as well as Rachmaninoff's *Rhapsody on a Theme of Paganini* and the American premieres of Stravinsky's *The Rite of Spring*, Mahler's Eighth Symphony, Berg's *Wozzeck*, and Schoenberg's *Guerrelieder*.

These sketches portray three very different figures. Toscanini was a passionate champion of the classics. While not averse to newer music, he dedicated himself most of all to performances of the music he considered the greatest. Koussevitzky was drawn less by classic scores and more by personal associations and new musical experiences. He cultivated friendships with composers, mediating between modernists and audiences in an attitude of respect for both. Stokowski came to hold an aggressively democratic philosophy, which he linked to technological progress. In a book called *Music for Us All* (1943), he wrote:

> Music is a universal language—it speaks to everyone—is the birthright of all of us. Formerly music was chiefly confined to privileged classes in cultural centers, but today, through radio and records, music has come directly into our homes no matter how far we may live from cultural centers. This is as it should be, because music speaks to every man, woman, and child—high or low, rich or poor, happy or despairing—who is sensitive to its deep and powerful message.

Stokowski's vision of a democratic musical culture depended on what he called "a progressive audience, versed in the acknowledged masterpieces yet open to the latest heresies." Believing that most adults had "difficulty in absorbing ideas and impressions," he did much of his proselytizing for new music at concerts aimed at young, presumably impressionable audiences.[5]

The contrasting careers of Toscanini, Koussevitzky, and Stokowski show the symphony orchestra between the two world wars as an arena with established norms that was also open to distinctive approaches. They also are a reminder that the most prominent names in the American classical sphere were performers—violinists Fritz Kreisler and Jascha Heifetz, pianists Artur Rubinstein and Vladimir Horowitz, and singers Amelita Galli-Curci, Rosa Ponselle, Ezio Pinza, and Kirsten Flagstad, for example. Most were foreign-born; all made their reputations presenting European masterworks to audiences in Europe and the United States. Live performance remained the public's chief point of contact with classical music, though after electrical recording replaced the acoustic process in the mid-1920s, record-buying listeners could experience something closer to concert-hall sound in their homes.

Radio introduced an unprecedented notion: that music, from symphony to popular song, was a form of entertainment suited to filling time in broadcast schedules. This voracious new medium broadcast a wide variety of music, most of it popular but by no means all. In 1926, NBC presented Serge Koussevitzky and the Boston Symphony in the first live network concert, attracting a million listeners. Five years later, the same network paid $100,000 for the right to broadcast grand opera live from the Metropolitan in New York; soon those broadcasts were the second-most popular on daytime radio. In 1938, 62.5 percent of respondents polled by *Fortune* Magazine said they liked opera or classical music on the radio, and 40 percent had heard of Toscanini, most of those identifying him as a conductor.[6] The classical sphere's ideal of transcendence had deep roots in the notion of exclusivity, but the music's appeal to listeners through the mass media opened it to new kinds of democratic access and interpretation. In the 1800s, musical changes—excerpting, simplifying, transcribing—had transformed operas and symphonies into fare for the general public. By the 1930s, thanks to new kinds of musical transmission, such works were being widely listened to in their original versions—as composers' music.

COMPOSERS, THE GOVERNMENT, AND THE MARKETPLACE DURING THE DEPRESSION

On August 17, 1937, Mexican composer Carlos Chávez conducted the Orquesta Sinfónica de México in the first performance of Aaron Copland's *El salón México*, inspired by a 1932 visit to a Mexico City dance hall. Copland labored over this work for several years—much longer than it usually took him to complete a composition. Its simpler style was a departure from the severe modernist stamp of a piece like his *Piano Variations*, composed earlier in the decade (1930). And Copland worried that his attempt to catch another country's flavor would miss the mark. Knowing that he lacked the experience to engage with "the more profound sides of Mexico," he found that his "thoughts kept returning to that dance hall."

> It wasn't so much the music or the dances that attracted me as the spirit of the place. In some inexplicable way, while milling about in those crowded halls, I had felt a live contact with the Mexican "people"—that electric sense one gets sometimes in far-off places, of suddenly knowing the essence of a people—their humanity, their shyness, their dignity and unique charm. I remember quite well that it was at such a moment I conceived the idea of composing a piece about Mexico and naming it *El Salón México.*

Copland went on to say that he often began his composing process "by collecting musical themes or tunes out of which a composition might eventually emerge," and in this work, he found it natural to use popular Mexican melodies. As if turning to Europe for permission, he justified his borrowing by citing Emmanuel Chabrier and Claude Debussy, both of whom had helped themselves "to the melodic riches of Spain."

Copland traveled to Mexico City for his work's premiere, "nervous about what the Mexicans might think of a 'gringo' meddling with their native melodies." But he was gratified by the warm response of orchestra players, audiences, and critics, who "seemed to agree that *El salón México* might well be taken for Mexican music—'as Mexican as the music of Revueltas,' which was like saying at that time, 'as American as the music of Gershwin.'" In the summer of 1938, *El salón México* was played in London, leading to publication by the English firm Boosey and Hawkes. The following October, Koussevitzky and the Boston Symphony Orchestra gave the work its first American performance. What happened next was a surprise. Copland recalled that Boosey's American agent

> called my piece an "American Bolero" and proceeded to fill orders for scores and rental parts that soon came in from all over. One year after publication in 1938, Boosey put together a list of orchestras that had played *El Salón México*: fourteen American orchestras ranging from the BSO to the Women's Symphony in Chicago; two radio orchestras; and five foreign ensembles. Never in my wildest dreams did I expect this kind of acceptance for the piece.[7]

From the start, however, Copland had sought to make *El salón México* audience-friendly. Using local melodies for themes, he kept them recognizable, and he stayed within the major-minor tonal system. The work has been connected to Copland's fourth stylistic period, the first being the formative years of 1920–25, followed by a second (1924–29) that emphasized jazz-derived works and a third devoted largely to more abstract music

Composer Aaron Copland (1900–1990) in the 1930s.

(1930–34). Composer-critic Virgil Thomson pointed out in the 1970s that Copland's ambition to enlarge his audience had forced him to learn "to speak simply," by following *his* example, not Debussy's or Chabrier's. In the later thirties and early forties, Thomson wrote, Copland "wanted populist themes and populist materials and a music style capable of stating these vividly. My music offered one approach to simplification; and my employment of folk-style tunes was, as Copland was to write me later about *The River*, 'a lesson in how to treat Americana.' "[8] In 1941, Copland offered his own explanation in *Our New Music:*

> During the mid- '30s I began to feel an increasing dissatisfaction with the re-
> lations of the music-loving public and the living composer. The old "special"
> public of the modern-music concerts had fallen away, and the conventional

concert public continued apathetic or indifferent to anything but the established classics. It seemed to me that we composers were in danger of working in a vacuum. Moreover, an entirely new public for music had grown up around the radio and phonograph. It made no sense to ignore them and to continue writing as if they did not exist. I felt that it was worth the effort to see if I couldn't say what I had to say in the simplest possible terms.[9]

Though Copland's words stress the impact of the mass media, his wish for a larger audience was also a response to a major socioeconomic change; for *El salón México* was composed at a time when the United States found itself in the grip of a deep economic depression.

The country had emerged from World War I as a creditor nation for the first time in history—one that took in more money from overseas than it spent. And the economy boomed during the 1920s, which saw a 50 percent increase in manufacturing output. By 1929, the United States was producing major shares of the world's coal (40 percent), petroleum (70 percent), hydroelectric power (30 percent), steel (50 percent), and natural gas (more than 90 percent). Domestic consumption kept pace with production; Americans used more electricity than the rest of the world combined. In 1919, earlier 6.7 million cars and 900,000 trucks were registered in this country; a decade later, the figures stood at 23 million cars and 3.5 million trucks. The market for cars and trucks fueled the growth of the petroleum and steel industries, and also the need for a wider network of highways as part of the national infrastructure. In October 1929, however, the stock market collapsed. And when many banks failed in the next couple of years, production, consumption, and investment declined, unemployment rose sharply, and confidence in the economic future crumbled. The Depression hit the United States with destructive force, though its impact varied from sector to sector. Agriculture, much of heavy industry, and the blue-collar workforce in general bore the brunt of the suffering. Those who managed to keep their jobs found buying power magnified as prices fell.[10]

The Depression made a deep impact on American musical life. Some larger institutions like symphony orchestras and the Metropolitan Opera survived on patronage and a bigger pool of listeners, recruited through radio broadcasts and recordings. In one resourceful move, the Metropolitan created an Opera Guild in 1934 to broaden its base of support in New York City. The guild sponsored lectures in such venues as New York University and public library branches, organized inexpensive concerts for schoolchildren, and involved local clubs and PTA groups in fund-raising, with an eye toward boosting the number of small donations. By 1940, its efforts had brought more than $300,000 into the company's coffers.[11] New-music activities, however, struggled to attract financial backing. (One faithful patron was Charles Ives, who supported *New Music*, a publishing venture started in 1927 by the composer Henry Cowell, centered on "noncommercial works of artistic value" by such composers as Carl Ruggles, Ruth Crawford, Arnold Schoenberg, and Ives himself.) With less money in the hands of audience members, work for performers began to evaporate. The size of the audience that could be reached by a broadcast or recorded performance greatly exceeded that for a live one, and broadcast performances were free to listeners within the sound of a radio. Moreover, the invention of sound film in 1927 did away with the need for the players who had previously accompanied silent films in orchestra pits from small-town theaters to urban movie palaces. Thus, economic decline and technological progress combined to bring performing musicians into a state of crisis.

Between 1929 and 1934, about 70 percent of all musicians in the United States were unemployed, a trend the American Federation of Musicians, the national musicians' union, was powerless to buck. In 1935, as part of a massive relief effort labeled Federal Project Number One, under the Works Progress Administration (WPA), the national government took action, establishing the Federal Music Project as a way of supporting unemployed musicians. At its peak, the program employed 16,000 musicians, who gave 5,000 performances drawing an estimated monthly attendance of 3 million. The project funded twenty-eight symphony orchestras, as well as numerous dance bands and folk-music groups. More than a million music classes were given to 14 million students. In addition, government funds were used to sponsor musicological research and to promote new music through the Composers' Forum-Laboratory. For the first time in the history of the United States, music was receiving systematic, comprehensive government support.

Federal Project One brought a new spirit to the nation's artistic life—a spirit that outlived the project itself. In contrast to wealthy patrons like banker J. P. Morgan, an avid art collector who was more interested in defining American taste in the fine arts than in making the works he acquired widely available, the WPA program, created with public money to keep artists from starving, tried to make their work accessible to as many Americans as possible. The program's policymakers saw Federal One as a democratic effort that exposed some parts of the country to original artworks, live theater, and symphony orchestras for the first time.[12] And so it was that classical music played a role in what has been called the cultural revolution of the thirties,[13] which created a vast, growing marketplace for live performances of composers from classic to avant-garde; radio broadcasts and recordings; and a government-sponsored effort to expose citizens from all walks of life to classical music. As a silver lining to economic hardship, the Depression years brought far more abundant access to music in the classical sphere than Americans had ever enjoyed before.

Depression-era adversity also fostered an environment of stylistic conservatism and an emphasis in art and music on regional and national subjects. But not all composers who in the 1930s wrote in an accessible idiom did so for the reasons that Aaron Copland gave. In fact, in the view of Virgil Thomson, who was not in the habit of connecting music with social causes, left-wing politics lay behind Copland's embrace of populist subjects and materials. While Copland himself never admitted as much, his colleague Marc Blitzstein openly espoused that political stance in works for the theater. The collaborations of Berthold Brecht and Kurt Weill, and especially *Die Dreigroschenoper* (based on *The Beggar's Opera* of 1728), strongly influenced Blitzstein, who translated Brecht and Weill's work as *The Threepenny Opera*. Blitzstein's own *The Cradle Will Rock* (1936–37), sponsored by the WPA's Federal Theater Project, centers on class warfare, with Mr. Mister, a hard-boiled capitalist, pitted against a group of workers trying to organize a union in the mythical Steeltown, U.S.A. Musically, the work takes the form of a modern ballad opera, couched in the musical idiom of the popular song and the linguistic one of the modern American city.

Thomson, a native of Kansas City who was trained at Harvard and then in Paris under Nadia Boulanger, displayed his own brand of modernism in the *Sonata da Chiesa*, a dissonant chamber work of 1926. Yet he held that aesthetic at arm's length in a pair of works that followed: *Variations on a Sunday School Tune*, for organ (1927), and *Symphony on a Hymn Tune* (1928). Scores for two WPA-sponsored films a decade later, *The Plow That Broke the Plains* (1936) and *The River* (1937), confirmed Thomson's credentials as an American-sounding composer. His most notorious effort was *Four Saints in Three Acts* (1934), an opera to a libretto by American expatriate writer Gertrude Stein, whom he met in Paris. Set in sixteenth-century Spain, the libretto celebrates the lives of St. Theresa, St. Ignatius, St. Settlement, and St. Chavez while following no perceptible plot. Thomson's method for composing this work was novel. As John Cage reported in a study of Thomson's music, "seated at his piano, text before him, and singing, he improvised an entire act at a time until it became clear to him that the vocal line and the harmony had taken stable form." Thomson himself declared his opera's style "simple, melodic, and harmonious . . . after twenty years of everybody's trying to make music just a little bit louder and more unmitigated and more complex than anybody else's." In one unforgettable moment, a soloist and male chorus alternate in singing "Pigeons on the grass, alas," words whose incongruity seems calculated to baffle and delight at the same time. (Humorist James Thurber once wrote of this passage that a pigeon is the *least* likely creature on earth to make anyone say "alas"!) "Like any other work of high comedy," Cage wrote, *Four Saints* "leaves few traces. It does not clutter up the memory, but it elevates the spirit."[14] Thomson's Midwestern roots and Harvard education were mixed with strong Gallic sympathies; he particularly admired French composer Erik Satie, noted for satire and musical simplicity.

Most Americans, philosopher John Dewey wrote in 1920, were "chiefly concerned with what goes on in their tenement house, their alley, their factory, their street," with not much interest in what "American" might mean in trans-local terms. The only things that seemed nationwide to Dewey were "the high cost of living, prohibition, and devotion to localisms."[15] During the 1930s, however, a sense of cultural unity grew among Americans as stronger connections were felt among the nation's regions. Economic hardship had something to do with this trend, for shared misery formed a bond among some citizens. But a sharp reduction in immigration was another factor; and social research was showing racial traits to be more culturally determined than inherited. White Protestants who spoke English as their first language tended to tone down earlier claims of ethnic superiority. And President Franklin D. Roosevelt was voted into power in 1932 by a coalition that crossed ethnic and class lines, including blacks as well as whites and many working people. Moreover, government-sponsored Federal One programs found artistic worth where it had been overlooked in the past, in folk culture and local life. Murals in post offices and WPA theater productions featured American themes. Painters and photographers in the mold of Thomas Hart Benton and Dorothea Lang took ordinary people in American settings as their subjects. While artistic works such as these portrayed the United States as an array of local settings, each with its own character, the national state encouraged citizens to think of such localities as expressions of a larger *American* consciousness. The state was finally responsible for the 1930s outpouring of diversity, from theater projects and the WPA's state historical guides to national labor laws and President Roosevelt's fireside chats on the radio.[16]

Such was the background for the nationalism of Roy Harris (1898–1971), who was born in Oklahoma, raised in California, and trained in Paris, and who aspired to compose on behalf of all Americans. An essay he wrote in 1933 claims that "wonderful, young, sinewy, timorous, browbeaten, eager, gullible" American society was at that very moment "slowly kneading consistent racial character from the sifted flour of experience and the sweat of racial destiny." In other words, Americans were in the process of finding a common racial identity that would override the local differences that divided them. In Harris's view, rhythm was the key that separated Americans from Europeans—especially the "asymmetrical balancing of rhythmic phrases." Moreover, he wrote, American music showed a tendency to avoid definite cadences and a fondness for modal harmony.[17] These traits appear in Harris's *Third Symphony in One Movement* (1939). Though not program-

Famed teacher Nadia Boulanger and students—Walter Piston, John Alden Carpenter, Boulanger, Roy Harris, conductor Serge Koussevitzky, violin soloist Zlatko Baloković, Mabel Daniels, Jean Françaix, and Edward Burlingame Hill—at the premiere of Piston's Violin Concerto No. 2, Symphony Hall, Boston, 1939.

matic, the work was laid out by the composer in five connected sections, which he labeled *Tragic, Lyric, Pastoral, Fugue,* and *Dramatic-Tragic.* Copland, who admired and wrote about the *Third Symphony,* described the pastoral section as a "seemingly endless succession of spun-out melodies."[18] But for endlessness, it would be hard to match the melody of the second section: highly chromatic avoiding a sense of tonic, and boundless in the way of a grand bit of rhetoric. Written in Harris's own populist vein, the melody fills some three-dozen bars, with barely a hint of repetition. It is easy to connect such a melody with Harris's ideas. For, following what he considered an American tendency to avoid cadences, the melody also suggests the vastness of the nation whose spirit Harris sought to evoke in this relatively brief but impassioned work.

Musically, Harris, Thomson, Blitzstein, and Copland all belong in the camp of conservatism suggested above. Yet each had his own sound, just as each employed a conservative musical idiom for different reasons, among them: a wish to contribute to a national style; a pro-French, anti-German leaning toward simplicity; a response to American geography or history; a hope of reaching the public through mass media; left-wing politics; and a borrowing of American folk and popular music. If in the *Third Symphony,*

Harris fancied himself as kneading an American product out of diverse ingredients, Copland put a New World stamp on four large-scale works of the period by borrowing folk and popular melodies, as he had done in *El salón México*. In two ballets about the West, *Billy the Kid* (1938) and *Rodeo* (1942), cowboy and Western tunes appear. *A Lincoln Portrait* (1942) for orchestra, featuring a narrator who speaks words of Abraham Lincoln, quotes Stephen Foster's *Camptown Races* and *Springfield Mountain*, a folk melody from eighteenth-century New England. *Appalachian Spring* (1944), a ballet set in rural Pennsylvania during the last century, contains a set of variations on the Shaker tune *Simple Gifts*.

While the idea of writing more accessible music attracted many composers of the 1930s, however, others scorned that notion. Roger Sessions, for one, warned against a retreat from "universal principle" into "the accident of locality" that he detected behind works like *El salón México*; and Sessions's dissonant, chromatic idiom was evidence of his belief in the universality of continuous stylistic evolution.[19] Moreover, during the 1930s and early 1940s, the rise in Europe of totalitarianism and fascism drove such eminent composers as Schoenberg, Stravinsky, Bartók, and Hindemith to the United States, where their presence did much to define contemporary music on these shores as a cosmopolitan endeavor.

Well before the 1930s, another member of the Copland-Sessions-Thomson generation had explored approaches to composition that owed little either to the cosmopolitan idea of stylistic evolution or the trend toward populist outreach. Henry Cowell, born in Menlo Park, California, in 1897, spent much of his early life in poverty and had little formal schooling. Yet by 1914, his unusual talent and intellect were recognized, and he began studying music with Charles Seeger, a composer and faculty member at the University of California at Berkeley, who encouraged Cowell's fondness for experiment. "Instead of studying one brand of harmony and counterpoint and applying this to every thought in music," Cowell wrote in the 1960s, he had determined to use "a different kind of musical material for each different idea that I have." The result was that, "even from the very start, I was sometimes extremely modernistic and sometimes quite old-fashioned, and very often in-between."[20]

The range of Cowell's modernistic ideas was remarkable. He won his reputation first as a composer-performer who treated the piano in unusual ways. *The Tides of Manaunaun* (ca. 1917) features tone clusters made by pressing down adjacent keys in blocks of sound spanning more than an octave. And *Dynamic Motion* (ca. 1916), conceived as a representation of the New York City subway, calls for the player to hammer out clusters with fists, forearms, and elbows in the manner of a virtuoso. *Aeolian Harp* (ca. 1923) and *The Banshee* (1925), on the other hand, use the piano more in a harplike than a percussive way, calling for the performer to play on the strings as well as the keyboard. Another of Cowell's unusual ideas had to do with relations between rhythm and pitch, and he composed a pair of string pieces, *Quartet Romantic* (1917) and *Quartet Euphometric* (1919), to investigate such connections. Between 1916 and 1919, he also worked on a treatise exploring fresh acoustical possibilities in the overtone series, published in 1930 as *New Musical Resources*.

By the latter 1920s, Cowell was drawing on the range of folk and non-Western music that had engaged him over the years, including Chinese, Japanese, African, South Indian, and Javanese as well as Irish. The *United Quartet* (1936) makes use of ostinatos, drones, and stratified textures in ways that help to explain his claim that the work "should be understood equally well by Americans, Europeans, Orientals, [and] higher primitives."[21] Cowell spent the years 1936–40 in San Quentin prison after being convicted on a morals charge for which he was later pardoned. He remained active there as a musician and composer, now with a practical spirit that turned him more toward Irish and American folk music as models. Yet collaborations with dancers, including the modernist pioneer Martha Graham, kept him active as a musical experimenter. In works for her and others during the late 1930s, Cowell tried out an "elastic" approach to musical form. He invented phrases that could be expanded or contracted on the spot, giving dancers freedom to shape the music during the act of performance. In 1939, Cowell also wrote several works for percussion ensemble at the behest of composer John Cage, who was then musical director for a dance company in Seattle.

Once released from prison, Cowell in 1941 married the ethnomusicologist Sidney Robertson, who introduced him to the music of William Walker's *Southern Harmony* (1835), a shape-note sacred tunebook compiled in South Carolina. Between 1944 and 1964, Cowell wrote, for various instrumental combinations, eighteen *Hymns and Fuguing Tunes*, inspired by early American hymnody, as well as eighteen of his twenty symphonies. And he and his wife traveled widely, in 1956 surveying the music of Ireland, Germany, Greece, Turkey, India, Pakistan, Iran, and Japan with the support of a Rockefeller Foundation grant, and in 1961 representing the United States at international conferences on music in Teheran and Tokyo. These travels led to such works as *Ongaku* (1957), in which Western instruments imitate traditional Japanese ones, and *Persian Set* (1957) for a chamber orchestra that includes the tar, a Persian string instrument.

While seeking as a composer to live "in the whole world of music," as he once put it, Cowell was also a tireless advocate for his fellow American composers. As editor of *New Music* from 1927 to 1936, he published the scores of many, including Charles Ives, whose biography he and his wife brought out in 1955. Cowell also promoted new music concerts through such organizations as the New Music Society and the Pan American Association of Composers. He wrote hundreds of articles, gave countless interviews on behalf of new music, and served as an overseas ambassador for the work of his American colleagues. And he taught composition, both privately and through institutions, counting among his pupils Burt Bacharach, John Cage, Dick Higgins, George Gershwin, and Lou Harrison.

Henry Cowell's career was living proof that neither European-based modernism nor American nationalism was broad enough in scope to encompass the imagination of American composers currently at work. Indeed, if confirmation of that point was needed, it came from the young California-born composer John Cage, a student of Schoenberg as well as of Cowell, who announced in a 1937 talk in Seattle: "I believe that the use of noise . . . to make music . . . will continue and increase until we reach a music produced through the aid of electrical instruments."[22] Cage's *Imaginary Landscape No. 1*, premiered in 1939, was scored for muted piano, a suspended cymbal, and two phonograph turntables—a hint that his imagination was taking a path that in the future would be linked with Ives, Cowell, and others whose appetite for musical experiment would be seen as another kind of American tradition.

This chronicle's main premise has been that music in America has evolved from an interplay of the classical, popular, and traditional spheres. Recent chapters have referred to Indian music, black oral traditions, and Spanish songs of the West and Southwest—all examples of music making in the third sphere. But not since our discussion in Chapter 4 of eighteenth-century ballads, songs, and dances in oral tradition has British-American traditional music been considered as a whole. Through all the musical activity described in the interim, that tradition was also developing in its own ways. Only where it came into contact with literate observers, however, is it possible to trace the tradition's historical development. The populist environment of the 1930s helped to bring Anglo-American folk music to wider public consciousness. And in the absence of a written record, one way to understand how and why that happened is to note the efforts of collectors who, from the late 1800s on, found enough significance in that music to gather, preserve, and study it.

29

All That Is Native and Fine

American Folk Song and Its Collectors

THE IDEA THAT FOLK SONGS differ from art songs and popular songs has led to a good deal of study, including speculation about their origins. German philosopher Johann Gottfried Herder in the latter eighteenth century, followed in the nineteenth by the philologist-folklorists Jacob and Wilhelm Grimm, understood folk song as a natural and spontaneous expression of peasant life, collectively composed. While that belief lay behind much of the collecting that followed, other students of folklore theorized that, however much collective transmission may have changed the songs, they had first been individually composed, and not necessarily by peasants.[1] The early twentieth-century argument between "communalists" and "individualists" points to mysteries: How did creation and transmission really work in folk traditions? And what did it mean that people low in the social order had preserved songs so ancient, powerful, and sometimes artful?

If folk songs were to be studied, they first had to be collected, and no collection of traditional song has been more influential than the five volumes of Harvard professor Francis James Child's *The English and Scottish Popular Ballads* (1883–98). This monumental work contains full texts and scholarly commentary on 305 ballads and all their known variants, a repertory that has come to be known as the Child ballads. For Child, a ballad was a literary text, not a song or a melody, and he did his collecting in libraries. Searching through printed sources—from books to broadsides—and manuscripts, he published the texts (not the tunes) of what he took to be the oldest English-language ballads in existence. One, *The Gypsy Laddie* (Child number 200), tells of a band of gypsies stopping by the dwelling of an absent nobleman and singing so sweetly that his wife falls in love, runs off with one of them, and is then pursued by her husband. Child prints eleven different versions, drawing on Scottish, English, Irish, and American sources. His commentary points to some of their differences. For example, the husband, unnamed in the earliest text, is called Lord Cassilis in three later ones; in other versions, Cassle, Castle, Corsefield, Cashan; and in the version collected in America, Garrick. The gypsy lover is variously known as Johnie, Jockie, Faa (a last name), Gipsy Davy, and Gypsie Geordie. In several versions, the husband finds his lady, then hangs gypsies—fifteen of them, or sixteen, or seven. In some, the lady regrets her change in status. "Last night," writes Child, "she lay with her lord in a well-made bed, now she must lie in an old barn." In one, which Child finds "ridiculously perverted in the interest of morals," the gypsy denies any interest in sex: "I swear that my hand shall never go near thee." Child also dismisses the claim that a real historical character, the wife of the Earl of Cassilis in the 1640s, was the ballad's heroine.[2]

The dignity of the ballads, together with their ancient lineage and the painstaking scholarship of Child and others, gave them a certain prestige in such academic fields as literary studies, philology, and historical poetics. And the debate about origins sparked plenty of intellectual effort. Since approximately one-third of the ballads in Child's canon claimed variants found in American sources, some scholars and collectors came to think of the ballad—especially the Child ballad—as this country's central Anglo-American folk repertory.

Folk-song study entered a new stage in the early twentieth century, when scholars realized that the ballad belonged to a living tradition. In one scholar's words: "The folk *speaketh*, not *spake*." Ballad collecting now moved beyond library research and theoretical speculation into fieldwork. The new collectors, called "Emersonians," turned to the folk themselves for material, in an attitude of respect for oral tradition and the people who were still carrying it on. And a key figure among them, at first in his native England but later in the United States, was Cecil Sharp, whose scholarly career took shape under the aegis of the Folk-Song Society.

That society was established in England in 1898 to collect and publish folk songs. As opposed to ballad scholars, who were chiefly interested in poetry, its founders were musicians determined, in the words of Sir Hubert Parry, the composer who gave the group's inaugural address, to "save something primitive and genuine from extinction" and "put on record what loveable qualities there are in unsophisticated humanity." Noting traditional folk music's remarkable ability to survive, Parry called it one of "the purest products of the human mind," though now in danger of being driven out by "the common popular songs of the day." For Parry and his colleagues, folk song "grew in the hearts of the people before they devoted themselves so assiduously to the making of quick returns."[3] Parry's themes—the primordial age of folk song, its deep-rooted authenticity, fear for its survival in a modern world, the virtues of the folk themselves, and nostalgia for an age before commerce had corrupted human endeavor—were sounded often by later collectors in Britain and the United States. And yet these notions obscured certain vital elements in the musical traditions that collectors such as Cecil Sharp encountered in the field.

A 1903 encounter with traditional English music had impressed Sharp enough to pique his interest in the Folk-Song Society, and he began to study the widespread oral tradition that still existed in England and Scotland. Sharp's way of collecting a song was standard for his time. Singers were asked to repeat what they had sung until Sharp had transcribed the melody accurately and written down a complete version of the text. In 1907, he published *English Folk-Song: Some Conclusions*, based on his own collection and analysis of some 1,500 examples. Sharp's study, which concentrates on music, concludes that folk melody is based on modal rather than major or minor scales and that folk songs were composed by individuals but transmitted by a communal process involving three steps: continuity, variation, and selection.

By continuity, Sharp meant that a song can exist in oral tradition only when it takes on a persistent form in singers' memories. As noted earlier, the narrative kernel of *The Gypsy Laddie* lies in a high-born wife's sudden departure in the company of gypsies and her husband's pursuit of her, although names, numbers, and details vary widely from version to version. Sharp's work convinced him that variation in verbal detail was seldom a matter of intention, seeming to spring "subconsciously from out of the heart of the singer." He also observed that although a folk song's words and music ought to be considered inseparable, singers thought much more about the words, and rarely changed a melody "from a conscious desire to improve." Rather, melodic variation might proceed from a desire to ornament, as in embellishing a sustained tone with turns or passing notes. Or a misremembered line might introduce irregularities that cause melodic change. Or a tune sung to a new set of words might be altered to fit them. Or a singer who favors one particular mode might change a song into that mode.[4]

Sharp discusses selection, his third element of transmission, as if folk song were a branch of Darwinian biology. Only variations attractive to the community will survive, he believes. In other words, the individual invents, but "the community selects." And Sharp separates the two in time.

> Every line, every word of the ballad sprang in the first instance from the head of some individual, reciter, minstrel, or peasant; just as every note, every phrase of a folk-tune proceeded originally from the mouth of a solitary singer. Corporate action has originated nothing and can originate nothing. Communal composition is unthinkable. The community plays a part, it is true, but it is at a later stage, after and not before the individual has done his work and manufactured the material.[5]

English folk song collector Cecil Sharp (1859–1924) paid several visits to America, transcribing songs from residents of Appalachia. Here, Sharp and his assistant Maud Karpeles (at right) collect from Mrs. Doc Pratt of Knott County, Kentucky, in 1917.

Yet whatever the role of individuals in creating folk music in the first place, it took a certain kind of community to keep it alive.

In 1915, Sharp learned that such a community existed in the mountains of North Carolina. On a visit to the United States, he made the acquaintance of Olive Dame Campbell, a Massachusetts native who some years earlier had begun collecting the words of traditional songs in Appalachia. Campbell urged Sharp, whom she met in New England, to come south. "There is a great amount of material untouched here," she wrote, including ballads, singing games, carols, and dances. After examining Campbell's own collection in early 1916, Sharp wrote a colleague: "She has just the combination of scientific and artistic spirit which work of this kind needs if it is to be of any use to posterity." And he found the value of material Campbell had already harvested "even higher than I had estimated." In July 1916, Sharp himself set out on a collecting expedition in western North Carolina. On August 1, he wrote to tell Campbell that he had already transcribed twenty-five tunes. "I found the singers very easy to handle," he reported, calling them "just English peasant folk [who] do not seem to me to have taken on any distinctive American traits. They talk English, sing English, behave English!" The next week found Sharp in an area northwest of Asheville, "the richest field" in which he had ever collected. The fruits of Sharp's expedition appeared in print in English *Folk Songs of the Southern Appalachians* (1917), a joint publication with Olive Campbell and the first major scholarly collection of the mountain people's music.[6]

One of the pleasures of Sharp's narrowly focused collecting policy was that he encountered the same songs over and over again. In Bertrand Bronson's *The Traditional Tunes of the Child Ballads* (1959–71), a giant four-volume work that includes both text and music of all known variants of every ballad in the Child canon, 128 versions of *The Gypsy Laddie* appear. And Sharp himself collected 28 of them in England and America. On September 1, 1916, in Flag Pond, Tennessee, just across the North Carolina border, he notated a version sung by Mrs. J. Gabriel Coates in seven stanzas, with an added refrain. Here the emphasis is less on the abduction and more on the conversation between husband and wife when he catches up with her. No revenge is taken; no gypsies—or gypsums, as they are called in this version—are hung. The wife refuses to return home with her husband, and then, in the last two stanzas, regrets her decision. The next day in nearby Rocky Fork, Tennessee, Mrs. Mary Norton sang for Sharp a five-stanza version of *The Gypsy Laddie* whose melody is quite different, drawing out the first and third lines, and repeating the fourth line of each stanza. The chase is missing from this version, which cuts from the lord's departure to the couple's confrontation. Here the wife has left a child as well as home and husband. And in the end he returns home alone, after repossessing her shoes "of Spanish leather."[7]

Together with differences introduced by oral transmission, these two examples illustrate narrative techniques typical of traditional ballads: (1) they focus on a single situation; (2) they are dramatic, in that action occurs during the course of the song; and (3) the narrator is impersonal, making no judgments. Ballads favor event over explanation, seldom beginning before the action is directed toward its outcome. In no version of *The Gypsy Laddie* are listeners told why the lady might want to leave, nor does either of these examples describe her departure. Instead, husband and wife are plunged into the consequences of her leaving. Dialogue is of central importance in these examples, filling four stanzas of each, with no transitions or pauses to indicate who is speaking. Protagonists speak in plain, formulaic language, with a stock of standard epithets and adjectives, such as the "milk-white" horse the squire rides in both versions and the lady's "lily-white hand" in the second. Repetition, present in both versions of *The Gypsy Laddie*, is another ballad technique linked to orality.

The impersonal tone of the texts may also have determined the way traditional singers performed them. Moreover, the presence of music tends to ensure a grave formality and ceremony to the texts, whether read or sung. With form as the top priority, a folk singer sings without innuendo or desire for any kind of connection with the audience.[8] The dignity and severity of traditional ballad singing recalls Charles Ives's remark that he had heard plain folk at camp meetings sing hymns "as the rocks were grown."

In 1916, Cecil Sharp found music in the southern Appalachians in a flourishing condition, which he linked to the social order. Having encountered ballads in England scattered among a few older singers, he suddenly found himself "for the first time in my life in a community in which singing was as common and almost as universal a practice as speaking," where music was "interwoven with the ordinary avocation of everyday life." Sharp had traveled to the United States hoping to observe the English ballad tradition in a healthy state of preservation, and that is what he found. Olive Campbell's collecting, in contrast, turned up some of the same songs but was not restricted to them. In 1908, Campbell had gone to the mountains with her husband, who had received a foundation grant to study the region's indigenous life. She collected all the music she found there regardless of its genre or character, including religious songs and hymns, popular music, instrumental tunes, and composed ballads and songs. But these other kinds of music held little interest for Sharp, who once told Campbell that "posterity will need the primitive songs and ballads to keep their two arts of music and dance real, sincere, and pure."[9]

Despite their differences, Campbell shared Sharp's belief that some of the songs in oral tradition were aesthetically better than others. She even imagined a social role that the better songs might play. In a letter to Sharp in 1916, she wrote that the folk movement in the mountains

> seeks the recognition and preservation of all that is native and fine. . . . We would like to have the people recognize the worth and beauty of their songs; we would like to have the singing of these songs encouraged in all the mountain schools and centers; we would like to have them displace the inferior music that is now being sung there. . . . The people have already begun to be somewhat ashamed of their songs; they need to have them appreciated by outsiders.[10]

Campbell writes here less as a collector than an activist looking for ways to improve the quality of mountain life. From her point of view, preserving the older songs was not enough: they were to be kept alive in the community to encourage people to take pride in what was "native and fine" instead of turning to lesser modern substitutes.

If a culture is viewed as an independent system best left alone by outsiders, Campbell's goal may seem high-handed. But what Campbell and Sharp considered inferior music was part of a much larger change that industrialization was bringing to Appalachia. Factories were fueled by coal, a resource the Appalachian mountains held in abundance. By 1900, companies outside the region were buying huge tracts of land there; within a decade, mines dotted the landscape, siphoning capital into the pockets of outside entrepreneurs. A way of life rooted in subsistence farming by land-owning mountain folk was being transformed into one dominated by the coal-mining industry.

Hindsight shows that the prospect of preserving traditional music with-out intervention was slim, for the life that had fostered it was disappearing. Cecil Sharp, who had little stake in the region except as a musical reposi-tory, cited examples of modern encroachment in a letter written in 1918. He had traveled to a small town in Franklin County, Virginia, expecting to find music ripe for collecting. But instead of English peasant folk living in a time warp, he encountered "a thoroughly respectable community living in com-fortable farm houses, owning, many of them, their own motor cars while the women we saw going to a weekend 'preaching' wore low-necked dresses, high-heeled shoes, talk[ed] in loud raucous voices and used face powder lavishly."[11] These rather sour comments were a sign that the musical inter-ests of mountain people were diverging from those of Sharp, the folk-song collector. Where the preservation-minded Sharp saw decline, however, an observer interested in new styles might well have found invigorating change. For at the time Sharp was traveling through Franklin, Henry, and Patrick counties, a remarkable blending was under way between southern West Vir-ginia and Virginia traditions of playing the fiddle and banjo.

Cecil Sharp made a stellar contribution to American folk-song study, yet the narrow scope of his song gathering was out of step with much of the other work going on in the United States at the time of his visit. For exam-ple, before Sharp ever set foot in America, Massachusetts-born scholar Phillips Barry had developed an inclusive philosophy of ballad collecting.

His work, carried on chiefly in New England, showed that whatever its origin, a song went through a process of communal re-creation when it en-tered oral tradition. By working to document that process, Barry refocused the issue of repertory. He and other collectors, taking the singers' own pref-erences as their starting place, recovered from oral tradition not only old ballads of English origin and their variants, but also ballads composed in America. Their work contradicted a widely held belief. In the first history of music in America, written in the 1880s, Professor Frédéric Louis Ritter of Vassar College had lamented the absence of folk music:

> The people's-song—"an outgrowth from the life of the people, the product of innate artistic instinct of the people, seeking a more lofty expression than that of every-day speech for those feelings which are awakened in the soul by the varied events of life"—is not to be found among the American people. The American farmer, mechanic, journeyman, stage-driver, shepherd, etc., does not sing,—unless he happens to belong to a church-choir or a singing-society.[12]

Many literate musicians took Ritter's claim as truth. And since he seems to have thought of white English speakers as the Americans lacking in folk music, their musical traditions played only a small role in the debate over musical nationalism that took place in the 1890s. In that debate, visiting Bohemian composer Antonín Dvořák had proposed indigenous folk music as the basis for an American art music, and he had been led to believe that only Native Americans and African Americans had such traditions. Now, however, the work of Phillips Barry and others was uncovering Anglo-American folk music in many regions, evidence that Americans had long been adding to and changing the Old World practices they inherited.

The late 1800s saw a steep rise of interest in indigenous American cultures. In 1888, the American Folklore Society was founded on the model of the Folklore Society of Britain, with the intent of gathering and publishing songs and stories from English, African-American, Indian, Mexican, and French-Canadian cultures. And after 1900, many state folklore societies were established, dedicated in large part to collecting and preserving folk song from the Old World, especially Child ballads. In the meantime (1914), the U.S. Department of Education itself declared a "rescue mission" for folk songs and ballads, in the belief that they were an endangered species.[13]

By mid-century, some twenty regional collections had resulted from this effort. One that represents the general type is *Folk-Songs of the South: Collected under the Auspices of the West Virginia Folk-Lore Society* (1925), by John Harrington Cox, the local society's archivist and general editor. The leaders of the enterprise worked through county teachers' institutes, which were held in the summer months. A call for old songs also went out in the *West Virginia School Journal and Educator*, a teachers' periodical. One teacher recruited her students in the effort:

> Miss Maud I. Jefferson, the teacher of English in the West Liberty Normal School, by talks on West Virginia folk-lore aroused the interest of thirteen girls. These girls, by searching the community and by writing home to their parents and friends, found a large number of valuable songs. They then prepared an original entertainment, made up in large part of songs, superstitions, and so forth, which they presented before the school and the people of the community. At this entertainment, the President of the Folk-Lore Society gave an address.[14]

Folk-Songs of the South begins with 33 Child ballads in 154 variants and continues with 152 other songs in 292 variants but no logical order. The collection's stock of tunes is modest: just 29 melodies for the 446 texts, and published in an appendix. As the collectors were volunteers, most of them with no musical training, perhaps that disparity should be no surprise. The collection contains four versions of *The Gypsy Laddie*, including one from

Cox himself—learned, he writes, "about 1880, from hired men, while living on a farm in Illinois." This eight-stanza version, with a refrain, centers on the husband, who saddles up his fastest (milk-white) horse, rides after his wife with tears "trickling down his cheeks," but ends up returning home alone, "For she remained by the river side, / In the arms of the Gypsy Davy." The rest of the songs range widely in genre and subject matter: a lumbering ballad from Maine; two cowboy laments; a number of Civil War songs, including George F. Root's *Just Before the Battle, Mother; Villikins and His Dinah*, which supplied the tune for *Sweet Betsey from Pike*; several temperance songs; *The Spanish Lady*, which Benjamin Franklin had mentioned a century and a half earlier; and the exuberant *Ground Hog Song*, an Appalachian favorite that traces a successful hunt and ends with a plump specimen skinned and boiling in the pot.

THE ARCHIVE OF AMERICAN FOLK SONG, COUNTRY MUSIC, AND THE RISE OF "URBAN FOLK" MUSICIANS

In 1922, the compiler of a collection of ballad texts wrote that the growing interest in such songs signaled "a trend toward democracy." As she put it, "the lowly may now serve as heroes and be paid attention to."[15] And by the latter 1920s, it was obvious to anyone paying heed that the United States was home to a rich, diverse assortment of music in the traditional sphere. One symbol of that recognition was the founding in 1928 of the Archive of American Folk Song at the Library of Congress in Washington, D.C. The idea seems to have come from Robert Winslow Gordon, a scholar and collector who was named the collection's first archivist. Gordon, born in Maine and a member of the Harvard College Class of 1910, did graduate work at Harvard with professors who were disciples of Francis J. Child. He taught for several years in the Harvard English Department and then in 1918 took a similar post at the University of California at Berkeley. During his years in Berkeley, academic duties increasingly took a back seat to his study of folk songs. Equipped with a portable cylinder recording machine, Gordon began his own career as a song collector. Between 1923 and 1927, he also wrote "Old Songs That Men Have Sung," a regular magazine column in *Adventure*, a popular journal devoted to the out-of-doors.

Gordon's column became part of the ambitious task he set for himself. Unlike most collectors, he refused to specialize—in texts over tunes, for example, or Child ballads, or the songs of one region or ethnic group. Rather, seeing himself as a research scientist, he focused on folk-song origin and development. By making a comprehensive collection, he believed, he could study and explain how folk songs grew. While the shape of that collection was still to be decided, Gordon hoped that the network set up by his column, which invited responses, would provide an unparalleled opportunity to gather songs from the magazine's estimated two million readers. Gordon imagined himself in contact with "the people," both as a field collector and a scholar who drew on the knowledge and experience of others. He trusted that contact, combined with his scientific bent, to point him toward a representative, truly American collection that would illuminate the character of the nation's folk song.[16]

In 1924, Gordon gave up his academic post at Berkeley. He spent the next several years collecting in the field, writing his column, and trying to support a family as a professional folklorist through grants and freelance writing. In 1927, he sent a complete set of his *Adventure* columns to Carl Engel, chief of the Library of Congress music division, and a lengthy correspondence followed. Persuaded by Gordon that the library was a logical place for such work to be centered, Engel was able the following year to raise money from private sources to fund a post for Gordon.

Well before interest in the study of folk music surfaced at the Library of Congress, however, the music business had discovered its commercial possibilities. For the genre now known as country music claims roots in Anglo-American traditions found in the South. The core of Southern culture was British, but the fiddlers, balladeers, and gospel singers who carried on its musical side as part of domestic and community life borrowed freely from other traditions, including nineteenth-century popular songs and dances and the music of black entertainers. In the years before 1920, local events evolved—fiddle contests, medicine shows, even vaudeville entertainment—that allowed talented white Southern performers for the first time to earn money for singing and playing.[17]

With a lively, indigenous, economically unstructured musical tradition at hand, together with the technological means of milking it for profit *and* a cultural reason to do so, the time was ripe for commercial intervention in the South. Through the two media of radio and phonograph record, many new customers could be reached, including people living in the southeastern rural and mountain regions. The record business had already proved adept at discovering and entering untapped markets. As early as 1909, the Columbia Phonograph Company had explained to its dealers that foreign-speaking immigrants formed one such market:

> Remember that in all large cities and in most towns there are sections where people of one nationality or another congregate in "colonies." Most of these people keep up the habits and prefer to speak the language of the old country. Speak to them in their own tongue, if you can, and see their faces light up with a smile that lingers and hear the streak of language they will give you in reply. To these people RECORDS IN THEIR OWN LANGUAGE have an irresistible attraction, and they will buy them readily.[18]

Early in the century, record companies had tended to regard the classical sphere as universal and to arrange "folk song" recordings, from ballads to spirituals, to meet a genteel standard of voice quality, diction, intonation, and blend. The marketplace, however, taught the companies two key lessons. First, ethnic audiences considered performance style part of any traditional music's identity. And second, recordings could be targeted toward any of a number of subcultures or ethnic groups, and people in those groups preferred recordings by other group members to those of outsiders. Record companies and radio stations competed in the 1920s to find such performers. A famous example was noted in Chapter 27: *Crazy Blues*, by Mamie Smith and Her Jazz Hounds, issued in 1920 on the OKeh label, the beginning of a flood of "race" records aimed at black customers. In the decade that followed, the blues was just one of many folk genres that, while being collected by scholars in the field, also circulated in the popular-music marketplace.

The evolution of country music into an industry began between 1920 and 1925, when show business discovered it. In 1922, radio stations in Atlanta and Fort Worth began to broadcast local performers. By 1925, so-called barn-dance programs were well established on the radio, with the WSM Barn Dance from Nashville, later the Grand Ole Opry, the most famous. In the meantime, Ralph Peer, the OKeh executive who in 1920 had supervised Mamie Smith's *Crazy Blues*, traveled south in 1923, and in Atlanta recorded "Fiddlin' John" Carson singing and playing. As the story goes, when Peer heard the songs Carson wanted to record—*The Little Old Log Cabin in the Lane* and *The Old Hen Cackled and the Rooster's Going to Crow*—he was unimpressed and decided that only Carson's fiddle tunes should be recorded. But a local distributor, recognizing that Georgia farmers and mill workers would appreciate Carson's singing as well as his playing, talked Peer into letting the fiddler sing. Sales proved the local man right, and later that year Carson was invited to OKeh's New York studios to make a dozen new recordings.[19]

In 1927, Ralph Peer traveled to the Clinch Mountains of Virginia, where he recorded the Carter Family—A. P. Carter, his wife Sara, and their sister-in-law Maybelle Glenn—who accompanied their singing with autoharp and guitar. Peer apparently suggested that the Carters record old songs, which they performed in the same informal style favored at family gatherings. Songs by A. P. Carter himself formed another part of the Carters' commercially successful mix. By the latter 1920s, Appalachian music was being circulated not only orally but by radio, on record, and even in print—in the sheet-music folios published for the Carter Family. As profits from record sales accumulated, questions of ownership and copyright cropped up. Claims for the purity of even the oldest songs could no longer be maintained, for recordings and radio broadcasts were now part of the process of transmission and selection.

The Carter family, including A. P. Carter, his sister-in-law Maybelle (left), and wife Sara (right, who usually played autoharp). Residents of the Clinch Mountains of Virginia, the family won fame in the South after they began to record their music making in 1927.

Even before he took up his post at the Archive of American Folk Song, Robert Winslow Gordon recognized that commercial invasion was affecting the Anglo-American traditions he was collecting and studying. Rather than simply deploring the new force, however, he tried to account for it in his scholarship, keeping a list of commercially recorded folk songs as part of his work at the library. But Gordon, who put his own fieldwork and analytical projects ahead of curatorial duties at the library, gradually lost the confidence of his superiors and left the archivist's post in 1933 with his collection no closer to being finished. Gordon's replacement, however, John A. Lomax, turned the Archive of American Folk Song into a force on the American music scene.

Born in 1867, John Lomax grew up in Texas with a deep interest in black music. Graduating from the University of Texas in 1887, he worked in that school's administration for some years. He also taught English at a Texas college between 1903 and 1910, with time off (1906–7) for M.A. study at Harvard, where Francis James Child's study of the ballads had made folk-song research respectable. Harvard professors urged Lomax to pursue his interest in cowboy songs, which led to a ground-breaking publication in 1910, *Cowboy Songs and Other Frontier Ballads* (from which Charles Ives took the text for the song *Charlie Rutlage*). Shortly after his book appeared, Lomax was elected president of the American Folklore Society and traveled and lectured widely, helping to boost the visibility of folklore studies, especially among teachers of English. By the early 1920s, Lomax had left the academic world for banking, though he continued to collect songs and ballads. In 1932, out of a job and a widower of sixty-five, he convinced Macmillan publishers in New York to sign him up for a comprehensive collection to be called *American Ballads and Folk Songs*. He then approached Carl Engel at the Library of Congress, who agreed that the library would furnish him with a state-of-the-art electric recording machine, blank records, and the use of their name as long as Lomax agreed to deposit his recordings at the library. In July 1933, Lomax was named honorary consultant to the Archive of American Folk Song at the Library of Congress for a stipend of $1 per year.

Lomax's long experience had introduced him to the major collections of folk-song materials in American libraries. His survey of these repositories and collections in print revealed that black folk songs were poorly represented. Therefore, he made these songs the focus of the collecting trip that he and his son Alan, eighteen years old and a student at the University of Texas, began in the summer of 1933. Eager to find African-American musicians insulated from white traditions, they visited mainly Southern penitentiaries and prison camps. The trip lasted four months, covered sixteen-thousand miles, and led to memorable experiences. John Lomax later described a moment at a lumber camp at Wiergate, Texas, when time seemed to stand still: the instant when a large tree that has just been cut begins its descent to the ground. "I heard for the first time the wail of the Negro woodsman," Lomax wrote, as the tree "sways and then falls to the earth with a shuddering crash. Shrill, swift, wavering, the shout swings to a sudden and dramatic conclusion." Lomax heard "music in that cry, and mystery, and wistful sadness" at the downfall of so huge a living thing. He also convinced the woodsmen to sing their "requiem of the falling pine into our recording machine."[20] Later, in Louisiana, the Lomaxes found the remarkable singer and guitarist Leadbelly (Huddie Ledbetter), who was then in jail. John Lomax arranged for his parole, and between 1935 and 1948 Leadbelly recorded many songs in his large repertory for the Library of Congress archive.

Chapter 28 noted how, during the Depression, folk culture was being evoked in the classical sphere. Borrowings from the traditional sphere by classical composers like Copland and Thomson required that the music be polished to fit in a realm where technical precision was taken for granted. Yet the idea that folk music carried its own kind of honesty and truth also gained currency in these years. Concert-hall composers who borrowed it were interested not only in broadening the appeal of their works but in grounding them in the basic stuff of human existence. At the same time, the latter 1930s marked a key period in the history of national collecting, with funds from the WPA being made available. In 1937, the Archive of American Folk Song, supported since 1928 by donations and outside monies, began receiving a small stipend from Congress. Alan Lomax was hired as a staff member, then went on collecting junkets of his own in Kentucky, Ohio, Michigan, Indiana, and Vermont. With their belief in folk song as a living force, not an antiquarian survival, John and Alan Lomax began to publish collections of folk songs depicting America as a populist democracy.

Alan Lomax, whose appetite for folk music blended political conviction with aesthetic appreciation, once traced the start of the folk-song revival back to 1933 and the early days of the New Deal in Washington. "The Roosevelts, the Tugwells, and the Hopkinses were interested in folk music," he claimed, because "they wanted to be identified with it as a democratic American art" that would give voiceless groups "a sense that they, too, contributed very much to the building of America."[21] In the Preface to a collection that he and his father published after World War II, Lomax set down his view of the collector's vocation. His words recall Olive Campbell's determination to promote music that was "native and fine." The collector, Lomax wrote,

> goes where book-learning is not. He lives with the underprivileged. He brings back the proof in their songs and stories and dances that these folks are expressive and concerned about the beautiful and the good. In doing so,

After accompanying his father, John Lomax, on a long folk-song-collecting trip in 1933, Alan Lomax (b. 1915) devoted himself to traditional music, including a 1948 radio program, "Your Ballad Man."

he continually denies the validity of caste lines and caste barriers. Malinowski says of the anthropologist, "He also has the duty to speak as the native's advocate." Just so, the folklorist has the duty to speak as the advocate of the common man.[22]

In other words, rather than a reporter or historical observer, a collector of folk song is an agent with a cultural goal. Unlike Campbell, Lomax leaned more toward advocacy than systematic intervention, and one of the goals of his advocacy was to make the Archive of American Folk Song a force in widening the music's audience. In 1941, he brought out a multirecord album that included black Southern convicts singing a field holler and a work song, one of the first field recordings to be commercially marketed. And in 1939–41, he produced two nationally syndicated radio programs for CBS: "Back Where I Come From" and a folk-music series for the "American

School of the Air." Less a scholar than a collector with great energy and discriminating taste, Lomax has been credited with the ability to elicit the finest performances from a community's best singers. As a writer and producer of programs, he cared less about authentic performances than about presenting American folk music at its best, even if that meant combining different versions of a song.[23]

Alan Lomax became a folk-song collector during troubled times. He reached maturity during the Depression and, just as the economy was recovering, saw war break out in Europe. From the time Germany invaded Poland in September 1939 until December 1941, when the United States entered World War II, questions about this country's role in the European conflict dominated American political life. Lomax came to perceive folk music as a means of rallying popular sentiment against evil forces. The political left, which won growing support during the 1930s, especially among immigrant groups, artists, and intellectuals, sympathized with the socialistic belief in a state-run economy rather than a more freely competitive one. The economic actions of President Roosevelt's New Deal government, which helped some Americans avoid economic disaster, brought that formerly radical notion closer to the political mainstream. Moreover, the ethnic diversity encouraged by the New Deal has also been shown to reflect the influence of the American Communist Party (CPUSA) among many liberal-minded Americans. The so-called United Front strategy adopted by the International Communist movement in 1935—setting aside temporarily the call for worldwide revolution and joining forces with a coalition of socialists, trade unionists, and liberals—allowed the CPUSA to identify itself with such democratic traditions as ethnic pluralism. At a time when the Party was trying to Americanize itself, the federal government was involved, through the WPA as well as the Archive of American Folk Song, with collecting and preserving folk culture in the name of democracy.

That context shaped Alan Lomax's stance as a collector and made him an influential figure in what has come to be called the folk revival. Convinced that he was working on behalf of true American patriotism, he made the most of his chance to speak as an advocate of the plain folk. If coaching informants, and becoming a folk singer himself, seem proof of a cultural outsider seizing control, the idea that folk music was the distilled political expression of American working people defused the issue of outsiders versus insiders. For Lomax in these years located the essence of folk music more in its political outlook—real or implied—and performance style than in the performer's personal history. Once folk music was separated from its native setting and invited into a movement claiming to represent "the common man," political outlook and musical skill could make an insider of an outsider. Lomax did what he could to make folk song an ideological popular music akin to the broadside ballads, abolition songs, temperance songs, and labor songs of earlier days. Thus its expressive power joined with left-leaning politics and a patriotic idealizing of plain folk in a blend that, with the help of mass-media distribution, made an impact in both the traditional and the popular spheres.

A good example of Lomax's eye for talent was his "discovery" in 1940 of folk singer and songwriter Woody Guthrie. In March of that year, a landmark concert was held at New York's Forrest Theater for the benefit of migrant farm workers. Billed as a "Grapes of Wrath Evening," after John Steinbeck's 1939 novel about the exploitation of farm laborers, the concert was historic because the featured artists were folk musicians, including Guthrie, Leadbelly, Burl Ives, Josh White, Richard Dyer-Bennet, the Golden Gate Quartet, Alan Lomax and his sister Bess, and "Aunt Molly" Jackson, a Kentucky native and songwriter long involved in pro-union activities. Festivals during the 1930s had established the precedent of folk singers and players performing for paying audiences, and many of these performers were experienced troupers, having sung on the radio, at union events and political rallies, and even in clubs. Nevertheless, to present them in an evening concert setting, on a New York theater stage, and in support of a political cause was a novel act of ideological entrepreneurship. Among the singers who appeared that night, Guthrie, newly arrived in the city, seems to have left the strongest impression.

Born in 1912 into an unstable Oklahoma family, Woody Guthrie was a talented, prolific writer who also sang and played guitar and managed to avoid formal schooling in any of these pursuits. From his teenage years he lived a wandering life, including stints as a laborer, street singer, and hobo. In 1937, he found himself a successful radio personality on station KFVD in Los Angeles as the star of a local show called "Here Comes Woody and Lefty Lou." In the course of his life, Guthrie wrote or adapted more than a thousand songs, reflecting his travels and emphasizing the Depression, the dust bowl drought of 1935, New Deal legislation, and union organization. Scornful of music with no message, Guthrie sang his politically hard-edged songs on picket lines, marches, and protest meetings. Alan Lomax, who heard Guthrie for the first time at the "Grapes of Wrath" concert, found him "miraculously" untouched by popular singing styles, and

> an unwitting classicist, someone who understood the power and integrity of the traditional forms and sang the old songs in an old-fashioned way, his voice droning and nasal and high-pitched. At the same time, and even more miraculously, he was a political radical, a living affirmation of Charles Seeger's theories of the activist potential of the music—those were *political* songs he was singing in traditional fashion. More important, though, Woody Guthrie was quite obviously a genius. His songs had the beautiful, easy-to-

Oklahoma-born Woody
Guthrie (1912–1967) parlayed
genuine folk roots and political
radicalism into a prominent
place in the folk revival
movement that began in the
latter 1930s.

remember simplicity of the best of folk art. . . . He was also very funny. Having introduced himself with several of his dust bowl songs, Woody was now telling . . . stories about his first few days in New York, and the audience was roaring. . . . "Trains were so crowded today, you couldn't even fall down. I had to change stations twice, and both times I came out with a different pair of shoes on."[24]

Lomax's respect increased even more as he experienced Guthrie's talent as a songwriter. During a cross-country trip whose last leg involved hitchhiking from Oklahoma to New York City in early 1940, Guthrie had come to hate a popular hit that seemed to be everywhere that winter, Irving Berlin's *God Bless America*. As Guthrie saw it, Berlin's song, whose text invoked the timeless phrase—or was it a cliché?—"home, sweet home," glossed over social inequality as if it were God's will. In February, shortly after reaching New York, Guthrie wrote a song in six stanzas that answered the falsely inspirational quality of Berlin's hit. A few years hence, and with changes, Guthrie's number became *This Land Is Your Land*, and anthem of national unity hardly less affirmative than Berlin's, though somewhat less formal. The original, however, reveals an edge of disenchantment in its fourth stanza:

Was a big high wall there that tried to stop me
A sign was painted said: Private Property.
But on the back side, it didn't say nothing—
God Blessed America for me.

And the sixth challenges Berlin's song directly:

> One bright sunny morning in the shadow of the steeple
> By the relief office I saw my people—
> As they stood there hungry,
> I stood there wondering if
> God Blessed America for me.[25]

After the "Grapes of Wrath" concert, Lomax invited Guthrie to Washington to record for the Archive of American Folk Song. He soon discovered that the singer had a huge repertory. (One song was *Gypsy Davy*, Child Ballad No. 200, which Guthrie sang to his own guitar accompaniment.) After several weeks with Guthrie as a house guest, Lomax also discovered that he used the phonograph to expand his repertory and refine his style. Bess Lomax, who shared a house with Guthrie in 1941, recalled how blues recordings by Blind Lemon Jefferson and T-Bone Slim helped him work on vocal delivery. "Woody had his own little record player upstairs with about eight records he listened to absolutely continuously," she remembered. "Sitting in the kitchen, you could hear him play the record, and at the end of the cut, he'd pick up the needle and move it back to the beginning. He'd play these songs maybe a hundred and fifty times, until he drove us crazy."[26]

It was also during this stay in Washington that Guthrie became the musical mentor of Pete Seeger, a young musician who, like Alan Lomax, came to folk music through inclination rather than birthright, and who was working at the Archive of American Folk Song when the two singers met. Born to a concert-violinist mother and a father (Charles) who was a modernist composer, teacher, and musicologist, Peter Seeger was introduced to folk music in the mid-1930s by his father and stepmother, the composer Ruth Crawford Seeger, who lived in Washington. Charles Seeger had gone to the nation's capital to work for the government's Resettlement Administration; in 1938, he was appointed assistant to the director of the WPA's Federal Music Project, joining with the Writer's Project chairman in a campaign of research and recording focused on American music. Ruth Crawford Seeger balanced motherhood and household duties with transcribing melodies that the Lomaxes had recorded for the archive. Pete, who had imbibed radical politics in his own family circle, dropped out of Harvard after two years, devoted himself to learning the five-string banjo, and after some cross-country wandering, settled in Washington. He arrived there at a time when a young man with his background, talent, work habits, and politics could make an impact as a folk musician, a career that until then had not existed.

The New York "Grapes of Wrath" evening in 1940 marked Pete Seeger's debut as a public performer, which he remembered as "a bust." "I didn't know how to play the five-string banjo," he later recalled. "I tried to do it too

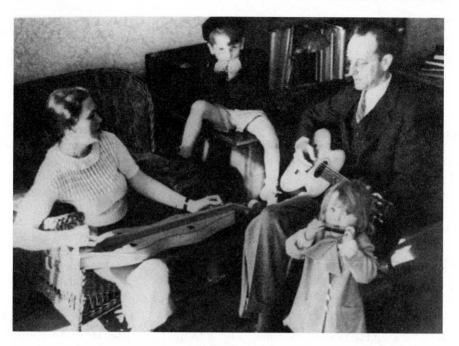

Ethnomusicologist Charles Seeger, his wife, the composer Ruth Crawford Seeger, and their children Michael and Peggy, pictured in Washington around 1937.

fast, and my fingers froze up on me. And I forgot words. It was the 'Ballad of John Hardy'; I got a polite applause for trying and retired in confusion." The occasion proved not to be a complete bust, however, for he saw Woody Guthrie in action and experienced the power of political folk music in a concert setting. Alan Lomax later said that from that night forward, "Pete knew it was his kind of music, and he began working to make it everybody's kind of music." Lomax went on to cite Seeger's "pure, genuine fervor, the kind that saves souls." And indeed, Seeger's zeal formed the core of his identity as a folk musician. As a teenager, that intensity had helped him meet the challenge of the five-string banjo, which, with no teacher available, he learned to play by listening to records. Seeger's banjo style was an amalgam built from the playing of Bascom Lamar Lunsford, Pete Steel, Dock Boggs, Buell Kazee, Wade Ward, Lilly Mae Ledford, and Uncle Dave Macon.[27] What especially fired Seeger's devotion in these years, however, was the idea that folk styles were perfectly suited to the political messages that he, Guthrie, Lomax, and others wanted to convey. Emanating from deep in the American grain, these styles manifested for Seeger true, unadorned, democratic expression, the opposite of Tin Pan Alley and Broadway offerings.

The 1930s was a time of growing academic interest in American culture,

The Almanac Singers, including (left to right) Woody Guthrie, Millard Lampell, Bess Lomax, Pete Seeger, Arthur Stern, and Sis Cunningham, around 1941.

and that interest linked up with leftist politics and the work of collectors to bring folk music to wider public attention. The convergence helped to create a fondness for folk music among middle-class youth, emanating from New York City, which was not only the entertainment industry's center but the place where, until the end of the 1950s, trends in popular folk song began. The "urban folk" musicians saw their music making as a passionate, principled avocation opposed to commercial popular music. Yet how were they to make a living selling their noncommercial music?

Early in 1941, Seeger—one of the first urban folk musicians and living proof of the artistic command such a performer could achieve—joined with Lee Hays, Millard Lampell, and Guthrie to form the Almanac Singers, a group devoted to practicing what its members preached. Singing songs about peace, war, and politics, the group set up Almanac House, a cooperative in Greenwich Village, where they lived together and held weekly musical gatherings. They did most of their singing in and around New York City, especially at union and political rallies, and occasionally on the radio. They also made recordings. They have been called the first urban folk-singing group, pursuing a goal stated by Millard Lampell: "We are trying to give back to the people the songs of the workers." The Almanacs used "the folk," "the people," and "the workers" as synonyms. Guthrie summarized the group's activist philosophy: "The biggest parts of our song collection are aimed at restoring the right amount of people to the right amount of land and the right amount of houses and the right amount of groceries to the right amount of working folks."[28]

Yet, however strongly the Almanac Singers rejected the label, they possessed the talent and charisma of successful entertainers. And as they sang for a widening range of audiences, their music struck a responsive chord, even with listeners who did not share their political outlook. After the United States entered the war, the Almanacs added anti-Nazi songs to their repertory. They even auditioned successfully at the Rainbow Room, a swanky nightclub atop a Rockefeller Center skyscraper, singing these words to the Appalachian tune *Old Joe Clark*:

> Round and round Hitler's grave
> Round and round we go,
> We're going to lay that poor boy down
> He won't get up no more.
>
> I wish I had a bushel
> I wish I had a peck
> I wish I had old Hitler
> With a rope around his neck.

The club owners loved the group for its novelty and impact, while complaining about their lack of showmanship. Bess Lomax, who was then part of the group, recalled how out of place the Almanacs felt as Rainbow Room entertainers. "We were absolutely unprepared for success of any kind," she explained. "The people running the club were sharp businessmen; they thought of us as an act, and treated us as one. . . . But if we were anything, it was *not* an act. . . . The Almanacs made it on sincerity." Yet she also recognized that the group's folk identity, though it might please a club audience, was not enough for "the workers we tried to reach." For "they were poor and didn't want to be," while "we were poor and didn't notice it"—or, rather, were poor by choice.[29]

Robert Winslow Gordon thought of folk music as coming from the past. In contrast, Pete Seeger, the Lomaxes, and the Almanac Singers approached it as a living force in the present. But in either case, "folklore" and "folk music" are distancing concepts. To Woody Guthrie, performing in something close to his native vernacular, such categories hardly existed. To urban folk musicians, on the other hand, the labels marked an identity that they had imagined into being. For folklore, ironically, springs more from dislocation than location, and occupies the margins of culture rather than its center. If the idea of folklore is understood as a conscious construction, then it is clear that the figures this chapter has shown in action—Sharp, Olive Dame Campbell, Gordon, and the circle of Lomax and Seeger—belong in the same company.

30

From New Orleans to Chicago

Jazz Goes National

As Paul Whiteman, proclaimed the King of Jazz, was dominating the popular music market, other dance musicians, chiefly black, were exercising another kind of freedom. By the late 1920s, cornetist (later trumpeter) Louis Armstrong was beginning to be recognized as a leader among them, a musician who brought individuality to the collective approach of New Orleans jazz. The warmth and strength of Armstrong's tone, his command of instrumental technique, the gravelly "grain" of his voice, the surge of his rhythm, and the richness of his melodic imagination gave his playing artistic authority. Armstrong's presence infused any setting in which he appeared with a spirit of freedom. To know and enjoy Armstrong's music was not necessarily to disdain Whiteman's. Yet the two—both jazz musicians according to the language of the day—were clearly doing different things, and in different settings.

Enter the jazz writer. From the time jazz came to public notice, it evoked a flood of written responses. Here was a new kind of expression—but what kind? What did it mean that performers made sounds that no classically trained musician would accept? that the jazz beat was so infectious? that audiences responded with sexy dancing? that the music seemed tied to "low" elements in society and flourished in cabarets and dives? Questions like these dominated early writing about jazz. But by the late 1920s, a few writers, perceiving the music as more than an entertainment fad or a symptom of civilization's decline, had begun to focus on what the musicians were actually doing. Perhaps no description of first encounters with jazz is more vivid than that of Roger Pryor Dodge. Before anyone tried to explain its musical workings to listeners, Dodge had discovered jazz and begun to explore it from the perspective of a serious layman in music who was also a professional dancer in New York City.

Dodge's process of discovery is traced in several articles published between 1929 and 1942. His perceptions are worth noting today because they focus on key traits of the music, brought to light by his unusual point of view. In a retrospective article published in 1942, for example, Dodge told readers that before he grew interested in jazz, his self-directed musical education had been evolving "by way of Chopin and Beethoven slowly back to Bach and his predecessors." And in 1934, he made a categorical statement owing much to his vocation as a dancer: "All great music, even church, leans upon and is developed by the dance." Against this background, certain moments in his listening life stood out. One was a New York concert in 1923 where Dodge encountered Stravinsky's *Piano Rag.* "Here, for the first time," he wrote, "I heard what I wanted Whiteman to do." Yet not until 1924 did Dodge hear his first "hot jazz record": white bandleader Ted Lewis's *Aunt Hagar's Blues,* which he found rhythmically simpler than Stravinsky but "far more real." Stravinsky "inclined me to look for nothing but startling rhythms," Dodge wrote, but *Aunt Hagar's Blues* seemed "more like 18th century music; it could grasp your attention by melodic significance."[1]

Dodge's comparison of jazz with earlier European music may seem off the mark to readers who know the music's African-American lineage. Yet he encountered jazz in the 1920s not as an intellectually packaged genre but a fresh approach to music making. To his ears, both jazz and Baroque music were based on "bare melodies, stripped to fundamentals"; dancer that he was, Dodge believed that, like a contrapuntal melody of Bach, "a jazz melody contains a rhythm that carries it through to its conclusion without pausing for false emotional effects." His comment that all great music was rooted in dance was audacious for suggesting that jazz, just then blossoming in the commercial arena, belonged in such company. Yet as early as 1929, he wrote that "the creative playing found in *low-down* jazz" had already established "a stronger form than any that has arisen for centuries."[2]

Music critics writing about jazz in mid-1920s New York concentrated chiefly on Whiteman and Gershwin. Dodge missed the Whiteman orchestra's Aeolian Hall concert in February 1924 but was in the audience when the program was repeated at Carnegie Hall in April. In his view, the musical form Gershwin chose for the *Rhapsody in Blue* doomed the composition, for its episodic structure went against what Dodge took to be "the genuine jazz ideal," which lay in "continuity and directness," and in carrying "a single musical idea" to completion. When Dodge read the critics' reactions to Gershwin's *Rhapsody in Blue,* he realized that none of them had grasped dance-based rhythmic continuity as a fundamental jazz trait. Yet his own understanding still showed major gaps. In the winter of 1924–25, for example, Dodge first heard Fletcher Henderson and his orchestra, an up-and-coming black dance band, at the Roseland Ballroom. He especially admired saxophonist Coleman Hawkins's solo on Henderson's recording of *Stutterer's Drag*—"so perfect and clearly laid out"—and trombonist Charlie Green's on *The Gouge of Armour Avenue*. But when Dodge asked Henderson when he had written "the hot choruses," the bandleader answered, "I don't write them. . . . They're played ad lib." Until that moment, it had never occurred to Dodge that jazz's vitality depended on improvisation. Dodge also asked about the band's arrangement of the *Rhapsody in Blue* and learned that Henderson considered the music outstanding. "It was quite a jolt," Dodge recalled, "to find out that solos which seemed so inventive and comparable to the great written music of other periods were not consciously plotted and composed, but were simply played *ad lib* by players who thought that Gershwin was a great composer."[3]

By 1927, Dodge had decided that the essence of jazz lay in "hot solos," the improvised sections of jazz performances. He began transcribing solos that he liked from his record collection and playing them "with one finger on the piano." This exercise had a professional payoff. As part of *Sweet and Low*, a 1930 Broadway revue, Dodge created an act in which he danced to trumpeter Bubber Miley's performance of the solos he had transcribed, including those in Duke Ellington's *East St. Louis Toodle-Oo* and *Black and Tan Fantasy* and Armstrong's *Potato Head Blues*. (Miley was an ex-member of Ellington's orchestra and the man who had first played some of his favorite solos.) The trumpeter's success at imitating the originals, Dodge wrote, proved "that a sympathetic reading of hot solos from notation, even on a different instrument from the original, lost nothing of the intrinsic beauty of the melodic line," for "a good solo is always a good solo."[4]

In view of comments made in a 1934 article, it may seem curious that Dodge danced to transcribed rather than improvised solos. But he had come to believe that superior art emanated from traditions where improvising was "so commonplace that every performer can avail himself of it with perfect ease." When musicians find it natural to vary every melody they hear, "or to invent new melody on a familiar harmony or to extemporize in general," then "we find a real freedom of invention." And Dodge discovered that freedom both in jazz and the music of eighteenth-century Europe, for both were based on the principle of variation.

> Instead of waiting months for a show piece to be composed and then interpreted (our modern academic procedure), then, in one evening, you could hear a thousand beautiful pieces, as you can now in jazz. Instead of going to a dance hall to hear Armstrong, in earlier times you might have gone to church and heard Frescobaldi; or danced all night to Haydn's orchestra; or attended a salon and listened to Handel accompany a violinist—with his extemporaneous variations so matter of course; or sneaked in on one of Bach's little evenings at home, when to prove his theory of the well-tempered

clavier he would improvise in every key, not a stunt improvisation in the manner of someone else, but preludes and fugues probably vastly superior to his famous notated ones.[5]

Dodge's willingness to approach music *as music* rather than an art tied to hierarchical categories is striking. His belief that improvisation and composition were stages within the same process points to an aspect of jazz that has received less attention than it deserves: the idea of melody composed *in the style of* an improvisation. Widespread improvising by early European instrumentalists, Dodge believed, had created a reservoir of melody ready to be tapped when musicians decided to write down their music. Thus, the melodic lines in many eighteenth-century European compositions owe much to improvisation, just as jazz composers take their cue from melody that was first improvised. By transcribing and dancing to the melodies of jazz solos, Dodge was showing that jazz improvisation could lead to a distinctive, written musical style.

In Dodge's view, the fountain that had long sustained Western music ran dry after Beethoven's death in 1827. For then the group spirit of the Baroque and Classical periods gave way to specialization, putting too much emphasis on "the creation of the solitary individual." Granting that works of outstanding composers deserved to be singled out for quality, Dodge warned against crediting artistic excellence too much to individuals.

> A school of art is based on the rank and file, and out of this rank and file rises the outstanding individual. The relation of their respective contributions is one of degree; the waters of genius rise higher, but they are part of the same fountain produced by the rank and file. From this point of view, the degree of his contribution, if he is working within a strong school, is never as great as it seems in isolation.[6]

As Dodge understood the matter, group spirit prevailed in eighteenth-century Europe *and* 1920s jazz because both were governed by ideals of severity, order, and discipline, providing a framework of accepted rules for musical practice.

Dodge found it strange that jazz musicians seemed to undervalue the importance of the music's "revolutionary melodic line." But if his insights about dance, improvisation, and the group spirit are examined in the context of African-based performance, the subject of jazz melody no longer seems quite so elusive. We saw in earlier chapters that the African ring shout preserved foundational elements through centuries of slavery in America, and that coon songs, show songs, ragtime, blues, and early jazz blended African-based elements with European ones. Dodge's writing about dance calls to mind the African notion of the time line, which gives jazz a metronomic beat, overlaid with polyrhythms and offbeat accents, sometimes in patterns.[7] His comments about improvisation may be linked to elements of texture (call and response, heterophony, foot patting), melody (blue notes, repeated figures, rhythmic-oral declamation), and timbre (cries, hums, hollers, moans, vocables) that appear spontaneously when jazz musicians perform. And when he writes about group spirit, we may perceive that as jazz musicians employ these techniques, they are "signifying" on the piece they are performing, the occasion, the mood of the moment, or all of these things together.

To "signify" is to make rhetorical use of preexistent material (melody, harmony, rhythm, form) as a gesture of respect or even fun. Signifying springs from the urge to vary rather than to repeat. It has been said that African-Americans show their love for a piece of music by changing it: by adding their own tropes—their figurative reinterpretations—to those of other musicians who have performed that music. And indeed, one of the joys of jazz performance is to play and sing in the company of other signifying musicians, carrying on a musical conversation within the framework of a given piece, trading lines, gestures, puns, and tropes that help to create the group spirit on which Dodge placed such high value.

The art and creative excitement of signifying lie in the space between the signifying performance and the original on which it is based. Jazz began and evolved around a limited repertory: blues songs, instrumental strains from ragtime with standard harmonic progressions, and a relatively small stock of songs and dance pieces—"standards"—that were performed repeatedly and that musicians and audiences were assumed to know. To play a blues number as a jazz musician is to signify musically so that the original, the varied form of it, and a consciousness of the dialogue between the two are all part of the performance. Therefore, a solo need not be improvised on the spot. For if it is convincingly and skillfully performed in the style of an improvisation, it may produce a similar effect. In the theme-and-variations format of many jazz performances, the solo will register as a variation on an original that has already been heard.

Dodge noticed, as an outside observer, certain traits fundamental to the artistic vitality of jazz. That he linked these traits to Europe rather than Africa says more about the state of musical knowledge in those days than about his own critical powers. Dodge's ideas provide a fresh perspective on two key jazz musicians who emerged in the 1920s: Ferd "Jelly Roll" Morton and Louis Armstrong, both New Orleans natives steeped in the city's musical traditions. Rooted in the foundational elements of African-American folk tradition, the music of Morton and Armstrong proved, well before the 1920s were over, that jazz was more than a matter of varying preexistent melodies, and that the signifying impulse could infuse many levels of a musical performance with the spirit of spontaneous commentary.

Ferd "Jelly Roll" Morton and the Red Hot Peppers, who recorded New Orleans–style jazz in Chicago in 1926–27.

MORTON, ARMSTRONG, AND CHICAGO

Born in 1890 of Creole parents by way of Haiti, Jelly Roll Morton began playing piano at ten and received his first professional experience as a pianist in New Orleans, some of it perhaps in Storyville, the city's red-light district. He grew up in contact with more than one of the city's different musical worlds, from European parlor and dance music to hard-driving stomps and blues, which he later disparaged but played with conviction. New Orleans may have been the cradle of Morton's art, but its nursery was black vaudeville and cabaret entertainment, in which he worked from 1907 to 1923. Morton in these years was an outstanding musician who lacked a forum for displaying his musical inventiveness, with the concept of jazz still new and recordings yet to become an effective means of musical dissemination and learning.[8]

Morton's long stint in vaudeville took him to many sections of the country. Driving expensive cars and wearing fancy clothes, he was full of braggadocio, but he usually managed to back up his claims of superiority at the keyboard. After a stay in Chicago during World War I, Morton returned there in the spring of 1923. Before the summer was over, he had made his first recordings, both as a solo pianist and a jazz band member. He also began to publish compositions through the Melrose Brothers Music Company in Chicago, and in 1926 he organized the Red Hot Peppers (cornet, clarinet, trombone, piano, banjo, bass, and drums) for an epic set of ensemble recordings for Victor. Recording sessions could be haphazard affairs in those days, but not when Morton was the leader. Baby Dodds, the group's drummer, recalled that Morton "used to work on each and every number" in rehearsal until he was satisfied.

> Everybody had to do just what Jelly wanted him to do. During rehearsal he would say, "Now that's just the way I want it on the recording," and he meant just that. We used his original numbers and he always explained what it was all about and played a synopsis of it on the piano. . . . You did what Jelly Roll wanted you to do, no more and no less. And his own playing was remarkable and kept us in good spirits. He wasn't fussy, but he was positive. He knew what he wanted and he would get the men he knew could produce it.[9]

Morton moved from Chicago to New York in 1928. But in a show-business environment dominated by large dance orchestras, his emphasis on New Orleans styles was considered old-fashioned. Work opportunities gradually dried up, and Morton fell into obscurity, convinced that he was the victim of a voodoo curse. He resurfaced in 1938, opening a small jazz club in Washington, D.C. Morton also presented himself at the Library of Congress, anxious that his role in the history of jazz—he claimed to have invented it—be documented. In a landmark encounter, he was interviewed by Alan Lomax, illustrating his recollections at the piano. While the book that Lomax based on these interviews did not appear until years after Morton died, a revival of interest in early jazz styles brought him back into the studio for more recordings (1938–40). After a trip to California in late 1940, however, he became ill with asthma and heart trouble and never recovered. His death in Los Angeles in July 1941, at fifty, was noticed by only a part of the jazz community.[10]

Louis Armstrong was born in poverty in New Orleans (1901), the son of a laborer who soon deserted the family and a mother who worked as a domestic and probably a part-time prostitute. While Armstrong grabbed some schooling as a boy, he claimed as his real diploma the common sense and consideration he learned from his mother. "I was taught to respect a man or woman until they prove in my estimation that they don't deserve it," he once wrote.[11] Armstrong went to work at the age of seven. He also formed a vocal quartet with friends that sang on street corners for tips. In 1913, the twelve-year-old Armstrong was declared delinquent and sent to the Colored Waif's Home, a local reform school, where he received his first instruction in music. He left the home two years later as a cornet player determined to make a career as a musician. By 1918, he was good enough that when cornetist King Oliver left New Orleans for Chicago, Armstrong took his place in a band led by trombonist Edmund "Kid" Ory. While playing with Ory's band in New Orleans bars and cabarets, Armstrong also began in the summer of 1919 to play with Fate Marable's band on Mississippi riverboats. Experience on these floating dance halls helped Armstrong develop the skills of a professional player.

In 1922, Oliver, who was leading his Creole Jazz Band in a South Side Chicago cabaret, invited Armstrong to join his group as a second cornetist. Oliver's band impressed musicians who heard them play, and Armstrong's reputation began to grow, especially after Oliver's band began recording in 1923. The next year, Armstrong left Oliver for the Fletcher Henderson Orchestra in New York. But late in 1925, he returned to Chicago and for the next several years performed in clubs and theaters there while also leading record dates with small groups. The sixty-five recordings that Armstrong and his Hot Five and Hot Seven groups made in 1925–28 on the OKeh label spread his reputation then and are now recognized as an enduring contribution to music history. Armstrong's virtuosity and genius transcended categorical boundaries to introduce a powerful new, utterly American mode of expression.[12]

In 1929, Armstrong moved from Chicago to New York and soon appeared in *Hot Chocolates*, a Broadway revue by Fats Waller and Andy Razaf. Then, under the direction of personal managers, he embarked on a career as a solo entertainer: a jazz trumpeter who also sang, led a big band, hosted his own radio show and guested on others, and appeared in films, all by virtue of supreme musicianship and a personality that seemed to welcome and embrace everyone. In 1947, his manager created Louis Armstrong and the All Stars, a group whose instrumentation followed that of a New Orleans ensemble. Armstrong toured the world for the U.S. State Department in the 1950s, proving an effective advocate for international friendship. A heart attack in 1959 curtailed his activities somewhat, but he kept performing until a few weeks before his death. When Armstrong died in 1971, he could claim an audience as large and varied as any musician in the world.

Except for their hometown, Morton and Armstrong seem to hold little in common. They were men of different generations and temperament. They took different approaches to music making, and Morton is known to have considered his Creole background evidence of racial superiority. The trajectories of their musical careers also differed sharply, and there is no record of the two men working together. Yet both of these New Orleans natives reached artistic fulfillment in Chicago: a Northern city whose environment allowed jazz, both commercially and artistically, to flourish.

Chicago's jazz scene was rooted in the African-American population on the city's South Side. In 1910, approximately 44,000 black residents lived there. Between 1916 and 1919, the great migration from Mississippi, Louisiana, Alabama, Arkansas, and Texas added thousands more, so that by

1920 the count stood at almost 110,000. This demographic shift, besides strengthening black political influence in the city, also ushered in the city's jazz age, widening the market for black musical entertainment. Cabarets, vaudeville and movie theaters, and dance halls were opened to serve that market. And by the later 1910s, some of these establishments were featuring the energetic, syncopated, often raucous-sounding dance music that, under the name of jazz, was gaining national attention. For musicians drawn to the city, Chicago meant jobs, decent wages, personal freedom, and the sparkle of nightlife. Jazz pianist Lillian Hardin, later Louis Armstrong's wife, re-called in later years Chicago's aura when she arrived there from Memphis in 1917. "I made it my business," she told an interviewer, "to go out for a daily stroll and look this 'heaven' over. Chicago meant just that to me—its beauti-ful brick and stone buildings, excitement, people moving swiftly, and things happening." In a bright-light district nicknamed The Stroll, which grew up around 35th Street, stores stayed open twenty-four hours a day, and at night the sidewalks rang with music and laughter.[13]

Although centered on the South Side, African-American entertainment in Chicago was not restricted to that area. Some black musicians played jazz in night spots on the North and West sides where black customers were not welcome. But the cabarets in which Chicago's jazz scene was grounded—the DeLuxe Cafe, Dreamland Cafe, Royal Gardens Cafe (renamed the Lincoln Gardens), the Apex Cafe, the Plantation Cafe, and the Sunset Cafe—were South Side "black-and-tans," presenting black entertainment in a setting where black and white customers mingled. Some of the clubs were black-owned, admitting whites but catering chiefly to neighborhood cus-tomers. Other black-owned clubs were designed with an interracial trade in mind. And still others were white-owned, seeking to attract white audiences with black entertainment and music.

A report published in 1913 claimed that a black business could succeed only if two-thirds of its customers were white.[14] Customers seeking excite-ment might find themselves in the middle of a police raid, for once Prohi-bition began, the liquor consumed in the cabarets was illegal. "Big Bill" Thompson, Chicago's mayor and no fan of the national law against drinking, enjoyed the political support of club owners and the gangsters who con-trolled the liquor trade. When reformers pushed for enforcement of the law, the mayor compromised by staging raids of clubs that violated city ordi-nances flagrantly, but most clubs were left alone.

Black customers included both tourists and South Side residents. Some clergymen condemned the cabarets as dens of iniquity, yet most South Side residents seem to have joined the black press in respecting the clubs as in-stitutions worthy of racial pride. They brought jobs, paying customers, and citywide attention to the South Side, whose residents they also supplied with polished professional entertainment, cast in familiar idioms of speech, humor, dancing, and music. The undisputed leaders of the Chicago jazz scene, however, were black musicians. Performing for black *and* white listeners, they learned to appeal to both. And the diversity of their audiences influenced the idiom of Chicago jazz musicians in the late 1910s and 1920s.

The Chicago careers of both Morton and Armstrong support this suggestion. In 1914–15, Morton served as music director at one South Side cabaret and led the orchestra at another. When he returned in 1923, however, it was as a champion of jazz, now an entertainment fad. As the composer of music that other jazz musicians were playing, Morton found his work in demand by the Melrose Brothers firm: entrepreneurs who made a specialty of linking black musicians with record companies. In addition to sheet music inspired by the jazz tradition, Melrose published jazz-band arrangements, known as "stocks," of numbers recorded by Chicago groups, some apparently transcribed from recordings. More widely than in print, however, jazz circulated on record. And by the time Morton came to town in the spring of 1923, black Chicago jazz musicians were being recorded in Richmond, Indiana, a five-hour train ride southeast of the city. The Starr Piano Company, located in Richmond, had recently entered the record business, and in 1922 began to record jazz groups from Chicago on its own Gennett label.

The irony of white performers being the first to record jazz, whose history and practice were shaped chiefly by black musicians, has been noted in earlier chapters. When the white Original Dixieland Jazz Band, who began recording in 1917, burst on the scene in New York, they were performing for a white audience that seems to have had little knowledge of black music making. Things were different in Chicago, where, as the ODJB's performances were inflaming New York's entertainment press, black jazz musicians were already playing for interracial audiences in South Side cabarets and theaters. When the ODJB and their recordings entered the orbit of Chicago, they had to compete with jazz shaped by black musicians. Moreover, the first Chicago-based white jazz ensemble to record took a black group as its model. The New Orleans Rhythm Kings, who in August 1922 visited the Gennett studios in Indiana, avoided ODJB-like comic effects and offered a polyphonic approach much like King Oliver's Creole Jazz Band, which was then playing at the Lincoln Gardens in Chicago. Made up of both New Orleans and Midwestern musicians, the NORK played for white audiences, knowing that the musical path they were following had been blazed by black innovators. In July 1923, the group made good on that knowledge, inviting Jelly Roll Morton to be their pianist on a recording date for Gennett—the first interracial recording sessions by Chicago musicians.[15]

Black jazz musicians playing in South Side cabarets also impressed an-

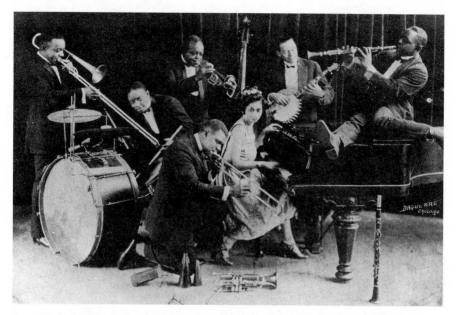

Joe "King" Oliver and the Creole Jazz Band, including Louis Armstrong (holding trombone in foreground) and Lilian Hardin (piano), who recorded in Richmond, Indiana, in 1923.

other group of local young white players, including banjoist and guitarist Eddie Condon, saxophonist Bud Freeman, and cornetist Jimmy McPartland. Condon's description of Oliver's band playing at the Lincoln Gardens in 1922 has often been quoted: "It was hypnosis at first hearing. Everyone was playing what he wanted to play and it was all mixed together as if someone had planned it with a set of micrometer calipers. . . . Freeman, McPartland and I were immobilized; the music poured into us like daylight running down a dark hole."[16] Lacking recordings, we can only guess what Oliver's group sounded like on this evening. But direct evidence exists to support such a guess. For on an April day in 1923, Oliver and his musicians took the long train ride to the Gennett Studios, made a total of twenty-seven recordings (including alternate takes), and then returned to Chicago, since no overnight lodging had been secured for them in Indiana.

Oliver's Gennett sides are a landmark in the history of jazz. Not only do they represent the first major set of recordings by black jazz musicians, but they seem to have broken the color barrier. From 1923 on, the music of black jazz performers as well as white was preserved and circulated on record. Moreover, the Oliver band's remarkable blend of freedom and discipline—playing what they "wanted to play" to achieve a precisely coordinated result—has been taken as another kind of landmark: an exemplar of classic New Orleans jazz.

Dippermouth Blues, recorded in April 1923 and itself considered a classic, is attributed to Oliver himself. The form is simple: a four-bar introduction and a two-bar final tag surrounding nine choruses based on the twelve-bar blues harmonic progression. (In jazz parlance, a chorus is the theme, including both melody and harmonic structure, that is stated and then varied, as in classical theme-and-variations form. The twelve-bar blues cycle in *Dippermouth Blues* is heard nine times, and each twelve-bar statement is called a chorus.) The first two choruses, plus the fifth and ninth, are played by the full ensemble, matching Eddie Condon's description of an intense free-for-all, with two cornets, a clarinet, and a trombone offering independent melodies while managing to stay out of each other's way. (This is the texture sometimes called "collective improvisation" and identified with New Orleans jazz.) The other five choruses are devoted to solos: by clarinetist Johnny Dodds (numbers three and four) and by Oliver (numbers six, seven, and eight), whose presentation ends with a two-bar "break" (a brief span of time during which the beat, while still present, is not played) and bass player Bill Johnson's shout: "Oh, play that thing!"

The impact of the Oliver band's rhythm could be especially compelling in person. As an aspiring young saxophonist, Bud Freeman heard the band often at the Lincoln Gardens, where it played for dancers who impressed Freeman with their grace. "When the Creole Jazz Band played," he later recalled, "each chorus seemed to swing more than the previous one until every bit of tension in you seemed to leave your body. That was the power of this music. There was nothing else like it on earth. If you couldn't dance, it made you dance."[17] The band's beat, articulated by the melody players and played continuously by the rhythm section, was so infectious that its temporary absence, always followed by a return, was an event. Two such events take place in *Dippermouth Blues*. The break at the end of the eighth chorus is one; the other is the "stop-time" accompaniment of Dodds's solo, where in each measure the rhythm section repeats a pattern of three quarter-note chords, plus a rest (the stop).

The most celebrated part of *Dippermouth Blues* is Oliver's cornet solo. For one thing, it is played with a variety of muted effects, an Oliver trademark. For another, it is accompanied by melody instruments as well as the rhythm section, so that Oliver's line is part of a web of counterpoint. Finally, it is a "set" solo: a melody in the style of an improvisation that Oliver worked out and repeated when his group performed this piece. A transcription of the first eight bars provides a glimpse of Oliver in action as a soloist; it also offers a sketch of how the instruments interact in collective improvisation.

Gennett's acoustic recording process, replaced in 1925 by electric recording using microphones, depended on large conical horns that picked up the sound best when players aimed their instruments directly into them. Al-

* A piano part is present on the recording, but the bass line is inaudible throughout most of it; no attempt at reconstruction has been made.

though a piano was part of the ensemble, on *Dippermouth Blues* only the four wind instruments and the banjo are heard clearly. Keeping in mind that Armstrong is silent on this chorus as Oliver moves into the spotlight, a listener notes that the trombone melody shares nothing with the cornet's. From the upbeat smear that kicks off the solo to the offbeat accents in

bars 3 and 4, to the vigorous pickup gesture in bar 8, the trombone's function is to keep momentum going at the ends of phrases, concentrating on
what would otherwise be dead spots between melodic statements. Honore
Dutrey's playing in *Dippermouth Blues* is a good example of the "tailgate"
trombone style.

Meanwhile, Dodds and Oliver carry on another kind of dialogue. Dodds's
melody could just as well be an independent solo, but with Oliver as the
featured player, he leaves windows through which the leader can be heard
against the trombone and rhythm section. Dodds also plays during Oliver's
rests; because this was a set solo in which Dodds knew what to expect, he
could plan phrases that dovetailed with Oliver's, in the manner of a call and
response. As for Oliver himself, the impact of his playing, which depended
heavily on sound variety, can only be suggested by the musical notation.
Nevertheless, certain typical traits are evident: a fondness for the middle register, a tendency to rhythmicize a line rather than inventing fresh
melodic material (mm. 1–4), and a strong rhythmic thrust. This eight-bar
transcription is nothing more than a brief sample of Oliver's Creole Jazz
Band in 1923. But it does show the balanced relationship among melodic
voices that is typical of New Orleans jazz, and that Louis Armstrong's emergence as a soloist would threaten.

To move from Armstrong's days as King Oliver's second cornetist
(1922–24) to his leadership of the Hot Five and Hot Seven groups, is to hear
him tapping a vein of vitality that made him one of the most influential of
all American musicians. In 1927, for example, Armstrong recorded *Struttin'
with Some Barbecue* with four other players. The piece begins and ends with
ensemble choruses in the New Orleans mode, full of call-and-response interchange. In between, the trombonist and clarinetist each play a solo half a
chorus long, accompanied by the rhythm section, and Armstrong plays a
complete solo chorus, backed by a stop-time accompaniment. Armstrong's
role in *Struttin'* is more prominent than was Oliver's in *Dippermouth Blues*.
His lead cornet in the ensemble sections takes center stage by virtue of its
powerful sound and rhythmic energy. And his solo's inventiveness outshines
that of his fellow players. Armstrong begins with an arching four-bar phrase
nearly two octaves wide, played with varied articulation and enlivened by
cross accents. He continues with a phrase that sounds like a refinement of
the first: similar in shape, higher in range, and parallel to the opening four
bars. The third phrase continues the shape of the first two so that when
Armstrong in the fourth uncorks a flourish that includes a flubbed note or
two, a listener may sense that statements and restatements have led him
into a musical situation he has not quite anticipated but still tackles fear-
lessly.

Armstrong's impact in these years could be magnetic. Trumpeter Max

Louis Armstrong and his Hot Five, including Lil Hardin (piano), Edmund "Kid" Ory (trombone), Johnny Dodds (clarinet), and Johnny St. Cyr, banjo.

Kaminsky, after hearing him live for the first time in 1929, recalled having felt "as if I had stared into the sun's eye." "Above all—above all the electrifying tone, the magnificence of his ideas and the rightness of his harmonic sense, his superb technique, his power and ease, his hotness and intensity, his complete mastery of his horn—above all this, he had the swing. No one knew what swing was till Louis came along."[18] With Armstrong on the scene, playing in clubs and theaters and heard widely on recordings, the group spirit that had dominated New Orleans jazz, and that Roger Pryor Dodge had celebrated in his writings, was now under siege.

Examples of Armstrong's solo artistry in these years are legion. Another can be heard on *West End Blues*, a tune by Oliver that Armstrong recorded in 1928 with pianist Earl Hines and three other musicians. Jazz historians, in singling out this performance for transcription, analysis, and discussion, may have taken the surprise out of the performance's most startling event: the unaccompanied fanfare in free tempo that begins the piece, ushering in what turns out to be a tender, contemplative blues number. This opening has been called a jazz counterpart to the cornet cadenzas of wind band soloists, from Pat Gilmore to Herbert L. Clarke of the Sousa band.

The first chorus of *West End Blues* begins gently, with Armstrong delivering Oliver's melody straight. His line through the entire chorus, however, shows restlessness creeping in. After a plain rendition of the first four-bar phrase, he turns the second into an unadorned call, followed by a florid response. And in the third phrase, Oliver's melody is dissolved by Armstrong's dazzling decorations. Later twelve-bar choruses include a solo by the trombonist, a delicate call-and-response duet between the clarinetist and Armstrong, who sings his responses rather than playing them, and a rippling solo chorus by Hines on piano. The last chorus, played by the whole ensemble, starts with another surprise: Armstrong sounds the beginning of Oliver's melody an octave higher than in the first chorus, sustaining a high B-flat for almost four bars. Then the tension is released in an improvised burst, based on a repetitive phrase that seems to break loose from rhythmic restriction, floating freely above the accompaniment. Armstrong's climactic conclusion manages to sound both spontaneous and structurally inevitable.[19]

Armstrong's *West End Blues* and other recordings he made in 1925–28 with the Hot Five and Hot Seven groups testify to his musical genius. Yet, together with God-given talent and imagination, the new musical synthesis that Armstrong achieved in the latter 1920s drew on three sources that were already present in the musical environment of Chicago's South Side. The first was the African-American oral tradition, with its practice of signifying on a given melody or harmonic framework. Linked by that tradition to a reservoir of melody and rhythm fed by improvisation, Armstrong was also gifted with an uncanny awareness of the moment that enabled him to make inspired musical choices. ("His mind worked so fast," his wife Lucille once commented, "he could hear gnats walking on cotton.")[20] The second influence came from the cabarets, where Armstrong learned, as an instrumental soloist, how to be an effective entertainer. The key lay in making an immediate impact. Those who aspired to work in Chicago's highly competitive show business needed to be able to distill their talents into artistic statements that would impress club managers, contractors, and bandleaders. Jazz musicians thus learned to work out solo statements representative of their own musical personality that would instantly grab the spotlight.[21]

The third influence, which helped jazz musicians in Chicago impress cabaret audiences, was the demand for virtuosity. According to songwriter Hoagy Carmichael, who was in Chicago during the 1920s, Armstrong owed much of his technical mastery to the prodding of conservatory-trained Lil Hardin, to whom he was married from 1924 until the 1930s. "Lil worked the fat off Louis," Carmichael wrote. "She got a book of the standard cornet solos and drilled him. He really worked, even taking lessons from a German down at Kimball Hall, who showed Louis all the European cornet clutches. Louis just took what he wanted. He got to be a good sight reader. When he began to record, he could use the music or wipe it off."[22] Although the claim of the classical teacher has not been verified, Carmichael's comments show Armstrong as a performer who, at this stage of his career, was eager to learn the tools of a cosmopolitan musician's trade and ready to draw on all available sources to do so.

Writers on jazz have sometimes assumed that the black oral tradition, the demands of audience taste, and formal musical training are incompatible, even mutually exclusive. Indeed, their differences are strong enough that each influence has been described here as if it belongs to a separate musical domain: the traditional, popular, and classical spheres. Yet even within these spheres, the values that infuse them—continuity, accessibility, and transcendence—do not exist in pure form. Rather, they are ideals or tendencies that can combine with each other and with other values as well. In Louis Armstrong's musical consciousness, these forces blended into a unique complementarity, each playing a role in the work of one of the century's most remarkable artists.

Armstrong's playing in the latter 1920s coalesced out of the energies of Chicago's nightlife. But the music of Ferd "Jelly Roll" Morton drew its strength from elsewhere, for Morton continued the New Orleans practice of collective improvisation long after it had ceased to be fashionable. Moreover, at a time when Armstrong's example was making solo *improvisation* increasingly important in jazz, Morton maintained *composition* as its vital force. "My theory," Morton once said, "is to never discard the melody." Thus his improvising concentrated on varying the melody, and his organizing principle was the varied *repetition* of whole sections. By around 1930, more and more jazz musicians, like Armstrong, were basing their improvisations chiefly on harmony, so that after an opening melodic statement only the piece's harmonic pattern mattered. This trend toward harmony-based improvising was a natural step as Broadway and Tin Pan Alley songs, with their colorful harmonies and audience appeal, made their way into the jazz repertory. Perhaps Morton's preference for melodic variation reflected his rootedness in ragtime, whose rhythm, melody, and multistrain forms he absorbed growing up. The diversity of material in the different strains, the textural contrasts Morton composed into them, and the pervasive improvising gave his music variety to balance the high value he placed on melodic repetition.[23]

Hyena Stomp, written for a Red Hot Peppers session in 1927 and recorded as a piano solo in 1938, illustrates Morton's technique of melodic variation. The structure—one sixteen-bar chorus presented eight times—shows an economy rare for Morton, who favored multistrain forms. And that chorus is based on a two-bar melodic statement resembling a riff: a simple, rhythmically pronounced melodic fragment that is repeated over and over. After two statements of the sixteen-bar theme, Morton begins to vary it. First, the emphasis moves from the right to the left hand. Then right-hand melodic decoration takes over. After another chorus in a similar vein, the melody moves back to the left hand, accompanied by right-hand polyrhythms. Finally, the last two choruses bring more widely spaced figures, suggesting an instrumental ensemble with trumpets and trombones. Yet the original melody never disappears. If Armstrong led the way in signifying on harmonic structures, Morton signified on melodies, proving that substance in jazz could emanate from composition as well as performance.

Morton's recordings with the Red Hot Peppers reveal his mastery of compositional form. In *Grandpa's Spells*, careful planning leads to wide diversity of sound, given that Morton had only seven instruments to work with.[24] And *Black Bottom Stomp*, one of Morton's finest compositions, moves at lightning speed through a formal structure whose outlines were still being debated forty years after the recording was made. Like most of Morton's music, the piece is cast in a strain form borrowed from ragtime, but instead of observing ragtime's sixteen-bar symmetries, Morton the composer takes them as a jumping-off point. After a four-bar introduction, he moves to an eight-bar first strain (**A**), a sixteen-bar second strain (**B**), repeated once, and a twenty-bar trio, or third strain, that is heard seven times. The trio section starts with an eight-bar phrase, then takes a harmonic detour so that what began as an eight-bar consequent phrase turns into a twelve-bar one. The first, sixth, and seventh choruses of the trio are played by the full ensemble; the rest are solos—first clarinet, then piano, cornet, and banjo—that lighten the texture. All seven choruses feature a break in bars 7–8. The sixth, with an ingenious cymbal break, shows the full ensemble playing softly but with high energy. The seventh, a climactic "stomp" chorus, features the whole ensemble in full cry, a trombone break of awesome comic vigor, and the drummer hitting the back beats hard.

BIX BEIDERBECKE: AMERICA'S FIRST JAZZ LEGEND

Although black musicians from New Orleans were the artistic leaders of the Chicago jazz scene, the social lives of many white Chicagoans were also energized by jazz that did not emanate from the South Side. Centered, as in New York, on modern social dancing in cabarets, clubs, and ballrooms, Chicago's cafe society was also served by white musicians who borrowed sounds from black jazz performers and emulated their peppiness, while steering clear of improvisation and blues-based rhythmic drive. The Benson Orchestra of Chicago, for example, was a successful, prestigious dance orchestra that also made records. From 1919 to 1925, Paul Beise led a syncopated novelty group in the city that was inspired by the Original Dixieland Jazz Band. In 1922, a lavish whites-only dance hall, named the Trianon after one of the Versailles palaces of King Louis XIV of France, was built on the

Leon "Bix" Beiderbecke (1903–1931), legendary jazz cornetist from Iowa.

far South Side and Paul Whiteman's orchestra hired from New York to play at its grand opening. In line with the Trianon's policy against "hot jazz," orchestra leader Meyer Davis sponsored a contest there to choose a new name for the music. "Synco-Pep" won out over a field of entries that included "Hades Harmonies," "Rhythmic-Reverie," "Glideola," and "Rhapsodoon."[25]

The Chicago jazz scene also gave birth to the career of Leon "Bix" Beiderbecke, a white jazz cornetist of whom Louis Armstrong once wrote: "The first time I heard Bix, I said these words to myself: There's a man as serious about his music as I am."[26] Born in 1903 into a prosperous family in Iowa, Beiderbecke showed an early interest in the piano and began lessons at the age of five. Finding his teachers' approaches to classical music unappealing, he lost interest and, in fact, never learned to read music fluently until late in life. As a teenager, recordings by Nick LaRocca and the ODJB caught his ear, and he taught himself cornet by playing along with them. His parents, unhappy with their son's musical taste and academic performance, sent him to Lake Forest Academy north of Chicago. Here he discovered the city's jazz scene; he also confirmed his indifference to school and fondness for alcohol. After being expelled from the academy in 1922, Beiderbecke stayed in the Midwest, living wherever he could find work playing jazz.

Catching on with other young white musicians who emulated black players, he began recording in 1924 with the Wolverines Orchestra. Over the next several years, pursuing a life of music and increasing self-neglect, he carved out a niche in the consciousness of some knowledgeable fans and jazz musicians.

With an uncommon ear but little formal training to draw on, Beiderbecke was admired from the start for his warm sound, melodic originality, and openness to modern classical music. In an appraisal published five years after Beiderbecke died, an admirer wrote that he heard in the recordings the spirit of "the man in the music, before the music was explained: the candor, force, personal soundness, good humor, and sheer love of the thing."[27] Bud Freeman, who knew and played with him, recalled near the end of his own life Beiderbecke's "love of the great composers of the day, such as Ravel, [Gustav] Holst, Schönberg, and Debussy." He speculated that "if Bix had lived longer he would have become one of America's greatest composers."[28]

In 1925–26, Beiderbecke lived for a time in St. Louis, playing in a band led by saxophonist Frank Trumbauer, with whom he joined the dance orchestra of Jean Goldkette in Detroit in May 1926. In 1927, Paul Whiteman hired both Beiderbecke and Trumbauer, in line with a policy of carrying a few jazz improvisers to enliven his band's performances. With Whiteman, and with various groups in New York between 1927 and 1929, Beiderbecke and Trumbauer made many influential recordings. By the time he left Whiteman in 1929, however, heavy drinking had taken its toll, and Beiderbecke was able to work only sporadically from then until he died in the summer of 1931.

Although Beiderbecke was little known by the general public while he was alive, his memory took on a mythic aura among some musicians and fans. A 1939 article, after tracing Beiderbecke's career to the time of his death, ends with the announcement "Then the legend began." It also includes fanciful stories then in circulation: the claim, for example, that after hearing Beiderbecke play, Louis Armstrong "broke down and cried, then admitted he could never play as well as that," and the romantic fable that the Whiteman band "kept an empty chair in the brass section when Bix was sick near the end."[29] Starting among musicians, the legend spread to the general public after the appearance of Dorothy Baker's novel *Young Man with a Horn* (Boston, 1938), based loosely on Beiderbecke's life and later made into a movie. Certain facts about Beiderbecke—his intuition, talent, alcoholic consumption, short life, and almost mystical devotion to music— helped to create the myth that would make him a symbol of the Roaring Twenties. But race was also a factor.

It was no accident that the first legendary jazz musician was white. In the 1930s, the general public would hardly have looked on a black figure as a positive symbol of anything. Moreover, the legend surely reflected the way white jazz musicians saw their own place in society. Although white musicians were spared racial prejudice, their social advantage did not necessarily carry over to the artistic realm. Armstrong, Morton, and Oliver could claim by birthright the African-American folk traditions whose abundant stock of melody and rhythm nourished their performances. But for whites, the process of becoming a jazz musician required a more self-conscious break with their social and musical background than it did for blacks. They had to construct their own artistic base. Moreover, as economic depression and the rise of radio and the movies changed the shape of popular entertainment in the 1930s, the marketplace for jazz changed with it. Bud Freeman recalled that white jazz musicians in these years had a tougher time finding work around Chicago than did black players. "There were some good-paying jobs on the North Side," he remembered, "but they didn't last as long as the South Side jobs did. Some South Side players, such as [clarinetist] Jimmie Noone, stayed with jobs that lasted years; we whites counted the length of ours by weeks, sometimes days."[30]

By the late 1930s, when the Swing Era had pulled big-band jazz into the forefront of American popular music, work for white jazz musicians was plentiful. But big-band work, based on written arrangements, lacked the spontaneity of the small New Orleans and Chicago jazz ensembles. Hence, a notion about jazz musicians took shape that had hardly existed during Beiderbecke's lifetime: jazz musicians who improvised well and resisted the formulas that popular success promoted could be more than entertainers, they could be artists. With the help of critics, a hierarchical standard was introduced into jazz that distinguished between commerce and art. Not everyone accepted this idea; Louis Armstrong, for example, seems to have considered commercial and artistic success as closely related goals. For some white jazz musicians, however, and for many critics, the two seemed mutually exclusive. As the audience for swing-band music grew, so did the belief that its attractions were artistically inferior to those of earlier jazz. From this perspective, the profession of jazz musician seemed to require a choice between work that demanded musical exploration and work that emphasized audience-pleasing formulas. Bix Beiderbecke became a symbol of one who had taken the artist's path, in spite of limited technique and a disorderly personal life. Moreover, his role on Whiteman's recordings, where he improvised briefly in elaborate, nonswinging arrangements, seemed to confirm his aesthetic distance from the formulas that made Whiteman's orchestra commercially successful.

The Beiderbecke legend has continued to evolve. One view has the cornetist actually refusing a musical education and aspiring to a kind of downward mobility, while another finds him more a victim of isolation than one who chose it, unable to connect with any tradition that spoke to his own sensibilities.[31] Both views assume that Beiderbecke thought of jazz in modern terms—as primarily a solo improviser's art—and that he never doubted the artistic worth of his own skills. While his recordings might seem to support these assumptions, however, there is also reason to question them. Against the claim of diseducation, for example, Beiderbecke is also known to have been full of pride after he flawlessly played the written trumpet solo on Whiteman's recording of Gershwin's *Concerto in F.* Nor is there doubt that he admired the wealth of musical knowledge commanded by Whiteman's organization.[32] Perhaps the conflict that haunted Beiderbecke lay in a lack of confidence that his chosen calling, an improvising jazz musician, was a worthy one. For while he rebelled against his upbringing, there is reason to question whether he ever transcended its values.

There is no denying the power of Beiderbecke as a symbol of bohemian artistry crushed by the music business's commercial demands, even though, on closer inspection, he looks more like a remarkable intuitive artist who lost faith in the instinct that first sustained him. Yet whatever the truth of the Bix legend, its existence suggests that by the latter 1930s, some white jazz musicians were finding it useful in helping them shape their own artistic identities, and fans of jazz were taking the music seriously.

31

Crescendo in Blue

Ellington, Basie, and the Swing Band

PAUL WHITEMAN WAS the most prominent of the white bandleaders who flourished in New York City, the nation's entertainment capital, during the 1920s and after. At the same time, a substantial number of black musicians launched careers there that succeeded artistically as well as commercially. First, the craze for blues singing set off in 1920 by Mamie Smith's recording of *Crazy Blues* encouraged many other female singers to follow suit—most notably Bessie Smith, who recorded a classic version of Handy's *St. Louis*

The Fletcher Henderson Orchestra, New York, 1924–25. The trumpet player in the middle of the back row is Louis Armstrong.

Edward Kennedy "Duke" Ellington (1899–1974), composer and bandleader, in a publicity photo taken in 1934.

Blues with Louis Armstrong in 1925, while he was with Fletcher Henderson's orchestra. Another important strain was virtuoso piano playing, as the "Harlem stride" school came to maturity. Taking up where ragtime performers had left off, James P. Johnson, Willie "The Lion" Smith, and Thomas "Fats" Waller, among others, honed their styles around multistrain pieces, fast tempos, and trademark technical flourishes.

In Prohibition-era New York City, however, dance orchestras seized artistic leadership in jazz. In 1924, the Fletcher Henderson Orchestra began a long-term engagement at the Roseland Ballroom in midtown Manhattan: a black band playing for white audiences in a white-dominated part of the city. Thanks to arrangements by Don Redman and talented soloists like Armstrong, trombonist Charlie Green, and tenor saxophonist Coleman Hawkins, Henderson could include jazz numbers in a menu of waltzes, popular songs, and more conventional dance music. Henderson's is considered the first dance orchestra that, while playing written arrangements, achieved the rhythmic lilt called swing. But by the end of the decade, another New York jazz orchestra had gained even more prominence. Led by Duke Ellington, this group was to be a presence on the American music scene from the 1920s into the 1970s.[1]

Edward Kennedy Ellington, born into a middle-class family in Washington, D.C., in 1899, once wrote from behind the mask he fashioned as a famous entertainer: "When I was a child, my mother told me I was blessed, and I have always taken her word for it." He started piano lessons at seven, studied commercial art in high school, and began playing piano professionally with Washington-area dance orchestras at seventeen. He seems always to have had a talent for leadership. Looking back over his life after seven decades of living it, Ellington saw a series of crossroads in which, whenever he needed a new skill or a push in a different direction, a friendly adviser had stepped forward. His autobiography identifies two traits that helped him excel: competitive drive, rooted in a hunger for personal achievement that he disguised behind a casual exterior, and a gift for finding the right collaborators.

In 1923, Ellington moved from Washington to New York with several other local musicians. For the next several years, he led groups in midtown clubs, touring New England in the summers with a dance orchestra. He also began to record. Late in 1926, Ellington hired as his manager Irving Mills, a sometime singer, active record producer, and member of a white music-publishing family. Personal connections with bootleggers enabled Mills to book Ellington and his musicians into the Cotton Club in Harlem, a prestigious nightspot where the band entertained white audiences, playing for floor shows and dancing over the next three years (1927–30). The group could also be heard over a radio broadcast hookup at the club, which introduced instrumental pieces and popular songs by Ellington, many of them with lyrics by Mills, across the country. The lordly manner that gave Ellington his nickname had already appeared by then.

It was at the Cotton Club that Ellington hit his stride as a composer. Working with such distinctive musicians as saxophonists Harry Carney and Johnny Hodges, clarinetist Barney Bigard, trumpeter Bubber Miley (replaced in 1929 by Cootie Williams), and trombonist Joe Nanton, he fashioned an ensemble that, while playing a varied repertory, specialized in original music. Between 1932 and 1942, Ellington traveled the United States, made two successful European tours (in 1933 and 1939), and recorded extensively with a fourteen-piece orchestra: six brass (three trumpets, three trombones), four reeds (two alto saxophones plus a tenor and a baritone, all doubling on clarinet), and a rhythm section of four (his own piano, plus double bass, guitar, and drums). Through these years, he composed larger works to complement his popular songs (*Mood Indigo, Sophisticated Lady*, and *Take the A Train*, the latter actually by Billy Strayhorn, who joined the band as a composer and arranger in 1939) and short instrumental pieces (*Concerto for Cootie, Ko-Ko*, and *Cotton Tail*). *Creole Rhapsody*, inspired by Gershwin's *Rhapsody in Blue*, appeared in 1931; *Reminiscing in Tempo* (1934), more than eleven minutes long, filled both sides of two ten-inch 78-rpm recordings. In 1943, Ellington began a series of annual Car-negie Hall concerts with *Black, Brown, and Beige*, a fifty-minute suite in five large sections, commemorating the history of African people in the New World.

After World War II, Ellington enlarged his orchestra to eighteen players. Large-scale pieces were now a regular part of his output, although he continued to write smaller ones too (e.g., *Satin Doll* in 1953). With Strayhorn's help, he had widened his range as a composer to the point of writing for occasional musical shows. But the Ellington band remained his artistic base, even as economic conditions and the appearance of new jazz styles forced most big bands out of business. Touring both at home and abroad, playing concerts, festivals, and dances, the band maintained a core of older favorites in its repertory as Ellington produced a flow of new compositions: the score to Otto Preminger's film *Anatomy of a Murder* (1959); new suites such as *Harlem (A Tone Parallel to Harlem)* (1950), *Suite Thursday* (1960), and the Shakespeare-inspired *Such Sweet Thunder* (1957); and the sacred music he wrote during his last decade. In the 1960s, Ellington began to be noticed in the halls of official American culture. He was awarded the Presidential Medal of Honor (1969), won honorary doctorates from Howard and Yale Universities, and was elected to the National Institute of Arts and Letters. He continued to compose and to lead the Ellington orchestra until his death in 1974. And in the years since, he has been more and more widely recognized, not only as a jazz musician but as an important composer of the twentieth century.

Billy Strayhorn, Ellington's close collaborator, observed that "Ellington plays the piano, but his real instrument is his band."[2] As leader of a band whose members, especially in the 1920s, were not all schooled musicians or secure readers of music, Ellington was also a composer who worked in an improvisatory tradition. Jelly Roll Morton faced a similar situation, yet as a pianist and small-ensemble leader, Morton did not have to compose for a full dance orchestra that, like Ellington's, also played floor shows and in theaters. With immediate impact as his goal, Ellington mastered musical forms more complex than dance music. And sound proved the shortest path to immediacy. Indeed, Ellington sought tonal "charisma" from his players, and he worked to discover fresh, unusual timbres that would seize listeners' attention. When he first worked in the band business, Ellington recalled, "the chief requisite was good personality of tone." Experience taught him that some musicians revealed their inner selves most deeply in their sound, and that audiences knew it. Alto saxophonist Johnny Hodges's "sultry solos," for example, were powerful because Hodges played them "in true character, reaching into his soul for them, and automatically reaching everybody else's soul. An audience's reaction to his first note was as big and deep as most applause for musicians at the end of their complete performance." Ellington also noticed that listeners' responses to Hodges, affirmed in "grunts, oohs, and aahs," with an occasional "Yes, daddy!" thrown in, were "never too loud to prevent their hearing the next note he played."[3]

These words point up Ellington's respect for audiences, whose collaborative role in performance he understood and appreciated. Sometimes he describes himself as something like a public servant: "I travel from place to place by car, bus, train, plane . . . taking rhythm to the dancers, harmony to the romantic, melody to the nostalgic, gratitude to the listener." Elsewhere he notes how rhythm can bring musicians and audience members into synchrony. "When your pulse and my pulse are together," he writes, "we are swinging, with ears, eyes, and every member of the body tuned in to driving a wave emotionally, compellingly, to and from the subconscious." In Ellington's view, musicians performed their best for knowledgeable listeners.

> When one is fortunate enough to have an extremely sensitive audience, and when every performer within the team on stage feels it, too, and reacts positively in coordination toward the pinnacle, and when both audience and performers are determined not to be outdone by the other, and when both have appreciation and taste to match—then it is indeed a very special moment, never to be forgotten.[4]

But again, sound—sometimes called "the Ellington effect" and a result of his ideas about music, the tonal personalities of his players, and his own explorations of the piano—was Ellington's trump card, making his band instantly recognizable and emotionally potent. By all accounts, the chief architect of the Ellington effect as it emerged in *East St. Louis Toodle-Oo*, a composition of the latter 1920s, was trumpeter Bubber Miley, who later accompanied Roger Pryor Dodge's dancing. Miley had discovered that by blowing, gargling, and humming at the same time and shaping the sound with a plunger mute, he could "growl" through his trumpet. Ellington loved this sound. For him, it was no technical trick but a call from Miley's heart. "He was raised on soul and saturated and marinated in soul," Ellington wrote of Miley. "Every note he played was soul filled with the pulse of compulsion."[5] After Miley left the band in 1929, his successors were required to master the growl, which shows up repeatedly in Ellington's later music.

On the road with Ellington. Gamblers in this candid railroad car
shot include singer Ivie Anderson, Drummer Sonny Greer, and
Ellington himself.

Within Ellington's storehouse of sounds, the trumpet growl could carry
programmatic implications as a feature of the "jungle music" the band
played to accompany the Cotton Club's exotic floor shows. In *Concerto for
Cootie* (1940), though, written to show off the talents of trumpeter Cootie
Williams, the trumpet growl is liberated from the minor mode and the jungle and used as one of many timbres at Williams's command. In *Ko-Ko*, a
blues number from the same year, the menacing sound at the beginning is
built on the foundation of Harry Carney's room-filling baritone sax, with the
trumpet section responding to Carney's rhythmicized E-flat. Then Juan
Tizol on valve trombone plays a riff-like call, responded to by the full saxophone section. Another kind of Ellington sound is heard in a family of
pieces slow in tempo, rich and often chromatic in harmony, and meditative
in atmosphere, of which *Mood Indigo* is the most famous. In *Dusk*, after
Ellington's piano introduction, the theme is played by a trio of instruments:
muted trumpet with the tune, muted trombone in the middle, and clarinet
on the bottom, as in *Mood Indigo*. In performance, the trio surrounds the

mike and plays quietly as one. By supporting two muted brass instruments with a low-range clarinet line, Ellington creates an unusual sound. But much of its impact also lies in the intense concentration required to produce such a delicate blend.

As well as a wide assortment of sounds, the Ellington orchestra produced musical effects that could be astonishing. Like jungle music, some are programmatic. *Daybreak Express* (1933) is just one of many Ellington pieces inspired by the sound of railroad trains. Other effects depend on the players' technical virtuosity. *Braggin' in Brass*, featuring the band's trumpet and trombone sections, begins with scurrying passagework for muted trumpets over the harmonies of the last strain of the early New Orleans favorite *Tiger Rag*. Next it is time for the three trombones to brag. And here Ellington shows the instrument's capacity for stinging attacks and the players' uncanny coordination with each other. He writes a descending broken-chord figure whose notes look conventional enough on paper; in performance, however, the line is chopped up so that each trombonist plays only every fourth note. Given the tempo, clocked at 316 quarter notes per minute, and the cross accents produced by Ellington's division of four-note groupings among three players, a lurching, spattering, hiccup-like melodic line results, drawing from listeners responses ranging from amusement to disbelief.

The New Black and Tan Fantasy (1938), based on the twelve-bar blues, contains another remarkable effect. Its third chorus begins as a trombone solo by Joe Nanton, with Ellington playing a stream of mysterious-sounding parallel chords in lagging quarter-note triplets behind him. Further in the background, at least at the start, is Barney Bigard's clarinet. At the very end of the preceding chorus, Bigard has swooped up to a high concert D-flat (the blue third in the key of B-flat), which he sustains softly, without vibrato, like a tiny beam of light. As Nanton's solo unfolds with Ellington's backing, the D-flat begins to increase in volume and, ever so slowly, to rise in pitch. By the tenth bar, Bigard's note has blossomed into a *fortissimo* F, ringing high above the orchestra.

Cornetist Rex Stewart, who played in the band from 1934 to 1945, left a memorable glimpse of Ellington in the act of creation. While he sometimes composed alone at the piano, he was also known to work new things out on the spot, with the musicians as collaborators. Stewart set the scene in a recording studio. Arriving late, Ellington would sit down at the keyboard and warm up, establishing the mood for the first number. He might then ask the musicians to "see if the piano is in tune," a signal that they were to tune up. Next, he might produce the score of his new composition, most likely written on "some scraggly pieces of manuscript paper." Stewart remembered one session at which Ellington pulled out "about one-eighth of a page on which he'd scribbled . . . some notes for the saxophones . . . but there was nothing for Johnny Hodges. Duke had the saxes run the sequence down twice, while Johnny sat nonchalantly smoking. Then, Duke called to Hodges, 'Hey, Rabbit, give me a long slow glissando against that progression.'" Next Ellington urged Cootie Williams to try entering on the second bar of the passage with a trumpet growl. Then the leader turned to trombonist Lawrence Brown. "You are cast in the role of the sun beating down on the scene," he prompted. When that announcement brought no response, Ellington went on: "What kind of a sound do you feel that could be? You don't know? Well, try a high B-flat in a felt hat, play it legato, and sustain it for eight bars." Then, with those elements as a starting point, Ellington gave the downbeat. The saxophone section played its melody, backed by the rhythm section and overlaid with Hodges's glissando, Williams's growl, and Brown's sun-warmed, muted B-flat. If the leader's guesses were on target and the men responded as he hoped, the Ellington effect might appear. "And," Stewart concluded, "that's the way things went—sometimes."[6]

As striking as Ellington's sounds and effects may be in isolation, they exist only as parts of whole compositions. *Old Man Blues* (1930) shows that his often playful approach to musical form appeared early in his career. For in this piece, which bears no connection in its phrase structure or harmonies to the twelve-bar blues, Ellington spars with listeners' expectations through extensions, ellipses, and the introduction of new melodic strains in the manner of Jelly Roll Morton. *Old Man Blues* also illustrates two other techniques common in Ellington's music. One is the quality of wordless singing that the plunger-mute technique produces, whether on trumpet or trombone. And this imitation of the voice, though bordering on the comic, leads us to hear many Ellington passages as conversations among instruments, often in the form of the call-and-response pattern lying at the heart of the blues. While the three groups in Ellington's orchestra—the reeds (clarinets and saxes), the brass (trumpets and trombones), and the rhythm (piano, guitar, bass, drums)—often play as units, a listener never knows when an individual voice will detach itself to comment on what other instruments are saying or singing.

After its introduction, *Old Man Blues* presents such an instrumental conversation, though perhaps it would be better to call it a series of statements by trombonist Nanton, around which clarinetist Bigard deftly dances. The piece teems with unexpected details. The second strain (**B**), for example, appears twice, and each time two bars early. The real tune is not introduced until the second **A** section. The trumpet solo in the fourth **A** section evokes a standard piece of stage business by beginning hopelessly behind the action and then catching up. And the brass section's break just before the last **A** is twice as long as expected. Even though the ending of *Old Man Blues*, a *ritard*, sounds a bit stilted, the quality of playing on the original recording is sharp, disciplined, crackling with excitement, and utterly convincing as an artistic statement.

Ellington's *Diminuendo and Crescendo in Blue* (1937) shows him working on a larger scale—too large to fit the three-minute limit imposed by the ten-inch 78-rpm recording. In fact, this work was written to fill an entire record, with the *Diminuendo in Blue* on one side and the *Crescendo in Blue* on the other. The title also refers to the twelve-bar blues, the jazz tradition's most familiar form, with its three four-bar phrases, its characteristic harmonic progression, and the implied call-and-response built into each phrase. Ellington uses this form, on which many players in the band were capable of improvising at length, as the basis for an ingeniously shaped piece in which improvisation plays only a small role.

Barney Bigard once said of Ellington: "At first, just after I joined Duke . . . I used to think everything was wrong, because he wrote so weird."[7] The opening of *Diminuendo and Crescendo in Blue* illustrates that side of Ellington, showing a capacity for formal play far beyond what his audience expected or his vocation as a dance band leader invited. On the one hand, the first four choruses function together as an adventurous introduction. On the other, they comment on the twelve-bar blues as an instrumental form. In each chorus, we hear the ingredients of standard blues form: the chord progression, the call-and-response pattern, and the principle of statement and restatement. Yet by changing some element in each—by delaying a harmonic arrival point, by switching the expected ordering of melodic statements or the character of calls and responses, or by adding measures—Ellington sows seeds of doubt in his listeners. Are we hearing blues choruses or not? We cannot be sure, until Chorus 5 arrives.

Thus, *Diminuendo in Blue* moves from dissonance to consonance, from loud to soft, from density to spareness, from rhythmic disruption to smoothness, and from formal opaqueness to formal clarity. Once Chorus 5 establishes the structure clearly, the ear is free to shift focus from form to the flow of events—changes in texture, sound, time intervals between calls and responses, melodic invention—leaving the rather frequent key changes as the main unusual feature. Beginning on a note of manic disconnection, as if Ellington were a cubist painter probing blues structure by pulling it apart, then putting the pieces back together in unexpected ways, the piece settles into a groove, hits a point of calm, and then reverses the process. And it is unified not only by the harmonic progression that underlies all twenty-two of its choruses but also by the melodic motive that begins the *Diminuendo*; returns in the seventh chorus in the saxes as the start of a longer melody (see example); begins the *Crescendo* and is heard through its first three choruses; and reappears at the beginning of both Chorus 8 and Chorus 11 of that section.

Alto and Tenor Saxophones

Baritone saxophone

Diminuendo and Crescendo in Blue and *Old Man Blues* are only two works among more than 1,100 that Ellington composed and copyrighted in the course of his career. In about 20 percent of these works, he shared authorship with musicians who played for him (chiefly Billy Strayhorn, but also including Barney Bigard, Johnny Hodges, Bubber Miley, Rex Stewart, Juan Tizol, and Cootie Williams), and he collaborated with others in the rest. As Stewart's peek into the recording studio suggests, even when Ellington was the sole composer of record, collaboration lay at the heart of his music making. For, as well as imagining fresh tone combinations, Ellington composed by working with his musicians so that their tonal personalities—their particular sound, way of playing, and inventiveness—actually helped to create the music. Perhaps a particular saxophone or trombone melody was his, perhaps not. When trumpeter Fred Stone spent a few months in the orchestra in 1970, he was struck by the unusual demands Ellington placed on his musicians:

> The Ellington Orchestra is the only musical outfit I know where the members are hired solely on the basis of their strength and individuality. It is the only orchestra I know where you are not required to become an exact percentage of the section you're playing with; where you are not required to match the sound of the previous member. You must function as an individual—and you are judged solely on your personal musicianship.[8]

That is what the eminent composer and jazz historian Gunther Schuller probably had in mind when he noted Ellington's unique partnership with his players—"unprecedented in the history of Western music."[9]

This undated photograph shows Ellington with W. C. Handy, the so-called Father of the Blues.

BASIE AND KANSAS CITY

In a region that might seem an unlikely place for jazz to have flourished, Kansas City, Missouri, boasted the wide-open nightlife that proved a key ingredient elsewhere. William "Count" Basie, a New Jersey–born piano player who had spent time in Harlem, recalled the evening around 1925 when he and a fellow musician first saw the city after dark. In town as part of a traveling theater company, they decided to have a look around after an evening performance. Walking away from downtown on Troost Avenue, they reached the corner of Eighteenth Street, "and wham! . . . It was one of the most fantastic sights I've ever seen in my life," Basie recalled. "There were joints all lit up and going full blast on both sides of the street for several blocks." Wherever he looked, "there was at least a piano player and somebody singing, if not a combo or maybe a jam session." Basie was struck by the contrast with New York. It took a while to find out where to go in Harlem, he explained, "because this was during Prohibition and there were all those speakeasies and hideaways and private clubs, also known as key clubs, and you couldn't just go in places like that unless you knew somebody." But in Kansas City, "all of those joints along that strip were wide open, and there were ambulances and police cars with sirens just sitting out there ready to roll." For Basie, the sight was completely unexpected. "There we were," he remembered more than half a century later, "way out there in the middle of nowhere, just looking around and hoping that we would find a little after-hours joint of some kind, and wham, we were coming into a scene where the action was greater than anything I'd ever heard of."[10]

Kansas City may have seemed the middle of nowhere to Basie. But for Americans who lived in the region bounded on the south by Houston, on the west by Albuquerque, and on the northwest and north by Cheyenne, Wyoming, and Sioux Falls, South Dakota, the city that stood at the inter-section of the Kansas and Missouri Rivers, near the edge of the Great Plains, was the center of commerce and gateway to the markets of the East. In the 1920s, half a million people lived in Kansas City, including a black population of between 10 and 15 percent. The local stockyards brought cat-tlemen, sheep farmers, and their herds to town; the city was also a hub for the railroads and a lively grain trade. Major theatrical circuits with head-quarters in New York reached as far west as Kansas City. And many West-erners went there in search of entertainment, which was plentiful because local officials wanted it to be. Early in the century, Democratic alderman Tom Pendergast had put together a political organization that, by trading jobs and personal favors for votes, took control of Kansas City. The Pender-gast machine ruled the local police, who in turn protected gambling and prostitution, and profits flowed toward the protectors. Pendergast also gov-erned the city's liquor distribution, and he continued to do so after Prohibi-tion made the selling of liquor illegal. With its variety of good-time venues, Kansas City was also a place where jobs for jazz musicians were plentiful, if low-paying.

As the musical capital of the Midwestern and Southwestern region known as the territories, Kansas City was the center of what amounted to a booking area of huge size and scattered population. By the latter 1920s, tour-ing bands were playing throughout the territories, and by the latter 1930s, many of the cities they visited were home to local bands that played some form of jazz. Bass player Gene Ramey, a native of Austin, Texas, remem-bered four or five such bands in Houston, eight or ten more in San Antonio, and perhaps twice that many in the Dallas/Fort Worth area and in Omaha alone. Traveling bands ranged widely, from Arkansas and Louisiana all the way north to British Columbia; and the territory bands played jazz because it was the day's popular social music.[11] In some locales, however, being a jazz band was not enough. A drummer recalled touring in Nebraska, Kansas, Wyoming, and South Dakota, where "we played for polkas, anything they'd want. We played for square dances, too. They had that type of dance during intermission, and they'd ask four or five of us to stay on the bandstand to play the music for 'em. There'd be a caller out there to call the dances." Jesse Stone, who led a territory band called the Blues Serenaders, believed that his group's versatility and entertaining skills explained their success. "We had a dance team in the band," he remembered, as well as a vocal quartet, a glee club, and three comedians, allowing the Serenaders to "do any kind of skits." Stone himself would play and sing at the piano, but he would also "do a lot of Cab Calloway–style jumping and dancing," including the splits.[12]

By 1930, a distinctive style of orchestral jazz was developing in Kansas City itself, especially in a band led by local native Bennie Moten. Based on a rhythm section that played a driving four beats to the bar, Moten's music relied heavily on the twelve-bar blues and on riff-based arrangements. The arrangements, written chiefly by Eddie Durham of the trombone section and Basie, the pianist, led to performances that blended solo and ensemble passages effectively. In 1932, Moten's band made a memorable set of recordings at the Victor studios in Camden, New Jersey. But in the Depression-plagued United States of the early 1930s, with the entertainment business at low ebb, conditions were not ripe for a black regional band without white management to succeed outside its own region. Moten and his men returned to Kansas City, which the Pendergast machine had made Depression-proof so that work was always available. In the spring of 1935, Bennie Moten died unexpectedly. And in August of that year, big-band jazz entered the public consciousness with a bang when a white dance band led by clarinetist Benny Goodman played at the Palomar Ballroom in Los Angeles.

Born in Chicago in 1909, Goodman was a virtuoso jazz improviser who had worked extensively in New York from 1928 until 1934, when he formed his own dance orchestra. The new Goodman band played in a New York theater, made records, and began appearing regularly on "Let's Dance," a radio series on the NBC network. Goodman commissioned arrangements from several professionals, most notably Fletcher Henderson, whose own orchestra had broken up. His exacting standards as a leader made the Goodman band a model of ensemble discipline and polish, playing a mixture of jazz tunes and popular songs of the day. In May 1935, the band began a cross-country tour with only mixed success. But the Los Angeles performance on August 21, broadcast nationwide to great acclaim, touched off a wave of enthusiasm and publicity so strong that it has been credited with launching the Swing Era, a new age of popular music. Whatever the truth of that claim, the jazz-oriented dance band was now the preferred popular music medium and would remain so for the next decade. Shortly after Goodman's success in Los Angeles, Basie formed a nine-piece group in Kansas City, hiring many of the Moten band's players and beginning a long-term engagement at the Reno Club. Before long, broadcasts on the club's radio hookup drew outside attention to the band. And by 1936, Basie's Midwest group, managed by a prominent white booking firm, was coming into its own as a swing band with a national following.

Basie was born in 1904 in Red Bank, New Jersey, to a father who did yard work and a mother who took in laundry. In later years, he described himself as a person of highly selective awareness. Indifferent to school, Basie was drawn from an early age to music. Although piano lessons taught him little about reading music, he learned quickly by ear. Basie quit school before finishing junior high to pursue a career in show business—not to get rich but because "I liked playing music, and I liked the life." He showed an instinct for getting ahead, first in New Jersey and then in Harlem, where he landed a job as pianist with a traveling theater company. When that tour ended, he returned to Harlem and worked in clubs there, meeting such local pianists as Fats Waller and Willie "The Lion" Smith. Basie recalled playing around 1925 in a club run by black entrepreneur Leroy Wilkins, where "you just tried to play better than anybody else, because some cat could come in there and sit in and take your job."[13]

In Harlem's competitive environment, musicians used any ploy that might gain them an advantage in the marketplace, as Basie observed wryly in explaining how he got his nickname.

> I knew about King Oliver, and I also knew that Paul Whiteman was called the King of Jazz. Duke Ellington was also getting to be one of the biggest new names in Harlem and also on records and the radio, and Earl Hines and Baron Lee were also important names. So I decided that I would be one of the biggest new names; and I actually had some little fancy business cards printed up to announce it. COUNT BASIE. Beware the Count is Here.

At first, "nobody really paid any attention to the name I had given myself," Basie recalled. But then one day he and saxophonist Ted Manning "got into an argument about something. And it went on and on until Ted finally said something like 'Basie you call yourself the Count, well, man, you're just about the most raggediest-assed count I've ever seen.'" From that time on, whenever "anybody mentioned anything about Count, everybody knew who that was."[14]

In 1926, Basie toured with another vaudeville act. When engagements ran out in Kansas City in 1927, he was hired at a theater there to accompany silent movies. He also got to know singer Jimmy Rushing and other members of the Blue Devils, a group led by bass player Walter Page. After a brief stint as the Blue Devils' pianist, Basie found himself "more and more tied up with music itself and less and less concerned with show business and entertainment in general."[15] By 1929, Basie had joined Moten's band. And in the next half dozen years, he gained the experience that made it possible after Moten died to recruit local players for his own group at the Reno Club. Almost everybody in that band was a good soloist, he remembered, and the group worked mostly off "head arrangements"—arrangements that, rather than being written down, were assembled from the ideas (out of the heads) of band members.[16]

"I really didn't think all that much about the airtime we were getting," Basie later recalled.[17] But the radio broadcasts proved decisive, for they were heard by John Hammond, who happened to be in Chicago toward the end of 1935, recording Benny Goodman's band as a producer for Columbia records. Hammond recalled the impact of the Basie band:

> One night . . . I went out to my car and I turned the dial all the way at the end of the dial at 1560 kilocycles and I heard some music that I couldn't believe. They said, "This is radio station W9XBY. . . . We are broadcasting from the Reno Club with Count Basie and His Orchestra." . . . They were on for an hour every night and on Saturday nights they were on for four solid hours. . . . When I heard Basie's rhythm section I've never been satisfied by any other rhythm section before or since.[18]

Basie's autobiography tells how the support of Hammond and Willard Alexander of the MCA booking agency helped to transform his local band into a polished, nationally known ensemble. Musicians were added to bring the group up to standard size—more than a dozen players. Female singer Billie Holiday was hired to join male singer Jimmy Rushing. The repertory was expanded to include new arrangements and greater musical variety. And the band learned to play in different venues and to please audiences outside the rough-and-ready confines of Kansas City's Reno Club. Yet the musical approach that Basie had worked out in Kansas City, and that had caught John Hammond's ear in the first place, remained intact. If Ellington sought players with a unique sound, Basie "knew how I wanted each section to sound" and therefore what each section member should sound like. "Even back when I was dictating those arrangements to Eddie Durham for Bennie Moten's band," he explained, "I could actually hear the band playing those passages while we were working on them. And that's the way Eddie wrote. We could write just like I heard it. He could voice each section just the way I wanted it." Basie followed Moten in keeping the blues prominent in the band's repertory. Soloists also played a key role in his strategy as a leader. "I have my own little ideas about how to get certain guys into certain numbers and how to get them out. I had my own way of opening the door for them to let them come in and sit around awhile. Then I would exit them. And that has really been the formula of the band all down through the years," he said late in life. Basie also admitted that while he was fond of fast tempos, loud volume, and "a good shouting brass section," he also liked "the band when the guys are just swinging their cans off down easy."[19]

If these comments tell us that Basie's musicians were steered by the leader's will and taste, they leave out an essential collaborative part of the band's sound: the rhythm section, especially after guitarist Freddie Green joined Basie in 1937. Walter Page's resonant walking bass kept the beat, which was given a top as well as a bottom by Green's even, on-the-beat guitar chords. The precision and firmness of Page and Green left drummer Jo Jones free to use the bass drum for accents instead of pulse marking. By moving his own timekeeping to the double "high-hat" cymbal, Jones lightened the rhythm section's sound without sacrificing intensity. Basie himself had arrived in Kansas City an experienced stride player who used his left hand as a rhythmic engine. But by the time he and the band headed east in 1936, he had worked out a new, stripped-down style that would remain his signature for the rest of his career. We can trace the transformation in a comparison of solos Basie played on *Moten Swing*, first in 1932 as Bennie Moten's pianist, and then in 1940 with his own outfit. The first solo projects self-sufficient, two-fisted liveliness; the second distills pianism down to delicate tracery. Rather than purposefully striding forward, Basie's left hand in the later example sustains whole notes or falls silent, while the right hand favors the high treble register and short phrases that end with light accents. Yet the second solo, with its economy and more relaxed pacing, ends up sounding more forceful than the first.[20]

Basie's rhythm section was a four-man accompanying unit, and within it he played his part as a group member to perfection. In opening the door for his soloists, inviting them in to hang around for a while, and then showing them the way out, Basie was all the while acting as accompanist-in-charge, a role that suited his temperament, character, and personal style. One of the great "comp artists" of all time—the jazz term means to play chords as a *comp*lementary ac*comp*anist to a featured soloist—Basie deftly blended artistic control with self-effacement, leading as well as following.

Though his style has been praised almost universally, nobody has yet claimed Basie as a master of melodic invention. His phrases have sometimes been called nothing more than clichés, perhaps abstracted from the work of other pianists. The power of Basie's playing lay not in melody but in rhythm and sound: in the way he placed, struck, shaded, and accented his notes and melodic gestures. Within the context of his band's rhythmic swing, Basie found a way to animate four- and eight-bar phrases and twelve-

In 1939, the Basie band played an engagement at the Apollo Theater in Harlem. Members pictured here include Lester Young (tenor sax, far right), Walter Page (bass), Freddie Green (guitar), Jo Jones (drums), and Basie (piano).

and thirty-two-bar cycles as only a consummate master of artistic form could do. One might call Basie the Swing Era's great democratizer of musical sophistication. On the one hand, he never wavered in making straight-ahead swing the goal of his band's performances. (Pressed for a definition, he once called swinging "some good things put together that you can really pat your foot by.")[21] On the other, he continually enhanced his band's ineffable rhythmic impulse by freshening his standard repertory of piano vamps, fills, obbligatos, and responses through off-center feints, jabs, and noodlings.

Basie honed his accompanying skills in collaboration with soloists as well as the whole band. And the chief soloist in the band's early years was tenor saxophonist Lester Young, a Mississippi native who played with Basie from 1936 until 1940. Young has been called the most original jazz improviser between Louis Armstrong and Charlie Parker: a musician of striking individuality. Playing with little vibrato, Young managed a sound both light and intense, and capable of carrying highly compelling ideas. He proved that swing did not require high volume and that understatement could be commanding. Young might improvise *against* a tune's phrase structure as well as with it, stay silent on beats where accents were expected, signify on musical clichés, and use strikingly original melodic intervals.[22]

Some of these traits may be heard in a solo that Young played in *Lester Leaps In* (1939), supported by Basie and the rhythm section. The tune is a riff-based head arrangement on the harmonies of Gershwin's popular song *I Got Rhythm*, whose chorus follows a standard thirty-two-bar form: state-

ment, restatement, contrast, and return (**aaba**). Young's solo has been transcribed and analyzed by more than one scholar, and each has found something different in it. (Gunther Schuller's transcription appears below.) One
has called attention to the melodic formulas that connect this solo to other
parts of the piece and to Young's solo style in general. Another takes the solo
as evidence of Young's fondness for asymmetry: his mission of breaking
down binary units of two, four, and eight bars with three- and five-bar
phrases, even to the point of shifting an entire eight-bar phrase ahead by
one bar.[23]

Young's solo in *Lester Leaps In*, while only a brief example, reveals something fundamental about his improvising technique. The solo seems to emanate from Young's act of locating himself vis-à-vis the original tune. One can almost imagine him taking a stance, figuratively speaking, at the edge of the tune—say with one foot inside the circle of its conventions and the other outside—and then signifying on any aspects that his nimble mind, sharp ear, and acute sense of awareness are moved at the moment to express. While most of his melodic material sounds newly invented, elements of the original also return as reference points. Except for the dissonant C at the start of the last section (8 measures from the end), Young follows the original harmonic structure, although he moves both into and away from the phrase structure. For all of Young's asymmetrical whimsy, however, his signifying never loses its secure rhythmic groundedness. His own gift for swinging is partly responsible, but so is the rhythm section of Page, Green, and Jones playing behind him. And Basie's punctuating dialogue with Young's solo line adds both to the swing and the asymmetry.

In an interview long after Young's death, Basie mentioned him as a player who could be counted on to swing. Pressed for details on the same subject, Freddie Green admitted that Lester "was my favorite, because of the way he played along with the rhythm section."[24] The disciplined rhythmic freedom and energy of the Basie band's rhythm freed Lester Young to explore asymmetry as a solo improviser. Or perhaps one could say that the rhythmic security provided by Basie allowed Young to signify on a more sophisticated, even structural level than would have been possible if the beat had not already been in secure hands. Young was a gifted improviser because he possessed a sovereign command of both vocabulary (melodic inventiveness) and syntax (the adroit placement of notes and phrases in the musical structure). With another supreme master of syntax behind him, he ventured as a soloist into terrain that no jazz soloist before him had visited.

EPILOGUE: THE SWING ERA AND THE HARLEM RENAISSANCE

When the United States entered World War II in 1941, swing bands were dominating the nation's popular music scene. From the ensemble led by the "King of Swing," Benny Goodman, to those of trombonist Tommy Dorsey, clarinetists Woody Herman and Artie Shaw, and saxophonist Charlie Barnet, many of the most successful were white. Broadcasting and recording, featuring both vocalists and instrumentalists, performing popular songs as well as jazz numbers with solo improvisations, serving long-term engagements in hotels and ballrooms, and touring to play dances and in theaters, these ensembles were loved by a wide range of Americans, especially younger ones. In 1939, a band led by trombonist Glenn Miller reached a pinnacle of popular success beyond that of any other group of the time. The Miller band's vogue continued into 1942, when Miller was inducted into the air force to lead a select service band. And a fondness for its sound survived the leader himself, who died in an air crash in 1944.

The commercial triumph of swing between 1935 and 1945 has been traced to two factors. The first was the creation, especially by Louis Armstrong, of a distinctive rhythmic language of jazz and the capturing of its improvisatory spirit in written arrangements for large dance bands. By the latter 1930s, whole bands were playing in the style of an improvisation, and audiences loved it, especially when they knew the original tunes. The second factor was the wide circulation of jazz-based styles, thanks to radio, recording, and film. The promise of interesting work and a good living lured many gifted musicians into the big-band field. Learning from such pioneers as Armstrong and Henderson, they helped to create a new professional environment for the music.[25] Thus, as the 1930s came to an end, the popular music that most Americans were dancing to, singing, and adapting as their own vernacular expression bore an African-American pedigree. Some black bandleaders, including Ellington, Basie, and Cab Calloway, were able to cash in on the big-band fad; and Louis Armstrong was now a full-fledged star. But white dominance in both the audience and the music's professional environment ensured that most of the chief icons and biggest money-makers would also be white. For many black jazz musicians, the Swing Era was a time when rewards in prestige and money fell short of the artistic influence they wielded.

This chronicle's discussions of African-American music have so far emphasized the folk and popular spheres. The careers of such composers as Will Marion Cook and Scott Joplin show that black musicians before World War I were allowed scant opportunity to work in the classical sphere. Yet there seems to have been little doubt among black artists and intellectuals that the concert hall and the classical sphere that served it deserved the high cultural prestige that both enjoyed. In the years after World War I, black musicians worked to establish a beachhead in the concert hall. Convinced that their music deserved such recognition, and that cultural prestige could be turned to social advantage, these men and women may be seen as part of the cultural movement known as the Harlem Renaissance.

Under way by around 1920, and led by black intellectuals, including philosopher Alain Locke, social scientist W. E. B. DuBois, and poet and author James Weldon Johnson, the Harlem Renaissance focused primarily on the arts, which distinguished it from earlier black efforts to move toward equality with whites through economic and social advancement. Cultural achievement, the leaders hoped, would crack the seemingly impregnable wall of racism, for once black writers, painters, and composers showed their mastery of classical techniques, whites would be compelled to give up the myth of inborn black inferiority.[26] The Harlem Renaissance ideal prescribed work that reflected the artists' black heritage, but in culturally prestigious (European) forms: not orally transmitted verse but poetry published in books and literary journals; not informal skits and dialect tales but stage dramas and novels; not spirituals sung by plain folk but artful settings fit for the concert hall. For example, *Go Down Moses*, a spiritual printed in a widely circulated choral arrangement of 1872, was turned into a composition for solo voice and piano in James Weldon Johnson and J. Rosamond Johnson's *The Book of American Negro Spirituals* (New York, 1925). This version imposes a dramatic shape and a mode of expression that the earlier one leaves to the performers.

Thick chords in the piano, rhythmic motion to suggest an inexorable march, precise dynamic inflections and accents, and a weighty sound that seems to call for a soloist with a big, resonant voice give the Johnson arrangement the trappings of an art song. The book's preface assures readers, however, that the arrangements have made no changes in the form of the songs, and that the "harmonizations have been kept true in character." It also claims that "an old-time Negro singer could sing any of the songs through without encountering any innovations that would interrupt him or throw him off."[27] Whether or not the Johnson arrangements actually fit such singers' performing habits, they met one goal of the Harlem Renaissance: to connect the African-American musical heritage with the concert stage. Tenor Roland Hayes, baritone Paul Robeson, and contralto Marian Anderson were among the African-American concert singers who made a mark in the 1920s and after, singing operatic and art-song repertory as well as spirituals. And black composers of this era—R. Nathaniel Dett was a prominent example—wrote choral and keyboard works based on African-American folk and popular music.

Perhaps the generation's most versatile black composer was William Grant Still. Born in 1895 in Woodville, Mississippi, Still grew up in Little Rock, Arkansas. He attended Wilberforce College in Ohio (1911–14) and the Oberlin Conservatory in 1917 and 1919. Later formal study included lessons with George W. Chadwick in 1922 and Edgard Varèse in 1923–24. Still earned his living in popular music, however, beginning in 1914 as a dance orchestra performer. In the summer of 1916, he worked as an arranger for W. C. Handy's music-publishing company in Memphis, producing the first band version of *St. Louis Blues*. In 1919, Still accompanied Handy to New York, where he continued in the publishing business and played in Handy's bands. He joined a black-owned recording firm in New York in 1921 as manager and arranger, and from 1921 to 1923 he played oboe in the pit orchestra of Noble Sissle and Eubie Blake's *Shuffle Along*, the decade's most success-ful black Broadway show. A polished professional arranger and composer who kept pace in later life with changing media, from dance bands to radio stations, film studios, and television shows, Still continued also to compose classical works, including ballets, operas, symphonies, orchestra suites, in-strumental chamber music, and vocal works, some with orchestra and some for voice and piano. His *Afro-American Symphony*, premiered in 1931 by the Rochester Philharmonic Orchestra with Howard Hanson conducting, marked the first time in history that a major orchestra had performed a black composer's symphony.

The performance of Still's symphony was a landmark for the aspirations of the Harlem Renaissance, crossing a boundary and creating a precedent for others to follow. (In this case, the others included black composer Florence Price's Symphony in E minor, premiered by the Chicago Sym-phony Orchestra in 1933, and William Dawson's *Negro Folk Symphony*, played in 1934 by the Philadelphia Orchestra.) Yet however symbolic this crack in the wall of racism, something was happening in the popular sphere during the 1930s that also testified to black achievement: the growing recog-nition of the artistic potential of jazz. Two related factors sparked that recog-nition. First, not only sheet-music publication and live performance but also recording, radio, and film were increasingly open to black jazz musicians. And second, jazz recordings could be imitated by other musicians, tran-scribed, studied, compared with other performances, and aesthetically eval-uated. Like a classical work, a jazz recording that rewarded such treatment could be said to have transcended the circumstances of its origin, moving into the realm of art.

Indeed, that very trend may be glimpsed in bits and pieces through the development of jazz's reception between the wars, starting with dancer-critic Roger Pryor Dodge's comparing jazz improvisation with the work of Girolamo Frescobaldi, Handel, J. S. Bach, and Haydn. By the end of the 1930s, jazz had inspired a number of journals, including *Down Beat*, a monthly magazine that marked current fashions in the band business. Books were also trying to place the music in American cultural life. In *Jazz, Hot and Hybrid* (1938), the classical musician and critic Winthrop Sargeant demonstrated through musical analysis that jazz repaid close listening, espe-cially its rhythm. *Jazzmen* (1939), a compendium of articles edited by Fred-erick Ramsey and Charles Edward Smith, discussed the music as the work of heroic figures. By 1940, fans were showing an interest in jazz history, a new field called discography was dealing with its recorded "documents," and a few European and American writers were reviewing jazz records critically in print. Jazz was also beginning to be heard in concert settings. In short, the music of many black jazz performers, rooted in folk practice and stylized according to the techniques of the popular sphere, had proved worthy of a level of critical attention that only music in classical forms had previously received.

It seems clear today that the recognition of jazz as an art form carries implications for African-American music broader than those imagined by the Harlem Renaissance leaders. If black-composed symphonies and art songs had poured forth during the 1920s and 1930s and been welcomed into the concert-hall repertory, that program of elevation would simply have endorsed the already powerful authority of the classical sphere. The perception of jazz as an art, on the other hand, challenged it. If certain recorded jazz performances rewarded close analysis—if a kinship really *did* exist between improvised music from the Baroque era and improvised music from twentieth-century Harlem or the South Side of Chicago—then sooner or later, the hierarchy of musical values in America would have to change. Determined to win a place for black artists in the existing hierarchy, Harlem Renaissance leaders can hardly have been expected to look beyond it. But if they had, they might have recognized that the perception of jazz that came out of the 1930s would help to alter the shape of musical life—especially the relations between the popular, classical, and traditional spheres—as the century continued. The consequences of that development, both for African-American musicians and American music in general, are hard to overestimate.

32

The Golden Age of the American Musical

ON THE FIRST TWO EVENINGS of December 1924, a pair of shows opened on Broadway that dramatize a split between the up-to-date and the old-fashioned. *Lady Be Good!*, with music and lyrics by George and Ira Gershwin—the brothers' first Broadway collaboration—was performed on December 1 at the Liberty Theater; the lighthearted tale about a stage brother and sister featured dancer Fred Astaire and his real-life sister Adele. And the next evening, *The Student Prince*, with music by Sigmund Romberg and lyrics by Dorothy Donnelly, received its New York premiere. Set in nineteenth-century Germany, this show tells the story of a crown prince who is sent to the university at Heidelberg to sample the life of a student. Seizing a rare chance for freedom, he falls in love, only to be called back to royal duty and an arranged marriage. The Hungarian-born Romberg, who immigrated to the United States in 1909, composed *The Student Prince* in the tradition of the Viennese operetta, with soaring melodies, rousing choruses, and an emphasis on idealized love. In contrast, the score of *Lady Be Good* took a modern tack. Earlier that year, George Gershwin had been proclaimed a musical innovator with his jazz concerto, the *Rhapsody in Blue*, and now he and Ira were trying their hand at a Broadway show with the flavor of the present. The result was groundbreaking. George's absorption of the musical vernacular, especially blues and jazz, was matched by Ira's felicitous skill at setting vernacular speech to music. The American musical theater had found a fresh native idiom.

Song lyrics proved a key partner in catching the spirit of the Jazz Age. By 1927, newspaper columnist Walter Winchell was designating the area around Broadway and Forty-Second Street "the slang capital of the world," for there the world of music and theater came together with the idiom of newspapers and magazines and the lingo of sports and gambling. A "talk of the town" emerged, featuring such terms as "ballyhoo," "click," "hit," "fan," "flop," "baloney," "turkey," "cinch," "phoney," "racket," and "squawk." H. L. Mencken later looked back on 1920s Broadway and declared it the chief producer of American slang.[1] In *Lady, Be Good!* and a series of musicals later in that decade, Ira Gershwin captured the language in lyrics for George's music.

Fascinating Rhythm, a song that Fred Astaire sang in this show, reflects the Gershwin brothers' fresh approach. Astaire's character complains of being distracted by a tricky rhythm. And the song's chorus, thirty-two bars long and in **abac** form, unveils that troublesome figure, which cuts across the standard accent patterns of four-bar phrases in duple time:

> Fas-ci-nat-ing rhy-thm! (*rest*) You've
> got me on the go! (*rest*) Fas-ci-
> na-ting rhy-thm! (*rest*) I'm all a-
> quiv-er (*rest*) (*rest*).[2]

Matched with George's springy melody, the colloquial turns in Ira's words give the song a distinctly modern, Jazz Age stamp. ("On the go" was a phrase new to the language, and "a-quiver" was rhymed with "flivver," a small, cheap car.) For those who heard it brand-new, *Fascinating Rhythm* embodied the Gershwin song's rootedness in present, crystallizing not timeless truths but the sights and sounds that seemed to be in the air at that aggressively post-Victorian moment.[3]

The spirit of Romberg's *The Student Prince* could hardly have been more different. The prince's tutor in Heidelberg sets the tone early in a song celebrating his own time as a student:

> Golden days in the sunshine of our happy youth,
> Golden days full of innocence and full of truth.

By the time he has finished, a familiar idea is planted: the past was a better time than the present. That nostalgic tone is matched by the music, which borrows its dramatic and musical styles from nineteenth-century opera. If *Oh, Lady Be Good*, a love song from the Gershwins' show, lent itself well to the clear diction and reedy voice of Fred Astaire, the ringing climaxes in Romberg's *Deep in My Heart, Dear* call for operatically trained tenors and sopranos. Before the decade was out, however, the gulf between *Lady, Be Good!* and *The Student Prince* was bridged by another composer-author team in a work that blended new elements effectively with older ones.

Show Boat, with a book and lyrics by Oscar Hammerstein II and music by Jerome Kern, received its New York premiere on December 27, 1927. Based on a popular novel by Edna Ferber, the show could lay claim to an illustrious theatrical heritage. Producer Florenz Ziegfeld was known for the lavish spectacles he brought to the Broadway stage, often in collaboration with Joseph Urban, the Austrian-born set designer who had been working with him since the *Ziegfeld Follies* of 1915. The publisher of the music, T. B. Harms of New York, was the most prestigious in the business, with most of the leading writers and composers of Broadway musicals under contract. Oscar Hammerstein II, already a successful author and lyricist in his

As with shows in the past, songs from Kern and Hammerstein's *Show Boat* (1927), including *Can't Help Lovin' Dat Man*, were sold as sheet music for amateur performers.

own right, belonged to a famous theatrical family as the grandson of operatic impresario Oscar Hammerstein I. And composer Jerome Kern brought a reputation for artistry to Broadway, where crass commercialism was often known to prevail.

Born in 1885 in New York City into a Bohemian-Jewish family that won financial prosperity in business, Kern was taught piano by a musical mother, received some formal training at the New York College of Music, published his first song in 1902, and in 1903 began working as a song plugger for Harms on Tin Pan Alley. Thanks to an inheritance, Kern was able to buy a share in the Harms firm around 1905; from then on, when the company prospered, so did he. Harms put Kern to work in the pre–World War I era interpolating new songs into operettas in London and New York. Then in 1915, a new phase of his career began. Together with librettist Guy Bolton and lyricist P. G. Wodehouse, Kern composed a series of small-scale shows for the three-hundred-seat Princess Theater that were more up-to-date than the operettas and song-and-dance musicals then in vogue. *Very Good Eddie* (1915), the second show in the series, marked Kern's first success as the composer of a whole score. By the time of *Show Boat*, the forty-two-year-old Kern was one of Broadway's most respected figures and the composer of several hit songs. His score to *Show Boat* added several more to that list: *Ol' Man River*, *Can't Help Lovin' Dat Man*, *Make Believe*, and *Why Do I Love You?*

Kern and Hammerstein's *Show Boat* is set in the Midwest, spanning an era from around 1890 to the 1920s. Rooted in American geography and history, the show tells the story of the uneasy romance between Gaylord Ravenal, a river gambler, and Magnolia, the daughter of a showboat captain. Act I centers on the boat, the *Cotton Blossom*, which travels the Mississippi piloted by Cap'n Andy Hawks, presenting shows in ports along the way. Since the first scene takes place in Natchez, Mississippi, with black stevedores unloading cargo, the issue of race is present from the start. The lifeblood of the Broadway stage, however, was the song of romantic love. And the first such number in this show is *Make Believe*, sung as a duet by Magnolia and Ravenal at their first encounter. Here the suave Ravenal charms the innocent Magnolia through a ploy. She has confessed her ambition of some day becoming an actress, for onstage, "you can make believe so many wonderful things that never happen in real life." Ravenal immediately suggests love as an example, and within moments the two are singing about a fancied romance between themselves. But while the words speak of pretending, the music conveys barely disguised passion. "Only make believe I love you," Ravenal sings, as Kern's melody launches them on a sea of fervent vocalism, with an octave leap by the second measure and a range of an eleventh in the first phrase alone. As the song reveals Magnolia and Ravenal to be "meant for each other," illusion becomes reality while the audience watches and listens.

Ravenal is called away at the end of *Make Believe*, leaving Magnolia starry-eyed. But when she asks a stevedore named Joe about Ravenal, he advises her to ask the river "what *he* thinks." As personified by Joe, the river is a mighty force, indifferent to human struggles. With the help of Hammerstein's lyrics, Kern composed a melody for the song's chorus (in thirty-two-bar **aaba** form) that set this number aside from the rest of the score. Taking their rhythmic impulse from "river," the words embody continuity and flow, avoiding the closure of regularly rhyming lines.

> Ol' Man River,
> Dat Ol' Man River
> He mus' know sumpin'
> But don't say nothin',
> He jes' keeps rollin',
> He keeps on rollin' along.

The repetition of the same four-note rhythmic motive—♩♩♩♩—in each of the first six bars of the song's **a** sections reinforces that idea. And the pentatonic movement in these measures, avoiding both the fourth and seventh scale degrees, adds to the folk-like character that Kern seems to have intended. (In *Show Boat*, a black dock worker's melodies differ in style from those of a white gambling man.) Yet Kern avoids monotony by giving each section its own curve, building to an impressive climax high in the baritone range in the song's final eight measures. The melody's sober tread and the text's philosophical cast lend authority to Joe, as if his view of the human trials and tribulations that swirl around the *Cotton Blossom* is bound to be wise.

If Kern's melody for *Ol' Man River* manages to be folk-like and dramatic at the same time, *Can't Help Lovin' Dat Man* borrows directly from the blues, a genre still popular in 1927. Julie La Verne, the show boat's sultry songstress, sings this number, whose verse is labeled "Tempo di Blues" and is set in twelve-bar blues form. These words are sung over Tin Pan Alley's standard blues accompaniment of repeated quarter notes. And the chorus that follows, again in thirty-two-bar **aaba** form, continues in a style spiced with blue notes. The singer confesses that however her man treats her, she is always ready to come back for more:

> Fish got to swim,
> Birds got to fly,
> I got to love one man till I die—
> Can't help lovin' dat man of mine.

Julie's number becomes a marker of racial identity. A black character named Queenie marvels that she has never heard "anybody but colored folks" sing that song. And soon, unmasked as a woman with African-American blood who has been passing for white, Julie is forced to leave the show boat.

The three songs cited here were all conceived for a particular character and a particular moment in *Show Boat*. Yet for all their differences in style— from operetta duet to hymnic, folk-like song, to blues number—each features a verse followed by a thirty-two-bar chorus. In other words, Kern wrote the songs of this integrated theatrical work so that they could circulate independently, in sheet-music form, as theatrical songs had been doing in the United States since the 1790s. Broadway songs were composed to contribute to a show *and* to appeal outside it, even to listeners and performers who knew nothing of their original context. By following popular-song conventions of the day, show songs of the Golden Age successfully entered the marketplace. And subject matter proved to be one of the most important conventions of all. *Ol' Man River* and *Fascinating Rhythm* aside, most show songs that won popularity in these years were songs about romantic love.

A view of romantic love appeared in songs during the 1920s that made innocent tunefulness seem Victorian and the passion of operetta generic. Courtship and love, treated almost as rituals in many earlier songs, now emerged as absorbing, sometimes mysterious personal adventures. In an earlier day, the question posed by Cole Porter's *What Is This Thing Called Love?* (1930) might have seemed hardly worth asking. But in the Jazz Age and after, romantic love was crowned the Feeling of Feelings, with little doubt that the subject deserved all the attention it received. "I was a humdrum person," Porter's verse confides, "leading a life apart," before "love flew in through my window wide, and quickened my humdrum heart." Love seizes this narrator in its grip. "Just who can solve its mystery?" he wonders. "Why should it make a fool of me?"

Since the plots of virtually all shows of the day involved characters seeking someone to love, the demand for love songs on Broadway was great. As one New York tunesmith put it, the songwriter's craft lay chiefly in saying "I love you" in thirty-two bars.[4] And with many talented composers and lyricists on the scene, words and music were joined again and again to register different states of the amorous mind. Two such states are caught in a pair of songs by top teams of the day. George and Ira Gershwin's *The Man I Love* (1924), composed for *Lady, Be Good!* but later cut for dramatic reasons, made its chief impact on its own. *My Heart Stood Still*, by Richard Rodgers and Lorenz Hart, was written for *A Connecticut Yankee* (1927), while also being sung independently. Both songs illustrate how masters of the genre could seize upon a detail—a fantasy or a fleeting moment—and make it a meditation on the workings of the human heart. *The Man I Love* is pure anticipation, as a woman reveals her romantic dream of a future love; *My Heart Stood Still* reflects on love at first sight. Both songs admit dependence on time-worn clichés, but these clichés are transcended by the songs' expression, which is graceful and self-aware.

For all the merit of Ira Gershwin's lyrics in *The Man I Love*, George's music gives the song its substance. By emphasizing the lowered-seventh scale degree, a note dissonant with the tonic harmony, the melody conveys restlessness. The fantasy is described in three eight-bar sections of an **aaba** form. Each begins by hovering around the seventh, then gradually works its way downward, from restlessness toward calm. And each describes a different stage of the imagined romance. The first vows confidence that Prince Charming will materialize:

> Some day he'll come along, the man I love:
> And he'll be big and strong, the man I love;
> And when he comes my way,
> I'll do my best to make him stay.

I took one look at you, That's all I meant to do;

And then my heart stood still!

The second section choreographs the meeting ("He'll take my hand," but "I know we both won't say a word"). Then, after an eight-bar speculation—in a new key and to a different tune—about the time of the meeting ("maybe Tuesday will be my good news day"), the last section imagines an idyllic future: "He'll build a little home, just meant for two, / From which I'll never roam, / Who would, would you?" In each **a** section, the same melodic figure is heard six times. And the parallel statements give a narrative quality to a text that, borrowing the well-worn "roam/home" rhyme from *Home, Sweet Home* and *Old Folks at Home*, seeks to be timeless as well as up-to-date.

The character who sings *The Man I Love* knows that listeners will find her fantasy a long shot. So the self-portrait she sketches is crucial. The

From 1924, when they wrote *The Man I Love*, to George's death in 1937, the Gershwin brothers collaborated on songs for musicals, movies, and the opera *Porgy and Bess*.

Prince Charming reference in the verse shows her lack of naïveté. Knowing the odds are stacked against her, she remains persistent, dedicated, and focused. The men she has met so far have not measured up, but that does not discourage her. Instead, by dwelling on one melodic figure ("the man I love"), she seems determined to stay the course. Unified but not overwhelmed by that repeated figure, the melody symbolizes confidence "that he'll appear." In this song, the music turns a romantic notion into a declaration of faith. Listeners are invited to believe, trusting that music as well shaped and solid as this could only come from a person worthy of respect.

Rodgers and Hart's *My Heart Stood Still* looks at a past instant rather than a dream of the future. By suspending time—freezing the frame, in effect—it explores the experience of love at first sight. Reliving the moment, the character remembers a feeling of physical shock:

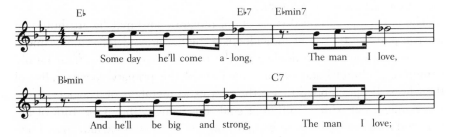

> I took one look at you,
> That's all I meant to do;
> And then my heart stood still!

Hart's lyrics, comprised of one-syllable words, suggest that the impact lingers on; Rodgers's melody confirms that suggestion. Each of the first two lines breaks off with a hint of breathlessness, with the last word falling on a short, unaccented quarter note. And the third line's melody mirrors the meaning, as downward quarter-note motion leads to three strokes (half note, half note, whole note) on the three final words. Just as the heart skips a beat, the melody "stands still" in this vivid moment of remembering.

The chorus of *My Heart Stood Still* shares the thirty-two-bar **aaba** form of *The Man I Love*, and three of its four sections also end with the title line. The second section elaborates the metaphor: "My feet could step and walk, / My lips could move and talk, / And yet my heart stood still!" In the release, or bridge (**b**) section, the focus shifts to the beloved's response, sung to a different melody:

> Though not a single word was spoken,
> I could tell you knew,
> That unfelt clasp of hands
> Told me so well you knew.

From this telepathic flash we return to the singer, who claims to have missed true happiness before the "thrill" (highest note of the song) of that "moment" (the first two-syllable word in any **a** section) "when my heart stood still."

These two songs share in the plenitude that American songwriters of the Golden Age discovered in male-female romance. A dream, a moment, a question, a metaphor, a phrase, a word, a name, anything could provide the idea around which a love song was built. In songs of earlier days, being in love was a general condition on a par with grieving or feeling patriotic. But as love took over the popular song, writers were challenged to discover fresh angles for portraying romantic involvement. The modern style of love blended devotion with evanescence, anxiety, and eroticism. Being in love was an exalted, delicious, yet precarious state, and there could be as many love stories as there were lovers.

The new emphasis on this variety of romantic love may be attributed, at least in part, to the rise of individualism. Before around 1880, most Americans had little reason to doubt that the ties linking people to their family, community, church, and occupation formed the primary social reality of their lives. People tended to see themselves as members of a society of the like-minded, not without different goals but living within a network of beliefs and relationships shared by many others. Between 1880 and 1900, however, these connections began to loosen. Attitudes changed especially in the cities, where industrial development brought rising prosperity, heightening competition and an awareness of class difference. From the 1920s on, Americans were more likely than before to downplay traditional social ties, seeking satisfaction beyond them and defining themselves in personal terms. One's beginnings could now be taken as a point of departure, perhaps to be left behind as identity was refashioned. Society in the Jazz Age was viewed as more a matter of choice than inheritance. Rather than a solid, enduring force, it was now impermanent, formed by shifting coalitions of individuals, each pursuing a personal destiny.[5]

By the end of World War I, songwriters were absorbing this spirit of individualism. The portrait of love that came to dominate the Broadway stage and Tin Pan Alley concentrated on lovers who are infatuated and preoccupied with each other beyond anything else, who dwell in a "world" of two, sometimes only one if the love affair has ended—or, as in *The Man I Love*, has yet to begin. Family, friends, society, and community barely exist in this world. The new individualism rules.

It is striking that so many songs took this approach in the years after World War I and so few before it. It also stands to reason that new subject matter would call for new musical expression. While the thirty-two-bar chorus preceded by a verse remained the norm for Broadway and Tin Pan Alley from the 1920s until mid-century and after, songwriters expanded and intensified their tonal vocabulary. In songs that risked tonal adventure, the release section of an **aaba** form offered ready opportunity. The releases of Kern's *Smoke Gets in Your Eyes* (1933) and Johnny Green's *Body and Soul* (1930), for example, jump into remote keys, then find their way back to the neighborhood of tonic in the **a** section's return. Such explorations were part of a more general trend toward harmonic enrichment. By the mid-1920s, Kern and Gershwin, among others, were using chords with sevenths, ninths, and added or altered tones almost anywhere in a song.[6]

The enriched harmony of Golden Age popular song came primarily from the songwriters' contact with the European classical sphere. Regular exposure to the music of Euroamerican stage composers such as Victor Herbert and Sigmund Romberg may have been a factor, but formal education played a role too, for Kern, Gershwin, Rodgers, and Porter all received classical training. Composers such as Liszt, Tchaikovsky, and Ravel had enlarged the harmonic vocabulary of Western music in general, and popular songwriters borrowed from their palette. The general kinship between European Romanticism and the idiom of American popular song is reflected in the way songwriters use chromaticism to intensify harmonic progressions that lead the listener, in a regular pattern of tension and release, from one phrase to the next. Piano miniatures of Edward MacDowell, which brought some-

thing of Richard Wagner's expressive chromaticism into the American concert hall and parlor, may also have played a role (see Chapter 19).

The release of Gershwin's *The Man I Love* (1924) offers a brief, clear
example of the enriched harmonic idiom at work. The melody begins in C
minor, moving in its two bars to E-flat, the relative major. There is nothing
in that relationship, or in the melody either, that would not have been commonplace a century earlier. Yet Gershwin's harmonization gives this eight-
bar passage a modern cast. In its first three measures, and again in its
second half, an inner voice in descending sixths adds complexity to the texture. So does the brief countermelodic figure that accompanies the pause
on the dominant harmony in the middle. These added lines introduce dissonances—nonharmonic tones—on almost every strong beat (beats one and
three of each four-beat measure). Forward momentum comes from harmonic progressions rooted in the bass line and the nonharmonic tones in-
flecting most of the chords. Even the cadential pause feels unsettled, for
the music cannot rest on such dissonances. Indeed, while this song, as well
as Gershwin's songs in general and the songs of his professional colleagues,
preserve traditional rhyme schemes and regular phrase structure, their harmonic instability reaches beyond that of any earlier popular-song style.

The songs of Broadway and Tin Pan Alley's Golden Age connect three
separate elements in a fusion that proved enduring: the social outlook of individualism, the subject of romantic love, and a musical idiom that blends
conventional form with nuanced, sometimes unstable harmony. Individualism allowed people to reject ancestral ties, to speak, dress, and behave as
they wished, and to pursue their own desires, including romantic involvement. But those who claimed such independence risked giving up the support and connection that ancestral ties provided. The new romantic love
song celebrated individuals who loved with a passion strong enough to overshadow these other social connections. And the musical idiom suggested
that love with such high expectations had to be more dynamic than stable.
Whatever the lyrics might say, the harmonic richness that bathed them reminded listeners that romance between "free" modern individuals could be
perilous.

To think of men and women as individuals is to recognize that they often
feel alone in the world. Even while coveting romantic attachment, such
people know that love will probably prove as temporary as it is enthralling
and that sooner or later they may again be by themselves. If, as historians
say, America lost its innocence in the World War I years, then surely the rise
of individualism, with the specter of solitude as one natural consequence,
played a role in the process. Although some Golden Age love songs explicitly
link romantic love with loneliness, many more suggest that connection
through their music. And since tragedy is hardly the stuff of popular expres-

sion, they treat loneliness as more poignant than tragic. To claim that Broadway and Tin Pan Alley songwriters probed the depths of the modern American consciousness would be an exaggeration. On the other hand, joined to sophisticated lyrics, the restless, complex harmonic idiom of many of their songs seems to point inward, as if toward an existential unknown, just as the simple diatonic idiom of an earlier age's parlor songs pointed outward to the network of home, family, and religious relations then assumed to surround the lives of right-thinking people.

What was the original audience for these songs? Like earlier theatrical numbers, they were written to appeal to theater audiences and to singers and players who performed them at home from sheet music. But beyond these customers, three developments of the 1920s make the question harder to answer. The first was the decline in sheet-music publication: a printers' strike and a paper shortage in 1920 caused the cost of production to triple, and the phonograph record, a growing presence in musical life through the 1910s, soon replaced sheet music as the primary means of selling popular music directly to consumers.[7] The second development was the rapid growth of radio broadcasting, which began as a commercial enterprise only after World War I. Radios could be found in about one-quarter of American homes by 1927, and sales grew even faster after that; by the end of 1928, nationwide broadcasting was an everyday reality, thanks to sixty-nine NBC affiliates.[8] The third change followed the advent of talking pictures in 1927. Silent films had long been accompanied by familiar old songs, classical excerpts, and melodies with associations that could be linked to images on the screen. But it did not take the music business long to recognize the marketing power of talking pictures, which claimed a weekly audience of 70 million. Hollywood and Tin Pan Alley joined forces to plug each other's products.[9]

Because recordings, radio, and the movies sold performances instead of printed music, their impact is hard to measure. For now songs of Broadway and Tin Pan Alley reached consumers far outside the original circle of theatergoers and amateur performers. And for many songs, consumers had a variety of performances to choose from. Moreover, Broadway and Tin Pan Alley were now competing with repertories that in earlier days had hardly been accessible in published form. To be sure, some blues and jazz tunes were published in sheet music and stock orchestrations, but recordings made performers, not songwriters, the artistic leaders in these traditions. And in the field of "hillbilly" music, centered in the South and involving publication only sporadically until the 1940s, regional performers gave a sense of coherence to the repertory. By 1930, a previously undreamed-of variety of music, including classical and even folk, was becoming available to listeners across a wide geographical, ethnic, and economic spectrum.

By recording and broadcasting performances of musicians in their inherited ethnic and regional styles, the new media made it possible for different communities to enjoy on record and the radio popular styles of "their own." Indeed, in the 1970s, Charles Hamm, the author of a groundbreaking history of American popular song, argued that Tin Pan Alley and Broadway songs were not the universal American vernacular of their day, as had long been assumed. Rather, as sophisticated songs for white, urban, middle- and upper-class Americans, they remained outside the experience of much of American society. They comprised a New York style, virtually uninfluenced by other regions of the country.[10] This was a striking idea in the history of American popular music. Yet while there is no denying that African Americans and white Southerners embraced styles of their own, it is hard to imagine how they avoided contact with New York–based songs, even if they had tried. For these songs were plugged and sold by a powerful media network in which black and Southern styles held only a marginal place during the 1920s and 1930s. Moreover, the claim that little cultural input reached New York from outside may apply to the writing of songs but hardly to performances, as more and more Americans were encountering popular songs through the distinctive personalities of Bing Crosby (from Spokane, Washington), Fred Astaire (Omaha), Guy Lombardo (London, Ontario), Louis Armstrong (New Orleans), Benny Goodman (Chicago), and dozens of others. There was no standard way to perform the "New York style" of popular song. Providing singers and players a framework for their own interpretations, Broadway and Tin Pan Alley continued the long line of performers' music that Alexander Reinagle and his fellow theater composers had begun publishing in America almost a century and a half earlier.

To imply that black and rural Americans resisted music from Broadway and Tin Pan Alley suggests that the menu of choices available was wide indeed. But recordings, radio, and the movies in the 1920s and 1930s produced nowhere near the variety that followed World War II. Moreover, just as "race" records were bought by white listeners, there is good reason to believe that Golden Age songs, emphasizing such universals as love, risk, and loneliness, resonated beyond their original audience. For example, black rock-and-roll singer "Little Richard" Penniman, who was born in 1935, noted: "I came from a family where my people didn't like rhythm and blues. Bing Crosby—'Pennies from Heaven'—Ella Fitzgerald, was all I heard."[11] As a Southern black household, the Pennimans might be assumed to have preferred styles more local than that of Bing Crosby, whose repertory ran heavily toward New York–made romantic love songs. Yet this family in Macon, Georgia, favored Crosby and Ella Fitzgerald: proof that however useful demographics and cultural inference may be in the marketing of music, they cannot account for the obdurate facts of personal taste.

THE MUSICAL STAGE AND SCREEN

Generally speaking, songs from Golden Age Broadway musicals have proved more enduring than the shows in which they appeared. Yet it is worthwhile to look at two classic stage works and a new genre—Gershwin's *Porgy and Bess* (1935), Rodgers and Hammerstein's *Oklahoma!* (1943), and the Hollywood film musical—as a reminder of how show music could function in a dramatic context.

George Gershwin called *Porgy and Bess* a "folk opera." His belief that a label was needed is understandable, for the work's precise nature was contested from the start. Gershwin's Broadway background raised doubts about whether he was up to a full-fledged operatic challenge. The score called for opera singers, but the show played nightly in a Broadway theater, raising further questions about whether it really was an opera. Knowledge that massive cuts took place before the New York premiere has also fed the view that the work is more a succession of musical numbers than an operatic whole, as has the subsequent popularity of some individual numbers. Moreover, commercial success for *Porgy and Bess* first came in 1941 when, stripped of its recitative, it was played as a Broadway musical: a drama of separate musical numbers linked with spoken dialogue.

If the "opera" half of Gershwin's label was challenged, so was the "folk." Based on the novel *Porgy* (1925), by DuBose Heyward, and with lyrics by Heyward and Ira Gershwin, *Porgy and Bess* depicts life in Catfish Row, a black ghetto in Charleston, South Carolina. A tale about Southern blacks by a white novelist, set to music by a New York–based, Jewish songwriter-lyricist team and played on the Broadway stage, was bound to draw criticism on grounds of authenticity. In addition, long after slavery and emancipation, the lives of African Americans were still affected by racial stereotyping: the notion that they were a superstitious, feckless, violent people, given to singing or brawling their troubles away. *Porgy and Bess*, which affirmed that stereotype, was seen in some quarters as an obstacle to black Americans' quest for social respect.

The plot centers on an improbable romance. Porgy, a crippled beggar, shows kindness to the beautiful but dissolute Bess when her lover, the stevedore Crown, is forced to flee after killing another Catfish Row resident in a drunken fight over a crap game. Porgy takes Bess in and falls in love with her. She becomes Porgy's woman, protected from community disapproval and the advances of Sportin' Life, the local dope peddler. Urged by Porgy to join a picnic excursion to Kittiwah Island, Bess encounters Crown, who is hiding there. Although she genuinely loves Porgy, Crown overcomes Bess's resistance, and after spending the night with him on the island, she returns to Catfish Row in a state of delirium. Porgy helps nurse her back to health, and though intuition tells him she has been with Crown, he reaffirms his love for her. A hurricane hits the coast while fishermen from Catfish Row are at sea. As the community prays for their safety, Crown reappears, mocks Porgy's physical shortcomings, and then rushes out into the storm in the vain hope of saving the fishermen. Surviving this onslaught of nature, he steals back to Catfish Row the next night to reclaim Bess. The waiting Porgy kills him in a brief struggle. When the police find Crown's body, they arrest Porgy as a witness. Freed a week later, he returns to Catfish Row, only to find that Bess, convinced by Sportin' Life that Porgy is gone for good, has sailed for New York with the dope peddler. The opera ends as Porgy leaves by goat cart to search for Bess. ("Which way New York?" he asks. "It's way up North, past the custom house," his neighbors reply.)

Porgy and Bess features songs of remarkable variety. The memorable melodies of the best known have made them enduringly popular. These songs include *Summertime*, a lullaby that invokes the spirituals of slavery times; *My Man's Gone Now*, sung by the widow of Robbins, whom Crown has killed; Porgy's banjo song *I Got Plenty o' Nuttin'*, in **aaba** form; and the love duet *Bess, You Is My Woman Now*. The principals of the opera are also members of a larger community virtually always onstage, whose character Gershwin portrays in communal songs. Instead of borrowing traditional spirituals, Gershwin wrote new ones, ranging in mood and technique from songful exaltation (*Leavin' for the Promise' Lan'*) and consolation (*Clara, Clara*) to stark desolation (*Gone, Gone, Gone*) and even simultaneously chanted prayers (*Oh, Doctor Jesus*), inspired by Gershwin's visits to black South Carolina churches while he was composing the work. On the secular side, Catfish Row's uninhibited social customs can be glimpsed in the fisherman Jake's commentary on romance (*A Woman Is a Sometime Thing*) and a barbaric episode, complete with vocables and tom-tom, during the Kittiwah Island excursion (*I Ain't Got No Shame*). At the picnic, the amoral Sportin' Life gets the community, softened up by a day of carousing, to join him in a mockery of biblical teaching, sung in call-and-response dialogue replete with blue notes (*It Ain't Necessarily So*).

Finally, Gershwin composed recitatives for *Porgy and Bess* that, in the tradition of performers' music, rely on the singer to reveal their full dramatic scope and songful potential. Bess's plea that Crown allow her to return from the picnic to Porgy's side is one of the most economically effective. Here, Bess's character stands revealed. Lacking a true moral compass, torn between love for the upright Porgy and lust for the formidable Crown, she moves in just eight bars from reasonable explanation ("It's like this, Crown") to the edge of despair. Gershwin restricts her to a word-bound vocal line that, as it rises over a static chordal background, calls more and more on the

Oklahoma! (1943) marked the start of a collaboration between composer Richard Rodgers (left) and lyricist-librettist Oscar Hammerstein II that continued until Hammerstein died in 1960.

singer's expressive powers. He leaves it to the performer to convey the precise moment in which Bess's good intentions collapse, then supports her admission of defeat with the opera's most tortured song of all, *What You Want Wid Bess?*

The choral numbers in *Porgy and Bess* firmly embed its tale of romantic love in a distinctive social setting. Much the same may be said of Rodgers and Hammerstein's *Oklahoma!* Based on *Green Grow the Lilacs*, a Broadway play by Lynn Riggs (1931), this show brought together a composer and a lyricist-librettist who had earlier worked successfully with other collaborators. The reception of *Oklahoma!* (1943), which ran on Broadway for 2,248 performances and for more than ten years on the road, surpassed by far anything previously achieved by a Broadway musical play. And later Rodgers and Hammerstein shows, including *Carousel* (1945), *South Pacific* (1949), *The King and I* (1951), and *The Sound of Music* (1959), not only enjoyed long New York runs but, like *Oklahoma!*, were made into film musicals. Set on a farm in the wide-open spaces of Indian territory just after the turn of the century, *Oklahoma!* explores the old-fashioned virtues of country folk, with

melodramatic touches added. Curly, a cowboy, is in love with Laurey, a virtuous young woman. Wanting to make Curly jealous, Laurey attends a box-
lunch social with Jud, a brooding ranch hand. But Curly bids everything he
owns in an auction for Laurey's picnic basket, and she marries him. Picking
a fight with Curly, Jud is killed by accident; and the bride and groom ride off
to begin their life together.

Why *Oklahoma!* won such extraordinary success has been the subject of
much speculation. But for Rodgers himself the key was that "everything in
the production was made to conform to the simple open-air spirit of the
story."[12] In the first place, the notion of locating a musical on the Western
prairies was unusual and the attempt to cultivate an "open-air spirit" even
more so. But most unusual of all was the decision to let the story, not
musical-comedy convention, govern what happened onstage. Fully aware of
the grip of such conventions, the creators of *Oklahoma!*—Rodgers, Hammerstein, director Rouben Mamoulian, and choreographer Agnes De-
Mille—resolved to bend them to fit their needs. Thus, no one would sing or
dance with the idea of stopping the show. By working forward from the setting and story rather than backward from standard musical-comedy ingredients, Rodgers, Hammerstein, and Company played with convention in a
way that gave *Oklahoma!* an atmosphere all its own.

Instead of a stage full of singers and dancers, the show's opening curtain
reveals a lone figure: Laurey's elderly Aunt Eller, who is churning butter.
Rodgers later wrote that the beginning warns the audience to "watch out!"
because "this is a different kind of musical." The landscape in *Oklahoma!* is
more protagonist than backdrop. Even before the audience meets the principal characters, it is invited to join in an appreciation of nature. The stage
directions of Lynn Riggs's play inspired this opening scene:

> It is a radiant summer morning . . . the kind of morning which, enveloping
> the shapes of earth—men, cattle in the meadow, blades of the young corn,
> streams—makes them seem to exist now for the first time, their images giv-
> ing off a visible golden emanation that is partly true and partly a trick of
> imagination focusing to keep alive a loveliness that may pass away.[13]

From offstage floats in the waltz melody of the show's first song, *Oh, What
a Beautiful Morning*, sung by Curly. On a morning like this one, even a cowboy, who knows how rare such moments are, is moved to sing about it. Indeed, the presence of the out-of-doors is felt throughout the show. And at
the end, with Laurey and Curly safely married, the company affirms a connection to nature in the show's title song:

> We know we belong to the land,
> And the land we belong to is grand.

That connection surely enhanced the appeal of *Oklahoma!* By placing the story in the heartland, where the characters often face challenges tougher than romantic ones, Rodgers and Hammerstein put their love story in a broader human perspective than most earlier musical comedies. It seems only natural for these characters, used to wrestling with forces beyond human control, to stop and savor the feel of a beautiful day. And it was surely no coincidence that Rodgers composed this mood-setting song as a waltz rather than a peppy production number. The waltz beginning helps to ease audiences into an appreciative frame of mind for a tale about an earlier age. Yet *Oklahoma!*, though set in the past, was also a product of its own time. In the classical sphere of Depression-era America, cosmopolitan sophistication had yielded in some circles to a focus on the common man in regional settings—a shift that took place in all the arts, from Thomas Hart Benton's murals to the novels of John Steinbeck. The notion of a "folk operetta," a label given *Oklahoma!* by one of its first reviewers, followed that trend.

Rodgers and Hammerstein's musical was also responding to something even more threatening: the United States' involvement in World War II, which dominated the national consciousness in 1943. When the Japanese bombed Pearl Harbor on December 7, 1941, the country was ill-prepared for the all-out war that followed. Once U.S. manpower and productive capacities were fully tapped, the tide turned. But in the early 1940s, the fate of Western civilization itself seemed in doubt. With so many men on active duty, millions of families were directly threatened. Radio and press accounts, together with photographs, brought information about the war into American homes. Tales of ground combat, naval battles, air raids, heroic and villainous deeds, and human tragedies came to be the stuff of everyday discourse. The production of many consumer goods was reduced or eliminated. Although North America was never invaded, foreign menace and domestic belt-tightening created a charged atmosphere that enhanced feelings of national unity.

While it may be exaggerating to call *Oklahoma!* a patriotic musical, Rodgers himself later commented that the show aimed to give wartime audiences both pleasure and optimism. Set in another time and place, it featured country folk with an uncomplicated view of life. These Oklahomans, the show implied, embodied the spirit that would carry the nation through bad times. Thus, at a historical moment when the world seemed mad with aggression and brutality, *Oklahoma!* struck a responsive chord by offering audiences a vision of Americans as good-hearted people in a land filled with promise for the future.

Director Rouben Mamoulian, who had filled the same role in *Porgy and Bess* and who was one of the first Hollywood film directors to blend acting, motion, sound effects, scenery, and lighting into one conceptual whole, con-

tributed much to *Oklahoma!*'s dramatic character. So did choreographer
Agnes DeMille, trained in classical ballet and modern dance, a onetime disciple of Martha Graham, who had recently choreographed *Rodeo* (1942), a
ballet with a score by Aaron Copland. In Hammerstein's scenario, Laurey's
doubts about marrying Curly were staged not in dialogue or songs but in a
"dream ballet." Judging that people in a frontier community like this one
would not be introspective, DeMille used dance to give audiences a fuller
understanding of Laurey's character, expressing emotions that words could
not convey. DeMille described her approach as "lyric, non-realistic and
highly stylized, but salted with detailed action that is colloquial, human,
recognizable."[14]

Oklahoma! combined entertainment, message, and local color in a fusion
of story, song, and dance that long outlived the war; in *People Will Say We're
in Love*, it also contained a hit song. But the show's open-air spirit pervaded
most of its other songs so thoroughly—*The Surrey with the Fringe on Top, I
Cain't Say No, Oh, What a Beautiful Morning*, and the title song are examples—that even when they circulated independently, they were still known
as songs from *Oklahoma!* Radio, road companies, and the long Broadway
run all helped to certify the connection. And so did the record business.
Rodgers later recalled:

> Jack Kapp, the president of Decca Records, came to us with a revolutionary
> idea. He wanted to use our cast, our conductor and our orchestra to repro-
> duce on records the same musical program that people heard in the theatre.
> It was the most exciting recording concept we'd ever heard of, and naturally
> we consented. From *Oklahoma!* on, the original-cast album has become a
> major by-product of Broadway musicals, but this was the first time it had
> been done.[15]

Thus, the identity of *Oklahoma!* as an artistic whole, built in to the show by
its creators, was also affirmed by the marketing of its music.

A new context for popular songs emerged at the end of the 1920s: the
movie musical. Having begun after the turn of the century on the East
Coast, the film industry had moved west to Southern California and by 1920
was established in Hollywood. Just as a few national circuits, most of them
New York–based, had controlled vaudeville and musical theater in the century's early years, Hollywood studios ruled the movie business. The most
prominent were Metro-Goldwyn-Mayer, Paramount, Warner Brothers, RKO
(Radio-Keith-Orpheum), and Twentieth Century Fox: all of them vertical
monopolies that controlled their own production, distribution, and exhibition in theaters. During the 1930s and 40s, these five studios plus three
others—United Artists, Columbia, and Universal—made several hundred
movies per year. In 1939 alone, for example, the studios released 376 films

and collected $673 million at the box office; in every week of that year, 52–55 million people watched at least one movie. With movie theaters outnumbering banks and department stores, movies had come to be one of the nation's largest industries.[16]

Factory-like organization enabled Hollywood studios to produce so many films. With few exceptions, Hollywood's goal was to crank out a profitable product intended for one-time viewing. Yet substantial profits gave studios the capital to recruit skilled actors, writers, directors, lyricists, and composers. Musicals comprised only a small part of the studios' output. Some, including the operetta and the revue, followed forms inherited from the Broadway stage. Others made music a key ingredient of films that broke new expressive ground: the animated cartoon, the story musical based on fantasy, and the dance musical.

In 1928, Walt Disney produced a short animated film picturing a character called Mickey Mouse as captain—with Minnie Mouse as crew—of a boat transporting a collection of animals down a river. At a time when the industry was changing from silent film to sound, the animation of *Steamboat Willie* was made to a metronome's beat, and rhythmic energy pulses through the assortment of whistles, cowbells, and tin pans featured in the sound track. The characters find musical instruments in unlikely places: Minnie Mouse cranks a donkey's tail to make the animal sing, Mickey plays on a bull's teeth as though on a xylophone.[17] Within a decade, Disney had begun making feature-length animated films, still relying on music to carry the action, as in *Snow White and the Seven Dwarfs* (1937).

Among movie musicals based on fantasy, perhaps the era's greatest achievement was MGM's *The Wizard of Oz* (1939), which dramatized the children's tale by L. Frank Baum and featured a score by Harold Arlen and E. Y. Harburg. The film, made for more than $2.5 million at a time when a loaf of bread and a gallon of gasoline cost six cents each, relied heavily on special effects. In the familiar story, twelve-year-old Dorothy is lifted up by a cyclone from the plains of Kansas and whirled into the magic land of Oz. There she meets several strange companions who join her in a visit to the Wizard, who helps her return home. The Kansas sequences are filmed in sepia-toned black and white, but Dorothy's adventures in Oz, where she encounters a yellow brick road and an Emerald City, appear in color.

Simultaneously with *The Wizard of Oz*, no fewer than eight other movies were being made on the MGM lot, which in 1939 employed more than three thousand artisans, craftsmen, laborers, and technicians, not to mention the six hundred actors, producers, directors, writers, and assistants who were also on the studio payroll. In an enterprise so vast, individual artistry could hardly be more than a small cog, and the talent of songwriters was no exception. While New York composers and lyricists stayed with a show

This image from *The Wizard of Oz* (1939) shows Judy Garland as Dorothy and Billie Burke as the Good Witch.

through out-of-town rehearsals and tryouts, in Hollywood they turned in their songs and picked up their paychecks. Songs for films were given to the studio's music director, who—working under the film's director, who answered to studio producers—farmed out the orchestration, arrangements, and connecting music to staff composers, or shouldered some of those duties himself. Hollywood songwriters lacked control over their music's use, but they were paid well for their work, and the American Society of Composers, Authors, and Publishers (ASCAP), which collected and dispensed performance royalties, added to their earnings. Lyricist and composer Johnny Mercer once noted that Hollywood songwriters who made $75,000 per year from their studios could expect a like amount in ASCAP royalties from performances of their songs.[18]

For *The Wizard of Oz*, Arlen and Harburg were asked to write not only songs but musical "sequences" that filled larger scenes. One of the film's major songs, *Ding Dong! The Witch Is Dead!*, comes directly out of a long "Munchkinland Musical Sequence." Another, *If I Only Had a Brain*, sung by the Scarecrow, also moves the plot forward. Even *Over the Rainbow*, the film's most famous song, has a clear function in the story: it shows the strength of Dorothy's imagination as she pictures a place more interesting to live than the Kansas flatland. Convinced that the film needed a melody here with breadth and sweep, Arlen filled the bill with a ballad based on bold upward leaps. Sung by the sixteen-year-old Judy Garland playing a preadolescent, the song could not revel in the kind of romantic love that dominated the day's popular music. But with Harburg's words sketching a vivid fantasy and Arlen supporting a mood of yearning with harmonies that feed the melodic line's expansiveness, the number projects its own kind of grandeur.

> Somewhere over the rainbow,
> Way up high,
> There's a land that I heard of
> Once in a lullaby.

Harburg later recalled that when Arlen had first unveiled the song for him at the piano, "he played with such symphonic sweep and bravura that my first reaction was: 'Oh, no, not for little Dorothy! That's for Nelson Eddy!'," Hollywood operetta's reigning baritone. The beginning octave leap seemed overblown to him until he got used to it. Arlen's publisher was afraid the leap would prove too daunting for most singers; sheet-music sales still figured in the popular-song trade's thinking.[19] But however unorthodox the start of its chorus, Arlen cast his ballad in standard thirty-two-bar **aaba** form, with a **b** section that emphasizes quiet, dreamy-sounding eighth-note declamation.

Now considered an icon of prewar American popular culture, *The Wizard of Oz* won that status only in the age of television. On its first release in 1939, the film fell almost $1 million short of making back MGM's investment, but in 1956 it appeared for the first time on television, and by the late 1960s broadcasts had become a near-annual event. Today the film is widely beloved by a vast number of Americans, whether for its vividness of story, characters, and visual settings; its reassuring pro-home message; its rout of

In this scene from the 1935 film *Top Hat*, Ginger Rogers and Fred Astaire are danc-ing to Irving Berlin's *Isn't This a Lovely Day?*

evil in the Wicked Witch's death; the chance it has given viewers to see the same film at different stages of life and to compare those experiences; or its catchy musical score.

By the late 1930s, the Hollywood musical had settled on a more or less standard framework: a modern-day romantic comedy that featured four or five songs and a dance or two. The so-called dance musical, especially as fashioned by Fred Astaire, did much to create this framework. Starting out in vaudeville, Astaire and his sister Adele played as a sibling pair in Broad-way revues and musical comedies—the Gershwins' *Lady Be Good* (1924) in-cluded—until 1931, when Adele quit the stage to marry. Fred set out for

Hollywood to market his talents, which included a feeling for light comedy, reliability as a singer, and utter perfection as a dancer, though not the handsomeness of a romantic screen idol.

In 1933, Astaire signed a contract with RKO studios, and before long he was paired with actress-dancer Ginger Rogers in a collaboration, now recognized as one of the miracles of Hollywood's studio era, that by 1939 had produced nine films and established the dance musical as a genre. Films starring Astaire and Rogers were sparked not by *more* dancing but by the use of dance to further narration and establish character. Astaire, who as a star won the right to choreograph these dances and even to help edit them, brought to his work the care of a perfectionist who might spend weeks on a three-minute dance routine.[20] He also brought an unparalleled dramatic flair. And the drama is contained within the dancing, the only really serious element in the Astaire-Rogers films. Only rarely do the characters they play show much distinctiveness; the interest and the fun lie in how the couple overcome misunderstandings and other obstacles to a romantic happy ending through singing and dancing.[21]

Songs were prime ingredients in the Astaire-Rogers dance musicals, and the leading songwriters supplied them—Irving Berlin, Rodgers and Hart, Cole Porter, Kern and Hammerstein, and the Gershwin brothers. One of the most celebrated of these collaborations is *Top Hat* (1935), with a score by Berlin, and with Astaire playing the irreverent Jerry Travers. Early in the movie, Travers folds his newspaper noisily enough in a stuffy London men's club to aggravate the members; he then makes sure they are truly shocked by tap dancing on his way out. Late-night dancing in his hotel room to Berlin's *No Strings* wakes up Dale Tremont, played by Rogers, who happens to be sleeping in the room below. Annoyed, she rushes upstairs to complain. When she leaves, the music returns quietly while Travers, appointing himself her personal sandman, sprinkles sand on the floor and dances on it caressingly.

The couple's declaration of love takes place silently during Travers's singing of *Cheek to Cheek*, for which Berlin composed a seventy-two-bar chorus without a verse. Travers sings his song while he and Tremont joint other couples in a standard fox-trot. He starts on an ecstatic note: "Heaven, I'm in heaven." And the lyrics go on to link his mood with dancing and the magic of her presence. Berlin's song begins with a remarkable sixteen-bar statement. Arch-like, it works its way upward to a high-note climax in the middle, descends to the lower octave in the next four bars, and spends its last four in a syncopated celebration of dance-floor romance. Berlin, who rather than accepting the standard Hollywood flat fee for a songwriter had managed to negotiate a share in the profits of *Top Hat*, visited the set regularly while the musical numbers were being filmed. According to a choreographer who helped with the dancing, Berlin showed an openness to Astaire's suggestions about the songs. *Cheek to Cheek* might have inspired some singers toward resonant vocalism, but when Astaire wanted to sing it "almost as though he were talking, Berlin said, 'Oh, that's great, I love it.' He loved the way Fred did that."[22]

Berlin's song follows the two sixteen-bar statements with a pair of eight-bar ones. Here the irrepressible Travers declares "dancing cheek to cheek" even more thrilling than mountain climbing or fishing. But then his jolly tone gives way to urgency. "Dance with me," he commands, "I want my arm about you." And Berlin's music shifts abruptly from C major to C minor, followed by an unexpected plunge into A-flat in the song's most dramatic tonal complication. This surge of open passion dissolves quickly, leading back to the home key of C major and a final statement of the opening sixteen bars. But while the musical return completes the song's formal circle—**aa** (16 + 16 bars) **b** (8 + 8) **c** (8) **a** (16)—on the screen Tremont has realized that she too has fallen in love. As the song is being sung, the couple pull gradually away from the crowd until, as it ends, orchestra music carries them off by themselves and into the big dance that follows. The unusual length of Berlin's song allows Astaire's character to complete his courtship of Rogers's, and the subsequent full-fledged dance marks the lovers' celebration of having found peerless partners for the dance of life that awaits them in the future.

The years after World War II saw the studios' decline and a crisis for the Hollywood film industry. Many factors contributed, but none more directly than the rise of television, as radio had challenged phonograph recordings in the 1920s. When studio leaders realized that they could not compete with television, they joined forces with the new medium. Studios began producing TV series as well as, even instead of, movies. Moreover, they sold off their backlist of old films for broadcast on the air, making television, in effect, a museum of film and introducing a new generation of Americans to films they would never have seen otherwise. The form in which these films appeared—reduced to tiny size and regularly interrupted by commercials—was far from the originals, and songs and dances in musicals, considered extraneous to the plot, were sometimes cut. Nevertheless, as the film industry struggled against its impact, television was broadcasting Astaire and Rogers as well as story musicals from MGM. Thus a postwar audience grew acquainted with films showing the Hollywood of an earlier day as a prolific creator of popular musical entertainment that, like some of its featured songs, occasionally approached elegance.[23]

33

Classical Music in
the Postwar Years

IN SEPTEMBER 1946, PETER YATES, an ardent music lover who earned his living working for the California State Employment office, published *Evenings on the Roof: Fourth Report*, a retrospective look at the concert series that he and his wife, the pianist Frances Mullen, had established and managed in Los Angeles for the past seven years. The Yateses' goal had been "to create an audience for that class of music which is always contemporary," from Paul Hindemith and Charles Ives in the twentieth century to William Byrd and Orlando Gibbons in the sixteenth. And they had launched the series on a financial shoestring, with performances taking place in their own house in a second-floor room with a plywood interior, windows overlooking the city, and space for about fifty listeners. Until 1942, when a hall was rented, concerts were held there on the fourth Sunday of each month. A yearly subscription cost three dollars for a dozen concerts, and a "contribution" of fifty cents bought admission to a single event.[1]

The first Evenings on the Roof concert, given on April 23, 1939, was devoted to music by Béla Bartók and the third to Charles Ives, featuring Frances Mullen's performance of the *Concord* Sonata for piano, a violin and piano sonata, and songs sung by Radiana Pazmore. Other concerts in the first season included a program of works by Ferruccio Busoni, an evening of music before Bach, and programs devoted to Mozart, Schoenberg, Roy Harris, and compositions from Henry Cowell's *New Music Quarterly*. In future years, and over a span of several seasons, the Yateses programmed all of Beethoven's piano works, plus the fifteen violin and cello sonatas and his only song cycle, in roughly chronological order. Audiences ranged from a high of forty or fifty at the Beethoven series to a low of eight for an all-viola program in 1941. A concert of Arnold Schoenberg's music in May 1941, which included movements from his Violin Concerto arranged for violin and piano, drew between fifteen and twenty customers, "sitting informally about the room," the soloist recalled, "some on the floor, some on a daybed in the corner." In the mid-1940s, after the series had been running for more than half-a-dozen years, Yates contrasted its priorities with those of the Music Guild of Los Angeles, a group that sponsored public concerts by noted virtuosi. "With them the audience comes first, the music second, their performers third," he wrote. "Our rule has been: performers first, music second, audience afterwards."[2]

The Canadian-born, Princeton-educated Yates, who in 1931 had gone west to court California native Mullen, was no great fan of Los Angeles, which he described in those years as a "veritable Sahara of artistic incomprehension." Nevertheless, by the time of World War II, the city was home to many distinguished musicians. Schoenberg himself and Igor Stravinsky, the two leading classical innovators of the first half of the twentieth century, both settled there during the 1930s. The local émigré community of composers also included Sergei Rachmaninoff, Mario Castelnuovo-Tedesco, Ernst Toch, Erich Wolfgang Korngold, and Ingolf Dahl. German-born conductor Otto Klemperer led the Los Angeles Philharmonic, the city's chief professional orchestra, from 1933 until 1939. And violinists Jascha Heifetz and Joseph Szigeti, pianists Artur Rubinstein and Vladimir Horowitz, and harpsichordist Alice Ehlers also lived there. Composer Ernst Krenek and cellist Gregor Piatigorsky arrived shortly after the war ended.

Of that distinguished group, Dahl, Toch, Szigeti, Ehlers, and Krenek performed in Evenings on the Roof concerts, and many of the others attended, some regularly. The orchestras at the Hollywood film studios also proved a ready source of performers, eager for challenges of the kind the Yateses' concerts provided. Moreover, some members of the Los Angeles Philharmonic Orchestra coveted more chances to play chamber music. The Evenings concerts offered performers only small fees or none at all, but they provided an outlet for unused artistic energies. Local performers in effect subsidized the series out of a love of music and an appetite for musical adventure.

These concerts, which in 1954 became the Monday Evening Concerts under different leadership, have won a niche in history for programming modern works in a city whose musical institutions generally ignored such works. But the series may also be seen as a critique of the American concert hall in general. Denying that performers had a duty to make their music accessible to a mass public, Yates charged both the concert hall and the media—radio and the phonograph alike—with seeking to do just that, plugging tried-and-true favorites and steering clear of more daring, less familiar music. Most of all, the Evenings on the Roof concerts were a critique of many classical performers' resistance to twentieth-century music. At the end of World War I, a gap had opened between the concert hall and living composers who conceived of music as an exploration of the contemporary world. That gap did not close with the passing of time. Moreover, historically minded performers and scholars were mining the past for lesser-known works and styles that had also been overlooked. The supply of music in the classical sphere was increasing much faster than the concert hall's demand.

Rooted in respect for the classics, but financially dependent on ticket sales and private patronage, the concert hall at the war's end followed values and tastes that had changed little since the days of Theodore Thomas. Its ruling formula combined edification and familiarity with an appreciation of virtuoso performance, and the notion that art could be glamorous as well as dignified. To change that formula—to question sanctioned genres, styles, composers, and works, or the dominance of prestigious conductors, singers, and players—would risk alienating an audience whose members found those ingredients appealing. Evenings on the Roof challenged the formula, rejecting the concert hall's link between art and glamour and edging away from familiarity. Performing in an unpretentious place, for listeners who had paid half a dollar or less to be there, the musicians were chosen for competence and availability, not charisma or fame. Would evenings like these influence the postwar concert hall? Might audiences be led to welcome more of the current musical supply? Was it still reasonable to expect the concert hall to do justice to the classical sphere as it now existed in the United States? And if not, what alternatives might be found?

These questions mapped out the territory in which composers in the United States worked after the war. And the ways they were answered did much to shape the classical sphere for the rest of the century.

THE UNITED STATES AFTER WORLD WAR II

As the leader of a force triumphant in both Europe and Asia, the United States in 1946 stood as the world's chief military power. And as manufacturers turned from weapons to new cars and new houses, the domestic economy began growing at an unprecedented rate. Public attitude was generally upbeat. Thousands of military veterans returned to school, supported by the GI "Bill of Rights." Perhaps the most telling social trend of the postwar era, however, was the increase in marriage rates and fertility; births rose from less than 2 million per year before the war to 3.8 million in 1947 and then edged higher, topping 4 million in every year between 1954 and 1964. Feeling more optimistic than their parents' generation, more and more young adults married, bought houses, and started families.[3]

But even as peace and prosperity promised a bright future, other legacies of the war clouded the postwar mood. One was the atom bomb, a symbol of American superiority in science and the dangers of scientific progress. In

August 1945, two bombs, one dropped on the city of Hiroshima and the other on Nagasaki, killed at least 135,000 Japanese and led to the enemy's surrender. Americans had discovered a way to destroy the world as a place where human beings could live. How would this power be controlled in the future?

Other outcomes of the war complicated the answer to that question. The Soviet Union, a wartime ally, now occupied much of Eastern Europe, and governments taking orders from the Communist regime in Moscow were set up in these countries against their will. Peace seemed even more fragile after 1949, when the Soviets began testing their own atom bombs. By this time, fear of communism pervaded American political life. From 1950 until 1953, U.S. soldiers fought in Korea in a conflict that started as a civil war but soon involved troops from China, which in 1949 had itself been taken over by a Communist regime. The sweetness of victory in 1945 had turned sour on the international front as the United States found itself in a global cold war. Moreover, the Nazi attempt to rid Europe of Jews—the Holocaust— left faith in human nature itself badly shaken. Evil on this scale was unprecedented in known human experience.

The war's aftermath brought new contradictions and ambiguities into American life. On one hand stood hopeful expectations, on the other, ominous doubts. The war's end also weakened the need for citizens to pull together. Peace and prosperity invited a growing emphasis on individual goals and the gratification of personal desires. With no crisis to focus on, Americans were free to pay more attention to their discontents. For example, World War II had brought many middle-class women into the workplace, but the GI Bill treated women's working role as temporary. The access it gave men to higher education ensured them a dominant place in the high-tech postwar economy. And the baby boom, together with the growth of suburbs, where life revolved around domesticity, created new pressures on American families that were borne chiefly by wives and mothers.

Peace and material abundance led in postwar America to a rising standard of living, and also to social restlessness. International unrest, fed by fears of annihilation and knowledge that a civilized culture like Germany's had allowed terrible atrocities, made the world seem precarious. The conflicting realities of prosperity and anxiety, of wealth and discontent, of moral purpose and corruption, led many postwar artists and intellectuals to a pessimistic outlook. On the international front, new enemies replaced old; at home, Americans were increasingly becoming conscious that there was no adversary more to be feared than the evil within themselves.

SCHOOLS, PATRONAGE, COMPOSERS, AND THE CONCERT HALL

With several leading European composers now living on American soil, the United States no longer seemed a provincial outpost of European musical life. Home-grown classical performers—soprano Eleanor Steber, conductor-composer Leonard Bernstein, and pianist William Kappell, for example—also contributed to that impression. And a growing number of professional schools were now serving the classical sphere, from conservatories to colleges and university departments that expanded their programs as military veterans returned to civilian life. High-level instruction was expanded partly in the spirit of edification and partly in the spirit of democratic access.

Teachers also benefited from Americans' support for music instruction. In a nation whose government offered no direct patronage, teaching subsidized musical activity that could not pay for itself. Such private universities as Harvard, Yale, and Columbia and tax-supported institutions as Indiana University, the Universities of Illinois and Michigan, and North Texas State University set up professional programs for aspiring performers, composers, teachers, and writers on music. Their curricula reflected the classical sphere's pedigree: students studied the history and theory of Western art music and received performance instruction chiefly in those repertories. Behind such endeavors, many faculty members also worked as scholars, composers, and performers. Their professional involvement was accepted because it was carried on in the name of education. More than any other calling, teaching has stretched the framework of musical employment in the United States, overlapping with, infusing, and in some cases subsuming other occupations for which demand has been less direct. By the mid-twentieth century, many musicians were finding college-level teaching a way to buy time for work of their own.

Performances are the main things musicians have to sell, and the classical sphere's primary marketplace has long been the concert hall: the infrastructure of orchestra and recital halls, opera houses, and the local, regional, and national agencies that recruit their customers. Composers in America have never played more than a small role in that marketplace; their postwar role may be shown by probing links between the concert hall and academic institutions. In these years, while academic musicians worked in the name of education, the concert hall framed its choices in the name of art. To make a general audience's artistic experience top priority was different from organizing musical experience to pass on to students. Engaging with the same tradition from a different point of view, the academy, while still tied to the work of the concert hall, diversified during the postwar

Five of America's leading classical composers of the postwar era were photographed
studiously avoiding each other's gaze: (from left) Samuel Barber, Virgil Thomson,
Aaron Copland, Gian Carlo Menotti, and William Schuman.

years into subdisciplines that together added up to an independent force.
Grounded in a changing conception of music history, some branches of the
academy welcomed the study and performance of repertories (pre-Bach and
modern) that the concert hall had excluded. And in a nation where home-
grown classical composers had long been culturally marginal and economically superfluous, the academy made living composers and their music part
of its institutional framework.

To understand where living composers fit in the postwar classical sphere,
it may be helpful to distinguish the composer's profession from the composer's role and place. The first remained largely a matter of survival. As
had been true since the 1790s, the profession of composer—a writer of
composers' music, in which scores provide the main authority for performances—was still linked only indirectly to a livelihood. Almost all postwar
classical composers earned their keep doing something else, especially
teaching. The rise of the academy brought a new commitment to supporting

the composer's role. Private patronage expanded to include support from foundations. And the federal government finally started funding composers directly after 1965, when the National Foundation on the Arts and Humanities was created. These programs indicated a respect for the composer's role in America and a democratic reluctance to favor particular individuals. If the role of composers grew more secure in the postwar world, however, their place in society remained small, and the shadow they cast in the American concert hall hard to detect. Composers were regularly commissioned to write new works for orchestras, chamber ensembles, recitalists, and opera companies, but as repeat performances were rare, few of these works entered the concert-hall repertory. Aspiring to be treated as artists whose works were heard, reheard, discussed, analyzed, and perhaps even relished, composers existed in the postwar concert hall more as representatives of a prestigious vocation.

The striking imbalance among the honored role, the neglected place, and the almost nonexistent profession of the American classical composer reflects society's acceptance in principle for what composers do but little interest in the results. In the decades after World War II, supported in large part by the academy, complemented by patronage in the form of commissions, prizes, and fellowships, new composers' music gained listeners more readily outside than inside the concert hall, thanks to an academic environment that began to share some features with scientific laboratories.

The lab analogy is borrowed from Milton Babbitt, who in 1958 likened himself and other "specialist" composers to theoretical mathematicians and physicists. Noting that nobody expects laypeople to understand these esoteric disciplines, Babbitt maintained that the music he wrote could only be grasped by listeners who had prepared themselves.[4] His comments point to a development with important consequences: some composers were claiming professional autonomy—the right to compose outside the strictures of general audience esteem, or critics' approval, or the skills of all but a few performers. Once composers had freed themselves from the need to engage with any but a specialist audience, they could develop their craft and ideas about music for their own sake, in the manner of researchers. At that point, the gap between the concert hall and the composer widened into a true split. From the specialist composer's point of view, the concert hall now looked more like foreign territory, an embodiment of commercial values and fear of new experience.

The concert hall in the 1920s and 30s, the one institution where the priorities of composers, performers, critics, impresarios, and audiences all had to be considered and reconciled, remained the chief public embodiment of the classical sphere. The academy's emergence after World War II challenged that position. As university teachers rewrote music history, and examples of specialized new music multiplied, the concert hall looked increasingly like part of a historical age that might be winding down. The academy could afford its new perspective by ignoring impresarios and the general audience—both key constituencies of the concert hall, which relied on the public for economic support. The notion that music written for specialist listeners might also be historically significant was one outcome of the academy's challenge to the concert hall. That idea could only have come from a quarter where the economics of public presentation was considered unimportant. To a large extent, composition in postwar America reflects the split of a more-or-less unified hierarchy, built around the concert hall, into complementary venues with different preferences and goals.

POSTWAR COMPOSITION

There is little question that the postwar academic environment steered some composers toward approaches that could be rationally explained. Foremost among these was the serial approach invented by Arnold Schoenberg in Vienna in the early 1920s, grounded in intellectual control. The first and most basic form of serialism is found in twelve-tone music, in which the composer orders all twelve pitches of the chromatic scale into a particular sequence, or series, also called the tone row. Here, twelve-tone technique substitutes for major-minor tonality, which Schoenberg abandoned around 1910, believing that music had long been evolving toward total chromaticism. Serialism offers a way to order pitches systematically without the gravitational pull of key centers.

Schoenberg rarely used the row to outline themes, employing it instead as an abstract structure for music in which all twelve pitches are equally important. A pitch could be sustained or even repeated; but once left, it was to be sounded again only after the other eleven pitches were heard. The twelve-tone technique's abstract character is also reflected in the ways Schoenberg brought variety into his rigorous use of pitch. As well as its principal, or prime, form (P), the row could be used in retrograde (R, which reverses the prime form's order), in inverted form (I, which reverses the direction of the intervals), and in retrograde inversion (RI, which reverses the order and inverts the intervals). Each of these forms could also be transposed to any of the other eleven pitches, offering the composer forty-eight forms of the row to work with.

While the twelve-tone technique's mathematical basis cannot be denied, composers have approached it in many different ways. Wallingford Riegger, whose first twelve-tone works date from 1931, won a prize in 1948 with his Third Symphony, which boasts serially organized themes. Roger Sessions, who taught composition at the University of California and Princeton, also employed the twelve-tone technique. Believing with Schoenberg that certain historical laws were "inherent in the nature of music itself," Sessions had been moving since the 1930s toward a more chromatic style.[5] In 1953, he wrote a Violin Sonata whose opening theme contained twelve different pitches; "I caught myself using the twelve-tone system," Sessions later reported.[6] Aaron Copland also explored twelve-tone technique in works of the postwar era—especially the *Quartet for Piano and Strings* (1950) and the *Piano Fantasy* (1957). The most dramatic proof of serialism's postwar reach, however, came from Igor Stravinsky, long considered the polar opposite of Schoenberg. In the early 1950s, Stravinsky discovered the music of Schoenberg's pupil Anton Webern and began writing twelve-tone music himself.

Yet perhaps no musician seized more eagerly than Milton Babbitt on the system-building potential of twelve-tone technique. Trained as a mathematician, and teaching both composition and music theory at Princeton University, Babbitt found beauty in the idea of a system of rationally ordered sounds. He took as his starting point the work of European composers (Schoenberg, Webern, and Alban Berg) who, when he began his own career in the 1930s, were still radical outsiders in the concert hall and the classical sphere in general. Babbitt extended his predecessors' innovations by serializing nonpitch elements as well: rhythm, dynamics, timbre, and register. His works were realizations of elaborate precompositional plans, based not only on tone rows but on patterns derived from them to order other musical elements. Babbitt's extensions of the serial principle produced music whose network of internal connections and relationships was formidably complex, despite such plain titles as *Three Compositions for Piano* (1947) and *Composition for Four Instruments* (1948). Indeed, those complex relationships are the essence of Babbitt's music. Having committed himself to opening up new frontiers of musical structure and perception, Babbitt did not hesitate to criticize uninformed listeners who judged his music by whether or not they liked the sound. Moreover, his passion for musical complexity and intellectual control would lead him during the late 1950s to reach beyond conventional instruments and live performance into the realm of electronic sound.

Serialism and its extensions broadened the possibilities for making and structuring musical sound. If a musical Rip Van Winkle had fallen asleep in 1940 and awakened twenty years later, the varieties of new music would surely have surprised him. What prewar commentators had sometimes lumped together as an "atonal school" had developed by 1960 into a range of idioms—freely chromatic, twelve-tone, systematically serialized, electronic, chance-based, or combinations thereof—with only atonality in common. Schoenberg's "emancipation of the dissonance" was now fully on display in the United States, as composers explored ways to make music out of previously excluded sounds. In tandem with the opening up of academic positions, this emancipation brought fresh energy and excitement to the contemporary music scene.

While composers who were exploring atonality took intellectual leadership in the postwar classical sphere, their music was most apt to be heard outside the traditional concert hall, especially in festivals devoted to new music. Yet new works featuring triads, tonal centers, and tuneful melodies had certainly not disappeared. The composers of such music often combined these traits with melodic angularity, harmonic dissonance, rhythmic asymmetry, and an expanded range of sound to express the unsettled temper of the times. Their place in the classical sphere is reflected in the list of winners of the Pulitzer Prize in music. The first was awarded in 1943, to a cantata by William Schuman, followed by a Howard Hanson symphony (1944) and in 1945 by Aaron Copland's *Appalachian Spring*. During the two postwar decades, only one atonal work—Elliott Carter's String Quartet No. 2 (1960)—won the prize. Awards in other years went to Charles Ives's Symphony No. 3 (in 1947, composed four decades earlier in a tuneful idiom); symphonies by Walter Piston; operas by Gian Carlo Menotti, Samuel Barber, Robert Ward, and Douglas Moore; and a film score by Virgil Thomson.

While works like these were representing contemporary American music in concert halls and opera houses, a small but influential academic establishment took shape on the East Coast, focused on atonality. In 1962, *Perspectives of New Music*, a journal funded by the Fromm Music Foundation, began publication out of an office in the Princeton University music department. The journal, which owed much to Babbitt's theorizing, spoke primarily for a group that linked aesthetic worth to complex analytical and compositional systems. And from the perspective of that circle, the concert hall's need for broad consensus made it seem an old-fashioned institution with little taste for artistic adventure.

Against this background of opposing outlooks and fragmented institutions, Elliott Carter emerged during the 1950s as a unique figure: a respected composer who worked his way toward a more and more complex atonal musical style while steering clear of musical systems. A native New Yorker born in 1908, Carter had grown up in the neighborhood where Charles Ives lived, attended concerts with him as a teenager, and came to know Ives well as a musician (see Chapter 25). Carter studied at Harvard College from 1926 to 1932, then went to Paris to continue his schooling in the liberal arts while also studying music with Nadia Boulanger. His works of the 1930s were generally considered "neoclassical," but after the war he began writing music of marked individuality: a piano sonata (1946), a sonata for cello and piano (1948), and his first string quartet (1951). From the piano sonata on, each new work by Carter seemed, at least to admirers, a daring

Elliott Carter (b. 1908) in the early 1970s outside Lincoln Center in New York.

advance in his development as a composer. And in 1962, Carter's music received a compliment that boosted his already solid reputation: Stravinsky, whose age, eminence, and acerbic views had made him an imposing presence on the musical scene, pronounced Carter's Double Concerto for piano, harpsichord, and small orchestra a masterpiece.

By the time Stravinsky's tribute was published (in a book of dialogues with conductor Robert Craft), Carter had already won distinction beyond the Pulitzer Prize, though his recent music remained unknown to the public at large. His innovative use of rhythm had drawn particular attention. Carter had worked out a way to change rhythm or tempo through a technique dubbed "metric modulation," which allowed the music to progress smoothly and with precise accuracy from one metronomic speed to another. In a 1959 visit to Princeton, Carter was invited to discuss metric modulation and other aspects of compositional craft. Urging his audience not to overemphasize matters of technique, Carter instead offered a cautionary view of recent musical developments. "One technical fad after another has swept over 20th-century music as the music of each of its leading composers has come to be intimately known," he warned. "Each fad lasted a few years, only to be discarded by the succeeding generation of composers, then by the music profession, and finally by certain parts of the interested public." Carter went on:

> Each of the trends of our recent past—primitivism, machinism, neo-Classicism, *Gebrauchsmusik,* the styles of Bartók and Berg, and now those of Schoenberg and Webern—has left and will leave in its trail numbers of really gifted composers whose music, skillful and effective as it is, is suffocated, at least for a time, by its similarity to other music of the same type. . . . The tendency to fad has been greatly encouraged by the promulgation of systems, particularly harmonic systems. . . . This kind of intellectual publicity can lead to a dead end even more quickly than the older fads derived from the actual sound of music.[7]

By calling recent stylistic trends fads, Carter was criticizing not the styles themselves but the tendency to employ them without the full commitment that a musical style demands of a composer. In his view, a composer's style ought to be grounded in a realm of irreducible artistic identity, beyond the reach of fashion or careerist aspiration. Indeed, Carter's belief that system and technique were means and not ends recalls the distinction that Ives, his first mentor, made between manner and substance. From a position outside the academy, Carter, whose independent income spared him the need to earn a living apart from being a composer, had learned that modern academic discourse was no more immune to trendiness than the views of concert-

hall critics. As for Carter's own music, its formidable complexity resisted explanation by any current theoretical system.

Half a century after its composition, Carter's String Quartet No. 1 seems
on its way to becoming part of the standard chamber music repertory. It is
also a work Carter has singled out as crucial to his own development as a
composer. "Up to this time," he wrote in 1970, "I had quite consciously been
trying to write for a certain audience—not that which frequented concerts
of traditional music, nor that which had supported the avant-garde of the
'20s (which in the '40s had come to seem elitist) but a new, more progressive
and more popular audience." In writing this work, however, he turned his
focus back on himself as a listener. As a well-schooled, experienced composer, Carter reasoned, the time had come to trust his own "private judgment of comprehensibility and quality," using his long-standing dedication
to "advanced" music as a starting point.

While preparing to compose the quartet, Carter, a close student of modern literature, found himself contemplating the question of "humanly experienced time" as imagined by German novelist Thomas Mann. In *The Magic
Mountain*, Mann writes: "It would not be hard to imagine the existence of
creatures, perhaps upon smaller planets than ours, practising a miniature
time-economy. . . . And, contrariwise, one can conceive of a world so spacious that its time system too has a majestic stride." The First Quartet is a
commentary on the passing of time itself, especially in the realm of dreams.
But how might one compose music whose subject is time, and the experiencing of time, in more spacious and majestic ways? Part of Carter's answer
was to abandon a steady beat and unchanging meter, standard devices
sometimes taken to represent clock time. Another was to "personalize" the
instruments in the hope that listeners might hear in their lack of synchrony
a conversation among contrasting musical voices. The result of Carter's
imaginative leaps is music whose emphasis on motion, change, and progression lead away from repetition and toward "many-layered contrasts of character—hence of theme or motive, rhythm, and styles of playing." In the
First Quartet, each instrument establishes its own character and rate of
speed, confronting listeners with a formidable complexity of texture.

In addition to Thomas Mann's ruminations on time, an idea from French
author Jean Cocteau's film *Le sang d'un poète* also helped to inspire the First
Quartet. This "dream-like" film is framed "by an interrupted slow-motion
shot of a tall brick chimney in an empty lot being dynamited. Just as the
chimney begins to fall apart, the shot is broken off and the entire movie follows, after which the shot of the chimney is resumed at the point it left off,
showing its disintegration in mid-air, and closing the film with its collapse
on the ground." With this effect in mind, the First Quartet begins with a ca-

denza for cello that is soon interrupted by the entrance of the other instruments, launching the main body of a work divided into three movements. At the very end of the third, a solo violin picks up where the beginning cello cadenza had long ago broken off, and the work ends quietly. In Carter's scenario, the cello and violin statements frame the quarter's main body, itself circular in the manner of many works of modern literature. Its "interlocked presentation of ideas parallels many characteristic devices" found in James Joyce and others, he writes: "the controlled 'stream of consciousness,' the 'epiphany,' the many uses of punctuation," and "grammatical ambiguities," including quotations from the music of Ives and of American composer Conlon Nancarrow. As in Cocteau's film, moreover, "the internal dream time" of the three long sections is imagined to last "but a moment" as the present world reckons external time.[8] In trying to follow Carter's complex musical textures, listeners may find it helpful to imagine that the composer has divided his authority among four performing rivals.

If Elliott Carter grounded his inspiration in humanistic modernism, another widely shared postwar impulse came from science. As early as 1917, Franco-American composer Edgard Varèse had proclaimed: "I dream of instruments obedient to my thought," able to capture "the exigencies of my inner rhythm." Two decades later, Varèse imagined the impact of technological progress on music he might compose in the future:

> When new instruments will allow me to write music as I conceive it, the movement of sound-masses, of shifting planes, will be clearly perceived in my work, taking the place of the linear counterpoint. When these sound-masses collide, the phenomena of penetration or repulsion will seem to occur. Certain transmutations taking place on certain planes will seem to be projected onto other planes, moving at different speeds and at different angles. There will no longer be the old conception of melody or interplay of melodies. The entire work will be a melodic totality.[9]

Varèse was one of many composers who in the century's earlier years dreamed of what is now called electroacoustic music, music made or altered electrically. Progress was slow until the magnetic tape recorder was perfected in the late 1940s; from then on, electroacoustic music came into its own. An international survey published in 1974 estimated that more than 2,000 composers, working in some 500 electronic music studios, had by then produced more than 10,000 electronic compositions, not to mention their wide use in popular genres.[10] The trends outlined in this survey have persisted into the 1990s: the increasing variety of sounds produced by electroacoustic music, the capacity to imitate standard instruments, and the technology's accessibility and appeal. Moreover, with one instrument able to

Edgard Varèse (1883–1965), French-born American composer, listening in 1959 to his *Poème électronique.*

produce the sound of many, the demand for acoustic music and its performers has dropped.

In the fall of 1952, two faculty members at Columbia University, Otto Luening and Vladimir Ussachevsky, presented the first American tape-music concert at the Museum of Modern Art in New York. The equipment used by these pioneering composers could hardly have been more different from the standard "hardware" of a musical education: tape recorders, a generator of sound signals, devices for filtering sound, scissors, razor blade, splicing block, and magnetic tape. Western music making had always involved some practical knowledge of acoustics—the science of the production, propagation, and perception of sound—but that knowledge centered on conventional instruments. Electroacoustic music posed different challenges. A new sound palette was available; but to control it required knowledge and experience that few musicians possessed. A concert stage filled with sound equipment rather than live performers carried a suggestion that

Milton Babbitt (b. 1917) at the RCA synthesizer.

technology's power might be outstripping humans' ability to govern it. How would the spatial properties of electronic sound affect compositional practice? Would long-held aesthetic principles such as the need to balance unity and variety still be useful to composers? Was technology bringing the art of music into a new age of heightened, extended human perception?

Although Varèse was nearing seventy when the technology he had imagined came into general use in the 1950s, he based two major works of that decade on electroacoustic sounds. *Déserts* (1954), written for twenty instrumentalists—piano, fourteen winds, and five percussionists—and a two-track tape, contrasts the different sound sources rather than blending them. The work is cast in a large **ABACABA** form, alternating live music (**A**) with taped and modified factory sounds (**B**), and revolving around a center section of taped and modified percussion sounds (**C**). In contrast to *Déserts*, written for concert-hall performance, Varèse conceived *Poème électronique* (1957–58), his last finished work, with a particular building in mind: a pavilion at the Brussels World's Fair of 1959. Collaborating with the eminent Swiss architect Le Corbusier, Varèse realized his longtime dream of creating music to exist in space as well as time. The work was tape-recorded and then played through 425 loudspeakers, arranged so that the sound could sweep across and around the curves of Le Corbusier's building. Varèse's achievement proved fleeting, however, for the pavilion was torn down after the fair closed.[11]

Composers of electroacoustic music in the early 1950s faced huge amounts of tedious labor: recording sounds on magnetic tape, rerecording them, and then manually splicing the bits of tape together to create the music itself. In 1959, however, the Radio Corporation of America installed in the Columbia University studio the Mark II, an advanced model of an electronic sound synthesizer that became the heart of the Columbia-Princeton Electronic Music Center, directed by Luening, Ussachevsky, and Babbitt. The synthesizer, which constituted and shaped the sounds, did away with the need to rerecord and to splice tape. Further, an instrument able to control precisely such elements as rhythm, dynamics, and timbre as well as pitch was perfectly suited to Babbitt's ideal of totally organized music. He used the Mark II to create his *Composition for Synthesizer* (1961) and *Ensembles for Synthesizer* (1964). He also combined live performance with synthesized sound in such works as *Vision and Prayer* (1961) and *Philomel* (1964).

The latter work was commissioned by soprano Bethany Beardslee, a contemporary music specialist, as part of a Ford Foundation program in which solo performers were invited to request pieces by composers of their choice. Sung to words by contemporary poet John Hollander, *Philomel* unites modern text with electronic wizardry and the skills of a virtuoso singer to offer a new version of an ancient myth. Philomela and Procne are daughters of the King of Athens. Procne, the wife of King Tereus of Thrace, asks Tereus to bring her sister Philomela from Athens for a visit. On the journey, the king grows enchanted with the grace and beauty of Philomela. Overcome by lust, he rapes her, then cuts out her tongue to guarantee her silence. After imprisoning Philomela in a secluded Thracian cottage, he tells Procne that her sister has died on the voyage. Philomela, however, weaves a tapestry depicting Tereus's crime and sends it to Procne, who correctly interprets its message. Procne rescues Philomela, and the two return to Athens. The sisters than avenge the rape by inviting Tereus to a banquet and serving him the cooked flesh of his own son. When Tereus discovers what he has eaten, he pursues the sisters into the forest. The gods protect Philomela by turning her into a nightingale.

Hollander's text is sung by the character Philomela, accompanied by the recorded voice of Beardslee and a score of synthesized sound. The work starts with Philomela fleeing her pursuer in the forest. Alternating with the tape, she tries out syllables, then forms words suggesting sounds in the name "Tereus." In the second section, which follows her transformation into a nightingale, she sings an "Echo Song," asking other birds—a thrush, a hawk, an owl, a raven, and a gull—for help in adjusting to her new form. But each request brings a refusal from the echoing tape. Finally, in the third section, Philomela finds her own true voice and, in Hollander's words, begins to reign "over a kingdom of song." Babbitt's score places great demands on the singer, who must speak as well as negotiating a range from F-sharp below middle C to B above the staff, and act as well as sing.

Although Varèse, Babbitt, and others explored the new medium vigorously during the 1950s, John Cage was the first American to complete a tape composition: *Imaginary Landscape No. 5* (1952). And later that year, Cage composed *Williams Mix*, a major work that lasts only four minutes and fifteen seconds. The example shows one page of the *Williams Mix* score, whose eight lines represent an eight-track reel-to-reel tape that runs at fifteen inches per second.

Cage began work on *Williams Mix* by gathering a "library" of sounds and dividing them into six categories. The letters on Cage's score indicate the

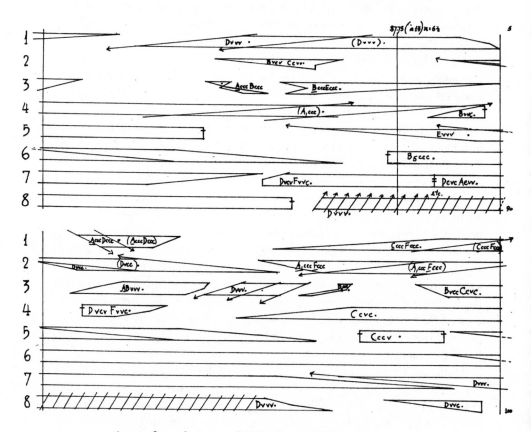

A page from the score of John Cage's *Williams Mix* (1952).

John Cage (1912–1992), composer and explorer of unintended sounds.

different sound categories; the shapes show how the tape was cut and spliced. Track 1 on this page, for example, begins with a D (manually produced) sound that gives way to a bit of A (city) sound mixed with D. After a brief silence, C (electronic) sound is mixed with F (small) sound. Underlined capital letters signify sounds that are given a patterned rhythm by rerecording a loop of tape. And sound categories are further modified by the small letters "c" and "v" that follow each capital. The first means that the sound has been controlled—from the standpoint of pitch, timbre (sound quality), and loudness. The second means that the sound has not been controlled. For track 1, for example, the first instruction, "Dvvv," calls for a manually produced sound whose pitch, timbre, and loudness have not been catalogued.

Cage produced the score by a process designed to bypass personal preference. Once the sounds were catalogued, his work focused on finding a system of choice that guaranteed random ordering. That system involved charts, chance, and the *I-Ching* (the Chinese *Book of Changes*, which Cage had encountered when he began to study Zen Buddhism in the late 1940s). The sounds were chosen by consulting sixteen charts built around the six sound categories with their controlled and uncontrolled permutations. The charts were constructed out of numbers arrived at by tossing coins and keeping track of the results (heads or tails), and the numbers were interpreted and transferred to the charts by consulting the *I-Ching*. If *Williams Mix* sounds like a random collection of sounds, that is exactly what Cage intended.

Williams Mix united Cage's interest in technology with a new philosophical outlook he adopted in the early 1950s. The philosophy, religion, and art of the West assumed that humans, created in the image of God, were destined to rule over nature. From a non-Western perspective, however, human beings were simply one of many species of life, and nature itself tended more toward randomness than order. The cumbersome process of composition that lay behind *Williams Mix*—255 seconds of music that took Cage and collaborators nine months to create—was inspired by a principle found in Indian philosophy: "Art is the imitation of Nature in her manner of operation."[12]

In Cage's earlier days, he had assumed that the opposite of sound was silence, and that duration was the one component of sound that could be measured against silence. That premise led him to believe that only duration offered a valid basis for musical structure. Then one day in 1951, Cage entered an anechoic chamber (one free from echoes), prepared to experience total silence. But what he in fact heard was the high sound of his nervous system in operation and the lower sound of his blood circulating. That lesson changed Cage's conception of sound. Having formerly understood the human situation as "objective," with sounds and silences alternating, he now saw it as "subjective," where sounds were always present, some intended and others not. Music had long been practiced as an art of intended sounds. But if one embraced unintended ones as well, the consequences could be profound. By refusing to discriminate between intention and nonintention, Cage also recognized that such binary formulations as "art-life" also disappeared, leading the way to sound itself rather than ideas about sound.[13] Once Cage decided that there was no real split between intention and nonintention, he avidly explored the latter. Much of his creative energy went toward setting up mechanical procedures that would bring sounds into compositions independent of his own will, hence with no deliberate link to other sounds.

4′33″, Cage's most famous work, was composed the same year as *Williams Mix* but emulated nature's manner of operation in an entirely different way. Conceived as a three-movement structure whose proportions— 30‴, 2′23″, and 1′40″—were determined by chance methods, 4′33″ prescribed no intentional sounds at all. Cage's "silent" piece invited listeners to pay attention to ambient sounds in the environment, in effect emptying themselves so that, following the injunction of Goethe's Meister Eckhart, they were ready to receive "the hidden word." Among other things, 4′33″could be viewed as a spiritual exercise, a means of quieting the will so that an infinite realm of possibilities may be experienced.[14]

It is no surprise that the concert hall rejected these ideas. Still, Cage had never counted on the concert hall for much support, nor did he enter academia. From almost the start of his composing career, he managed to scrape together a living by collaborating with other artists, chiefly dancers. Many of his percussion works of the 1930s were written as dance pieces. In the 1940s, he served as accompanist for a dance company headed by Merce Cunningham, later becoming its music director (1953). The early 1950s found him involved in another collaboration—the privately funded Project for Music for Magnetic Tape—that included composers such as Morton Feldman (*Intersection*), Christian Wolff (*For Magnetic Tape*), Earle Brown (*Octet*), and David Tudor. Cage was the central figure in this group, sometimes referred to as the "New York School," all of whom remained in close contact between 1950 and 1954. By introducing the other four composers to Cunningham, who used their scores for his dances, Cage lent important assistance to his collaborators. In 1949, moreover, he had traveled to Europe and established a friendship with the French composer Pierre Boulez. A lively correspondence between the two took place over the next several years, as Cage was able to secure more European performances for his music and that of several New York colleagues. Meanwhile, at home Cage had also become a friend and champion of the painters Robert Rauschenberg and Jasper Johns, whose rise to fame as members of the New York School of Abstract Expressionism would help to further Cage's own work, though indirectly. Many years later, the composer Lou Harrison, a longtime colleague and friend of Cage, told an interviewer: "I hesitate to say this . . . but John liked famous people."[15]

One of Cage's most notorious collaborations took place at Black Mountain College in North Carolina in August 1952. Inspired by writings of the French surrealist poet and theatrical theorist Antonin Artaud, Cage created *Black Mountain Piece*, a theatrical experience that was a precursor of the "happenings" of the 1960s. The event was held in the college dining room, with chairs set up in the middle for the audience. Though no written scenario survives, a report has been compiled of what people who were there remembered about the first and only performance:

> Cage was located: standing on a step ladder/sitting on a step ladder/at a raised lectern to one side of the room; where he was reading the Bill of Rights/a lecture from Meister Eckhart/the Declaration of Independence;
>
> Charles Olson read poetry from a ladder/was "planted" in the audience, standing up and saying a line or two at the appropriate times/talked or laughed on cue from the audience;

Hanging from the rafters were: [Robert] Rauschenberg's white paintings /Rauschenberg's black paintings/a recent painting by Franz Kline;

Nick Cernovich (and perhaps dance student Tim LaFarge) projected movies and slides on the walls. Some recall images of the school cook, then the sun, and, as the image moved from the ceiling down the wall, the sun sank; others are sure only abstract images were used;

Merce Cunningham danced around, in the middle of, and through the audience (a dog apparently joined in and followed Cunningham around for a time);

David Tudor played piano and/or a radio;

M[ary] C[atherine] Richards read poetry (perhaps Edna St. Vincent Millay); and may have recited from a ladder as well;

Robert Rauschenberg played scratchy records on an old wind-up phonograph with horn loudspeaker;

student Jay Watt performed a musical work in a corner using some of Lou Harrison's Asian instruments;

at the conclusion of the event, cups, which had been placed upon all the seats before the performance began, were filled with coffee by girls (or in some accounts, boys) dressed in white. Many of the cups had been dirtied in the course of the event with ashes and cigarette butts but were filled with coffee nonetheless.[16]

As news of events such as this one spread, so did Cage's notoriety—if not as a composer then as either a gag artist or satirist, or perhaps a musical anarchist working to undermine the foundations of Western musical endeavor. These opinions persisted well into the 1960s and, in some quarters, even up to Cage's death in 1992. Yet, though often scorned and attacked, Cage also found himself in increasing demand as a lecturer and performer. In Europe, under Cage's influence, the German composer Karlheinz Stockhausen began in the mid-1950s to experiment with chance operations. Many younger Americans—including Dick Higgins, Jackson MacLow, and others who took Cage's courses at the New School for Social Research in New York during the 1950s, and Gordon Mumma, Robert Ashley, and other members of the Ann Arbor ONCE group in the early 1960s—took his example as a jumping-off point for work of their own. *Silence* (1961), the first of several compilations of Cage's lectures and writings, established him as a significant writer on music; winning a wide readership, it has remained in print to this day.

In public, however, Cage's works sometimes provoked open disrespect. The performance of the *Concert for Piano and Orchestra* at Cage's Twenty-Five-Year Retrospective concert in New York's Town Hall (1958) sparked a noisy response that was recorded for posterity. In an even more infamous display in 1961, the performers themselves produced much of the disturbance. Leonard Bernstein and the New York Philharmonic Orchestra commissioned a work entitled *Atlas Eclipticalis*, but the premiere was a disaster during which many audience members walked out. In later performances, members of the orchestra actually hissed the composer. Cage himself later told an interviewer that the New York Philharmonic was "a bad orchestra. They're like a group of gangsters. . . . They would tear the microphones off the instruments and stamp on them, and the next day I would then have to buy new ones to replace them for the next performance."[17]

That such behavior led to no strong retaliation or outrage shows that Cage was still considered a marginal figure in the early 1960s. Indeed, that fact is not surprising, for music in the Western world has long been considered an art of expression, and Cage wrote his last "intentionally expressive" music in 1951. As he later explained: "I had been taught in the schools that art was a question of communication. I observed that all of the composers were writing differently. If art was communication, we were using different languages. We were, therefore, in a Tower of Babel situation where no one understood anyone else." Against that background, Cage discovered in early texts from both East and West what he considered a better reason to compose music than either expression or communication: "to quiet the mind thus making it susceptible to divine influences."[18] In a 1957 address to the Music Teachers National Association (MTNA) on "Experimental Music," he ended with the following paragraph, part or all of which has often been quoted as the essence of his composing philosophy:

> And what is the purpose of writing music? One is, of course, not dealing with purposes but dealing with sounds. Or the answer must take the form of paradox: a purposeful purposelessness or a purposeless play. This play, however, is an affirmation of life—not an attempt to bring order out of chaos nor to suggest improvements in creation, but simply a way of waking up to the very life we're living, which is so excellent once one gets one's mind and one's desires out of its way and lets it act of its own accord.[19]

This statement's affirmative tone, counseling an acceptance of life as it is, may at first make these words seem less subversive than they actually are. In fact, however, the notion of replacing intellectual analysis and the pursuit of one's desires with "purposeless play" offers a radical prescription for emptying the mind, in contrast to academic instruction and the Western musical tradition itself, which both strive to fill it. On the strength of that liberating prescription, Cage was often proclaimed, as the millennium approached, a key figure in twentieth-century music.

In 1959, Igor Stravinsky (center, foreground) conducted a New York performance of his earlier work *The Wedding*, with composers (left to right) Samuel Barber, Lukas Foss, Aaron Copland, and Roger Sessions as Pianists.

EPILOGUE

On April 6, 1964, a musical work was premiered in California whose symbolic weight belies both its brevity (barely ninety seconds long) and the small size of its forces (baritone voice and three clarinets). *Elegy for J.F.K.*, composed by the eighty-one-year-old Igor Stravinsky, mourned the assassination of November 22, 1963, of President John F. Kennedy. The premiere, conducted by Robert Craft, took place in Santa Monica at the Monday Evening Concerts, which continued the Evenings on the Roof series that Peter Yates and Frances Mullen had established in 1939. Stravinsky, who died in 1971, filled a key place in postwar American musical life as the survivor of an era governed by musical axioms that commanded general agreement because they seemed historically necessary. In fact, his embrace of twelve-tone technique in the early 1950s had raised the stock of serialism in some circles to near-axiomatic status. And the *Elegy* seemed a fitting gesture: the Russian-born master, long an American citizen, composing music to mark the death of the nation's leader.

Yet even while noting the *Elegy*, a historical observer cannot miss the widening range of styles that would soon overwhelm the idea of historical necessity. It is true that serialism and atonality were well established in the classical sphere. But so were diatonic approaches, as practiced by Samuel Barber, whose *Antony and Cleopatra* opened New York's new Metropolitan Opera House in 1966, and William Schuman, who continued composing after assuming the presidency in 1962 of Lincoln Center for the Performing Arts. In April 1965, Charles Ives's Symphony No. 4, composed between 1910 and 1916, was heard in full for the first time. That event enriched the context for considering Henry Cowell, Harry Partch, Lou Harrison, Conlon Nancarrow, and John Cage himself as part of an American "experimental" tradition, breaking ranks with the European past. Electroacoustic possibilities were also being explored. And in 1964, Terry Riley composed *In C*, whose obsessive repetition of simple diatonic fragments outlined a style that was soon labeled "minimalist." Finally, with only Igor Stravinsky left from a past when great composers were thought to define the heart of musical endeavor, other kinds of music were also challenging the classical sphere's place atop the nation's musical hierarchy.

34

Rock Around the Clock

The Rise of Rock and Roll

IN 1959, A PRESTIGIOUS UNIVERSITY PRESS published a book of essays called *The Art of Jazz*, a title meant to make a statement. The critical response an artistic activity received, the editor told his readers, was a true measure of its quality. And over the past two decades, "a small but respectable body of criticism" had accumulated around jazz—the kind of writing "that only an art can inspire and that only an art deserves." Gathered in *The Art of Jazz*, these writings focused chiefly on the music itself, especially as preserved on record.[1]

Why begin a chapter on rock and roll with a statement about jazz criticism? Because critical writing sets jazz apart from other popular music of the period. While far from the most lucrative popular genre in the postwar years, jazz was the only one then being taken seriously by critics. This is not to deny that popular music received plenty of publicity. Popular-music figures were show-business celebrities and therefore newsworthy, winning notice from magazines and newspapers, the trade press, and sometimes biographers. But these writings treated them more as unique, charismatic individuals than as artists. Where writers on jazz showed an eagerness to explain the artistry of performers they admired, writers on other popular genres were much less likely to try to analyze their subjects' aesthetic achievements.

For example, although theater reviewers assessed every new Broadway musical, not until much later did critical histories of the musical begin to appear. Postwar books on Broadway tended toward celebration, concentrating on the longest-running shows and their performers, and centered on their crowd-pleasing features. Commentators seldom went beyond citing the best-known songs and reminding readers of their impact or charm. Like the notion of the musical as a historical form in its own right, the idea of the

Broadway and Tin Pan Alley song as a genre of musical composition had to await studies published in the 1970s and after.

Much the same may be said about other music in the popular sphere. Mainstream pop stars such as Bing Crosby, Frank Sinatra, Nat "King" Cole, Doris Day, Patti Page, and Rosemary Clooney, among others, received uncritical appreciation for their song hits from recordings, radio, television, and in some cases movies. And written accounts of other genres emphasized performers and numbers that had won the biggest audiences: in country and western music, for example, Gene Autry and Hank Williams; in gospel music, Mahalia Jackson; in rhythm and blues, Ray Charles; and in "urban" folk music, the Kingston Trio and Joan Baez. The advent of rock-and-roll performers such as Elvis Presley and Chuck Berry in the mid-1950s, now recognized as a key event in American cultural history, was treated as big news by the mainstream press but received little notice from musically informed commentators.

That situation changed after 1965. Today, many scholars are critiquing popular music and exploring its history. This new inclination owes much to the example of jazz critics, who long ago bridged the gap between the popular sphere's impermanence and the classical sphere's investment in history and criticism. By discussing jazz in a way that only an art deserves, critics vouched for the music's aesthetic power. But only *by treating performances as the equivalent of compositions* were they able to claim authority for their judgments. Phonograph records made that possible by turning onetime performances into permanent works. Fashioned on the spot by singers and players in collaboration with composers, arrangers, producers, and technicians, recordings were defined not by musical notation but by their sound; they became the artifacts through which historical trends could be traced, first in jazz, then in other popular genres.

YOUTH AND IDENTITY

As well as entertaining them, popular music in the years after World War II proved a source of identity for growing numbers of Americans. The phenomenon was not new to the record business, which after World War I had profited by selling recordings of ethnic groups in their own communities. Another example was the music trades' discovery and marketing of local styles from the South's traditional sphere. A third was Broadway and Tin Pan Alley's celebration in the years between the wars of individualistic romantic love. Ethnic, regional, and class-based markers in these genres confirmed the identity of the music's original creators and fans. They also appealed more widely, as people from other walks of life heard the music. And while ethnicity, locality, and class continued to play important roles in

Frank Sinatra (1915–1999) in the early 1940s, as singer with the Tommy Dorsey Orchestra.

the popular sphere, now another new factor—age—came into prominence. No social fact about postwar American music is more noteworthy than the growing influence of teenagers in the musical marketplace.

The rise of the youthful popular music fan has often been linked to the advent of rock and roll in the 1950s, when white teenagers began connecting with black-oriented styles. Yet teenagers had entered the popular sphere's marketplace with a bang at least a decade earlier. In 1944, when the twenty-nine-year-old crooner Frank Sinatra played an engagement at New York's Paramount Theater, his popularity was so great that his fans—mostly females belonging to the "bobby-socks brigade," ages twelve to sixteen—packed the theater long before the show began. When he appeared onstage, their screams of adoration rose hysterically. "Girls have plucked hairs from his head and, at somewhat less trouble to him, have collected clippings of his hair from the floors of barbershops," a magazine article reported. "One Sinatra fan carried around in a locket what she insists is a Sinatra hangnail."[2]

What gave a popular singer the power to inspire such adoring reverence? To experts of the time, generational conflict seemed the best explanation. The winner of a "Why I Like Frank Sinatra" essay contest, held in 1946 in Detroit, called Sinatra "one of the greatest things that ever happened to Teen Age America," because he made up for feelings of neglect. "We were the kids that never got much attention," the author explained. "But he's made us feel like we're something. . . . He gives us sincerity in return for our faithfulness."[3] Feeling excluded from their parents' world, many young women and girls found solace in the mildly subversive ritual of swooning over Frank Sinatra. Indeed, in the postwar era, a growing "generation gap" did much to transform the popular sphere, especially as a business enterprise. Its cause was simple: American youth in those years was searching for social identity. To understand why, it will help to look first at an earlier youth culture.

The peer-group culture of the 1920s took shape within college life and found its expression chiefly through college institutions, such as fraternities, sororities, and athletic societies. With social conformity as the unifying factor in campus life, even the few who rebelled against the norm did so in the spirit of "slumming": seeking thrills in capers they considered socially beneath themselves. The collegiate youth culture also gloried in consumption. So-called flappers in the 1920s pursued instant gratification, placing a high priority on fashion and style and valuing personal liberty above all else. Created by and for upper- and middle-class youth, this culture attracted working-class young people as well. Its musical parallel was found in ensembles such as Fred Waring and the Pennsylvanians, which in 1925 scored commercial success with a recording of *Collegiate*, a peppy Tin Pan Alley tribute to undergraduate fashion ("C'llegiate, c'llegiate, / Yes! we are collegiate. / Nothing intermedjate, / No ma'm. / Trousers baggy, / And our clothes look raggy, / But we're rough and ready, / Yes!"). Together with Paul Whiteman and other bandleaders, Waring was linked in the white public's mind with jazz. In 1927, *Good News*, a campus musical with songs by Ray Henderson, Lew Brown, and Buddy DeSylva, began a run of 557 New York performances, with an up-tempo dance number called *The Varsity Drag* as one of its hit songs. Theater ushers for the show wore collegiate jerseys, while the band members, led by conductor George Olsen, entered shouting collegiate cheers, then ran down the aisle into the orchestra pit.[4]

By all indications, the youth culture of the 1920s was more interested in upward mobility than rebellion. While offering modes of consumption and style that broke with the older generation, the collegiate subculture shared mainstream society's economic values and many of its social ones. The opposition to jazz voiced by their parents as well as educators and clergymen was rooted in uncertainty and fear: fear of racial difference, uninhibited dancing, and the aura of vice that surrounded many jazz venues during the Prohibition Era. The Fred Waring–Paul Whiteman–*Good News* approach to jazz, however, answered some of these objections by denying the music's black roots and treating it as a smart new form of emotional release. Young Americans' desire to escape Victorian restraints fed their enthusiasm for jazz, but not until the 1950s was a rebellious youthful identity, founded on resentment against elders, defined and crystallized strongly enough to spark a commercially successful youth movement in music.

The decade of the 1950s established generational conflict as a major theme in American popular culture. Novelist J. D. Salinger's *The Catcher in the Rye* (1951), written from an adolescent's perspective, seemed to speak for the whole postwar generation. Its hero, sixteen-year-old Holden Caulfield, experiences growing up as a process of disillusionment. The adult society described in the book is so corrupt—"phony" is a key word—that only through a teenager's eyes can innocence be glimpsed. Movies also took up the theme, with a young Marlon Brando and an even younger James Dean playing characters who sullenly resisted adult notions of virtue and re-spectability. A 1954 film, *The Wild One*, casts Brando as a member of a mo-torcycle gang. Asked by a waitress what he's rebelling against, he replies: "Whattaya got?" Dean's career involved starring roles in only three films be-fore he was killed in a car crash at age twenty-four. But in *Rebel Without a Cause* (1956), Dean portrayed misunderstood youth with a conviction that resonated into the future. The screenplay cast him as the victim of insensi-tive parents. Notes accompanying the script read:

> At seventeen he is filled with confusion about his role in life. Because of his "nowhere" father, he does not know how to be a man. Because of his wound-ing mother, he anticipates destruction in all women. And yet he wants to find a girl who will be willing to receive his tenderness. . . . [At one point, Dean's character muses:] "If I could have just one day when I wasn't all con-fused . . . I wasn't ashamed of everything. If I felt I belonged someplace."[5]

Here are the earmarks of postwar teenage angst: a general feeling of confu-sion; a lack of adult role models; an appetite for sexual activity but no ap-proved outlet; and a feeling of being out of place and of belonging nowhere. If popular culture in the 1950s seized on these themes, it was because many youngsters already shared the feelings they aroused. And as American youth found reasons to blame older generations for creating a society that evoked such feelings, mistrust between older and younger Americans increased.

Postwar teenagers grew up with views different from those of their par-ents. Much of that difference lay in the enormous expansion of the pur-chasing power of consumers, and the influence of electronic mass media. The first brought teenagers fully into the marketplace, with money to spend; and the money gave them the freedom to reject their parents' tastes and val-ues. The second added television to an array of mass media that already in-cluded recordings, movies, newspapers and magazines, and radio. By the 1950s, the mass media were introducing Americans to experiences far be-yond their own. Within popular music, many middle-class youngsters chose the cultural alternative of downward mobility to claim turf that was supposedly more authentic than that of their elders, and surely separate from it. "If rock 'n' roll had had no other value," declared a writer who was a teenager in those years, "it would have been enough merely to dent the smug middleclass consciousness of that time and throw into confusion some of the deadening rigidity of that world."[6]

ECONOMICS AND HIERARCHY IN THE MUSIC BUSINESS

Buyers of sheet music are presumably performers who can read musical notation and who intend to sing or play it themselves. Buyers of recordings are primarily listeners. In broadcasting, however, there is no artifact to buy, nor do listeners control *when* they hear any particular piece of music. Yet they do hear music, and when it becomes familiar and pleasing, listeners may buy the records or even the sheet music. Further, because broadcasting time is paid for by advertisers, the music becomes part of a vast marketing enterprise. A look at radio's place in the history of American advertising shows that although its future was briefly in doubt during the early 1920s, by 1925 the airwaves were full of national ads, and by 1928 buying radio time was as much a part of the big agencies' strategy as was newspaper and magazine space. In radio, moreover, advertisers had control over the entertainment. And the content of television, which arrived in the late 1940s, was shaped from the start by marketplace imperatives.

As television became the main arena for general family entertainment, radio grew more specialized. Radio may even have taken a cue from the record business, which had long been targeting particular groups as buyers. And once the popular music business in the early 1950s recognized teenagers as a social group with distinctive musical tastes, recording companies and radio stations looked for ways to connect with these new customers.

The commercial process that made teenage listeners a force in the musical marketplace could trace its roots at least as far back as 1914, when the American Society of Composers, Authors, and Publishers (ASCAP) was founded. The purpose of this first American performing-rights society was to license the published music of its members and then collect fees from anyone who performed that music for profit in any medium. Virtually all the leading composers, songwriters, and publishers joined ASCAP, and a mechanism was worked out to pay them when their music was played or sung in theaters, concert halls, restaurants, and dance halls. In 1932, ASCAP turned its attention to radio, agreeing with the National Association of Broadcasters (NAB) to collect a blanket license fee: 3 percent of the networks' gross revenue in 1933, which rose in 1935 to 5 percent.[7]

In the meantime, the practice of playing recorded music over the air had begun in earnest, monitored by "disc jockeys" who introduced the selections and filled the time between them with conversation and commercial plugs. A survey by the Federal Communications Commission in 1938 found that 51.6 percent of all programs were based on popular music recordings, chiefly selected by disc jockeys, and licensed by ASCAP. In 1939, ASCAP announced that when the current agreement expired, it would demand 7.5 percent of the networks' gross receipts. Unwilling to agree, the networks formed their own performing-rights society, which, under the name of Broadcast Music Incorporated (BMI), scurried to license music that ASCAP had overlooked. For several months at the start of 1941, the networks did without the music of Tin Pan Alley, Broadway, and Hollywood (all of which ASCAP had licensed) and substituted Latin, hillbilly, folk music, black popular music that would later be called rhythm and blues, and music in the public domain.

The struggle over radio revenues reflects not only economic rivalry but a musical hierarchy within the popular sphere. ASCAP, formed in New York to protect the interests of the city's composers and publishers in both the classical and popular spheres, saw itself as an upholder of professional standards. From ASCAP's perspective, BMI's interest in genres outside the standard professional circle betrayed a willingness to put economics above craftsmanship. Indeed, Tin Pan Alley now saw itself as supporting an apprenticeship system like the old European guilds: guiding young professionals who came up through the ranks and were allowed to publish songs only after they learned their trade. The new situation fostered by BMI put record producers, not publishers, in control, and they showed little inclination to invest in the development of songwriters.[8]

When BMI was founded in 1939, the two organizations were sharply divided by musical genre, though the gulf soon narrowed. With a virtual monopoly on mainstream pop, Broadway musicals, and Hollywood film scores, ASCAP genres could claim kinship with the classical sphere. (As Chapter 32 has shown, these genres were grounded in nineteenth-century European Romanticism.) In contrast, the genres licensed by BMI showed more African-American than Euroamerican influence, favoring informality over elevation. Rhythm and blues, black gospel and white gospel, the blues, and eventually rock and roll were developed chiefly by musicians on the BMI side of the spectrum. Jazz was a special case: luminaries such as W. C. Handy, Fats Waller, Duke Ellington, and Louis Armstrong were invited to join ASCAP, but most jazz musicians were not. It follows that BMI was more likely to license the work of urban folk performers, who borrowed directly from the traditional sphere and reveled in a plainness of manner that their fans found authentic. And with such publishing firms as M.M. Cole, Southern Music, and Acuff-Rose joining as members by 1942, all of them boasting large catalogues of rural and "race" music, country and western music also became identified with BMI.[9]

The breaking of ASCAP's stranglehold on performing-rights money decentralized the popular music business, made it more diverse, and called the industry's hierarchy into question. Technological progress contributed to these trends. Thanks to the new portable tape recorder, small companies now began to enter the business. By 1954, the number of record companies was approaching two hundred, and regional centers for recording had opened up in Chicago, Cincinnati, Houston, Memphis, and Los Angeles. While the major companies continued strong in their specialties, many of the new independent ones concentrated on black rhythm and blues or white country and western markets, which were now appealing to more and more listeners. In the same period, 45- and 33-rpm recordings began to replace the long-standard 78-rpm speed, with singles at 45-rpm becoming the favored popular disc format.

The outpouring in the late 1940s of rhythm and blues, gospel, and country and western music recordings, plus the rising influence of television, made a major impact on radio. Independent stations were licensed in growing numbers, and station owners found recorded music a good way to fill air time at low cost while also attracting advertisers. Programming was built around disc jockeys who played records and provided a mix of talk and advertising aimed at particular groups of listeners—heralding the arrival of "format" radio, whose musical spectrum was limited, sometimes even to single genres. Some disc jockeys ("deejays") gained a following as personalities and superfans of the genres they played on the air. They made themselves experts in the thing that broadcasters valued most: a knowledge of their audience's preferences as consumers. For deejays, first and foremost, were salesmen—for their station, the records they played, the styles and artists they favored, the products they hawked, and ultimately for their own authority as cultural spokesmen who had something more than culture to sell.

In a commercial environment like this one, it seems almost inevitable that popularity itself would come to be big news. In 1940, *Billboard* magazine, a weekly show-business trade journal, began to publish "charts" of the best-selling records in different categories. And from then on, popularity contests between recordings loomed large on the airwaves, giving listeners a sense that buying records signaled participation in the process of choosing the best artists and songs. Since on-the-air plugging proved a hugely effective way to promote record sales, companies by the late 1940s were competing hard to win time on the radio for their releases. That competition put disc jockeys in a position of power. One of the most respected, Cleveland deejay Bill Randle, told *Variety* magazine in 1952 that musical factors now had less to do with making a hit record than did salesmanship. In Randle's view, about one hundred disc jockeys "really controlled the popular-music business." Without "their concentrated action no song could become a major song and no artist could remain a major artist, nor could a new name be made."[10]

FROM RHYTHM AND BLUES TO ROCK AND ROLL

A key moment in American music history took place when teenagers' hunger for a music they could call their own combined with the popular music business's hunger for profits. Two developments brought that intersection about: the appearance of a style that appealed to white youngsters and the advent of performers who could take the role of teen icons, as Frank Sinatra had done for young females in the 1940s. From the mid-1950s on, Elvis Presley embodied the second. And the first was rock and roll, based on black rhythm and blues but packaged and marketed for white teenage audiences, chiefly by white performers.

Whether or not rock and roll was a truly revolutionary musical style, it certainly posed a revolutionary challenge to the structure of the popular music trade. Hierarchy in that trade is reflected not only in the existence of two major performing-rights societies—ASCAP and BMI—but in the different premises on which they were founded. The first took a musical work to be a composition that is written down, published, and *then* circulated through various media; the second accepted the idea that a musical work might be conceived in live performance or a sound studio, and written down only after the fact. If the first valued professional standards and musical expertise, the second was more interested in communication and audience response. If the first held formal training in high respect and saw musicians as its best advocates, the second was less choosy and perhaps more comfortable with the role now filled by nonmusicians—disc jockeys—as salesmen. Both societies were organized for commercial gain, and the genres in which their members worked converged more and more as time passed. But ASCAP's more exclusive attitude reflected a belief in "higher" and "lower" values that harked back to an era when sheet music had been the trade's main commodity. Recordings had left that hierarchical view more or less intact. But broadcasting, financed by advertisers and devoted to the marketing of other products, carried music into a realm that was beyond the power of any group of music makers to control.

In the two decades that followed World War II, American musicians gradually woke up to a new reality: that the broader a musical organization's reach, the more fully it would be controlled by economic priorities. What had been seen as a *musical* marketplace was being taken over by the much larger *general* marketplace created by the broadcast media. In fact, by the last third of the century, a majority of Americans would accept TV and radio as the main arena of the nation's cultural life. In that arena, music—the classical, popular, and traditional spheres taken together—would need to compete for audience attention with news, sports, variety, comedy, drama, movies, and advertising. Power in the popular music trade shifted away from the musicians who made the music toward company personnel who were perceived to be expertly tuned to the marketplace. By the 1950s, the A&R (artists and repertoire) people who supervised a company's recording sessions held sway.

After 1965, the hierarchy that had long supported the values asserted by ASCAP looked somewhat old-fashioned. In the 1950s, however, popular music was still protected by its own professional organizations, whose ranking of genres carried a certain amount of clout. And as the decade began, rhythm and blues (R&B), the industry term for black popular music, stood rather low in that hierarchy.

Billboard magazine used the rhythm-and-blues label from 1949 through 1964 to refer to recordings by black musicians that were popular in black communities, replacing the older categories of "race" records and "Harlem hit parade." Rhythm and blues has sometimes been described as a musical genre, but it has also been seen as an economic, sociological, and chronological term. There is no disagreement that rhythm and blues emanates from the traditional sphere: a transformation and updating of the older Southern folk blues for black audiences. Its lineage has been traced to styles of the Mississippi Delta as modified in Chicago and other cities, but with influence from black swing bands, such as that of Lionel Hampton, and the small-band "jump-blues" approach of Louis Jordan, with elements of piano boogie-woogie mixed in. The ensemble makeup was far from standard. Groups might feature a lead singer or an instrumentalist or both, plus an assortment of other instruments. The rhythm section might include double bass or electric bass guitar, plus drums, guitar, and a keyboard instrument (piano or organ). The backup group might also include any combination of voices, wind instruments, guitar, or organ. While the rhythm section was paramount, all the performers in this primarily vocal genre helped maintain the beat that made the music danceable. The meter was always duple, with the so-called back beats—the second and fourth of a four-beat measure—often accented. Beyond these fundamentals, R&B featured lead singers (e.g., Clyde McPhatter, Sam Cooke) who might work alone or as part of a group (the Drifters, the Orioles, the Coasters). The words of R&B songs, mostly about love life, gravitated during the 1950s increasingly toward teenagers. Twelve-bar blues and thirty-two-bar song forms predominated.

An increase in the number of companies that produced rhythm and blues records points to the music's growing strength in the postwar market-place. Famous bandleaders like Hampton and Jordan recorded on major la-bels. But much of the music came from new independent firms, including Savoy (founded in 1942 in Newark, New Jersey), King (1944, Cincinnati), Modern (1945, Los Angeles), Atlantic (1947, New York), Aristocrat-Chess (1947, Chicago), Peacock (1949, Houston), and Sun (1952, Memphis). To-day, when music of all kinds is so readily available, it may not be easy to imagine the impact on white listeners of records by black artists who were drawing straight from the African-American traditional sphere. The primal rhythmic churning of Wynonie Harris's *Good Rockin' Tonight*; the gospel-like call and response of the Ravens' *Bye Bye Baby Blues*; the shouting and stomping propulsion of John Lee Hooker on *Boogie Chillen'* and *Crawling Kingsnake*; the honking tenor sax sound on Big Jay McNeely's *Deacon's Hop* or Paul Williams's *The Hucklebuck*—there were simply no white equivalents for numbers like these.[11]

Direct, unself-conscious, celebrating bodily joys, rooted in black tradi-tions, yet stylized for distribution in the modern marketplace, postwar "race" music communicated with American listeners. While most company owners and producers were white, they targeted black listeners, as record compa-nies had been doing since Mamie Smith's *Crazy Blues* of 1920. Producer Jerry Wexler recalled the words of Ahmet Ertegun, his boss, when he first went to work for Atlantic Records in the early 1950s:

> There's a black man living in the outskirts of Opelousas, Louisiana. He works hard for his money; he has to be tight with a dollar. One morning he hears a song on the radio. It's urgent, bluesy, authentic, irresistible. He be-comes obsessed. He can't live without this record. He drops everything, jumps in his pickup, and drives twenty-five miles to the first record store he finds. If we can make that kind of music, we can make it in the business.[12]

Wexler's story signals a key development in broadcasting. During the 1930s, there had been no such thing as a radio station aimed at black listen-ers, nor any that specialized in black musical forms other than swing. As black radio began to take shape, however, the new record labels began to serve them. And after the war, across the southern United States—in St. Louis, Atlanta, Louisville, Memphis, Los Angeles, New Orleans, Miami, and Nashville—black radio matured, with the founding of stations centered on rhythm and blues and also, depending on their location, offering gospel, traditional blues, or jazz.[13]

In the late 1940s, then, rhythm and blues enjoyed a substantial but still largely segregated presence in America. The R&B artists active in recording and broadcasting were also experienced live performers who learned their trade in the theaters, dance halls, clubs, tent shows, and other black venues

Alan Freed, who, working in Cleveland in the early 1950s, became one of the first white disc jockeys to play rhythm-and-blues recordings for white youth.

that comprised the "chitlin circuit." But broadcasting increased the diversity of their audience while expanding its size. Whites could listen to black radio, and they could then buy records by black artists. As one industry figure put it, "you could segregate schoolrooms and buses, but not the airwaves."[14] Black disc jockeys, who developed their own ways of talking about the music they played on the air, had a lot to do with recruiting white fans. "Wild Bill" Curtis in the early 1950s, for example, would tell listeners about a group called the Drifters he had met when they were still unknown, then put their record on, rave ecstatically, play the record again, and watch the phones light up as listeners and record stores called to ask where they could find this new release.[15]

Another avenue to rhythm and blues opened up in 1951 when white Cleveland disc jockey Alan Freed learned from a local record store owner that white youngsters were now buying records previously thought to be exclusively "Negro music." Freed, then working as a classical-record host, responded by starting "The Moondog Show," a youth-oriented program centered on rhythm and blues recordings and broadcast on a clear-channel station whose signal could be heard across the Midwest. As Moondog, Freed won immediate success, speaking the language of his mostly teenage audience. Before long, he was organizing live rhythm and blues shows in Cleveland. In March 1952, for example, Freed staged an event featuring black artists at the Cleveland Arena that drew a mixed-race crowd of around 25,000 teenagers to a facility that could accommodate less than half that number, resulting in the first rock-and-roll riot.[16]

Alan Freed would soon win national prominence as one of the first white disc jockeys to introduce teenagers to rhythm and blues. But no contribution was more lasting than the label he gave this music: "rock and roll." Freed did not invent the phrase; he borrowed it from African-American song, where it was sometimes used to mean sexual intercourse. Only insiders knew that, however. The general public accepted "rock and roll" as a name that was free of racial overtones and fit the style. In fact, the label has been claimed as a key to the racial crossover. For when white show-business entrepreneurs, following Freed's example, began substituting "rock and roll" for "rhythm and blues," racial identification was glossed over, and young white fans of the music were spared a certain amount of conflict.[17]

Readers of this history will recall earlier parallels in black-white musical interaction that worked to white economic advantage. In the early 1910s, Irving Berlin took the lead in transforming ragtime from a black genre into a "universal" one by disconnecting it from black dialect and characters. And in the mid-to-late 1920s, Paul Whiteman and others performed a similar operation on jazz. In both cases, though the cultural and musical emphasis shifted, the name stayed the same. In the 1950s marketplace, however, with its mass-media salesmanship and quick distribution, the new name helped the music find its audience. But the music's black creators were not cut in on the profits. One black critic has judged the artistic product of rock and roll a watered-down version of the real thing. He cites its "pseudo rebellion akin to the blues but without the mature battle of the sexes essential to that black expression." And he accuses Alan Freed of trivializing an African-American genre. "Rock & roll wasn't a music," he writes, "but a marketing concept that evolved into a life-style."[18]

The eyewitness account by a white author who was twelve years old in 1955 offers a different view. For him, unruliness was an important if ambiguous part of growing up. "For all the youthful gestures of rebellion," he says, "you expected some day to take your place in adult society." And he understood that his parents would tolerate a certain amount of nonconformity. Rock and roll "provided us with a release and a justification that we had never dreamt of." No force on earth made it easier to offend grown-ups, to mock "the sanctimoniousness of public figures," or to draw a "clear line of demarcation between *us* and *them*."[19]

Together with excitement, the new music offered a chance to redefine "us" and "them." Inherited boundary lines gave low prestige to the likes of Chuck Berry, Little Richard, Jerry Lee Lewis, Elvis Presley, and the groups they represented. By casting their lot with these performers, white middle-class teenagers could feel as if they were taking a stand for freedom, high spirits, emotional truth, and fun, and against the confining proprieties of middle-class life. The music testified that youth now constituted a community with its own modes of expression. Though not couched in political terms, rock and roll declared an independence that gave teenage identity a political edge. Moreover, the freedom to draw lines was granted not by parents, teachers, or clergy but by the consumer marketplace. Youngsters in comfortable middle-class circumstances could now try on a less privileged identity for size. They now could get a taste of feeling rebellious without actually having to rebel. And in the mid-1950s, no entertainer was better known for redrawing the boundary lines than Elvis Presley.

Elvis Presley in Memphis

That story begins with Presley, born in 1935 in Mississippi, as a teenager in Memphis, where he and his parents had moved in the late 1940s. Living at the edge of poverty, Presley's mother and father had little money to spare for their son's musical education, though they did buy him a guitar. But as a youth with an avid appetite for music, he sampled a wide variety. There is evidence that the young Elvis was a fan of black radio, especially WDIA in Memphis, where B. B. King, a singer and guitar player from the Mississippi Delta, was just starting out as a disc jockey. He sometimes hung out at Charlie's record store on Main Street, where a jukebox offered a variety of recordings for listeners willing to spend a nickel.[20] Memphis was also a place where white gospel quartet singing flourished. That tradition, which grew out of singing schools of the nineteenth century, had been started by publishing firms that hired male quartets to travel and perform from the company's sacred tunebooks. By the mid-twentieth century, some of the quartets were making records and singing on the radio. Their repertory, rooted in the nineteenth-century gospel-hymn style first popularized by Dwight L. Moody and Ira Sankey, was all sacred. But they were polished performers who bantered with their crowds and entertained them while singing emotionally charged spiritual songs that listeners could tap their feet to. Gospel quartet music was the center of Presley's musical universe in those days, with a group called The Statesmen a particular favorite. Featuring a tenor named Hovie Lister, this quartet was sometimes criticized for being too showy and too "black-sounding" to be convincing spokesmen for the Christian religion. Presley and his first girlfriend, though, fast became Statesmen groupies.

While black R&B and white gospel both left a deep and lasting impression on the young Elvis Presley, there seems to have been no kind of music that he did not love. He listened not only to Eddy Arnold, Hank Williams, and other country stars but to such mainstream pop artists as Teresa Brewer, Kay Starr, Joni James, Bing Crosby, Eddie Fisher, and Perry Como. He attended classical orchestra concerts at the outdoor Overton Park in Memphis. Dramatic tenor Mario Lanza and the Metropolitan Opera radio broadcasts were also on his menu of listening favorites. Biographical accounts of Presley's early years in Memphis leave the impression of a loner: a painfully shy youngster with a rich fantasy life revolving around music. "I just loved music. Music period," he later told an interviewer. Though without formal training or experience as a performer, he nursed an obsessive wish to become a singer. And that desire led him, shortly after he graduated from high school, to the office of Sun Records, founded and run in Memphis by Sam Phillips.

Phillips, a native of Florence, Alabama, had moved to Memphis and in 1950 opened a recording studio with a remarkably idealistic purpose in mind:

> I thought to myself: suppose that I would have been born *black*. Suppose that I would have been born a little bit more down on the economic ladder. I think I felt from the beginning the total inequity of man's inhumanity to his brother. And it didn't take its place with me of getting up in the pulpit and preaching. It took on the aspect with me that *someday I would act on my feelings, I would show them on an individual, one-to-one basis.*[21]

Phillips's assistant at Sun Records, a woman named Marion Kiesker, confirmed his determination to run a business with more than economic gain in mind. "He would talk about this idea that he had, this dream, I suppose, to have a facility where black people could come and play their own music, a place where they would feel free and relaxed to do it." By 1953, that dream had led to rhythm and blues hits on the Sun label by such black artists as Rufus Thomas and Junior Parker. In that year, the eighteen-year-old Elvis Presley showed up at the Sun studio and paid $3.98 plus tax for the chance to be recorded, singing to his own guitar accompaniment. Presley chose a pair of sentimental ballads for the occasion, and Phillips's assistant made a note next to the boy's name: "Good ballad singer. Hold."[22] And that was where Elvis Presley's singing career rested for about a year.

In the summer of 1954, Scotty Moore, a guitarist who led a country music band in Memphis, was looking for a singer to record with, and Sam Phillips suggested Presley. An audition was set up at the Sun studio. Toward the end of the session, "this song popped into my mind that I had heard years ago," Elvis later recalled, "and I started kidding around with it." The song was *That's All Right*, a rhythm and blues number by Arthur Crudup, a Mississippi-born bluesman. Moore remembered the occasion well:

All of a sudden . . . Elvis just started singing this song, jumping around and acting the fool, and then Bill [Black] picked up his bass, and he started acting the fool, too, and I started playing with them. Sam, I think, had the door to the control booth open—I don't know, he was either editing some tape, or doing something—and he stuck his head out and said, "What are you doing?" And we said, "We don't know." "Well, back up," he said, "try to find a place to start, and do it again."[23]

Surprised that Presley even knew a song by Arthur Crudup, Sam Phillips was struck even more with the originality, freshness, and exuberance of the performance.

Artistic breakthroughs of such consequence are rare, and eyewitness accounts even rarer. This story pinpoints the moment when an artist who would soon number his fans in the millions first unlocked the door to a fresh realm of personal expression. But if the connection that forged the key was made by the creative mind of Elvis Presley, he stumbled on it during a process of musical collaboration. The creative spark lit by Presley's clowning was fanned by the musicians in the studio with him and also by Sam Phillips, who was able to judge the significance of the moment and capture it on tape. While only a musician could have taken the leap of imagination that Presley took, without Phillips's response, the breakthrough now traced to that evening might have been postponed indefinitely. The musical process behind *That's All Right* contradicts the assumption that the role of creator is always filled by a composer. For what was actually composed in the Sun studio was a *record*: a recording of a performance whose elements included Arthur Crudup's song, Elvis Presley's singing, Scotty Moore and Bill Black's accompaniment, and Sam Phillips's response to the result.

It is true that recordings had been on the scene for decades and had long ago surpassed sheet music as the most profitable way to circulate popular music; yet the aim of recording was to represent musicians as they sounded in live performance. Popular singing was an exception. Indeed, behind Elvis Presley's breakthrough lay several decades of sound enhancement that began in the mid-1920s, with the invention of the electric microphone. The microphone could carry a soft, nuance-filled sound to all corners of a large space. Crooners developed a singing style that relied on technology, and from that time on, technology was integrated into popular singing, heightening and polishing the sound of the recorded voice.[24]

Rhythm and blues performers used electricity chiefly to boost the level of excitement. A player such as T-Bone Walker or Muddy Waters could dominate a noisy barroom with the sound of his electric guitar. Yet for all of its reliance on technology, R&B remained chiefly a mode of live performance. In

Elvis Presley (1935–1977), singing in Memphis in 1956 to an audience of ecstatic young listeners.

contrast, rock and roll, whose aesthetic foundations lay in R&B's energetic performing style and exaggerated sonic presence, was grounded in the recording process. It became popular not so much through live performances but through records played on the radio. That the makers of rock and roll embraced technology from the start is dramatized by Presley's Memphis audition, which took place in a recording studio and used its tools as part of the artistic process. Sam Phillips was interested in how Elvis Presley sang, but also in how he sounded on tape.[25]

Phillips sensed that something important had happened in Elvis's first recording session. In 1959, he told a Memphis reporter that in the early 1950s "you could sell a half million copies of a rhythm and blues record" but no more, because the appeal to white youngsters was limited. "There was something in many of those youngsters that resisted buying this music. The Southern ones especially felt a resistance that even they probably didn't quite understand. They liked the music, but they weren't sure whether they ought to like it or not. So I got to thinking how many records you could sell if you could find white performers who could play and sing in this same exciting, alive way."[26] In Elvis Presley, Phillips found what he had been looking for: a singer who discovered in a black performing style a catalyst for an exciting, alive style of his own.

Considering the obscurity in which his musical career began, Presley's rise to fame took place with amazing speed. The professional network open to a singer of his background was that of country music, so after his first Sun recording was released, he began touring the South with a troupe headlined by country star Hank Snow. Radio appearances on the Grand Ole Opry from Nashville and the Louisiana Hayride from Shreveport were also sandwiched in. The role of professional performer encouraged the shy young man to shed some of his natural inhibitions, unleashing a magnetic, sexually charged onstage presence that worked young audiences into a state of frenzy. A seventeen-year-old Texan who would later become a country singer described Elvis's impact on the teenage girls of Kilgore, Texas, and on himself too. "This cat came out," he recalled,

> in red pants and a green coat and a pink shirt and socks, and he had this sneer on his face and he stood behind the mike for five minutes, I'll bet, before he made a move. Then he hit his guitar a lick, and he broke two strings. Hell, I'd been playing ten years, and I hadn't broken a *total* of two strings. So there he was, these two strings dangling, and he hadn't done anything except break the strings yet, and these high school girls were screaming and fainting and running up to the stage, and then he started to move his hips real slow like he had a thing for his guitar. . . . For the next nine days he played one-nighters around Kilgore, and after school every day me and my girl would get in the car and go wherever he was playing that night. That's the last time I tried to sing like Webb Pierce or Lefty Frizzell.[27]

If Presley's showmanship seemed to spring from God-given talent and an innate grasp of audience psychology, he also showed a keen interest in self-improvement, as if determined to make up for his lack of training and experience. His first manager recalled a time in 1955 when Elvis was home in Memphis on a break from touring. Dropping by the Presley house, he found the singer "with a stack of records—Ray Charles and Big Joe Turner and Big Mama Thornton and Arthur 'Big Boy' Crudup—that he studied with all the avidity that other kids focused on their college exams." Winning more attention as his recordings circulated, Presley soon left Sam Phillips's Sun

Records for RCA Victor and found a new manager. *Billboard* magazine's comment on the move recognizes Elvis's challenge to the industry's marketing structure: "Altho Sun has sold Presley primarily as a c.&w. [country and western] artist, Victor plans to push his platters in all three fields—pop, r.&b., and c.&w."[28]

Another factor in Presley's rise to fame was his presence on national television. In January 1956, he made the first of several appearances on "Stage Show," a CBS variety program featuring the swing musicians Tommy and Jimmy Dorsey and their big band. Elvis raced onto the stage and swung into a performance of Joe Turner's *Shake, Rattle, and Roll*, complete with acrobatic gyrations and full of confidence and the sheer enjoyment of performing. By the time he made his last appearance on "Stage Show" in March, he was riding a wave that carried him to Hollywood for a screen test with film producer Hal Wallis. Records, radio, television, and press coverage had made a national star of a young man who, less than two years earlier, had discovered his musical persona in a recording studio in Memphis. At twenty-one, Presley in early 1956 was the hottest act in show business, though what *kind* of an act was still open to debate.

RACE, GENRE, AND ROCK AND ROLL

Elvis Presley's talent, charisma, and animal energy go a long way toward explaining his quick rise to fame. Yet he also benefited from changes taking place in the popular music business before he appeared on the scene. His audition at the Sun studio was a key moment in one important career, not the "invention" of rock and roll itself. In fact, Presley's place in rock-and-roll history is far from settled. According to some, Elvis rode to stardom on the tide of a cultural phenomenon so strong and inevitable that the music would have happened even without him. His main achievement was the huge audience of teenagers that he captured for rock and roll almost overnight.

Rock and roll owed much of its popularity to differences from the music of Tin Pan Alley. Musical traits included a driving 4/4 time, accenting the first beat of each bar and some backbeats; a fondness for twelve-bar blues form; the use of amplified instruments, especially electric guitar; blues-influenced singing; and alternating vocal sections with instrumental ones played by tenor sax, electric guitar, or keyboard soloists. Many early rock-and-roll hits were white performers' versions of rhythm-and-blues songs, with lyrics about love and sex. The rather grating singing style, wholly unsuited to Western art music or even Tin Pan Alley, derived from rural music, both white and black.[29]

Thus, in musical approach, repertory, sound, and singing style, rock-and-

Bill Haley and the Comets, whose hit *Rock Around the Clock* helped to start the national craze for rock and roll in the mid-1950s.

roll performers drew a hard line between themselves and the Broadway–Tin Pan Alley kinship with the classical sphere. They also distanced themselves from folk and blues singers by embracing technology and avidly pursuing commercial success; from jazz musicians by emphasizing fixed versions of pieces and audience accessibility; and from gospel performers through their secular subject matter. The line between "us" and "them" grew less clear, however, when it came to rhythm and blues and country music: unlike rock and roll, they were intended for grown-up listeners. Ray Charles, whose recordings ranked high on rhythm and blues popularity charts of the day, insisted that "I never considered myself part of rock 'n' roll." Charles thought of Chuck Berry, Little Richard, and Bo Diddley as the leaders in that style, and he found "a towering difference" between their music and his own. "My stuff was more adult," he explained. "It was more difficult for teenagers to relate to . . . more serious, filled with more despair than anything you'd associate with rock 'n' roll."[30]

Rock and roll's impact on the popular music business was revealed by its domination of *Billboard*'s popular, or "Top 100," record-sales chart. But that was only the start. Until the mid-1950s, each *Billboard* chart reflected a distinct market with its own performers, radio stations, and retail outlets; the idea of a disc crossing over from one chart to another was unheard of. Record industry professionals were caught off guard in the summer of 1955, when *Rock Around the Clock*, by Bill Haley and the Comets, the top single on the popular (i.e., white) chart, also appeared on the rhythm and blues chart. Then *Maybellene*, by Chuck Berry, which topped the rhythm and blues charts, appeared in the fall on the popular chart and remained there for fourteen weeks. And then *Heartbreak Hotel*, by Elvis Presley, topped *both* the popular and country-western lists, while also rising to the No. 5 spot on the rhythm and blues chart. Rock and roll was proving to be a truly interracial expression. Barriers that had long separated country music, rhythm and blues, and pop seemed in danger of collapsing.

The spectacle of eroding barriers in the music business mirrored a historic change that was under way in American society. For as young white listeners reveled in a new, black-inspired popular music, black Americans had entered a new phase in their fight to secure the rights of citizenship. *Brown vs. Board of Education* (1954), the Supreme Court decision that declared school segregation illegal, touched off a period of intense, sometimes violent conflict. Within a year, white Southern opposition was organized. White citizens' councils were formed that, while denying violent intent, fueled an environment that condoned violence. And politicians also found ways to encourage the defiance of court orders without actually advocating it.

In the civil rights movement, black Southerners fought with dignity for civil liberties, using the weapons at their disposal, including civil disobedience and nonviolent confrontation. They also educated whites about the evils of segregation. The movement dramatized black civil discontent while stressing possibilities for interracial collaboration. In 1955, a boycott led by the twenty-six-year-old Reverend Martin Luther King Jr. succeeded in desegregating public transportation in Montgomery, Alabama. And in the early 1960s, "sit-ins" and "freedom marches" came to be standard nonviolent tactics. Black citizens, with some white support, joined forces to secure the equality guaranteed in principle by federal court decisions, and eventually by the landmark Civil Rights Act that Congress passed in 1964, followed by the Voting Rights Act of 1965.

The mass media also helped to weaken racial barriers. In the Montgomery boycott's early days, the city's white-owned newspapers either ignored the story or attacked the nonriders for financially undermining the bus system. But a local TV station whose news director covered the boycott drew attention to Montgomery when the national network began picking up its telecasts. Before long, reporters were arriving to follow what seemed to many non-Southerners a modern morality play: an example of ordinary Americans standing up for basic rights. With outside witnesses on the scene, white authorities were constrained from using physical violence. At the same time, their presence encouraged the black leadership and its followers.[31]

Meanwhile, Southern white youngsters were beginning to cross the color line to embrace so-called race music—at least as embodied in the new style called rock and roll. And that fact makes it seem no coincidence that in 1954–55, when the laws supporting segregation in the South were challenged, young white audiences around the country were embracing black-derived musical styles as their own. Teenagers who bought rock-and-roll records surely did so more as fans of the music than as champions of racial equality. Yet by accepting rock and roll with enthusiasm, white teenagers endorsed a sensibility shaped by black Americans. The rise of rock and roll turned the cultural identity of American youth in an interracial direction. The tide that carried rock and rollers to fame was grounded in a process of social change that reached far beyond music.

35

Songs of Loneliness and Praise

Postwar Vernacular Trends

THE IMAGE OF TUMBLING BARRIERS in popular music and society is a powerful one. And the arrival of rock and roll has often been seen as cause for celebration: a populist triumph over elitism. From this perspective, the winning blend grew out of a fusion of Southern white (country) music with urban black (rhythm and blues). Key figures included Elvis Presley, who "sang black," and Chuck Berry, a black, Missouri-raised singer who sometimes sounded white. The notion of populism on the march was enhanced by news that the ASCAP-dominated New York/Hollywood axis of the music business had been caught off guard by the new music's sudden popularity and its emanation from studios in such places as Memphis. It was certainly true, too, that sexuality, long suppressed or veiled in commercial popular music, was thrust into prominence by the music's openly pelvic beat. White youngsters, to whom no style in the popular sphere had ever before been addressed, were now the intended audience for a kind of music that seemed to glory in its ungenteel, lower-class origins. Finally, rock and roll was quintessentially American, owing little to European antecedents or the classical sphere—whose prestige, however, still stood high enough in 1956 for Chuck Berry to sing "Roll over, Beethoven, and tell Tchaikovsky the news."

There is no question that rock and roll replaced Tin Pan Alley songwriting as the dominant force in the popular music marketplace. But this phenomenon reflected a new *type* of marketplace, changed by technology, demographics, and economic competition. The advent of television, microgroove recordings, and the 45-rpm single had already transformed musical distribution. Demographically, black radio and youth-oriented programs helped to bring new groups of customers to the fore. And once the new style's economic potential was revealed, the record business boomed. A tally of gross revenues from record sales shows an increase from $191 million in

1951 to $514 million in 1959. The first big leaps took place in 1955 and 1956, when teenagers entered the marketplace in droves.[1] From 1955 on, in other words, the Top 100 *Billboard* chart measured the preferences of a younger, more specialized segment of the population than it had before.

Yet the pop single was only one of many products in a market that was also being changed by the advent of the long-playing record (33 1/3 rpm). And if we look beyond single hit records, we see that the Tin Pan Alley songwriting tradition was also alive and well after the war, now emphasizing consolidation and refinement over exploration and discovery. Experienced, talented songwriters and performers in this idiom were plentiful, and a widespread infrastructure of publishing, recording, broadcasting, and live performance stood at these musicians' disposal. Furthermore, the Broadway musical enjoyed one of its most illustrious decades in the 1950s with such shows as Rodgers and Hammerstein's *The King and I* (1951) and *The Sound of Music* (1959), Lerner and Loewe's *My Fair Lady* (1956), Laurents, Sondheim, and Bernstein's *West Side Story* (1957), and Frank Loesser's *Guys and Dolls* (1950) and *The Most Happy Fella* (1956), all of which (except for *West Side Story*) were successfully revived on Broadway in the 1990s.

This book has made a refrain of the dogma that the popular sphere's main goal is accessibility: an investment of ultimate authority in the present-day audience. It has also been assumed that Broadway's preoccupation with audience approval separates it from opera, which aspires to transcendence in line with its classical pedigree. Yet the shows listed above, among others, accessible enough to be hits in the 1950s, were showing clear signs of transcendence in the 1990s. Moreover, during "The Age of Rock," beginning around 1955, some songs—standards—written as early as the 1920s by Broadway and Tin Pan Alley tunesmiths were still being performed.

Standards were fundamental to the popular-song trade's notion of a healthy business, and economics suggests why. Around 1960, the annual income received by Irving Berlin and Cole Porter from ASCAP, mostly for songs they'd written in the past, was $90,000–$100,000; Rodgers and Hammerstein took in around $75,000; the Gershwin, Kern, and Hart estates around $50,000; and Lerner and Loewe, Johnny Mercer, Ira Gershwin, Jule Styne, Frank Loesser, Sammy Cahn, Dorothy Fields, and Harry Warren, $30,000–$50,000.[2] With rewards like these available to those who succeeded, the songwriting business held plenty of attraction for talented lyricists and composers.

Readers will recall earlier examples of popular songs that transcended the time and place of their origin. Yet in the years after World War II, the mainstream popular repertory as a whole took on a somewhat historical cast: grounded in a core of standards that endured even as new songs were being composed and circulated. New songs remained important, and competition to catch the public ear never slackened. But songs of the twenties, thirties, and forties and the vein of romantic individualism they explored provided a yardstick against which newer ones were measured.

One cause of the older tradition's durability was that many of its leading songwriters were still on the scene and active; Harold Arlen, Burton Lane, E. Y. ("Yip") Harburg, and Duke Ellington may be added to those named above. Another was the presence of expert interpreters who had learned their trade with Swing Era big bands: not only Bing Crosby and Louis Armstrong—jazz singers before the Swing Era began—but Frank Sinatra, Perry Como, Jo Stafford, Ella Fitzgerald, Dinah Shore, Dick Haymes, Peggy Lee, Billie Holiday, Margaret Whiting, Nat "King" Cole, and Kay Starr. A third cause was the large adult audience, people who had grown up with the music and still considered it theirs. A fourth was that jazz musicians had drawn on popular song for their own repertory of standards; multiple arrangements had kept the songs fresh through variation, and listeners were used to hearing their favorites in a variety of settings. Finally, there was the issue of quality. As early as 1925, *Variety* had recognized the uncanny match between words and music that American songwriters were achieving. Lyricist Yip Harburg later summed up their credo in a deft syllogism: "Words make you think thoughts; music makes you feel a feeling; and a song makes you feel a thought."[3]

In the postwar era, then, well before the advent of rock and roll, the classical sphere's ideal of transcendence had won a beachhead within the Tin Pan Alley and Broadway genres. And one of the main figures in perpetuating the notion of a standard repertory of classic popular songs was Frank Sinatra, whose commanding position in the marketplace pointed to the rise of singers, as opposed to bandleaders, as its dominant force. Between 1953 and 1961, working with skilled arrangers, Sinatra recorded no fewer than sixteen "concept albums." Here was proof that the single-song disc on which *Billboard* based its popularity charts was no longer the only way for a pop singer to reach the public on record. An LP album might include eight or ten selections, any of which could be issued separately. Aimed chiefly at adults, concept albums connected songs that had been written separately, and in Sinatra's case, reflected the artistic quality he found in the work of American songwriters.

The songs included on *Frank Sinatra Sings Only the Lonely*, for example, an album of Nelson Riddle arrangements recorded in 1958, span almost three decades, starting in the early 1930s. As a group, they show variety within a generally melancholy mood, with Riddle's orchestral arrangements providing a more contemporary sound. One of the songs, Harold Arlen and Johnny Mercer's *One for My Baby* (1943), is a sophisticated blues-oriented ballad that blends respect, sentiment, denial, pain, resignation, and a musical richness to match. Written for a film performance by Fred Astaire and set in a barroom late at night, the song is sung by a customer who pours his heart out to Joe, the silent bartender, drinking "to the end of a brief episode" while Joe sets up "one for my baby, and one more for the road." The composer once called this song "another Arlen tapeworm" because its fifty-eight-bar chorus almost doubles the standard thirty-two-bar length.[4] As arranged by Riddle, the song breathes a saloon atmosphere in which Sinatra sounds at home. By 1958, Sinatra's image was far removed from that of the bobby-soxer idol of earlier years. Marital and vocal problems, a public fistfight, and rumors of mob connections had set his career on a downward course in the late forties and early fifties, followed by an upturn only after he won an Academy Award for a film role in 1953. More than forty years old when he recorded this album, Sinatra brought the stamp of authenticity to its mood of urban loneliness. In the public's perception, he sang with a voice that knew how it felt to be driven to late-night drinking by an unhappy love affair.

Riddle's arrangement adds a note of grandeur and a deft layer of instrumental commentary to Arlen and Mercer's song. Using strings here and there for organlike effects, he underscores the depth and poignancy of the singer's distress. At the same time, starting with a bluesified piano introduction and using a figure from that intro as the piano's response to many of the singer's "calls," Riddle suggests the presence of another, nonsinging character: a barroom piano player whose job it is to play into the wee hours every evening, and for whom tales of heartbreak are all in a night's work. When Sinatra's voice trails off at the end, imagining "the long, long road" that lies ahead, the blues-tinged figure that began the song continues in the piano. Personal stories come and go, the performance seems to say, but the blues are always with us. The Sinatra-Riddle version of *One for My Baby* draws back the curtain on an adult venue where bartenders and musicians are the healers, doling out balm for the aching heart by the glass and by the tune.

While postwar mainstream pop grew more fragmented, country music was in a robust condition. With prosperity growing in the South, the demand for amusement quickened. The Grand Ole Opry now had radio competition from other barn-dance programs such as Louisiana Hayride, and jukeboxes reverberated with songs by such country entertainers as Eddy Arnold, Kitty Wells, Lefty Frizzell, and Hank Williams. Then in 1951, a number by the country writer and performer Pee Wee King, published by Acuff-Rose of Nashville, became a major hit record: the song was *Tennessee Waltz*, a nostalgic thirty-two-bar ballad about the night the singer lost her lover to another woman. The recording by Patti Page that made this song nationally popular shows little of the character of traditional country music performance. In fact, in a studio production innovative for its time, the record fea-

Hank Williams (1923–1953), singer, guitarist, and songwriter whose songs continued to be a presence in country music long after his early death.

tures the Oklahoma-born Page singing a sweet-sounding overdubbed duet with herself in a voice and diction essentially free of regional traits. The song's mainstream success seemed to indicate that Southern songwriters' emotional directness could jump barriers of social class and geography.

Country musicians have been praised for tackling such subjects as adultery, divorce, and drunkenness when other traditions were avoiding them, for writing about the world in which people live from week to week and are given to drowning their sorrows in the kind of taverns and bars where singers like Hank Williams served their apprenticeship. The music was chiefly a male enterprise until after the war, when female stars began to emerge. In 1952, *It Wasn't God Who Made Honky Tonk Angels*, a song sung by Kitty Wells, answered Hank Thompson's *The Wild Side of Life*, which contains the line "I didn't know God made honky tonk angels." The first song brings a female perspective to the assumption that men are forever being "done wrong" by women. Set in a roadhouse, the lyrics view the woman's position as riskier than that of the man, whose wild tendencies are deemed socially acceptable by Hank Thompson's song—and the Arlen-Mercer *One for My Baby*. Wells's number uses one inequity to suggest a broader attitude of social discrimination: men may visit bars alone, but a woman who does so forfeits her claim to virtue. From the song's point of view, women are victims of the faithlessness and aggression of male desire.

In the years following the war's end, country music was living proof of the staying power of old forms, styles, themes, and sounds, as the fiddle and steel guitar remained basic instruments. In the fall of 1947, the Grand Ole Opry sent a unit headed by singer Ernest Tubb to New York's Carnegie Hall, the first country group to be featured there. By mid-century, some 650 radio stations were broadcasting live hillbilly talent, and *Billboard* could report the widespread box-office appeal of country performers, even in "sedate New England." Saturday night broadcasts of several hours on Nashville's WSM, including a half-hour segment on the NBC network, made the Opry the undisputed leader of barn-dance radio programs. The immensely popular singer and fiddler Roy Acuff transformed the Opry from a local barn dance into a national showcase that represented country music's pinnacle of success.[5]

One performer who established himself at the Opry as early as 1939 was mandolin virtuoso Bill Monroe, born in 1911 in the bluegrass state of Kentucky. In the world of country music, where borrowing from mainstream pop was considered forward-looking, Monroe's string-band instrumentation and preference for acoustic instruments—mandolin, five-string banjo, fiddle, guitar, double bass—gave his group an old-fashioned flavor. Monroe cultivated complexity; instruments in his group played solo breaks between verses of songs, and their harmonic and rhythmic background often responded to calls in the singing. Most of his music was vocal, but in instrumental numbers the melody instruments took solo choruses, in the manner of jazz musicians. The up-tempo numbers were faster than anything else in country music. And he pitched his music high, with the tenor—which he sang himself—set above the melodic lead and sometimes reaching as far up as the C above middle C.

Within postwar country music, Monroe and his musicians were an un-

Bill Monroe (1911–1996), a key figure in the founding of bluegrass music, performs in the 1970s with the Bluegrass Boys, consisting of his own mandolin, plus fiddle, banjo, guitar, and double bass.

common blend of the ancient with the modern. The band's audience recognized the music, with its black-inspired rhythmic drive, as exciting, but the songs themselves were generally old-fashioned. Love songs ran toward despair. Marriage was treated, both seriously and humorously, as a conflict zone. Blues songs took an independent, sometimes hostile male point of view. Monroe and those who followed his path resisted country music's appetite for modern pop conventions. Though solidly grounded in the popular sphere, they projected a historical image that reached into the traditional sphere.

Asked in 1977 to define his style, dubbed "bluegrass" in the latter 1950s, Monroe called it "the old southern sound, that was heard years ago, many, many years ago in the backwoods, at country dances." While this comment may seem fanciful, it provides a key to Monroe's artistic imagination. Elsewhere he recalled that in writing a fiddle tune called *Land of Lincoln*, he made the piece "go the way I thought Abraham Lincoln might have heard it—a tune like he might have heard when he was a boy from some old-time fiddler." Here is a mythic image of the past disconnected from time. For Monroe meant by oldness the kind of simplicity that only folk traditions can preserve. Bluegrass, therefore, was a musical style that also served as a frame for distancing traditional songs or tunes from the present. More broadly, it may be seen as a modern *representation* of Appalachian folk music, reconstituted for the concert stage.[6]

Monroe's music exhibited links with the past that were more than mythic. The subject matter, ethos, choice of instruments, and manner of singing all looked backward to continuities with the traditional sphere. The vocal style was impersonal and stylized in the manner of Anglo-American folk singing, and the high range favored by many singers can be traced back to a number of folk practices, from black field hollers to Primitive Baptist hymnody. The piercing vocal tone is a direct legacy from Bill Monroe: the "high lonesome sound" that for many listeners has balanced the music's impersonal side with an impassioned edge.

Beginning in the middle 1950s, the music's mix of ancient and modern traits caught the fancy of young fans who were to play a role in its future development. They were not country-music lovers but folk music performers, including Mike Seeger—son of Charles and Ruth Crawford Seeger, and Pete Seeger's half-brother—and Ralph Rinzler, who would become a major promoter of bluegrass. "Mike and I," Rinzler later said, "would go to various parks sorting out who we liked—Bill [Monroe], the Stanley Brothers, Grandpa Jones, Don Reno." Approaching an unfamiliar music with other styles in their ears, these musicians heard bluegrass as a new musical genre with Anglo-American folk roots. Their folk music education had centered on Library of Congress and Folkways recordings, which emphasized Appalachian styles. And they were fascinated with performances in this style chiefly because of the traditional Appalachian elements they heard in them.[7]

Inspired by their own performing interests, these young champions of the music moved to make it accessible to others who shared their tastes. One element that thrilled them especially was the banjo playing of Earl Scruggs, with Monroe and the Bluegrass Boys from 1945 to 1948, then with the Foggy Mountain Boys, and then as emulated by Ralph Stanley, Don Reno, and other five-string banjoists. Scruggs has been credited with two key contributions to banjo playing. First and foremost, he was admired and copied for his three-finger "up-picking" style with metal picks, which allowed him to play a continuous stream of fast-moving notes while maintaining a loud, powerful tone. Second, he refused to take up the role of comedian that banjo players had often filled in country music ensembles. Scruggs's musical persona and his virtuosity introduced a new era in which banjo players were valued more for their playing than their clowning. In the music of bluegrass bands, the most exciting and virtuosic solos were often the ones taken by the banjo.[8]

In 1957, Earl Scruggs and the still-unnamed musical genre he had helped to create were recognized when Mike Seeger, who produced records as well as performing on them, brought out on Folkways Records the first bluegrass LP, *American Banjo Scruggs Style*. Seeger's recording offered an anthology of fifteen different banjo players' work, and its format lent new prestige and permanence to the music. *American Banjo Scruggs Style* was educational and practical, aimed at an audience ready for something different. The accompanying brochure's introduction, written by Ralph Rinzler, told how in 1945 "a well known mandolin picker and singer in Kentucky, Bill Monroe, organized a different type of band from those already in existence." After mentioning Scruggs and his banjo style briefly, Rinzler continued: "The banjo along with many of the 'old-time' songs, had been revived and numerous 'bluegrass' bands, patterned on those of Scruggs and Monroe, were soon doing performances and making recordings for well-known companies."[9] This sentence is important, for both the notion of revival and the "bluegrass" tag it applies to the music. The first implied that Scruggs's music was old: a *re*discovery within the traditional sphere of something temporarily set aside, perhaps in the name of progress. The second is the earliest known use of the label that stuck to Bill Monroe's musical style and that of his followers.

Earl Scruggs in 1957 was a musician working successfully in the country music business. And that makes *American Banjo Scruggs Style* a crossover record, taking music made in the popular sphere's country genre and relocating it in the traditional sphere's Appalachian folk genre. The idea that bluegrass was folk, not popular, music gained ground in the late 1950s, as shown by its presence in *Folksong '59*, a concert staged in April of that year by Alan Lomax in New York's Carnegie Hall. A few months later, a second Folkways LP compiled by Mike Seeger was released: *Mountain Music Bluegrass Style*. By this time, young folk revivalists had noticed bluegrass, and Seeger's album and accompanying brochure served them as a primer and a guidebook to the style. In the fall of that year, an article by Lomax in *Esquire* magazine introduced the music to a broader readership. According to Lomax, bluegrass was "folk music with overdrive" and "the brightest and freshest sound in American popular music today." By describing it as "a sort of Southern mountain Dixieland," he related bluegrass to a jazz style his readers would know. He also gave the music a pedigree, noting its roots in traditional mountain styles. And if readers questioned the music's importance, Lomax was ready with a dramatic historical claim: "The bluegrassers," he wrote, "have developed the first true orchestral form in five hundred [i.e., three hundred plus] years of Anglo-American music, and their silvery, pinging sound provides a suitable, yet modern and 'hot,' setting for the songs of the frontier with which American has recently fallen in love."[10]

Lomax's remarks indicate that as the 1950s drew to a close, a music other than jazz was helping to bring historical consciousness into the popular sphere. Echoes from that consciousness, revealed in the popular sphere's links to the traditional sphere, would help to reshape American musical life during the last third of the twentieth century.

THE FOLK REVIVAL AND THE POPULAR SPHERE

Our story has moved from the heart of the popular sphere toward its borders and the notion of revival: the embrace of traditional music by people outside the communities in which it originated. "Folk revival" is now a familiar idea, linked especially to the Depression and postwar years. Although centered on music in the traditional sphere, the folk revival cut across the ideals of all three spheres—the transcendence of the classical, the accessibility of the popular, and the continuity of the traditional—in a way that invited flexibility and realignment. Other than live singing and playing, its chief medium was the LP recording. The LP's length and room for explanatory notes enabled musicians and scholars to shape folk repertories into the equivalent of new works: selected performances to be appreciated and studied, such as Mike Seeger's two bluegrass recordings. Packages like these revealed transcendent value in music that had taken shape without three standard agents of transcendence: notation, formal training, or aesthetic criticism. The recordings also confirmed that, as American musicians had been proving for generations, not all music made in the name of commercial accessibility was ephemeral. The folk revival put music that had seemed to stand outside history into historical perspective, and as the historical frame was expanded, the three spheres appeared less separate than they had before. Not until after 1965 did the idea take hold that the classical, popular, and traditional spheres were separate branches of musical activity *and also* parts of one interdependent whole: a whole with a history.

In the early 1970s, the folk singer Pete Seeger gave five reasons why many young Americans had chosen folk music as their favorite form of musical expression:

1. The desire of postwar Americans to learn more about their country's heritage;
2. An increase in "do-it-yourself" activities, counteracting the passive attitude that television was supposedly producing;
3. A belief in the excellence of American folk songs, collected by folklorists and recorded by knowledgeable performers;
4. An understanding that folk songs do not necessarily stigmatize or condescend to the social groups that were often their subjects;
5. The opportunity that folk songs offer performers to comment on current events in song rather than speech.

Seeger's analysis also joins an issue that folk music fans were sometimes inclined to overlook: the difference between revivalists and people making the same music by birthright. "It takes a certain sophistication," Seeger wrote, "to sing an old spiritual without wondering if someone will call you

Publicity shot of William Lee Conley, a.k.a. Big Bill Broonzy (1893–1958), an early representative of the blues revival that blossomed in the late 1950s.

an Uncle Tom." Revivalists, already distanced from their material and accustomed to judging it aesthetically, were not much troubled by problems like these. "Maybe we had to wait a few years," Seeger suggested, "till we were far enough away from our past to be able to pick and choose the good from the bad."[11] In other words, the folk revival was a modern historical representation of a folk milieu less sophisticated than that of the revivalists themselves. Inspired by traditional music, revival musicians attributed countercultural values to it and used the combination to sketch a sound portrait of an alternative national past and present. That portrait appealed to some Americans, especially young ones, who heard in it an authenticity and directness that seemed to be missing from other popular music and, indeed, from modern life itself.

Perhaps nothing reveals more vividly the conflicts behind the folk revival than its approach to the blues. The history of the blues before World War II traces a winding path through traditional and popular music. Originating in African-American oral tradition, blues by the 1910s had begun to appear as published songs in the popular sphere. Bessie Smith and other classic female blues singers after 1920, although their roots were folk, were skilled entertainers whose race records found white buyers as well as black. Moreover, both black and white jazz musicians incorporated blues numbers into their repertory. Meanwhile, "down-home blues," an older strain, continued to flourish in the Mississippi Delta, where it had originated. Its performers were male, not female; and where classic blues artists usually performed with a piano or small jazz ensemble, these men accompanied themselves on guitar. In contrast to the theaters and clubs in which female blues artists performed, Charlie Patton and Robert Johnson worked during the 1930s in juke joints, logging camps, fish fries, and on street corners for tips.

By the late 1930s, Chicago, a magnet for Southern blacks traveling north to find work, was also a center for blues performance. "Big Bill" Broonzy, a black singer, guitar player, and songwriter, had come to the city from Arkansas in 1920, and in the 1930s began making records and singing in South Side nightspots for black audiences. Yet when Broonzy worked outside that milieu, he sometimes found himself treated more as a symbol of racial politics than the musician and entertainer he had come to be. In a New York concert in 1939, for example, he heard himself introduced as "an ex-sharecropper"—an unaccustomed label for one who had not farmed since 1916. As an entertainment professional, Broonzy, rather than trying to reconcile the expectations of his different audiences, accommodated both. For black audiences, he sang and recorded blues numbers (260 by 1952); for white audiences, he sang work songs and back-country blues he learned from records and books on country music.[12]

So began the blues revival, whose first phase peaked around 1969. Its achievements were many, including the reissue of early blues recordings; the launching of further research; the founding of blues journals; the discovery of new singers in the older folk tradition; the rediscovery of older singers who had fallen into obscurity; the staging of public events featuring blues artists; the emulation of their styles by young performers, chiefly by copying recordings; and the growth of a mystique around what were perceived as the true folk elements in the blues. The revival was thus a cultural intervention by white devotees who then became the chief consumers of its results. Looking back recently on his own involvement, one participant noted the blues revival's unforeseen result. While championing a music by and for black Americans, revivalists turned it into a music chiefly for white Americans and Europeans. The writer lays responsibility on himself and his fellow revivalists:

> By our interpretive acts, we constructed the very thing we thought we had found. This is not to say there was nothing "out there" called blues. . . . Rather, I am saying that the various activities of the blues revivalists constituted a commodity called "blues" that came to be consumed as a popular music and a symbol of stylized revolt against conservative politics and middle-class propriety.[13]

It was no coincidence that the blues revival was launched during the civil rights struggle—halfway between the Supreme Court's 1954 decision to desegregate public schools and Congress's 1965 passage of the Voting Rights Act. Against the background of a campaign that pitted Southern black activism against Southern white resistance, the music was hard to separate from racial politics. And once traditional blues performers won appreciation as artists, the injustice of their low rank in society seemed to symbolize the plight of black Americans in general. In response, blues revivalists constructed an African-American identity conspicuously like the one they envisioned for themselves. While taking up the cause of traditional blues artists in the name of rescuing them and their art from poverty and obscurity, they ended up using the blues symbolically to wage battles of their own.

The revivalists deserve credit for recognizing the artistic importance of traditional blues performers, past and present. For those who were still active, they also found opportunities to perform and record, and they promoted musicians' work by emulating their playing and singing, often with sensitivity and skill. Nevertheless, their music was a modern historical representation of a folk milieu, scrupulous in details of musical authenticity and made accessible to a new audience, chiefly white, by the layer of political implication that the blues context was now believed to carry.

GOSPEL MUSIC IN CHICAGO

The blues revival offers a good starting point for approaching black gospel music. While blues and gospel share a tonal idiom, a rhythmic approach, and a rootedness in traditional black culture, their functions, messages, and cultural positions differ fundamentally. Blues is a secular music, tied to work and entertainment; gospel is a sacred music, performed in public worship. Blues speaks for individuals, gospel for communities. Where blues states problems of human existence, gospel solves them through Christian doctrine. Blues fits in many settings; gospel, as part of black religious life, has proved less adaptable. In the commercially driven culture of the United States, where religious sentiments might alienate customers, entertainers have tended to stick to secular expression. Gospel music did not circulate widely outside black communities during the early postwar years.

Black gospel music exemplifies the attitude of *praise*, in contrast to *edification*. Praise is directed not toward worshipers but to the Almighty, whom it seeks to glorify by offering the best in human expression: the most heartfelt, ecstatic, artful, and therefore worthy. The emotionally direct yet disciplined musical stylizations of black gospel performers have proved to be among the most powerful agents of praise in the modern Christian church.

Antiblack prejudice in America has sometimes encouraged racial unity, but it has also sharpened black class consciousness. And religious life has mirrored the black community's social divisions. In Chicago, for example, middle-class blacks gravitated toward African Methodist Episcopal (AME) and Baptist churches, while working-class blacks—including migrants from the South—were more likely to join pentecostal, or "sanctified," congregations. Middle-class black denominations modeled their worship customs on white churches: in the latter 1920s, for example, the choirs at Olivet Baptist and Pilgrim Baptist, two of black Chicago's largest congregations, were singing sacred music by the likes of Bach, Handel, Mendelssohn, Haydn, and Rossini. The ministers of these churches designed worship services to keep congregational participation under control, which required a restrained preaching style and an avoidance of traditional black worship music, except for arranged, notated Negro spirituals. A very different spirit was found in pentecostal denominations such as the Church of God in Christ. Congregational hymns in their services were "gospelized" and the mood ecstatic, with jubilant singing to drums and tambourines (or even pots and pans), hand clapping and foot stomping, shouting and fainting, as in the days before Emancipation.[14]

Modern black gospel music took shape before World War II as mainstream denominations brought sanctified musical styles into their worship. A key step took place in August 1930 at a convention of black Baptists in Chicago when a singer stirred the delegates with her performance of *If You See My Savior*, composed in 1928 by Thomas A. Dorsey. Sometimes called "Georgia Tom," Dorsey was an active Chicago musician and songwriter whose performing credits included a stint as pianist for blues singer

Gertrude "Ma" Rainey. The son of a sometime clergyman, Dorsey experienced a spiritual crisis around this time and, from the early 1930s on, devoted himself entirely to sacred music. His song's success at the 1930 Baptist conference proved a turning point in his career.[15]

A change in leadership at Chicago's Ebenezer Baptist in 1931 created an opening there for the pentecostal approach. The Reverend J. H. L. Smith, who had left Alabama to become minister at Ebenezer, hoped to relax the music program's formality by featuring songs like those he had heard in the South. In January 1932, a new choir of more than a hundred, directed by Theodore Frye and accompanied by Dorsey himself, made its debut during a worship service at Ebenezer Baptist, singing the kind of songs that Smith favored.[16] Later that year, Dorsey joined with others to form the National Convention of Gospel Choirs and Choruses, dedicated to teaching the gospel style to other church musicians and choral groups. And 1932 also saw the founding of the Dorsey House of Music, the first publishing company devoted to black gospel music.

Dorsey, who remained active into the 1980s, has been dubbed the "Father of Gospel Music." Indeed, his ability to compose, improvise, and notate music, his command of blues-derived rhythmic drive, commitment to the church, and understanding of sacred and secular music as two sides of the same coin make Dorsey the very model of a black gospel musician. Moreover, the early 1930s was a time of tension in Chicago's churches between Northern urban and Southern black culture, and Dorsey came forward with music that was authentically Southern yet urbanized enough to counter the northern culture's push for Mozart and Beethoven.[17]

If Thomas A. Dorsey was its father, however, gospel music offered rich opportunities for women as well as men, including solo singers Sallie Martin, Bessie Griffin, Marion Williams, Clara Ward, and Mahalia Jackson. Jackson, born in New Orleans and raised chiefly in Chicago, was introduced to audiences far beyond the circle of black churches during the 1950s and 60s, through recordings, tours, and broadcasts. Her voice, artistry, and Christian conviction made her the world's leading gospel singer, a judgment that still stands today.

And the career of Roberta Martin proved that singing was not the only role open to women in gospel music. Born in 1907 in Arkansas, Martin moved with her family at age ten to Chicago, where private piano study gave her a solid musical background. At Ebenezer Baptist in the early 1930s, she worked with Dorsey and Theodore Frye, and accompanied a choir of youngsters. She also began to realize that gospel music offered many opportunities to a person with her skills. First and foremost was performance. In 1933, Martin recruited several male singers to form the Frye-Martin Quartet, reflecting a gender split in gospel groups, which then consisted either of male

The Roberta Martin Singers, a Chicago-based gospel ensemble, photographed in 1969.

quartets wearing business suits or female choruses wearing choir robes. By 1936, she was adding her own alto voice to the group, now called the Roberta Martin Singers, which she accompanied on piano. In the mid-

1940s, she added two women singers, marking the first combination of male and female voices in one ensemble. By then, Martin and her singers were also recording for independent labels around New York that specialized in rhythm and blues and jazz. The group spent part of the year in and around Chicago, singing in churches, meeting halls, and religious revivals. They also toured, always by car. One member recalled a typical itinerary, lasting from January to June.

> In the winter we would go to California or Florida. We would work from Jacksonville all the way down to Key West. By the time we would come out of Florida, the weather would be nice in this area, and we would go into Philadelphia, where for a number of years we sang at Mount Carmel Baptist Church from Palm Sunday to Easter Sunday.[18]

Roberta Martin sang, played, and traveled with her singers until the late 1940s. From then on, she concentrated more on writing and arranging music and running her own publishing business. For indeed, as well as a performing style rooted in African-American oral tradition, gospel was also a musical repertory. Performers often sang items from the nineteenth-century Moody-Sankey hymnbook called *Gospel Hymns*, or even traditional spirituals. Yet new songs also boosted the music's appeal for singers and congregations. As the composer of some fifty gospel songs whose religious sentiments spoke more to contemporary audiences, and as the arranger of many more, Roberta Martin put her stamp on the genre's entry into a written tradition. And as the publisher of nearly three hundred pieces of gospel sheet music between 1939 and her death in 1969, she found another way to realize income from her musical labors. Unlike Dorsey, who published only his own music, Martin advertised her inventory by publishing the songs her group sang, regardless of the composer. Alone among musicians of her era, she seems to have recognized gospel music as an endeavor that linked spirituality, music making, and commerce in a single enterprise. (The example of the musician-businessman Lowell Mason in the 1830s and 40s comes to mind.)

Lawrence Roberts, the producer of her Savoy records, recalled after her death: "Miss Martin was the first and only individual on that label—and our roster of artists reads like a 'Who's Who' of American gospel—who maintained her own publishing rights." Roberts also remembered her persuasive powers as the only Savoy artist who could wangle a cash advance of any size out of the company. Herman Lubinsky, the firm's owner, was known as a tough negotiator; yet Martin, according to Roberts, could walk into his office, say "a very few words, flash her famous smile, and get Lubinsky to pull out the checkbook and begin to write. Sometimes two days later, he would say affectionately, 'Roberts, how much did I give her?' " In tribute to her skill at playing the role of artist-in-need, Lubinsky sometimes referred to Martin as the "Helen Hayes of gospel."[19]

God Specializes, written by Gloria Griffin of the Roberta Martin Singers and arranged by Martin, is one example of a gospel-style number in published form. But as was typical of published performers' music in all genres, the written arrangement was intended only as a starting point for singers and players, who embellished the written version in performance. The song's premise is that, like a doctor, God is a specialist at rescuing people from their troubles, including physical ills, pessimism about the future, and bereavement. The opening verse, sung "slow and with feeling"—i.e., in a free tempo—invites the talents of a soloist with the energy and conviction that good gospel singers radiate:

> Have you any rivers that you think are uncrossable?
> Have you any mountains that you can't tunnel thru?
> God specializes in things thought impossible
> And he will do what no other power can do.

Three more verses follow, each paralleling the first. The climax comes in the "special chorus" that follows the verses. This chorus is sung in freely swung rhythm backed by a driving keyboard accompaniment—perhaps piano, plus an electric Hammond organ, which was introduced to gospel in the late 1940s and became part of the standard sound. Though far from prescriptive, the notation illustrates three techniques that lie at the heart of the gospel style: call and response between soloist and chorus; the chorus's reiteration of "God specializes," the song's core idea; and the "vamp," which in gospel music means a short, repeated musical section. In the vamp of *God Specializes*, the soloist lists troubles that we can imagine multiplying in the heat of performance, each addition heightening the excitement and raising the level of the listeners' and the participants' delight.

Gospel music commentators generally agree that Roberta Martin's enterprise was unmatched in the field, and that she died a rich woman, though a business associate denied the second claim. But whatever her financial status, Martin's funeral has been seen as a symbol of black gospel music's place in American life: a blend of acceptance and obscurity. When she died in January 1969 at the age of sixty-two, fifty-thousand Chicagoans passed through Mount Pisgah Baptist Church, where she was music director, to view the body, although no national newspaper or journal covered the event. Across the United States, gospel fans heard the news through word of mouth and radio broadcasts.[20]

Gospel music's roots in the heritage of spirituals, ring shouts, and the

blues have made it the wellspring from which other African-American musical traditions have flowed. Many who have excelled in jazz, blues, rhythm
and blues, and soul have served their apprenticeship in the black church.
And partly because participation in gospel music making has been widely
accessible to black Americans, its influence has been broad as well as deep.
Gospel music was responsible for much of what came to be considered emblematic in American culture of the 1960s: from rock and roll's beat, drama,
and group vibrations to the hymn singing at sit-ins and freedom marches,
and the "brother-and-sister" fraternity of revolution.[21]

36

Jazz, Broadway,
and Musical Permanence

IF GOSPEL MUSIC WAS a wellspring that nourished popular music making in postwar America, jazz was the most highly regarded distillation to emerge from the reservoir of African-American practices. By the 1940s, the notion of jazz as a true art form was well established among its fans. Jazz books, journals, discographies, and concerts in increasing number signaled that the music was being listened to seriously, reflected upon, and viewed historically. As World War II neared its end, a musical revolution burst on the jazz scene, sparked by a new generation of innovators. The modern jazz that such players as trumpeter John Birks "Dizzy" Gillespie, alto saxophonist Charlie Parker, and drummer Max Roach brought to public attention differed enough from earlier jazz to earn a name of its own: bebop.

It is true that bebop maintained elements of earlier jazz styles, including rhythmic swing, a tonal idiom based on triads, and some of the same tune repertory. Yet the differences were more conspicuous: a tendency toward faster tempos, more virtuosity and rhythmic discontinuity, less tunefulness, and bolder harmonic choices. Bebop was usually played by small groups: quartets, quintets, or sextets with one or more horns (trumpet, sax) and a rhythm section (piano, bass, drums, and sometimes guitar). A typical performance began and ended with the tune, usually played by the horns in unison. In between, each horn improvised on the tune's harmonic structure, playing one or more choruses depending on the tempo. The piano did the same, and sometimes the bass, the drummer, or both were also given solo space. In medium- or up-tempo numbers, soloists sometimes "traded fours" with each other or with the drummer or the bass player, alternating improvised four-bar sections in call-and-response fashion.

Perhaps the biggest change from earlier jazz lay in the emphasis bebop placed on improvisation. Though jazz had been recognized for its spontane-

John Birks "Dizzy" Gillespie standing with friend at New York's 52nd Street and Sixth Avenue, a corner marking one end of what jazz musicians came to call "The Street."

ity since the 1920s, bebop made solo improvisation *the* fundamental aspect of jazz performance and the main measure of a performer's standing. Such elements as the choice of tune, the expressiveness of the sound, the quality of the rhythmic groove or feel, and the interaction among performers were still important, but the bebop aesthetic treated them as secondary. Solo statements were now the main events. Hence the leaders of the new style were the best improvisers: those who could most reliably invent fresh-sounding melodic variations on given harmonic structures. The art of jazz was linked more and more to the highly demanding skill of solo improvisation.

The story of bebop's birth in Harlem during the early 1940s is well-known in the lore of American music making. Beginning around 1941, a group of young musicians, many of them big-band members, made a nightspot called Minton's Playhouse their headquarters for after-hours jamming. In this free environment, musicians experimented with new techniques and approaches, trading ideas with others of an innovative bent, including house pianist Thelonious Monk. A new style gradually took shape in Minton's workshop atmosphere, rooted in Swing Era practice but pushing beyond its norms of tonality and velocity, and expecting listeners to take the music on its own terms. As long as the new style remained an off-hours activity in Harlem, its public reception hardly mattered. But in the winter of 1943–44, white listeners got a taste of bebop when Dizzy Gillespie led a quintet—trumpet, sax, piano, bass, and drums—into the Onyx Club, a midtown Manhattan nightspot. The year 1944 also saw the end of a recording ban invoked in mid-1942 by the American Federation of Musicians to protest the broadcasting of recorded music. And in that year, the first bebop recordings were made.

To many ears accustomed to Swing Era sounds, bebop seemed a radical departure. Further, Gillespie, the first musician to win fame as a bebopper, cultivated the eccentric side of his personality in public (telling jokes at the microphone, for example, that only aficionados could understand), as if to stress that the new jazz was not for everybody. Wearing a beret and dark glasses and sporting a goatee, Gillespie also affected a look that encouraged the mainstream press, when it noticed bebop at all, to portray it as an off-beat musical cult. Whether in public or on record, then, bebop was a provocative music, performed by a new breed of musician. Rather than courting audience members, beboppers seemed almost eager to separate listeners who "dug" the music from those who did not. Indeed, the mid-1940s division of the jazz audience had much in common with a split that had occurred a few years earlier between so-called moldy-fig listeners, who loved older New Orleans–based styles, and those who preferred the straight-ahead excitement of the swing band.

In 1948–49, hoping to heal such divisions, a white critic and record producer published in a jazz journal a series of four articles that spelled out the connections between bebop and earlier jazz. And in doing so, he advanced the view that the different jazz styles—New Orleans, Chicago, Kansas City,

swing, and bebop itself—sprang from one basic impulse and were connected in a single evolutionary jazz tradition.

> Just as Armstrong, growing out of the great New Orleans tradition, sounds a
> new style, Roy Eldridge stems from Louis, and Dizzy Gillespie from El-
> dridge. These are the three great trumpet stylists of the past thirty years. The
> same trends appear on the other instruments. The contemporaries are prod-
> ucts of the past which they have absorbed. The total picture of instrumental
> change and individual experiment equals a musical language which con-
> stantly extends, reaffirms, and replenishes itself. From Jelly Roll Morton to
> Max Roach, our music is a whole art extended across the time and space of
> twentieth-century America, and back into the roots of African culture.[1]

Several ideas basic to later jazz historiography are touched on here: that
each instrument has taken its own path of development; that certain players
have served as models at certain times; that the most important jazz musicians absorb the past, then find ways to move beyond it; and that jazz musicians are all part of the same collaborative process—a twentieth-century
American music with African roots. Like Western classical music, jazz is
said here to be based on a musical language inherited, extended, and
changed over time by creative musicians. In another parallel with the classical sphere, the introduction of modern style changes, leaving some audience members baffled, provides a role for critics who can explain the notion
of an evolving style—i.e., conventions of melody, harmony, rhythm, timbre,
and texture that exist in any historical moment. The parallel is strengthened
further when the author, insisting on the continuity of jazz, warns listeners
"who cannot enjoy the music of Morton and Armstrong" that they are "truly
as poor as those" who cannot understand Lester Young and Charlie Parker.
Just as musical style in Western written composition changed but did not
necessarily improve from Beethoven's era to Stravinsky's, the evolution from
Armstrong in the 1920s to Parker in the 1940s carried from one generation to
the next a similar artistic impulse in the primarily oral tradition of jazz.

Having made the case for continuity, the author reveals his belief in
progress, declaring certain aspects of bebop superior to anything in earlier
jazz. He finds the music's rhythmic sophistication worth an article in itself.
He also finds the performers' technical virtuosity high enough to have raised
jazz to a new level. Moreover, a contemporary player "has more harmonic
material at his disposal than a Dodds, Armstrong, Hawkins, or even a Lester
Young." Harmonic advances have "filtered into jazz language," whether by
way of swing arrangers or European borrowings, because of the musicians'
increasingly cosmopolitan attitude. Bebop, the author writes, "reasserts the
individuality of the jazz musician as a creative artist."[2] Here is an idea found
in many accounts of jazz history: that although born in the realm of popular

entertainment and often threatened by the possibility of commercial sell-out, the jazz tradition was the work of musicians who put art before money. From this point of view, the commercial success of Swing Era big bands had brought to jazz corrupting influences that bebop had purged. Jazz flourished best as an art in noncommercial environments, the author claimed. Consequently, earlier creative peaks in jazz had occurred in places that provided them: New Orleans before 1917, Chicago in the early 1920s, Kansas City in the early 1930s, and Manhattan in the early and mid-1940s.

Charlie Parker, born in Kansas City, Kansas, in 1920, was a central figure whose rhythmic originality, harmonic complexity, virtuoso technique, and inventiveness as an improviser helped to bring about changes in style that much of the jazz audience disapproved. Popular music has been created chiefly to attract audiences. The audience for swing bands, which defined mainstream popular music during the war years and in which Parker began his professional life, was enormous. Yet Parker's playing was geared not to that audience but to a musical logic of his own, and to listeners who liked the result. In making a style change that reduced the audience's size, Parker seized an artistic freedom that few earlier jazz musicians had enjoyed. But that freedom imposed a burden: how to survive as a popular artist who played music that only a fraction of the jazz audience would accept.

As World War II came to an end, the idea that music could have an essence separate from the way it sounded in performance carried little or no weight in the popular sphere. That idea, basic to the claim of transcendent artistry, belonged to the classical sphere. Parker and his contemporaries were the first generation of jazz musicians to believe that in jazz, as in the classical sphere, musical creation, presentation, and reception could be different things. Instead of thinking backward from reception to creation, tailoring their music to an idea of what audiences would relish and buy, they devoted themselves to creation and performance, in the manner of classical musicians letting reception take care of itself.

As jazz has evolved, so have the musicians' links with their audiences. In early twentieth-century New Orleans, the music that came to be called jazz belonged to communal activity, played chiefly by nonprofessionals. It was functional music for dancing, parades, picnics, and other events. As jazz found its way onto stages, musicians learned to tailor their performances for theaters and nightclubs, where it belonged to a larger spectacle: a floor show, a variety program, or a movie screening. In those settings, they were encouraged to feature audience-pleasing routines, as Louis Armstrong did with great success. As late as the 1950s, an ad in *Down Beat* magazine, the premier trade journal, warned performers to "remember today you not only must be able to play, you must be able to do some acting, singing, dancing and also speak lines."[3] In other words, jazz belonged to show business.

Trade professionals, however well they played, had better be able to keep the customers entertained.

Bandleaders like Ellington and Basie proved during the Swing Era that customers could be kept dancing to music that was artistically satisfying to compose and perform. When the war ended and many big bands broke up, a cadre of modern players remained who were eager to emphasize the listening side of jazz. But when they began to be booked into Manhattan clubs without dance floors, they had no tradition of presentational manner, stage deportment, or programming to guide them. Avoiding both standard tricks of showmanship and the formality of concert-hall performers, Parker and most of his colleagues brought a stage manner that might be irreverent, nonchalant, or standoffish into a nightclub setting where audiences were primed for entertainment and managers for financial profit.

In the early postwar years, the musicians' coupling of uncertain show business skills with artistic originality sparked a unique excitement. Though pared down to a small fraction of the Swing Era's scale, New York's modern jazz scene blossomed: uptown in Harlem, downtown in Greenwich Village, but most of all in the heart of midtown, on 52nd Street between Fifth and Sixth Avenues. Tenor saxophonist Dexter Gordon later described "The Street," where all the top jazz clubs were located, as "the most exciting half a block in the world. Everything was going on—music, chicks, connections . . . so many musicians working down there, side by side"—a milieu, in other words, where women who were drawn to jazz musicians could be found, as could drug dealers.[4] (Parker had been a heroin user since his teenage years and was also a heavy drinker. Many others followed his example, partly in the belief that drug use sparked Parker's creative imagination.) Fans of the music made up in passion what they lacked in numbers. Those who "dug" modern jazz gloried in being "hip" to the music's aura of freedom, intensity, and sense of self-assertion by a group of young performers, chiefly black, who radiated command and independence of spirit.

Public debate about what bebop musicians were "saying" was led by white commentators. Some suggested parallels to modern music in the classical sphere. Reflecting later on that notion, however, the writer Albert Murray saw the music's complexity in a different light. Rather than "a theorist dead set on turning dance music into concert music," Murray wrote, Parker was an innovator "adding a new dimension of elegance to the Kansas City drive, which is to say to the velocity of celebration." To Murray's ears, Parker's adventures in melody, harmony, and rhythm demonstrated that he "was out to swing not less but more." "Sometimes he tangled up your feet but that was when he sometimes made your insides dance as never before."[5]

Parker's Mood, a blues number recorded for the Savoy label in 1948, reveals the saxophonist's artistry in full bloom. In the half century since he, pi-

Alto saxophonist Charlie "Bird" Parker and trumpeter Dizzy Gillespie, with bassist Tommy Potter (1950).

anist John Lewis, bassist Curly Russell, and drummer Max Roach made this record for 78-rpm release, it has been reissued, transcribed, written about, discussed, and canonized. Today, hearing the music on record and in a context created by jazz historians and critics, it is easy to imagine that Parker and his colleagues recorded *Parker's Mood* in a line of instrumental performances reaching back to Jelly Roll Morton and King Oliver, not to mention Louis Armstrong, who was still active and musically vigorous. But for Parker, his collaborators, and the staff of Herman Lubinsky's Savoy record company, far more important than who might be listening five decades hence was the question of who would buy a recording in 1948.

Parker's Mood might have been heard in its own day as related to any one of several branches of the blues family, including (1) the down-home oral tradition from the rural South that would soon spark the blues revival; (2) a written classic stage tradition that singers had been performing with jazz ensembles since the day of Ma Rainey and Bessie Smith; (3) a newer urban practice featuring the electric guitar that was gaining black fans from

Chicago in the North to Texas in the South; (4) the style of black urban popular music soon to be dubbed rhythm and blues that by the mid-1950s would inspire the white teenage music called rock and roll; and (5) the so-called gospel blues, emphasizing a sixteen-bar form closely related to the twelve-bar blues, popularized by Thomas A. Dorsey. Each of these genres had its own audience, but those audiences were not mutually exclusive, nor were they necessarily distinct from the audience for modern jazz. As a series of choruses based on a blues feeling and structure that all these genres held in common, *Parker's Mood* in 1948 would not have sounded out of place coming from a jukebox in a black neighborhood barbershop, café, or bar.

But for all the accessibility that it offered different audiences of the late 1940s, *Parker's Mood* also emphasizes invention in a way that targeted fans of modern jazz, whether black or white. Four improvised choruses in B-flat are played: two by Parker, one by Lewis, and a final one by Parker. A typical be-bop performance begins and ends with the "head" (composed melody); but this work presents no returning melody at all, except an introductory two-bar figure that returns after the last chorus as a tag. Perhaps the slow tempo explains why. Given Parker's skill as a blues improviser, it would have seemed perverse to devote two choruses (half the performance) to a com-posed melody, whose usual function is to act as a springboard for the im-provised choruses. (A fifth chorus would have made the performance too long to fit on a standard 78-rpm disc.) Hence, the composition recorded and circulated as *Parker's Mood* consisted of a tempo, a chord progression, and a soulful spirit, but no precomposed melody.

Still, the lack of a standard twelve-bar head does not leave *Parker's Mood* short on tunefulness, for the saxophonist fits plenty of melody into his dec-oration of the harmonic structure. In fact, each chorus begins with a melodic statement that is hard to forget. In the first, Parker opens with a pair of complementary two-bar phrases. In the second, he offers a shorter statement that, ignited by a bold upbeat octave leap, lands with a turning gesture on the downbeat and then, after a brief stutter on B-flat, dissolves into a long descending cascade. John Lewis's piano provides a lyric interlude on the third chorus. Then Parker returns with another arresting statement, in which he outlines first the tonic triad (B-flat) and then the subdominant (E-flat), separated by another B-flat stutter.

Parker's Mood is remarkable in many ways, but perhaps especially for its summarizing of blues technique, from the straightforward tunefulness that begins each chorus to the asymmetrical tracery that follows. In the second phrase of the last chorus, for example, drummer Max Roach shifts suddenly into a high-hat cymbal pattern in double time—a suggestion that the beat is suddenly moving twice as fast as before—and Parker responds with grace and balance.

Parker's Mood is the kind of performance that can reward many different kinds of listening. The intro and tag and the chorus beginnings suggest a soloist in the role of singer or preacher, "telling it like it is." But the asymmetrical, muttering, prose-like side of Parker's velocity of celebration is present too—in every chorus, and especially the second, where pauses overlay the four-bar phrases with melodic gestures of varying, unpredictable length. For the scholarly analyst eager to test the saxophonist's invention against composers who write their music rather than improvising it, transcribing the performance into musical notation shows the worthiness of *Parker's Mood* on that front as well. In three minutes flat, Parker explores a range of techniques and shadings of a mood that testify to the breadth and richness of the blues sensibility in the hands of an expert practitioner of modern jazz.

For all the disorderliness of Parker's personal life, contemporaries recognized his superior musicianship and originality, and by 1950 jazz already bore clear signs of his influence. Some of his compositions were by then standards. His recordings were widely known, and saxophonists were not the only players who wore them out with repeated listening, trying to learn from his unique style of improvising. Finally, Parker's bold artistic spirit, ready to follow musical logic wherever it might lead, inspired other musicians to push the boundaries further, which in turn distanced modern jazz even more from the center of the popular sphere, on which it relied for economic support.

Another aspect of Parker's legacy was the recognition that high technical skill was needed to perform modern jazz. And here it may be helpful to turn to Martin Williams's *The Jazz Tradition*, published in 1970: a book of chronologically arranged essays by a critic who in the 1950s was working out his own understanding of the art of jazz, as Roger Pryor Dodge had done in the 1920s and 30s.[6] Williams notes the virtuosity of most first-generation modernists, including Gillespie, Roach, and pianist Bud Powell. Yet those who dominated the music's second decade (1955–65), he says, made their mark in other ways. He cites Thelonious Monk, John Lewis, and Miles Davis as prime examples of musicians who turned their lack of virtuoso technique into avenues for exploration. And each contributed to a general "cutting back, opening up, and airing out of the density of modern jazz." Monk's roots as a pianist lay in the Harlem stride school of James P. Johnson and Fats Waller. As the first major jazz composer since Ellington, however, Monk developed a performing style that put gesture above facility. His lean-textured compositions seem to have originated out of that style—hence from instrumental rather than vocal sounds. And they are grounded in a rhythmic sense as asymmetrical as Parker's. In mastering "displaced accents, shifting meters, shaded delays, and anticipations," Monk's ear grasped the artistic potential of "effective pause and of meaningfully employed space, rest, and silence." By placing a Monk blues like *Misterioso* (1947) in a line with Duke Ellington and Jelly Roll Morton, Williams suggests a jazz background for such distilled expression. Yet Monk's sound, with melody and harmony organized around the rhythm, was a uniquely modern one.[7]

John Lewis, like Monk a pianist-composer, made his mark as music director of the Modern Jazz Quartet (MJQ, with piano, vibraharp, bass, and drums), formed in the early 1950s in the hope of expanding the audience for modern jazz. Rather than building their performances solely around improvising, Lewis and his three colleagues set out to provide music that could be listened to attentively in a concert hall.[8] Lewis wrote pieces for the quartet that combined composition and improvisation in ways that repaid close listening.

Django, for example, honors the memory of the European gypsy guitarist-turned-jazzman Django Reinhardt. And Lewis's composition, in **ABA** form, begins and ends with a dirge-like melody twenty bars long, played in a slow, free tempo. The faster main body of the piece (**B**) offers a series of choruses over which vibraharpist Milt Jackson and Lewis solo. The thirty-two-bar chorus, however, does not follow the standard **aaba** or **abac** plan but is in the form **aa** (6 + 6 measures) **b** (8 measures) **a** (4 measures) **c** (8 measures), with **a** based on a minor-mode harmonic progression, **b** on a single repeated pitch in the bass (pedal point), and c on a blues-derived riff-like figure played by bassist Percy Heath. Because each chorus offers three distinct changes of material and mood, the players are invited to respond in kind. In a 1960 performance, recorded live in Sweden, the transition from the **B** section to the return of the dirge (**A**) takes place in a long *diminuendo* whose delicacy proves that modern instrumental jazz can achieve tenderness.[9]

In works like *Django*, John Lewis is credited with bringing order and form to the materials that brilliant first-generation improvisers like Parker had discovered. The Modern Jazz Quartet, with its relatively soft, "cool" sound and the serious demeanor of the players, who dressed in dark business suits and ties, opened the concert hall to a kind of jazz akin to classical chamber music. And Lewis explored that link further by composing Baroque-style "suites" and jazz fugues for the MJQ. Other groups, notably the Gerry Mulligan Quartet and especially the Dave Brubeck Quartet, tapped into and expanded further the chiefly white audience that embraced the restrained musical intensity that Lewis and the MJQ pioneered. And in the latter 1950s, trumpeter Miles Davis made a series of recordings with an ensemble led by arranger Gil Evans that also worked similar emotional territory.

Davis, the third of the key second-generation masters, emerged in the latter 1940s with an introspective lyric approach that contradicted the image

Trumpeter Miles Davis (1926–1991) was a magnetic presence on the jazz scene from the mid-1940s through the 1980s.

of modern jazz as virtuoso music. By 1954, he had discovered an intensely personal sound that was often heard in tightly muted playing, close to the microphone. Williams thinks that the Davis sound's combination of low volume and distinctive color became popular partly because it made good background music. Yet he finds the sound "a triumph of human feeling over its electronic vehicle." By the mid-1950s, Davis's growing technical command of the trumpet was also enabling him to vary his sound and to execute unexpected rhythms cleanly.[10]

In *Walkin'*, a blues number recorded in 1954 with a group including trombonist J. J. Johnson, pianist Horace Silver, and drummer Kenny Clarke, Davis exhibited new interest in melodic development and a style in which silences became fundamental to his musical vocabulary. From then on, "one passionate note from Miles Davis seemed to imply a whole complex of expressive sounds, and three notes a ravishing melody." By the decade's end, on a Gil Evans–arranged album called *Sketches of Spain* (1959–60), Davis could play a Holy Week lament for the tragedy of the crucifixion reflecting "a stark, deeply felt communal anguish that jazz has not heard since King Oliver." In 1959, on the album called *Kind of Blue*, made with saxophonists Julian "Cannonball" Adderley and John Coltrane and pianist Bill Evans, among others, Davis pursued simplicity and directness of statement in another way, basing the thirty-two-bar structure of *So What* not on a chord pattern but an eight-note Dorian, or modal, scale. And in 1965, in a group with tenor saxophonist Wayne Shorter and the young virtuoso drummer Tony Williams, Davis again found the cutting edge of jazz innovation with a set of his own unusual compositions, including *Circle*. For Williams, however, the move toward fusion with rock music that Davis made in the next stage of his career was an artistic failure, chiefly "because of the doggedly static nature of the rhythm." But there is no doubt of Williams's respect for Davis's artistry. "The lightness of his trumpet sound had something to do with his broad acceptance, to be sure," he writes, "and because of that lightness he has been called 'a man walking on eggshells.' But Davis the musician walked firmly and sure of foot; if he ever encountered eggshells, his intensity would probably grind them to powder."[11]

Miles Davis's 1954 recording of *Walkin'* was issued on a 33-1/3-rpm record, a format developed for classical music. The flexible length that LP recording offered jazz musicians influenced the content of their music as well as boosting its prestige. And by emphasizing kinship to the classical sphere, the LP influenced the public perception of jazz as an art. Where a popular single contained just two numbers—one on either side of a 78- or 45-rpm disc—an LP offered many more. The relatively high price encouraged repeated listening, which helped fans absorb unfamiliar styles. By reissuing recordings from earlier times, LPs invited listeners to think about jazz's historical continuity, and they came with liner notes by a writer who might suggest a frame for listening. Thanks in part to LP recordings, fans of modern jazz began to include more concertgoers and readers of the journals for which jazz critics now commonly wrote. Growing numbers of white college-age youngsters embraced jazz as their own. And in the summer of 1954, the Newport Jazz Festival, modeled on classical festivals, was founded in Newport, Rhode Island. Jazz was finding a new place on the American cultural scene.

But what was that place? Did jazz in the middle 1950s and after still belong to a popular sphere that rock and roll was reshaping? By transcending the circumstances of their origin and enduring as admired pieces of music, did not classic jazz performances undermine the three-sphere structure of American music making? These are legitimate questions flowing from the situation of jazz musicians in postwar America, who made music in a realm built around accessibility. To widen access further, jazz musicians also made records. Writers on jazz, looking beyond the recordings' commercial purpose, treated them as an artistic legacy. And especially from the early 1950s on, they shaped that commercial outpouring into a *body of work*, centered around examples like *Parker's Mood* and *Django*. Indeed, as noted earlier in this chapter, jazz writers conceptualized an artistic tradition in jazz that, with its great figures, canonic works, and style periods, paralleled the tradition of the Western classical sphere. And they did so before many of the musicians began to describe themselves publicly as artists, and *long* before most musicians, critics, teachers, and writers in the classical sphere showed more than passing interest in the idea of jazz as an art form. In a day when such labels as "new music" and "contemporary music" pointed to a Europe-centered classical sphere centered in academia and the concert hall, jazz musicians lacked the intellectual prestige to convey their own artistic ideas beyond the circle of jazz fans, though that circle was widening. Therefore, even though modern jazz musicians scorned the popular sphere's emphasis on easy accessibility, their informal customs of training, repertory, notation, and intellectual exchange—and the general tone of the music itself—held more in common with the commercial marketplace than the institutions of the classical sphere.

These facts provide a background against which the ideas in Martin Williams's *The Jazz Tradition* may be viewed. The book portrays jazz as a Western art conceived and shaped by black American musicians. As a white Southerner, born in Richmond, Virginia, in 1924, Williams recognized that some would reject his portrayal; and as an author with no formal training in music, he also realized that his own credentials would be questioned. Nevertheless, armed with sharp ears, an excellent memory, and a profound trust in the communicative power of music, he showed a talent for getting at what made the musicians tick as artists. Tenor saxophonist Sonny Rollins is discussed as a master of extended improvised solos, unified not just by mood and harmonic structure but by the continual reworking of repeated fragments of melody. Pianist Horace Silver, proponent of a mid-1950s trend toward "funk" that subordinated melody and harmony to the rhythmic groove, is described as a dedicated professional craftsman. Pianist Bill Evans, "the most important and influential white jazz musician after Bix Beiderbecke," is recognized for recording some of the most emotionally exposed lyric performances ever conceived in jazz. Bass player and composer Charles Mingus is cited as a musician who through interviews, liner notes, speeches, and an autobiography, "seemed to offer us himself . . . as a part of his music." And saxophonist Ornette Coleman is credited with "the first fundamental reevaluation of basic materials and basic procedures for jazz since the innovations of Charlie Parker."[12]

The essays in *The Jazz Tradition* point to another subject that deserves comment: jazz composing, arranging, and instrumental playing have a long history as male preserves. The only role readily open to women before the recent past was as a singer—Billie Holiday and Ella Fitzgerald are well-known examples—featured in a big band, partly for musical variety and partly for show-business glamour. In recent years, as women have increased their presence in jazz, there has been debate about whether their past contributions have been properly recognized. Whatever the answer, Williams's essays on Holiday and Sarah Vaughan are the only ones in his book about modern female jazz performers. Subtitled "The Meaning of Self-Discovery," the Vaughan essay sketches a portrait of a remarkable musician.

Williams notes Vaughan's arrival on the scene in the 1940s, without for-

Sarah Vaughan (1924–1990), a remarkable singer by any
standard, could use her capacious voice as a jazz instrument
or a vehicle for words, or both.

mal training but with a voice of exceptional range, body, volume, and "variety of vocal textures," to which she added excellent control, plus an ear and
sense of pitch that "were just about perfect." Vaughan's achievements are
summed up in a pair of different challenges she met: (1) adopting her vocal
techniques "to the subtler demands and nuances of swing," and (2) "exploring and sustaining the mood and potential drama of each song while not in-
hibiting herself vocally or musically." The essay ends with a tribute that
places Vaughan's work in a context beyond jazz, popular music, or American
music: she is seen as a contributor to the history of singing. "It took several
generations of singers in seventeenth- and eighteenth-century Italy to explore the potential of the human voice and arrive at what we call the *bel
canto* style," Williams writes. "Sarah Vaughan accomplished the virtual
equivalent of those explorations in a contemporary American style, in less
than one lifetime, and in a single voice."[13]

Mixed evaluations are rare in the essays that make up *The Jazz Tradition*.
Yet mixed treatment is given to saxophonist John Coltrane, considered by
many listeners to be the dominant figure in the history of jazz. Williams
grants Coltrane's virtuosity and inventiveness, but he believes that style

changes in the last years of Coltrane's career—especially his attempts to reconcile jazz with expressions of non-Western spirituality—forced him sometimes into a state of "personal indecision or frustration." "Coltrane's authentically wild passion" in some performances "seems not so much a part of the music as a part of the musician." Indeed, Coltrane's explorations could carry him beyond the reach of jazz's power to identify basic human conflicts and resolve them within the same musical framework, a power fundamental to the jazz tradition as Williams understands it. Creating music that sounded to Williams more static than dynamic, the saxophonist sometimes left conflicts unresolved. The essay on Coltrane ends with an unusually personal comment, part credo and part confessional. It was not, Williams writes, that Coltrane was anything less than "a true artist."

> I think he was, and I think that like all true artists he spoke of matters of the spirit, not of society and politics. Indeed, the deeper purpose of the incantatory sections in his music has to be—as with any incantation—to evoke the gods and the demons whose ways are timeless and yet always contemporary. Perhaps, if his music does not quite reach me and satisfy me as it has reached some others, the answer is that the gods he sought to invoke are not my gods.
>
> In any case, Coltrane was bold enough to state his message so that the future must acknowledge that he has been with us.[14]

The rising artistic status of jazz had encouraged some musicians to focus their energies on the common ground held with the Western classical tradition. In 1957, classical composer and French horn player Gunther Schuller, long involved with jazz and just beginning to write seriously about it, coined the term "third stream" for music that brought jazz techniques into the classical sphere, or vice-versa. "Through improvisation or written composition or both," the goal of third-stream music, Schuller wrote, was to synthesize "the essential characteristics and techniques" of the two established styles into a new hybrid.[15] John Lewis and the Modern Jazz Quartet were already working that territory in compositions like *Django*, recorded first in 1954–55. And Schuller himself explored third-stream possibilities in such works as *Transformation* (1957) for jazz ensemble, *Concertino* (1959) for jazz quartet and symphony orchestra, and *Variants on a Theme of Thelonious Monk* (1960), for thirteen instruments, recorded with Ornette Coleman, Eric Dolphy, and Bill Evans among the performers.

Around 1960, then, jazz musicians were borrowing classical forms and techniques; classical musicians were cultivating jazz fusions and intersections; jazz performers were playing regularly in concert halls and at festivals; classical composers were introducing jazz improvisation into written concert works; and critics were debating the merits of such blendings. But even as modern jazz was being pulled toward the classical sphere's orbit, a counter-pull was taking place, led by black musicians and activists, toward the African traditions of the music. Spurred by the black struggle for social equality, these men and women believed that some modern jazz performers were working out a characteristically black mode of expression whose deepest spirit was not accessible to whites. Music like Coltrane's, they argued, was best understood from a black perspective, and a white critic like Williams was therefore unqualified to judge his work (though Coltrane himself never made any such claim). The rise of black nationalism during the 1960s brought an ideology into the discourse on jazz that would influence its creation, presentation, and reception deeply in the years to come.

Meanwhile, although jazz remained unique in the serious critical attention it received, it was not the only genre outside the classical sphere that was being touted for classic status and higher intellectual respect.

BROADWAY MUSICALS IN THE POSTWAR ERA

On October 7, 1956, the thirty-nine-year-old composer and conductor Leonard Bernstein surveyed the American musical theater in a national television broadcast. "For the last fifteen years," he told viewers, "we have been enjoying the greatest period our musical theater has ever known." Bernstein supported his statement with a list of recent classic Broadway shows: *Pal Joey, Annie Get Your Gun, Oklahoma!, South Pacific, Guys and Dolls, Kiss Me, Kate.* And he credited the blossoming to the talent of these shows' creators, illustrating his claim with examples from Rodgers and Hammerstein's *South Pacific.*[16]

Bernstein's experience as a classical musician had taught him that opera deserved its high place in the musical and theatrical hierarchy. Yet the works featured in his broadcast had found a balance point between operatic grandeur and the easy accessibility of standard show-business musical forms. The shows he called young classics all belonged "to an art that arises out of American roots, out of our speech, our tempo, our moral attitudes, our way of moving." And the placement of this American art, as with jazz, was no small issue. As Bernstein saw it, the best recent shows were neither opera nor light entertainment, but a new form somewhere between the two. "We are in a historical position now similar to that of the popular musical theater in Germany just before Mozart came along," Bernstein announced. "In 1750, the big attraction was what they called the *Singspiel*," a popular form that "took the leap to a work of art through the genius of Mozart" in *The Magic Flute* of 1791. American musical theater needed only "for our Mozart to come along. . . . And this event can happen any second. It's almost as though it is our moment in history, as if there is a historical neces-

Composer and conductor Leonard Bernstein (1918–1990) made a strong impact on the public with television appearances that took up serious musical matters in an engaging way.

sity that gives us such a wealth of creative talent at this precise time."[17] Less than a year later, Bernstein himself stepped into the role he had outlined for the new American Mozart. In September 1957, *West Side Story*, with a book by Arthur Laurents, choreography by Jerome Robbins, and lyrics by Stephen Sondheim set to Bernstein's music, opened in New York to the acclaim of critics and audiences.

The high value Bernstein placed on American musicals seemed calculated to surprise 1956 viewers, for their artistic prestige was then rather low. Musicals were ignored by music critics, who saw the classical and popular spheres—art and light entertainment, to use Bernstein's terms—as separated by a firm barrier. This is not to say that the musical was free of aesthetic ideology. Since the success of *Oklahoma!* (1943), writers had generally agreed that shows emphasizing songs, dances, and high-spirited romance lacked the impact of integrated shows whose musical numbers were rooted in the drama. Beyond that idea, however, there was nothing comparable to the sustained, written, public discourse that for centuries had been focused on operatic drama, music, characters, and aesthetics.

In opera, the act of bringing artistic transcendence to modern audiences called for regular historical explanation and reinterpretation of the works themselves. If a work was new, both its quality and its connection to earlier operas received critical discussion. The Broadway musical, however, needed no such go-betweens. Authors and composers submitted their work directly to the judgment of audiences, whose verdict, registered at the box office, was equally direct. Aesthetic decisions were made to trigger positive public responses. If the audience seemed pleased, the decision was right; if not, changes were made. A tryout run preceded a show's Broadway opening so that out-of-town audience response could be used to identify problems, but the makers of musicals took the public pulse even earlier. Alan Jay Lerner, the librettist and lyricist of *My Fair Lady* and *Brigadoon*, wrote that when he and composer Frederick ("Fritz") Loewe finished a song, "we would dash around the neighborhood, looking for 'customers,' as Fritz would say, meaning neighbors for whom to play it. Naturally, our captive audience was complimentary, but somehow we could always tell if the compliments were because of the song or because of the friendship. Very often it influenced us and made us aware of a weakness." Lerner also related that when Irving Berlin was working on a musical film, he would sometimes show up at the studio to play a new song for the crew. "The moment he finished he would look around the room and if he did not see the exact reaction he wanted in the eyes of his listeners, no matter how they may have raved, the song was never heard again."[18]

When placed against the perspective laid out by Leonard Bernstein's 1956 telecast, these comments point to a contradiction. On one hand, an experienced classical musician and Broadway composer was comparing musicals with Mozart. On the other, leading figures of the Broadway stage were deferring to public taste in a way that no classical composer would do. Bernstein tuned his idealism to catch Broadway's transcendent possibilities. Lerner, Loewe, and Berlin, for whom such idealism was a distraction from the task at hand, took the pragmatic stance of craftsmen. And thus a prominent American art form developed with no clear idea of itself as an art.

In his 1967 book *The American Musical Theater: a Consideration*, Lehman Engel offers an intellectual framework to define the musical's particular brand of artistry. Rather than a scholar or critic, the author was a working musician who spent much of his life composing for the stage and television and conducting Broadway shows. Engel names eleven shows from the years 1940–57 that represented "that theater in its most complete and mature state." Noting that no one had ever adequately defined what makes a good musical, he searches for common elements in these shows, hoping to distill "certain working principles—not rules or formulas—imposed by the nature of the genre and the world in which we live."[19]

Engel's impulse to write about the Broadway musical sprang from a sense of mission: a desire to promote the writing of better musical shows. His list of eleven includes the six Bernstein praised in 1956, plus *Brigadoon, My Fair Lady, West Side Story, Carousel,* and *The King and I.* What traits, if any, do these musicals have in common? As a composer, Engel might have been expected to find his answer in the music. But years in rehearsal rooms and theater pits taught him that in the musical, for all its links to opera, the librettist carried "the largest single share of the responsibility for a show's success," and he proceeds to illustrate why the best Broadway musicals were based on a preexistent story, play, novel, or historical character. In the opening scene of each model show, "the author introduces, as such, his two principal characters, indicates directly or implicitly some conflict of position or personality that separates them, and sets up a *need* in the audience to see a genuine resolution of their differences." The audience's need is rooted in character, which is also the librettist's responsibility. The romantic hero and heroine must be convincing and recognizable so that audiences will identify with them. The universal condition of humankind is therefore simplified and expressed through just two people. And audience members, "belonging to the same human race, understand, feel, laugh at, and celebrate" the pair, participating in their drama because they are, "in reality, ourselves."[20]

To Engel, what separated the great contemporary musicals from those of the 1920s and 30s was not so much the music, choreography, or acting, but the more realistic stories and better-rounded characters. And characters who could be "at once romantic, 'serious,' and funny" were hard to create from scratch.[21] Alan Jay Lerner wrote that "any character in a play is a condensation." And he added: "From the mass of mosaic pieces that form the pattern of each human being, the author selects the few predominant ones that he wishes the audience to know and that makes it possible to tell the story."[22] It is simpler to create convincing stage characters out of existing ones than to conceive of whole characters who will never be shown onstage in more than a fragmentary way.

In successful musicals, as in opera, personal traits only hinted at in the dialogue could be revealed in a song. As Lerner put it, his goal was "to write musical plays in which the songs would be witty and tender because the characters were witty and tender."[23] And Engel's *American Musical Theater* concludes that the best Broadway musicals were romantic fantasies whose heroes and heroines invited audience members to catch glimpses of themselves, as if in a mirror. A proper flow of story, dance, and song was essential, but success depended on the audience caring that the main conflict be resolved happily. Characters who could be imagined as one's own alter egos were the key to that caring.

All the shows on Engel's list succeeded as dramatic wholes. At the same time, like shows of the earlier Golden Age, they contained hit songs that circulated independently. The list leaves no doubt that Rodgers and Hammerstein were supreme masters of the kind of musical play that swept audiences up in its aura. It also testifies to the creative powers of two leading composer-lyricists of an earlier day who survived in the postwar era, when they found the right book. One was Irving Berlin, whose *Annie Get Your Gun* proved to be the leading hit of 1946. The other was Cole Porter, whose *Kiss Me, Kate* (1948) took Shakespeare's *The Taming of the Shrew* as its starting point.

If *Oklahoma!* was the most popular musical of the 1940s, Lerner and Loewe's *My Fair Lady* (1956) claimed that honor for the 1950s, breaking the earlier show's record by running on Broadway for six years and a total of 2,717 performances. And since *My Fair Lady* is one of the shows that Lehman Engel studied with care, it is no surprise that the work fits his description of what makes a good musical. Lerner's book is based on George Bernard Shaw's *Pygmalion*, a play inspired by the classical legend of a sculptor who fell in love with his own statue. The show starts by introducing the two main characters and the gulf between them: a conflict that is resolved at the end by love.

In the opening scene, set in a London market, Professor Henry Higgins, a phonetics expert, encounters Eliza Doolittle, a raucous, uneducated flower seller. Lerner later explained: "What Shaw wanted us to know about Higgins was that he was passionate about the English language, believed it to be the principal barrier separating class from class, and that he was a misogynist."[24] And these traits are established immediately. After overhearing Eliza's speech, Higgins scolds her for the coarseness of its sound, and then launches into his first song: *Why Can't the English (Teach Their Children How to Speak)?* At the song's end, he bets an acquaintance that he can turn Eliza into a lady in six months, simply by improving her speech. He then leaves the stage. And now, having sketched the sharp-tongued, language-loving, woman-hating Higgins, Lerner and Loewe use music to fill out the character of the woman who has aroused his disapproval. In *Wouldn't It Be Loverly?*, sung with an ensemble of other market folk, Eliza imagines a life of comfort to replace the harsh one she knows. The song's quiet charm shows another side of Eliza. And by the end of it, two conflicts have been laid out: Will Higgins turn this untutored girl into a speaker of proper English? and how could romance bloom between such an ill-matched pair?

The first is resolved before the second, which is heightened by Higgins's antifemale harangues and his insensitivity to Eliza's feelings. Act I revolves around Eliza's language study, whose progress is slow. Late one evening, a crisis is reached as Higgins tries to teach her the long "a," as in "take instead

As Professor Henry Higgins in Lerner and Loewe's *My Fair Lady* (1956), Rex Harrison coaches Julie Andrews (Eliza Doolittle) on English pronunciation while Robert Weede as Col. Pinkerton listens.

of tyke." Neither bullying nor endless repetition has worked, so Higgins gives persuasion a try.

> HIGGINS: Eliza, I know you're tired. I know your head aches. . . . But . . . think what you're dealing with. The majesty and grandeur of the English language. It's the greatest possession we have. The noblest sentiments that ever flowed in the hearts of men are contained in its extraordinary, imaginative and musical mixtures of sounds. That's what you've set yourself to conquer, Eliza. And conquer you will. (*He rises, goes to the chair behind his desk and seats himself heavily.*) Now try it again.
> ELISA: The rain in Spain stays mainly in the plain.

The line, delivered haltingly at first, then repeated with more confidence, marks a breakthrough in Eliza's lessons. Her ear has finally caught the sound of correct pronunciation, and her tongue has imitated it. The magic of the moment is celebrated in a song based on Eliza's properly pronounced line. Heroine and hero finally discover common ground; the tango rhythm of

The Rain in Spain allows them to revel in singing, dancing, and the joy of shared achievement.

From this point on, Eliza proves herself a brilliant student, and Higgins passes her off at a formal ball as a person of high birth. But with this conflict solved, the drama moves into deeper waters. Eliza, who by now has won the audience's heart, is in love with a man so self-absorbed that he remains oblivious to her feelings. Lerner and Loewe crystallize Higgins's chauvinism in *A Hymn to Him*, a song shared with his friend and professional colleague Colonel Pickering. The number ends with the two middle-aged bachelors in full agreement about how women should act.

> HIGGINS: Why can't a woman behave like a man?
> Men are so friendly, good-natured and kind;
> A better companion you never will find.
> If I were hours late for dinner, would you bellow?
> PICKERING: Of course not.
> HIGGINS: If I forgot your silly birthday, would you fuss?
> PICKERING: Nonsense.
> HIGGINS: Would you complain if I took out another fellow?
> PICKERING: Never.
> HIGGINS: Why can't a woman be like us?

In the end, however, Higgins, who claims credit for Eliza's transformation, realizes that he has "grown accustomed to her face" and feels lonely without her. And when she appears unexpectedly at his house, he delivers the show's last line to a character who hears it as the equivalent of "I love you too." "Eliza?" he asks. "Where the devil are my slippers?"[25] With irony instead of a romantic speech, Higgins preserves his character, Eliza gets the man she fell in love with, and the audience is invited to assume that the gulf between them has been dissolved by his (indirect) expression of approval.

Shaw's play *Pygmalion* (1912) ends with Henry Higgins still a smug bachelor and Eliza Doolittle prepared to make her own way in life. But musical comedy relies on the blossoming of romantic love. Musicals pay far more attention to falling in love than to its long-term consequences. Once the conflict is resolved, the adventure is over, and living happily ever after is assumed. In the postwar era, such fairy-tale expectations kept the Broadway musical in its niche as a fantasy geared to mass audience taste, no matter how sophisticated its musical techniques. Even the near-operatic *West Side Story*, the only tragic example in Engel's canon, which ends with the hero being shot dead, seems the exception that proves the rule. Modeled after Shakespeare's *Romeo and Juliet*, the story turns on unconditional, idealized, almost mystical love at first sight. While most musicals end with the hero and heroine poised to begin a life together, Maria and Tony are denied that chance by the hate-filled society in which they live. Yet before he dies, they experience their moment of perfect bliss, musical-theater-style.

If we are seeking one more reason that the musical comedy of the postwar era was not taken as a serious art form by critics, perhaps this is it. Although stories and characters grew more realistic, reliance on an old-fashioned view of romantic love persisted. Convinced that audiences came to the theater to watch two lovers find their way into each other's arms, the makers of musicals held to that time-tested formula, showing little inclination to explore beyond it.

37

Melting Pot or Pluralism?
Popular Music and Ethnicity

A SCENE IN OSCAR HIJUELOS's *The Mambo Kings Play Songs of Love*, a prize-winning novel published in 1989, depicts Cesar Castillo, Cuban-born and almost sixty years old, shedding the uniform of his day job and preparing to sing and play at a wedding reception. The setting is New York City around 1977.

> First, cologne behind his ears and neck; then talcum powder under his arms and on his hairy chest, with its scar over the right nipple. Clean pair of striped boxer shorts, then high silk socks with garters. On with his flamingo-pink shirt and fading white suit, tight around the middle. . . . Then on with his sky-blue tie and silver tie clip. He rubbed slick Brylcreem into his hair, put a little Vaseline under his eyes to help disguise the wrinkles, then applied a wax pencil over his wisp of a mustache, like Cesar Romero's in the old movies. Then he put on his white golden-buckled shoes and spit-polished the soft leather with a chamois cloth. When he finished that, he looked himself over. Satisfied that he had not left a stitch out of place, he was ready to go.[1]

The mambo, dance music that combined Afro-Cuban rhythms with the Swing Era's big-band format, was popularized in the United States by Cuban-born musicians during the 1940s; in the 1950s, the dance won national popularity. In Hijuelos's novel, Castillo and his brother arrive in New York in 1949. Soon they form the Mambo Kings, a group including flute, violin, piano, bass, saxophone, two trumpets, and two drummers, one playing an American kit and the other a battery of congas. The band peaks in the mid-1950s, then disbands in 1957 after the brother's death in a car wreck. In the 1970s, Cesar Castillo is working as an apartment building superintendent who still performs occasionally with Cuban bands around New York.

Tito Puente (1923–2000), Latin band leader and percussionist, pictured at a 1998 festival in the Bahamas.

Thinking back later on this particular evening, Castillo remembers the end of the second set, when such "classics" as *El Bordeguero* and *Cachita*

> had gotten even the old grandmothers and grandfathers to shake their bodies and laugh gaily as if they were young again. He had watched a wisp of a woman, thin and bent over like a branch, in a many-layered black dress from another age, turning into a twelve-year-old girl, her arthritic shoulders pulsing forward as if she'd just joined a conga line. Inspired, the Mambo King had blown his trumpet hard, winked, and shouted *"Vaya!"* the notes of his solo sailing the rippling sea of 3/2 time, and the music had sounded so good that even his drowsy bass player Manny, tired from his day's work, began to awaken.

Clicking off the microphone, Castillo steps down from the bandstand and heads for the men's room. When he feels a tug at his sleeve, he finds himself looking into the face of an attractive woman of thirty or thirty-five. She introduces herself, as Lydia Santos and tells him: "I really like your music. You know, I have seen you before, years ago, when I was a young girl. My father would take me to the Teatro Hispano to see all the shows. I saw you there and in Brooklyn. And sometimes up in the Bronx." Her attention delights Castillo. Most of the younger women he meets at this stage in his life have never heard of the Mambo Kings, or perhaps they know the name only as "one out of dozens of other antique orchestras whose records their parents played when they were feeling nostalgic." He promises to return later in the evening to talk. Then, in line at the men's room, a young man asks him what he thinks of the rising Panamanian Rubén Blades: "You must have known a lot of the greats in your time, huh?" Cesar replies: "Yes, you name 'em . . . [Tito] Puente, Eddie Palmieri, Ray Barretto, Pérez Prado. I knew a lot of guys going back a long time. Talented guys with style and good musical ideas who vanished into thin air. . . . Don't get me wrong, my friend," he continues. "You can make a living, but it's not easy, and forget getting rich."

Later that evening Castillo sings *Beautiful Maria of My Soul*, a song he and his brother composed in 1955 that is still their most popular number.

> As he had for years and years, the Mambo King sang that bolero, his vocal cords quivering, his face radiant with sincere, love-drenched emotion: arms spread wide before his corpulent body, he sang to the women with all his heart. And looking at the crowd, his eyes found Lydia: she had been staring at him, a bent straw dangling from between her cherry-red lips. He sang the last verse of the song to her, and only her. While navigating the melancholic beauty of that melody, he had thought to himself: There goes that young chick again, looking at me.

The band plays until 3:30 A.M. When the father of the bride hands him an envelope containing $300, he considers it a good night: $50 for each of the five musicians, "for seven and a half hours of live music, plus a fifty-dollar tip to split among themselves." And when he heads home with Lydia's phone number in his pocket, the Mambo King is feeling "far from tired," stirred by the possibility of romance with an attractive younger woman who thinks of him as an artist.[2]

Fiction can mix facts with an exploration of feelings that historical writing cannot reach. Hijuelos's novel describes New York's Cuban musical scene in the years after World War II. It also reveals aspects of a popular performer's experiences that are hard to document: the unspoken messages that pass between the performer and audience members, for example, and the links between a musician's private thoughts and public functions. Castillo's modest pay and his remarks about the musician's lot point to a blue-collar vocation. On the other hand, the careful grooming, sexual undercurrent, and joyous, rapt response of listeners point to something closer to the rituals of a worldly priest. Cesar Castillo is a mythic figure in a walk of life that, for all its mundane side, also awakens deep human feelings and has its own ways of dealing with them. The blend of historical and emotional truth behind his character makes Hijuelos's Mambo King a good entrée to American popular music outside the circle of English-language traditions.

One of the novel's historical themes is that of music making as an occupation. Castillo and his band members, like most popular musicians, are part-timers with day jobs; even in a city like New York, many such performers have worked outside the official structure of unions, standard wages, and taxable income. Another theme is the matter of costume and its effects on the performer-audience connection; in Castillo's case, elegance of dress sets him apart as a charismatic, romantic figure. Yet another is the range of skills Castillo has developed as an entertainer courting public favor: master of ceremonies, trumpeter, graceful dancer (despite his bulk), and vocalist who, in pouring out songs of impassioned love, convinces audience members that he is singing from the heart. Spanish-language song he addresses to the women in the audience, especially Lydia Santos, dwells on a lover's confusion:

> . . . How can I hate you
> if I love you so?
> I can't explain my torment,
> for I don't know how to live
> without your love . . .
> What delicious pain
> love has brought to me
> in the form of a woman.
> My torment and ecstasy,
> María, my life,
> Beautiful María of my soul.[3]

One can surely imagine a more upbeat message for a couple about to begin married life together. Yet songs about love's ecstatic torment loom large on the Hispanic side of Cuban culture. Singing them helps Castillo fulfill his "ambassadorial" role at a gathering where musicians are expected to bridge the generation gap. At the same time, that role suggests how the passing of the years might affect a professional singer of love songs. Rather than updating his repertory and style, Castillo tries to appeal across generations by embodying elegance; and he is mindful of the gulf between his grandfatherly age and the lustful state of his consciousness. To the question of what popular singers think about when they are performing, the image of Cesar Castillo offers a double-edged answer. From behind a face "radiant with sincere, love-drenched emotion" he coolly reflects on the gaze of a prospective sexual partner.

Most of all, Hijuelos's novel offers a glimpse of music making in one of the many ethnic groups in America. Castillo represents foreign-born musicians who reach maturity in their homeland, emigrate to the United States, join a network of musicians with similar backgrounds, and spend much of their musical life in that network. The tradition of Castillo and his compatriots, chiefly Cubans, boasts a history of wide commercial appeal, as shown by the mambo's appearance in mainstream (English-speaking) popular music during the 1950s. Twenty years later, the impact of the mambo could still be felt in celebrations such as this post-wedding party: an event held at a club in a Latino neighborhood whose owners are Puerto Rican, honoring a bride, groom, and guests of Latino extraction, and featuring the sounds of Latino musicians grounded in a Cuban blend of Hispanic and African influences. Yet while Spanish speakers in New York hold cultural turf in common, separate communities of Cubans, Puerto Ricans, and Dominicans exist in the city, each with its own music and dances. Boosted in New York by an infrastructure of recording and broadcast media, these Latin traditions also enjoy a strong presence in southern Florida, especially Miami. And to the west, many other Spanish-speaking Americans from Texas to California are involved in Mexican musical traditions.

Performers, dancers, and listeners to Latin-based traditions make up only a fraction of those who participate in the full range of ethnic musics that have flourished in America. Our chronicle began with American Indian tribes and the first music known to exist on this continent. And we have returned often to the intersections and blendings of African-American and Euroamerican traditions. But many other ethnic groups, including eastern, western, northern, and southern European ones, Caribbean immigrants from outside the Spanish-language orbit, and Asians (especially Chinese), have also carried on their own separate musical traditions. Where do such ethnic traditions belong in American music history?

Three eminent historians of music in the United States have answered this question differently. Gilbert Chase shows that ethnic pluralism, though basic to musical life in this nation of immigrants, was not welcomed by all musicians in the classical sphere. He quotes from a 1931 essay by Daniel Gregory Mason (the grandson of Lowell Mason), a composer and prominent writer on music who believed that America's true ethnic character was embodied in Anglo-Celtic stock. "Our whole contemporary aesthetic attitude toward instrumental music, especially in New York," Mason complained, "is dominated by Jewish tastes and standards, with their Oriental extravagance, their sensuous brilliancy and intellectual facility and superficiality."[4] Chase then describes how Jewish-American composers such as George Gershwin, Aaron Copland, and Leonard Bernstein combined elements from the classical and popular spheres. From there he moves on to popular-sphere blendings with the traditional sphere, including Tex-Mex in

the Southwest, Jewish popular music in New York City, and Balkan traditions in Chicago. His discussion reaches a climax of sorts in his description
of a 1982 Ethnic Heritage Festival in Memphis that featured local performers. One might have expected such an event—held in the media capital
closest to the fabled "land where the blues began"—to center on black musicians; but this one had a different emphasis:

> One of the featured artists was Tsilya Sadetsky, a Jewish-American singer
> who in 1976 migrated to Memphis together with her son Igor, who accompa-
> nied her on the piano. Many of the Yiddish and Russian folksongs that she
> present[ed] were learned from older family members. Other performers in
> the festival included Israeli, Greek, Scottish and Laotian folk dance groups,
> an Irish accordionist, a Scottish bagpiper, a Chinese folk singer, a Polish
> polka band, and Greek bouzouki players. Who could ask for anything more?[5]

Another historian, H. Wiley Hitchcock, omits the traditional sphere almost entirely, for the series in which his book appears contains a separate
volume on folk and traditional music of Europe and North America.[6]
Charles Hamm, whose study provides more detail than any earlier history of
the subject, also admits that much has been left out. He justifies the omissions by explaining his approach: "I have not dealt with music which did not
change in significant ways in the New World, music which remained identified with the national and ethnic groups who brought it to America, music
which did not interact with other forms of music." Hamm's account therefore centers on music that "has changed in style and form after being
brought to the New World."[7]

The lack of consensus among these three historians shows that the place
of ethnic musical traditions in the United States remains uncertain. Chase's
study, however, proves especially helpful for recognizing that both acculturation (the melting pot) and resistance to it (cultural pluralism) hold significance in American musical life. The first is surely among the most powerful of all New World metaphors. According to melting-pot ideology, the
strength of American institutions reshapes ethnic practices into new hybrids. From language and regional cooking to the arts, these hybrids form
the heart of a common American culture. Yet for all its impact, the melting
pot has been countered at many points by the power of cultural pluralism,
or, to use a more current term, ethnicity.

The historian Rudolph J. Vecoli has sought to explain why, in the face of
the melting-pot image of *e pluribus unum*, attachment to one's own kind has
shown such resilience. Most immigrants in the late 1800s were country folk,
Vecoli explains, more likely to think of themselves as part of a family or a local group than a nationality. However, as they found niches in particular occupations, such pioneers

recruited family and friends through chain migrations. These nuclei in time became neighborhoods serving as a buffer against insecurity, culture shock, and hostile strangers. Mutual aid societies . . . were formed, saloons and groceries established, and synagogues and churches erected. Such small-scale communities became building blocks for more encompassing ethnicity. Working with and living among others engendered a sense of peoplehood among those who shared a familiar language, religion, and culture. Immigrants quickly learned a basic rule of American pluralism: strength lies in numbers. Whether defending neighborhood turf, cultivating business clientele, or trading votes for jobs, ethnic solidarity served as the organizing strategy.

Regional patterns of ethnicity have persisted throughout the twentieth century: "Irish and French Canadian concentrations in New England; Italian and Jewish in the Middle Atlantic states; German and Scandinavian in the Midwest; Slavic in the industrial heartland from Pennsylvania west to Illinois; old-stock Americans (black and white) in the South; Mexicans in the Southwest; and Asians on the Pacific Coast." While practicalities bound group members to each other, ethnicity also had an ideological side. "As an imagined community," Vecoli writes, "ethnicity required symbolic representations of 'our people,' thus the importance of rhetoric and rituals, of flags and uniforms, of music and poetry."[8]

Few symbols of national identity are more potent or immediate in their impact than music, which can create collective consciousness on the spot. While some ethnic groups adapted traditional repertories to New World situations, several of the more conservative maintained music orally that in Europe had been abandoned much earlier. Non-English-speaking groups have tended to be more conscious of their folk heritage than native-born Americans, and music has helped these immigrants keep the cohesion of their group while also gaining the respect of mainstream society. Many have seen fit to promote their folk heritage through modern means, with books and cassette tapes replacing oral tradition.

The oldest music preserved by such groups as the Amish (in Pennsylvania, Ohio, Indiana, Illinois, Iowa, and Maryland) is mostly religious. In contrast, Jewish-American traditions are chiefly secular and wildly eclectic. French Cajun-American music of southern Louisiana, also secular, dates from the mid-eighteenth century, when Acadians were forcibly deported from Nova Scotia to the English colonies. After World War II, Italian singers and entertainers entered the popular sphere with examples of a modern Italian-American musical identity that complemented the Latin rumba and mambo, and later the Brazilian bossa nova. (Italian-American singers such as Louis Prima, Julius LaRosa, and Dean Martin were among the shapers of this identity.) Scandinavian immigration took place chiefly between 1850 and World War I, with substantial settlements in Minnesota, Wisconsin, and Michigan, where Norwegian, Swedish, and Finnish music making all continued. Slavic and Polish-American music have also taken root in some regions. And the 3.5 million Asian Americans, including Chinese, Japanese, Koreans, Indians, Pakistanis, Filipinos, and recent arrivals from Vietnam, Cambodia, and Laos have similarly been preserving native customs while assimilating into American society.[9] Reflecting the contrary pulls of ethnicity and the melting pot, immigrants are likely to feel both a desire to adapt to their new environment and a drive to maintain their ethnic heritage and individuality. Singing societies and theaters—especially theaters founded by Eastern European Jews—have furthered ethnic music in America, as have the record industry, and the commercial media.

This brief overview of ethnic music leads back to one of our chronicle's main premises: that the history of music in America revolves chiefly around performance. Only after studying performance contexts, which have relied heavily on music originating elsewhere in the world, can we come to grips with the role of composition, written or oral, in American musical life. Indeed, all the ethnic traditions named so far belong to American music history. Traditions cited here should be understood as examples chosen from among many possibilities. Beyond the issue of inclusion and exclusion, however, lies one of chronology, for all the musical traditions mentioned so far could have appeared earlier in our story. The reason we deal with them now has to do with the way these traditions have been perceived outside their own communities. (And it should be remembered that not until the 1960s did the word "ethnicity" come into common use.)

YOUTH, ETHNICITY, AND THE FOLK REVIVAL IN THE EARLY 1960S

The decade of the 1960s saw a social and cultural shift that left few aspects of American life untouched. And music played a role in that shift. During the latter 1960s, the links between popular music and social change lent the popular sphere more prestige than it had ever enjoyed before. While other factors enhanced that prestige, ethnicity offers a good starting place. For one thing, it evokes the traditional sphere, and the new popular music drew support from its folk connections. For another, ethnicity came to be seen as a form of political resistance at a time when questioning mainstream American values, including those of the melting pot, was touted as a virtue.

Before the 1960s, most Americans recognized a patriotic duty to place the national interest above the wishes of their own faction. When President John F. Kennedy urged people in 1961 to "ask not what your country can do for you; ask what you can do for your country," patriotism seemed alive and well. Yet during the decade, the notion of "your country" lost much of its power to command allegiance. And group identity challenged the melting-pot ethos, which was rooted in patriotic feelings of an earlier day.

Though not universal, the shift away from a collective American identity was widespread among ethnic groups. Black Americans had never been candidates for the melting pot anyway, and some black leaders now called for racial separation as an alternative to the civil rights movement's drive for integration. American Indians banded together, sometimes across tribal lines, to claim political rights lost long ago in the settlement of North America. Mexican Americans formed a "Chicano" movement that opposed assimilation, took pride in Mexican culture and the Spanish language, and declared solidarity with Mexican immigrants. And then there was the so-called generation gap, which divided Americans by age.

We have seen how white teenagers in the mid-1950s distanced themselves from their parents' generation by embracing rock and roll, changing the musical marketplace in the process. Once established as a community of consumers whose tastes could not be ignored, American youth found other ways to exert its independence, including social and political activism. The youth revolt of the 1960s encouraged college students to take a critical view of their own country. Having experienced neither economic depression nor a world war, the new generation tended to think of the Cold War as having little to do with them. Their viewpoint also owed much to postwar affluence: to consumer culture and to television's homogenizing influence. Moreover, college enrollment in 1970 was four times that of 1945, and many universities had become giant institutions whose dependence on research contracts from corporations and the government invited students' resistance. Gradually, baby boomers latched on to the notion that their parents' generation had not managed the country well.

An ethnic issue lay at the heart of this verdict. The civil rights struggle proved that African Americans were still being denied basic rights of citizenship, especially in the South. By 1960, a few white college students had begun to join in the campaign for equality under the law, and that campaign fostered a political outlook that encouraged radicalism. The chief foes of democratic ideals, rather than foreign enemies, were now seen to be American institutions and a power structure that steered them toward undemocratic ends. Student activism increased sharply after 1965, when, in a bid to stop the spread of communism, the United States entered a long-simmering civil war in Vietnam. By the end of the decade, the student generation's quarrel with its elders had erupted on many campuses into episodes of open revolt.

It was a long way, however, from Peace Corps volunteering and civil rights organizing in the early 1960s to the revolts that followed. Respectful of the political power that was flowing into their hands, college-age activists of the early 1960s hoped to use it for idealistic ends. Even if older Americans had defaulted as charged on their commitment to democracy, they had endowed their sons and daughters with high purposes.[10]

The folk music revival provided a source of identity for many of the young men and women who shared these high purposes. Rejecting commercial mass culture, they became singers and players, borrowing, performing, and if necessary reshaping music from the traditional sphere to address concerns of their own. But how, precisely, did the folk revival connect with the student movement's crusade to renew democracy? Why, an article in *Mademoiselle* asked, did college students want to make music that expressed "the ideas and emotions of the downtrodden and the heartbroken, of garage mechanics and millworkers and miners and backwoods farmers"? One answer was that students found the world brutal and threatening, and that such songs also reflected their own state of mind.[11] Focusing on the realities that underlay American life in the present, folk revivalists had already claimed their own outsider's status. And songs from many oral repertories had expressed the sensibilities of other outsiders, using the idioms of plain people rather than formally trained artists. By learning these songs and mastering the styles of traditional performers, revivalists saw themselves as renewing connections with a strain of democratic experience that modern life was threatening to destroy. Folk music's window on the world made it appealing to revivalists on both political and aesthetic grounds.

Having claimed common ground with music makers in traditional cultures, revival musicians mixed with them more often as social equals. This approach was encouraged by the rise of ethnomusicology, an academic field centered on the study of both Western and non-Western traditional music. Such practical contact helped the revivalists gain competence in re-creating folk styles and lent authenticity to their efforts. It also led beyond Anglo-American and African-American traditions, which had so far dominated the revival. A movement that had begun with ballads, bluegrass, and blues grew to encompass New England contradances and Cajun, Klezmer, and Irish music. By the 1990s, folk styles from Latin America, Africa, Indonesia, eastern Europe, and the Middle East had turned the traditional sphere into a continuous, spiraling process of musical globalization.[12] The blendings, and the commercial stakes involved, called older notions of folk purity and authenticity into question. At the same time, many ethnic styles preserved their distance from the musical melting pot, and therefore performers in these traditions, from Latino salsa players in New York City to Chinese opera singers in San Francisco, were sometimes claimed as allies by those with a political agenda.

In 1962, activist Tom Hayden drafted a statement on behalf of the Students for a Democratic Society (SDS), offering reasons to reject the political status quo. "We are the people of this generation, bred in at least moderate comfort," the text declared, "housed in universities, looking uncomfortably to the world we inherit." Hayden's manifesto focused on the decline of individual freedom in modern America. He saw the country as being dominated by large institutions, from governments to universities, that oppressed individuals and left them alienated. Inspired in part by black activism in the South, his statement urged students to restore "participatory democracy" by wresting "control of the educational process from the administrative bureaucracy" and then finding common political ground with other dissident movements.[13] Hayden's diagnosis offered an idealistic goal, a collective strategy for pursuing it, and a strong, faceless foe. It was chiefly the second of these elements that allowed ethnic traditions to be considered part of the folk revival, and therefore linked to the student movement's politics.

The folk revival used old and new forms to comment on current issues. One who in the early 1960s provided a link to the political heritage of the 1930s was Bob Dylan. Born in Hibbing, Minnesota, in 1941, Dylan picked up the guitar in high school and briefly attended the University of Minnesota. Late in 1960, he made a pilgrimage to New York to the bedside of an ailing Woody Guthrie. Donning the mantle of Guthrie, who a generation earlier had used the Anglo-American folk idiom to write topical songs with political messages, Dylan in 1963 recorded *The Times They Are a-Changing*, an anthem to the generation gap that threw down the gauntlet to older Americans. Set in strophic form and 3/4 time, the words declare that parents cannot really know daughters and sons who have already joined other young comrades in rejecting older values, in language that blends poetic economy with colloquial diction. Dylan accompanies himself on acoustic guitar. Wearing a harmonica supported by a shoulder brace, he fills out the ends of stanzas with its edgy timbre. His voice—nasal, a bit thin, uncultivated in sound but with clear declamation of the words—conjures up the spirit of Woody Guthrie.

By the time Dylan wrote this song, he had already made a mark as a folk revival musician, admired especially for such topical numbers as *Blowin' in the Wind*. While clearly inspired by Guthrie and valued for the political impact of his music, however, Dylan did not fit comfortably into the revival movement. His imagination ranged beyond politically charged subjects; for example, he showed a special affinity for love songs whose bitter tone was tied neither to folk tradition nor any apparent social cause. Using the folk revival's acoustic guitar accompaniments, and singing in a somewhat strident voice, Dylan offered songs that showed a high standard of professional

The final concert in the 1963 Newport Folk Festival ended with the singing of the spiritual *We Shall Overcome* by many of the participants, including (left to right): Paul Stookey, Mary Travers, Peter Yarrow, Joan Baez, Bob Dylan, Rutha Mae Harris, Charles Neblett, Cordell Reagon, Bernice Johnson, and Pete Seeger. Theodore Bikel, who stands at Seeger's left, is cropped from this picture.

skill, challenging audiences rather than offering them easy listening pleasures.

We can recognize Dylan as an artist in transition by glimpsing him in action at the Newport Folk Festivals of 1963, 1964, and 1965. In the 1963 festival, he was introduced to the audience at an afternoon workshop by Joan Baez, and that evening sang a set of his own topical songs to an appreciative audience. The evening concert ended with Dylan, Baez, Pete Seeger, Theodore Bikel, the folk trio Peter, Paul, and Mary, and the Freedom Singers, an African-American group from the South featuring Cordell Reagon and Bernice Johnson, joining together for a grand finale on *We Shall Overcome*, the anthem of the civil rights movement. In August of that year, the same group of performers cemented the folk revival's link with the civil rights movement as they gathered to sing during a march on Washington, which culminated in the Reverend Martin Luther King's historic "I have a dream" speech on the steps of the Lincoln Memorial.

At the 1964 Newport Festival's topical song workshop, however, Dylan's contribution consisted of two new songs that could have been topical only to him: *It Ain't Me, Babe* and *Mr. Tambourine Man*. And the subpar quality of his performance at an evening concert was noticed and commented on. But whether or not Dylan was in top form, the festival this year broadened its range to include musicians and styles outside the usual folk circle whose work would influence him. One was the country singer Johnny Cash, who was little known by the folk crowd. After giving a stunning concert performance, Cash got together backstage with Dylan, and they spent the rest of the evening together taping songs. Another boundary crosser was Muddy Waters, a bluesman from the Mississippi Delta who performed at the festival with amplified instruments. These two musicians plus Dylan's own determination to move beyond topical songs, pointed the way to elements that the young singer would soon integrate in a fresh personal idiom.

Dylan's performance with rock-and-roll backing at the Newport Folk Festival of 1965 has long been recognized as a landmark event. Yet within his own career it was not the radical change that most folk revivalists took it to be. "Electric songs" were for him more a return than a departure, for Dylan had grown up listening to and playing rock and roll. Not until 1959 had he turned toward folk music, after encountering the writings and music of Woody Guthrie. As Dylan later admitted, he had latched on to folk singing when he got to New York City "because I saw a huge audience was there." Yet he knew that the folk scene "wasn't my thing" because he felt out of step with the organizations that supported the music. Constructing a folk singer's persona, he won both artistic and commercial success, but without sharing the folk revival's devotion to musical boundaries. When Dylan decided at Newport to sing a few numbers with the Butterfield Blues Band, he thought he had laid the groundwork for a "plugged-in" performance.[14]

But when he appeared onstage with an electric guitar and launched a rocking version of *Maggie's Farm*, the audience registered its disapproval. And when he led the band into *Like a Rolling Stone*, the outcry grew noisier: "This is a folk festival! Get rid of that band!" Pete Seeger is said to have turned purple, perhaps even to have threatened to destroy the stage wiring system. After one more number, Dylan and his musicians left the stage. Returning alone with an acoustic guitar, he sang *Mr. Tambourine Man*, an established favorite that calmed the crowd. But when he signed off with *It's All Over Now, Baby Blue*, Dylan was bidding farewell to the folk audience.[15]

Dylan's performance at Newport '65 carried him into the openly commercial arena of the popular sphere, where a family of idioms soon to be known as "rock" music was developing out of rock and roll. This move brought added pressure to succeed in the marketplace, yet it also freed him from the folk revival's tendency to view human affairs as a struggle between honorable friends and evil enemies. In the political climate of the early 1960s, protest songs fostered categorical thinking. As folk singer Dave Van Ronk once put it, the danger of a protest song was that it ultimately served to "dissociate you and your audience from all the evils of the world"—a naive position in his view, and in Dylan's too, for both understood good and evil to be intertwined in ways that involve everyone.[16]

By 1965, social change was opening the realm of popular song to the

Bob Dylan sings at the piano with harmonica at the ready.

kinds of complexities and ambiguities that filled Bob Dylan's imagination. Woody Guthrie had not been the only discovery of Dylan's teenage years, for the young singer was also drawn to poetry by the French symbolist Arthur Rimbaud and by such beat poets as Allen Ginsberg and Jack Kerouac. And now Dylan's move away from a folk idiom deepened his engagement with the grotesque and the absurd in art, with existentialism, and with dreams and hallucinations.[17] In an earlier day, such mental terrain would never have inspired popular songs. But never before had the popular music audience included so many educated young people who were avidly searching for messages.

Like a Rolling Stone, released first as a single and then featured as the first song on Dylan's album *Highway 61 Revisited*, shows the singer exploring a realm of expression in which caustic words are declaimed to a joyous, almost hymnlike instrumental accompaniment. Electric guitars, piano, and organ play over a foundation of bass guitar, drums, and tambourine. Dylan's voice slices in with brusque declamation over the rolling tide of electrified sound. He is rebuking someone in statements that erupt after forty bars into a litany of gibes: "How does it feel? / To be without a home? / Like a complete unknown? / Like a rolling stone?" This section turns out to be the chorus, which repeats a four-bar harmonic cycle—one bar of tonic harmony, one of subdominant, and two of dominant—over and over, each cycle introduced by a line of text. Except for the title line, which Dylan sings to a five-note figure (do-do-fa-*mi*-do), all the melody present is instrumental.

Too free in form, redundant in material, and scarce in vocal melody to pass in 1965 as a standard pop, country, or folk song, *Like a Rolling Stone* is an early example of a rock song. And Dylan's performance succeeded so well that a trade paper proclaimed it in 1976 the top rock single of all time. Made up of a series of paired verbal statements, the forty-bar verse—which may be diagrammed **a** (8 + 8 measures) **b** (4 + 4) **c** (4 + 4) **d** (8)—is complex enough to make the chorus's looping repetitiousness welcome. And the song's musical character is ecstatic. Volume is one reason. Not only is it possible to start loud and grow even louder, but amplification allows players to relax while projecting their sound. The musical form also plays a key role. In the chorus, Dylan delivers each line of his litany just before the start of a new four-bar cycle. Therefore, the instruments sound as if they are playing responses to his calls: driving, bluesified figures over which a short, patterned organ melody soars. Call and response is also built into the verse.

Like a Rolling Stone lasts six minutes, unusually long for a single in the pop music marketplace. The subject is also unusual: an overprotected person being forced out into a cruel world. The song taunts middle-class American youth with images showing that it takes a tough, resilient spirit to give up the props of middle-class life. But even as his song lays out a scenario of existential loneliness, Dylan offers a counternarrative in sound: the undisguised camaraderie of musicians who are having a wonderful time playing together.

BLACK-WHITE INTERACTIONS

"Little Richard" Penniman, black rock and roller of the 1950s, once made an extravagant claim: "I believe my music can make the blind see, the lame walk, the deaf and dumb hear and talk, because it inspires and uplifts people. It uplifts the soul, you see everybody's movin', they're happy, it regenerates the heart and makes the liver quiver, the bladder splatter, the knees freeze."[18] This mix of preaching, versifying, and hyperbole unites several elements that gave rock and roll—and, from the mid-1960s on, rock—a key place in the era's social turbulence. Little Richard's words testified that the new popular music, connecting sound and movement, was capable of exploding into the realm of the spirit.

In a like-minded vein, Robert Palmer, in *Rock & Roll: An Unruly History* (1995), outlines his own thirty-five-year involvement with the music that became his religion.[19] His account dwells on the theme of ineffable experience. Rather than a style, he says, rock and roll is a culture granting musicians "access to an unprecedented heritage of live and recorded music, and the creative freedom to take what they want from it." Rock-and-roll culture, whose presence still surrounds Americans in the 1990s, has enabled newer popular artists and genres to tap a strain of rebelliousness dating at least back to Little Richard. These genres, Palmer says, could not have evolved out of pre-rock popular song.

> Rap, metal, thrash, grunge, have different attitudes toward the organization of sound and rhythm, different ideas concerning the nature of *the song*. Their distance from pre-r&r norms cannot be explained by advances in musical instruments and recording technology alone. Far more than musical hybrids, these sounds proceed from what amounts to a different tradition, different from the old mainstream pop and different right on down to the most basic musical values.

Palmer locates that difference in rock and roll's intent. *"The music wants to rock you,"* he writes, not simply touching the emotions but shaking up the consciousness and body of the listener. And he includes in his rock-and-roll family all popular genres up to the present (including hip-hop) that, in Little Richard's words, try to make your liver quiver.[20]

The notion that rock and roll is a music with an attitude—an expressive form seeking to provoke, disrupt, and shock—helps to explain why it found a willing audience in the 1960s. The year of Bob Dylan's *Like a Rolling Stone* (1965) was also the year the U.S. government began sending troops to Southeast Asia. Many younger Americans saw the war in Vietnam, which would cost more than 58,000 American lives, as a symbol of national failure. The older generation was attacked for forcing young Americans to fight in an undeclared foreign war. Targets ranged from individuals (parents, teachers, and clergy) to institutions (schools, churches, the government), to manners, norms, and laws of society, and to personal sensibilities. Rock musicians helped fans hone a vocabulary of disrespect for elders and the status quo. Their personalities, costumes, and hair styles seemed calculated to widen the generation gap. Aggressively loud volume, harsh singing, raucous guitar playing, and a fondness for repetition signaled that these musicians meant to overturn musical refinement itself. Song lyrics, behavior, and the publicity surrounding the new breed called "rock star" flaunted restrictions on sex and on drug use, seeming to invite young fans into risky lifestyles. ("Would you want your daughter to date a Rolling Stone?" an ad for that group asked suggestively.) With young Americans' esteem for authority running low, rock-and-roll musicians won audiences of great size and enthusiasm by appealing to countercultural sentiments. A young writer of the day commented in 1971: "There was a fantastic universal sense that what-ever we were doing was *right*, that we were winning. And that, I think, was the handle—that sense of inevitable victory over the forces of Old and Evil. . . . We were riding the crest of a high and beautiful wave."[21]

But while lending itself well to academic discussion, politics has proba-bly not been uppermost in the minds of most people who, since Elvis Pres-ley's early days, have listened and danced to rock and roll. Indeed, behind the cutting edge of unruliness, a vast expressive territory has opened up in which singers, players, and songwriters have found the idiom's possibilities almost limitless—a territory filled with songs of many styles, moods, and persuasions. Most of these songs have left listeners' livers, bladders, and knees undisturbed, though their celebration of bodily pleasures cannot be denied.

Robbie Robertson, who worked with Bob Dylan and with his own group, The Band, recalled the mid-sixties as a charmed musical age.

> The Beatles were making very interesting records, there was a whole wave of amazing music coming from Motown and Stax, and Dylan was writing songs with much more depth than what had come along before. Everything was changing, all these doors were being opened, and it made you think, "I could try *anything, right now.*" Revolutionary times are very healthy for experiment-ing and trying stuff—and for being fearless in what you try.[22]

Robertson's words apply to an era when a young musician could aspire to being artistically serious *and* commercially successful. And the artistic fuel for these revolutionary times came chiefly from black musicianship, the source that powered the Motown record company in Detroit and the Stax firm in Memphis.

New patterns of black-white musical exchange in the 1960s transformed the popular sphere. Until then, white ownership and control of the music business had been taken for granted. Mainstream pop presented many white stars and a few black ones to predominantly white audiences, while rhythm and blues marketed black artists to black audiences. In the 1960s, however, star performers won more independence, and the balance of power began to shift. Racial interaction changed too. Listening to records by black musicians and cultivating personal contact with them led more white singers and players to try to match the emotional intensity of black gospel and blues singers and led more white listeners to become fans of black mu-sicians. Motown and Stax flourished in this climate through racial ex-changes rarely seen before civil rights activity began coaching white and black Americans toward equality before the law.

Founded in 1959 by black songwriter and record producer Berry Gordy Jr., the Motown record company in the 1960s came to be one of the most influential in the history of popular music. Gordy drew performers chiefly from Detroit's black community, at least during Motown's early years. The company's records combined elements from rhythm and blues, gospel, blues, and rock and roll with the aim of attracting white listeners as well as black. To teach stage presence, Gordy hired the proprietor of a Detroit modeling school, who treated the singers as though they were being groomed for the White House and Buckingham Palace. And in 1965, veteran tap dancer Cholly Atkins was named staff choreographer. As Atkins described his work at Motown: "I take R&B artists and teach, educate, and prepare them for that transition from the chitlin circuit to Vegas."[23] The Motown sound relied heavily on mainstream pop trappings, including studio orchestras with string sections. At the same time, Motown recordings boasted a vital rhythmic core, supplied by jazz-oriented musicians sometimes called "the Funk Brothers": pianist Earl Van Dyke, bassist James Jamerson, and drummer Benny Benjamin. The company's blend of pop lushness with rhythmic bite and imaginative harmonies proved appealing to white and black listeners alike. In the racial climate of the 1960s and after, white teenage audiences were ready to respond to black performers. Such Motown stars as Diana Ross and the Supremes, Smokey Robinson and the Miracles, Marvin Gaye, Stevie Wonder, and the Jackson Five enjoyed great success in the marketplace, performing under the aegis of a black capitalist who kept a tight rein on all aspects of his enterprise.

Meanwhile, white-owned Stax/Volt Records in Memphis was making rhythm and blues hits with black singers backed by Booker T. and the MGs, a racially mixed studio rhythm section. In 1962, the label released its first record by Otis Redding, a singer from Macon, Georgia, who soon became Stax's best-selling artist as well as a favorite with the company's musicians. In ballads, he often took a tone of pleading vulnerability. But he also mastered a rhythmic, up-tempo style that often carried his performances far beyond the song's original words and music. In 1965, Jerry Wexler of New York's Atlantic label, ready for a change from his own company's reliance on written arrangements, traveled to Memphis with Wilson Pickett and other Atlantic artists and recorded them with Stax's Booker T. and the MG's. The link with Wexler and Atlantic allowed Stax to improve its distribution. Thus a Memphis firm's combination of black singers, Southern white ownership, national marketing network, and mix of white and black instrumentalists gave rise to "soul" music, which by the latter 1960s was being perceived as quintessentially black.

The career of singer-songwriter-dancer-bandleader James Brown, raised in and around Augusta, Georgia, reflects another kind of black-white interaction. According to Brown's autobiography, even as a five-year-old he disliked the blues, an opinion that he says never changed. By the time he was

James Brown (at the microphone) and the Famous Flames perform in 1967 with the James Brown Orchestra.

a teenager, he realized that he "liked gospel and pop songs best of all." In the course of learning piano to supplement his drumming and guitar playing, Brown "got all the Hit Parade books and learned all the pop tunes," admiring especially numbers by Bing Crosby and Frank Sinatra. Another inspiration came from the black church, and especially from worship that featured singing and hand clapping. More than the doctrine, Brown was impressed by the atmosphere. He remembered one revival service featuring "a preacher who really had a lot of fire. He was just screaming and yelling and stomping his foot and then he dropped to his knees. The people got into it with him, answering him and shouting and clapping time." The experience stuck with Brown, who from then on studied preachers closely so that he might imitate them.[24] These recollections point to Brown's lifelong hunger for the spotlight and to please audiences. The strength of his desire to succeed provided drive and discipline and his imagination discovered skills he could borrow from popular music and the black church to make his act unique.

Brown's entertainment career began as a member of a vocal quartet in Toccoa, Georgia. His first big break came in the mid-1950s, when he began recording for King Records in Cincinnati. Having scored a national hit with *Please, Please, Please* (1956), he and his group hired a touring band. By the early 1960s, the James Brown Show was an evening-length revue, built around the star's energy and honed chiefly on the road. According to Brown, he was now performing as many as 350 days a year, "most of them one-night stands. I played every place—arenas, auditoriums, clubs, ball parks, armories, ballrooms, any place that had a stage or a place you could put one." Billed as "the hardest-working man in show business," Brown took a blue-collar approach to his profession. "When you're on stage," he wrote, "the people who paid money to get in are the boss, even if it cost them only a quarter. You're working for them."[25] An LP of Brown and his troupe playing at the Apollo Theater in Harlem was released in 1963, selling over a million copies—an astounding figure for a black performer in a market built on singles. The live recording presents a pop star working a crowd in a way that makes the customers partners in a communal experience. Brown by now was a commanding presence: not only a singer but an accomplished, athletic dancer who mesmerized audiences with his splits, leaps, and other exuberant steps.

By 1964, James Brown was supervising his recordings for King, whose boss never showed much fondness for his star's innovative streak. One result was a move away from conventional song structures and toward a new emphasis on movement and dance. The breakthrough recording was *Papa's Got a Brand New Bag* (1965), a number more than four minutes long that devotes less than half its length to a sung delivery of the lyrics, which celebrate dancing. *Papa* begins with the briefest of intros: a sustained full-volume blast from a band—three trumpets and a trombone, four saxes, and a rhythm section of organ, guitar, bass, and drums—that plays with fierce precision from start to finish. With similar edge and bite, Brown sings a pair of vocal choruses in twelve-bar blues form, followed by an eight-bar bridge and another two choruses. But at this point, well short of the two-minute mark, the blues structure disappears to be replaced by a vamp—here a repeated four-beat unit built on a rhythm in the bass: ♩. ♪♫♫ . The melody instruments interlock with that figure by attacking the second beat with an explosive accent: ♪ ♫♪♪ . The drummer, who also accents the backbeats (two and four) regularly, maintains an eighth-note subdivision on cymbal. This lurching, effortful vamp churns ahead for the next two and a half minutes to the final fadeout, overlaid by Maceo Parker's long tenor sax solo and Brown's occasional shouts of encouragement, turning every second beat into an event. (In live performance, the singer danced this part of the number.) Brown's commitment to rhythm is made unmistakable by *Papa's* two-part form, which uses song to introduce the vamp—normally a short, repetitive interlude leading into or out of the song's main musical statement—instead of the other way around. Brown later wrote that by this time in his career, "I was hearing everything, even the guitars, like they were drums."[26]

In *Papa's Got a Brand New Bag* and other recordings that followed, Brown virtually invented the style we now call "funk," and in the process became the best-selling rhythm and blues artist of the day. He was the only 1950s rhythm and blues artist to bridge the gap successfully to soul artist in the 1960s and funk artist in the 1970s. Echoes of Brown's techniques were inescapable on black radio of the 1980s. And his influence has proved international, extending to European new wave music, West African Afro-beat, and West Indian reggae.[27] It is noteworthy that this highly original performer, accepted as a distiller of true black artistry, began life with an aversion to blues—not the musical form but its fixation on melancholy—and a deep attraction to mainstream pop.

38

From Accessibility to Transcendence

The Beatles, Rock, and Popular Music

By the late 1950s, rock and roll had gained a prominent place in the youth culture of the United Kingdom as well as the United States. A few British youngsters encountered African-American styles through recordings by Southern blues artists, including Sonny Boy Williamson, Bill Broonzy, and the duo of Sonny Terry and Brownie McGee. Many more took in the sounds of Chuck Berry, Fats Domino, and Elvis Presley. By around 1960, the city of Liverpool and its environs alone boasted almost three hundred rock-and-roll clubs and about the same number of local bands. The most successful British band began, in fact, in Liverpool as the Quarrymen. The group was founded in 1956 by singer and guitarist John Lennon—rhythm guitarist Paul McCartney joined the same year, lead guitarist George Harrison joined in 1957, and drummer Ringo Starr was added later—was reincarnated as Johnny and the Moondogs and finally as the Beatles, who did not single out any one member as the star. In their early days, the Beatles played rough-and-tumble clubs in Hamburg, Germany, as well as the Cavern Club in Liverpool, honing their craft but also experimenting freely with drugs, as did many in show business.

The band's image shifted to clean in 1961, when they hired Brian Epstein as manager. And the next year, after several other companies had rejected their demonstration tape, the Beatles won a recording contract with EMI. George Martin, the classically trained producer who signed them, admitted that neither the group's singing nor their original songs impressed him much at first, but he was taken with their engaging personalities. He was more impressed after traveling to Liverpool for a performance at the Cavern Club, which he described as "a sweaty little railway-arch kind of place" that reminded him of a dungeon. The Beatles "sang all the rock-and-roll numbers that they'd copied from American records, and it was very raucous, and the kids loved every minute of it." Martin saw at once that the gyrations of other British rockers "were clinical, anaemic, even anaesthetic, compared with the total commitment of the Beatles, which somehow got down to the very roots of what the kids wanted." During 1963, the Beatles, now featuring more original songs by Lennon and McCartney, won such ardent, widespread popularity in Britain that their reception earned its own label: "Beatlemania." The group's success in the marketplace for hit singles in 1964–65 had no precedent, and the hits were all songs of their own. Martin recalls:

> Starting with "Please Please Me" we had twelve successive number ones. It was a unique achievement, so perhaps it is worth listing them: "From Me to You," "She Loves You," "I Want to Hold Your Hand," "Can't Buy Me Love," "A Hard Day's Night," "I Feel Fine," "Ticket to Ride," "Help!" "Day Tripper," "Paperback Writer," and "Yellow Submarine." It became almost an accepted fact of nature. The question was not whether a record would get to number one, but how quickly. In the end, it was happening in the first week, with advance sales around the million mark.[1]

The Beatles' impact in the United States was sudden, far-reaching, and at first dependent on adolescent girls. American Beatlemania made itself felt in February 1964 in a legendary appearance by the group on the Ed Sullivan television show. The screaming teenagers with their constant shrieks of excitement recalled Frank Sinatra's performances in the 1940s and Elvis Presley's in the 1950s. And their enthusiasm helped to enrich the record industry's coffers through a remarkable sales development: the Beatles' first LP, "Meet the Beatles," outsold the group's first single by a margin of 3.6 million to 3.4 million, the first time an album had ever sold more copies than its single counterpart.[2] The craze for the group also produced a rash of spinoff T-shirts, wigs, books, and other items.

The Beatles' American reception, a subject that received wide attention in its own day and after, may be boiled down to a chronology:

> 1964 Appearance on "Ed Sullivan Show" on February 9 achieves highest Nielson rating in TV history, with an audience of 73 million.
> *I Want to Hold Your Hand* becomes No. 1 record in United States Eight other Beatles recordings are top sellers for the year. The movie *A Hard Day's Night* released, winning critical acclaim and financial success.
> 1965 Beatles concert fills New York's Shea Stadium on September 16.
> 1966 Last live Beatles concert given in San Francisco on August 29.
> 1967 *Sergeant Pepper's Lonely Hearts Club Band* recording released;

> *Magical Mystery Tour* album released, tying in with TV movie of same name.
>
> *1968* Total record sales calculated at more than 200 million worldwide.
>
> *1969* John Lennon marries Yoko Ono on March 20.
>
> *1970 Abbey Road* recording released, the Beatles' last LP; Paul McCartney announces in April his departure from the group.
>
> *1975* Beatles partnership legally dissolved in January.[3]

These events outline a fairly clear path: immediate public acceptance on a grand scale; a retreat from public life; a new trajectory of artistic growth; a continuing appeal to record buyers; and the growing pressures of wealth and fame, leading to a breakup. From an artistic standpoint, the 1966 entry marks a basic shift in the life of the group. The Beatles' audience had grown so enormous that touring and live performance lost their appeal. Therefore, the group concentrated on the recording studio. The new musical ideas they explored, especially in the years 1965–67, led them away from their early stage-band sound; they experimented with new textures and forms, with a breadth of view that came to include avant-garde techniques from the classical sphere and even the music of India, which entered the Beatles' orbit after George Harrison's study with the sitar virtuoso Ravi Shankar. With each new album in these years, the group broke new musical ground—especially in *Rubber Soul* (1965), *Revolver* (1966), and *Sergeant Pepper's Lonely Hearts Club Band* (1967).

If the Beatles' success was remarkable in the 1960s, it came to be even more so for the way the music outlived the group itself. Even today, three decades after the members' last collaboration, their recordings are still heard on the radio and are readily available in record stores. Beatles songs, now standards, are widely sung and played by others. Music and book stores carry them in sheet-music folios and fake books; and in 1989, *The Beatles: Complete Scores* appeared in print; a 1,136-page volume containing full transcriptions of 213 songs recorded by the group, published by the commercial firm that owns the copyrights. Historical chronicles, biographies, and iscographies document the Beatles' career, and critical interpretations of their music abound. With their presence preserved on record and film, in photographs and words, and in musical notation, the Beatles can claim devoted fans who were not yet born when their partnership dissolved. In pursuing the popular sphere's goal of accessibility, the Beatles created a body of recorded music that now seems on the brink of achieving artistic transcendence.

The Beatles are not the only popular musicians of the 1960s to approach this position. Indeed, the notion of claiming transcendence for musicians who have also won great success in the marketplace suggests a sea change

in the priorities of American music making as a whole. But before addressing this matter, we need to consider the Beatles from two more perspectives: the place they carved out for themselves within the popular sphere
and their achievement as musicians.

As a rock-and-roll band in both pedigree and instrumentation, the Beatles belonged to a tradition that offered access to an unprecedented heritage
of live and recorded music, much of it the fruit of black-white interaction. If
the Beatles' first fans were teenage girls, their base broadened to cross generational and gender (though seldom racial) lines. Because many of their
earlier songs were tuneful tributes to the joys of young love, the Beatles
seemed at first to stand apart from the American counterculture's political
side. On the other hand, as their music moved toward less conventional
forms and more ambiguous poetic images (some suspected of being drug
references), the Beatles were seen increasingly as part of the general rebellion against authority, especially after news of their marijuana and LSD use
circulated. Yet their matchless financial success, breadth of appeal, and
slant on the issue of social class seemed to put them in a category by themselves. The tales and numbers documenting their popularity in the United
States surely helped create the aura that surrounded them, but to understand what made the Beatles different, we also have to look overseas.

An early historian of rock and roll, Charlie Gillett, himself an Englishman, took on the question of the Beatles' distinctive appeal not long after
the group broke up. He traces their stylistic roots to Little Richard's hard-
edged rocking and Motown's softer call-and-response style, two approaches
that had never before been combined. Because they played their own instruments and were talented songwriters, they were able to maintain control
of their music in the recording studio, where musicians were sometimes
ruled by producers. Most of all, however, Gillett found their social outlook
crucial to their success, especially for the way they played on the incon-
gruities in the British class system. The context for that play lay in a body of
social discourse that in the latter 1950s was translated to the screen in such
films as *Saturday Night and Sunday Morning* and *The Loneliness of the Long
Distance Runner*. These films depicted working-class life as more honest,
real, and interesting than life in the middle class, a belief long touted by
middle-class British socialists. Coming from working-class backgrounds
themselves, the Beatles might have made perfect spokesmen for that attitude. Instead, they undermined it, by delivering whatever social commentary they had to offer in a spirit of nonchalant, irreverent humor and
disrespect for social convention.

Most tellingly, the Beatles seemed to enjoy wealth and fame. They presented an image of working-class youth as loose, free, and irrepressibly playful, showing no more respect for the newer image of class-based virtue than

for the older aristocratic hierarchy. And audiences found their expressions of hedonism charming. Indeed, both male and female audiences seemed to love the Beatles, one of very few groups who turned out to be as musically interesting as they were fun to watch.[4]

Susan Douglas, an American who herself experienced Beatlemania as a teenager in the 1960s, explores the female response and concludes that for girls, the Beatles "perfectly fused the 'masculine' and 'feminine' strains of rock 'n' roll in their music, their appearance, and their style of performing." Part of the appeal lay in their use of the male falsetto, which she credits to the influence of "girl groups" such as the Shirelles. By singing in a range more conventionally female than male, groups like the Beatles encouraged girls to assume male roles, and thus challenged macho masculinity. At the same time, Douglas recalls,

> when we watched these joyful, androgynous young men, we saw not just a newly feminized, distinctly friendlier form of manhood. We also saw our *own* reflection. In these boys were glimpses not only of a new masculinity but also of the best part of 1960s adolescent femininity—an eagerness to reach out to others, a faith in love, a belief in progress, and a determination to leave behind hoary conventions about staying in one's own place.[5]

Three points need to be kept in mind in any consideration of the Beatles' music. First, the group's charismatic appeal to teenage fans formed the cornerstone of their career. Second, the originality and freshness of their songwriting help to explain their staying power in the marketplace. And third, the Beatles' claim to lasting importance—to artistic transcendence—owes much to their use of studio resources and the idea that an LP album can make a unified statement through related songs. A musical example illustrating each of these points will help us understand the group's impact in the 1960s, as well as the reasons for the music's continuing appeal.

In 1964, Lennon and McCartney's *Can't Buy Me Love* appeared as a single record, quickly earning number-one hit status on both sides of the Atlantic. The last couplet of each verse repeats the song's message. The title line also forms the basis of the chorus, though sung to a different tune (do-mi-sol-*sol*-mi). The tempo is quick, the singing youthful, exuberant, and easy sounding. Though the verses follow the twelve-bar blues chord progression, this is not a song about a problem. Rather, it sounds more like an enactment of the spirit-lifting, life-affirming, joyous feelings that go along with being in love, which makes jewelry, cash, and other material goods seem trivial. In *Can't Buy Me Love*, the Beatles are working out of the direct, uncomplicated, youth-oriented approach they developed while absorbing American influences during their years in Liverpool and Hamburg.

A more musically adventurous side of the group comes to light in *You're*

Going to Lose That Girl, written for the movie *Help!* (1965). The song blends unconventional and conventional elements from the start: a statement of the chorus with no instrumental intro. The chorus text consists of the title line, sung by the lead and backup singers as a call and response, over a familiar, vamp-like harmonic progression (I-vi-ii-V). But the chorus is also unusually short, four bars, and open-ended. Finishing on a dominant chord after a striking upward leap of a sixth, it sounds more like half a statement than a whole one. Next comes an eight-bar verse sung by Lennon and echoed by McCartney and Harrison:

> If you don't take her out tonight
> She's going to change her mind,
> And I will take her out tonight
> And I will treat her kind.

The chorus is repeated, then followed by a second verse of warning. Again the chorus returns, with its call-and-response vocal exchange. But now a twist brings the open-endedness into play. In a two-bar extension, the lead vocal unexpectedly leaps upward a seventh instead of a sixth, to A. Sustaining and decorating that pitch, Lennon's voice seems to pull the instrumental bass toward D-natural, a fifth below it. And now, with the original key of E major undercut, a D-major chord is made the jumping-off point for a new section: a stomping eight-bar statement in G major. The text of the new section poses a direct challenge:

> I'll make a point
> Of taking her away from you,
> (What would you do?) Yeah!
> The way you treat her
> What else can I do?

The new section ends on an F-major chord that is as unexpected as any other tonal surprise in this harmonically daring song. But the level is then ratcheted down to the home key of E major and a return of the verse material, heard now as a guitar solo with vocal responses ("You're going to lose that girl"). From there to the colorful final cadence (VII-IV-I), earlier sections are repeated often enough to make the harmonic shifts sound less strange, if still offbeat and fresh. Standard rock-and-roll elements abound in *You're Going to Lose That Girl*, from the straightforward words to the I-vi-ii-V harmonic progression, the call-and-response vocalism, and the simple guitar solo. But the harmonic plan—a key of E major pitted against the remote key of G major—and the unfolding of the form lend an air of musical adventure.

The thirteen musical numbers of *Sergeant Pepper's Lonely Hearts Club*

The cover of the Beatles' album *Sergeant Pepper's Lonely Hearts Club Band* is one of the enduring icons of the 1960s.

Band have been called a song cycle that is also a work of musical genius. According to producer George Martin, the idea of a unified album came from Paul McCartney. After writing one song—in Martin's view "just an ordinary rock number and not particularly brilliant as songs go"—about a military band led by a mythical character named Sergeant Pepper, McCartney suggested: "Why don't we make the album as though the Pepper band really existed, as though Sergeant Pepper was making the record? We'll dub in effects and things." Martin recalled: "I loved the idea, and from that moment it was as though *Pepper* had a life of its own, developing of its own accord rather than through a conscious effort by the Beatles or myself to integrate it and make it a 'concept' album."[6] Looking back in 1979, Martin remembered *Sergeant Pepper* not only as their top seller but the album that turned the group "from being just an ordinary rock-and-roll group into being significant contributors to the history of artistic performance. It was a turning-point—*the* turning-point." Martin also made a strong claim for the influence of *Sergeant Pepper* on the popular sphere in general, calling it the watershed that changed the art of recording into something capable of standing "the test of time as a valid art form: sculpture in music, if you like."[7] Having taken over 900 hours of studio time to put together, the *Sergeant Pepper* album is unperformable in a live setting.

For George Martin, *A Day in the Life* by Lennon and McCartney, sung by Lennon, was "the major piece of the whole album."[8] But this composition cannot be summarized in the way *Can't Buy Me Love* and *You're Going to Lose That Girl* can, for they are both independent love songs written to stand on their own. *A Day in the Life* reached the public as the last of a series of songs in an album intended to make a cumulative impression. And that impression depended not only on the sound but the other materials that came with the record. All the lyrics of all the songs are included in the package; and so are many color photos of the Beatles, dressed in fancy satin band uniforms, as if ready to take up their instruments at Sergeant Pepper's command. Another striking feature is the cover photograph, now a familiar icon of the era: the Beatles are shown in their role as bandsmen, standing behind the bass drum and surrounded by effigies of several dozen historical figures, living and dead, including Karl Marx, Marilyn Monroe, W. C. Fields, Oscar Wilde, Marlon Brando, T. H. Lawrence, Bob Dylan, Mohandas K. Gandhi, Shirley Temple, Karlheinz Stockhausen, and Albert Einstein. And the ways the lyrics of the thirteen songs are connected with each other are no more straightforward than are the links among this assortment of characters.

A Day in the Life, which begins with the voice of John Lennon singing, "I read the news today, oh boy," offers a meditation on the impersonality, disconnectedness, and menace of the modern world. Sounding a bit bewildered, the singer notes a few of a single day's experiences: hearing news of a traffic fatality, seeing a war film, and reading about the nation's deteriorating roads, sandwiched around the problem of getting to work in the morning. Where *Can't Buy Me Love* and *You're Going to Lose That Girl* support their lyrics' clear sentiment with catchy tunes and plenty of rhythmic drive, *A Day in the Life* is more discontinuous, less tuneful, and built around studio effects. The song's only direct statement of personal feeling, the line "I'd love to turn you on," which Lennon sings near the middle and again at the end, is answered both times by a long, slow, somewhat discordant *crescendo*, filling twenty-four bars and played by a symphony orchestra, which George Martin hired and conducted for this recording. According to Martin, the orchestra *crescendo* was Lennon's idea. But it fell to Martin, the only literate musician on the production team, to show the players how to achieve it. He solved the problem of notation by writing at the beginning of the twenty-four bars, the lowest possible note for each of the instruments in the orchestra. At the end of the twenty-four bars, I wrote the highest note each instrument could reach that was near a chord of E major. Then I put a squiggly line right through the twenty-four bars, with reference points to tell them roughly what note they should have reached during each bar. The musicians also had instructions to slide as gracefully as possible between one noted the next. . . . I marked the music "pianissimo" at the beginning and "fortissimo" at the end."[9]

Once recorded, this passage was spliced into the final version, illustrating what Martin meant when he called the album a "sculpture in music."

Sergeant Pepper's Lonely Hearts Club Band, and *A Day in the Life* in particular, were received in some quarters as serious works of art—a reception unimaginable for a popular number of an earlier era. One critic even compared *A Day in the Life* to the poet T. S. Eliot's masterpiece *The Waste Land*. Another likened the song to Picasso's *Guernica*, the monumental 1937 painting that depicts the horrors of the Spanish Civil War, hearing echoes of nuclear disaster in the orchestra *crescendo* and the reverberation of the last chord (which, thanks to George Martin's sound sculpturing, takes almost a minute to die away).[10] These judgments point to a shift in perspective. We have seen that recordings turn musical performances into permanent works, and that critical writing can lend an aura of artistic worthiness to any form of expression it addresses. Through the 1950s and early 1960s, jazz was the only idiom in the popular sphere to inspire its own body of criticism. But in the mid-1960s, as vivid poetic images, social critiques, and the ambiguities of modern art found their way into some popular music, *and* growing numbers of young, literate listeners heard the sensibilities and concerns of their generation being expressed there, the work of Dylan, the Beatles, and other popular stars suddenly seemed worthy of critical treatment. A new kind of connection was forming between these musicians and their audiences. And a new breed of writer, the rock critic, appeared on the scene to take the measure of that connection.

The periodical *Rolling Stone*, begun in 1967, was one of several journals founded in the latter 1960s to celebrate the countercultural spirit, including the work of rock musicians. Those who wrote on the subject were chiefly young men (as opposed to women) suspicious of older elite values: believers in populism tuned to an ethos of youthful self-assertion. Most lacked either a technical knowledge of music or formal grounding in the principles of criticism, but they understood the music's role on the current scene, drawing assurance from enthusiasms they shared with other fans on the same side of the generation gap. And they embraced with conviction and gusto the task

Janis Joplin (1943–1970), one of the 1960s' outstanding female rock singers, onstage.

of interpreting both live performances and recordings. Jon Landau, Lester Bangs, Greil Marcus, Dave Marsh, and Robert Christgau have been singled out for special notice; the last three are still active and influential on the current scene.

Rock's varied menu of styles gave critics one way of approaching their subject aesthetically and historically. Subgenres abounded: hard rock, soft rock, folk rock, progressive rock, rockabilly, heavy metal, jazz rock, acid rock, and others. And each had its own lineage, based on links with other genres in the popular, traditional, and even the classical sphere, that needed explaining. Another approach, stemming from the notion "the music wants to rock you," took musicians' battles against stagnation on one hand and their self-destructiveness on the other as a theme. The rapid growth of the popular music audience, together with the countercultural stance of many rock stars, brought influence and power increasingly into the hands of a select group of performers. Yet wealth and fame could be as burdensome, even dangerous, as they were desirable. The example of such stars as Jim Morrison of the Doors, Janis Joplin of Big Brother and the Holding Company, and guitarist Jimi Hendrix, all of whom lived hard, sometimes behaved outrageously onstage, and died young, embodied the destructive side of success. But those like Elvis Presley, who succeeded, thrived, and eventually outlived his early fame, faced the risk of growing so rich and reclusive that they might lose the edge that had made listeners' livers quiver in the first place. Thus punk rock, a mid-1970s genre in which inexpert but passionate performers offered a radically nihilistic view of society, was understood as an attempt to purge rock of greed and musical professionalism. According to this view, performers' perpetual search for fresh ways to register unruliness has allowed rock and roll to maintain a rebellious edge despite its grounding in the commercial marketplace.

In the latter 1960s, then, rock music began to win intellectual respectability. In fact, the *Sergeant Pepper* album has been called the first "art rock" album.[11] And it was followed by other performances and recordings in which rock musicians put their own spin on classical elements, or even on works from the classical sphere. (An example of the latter is Emerson, Lake, and Palmer's 1972 version of *Pictures at an Exhibition*, a piano work from 1874 by Russian composer Modest Musorgsky that is best known in an arrangement for orchestra by Maurice Ravel.) But perhaps more crucial to rock music's growing intellectual prestige was that, to use a catchword of the day, it was considered more socially "relevant" than earlier popular music. That relevance, reflected in the lyrics, centered chiefly on personal issues. Even though rock music was rooted in a youth culture that was rejecting society's traditional attitudes and values, only rarely were its lyrics direct political statements; rather, they mirrored the internal struggles that individuals faced as they interreacted with others. Where folk revivalists sang songs of protest in the name of "the people," rock musicians explored how it felt to belong to a generation searching for other kinds of human connection.

So far in this chronicle, "rock and roll" and "rock" have been treated as if they were synonymous, but it is now time to distinguish between them. Until the middle 1960s, the term "rock and roll" had been applied generally to post–Tin Pan Alley popular styles. By 1967, however, when such San Francisco–based groups as Big Brother and the Holding Company, Quicksilver Messenger Service, Moby Grape, the Jefferson Airplane, the Grateful Dead, and Country Joe and the Fish gained national attention, the term "rock" was coming into use for their music. A *Newsweek* article from December 1966 describes a new kind of youthful entertainment in the Bay Area:

> Every weekend in such immense halls as the Fillmore and the Avalon Ballroom, and college auditoriums like the Pauley Ballroom at Berkeley, the music assaults the ears; strobe lights, pulsating to the beat, blind the eyes and sear the nerves. Psychedelic projections slither across the walls in protoplasmic blobs. Two or three thousand young people jam the floor, many in "ec-

static" dress—men with shoulder-length locks and one earring, cowboy outfits, frock coats, high hats; women in deliberately tatty evening gowns, rescued from some attic, embellished by a tiara and sneakers. Arab kaftans are
worn by both sexes, who also affect bead necklaces, the high sign of LSD
initiation.[12]

In addition to a heavy reliance on electricity (for amplification and the mixing of instruments and voices, which requires manipulation in a sound studio), traits of the new style included a wider variety of musical instruments,
more flexible song forms, and intensely subjective lyrics. By the early 1970s,
"rock" had changed from a stylistic term into an umbrella, incorporating a
myriad of musical styles, with only the audience as common denominator.
The idioms and artists that attracted rock audiences in these years include
the classical Indian music of Ravi Shankar, the fusion of jazz and rock by
Miles Davis, Joan Baez's folk revival songs, organist Virgil Fox, who sometimes superimposed a light show on his performances of J. S. Bach, and
avant-garde composer John Cage.[13]

What was the connection between rock music and the umbrella it offered to such a range of other styles in these years? The British sociologist
and popular-music lover Simon Frith draws a social and chronological
distinction between rock and roll, a working-class idiom that appealed to
working-class people *and* teenagers across the economic spectrum, and
rock, which he sees as tailored for white suburban youth. Rock and roll offered listeners "a sense of freedom that was, simultaneously, a sense of root-
lessness and estrangement," focused on "the youth rebel, the loner who
cannot settle down because he's got no place to go." But rock music of the
latter 1960s and early 1970s packaged that ethos for the sensibilities of
middle-class audience members, many of them born and bred in the suburbs. Familiar with feelings of estrangement and rebellion, these listeners
had nevertheless been raised in a culture that measured self-worth by success. They tended to be "disciplined and creative, rational and ambitious,"
Frith writes. "They have to be, simultaneously, satisfied and dissatisfied with
their lot." And rock music helped them maintain that balance, while in-
jecting what felt like a dose of gritty reality into their lives. "Part of the
middle-class use of rock, in short, has been as a way into working-class
adolescence. What is on offer is the fantasy community of risk."[14]

In Frith's view, the communal experience offered by rock music consisted simply of enjoying the music while at the same time believing that
others of like mind were enjoying it too. To quote Greil Marcus, another
prominent rock critic: "We fight our way through the massed and leveled
collective taste of the Top 40, just looking for a little something we can call
our own. But when we find it and jam the radio to hear it again it isn't just

ours—it is a link to thousands of others who are sharing it with us. As a matter of a single song this might mean very little; as culture, as a way of life, you can't beat it."[15] In other words, the rock community "refers not to an institution, to a set of people, but to a sensation." The notion was fabricated by choosing elements of working-class culture and fashioning from them "a romantic idea for 'rebel' suburban kids" that could then be consumed.

Having shown that the idea of the rock community turns under inspection into a myth, Frith goes on to affirm the power of that myth. "The significance of magic," he writes, "is that people believe it."[16] He describes the sensation of community well enough to suggest how rock fans might well have included the likes of Ravi Shankar, Miles Davis, Virgil Fox, and John Cage in their purview—partly on the basis of musical sound and style, but partly too because many listeners outside the rock community would find something in each one to object to.

A recent survey of popular music from the 1950s to the 90s takes the notion of community and the rock umbrella in a different direction. Rock in the latter 1960s, when social barriers that divided groups in America seemed to be breaking down, is seen more as an attitude than a style or a set of musical practices—a time when "musicians as different as the Grateful Dead, the Beatles, Bob Dylan, and James Brown demonstrated that they had fans in common." Many members of the rock audience also embraced Eastern religions and social activism, seeking to discover new facets of the self.

> The counter-culture emphasized not only personal expansion of awareness and options, but also collective experimentation with free living and free loving (enabled by recent advances in contraception). Non-competitiveness and harmony were symbolized in 1967 by the "Summer of Love" and the first large rock festival, the Monterey Pop Festival. However, men and women were not equally freed by the sexual revolution.[17]

These comments point to perhaps the most far-reaching change of all: the new emphasis Americans were placing on personal identity. Rooted in the generation gap, the civil rights movement, the rise of ethnic pride, the gay rights movement, and a women's movement that was just getting started, the notion of identity as a key element of life—and one subject to constant negotiation—entered the American consciousness with full force in the late 1960s. And rock music, with its concern for individuals and knack for getting at serious issues, offered a ready means for expressing identity and trying out new ones.

This chapter began with the observation that the Beatles' music and the public response to it traced a path from accessibility to transcendence. Two facts have been offered to support that idea: almost three decades after their breakup, commercial demand for Beatles' recordings continues; and rock critics have advanced claims for the music's artistic and intellectual worth that until the latter 1960s had never been made for repertories outside the classical sphere, except for jazz. Yet survival in the marketplace and writer's claims of aesthetic achievement constitute a different kind of transcendence from that which, since the early 1800s, has served as the classical sphere's ideal. The earlier ideal was built around formal traits of the works themselves, preserved in scores. Rock experience, in contrast, has centered on listeners' responses.

Tailored to circulate in a consumer marketplace that today belongs to an international entertainment enterprise, rock aims to succeed there through precise cultural placement. With its many offshoots, the music has defined the popular sphere's mainstream for the last several decades. Many middle-class Americans continue to find its populist stance authentic and engaging. Moreover, the exclusion of nonfans—listeners thought to be out of step with rock's sensibilities—lends another provocative edge to the experience. To conclude that rock's musical substance lacks richness or is incidental to its appeal would be wrong. On the other hand, as the rock umbrella shows, it would also be wrong to link the music's appeal *only* to its sound and style. The myth of the rock community has shown an uncanny power to compel belief in a group identity that many rock fans have experienced as tribal: based on shared customs and tastes, and more choosy than welcoming in tone. As for rock transcendence, it may have more to do with social attitude than with the music that evokes it. As long as a sizable audience believes in the sensation of a community favoring "rebellious" personal identities and ready to scorn those outside the tribe, the music seems likely to maintain its powerful place in the American popular sphere.

39

Trouble Girls, Minimalists, and The Gap

The 1960s to the 1980s

IN THE LATE TWENTIETH-CENTURY UNITED STATES, no social issue has sparked more widespread discussion than identity. And as the ground of male-female relations has shifted, American women especially have explored a widening range of identities. Music has been involved in that exploration. Popular female vocal ensembles ("girl groups"), for example, spoke powerfully to the experience of gendered identity in the early 1960s. As girls and young female teenagers were bombarded with contradictory messages from parents, teachers, and the mass media, the songs of girl groups straddled many of those contradictions, and especially the tension between restraint and freedom. Girls could play at being the defiant rebel as well as the docile girlfriend.[1]

Sweet Talkin' Guy, by the Chiffons, a recording from 1960, offers an example. The song, which young female listeners loved, is about a deceitful, irresistible male charmer; its message is that it's normal to want to yield to such boys as well as try to resist them.[2] By the 1970s, the sense of that dividedness had given rise to the political movement called women's liberation. Rather than assuming that they themselves could resolve the contradictions they lived with, women began to advocate changes in society.

Among the warring pieces of late twentieth-century female identity was a changing attitude toward sex. Americans today are far more likely than in the past to live alone, delay marrying, and engage in sexual intercourse outside marriage. Since 1960, the number of unmarried couples living together has quadrupled. The notion of "saving oneself"—especially if one is female—for sex within marriage has lost both moral authority and social appeal.

The shift has been traced to the early 1960s, when movies, literature, and fashion proclaimed a new openness about sexuality. That openness followed a biological breakthrough: the 1960 appearance on the market of the birth-control pill. Women could now engage in sexual activity without worrying about unwanted pregnancies, and could thus create sexual identities before marriage and apart from it. At the same time, new ideas about sex affected marriage itself. With fertility under control through contraception and abortion, growing numbers of married women pursued careers outside the home, and family roles and expectations changed accordingly. This development had many causes, from economic (the desire for a higher standard of living) to personal (the wish for a more stimulating life). Since the 1970s, it has been fueled ideologically by the women's movement, which has criticized the idea that a woman's only proper sphere of fulfillment lay in child care and housework. The notion that women must put the needs of spouses and children before their own also came under heavy attack.

The sexual revolution of the 1960s left few corners of American life untouched. In fact, however, it amounted to a *second* sexual revolution—a follow-up to one that took place after World War I.[3] The Nineteenth Amendment to the U.S. Constitution, granting women the right to vote, was ratified in 1920, when female identity had already begun moving away from traditional patterns. The Victorian principle that male and female activity—work, play, and family interaction—should be pursued separately was breaking down; a symptom of its weakening lay in the century's early years, when men and women began more and more to pursue recreation together. Leisure was linked to sexuality by new fashions and attitudes: for young women, bobbed hair, short skirts, and makeup, and for young men, owning a car and being a good dancer. Movies provided sexual models not only on the screen but in the audience.

If the sexual revolution of the 1920s had already introduced same-sex socializing, recognized female sexuality, approved contraception, and advocated companionate marriage, why was another revolution needed in the 1960s? One reason is that while the 1920s idea of "new" women affected chiefly the white middle class and the affluent, the 1960s idea was embraced by working-class women too. Another is that many middle-class women reconnected with an older model of female identity. From the early 1940s on, young Americans married at record rates. Fertility, declining since the early twentieth century, now began to rise; families with three or more children grew more common. The growth of suburbs also affected gender roles. Suburban culture revolved around domesticity, and women were encouraged to embrace a domestic role as their fitting place in the natural order of things. Yet even as domesticity was being affirmed, more wives were moving into the workforce. The sexual revolution of the 1960s could claim continuity with earlier feminist movements while at the same time declaring a break with a past that had taken male dominance for granted.

As we saw in Chapter 32, songwriters in the 1920s began celebrating romantic love between free individuals. But rock-and-roll and rock songs, including those of 1960s girl groups, brought other views of love into the popular sphere. Romance, with its suggestions of idealism and mystery, may seem old-fashioned in an age when love is often demystified. While many songs of the earlier era bathed listeners in charm that could turn erotic, they also treated eroticism as a male impulse that females were obliged to control. Romantic love between free individuals in that era took place on an obviously uneven playing field.

For young men and women of recent generations, however, sexuality was no longer an undercurrent but a realm of self-assertion—even rebellion, as turf was staked out around the generation gap. Once domestic ideology was set aside and sexuality detached from marriage, romantic love took on more hedonistic overtones. Some youth of the early 1960s saw the change in racial terms, suggesting that unhealthy sexual inhibitions had plagued white Americans more than black ones. One male student activist praised his cohorts as a generation "with a new, less repressed attitude toward sex and pleasure," adding that popular music had liberated them. But how did females respond to the popular sphere's new openness about sex? In some cases, positively. One young woman called the music's realism "a great release after all those super-consolation ballads." Another commented that rock had "provided me and a lot of women with a channel for saying 'want,' and for asserting our sexuality without apologies and without having to pretty up every passion with the traditionally 'feminine' desire for true love and marriage." Rock performers such as the Rolling Stones appealed precisely because of their antiromanticism.[4]

Although rock musicians have played a key role in circulating images of sexually independent women, they did not introduce them to the popular music scene. For the 1920s had already witnessed a trend in popular song that treated sex with unsentimental frankness. The vehicle was the blues: Gertrude "Ma" Rainey and Bessie Smith sang about the experiences of black working-class women in ways far removed from the songs aimed at the white middle class. Blues-style love was no idealized realm where dreams for future happiness were stored. Rather, blues songs were often linked with possibilities for greater social freedom. The notion of marriage as the goal that defined the lives of women contradicted black social realities of the day. Indeed, the lyrics of songs sung by Rainey and Smith reveal women's blues of the 1920s and 30s as a working-class form that anticipates the consciousness-raising of the 1970s women's liberation movement. These songs have the effect—with hindsight, at any rate—of turning personal matters into political ones.[5]

Blues protagonists in the songs of Rainey, Smith, and other early

blueswomen are seldom married women and almost never mothers. Subjects include death, disease, homosexuality, poverty, infidelity, depression,
prison, alcohol, and abandonment.[6] In a segregated society whose popular
entertainment idealized romance, African Americans probably provided
most of the audience for these singers. But by the 1960s, the civil rights
movement had breached some of the racial barriers; jazz, rock and roll, and
other kinds of blues had introduced whites to that tradition's blend of hard
truth and playfulness; and the sexual revolution was undermining older romantic stereotypes while also showing that male-female relationships could
explore love and sex separately. Where the protagonists in earlier love songs
longed for ineffable connection, those of rock songs had a greater tendency
to perceive that male-female connections involved power. While love tends
to mask the issue of power relations or dodge it altogether, sex detached
from love is an arena where the partners' priorities are likely to clash.

The *quality* of sexual experience, once a subject too intimate for public
airing, was now openly discussed. As a realm unto itself, sex could now be
thought of as the ultimate leisure activity. And the best sex was said to happen *outside* marriage, without its distractions of love and commitment. The
expansion of sexual opportunity during the 1960s was part of the culture's
acceptance of hedonism.

With sex detached from reproduction, a realistic outlook was believed to
dispel the mystique of romance and reintegrate elements of the fragmented
female identity. Yet even as women's identity changed, sex remained gender-
bound, with men still the main sexual consumers and women the sexual
commodities. Though freed from earlier stereotypes, women were assigned
new ones, still subordinate to men. The roots of these stereotypes have
been detected in the bohemian rebellion of young men against the family,
specifically against their mothers and sisters as representative of a confining
domesticity.[7] New female paradigms in the counterculture responded to
this notion of male character, including the flower child, earthmother, and
idealized prostitute. After the sexual revolution, sex as self-expression was
still a male prerogative; for women, the tension between sexual freedom and
restraint persisted.[8]

Whatever the balance of power between males and females today, the
image of modern women—especially *young* modern women—as independent and often untamable is widespread. Today's ideal of the sassy, spunky,
unencumbered female surely rejects the view that female identity revolves
around duty and obligation. That rejection is found throughout *Trouble
Girls: The Rolling Stone Book of Women in Rock* (1997), written and edited
entirely by women and claiming for its subjects a line of predecessors
reaching back to Ma Rainey. The cover features P. J. Harvey, a young British
rock-and-roll performer, representing the spirit of independent young

British rock singer P. J. Harvey graces the cover of this landmark publication of 1997.

womanhood in a pose that is stylized and ambiguous in the manner of a fashion photo. Harvey's image, caught in motion, invites the male gaze while at the same time repelling it, mocking any hope of connection, emotional or physical. ("Stare all you want," the image seems to say, "but try to touch me, and I'm outta here.") Harvey glories in her attractiveness, aware of the power that looks like hers can wield. But the image seems to signify that this cover girl needs no one—especially not a man who might try to take her under his wing.

Although less famous than many other songwriters and singers discussed in *Trouble Girls*, Harvey is apparently featured to suggest that the book's focus is more current than historical. She appears not only on the cover but in the final essay, written by the volume's general editor and giving readers a glimpse of what *Rolling Stone*'s editors consider cutting-edge artistry. While saying little about P. J. Harvey as a musician, it celebrates her emotional authenticity. The singer's "hard-headed songs," said to be "full of slash-and-burn exuberance," are praised. And Harvey's second album (1993) is called "a raw-throated, mud-soaked woundfest" whose songs form "a brilliant miasma of tortured love and fractured fables," as well as "a roiling ball of gorgeous aggression."[9]

The themes of realism, suppressed rage, and the therapeutic benefits of women speaking their mind loom large in *Trouble Girls*, which also confronts rock music's long-standing misogyny. In the preface, a prominent female rock critic of the 1960s, explaining how a feminist managed to stomach the rock music of that era, pays tribute to truth telling, wherever it leads: "Music that boldly and aggressively laid out what the singer wanted, loved, hated—as good rock & roll did—challenged me to do the same, and so, even when the content was antiwoman, antisexual, in a sense antihuman, the form encouraged my struggle for liberation."[10] *Trouble Girls* sees personal matters in political terms. The responsibilities of marriage and motherhood are seldom mentioned. A woman's right to live life in accord with personal priorities and wishes is assumed, free from any program dictated by earlier social custom or even by biology.

More than five hundred pages long, *Trouble Girls* covers a wide range of musicians and genres. Profiles on the varied group of women who followed such 1960s pioneers as Carole King, Aretha Franklin, Diana Ross, Laura Nyro, and Grace Slick show us how they broadened rock's expressive possibilities. From blues-based performers (Janis Joplin, Bonnie Raitt) to the cabaret, theater, and screen (Bette Midler); from writers of their own material (Raitt, Joni Mitchell) to interpreters of the songs of others (Midler, Linda Ronstadt); and from black-influenced (Raitt, Joplin, Tina Turner) to Mexican and Hispanic (Ronstadt), these women dramatize rock music's diversity. Their treatment in *Trouble Girls* emphasizes boundary crossing and rebellion. If the book has one theme, it is that rock music is an arena where modern identities for women are being proposed and constructed.

The authors of *Trouble Girls* are not endorsing a program of social action. Rather, their aim is to register a vibrant, stylish, modern female consciousness. Whereas the women's movement has evolved around a political agenda, the book emphasizes images and symbolic gestures that repudiate a sexist past. Perhaps just as youth and maturity have different ways of expressing aspiration, the agenda and the book are natural complements. At the same time, the gap between the two suggests that more than a sexual revolution and a liberation movement are needed to unify the fragmented sense of personal identity that many American women take to be a condition of life in today's world.

In the popular sphere, changing views of romance have helped to bring female musicians to the fore. But in the classical sphere, opportunity for women has been limited until recent years. Before World War II, almost all performers in major symphony orchestras were male; although separate women's orchestras also existed, they disappeared almost entirely after the war, and since then integration has been the pattern. In 1947, female employment in major symphony orchestras stood at 8 percent; by 1982, that figure had risen to 26.3 percent.[11] Such changes reflect the belief that women's past exclusion was based on prejudice.

Women also made small gains in classical composition, a field monopolized even more fully by men. Commissions and prizes awarded by foundations have overwhelmingly favored men, though a pattern of growing inclusiveness could be found in the Guggenheim, Koussevitsky, and Fromm Foundation awards to composers after the mid-1960s. The first gave twice as many awards to women in the 1970s as in the preceding forty years; the second gave no awards to women between 1941 and 1966, but five between 1967 and 1986; and the third, after awarding all its prizes to males between 1952 and 1969, gave six to women in the next fifteen years.[12]

That female composers are gaining in prominence is confirmed by a 1991 book on women in music. Classifying their work according to style, this study proposes seven categories: serial music (Louise Talma, Joan Tower, Barbara Kolb), sound-mass (Kolb, Nancy Van de Vate), sonic exploration (Annea Lockwood, Lucia Dlugoszewski, Darleen Cowles Mitchell, and Julia Perry), performance art (Pauline Oliveros, Laurie Anderson, Joan La Barbara, Meredith Monk), electronic and computer music (Emma Lou Diemer, Jean Eichelberger Ivey), symphonic music (Ellen Taaffe Zwilich), and "post-avant-garde synthesis" (Elaine Barkin, Libby Larsen, Joyce Mekeel). The list suggests that the music of women rock singers and women classical composers is equally diverse.

Women have often been said to approach music making and composing differently from men. Symphonic conductor Joanne Falletta told an interviewer in the early 1980s that "the more I got into conducting, the more I had to come to terms with how I was raised as a young Catholic girl. We were taught to be supportive, nurturing, gentle, kind."[13] And in a 1984 essay, Pauline Oliveros, who has won a prominent place in avant-garde music circles, describes contrasting creative modes: "(1) active, purposive creativity, resulting from cognitive thought, deliberate acting upon or willful shaping of materials, and (2) receptive creativity, during which the artist is like a channel through which material flows and seems to shape itself." According

Composer Pauline Oliveros (b. 1932) has pioneered the exploration of musical sound and the presence of women in avant-
garde musical circles.

to Oliveros, society has valued the first mode—analytical and "identified
with aggression and masculinity"—more highly than the second, which she
calls intuitive. She has proposed women's liberation as an antidote to such
one-sidedness. Women, she believes, are more likely than men to recognize
the intuitive mode as equal to the analytical. In her view, the oppression of
women has devalued intuition, "which is culturally assigned to women's
roles."[14]

Oliveros has been called the female counterpart of John Cage, with each
of her works a kind of meditation on sound itself. During the 1970s, in fact,
she composed a series of *Sonic Meditations*: collective improvisations that
can involve the audience ("My feeling was that if somebody wanted to participate they were welcome, but if they didn't there was no obligation").

Compositions of this kind are attuned toward intuition and receptivity and away from analytical modes. Indeed, Oliveros has admitted that people who "dismiss such pieces as nonmusic . . . may be quite right," though she does not.[15] Oliveros has helped to make audiences more aware of sound, while at the same time raising consciousness about women as creators of music.

Pauline Oliveros is also recognized for helping to found a new genre: so-called performance art, linked chiefly with female composers who came on the scene in the 1970s. Women composers have shown more inclination than men to consider their own bodies and voices as material for the making of music. These composers—often called performance artists to distinguish them from those who write conventional composers' music, though they still create musical structures—include Diamanda Galás, Laurie Anderson, Joan La Barbara, and many more. A prime example is the dancer-filmmaker-singer-composer Meredith Monk, linked by some critics to a minimalist style of composition. Monk rejects that label:

> I come from a folk music tradition. I was a folk singer with a guitar. The repetition in my music I think of as being like folk music: you have your chorus and verse. I'm more interested in how the voice digs down into emotional reality. It's like the freedom of a jazz singer, it's not a patterning impulse. The minimalist thing is about reduction. Vocally, I always thought about magnification, expansion. The repetitions are just a layer for the voice to take off from and go somewhere, and also to land on again.[16]

Monk's words point beyond female identity to the idea of creating music that sustains interest by involving listeners in the sensuous experience of sound itself. Born in 1942, Meredith Monk was one of a number of younger American composers who gravitated to New York City during the 1960s, working out alternative approaches to music and sound. And because they reversed an influential postwar trend toward complexity and the analytical mode, their work invites a consideration of fresh notions of identity that began to take shape around the idea of being an American composer.

The Gap and the Identity of American Composers

"No other single aspect of twentieth-century music seems so central as the celebrated and oft-trotted-out 'gap between composer and audience,'" writes the author of a 1997 study of American composition in the classical sphere. And he then adds:

> If the name hadn't already been appropriated by a popular clothing store chain, one might expect that future music historians will refer to this century simply as The Gap. It is our defining neurosis. We pretend to lament its existence, but actually, we have become so proud of it that, when music

doesn't put up barriers to the audience's comprehension or patience, we accuse it of not being authentically twentieth-century. There's something tough and puritan about living with The Gap, like doing without running water or television.[17]

This comment appears halfway through a book whose author understands the historical circumstances from which The Gap emerged. For he himself is a composer: a receiver of The Gap's protection, though he now makes it a target for playful scorn. What can be learned from the perspective of a composer and writer whose broad-ranging study views with irony a situation relied on and endorsed by many twentieth-century American composers as the root of their artistic freedom?

The writer is Kyle Gann, born in 1955 in Dallas. Readers get a clear view of his outlook from the final chapter, which boldly claims that a particular style of music written by composers of his generation, himself included, has already made the decade of the 1990s "the most fertile in American music" since the 1920s. Gann labels that compositional approach "totalism," combining visceral audience appeal with a complexity that can hold the interest of the sophisticated expert.[18] As Gann sees it, the autonomy won by American composers in the classical sphere has proved hollow. The presence of an independent academic venue has favored the intellectual side of composition, he contends, while effacing spontaneity, putting a damper on expression and ignoring audience response. In recent years, more accessible approaches have attracted new audiences—especially to so-called minimalism and its spinoffs. Some observers have disparaged that trend as artistically shallow, perhaps even commercially opportunistic. But a totalist approach has given composers a response to the charge of triviality. Combining the intellectual rigor of complex twentieth-century systems (e.g., serialism) with a beat, while seeking to engage the emotions of listeners, totalism holds out promise for a classical sphere in the new millennium that is not so sharply divided against itself.

There is no denying Gann's mythic tone here, which casts totalism and his own generation in a starring role. At the book's very end he lets his imagination range into the future. "Say for a minute," Gann writes, that artists are "the antennae of the race, the first people to register and reflect undercurrents of collective psychological change." If that is true, perhaps composers of the 1990s, who are "once again creating music in which the intellectual, physical, and emotional appeal are no longer separated," are pointing toward a "rebirth in American society." It may be, he says, that the route from John Cage's 4'33" to John Luther Adams's *Dream of White on White* (1992, for instrumental ensemble) and such operas as Meredith Monk's *Atlas* (1991) and Mikel Rouse's *Dennis Cleveland* (1996) "is a road that society itself is slowly and belatedly traversing, a road that starts with the simple, egoless act of stopping to listen, and that points toward a reintegration of personality, toward restoring playfulness and emotiveness to creativity."[19]

While this prophecy may strike some readers as inspirational, others will object to the suggestions that (1) American composers before the 1990s had avoided personality, playfulness, and emotiveness; (2) it is a new idea in modern music to connect intellectual, physical, and emotional appeal; and (3) these traits can be achieved by choosing a particular approach to composition. Many American composers of the last half century have valued and pursued the very things they are said here to have rejected. Thanks in large part to The Gap, however, and the remarkable autonomy composers have enjoyed, agreement on *which* works composed since World War II have achieved greatness, if any, has proved elusive. Autonomy fosters a relative attitude that undercuts the notion that such judgments are possible. Many composers would probably agree with George Rochberg, who in 1980 said that rather than trying to enlarge his audience, he relies on listeners ready to deal with what he has to say.[20] But the number of such listeners is small. Gann's prophecy aside, The Gap has surely encouraged composers to write music that most listeners find esoteric.

Gann maintains that any serious consideration of the 1990s must start "with the overwhelming fact that there are far more active composers today than at any previous time in history."[21] He admits that the range of styles is too broad to provide a framework for discussing music in the 1990s, but chronology reveals a pattern. He then lists seven social conditions common to composers born in the 1950s:

1. The increased contact with non-Western music, together with the teaching of jazz and the large amount of pre-Baroque European music available on records, has shown "that European music of the common-practice period is just one music among many, with no privileged position."
2. The phasing out of music education in many school districts has made it difficult for Americans to create a common musical culture, except for what is heard on the radio.
3. Since the middle 1980s, sequencing software has become so common that notation has faded in importance. "Much music today is made, even by amateurs, directly on the computer screen."
4. Music publishers now bring out so little new music that composers find it nearly impossible to obtain commercial circulation of their scores. On the other hand, compact discs are fairly cheap to produce and easy to distribute. New music today is more likely than ever before to "be judged only for how it sounds, for the score may either not exist or be practically unavailable."
5. The easy availability of sound samplers has redefined "the musical atom."

The most elemental musical unit, formerly the individual note, may now be "a sound complex or quotation."

6. "Growing up in an environment pervaded with rock music has become an almost universal experience. It is increasingly rare, then, for composers to write without taking the rhythms, instrumentation, or performance conventions of rock into account," especially if they hope to reach a live audience.

7. Finally, "a drastic splintering of audiences" has taken place, producing "a daunting multiplicity of subcultures," each increasingly cut off from the others. "The number of routes toward a successful career has increased proportionately with the impossibility of getting a significant hearing outside one's subculture," as "the orchestral circuit, the opera circuit, the improvisation scene, the new-music community, the theater music world, [and] the academic music world" have grown more distant from each other.[22]

These factors have shaped a common outlook among many composers Gann's age and younger, for whom The Gap looks more like a self-imposed handicap than a bulwark for creative freedom. The new outlook rests on three basic shifts: a growing belief in present-day American aesthetic approaches, an enlivened appreciation of musical sound, and less resistance to popular music and marketplace values. Gann's seven conditions help to explain these shifts. The first two reflect a decline in the authority of the European classical sphere, whose establishment in the United States has long been considered this country's ticket to a place in the family of Western musical nations. The third, fourth, and fifth, sparked by easier access to sound-making technology, follow a trail blazed by Cage, Oliveros, and others who have located the essence of music in sound itself. The sixth, challenging the assumption that music in the popular sphere is artistically inferior, reveals a growing interest in audience appeal. And the seventh is also tied to the marketplace, accepting the notion that composers should feel free to specialize and to target particular groups of consumers.

Laurie Anderson, a slightly older composer (b. 1947) and confirmed boundary crosser, has criticized The Gap and then defended it. The classical sphere's attitude, she has said, can be "a pretty snobbish kind of thing." On the other hand, that stance has made possible "an environment for people to invent and go beyond what is on the airwaves, which is for twelve-year-olds it's so stupid." To avoid misunderstanding, Anderson, noting that in recent years she has owned neither a radio nor a TV set, clarified her remark: "Not that twelve-year-olds are stupid, but pop music and popular culture are pretty inane. So the avant-garde has an obligation to be very closed."[23] In other words, The Gap's exclusive attitude has protected artists from being overwhelmed by voracious commercialism.

The trend that Gann outlines signals a growing inclination by younger classical composers to accept the world as they find it and to ground their work in conditions they encounter in everyday life. This tendency points toward a new identity for American composers. For each of Gann's seven conditions departs from what many earlier composers have accepted as axioms: the privileged position of European classics, the need for a common classical music culture, the idea of composition as a written practice, the primacy of score over sound, the fundamental importance of the individual note, the inferiority of commercially successful popular music, and the idea that it is natural for a composer to work in a variety of genres. That these claims are losing their status as axioms suggests the passing of influence away from composers who see themselves as champions of quality in an age of quantity, and toward those who find today's democratic, technological, market-driven society a fertile arena for their creative imagination.

History is often said to support the view that, although sometimes misunderstood or vilified at first, work of quality will eventually be recognized. (Nicolas Slonimsky's *A Lexicon of Musical Invective*, which collects wrongheaded criticisms of composers from Beethoven to Bartók, is sometimes cited to demonstrate that in the end artistic worthiness is all that really matters.) Gann's analysis, however, says that many younger composers no longer trust that scenario. As they see it, the United States is home today to more good composers than ever before. Traditional barriers of nationality, culture, and economics are wearing down, and the supply of music grows increasingly out of proportion to the demand. An almost limitless capacity exists to gather, record, reshape, and circulate musical sound. Moreover, film, television, and MTV have linked music with images, which mass circulation has made widely familiar. In a musical culture of such abundance and diversity, the idea of composing as a private activity, walled off within the classical sphere's contemporary wing, can look more parochial than lofty and admirable.

The roots of the change outlined here extend back to the 1960s and before, in part to John Cage and his experimental outlook, but also to the rise of musical styles that have come to be grouped under the heading of "minimalism." As a musical style, minimalism drew criticism for lacking eventfulness, yet it attracted an audience of enthusiastic listeners. And some of its pioneering figures—Philip Glass, Steve Reich, and John Adams—showed that it was possible to reach an audience much larger than the usual one for new music.

According to Philip Glass, by 1967 modern music in New York was being transformed by "a generation of composers who were in open revolt against the academic musical world." Glass had by then encountered northern Indian music in Paris through performances by Ravi Shankar, which led him to "a whole different way of thinking about music." Musical events, he learned, could be created by tension between melody and rhythm, as well as by the Western tension between melody and harmony. In a like-minded spirit, Steve Reich described a busy New York new-music scene in 1965 that made him feel like a complete outsider. "I was not very much in touch with composers of the type that would be doing new music," he remembered. "On the one hand there were people up at Columbia-Princeton who I felt totally out of touch with and unsympathetic towards, and on the other hand there was the John Cage group who I felt totally out of sympathy with. So there was really no place for me." Reich was trying to find ways to build on his first musical loves: jazz, Bach, and Stravinsky. ("That's really why I became a composer," he later recalled. "It was that kind of music that brought me to tears, and nothing else. Still is.")[24] His discovery in 1962 of African rhythmic concepts helped him find his own creative path. The stylistic interests and pedigrees of Reich and Glass were entirely out of step with those favored by leaders of New York's musical life.

Three distinct models of composers' identity dominated the New York classical scene in the mid-1960s: the composer as intellectual, the composer as experimentalist, and the composer as creator of works for the concert hall. Serial composers, many of whom were now using electroacoustic sound, dominated academia. The composer Charles Wuorinen, for example, declared in 1975 "the twelve-tone system in all its ramifications . . . the legitimate successor to the tonal system." Serialism's technical and historical authority meant to him that there was really only one way of composing, based on an analytical mode of creativity. With less dogmatic solemnity, composer Jacob Druckman remembered that "not being a serialist on the East Coast of the United States in the sixties was like not being a Catholic in Rome in the thirteenth century."[25] Though their audience was small, serialists engaged with artistic issues emphasized by influential Europeans such as Pierre Boulez and Karlheinz Stockhausen, and that engagement carried enough intellectual prestige to ensure support for academic teaching and composing. As for Cage and his fellow experimenters, they enhanced their position in these years by questioning boundaries between life and art. Challenging the very idea of an artwork, they tapped patrons who supported modern dance and avant-garde painting.

As the classical music establishment's public arm, the concert hall has often been accused of hostility or indifference to contemporary expression. Yet its leaders have also recognized composition as a part of any vital musical culture, sustaining the active role of composers with commissions and occasional performances of their music. Pulitzer Prizes were awarded in the latter 1960s to works by younger composers who earned their living in academia: Leslie Bassett's *Variations* for orchestra (1966), Leon Kirchner's String Quartet No. 3 (1967), George Crumb's *Echoes of Time and the River* for orchestra (1968), and Karel Husa's String Quartet No. 3 (1969). Moreover, a number of composers including George Rochberg, Crumb, Jacob Druck-man, William Bolcom, Lukas Foss, and David del Tredici began writing mu-sic that harked back to the European past, called the New Romanticism. These composers sought to connect with a classical establishment that had never accepted serial music in the first place. They, and more recently Christopher Rouse, Ellen Taaffe Zwilich, John Harbison, Joseph Schwant-ner, and Joan Tower, among others, have benefited from the resources that orchestras and opera houses can place at a composer's disposal.

By 1965, LaMonte Young and Terry Riley, two composers from the west-ern United States, were writing lengthy works based on severely reduced amounts of musical material that would point the way for Glass, Reich, and other young composers who fit none of the three composers' niches. A radi-cal example, and the first in what is now defined as a minimalist line, was Young's *Trio for Strings*, composed in 1958 from tones held for enormous lengths of time. (In a London performance of 1989, the opening section of this piece for violin, viola, and cello, containing only three different notes, lasted five minutes and eighteen seconds.) What inspired a young composer in the late 1950s to write such music? Young's answer was that he discovered "a *feeling* involved in these long spaces of time that really meant a lot to me." Recognizing that "these sustained tones dealt with frequency—rhythms on a much higher level," he also found that the musical sound opened the door to a kind of spiritual understanding that he would go on to explore in the future.[26]

Terry Riley, a Californian and close colleague of Young's since the 1950s, was another key figure in the fashioning of a minimalist approach. In the past, Kyle Gann has written, "if you asked composers what one piece made them decide they wanted to become a composer, dozens of them, as diverse as Conlon Nancarrow and William Schuman, would reply: 'The Rite of Spring.' Today, ask the same question to composers born after 1940, and you'll often get one or both of two answers: Terry Riley's *In C* and Steve Reich's *Come Out*."[27] Written in San Francisco in 1964, *In C* gave the minimalist movement in America a public profile, becoming in some ways its anthem.

Questioned often over the years about this work's genesis, Riley has de-scribed improvisation as one of its main influences. The fifty-three short motives that make up *In C*—repeated constantly over a fast pulse high in the piano—must be played in order, but the performers decide how long each one is played and therefore how they fit together. Having grown up playing jazz, Riley was comfortable with the idea of on-the-spot creation. Technology was another influence. Riley spent 1962–63 in Paris, where, working as a jazz pianist, he began experimenting with tape loops. *In C* is written for live performers playing an unfixed number of unspecified instruments, but its repetitions sound electronically inspired. A third influence was Riley's outlook on life, which took music as a way of approaching a new mode of consciousness. "I was a beatnik, and then I turned into a hippie," Riley told an interviewer. In the mid-sixties, he had been

> very concerned with psychedelia and the psychedelic movement of the sixties as an opening toward consciousness. For my generation that was a first look towards the East, that is, peyote, mescaline, and the psychedelic drugs which were opening up people's attention towards higher consciousness. So I think what I was experiencing in music at that time was another world. Besides just the ordinary music that was going on, music was also able to transport us suddenly out of one reality into another. Transport us so that we would almost be having visions as we were playing. So that's what I was thinking about before I wrote *In C*. I believe music, shamanism, and magic are all connected, and when it's used that way it creates the most beautiful use of music.[28]

In C was premiered in November 1964 at the San Francisco Tape Music Center by an ensemble of thirteen: six keyboards including an electric organ, two saxophones, accordion, two trumpets plus a third doubling on recorder, and clarinet. (Riley and Steve Reich were two of the keyboard players, Pauline Oliveros the accordionist, and the composer Morton Subotnick the clarinetist.) Light projections also accompanied the performance. A respected local critic reviewed the piece enthusiastically. He found Riley's music primitivistic, with relentless continuity, yet full of "melodic variations and contrasts of rhythm," and even climaxes that "appear and are dissolved in the endlessness." "At times," he wrote, "you feel you have never done anything all your life long but listen to this music and as if that is all there is or ever will be, but it is altogether absorbing, exciting, and moving too."[29]

Steve Reich's role in the premiere is also part of the story of minimalism's beginnings. Though not a jazz musician himself, Reich has noted the effect of listening as a teenager to trumpeter Miles Davis, drummer Kenny Clarke, and a bit later to saxophonist John Coltrane, especially while studying composition at Mills College in Oakland, California (1961–63). "The jazz influence that's all over my work is not so specific," he said in 1987, "but without the rhythmic and melodic gesture of jazz, its flexibility and nuance, my work is *unthinkable*."[30] Reich remembered learning "a tremendous amount from putting [*In C*] together, and I think it had a very strong influence on me."[31]

Reich has described how he stumbled onto the process behind his own breakthrough piece, *Come Out*. In 1965, he had made tape loops from a short passage of a street preacher's sermon he had recorded in San Francisco. The loops were intended as a way of superimposing one phrase upon another for musical effect, with the help of two tape machines.

Composer-percussionist Steve Reich performs in New York, 1971.

I put headphones on and noticed that the two tape recorders were almost exactly in sync. The effect of this aurally was that I heard the sound jockeying back and forth in my head between my left and right ear, as one machine or the other drifted ahead. Instead of immediately correcting that, I let it go . . . took my hands off it for a bit. What happened was that one of the machines was going slightly faster, and the sound went over to the left side of my head, crawled down my leg, went across the floor, and then started to reverberate, because the left channel was moving ahead of the right channel. I let it go

further, and it finally got to precisely the relationship I wanted to get to. . . .
It was an accidental discovery.[32]

Come Out (1966) used that discovery in a different way. From an interview
with a victim of a police beating in Harlem, who had been told he could
only receive hospital care if he was bleeding, Reich chose a single sentence:
"I had to, like, let some of the bruise blood come out to show them." Then
he tape-looped the last five words. Repeated for more than twelve minutes,
and *very* slowly pulled out of phase on several sound channels, the words
are gradually transformed from one kind of sound material into another:
short, blurred melodic gestures impossible to recognize as human speech.[33]
Reich has likened "performing and listening to a gradual musical process"
such as this one to "pulling back a swing, releasing it, and observing it gradually come to rest; turning over an hour glass and watching the sand slowly
run through to the bottom; placing your feet in the sand by the ocean's edge
and watching, feeling, and listening to the waves gradually bury them." And
he adds: "While performing and listening to gradual musical processes one
can participate in a particular liberating and impersonal kind of ritual. Focusing in on the musical process makes possible that shift of attention away
from *he* and *she* and *you* and *me* outwards towards *it*."[34]

Reich has also explained that while fond of the possibilities of taped
speech, he preferred live instrumental performance. He pointed to a discovery along those lines in 1966:

> I finally sat down at the piano and made a tape loop of myself playing a re-
> peating pattern. Later it became one of the patterns of *Piano Phase*. And I
> played it back and just started to play against the loop myself. I found, to my
> pleasant surprise, I could do it. I could control it. And what's more, it was a
> very interesting way of performing because it wasn't improvising and yet it
> wasn't really reading either. That seemed very exciting indeed.[35]

Early in 1967, Reich organized a pair of concerts at the Park Place in New
York, a cooperative gallery associated with the geometric, nondecorative
minimal art of such painters and sculptors as Ellsworth Kelly, Sol LeWitt,
and Richard Serra. Reich's concerts were part of an effort by the gallery to
promote interchange among experimental artists in different media. The
featured new work was a version of *Piano Phase* for four electric pianos,
played by Reich and three colleagues, an outcome of the composer's experiment in playing live against a tape loop. In its published two-piano version,
Piano Phase is based on a short phrase of melody made up of running sixteenth notes. The phrase is repeated over and over, first in unison but then
with the second player accelerating very slightly until, Reich's instructions
read, "he is one sixteenth ahead," a "shift of phase relation between himself

The Philip Glass Ensemble, with the composer at the left, plays at New York University, 1971.

and the first pianist."[36] A listener hears the piece as a practically seamless, seemingly endless parade of tiny changes in detail. The rock-steady tempo, almost imperceptible rhythmic shifts, and ceaseless repetition create a busy-sounding texture that is sometimes transparent and sometimes less so, with unexpected bits of melody being thrown off from the contrapuntal interaction of the different lines.

Reich met Philip Glass, a former Juilliard colleague, after the second Park Place Gallery concert, and before long the two, along with saxophonist Jon Gibson and several other musicians, had formed an ensemble to play music by its members. Their doing so ran counter to a trend toward specialization that, in academic and concert-hall circles, had made twentieth-century composers who played their own works more the exception than the rule. The minimalists did much to reverse that trend. In fact, the composer-led ensemble was a key part of their contribution to the late twentieth-century musical scene.

Composers have long complained that standard ensembles such as orchestras do a substandard job with new music, especially when it calls for unusual sounds or playing techniques. Forming one's own group ensures not only adequate rehearsal but sympathetic interpreters ready to pour their heart and soul into the music and its performance. Reich and Glass split up in 1971 to form separate ensembles. Made up of between five and eight players, these groups sounded more like an orchestra than chamber music, for players doubled each other's lines, and, especially in Glass's works, the music was amplified by the use of synthesizers and microphones. The clear-cut lines of that sound, together with the music's tonal simplicity and rhythmic interest, proved a key to the public appeal of minimalism.[37]

Glass has described the Philip Glass Ensemble as the cornerstone of his musical enterprise, attributing its success to business know-how, artistic confidence, and personal ambition. The business part came naturally to Glass, the son of a record-store owner. "The first thing I knew about music," he has said, "was that you sold it." He supported the ensemble by working as a cab driver, plumber, and furniture mover rather than teaching. "After the first concert, I began paying people. Now, that was very hard to do; it usually meant that I never got paid myself." But paying his players kept the ensemble together, while guaranteeing concerts of high quality. Glass also bet on his music's appeal by refusing to let anyone but his own ensemble perform it. "I felt that if I had a monopoly on the music, that as the music became known there would be more work for the ensemble." He committed the group to twenty concerts a year after discovering that this would qualify his players for unemployment insurance. Glass worked day jobs until 1978, when grants and commissions finally allowed him to concentrate on composition.[38]

Comfortable with the idea of making art that makes money, Glass has also argued that he and his compatriots have restored something valuable to American musical life by coming "back to the idea that the composer *is* the performer." Rather than setting themselves apart, he has said, "we became real people again to audiences. We learned to talk to people again." Glass has also claimed a long-standing desire to transcend The Gap. "I personally knew that I didn't want to spend my life writing music for a handful of people. . . . I wanted to play for thousands of people; I was always interested in a larger audience. I saw that possibility from a very early age and I unswervingly set myself that goal." And when prodded to explain his music's appeal, Glass once responded: "For one thing, I'm out there playing it all the time. Also I tend to pick projects that get heard a lot; *Koyaanisqatsi* is a film that millions of people saw."[39]

In November 1976, *Einstein on the Beach*, a "portrait opera" and collaboration between Glass and theater director Robert Wilson, was staged in two sold-out performances at New York's Metropolitan Opera House, which had been rented for the occasion. Wilson's concept was to wean theater away from literature and narrative, reorienting it more toward visual imagery and spectacle, an approach that squared with Glass's own theatrical ideas. As a result, the opera offers neither a plot nor any singing characters. Glass has reported that he and Wilson chose Albert Einstein as a subject because he was known to the public: recognizable from photographs—distinctive face, untamed mass of white hair—and acknowledged as a genius. Einstein also enjoyed playing the violin, and so a solo violinist dressed as Einstein functions both as a musician and a character in the opera. Singing is prominent in the work, but the soprano soloist and the chorus sing only numbers and solfege syllables. According to Glass, people who attended performances could be counted on to bring their own story with them.[40]

Einstein on the Beach's penultimate scene is the high point, reached through spectacle and sound. The scene features a bar of light, earlier used to represent a bed, that is suddenly transformed into a spaceship. Over a six-minute interval, the bar gradually rises, as if lifting off into space. The plot summary reports: "The sense of an atomic explosion is overwhelming. A curtain descends, cutting off the scene. It bears Einstein's equation for atomic energy: $E=Mc^2$."[41] The music is delivered by the whole ensemble at full volume and at breakneck speed, with a chorus chanting numbers to keep the rhythm. A five-chord progression—one heard earlier in the work at slower tempos—harmonizes the choral singing, sounding like a cadence formula but never settling in on its point of harmonic resolution.

The effect of all this activity, speed, and volume is static and incantatory. Glass has said that only when audiences shed their usual listening habits and become free from memory and anticipation will they "be able to perceive the music as a 'presence,' freed of dramatic structure, a pure medium of sound."[42] These words apply especially well to the scene described here. Convincingly and precisely articulated in performance, the gyroscopic energy of its music, driving performers and listeners obsessively around the same loop, succeeds by sheer weight of sound and accumulation in achieving a grand, even monumental solemnity.

The success of Glass's opera may be measured by later performances, recordings, international impact, and reputation. And it has turned out to be historically significant. For one thing, while opera has long enjoyed a prominent place in American musical life, American-composed operas have won only a small niche in the standard repertory. *Einstein* was different. The Wilson-Glass collaboration brought to the musical stage a brand of theatricality that, while reflecting a contemporary spirit, was also musically accessible. And if not all operagoers appreciated the work, a new population of listeners, including theatergoers and a number of rock fans, now found reason to attend an opera. (Glass recalled audience watching at one of the Metropolitan Opera *Einstein* performances with an administrator there, who wondered: "Who are these people? I've never seen them here before.")[43] The work can be seen, too, as part of a larger international trend, beginning in Europe in the 1960s, to bring new theatrical energy to opera by giving more authority to directors and staging older works in modern settings. At the same time, the idea of a new American opera drew audiences, sparked debate, and made the opera house a center for artistic ferment. Commissions for other composers followed, including John Adams, who had written such minimalist instrumental works as *Shaker Loops* and *Harmonium*. In 1987, the Houston Grand Opera premiered *Nixon in China*, in which Adams collaborated with librettist Alice Goodman and stage director Peter Sellars. That work established Adams as a composer with an international reputation and a distinctive musical style. The Nixon opera, Adams's next (*The Death of Klinghoffer*), and several more operas by Glass have been credited with introducing contemporary issues into a traditional venue.[44]

More generally, the public attention given the music of Riley, Reich, Glass, and Adams reflects a broader Gap-closing trend that has accelerated in the 1990s, reflecting the growth of mutual interest between the concert hall and living composers. Several minimalist composers—all of whom, like Meredith Monk, disavow that label, by the way—have proved to be pioneering agents in this trend. But composers with other stylistic approaches have contributed too: the so-called New Romanticists, for example, a group of "postminimalists" (including William Duckworth, Janice Giteck, Daniel Lentz, and others), *and*, most directly and explicitly, perhaps, the younger group referred to earlier as totalists. All have challenged The Gap. All have worked to find a place in the mix of institutions that make up the present-day concert hall: an environment where the preferences of paying customers, scorned by some in the postwar era, are treated with respect.

In a 1980 interview, George Rochberg made an anti-Gap statement that takes the listener's point of view into account as well as the composer's. Rochberg had spent his working life in academia, yet while sometimes dismayed by the audience's small size, he also mistrusted the academy's exclusive attitude. Rochberg found himself standing up for a much-maligned group: music lovers, by which he seems to have meant concertgoers and admirers of the European (and American) classics. This group, he believed, comprised a "quite intelligent and often very sensitive" body of listeners.

> As I like to tell my students, they're easily as intelligent as any group of composers you might assemble. They know just as much about life, certainly as much about the problems of reality, and sometimes as much about music—

except that they don't compose it. You cannot start out with the adversary notion that the audience is made up totally of ignoramuses and you've got to educate them. . . . Nor have you the right to demand of audiences that they spend a lifetime listening to or studying a handful of pieces because you say they're good. They don't have time.[45]

By recognizing listeners as individuals with their own legitimate stake in the experience and limited time to pursue it, Rochberg brings the question of demand into a discussion usually dominated by issues of supply. His perspective on The Gap complements a broader one proposed by a cultural theorist in the latter 1980s: "A creative culture is a triangle requiring three points: individual artists, a tradition to work within and against, and a public with an adequate amount of disposable attention."[46]

The late twentieth-century American creative triangle in the classical sphere is one with a severely undernourished third point. This country has been blessed with a wealth of composers and a ready assortment of musical traditions; the problem lies in the amount of public attention a composer may hope to claim. Today, consumption fueled by advertising is pervasive and competition for public notice fierce. The choices of so-called leisure activities are widely varied: music, drama, literature, and the visual arts, of course, but also television, radio, movies; sports as participation and spectatorship; travel; cookery and restaurant-going; even shopping. Within the field of music, the popular sphere clearly overshadows the classical with the sheer weight of its presence. And since the classical sphere's performers devote much of their energy to European music of the past, the corner devoted to contemporary composition is barely known to the general public, including even many avowed music lovers. A new work in a complex, unfamiliar idiom has only a tiny chance of winning public attention beyond a small circle of connoisseurs.

Yet that situation has not dampened the impulse to compose, thanks in large part to The Gap, which asserts that art is autonomous, potentially transcendent, and vitally important—among the most worthwhile things a human being can do. Artists are key figures in society, whether they are so recognized or not. Further, because posterity has often judged artists more truly than their own contemporaries, present-day indifference may not be fatal to the life of one's work. Artists must therefore follow their own creative path, undeterred by reception, which they cannot control anyway. To believe in The Gap is to be convinced that the wellsprings of artistic creation lie deep in the human consciousness. Composers who let ephemeral things influence artistic decisions risk compromising their calling for the sake of temporary reward.

Implicit in this outlook is an image of identity built around exclusiveness, idealism, and a long view of history. It has inspired many composers in the past and will doubtless sustain more in the future. But that image has seemed less attractive to many other composers, who were raised in America's consumer culture and are unashamed to claim its interest in sound, popular expression, and technology for their own. These musicians, while classically trained, have also accepted the United States as a consumption-driven marketing mecca. Folding that idea into their identity as artists, they have explored ways of writing music that strengthens their claim on the public's limited store of disposable attention—not in some indeterminate future, but *now*. For them, the question of how much time a listener must spend to connect with their music is crucial. Therefore, composers may use a regular beat, synthesized sound, and amplified volume in their music to quicken connections with listeners.

Minimalism reaffirmed an axiom out of favor in the classical sphere during much of the twentieth century: that composers may honorably seek common ground with nonspecialist listeners. By reducing the amount of musical material a listener had to digest, Young, Riley, Reich, Glass, Monk, and Adams moved the focus of listening away from perceiving and remembering local events and toward the experience of sound in the moment and change on an expanded time scale. That scale invited a contemplative response that could connect with spirituality, ritual, and, in Riley's case, an expanding consciousness linked to drug use. Each of these possibilities opened up common ground with the youthful counterculture of the 1960s and helped mold the tastes of younger generations. By performing music as well as inventing and writing it, by mixing with the crowd, à la Philip Glass, by showing respect for listeners' intuitive responses, and by seeming as concerned with their work's reception as with the way it was composed, these musicians seemed readier than many of their Gap-observing colleagues to embrace the spirit of their own place and time. And by bringing to bear on their composing not only Europeanized training but what they had learned from vernacular (especially jazz) and non-Western music, they infused their work with a more inclusive sensibility. The minimalists were by no means the only agent in the Gap-closing process. But the impact of their presence and their music, like a warm wind thawing barriers that had sometimes seemed frozen into place, has helped to instill a spirit of democratic possibility and excitement in the classical music scene today.

40

Black Music and American Identity

READERS MAY HAVE NOTICED PARALLELS with African-American music in Kyle Gann's list of conditions that have influenced recent classical composers in America. The waning reliance on notation, the judging of works by the way they sound, and the use of sound complexes rather than single notes as musical "atoms" all overlap with black practices. Rock music, whose presence is near-universal, is grounded in the rhythms, instrumentation, and performance conventions of rhythm and blues, an African-American genre. And if such aesthetic notions as music's autonomy and the historical timelessness of individual works are losing prestige in the concert hall, perhaps black music's impulse to tailor performances to the occasion has something to do with that as well. Gann's list also notes the splintering of audiences in the classical sphere. Yet musical exchange among the classical, popular, and traditional spheres has never been more open than it is today. And that openness, which counters the divisive trend, owes much to the wide appeal of black musical idioms.

Through much of the twentieth century, there has been no more efficient signifier of American music than the sound of African-American music. Yet, as shown repeatedly in this chronicle, white Americans have often embraced black musical styles without addressing the cultural implications of that embrace.[1] Even many leading African-American musicians have found themselves in a weak position to be credited for their achievement or to win economic rewards proportional to the impact their music has made.

Throughout this book, we have seen how different African-American styles came about—from minstrel songs and dances, spiritual songs, and ragtime in the nineteenth century to blues, early jazz, swing, modern jazz, rhythm and blues, rock and roll, soul, and rock; and we have seen how such ring-shout practices as call and response, improvisation, timbral variation, rhythmic variety tied to a metronomic pulse, and signifying give African-derived music its continuity from one genre to another. Our tour of American music history has led in these final chapters to the subject of identity: personal and group identity, ethnic identity, generational and gendered identity, and the artistic identity of American composers. And therefore it seems fitting to note an aspect of black identity that has not been stressed so far: a spirit of cooperative interplay that has helped make black music irresistible to listeners and musicians outside black culture. It has recently been suggested that for all the variety of civilizations native to Africa, a collaborative attitude toward cultural performance is common to many of them. African identity itself develops within a system of interrelationships among family and community. For contemporary Africans, identity can be defined only in relation to others.[2]

The idea that black music making in the traditional sphere has depended on creative interaction is familiar. Ring-shouters, congregations, and work crews are just three groups in African-American culture noted for collaborative musical expression. But as black musicians have moved into more formal and professional settings, writers about their music have tended to take group interaction for granted or even to ignore it altogether. Jazz criticism and history, for example, have stressed individual achievement. Singling out such greats as Louis Armstrong, Duke Ellington, Art Tatum, Charlie Parker, and John Coltrane, writers have tended to stress technical virtuosity, improvisatory invention, and structural imagination, each a skill valued in Western art music. There is nothing surprising in that emphasis. Since the classical sphere, respected as a locus of artistic quality, was slow to appreciate jazz artistry, many jazz writers have framed their work around the idea that the best jazz musicians deserve a place in the pantheon as recognized peers of classical artists.

We get a different perspective from Michael Carvin, an African-American jazz drummer who, in an interview with the jazz scholar Ingrid Monson, holds forth on the drummer's function in a small ensemble: in this case trumpet, saxophone, and a rhythm section of piano, bass, and drums. "A drum is a woman," Carvin announces:

> You take a woman that has four kids, and all four of them come home from school together. One of them made an A; he's very happy. One made an F; he's very sad. One caught a cold today; he's upset. And one lost his jacket and he's *very* upset. Now when they hit the house, all four of them is hittin' the mother at the same time. The one that got an A'll say, "Mommy look I got an A," and he's excited; and the one that got an F, say [crying tone of voice], "Oh mommy, I got an F;" the one that got a cold, "Mommy, I'm catching a cold," but she have to, at the same time, deal with *all* of them at the same time and cool each one of them out for the energy level that they

are *dealing* with. And that's why they say the drum is a *woman* . . . cause that's the same thing a drummer has to do. You come to the gig, [pace of speaking increases] the trumpet player's *up*, boy he feel like playing it. The saxophone, you know, he don't feel too good. The piano player say, "Aw, man, I shouldn't have ate so much, man, I'm feeling a little sluggish." It's the same thing. And . . . they all coming to you at the same time, so you're getting the news from all four of them at the same time. Right? Cause you're the bandleader, right? And you have to say, "Aw, man, damn you ate too much? [high tone of voice] Why, man, you big as a house." And you got to try to get him happy and the other guy that's *already* stretching, then you want to kind of cool him *down*, cause he's stretching *too* much. He got too much energy. And then the guy that is not feelin' so good, then you got to [give him] a pep talk . . . before you go play. And they never ask you, "How do *you* feel?"[3]

Of all the traits of black musical identity touched on here, none is more striking than the sociability of jazz improvisation—a trait stressed repeatedly by Monson, whose questions prompted the comparison in the first place. Looking beyond melody players (the trumpeter and saxophonist) to the interactive process that supports them, her study centers on the rhythm section, with bass players, piano players, and drummers her chief subjects. In interviews, she has pressed them to talk about the quality of attention paying, the way of responding to each other during performance, the near-telepathic communication that can take place when chemistry and sociability are right. Veteran pianist Sir Roland Hanna tells her: "We train ourselves over a period of years to be able to hear rhythms and anticipate combinations of sounds before they actually happen."[4]

The drummer is a key to establishing a sociable environment for playing jazz. Indeed, drummers come by that role honestly as they learn to master the drum kit, for jazz drumming has been described as a musical exercise for four limbs, each with a separate function. The right hand keeps time on the ride cymbal; the right foot tends the bass drum pedal, chiefly for punctuation and accents; the left hand is free for hits and "fills" on the snare drum, tom-tom, or cymbals, in response to the musical moment; and the left foot is on the pedal controlling the high-hat cymbals, usually played on beats two and four of a four-beat measure. Thus, the drummer forms a complete ensemble. In performance, each limb's prescribed function serves as a starting point that might lead almost anywhere. Just as a mother looks for ways to balance tensions among family members whose emotions are all over the map, a drummer tries to unite individual musicians (sometimes by guiding an out-of-sync player back on track with a foot or hand) in a spirit of sociable interdependence that promotes creative improvising.

But no drummer can accomplish that feat alone. Monson quotes the

Bassist Cecil McBee in his role as teacher in the jazz program at Boston's New England Conservatory.

bass player Cecil McBee on what can happen when the interactive spirit takes hold.

> We are all individuals. . . . When we approach the stage . . . we are collectivized there. . . . the band begins to play, history is going to take place. This energy proceeds to that area and it says, "All right, I'm here, I will direct you and guide you. You as an individual must realize that I am here. You cannot control me; you can't come up here and say, 'Well, I'm gonna play this,'" unless you're reading [from a written arrangement]. . . . You can't go there and intellectually realize that you're going to play certain things. You're not going to play what you practiced. . . . Something else is going to happen . . . so the individual himself must make contact with that and get out of the way.

It seems fitting that in dealing with such a complex, ineffable subject, Ingrid Monson has talked at length to musicians whose professional lives revolve around improvising with other musicians. The study of black music has suffered in the past from the reluctance of writers and scholars, often white, to consult more than casually with players and singers themselves, perhaps on the assumption that nothing important would be learned from such conversations. That prejudice has grown directly out of the social and economic asymmetry between whites and blacks. The insight conveyed by McBee's statement gives reason to be glad that such prejudice has faded.

McBee starts with something fundamental that is often overlooked or taken for granted. If jazz musicians are to play well together, each must bring something unique and personal to the experience; at the same time, each must know how to let musical exchange direct individual effort. Since no member of the group knows, when a piece begins, how long it will last, or what notes he or she will play in the course of it, or the rhythmic effect, harmonic voicing, or sound quality that will be needed at any particular moment, the musicians must make all those choices as the piece unfolds—on the spot, and according to cues from each other. That process is the history that is about to be made. Performing jazz, then, can be the most delicate of cooperative exercises: a group of artistic peers, working together in a sound environment where individual and group identity are constantly being asserted, negotiated, and redefined as the demands of the musical moment change. On the other hand, the basic elements of jazz are simple enough that many performers have learned to use them. Without denying the mystique that surrounds jazz artistry, we would also not want to overlook the music's origins in the popular sphere or its workmanlike side, whose discourse and spirit are more democratic and inclusive than esoteric and rarefied.

The next part of McBee's testimony comes straight out of performing experience. When the band starts playing, he says, a new entity comes into being. Created by the performers together, it stands beyond the reach of any one of them. McBee personifies this new force as "energy," and he gives it a voice that promises to guide the musicians. The players' job, first, is to recognize the new entity when it appears, and second, to maintain its presence. But the latter calls for discipline and delicacy. For if any player tries to control the flow by venturing outside the zone of collaboration ("Well, I'm gonna play *this*"), energy will most likely disappear. "You're not going to play what you practiced," McBee says, pointing to a common cause of interactive dissonance. The musicians create something rare and valuable together; each of them engages with it, and then they "get out of the way." Having transformed individual effort into group energy, the players must together follow that energy wherever it leads.

While most of the jazz musicians Monson interviewed had extensive training in music theory—chords, scales, and harmonic progressions—and had mastered its technical discourse, they usually turned to metaphors when discussing aesthetic issues. McBee's was "energy," but a more widespread term is "groove" (synonymous with "swinging" or "cooking"). One clarinet player called grooving "a euphoria that comes from playing good time *with* somebody."[5] And a piano player described it "as a type of personal and musical chemistry." The term signifies an emotional response as well as a rhythmic keeping time; in fact, the groove can be said to lie in the tiny discrepancies between musicians (or between a drummer's hand and foot)

playing to a strict beat. Moreover, that feeling—centered on rhythm and affirming the place of collaborative interaction—is all-important to performers
and listeners alike. An avid listener has put it this way: "Being together and
tuning up to somebody else's sense of time is what we're here on the planet
for."[6]

The connection of jazz to African-American ethnic identity is a broader
question, complicated by the economic and social asymmetry between
whites and blacks. In fact, that asymmetry has often been taken as a defining condition, as in a well-known interpretation by black author LeRoi Jones
(Amiri Baraka), published in 1963. Baraka's three overlapping arguments are
as follows. First, both the roots and the meaning of blues and jazz lie in "the
social and political struggles of black Americans to escape slavery and oppression." Second, the pervasiveness of white-controlled institutions threat-
ens "the black struggle for cultural self-awareness." And third, black
solidarity in these struggles is undermined by "the class aspirations of the
black bourgeoisie," and by the failure of some black creative artists to participate in them. These ideas remain part of today's discussions of the subject, testimony to the book's seminal quality. Baraka's *Blues People* seems
especially to demand a response because its conclusion is pessimistic: that
"white Euro-American hegemony has robbed African-Americans of their
culture," and that only black solidarity and black control of independent
cultural and economic institutions will allow black musicians to express the
true ethnic identity of African Americans.[7]

Baraka's perspective bears the stamp of the 1960s, when the idea of ethnicity was framed to challenge that of the melting pot. It is hardly surprising
that some black Americans took cultural nationalism as an alternative to the
civil rights movement, whose ideal of racial integration was proving a
painfully slow way to battle racism. Yet some observers found the book's
main thesis more a reflection of social theorizing than an evenhanded analysis of African-American music history. If white control had been so thorough, why had so many African musical techniques flourished, and how had
black music making come to mean so much to listeners, black and white
alike? (Were Bessie Smith, Billie Holiday, Lester Young, Miles Davis, and
other outstanding black artists to be considered flawed products of a white-
dominated system?) Blues and jazz, rather than fragments of a weakened
African-American tradition, looked more like potent presences in American
culture as a whole. The glass could be seen as half full, not half empty.
Rather than putting authentic black music in a reactive posture where it
could only function as a form of protest, the novelist and critic Ralph Ellison, for example, looked beyond injustice and oppression to a remarkable
triumph: the story "of enslaved and politically weak men [and women] successfully imposing their values upon a powerful society through song and

dance."[8] Black intellectuals led by Ellison and Albert Murray have concentrated on qualitative aspects of the music, and especially the kind of experience it offers to performers and listeners; in doing so, they have shed light not only on music's connection to black ethnic identity but on the issue of American identity as a whole.

Jazz musicians are lordly, commanding figures in the blues tradition celebrated by Murray, who in the 1970s put forward a far-reaching interpretation of African-American music.[9] For Murray, the heart of jazz lies in the blues tradition, which has managed to confront and balance the bewildering array of contradictions and complexities of African-American life. The blues is part of a larger cultural process that involves individuals determined to keep details of painful experience alive; the ability to squeeze out of that experience not a consoling message but a "near-tragic, near-comic lyricism"; and the use of that lyricism not to lament but to celebrate life.[10] And the marvel is that an idiom so all-embracing, accessible, and capable of further development came into being in the first place.

The blues sensibility as Murray sees it takes shape in a context of performance—by singers and players, to be sure, but also by listeners. The knowledge a performing audience brings to an event, expressed through dancing and responding, is fundamental to the experience. Such settings embody the blues tradition's reliance on collaboration:

> ragtime and barrelhouse piano players confronting the challenge of entertaining an extremely discerning clientele, people trading the downhome workweek for a downhome goodtime; people expecting . . . to dance the whole night long. It is young saxophone players confronting the rigorous demands of their craft, trying to establish their identity by spinning a fresh two-chorus variation on a theme that has been worked over for years by the very best players of the instrument. It is, in its ultimate statement, the crowning aesthetic achievement of swing, a code for living and a profound insight into the human condition of modern man.[11]

The last sentence's reference to swing brings to mind something too basic to go out of date: the idea of jazz musicians' interactive collaboration under the aegis of the groove. The musicians' ultimate goal is to achieve a state of euphoric interaction, centered on rhythm, that demands at all costs to be sustained. Murray turns that idea into a cultural principle.

> When the Negro musician or dancer swings the blues, he is fulfilling the same fundamental existential requirement that determines the mission of the poet, the priest, and the medicine man. He is making an affirmative and hence exemplary and heroic response to that which André Malraux describes as *la condition humaine*. Extemporizing in response to the exigencies of the situation in which he finds himself, he is confronting, acknowledging, and

contending with the infernal absurdities and ever-impending frustrations inherent in the nature of all existence by *playing with the possibilities that are
also there*. Thus does man the player become man the stylizer and by the
same token the humanizer of chaos; and thus does play become ritual, ceremony, and art; and thus also does the dance-beat improvisation of experience in the blues idiom become survival technique, esthetic equipment for
living, and a central element in the dynamics of U.S. Negro life style.[12]

The blues tradition makes no claim for life's coherence or logic. Nor does
it hold out hope, like religion, that change or deliverance is possible. It sees
human existence as an enterprise fraught with absurdities and frustrations,
and only by accepting that fact can one begin to know the power of the
blues tradition. Playing does not mean restructuring, but it does offer tools
for stylizing and humanizing the conditions in which people lead their lives.
The secular ritual of blues is manifested most directly in the rhythmic
groove, which ties the dance-beat improvisation of experience to collaborative interaction. Perhaps that interactive spirit helps to explain what the
American poet William Carlos Williams, a white physician who lived in a
working-class neighborhood in New Jersey, admired in his black neighbors
when he wrote, in the 1920s: "There is a solidity, a racial irreducible minimum, which gives them poise in a world where they have no authority."[13]

Music making in the jazz tradition is a multilayered enterprise, demanding insight into the human condition and plenty of technical skill. As artistic
recognition of jazz blossomed in the 1960s, the music splintered into a
widening range of styles. Earlier ones, from New Orleans to bebop, were
maintained; and new styles also came to the fore, including free jazz (Ornette Coleman), modal jazz (Miles Davis, John Coltrane), fusion with rock
elements (Davis, John McLaughlin, Herbie Hancock, Chick Corea), intersections with non-Western music (Art Ensemble of Chicago, Coltrane,
Keith Jarrett), and even connections with the classical avant-garde (Anthony Braxton). At the same time, as rock's appeal for young listeners re-
structured the music business, jazz's economic base declined. A symptom of
that decline was the number of new organizations, formed chiefly by musicians themselves, to promote and sustain music making that could not
support itself in the marketplace: in Chicago, the Association for the Advancement of Creative Musicians (AACM; Muhal Richard Abrams, 1965)
and the Jazz Institute of Chicago (Don DeMicheal and others, 1969); and in
New York, the Jazz Artists Guild (Max Roach, Charles Mingus, Jo Jones,
1960), the Jazz Composers Guild (Bill Dixon, 1964), Jazzmobile (Billy Taylor,
1964), the Jazz Composer's Orchestra Association (Carla Bley and Mike
Mantler, 1966), and Collective Black Artists (CBA; Reggie Workman, 1970).
Another symptom of jazz's changing place in American culture was the

New York's Lincoln Center Jazz Ensemble, directed by trumpeter-composer Wynton Marsalis, performs music from all periods of jazz history.

spread of formal instruction and patronage. In the latter 1960s, schools and colleges began to set up programs of jazz study. By the late 1970s, according to *Down Beat* magazine, a quarter of a million people were studying jazz formally. Moreover, in a move unprecedented for any music in the popular sphere, musicians and institutions devoted to jazz began receiving grants from government agencies and foundations. (In 1968, the National Association of Jazz Educators was formed from within the Music Educators National Conference.) The idea of grants for jazz musicians is a double-edged commentary on the music's new position: recognized as artistically important but largely overlooked by the huge audience for popular music.

Academic institutions were not the only ones to embrace jazz. In 1970, the Smithsonian Institution, now also called the National Museum of American History, hired the jazz critic Martin Williams to direct a jazz program. Important record reissues followed—especially *The Smithsonian Collection of Classic Jazz*, a canon in the form of a record anthology, selected and annotated by Williams—and so did Smithsonian-sponsored concerts by "repertory" ensembles, reconstructing significant performances of the past. Another powerful endorsement was the creation in 1991 of a permanent jazz department at New York's Lincoln Center for the Performing Arts, perhaps the nation's flagship classical-music institution, being home to the Metropolitan and New York City Opera companies as well as Avery Fisher Hall, where the New York Philharmonic Orchestra plays, and the Juilliard School of Music. The 1997 Pulitzer Prize in music composition was awarded for the first time to a jazz composition: *Blood on the Fields,* an oratorio for jazz ensemble and vocalists and set in slavery times, by Wynton Marsalis, trumpeter, composer, and director of Lincoln Center's jazz program.

New Orleans native Marsalis, part of a musical family and an outspoken presence since he burst onto the national scene in the early 1980s, has taken the view that, as well as an African-American inheritance, jazz is also a broader reflection of American character. In this belief, he follows the lead of his intellectual mentors, Albert Murray included. Further, accusing popular music of excessive commercialism and a lack of artistic integrity, he has proposed that jazz be taught to youngsters as an alternative to hip-hop music, which has rhythm but "no message." Marsalis has shown a strong tendency to preach the principles of his own taste. Indeed, a comment like this one might indicate a lack of faith in young people's ability to cope with popular culture on their own, finding worthwhile meanings within it. For in fact, Marsalis makes a clear qualitative distinction between popular music in general and the kinds of music he plays. Backed by a pedigree that includes professional training at the Juilliard School and performances of classical works, Marsalis has presented himself as an artist working within the jazz tradition's strict standards—that is, the evolutionary stream beginning with ragtime and blues and followed by such styles as New Orleans, Chicago, New York (the dance orchestras of Duke Ellington and Fletcher Henderson), Kansas City swing, bebop, hard bop, and more recent spinoffs from the bop mainstream of the 1940s and 50s (mapped out, for example, by *The Smithsonian Collection of Classic Jazz*).[14]

In a milieu full of strong-minded individuals, it is no surprise that Marsalis's stance as a player and spokesman for jazz has drawn criticism from other musicians, especially since he has become a dispenser of patronage through Lincoln Center. Many have disagreed with his restrictive, historical approach to a tradition that since the 1950s has evolved into a broad range of musical styles, linked chiefly by improvisation. Some have also challenged his image of jazz musicians' identity. As clarinetist Don Byron has put it: "One of the fallacies of the Wynton era is that jazz cats don't listen to rap." For trumpeter Lester Bowie, a member of Chicago's AACM, the tradition was much more diverse than Marsalis granted. Jazz, said Bowie, is "not simple music anymore. So it does belong in the concert hall. But it also belongs in the street, on the farm, it needs equal access everywhere, the same as country western, rap, anything. Because jazz is all of these."[15]

"Most great music is in some sense nationalistic," Marsalis told an interviewer in 1984, and "the ultimate achievement of a society is the establishment of an art form that is indigenous to that society. . . . Cultural awareness is what gives people a sense of self-pride as a group, and what defines the national character." As Marsalis saw it, European composers have been esteemed for works that circulate in musical notation, which implies intellectual control, and Americans have tended to look to Europe for models of musical greatness. Because jazz involves improvisation, it has sometimes been thought to owe more to emotion than intellect, a notion that has limited its artistic prestige. Yet improvisation draws as much on intellect and formal control, Marsalis argued, as on intuition. Moreover, in the 1940s, musicians such as Armstrong, Parker, Ellington, and Monk "introduced an entire range of mood and emotion into the vocabulary of Western music, an entirely new way of phrasing, an entirely new way of thinking in the language of music," and this breakthrough "perfectly captures the spirit and tone of America." But it has gone largely unrecognized for two reasons. First, racism and economic inequality have marginalized jazz. And second, cultural standards have slipped to the point that "anything can pass for art." Marsalis blamed the mass media for promoting a popular culture "with everything reduced to the lowest common denominator." And he challenged his fellow musicians to restore and uphold standards: "We musicians should never forget that it is our job to educate people, to stand up for excellence and quality." In his view, the excellence and quality of jazz were democratic and characteristically American because the music combined a vernacular base with a hunger for artistic exploration.[16]

In another article from 1984, Marsalis used the rhythmic groove as a starting point for another comment on jazz musicians' need for intellectual understanding and control: He maintained that "the rhythm of the notes" had to make sense to listeners, once again singling out Armstrong and Parker for their ability to communicate while improvising, and Ellington and Monk for their harmonic logic.[17]

The statements made in these two articles are arresting, especially for their highly unusual example of a black jazz musician taking on the role of intellectual spokesman in a national forum and pushing an educational agenda from within the popular sphere. Another belief behind Marsalis's stance is that musical quality is hierarchical, and that the artistry of some jazz masters (Ellington) places them on an equal footing with illustrious European composers (Beethoven and Stravinsky). But perhaps the most striking notion of all is that *no music is more thoroughly American than jazz*—that is, the blues-based strain championed by Marsalis—whose civilizing force and ritualistic expression have provided a much-needed boost to the nation's sense of humanity. That idea is grounded in the blues-based interpretation of black culture itself, which in 1970 led Albert Murray to dub black citizens "the omni-Americans," possessors of "the most complicated sensibility in the modern world."[18]

The artistic recognition that jazz has received in recent years testifies not only to its repositioning among the three spheres of American musical activity but to the way the music's elements cut across those categories. For the idiom of jazz, rooted in the African-American traditional sphere, has also relied on the popular sphere for repertory and forms; the careers of jazz musicians are still mostly carried on in the popular sphere's marketplace, but some have identified with the traditional sphere (chiefly African) and others more with the classical concert hall. Finally, once jazz is recorded, it is likely to be analyzed historically, culturally, or technically with the help of approaches developed in the classical sphere. Works that pass muster may then be treated as part of a permanent, hence transcendent, musical legacy. That legacy, and the rootedness of jazz in black vernacular music making, help to explain why a number of black classical composers born before World War II—T. J. Anderson, David Baker, Hale Smith, and Olly Wilson come to mind—developed their musical talents in younger years as jazz performers and have drawn on that experience ever since. Thus a music that was once socially controversial, linked in the minds of many white Americans with unsavory conduct and a lack of schooled musicianship, enjoys today the respected status due a full-fledged art form.

IDENTITY AND HIP-HOP CULTURE

While jazz matured in a climate of segregation, and rhythm and blues out of the inequality that fueled the civil rights movement's push for racial integration, the newer form of black expression known as hip hop took shape during the 1970s and 80s as the American economy was being deindustrialized. In the new global economy, resources were transferred away from local business and national companies into the hands of international corporations; as these corporations gained power in the marketplace, manufacturing jobs were moved out of cities to locations where labor was cheaper. As a result, many Americans who lacked education and technical skills found themselves consigned to low-paying jobs in the service sector. In a time of generally rising prosperity, the gap between rich and poor widened. For those at the lower end of the economic scale (mostly Hispanics and blacks), low-paying jobs, joblessness, and rising crime rates, often linked to the use of drugs, were the legacy of deindustrialization. Moreover, many of the same people suffered ill effects from urban renewal, which in some neighborhoods meant the tearing down of affordable housing to build expressways.

The South Bronx area of New York City was hit especially hard by deindustrialization and urban renewal. And hip hop culture was born there in the late 1970s as a resistance to those forces. Hip hop sprang from the tension between postindustrial oppression and the positive bonds of black expressiveness. Both sides of the ledger are reflected in an excerpt from *The Message*, a rap number about life in the ghetto, recorded in 1982 by Grandmaster Flash and the Furious Five:

> Got a bum education, double-digit inflation
> Can't take the train to the job, there's a strike at the station
> Don't push me cause I'm close to the edge
> I'm tryin' not to lose my head
> It's like a jungle sometimes it makes me wonder
> How I keep from going under.[19]

The words register the destructive effects of unequal opportunity: poor schooling, unreliable public services, and a feeling that the jungle of urban life is about to claim another victim. On the other hand, rap's combining of rhythmic declamation with a beat allows it to draw on preaching and music, two of the most potent black cultural traditions. Further, the words suggest a parallel with blues singers, who keep painful experience alive in their consciousness by placing it in an artistic frame, though *The Message* is less a lyric statement than an angry diatribe. That *The Message* was heard by outsiders at all was a tribute to the resourcefulness of Grandmaster Flash and his cohorts, who, working in a blighted part of the city, found a local company willing to record and distribute their music. Indeed, some of rap's original creators and producers fared rather well in their dealings with the mainstream music business. Rap's appeal led to the creation of independent record labels, which allowed young black entrepreneurs, mostly men, to gain valuable business experience as managers. Flourishing outside the artistic and economic constraints that the larger music corporations impose, some of these companies have been able to control their own artistic destinies.

Rather than being performed live, the musical background to *The Message* is a collage of excerpts from earlier recordings, a technique Grandmaster Flash perfected on two turntables that would lead eventually to the use of "samplers": computers able to duplicate any existing sound digitally, play it back at any speed or pitch, and loop it endlessly. The powerful beat, though very different in sound from a jazz groove, provides a matrix for the delivery of the words. People growing up in the South Bronx in the 1970s, we may assume, had little contact with standard musical instruments. Yet many were avid listeners and a few learned to "play" electronic devices—

The rap group Run-D.M.C., pictured in 1988 after winning a Grammy Award (left to right: Joseph Simmons, Darryl McDaniels, Jason Mizell).

turntables, then tape decks, synthesizers, mixers, drum machines, and samplers—with virtuoso control. Like other early rappers, Grandmaster Flash came to this branch of music making not as a musician in the traditional sense but as a disc jockey with a charismatic line of talk.

From the 1980s on, the themes of rap videos have centered on local neighborhoods. Asked to define the three most important themes in representing rap visually, an experienced video director answered: "Posse, posse, and posse"—in other words, setting the action in the artists' locale and feeding off the sense of tight connectedness with their sidekicks. "If you have an artist from Detroit," this director explains, "the reason they want to shoot at least one video on their home turf is to make a connection with, say, an East Coast New York rapper. It's the dialogue. It's the dialogue between them and where they're from."[20] To be grounded on one's home turf and in the company of a "posse" of like-minded cohorts is a source of strength and confirms the musicians' unambiguous identity. At the same time, rap's cutthroat competitiveness stimulates the energy and assertiveness that go into rappers' performing, boosting its appeal for some listeners in part because the sound, tone, and stance are offensive to others.

Rap music has been sharply criticized for its content: the often obscene language, images of violence against women and authority (especially the police), and, in the case of Marsalis's critique, thinness of musical interest. The story of the music's evolution in the marketplace is one of local entrepreneurship, emergence in other locales, unexpected commercial success, and an appeal to audiences far beyond ghetto communities. It is also a story of growing diversity. Since 1990, together with gangsta rap and such familiar subjects as sexual boasting, Afrocentric emphases, and protest raps, rap music has embraced the experience of blacks in the South, jazz samples, live instrumentation (including folk guitar), introspective lyrics, and New Age/soul fusions.[21]

It has been noted that young white males from the suburbs are among rap's most avid fans, though their interest does not seem to extend to political involvement. Perhaps part of the appeal has to do with the fantasy of downward mobility that earlier made rock music so widely appealing: white youngsters geared for success in competitive academic settings seeking temporary release from those responsibilities. It is probably fair to say that what these fans appreciate most about rap is its "edge," its sense of entitlement and open defiance. But from a historical point of view, rap may also be seen as the latest in a line of African-American styles that have broadened the world's idea of music. For whatever the words may be saying, the *sound*—the cranked-up dominance of the bass drum machine, the pulsating rhythmic grooves, the sense that vast technological power is being tapped, the high volume at which the music is played, the ranting, in-your-face tone of the voices—testifies to an ever-broadening conception of what music is and does, continuing an expansion in which twentieth-century American music deserves pride of place.

Epilogue ⨪

IN OCTOBER 1995, I TRAVELED to Calumet, in Michigan's Upper Peninsula, to attend a concert of the Keweenaw (pronounced KEY-wa-naw) Symphony Orchestra. Nearly six hundred miles northwest of Ann Arbor, where I
live, Calumet lies in Michigan's Copper Country, home of a mining industry
that flourished from the late 1800s into the 1920s, bringing prosperity to the
region. Today the copper mines are closed. The population of Calumet
Township, once close to 100,000, is now below 7,500. But the Calumet Theater, a two-balcony structure of some elegance built around the turn of the
century to seat 800, testifies to a lively past. Further evidence of bygone
glory may be found in Laurium, an adjoining town. The hometown of
George Gipp, "the Gipper" of 1920s Notre Dame football legend, Laurium
boasts a number of lavish houses built for mining-company executives. The
bed-and-breakfast where I stayed was such a place, featuring huge upstairs
bedrooms and wallpaper that turned out to be elephant hide. Aside from the
tourist trade, however, what keeps the Keweenaw Peninsula economically
vital today is Michigan Technological University, a state-supported institution founded in 1885, now with a student body of 6,500 and located in
Houghton, a dozen miles south of Calumet.

The Keweenaw Symphony is a community orchestra. Established in
1970, it boasts between fifty and sixty members and in a typical season prepares four different concert programs. The orchestra's only paid player is the
concertmaster, the violin section's leader. The rest are volunteers, some
from the Michigan Tech faculty and student body and others from the region at large, including a few youngsters barely in their teens. Without the
school, there would obviously be no Keweenaw Symphony. And the university supports the orchestra in official as well as unofficial ways. For one
thing, it makes the conductor's post part of the teaching assignment of a

853

The Calumet Theater in Calumet, Michigan, a two-balcony hall seating approximately eight hundred, opened its doors in 1900.

Fine Arts Department faculty member; for another, it offers rehearsal space and staff support. During the orchestra's 1995–96 season, the KSO's conductor was Jeffrey Bell-Hanson, also the band director at Michigan Tech, who was then in his seventh year on the job.

The program I heard was built around a pair of works for two pianos and orchestra. The featured compositions, played between an overture by Beethoven and ballet music from Charles Gounod's opera *Faust*, were *Infinity Variations 2* by American composer David Borden and Mozart's Concerto for Two Pianos in E-flat (K. 365). The keyboard soloists were brought in for the concert, their fees paid by a grant to the orchestra from the Michigan Council for the Arts. What made this concert unusual was that the soloists played fortepianos: copies of Viennese instruments used in Mozart's time (1780s) and transported to Calumet by the players. I attended because one of the soloists was Penelope Crawford, my wife. Since the fortepiano is a rare artifact today and requires constant maintenance, Penny performs on her own instrument. For most of her out-of-town engagements, we load the piano into our van, and she heads out by herself. On this trip, I accompanied her and David Breitman, the other piano soloist, to help with logistics and hear the music. But most of all, I took the trip because of the concert's location.

My mother is a native of Michigan's Upper Peninsula. Snapshots from her childhood, together with stories of Hiawatha, logging camps, trout fishing, and long cold winters, made a strong impression when I was a boy. I first set foot there in 1948, when a trip to "the U.P." still required a ferry ride across the Straits of Mackinac. As a college student in the middle 1950s, I managed several summer trips there with friends, and later my wife and I, both native Michiganians and now with offspring of our own, enjoyed more Upper Peninsula camping. In the winter of 1976, I visited Michigan Tech to conduct a choir and was shown the Calumet Theater, where, my host reported, opera performances had been given in the early 1900s. From that time on, the notion of the remote, rugged Copper Country as a place with a storied musical past carried a fascination for both of us. When Penny's Ann Arbor–based manager raised the prospect of her playing in Calumet, therefore, she promptly accepted.

The use of antique-style pianos in the Keweenaw Symphony's October 1995 concert, more than a colorful detail, may be seen as a statement of artistic principle. To summarize a complex subject, starting in Europe in the 1960s and soon finding a niche in the United States, an early-music revival movement questioned basic assumptions behind classical performance. By the 1980s, the movement had challenged the belief that the entire concert repertory, built around a core of classic works from the 1700s, 1800s, and 1900s, may be performed on the same instruments and with basically the same vocabulary of musical expression. According to early-music advocates, a work is best served when performers draw their vocabulary of expression from the sound palette that was available to the composer. And so builders have worked to restore and copy older instruments that were once thought obsolete. Revivalists believe that using technology of the period—playing Mozart, for example, on a five-octave, wood-framed fortepiano of his era rather than on today's seven-octave, cast-iron-framed grand piano—improves their chance of catching the spirit behind that era's music.

The early-music revival has stirred controversy. Revivalists have sometimes referred to the feeling of liberation that using a period instrument can kindle in a performer. They have also taken pride in reclaiming an older realm of sound, fresh to modern ears and almost surely closer to what the composer heard. The teaching of performers, however, remains generally under the control of musicians who are not closely informed about the debate. When responding to early-music advocates at all, they have often charged that the revivalist approach promotes an ideal of historical authenticity over "the music," by which they mean interpretative approaches long accepted as convincing and beautiful. Crawford and Breitman, each trained first on the modern grand piano, both find the fortepiano ideally suited to Mozart's music—especially its responsiveness to a player's touch and the clarity and delicacy of its sound. I can also report that audience members and musicians in Calumet seemed to appreciate the fortepianos, not because they made the Mozart performance more authentic but because their sound palette proved unusual, varied, and satisfying to the ear.

The Keweenaw Symphony concerts made a strong impression on me: the only audience member who, as far as I know, was engaged in writing about the history of American music. Personal factors—my wife's involvement, for example, and the fascination that the U.P. had long carried in my mind—explain some of that impact. What I also encountered in Calumet, however, were two things that seemed to deserve a place in this chronicle: first, a commitment to classical music making as a community endeavor, and second, a confidence that built-in shortcomings would not prevent the orchestra from achieving powerful musical moments in performance. The first point taps into a strain with a long history in the United States. Operating on a largely amateur basis, granting membership even to players struggling to control their instruments, and though severely restricted in rehearsal time still programming works that would challenge any orchestra to play well, the Keweenaw Symphony stands in a tradition of community performance whose pedigree reaches back to a time when Mozart, Beethoven, and Gounod could *only* be heard live. Through several rehearsals and two performances that I attended, this collection of people, disparate in age, background, and skill, managed to maintain a feeling of shared purpose as they made music together. It is hard to imagine the group performing in public without a core of hired professionals (conductor, concertmaster, soloists). But with these experienced musicians to lead them, the orchestra was able to project an attitude toward performing that did honor to the art of music.

Nevertheless, a good attitude would not have justified bringing the Keweenaw Symphony Orchestra into this story had not the concert contained moments of enthralling musical sound. To my ears, the most striking was the start of Borden's *Infinity Variations 2*. When Penny received the KSO's invitation, she also suggested performing a composition by Borden, a long-time friend whose music she had played and admired. Conductor Bell-Hanson, keen on the idea of keeping the KSO's repertoire contemporary, liked the suggestion. Familiar with some of Borden's music, he thought that its style—emphasizing strong continuity, slow harmonic change, limited dissonance, and a constant percolation of rhythms—might appeal to the local audience, although his players were sure to find the rhythms difficult. Moreover, Borden's fondness for keyboard figuration seemed well matched to the fortepiano's capabilities.

To set the scene for the concert's crowning moment, we may focus on the end of its first number: Beethoven's *Egmont* Overture, written for an orchestra of the early 1800s. As the applause dies down, the stage of the Calumet Theater dissolves into the bustle of movement that a new setup requires. The two fortepianos are carried in and placed at the front of the stage; and the orchestra, now comprising more instruments than Beethoven's piece calls for, is reseated around them. The audience's peak of expectation is now at hand, sparked by uncertainties. Fortepianos are obviously related to "normal" pianos, but what do these instruments actually sound like? And what can be expected from this contemporary composer whose music is about to be heard for the first time in the Copper Country?

For the record, Borden—himself a keyboard player and jazz pianist trained in composition at the Eastman School, Harvard University, and in Germany—places a high priority on connecting with audiences. From 1968 into the late 1980s, he served as composer and accompanist in Cornell University's Dance Department in Ithaca, New York, then joined the Cornell Music Department as director of its electronic music studio. In 1969, he founded Mother Mallard's Portable Masterpiece Company, a synthesizer-based group and composer-led ensemble akin to the ones formed in the latter 1960s by Steve Reich and Philip Glass. Borden's works, published under the rubric of Lameduck Music and circulated on the Earthquack recording label, feature steady beats and repeated patterns, a strong rhythmic drive, and an emphasis on counterpoint. The last of these traits is reflected in *The Continuing Story of Counterpoint*, a title under which Borden has grouped many compositions he has written since the mid-1970s, now adding up to several hours of music. In programming a work by David Borden, the conductor and soloists chose new music better suited than most to fit on a concert featuring old instruments.

And now, back on the Calumet Theater stage, the soloists have taken their places, the audience is ready, and conductor Bell-Hanson gives the downbeat to begin Borden's piece. Its mood is gentle and the sound hushed and transparent: fortepianist Crawford plays continuous octave eighth notes in the left hand with the orchestra's lower strings providing quiet punctuation. In measure 9, a soft, spare, melodic figure is heard. Motion and sound are emerging out of silence, and the shape they are taking is foursquare and predictable. The left-hand murmur fills eight bars before the melodic figure enters. The first real stirring in the orchestra begins four bars later. Once the melodic figure is introduced, it is repeated, establishing a pattern of entrances every two bars, always on the downbeat. In short, the beginning of *Infinity Variations 2* creates an aura of contemplative restraint, contemporary in tone yet as regular in its phrase structure as something an eighteenth-century composer might have written.

Before long, however, the foursquare predictability unravels; for Borden, whose artistic personality is far from gentle, has set up the opening mood only to shatter it. The other fortepiano enters with a bang: a dense, dissonant texture, where all before has been open, spacious, and consonant; a pair of five-beat measures after nothing but four-beat ones; and soon the sound of two keyboards playing in jangling, clashing layers. *Infinity Variations 2*, set in three sections, lasts for more than twenty minutes, seeming to hold the audience's attention and winning a warm response when it ends. But as a member of the audience both on Saturday night and Sunday afternoon, I can testify that the concert's most electric moment—the time when musicians and audience members came most fully into a synchronicity of spirit—was this beginning: bone simple, requiring little from the orchestra, and basically in the hands of a soloist able to play, softly and steadily, music that sounds like a serene preparation for something to come.

It was that synchronicity of spirit, perceptible at the first rehearsal of Borden's piece and every time it was played thereafter, that convinced me to mention the Calumet concert in this book. Engaged then in writing about the classical sphere's struggle to establish itself in the latter nineteenth century, I had been reading and hearing a lot about its supposed decline in the late twentieth. But the Keweenaw Symphony concert contradicted the idea that an enterprise as vast and various as classical music making in America could ever be characterized by a concept as fuzzy and subjective as "decline." That feeling was strengthened by the circumstances: a community ensemble playing the work of a living American composer in a corner of the world where such an endeavor can inspire raptly attentive responses, though perhaps of no significance to a demographic trend spotter.

On what grounds does such an event deserve a place in history when many other noteworthy ones have gone unmentioned? Does not the Calumet concert's appearance in this chronicle cross a line between the anecdotal and the historical? My reply is that that line, not always clear to start with, can grow even more indistinct as the subject nears the present. People tend to value experiences less for their general drift than for their specific flavor and feel, which may remain vivid long after the fact. The impact of the Calumet concert, which lingers in my mind, taught me something about writing music history that I had not put into words before: in the gap between specific events and the broader processes we recognize as historical lie the wellsprings of narrative energy. As one thinks hard about why certain details refuse to be forgotten, their place in the larger scheme of things may start to reveal itself. On the other hand, by continually testing accepted beliefs against new evidence, one may complement them with fresh meanings, or perhaps even change them. Without stories that give life to such revelations and changes, historical reports of the past would have little appeal in the present.

In choosing to end a long historical narrative with personal, local experience, I have felt obliged to argue for the Calumet concert's connectedness to broader issues. At the same time, making that choice has also helped me realize how often in the course of this project the impulse to write has been triggered by a general comment, encountered in reading or conversation, that did not square with my understanding of the specifics of the case: a particular situation, for example, or a musician, a piece of music, or even a performance. Nothing, in other words, engages a historian's mind quite like disagreement—the gut-level feeling that says, "It wasn't like that." Perhaps that is why interweaving the specific with the general proves to be such a humanly satisfying endeavor. For just as reaching a general conclusion forces an author to write *against* the narrowness of focus that specific facts impose, so the recounting of details ensures that he or she is always considering the broader framework in which those details take on historical significance. Thus, embroiled in the tensions caused by the perpetual need to cut across the grain, historians work in the hope of reconciling those tensions in a synthesis respectful of both the general and the specific dimensions of their subject.

In writing this book, I have aimed for such a synthesis, hoping that its example will encourage readers to reflect on their own musical experiences and where they might fit in the vast, diverse, interconnected landscape of American music making.

Notes

Introduction

1. Ellison 1986, 42.
2. Quoted from Hitchcock 1988, 54, the third edition of *Music in the United States*.

1. The First Song: Native American Music

1. Mitchell 1978, 168.
2. Todorov 1984, 133.
3. Meinig 1986, 70.
4. Berkhofer 1978, 28.
5. Stevenson 1973a, 2.
6. Quoted ibid., 4.
7. Parkman 1983, 1:425.
8. Quoted in D. Crawford 1967, 199.
9. Quoted in Stevenson 1973a, 20.
10. Quoted ibid., 21.
11. Quoted ibid., 20.
12. Quoted in Crawford 1967, 202.
13. Quoted in Stevenson 1973b, 404.
14. Quoted ibid., 408–9.
15. Quoted ibid., 405–6.
16. Ibid., 406–7. English compiler Joseph Ritson included this item in *Scotish Songs, in Two Volumes* (London. 1794), which attributes the text to Anne Hunter (1742–1821) and the tune to "a gentleman named Turner, who had (owing to some singular events in his life) spent nine years amongst the natives of America." According to Ritson, Turner told Hunter that the melody "was peculiar to that tribe or nation called the Cherokees, and that they chanted it to a barbarous jargon, implying contempt for their enemies in the moments of torture and death." Hunter's words were intended to convey the "mixture of respect, pity and horror" with which she believed whites looked "upon the fierce and stubborn courage of the dying Indian." See also Koegel 1997.

2. *European Inroads: Early Christian Music Making*

1. Meinig 1986, 44, 51.
2. Housewright 1991, 16.
3. Béhague in *NGDAM* 1986, 2:395–96.
4. Summers in *NGDAM* 1986, 1:346.
5. Meinig 1986, 58.
6. Ibid., 66–69.
7. Parkman 1983, 1:755–57.
8. Stevenson 1966, 3.
9. Quoted ibid., 8.
10. Crawford 1984, contains a summary of the tune's printings in American sacred tunebooks, 1698–1810.
11. Quoted from Stevenson 1966, 12–13.
12. Quoted in Hood 1846, 20.
13. Two more psalms were set in so-called "Hallelujah" meter: 6.6.6.6.4.4.4.4., and one in "six eights" 8.8.8.8.8.8.
14. Cotton 1647, 62.
15. Symmes 1720, 8.
16. Ibid.
17. *Brief Discourse* 1725, 7.
18. Boston, *New England Courant*, February 17/24.
19. Gould 1853, 160.

3. *From Ritual to Art: The Flowering of Sacred Music*

1. Quoted from Hood 1846, 106–8.
2. Mather 1721, 13.
3. Quoted in Hood 1846, 103n.
4. The appendix of the ninth and tenth editions contained thirteen tunes harmonized for two voices. See Britton 1990, 107–8.
5. The first edition was published in 1721; no copies before the third edition (1723) have survived, however, See Britton 1990, 583–84.
6. *Boston Weekly News-Letter*, April 12–19, 1714.
7. Symmes 1720, 20.
8. Osterhout 1986, 130–33, recounts the Farmington congregation's battle over Regular Singing.
9. Symmes 1723, 58, 49, 12: Symmes 1720, 20, 17.
10. Quoted in Lowens 1964, 282.
11. Gould 1853, Chapter 7.
12. *New Hampshire Gazette*, January 13, 1764.
13. Greenland (New Hampshire) and Rowley, Massachusetts, had choirs in 1762, followed by Ipswich and Medford (1763), Beverly and Hamlet (1764), Dedham

(1766), Westford (1767), Essex, Framingham, Leicester, and Sturbridge (1768), and Worcester (1769). Britton 1990, 49 n. 56.

14. Parkman 1983, 2:1276.
15. Silverman 1984, 326.
16. Meinig 1986, 295, 298.
17. Material on Billings is taken here chiefly from McKay 1975. See also Billings 1977–90.
18. Billings 1794, xxxi.
19. In *The Singing Master's Assistant*, Billings set fourteen texts from Watts's *Hymns*, eleven from Watts's *Psalms*, and eleven more from Brady and Tate's *New Version of the Psalms*, as well as another eleven of his own texts.
20. The upbeat to m. 9, where the treble enters, is also a fifth; so is most of mm. 11–12, all of m. 13 and the sustained note supporting the last singing of the word "glory" (m. 18).
21. Capen 1805. [iii].
22. Gould 1853, 58–59.
23. Housewright 1991, 60–61.
24. Quoted in Sonneck 1905, 59.
25. Quoted in ibid., 60.
26. Quoted in Stevenson 1966, 48–49.
27. Mann 1966, 64.
28. Jacob Duché, quoted in Stevenson 1966, 34.
29. Ellinwood 1953, 37.
30. Ochse 1975, 51–62.
31. Ellinwood 1953, 36.
32. Ibid., 37.
33. Kroeger in *NGDAM* 1986, 3:273.
34. Richard Franko Goldman, quoted in Stevenson 1966, 42.

4. *"Old, Simple Ditties": Colonial Song, Dance, and Home Music Making*

1. Quoted from Sonneck 1916, 81.
2. Quoted from Carleton Sprague Smith in Lambert 1980. 297n.
3. Quotations here and below are from a facsimile, ibid., 296.
4. Quotations here and below are from a Salem, Massachusetts, broadside, ibid, 308.
5. Quoted from Carleton Sprague Smith in Lambert 1980, 312.
6. Quoted from a facsimile of *A Spanish Lady's Love for an English Gentleman*, ibid, 310.
7. Quoted from Cynthia Adams Hoover in Lambert 1985, 767–68.
8. Quotations here and below are taken from a facsimile in Carleton Sprague Smith in Lambert 1980, 189.

9. Smith, ibid., 192n, makes that suggestion.

10. As noted on the broadside, the battle was fought on August 12, and on August 24 James Franklin's newspaper advertised: "On Wednesday next will be publish'd . . . an Excellent new Song, Entituled, The Rebels Reward."

11. Parkman 1983, 2:500–1. William Carlos Williams offers a far more sympathetic view of the priest in Williams 1956, 105–29.

12. Ibid., 2:484.

13. Quoted from a facsimile in Smith in Lambert 1980, 348.

14. Quoted in Isaac 1982, 79.

15. Quoted from a facsimile in Arthur Schrader in Lambert 1980, 118.

16. The text below is quoted from Schrader, ibid., 139–40. On the British occupation of Boston, the song's Irishman asks: "And what have you got now, with all your designing / But a town without victuals to sit down and dine in?"

17. Mather 1684, 24.

18. Sonneck 1907, 9n.

19. *Boston News-Letter*, March 2, 1713.

20. See Cynthia Adams Hoover in Lambert 1985, 749.

21. Quoted in Isaac 1982, 78–79.

22. Housewright 1991, 65–66.

23. Quoted from Hoover in Lambert 1985, 744n.

24. Quoted from Hoover, ibid., 744–45, 770.

25. Joy Van Cleef and Kate Van Winkle Keller in Lambert 1980, 47–49.

26. *Wright's Compleat Collection of Celebrated Country Dances*, vol. 1 (London, ca. 1742), reproduced ibid., 1980, 27.

27. Clement Weeks' dance MS (Greenland, N.H., 1783), reproduced ibid., [23].

28. See Wolfe 1964; Board of Trade 1871.

29. Lambert 1985a, 409–514, presents the results of the search in meticulous detail, with many illustrations.

30. Quoted in Lambert 1985a, 469, 479.

31. Silverman 1976, 33.

32. Talley 1988, 47, 58.

33. Cripe 1974, 97–128, lists the contents of the Jefferson musical collection.

34. Jefferson 1984, 761–62.

35. Quoted from Sonneck 1905, 3.

36. Gillian Anderson discovered the musical sources for this work and has made a modern edition. Quoted here from Sonneck 1905, 108–9.

37. Silverman 1976, 414.

38. Sonneck 1905, 113.

39. See Silverman 1976, 673; Chase 1987, 90–91.

40. As further bibliographic digging has revealed, after ratification but before *Seven Songs* reached print, a sacred tunebook called *The Federal Harmony* was published in Boston (it was advertised in late September 1788), with eight new American sacred compositions, two of them attributed to Massachusetts

composer Oliver Holden, who might therefore deserve the credit Hopkinson claimed for himself.

41. Hamm 1979, 93; Jefferson 1984, 940.

5. *Performing "By Particular Desire": Colonial Military, Concert, and Theater Music*

1. Quoted in Yellin 1969, 285.
2. Quoted from Cynthia Adams Hoover in Lambert 1985, 715–16.
3. Ibid., 726.
4. Camus 1976, 3.
5. Ibid., 4f.
6. Ibid., 48, 50.
7. Lambert in Lambert 1985a, 410.
8. Sonneck 1907, 253n; Hoover in Lambert 1985, 806.
9. Sonneck 1907, 61.
10. Ibid., 14, 74, 75, 20.
11. Ibid., 109, 39.
12. Ibid., 70–73.
13. Ibid., 73.
14. Ibid., 315–16.
15. Barish 1981, 1.
16. Lowens 1964, 100–1. *Ça ira* was a fiery song of the French Revolution; *La Marseillaise*, composed in 1792, was also connected with the revolution and is now the French national anthem.
17. Quotations are from Gay 1922, a facsimile of the original 1729 edition.
18. Porter 1991 describes the work's musical numbers on 59–71; see also 74–75
19. Ibid., 70.

6. *Maintaining Oral Traditions: African Music in Early America*

1. Jefferson 1984, 264.
2. Ibid., 288.
3. Meinig 1986, 226, 231.
4. Epstein 1977, 6.
5. Levine 1977, 8.
6. Ibid., 12.
7. Epstein 1977, 82.
8. Levine 1977, 31–32.
9. Southern 1997, 25.
10. Southern 1983, 32.
11. Southern 1997, 27–29, 34.
12. Epstein 1977, 80.
13. Southern 1997, 43.

14. Ibid., 37.
15. Quoted in Ahlstrom 1972, 701.
16. Quoted from Southern 1983, 54, 58–59. See also Southern 1997, 75–80.
17. Southern 1997, 53.
18. Southern 1983, 44–46.
19. Wilson in Wright 1992, 328.
20. Ibid., 328–29, 333.
21. Ibid., 328.
22. Southern 1982, 243–44.
23. Meinig 1986, 153–54, 229.
24. Epstein 1977, 39, 104.
25. Ibid., 107.
26. Southern 1997, 168.
27. Chernoff 1979, 141.
28. Epstein 1977, 39–40.
29. Wood 1974, 324–25.
30. Epstein 1977, 114–15.
31. Ibid., 107, 84.
32. Meinig 1986, 229.
33. Kmen 1966, 226.
34. Epstein 1977, 32.
35. Ibid., 92.
36. Ibid., 84, 92–93.
37. Ibid., 97–98.
38. Bruce 1974, 51.
39. Quoted ibid., 4n. The term was used by historian Frank Lawrence Owsley to refer to "the great mass of ante-bellum Southern farmers and townspeople who were neither rich nor starving."
40. Bruce 1974, 52; Ahlstrom 1972, 437.
41. Eileen Southern, however, has located possible versions of "Go shouting all your days" and the other camp-meeting chorus Watson quotes in *Slave Songs of the United States* (New York, 1867), further strengthening the case for black-white exchange, though the publication date follows Watson by almost half a century. See Southern 1997, 86–87; see also Southern 1983, 62–64, for the full text of Watson's denunciation of the camp-meeting hymn.

7. Correcting "the Harshness of Our Singing": New England Psalmody Reformed

1. Quoted from Bailyn 1986b, 8–10.
2. Ibid., 10, 21.
3. Meinig 1986, 343–44.
4. Law 1794, 8.

5. Law 1800, [6].
6. Quoted in Crawford 1968, 132.
7. Crawford 1968, 158–76, tells the story of Law and shape notes.
8. Gould 1853, 69.
9. Law 1821, 26.
10. Emmons 1806, 12.
11. Brown 1974, 29ff.
12. The result is documented by Richard Crawford in Crawford 1990, 240–46.
13. Dahlhaus 1989, 178f.
14. Billings 1794, 39–41.

8. *Edification and Economics: The Career of Lowell Mason*

1. Tocqueville 1969, 295, 292–93.
2. Britton 1990, 21.
3. Pemberton 1985, 32.
4. Nineteenth-century American writers often described music grounded in theoretical expertise as "scientific." A British source of 1725 reflects that meaning: "the word science is usually applied to a whole body of regular or methodical observations or propositions . . . concerning any subject of speculation." See Williams 1976, 232–35, which traces the word's history in the vocabulary of culture.
5. Perkins 1893, 39.
6. Rich 1946, 9.
7. H. Mason 1944. The study also notes that Mason's habit of publishing without attribution makes a complete list impossible to compile. See also Sanjek 1988, 2: 206, which reports 1,126 original tunes and 497 reharmonizations and arrangements.
8. Mason's tune is the basis for the fugue, called "Chorale," that begins Ives's quartet (1896). In 1909, Ives revised that movement for orchestra and transferred it to the Fourth Symphony, where it serves as the third movement. See Ives 1972, 154–55.
9. Stevenson 1966, 81.
10. Quoted in Pemberton 1985, 70–71.
11. Boston Academy 1834, 18.
12. Birge 1966, 38.
13. Root 1891, 52.
14. Ibid., 85–86.
15. Pemberton 1985, 121.
16. Sanjek 1988, 2:206; Crawford 1993, 259, summarizes the findings of other scholars, especially Broyles 1992.
17. A loan from his father of $5,000 helped Henry Mason to get started in the instrument-making business. Mason's benefactions include the purchase of an

important German music library that eventually went to Yale University, and support of the studies and work of Alexander Wheelock Thayer, Harvard College graduate and noted biographer of Beethoven. See also Pemberton 1985, 179–81.

18. Quoted in Stevenson 1966, 82.
19. Sanjek 1988, 2:208.
20. Reynolds 1964, 104.
21. Jones 1886, 178; Lawrence 1988, 538.
22. Lawrence 1988, 538, 600.
23. Quoted ibid., 43n.
24. Root 1891, 9.
25. Ibid., 26–27.
26. Ibid., 42–43, 52–54.
27. Ibid., 98.

9. *Singing Praises: Southern and Frontier Devotional Music*

1. Jackson 1933, 122–23.
2. Ibid., 123.
3. Ibid., 44, 119–20.
4. Ibid., 120–22.
5. Meinig 1993, 269, 275–76.
6. Jackson 1933, 213.
7. Meinig 1993, 275–78.
8. Davisson 1816, 22.
9. Jackson 1937, 6.
10. Hatch 1989, 128–29.
11. For example, FREE GRACE in Ingalls's book sets to music a text with refrain quoted in Chapter 6 from black Philadelphia minister Richard Allen's hymn collection of 1801.
12. Ingalls 1805, ix.
13. Jackson 1937, 10.
14. Jackson 1933, 313.
15. Hatch 1989, 143.
16. Quoted in Steel 1988, 129, and Cobb 1978, 71–72. Jackson 1933, 81–82, describes James, "a lawyer of the old-time rural type," as a Southerner whose father had known B. F. White personally. James's *Brief History of the Sacred Harp*, he goes on to say, "is poorly organized, its language is often hard to understand, and in the few instances where I have been able to check up on his data, I have found a quite considerable number of errors." Nevertheless, he acknowledges James's account "as the work of one who was on the inside," who loved *The Sacred Harp* almost as much as the Holy Bible, and who regarded "those who had a hand in

its making as apostles of light, and those who taught the singing of its songs as near-saints." My comments on *The Sacred Harp* owe much to Steele's article.

17. Quoted in Cobb 1978, 69; quoted in Jackson 1933, 86.
18. Quoted in Cobb 1978, 72.
19. White 1968, vii.
20. Walters 1978, 23.
21. Hammond 1974, 79.
22. Echols in *NGDAM* 1986, 2:448.
23. The evaluation is Hammond's. Millennialism is the belief that a one-thousand-year period of holiness in which Christ returns to rule the world is just around the corner.
24. Cross 1950, 3.
25. Hatch 1989, 196.
26. Cross 1950, 152; Hatch 1989, 196–97.
27. Bushman 1992, xiii, presents this roster of middle-class callings.
28. Broyles 1992, 78. Finney apparently did not answer Leavitt's letter.

10. *"Be It Ever So Humble": Theater and Opera, 1800–1860*

1. Porter 1991, 174–75.
2. Ibid., 170–71.
3. Quoted ibid., 179.
4. Ibid., 179.
5. Ibid., 191–92.
6. Quoted ibid., 208.
7. Ibid., 312.
8. McConachie 1992, 37–38, 41.
9. Quoted in Hamm 1979, 167.
10. The melody of the song first appeared in 1821, under the title *To the Home of My Childhood*, with words by Thomas Bayley; identified then as a Sicilian air, it may well have been composed by Bishop and adapted to Payne's text in 1823. Fuld 1971, 275.
11. Ahlquist 1997, 77–81; Dizikes 1993, 3, 100.
12. Wood 1855, 94.
13. Ahlquist 1997, 145–46.
14. Quoted in Grimsted 1968, 64.
15. Lawrence 1988, 61, 133, 135, 218.
16. Whitman 1982, 523. The poem was first published in 1881.
17. Ahlquist 1997, 68, 75–76.
18. Preston 1993, 10–13.
19. Dwight's Journal, February 5, 1853.
20. Quoted in Ware 1980, 54.

21. Ibid., 118.
22. Dizikes 1993, 135–37.
23. Ibid., 25–26. Kmen 1966, Chapters 3–9, traces New Orleans Operatic life in detail.
24. Quoted in Kmen 1966, 198.
25. Preston 1993, 280.
26. Martin 1993, xix, 47.
27. Martin 1993, 3, 93; Dizikes 1993, 119.
28. Dizikes 1993, 112–15.
29. Martin 1993, 199.
30. Thomas 1905, 24–25.

11. Blacks, Whites, and the Minstrel Stage

1. Quoted in M. Watkins 1994, 51–52.
2. Frederickson 1971, 57.
3. Quoted in M. Watkins 1994, 51.
4. Nathan 1962, 145.
5. Lott 1993, 140.
6. Nathan 1962, vii–viii.
7. Quoted in M. Watkins 1994, 65–66.
8. Lott 1993.
9. Quoted in Dennison 1982, 58.
10. Quoted from sheet music in Jackson 1976.
11. Quoted in Dennison 1982, 38–40.
12. Lott 1993, 117–18.
13. The dictionary defines "charivari" as "a noisy mock-serenade to newlyweds." If the target of this "charivari" was not a bridegroom but a theater manager, the choice of word reflects the spirit of the attempt: to parody so outrageously the idea of a lover's serenade that it compels attention even from those who wish you would go away.
14. Nathan 1962, 117.
15. Toll 1974, 52, 34.
16. Ibid., 32.
17. Rice 1911, which presents brief biographies of all blackface entertainers known to the author, shows that a fairly large number were of English birth. In other words, once American performers created the conventions and took them to the British Isles, performers there quickly mastered them.
18. Sacks 1988, 409 ff.; Nathan 1962, 110–11.
19. Nathan 1962, 64–65, 113.
20. Winans in Loney 1984, 71–73.
21. Board of Trade 1871 lists seven different editions of the song. That seven different publishers were keeping *Old Dan Tucker* in print more than twenty-five

years after its first publication shows that no effective copyright existed on the music; either it was a foreign composition, hence ineligible for copyright protection, or it was taken from folk tradition and thus fair game for any publisher. The latter is much more likely.

22. Quoted from Jackson 1976.
23. *Knickerbocker* Magazine, 1845; quoted in BPIM 1975, 87–88.
24. Wilentz 1984, 259.
25. Lawrence 1988, 417; Sanjek 1988, 2:173–74.
26. Austin 1975, 16.
27. Ibid., 203.
28. Quoted from Howard 1934, 196–97.
29. Christy seems also to have paid Foster $15 for the privilege of claiming authorship. Foster's letter promises: "I will if you wish, willingly refund you the money which you paid me on that song." Howard 1934, 197, 199–201.
30. Hamm 1979, 57.
31. Austin 1975, 246–47.
32. Note the survey by Winans in Loney 1984, 81–84, 91–92, which shows the declining emphasis on comic songs and songs about black life in favor of sentimental and tragic songs and opera parodies.
33. Toll 1974, 87.
34. Ibid., 88.
35. Stowe 1982, 9.
36. Ibid., 12.
37. Toll 1974, 94.

12. Home Music Making and the Publishing Industry

1. Wolfe 1980, 108–20.
2. Crawford 1993, 59–60.
3. Sonneck 1907, 223–24.
4. Reinagle 1978.
5. Hitchcock 1988, 53ff., discusses the Great Divide, using these terms.
6. See G. Watkins 1994.
7. D. W. Krummel, quoted in Sanjek 1988, 2:137–38.
8. Royalties could be a percentage of the retail price (10 percent was standard) or a fixed amount for every copy sold (2 cents was typical).
9. Wolfe 1980, 210.
10. Board of Trade 1871, xi.
11. Quoted in Hoover in *NGDAM* 1986, 3:560.
12. Hinson and Hitchcock in *NGDAM* 1986, 3:562.
13. Bushman 1992, 442.
14. Quoted ibid., 445.
15. According to Richard Leppert's research: "Throughout the history of domestic

keyboard instruments the vast majority of players are known to have been women" (1993, 133).

16. Bushman 1992, 440–41.
17. Dahlhaus 1989, 313.
18. Strobel in *IED* 1998, 5:221–23.
19. Lawrence 1988, 324.

13. *From Ramparts to Romance: Parlor Songs, 1800–1865*

1. For the following information and analysis I am indebted to the work of Jon Finson.
2. From *Rokeby*. Quoted from Finson 1994, 14.
3. Finson proposes Scott's "The Crusader's Return," a poem in Chapter 17 of *Ivanhoe*, as Hewitt's model for this text. See ibid., 19–20.
4. Quoted ibid., 20.
5. Quoted in Kasson 1990, 63–64. Twain also offers alternative versions for floods, shipwrecks, hurricanes, and other disasters.
6. Finson 1994, 25, 34. Although Morris's poem deals with the present, some American chivalric courtship songs feature a lute-playing knight serenading a lady who looks down from her tower.
7. Austin 1975, 133.
8. Quoted in American Poetry 1993, 1:70.
9. Compare, however, Fats Waller's recording, in which Waller seems to find his own "exquisite pleasure" in ridiculing the very notion of a song about a bucket.
10. Hamm 1979, 178.
11. Quoted ibid., 178.
12. Root 1891, 18.
13. Quoted in Jackson 1976, 287.
14. Quoted in Lawrence 1988, 229.
15. Quoted in Walters 1978, 124.
16. Cockrell 1989, 9–10.
17. Quoted ibid., 149.
18. Ibid., 254.
19. Royster 1991, xi–xii.
20. Quoted from *American Poetry* 1993, 2:390–92.
21. Meinig 1993, 487–89; NB map on 488.
22. Quoted in Linderman 1987, 100.
23. Scholars have yet to agree on who composed the melody. See Fuld 1971.
24. Root 1891, 136, 133.
25. Sacks and Sacks 1988 raise the distinct possibility that the song was created by African Americans, perhaps one or more members of the Snowden family of Knox County, Ohio, who were claimed in local sources to have "taught 'Dixie' to Dan Emmett" (409).

26. Quoted from *American Poetry* 1993, 1:646.
27. Nathan 1962, 265–66.
28. Lincoln 1989, 2:696.
29. Quoted from facsimile in Crawford 1977, 105–7.
30. The same pattern later served as the basis for the hymn tune CONVERSE, by Charles C. Converse (1868), sung to the words, "What a friend we have in Jesus."
31. Quoted from facsimile in Crawford 1977, 59–61.
32. Quoted in Linderman 1987, 209.
33. Ibid., 194.

14. *Of Yankee Doodle and Ophicleides: Bands and Orchestras,* *1800 to the 1870s*

1. Quoted from Newsom 1976, [4].
2. Ibid. [5].
3. Preston 1992, xxii–xxiv.
4. Founded in the 1830s, this band continued as a performing ensemble well into the twentieth century. Its best-known leader, David Wallis Reeves, took that post in 1866 and held it almost continuously until his death in 1900.
5. Goldman 1961, 45.
6. The American Band's concert of March 10 gave local composers an even more prominent place. Marshall wrote a set of "Grand Concert Waltzes," which he dedicated "to the subscribers and patrons" of the band's 1850–51 concert series. And the program also included two pieces by Francis H. Brown, organist of the First Baptist Church and a prolific composer, who contributed a song sung by Miss Carpenter and a quickstep for band. Neither Carl Lobe nor Romaine can be further identified.
7. Hazen 1987, 121.
8. Ibid. 114.
9. Quoted from Hitchcock 1988, 46.
10. Waters 1955, 100.
11. Hazen 1987, 118.
12. Ibid., 121.
13. *Homespun America* 1993, 15.
14. Foster 1990, 1:289.
15. *Homespun America* 1993, 19.
16. Gottschalk 1964, 45.
17. Lott in Crawford 1990, 176.
18. Starr 1995, 123.
19. Ryan 1899, 56.
20. Lawrence 1988, 545.
21. Johnson 1953, 79.

22. Lawrence 1988, 546. Johnson in *NGDAM* reports that they played the Mendelssohn work over a thousand times in the United States.
23. Ryan 1899, 60–62.
24. Ibid., 62.
25. Carse 1951, 32. The French phrase means "Turkish garden."
26. Ibid., 79.
27. Quoted from Sablosky 1986, 36, 35.
28. Graziano in Crawford 1990, 198f., 206f.
29. Darlington 1956, 34.
30. Quoted from Sablosky 1986, 60–70.

15. *From Church to Concert Hall: The Rise of Classical Music*

1. Perkins 1883, 39, 44–45.
2. Mason 1901, 5.
3. Hastings 1853, 111.
4. Broyles writes: "Although the Handel and Haydn Society did have some members from the working class, it was predominantly a middle-class organization in its early years. Dwight correctly observed that 'first families [of Boston] were not much represented in the ranks' " (1992, 140).
5. Quoted in Ellinwood 1953, 109.
6. Hastings 1853, 245, 109.
7. At Christ Episcopal Church, for example, on Fifth Avenue at 35th Street, the choir director was James M. Mozart, the soprano Mrs. J. M. Mozart, and the tenor Harrison Millard, a well-known songwriter. See *American Musical Directory* 1861, 220.
8. Porter 1834, 288.
9. *American Musical Directory* 1861, 247.
10. Lawrence 1988, 247.
11. Gould 1853, 180.
12. Hastings 1853, 122–23, 128.
13. Quoted in Ellinwood 1953, 124 and Ogasapian 1977, 82–83.
14. Saloman 1995, 31, 41–42, 47, 54, 68.
15. Broyles 1992, Chapter 7, especially 199–200.
16. Ibid., 203.
17. See Levine 1988, Part Two, and DiMaggio in Mukerji and Schudson 1991, 374ff. For a dissenting view, Locke and Barr 1997, 296ff.
18. Saloman 1995, 41.
19. Broyles 1992, 235. The phrase, which comes from the period, serves as the title for Broyles's book, on which much of my treatment of this subject relies.
20. Thomas 1905, 127, 216, 286.
21. Ibid., 33.

22. Schabas 1989, 36–38. The New York Philharmonic Society in these years played no more than half a dozen programs in a season.
23. Ibid., 52.
24. Hart 1973, 22.
25. Schabas 1989, 244.
26. Hart 1973, 30.
27. Russell 1927, 3.
28. See Levine 1988, 85–146.
29. Hart 1973, 32.
30. Schabas 1989, 182–83.
31. Ibid., 253.

16. *From Log House to Opera House: Anthony Philip Heinrich and William Henry Fry*

1. See Chase 1987, Chapter 15.
2. Plantinga 1984, 21.
3. Upton 1939, 40.
4. Ibid., 40, 66.
5. Ibid., 75.
6. Ibid., 103.
7. Parker 1975, 114, 116.
8. Upton 1939, 67.
9. Ibid., 143.
10. Ibid., 193, 182.
11. Commenting on the Romantic notion of artists as visionaries, Leon Plantinga writes: "This view of the artist as a kind of Promethean figure in society, as a firebringer from the gods to man—and yet rejected by that society he is bound to serve—gained wide currency among musicians and music critics of the earlier nineteenth century. Flattering in a way to the composer, it also placed upon him a special burden to prove worthy of his calling" (1984, 16).
12. Quoted from Lawrence 1988, 628–30.
13. Ibid., 630–31.
14. Quoted from Chase 1966, 47, 49, 50.
15. Writing in 1882, critic Richard Grant White, who had worked in New York from the 1850s on and had heard an 1858 performance, praised Fry as "an accomplished musician and critic" and "a man born with the creative musical faculty and also with fine perceptions in musical rhetoric and the requirements in this respect of the lyric drama." As for *Leonora*, he found that, "like the early work of all artists," it "was so colored by the tone of his predecessors as to seem almost an imitation." Yet it "also showed a constructive power and a mastery of the resources of the opera, vocal and instrumental, which promised, with encourage-

ment and time to produce something of which musical Americans might have been proud. But he did not have encouragement, nor yet time." Quoted from Upton 1954, 159.

16. Dizikes 1993, 99–100.
17. Upton 1954, 25–27, 30, 34.
18. Lawrence 1995, 390.
19. Ibid., 766, 258n. He is reported to have recovered about $6,000 from receipts.
20. Lawrence 1988, 408n., advises: "It is indeed remarkable that in 1853 a mixed audience of some two thousand New Yorkers were willing to congregate for eleven consecutive weeks, braving weather and insults, to imbibe the last in esoteric musical enlightenment."
21. Lawrence 1995, 386.
22. Quoted from Lowens 1964, 217–18.
23. Upton 1954, 132.
24. Quoted ibid., 337–38.
25. Quoted from Shanet 1975, 112.
26. Ibid., 113–14.
27. See Johnson 1995.

17. A New Orleans Original: Gottschalk of Louisiana

1. Starr 1995, 150.
2. Gottschalk 1964, 10–11.
3. Starr 1995, 50, 51–55, 60.
4. Ibid., 65–70.
5. Gottschalk, "The Last Hope," Dover edition (1854).
6. Gottschalk 1964, 96.
7. Reynolds 1964, 67.
8. Gottschalk 1964, 244.
9. Starr 1995, 164.
10. Ibid., 160.
11. Gottschalk 1964, 75.
12. Ibid., 173–75.
13. Doyle 1983, 12, traces Gottschalk's itinerary for 1862, starting with "the principal cities of the East: Philadelphia, Newark, Baltimore, Washington, Worcester, Providence, Portsmouth, Portland, Salem, Springfield, Burlington, New Haven, and Boston; in New York State he appeared in Lockport, Ogdensburg, Watertown, Batavia, Rochester, Auburn, Canandaigua, Geneva, Elmira, Oswego, Rome, and Utica; in the West he was heard in Cincinnati, Louisville, St. Louis, Chicago, Milwaukee, Toledo, Cleveland, Detroit, Erie, Sandusky, Zanesville, Columbus, Madison, and Indianapolis; in Canada, Kingston, Hamilton, Montreal, Quebec, Ottawa, and Toronto. There was a concert in August for wounded soldiers in Saratoga. In October Gottschalk played with Theodore

Thomas in chamber concerts in New York and met the young prodigy Teresa
Carreño."

14. Gottschalk 1964, 307.
15. Starr 1995, 439–40, 444, 450.
16. See Offergeld 1969, xiii–xiv.
17. Gottschalk 1964, 48–49.

18. *Two Classic Bostonians: George W. Chadwick and Amy Beach*

1. See Horowitz 1994.
2. Hubbard 1908, 13.
3. Block 1994, xiv.
4. Foote 1946, 54.
5. Charles Martin Loeffler, firmly anti-German in his personal outlook, was an exception to this claim.
6. Lowens 1971, 48.
7. Hubbard 1908, 1.
8. Kearns 1965, 87.
9. Meinig 1993, 421.
10. Yellin 1990, 33.
11. Bomberger 1991, 75–76.
12. Quoted in Crawford 1993, 244.
13. Yellin 1990, 5.
14. Ibid., 68–69.
15. Quoted ibid., 94.
16. Ibid., 113–14.
17. Ibid., 115–16.
18. Block in Cook and Tsou 1993, 108.
19. Jenkins 1994, 78, 37.
20. Block 1994, xv.
21. Elson 1904, 293–94.
22. Chapter 15 of Elson's *History* is entitled "American Women in Music."
23. Jenkins 1994, 29.
24. Ibid., 29.
25. Ibid., 77–78 and note.
26. Ibid., 78.

19. *Edward MacDowell and Musical Nationalism*

1. Unless otherwise noted, the biographical material below is taken from Gilman 1908 and Lowens 1971.
2. Bomberger 1991, 200.
3. Other composers represented on this landmark program were Paine, Foote, Chadwick, Dudley Buck, Henry Holden Huss, and the conductor himself.

4. Gilman 1908, 32.
5. Ibid., 63.
6. Sonneck 1916, 90.
7. Lowens 1971, 103, 105.
8. Ibid., 280.
9. Parakilas 1992, 24; Dahlhaus 1989, 36–37.
10. Lowens 1971, 95.
11. Shi 1995, 205.
12. Lowens 1971, 95–96.
13. MacDowell 1912, 254.
14. Gilman 1908, 82–83.
15. MacDowell 1912, 271.
16. Ibid., 270.
17. Gary Tomlinson in Floyd 1995, 276–77.
18. Lowens 1971, 55.
19. Gilman 1908, 133; Farwell and Darby 1915, 366.
20. Block in Crawford 1990, 257.
21. As noted in Irving Lowens's introduction to MacDowell 1912, xxiv, his comments on Dvořák's involvement in American nationalism were cut from the published lectures, but Gilman 1908, 83–85, quotes them in full. Historians have sometimes given the impression that MacDowell's disagreement with Dvořák over nationalism took place in a public debate. See Hamm 1983, 415–16, for example, where Dvořák is called MacDowell's "competitor."
22. Gilman 1908, 83–84.
23. Ibid., 84–85.
24. Ibid., 1989, 148.
25. Lowens 1971, 278.
26. Gilman 1908, 15.

20. *"Travel in the Winds": Native American Music from 1820*

1. Welch 1986, 354–60.
2. *American Poetry* 1993, 2: 662, 982.
3. Another collector wrote in 1822 about a pair of Cherokee songs with about the same number of words: "These consist of but one sentence each, with a chorus. Nothing of length seems to exist among them. They repeat the song and the chorus until they are tired." Ibid., 2:982.
4. Ibid., 2:989.
5. Ibid., 2:990.
6. Quotes from Hiawatha taken from Longfellow 1962.
7. Dana Gioia in Parini 1993, 88.
8. Quoted in Pisani 1996, 314.
9. "The recording of Indian music on the phonograph was first done successfully

by Jesse Walter Fewkes, with songs of the Passamaquoddy tribe in Maine. Benjamin Ives Gilman made use of Fewkes's phonograph recordings of songs of the Zuñi tribe for his monograph on their music; and Frances Densmore, for many years at the Bureau of American Ethnology of the Smithsonian Institution in Washington, recorded and analyzed hundreds of Indian songs." Hamm 1983, 9.

10. Nettl in *NGDAM* 1986, 2:464–68.
11. These characteristics are laid out in Hamm 1983, 9–10, from which some of the wording is quoted.
12. Lee in Myers 1993, 25.
13. Quoted ibid., 23.
14. Quoted ibid., 23.
15. Quoted from Pisani 1996, 319.
16. Natalie Curtis, quoted in Hamm 1983, 22.
17. Lewis in *EUSTC* 1996, 143.
18. Browner 1995, 1999.
19. Quoted from Lucy Maddox in Parini 1993, 734. The poem is called "Anchorage."

21. *"Make a Noise!": Slave Songs and Other Black Music to the 1880s*

1. Douglass 1994, 183–84.
2. Ibid., 183–85.
3. Southern 1983, 89–90.
4. Epstein 1977, 165.
5. Ibid., 174.
6. Southern 1983, 73.
7. Mathews 1889, 98.
8. Epstein 1977, 188–89.
9. Quoted ibid, 244.
10. The foregoing is taken from ibid., 243–48.
11. Floyd 1995, 41–42.
12. Epstein 1977, 304–20.
13. Allen 1867, iv–v.
14. Ibid., x, iv.
15. Quoted ibid., xiii–xiv.
16. Ibid., xiv.
17. Stuckey 1987, 16.
18. Paraphrased from Floyd 1995, 6.
19. Marsh 1892, Chapters 2–5; Southern 1982, 132–33.
20. Marsh 1892, 38.
21. Epstein in Crawford 1990, 38.
22. Lovell 1972, 367.
23. Trotter in Southern 1983, 147.
24. Southern 1971, 123–24; Southern 1977b, 7.

25. Southern 1977b, 7–8, 12–13.
26. Southern 1983, 124.
27. Southern 1997, 113.
28. Cockrell 1989, 80.
29. Southern 1997, 94–95.
30. Magriel 1978, 50–52; Floyd 1995, 55.
31. Quoted from Trotter 1878, 82–83.
32. Trotter 1878, 120–21.

22. *Songs of the Later Nineteenth Century*

1. Lingenfelter 1968, 42–43.
2. Logsdon 1989, 284.
3. Lingenfelter 1968, 334–35.
4. Ibid., 5.
5. Quoted in Koegel 1994, 2:206
6. Ibid., 1:19.
7. Farwell 1995, 105, 111.
8. The two men at one point apparently envisioned a book of fifty songs, and in the published songbook's introduction in 1923, Lummis writes: "I hope to be able to follow this book with others, each of about the same number of songs, until we have preserved a fair showing of the quaint, heartfelt and heart-reaching Folksong which flowered in the California That Was." See Koegel 1994, 1:41n; 2:207.
9. Ibid., 2:207.
10. Garcia recorded thirteen of the songs, including the two discussed below. Adalaida Kamp, who recorded the other one, was in her middle sixties when she did so. See ibid., 1:962–66.
11. Ibid., 2:208. Quoted from Farwell's prefatory note in *Spanish Songs*.
12. Farwell 1995, 108–9.
13. Root 1891, 151.
14. Sheet-music sales were reported to have reached 300,000 copies in the ten years after publication. *Silver Threads* enjoyed an even more lucrative afterlife. "As a result of its constant performance by the minstrel-show singer Richard Jose," it sold "more than two million copies by 1900, and an additional one million in 1907, when it was revived, and concentrated song plugging by its publishers led to far greater and immediate sales" (Sanjek 1988, 2:255; see also Jackson 1976, 281).
15. Schlereth 1991, 55–56.
16. Marsden 1980, 35.
17. Ibid., 32.
18. Sanjek 1988, 2:250–51.

19. Foner 1975, 270.
20. Ibid., 130, 217, 152.

23. *Stars, Stripes, and Cylinders: Sousa, the Band, and the Phonograph*

1. Kreitner 1990, 97–98.
2. Ibid., 187–88.
3. Hazen 1987, 41.
4. Bierley 1984, 66.
5. Bierley 1973, 156.
6. Ibid., 139–40.
7. Ibid., 140.
8. Ibid., 50, 138–39.
9. Bierley 1984, 72.
10. Bierley 1973, 120, 142.
11. Bierley 1984, 69.
12. Ibid., 89. These words are sung to the second half of the trio.
13. Ibid., 95.
14. Hazen 1987, 186–89.
15. Floyd 1977, 174.
16. Ibid., 178.
17. Smart 1970, 3.
18. Quoted ibid., 4.

24. *"After the Ball": The Rise of Tin Pan Alley*

1. Hamm 1979, 287.
2. Sanjek 1988, 2:315.
3. Marks 1934, 3.
4. Ibid., 38–40.
5. Ibid., 23, 25.
6. Ibid., 4.
7. Marks 1934, 295, locates this establishment at 50 Bowery, near Canal Street. The women's orchestra is said to have been the first in the country.
8. Ibid., 7–8.
9. Ibid., 9–10, 17–18.
10. Gilfoyle 1992, 224–25. This work also quotes an observer who in 1900 called Theiss's and two other concert saloons "three of the largest markets for women which the city ever had" (212).
11. Marks 1934, 18.
12. Ibid., 20–21.
13. Sanjek 1988, 2:324–25.

14. Walters in *EUSTC* 1996, 1463–64.
15. Dreiser, quoted in Hamm 1979, 289.
16. Sanjek 1988, 2:321–22; Jasen 1988, 13.
17. Hamm 1979, 291.
18. Marks 1934, 45. He adds that theater audiences "were Irish too. [New York] had the largest Irish population in the world. They had acquired some money and would spend it, while the new waves of immigrants picked up the shovels, which now became subject for comic ballads." Edward Harrigan, the leading playwright-actor-songwriter of New York's Irish musical stage in the pre–Tin Pan Alley era, wrote with composer Dave Braham many memorable songs for his plays, though none won the popularity of the hits on our list. See Finson 1997.
19. Marks 1934, 44.
20. Ibid., 38, 51.
21. Sundquist 1993, 283–84.
22. Quoted in Finson 1994, 227.
23. Marks 1934, 96.
24. Ibid., 86–87.
25. Compare Marks's comment: "Hogan became an object of censure among all the Civil Service intelligentsia, and he died haunted by the awful crime he had unwittingly committed against the race" (91). The quote is from Sundquist 1993, 284.
26. Southern 1997, 317–18.

25. *"To Stretch Our Ears": The Music of Charles Ives*

1. General histories of music from that era include Ritter 1883 and 1890, Mathews 1889, and Elson 1904. See Crawford 1993, Chapter 1.
2. Sessions 1979, 157.
3. Tocqueville 1969, 458.
4. Sherwood 1995, 2–3.
5. Charles Seeger, composer Henry Cowell's teacher and head of the music department at the University of California, owned both of Ives's publications and talked to Cowell about Ives in the 1920s. According to Sidney Robertson Cowell, Seeger and Carl Ruggles (later one of Ives's closest friends) felt strongly at the time that "one shouldn't waste time on this music: it was the work of an amateur, a dilettante and a clown." See Feder 1992, 320.
6. Ibid., 98. The book was John Tasker Howard, *Our American Music* (1931).
7. Ives 1972, 45, 115.
8. Ibid., 115.
9. Swafford 1996, 64–65.
10. Ives 1972, 45.
11. Hitchcock 1993, 320, summarizing Feder.

12. Ives 1962, 84.
13. Compare Emerson's "Plato, or, the Philosopher:" "These things we are forced to say, if we must consider the effort of Plato, or of any philosopher, to dispose of Nature,—which will not be disposed of." Emerson 1983, 653.
14. Perlis 1974, 220.
15. Swafford 1996, 332–33; Carter 1977, 48–49.
16. Ives 1972, 87; the walk took place in 1908.
17. Ives manuscript, as quoted in Swafford 1996, 242.
18. Ives 1962, 4.
19. Burkholder 1995, 327–30. For another analysis, see Starr 1992, which devotes most of a chapter on "Layering" to *The Housatonic at Stockbridge*, 115–26.
20. Ives 1972, 132–33.
21. Ibid., 132.
22. Ibid., 115. Ives attributed this belief to his father.
23. As summarized in Hitchcock 1988, 168–69.
24. Quoted from Hitchcock 1977, 93.
25. Ives 1962, 1. The *Essays* are not a program for the sonata but a full discussion of Ives's aesthetic beliefs. However, they do supply a narrative program for *Thoreau*.
26. In the Baroque and Classical eras, sonatas were made up of thematically independent movements. In the 1800s, composers sometimes pursued overall musical unity by presenting the same theme in more than one movement, a practice that has been called "cyclic." Ives's use of the same theme in all four movements carries the device further than most European composers had done.
27. Ives 1972, 44.
28. Cowell 1955, 142.
29. Ives 1962, 68.
30. Ibid., 128.

26. *"Come On and Hear": The Early Twentieth Century*

1. Wharton 1920. Soprano Christine Nilsson was a real singer, and the Academy of Music was New York's main opera house from the 1850s into the 1880s. Wharton was wrong about the size of the academy, however, which had a seating capacity of 4,600.
2. Ibid., 2–3.
3. Quoted from Slonimsky 1971, 100.
4. Furia 1990, 182.
5. Bordman 1978, 236; Sanjek 1988, 2: 334.
6. According to Whitburn 1986, 328, vocalist Billy Murray's recording was "the biggest-selling record of Victor's first decade" and led national record sales for a ten-week period in 1906. Sanjek 1988, 2:333, says that Cohan's song sold more than one million copies of sheet music.

7. McConnell in *EUSTC* 1996, 253–54.

8. Ibid., 255–56.

9. Johnson 1933, 173.

10. The music and scripts of *In Dahomey* are published in Riis 1996.

11. Badger 1995, 42.

12. Sanjek 1988, 2:335–36, 289.

13. Handy 1941, 80–81.

14. Berlin 1994, 7.

15. The information on Sedalia is from Berlin 1994, 13–23.

16. Floyd 1995, 70.

17. See Joplin 1971, 283–86.

18. James Scott's *Grace and Beauty (a classy Rag)* was published in New York in 1909. See Scott 1992, 95.

19. The period of time within which those copies were sold has never been specified. Black songwriter Chris Smith is supposed to have said about the *Maple Leaf Rag*'s difficulty, "Ain't nobody can play it, but lots likes to play at it." Marks 1934, 159.

20. Morton once called Joplin "the greatest ragtime writer who ever lived and the composer of *Maple Leaf Rag*." Johnson, speaking of rags he was playing in New York around 1912, said that "everybody knew [the piece] by then." And recalling the period around 1908, Robinson, a white musician, called Joplin's piece "one of the finest tunes ever written . . . the King of Rags, and in my way of thinking, nothing that Joplin or any other rag writers wrote ever came close to it." See Berlin 1994, 56.

21. Its arrival there coincides with a standard harmonic progression, alternating two bars of dominant harmony with two bars of tonic until bar 13, where a four-bar cadence pattern sets in. This harmonic plan proved so serviceable, according to James Dapogny, an experienced pianist in the tradition, that it was used again and again—perhaps, he estimates, in as many as half of the second strains of piano rags published in the ragtime era.

22. See Berlin article, 51–65 in Crawford 1990.

23. Berlin 1994, 202–5, 226.

24. Marks 1934, 159–60.

25. Berlin 1980, 2.

26. Hamm 1994, xliii.

27. Erenberg 1981, 150–53.

28. Ibid., 146–47.

29. Hamm 1994, xxii; Bergreen 1990, 142.

30. Hamm 1994, xxix, xxxiv, xli, xliv.

31. May 1959, ix.

32. Hamm 1994, xxxvii.

33. Southern 1982, 73, 128–29. Vernon Castle died in 1917.

34. Anderson 1982, 77–78.

35. Badger 1995, 167.
36. Ibid., 221.
37. Morgan 1991, 46–47.

27. *The Jazz Age Dawns: Blues, Jazz, and a Rhapsody*

1. Ellison 1964, 78.
2. Murray 1970, 58 (italics in original). See also 843–44 of the present volume.
3. Handy 1941, 124–26.
4. Jeff Todd Titon has applied the "down-home" label in preference to the older "country blues." For, he explains, although the blues originated in "a rural landscape with a low population density," oral blues performance came to refer "not to a place but to a spirit, a *sense* of place evoked in singer and listener by a style of music" (1977, xiii).
5. Peretti, 1992, 30–31.
6. Gushee 1994, 22; *NGDAM* 4:427.
7. Gushee 1994, 10.
8. Bechet 1960, 50, 3.
9. *NGDJ* 2: 168.
10. Bushell, 1988, 25.
11. Williams 1967, 30.
12. Moore 1985, 84–85.
13. Oja 2000 is the basis for the information here and on the following pages.
14. Schwartz and Childs 1967, 196.
15. Quoted in Slonimsky 1971, 342, 371.
16. Copland 1968, 105.
17. Payne 1960, 45; Jablonski 1987, 59–60.
18. Oja 1994, 650–51. Sales of the *Rhapsody in Blue* disc are said to have totaled one million copies.
19. The labels in this and later examples are from Gilbert 1995, 58–59.
20. Oja 1994, 656.
21. Ibid., 657.

28. *"The Birthright of All of Us": Classical Music, the Mass Media, and the Depression*

1. Copland 1968, 9.
2. Matthew Arnold's words are quoted from Kronenberger 1971, 19.
3. Horowitz 1987, 3.
4. Copland 1968, 157.
5. Horowitz 1987, 172–73.
6. Marquis 1986, 38.
7. Copland 1984, 245–47.
8. Thomson 1971, 53–55.

9. Copland 1968, 160.
10. Bernstein in *EUSTC* 1996, 1192–97.
11. McCarthy in *EUSTC* Kutler 1996, 1731.
12. Ibid., 1730.
13. Marquis 1986, 13.
14. Hoover and Cage 1959, 157.
15. McConnell in *EUSTC*, 257–58.
16. Ibid., 261–62.
17. Quoted in Chase 1966, 148–51.
18. Copland 1968, 124.
19. Sessions 1979, 135.
20. Quoted from Johnson in Nicholls 1998, 16.
21. Quoted ibid., 57. In 1931, Cowell received a fellowship from the John Simon Guggenheim Foundation to study non-Western music in Berlin with the ethnomusicologist and acoustician Erich von Hornbostel.
22. Cage 1961, 3.

29. *"All That Is Native and Fine": American Folk Song and Its Collectors*

1. Myers 1993, 36–37.
2. Child 1898, iv, 61–65.
3. Quoted in Wilgus 1959, 57.
4. Ibid., 59, 62.
5. Quoted ibid., 63.
6. Whisnant 1983, 113–18.
7. These two versions are Nos. 35 and 21 of child ballad 200 in Bronson 1959.
8. Bronson 1959, x–xi.
9. Whisnant 1983, 117, 115.
10. Ibid., 103.
11. Ibid., 124.
12. Ritter 1890, 421.
13. Myers 1993, 38–39.
14. Cox 1925, xvii–xviii.
15. Louise Pound, quoted in Kodish 1986, 7.
16. Kodish 1986, 33–34.
17. Malone, *ESC* 1989, 1002–3.
18. *Ethnic Recordings* 1982, 3.
19. Malone 1968, 38–41.
20. Wolfe and Lornell 1992, 112.
21. Quoted in Lieberman, 1989, 38.
22. Lomax 1947, ix.
23. Cohen 1991, 22–23.
24. Klein 1980, 149–50. Charles Seeger, whose career evolved from that of a com-

poser to an ethnomusicologist, was an important intellectual and political figure in music, as well as the father of folk singer Pete Seeger and the husband of composer Ruth Crawford Seeger.

25. Quoted ibid., 140–41.
26. Dunaway 1981, 93.
27. Ibid., 63–64, 50.
28. Quoted from Lieberman 1989, 53.
29. Dunaway 1981, 100.

30. *From New Orleans to Chicago: Jazz Goes National*

1. Dodge 1995, 99, 13, 100.
2. Ibid., 5, 7.
3. Ibid., 6, 100–1.
4. Ibid., 102.
5. Ibid., 14–15.
6. Ibid., 67.
7. Floyd 1995, 28–29.
8. Gushee 1985, 394, 407.
9. Quoted from Williams 1967, 60.
10. Dapogny 1982, 21–22.
11. Giddins 1988, 60.
12. Ibid., 85–86.
13. Kenney 1993, 11–15.
14. Ibid., 6.
15. Kenney 1993, 130; Kennedy 1994, 75–76.
16. Kenney 1993, 105.
17. Freeman 1989, 8.
18. Quoted from Kenney 1993, 105.
19. Schuller 1968, 115–19.
20. Giddins 1988, 168.
21. Kenney 1993, 59.
22. Carmichael 1965, 203.
23. Dapogny 1982, 7–8.
24. Schuller 1968, 164–65, counts eight different combinations, heard not only from one chorus to the next but also in smaller units, including even two-bar and four-bar phrase groups.
25. Kenney 1993, 67, 71, 77–80.
26. DeFaa 1990, 59.
27. Ferguson 1982, 20.
28. Freeman 1989, 12.
29. Ramsey and Smith 1939, 160, 144.
30. Freeman 1989, 33.

31. See Douglas 1995, 430–31; Williams 1993, 69–70.
32. Sudhalter and Evans 1974, 255–56.

31. *"Crescendo in Blue": Ellington, Basie, and the Swing Band*

1. The following material on Ellington is adapted from Crawford 1993, Chapter 5, which draws on Tucker 1991 and Ellington 1973.
2. Shapiro and Hentoff 1955, 237.
3. Ellington 1973, 462, 118.
4. Ibid., 261, 227, 453.
5. Ibid., 106.
6. Stewart 1972, 97–98.
7. Quoted from Dance 1970, 84.
8. Quoted from Rattenbury 1990, 23.
9. Schuller 1989, 48.
10. Basie 1985, 64–65.
11. Pearson 1987, 39.
12. Ibid., 39, 49.
13. Basie 1985, 46, 68–69.
14. Ibid., 17, 20.
15. Ibid., 108.
16. Schuller in *NGDJ* 1988, 1:33.
17. Basie 1985, 161.
18. Pearson 1987, 142.
19. Basie 1985, 170–71.
20. Tucker 1985, 46.
21. Dance 1974, 13.
22. Williams 1993, 122–24.
23. Porter 1985, 58–61; Schuller 1989, 251.
24. Dance 1974, 16.
25. Schuller 1989, 661–63.
26. Floyd 1990, 1–3.
27. Johnson 1925, 50.

32. *The Golden Age of the American Musical*

1. Furia 1996, 45.
2. Ibid., 47–48.
3. Douglas 1995, 483.
4. Furia 1990, 14.
5. Bellah 1985, 35–44.
6. Hamm 1979, 361–66.
7. Numbers tell the story. During one seventy-five-week period beginning in 1922, Irving Berlin's *Say It with Music* sold 375,000 printed copies—a healthy amount

but barely a tenth as large as the 3.5 million sold by Ray Egan and Richard Whiting's *Till We Meet Again* in 1918. Berlin's *Say It with Music* was nevertheless a hit, from its sale during the same seventy-five weeks of 1 million records and 100,000 piano rolls. See Crawford 1993, 216.

8. Sanjek 1988, 3:87, 95–96. The rise of radio is said by Sanjek to have changed "the profile of the average sheet-music buyer." The "young women who tried out new songs by playing on the piano the few bars printed on the back of all sheet music and then ordered them from New York" now seemed old-fashioned when compared with "the bobbed-hair, short-skirted, gum-chewing flappers who dialed around the radio frequencies looking for a new song to learn."

9. Ibid., 3:106–8. Publishers printed orchestrations of movie songs and made them available to radio bands, movie-house stage bands, and organists, then sat back and let the screen do the work. And film studios began to make musical films. *Broadway Melody*, released in 1929 by Metro-Goldwyn-Mayer, was the first. Its songs were published by Robbins Music, which sold sheet music and recorded versions in the lobbies of MGM-owned theaters where the movie ran. In the same year, the show business journal *Variety* explained how the movies were bringing new "affluence and influence" to songwriters, not always an admired breed. Lyricists and composers now worked in teams in Hollywood, producing songs that, according to *Variety*, didn't even need to be very good, "in view of the screen's power to carry mediocre song material to hitdom, providing the picture is strong."

10. Hamm 1979, 377–79.

11. Ibid., 391. *Pennies from Heaven* was introduced by a 1936 film of the same name in which Bing Crosby and Louis Armstrong appeared.

12. Rodgers 1975, 252.

13. Quoted from Green 1963, 106–7.

14. Easton 1996, 201.

15. Rodgers 1975, 264.

16. Roberts in *EUSTC* 1996, 1754.

17. Mordden 1981, 11.

18. Harmetz 1977, 206, 90.

19. Jablonski 1996, 131, 133.

20. Mordden 1981, 114–15.

21. Croce 1972, 6–7.

22. Bergreen 1990, 346.

23. Mordden 1981, 199–200.

33. *Classical Music in the Postwar Years*

1. D. Crawford 1995, 76–77, 36.

2. Ibid., 43, 48–49, 71.

3. J. Patterson 1996, 77–79.

4. Chase 1966, 238–39.
5. Quoted from Austin 1966, 438.
6. Quoted from Hitchcock 1988, 246.
7. Carter 1977, 201.
8. Ibid., 274–77.
9. Quoted from Schwartz and Childs 1967, 196–98.
10. Davies in Vinton 1974, 212.
11. Hitchcock 1988, 260–61.
12. D. Patterson 1996, 68–69, 95–99. The words are those of Ananda K. Cooma-raswamy.
13. Hitchcock 1988, 265–66.
14. Pritchett 1993, 60.
15. D. Patterson 1996, 33.
16. Ibid., 230–31.
17. Gagne and Caras 1982, 75.
18. Quoted from Kostelanetz 1987, 41.
19. Cage 1961, 12.

34. *"Rock Around the Clock": The Rise of Rock and Roll*

1. Williams 1959, introduction.
2. Petkov 1995, 37–38.
3. Ibid, 35, 36.
4. Frith 1981, 191–92; Bordman 1978, 427–28
5. Halberstam 1993, 485.
6. Guralnick 1971, 18.
7. Shaw 1982, 12.
8. Jasen 1988, 285.
9. Malone 1979, 91.
10. Sanjek 1988, 3:247.
11. George 1988, 26–28.
12. Wexler 1993, 78–79.
13. George 1988, 18–29.
14. Wexler 1993, 90.
15. George 1988, 43.
16. Halberstam 1993, 465–66; Palmer 1979, 2.
17. George 1988, 67.
18. Ibid., 67.
19. Guralnick 1971, 17–20.
20. Guralnick 1994, 45. Much of the following account is taken from this source.
21. Ibid., 60 (italics in original).
22. Ibid., 61, 64.
23. Ibid., 95.

24. Zak 1997, 4, 6.
25. Ibid., 10–14.
26. Guralnick 1994, 96.
27. Hemphill, 1970. 192–93.
28. Ibid., 195, 233.
29. Hamm 1979, 395.
30. Charles 1978, 196–97.
31. Halberstam 1993, 560.

35. *Songs of Loneliness and Praise: Postwar Vernacular Trends*

1. Sanjek 1988, 3:355.
2. Mattfeld 1962, xiii.
3. Furia 1997, 386.
4. Jablonski 1996, 162–63.
5. Malone 1968, 209–13.
6. Cantwell 1984, 14–15, 34, 71.
7. Rosenberg 1985, 109.
8. Linn 1991, 140–42.
9. Rosenberg 1985, 111.
10. Quoted ibid., 154.
11. Seeger 1972, 11.
12. Charters 1975, 177, 179.
13. Titon in Rosenberg 1993, 222–23.
14. Harris 1992a, 103, 106–8; Boyer 1995, 19.
15. Harris 1992b, 180–81.
16. Harris 1992a, 192–96.
17. Harris 1992b, 182.
18. Eugene Smith quoted in Reagon 1992, 303–4.
19. Lawrence Roberts quoted in Reagon 1992, 304.
20. Heilbut 1985, ix–x.
21. Ibid., x.

36. *Jazz, Broadway, and Musical Permanence*

1. Williams 1959, 195–96. The author was Ross Russell.
2. Ibid., 200–2.
3. Quoted in Rosenthal 1992, 23.
4. Quoted ibid., 17.
5. Murray 1976, 164–66.
6. Later editions appeared in 1983 and 1993, with new chapters added and some reworking of earlier material. Quotations here are from the second revised edition (1993).
7. Williams 1993, 205, 152, 157.

8. Ibid., 169.

9. Ibid., 175–76; Smithsonian Collection 1987.

10. Williams 1993, 199–202.

11. Ibid., 202–7.

12. Ibid., 197, 219, 222, 236.

13. Ibid., 210–14.

14. Ibid., 265–67, 234–35.

15. Schuller in *NGDJ* 1988, 2:531.

16. Bernstein 1959, 174.

17. Ibid., 178–79.

18. Lerner 1978, 54.

19. Engel 1967, 75.

20. Ibid., 96, 80, 78.

21. Ibid., 79.

22. Lerner 1978, 44.

23. Ibid., 33–34.

24. Ibid., 44.

25. Quotations of *My Fair Lady* taken from Citron 1995, 264–79.

37. *Melting Pot or Pluralism?: Popular Music and Ethnicity*

1. Quotations here and below are from Hijuelos 1989, 341–58.

2. Ibid., 155, 341–58.

3. Ibid., 125.

4. Quoted in Chase 1987, 47 (the third edition of Chase 1955); the author died in the early 1990s.

5. Ibid., 481–84.

6. Hitchcock 1988, in Prentice Hall series, which also includes a separate volume on Latin America.

7. Hamm 1983, 656.

8. Vecoli in *EUSTC* 1996, 167–68.

9. Myers 1993, 453–57; Chase 1987, 484.

10. Cantwell 1996, 324.

11. Quoted ibid., 327–28.

12. Ibid., 36.

13. Tindall 1996, 1439.

14. Shelton 1986, 356, 301.

15. Ibid., 301–2.

16. Ibid., 100.

17. Ibid., 267.

18. Quoted in Hamm 1983, 618.

19. Palmer 1995, 147.

20. Ibid., 8–9.

21. Thompson 1971, 68.

22. Palmer 1995, 110–11.

23. Malone 1996, 121, 124.

24. Brown and Tucker 1986, 6, 18.

25. Ibid., 109.

26. Ibid., 158.

27. Bowman, *ESC* 1989, 1046.

38. *From Accessibility to Transcendence: The Beatles, Rock, and Popular Music*

1. Martin 1979, 122–25, 168. He went on to say that the Beatles' next recording, "in my estimation . . . the best record we ever made—'Penny Lane' and 'Strawberry Fields,'" reached No. 2 on the sales charts.

2. Sanjek 1988, 3:382–83. Sanjek adds that only two singles in 1963 topped one million in sales, and sales of the Beatles album "quickly surpassed the two previous major LP sellers, 'The First Family,' a spoof of the Kennedys, and the cast album of *My Fair Lady*."

3. See Lax and Smith 1989.

4. Gillet 1970, 312–13.

5. Douglas 1994, 96, 116, 119.

6. Martin 1979, 202.

7. Ibid., 214.

8. Ibid., 208.

9. Ibid., 209–10.

10. Hertsgaard 1995, 10; Gracyk 1996, 112.

11. Rockwell in *NGDAM* 1986, 1:74.

12. *Newsweek* for December 19, 1966.

13. Ibid., 646, 649–50.

14. Frith 1985, 165, 167.

15. Quoted ibid., 164.

16. Ibid., 168.

17. Walser 1998, 363–64. This analysis also dramatizes the male dominance that accompanied the rock revolution. The presence of female artists on the singles charts, the author writes, "declined from 32% in 1963 to only 6% in 1969."

39. *Trouble Girls, Minimalists, and The Gap: The 1960s to the 1980s*

1. Douglas 1994, 87–88.

2. Ibid., 89.

3. Cohen and Tebeau in *EUSTC* 1996, 114.

4. Frith 1981, 238–39.

5. Davis 1998, 42.

6. Ibid., 12–13.

7. Frith 1981, 241.
8. Ibid., 242.
9. O'Dair 1997, 544–46.
10. Willis in O'Dair 1997, xvi.
11. Tick in *NGDAM* 1986, 4:554.
12. Ibid., 555.
13. Edwards in Pendle 1991, 219–43, 248.
14. Gann 1997, 162–63.
15. Duckworth 1995, 172–73.
16. Gann 1997, 208–9, from a 1996 interview.
17. Gann 1997, 184.
18. Ibid., 384, 355.
19. Ibid., 385–86.
20. Gagne and Caras 1982, 341.
21. Gann 1997, 352.
22. Ibid., 353–55.
23. Duckworth 1995, 380, 383.
24. Ibid., 335, 330–31, 299–300.
25. Gagne and Caras 1982, 393–94, 156.
26. Duckworth 1995, 228.
27. Gann 1997, 325.
28. Duckworth 1995, 275, 269.
29. Strickland 1993, 174. The critic was Alfred Frankenstein.
30. Strickland 1991, 38.
31. Duckworth 1995, 296.
32. Ibid., 296–97.
33. Duckworth 1995, 297–98; Gann 1997, 198; Strickland 1991, 39–40.
34. Reich 1974, 9, 11.
35. Duckworth 1995, 298.
36. Quoted from Gann 1997, 199.
37. Ibid., 199.
38. Duckworth 1995, 335–36, 338.
39. Ibid., 335, 337, 339.
40. Glass 1987, 32–34.
41. Ibid., 83.
42. Quoted in Morgan 1991, 433.
43. Glass 1987, 47, 53.
44. Dizikes 1993, 541–42.
45. Gagne and Caras 1982, 343–44.
46. Gann 1997, 385.

40. *Black Music and American Identity*

1. Monson 1996, 103.
2. Caponi 1999, 12.
3. Michael Carvin in Monson 1996, 64–65.
4. Monson 1996, 69, 49.
5. Ibid., 67–68.
6. Keil and Feld 1994, 98, 24.
7. As summarized in Gennari 1993, 232–34.
8. Quoted ibid., 234–35.
9. *The Omni-Americans* (1970) and *Stomping the Blues* (1976).
10. Ellison 1964, 78.
11. Gennari 1993, 249.
12. Murray 1970, 58.
13. Williams 1956, 209.
14. Porter 1997, 317–18, 282.
15. Whitehead 1993, 18.
16. Marsalis 1984, passim.
17. Ibid.
18. Murray 1970, 166.
19. Quoted in Rose 1994, 21.
20. Ibid., 10–11.
21. Ibid., 59.

Bibliography

Abbreviated Entries

BPIM. 1975. *The Black Perspective in Music.*

ESC. 1989. *Encyclopedia of Southern Culture.* Ed. Charles Reagan Wilson and William Ferris. Chapel Hill: University of North Carolina Press.

EUSTC. 1996. *Encyclopedia of the United States in the Twentieth Century.* 4 vols. Ed. Stanley I. Kutler. New York: Charles Scribner.

Harvard. 1986. *The New Harvard Dictionary of Music.* Ed. Don Michael Randel. Cambridge, Mass.: Harvard University Press.

IED. 1998. *International Encyclopedia of Dance: A Project of Dance Perspectives Foundation.* 6 vols. Ed. Selma Jeanne Cohen. New York: Oxford University Press.

JAMS. Journal of the American Musicological Society.

NGDAM. 1986. *The New Grove Dictionary of American Music.* 4 vols. Ed. H. Wiley Hitchcock and Stanley Sadie. London and New York: Macmillan.

NGDJ. 1988. *The New Grove Dictionary of Jazz.* 2 vols. Ed. Barry Kernfeld. London and New York: Macmillan.

NGDMM. 1980. *The New Grove Dictionary of Music and Musicians.* 20 vols. Ed. Stanley Sadie. London and New York: Macmillan.

NGDO. 1992. *The New Grove Dictionary of Opera.* 4 vols. Ed. Stanley Sadie. London: Macmillan; New York: Grove's Dictionaries of Music.

Books, Articles, Liner Notes, Newspapers

Ahlquist, Karen. 1997. *Democracy at the Opera: Music, Theater, and Culture in New York City, 1815–60.* Urbana: University of Illinois Press.

Ahlstrom, Sydney E. 1972. *A Religious History of the American People.* New Haven: Yale University Press.

Allen, William Francis. [1867] 1951. *Slave Songs of the United States.* Reprint, New York: Peter Smith.

American Musical Directory. [1861] 1980. Reprint, New York: Da Capo.

American Poetry: The Nineteenth Century. 1993. 2 vols. Ed. John Hollander. New York: Library of America.

Anderson, Donna K. 1986. "Charles Tomlinson Griffes." 2:286f. in *NGDAM*.

Anderson, Jervis. 1981. *This Was Harlem: A Cultural Portrait, 1900–1950.* New York: Farrar, Straus, Giroux.

Austin, William W. 1966. *Music in the 20th Century, from Debussy through Stravinsky.* New York: Norton.

————. 1975. *"Susanna," "Jeanie," and "The Old Folks at Home": The Songs of Stephen C. Foster from His Time to Ours.* New York: Macmillan.

Avakian, George. 1959. Program notes for sound recording: John Cage, *The 25-Year Retrospective Concert of the Music of John Cage.* New York: distributed by George Avakian.

Badger, Reid. 1995. *A Life in Ragtime: A Biography of James Reese Europe.* New York: Oxford University Press.

Bailyn, Bernard. 1986a. *The Peopling of British North America: An Introduction.* New York: Knopf.

————. Bernard. 1986b. *Voyagers to the West: A Passage in the Peopling of North America on the Eve of the Revolution.* With the assistance of Barbara DeWolfe. New York: Knopf.

Baker, Theodore. 1978. *Baker's Biographical Dictionary of Musicians.* 6th ed. Rev. Nicolas Slonimsky. New York: Schirmer.

Barish, Jonas A. 1981. *The Antitheatrical Prejudice.* Berkeley and Los Angeles: University of California Press.

Barrett, Mary Ellin. 1994. *Irving Berlin: A Daughter's Memoir.* New York: Simon and Schuster.

Basie, Count. 1985. *Good Morning Blues: The Autobiography of Count Basie.* As told to Albert Murray. New York: Random House.

The Beatles Complete Scores. 1989. Milwaukee: Hal Leonard.

Bechet, Sidney. [1960] 1978. *Treat It Gentle.* Reprint, New York: Da Capo.

Behague, Gerard H. 1986. "Hispanic-American Music." 2:395ff. in *NGDAM*.

Bellah, Robert N., et al. 1985. *Habits of the Heart: Individualism and Commitment in American Life.* Berkeley and Los Angeles: University of California Press.

Berger, Arthur. 1953. *Aaron Copland.* New York: Oxford University Press.

Bergreen, Laurence. 1990. *As Thousands Cheer: The Life of Irving Berlin.* New York: Viking.

Berkhofer, Robert F. 1978. *The White Man's Indian: Images of the American Indian from Columbus to the Present.* New York: Knopf.

Berlin, Edward. 1990. "On the Trail of a Guest of Honor." Pp. 51ff. in Crawford et al., eds., 1990.

————. Berlin, Edward A. 1994. *King of Ragtime: Scott Joplin and His Era.* New York: Oxford University Press.

Bernstein, Leonard. 1959. *The Joy of Music.* New York: Simon and Schuster.

Bernstein, Michael A. 1996. "Depressions and Recessions: The Business Cycle." 3:1183ff in *EUSTC*.

Bierley, Paul E. 1973. *John Philip Sousa, American Phenomenon.* Englewood Cliffs, N.J.: Prentice Hall.

———. 1984. *The Works of John Philip Sousa.* Columbus, Ohio: Integrity Press.

Billings, William. 1794. *The Continental Harmony.* Boston: Thomas and Andrews.

———. 1977–90. *The Complete Works of William Billings.* 4 vols. Ed. Karl Kroeger and Hans Nathan. Boston: The American Musicological Society and The Colonial Society of Massachusetts.

Birge, Edward Bailey. [1928] 1966. *History of Public School Music in the United States.* New and augmented ed. Boston: Oliver Ditson. Reprint, Washington, D.C.: Music Educators National Conference.

Block, Adrienne Fried. 1990. "Dvořák, Beach, and American Music" Pp. 256ff. in Crawford et al., eds. 1990.

———. 1993. "The Child Is Mother to the Woman." Pp. 107ff. in Cook and Tsou, eds. 1993.

———, ed. 1994. *Quartet for Strings (in One Movement), Opus 89,* by Mrs. H. H. A. Beach. Recent Researches in American Music, 23. Music of the United States of America, 3. Madison, Wis.: A-R Editions.

Block, Geoffrey. 1997. *Enchanted Evenings: The Broadway Musical from "Show Boat" to Sondheim.* New York: Oxford University Press.

Board of Music Trade of the United States of America. [1871] 1973. *Complete Catalogue of Sheet Music and Musical Works, 1870.* Introduction by Dena J. Epstein. Reprint, New York: Da Capo.

Bohlman, Philip V., et al. "European-American Music." 2:64ff. in *NGDAM*.

Bomberger, E. Douglas. 1991. *The German Musical Training of American Students, 1850–1900.* Ph.D. diss., University of Maryland.

Booth, Mark W. 1981. *The Experience of Songs.* New Haven: Yale University Press.

Bordman, Gerald. 1978. *American Musical Theatre: A Chronicle.* New York: Oxford University Press.

———. 1980. *Jerome Kern: His Life and Music.* New York: Oxford University Press.

———. 1981. *American Operetta: From "H.M.S. Pinafore" to "Sweeney Todd."* New York: Oxford University Press.

Boston Academy. 1834. Boston Academy of Music, *Annual Report* II.

Boston, New England Courant, 1724.

Boston News-Letter, 1713.

Boston Weekly News-Letter, 1714.

Bowman, Robert 1989. "James Brown." Pp. 1046 in *ESC*.

Boyer, Horace Clarence. 1995. *How Sweet the Sound: The Golden Age of Gospel.* Washington, D.C.: Elliott and Clark.

Bradbury, Malcolm, and Richard Ruland. 1991. *From Puritanism to Postmodernism: A History of American Literature.* New York: Penguin.

Braithwaite, J. Roland. 1992. "Originality in the 1801 Hymnals of Richard Allen." Pp. 71ff. in Wright and Floyd, eds., 1992.

Brancaleone, Francis. 1989. "Edward MacDowell and Indian Motives." *American Music* 7 (winter 1989): 359.

A Brief Discourse Concerning Regular Singing. 1725. Boston: B. Green, Jr.

Britton, Allen Perdue, and Irving Lowens, completed by Richard Crawford. 1990. *American Sacred Music Imprints, 1698–1810: A Bibliography.* Introduction by Crawford. Worcester, Mass.: American Antiquarian Society.

Bronson, Bertrand Harris, ed. 1959–72. *The Traditional Tunes of the Child Ballads, with their Texts.* 4 vols. Princeton, N.J.: Princeton University Press.

Brown, James, with Bruce Tucker. 1986. *James Brown, the Godfather of Soul.* New York: Macmillan.

Brown, Richard D. 1974. "The Emergence of Urban Society in Rural Massachusetts." *Journal of American History* 41 (June): 29ff.

Browner, Tara C. 1995. *Transposing Cultures: The Appropriation of Native North American Musics, 1890–1990.* Ph.D. diss., University of Michigan.

———. 1999. "American Indian Music and Dance." In *The 1999 Grolier Multimedia Encyclopedia.*

Broyles, Michael. 1992. *Music of the Highest Class: Elitism and Populism in Antebellum Boston.* New Haven: Yale University Press.

Bruce, Dickson D. 1974. *And They All Sang Hallelujah: Plain-Folk Camp-Meeting Religion, 1800–1845.* Knoxville: University of Tennessee Press.

Bruchey, Stuart. 1990. *Enterprise: The Dynamic Economy of a Free People.* Cambridge: Harvard University Press.

Buechner, Alan Clark. 1960. *Yankee Singing Schools and the Golden Age of Choral Music in New England, 1760–1800.* Ed.D. diss., Harvard Graduate School of Education.

Burkholder, J. Peter. 1995. *All Made of Tunes: Charles Ives and the Uses of Musical Borrowing.* New Haven: Yale University Press.

Bushell, Garvin, as told to Mark Tucker. 1988. *Jazz from the Beginning.* Ann Arbor: University of Michigan Press.

Bushman, Richard L. 1992. *The Refinement of America: Persons, Houses, Cities.* New York: Knopf.

Cage, John. 1961. *Silence: Lectures and Writings.* Middletown, Conn.: Wesleyan University Press.

Camus, Raoul. 1986. "Bands." 1:127ff. in *NGDAM.*

Camus, Raoul François. 1969. *The Military Band in the United States prior to 1834.* Ph.D. diss., New York University.

———. 1976. *Military Music of the American Revolution.* Chapel Hill: University of North Carolina Press.

Cantwell, Robert. 1984. *Bluegrass Breakdown: The Making of the Old Southern Sound.* Urbana: University of Illinois Press.

————. 1996. *When We Were Good: The Folk Revival.* Cambridge: Harvard University Press.

Capen, Samuel. 1805. *Norfolk Harmony.* Boston: Manning and Loring.

Caponi, Gena Dagel, ed. 1999. *Signifyin(g), Sanctifyin', and Slam Dunking: A Reader in African American Expressive Culture.* Amherst: University of Massachusetts Press.

Carmichael, Hoagy, with Stephen Longstreet. [1965] 1976. *Sometimes I Wonder: The Story of Hoagy Carmichael.* Reprint, New York: Da Capo.

Carse, Adam von Ahn. 1951. *The Life of Jullien, Adventurer, Showman-Conductor, and Establisher of the Promenade Concerts in England.* Cambridge, Eng.: Heffer.

Carter, Elliott. 1977. *The Writings of Elliott Carter: An American Composer Looks at Modern Music.* Compiled, edited, and annotated by Else Stone and Kurt Stone. Bloomington: Indiana University Press.

Charles, Ray, and David Ritz. 1978. *Brother Ray: Ray Charles' Own Story.* New York: Dial Press Paperback, New York: Warner Books.

Charters, Samuel B. [1959] 1975. *The Country Blues.* Reprint, with a new introduction by the author. New York: Da Capo.

Charters, Samuel B., and Leonard Kunstadt. [1962] 1981. *Jazz: A History of the New York Scene.* Reprint, New York: Da Capo.

Chase, Gilbert. 1955. *America's Music, from the Pilgrims to the Present.* New York: McGraw-Hill.

————. Gilbert, 1987. *America's Music, from the Pilgrims to the Present.* 3rd. ed. rev. Urbana: University of Illinois Press.

————, ed. 1966. *The American Composer Speaks: A Historical Anthology, 1770–1965.* Baton Rouge: Louisiana State University Press.

Chernoff, John Miller. 1979. *African Rhythm and African Sensibility: Aesthetics and Social Action in African Musical Idioms.* Chicago: University of Chicago Press.

Child, Francis James, ed. [1882–98] 1965. *English and Scottish Popular Ballads.* 5 vols. Reprint, New York: Dover.

Citron, Stephen. 1995. *The Wordsmiths: Oscar Hammerstein 2nd and Alan Jay Lerner.* New York: Oxford University Press.

Clarke, Donald. 1995. *The Rise and Fall of Popular Music.* New York: St. Martin's Press.

Cobb, Buell E. 1978. *The Sacred Harp: A Tradition and Its Music.* Athens: University of Georgia Press.

Cockrell, Dale. 1986. "Beatles." 1:171f. in *NGDAM.*

————, ed. 1989. *Excelsior: Journals of the Hutchinson Family Singers, 1842–1846.* Stuyvesant, N.Y.: Pendragon Press.

Cohen, Lizabeth, and Mark Tebeau. 1996. "Gender Issues." 1:101ff. in *EUSTC.*

Cohen, Norm. 1991. *Folk Song America: A Revival.* Booklet with Smithsonian Collection of Recordings. RD 046–1, 2, 3, 4. Washington, D.C.: Smithsonian Institution Press.

Collier, James Lincoln. 1989. *Benny Goodman and the Swing Era.* New York: Oxford University Press.

Cook, Susan C., and Judy S. Tsou, eds. 1993. *Cecilia Reclaimed: Exploring Gender and Music.* Urbana: University of Illinois Press.

Copland, Aaron. [1941] 1968. *The New Music, 1900–1960.* Revised and enlarged edition. New York: Norton.

Copland, Aaron, and Vivian Perlis. 1984. *Copland: 1900 through 1942.* New York: St. Martin's Press.

Cotton, John. 1647. *Singing of Psalmes a Gospel-Ordinance.* London: M. S. for Hannah Allen.

Cowell, Henry, and Sidney Cowell. 1955. *Charles Ives and His Music.* New York: Oxford University Press.

Cox, John Harrington, ed. [1925] 1967. *Folk-Songs of the South.* Reprint, New York: Dover.

Crawford, David E. 1967. "The Jesuit Relations and Allied Documents." *Ethnomusicology* 11:199ff.

Crawford, Dorothy Lamb. 1995. *Evenings on and off the Roof: Pioneering Concerts in Los Angeles, 1939–1971.* Berkeley and Los Angeles: University of California Press.

Crawford, Richard. 1968. *Andrew Law: American Psalmodist.* Evanston, Ill.: Northwestern University Press.

———. 1977. *The Civil War Song-book.* New York: Dover.

———. 1986."George Gershwin." 2:199ff. in *NGDAM.*

———. 1992. "Notes on Jazz Standards by Black Authors and Composers." Pp. 245ff. in Wright and Floyd, eds., 1992.

———. 1992a. "Porgy and Bess." 3:1061–63 in *NGDO.*

———. 1993. *The American Musical Landscape.* Berkeley and Los Angeles: University of California Press.

———. 1996. "Music." 4:1609ff. in *EUSTC.*

———, ed. 1984. *The Core Repertory of Early American Psalmody.* Recent Researches in American Music, 11–12. Madison, Wis.: A-R Editions.

Crawford, Richard, R. Allen Lott, and Carol J. Oja, eds. 1990. *A Celebration of American Music: Words and Music in Honor of H. Wiley Hitchcock.* Ann Arbor: University of Michigan Press.

Cripe, Helen. 1974. *Thomas Jefferson and Music.* Charlottesville: University Press of Virginia.

Croce, Arlene. 1972. *The Fred Astaire and Ginger Rogers Book.* New York: Galahad.

Cross, Whitney R. 1950. *The Burned-Over District: The Social and Intellectual History of Enthusiastic Religion in Western New York, 1800–1850.* Ithaca: Cornell University Press.

Crouch, Stanley. 1995. *The All-American Skin Game; or, The Decoy of Race: The Long and Short of It. 1990–1994.* New York: Pantheon.

Curtis, Natalie. 1907. *The Indian's Book.* New York: Harper.

Dahlhaus, Carl. 1989. *Nineteenth-Century Music.* Berkeley and Los Angeles: University of California Press.

Dallek, Robert. 1996. Introduction. 1:247ff. in *EUSTC.*

Dance, Stanley. 1970. *The World of Duke Ellington.* New York: Scribner.

———. 1974. *The World of Swing.* New York: Scribner.

Dapogny, James, ed. 1982. *Ferdinand "Jelly Roll" Morton: The Collected Piano Music.* Washington, D.C.: Smithsonian Institution Press.

Darlington, Marwood. 1956. *Irish Orpheus: The Life of Patrick S. Gilmore, Bandmaster Extraordinary.* Philadelphia: Olivier-Maney-Klein.

Davies, Hugh. 1974. "Electronic Music: History and Development." Pp. 212ff. in *Dictionary of Contemporary Music.* Ed. John Vinton. New York: Dutton.

Davis, Angela Y. 1998. *Blues Legacies and Black Feminism: Gertrude "Ma" Rainey, Bessie Smith, and Billie Holiday.* New York: Pantheon.

Davisson, Annanias. [1816] 1976. *Kentucky Harmony.* Reprint, Minneapolis: Augsburg.

Deffaa, Chip. 1990. *Voices of the Jazz Age: Profiles of Eight Vintage Jazzmen.* Urbana: University of Illinois Press.

Dennison, Sam. 1982. *Scandalize My Name: Black Imagery in American Popular Music.* New York: Garland.

Dickstein, Morris. [1977] 1989. *Gates of Eden: American Culture in the Sixties.* Reprint, New York: Penguin.

Diggins, John P. 1988. *The Proud Decades: America in War and in Peace, 1941–1960.* New York: Norton.

DiMaggio, Paul. 1991. "Cultural Entrepreneurship in Nineteenth-Century Boston." Pp. 374ff. in Mukerji and Schudson, eds., 1991.

Dizikes, John. 1993. *Opera in America: A Cultural History.* New Haven: Yale University Press.

Dodge, Roger Pryor. 1995. *Hot Jazz and Jazz Dance: Collected Writings, 1929–1964.* New York: Oxford University Press.

Douglas, Ann. 1995. *Terrible Honesty: Mongrel Manhattan in the 1920s.* New York: Farrar, Straus, Giroux.

Douglas, Susan. 1994. *Where the Girls Are: Growing Up Female with the Mass Media.* New York: Times Books.

Douglass, Frederick. 1994. *Autobiographies.* New York: Library of America.

Doyle, John Godfrey. 1983. *Louis Moreau Gottschalk, 1829–1869: A Bibliographical Study and Catalog of Works.* Detroit: Information Coordinators.

Duckworth, William. 1995. *Talking Music: Conversations with John Cage, Philip Glass, Laurie Anderson, and Five Generations of American Experimental Composers.* New York: Schirmer.

Dunaway, David King. 1981. *How Can I Keep from Singing: Pete Seeger.* New York: McGraw-Hill.

Dwight's Journal of Music, 1853. Boston.

Dyson, Michael Eric. 1993. *Reflecting Black: African-American Cultural Criticism.* Minneapolis: University of Minnesota Press.

Easton, Carol. 1996. *No Intermissions: The Life of Agnes de Mille.* Boston: Little, Brown.

Echols, Paul C. 1986. "Hymnody." 2:446ff. in *NGDAM.*

Edwards, J. Michele, with contributions by Leslie Lassetter. 1991. "North America since 1920." Pp. 211ff. in Pendle, ed., 1991.

Eliason, Robert E. 1972. *Keyed Bugles in the United States.* Washington, D.C.: Smithsonian Institution Press.

Ellington, Duke. 1973. *Music Is My Mistress.* Garden City, N.Y.: Doubleday.

Ellington, Mercer, with Stanley Dance. 1978. *Duke Ellington in Person: An Intimate Memoir.* Boston: Houghton Mifflin.

Ellinwood, Leonard W. [1953] 1970. *The History of American Church Music.* Reprint, New York: Da Capo.

Ellison, Ralph. 1964. *Shadow and Act.* New York: Random House.

———. 1986. *Going to the Territory.* New York: Random House.

Elson, Louis Charles. 1904. *The History of American Music.* New York: Macmillan.

Emerson, Ralph Waldo. 1983. *Essays and Lectures.* New York: Library of America.

Emmons, Nathanael. 1806. *A Discourse . . . at a Publick Meeting of a Number of Singers.* Providence, R.I.: Hawkins.

Engel, Lehman. 1967. *The American Musical Theater: A Consideration.* CBS Legacy Collection Book. New York: Macmillan.

———. 1974. *This Bright Day: An Autobiography.* New York: Macmillan.

Epstein, Dena J. 1977. *Sinful Tunes and Spirituals: Black Folk Music to the Civil War.* Urbana: University of Illinois Press.

———. 1990. "Theordore F. Seward and the Fisk Jubilee Singers." Pp. 36ff. in Crawford et al., eds., 1990.

Erenberg, Lewis A. 1981. *Steppin' Out: New York Nightlife and the Transformation of American Culture, 1890–1930.* Westport, Conn.: Greenwood Press.

Ethnic Recordings in America: A Neglected Heritage. 1982. Washington, D.C.: American Folklife Center, Library of Congress.

Evans, David. 1989. "Blues." Pp. 995ff. in *ESC.*

Farwell, Arthur. 1995. *"Wanderjahre of a Revolutionist" and Other Essays on American Music.* Ed. Thomas Stoner. Rochester, N.Y.: University of Rochester Press.

Farwell, Arthur, and W. Dermot Darby. 1915. *Music in America.* Vol. 4 in *The Art of Music: A Comprehensive Library of Information for Music Lovers and Musicians.* Ed. Daniel Gregory Mason. New York: The National Society of Music.

Feder, Stuart. 1992. *Charles Ives, "My Father's Song": A Psychoanalytic Biography.* New Haven: Yale University Press.

Ferguson, Otis. 1982. *The Otis Ferguson Reader.* Ed. Dorothy Chamberlain and Robert Wilson. *December Magazine,* vol. 24, no. 1/2. Highland Park, Ill.: December Press.

Finson, Jon W. 1994. *The Voices That Are Gone: Themes in Nineteenth-Century American Popular Song.* New York: Oxford University Press.

————, ed. 1997. *Collected Songs: Edward Harrigan and David Braham.* Recent Researches in American Music, 27. Music of the United States of America, 7. Madison, Wis.: A-R Editions.

Fiske, Roger. 1973. *English Theatre Music in the Eighteenth Century.* London and New York: Oxford University Press.

Floyd, Samuel A., Jr. 1977. "Alton Augustus Adams." Pp. 173ff. in *BPIM.*

————. 1991. "Ring Shout! Black Music, Black Literary Theory, and Black Historical Studies." *Black Music Research Journal* 11/2 (Fall):267ff.

————. 1995. *The Power of Black Music: Interpreting Its History from Africa to the United States.* New York: Oxford University Press.

————, ed. 1990. *Black Music in the Harlem Renaissance: A Collection of Essays.* Westport, Conn.: Greenwood Press.

Foner, Philip S. 1975. *American Labor Songs of the Nineteenth Century.* Urbana: University of Illinois Press.

Foote, Arthur. [1946] 1979. *Arthur Foote, 1853–1937: An Autobiography.* Reprint, New York: Da Capo.

Foster, Stephen Collins. 1990. *The Music of Stephen C. Foster: A Critical Edition.* Prepared by Steven Saunders and Deane L. Root. 2 vols. Washington, D.C.: Smithsonian Institution Press.

Fredrickson, George M. 1971. *The Black Image in the White Mind: The Debate on Afro-American Character and Destiny, 1817–1914.* New York: Harper and Row.

Freeman, Bud. 1989. *Crazeology: The Autobiography of a Chicago Jazzman.* Urbana: University of Illinois Press.

Friedwald, Will. 1995. *Sinatra! The Song Is You: A Singer's Art.* New York: Scribner.

Frith, Simon. 1981. *Sound Effects: Youth, Leisure, and the Politics of Rock 'n' Roll.* New York: Pantheon.

————. 1985. "The Magic That Can Set You Free: The Ideology of Folk and the Myth of the Rock Community." *Popular Music* 1:159ff.

Fuld, James J. 1971. *The Book of World-Famous Music: Classical, Popular, and Folk.* Rev. ed. New York: Crown.

Furia, Philip. 1990. *The Poets of Tin Pan Alley: A History of America's Great Lyricists.* New York: Oxford University Press.

————. 1996. *Ira Gershwin: The Art of the Lyricist.* New York: Oxford University Press.

————. 1997. "Something to Sing About: America's Great Lyricists." *American Scholar* (summer), pp. 379ff.

Gagne, Cole, and Tracy Caras. 1982. *Soundpieces: Interviews with American Composers.* Metuchen, N.J.: Scarecrow Press.

Gann, Kyle. 1997. *American Music in the Twentieth Century.* New York: Schirmer.

Gates, Henry Louis. 1996. "King of Cats." *The New Yorker,* April 8, pp. 70ff.

Gay, John. [1922] 1973. *The Beggar's Opera.* Fascimile reprint of 1729 edition. London: Daniel O'Connor. Reprint, New York: Dover.

Gennari, John Remo. 1993. *The Politics of Culture and Identity in American Jazz Criticism.* Ph.D. diss., University of Pennsylvania.

George, Nelson. 1988. *The Death of Rhythm & Blues.* New York: Pantheon.

———. 1985. *Where Did Our Love Go?*

Giddins, Gary. 1988. *Satchmo.* New York: Doubleday.

Gilbert, Steven E. 1995. *The Music of Gershwin.* New Haven: Yale University Press.

Gilfoyle, Timothy J. 1992. *City of Eros: New York City, Prostitution, and the Commercialization of Sex, 1790–1920.* New York: Norton.

Gillett, Charlie. 1970. *The Sound of the City: The Rise of Rock and Roll.* New York: Outerbridge and Dienstfrey.

Gilman, Lawrence. [1908] 1969. *Edward MacDowell: A Study.* Reprint, New York: Da Capo.

Gilmore, Mikal, and Robert Witmer. 1986. "Motown." 3:283 in *NGDAM.*

Gioia, Dana. 1993. "Longfellow in the Aftermath of Modernism." Pp. 64ff. in Parini, ed., 1993.

Glass, Philip. 1987. *Music by Philip Glass.* New York: Harper and Row.•

Gold, Robert S. 1964. *A Jazz Lexicon.* New York: Knopf.

Goldfield, David R. 1996. "The South." 1:61ff. in *EUSTC.*

Goldman, Richard Franko. 1961. *The Wind Band, Its Literature and Technique.* Boston: Allyn and Bacon.

Gottschalk, Louis Moreau. 1964. *Notes of a Pianist.* Ed. Jeanne Behrend. New York: Knopf.

———. 1973. *Selected Piano Works.* Ed. Richard Jackson. New York: Dover.

Gould, Nathaniel D. [1853] 1972. *Church Music in America, Comprising Its History and Its Peculiarities at Different Periods, with Cursory Remarks on Its Legitimate Use and Its Abuse.* Reprint, New York: AMS Press.

Gracyk, Theodore. 1996. *Rhythm and Noise: An Aesthetics of Rock.* Durham, N.C.: Duke University Press.

Graziano, John. 1990. "Jullien and His Music for the Million." Pp. 192ff. in Crawford et al., eds., 1990.

Green, Stanley. [1963] n.d. *The Rodgers and Hammerstein Story.* Reprint, New York: Da Capo.

Greene, Victor. 1992. *A Passion for Polka: Old-Time Ethnic Music in America.* Berkeley and Los Angeles: University of California Press.

Griffiths, Paul. 1995. *Modern Music and After.* New York: Oxford University Press.

Grimsted, David. 1968. *Melodrama Unveiled: American Theater and Culture, 1800–1830.* Chicago: University of Chicago Press.

Guralnick, Peter. [1971] 1981. *Feel Like Going Home: Portraits in Blues & Rock 'n' Roll.* New York: Outerbridge and Dienstfrey. Paperback, ed., New York: Vintage.

———. 1986. *Sweet Soul Music: Rhythm and Blues and the Southern Dream of Freedom.* New York: Harper and Row.

———. 1994. *Last Train to Memphis: The Rise of Elvis Presley.* Boston: Little, Brown.

Gushee, Lawrence. 1985. "A Preliminary Chronology of the Early Career of Ford 'Jelly Roll' Morton." *American Music* 3 (1985): 389ff.

———. 1988. "New Orleans." 2:168 in *NGDJ*.

———. 1994. "The Nineteenth-Century Origins of Jazz." *Black Music Research Journal* 14/1 (spring): 1ff.

Hajdu, David. 1996. *Lush Life: A Biography of Billy Strayhorn*. New York: Farrar, Straus, Giroux.

Halberstam, David. 1993. *The Fifties*. New York: Villard.

Hamm, Charles. 1979. *Yesterdays: Popular Song in America*. New York: Norton.

———. 1983. *Music in the New World*. New York: Norton.

———. 1986. "John Cage." 1:334ff in *NGDAM*.

———. 1986. "Popular Music." 3:569ff in *NGDAM*.

———. ed. 1994. *Early Songs by Irving Berlin*. Music of the United States of America, 2. Madison, Wis.: A-R Editions.

Hammond, Paul Garnett. 1974. "Music in Urban Revivalism in the Northern United States, 1800–1835." DMA diss., Southern Baptist Theological Seminary.

Handy, W. C. 1941. *Father of the Blues: An Autobiography*. New York: Macmillan.

Harmetz, Aljean. 1977. *The Making of "The Wizard of Oz": Movie Magic and Studio Power in the Prime of MGM, and the Miracle of Production #1060*. New York: Knopf.

Harris, Michael W. 1992a. *The Rise of Gospel Blues: The Music of Thomas Andrew Dorsey in the Urban Church*. New York: Oxford University Press.

———. 1992b. "Conflict and Resolution in the Life of Thomas Andrew Dorsey." Pp. 165ff. in Reagon, ed., 1992.

Hart, Philip. 1973. *Orpheus in the New World: The Symphony Orchestra as an American Cultural Institution*. New York: Norton.

Hartnoll, Phyllis, ed. 1967. *The Oxford Companion to the Theatre*. 3rd ed. London and New York: Oxford University Press.

Hastings, Thomas. 1853. *Dissertation on Musical Taste*. New York: Mason.

Hatch, Nathan O. 1989. *The Democratization of American Christianity*. New Haven: Yale University Press.

Hazen, Margaret Hindle, and Robert M. Hazen. 1987. *The Music Men: An Illustrated History of Brass Bands in America, 1800–1920*. Washington, D.C.: Smithsonian Institution Press.

Heilbut, Anthony. 1985. *The Gospel Sound: Good News and Bad Times*. Updated and revised. New York: Limelight.

Heinrich, Anthony Philip. [1820] 1972. *The Dawning of Music in Kentucky; or, The Pleasures of Harmony in the Solitudes of Nature*. Reprint, New York: Da Capo.

Hemphill, Paul. 1970. *The Nashville Sound: Bright Lights and Country Music*. New York: Simon and Schuster.

Hertsgaard, Mark. 1995. *A Day in the Life: The Music and Artistry of the Beatles*. New York: Delacorte Press.

Hijuelos, Oscar. 1989. *The Mambo Kings Play Songs of Love.* New York: Farrar, Straus, Giroux.

Hinson, Maurice, and H. Wiley Hitchcock. "Piano Music." 3:562ff. in *NGDAM.*

Hitchcock, H. Wiley. 1988. *Music in the United States: A Historical Introduction.* 3rd ed. Englewood Cliffs, N.J.: Prentice-Hall.

———. 1993. "Reviews—Charles Ives: 'My Father's Song,' A Psychoanalytic Biography by Stuart Feder," *JAMS* 46/2 (summer): 319.

Hitchcock, H. Wiley, and Vivian Perlis, eds. 1977. *An Ives Celebration: Papers and Panels of the Charles Ives Centennial Festival-Conference.* Urbana: University of Illinois Press.

Homespun America: Music for Brass Bands, Social Orchestra and Choral Groups from the Mid-19th Century. 1993. Eastman Wind Ensemble. Notes by Donald Hunsberger. Vox Box CDX 5088.

Hood, George. 1846. *A History of Music in New England: With Biographical Sketches of Reformers and Psalmists.* Boston: Wilkins, Carter.

Hoover, Cynthia Adams. 1985. "Epilogue to Secular Music in Early Massachusetts." Pp. 715ff. in Lambert, ed., 1980–85.

———. "Piano (forte)." 3:559ff. in *NGDAM.*

Hoover, Kathleen O'Donnell, and John Cage. 1959. *Virgil Thomson: His Life and Music.* New York: T. Yoseloff.

Hopkinson, Francis. 1788. *Seven Songs for the Harpsichord or Forte Piano.* Philadelphia: T. Dobson.

Horowitz, Joseph. 1987. *Understanding Toscanini: How He Became an American Culture-God and Helped Create a New Audience for Old Music.* New York: Knopf.

———. 1994. *Wagner Nights: An American History.* Berkeley and Los Angeles: University of California Press.

Horstman, Dorothy. 1975. *Sing Your Heart Out, Country Boy.* New York: Dutton.

Housewright, Wiley L. 1991. *A History of Music and Dance in Florida. 1565–1865.* Tuscaloosa: University of Alabama Press.

Howard, John Tasker. 1931. *Our American Music: Three Hundred Years of It.* New York: Crowell.

———. 1934. *Stephen Foster: America's Troubadour.* New York: Crowell.

Hubbard, William Lines, ed. 1908. *History of American Music.* Vol. 4 in *The American History and Encyclopedia of Music.* Toledo: Irving Squire.

Hughes, Robert. 1997. *American Visions: The Epic History of Art in America.* New York: Knopf.

Ingalls, Jeremiah. [1805] 1981. *The Christian Harmony: Or, Songster's Companion.* Reprint, New York: Da Capo.

Isaac, Rhys. 1982. *The Transformation of Virginia, 1740–1790.* Chapel Hill: University of North Carolina Press.

Ives, Charles. 1962. *Essays Before a Sonata, and Other Writings.* Ed. Howard Boatwright. New York: Norton.

———. 1972. *Memos*. Ed. John Kirkpatrick. New York: Norton.

Jablonski, Edward. 1987. *Gershwin*. New York: Doubleday.

———. 1992. *Gershwin Remembered*. Portland, Ore: Amadeus Press.

———. 1996. *Harold Arlen: Rhythm, Rainbows, and Blues*. Boston: Northeastern University Press.

Jackson, George Pullen. [1933] 1965. *White Spirituals in the Southern Uplands: The Story of the Fasola Folk, Their Songs, Singings, and "Buckwheat Notes."* Reprint, New York: Dover.

———. [1937] 1964. *Spiritual Folk-Songs of Early America: Two Hundred and Fifty Tunes and Texts, with an Introduction and Notes*. Reprint, New York: Dover.

Jackson, Richard. 1976. *Popular Songs of Nineteenth-Century America: Complete Original Sheet Music for 64 Songs*. New York: Dover.

Jairazbhoy, Nazir A., et al. 1986. "Asian-American Music." 1:79ff. in *NGDAM*.

Jasen, David A. 1988. *Tin Pan Alley . . . The Golden Age of American Popular Music from 1886 to 1956*. New York: Fine.

Jefferson, Thomas. 1984. *Writings*. New York: Library of America.

Jenkins, Walter S. 1994. *The Remarkable Mrs. Beach, American Composer*. Warren, Mich.: Harmonie Park Press.

Johnson, H. Earle. 1953. "The Germania Musical Society." *Musical Quarterly* 39 (1953): 75ff.

———. [1965] 1981. *Hallelujah, Amen! The Story of the Handel and Haydn Society of Boston*. Reprint, New York: Da Capo.

Johnson, James H. 1995. *Listening in Paris: A Cultural History*. Berkeley and Los Angeles: University of California Press. 1995.

Johnson, James Weldon. 1933. *Along This Way: The Autobiography of James Weldon Johnson*. New York: Viking.

Johnson, James Weldon, and J. Rosamond Johnson. [1925–26] 1969. *The Books of American Negro Spirituals: Including the Book of American Negro Spirituals and the Second Book of Negro Spirituals*. Reprint, New York: Da Capo.

Johnson, Steven. 1998. " 'Worlds of Ideas': The Music of Henry Cowell." Pp. 15ff. in Nicholls, ed., 1988.

Jones, F. O., ed. [1886] 1971. *A Handbook of American Music and Musicians: Containing Biographies of American Musicians and Histories of the Principal Musical Institutions, Firms, and Societies*. Reprint, New York: Da Capo.

Jones, Leroy, a.k.a. Imamu Amiri Baraka. 1963. *Blues People: Negro Music in White America*. New York: Morrow.

Joplin, Scott. 1971. *The Collected Works of Scott Joplin*. New York: The New York Public Library.

Jordan, Winthrop D. 1968. *White over Black: American Attitudes toward the Negro, 1550–1812*. Chapel Hill: University of North Carolina Press.

Kasson, John F. 1990. *Rudeness and Civility: Manners in Nineteenth-Century Urban America*. New York: Hill and Wang.

Kearns, William Kay. 1965. *Horatio Parker (1863–1913): A Study of His Life and Music.* Ph.D. diss., University of Illinois.

Keil, Charles, and Steven Feld. 1994. *Music Grooves: Essays and Dialogues.* Chicago: University of Chicago Press.

Keil, Charles, and Angeliki Keil. 1992. *Polka Happiness.* Philadelphia: Temple University Press.

Kennedy, Rick. 1994. *Jelly Roll, Bix, and Hoagy: Gennett Studios and the Birth of Recorded Jazz.* Bloomington: Indiana University Press.

Kenney, William Howland. 1993. *Chicago Jazz: A Cultural History, 1904–1930.* New York: Oxford University Press.

Klein, Joe. 1980. *Woody Guthrie: A Life.* New York: Knopf.

Kmen, Henry A. 1966. *Music in New Orleans: The Formative Years, 1791–1841.* Baton Rouge: Louisiana State University Press.

Knickerbocker Magazine. 1845. New York. In *BPIM* 1975, pp. 83ff.

Kodish, Debora G. 1986. *Good Friends and Bad Enemies: Robert Winslow Gordon and the Study of American Folksong.* Urbana: University of Illinois Press.

Koegel, John. 1994. *Mexican-American Music in Nineteenth-Century Southern California: The Lummis Wax Cylinder Collection of the Southeast Museum, Los Angeles.* Ph.D. diss., Claremont Graduate School.

———. 1997. "'The Indian Chief' and 'Mortality': An Eighteenth-Century British Popular Song Transformed into a Nineteenth-Century American Shape-Note Hymn." Pp. 437ff. in *Music in Performance and Society: Essays in Honor of Roland Jackson.* Ed. Malcolm Cole and John Koegel. Warren, Mich.: Harmonie Park Press.

Kostelanetz, Richard. 1987. *Conversing with Cage.* New York: Limelight Editions.

Kreitner, Kenneth. 1990. *Discoursing Sweet Music: Town Bands and Community Life in Turn-of-the-Century Pennsylvania.* Urbana: University of Illinois Press.

Kroeger, Karl. 1986. "Moravian Church, Music of the." 3:271ff. in *NGDAM.*

Kronenberger, Louis, ed. 1971. *Atlantic Brief Lives: A Biographical Companion to the Arts.* Boston: Little, Brown.

Lambert, Barbara. 1985. Appendix C. Pp. 935ff. in Lambert, ed., 1980–85.

———. 1985a. "Social Music, Musicians, and Their Musical Instruments in and around Colonial Boston." Pp. 409ff. in Lambert, ed., 1980–85.

———, ed. 1980–85. *Music in Colonial Massachusetts, 1630–1820: A Conference Held by the Colonial Society of Massachusetts, May 17 and 18, 1973.* 2 vols. Publications of the Colonial Society of Massachusetts, 53–54. Boston: Colonial Society of Massachusetts. Charlottesville: University Press of Virginia.

Law, Andrew. 1794. *The Art of Singing: Part 1. The Musical Primer.* Cheshire, Conn.: William Law.

———. 1800. *The Art of Singing.* 3rd ed. Cheshire, Conn.: Samuel Andrews.

———. 1821. *Essays on Music.* Hartford: Bowles and Francis.

Lawrence, Vera Brodsky. 1988. *Resonances, 1836–1850.* Vol. 1 in *Strong on Music: The New York Music Scene in the Days of George Templeton Strong, 1836–1875.* New York: Oxford University Press.

————. 1995. *Reverberations, 1850–1856.* Vol. 2 in *Strong on Music: The New York Music Scene in the Days of George Templeton Strong, 1836–1875.* Chicago: University of Chicago Press.

Lax, Roger, and Frederick Smith. 1989. *The Great Song Thesaurus.* 2nd ed., updated and expanded. New York: Oxford University Press.

Leach, William. 1993. *Land of Desire: Merchants, Power, and the Rise of a New American Culture.* New York: Pantheon.

Lears, T. J. Jackson. 1994. *Fables of Abundance: A Cultural History of Advertising in America.* New York: Basic.

Lee, Dorothy Sara. 1993. "North America: Native American." Pp. 19ff. in Myers, ed., 1993.

Lemann, Nicholas. 1991. *The Promised Land: The Great Black Migration and How It Changed America.* New York: Knopf.

Leppert, Richard D. 1993. *The Sight of Sound: Music, Representation, and the History of the Body.* Berkeley and Los Angeles: University of California Press.

Lerner, Alan Jay. 1978. *The Street Where I Live.* New York: Norton.

Levine, Lawrence W. 1977. *Black Culture and Black Consciousness: Afro-American Folk Thought from Slavery to Freedom.* New York: Oxford University Press.

————. 1988. *Highbrow/Lowbrow: The Emergence of Cultural Hierarchy in America.* Cambridge: Harvard University Press.

Lewis, Earl. 1996. "Race." 1:129ff. in *EUSTC.*

Lieberman, Robbie. 1989. *My Song Is My Weapon: People's Songs, American Communism, and the Politics of Culture, 1930–1950.* Urbana: University of Illinois Press.

Limerick, Patricia Nelson, and Jon Coleman. 1996. "The West." 1:81ff. in *EUSTC.*

Lincoln, Abraham. 1989. *Speeches and Writings, 1859–1865.* New York: Library of America.

Linderman, Gerald F. 1987. *Embattled Courage: The Experience of Combat in the American Civil War.* New York: Free Press.

Lingenfelter, Richard, Richard A. Dwyer, and David Cohen, eds. 1968. *Songs of the American West.* Berkeley and Los Angeles: University of California Press.

Linn, Karen. 1991. *That Half-Barbaric Twang: The Banjo in American Popular Culture.* Urbana: University of Illinois Press.

Lipsitz, George. 1990. *Time Passages: Collective Memory and American Popular Culture.* Minneapolis: University of Minnesota Press.

Locke, Ralph P., and Cyrilla Barr, eds. 1997. *Cultivating Music in America: Women Patrons and Activists since 1860.* Berkeley and Los Angeles: University of California Press.

Loesser, Arthur. 1954. *Men, Women, and Pianos: A Social History.* New York: Simon and Schuster.

Logsdon, Guy, ed. 1989. *"The Whorehouse Bells Were Ringing" and Other Songs Cowboys Sing.* Urbana: University of Illinois Press.

Lomax, John Avery, and Alan Lomax, arrs. and eds., 1947. *Folk Song U.S.A.: The III Best American Ballads*. New York: Duell, Sloan and Pearce.

Loney, Glenn, ed. 1984. *Musical Theatre in America: Papers and Proceedings of the Conference on the Musical Theatre in America*. Westport, Conn.: Greenwood Press.

Longfellow, Henry Wadsworth. 1962. "Song of Hiawatha," excerpt. P. 87 in *The Mentor Book of Major American Poets*. Ed. Oscar Williams and Edwin Honig. New York: New American Library, 1962.

Lott, Eric. 1993. *Love and Theft: Blackface Minstrelsy and the American Working Class*. New York: Oxford University Press.

Lott, R. Allen. 1990. "Bernard Ullman: 19th-Century American Impressario." Pp. 174ff. in Crawford et al., eds., 1990.

Lovell, John. 1972. *Black Song: The Forge and the Flame; The Story of How the Afro-American Spiritual Was Hammered Out*. New York: Macmillan.

Lowens, Irving. 1964. *Music and Musicians in Early America*. New York: Norton.

Lowens, Margery Morgan. 1971. *The New York Years of Edward MacDowell*. Ph.D. diss., University of Michigan.

MacDowell, Edward. [1912] 1969. *Critical and Historical Essays: Lectures Delivered at Columbia University*. Ed. W. J. Baltzell. Reprint, New York: Da Capo.

Maddox, Lucy. 1993. "Native American Poetry." Pp. 728ff. in Parini, ed., 1993.

Magriel, Paul David, ed. [1948] 1978. *Chronicles of the American Dance: From the Shakers to Martha Graham*. New York: Da Capo.

Malitz, Nancy. 1992. "New York." 3:361ff. in *NGDO*.

Malone, Bill C. 1968. *Country Music USA: A Fifty-Year History*. Austin: University of Texas Press.

———. 1979. *Southern Music, American Music*. Lexington: University Press of Kentucky.

———. 1986. "Country Music." 1:516f. in *NGDAM*.

———. 1993. *Singing Cowboys and Musical Mountaineers: Southern Culture and the Roots of Country Music*. Athens: University of Georgia Press.

Malone, Jacqui. 1996. *Steppin' on the Blues: The Visible Rhythms of African American Dance*. Urbana: University of Illinois Press.

Mann, Thomas. [1948] 1966. *Doctor Faustus: The Life of the German Composer, Adrian Leverkuhn, as Told by a Friend*. New York: Modern Library.

Manuel, Peter. 1995. *Caribbean Currents: Caribbean Music from Rumba to Reggae*. Philadelphia: Temple University Press.

Marcus, Greil. 1997. *Invisible Republic: Bob Dylan's Basement Tapes*. New York: Holt.

Marks, Edward B. 1934. *They All Sang: From Tony Pastor to Rudy Vallee*. New York: Viking.

Marquis, Alice Goldfarb. 1986. *Hopes and Ashes: The Birth of Modern Times, 1929–1939*. New York: Free Press.

Marsalis, Wynton. 1984. "In Defense of Standards." *Keynote*. December, 8–12.

Marsden, George M. 1980. *Fundamentalism and American Culture: The Shaping of Twentieth Century Evangelicalism, 1870–1925*. New York: Oxford University Press.

Marsh, J. B. T. 1892. *The Story of the Jubilee Singers*. Cleveland: Cleveland Printing & Publishing Co.

Martin, George. 1979. *All You Need Is Ears*. New York: St. Martin's Press.

Martin, George Whitney. 1993. *Verdi at the Golden Gate: Opera and San Francisco in the Gold Rush Years*. Berkeley and Los Angeles: University of California Press.

Mason, Henry L., comp. 1944. *Hymn-Tunes of Lowell Mason: A Bibliography*. Cambridge, Mass.: The University Press.

Mason, William. [1901] 1970. *Memories of a Musical Life*. Reprint, New York: Da Capo.

Mather, Cotton. 1721. *The Accomplished Singer*. Boston: B. Green.

Mather, Increase. 1684. *An Arrow Against Profane and Promiscuous Dancing, Drawn out of the Quiver of the Scriptures*. Boston: Printed by S. Green.

Mathews, W. S. B., ed. [1889] 1970. *A Hundred Years of Music in America: An Account of Musical Effort in America During the Past Century*. Reprint, New York: AMS Press.

Mattfeld, Julius. 1962. *Variety Music Cavalcade 1620–1961: A Chronology of Vocal and Instrumental Music Popular in the United States*. Rev. ed. Introduction by Abel Green. Englewood Cliffs, N.J.: Prentice-Hall.

May, Henry F. 1959. *The End of American Innocence: A Study of the First Years of Our Own Time, 1912–1917*. New York: Knopf.

McCarthy, Kathleen. 1996. "Patronage of the Arts." 1:725ff. in *EUSTC*.

McConachie, Bruce A. 1992. *Melodramatic Formations: American Theatre and Society, 1820–1870*. Iowa City: University of Iowa Press.

McConnell, Stuart. 1996. "Nationalism." 1:251ff. in *EUSTC*.

McKay, David P., and Richard Crawford. 1975. *William Billings of Boston: Eighteenth-Century Composer*. Princeton, N.J.: Princeton University Press.

Mead, Rita, and Ned Sublette. 1986. "Broadcasting." 1:296ff. in *NGDAM*.

Meinig, D. W. 1986. *The Shaping of America: A Geographical Perspective on 500 Years of History*. Vol. 1, *Atlantic America, 1492–1800*. New Haven: Yale University Press.

———. 1993. *The Shaping of America: A Geographical Perspective on 500 Years of History*. Vol. 2, *Continental America, 1800–1867*. New Haven: Yale University Press.

Mellers, Wilfrid. 1966. *Music in a New Found Land: Themes and Developments in the History of American Music*. New York: Knopf.

The Middlesex Collection of Church Music: or, Ancient Psalmody Revived. 1807. Boston: Manning and Loring.

Miller, Jim. 1986. "James Brown." 1:307–8 in *NGDAM*.

Miller, Marc H., ed. 1994. *Louis Armstrong: A Cultural Legacy*. Seattle: University of Washington Press.

Mintz, Steven. 1996. "Family." 1:221ff. in *EUSTC*.

Mitchell, Frank. 1978. *Navajo Blessingway Singer: The Autobiography of Frank Mitchell, 1881–1967*. Ed. Charlotte J. Frisbie and David P. McAllester. Tucson: University of Arizona Press.

Monson, Ingrid. 1996. *Saying Something: Jazz Improvisation and Interaction*. Chicago: University of Chicago Press.

Moore, MacDonald Smith. 1985. *Yankee Blues: Musical Culture and American Identity*. Bloomington: Indiana University Press.

Moraga, Cherrie. 1993. *The Last Generation: Prose and Poetry*. Boston: South End Press.

Mordden, Ethan. 1981. *The Hollywood Musical*. New York: St. Martin's Press.

Morgan, Robert P. 1991. *Twentieth-Century Music: A History of Musical Style in Modern Europe and America*. New York: Norton.

Morris, Richard, ed. 1970. *Encyclopedia of American History*. Enlarged and updated. New York: Harper and Row.

Moss, Harold Gene. 1970. *Ballad-Opera Songs: A Record of the Ideas Set to Music, 1728–1733*. Ph.D. diss., University of Michigan.

Mueller, John Henry. 1951. *The American Symphony Orchestra: A Social History of Musical Taste*. Bloomington: Indiana University Press.

Mukerji, Chandra, and Michael Schudson, eds. 1991. *Rethinking Popular Culture: Contemporary Perspectives in Cultural Studies*. Berkeley and Los Angeles: University of California Press.

Murray, Albert. 1970. *The Omni-Americans: New Perspectives on Black Experience and American Culture*. New York: Outerbridge and Dienstfrey.

———. 1976. *Stomping the Blues*. New York: McGraw-Hill.

———. 1996. *The Blue Devils of Nada: A Contemporary American Approach to Aesthetic Statement*. New York: Pantheon.

Myers, Helen, ed. 1993. *Ethnomusicology: Historical and Regional Studies*. New York: Norton.

Nabokov, Peter, ed. 1991. *Native American Testimony: A Chronicle of Indian-White Relations from Prophecy to the Present, 1492–1992*. New York: Viking.

Nathan, Hans. 1962. *Dan Emmett and the Rise of Early Negro Minstrelsy*. Norman: University of Oklahoma Press.

National Cyclopedia of American Biography. 1891. New York: James T. White.

Nettl, Bruno. 1956. *Music in Primitive Culture*. Cambridge: Harvard University Press.

———. 1986. "Indians, American." 2:460ff. in *NGDAM*.

———. 1983. *The Study of Ethnomusicology: Twenty-Nine Issues and Concepts*. Urbana: University of Illinois Press.

———. 1989. *Blackfoot Musical Thought: Comparative Perspectives*. Kent, Ohio: Kent State University Press.

New Hampshire Gazette, 1764.

Newsom, Jon. 1976. "Our Musical Past: A History of the Instruments and the Musical Selections." Notes to sound recording *Our Musical Past*. Washington, D.C.: Library of Congress.

Nicholls, David, ed. 1998. *The Cambridge History of American Music*. Cambridge and New York: Cambridge University Press.

——, ed. 1998. *The Whole World of Music: A Henry Cowell Symposium*. Amsterdam: Harwood.

Norton, Pauline Elizabeth Hosack. 1983. *March Music in Nineteenth-Century America*. Ph.D. diss., University of Michigan.

Ochse, Orpha Caroline. 1975. *The History of the Organ in the United States*. Bloomington: Indiana University Press.

O'Dair, Barbara, ed. 1997. *Trouble Girls: The Rolling Stone Book of Women in Rock*. New York: Random House.

Offergeld, Robert. 1969. Introduction to *The Piano Works of Louis Moreau Gottschalk*. Ed. Vera Lawrence. New York: Arno Press and *The New York Times*, 1969.

Ogasapian, John. 1977. *Organ Building in New York City, 1700–1900*. Braintree, Mass: Organ Literature Foundation.

Oja, Carol J. 1994. "Gershwin and American Modernists of the 1920s." *Musical Quarterly*. 78/4: 646ff.

——. 2000. *Making Music Modern: New York in the 1920s*. Forthcoming.

Oliver, Paul. 1986. "Blues." 1:242ff. in *NGDAM*.

Osterhout, Paul, R. 1986. "Note Reading and Regular Singing in Eighteenth-Century New England." *American Music* 4/2 (summer): 125ff.

Palmer, Robert. 1979. *A Tale of Two Cities: Memphis Rock and New Orleans Roll*. Brooklyn: Institute for Studies in American Music.

——. 1995. *Rock & Roll: An Unruly History*. New York: Harmony.

Parakilas, James. 1992. *Ballads Without Words: Chopin and the Tradition of the Instrumental Ballade*. Portland, Ore.: Amadeus Press.

Pareles, Jon. 1986. "Bob Dylan." 1:669ff. in *NGDAM*.

Parini, Jay, ed. 1993. *The Columbia History of American Poetry*. New York: Columbia University Press.

Parker, John Rowe. [1824] 1975. *A Musical Biography: or, Sketches of the Lives and Writings of Eminent Musical Characters. Interspersed with an Epitome of Interesting Musical Matter*. Reprint, Detroit: Information Coordinators.

Parkman, Francis. 1983. *France and England in North America*. 2 vols. New York: Library of America.

Patterson, David Wayne. 1996. *Appraising the Catchwords, c. 1942–1959: John Cage's Asian-Derived Rhetoric and the Historical Reference of Black Mountain College*. Ph.D. diss., Columbia University.

Patterson, James T. 1996. *Grand Expectations: The United States, 1945–1974*. New York: Oxford University Press

Payne, Robert. 1960. *Gershwin*. London: Hale.

Pearson, Nathan W. 1987. *Goin' to Kansas City*. Urbana: University of Illinois Press.

Pemberton, Carol Ann. 1985. *Lowell Mason: His Life and Work.* Ann Arbor: UMI Research Press.

Pendle, Karin, ed. 1991. *Women and Music: A History.* Bloomington: Indiana University Press.

Peretti, Burton William. 1992. *The Creation of Jazz: Music, Race, and Culture in Urban America.* Urbana: University of Illinois Press.

Perkins, Charles Callahan, and J. S. Dwight, eds. [1883–93] 1977. *History of the Handel and Haydn Society, of Boston, Massachusetts.* Reprint, New York: Da Capo.

Perlis, Vivian. 1974. *Charles Ives Remembered: An Oral History.* New Haven: Yale University Press.

Petkov, Steven, and Leonard Mustazza, eds. 1995. *The Frank Sinatra Reader.* New York: Oxford University Press.

Pisani, Michael V. 1996. *Exotic Sounds in the Native Land: Portrayals of North American Indians in Western Music.* Ph.D. diss., Eastman School of Music, University of Rochester.

Plantinga, Leon. *Romantic Music: A History of Musical Style in Nineteenth-Century Europe.* New York: Norton, 1984.

Porter, Eric C. 1997. *"Out of the Blue": Black Creative Musicians and the Challenge of Jazz, 1940–1995.* Ph.D. diss., University of Michigan.

Porter, Lewis. 1985. *Lester Young.* Boston: Twayne.

Porter, Susan L. 1991. *With an Air Debonair: Musical Theatre in America, 1785–1815.* Washington: Smithsonian Institution Press.

Porter, William Smith. 1834. *The Musical Cyclopedia.* Boston: J. Loring.

Preston, Katherine K. 1992. *Music for Hire: A Study of Professional Musicians in Washington, 1877–1900.* Stuyvesant, N.Y.: Pendragon Press.

————. 1993. *Opera on the Road: Traveling Opera Troupes in the United States, 1825–60.* Urbana: University of Illinois Press.

Pritchett, James. 1993. *The Music of John Cage.* Cambridge and New York: Cambridge University Press.

Ramsey, Frederic, and Charles S. Smith, eds. 1939. *Jazzmen.* New York: Harcourt, Brace.

Rattenbury, Ken. 1990. *Duke Ellington, Jazz Composer.* New Haven: Yale University Press.

Reagon, Bernice, ed. 1992. *We'll Understand It Better By and By: Pioneering African American Gospel Composers.* Washington, D.C.: Smithsonian Institution Press.

Reich, Steve. 1974. *Writings About Music.* Halifax: Press of Nova Scotia College of Art and Design. New York: New York University Press.

Reid, Jane Davidson. 1993. *The Oxford Guide to Classical Mythology in the Arts, 1300–1990s.* 2 vols. New York: Oxford University Press.

Reinagle, Alexander. 1978. *The Philadelphia Sonatas.* Ed. Robert Hopkins. Recent Researches in American Music, 5. Madison, Wis.: A-R Editions.

Reynolds, William Jensen. 1964. *Hymns of Our Faith: A Handbook for the Baptist Hymnal*. Nashville: Broadman Press.

Rice, Edward Le Roy. 1911. *Monarchs of Minstrelsy: From "Daddy" Rice to Date*. New York: Kenny.

Rich, Arthur Lowndes. 1946. *Lowell Mason, "The Father of Singing Among the Children."* Chapel Hill: University of North Carolina Press.

Riis, Thomas L. 1989. *Just before Jazz: Black Musical Theater in New York, 1890–1915*. Washington, D.C.: Smithsonian Institution Press.

———, ed. 1996. *The Music and Scripts of In Dahomey,* by Will Marion Cook. Recent Researches in American Music, 25. Music of the United States of America, 5. Madison, Wis.: A-R Editions.

Ritter, Frederic Louis. 1883. *Music in America*. New York: Scribner.

———. [1890] 1970. *Music in America*. Reprint, New York: Johnson.

Roberts, Randy. 1996. "Leisure and Recreation." 4:1743ff. in *EUSTC*.

Rockwell, John. 1983. *All American Music: Composition in the Late Twentieth Century*. New York: Random House.

———. 1986. "Art Rock." 1:74 in *NGDAM*.

Rodgers, Richard. [1975] 1978. *Musical Stages: An Autobiography*. New York: Random House.

Root, George Frederick. 1891. *The Story of a Musical Life: An Autobiography*. Cincinnati: John Church.

Rose, Tricia. 1994. *Black Noise: Rap Music and Black Culture in Contemporary America*. Hanover, N.H.: Wesleyan University Press and University Press of New England.

Rosenberg, Neil V. 1985. *Bluegrass: A History*. Urbana: University of Illinois Press.

———, ed. 1993. *Transforming Tradition: Folk Music Revivals Examined*. Urbana: University of Illinois Press.

Rosenthal, David. 1992. *Hard Bop: Jazz and Black Music, 1955–1965*. New York: Oxford University Press.

Rossiter, Frank R. 1975. *Charles Ives and His America*. New York: Liveright.

Rourke, Constance. 1942. *The Roots of American Culture and Other Essays*. New York: Harcourt, Brace.

Royster, Charles. 1991. *The Destructive War: William Tecumseh Sherman, Stonewall Jackson, and the Americans*. New York: Knopf.

Russell, Charles Edward. 1927. *The American Orchestra and Theodore Thomas*. Garden City, N.Y.: Doubleday, Page.

Russell, Ross. 1971. *Jazz Style in Kansas City and the Southwest*. Berkeley and Los Angeles: University of California Press.

Ryan, Thomas. 1899. *Recollections of an Old Musician*. New York: Dutton.

Sablosky, Irving. 1986. *What They Heard: Music in America, 1852–1881, from the Pages of Dwight's Journal of Music*. Baton Rouge: Louisiana State University Press.

Sacks, Howard L., and Judith R. Sacks. 1988. "Way Up North in Dixie: Black-White Musical Interaction in Knox County, Ohio." *American Music* 6/4 (winter): 409ff.

Salem. 1805. *The Salem Collection of Classical Sacred Musick.* Salem, Mass.: Cushing.

Saloman, Ora Frishberg. 1995. *Beethoven's Symphonies and J. S. Dwight: The Birth of American Music Criticism.* Boston: Northeastern University Press.

Sandow, Gregory. 1986. "Philip Glass." 2:228ff. in *NGDAM.*

Sanjek, Russell. 1988. *American Popular Music and Its Business: The First Four Hundred Years.* 3 vols. New York: Oxford University Press.

Schabas, Ezra. 1989. *Theodore Thomas: America's Conductor and Builder of Orchestras, 1835–1905.* Urbana: University of Illinois Press.

Schlereth, Thomas J. 1991. *Victorian America: Transformations in Everyday Life, 1876–1915.* New York: HarperCollins.

Schrader, Arthur F. 1980. "Songs to Cultivate the Sensations of Freedom." Pp. 105ff. in Lambert, ed., 1980–85.

Schuller, Gunther. 1968. *Early Jazz: Its Roots and Musical Development.* New York: Oxford University Press.

———. 1988. "Arrangement." 1:33/00 in *NGDJ.*

———. 1988. "Third Stream." 2:531 in *NGDJ.*

———. 1989. *The Swing Era: The Development Of Jazz, 1930–1945.* New York: Oxford University Press.

Schwartz, Elliott, and Barney Childs, eds. 1967. *Contemporary Composers on Contemporary Music.* New York: Holt, Rinehart and Winston.

Scott, James. 1992. *The Music of James Scott.* Ed. Scott DeVeaux and William Howland Kenney. Washington, D.C.: Smithsonian Institution Press.

Seeger, Pete. 1972. *The Incompleat Folksinger.* New York: Simon and Schuster.

Sessions, Roger. 1979. *Roger Sessions on Music: Collected Essays.* Princeton, N.J.: Princeton University Press.

Shanet, Howard. 1975. *Philharmonic: A History of New York's Orchestra.* New York: Doubleday.

Shapiro, Nat, and Nat Hentoff, eds. [1955] 1966. *Hear Me Talkin' to Ya: The Story of Jazz as Told by the Men Who Made It.* Reprint, New York: Dover.

Shaw, Arnold. 1982. *Dictionary of American Pop/Rock.* New York: Schirmer.

Shelton, Robert. 1986. *No Direction Home: The Life and Music of Bob Dylan.* New York: Morrow.

Sherwood, Gayle D. 1995. *The Choral Works of Charles Ives: Chronology, Style, and Reception.* Ph.D. diss., Yale University.

Shi, David E. 1995. *Facing Facts: Realism in American Thought and Culture, 1850–1920.* New York: Oxford University Press.

Silverman, Kenneth. 1976. *A Cultural History of the American Revolution: Painting, Music, Literature, and the Theatre in the Colonies and the United States from the Treaty of Paris to the Inauguration of George Washington, 1763–1789.* New York: Crowell.

————. 1984. *The Life and Times of Cotton Mather.* New York: Harper and Row.

Slonimsky, Nicolas. 1971. *Music since 1900.* 4th ed. New York: Scribner.

Smart, James 1970. *The Sousa Band: A Discography.* Washington, D.C.: Library of Congress.

Smith, Carleton Sprague. 1980. "Broadsides and Their Music in Colonial America." Pp. 157ff. in Lambert, ed., 1980–85.

Smithsonian Collection of Classic Jazz. 1987 Rev. ed. Selected and annotated by Martin Williams. Washington, D.C.: Smithsonian Institution.

Sonneck, Oscar G. [1905] 1967. *Francis Hopkinson, the First American Poet-Composer, (1737–1791), and James Lyon, Patriot, Preacher, Psalmodist (1735–1794): Two Studies in Early American Music.* Reprint, New York: Da Capo.

————. [1907] 1978. *Early Concert-Life in America (1731–1800).* Reprint, New York: Da Capo.

————. 1916. *Suum Cuique: Essays in Music.* New York: Schirmer.

Southern, Eileen. 1977a. "Musical Practices in Black Churches of Philadelphia and New York." *JAMS* 30/2: 296ff.

Southern, Eileen. 1977b. "Frank Johnson and his Promenade Concerts." *BPIM* v. 3ff.

————. 1982. *Biographical Dictionary of Afro-American and African Musicians.* Westport, Conn.: Greenwood Press.

————. 1997. *The Music of Black Americans: A History.* 3rd ed. New York: Norton.

————, ed. 1983. *Readings in Black American Music.* 2nd ed. New York: Norton.

Spiller, Robert, et. al., eds. 1963. *Literary History of the United States.* 3d ed., rev. New York: Macmillan.

Starr, Larry. 1992. *A Union of Diversities: Style in the Music of Charles Ives.* New York: Schirmer.

Starr, S. Frederick. 1995. *Bamboula!: The Life and Times of Louis Moreau Gottschalk.* New York: Oxford University Press.

Steel, David Warren. 1988. "Lazarus J. Jones and *The Southern Minstrel* (1849)." *American Music* 6/2 (summer): 123ff.

Stevenson, Robert. 1966. *Protestant Church Music in America: A Short Survey of Men and Movements from 1564 to the Present.* New York: Norton.

————. 1973a. "Written Sources for Indian Music until 1882." *Ethnomusicology* 17:1ff.

————. 1973b. "English Sources for Indian Music until 1882." *Ethnomusicology* 17:339ff.

Stewart, Rex. 1972. *Jazz Masters of the Thirties.* New York: Macmillan.

Stowe, Harriett Beecher. 1982. *Three Novels: Uncle Tom's Cabin or, Life Among the Lowly, The Minister's Wooing, Oldtown Folks.* New York: Library of America.

Strickland, Edward. 1991. *American Composers: Dialogues on Contemporary Music.* Bloomington: Indiana University Press.

————. 1993. *Minimalism: Origins.* Bloomington: Indiana University Press.

Strobel, Desmond F. 1998. "Polka." 5:221ff. in *IED.*

Stuckey, Sterling. 1987. *Slave Culture: Nationalist Theory and the Foundations of Black America*. New York: Oxford University Press.

Sudhalter, Richard M., and Philip Evans. 1974. *Bix: Man and Legend*. New Rochelle, N.Y.: Arlington House.

Summers, William. 1986. "California Mission Music." 1:345ff. in *NGDAM*.

Sundquist, Eric J. 1993. *To Wake the Nations: Race in the Making of American Literature*. Cambridge: Harvard University Press.

Swafford, Jan. 1996. *Charles Ives: A Life with Music*. New York: Norton.

Symmes, Thomas. 1720. *The Reasonableness of, Regular Singing*. Boston: B. Green.

————. 1723. *Utile Dulci. Or, A Joco-Serious Dialogue, Concerning Regular Singing*. Boston: B. Green.

Talley, John Barry. 1988. *Secular Music in Colonial Annapolis: The Tuesday Club, 1745–56*. Urbana: University of Illinois Press.

Thomas, Theodore. [1905] 1964. *Theodore Thomas: A Musical Autobiography*. 2 vols. Ed. George P. Upton. Reprint, New York: Da Capo.

Thompson, Hunter S. 1971. *Fear and Loathing in Las Vegas: A Savage Journey to the Heart of the American Dream*. New York: Random House.

Thomson, Virgil. 1971. *American Music since 1910*. New York: Holt, Rinehart and Winston.

Tibbetts, John C., ed. 1993. *Dvořák in America, 1892–1895*. Portland: Amadeus Press.

Tick, Judith. 1986. "Women in Music." 4:550ff. in *NGDAM*.

Tindall, George Brown, and David Shi. 1996. *America: A Narrative History*. 2 vols. 4th ed. New York: Norton.

Titon, Jeff Todd. 1977. *Early Downhome Blues: A Musical and Cultural Analysis*. Urbana: University of Illinois Press.

————. 1993. "Reconstructing the Blues: Reflections on the 1960s Blues Revival." Pp. 220ff. in Rosenberg, ed., 1993.

Tocqueville, Alexis de. 1969. *Democracy in America*. Ed. J. P. Mayar. Trans. by George Lawrence. Garden City, N.Y.: Doubleday.

Todorov, Tzvetan. 1984. *The Conquest of America: The Question of the Other*. New York: Harper and Row.

Toll, Robert C. 1974. *Blacking Up: The Minstrel Show in Nineteenth Century America*. New York: Oxford University Press.

————. 1982. *The Entertainment Machine: American Show Business in the Twentieth Century*. Oxford and New York: Oxford University Press.

Trotter, James M. [1878] 1968. *Music and Some Highly Musical People*. Reprint, New York: Johnson.

————. 1983. From "Music and Some Highly Musical People." Pp. 142ff. in Southern, ed., 1983.

Tucker, Mark. 1985. "Count Basie and the Piano That Swings the Band." *Popular Music* 5:45ff.

———. 1991. *Ellington: The Early Years.* Urbana: University of Illinois Press.

Upton, William Treat. 1939. *Anthony Philip Heinrich: A Nineteenth-Century Composer in America.* New York: Columbia University Press.

———. 1954. *William Henry Fry: American Journalist and Composer-Critic.* New York: Crowell.

Van Cleef, Joy, and Kate Van Winkle Keller. 1980. "Selected American Country Dances and Their English Sources." Pp. 3ff. in Lambert, ed., 1980.

Van der Merwe, Peter. 1989. *Origins of the Popular Style: The Antecedents of Twentieth-Century Popular Music.* Oxford: Clarendon Press.

Vecoli, Rudolph J. 1996. "Ethnicity and Immigration." 1:161ff. in *EUSTC.*

Vinton, John. 1974. *Dictionary of Contemporary Music.* New York: Dutton.

Walser, Robert. 1998. "The Rock and Roll era." Pp. 345ff. in *Cambridge History of American Music.*

Walter, Thomas. 1721. *The Grounds and Rules of Musick Explained.* Boston: J. Franklin.

Walters, Ronald G. 1978. *American Reformers, 1815–1860.* New York: Hill and Wang.

———. 1996. "The Mass Media and Popular Culture." 4:1461 in *EUSTC.*

Ware, W. Porter, and Thaddeus C. Lockard, Jr. 1980. *P. T. Barnum Presents Jenny Lind: The American Tour of the Swedish Nightingale.* Baton Rouge: Louisiana State University Press.

Waters, Edward N. 1955. *Victor Herbert: A Life in Music.* New York: Macmillan.

Watkins, Glenn. 1994. *Pyramids at the Louvre: Music, Culture, and Collage from Stravinsky to the Postmodernists.* Cambridge: Harvard University Press.

Watkins, Mel. 1994. *On the Real Side: Laughing, Lying, and Signifying: The Underground Tradition of African-American Humor That Transformed American Culture, from Slavery to Richard Pryor.* New York: Simon and Schuster.

Welch, James. 1986. *Fools Crow.* New York: Viking.

Wentworth, Harold, and Stuart Berg Flexner, eds. 1960. *Dictionary of American Slang.* New York: Crowell.

Wexler, Jerry, and David Ritz. 1993. *Rhythm and the Blues: A Life in American Music.* New York: Knopf.

Wharton, Edith. 1920. *The Age of Innocence.* New York: Grosset and Dunlap.

Whisnant, David E. 1983. *All That Is Native and Fine: The Politics of Culture in an American Region.* Chapel Hill: University of North Carolina Press.

Whitburn, Joel. 1986. *Joel Whitburn's Pop Memories, 1890–1954: The History of American Popular Music, Compiled from America's Popular Music Charts.* Menomonee Falls, Wis.: Record Research.

White, B. F., and E. J. King. 1968. *The Sacred Harp.* Facsimile ed. Introduction by George Pullen Jackson. Nashville: Broadman Press.

White, Eric Walter. 1979. *Stravinsky: The Composer and His Works.* 2nd ed. Berkeley and Los Angeles: University of California Press.

Whitehead, Kevin. 1993. "Jazz Rebels: Lester Bowie & Greg Osby." *Down Beat,* August, 16ff.

Whitman, Walt. 1982. *Complete Poetry and Collected Prose*. New York: Library of America.

Wilentz, Sean. 1984. *Chants Democratic: New York City and the Rise of the American Working Class, 1788–1850*. New York: Oxford University Press.

Wilgus, D. K. 1959. *Anglo-American Folksong Scholarship since 1898*. New Brunswick, N.J.: Rutgers University Press.

Williams, Martin T. 1967. *Jazz Masters of New Orleans*. New York: Macmillan.

————. 1993. *The Jazz Tradition*. 2nd rev. ed. New York: Oxford University Press.

————, ed. 1959. *The Art of Jazz: Essays on the Nature and Development of Jazz*. New York: Oxford University Press.

Williams, Raymond. 1976. *Keywords: A Vocabulary of Culture and Society*. New York: Oxford University Press.

Williams, William Carlos. 1925 [1956]. *In the American grain*. New York: New Directions.

Williams-Jones, Pearl, and Bernice Johnson Reagan, eds. 1992. "Conversations: Roberta Martin Singers Roundtable." With comments by Eugene Smith and Lawrence Roberts. Pp. 287ff. in Reagon, ed., 1992.

Willis, Ellen. 1997. Preface to O'Dair 1997.

Wilson, Olly. 1992. "The Heterogenous Sound Ideal in African-American Music." Pp. 327ff. in Wright and Floyd, eds., 1992.

Winans, Robert. 1984. "Early Minstrel Show Music, 1843–1852." Pp. 71ff. in Loney, ed., 1984.

Witmer, Robert, and Anthony Marks. 1986. "Rhythm-and-Blues." 4:36–37 in *NGDAM*.

Woideck, Carl. 1996. *Charlie Parker: His Music and Life*. Ann Arbor: University of Michigan Press.

Wolfe, Charles, and Kip Lornell. 1992. *The Life and Legend of Leadbelly*. New York: HarperCollins.

Wolfe, Richard J. 1964. *Secular Music in America, 1801–1825: A Bibliography*. 3 vols. New York: New York Public Library.

————. 1980. *Early American Music Engraving and Printing: A History of Music Publishing in America from 1787 to 1825 with Commentary on Earlier and Later Practices*. Urbana: University of Illinois Press.

Wood, Peter H. 1974. *Black Majority: Negroes in Colonial South Carolina from 1670 through the Stono Rebellion*. New York: Knopf.

Wood, William B. 1855. *Personal Recollections of the Stage, Embracing Notices of Actors, Authors, and Auditors, During a Period of Forty Years*. Philadelphia: H. C. Baird.

Wright, Josephine, ed., with Samuel A. Floyd, Jr. 1992. *New Perspectives on Music: Essays in Honor of Eileen Southern*. Warren, Mich.: Harmonie Park Press.

Yellin, Victor Fell. 1969. "Musical Activity in Virginia Before 1620." *JAMS* 22: 284–89.

————. 1990. *Chadwick, Yankee Composer.* Washington, D.C.: Smithsonian Institution Press.

Yoder, Don. 1961. *Pennsylvania Spirituals.* Lancaster: Pennsylvania Folklife Society.

Zak, Albin J., III. 1997. *Multitrack Recording as a Compositional Process: The Poetics of Rock Composition.* Ph.D. diss., City University of New York.

$\mathcal{C}$redits

Music and Text

Arlen, Harold and E. Y. Harburg, "Over the Rainbow." *Over the Rainbow*, by Harold Arlen and E. Y . Harburg. © 1938 (Renewed 1966) Metro-Goldwyn-Mayer Inc. © 1939 (Renewed) EMI Feist Catalog Inc. All Rights Reserved. Used by Permission. Warner Bros. Publications U.S. Inc., Miami, FL 33014.—p. 685

Browner, Tara, "American Indian Music and Dance." From the *Grolier Multimedia Encyclopedia*, 1999 Edition. Copyright © 1999 by Grolier Incorporated. Reprinted by permission.—pp. 405–6

Donnelly, Dorothy and Sigmund Romberg, *The Student Prince*. *The Student Prince*, by Dorothy Donnelly and Sigmund Romberg. © 1932 (Renewed) Warner Bros. Inc. All Rights Reserved. Used by Permission. Warner Bros. Publications U.S. Inc., Miami, FL 33014.—p. 665

Duckworth, William, *Talking Music: Conversations with John Cage, Philip Glass, Laurie Anderson, and Five Generations of American Experimental Composers*. From *Talking Music: Conversations with John Cage, Philip Glass, Laurie Anderson, and Five Generations of American Experimental Composers*, by William Duckworth (Schirmer, 1995). Reprinted by permission of The Gale Group.—pp. 821, 824, 826–28, 830, 832

Dylan, Bob, "Like a Rolling Stone." © 1965 by Warner Bros., Inc. Copyright renewed 1993 by Special Rider Music.—pp. 791–92

Ellington, Edward Kennedy, "Diminuendo and Crescendo in Blue." Used by Permission of Famous Music Corporation. All Rights Reserved.—p. 650

Floyd, Samuel, "Alton Augustus Adams." Reprinted by permission of The Black Perspective in Music.—pp. 466–67

Gann, Kyle, *American Music in the Twentieth Century*. From *American Music in the*

Twentieth Century, by Kyle Gann (Wadsworth Publishing Co., 1997). 1997. Reprinted by permission of The Gale Group.—pp. 821–24, 830, 835

Gershwin, George, "Fascinating Rhythm." © WB Music Corp.; Copyright Renewed. All Rights Reserved. Used by Permission.—p. 665

Gershwin, George, *Rhapsody in Blue*. *Rhapsody in Blue*, by George Gershwin. © 1924 (Renewed) WB Music Corp. All Rights Reserved. Used by Permission. Warner Bros. Publications U.S. Inc., Miami, FL 33014.—p. 576

Gershwin, George and Ira, "The Man I Love." *The Man I Love*, by George Gershwin and Ira Gershwin. © 1924 (Renewed) WB Music Corp. All Rights Reserved. Used by Permission. Warner Bros. Publications U.S. Inc., Miami, FL 33014.—p. 670

Glass, Philip, *Einstein on the Beach*. © 1976 Dunvagen Music Publishers, Inc.— p. 833

Grandmaster Flash, "The Message." © by Sugar Hill Music Publishing. All Rights Reserved. Used by permission.—p. 849

Guralnick, Peter, "Last Train to Memphis: The Rise of Elvis Presley." From *Last Train to Memphis: The Rise of Elvis Presley*, by Peter Guralnick. Copyright © 1994 by Peter Guralnick. By permission of Little, Brown and Company, (Inc.).— pp. 728–29, 731

Guthrie, Woody, "This Land Is Your Land."* *This Land Is Your Land*. Words and Music by Woody Guthrie. TRO-©-Copyright 1956 (Renewed) 1958 (Renewed) 1970 (Renewed) Ludlow Music, Inc., New York, NY. Used by Permission.— pp. 614–15

Hammerstein, Oscar, "Can't Help Lovin' Dat Man." © 1927 Universal-Polygram International Publishing, Inc. Copyright renewed. All rights reserved. International copyright secured [ASCAP].—p. 668

Hammerstein, Oscar, "Ol Man River." © 1927 Universal-Polygram International Publishing, Inc. Copyright renewed. All rights reserved. International copyright secured [ASCAP].—p. 668

Harjo, Joy, "Anchorage." From the book *She Had Some Horses*, by Joy Harjo. Copyright © 1983, 1997 by Thunder's Mouth Press. Appears by permission of the publisher, Thunder's Mouth Press.—p. 406

Hart, Lorenz, and Richard Rodgers, "My Heart Stood Still." *My Heart Stood Still*, Words by Lorenz Hart, Music by Richard Rodgers. © by Williamson Music and The Estate of Lorenz Hart administered by WB Music Corp. International copyright secured. All rights reserved.—pp. 671–72

Hijuelos, Oscar, *The Mambo Kings Play Songs of Love*. Except from Side A: "In the Hotel Splendour 1980" and "Toward the end, while listening to the wistful 'Beauti-

---

*The excerpt used in this book was taken from Woody Guthrie's original manuscript and is different from the published words.

Illustrations

P. 6: Collection of Wiley L. Housewright; p. 42: New York Public Library at Lincoln Center; p. 46: Brown University Library; p. 49: Courtesy Congregational Church, South Dennis, Massachusetts; p. 53: Library of Congress; p. 54: From the collection of the Moravian Historical Society, Nazareth, Pennsylvania; p. 63: Courtesy Henry E. Huntington Library and Art Gallery; p. 68: Library of Congress; p. 72: Library of Congress; p. 75: Library of Congress; p. 77: © Christie's Images; p. 79: New York Public Library, Music Division; p. 91: Corbis; p. 98: © Collection of The New-York Historical Society; p. 109: Bettmann/Corbis; p. 114: Abby Aldrich Rockefeller Folk Art Center, Williamsburg, Virginia; p. 119: Maryland Historical Society, Baltimore, Maryland; p. 130: Library of Congress; p. 130: Library of Congress; p. 146: New York Public Library, Music Division; p. 157: From *White Spirituals in the Southern Uplands*, Dover Publications, Inc., New York; p. 160: Library of Congress; p. 168: Library of Congress; p. 170: Library of Congress; p. 183: New York Public Library, Music Division; p. 187: New York Public Library, Music Division; p. 188: New York Public Library, Music Division; p. 200: From *Popular Songs of Nineteenth-Century America*, Dover Publications, Inc., New York; p. 207: From *Popular Songs of Nineteenth-Century America*, Dover Publications, Inc., New York; p. 209: Bettmann/Corbis; p. 211: From *Song Book*, selected by Richard Jackson, Dover Publications, Inc., New York; p. 214: From *Popular Songs of Nineteenth-Century America*, Dover Publications, Inc., New York; p. 224: Library of Congress; p. 225: New York Public Library, Music Division; p. 231: New York Public Library at Lincoln Center; p. 234: Culver Pictures; p. 238: © Collection The New-York Historical Society; p. 252: From *Popular Songs of Nineteenth-Century America*, Dover Publications, Inc., New York; p. 254: Bettmann/Corbis; p. 256: New York Public Library, Music Division; p. 262: Bettmann/Corbis; p. 265: Photograph by permission of the Buffalo & Erie County Public Library, Rare Book Room; p. 268: From *The Civil War Songbook*, selected by Richard Crawford, Dover Publications, Inc., New York; p. 274: Library of Congress; p. 278: Library of Congress; p. 283: © Collection The New-York Historical Society; p. 288: Bettmann/Corbis; p. 297: © Collection The New-York Historical Society; p. 298: © Collection The New-York Historical Society; p. 301: Courtesy of the Harvest University Archives; p. 306: Bettmann/Corbis; p. 309: Cincinnati Museum Center; p. 318: Library of Congress; p. 325: Daguerreotype Collection, Library of Congress; p. 328: The New York Philharmonic Archives; p. 336: From *Piano Music of Louis Moreau Gottschalk*, Dover Publications, Inc., New York; p. 346: Bettmann/Corbis; p. 348: From *The Banjo in the Music of Gottschalk*, ed. Richard Jackson, Dover Publications, Inc., New York; p. 355: Bettmann/Corbis; p. 357: Courtesy New England Conservatory, Boston, Massachusetts; p. 362: Courtesy of the heirs of George Whitefield Chadwick; p. 366: Library of Congress; p. 369: Corbis; p. 375: New York Public Library, Music Division; p. 377: Bettmann/Corbis; p. 391: National Museum of American Art, Smithsonian Institution, Gift of Mrs. Joseph Harrison, Jr. Photo: National Museum of American Art, Washington, D.C./Art Resource, New York; p. 393: National Museum of American History, Smithsonian Institution, Washington, D.C.; p. 397: Photo by Melvin Gilmore, Courtesy Nebraska State Historical Society, Lincoln; p. 399: Idaho State Historical Society, #3771; p. 409: Abby Aldrich Rockefeller Folk Art Center, Williamsburg, Virginia; p. 420: Courtesy New York Public Library, Schomburg Center for Research in Black Culture; p. 424: Charles L. Blockson Collection; p. 426: Harvard Theatre Collection, The Houghton Library, Frederic Woodbridge Wilson, Curator; p. 436: Courtesy of the Southwest Museum, Los Angeles. Photo #24536; p. 437: Courtesy of the Southwest Museum, Los Angeles. Photo #42036; p. 442: From *Popular Songs of Nineteenth-Century America*, Dover Publications, Inc., New York; p. 445: New York Public Library, Music Division; p. 454: (bottom) State Historical Society of Wisconsin, WHi (X3) 12673; (top) State Historical Society of Wisconsin, WHi (X3) 38436; p. 456: Library of Congress; p. 457: Courtesy U.S. Geological Library, Reston, Virginia; p. 461: New York Public Library, Music Division; p. 466: Brown Brothers, Sterling, Pennsylvania; p. 468: U.S. Martin Archives; p. 472: (detail of photo) © Collection of The New-York Historical Society; p. 476: Charles W. Stein Collection; p. 477: Daniel C. Harter Collection; p. 480: From *Favorite Songs of the Nineties*, Dover Publications, Inc., New York; p. 485: From *Favorite Songs of the Nineties*, Dover Publications, Inc., New York; p. 491: From 36 *Song Hits by Great Black Songwriters*, Dover Publications, Inc., New York; p. 500: The Charles Ives Papers, Yale University Music Library; p. 502: The Charles Ives Papers, Yale University Music Library; p. 505: The Charles Ives Papers, Yale University Music Library/photo: Bill Joli; p. 507: Bettmann/Corbis; p. 522: The Charles Ives Papers, Yale University Music Library; p. 526: The New York Public Library, Music Division; p. 534: Courtesy New York Public Library, Schomburg Center for Research in Black Culture; p. 540: Bettmann/Corbis; p. 548: Baldwin H. Ward/Corbis; p. 553: Bettmann/Corbis; p. 561: Bettmann/Corbis; p. 572: Bettmann/Corbis; p. 583: Hulton-Deutsch Collection/Corbis; p. 584: Bettmann/Corbis; p. 588: Corbis; p. 600: Courtesy English Folk Dance and Song Society; p. 608: Bettmann/Corbis; p. 611: Smithsonian Institution, Courtesy of The Alan Lomax Archive, New York; p. 614: Bettmann/Corbis; p. 616: New York Public Library, Music Division; p. 617: Courtesy of the Woody Guthrie Archives; p. 624: William Ransom Hogan Jazz Archives, Tulane University Library; p. 629: William Ransom Hogan Jazz Archives, Tulane University Library; p. 633: Bettmann/Corbis; p. 637: Corbis; p. 642: Bettmann/Corbis; p. 646: New York Public Library, Music Division; p. 651: New York Public Library, Music Division; p. 657: Bettmann/Corbis; p. 671: New York Public Library, Music Division; p. 679: Bettmann/Corbis; p. 684: Bettmann/Corbis; p. 686: Photofest; p. 694: Bettmann/Corbis; p. 699: © 1999 Nancy Crampton; p. 703: Bettmann/Corbis; p. 707: Hulton-Deutsch Collection/Corbis; p. 712: Archive Photos; p. 716: New York Public Library, Music Division; p. 725: Photofest; p. 730: Bettmann/Corbis; p. 733: Courtesy Retna, Ltd., photograph by David Redfern; p. 740: Bettmann/Corbis; p. 742: Courtesy Country Music Hall of Fame; p. 746: © Frank Driggs/Archive

Index

Italic page numbers indicate an illustration.